The Scholarship Book 2001

The Complete Guide to Private-Sector Scholarships, Fellowships, Grants, and Loans for the Undergraduate

DANIEL J. CASSIDY

PRENTICE HALL

ISSN 1528-9079

National Scholarship Research Service (NSRS)™
A Division of Cassidy Research Corporation
5577 Skylane Boulevard, Suite 6A
Santa Rosa, California 95403
Phone: 707/546–6777
FAX: 707/546–6785

Printed in the United States of America
10 9 8 7 6 5 4 3 2 1   *10 9 8 7 6 5 4 3 2 1*

ISBN 0-13-088008-6 (PPC)   ISBN 0-13-027561-1 (w/CD)

PRENTICE HALL
Paramus, NJ 07652

On the World Wide Web at http://www.phdirect.com

I wish to thank all of those who have made this 8th edition of *THE SCHOLARSHIP BOOK 2001* the best ever. My sincere thanks and gratitude go to:

The staff at NSRS

especially:

My wife, Deirdre Carlin Cassidy, Vice President/Controller

Research & Computer Engineering heads
Tammy M. Parnell & Richard E. Merwin

Administration & Public Relations heads
Jean E. Van Dyke & Joseph D. Gargiulo

A very special thank you to
Jim Eason
ABC's KGO & KSFO Radio, San Francisco
The man who made NSRS possible!

And Larry King for taking NSRS national!

And Prentice Hall, et al.

Especially
Eugene Brissie and Tom Power . . . and, as always, Barbara Palumbo

Contents

INTRODUCTION vii

HOW TO USE THIS BOOK xxxiii

QUICK FIND INDEX xxxv

FIELD OF STUDY INDEX liv

SCHOLARSHIPS AND AWARD LISTINGS 1

HELPFUL PUBLICATIONS 461

CAREER INFORMATION 482

ALPHABETICAL INDEX 493

Introduction

The information in *THE SCHOLARSHIP BOOK 2001* was compiled from the database of the largest private sector financial aid research service in the world. Located in Santa Rosa, California, NATIONAL SCHOLARSHIP RESEARCH SERVICE (NSRS)™ began tracking private sector scholarships in the late 1970s, using a specialized computer system. As awards increased and research uncovered new sources for today's students, the addition of the INTERNATIONAL SCHOLARSHIP RESEARCH SERVICE (ISRS) doubled the size of this independently developed database. Prospective college students and present undergraduates will find the information in this book valuable in directing their applications and broadening their prospects for scholarship selection.

THE FACTS

According to the Association of Fund Raising Counsel, more than 80 percent of the grant applications that went to more than 44,000 foundations in the United States were either misdirected or filled out improperly. Many scholarships, fellowships, grants, loans, and internships go unclaimed each year—not because students do not qualify, but because they don't know that the money is available. In 1997, NSRS surveyed the private sector scholarship sources and the results found that 3.5 percent or almost 1 billion dollars of these private sector monies went undistributed. There is a great need to organize this "paper-chase" of information into a workable source for today's student. Utilizing the data collected in this book, students will have a broad base of information to convert to their advantage. The monies are there. Apply for them!

PRIVATE SECTOR FUNDS

Philanthropy in the United States is alive and well. These funds, which totaled $58.67 billion in 1982, increased to a whopping $329.91 billion in 1997. Of that amount, nearly 15 percent (or $49.49 billion) goes into the United States educational system, making the private sector the leader in funding at 55 percent of the available scholarships, fellowships, grants, and loans domestically. An additional $30-plus billion is dispersed by other countries worldwide.

And that amount increases daily. The interest alone on a properly invested $2 million is easily $100,000 annually. Private sector resources for higher education are as varied as the awards themselves.

Many scholarships are renewable. You simply sign for them year after year. Most allow you to "piggy-back" several individual scholarships. The average undergraduate scholarship is $5,000 per year, ranging from a low of $100 to a high of $25,000. Graduate-level fellowships range from $10,000 to over $60,000. If you are a graduate student or planning to go on to graduate school for a master's, doctorate, or post-doctorate study, be sure to get a copy of *Dan Cassidy's Worldwide Graduate Scholarship Directory,* 5th Ed. © 2000/2001 by Career Press. Order from NSRS at 800-HEADSTART or Career Press at 800-CAREER-1. Some graduate and post-graduate research projects can yield a quarter of a million dollars or more to fund your project. As inflation spirals, so does the cost of education and the need for financial assistance.

INVESTIGATE THE POSSIBILITIES

Don't think you can't apply because you earn too much money; **80 percent of the private sector does not require a financial statement or proof of need.** Don't think that application deadlines occur only in the fall; **private sector deadlines are passing daily** because often they are set to coincide with the tax year or organizational meeting dates. Don't believe that grades are the only consideration for an award; many application questions deal with personal, occupational, and educational background; organizational affiliation; talent, or ethnic origins; **90 percent are not concerned with grades.** Don't be concerned with age; many organizations are interested in the re-entry student and the mid-career development student. **In fact age is not a restriction,** especially since 1 out of 2 students are now over the age of 25. This is a big jump from 3 years ago when 1 out of 4 were over 25. This is because many students are going back to school after starting families or changing careers as we shift from the industrial wave to the high-tech wave. The Business and Professional Women's Foundation awards hundreds of scholarships to applicants who must be older than 25 or even 35. There is a scholarship at the California state colleges for students over the age of 60 for life-long learning.

PLAN TO COMPETE AND QUALIFY

The plan is simple—use this book and every other resource you can find. Inquire at your institution's financial aid office about government assistance and private endowments at the school. If you are a high school student in any year, begin by writing to ten or more schools. Select a range of institutions that interest you, both large and small, public and private. Request the application materials and school catalogs—many private endowments are available in the forms of scholarships and fellowships bequeathed by alumni and are listed in the school catalog under financial aid. A significant number of these go unclaimed because qualified students do not know they exist! The information is available, but the commitment and determination to find it belongs to the individual.

The private sector is easily accessed with this book. The student can use the tables provided to cross-reference the scholarships applicable to his or her personal background and educational goals. Choose as many as you qualify for, and request application forms and any pertinent materials. Some have specific requirements for applicants such as a personal interview, the submission of an essay or related work, or a promise to work for the company on completion of study and/or the earning of a degree. Others may have paid internships or work advancement programs. Still others may simply require that you fill out an application form.

The money is there. Many go unclaimed. Even the most common scholarship source, such as Rotary, Lions, Elks, Zonta, etc., are complaining that students are not requesting their scholarship application forms, nor applying. Students who do not take the time to inquire lose every advantage. The opportunity to advance to a graduate degree will widen many avenues for your future, and the rewards are incalculable. Information is merely a passage waiting to be used. The resources to achieve your goals are available to you; you need only pursue them.

A human mind, once stretched to a new idea,
never returns to its former dimension.

—Oliver Wendell Holmes, Sr.

Good Luck! And remember:

There's nothing to it
but to do it!

Sincerely,
Daniel J. Cassidy
Founder and Author

Just for Fun: A Potpourri of Scholarships

Note: Most of the following sources are detailed in this book. Just find them in the alphabetical index in the back of the book, and look up their record numbers for details. Those not listed either are for graduate or international study only, or the sources wished not to appear in this book, primarily because they are at a particular school. In order to find out more about the sources not detailed in this book, call NSRS at 707/546-6777.

1. The **Countess of Munster Musical Trust** has scholarships in varying amounts to British and Commonwealth citizens studying music.

2. Don't be bugged by a lack of funds. Money really does grow on trees. The **International Society of Arboriculture** invites horticulturists, plant pathologists, and entomologists to pluck a grant for the study of shade trees.

3. Your tuition troubles could be gone with the wind! If you are a lineal descendant of a worthy Confederate soldier, contact the **United Daughters of the Confederacy** about their $400 to $1,500 scholarships.

4. If you or your parents are actively involved in Harness Racing, you just might hitch yourself to one of the **Harness Tracks of America** scholarships worth $2,500 to $3,000.

5. You could lace up a scholarship of up to $2,000 for undergraduate study if you are a dependent child of a worker in the footwear industry. It's a patent idea from **Two/Ten International Footwear Foundation**.

6. Don't let financial woes cast a pall over your dreams. Bury those worries with a **Hilgenfeld Foundation for Mortuary Education** scholarship! It's available to qualified individuals interested in the funeral service or funeral education fields.

7. Jen unu mil pundo nun EK! (Here's a thousand pounds—now go!) If you understood that you might be eligible for a **Norwich Jubilee Esperanto Foundation** scholarship paying $500 to study Esperanto in the United Kingdom.

8. For a left-handed freshman enrolled at Juniata College and who needs the money, **Beckley Scholarship Foundation** offers $700.

9. For students whose ancestors put their John Hancocks on the Declaration of Independence, scholarships worth $1,200 to $2,000 are given by **Descendants of the Signers of the Declaration of Independence.**

10. Investigating scholarship possibilities? The **Association of Former Agents of the U.S. Secret Service** offers scholarships of $500 to $1,500 to undergraduate law enforcement and police administration students. You do have to give your real name, but fingerprints won't be necessary.

THE TOP TEN INTERNATIONAL SCHOLARSHIPS FOR NON-U.S. STUDENTS

1. Like sushi? Then you may want to contact the **Association of International Education** in Japan. Programs of six months to one year are offered to international undergraduate and graduate students to pursue studies in Japan.

2. Fish and chips anyone? Female graduate students from any country may contact **The British Federation of Women Graduates** if they wish to pursue study and/or research in Great Britain.

3. Graduate students under age 31 can receive a stipend to spend one academic year in South Africa through the **South African Department of Arts, Culture, Science, and Technology.** Available to those who wish to gather information for a thesis or study project which they are working on for their home university.

4. Want to study somewhere between the Statue of Liberty and the Golden Gate Bridge? The **American Association of University Women Educational Foundation** offers non-U.S. citizens the opportunity to pursue full-time study or research in the U.S. Must be female graduate or postgraduate students.

5. Do you speak German? If so, and you are between 20 and 35, the **Austrian Cultural Institute** offers awards to doctoral and advanced graduate students from around the world to pursue study and research in Austria.

6. If you have ever written a letter to a friend about your experience in a foreign country, then you should contact **World of Knowledge.** This was one of their past contests, and new ones are created each year for international graduate students who will be attending college in the U.S.

7. Danish citizens wishing to study in the U.K. should contact the **Anglo-Danish Society.** Awards of up to 175 pounds/month are given for up to six months of study.

8. Students in various European countries can apply to the **Netherlands Organization for International Cooperation in Higher Education.** Grants are given for study in the Netherlands.

9. The **International Council for Canadian Studies** offers many opportunities for Canadian citizens to pursue study or research at the graduate or postgraduate level in various countries. Must have a working knowledge of the relevant language of instruction.

10. Students of Mongolian heritage who are citizens of Mongolia, the People's Republic of China, and the former Soviet Union can receive a scholarship from the **Mongolia Society.** Awards allow students to pursue studies in the U.S.

THE TOP TEN INTERNATIONAL SCHOLARSHIPS FOR U.S. STUDENTS

1. Ever wondered what school is like in another country? College students may apply to the **Rotary Foundation of Rotary International** for the opportunity to study in a foreign country. Both student's home country and country of intended study must have Rotary Clubs.

2. Gesundheit! U.S. citizens who are sophomores or juniors in high school don't even have to know what that means if they join **Youth for Understanding International Exchange** to Germany. Students with a minimum 3.0 GPA live with a host family in Germany, and there is no language requirement.

3. Mama Mia! Undergraduate and graduate students of Italian ancestry can receive $2,000 from the **National Italian American Foundation** to pursue studies in Italy. Academic merit, community service, and financial need are considered.

4. **Zeta Phi Beta Sorority Educational Foundation** provides $500-$1,000 to U.S. undergraduate and graduate students planning to study abroad. Awards also given to foreign students wishing to study in the U.S.

5. Ever wondered what living with an international family would be like? High school students wishing to attend secondary school in another country should contact **AFS Intercultural Programs.** Students from fifty different countries live with host families in this international exchange.

6. Bundle up and head to Scandinavia with the **Centre for International Mobility.** CIMO and The Fulbright Center offer graduate scholarships to U.S. citizens under 35 years of age to study and carry out research in Finland.

7. Bienvenue a France! U.S. citizens accepted to or enrolled full-time at the **Institute for American Universities** in Cedex, France may receive $500 to aid with tuition.

8. You'll be smashing plates you're so excited when you hear from the **Cyprus Children's Fund.** They award scholarships to U.S. citizens and U.S. residents of Greek or Greek Cypriot heritage who wish to pursue studies in Greece or Cyprus. Greek and Cyprus citizens may receive awards to study in the U.S.

9. The **Youth Foundation, Inc.** offers scholarships for a U.S. undergraduate's junior year abroad. Selection is based on character, need, scholastic achievement, objective, motivation, potential for leadership, and good citizenship.

10. Want to get away? Various scholarships are awarded by the **Institute for the International Education of Students** for studying abroad in many different countries. Organization encourages students with a wide variety of interests and abilities and who represent a wide range of social and economic backgrounds.

THE TOP TEN CELEBRITY SCHOLARSHIPS

1. The proof is in the pudding! **Bill Cosby** and his wife, Camille, have been acclaimed "The First Family of Philanthropy" for their generous donations to various colleges in excess of $28 million dollars. Contact Spellman College.

2. The **Eddie Murphy/Paramount Pictures $25,000 Writing Fellowship.** Silver Screen? Let your talent shine with a postgraduate film and television writing internship at Paramount Pictures presented to eligible bachelor-degree grads of Hampton and Howard Universities who are tuned into television and screen writing. Check with these colleges.

3. The cost of college doesn't go for the price of peanuts these days, so **The Scripps Howard Foundation** is offering the **Charles M. Schultz Award.** $2,500 for an outstanding college cartoonist working at a college newspaper or magazine. Don't be a Blockhead! Apply!

4. "Average yet creative" is the punchline for junior telecommunications majors at Ball State University. **The David Letterman Telecommunications Scholarship Program** could pay your way to graduation if you are an average student with a very creative mind.

5. Don't make a big production out of the high cost of filmmaking! All it takes is "Forty Acres and a Mule"! **Spike Lee** and **Columbia Pictures** offer production fellowships to students in their second or third year of graduate study at the New York University Tisch School of Film. Two $5,000 fellowships are awarded per year to graduates rolling in action in production, filmmaking, and acting. Contact Tisch School of Film.

6. This is certainly one house with high equity! Morehouse College received $1 million dollars from celebrity Oprah Winfrey to establish the **Oprah Winfrey Endowed Scholarship Fund.** Contact Morehouse College.

7. Is the cost of college a dramatization? The right stage for you could be **Debbie Allen** and **Phylicia Rashad's** applause for their father in the **Dr. Andrew Allen Creative Arts Scholarship** of $15,000. A command performance is requested from undergraduate juniors and seniors at Howard University who portray excellence in drama, song, and dance.

8. Are you between the ages of 17 and 22 living in the Golden State or the Lone Star State? If you are a Mexican-American resident of California or Texas and in an undergraduate program, you may just strike gold with the **Vikki Carr Scholarship** of up to $3,000!

9. College costs driving you up the wall? Go ahead and dance on the ceiling! **Lionel Richie** has made students of Tuskegee University lighter than air with his $500,000 donation for an endowment in the business school at Tuskegee. Contact Tuskegee University.

10. Well Hee-Haw, Y'all! Miniere's Network offers the **Minnie Pearl Scholarships** to financially needy high school seniors who have a significant bilateral hearing loss, good grades, and who have been accepted for enrollment by an accredited university, college, or technical school.

THE TOP TEN CORPORATE SCHOLARSHIPS

1. How sweet it is! **Sara Lee Corporation** employees and their children can apply for a student loan of up to $2,500 for study at an accredited institution.

2. Calling all high school seniors! **GTE** offers scholarships to dependents of full-time employees who are planning to begin full-time study at an accredited undergraduate college or university.

3. Would you like fries with that? **McDonald's Golden Arches Scholarships** are served to New York Tri-State residents planning to attend their first year of college full-time. Must be U.S. citizens/permanent residents and show evidence of either community service or employment.

4. Are you a high school senior searching for college tuition? You CAN go to school with help from the **American National Can Company** scholarship program. These scholarships are available for undergraduate study to dependents of company employees.

5. You'll know more than your ABC's if you take advantage of the **Capital Cities / ABC, Inc.** Merit Scholarship Programs. These awards are open to dependent children of Capital Cities / ABC employees.

6. Need a Midas touch in searching for scholarships? The **Midas International Corporation** offers scholarships to dependents of current Midas employees.

7. Want to "bank" on your college education? If you are a high school senior and are a dependent of a **Citibank** employee, you can receive a scholarship of up to $5,000 for undergraduate study.

8. **Philip Morris** offers a scholarship program "to-bacc-you" in your scholarship quest. Open to children of full-time employees.

9. Don't be derailed by the cost of a college education! The **Union Pacific Railroad** offers an Employee Dependent Scholarship Program to high school seniors in the top 1/4 of their class.

10. Dependents of **Levi Strauss & Company** employees aren't blue! They can apply for scholarships of up to $1,000 for full-time undergraduate study.

THE TOP TEN SCHOLARSHIPS FOR WOMEN

1. The **California Junior Miss Program** scholarship competition is open to girls in their junior year of high school who are U.S. citizens and California residents. Winner receives $15,000 for books, fees, and tuition at any college in the world.

2. Fore! The **Women's Western Golf Foundation** has $2,000/year awaiting female high school seniors who are U.S. citizens and who have high academic standing, financial need, and an involvement with golf—skill is NOT a criterion!

3. You don't need to see it to believe it! The **National Federation of the Blind** (Hermione Grant Calhoun Scholarship) offers $3,000 to legally blind women who are undergraduate or graduate students studying in any field.

4. For women re-entry students, the **Jeanette Rankin Foundation** awards $1,000 to the winning woman aged 35 or older who is a U.S. citizen enrolled in a program of voc-tech training or in an undergraduate program.

5. Are you a female undergraduate in the field of science or social science? If so, you can apply to the **Association for Women in Science Educational Foundation's** *Dr. Vicki L. Schechtman Scholarship.* Award for U.S. citizens with a minimum 3.0 GPA, and may be used for tuition, books, housing, research, equipment, etc.

6. Don't beat around the bush. Contact the **Landscape Architecture Foundation** (Harriett Barnhart Wimmer Scholarship), which offers $1,000 to women who have demonstrated excellent design ability in landscape architecture, have sensitivity to the environment, and who are going into their final year of undergraduate study.

7. For modern-day Rosie the Riveters, the **Society of Women Engineers** (General Electric Foundation Scholarship) offers $1,000 to women who are U.S. citizens studying engineering or computer science. Must be high school seniors entering an accredited school as freshmen.

8. The **Astrae National Lesbian Action Foundation** (Margot Karle Scholarship) gives $500 to women students whose career path or extracurricular activities demonstrate political or social commitment to fighting for the civil rights of gays and lesbians.

9. Are you a college-bound high school senior girl? **Mervyn's California/Women's Sports Foundation Scholarship Fund** has $1,000 for you if you're involved in athletics. The program is not limited to California residents.

10. Love to fly? The **International Society of Women Airline Pilots** (ISA International Career Scholarship) offers $500-$1,500 to women throughout the world who are pursuing careers as airline pilots and have at least 750 hours of flight experience.

THE TOP TEN SCHOLARSHIPS FOR MEN

1. Have you earned your merit badge? The **Fred A. Bryan Collegiate Students Fund** (Trust Fund Scholarships) offers scholarships for male graduates of South Bend High School in Indiana with preference to those who have been Boy Scouts. Recipients receive between $1,400 and $1,600 for undergraduate study at an accredited college or university.

2. The **Phi Kappa Theta National Foundation** (Scholarship Program) offers undergraduate scholarships to members of the Phi Kappa Theta fraternity. Five scholarships are awarded based on financial need.

3. Male opera singers who are from the land down under may apply for the *Sir Robert Askin Operatic Travelling Scholarship* offered by **Arts Management P/L.** Australian citizenship is required, and you must be between the ages of 18-30.

4. Do you belong to the NAACP? The **NAACP National Office** offers the *Willems Scholarship* for male members of the NAACP studying engineering, chemistry, physics, or mathematics. Undergraduates receive $2,000, and the graduate award is $3,000.

5. American males of Anglo-Saxon or German descent should contact the **Maud Glover Folsom Foundation, Inc.** which offers $2,500 to those under age 35. For use in prep school, high school, college, and advanced education.

6. The **Boys & Girls Clubs of San Diego** (Spence Reese Scholarship Fund) offer scholarships to male high school students planning a career in medicine, law, engineering, or political science. Preference to students who live within a 250-mile radius of San Diego. Boys Club affiliation is not required.

7. Your prayers have been answered! The **Elmer O. & Ida Preston Educational Trust** (Grants and Loans) offers an award that is half-grant and half-loan to male residents of Iowa who are pursuing a collegiate or professional study at an Iowa college or university. Applicants must be planning on a career in Christian ministry and must provide a recommendation from a minister commenting on the student's potential.

8. Strike! The **Young American Bowling Alliance** offers the *Chuck Hall Star of Tomorrow Scholarship* of $4,000 to male students who are amateur bowlers and members of ABC or YABA up to age 21. Must be a high school senior or an undergraduate attending college.

9. The **Raymond J. Harris Education Trust** offers scholarships of various amounts to Christian males for use at nine Philadelphia area colleges. Students must be studying medicine, law, engineering, dentistry, or agriculture.

10. Fill your financial cavities with funds from the **American Dental Hygienists Association.** They have several scholarships designated for under-represented groups in that field, specifically minorities and men.

THE TOP TEN SCHOLARSHIPS FOR MINORITIES

1. The **Council on International Educational Exchange** offers *Bailey Minority Scholarships* of $500 for minorities studying in any field. Awards are for study, work, volunteer, and home-stay programs almost anywhere in the world.

2. Ethnic minority students enrolled at accredited colleges or universities who can demonstrate financial need and academic excellence may qualify for $2,500 *Lena Chang Scholarship* awards from the **Nuclear Age Peace Foundation.** Two letters of recommendation and an essay on ways to achieve peace in the Nuclear Age and how one hopes to contribute to that end are required.

3. Minority undergraduates with at least a 3.0 GPA desiring to spend a semester or summer studying in a participating foreign university and who demonstrate leadership potential and extracurricular involvement in multicultural or international issues may qualify for *International Scholarships for Minorities* from the **American Institute for Foreign Study.** There is one scholarship that consists of full program fees and transportation, and there are also five semester scholarships of $1,000.

4. The **Jackie Robinson Foundation** offers scholarships of $5,000 per year for four years to minority high school seniors who are college-bound. The program includes counseling, assistance in obtaining summer jobs, and permanent employment after graduation.

5. Ethnic minorities with disabilities and ethnic minorities with disabilities who are gifted and talented meet the criteria for *Stanley E. Jackson Scholarship Awards* of $500 from the **Foundation for Exceptional Children.**

6. The **Aviation Scholarship Foundation** offers opportunities for minority or low-income students in the Chicago area to take a one-year-long program of weekend flight training.

7. Women of color who are interested in the fields of sports, physical education, and other sports-related careers have the opportunity to receive *Jackie Joyner-Kersee/Zina Garrison Minority Scholarships* of $4,000-$5,000 from the **Women's Sports Foundation.**

8. High school seniors have new windows of opportunity with the **Gates Millennium Scholars Program.** School faculty may nominate African American, Native American, Hispanic, and Asian American students planning to enter college. Awards are based on academic performance in math and science, school activities, leadership potential, and need. Must be U.S. citizen.

9. Disadvantaged and/or minority students entering a program leading to a B.A. or M.A. in architecture may have the ability to receive scholarships from the *Minority/Disadvantaged Scholarship Program* offered by the **American Institute of Architects/American Architectural Foundation.**

10. The **American Association of Law Libraries** offers a *George A. Straight Minority Stipend Grant* of $3,500 to a minority group member who is a college graduate with library experience and is working toward an advanced degree that could further his or her law library career.

THE TOP TEN RELIGIOUS SCHOLARSHIPS

1. The **David and Dovetta Wilson Scholarship Fund** offers scholarships of $1,000 to college-bound high school seniors who are U.S. citizens and are selected for their academic achievement, involvement in the community, and religious activities.

2. The **Memorial Foundation for Jewish Culture** offers an *International Scholarship Program for Community Service,* which is open to any individual, regardless of country of origin, for undergraduate study that leads to careers in the Rabbinate, Jewish education, social work, or religious functionaries outside the U.S., Israel, and Canada. Must commit to serve in a community of need for three years.

3. Scholarships are being offered to high school graduates who are from the southeastern U.S. and who wish to study ministry, missionary work, or social work by **The Heath Education Fund.**

4. The **American Foundation for the Blind** offers a *Gladys C. Anderson Memorial Scholarship* of $1,000 to a woman who is legally blind and studying religious or classical music at the college level. A sample performance tape of voice or instrumental selection is required.

5. Various scholarships for students in the field of pastoral (religious) music are available from the **National Association of Pastoral Musicians.** Applying students must be a member of this organization in order to receive a scholarship.

6. **Women of the Evangelical Lutheran Church in America** offers *Belmer-Flora Prince Scholarships* for women who are ELCA members planning on studying for ELCA service abroad that does not lead to a church-certified profession. Women must be U.S. citizens, over the age of 21, and have experienced an interruption in schooling for at least two years since high school.

7. The *Leonard M. Perryman Communications Scholarship for Ethnic Minority Students* of $2,500 is offered by the **United Methodist Church** to an ethnic minority undergraduate junior or senior who is enrolled in an accredited school of communications or journalism. The student must have a Christian faith and be pursuing a career in religious communications.

8. Ministerial students who are enrolled in a master's program in theology that may be leading to ordination in a main-line Christian denomination could possibly qualify for **Harding Foundation** grants of $2,400/year.

9. The **Presbyterian Church (U.S.A.)** offers its members scholarships if they are high school seniors planning to pursue full-time studies at participating colleges. Must be U.S. citizens/permanent residents and show financial need.

10. The *Earnest and Eurice Miller Bass Scholarship Fund* offers scholarships to undergraduate students who are members of the **United Methodist Church** and planning careers in the ministry or other religious careers.

THE TOP TEN KINDERGARTEN TO 12TH-GRADE SCHOLARSHIPS

1. Students in grades 7-12 have the opportunity to win up to $5,000 from **Alliance for Young Artists and Writers, Inc.** All that is required is the ability to demonstrate a talent in art, photography, writing, or interdisciplines. Cash grants are awarded and can be used for any field of study.

2. Have you ever had the desire to fly? The **Stephen M. Price Foundation** is giving boys and girls between the ages of 14 and 16 who are economically disadvantaged and reside in the area of Jacksonville, Florida, the opportunity to earn a private pilot's license.

3. The **Veterans of Foreign Wars of the United States** have an annual *Voice of Democracy Audio-Essay Scholarship Contest.* The contest is open to students in tenth, eleventh, and twelfth grades who attend public, private, and parochial high schools. Awards range from $1,000 to $20,000.

4. It has become easier for needy students in Washington to attend private schools. The **Washington Scholarship Fund** is offering up to $1,700 per year to students in grades K-12.

5. **AFS Intercultural Programs** has created the *International Exchange Student Program* to give high school students the opportunity to study abroad for a semester or a year with financial assistance. Students live with host families and attend local secondary schools.

6. Students between the ages of 6 and 21 and who have moderate to profound hearing loss are being given the opportunity to win scholarships by the **Alexander Graham Bell Association for the Deaf.** In order to qualify, students must use speech and residual hearing and/or speechreading as a primary form of communication.

7. The **John Edgar Thomson Foundation** is offering financial assistance to the daughters of deceased railroad workers between the ages of infancy and 22 depending on whether or not a higher education is sought.

8. Financially needy Hawaiian residents who are orphans, half-orphans, social orphans (neglected or abused), or children born out-of-wedlock are being offered scholarships for preschool, summer programs, private schools, and college by the **Teresa F. Hughes Trust.**

9. Scholarships and awards can be earned by students who participate in a sewing, knitting, or crocheting competition. **The National Make It Yourself with Wool Competition** involves creating a wool garment from a current pattern. The fabric must contain at least 60% wool.

10. Students in grades 4-12 can enter an essay competition and possibly receive an award to help with full to partial tuition to Space Camp. This competition was created by the **U.S. Space Camp Foundation.**

THE TOP TEN TRAVEL SCHOLARSHIPS

1. Have you completed two years of university coursework or the equivalent in professional experience? If so, the **Rotary Foundation of Rotary International** is offering to pay up to $23,000/year for you to travel and study internationally.

2. If you are a female athlete and you enjoy to travel, then here is the perfect opportunity for you. The **Women's Sports Foundation** is giving up to $1,500 to individual athletes and up to $3,000 to teams. These grants are available for training, coaching, equipment, and travel.

3. You may get starry eyed just thinking about it. The **International Astronomical Union** is offering to pay for the travel expenses of graduate students, postdoctoral fellows, or faculty-staff members at any recognized educational research institution or observatory in order to visit institutions abroad for at least three months.

4. **Woods Hole Oceanographic Institute** is awarding a $3,900 stipend and possible travel allowance to students who have completed their junior year of college or are beginning graduate school. They must be studying in any field of science with an interest in oceanography. The students will travel to Woods Hole, MA, and study there for twelve weeks during the summer.

5. The **Archaeological Institute of America** is offering $3,000 to a college graduate who is interested in working on a scholarly project relating to Aegean Bronze Age archaeology. Preference goes to the projects that require travel to the Mediterranean.

6. Are you interested in studying leprosy or tuberculosis? The **Heiser Program for Research in Leprosy and/or Tuberculosis** is coughing up as much as $28,000 plus travel allowance in postdoctoral fellowships and research grants.

7. If you can speak and read French, German, or Dutch, then you just might qualify for a graduate fellowship in Belgium. The *Belgian American Educational Foundation* is offering ten awards per year to applicants who have a master's degree or who are working toward a Ph.D. The award includes round-trip travel to Belgium, living expenses, tuition, and fees.

8. Do you ever feel the need to escape to a foreign country for a few months? If you are a minority student with a 2.0 GPA or higher, you just might qualify to spend the summer abroad. **Youth for Understanding International Exchange** chooses forty students every year to spend a summer in select countries where they will live with host families.

9. Have you ever wondered what it would be like to live in a castle? The **Giacomo Leopardi Center** is offering to pay the tuition and travel expenses for the first three hundred students who apply. The school is located in Italy and it teaches the Italian language and culture.

10. High school sophomores, juniors, and seniors are being given the opportunity to spend two or three weeks at sites in North or Central America by the **Earthwatch Student Challenge Awards.** This gives them the opportunity to have an intimate look at the world of science and state-of-the-art technology.

THE TOP TEN ARTS SCHOLARSHIPS

1. Action! **The Christophers** offers a film and video contest for college students to create an image expressing an annual topic. Awards are based on ability to capture theme, artistic/professional proficiency, and adherence to rules.

2. Calling all Americans! The **Ladies Auxiliary to the Veterans of Foreign Wars of the United States** gives high school students an opportunity to express their patriotism through art. Annual awards are given for works on paper or canvas in a variety of styles.

3. U.S. citizens of Japanese ancestry may wish to join the **Japanese American Citizens League** to be eligible for their creative arts award. Undergraduate and graduate students should create projects that reflect the Japanese-American experience and culture.

4. Are you a drama geek? The **Princess Grace Foundation** offers scholarships for students under age 25 in acting, directing, and design at U.S. schools.

5. Aspiring Austrian artists and architects who wish to ply their trade in the U.S. should contact the **Austrian Cultural Institute.** Grants are available to spend time at the Mak Center in Los Angeles, which has a year-round schedule of exhibitions, symposia, lectures, performances, workshops, and publications.

6. Want to see how Buzz and Woody came to life? **Pixar Animation Studios** offers summer internships for college and university students to obtain "hands on" experience in animation.

7. Playwrights and composers should submit an original full-length play or musical to the **Stanley Drama Award Competition.** Work must not have been professionally produced or received tradebook publication.

8. Are you the next Picasso? The **Canada Council for the Arts** offers grants to young and established professional Canadian artists. Program is designed to give artists free time necessary for personal creative activity and to help them improve their skills in performing arts, visual/media arts, or creative writing.

9. High school seniors and 17- to 18-year-olds in the creative and performing arts should contact **The National Foundation for Advancement in the Arts** to enter their talent contest. Areas include dance, jazz, music, photography, theatre, visual arts, voice, and writing.

10. **National Scholarship Trust Fund of the Graphic Arts** provides high school seniors, undergraduates, and graduate students with scholarships and fellowships in printing, publishing, and graphic technology. Minimum 3.0 GPA required.

THE TOP TEN ATHLETIC SCHOLARSHIPS

1. Fore! U.S. high school seniors who have served as a caddie at a WGA member club may apply for a scholarship from the **Western Golf Association.** Must be in the top 25% of your class, have outstanding personal character, and demonstrate financial need.

2. The **Francis Ouimet Scholarship Fund** offers scholarships to Massachusetts residents who have worked as golf caddies, in pro shops, or as superintendents of operations at a Massachusetts golf course.

3. NCAA student-athletes can receive scholarships from the **National Collegiate Athletic Association** for graduate or undergraduate study, depending on GPA and financial need. Must be nominated by a faculty athletics representative at your school.

4. Do you want to be the next Picaboo Street? The **Women's Sports Foundation** provides financial assistance to female athletes and women pursuing sports-related careers.

5. Kansas students who have participated in high school athletics may apply to the **American Legion of Kansas** for their scholarship to be used at any Kansas college, university, or trade school.

6. Whoa! The **National Horseshoe Pitchers Association** gives awards to students under age 18 who compete in a horseshoe pitching league.

7. The **Community Foundation of Western Massachusetts** offers scholarships to graduating seniors of Gateway Regional High School in Huntington, MA, and Longmeadow High School in Longmeadow, MA. Must have a strong interest in and have excelled in athletics.

8. Caddies at New Jersey golf clubs can receive undergraduate scholarships from the **New Jersey State Golf Association.** Awards based on scholastic achievement, financial need, and length of service as a caddie.

9. Are you a high school jock? Seniors who are involved in some type of athletics can apply to **Footaction USA** if they have a minimum 2.0 GPA and are U.S. citizens.

10. The **Aromando Family Educational Foundation** offers scholarships to aspiring teachers and theologians of Italian ancestry who are practicing Roman Catholics with a minimum 3.0 GPA. Must have at least two varsity letters in one or more high school sanctioned athletic or extracurricular programs.

TOP TEN AVIATION SCHOLARSHIPS

1. Love to fly? Scholarships are being made available for students studying in the fields of aviation and aerospace by the **Ninety-Nines, Inc. International.** Eligibility requirements vary.

2. Calling all Amelia Earharts! The **International Society of Women Airline Pilots** offers scholarships to women who are interested in pursuing careers in flying the world's airlines. Applicants must have a U.S. FAA Commercial Pilot Certificate with an Instrument Rating and a First Class medical. They also must have 750 flight hours.

3. Undergraduate juniors and seniors who have scholastic plans leading to future participation in the aerospace sciences and technologies have the ability to win the *Dr. Robert H. Goddard Space Science and Engineering Scholarship* from the **National Space Club.**

4. Do you prefer the business end of aviation? Then contact the **Aviation Distributors and Manufacturers Association International.** They offer scholarships to students pursuing careers in aviation management or as professional pilots.

5. Do you prefer whirlybirds? The **Vertical Flight Foundation** is giving scholarships to undergraduate and graduate students who have proven interests in pursuing careers in some aspect of helicopter or vertical flight. The scholarships are up to $2,000.

6. The Eagle has landed! Minority graduate students who are studying in the fields of science and engineering qualify for **National Aeronautics and Space Administration Scholarships** if they are considering a career in space science and/or aerospace technology.

7. Stand at attention! CAP cadets pursuing studies in Ground and Air Training for FAA private pilot licenses qualify for a $2,100 *Major Gen. Lucas V. Beau Flight Scholarship* which is being offered by the **Civil Air Patrol.**

8. Do you copy, 10-4? The **Aircraft Electronics Association Educational Foundation** offers scholarships to students who are studying avionics and/or aircraft repair and who are attending post-secondary institutions, including technical schools.

9. Fasten your seatbelts! Students who have a GPA of at least a 3.0 and have completed half of their course of study may qualify for an *Al and Art Mooney Scholarship* of $1,000 which is offered by **Mooney Aircraft Pilots Association Safety Foundation.** Applicants must be a member of MAPA and have a career objective that would promote flight safety.

10. Are you a daredevil? The **EAA Aviation Foundation** offers two *Aviation Achievement Scholarships* of $500 and up annually to individuals who are active in sport aviation. The scholarships are to be used in order to further the recipients' aviation education training.

Recommendations by Dan Cassidy and Colleagues

By using this book to track down all your potential sources of funding, you may need additional help. Following are some excellent sources that NSRS recommends. (Note: These are also listed in the "Helpful Publications" section.)

LAST-MINUTE COLLEGE FINANCING, $20. Whether your child starts college in 15 years or next semester, this helpful guide answers such questions as "How do I get the money together in time?" "How do I locate quality low-cost colleges?" and "How do I find sources of financial aid that I may have overlooked?"

KIT: LAST-MINUTE COLLEGE FINANCING (book), SCHOLARSHIP RADIO SHOW (audio cassette), KIDS, COLLEGE, & CASH (VHS tape), $35. Resources to help students in their search for financial aid.

COLLEGE-BOUND FAMILY LIBRARY, $142. A package of books, booklets, audio, and video tapes that should be in the library of every family who has children. What colleges have the programs best suited for your child? What resources are available to you to help you pay for college? Contact NSRS for a complete list of this package.

GUIDE TO TRAVEL GRANTS, $20. An eighty-page booklet containing hundreds of sources of funding for travel in various fields of study and professions.

FLY BUCKS, $20. A thirty-page booklet containing over eighty sources of funding for education in aeronautics, aviation, aviation electronics, aviation writing, space science, aviation maintenance technology, and vertical flight.

GUIDE TO PRIVATE SECTOR KINDERGARTEN-12TH GRADE SCHOLARSHIPS, $20. A 90-page booklet of scholarships for elementary and secondary private schools with introduction on how to apply.

Write or phone:
National Scholarship Research Service
Box 6694
Santa Rosa, California 95406-0694
707/546-6777

THE MEMORY KEY, $12.99. Practical, easy-to-use handbook helps students with study skills and anyone dealing with information overload, shedding light on how memory works and what you need to do to achieve memory improvement.

DEBT-FREE GRADUATE: HOW TO SURVIVE COLLEGE WITHOUT GOING BROKE, $13.99. Tells students how they can stay out of debt while taking simple and easy measures, while still having the time of their lives at college.

HOW TO STUDY, $12.99. Includes how to create work environment, excel in class, use the library, do research online, and more.

GREAT BIG BOOK OF HOW TO STUDY, $15.95. More than 400 pages of useful information and advice, written in a direct, motivational style that will help students regain the confidence they need to succeed in school.

ADVENTURE CAREERS, $11.99. This comprehensive source for information about completely different and decidedly unroutine career paths is packed with practical how-to's, lists of contacts, and first-hand experiences.

THE CAREER ATLAS, $12.99. Details education and experience requirements for 400 career paths within 40 occupational areas.

COLLEGE SURVIVAL INSTRUCTION BOOK, $6.99. Filled with tips, advice, suggestions, and secrets for making your college life more interesting and rewarding.

101 GREAT ANSWERS TO THE TOUGHEST INTERVIEW QUESTIONS, $11.99. For part-time job seekers or those seeking permanent careers, this guide includes overview of the interviewing process and covers a full range of possible interview topics.

CREATIVE GUIDE TO RESEARCH, $16.99. Guide for students, professionals, and others pursuing research, describing how to find what you need, online or offline.

"ACE" ANY TEST, $8.99. Walks test-takers through successful test preparation, including reading for maximum retention, researching the teacher's test-giving history, and "psyching up" for test day.

Write or phone:
Career Press, Inc.
3 Tice Road, P.O. Box 687
Franklin Lakes, NJ 07417
800/CAREER-1

ACADEMIC YEAR ABROAD, $44.95 and $5.00 handling. The most complete guide to planning study abroad describes over 1,900 postsecondary study programs outside the U.S. Concise descriptions provide the information you need on costs, academic programs and credits, dates and application, and more.

VACATION STUDY ABROAD, $39.95. Describes over 1,800 summer or short-term study abroad sponsored by United States colleges and universities and foreign institutions. All orders must be prepaid. IIE pays domestic postage.

If you have questions write or phone:
Institute of International Education (IIE)
Publications Service, IIE
809 United Nations Plaza, New York, NY 10017
212/984-5330

MAKING IT THROUGH COLLEGE, $1.00. Handy booklet describing how to make it through college. Includes information on how to cope with competition, getting organized, study techniques, solving work overloads, and much more.

Write to:
Professional Staff Congress
25 West 43rd Street, 5th Floor
New York, NY 10036

TEN STEPS IN WRITING THE RESEARCH PAPER, $9.95. Arranged to lead the student step-by-step through the writing of a research paper from finding a suitable subject to checking the final copy. Easy enough for the beginner, complete enough for the graduate student. 177 pages.

Write to:
Barron's Educational Series Inc.
250 Wireless Blvd.
Hauppauge, NY 11788

NEED A LIFT? $3. Outstanding guide to education and employment opportunities. Contains complete information on the financial aid process (how, when, and where to start), scholarships, loans, and career information addresses.

Write to:
American Legion National Emblem Sales
P.O. Box 1055
Indianapolis, IN 46206

COLLEGE FINANCIAL AID EMERGENCY KIT, $6.95 (prepaid). 40-page booklet filled with tips on how to meet the costs of tuition, room and board, and fees. Tells what is available, whom to ask, and how to ask!

Write to:
Sun Features Inc.
Box 368 (Kit)
Cardiff, CA 92007

COLLEGE FINANCIAL AID FOR DUMMIES, $19.99. Dr. Herm Davis and Joyce Lain Kennedy suggest "great ways to pay without going broke." For high school and college students and adults returning to school.

See website, call, or write:
IDG Books Worldwide, Inc.
919 E. Hillsdale Blvd., Suite 400
Foster City, CA 94404
800/762-2974
www.dummies.com

THE CARE BOOK (College Aid Resources for Education), $29.95. This publication was developed by Dr. Herm Davis to be a hands-on daily reference for counselors as well as for families. It assists students in finding statistics on colleges and comparing college costs, enrollments, form requirements, etc. Includes a CD-ROM money planner.

Write or phone:
National College Scholarship Foundation, Inc. (NCSF)
16728 Frontenac Terrace
Rockville, MD 20855
301/548-9423

FISKE GUIDE TO COLLEGES, $18. Describes the 265 top-rated four-year colleges in the U.S. and rates for academics, social life, and quality of life.

Write to:
Times Books
400 Hahn Road
Westminster, MD 21157

INDEX OF MAJORS AND GRADUATE DEGREES, $18.95 plus $4.00 postage and applicable tax. Describes over 600 major programs of study at 3,200 undergraduate and graduate schools. Also lists schools with religious affiliations, special academic programs, and special admissions procedures.

Write to:
College Board Publications
Two College Way
Forrester Center, WV 25438

PETERSON'S GUIDE TO FOUR-YEAR COLLEGES, $24.95. Detailed profiles of over 1,900 accredited four-year colleges in the U.S. and Canada. Also includes entrance difficulty directory, majors directory, and college cost directory.

PETERSON'S GUIDE TO TWO-YEAR COLLEGES, $19.96. Includes information on 1,600 junior and community colleges in the U.S. and Canada, listing programs offered, tuition costs, and financial aid available.

If you are somewhat undecided on the question of a career,
simply browsing through the myriad possibilities may spark an unexpected interest.
—Business Week

See website or write to:
Peterson's Inc.
P.O. Box 2123
Princeton, NJ 08543-2123
www.petersons.com

COLLEGE DEGREES BY MAIL AND MODEM, $12.95 plus $4.50 shipping and handling. John Bear, Ph.D., describes every approach known to earning a degree without ever taking a single traditional course! It lists 100 reputable colleges that offer bachelors, masters, doctorates, and law degrees through home study. The book also lists colleges reputed to be diploma mills and cautions against them.

Write to:
Ten Speed Press
P.O. Box 7123
Berkeley, CA 94707

HOW TO WIN A SPORTS SCHOLARSHIP, $19.95 plus $3.00 shipping and handling. This is an easy-to-use workbook that teaches high school students and their families a step-by-step process for winning sports scholarships. You don't have to be a superstar! $100,000 scholarships offered in 35 sports each year! Over $500 million awarded annually! There is a special section for female athletes. 250 pages.

Write to:
Hastings Communications
P.O. Box 14927
Santa Rosa, CA 95402

SPORTS FOR HER, $45.00 plus $4.00 shipping and handling. This reference guide for teenage girls explores high school sports from a girl's perspective and examines sports issues as they pertain to young women. Provides practical advice on training and practicing techniques, trying out for the team, and organizing school teams. Includes advice on possible sports-related problems for girls. 264 pages.

Write to:
Greenwood Publishing Group
88 Post Road West, P.O. Box 5007
Westport, CT 06881-5007

LANGUAGE LIAISON PROGRAM DIRECTORY, Free. Want to learn another language? Learn it like a native in the country where it is spoken. New programs start every week year-round from two weeks to a year long. Programs are open to students, teachers, executives, teens, seniors, families, and leisure travelers. Includes activities, excursions, and homestays.

See website or write to:
Language Liaison
1610 Woodstead Ct., Suite 130
The Woodlands TX 77380
www.languageliaison.com

WHERE THERE'S A WILL, THERE'S AN A, $44.95. Videotape seminars for college and high school students on how to get better grades.

See website or write to:
Olney "A" Seminars
P.O. Box 686
Scottsdale, AZ 85252-0686
www.wheretheresawill.com

HOMESCHOOLING ALMANAC, $24.95. Mary & Michael Leppert's all-encompassing guide includes more than 900 educational products, such as books/magazines, software, videos, games, crafts, science kits, prepackaged curricula, cybersources, methods, etc. Provides state-by-state breakdown of legal requirements, support groups, and organizations.

See website or write to:
Prima Publishing
P.O. Box 1260BK
Rocklin, CA 95677
www.primalifestyles.com

FINANCIAL AID FOR MINORITIES, $5.95 each. Several booklets with hundreds of sources of financial aid for minorities. When ordering, please specify which of the following you are interested in: Students of Any Major; Business & Law; Education; Journalism & Mass Communications; Health Fields; or Engineering & Science.

Call or write to:
Garrett Park Press
P.O. Box 190
Garrett Park, MD 20896
301/946-2553

OCCUPATIONAL OUTLOOK HANDBOOK, $16.95. Annual publication designed to assist individuals in selecting appropriate careers. Describes about 250 occupations and includes current and projected job prospects.

CFKR CAREER MATERIALS CATALOG, Free. A catalog of printed materials, software, and videotapes covering career planning, college financing, and college test preparation. For primary grades through graduate school.

See website, call, or write:
CFKR Career Materials
11860 Kemper Road, #7
Auburn, CA 95603
800/525-5626
www.cfkr.com

JOURNALIST'S ROAD TO SUCCESS, $3.00. Comprehensive source book for high school and college students who are interested in journalism careers. Helps choose colleges that offer the best combination of academic programs, practical experience, and scholarships.

NEWSPAPERS, DIVERSITY, AND YOU, Free. Information on grants, scholarships, and internships specifically for minority high school and college students, along with articles written by professional journalists of color.

See website, call, or write:
Dow Jones Newspaper Fund
P.O. Box 300
Princeton, NJ 08543-0300
800/DOW-FUND
www.dj.com/newsfund

HOW TO FIND OUT ABOUT FINANCIAL AID, $37.50. In addition to this guide, Gail Ann Schlachter has written several books on financial aid. Subjects include The Disabled & Their Families; Veterans, Military Personnel, & Their Families; Women; and Minorities.

Call or write:
Reference Service Press
5000 Windplay Drive, Suite 4
El Dorado Hills, CA 95762
916/939-9620

SAMPLE TIME-SAVING FORM LETTER
REQUESTING APPLICATION INFORMATION

Use this sample letter as a guide to create a general letter requesting information. Photocopy your letter and address the envelopes for mailing. Include the name of the scholarship you are applying for with the address on the envelope, so they will know which scholarship(s) you are requesting. Because this information is on the envelope, which you have to personally address anyway, it is not necessary to also include it on the letter. Just make sure your name and address are included, and photocopy the same request to be mailed to all the different sources, keeping it as generic as possible. It isn't time to introduce yourself until you send in the application. Enclosing a self-addressed, stamped envelope may give you a speedier response. Remember to apply well in advance of the deadlines. You should keep a calendar to keep track of them.

Date

Scholarship Program Office

Dear Scholarship Director:

Please send me application forms for any scholarships or fellowships that you might offer. I am enclosing a self-addressed, stamped envelope for your convenience in replying.

Sincerely,

Dick Merwin
5577 Skylane Blvd., Suite 6A
Santa Rosa, California 95403
707/546-6777

THE PLAN

Once you have written to scholarship sources for complete information, you might consider starting three financial aid boxes to maintain your information. You might call them "Government Funding," "School Endowments," and "Private Sector."

The Government Funding Box

Put all information from state and federal programs in this box.

Remember:
Dept. of Education 800/4FED-AID.
800/433-3243

The Coordinating Board for your state is in your phone book under "Government" or call your school.

The School Endowments Box

The college catalog's financial aid section will usually list the endowments and scholarships from alumni and local businesses. Put the catalogs in this box.

The Private Sector Box

This box should contain material you have gleaned from this book and/or from your NSRS personalized and expanded computer printout.

Call 707/546-6777

THE SEARCH

Believe it or not, just about everything about you will come into play in your search for scholarships—your ancestry, religion, place of birth and residence, parent's union or corporate affiliation, your interest in a particular field, or simply by filling out the applicatio—can all be eligibility factors.

Using the tables in this book, the average student will find at least 20 to over 100 different private sector scholarship sources. Next, write to them and ask for their scholarship applications and requirements. *The letter can be a general request for information "form" letter that can be photocopied, but you should be specific about the name of the scholarship you are inquiring about on the envelope. For example, The Cassidy Endowment for Education (XYZ Scholarship).*

Write to each source as far in advance of their scholarship deadline as possible, and don't forget to send a self-addressed, stamped envelope—it not only expedites their reply, it is polite and shows that you care about applying and some organizations do require one.

Remember, on the outside of the envelope, list the name of the specific scholarship you are inquiring about. That way the person opening the mail will know where to direct your inquiry. Replies to these letters should be sorted into the appropriate boxes.

THE GOVERNMENT BOX

Please, please fill out the Free Application for Federal Student Aid (FAFSA) from the federal government. You can get a FAFSA from any high school, junior college, college, university or phone 800/4FED-AID (800/433-3243) or *http://www.fafsa.ed.gov* for web access. Note, the nice thing about this phone number is that you can track your information regarding it being processed and to what schools it was sent to per your request and when. At the very least these state and federal forms are the beginning of your scholarship profile at the financial aid office at the school. Most of the schools are now using these forms for their private endowment-based scholarship. So, even if you do not receive government funding, you will be ready to apply for loans from various outside school sources, such as banks, and the school-based programs, such as school endowments, scholarships, fellowships, grants, loans, college work study, athletic, military ROTC, etc. *So the FAFSA is a must, no matter what!*

On a quiet Saturday or when you have time, sit down and review the information. In the "Government" box, you will find that the state and federal forms are very similar, asking a multitude of questions regarding income, assets, and expenses. Don't automatically exclude yourself from state and federal funding thinking that you or your family make too much money. These programs vary tremendously from state to state and the federal programs have changed quite a bit. For example, there is no longer a $32,500 limit on the amount parents can earn in order to qualify for a student loan; but since that limit has been raised to $45,000, there will be less federal money to go around, so be sure to get in line quickly.

A bit of good news in the student loan arena is that the federal government no longer will consider the value of your house or farm in determining the amount of aid for which you qualify. I cannot stress enough the importance of filing the FAFSA, so please do it no matter what!

THE SCHOOL ENDOWMENTS BOX

You will usually find a list of endowments from alumni listed in the financial aid section of the college catalog. Often endowments to schools are not advertised and may go unclaimed. For example, at a small school like the University of San Francisco, the total endowments average $20 million to $30 million per year. At Ivy League schools, endowments range from $100 million to $200+ million each year. Of those endowments, 10 percent to 15 percent go to the financial aid office in the form of scholarships, fellowships, grants, and loans.

You will discover that sources in the "School Endowments" box are really just other forms of private sector scholarships. The difference is that endowment money is given directly to the school and is administered exclusively by the school's financial aid office, so you must deal directly with the college. You'll find that the myths I talked about earlier also apply to these private endowments—again, don't exclude yourself because of those old clichés regarding your grades, financial status, deadlines, or age.

THE PRIVATE SECTOR BOX

With your "Private Sector" box, you will find that once you have seen one or two forms, you have pretty much seen them all. Usually they are one or two pages asking where you are going to school, what you are going to major in, and why you think you deserve the scholarship. Some scholarship sources require that you join their organization. If the organization relates to your field of study, you should strongly consider joining because it will keep you informed (via newsletters, magazine, etc.) about developments in that field.

Some scholarship organizations may want you to promise that you will work for them for a period of time. The Dow Jones Newspaper Fund offers up to $80,000 in scholarships annually for journalism and mass communications students. In addition, a two-week intensive course (equivalent to advanced editing courses at most journalism departments) is followed by summer employment at a newspaper—interns receive a weekly salary. This could even yield a permanent job for the student.

Source: Discover Card Tribute Award (Scholarship) American Association of School Administrators P.O. Box 9338 Arlington, VA 22219 Telephone: 703/875-0708 Amount(s): $1,000–$20,000 Deadline(s): January Area(s): All fields of study	Include scholarship name as well as organization name & address on envelope. Call if you don't receive application by a month or so before deadline. Don't request info too late! Write at least a month before deadline for an application.
Description: Open to high school juniors whose freshman and sophomore GPA was at least 2.75. Award is based on *financial* merit, not on financial need. Applicants must have achievement in 4 of these 5 areas: special talent, leadership, obstacles overcome, community service, and unique endeavors.	Different foundations have different definitions of need, academic achievement, etc. Don't rule yourself out until you have exact descriptions from the foundations themselves.
Information: A total of 9 scholarships are available in each of the fifty states. Write to Shirley Kennedy Keller at above address for an application.	Don't forget to include contact name if given.

THE ESSAY

Most organizations awarding scholarships require an essay as part of the application process. The essay is the most important part of the private sector scholarship search.

The following excerpt from the University of California at Los Angeles (UCLA) application material emphasizes the importance of the essay and contains good advice no matter where you are going to college:

The essay is an important part of your application for admission and for scholarships.
For these purposes, the University seeks information that will distinguish you from other applicants. You may wish, therefore, to write about your experiences, achievements, and goals. You might, for example, discuss an important life experience and what you learned from it. You might also describe unusual circumstances, challenges, or hardships you have faced. School activities and experiences are also topics to discuss in your essay but they do not need to be the focus.

Rather than listing activities, describe your level of achievement in areas you have pursued—including employment or volunteer activities—and the personal qualities revealed by the time and effort you have devoted to them.

Also, discuss your interest in your intended field of study. If you have a disability, you may also include a description of its impact on your experiences, goals, and aspirations.

The University seeks information about any exceptional achievements such as activities, honors, awards, employment, or volunteer work that demonstrates your motivation, achievement, leadership, and commitment.

Make sure your essay is neatly typed, is well written, and does not contain grammatical errors or misspelled words.

THE APPLICATION

When filling out scholarship application forms, be complete, concise, and creative. People who read these applications want to know the real you, not just your name. Scholarship applications should clearly emphasize your ambitions, motivations, and what makes you different from everyone else. Be original!

Your application should be neatly handwritten or typewritten, and neatness counts. I had a complaint from one foundation about a student who had an excellent background and qualifications but used a crayon to fill out the application.

Once your essay is finished, make a master file of it and other supporting items. Photocopy your essay and attach it to each application. If requested, also include: a resume or curriculum vitae, extracurricular activities sheet (usually one page), transcripts, SAT or ACT scores, letters of recommendation (usually one each from a teacher, employer, and friend) outlining your moral character, and if there are any newspaper articles, etc., about you, it is a good idea to include them, as well.

Application Checklist

The following supporting documents may be requested with your application. I suggest you make a master file for these documents and photocopy them. You can then just pull a copy from your file and attach it to the application upon request.

- ❑ 1. Include your essay.
- ❑ 2. Include extracurricular activities sheet, or
- ❑ 3. Include curriculum vitae if in college, or resume if you are in the job market.
- ❑ 4. Include transcripts.
- ❑ 5. Include SAT or ACT scores.
- ❑ 6. Include letters of recommendation.
- ❑ 7. Include any newspaper articles, etc., about yourself (if you have any).

You might also include your photograph, whether it's a high school picture or a snapshot of you working at your favorite hobby. This helps the selection committee feel a little closer to you. Instead of just seeing a name, they will have a face to match it.

Mail your applications early, at least a month before the deadline.

THE CALENDAR

I also find it helpful to keep a calendar with deadlines circled so you can stay organized. You can hang it above your three scholarship boxes so it is easily visible. Each application should have its own file. On the outside of the file, you might rate your chances of getting the scholarship on a scale of 1 to 10.

If a scholarship application deadline has passed, save it for the next year. If you are turned down for a scholarship, don't worry. Some organizations want to see if you will apply a second time. The important point is to stay motivated and be persistent.

Calendar

Sun	M	T	W	Th	F	Sat
1	2	3	4	5	6	7
8	9	10	11	12	13	14
15	16	17	18	19	20	21
22	23	24	25	26	27	28
29	30	31				

Government Box

Endowment Box

Private Sector Box

Box With Master Files 1–7.

WHERE THE INFORMATION IN THIS BOOK CAME FROM

The information in this book was compiled from the database of the largest private sector college financial aid research service in the world: National Scholarship Research Service (NSRS)™ located in Santa Rosa, California.

Since the late 1970s, NSRS had been using computers to research and update information on potential sources of financial assistance for college students. Many thousands of students have used NSRS's services to locate sources offering financial aid.

NATIONAL SCHOLARSHIP RESEARCH SERVICE (NSRS)™

NSRS computers store information on thousands of private sector aid programs worldwide for all levels of study: from high school freshmen, high school students preparing to enter college, undergraduates doing an associate or bachelors degree, graduate students doing a master's, doctorate, to postdoctoral researchers. Note that there are even scholarships for junior high school 7th and 8th graders, usually contests from groups such as Duracell, DuPont, General Learning Corporation, and many more

NSRS is the only service since 1979 that serves high school freshmen through postdoctorates worldwide! It also is the only service with **Dan Cassidy's Scholarship Alert℠ which automatically informs the scholarship sources for you of your eligibility.** Scholarships will notify you directly of application deadlines and requirements and will mail you their application materials automatically.

Applicants for NSRS services first complete a biographical questionnaire, indicating their particular area(s) of interest. This information is entered into the computer, which searches NSRS files for the scholarships for which the applicant may qualify. Since each applicant has a different background and each of the thousands of aid programs has different requirements, this computer search can save valuable time, money, and often provides students with potential sources of aid for which they might never have considered applying.

If you consider that all the financial aid programs listed in this book are constantly changing—with new application dates, qualifying requirements, etc.—you may want to utilize these services.

Since NSRS is a division of *Cassidy Research Corporation, a California Corporation* since 1979, there is a modest fee for the services provided. For a product list, write or call:

NATIONAL SCHOLARSHIP RESEARCH SERVICES
Box 6694
Santa Rosa, California 95406-0694
24-Hour Phone: 707/546-6777
24-Hour Fax: 707/546-6785
E-mail: NSRS@MSN.COM
Internet: http://www.1800headstart.com

THE WORLDWIDE WEB

National Scholarship Research Service (NSRS)™ is traveling on the World Wide Web's super highway.

Throughout the world you can communicate with "Mr. Scholarship," Daniel J. Cassidy, president and founder of NSRS, by using the worldwide highway at the following NSRS addresses:

NSRS Internet
1800HEADSTART.COM
Example: www.1800headstart.com

Cassidy Endowment for Education (CEE) Internet
a nonprofit public benefit corporation
FASTAP.ORG
Example: www.fastap.org

The Cassidy Endowment for Education (CEE), a public benefit nonprofit organization, is pleased to announce this year that it will be providing scholarships for graduate studies. Please call 707/546-6898 for an application, or visit the website at www.gradstudies.com. If you need help in starting or managing a scholarship, or would just like to donate to the Cassidy Endowment for Education's scholarship program, please phone or write:

Cassidy Endowment for Education
5577 Skylane Blvd., Suite 6A
Santa Rosa, CA 95403
Phone: 707/546-6898
Fax: 707/546-6897

America Online E-mail
nsrs@aol.com

MicroSoft Network E-mail
nsrs@msn.com

IMPORTANT NOTE

This book is an abridged version of the NSRS worldwide database, serving high school freshmen through postdoctorates worldwide and now kindergarten through 12th grade (K-12) at private schools. For a more comprehensive search for sources of educational financing, write to NSRS, *now with Scholarship Alert^SM auto-notification to the scholarship source, saving you time and money! You just wait for the scholarship applications to arrive in the mail at your doorstep.*

Every effort has been made to supply you with the most accurate and up-to-date information possible, but—even as this book goes to print—awards are being added and application requirements are being changed by sponsoring organizations. Such circumstances are beyond our control.

Since the information we have supplied may not reflect the current status of any particular award program you are interested in, you should use this book only as a guide. Contact the source of the award for current application information.

If questions arise during your search for educational funding, you are welcome to call an NSRS counselor at 707/546-6777.

SCHOLARSHIP SEARCH SCAMS

If they guarantee a scholarship or if the information is free, buyer beware! Think about it. The decision for scholarship selection is decided only by the scholarship organization itself, not by someone selling you the information. And, most of these online organizations with free information on the World Wide Web are just selling your very personal information to mailing houses. It's like Grandma used to say, *"Nothing is free, and you get what you pay for!"*

A disturbing number of scholarship-sponsoring organizations have reported in recent months that they are receiving a high volume of inquiries from students who are *unqualified* for the awards about which they are asking.

Because of the number of these types of reports, we are investigating the origins of the misguided inquiries. Most often we find that someone has taken only names and addresses from our scholarship books and is selling the information—a general listing of scholarships available in a particular field of study—to students without regard to the student's qualifications. Most of these "operations" make no effort to match the student's educational goals and personal background with the requirements of the scholarships.

The books that we publish contain 40 tables in the front of the book, along with the source description, providing accurate cross-matching of the student's characteristics to the requirements of scholarship sources. National Scholarship Research Service (NSRS)™ and the publishers of our books are doing all we can to stop any abuse of our copyright which might result in an inconvenience to our scholarship-sponsoring organizations. We've assisted the Federal Trade Commission in closing down some of these "operations," and we are currently pursuing others.

Lastly, if any scholarship service is so-called FREE or guarantees a scholarship, savings bond, or a fountain pen, "buyer beware!" If it sounds too good to be true, then it probably is. Since it is solely at the discretion of the scholarship-sponsoring organizations to choose their scholarship recipients each year, these scholarship search scams cannot guarantee that users of their service will get a scholarship. Use this book to accurately cross-match scholarship sources for which you are eligible and avoid those scholarship search scams who merely copy information from our books.

Be sure to check out our Education Round Table to be safe in finding good, honest information from reliable sources at www.1800headstart.com or call us at 707/546-6777.

How to Use This Book

Each award, book, and resource listed has a record number preceding it. All of our indexes are based on these record numbers.

Here is a short guide to finding the information you need:

"QUICK FIND" INDEX

Most private-sector awards have certain eligibility qualifications. We have selected several of the most common requirements for this "Quick Find" index.

Here you can find awards targeted for people of a particular race, religion or family ancestry, for people who will be studying in a particular state or community, for the physically handicapped, and much more. Simply go through each of the tables and write down the reference numbers that apply to you. Then proceed to those sources and read each one carefully to see if you qualify.

FIELD OF STUDY INDEX

Since the awards listed in this book are also based on your intended field of study, we have structured this index along the lines of a college catalog.

First, look under your particular field of study (e.g., "School of Business"). Then, look under your area of interest (e.g., "Accounting") and, finally, under your specific subject (e.g., "Banking"). In this section, you will find record numbers that reference both financial aid awards and other resources that can help you in your career. Again, since there might be several eligibility requirements you must meet in order to be able to qualify for any listed award, be sure you read each listing *carefully and that you meet the requirements of the award* before requesting an application.

SCHOLARSHIP AND AWARD LISTINGS

Each listing contains a very condensed description of the award, its eligibility requirements, deadline dates, and where to get more information or an application.

You will notice a large "General" section. These are awards that do not usually specify a particular field of study in their eligibility requirements. You need to use the indexes provided and read each listing carefully to see if you might qualify for one of these awards.

Use the information we have provided only as a guide. Write to the source for a complete description of qualifications.

HELPFUL PUBLICATIONS

This section contains a selection of books and pamphlets that we consider helpful to the student. These publications are excellent sources of information on a wide variety of college and financial aid subjects.

If you discover a publication you find particularly helpful, let us know so we can share the information with others.

CAREER INFORMATION

This is a list of organizations that can help you decide where to study, give you information on job opportunities available in your field of study, and much more. We encourage you to write to these organizations for information.

ALPHABETICAL INDEX

A to Z, this index lists the reference number of every award, book, and career organization included in this book.

LEGEND FOR "QUICK FIND INDEX" AND "FIELD OF STUDY" INDEX:

D = Dependent
DIS = Disabled
DEC = Deceased
NOT D = Not Dependent
G = for Graduate Study only

Examples:

Choose Fireman if you are a Fireman.
Choose **Fireman-D-DIS** if you are a **dependent** of a **disabled** Fireman.
Choose **Fireman-D-DEC** if you are a **dependent** of a **deceased** Fireman.
Choose **Fireman-NOT D** if you are a **dependent** of a fireman but are **not** a fireman yourself.
Choose **Fireman-G** if you are a **graduate** student who is a fireman.

B = Booklet source in "Helpful Publications" section.
C = Career source in "Career Information" section.

Quick Find Index

ARMED FORCES

A Current Member, 592, 673, 1598, 2485, 2490, 3066, 3097, 3186, B3684

A Dependent-Current Member, 592, 673, 1511, 1598, 1639, 1980, 2477, 2490, 2491, 2495, 2541, 2573, 2581, 2646, 2654, 2695, 2755, 2767, 2776, 2814, 2824, 2921, 3051, 3096, 3097, 3178, 3179, 3183, 3184, 3187, 3199, 3301, 3341, 3372, 3469, B3680, B3684

A Dependent-Former Member, 592, 673, 1511, 1598, 1639, 1980, 2476, 2477, 2490, 2495, 2497, 2540, 2541, 2542, 2563, 2573, 2611, 2622, 2646, 2695, 2750, 2767, 2776, 2810, 2814, 2824, 2921, 2999, 3003, 3025, 3044, 3051, 3052, 3084, 3096, 3097, 3178, 3179, 3199, 3207, 3220, 3238, 3272, 3301, 3341, 3358, 3366, 3414, 3469, 3477, 3523, 3563, 3577, B3680, B3684

A Dependent-Retired Member, 1980, 2654, 2750, 2921, 3052, 3183, 3184, 3301, 3469

A Former Member, 592, 673, 1598, 2564, 2750, 2929, 3052, 3064, 3091, 3097, 3186, 3198, 3211, 3245, 3370, 3522, 3578, B3680, B3684

A Spouse-Current Member, 592, 673, 1598, 2490, 2491, 2498, 2541, 2573, 2767, 2814, 3097, 3183, 3184, 3185, 3301, 3372, B3684

A Spouse-Former Member, 592, 673, 1598, 2490, 2573, 2611, 2622, 2750, 2814, 3003, 3025, 3044, 3097, 3301, B3684

A Widow-Former Member, 2490, 2498, 2541, 2573, 2622, 2631, 2750, 2767, 3003, 3025, 3097, 3301, 3577, B3684

Officer, 2755

State National Guard, 2631, 2928, 3066, 3487

Stationed Overseas, 3185

US Air Force (any branch), 593, 674, 1599, 2485, 2490, 2491, 2495, 2755

US Air Force ROTC, 486

US Air Force-Air Natl Guard, 2485, 2495, 3066

US Air Force-Reserve, 2495

US Army (any branch), 2581, 2755

US Army-1st Cavalry Div Assn, 2810

US Army-1st Inf Div, 3358

US Army-37th Div, 2477

US Army-ROTC, 593, 674, 1599

US Coast Guard (any branch), 2755, 3179

US Marines (any branch), 2755, 3051, 3179, 3180, 3181, 3182, 3183, 3184, 3185, 3186, 3187

US Marines-1st Div, 2476

US Marines-3rd Div, 3477

US Marines-Corpsman (NOT D), 3052

US Marines-Marine Tanker, 3052

US Navy (any branch), 2755, 3179, 3180, 3181, 3182, 3183, 3184, 3185, 3186, 3187, 3477

US Navy ROTC, 593, 674, 1599

US Navy-Civil Eng Corps-D, 3341

US Navy-Corpsman (NOT D), 3052

US Navy-Fleet Reserve Assn, 2814

US Navy-Seabees, 3341

US Navy-Submarine Force, 2776, 3523

US Navy-Supply Corps, 3178

Vet Deceased in Retir-D, 2490, 2824, 3003, 3182, 3301

Vet-Blind, 2611

Vet-Deceased, 2476, 2581, 2767, 2810, 2824, 3003, 3025, 3044, 3238, 3577

Vet-Deceased in Service-D, 2490, 2622, 2631, 2767, 2776, 2824, 2948, 2999, 3003, 3010, 3060, 3063, 3090, 3097, 3180, 3181, 3182, 3232, 3301, 3366, 3371, 3477

Vet-Desert Shield/Desert Storm, 2540, 2810, 3097, 3211, 3245, 3272, 3370, 3477

Vet-Disabled, 2476, 2497, 2498, 2631, 2695, 2767, 2810, 2824, 3003, 3025, 3044, 3084, 3220, 3238, 3272, 3366, 3370, 3522

Vet-Disabled in Service-D, 2622, 2824, 3003, 3010, 3060

Vet-Duty on Aircraft Carrier-D, 3397

Vet-KIA-D, 2497, 2498, 2573, 2622, 2631, 2695, 2824, 2999, 3084, 3090, 3207, 3220, 3272, 3301, 3366, 3563, 3590

Vet-MIA-D, 2497, 2498, 2573, 2622, 2695, 2767, 2824, 2999, 3003, 3096, 3199, 3220, 3301, 3366, 3372, 3590

Vet-POW-D, 2497, 2498, 2573, 2695, 2767, 2824, 2999, 3003, 3096, 3199, 3220, 3301, 3366, 3372, 3590

Vet-Retired, 2490, 2581

Vet-Vietnam, 2540, 2750, 2810, 2999, 3096, 3211, 3245, 3272, 3370, 3477

Vet-WWII or Korea, 2477, 2540, 3245, 3272, 3370, 3523

CITY/COUNTY INTENDED STUDY

Atlanta GA/USA, 59, 879, 880

Boston MA/USA, 1078

Chicago IL/USA, 75, 216, 840, 889, 969, 1077, 2103

Los Angeles Metro CA/USA, 59, 77, 841, 879, 880, 886, 974, 2137, 2138, 2139, 2140, 2218, 2561

New York City NY/USA, 83, 118, 145, 146, 518, 544, 545, 913, 2127, 2164, 2326, 2327, 2392, 2393, 2590, 3298

Orange CA/USA, 2137, 2138, 2139, 2140

Orange FL/USA, 3532

Orlando FL/USA, 3532

Philadelphia Metro PA/USA, 2747

Ross OH/USA, 3275

San Diego Co/CA/USA, 1656, 1741, 1804, 1880, 1955

San Francisco CA/USA, 198, 1154, 3395, 3473

St. Louis MO/USA, 2849

Ventura CA/USA, 2137, 2138, 2139, 2140

Washington DC/USA, 144, 197, 267, 822, 926, 1240, 1459, 1495, 2232

Wilkes-Barre PA/USA, 3150

COMPANIES

American Express-D, 2519

American Natl Can Co.-D, 2545

Basin Electric Power Co.-D, 2602

Bedding Plants-D/S/P, 2606

Chrysler Corp.-D, 2677

Cigna-D, 2676

Corporate Employee-D, 2773

Deerfield Plastics-D, 2706

Dixie Yarns, 2773

Gerber Products-D, 3435

Haggar-D, 2889

JCPenney, 12, 120

JCPenney-D, 12, 120

Johnson Controls-D, 2988

McDonald's Emp, 3069

Nat Arts Matrls Trd Assn-D/S/P, 3116

Nat Arts Matrls Trd Assn NAMTA, 3116

National Roofing Fdn/NRCA-D/S, 3165

National Roofing Foundation, 3165

North American Philips-D, 3279

Northeastern Loggers-D, 3227

Sara Lee, 3332, 3333

Sara Lee-D, 3332, 3333

State Farm-D, 3379

Tektronix-D, 106, 3403

The West Co-D, 2903

Tri-State Gen/Trans Assn-D, 3483

United Parcel Service-D, 3471, 3472

Wal-Mart, 3551

Wal-Mart Distribution, 3550

Wal-Mart-D, 3551, 3552

Wyoming Dept of Corrections, 3588

Wyoming Dept of Corrections-D, 3588

CONTINENT OF INTENDED STUDY

North America, 142, 362, 629, 730, 731, 732, 749, 800, 835, 1041, 1169, 1526, 1530, 2047, 2418

COUNTRY OF INTENDED STUDY

Canada, 43, 44, 63, 76, 169, 245, 279, 476, 513, 690, 715, 730, 731, 732, 786, 833, 844, 876, 891, 943, 958, 970, 1079, 1133, 1228, 1250, 1258, 1262, 1332, 1394, 1433, 1456, 1520, 1526, 1539, 1671, 1691, 1739, 1760, 1828, 1902, 1927, 1981, 2106, 2155, 2156, 2157, 2158, 2159, 2160, 2185, 2281, 2363, 2409, 2417, 2466, 2606, 2808, 2809, 2935, 3008, 3333, 3348, 3519, B3655, B3667, B3671, B3739, B3755, B3758

Mexico, 170, 730, 731, 732, 786, 1042, 1526, 1539

United States, 5, 7, 13, 15, 24, 25, 26, 27, 28, 29, 30, 31, 32, 33, 34, 35, 36, 37, 38, 40, 41, 43, 44, 49, 58, 59, 60, 63, 64, 68, 69, 76, 78, 82, 93, 96, 106, 112, 113, 121, 123, 129, 139, 140, 141, 143, 155, 156, 162, 166, 169, 170, 174, 175, 176, 190, 199, 203, 205, 217, 240, 244, 245, 257, 259, 260, 263, 275, 279, 284, 308, 311, 314, 319, 327, 334, 337, 339, 342, 343, 344, 345, 348, 349, 355, 358, 444, 445, 446, 447, 448, 449, 450, 451, 452, 453, 454, 455, 456, 457, 458, 460, 461, 465, 466, 468, 469, 476, 481, 488, 495, 496, 505, 507, 513, 521, 522, 530, 532, 537, 539, 540, 548, 549, 555, 563, 564, 565, 566, 568, 570, 575, 576, 582, 583, 585, 591, 592, 593, 594, 595, 599, 602, 607, 615, 617, 620, 622, 625, 628, 630, 636, 637, 638, 639, 640, 641, 642, 643, 644, 645, 646, 647, 648, 649, 650, 651, 672, 673, 674, 675, 676, 684, 690, 691, 692, 696, 698, 704, 706, 707, 708, 709, 710, 715, 716, 725, 730, 731, 732, 735, 736, 739, 742, 743, 746, 747, 764, 769, 771, 776, 783, 786, 787, 794, 795, 799, 806, 808, 813, 816, 819, 820, 821, 825, 827, 828, 833, 839, 842, 844, 846, 865, 868, 874, 875, 876, 879, 880, 882, 883, 884, 885, 891, 898, 905, 916, 929, 930, 933, 934, 937, 938, 942, 943, 951, 958, 967, 970, 986, 989, 996, 997, 1001, 1002, 1017, 1020, 1021, 1033, 1047, 1061, 1067, 1068, 1069, 1079, 1092, 1098, 1102, 1105, 1116, 1120, 1123, 1127, 1131, 1131, 1133, 1140, 1148, 1150, 1151, 1156, 1191, 1212, 1215, 1218, 1219, 1228, 1239, 1241, 1243, 1248, 1250, 1258, 1262, 1266, 1275, 1281, 1283, 1285, 1287, 1292, 1299, 1309, 1310, 1311, 1312, 1313, 1314, 1315,

1316, 1317, 1318, 1319, 1320, 1321, 1322, 1326, 1328, 1332, 1334, 1336, 1341, 1351, 1355, 1356, 1371, 1372, 1374, 1376, 1378, 1380, 1381, 1383, 1388, 1391, 1392, 1393, 1394, 1398, 1405, 1411, 1412, 1413, 1415, 1416, 1418, 1419, 1428, 1433, 1444, 1448, 1450, 1454, 1455, 1456, 1458, 1461, 1462, 1467, 1470, 1472, 1478, 1481, 1493, 1494, 1514, 1515, 1518, 1519, 1520, 1526, 1532, 1535, 1537, 1539, 1542, 1546, 1547, 1550, 1552, 1555, 1559, 1570, 1573, 1575, 1582, 1583, 1586, 1588, 1592, 1593, 1595, 1598, 1599, 1600, 1601, 1604, 1608, 1617, 1622, 1626, 1628, 1634, 1637, 1642, 1644, 1646, 1647, 1652, 1658, 1665, 1671, 1675, 1678, 1681, 1682, 1683, 1685, 1691, 1699, 1700, 1701, 1702, 1703, 1714, 1715, 1730, 1738, 1739, 1743, 1744, 1752, 1754, 1760, 1768, 1769, 1771, 1785, 1786, 1787, 1796, 1799, 1810, 1811, 1814, 1817, 1820, 1823, 1824, 1828, 1835, 1836, 1845, 1846, 1847, 1848, 1849, 1850, 1851, 1852, 1853, 1854, 1855, 1856, 1857, 1863, 1874, 1883, 1889, 1902, 1906, 1913, 1914, 1915, 1916, 1918, 1924, 1927, 1936, 1937, 1944, 1945, 1954, 1964, 1969, 1971, 1981, 1988, 1990, 1996, 1997, 1998, 2000, 2002, 2014, 2015, 2016, 2017, 2018, 2019, 2020, 2021, 2022, 2023, 2024, 2025, 2026, 2027, 2028, 2029, 2034, 2035, 2040, 2050, 2055, 2057, 2062, 2063, 2070, 2071, 2076, 2077, 2078, 2081, 2085, 2086, 2087, 2091, 2096, 2102, 2106, 2108, 2110, 2112, 2113, 2114, 2115, 2116, 2122, 2126, 2134, 2144, 2146, 2147, 2148, 2149, 2155, 2156, 2157, 2158, 2159, 2160, 2161, 2171, 2179, 2180, 2185, 2196, 2203, 2204, 2208, 2211, 2212, 2217, 2219, 2222, 2227, 2229, 2230, 2235, 2236, 2238, 2239, 2241, 2245, 2248, 2249, 2250, 2254, 2256, 2264, 2265, 2275, 2281, 2282, 2304, 2306, 2308, 2310, 2315, 2316, 2325, 2331, 2332, 2337, 2341, 2344, 2348, 2351, 2355, 2363, 2365, 2366, 2371, 2376, 2378, 2395, 2397, 2399, 2400, 2404, 2405, 2406, 2409, 2416, 2417, 2423, 2425, 2431, 2434, 2435, 2444, 2446, 2451, 2466, 2474, 2481, 2484, 2488, 2496, 2502, 2543, 2562, 2565, 2579, 2580, 2601, 2604, 2605, 2606, 2609, 2627, 2635, 2639, 2642, 2648, 2666, 2670, 2671, 2676, 2682, 2685, 2686, 2688, 2737, 2738, 2739, 2744, 2747, 2750, 2751, 2753, 2759, 2762, 2768, 2772, 2778, 2782, 2788, 2792, 2796, 2808, 2809, 2829, 2831, 2842, 2850, 2857, 2864, 2867, 2889, 2893, 2894, 2906, 2935, 2948, 2957, 2960, 2975, 2988, 3006, 3014, 3018,

3022, 3035, 3045, 3047, 3048, 3050, 3057, 3082, 3097, 3099, 3100, 3101, 3102, 3110, 3112, 3113, 3118, 3126, 3129, 3130, 3131, 3132, 3133, 3134, 3135, 3163, 3170, 3175, 3189, 3191, 3194, 3200, 3202, 3214, 3219, 3222, 3228, 3233, 3234, 3235, 3236, 3237, 3247, 3248, 3249, 3252, 3268, 3277, 3282, 3289, 3298, 3299, 3300, 3302, 3303, 3304, 3332, 3340, 3345, 3347, 3348, 3351, 3370, 3378, 3384, 3385, 3395, 3397, 3403, 3408, 3410, 3411, 3421, 3425, 3468, 3471, 3472, 3473, 3479, 3485, 3487, 3488, 3508, 3516, 3517, 3520, 3530, 3531, 3549, 3550, 3551, 3552, 3557, 3566, 3574, 3579, B3615, B3655, B3656, B3664, B3666, B3667, B3671, B3676, B3708, B3709, B3739, B3740, B3755, B3758, B3760, B3761, B3780, B3793, B3803

COUNTRY OF RESIDENCE

Canada, 44, 63, 105, 151, 274, 328, 724, 777, 778, 781, 833, 876, 958, 982, 1133, 1145, 1188, 1189, 1228, 1250, 1258, 1332, 1394, 1433, 1456, 1487, 1520, 1526, 1795, 2160, 2519, 3168, 3333, B3721, B3721

Mexico, 777, 778, 781, 1526, 3249

United States, 16, 18, 19, 44, 48, 49, 60, 63, 69, 81, 89, 95, 103, 104, 105, 106, 124, 128, 133, 134, 135, 136, 137, 138, 143, 146, 147, 151, 172, 186, 191, 194, 220, 221, 226, 227, 229, 236, 251, 254, 256, 270, 274, 291, 292, 297, 299, 310, 312, 315, 316, 322, 323, 324, 328, 331, 340, 341, 342, 347, 350, 355, 357, 359, 361, 399, 462, 463, 470, 471, 478, 479, 482, 487, 514, 523, 541, 545, 546, 547, 556, 560, 561, 563, 564, 565, 566, 567, 568, 569, 571, 573, 581, 586, 587, 596, 600, 605, 606, 618, 623, 652, 654, 655, 677, 679, 681, 683, 693, 699, 700, 702, 709, 710, 717, 718, 719, 721, 722, 724, 733, 742, 748, 765, 768, 769, 773, 774, 777, 778, 781, 788, 789, 810, 811, 812, 815, 823, 833, 836, 850, 856, 860, 861, 861, 862, 863, 865, 869, 871, 873, 876, 892, 894, 896, 898, 906, 915, 917, 919, 920, 921, 924, 925, 930, 942, 948, 950, 952, 954, 958, 960, 962, 975, 978, 982, 987, 995, 998, 999, 1005, 1008, 1014, 1017, 1024, 1029, 1032, 1040, 1046, 1048, 1049, 1057, 1058, 1067, 1068, 1069, 1075, 1082, 1085, 1091, 1094, 1095, 1106, 1109, 1116, 1117, 1122, 1132, 1133, 1134, 1135, 1136, 1137, 1138, 1145, 1150, 1151, 1161, 1163, 1164, 1165, 1171, 1172, 1173, 1177, 1179, 1183, 1188, 1189, 1196, 1197, 1204, 1209, 1210, 1216, 1217, 1221, 1228, 1231, 1233, 1234, 1239, 1249, 1250, 1258, 1289, 1332, 1346, 1347, 1348,

1349, 1350, 1353, 1358, 1373, 1380,
1387, 1388, 1394, 1418, 1427, 1428,
1433, 1439, 1443, 1450, 1456, 1467,
1479, 1480, 1483, 1484, 1485, 1487,
1491, 1493, 1496, 1501, 1512, 1515,
1516, 1520, 1525, 1526, 1527, 1528,
1529, 1531, 1533, 1555, 1559, 1564,
1569, 1571, 1576, 1590, 1593, 1596,
1602, 1605, 1606, 1610, 1620, 1640,
1644, 1650, 1653, 1659, 1667, 1668,
1672, 1675, 1683, 1686, 1693, 1695,
1699, 1700, 1707, 1712, 1717, 1718,
1720, 1721, 1726, 1727, 1728, 1729,
1735, 1746, 1753, 1754, 1755, 1772,
1773, 1780, 1795, 1815, 1817, 1834,
1844, 1864, 1865, 1866, 1867, 1868,
1869, 1870, 1871, 1872, 1885, 1886,
1888, 1889, 1889, 1898, 1903, 1910,
1914, 1920, 1921, 1943, 1960, 1962,
1964, 1969, 1969, 1976, 1977, 1978,
1983, 1987, 1992, 1995, 2005, 2007,
2008, 2032, 2039, 2040, 2043, 2044,
2045, 2049, 2058, 2061, 2062, 2063,
2064, 2065, 2074, 2090, 2097, 2105,
2116, 2118, 2134, 2141, 2160, 2174,
2186, 2199, 2202, 2208, 2212, 2225,
2228, 2238, 2241, 2243, 2247, 2248,
2250, 2260, 2276, 2277, 2286, 2289,
2302, 2319, 2324, 2327, 2338, 2346,
2350, 2356, 2358, 2374, 2379, 2382,
2385, 2393, 2394, 2403, 2410, 2415,
2424, 2426, 2427, 2428, 2430, 2434,
2442, 2447, 2448, 2449, 2457, 2460,
2470, 2476, 2477, 2480, 2487, 2490,
2491, 2496, 2497, 2498, 2499, 2500,
2504, 2505, 2515, 2518, 2519, 2521,
2524, 2527, 2531, 2532, 2540, 2542,
2561, 2574, 2581, 2585, 2595, 2600,
2603, 2607, 2615, 2619, 2620, 2623,
2624, 2626, 2631, 2636, 2637, 2638,
2639, 2651, 2654, 2655, 2656, 2658,
2659, 2661, 2663, 2665, 2676, 2682,
2683, 2684, 2685, 2689, 2691, 2695,
2697, 2698, 2699, 2700, 2701, 2703,
2704, 2705, 2706, 2708, 2709, 2710,
2711, 2712, 2713, 2714, 2715, 2717,
2718, 2719, 2720, 2721, 2722, 2723,
2724, 2725, 2726, 2727, 2728, 2729,
2730, 2732, 2733, 2734, 2735, 2737,
2738, 2739, 2743, 2747, 2748, 2749,
2755, 2756, 2760, 2762, 2767, 2772,
2776, 2778, 2779, 2781, 2786, 2787,
2791, 2794, 2806, 2807, 2810, 2814,
2816, 2820, 2823, 2826, 2828, 2833,
2834, 2837, 2840, 2842, 2843, 2850,
2856, 2859, 2860, 2864, 2867, 2872,
2887, 2888, 2892, 2895, 2899, 2905,
2909, 2911, 2912, 2918, 2919, 2920,
2924, 2925, 2932, 2933, 2939, 2945,
2946, 2948, 2949, 2952, 2953, 2954,
2959, 2962, 2963, 2970, 2972, 2973,
2974, 2976, 2979, 2980, 2987, 2994,
2996, 2997, 2998, 2999, 3004, 3005,
3006, 3010, 3012, 3014, 3019, 3021,

3022, 3024, 3026, 3027, 3028, 3035,
3044, 3049, 3050, 3054, 3055, 3058,
3062, 3063, 3064, 3066, 3067, 3070,
3071, 3072, 3073, 3077, 3079, 3080,
3081, 3082, 3083, 3086, 3088, 3089,
3090, 3091, 3095, 3096, 3101, 3102,
3107, 3109, 3110, 3117, 3118, 3119,
3120, 3122, 3137, 3139, 3140, 3141,
3142, 3143, 3144, 3145, 3146, 3147,
3148, 3149, 3150, 3151, 3152, 3153,
3154, 3155, 3156, 3157, 3158, 3159,
3160, 3161, 3162, 3167, 3168, 3172,
3175, 3178, 3192, 3194, 3196, 3197,
3198, 3199, 3201, 3202, 3204, 3205,
3206, 3207, 3208, 3209, 3212, 3216,
3219, 3220, 3221, 3226, 3233, 3234,
3235, 3236, 3237, 3238, 3239, 3243,
3245, 3246, 3247, 3248, 3249, 3250,
3251, 3252, 3265, 3274, 3281, 3284,
3286, 3287, 3288, 3290, 3291, 3292,
3298, 3301, 3304, 3304, 3305, 3312,
3313, 3318, 3320, 3325, 3330, 3331,
3332, 3334, 3339, 3345, 3351, 3354,
3357, 3359, 3360, 3367, 3368, 3370,
3371, 3372, 3376, 3380, 3381, 3382,
3383, 3384, 3388, 3389, 3391, 3395,
3398, 3400, 3401, 3408, 3409, 3410,
3411, 3413, 3416, 3418, 3419, 3424,
3425, 3430, 3449, 3453, 3454, 3455,
3456, 3457, 3458, 3459, 3460, 3461,
3462, 3463, 3464, 3465, 3470, 3475,
3477, 3478, 3482, 3487, 3489, 3490,
3491, 3492, 3497, 3500, 3503, 3504,
3507, 3510, 3515, 3516, 3517, 3523,
3530, 3537, 3538, 3541, 3542, 3545,
3546, 3548, 3559, 3563, 3571, 3573,
3574, 3575, 3577, 3578, 3579, 3601,
3604, 3605, B3618, B3626, B3680,
B3681, B3719, B3721, B3745, B3806

CURRENT GRADE POINT AVERAGE

Low (under 2.0), B3811

Average (2.0–3.0), 6, 38, 42, 63, 79, 80, 82,
83, 103, 128, 132, 191, 210, 221, 225,
231, 234, 235, 258, 282, 283, 285, 289,
290, 301, 321, 345, 378, 402, 408, 463,
473, 485, 512, 562, 588, 593, 603, 656,
674, 701, 715, 737, 768, 775, 832, 873,
886, 946, 947, 1035, 1037, 1154, 1223,
1224, 1232, 1276, 1304, 1306, 1307,
1308, 1323, 1327, 1331, 1366, 1409,
1442, 1471, 1482, 1516, 1545, 1558,
1563, 1583, 1594, 1599, 1622, 1698,
1725, 1746, 1782, 1784, 1832, 1840,
1895, 1907, 1930, 1933, 1935, 1956,
1957, 1978, 2012, 2013, 2035, 2049,
2051, 2052, 2053, 2062, 2063, 2146,
2147, 2198, 2213, 2270, 2274, 2298,
2299, 2300, 2345, 2417, 2421, 2452,
2490, 2491, 2540, 2549, 2569, 2570,
2580, 2582, 2603, 2608, 2617, 2632,

2675, 2748, 2763, 2770, 2772, 2829,
2831, 2845, 2846, 2858, 2864, 2886,
2905, 2914, 2953, 2954, 2959, 2982,
3016, 3017, 3026, 3046, 3061, 3072,
3076, 3112, 3113, 3119, 3120, 3124,
3128, 3182, 3183, 3184, 3190, 3203,
3215, 3241, 3267, 3275, 3330, 3331,
3338, 3353, 3387, 3435, 3441, 3498,
3507, 3514, 3527, 3528, 3529, 3536,
3542, 3544, 3561, 3565, 3601, 3604,
3605, 3606, B3811

High (3.0–3.5), 1, 6, 10, 22, 23, 38, 39, 41,
42, 44, 48, 49, 50, 51, 52, 57, 63, 66, 67,
79, 80, 82, 83, 86, 87, 88, 101, 103, 104,
107, 108, 118, 127, 128, 131, 132, 134,
139, 140, 141, 142, 143, 155, 159, 160,
161, 177, 182, 191, 192, 199, 202, 210,
211, 221, 225, 227, 228, 229, 231, 234,
235, 240, 256, 258, 259, 260, 263, 272,
274, 276, 281, 282, 283, 285, 286, 289,
290, 294, 296, 301, 302, 304, 313, 316,
321, 325, 332, 344, 345, 346, 347, 348,
349, 355, 361, 367, 368, 370, 371, 373,
374, 375, 378, 380, 384, 388, 391, 396,
400, 402, 404, 405, 407, 408, 409, 440,
444, 463, 464, 465, 467, 470, 471, 473,
478, 479, 480, 485, 496, 498, 508, 510,
512, 524, 525, 527, 538, 539, 540, 547,
556, 560, 561, 562, 576, 578, 586, 587,
588, 592, 593, 594, 598, 603, 609, 610,
612, 621, 622, 625, 634, 635, 653, 654,
655, 656, 662, 670, 673, 674, 675, 685,
686, 692, 699, 700, 701, 702, 711, 712,
713, 715, 719, 726, 730, 731, 732, 736,
737, 738, 740, 742, 743, 751, 752, 753,
754, 756, 768, 769, 773, 774, 775, 795,
796, 803, 810, 811, 812, 816, 821, 826,
832, 836, 838, 855, 856, 860, 865, 873,
875, 877, 886, 900, 916, 923, 942, 946,
947, 952, 959, 966, 985, 997, 1001, 1035,
1037, 1047, 1052, 1053, 1061, 1062,
1085, 1154, 1167, 1178, 1179, 1190,
1193, 1194, 1195, 1212, 1214, 1217,
1223, 1224, 1231, 1232, 1247, 1265,
1269, 1270, 1274, 1276, 1286, 1298,
1302, 1304, 1306, 1307, 1308, 1323,
1324, 1327, 1331, 1336, 1340, 1354,
1358, 1362, 1363, 1364, 1366, 1367,
1371, 1376, 1380, 1385, 1388, 1389,
1402, 1403, 1409, 1410, 1415, 1418,
1422, 1424, 1428, 1429, 1439, 1440,
1441, 1442, 1448, 1450, 1451, 1457,
1467, 1471, 1472, 1473, 1482, 1484,
1494, 1502, 1509, 1515, 1516, 1523,
1526, 1534, 1540, 1541, 1545, 1546,
1548, 1551, 1555, 1558, 1559, 1560,
1563, 1564, 1567, 1572, 1577, 1581,
1582, 1583, 1584, 1585, 1587, 1590,
1593, 1594, 1595, 1596, 1598, 1599,
1600, 1603, 1606, 1619, 1622, 1623,
1627, 1636, 1644, 1645, 1669, 1680,
1681, 1685, 1687, 1695, 1697, 1698,
1724, 1725, 1737, 1746, 1754, 1756,
1767, 1769, 1771, 1776, 1780, 1781,

1782, 1783, 1784, 1788, 1789, 1817, 1822, 1823, 1825, 1830, 1832, 1840, 1846, 1847, 1848, 1850, 1852, 1853, 1854, 1855, 1856, 1857, 1859, 1861, 1864, 1865, 1866, 1867, 1873, 1886, 1888, 1895, 1906, 1907, 1912, 1913, 1914, 1916, 1918, 1929, 1930, 1931, 1933, 1935, 1943, 1954, 1956, 1957, 1958, 1978, 1987, 1994, 1995, 1996, 1999, 2000, 2011, 2012, 2013, 2034, 2035, 2037, 2049, 2051, 2052, 2053, 2061, 2062, 2063, 2072, 2074, 2075, 2084, 2099, 2100, 2104, 2123, 2127, 2134, 2146, 2147, 2150, 2162, 2191, 2198, 2200, 2213, 2216, 2223, 2227, 2229, 2230, 2238, 2247, 2252, 2256, 2258, 2261, 2270, 2274, 2275, 2291, 2296, 2298, 2299, 2300, 2302, 2305, 2312, 2313, 2322, 2325, 2336, 2342, 2345, 2346, 2347, 2350, 2353, 2357, 2374, 2375, 2380, 2382, 2415, 2417, 2421, 2452, 2456, 2464, 2465, 2469, 2481, 2484, 2490, 2491, 2492, 2503, 2520, 2531, 2532, 2540, 2549, 2550, 2559, 2565, 2569, 2570, 2577, 2580, 2582, 2583, 2585, 2601, 2603, 2607, 2608, 2609, 2617, 2625, 2627, 2630, 2632, 2635, 2639, 2675, 2681, 2686, 2704, 2715, 2723, 2733, 2737, 2738, 2742, 2746, 2748, 2763, 2765, 2766, 2771, 2772, 2774, 2783, 2788, 2789, 2803, 2817, 2820, 2822, 2826, 2829, 2831, 2845, 2846, 2847, 2848, 2853, 2858, 2863, 2864, 2867, 2868, 2870, 2871, 2874, 2885, 2886, 2902, 2905, 2907, 2908, 2909, 2914, 2918, 2930, 2938, 2951, 2953, 2954, 2955, 2959, 2967, 2982, 2996, 3014, 3016, 3017, 3021, 3026, 3027, 3028, 3030, 3031, 3035, 3037, 3046, 3047, 3061, 3071, 3072, 3076, 3092, 3093, 3119, 3120, 3124, 3128, 3129, 3130, 3131, 3132, 3133, 3134, 3135, 3138, 3142, 3164, 3170, 3171, 3178, 3182, 3183, 3184, 3190, 3203, 3204, 3205, 3209, 3215, 3218, 3229, 3231, 3237, 3241, 3242, 3250, 3267, 3268, 3275, 3288, 3295, 3300, 3302, 3303, 3307, 3316, 3330, 3331, 3335, 3338, 3344, 3348, 3353, 3359, 3380, 3382, 3385, 3387, 3393, 3394, 3402, 3405, 3428, 3429, 3435, 3438, 3441, 3443, 3469, 3491, 3497, 3498, 3507, 3514, 3516, 3517, 3524, 3527, 3528, 3529, 3536, 3542, 3544, 3561, 3564, 3565, 3597, 3599, 3600, 3601, 3602, 3604, 3605, 3606

Excellent (above 3.5), 6, 7, 10, 22, 23, 38, 39, 41, 42, 44, 48, 49, 50, 51, 57, 63, 66, 67, 79, 80, 82, 83, 84, 85, 86, 87, 88, 93, 101, 103, 104, 107, 108, 118, 127, 128, 131, 132, 134, 139, 140, 141, 142, 143, 155, 159, 160, 161, 162, 177, 182, 191, 192, 199, 202, 210, 211, 221, 225, 227, 228, 229, 230, 231, 234, 235, 240, 256,

258, 259, 260, 263, 272, 274, 276, 278, 279, 280, 281, 282, 283, 285, 289, 290, 294, 296, 301, 302, 313, 316, 321, 325, 327, 332, 344, 345, 346, 347, 348, 349, 355, 361, 366, 367, 368, 369, 370, 371, 373, 374, 375, 376, 378, 380, 383, 384, 387, 388, 390, 391, 393, 395, 396, 397, 399, 400, 401, 402, 403, 404, 405, 407, 408, 409, 415, 416, 417, 419, 420, 421, 422, 423, 424, 425, 426, 427, 428, 430, 431, 432, 434, 435, 436, 438, 440, 463, 464, 465, 467, 470, 471, 473, 478, 479, 480, 485, 496, 498, 508, 510, 511, 512, 524, 525, 527, 538, 539, 540, 547, 558, 560, 561, 562, 576, 578, 586, 587, 588, 592, 593, 594, 598, 603, 609, 610, 612, 621, 622, 625, 633, 634, 635, 636, 653, 654, 655, 656, 662, 670, 673, 674, 675, 685, 686, 692, 699, 700, 701, 702, 711, 712, 713, 715, 719, 726, 730, 731, 732, 734, 736, 737, 738, 740, 742, 743, 751, 752, 753, 754, 755, 756, 768, 769, 773, 774, 775, 795, 796, 803, 807, 810, 811, 812, 816, 821, 826, 832, 836, 838, 855, 856, 860, 865, 873, 875, 877, 886, 900, 916, 923, 942, 946, 947, 959, 966, 985, 997, 1001, 1035, 1037, 1047, 1052, 1053, 1061, 1062, 1085, 1154, 1167, 1178, 1190, 1193, 1194, 1195, 1212, 1214, 1217, 1223, 1224, 1231, 1232, 1247, 1265, 1269, 1270, 1274, 1276, 1286, 1298, 1302, 1304, 1306, 1307, 1308, 1323, 1324, 1325, 1327, 1331, 1336, 1337, 1340, 1354, 1358, 1362, 1363, 1364, 1366, 1367, 1371, 1376, 1380, 1383, 1385, 1388, 1389, 1402, 1403, 1409, 1410, 1415, 1418, 1422, 1424, 1428, 1429, 1439, 1440, 1441, 1442, 1448, 1450, 1451, 1457, 1467, 1471, 1472, 1473, 1482, 1484, 1494, 1502, 1509, 1515, 1516, 1523, 1526, 1534, 1540, 1541, 1545, 1546, 1548, 1551, 1555, 1558, 1559, 1560, 1563, 1564, 1572, 1577, 1581, 1582, 1583, 1584, 1585, 1587, 1590, 1593, 1594, 1595, 1596, 1598, 1599, 1600, 1603, 1606, 1619, 1622, 1623, 1627, 1636, 1637, 1644, 1645, 1648, 1652, 1669, 1676, 1680, 1681, 1685, 1687, 1690, 1691, 1692, 1695, 1697, 1698, 1713, 1724, 1725, 1737, 1746, 1754, 1756, 1767, 1769, 1771, 1776, 1780, 1781, 1784, 1788, 1789, 1817, 1822, 1823, 1825, 1827, 1828, 1829, 1830, 1832, 1840, 1845, 1846, 1847, 1848, 1849, 1850, 1851, 1852, 1853, 1854, 1855, 1856, 1857, 1864, 1865, 1866, 1867, 1873, 1886, 1888, 1895, 1906, 1907, 1912, 1913, 1914, 1916, 1918, 1926, 1927, 1928, 1929, 1930, 1935, 1942, 1943, 1954, 1956, 1957, 1958, 1978, 1987, 1994, 1995, 1996, 1999, 2000, 2011, 2012, 2013, 2035, 2037, 2049, 2051, 2052, 2053, 2061, 2062, 2063, 2072,

2073, 2074, 2075, 2084, 2099, 2104, 2110, 2123, 2127, 2134, 2146, 2147, 2150, 2162, 2191, 2198, 2213, 2216, 2223, 2227, 2229, 2230, 2238, 2247, 2249, 2252, 2256, 2258, 2261, 2270, 2274, 2275, 2291, 2296, 2298, 2299, 2300, 2302, 2305, 2310, 2312, 2313, 2322, 2325, 2336, 2342, 2345, 2346, 2347, 2350, 2353, 2357, 2362, 2363, 2364, 2374, 2375, 2380, 2382, 2415, 2417, 2421, 2452, 2456, 2464, 2465, 2469, 2473, 2481, 2484, 2490, 2491, 2492, 2503, 2531, 2532, 2540, 2549, 2550, 2559, 2565, 2569, 2570, 2571, 2577, 2580, 2582, 2583, 2585, 2601, 2603, 2607, 2608, 2609, 2613, 2617, 2621, 2625, 2626, 2627, 2630, 2632, 2635, 2639, 2663, 2664, 2680, 2681, 2686, 2704, 2705, 2715, 2723, 2733, 2737, 2738, 2742, 2746, 2748, 2763, 2765, 2766, 2771, 2772, 2783, 2788, 2789, 2803, 2817, 2820, 2822, 2826, 2829, 2831, 2835, 2845, 2846, 2847, 2848, 2853, 2858, 2860, 2863, 2867, 2868, 2870, 2871, 2874, 2885, 2886, 2902, 2905, 2907, 2908, 2909, 2914, 2918, 2930, 2938, 2947, 2950, 2951, 2953, 2954, 2955, 2959, 2967, 2982, 2996, 3014, 3016, 3017, 3021, 3026, 3027, 3028, 3029, 3030, 3031, 3035, 3037, 3046, 3047, 3061, 3071, 3072, 3076, 3086, 3092, 3093, 3105, 3114, 3124, 3125, 3128, 3129, 3130, 3131, 3132, 3133, 3134, 3135, 3138, 3142, 3152, 3164, 3170, 3171, 3178, 3183, 3190, 3191, 3203, 3204, 3205, 3206, 3209, 3215, 3229, 3231, 3232, 3237, 3241, 3242, 3243, 3250, 3267, 3268, 3273, 3275, 3278, 3288, 3297, 3300, 3302, 3303, 3307, 3316, 3330, 3331, 3335, 3338, 3344, 3348, 3353, 3364, 3380, 3382, 3385, 3387, 3393, 3394, 3402, 3404, 3408, 3410, 3428, 3429, 3432, 3435, 3438, 3441, 3443, 3469, 3489, 3491, 3497, 3498, 3507, 3514, 3516, 3517, 3519, 3524, 3527, 3528, 3529, 3536, 3542, 3544, 3556, 3561, 3564, 3565, 3599, 3600, 3601, 3602, 3604, 3605, 3606

CURRENT SCHOOL PROGRAM

Camp, 2796, 3406, B3783
Homeschool, B3706, B3710
Preschool, 2799, 2910, 3322, B3666, B3700, B3710, B3783
Kindergarten, 2510, 2644, 2653, 2656, 2667, 2799, 2800, 2849, 2910, 2981, 3127, 3166, 3168, 3224, 3264, 3319, 3322, 3374, 3406, 3419, 3423, 3439, 3484, 3557, 3576, B3666, B3699, B3700, B3710, B3721, B3783, B3789, B3799

Elementary School, 1088, 1170, 2503, 2506, 2510, 2644, 2645, 2653, 2656, 2667, 2693, 2753, 2799, 2910, 2981, 3056, 3127, 3163, 3224, 3255, 3264, 3322, 3374, 3406, 3419, 3423, 3430, 3439, 3448, 3476, 3484, 3557, 3576, B3639, B3666, B3699, B3700, B3708, B3710, B3721, B3728, B3747, B3789, B3799, C3901

1st Grade, 2800, 2849, 3166, 3168, 3319, 3476

2nd Grade, 2800, 2849, 3166, 3168, 3319, 3476

3rd Grade, 2800, 2849, 3166, 3167, 3168, 3319

4th Grade, 2800, 2849, 2978, 3166, 3167, 3168, 3319, 3499, 3567

5th Grade, 1146, 2800, 2978, 3111, 3166, 3167, 3168, 3442, 3451, 3466, 3499, 3567

6th Grade, 1146, 2745, 2778, 2800, 2978, 3111, 3166, 3167, 3168, 3324, 3442, 3451, 3466, 3499, 3567

7th Grade, 328, 724, 833, 876, 958, 982, 1146, 1228, 1250, 1332, 1394, 1433, 1456, 1487, 1520, 2745, 2778, 2799, 2800, 2978, 3075, 3089, 3111, 3166, 3167, 3168, 3324, 3442, 3451, 3466, 3486, 3499, 3567

8th Grade, 328, 724, 833, 876, 958, 982, 1146, 1228, 1250, 1332, 1394, 1433, 1456, 1487, 1520, 2673, 2745, 2778, 2799, 2800, 2870, 2978, 3075, 3089, 3111, 3166, 3167, 3168, 3240, 3324, 3428, 3434, 3442, 3451, 3466, 3486, 3499, 3567

9th Grade, 962, 1146, 2536, 2778, 2870, 2978, 3089, 3094, 3111, 3166, 3167, 3168, 3240, 3451, 3486, 3499

Junior High/Middle School, 833, 876, 958, 1083, 1088, 1170, 1228, 1250, 1332, 1394, 1433, 1456, 1520, 2506, 2510, 2644, 2653, 2656, 2667, 2753, 2866, 2910, 2981, 3056, 3127, 3163, 3166, 3224, 3255, 3264, 3322, 3324, 3374, 3386, 3406, 3419, 3423, 3430, 3439, 3476, 3484, 3557, 3576, B3639, B3666, B3699, B3700, B3706, B3710, B3728, B3747, B3783, B3784, B3789, B3792, B3799, B3805, C3901

High School, 13, 121, 129, 257, 297, 328, 337, 341, 353, 359, 364, 460, 502, 615, 724, 757, 814, 820, 833, 834, 872, 876, 887, 909, 912, 958, 960, 962, 982, 999, 1014, 1030, 1039, 1040, 1046, 1054, 1083, 1088, 1094, 1095, 1146, 1147, 1162, 1170, 1184, 1228, 1234, 1250, 1283, 1332, 1373, 1383, 1394, 1433, 1443, 1456, 1487, 1491, 1498, 1501, 1505, 1514, 1520, 1547, 1631, 1642, 1961, 1990, 2055, 2095, 2116, 2124, 2153, 2231, 2244, 2339, 2355, 2444, 2451, 2459, 2501, 2503, 2506, 2510,

2536, 2537, 2578, 2582, 2589, 2644, 2645, 2650, 2653, 2656, 2667, 2673, 2681, 2691, 2693, 2703, 2743, 2745, 2753, 2778, 2789, 2799, 2800, 2809, 2843, 2866, 2870, 2898, 2900, 2906, 2907, 2910, 2911, 2941, 2944, 2949, 2981, 2985, 2986, 2987, 3016, 3056, 3075, 3108, 3111, 3127, 3138, 3163, 3166, 3167, 3168, 3176, 3224, 3230, 3237, 3240, 3251, 3254, 3255, 3264, 3279, 3280, 3285, 3318, 3320, 3321, 3322, 3326, 3339, 3374, 3386, 3402, 3406, 3419, 3421, 3423, 3430, 3434, 3439, 3442, 3447, 3448, 3451, 3466, 3470, 3473, 3474, 3476, 3481, 3484, 3486, 3492, 3493, 3521, 3524, 3537, 3539, 3541, 3557, 3566, 3567, 3576, 3579, 3601, 3603, 3604, 3605, B3608, B3638, B3654, B3655, B3658, B3661, B3666, B3674, B3679, B3695, B3699, B3700, B3704, B3706, B3708, B3710, B3712, B3717, B3726, B3728, B3731, B3738, B3746, B3748, B3749, B3752, B3755, B3756, B3757, B3758, B3784, B3789, B3792, B3793, B3799, B3809, C3845, C3846, C3901, C3917, C3973

High School Freshman, 849, 960, 1007, 1472, 1595, 2486, 2596, 2691, 2857, 2924, 2925, 2944, 3138, 3223, 3324, 3421, 3450, 3499, 3541, B3805

High School Sophomore, 324, 487, 849, 960, 962, 1007, 1233, 1472, 1485, 1595, 1610, 2426, 2486, 2513, 2536, 2596, 2634, 2691, 2779, 2857, 2924, 2925, 2944, 2978, 3089, 3094, 3138, 3164, 3223, 3324, 3362, 3421, 3450, 3499, 3541, 3599

High School Junior, 60, 324, 377, 390, 487, 558, 766, 807, 849, 880, 960, 962, 1007, 1233, 1325, 1425, 1472, 1485, 1502, 1551, 1587, 1595, 1610, 1627, 1687, 1776, 1825, 2073, 2230, 2426, 2472, 2486, 2489, 2513, 2536, 2597, 2601, 2634, 2691, 2771, 2779, 2828, 2881, 2901, 2913, 2924, 2925, 2941, 2944, 2978, 3089, 3098, 3138, 3164, 3170, 3172, 3223, 3324, 3332, 3333, 3354, 3362, 3364, 3421, 3499, 3531, 3541, 3564, 3574, 3599, 3602, B3615, B3618, B3626, B3692, B3778, C3974, C3975

High School Senior, 1, 2, 7, 8, 12, 13, 14, 15, 16, 21, 23, 42, 43, 46, 52, 59, 60, 67, 84, 86, 89, 93, 95, 97, 99, 101, 111, 120, 121, 122, 123, 124, 133, 137, 138, 149, 152, 159, 160, 163, 165, 178, 179, 189, 199, 200, 204, 211, 214, 215, 218, 227, 230, 231, 236, 237, 238, 240, 258, 259, 268, 270, 272, 273, 274, 275, 284, 285, 291, 293, 295, 301, 304, 306, 313, 317, 324, 327, 330, 332, 337, 338, 339, 340, 343, 344, 345, 346, 347, 363, 365, 366, 367, 368, 369, 370, 371, 372, 373, 374, 375, 376, 377, 378, 379, 380, 381, 382, 383, 384, 385, 386, 387, 388, 390, 391,

392, 393, 394, 395, 396, 397, 398, 399, 400, 401, 402, 403, 404, 405, 406, 407, 408, 409, 413, 414, 418, 424, 429, 433, 437, 439, 442, 459, 462, 463, 473, 476, 487, 495, 496, 506, 510, 511, 512, 514, 525, 537, 554, 558, 562, 573, 575, 576, 584, 588, 598, 605, 608, 615, 616, 617, 618, 620, 622, 631, 632, 634, 635, 656, 681, 682, 685, 691, 692, 701, 702, 705, 722, 723, 725, 733, 735, 736, 739, 751, 752, 753, 754, 755, 756, 758, 759, 760, 761, 766, 768, 775, 791, 794, 795, 802, 803, 805, 807, 816, 817, 822, 824, 827, 828, 829, 832, 838, 853, 855, 862, 873, 875, 877, 879, 880, 894, 897, 900, 901, 902, 917, 919, 920, 923, 927, 932, 933, 934, 935, 945, 947, 953, 959, 960, 962, 966, 981, 991, 998, 1004, 1005, 1007, 1019, 1020, 1021, 1022, 1027, 1036, 1037, 1061, 1062, 1070, 1085, 1092, 1093, 1096, 1099, 1102, 1103, 1104, 1107, 1108, 1122, 1132, 1138, 1143, 1148, 1152, 1157, 1158, 1159, 1163, 1164, 1165, 1178, 1180, 1181, 1187, 1190, 1192, 1198, 1201, 1204, 1205, 1215, 1218, 1219, 1220, 1221, 1223, 1224, 1225, 1233, 1235, 1236, 1240, 1242, 1244, 1245, 1246, 1251, 1262, 1265, 1270, 1271, 1275, 1279, 1282, 1284, 1288, 1290, 1293, 1295, 1297, 1299, 1300, 1305, 1306, 1307, 1325, 1326, 1331, 1343, 1347, 1354, 1358, 1363, 1375, 1377, 1379, 1382, 1384, 1386, 1399, 1403, 1410, 1414, 1417, 1420, 1425, 1426, 1430, 1435, 1439, 1441, 1446, 1447, 1449, 1457, 1460, 1461, 1462, 1463, 1464, 1468, 1469, 1471, 1473, 1476, 1484, 1485, 1486, 1489, 1494, 1495, 1502, 1503, 1504, 1506, 1507, 1509, 1510, 1513, 1516, 1530, 1534, 1541, 1546, 1551, 1553, 1554, 1557, 1558, 1563, 1564, 1566, 1567, 1572, 1577, 1578, 1582, 1583, 1584, 1587, 1589, 1591, 1594, 1597, 1603, 1609, 1610, 1611, 1612, 1617, 1622, 1623, 1627, 1629, 1630, 1632, 1633, 1636, 1638, 1641, 1656, 1657, 1669, 1687, 1689, 1698, 1723, 1737, 1741, 1742, 1745, 1756, 1773, 1776, 1777, 1784, 1804, 1805, 1825, 1826, 1832, 1840, 1863, 1880, 1881, 1882, 1886, 1887, 1891, 1906, 1921, 1925, 1935, 1955, 1960, 1962, 1966, 1980, 2010, 2013, 2035, 2045, 2047, 2051, 2054, 2055, 2056, 2057, 2058, 2063, 2066, 2068, 2073, 2075, 2086, 2087, 2088, 2096, 2109, 2110, 2111, 2118, 2119, 2121, 2131, 2135, 2136, 2141, 2143, 2146, 2148, 2154, 2162, 2166, 2170, 2171, 2174, 2179, 2180, 2181, 2182, 2188, 2190, 2191, 2193, 2195, 2198, 2199, 2205, 2208, 2216, 2230, 2235, 2236, 2237, 2242, 2253, 2256, 2257, 2261, 2273, 2276, 2283, 2288,

2300, 2305, 2307, 2310, 2322, 2324, 2331, 2332, 2333, 2334, 2336, 2341, 2345, 2347, 2365, 2366, 2367, 2375, 2379, 2381, 2397, 2399, 2400, 2401, 2403, 2409, 2418, 2424, 2425, 2426, 2430, 2432, 2435, 2441, 2442, 2444, 2445, 2446, 2447, 2448, 2457, 2460, 2463, 2467, 2468, 2472, 2473, 2477, 2478, 2479, 2481, 2482, 2484, 2487, 2488, 2489, 2490, 2491, 2496, 2499, 2505, 2509, 2511, 2512, 2519, 2520, 2521, 2522, 2524, 2526, 2534, 2535, 2536, 2538, 2539, 2540, 2541, 2542, 2544, 2545, 2555, 2558, 2563, 2565, 2567, 2570, 2571, 2577, 2582, 2592, 2597, 2598, 2599, 2600, 2601, 2604, 2605, 2608, 2612, 2613, 2614, 2615, 2616, 2617, 2618, 2619, 2621, 2623, 2625, 2626, 2628, 2630, 2632, 2633, 2635, 2636, 2637, 2639, 2640, 2642, 2643, 2647, 2648, 2651, 2654, 2657, 2659, 2660, 2661, 2662, 2663, 2664, 2665, 2668, 2671, 2672, 2675, 2676, 2677, 2680, 2686, 2689, 2690, 2691, 2695, 2696, 2697, 2698, 2701, 2705, 2707, 2711, 2712, 2715, 2723, 2725, 2728, 2730, 2731, 2733, 2734, 2735, 2737, 2738, 2739, 2746, 2752, 2754, 2755, 2759, 2760, 2764, 2765, 2766, 2775, 2776, 2777, 2779, 2781, 2782, 2784, 2785, 2791, 2803, 2807, 2812, 2813, 2816, 2817, 2820, 2822, 2826, 2828, 2830, 2831, 2835, 2836, 2840, 2842, 2847, 2850, 2851, 2852, 2853, 2855, 2859, 2861, 2864, 2868, 2869, 2873, 2875, 2878, 2879, 2881, 2882, 2883, 2884, 2885, 2886, 2887, 2897, 2899, 2903, 2908, 2909, 2912, 2913, 2915, 2917, 2918, 2919, 2920, 2921, 2922, 2923, 2924, 2925, 2926, 2927, 2930, 2931, 2934, 2935, 2936, 2938, 2939, 2944, 2947, 2951, 2953, 2954, 2955, 2956, 2958, 2959, 2961, 2962, 2965, 2967, 2974, 2975, 2977, 2978, 2980, 2984, 2994, 2995, 2996, 2998, 3002, 3006, 3007, 3009, 3010, 3011, 3013, 3015, 3018, 3019, 3022, 3024, 3029, 3030, 3031, 3032, 3033, 3034, 3035, 3038, 3040, 3041, 3046, 3047, 3051, 3052, 3054, 3061, 3068, 3069, 3071, 3072, 3073, 3076, 3080, 3087, 3088, 3092, 3093, 3098, 3099, 3110, 3112, 3113, 3114, 3115, 3117, 3118, 3119, 3120, 3121, 3122, 3123, 3137, 3138, 3139, 3140, 3142, 3146, 3147, 3148, 3149, 3150, 3153, 3155, 3156, 3162, 3165, 3169, 3170, 3171, 3172, 3177, 3190, 3195, 3196, 3197, 3201, 3204, 3209, 3210, 3215, 3216, 3217, 3218, 3227, 3233, 3234, 3239, 3242, 3243, 3246, 3247, 3248, 3250, 3253, 3256, 3257, 3259, 3260, 3261, 3262, 3263, 3265, 3266, 3267, 3268, 3270, 3271, 3273, 3282, 3283, 3284, 3288,

3291, 3299, 3302, 3307, 3308, 3312, 3328, 3329, 3330, 3333, 3335, 3343, 3351, 3352, 3353, 3354, 3358, 3362, 3363, 3364, 3373, 3376, 3379, 3380, 3381, 3382, 3385, 3391, 3392, 3397, 3399, 3400, 3403, 3404, 3405, 3408, 3409, 3410, 3411, 3412, 3414, 3416, 3417, 3418, 3420, 3421, 3422, 3424, 3426, 3427, 3428, 3429, 3431, 3432, 3435, 3436, 3440, 3441, 3443, 3446, 3452, 3453, 3454, 3455, 3456, 3457, 3458, 3459, 3460, 3461, 3462, 3463, 3464, 3465, 3467, 3471, 3475, 3482, 3485, 3489, 3491, 3497, 3498, 3499, 3501, 3504, 3505, 3509, 3513, 3515, 3516, 3517, 3523, 3532, 3536, 3538, 3541, 3549, 3550, 3551, 3552, 3556, 3559, 3561, 3563, 3564, 3565, 3568, 3571, 3574, 3583, 3585, 3586, 3587, 3589, 3592, 3595, 3596, 3597, 3598, 3600, 3607, B3615, B3618, B3626, B3639, B3640, B3641, B3642, B3645, B3653, B3679, B3688, B3692, B3721, B3747, B3748, B3768, B3777, B3778, C3938, C3974, C3975, C3976

High School Dropout, 2575, 3269, 3496, B3694

Private K-12 School, 499, 1088, 1171, 1172, 2458, 2465, 2501, 2510, 2644, 2645, 2653, 2656, 2667, 2673, 2691, 2693, 2745, 2799, 2809, 2849, 2857, 2866, 2870, 2900, 2906, 2907, 2910, 2985, 2986, 3056, 3075, 3108, 3111, 3224, 3230, 3240, 3255, 3264, 3280, 3319, 3320, 3321, 3322, 3326, 3374, 3406, 3419, 3421, 3423, 3430, 3439, 3442, 3447, 3450, 3451, 3466, 3470, 3473, 3476, 3484, 3486, 3539, 3557, 3566, 3567, B3666, B3699, B3700, B3708, B3756, B3789, B3799

Associates, 5, 9, 12, 24, 25, 26, 27, 28, 29, 30, 31, 32, 33, 34, 35, 36, 37, 41, 43, 44, 46, 51, 53, 55, 58, 63, 65, 67, 75, 76, 77, 78, 79, 81, 83, 85, 87, 88, 96, 99, 100, 103, 106, 111, 112, 114, 120, 125, 131, 133, 137, 138, 140, 141, 144, 149, 157, 160, 167, 168, 169, 170, 171, 172, 173, 183, 184, 185, 186, 190, 191, 195, 197, 200, 202, 203, 208, 212, 213, 216, 217, 221, 222, 223, 224, 237, 252, 255, 258, 263, 267, 268, 270, 271, 272, 278, 279, 280, 282, 284, 285, 294, 298, 299, 300, 303, 305, 313, 319, 323, 329, 332, 348, 349, 353, 358, 362, 411, 412, 415, 417, 434, 445, 446, 447, 448, 449, 450, 451, 452, 453, 454, 455, 456, 457, 458, 464, 472, 476, 477, 483, 487, 488, 489, 499, 502, 505, 514, 539, 540, 552, 565, 577, 578, 579, 582, 589, 590, 597, 598, 602, 613, 625, 628, 629, 631, 635, 637, 638, 639, 640, 641, 642, 643, 644, 645, 646, 647, 648, 649, 650, 652, 657, 659, 661, 667, 669, 678, 685, 689, 702, 709, 711, 714, 715, 721, 727, 729, 734, 740, 746,

749, 757, 762, 765, 770, 772, 777, 780, 786, 796, 800, 809, 813, 814, 817, 821, 822, 837, 838, 840, 845, 851, 852, 858, 862, 865, 874, 884, 885, 887, 889, 891, 897, 903, 907, 913, 916, 919, 920, 923, 926, 927, 928, 929, 931, 937, 941, 942, 944, 954, 966, 969, 970, 973, 980, 981, 997, 1004, 1005, 1006, 1007, 1028, 1033, 1042, 1045, 1047, 1048, 1050, 1054, 1065, 1075, 1077, 1079, 1081, 1088, 1101, 1113, 1121, 1122, 1128, 1129, 1138, 1143, 1147, 1162, 1168, 1171, 1172, 1184, 1190, 1198, 1199, 1202, 1205, 1206, 1209, 1211, 1212, 1216, 1225, 1226, 1227, 1229, 1230, 1234, 1235, 1240, 1258, 1273, 1278, 1280, 1282, 1288, 1291, 1294, 1307, 1308, 1309, 1310, 1311, 1312, 1313, 1314, 1315, 1316, 1317, 1318, 1319, 1320, 1321, 1322, 1323, 1334, 1335, 1338, 1342, 1344, 1350, 1352, 1354, 1361, 1364, 1366, 1369, 1371, 1372, 1380, 1387, 1390, 1395, 1400, 1401, 1409, 1412, 1418, 1427, 1431, 1432, 1434, 1436, 1437, 1442, 1445, 1452, 1453, 1457, 1459, 1467, 1470, 1474, 1475, 1480, 1481, 1486, 1488, 1495, 1498, 1508, 1509, 1511, 1517, 1521, 1523, 1524, 1525, 1530, 1534, 1537, 1544, 1545, 1548, 1549, 1550, 1555, 1558, 1561, 1564, 1565, 1572, 1577, 1579, 1580, 1585, 1586, 1603, 1608, 1613, 1616, 1618, 1626, 1636, 1639, 1648, 1649, 1651, 1655, 1656, 1658, 1660, 1664, 1666, 1669, 1672, 1673, 1679, 1681, 1690, 1691, 1692, 1698, 1699, 1700, 1710, 1711, 1713, 1719, 1722, 1725, 1737, 1740, 1741, 1743, 1744, 1746, 1747, 1750, 1751, 1756, 1757, 1758, 1762, 1766, 1769, 1773, 1774, 1775, 1778, 1784, 1789, 1793, 1794, 1797, 1798, 1803, 1804, 1806, 1809, 1812, 1813, 1818, 1820, 1823, 1824, 1827, 1828, 1829, 1832, 1838, 1839, 1844, 1858, 1862, 1863, 1864, 1865, 1872, 1873, 1879, 1880, 1884, 1885, 1887, 1889, 1890, 1893, 1894, 1895, 1896, 1897, 1899, 1900, 1903, 1904, 1907, 1908, 1911, 1916, 1919, 1921, 1922, 1923, 1924, 1926, 1927, 1928, 1930, 1931, 1933, 1935, 1939, 1940, 1941, 1942, 1945, 1946, 1947, 1948, 1953, 1955, 1958, 1959, 1963, 1966, 1969, 1970, 1972, 1973, 1974, 1975, 1977, 1980, 1983, 1984, 1986, 1993, 1996, 1997, 1999, 2000, 2001, 2002, 2004, 2006, 2007, 2012, 2013, 2014, 2015, 2016, 2017, 2018, 2019, 2020, 2021, 2022, 2023, 2024, 2025, 2026, 2027, 2036, 2037, 2038, 2041, 2042, 2044, 2046, 2047, 2048, 2049, 2050, 2054, 2062, 2067, 2075, 2077, 2079, 2091, 2093, 2095, 2096, 2097, 2098, 2103, 2106, 2111, 2121, 2124, 2130,

2132, 2133, 2142, 2143, 2144, 2145, 2148, 2150, 2160, 2164, 2166, 2168, 2176, 2187, 2190, 2191, 2199, 2201, 2202, 2211, 2214, 2216, 2220, 2227, 2231, 2232, 2233, 2234, 2238, 2245, 2248, 2254, 2255, 2261, 2264, 2267, 2269, 2274, 2275, 2276, 2289, 2294, 2295, 2298, 2299, 2301, 2305, 2311, 2315, 2320, 2321, 2324, 2336, 2347, 2361, 2362, 2363, 2364, 2369, 2372, 2373, 2375, 2379, 2381, 2384, 2389, 2390, 2407, 2408, 2409, 2410, 2411, 2412, 2417, 2418, 2419, 2423, 2424, 2426, 2427, 2428, 2431, 2433, 2437, 2438, 2439, 2441, 2448, 2450, 2453, 2455, 2458, 2459, 2460, 2464, 2465, 2475, 2476, 2479, 2482, 2489, 2490, 2491, 2492, 2495, 2496, 2497, 2499, 2500, 2505, 2507, 2514, 2516, 2517, 2518, 2519, 2522, 2527, 2530, 2540, 2542, 2544, 2546, 2548, 2549, 2551, 2552, 2553, 2554, 2556, 2557, 2558, 2559, 2562, 2568, 2569, 2572, 2573, 2574, 2576, 2581, 2583, 2588, 2595, 2598, 2600, 2602, 2603, 2606, 2608, 2610, 2611, 2612, 2618, 2620, 2622, 2623, 2625, 2626, 2627, 2628, 2630, 2631, 2635, 2636, 2637, 2638, 2640, 2641, 2642, 2652, 2660, 2661, 2662, 2665, 2666, 2672, 2675, 2676, 2677, 2678, 2679, 2682, 2683, 2684, 2685, 2687, 2695, 2696, 2699, 2701, 2702, 2703, 2704, 2705, 2706, 2708, 2709, 2710, 2711, 2712, 2713, 2714, 2716, 2717, 2718, 2719, 2720, 2721, 2722, 2725, 2728, 2729, 2732, 2733, 2734, 2735, 2739, 2740, 2744, 2747, 2749, 2750, 2751, 2752, 2753, 2757, 2758, 2760, 2761, 2767, 2780, 2786, 2788, 2798, 2800, 2803, 2804, 2807, 2808, 2811, 2818, 2819, 2823, 2827, 2829, 2830, 2832, 2836, 2844, 2848, 2851, 2852, 2854, 2856, 2859, 2860, 2863, 2865, 2871, 2873, 2876, 2877, 2879, 2880, 2890, 2891, 2898, 2899, 2905, 2908, 2914, 2915, 2919, 2920, 2926, 2928, 2929, 2931, 2932, 2936, 2940, 2942, 2943, 2944, 2946, 2948, 2954, 2955, 2961, 2963, 2964, 2966, 2967, 2968, 2971, 2974, 2976, 2979, 2981, 2982, 2995, 2996, 3001, 3004, 3010, 3012, 3015, 3019, 3022, 3025, 3026, 3027, 3028, 3032, 3033, 3034, 3035, 3036, 3037, 3043, 3044, 3046, 3048, 3049, 3051, 3052, 3054, 3057, 3058, 3060, 3062, 3064, 3065, 3073, 3077, 3078, 3079, 3080, 3084, 3085, 3086, 3087, 3088, 3090, 3096, 3098, 3104, 3105, 3106, 3114, 3115, 3116, 3122, 3128, 3129, 3130, 3131, 3132, 3133, 3134, 3135, 3136, 3139, 3140, 3141, 3143, 3148, 3150, 3152, 3153, 3155, 3156, 3162, 3165, 3169, 3173, 3174, 3178, 3179, 3183, 3184, 3189, 3190,

3193, 3195, 3198, 3199, 3203, 3208, 3211, 3212, 3215, 3216, 3220, 3225, 3227, 3231, 3232, 3238, 3241, 3243, 3244, 3246, 3247, 3248, 3252, 3258, 3259, 3263, 3266, 3268, 3276, 3278, 3282, 3283, 3285, 3286, 3287, 3292, 3293, 3296, 3301, 3305, 3308, 3313, 3315, 3323, 3328, 3329, 3330, 3331, 3337, 3339, 3340, 3341, 3344, 3346, 3347, 3349, 3350, 3352, 3356, 3357, 3361, 3365, 3366, 3369, 3370, 3371, 3372, 3377, 3383, 3387, 3389, 3390, 3392, 3394, 3396, 3398, 3400, 3413, 3415, 3418, 3420, 3427, 3434, 3435, 3441, 3444, 3452, 3453, 3454, 3455, 3456, 3457, 3458, 3459, 3460, 3461, 3462, 3463, 3464, 3465, 3469, 3480, 3483, 3489, 3491, 3495, 3496, 3498, 3506, 3507, 3521, 3532, 3534, 3535, 3538, 3542, 3545, 3555, 3558, 3563, 3565, 3568, 3569, 3573, 3579, 3580, 3581, 3588, 3590, 3591, 3593, 3594, 3607, B3608, B3615, B3618, B3626, B3638, B3640, B3641, B3644, B3645, B3648, B3654, B3655, B3658, B3661, B3666, B3679, B3681, B3688, B3695, B3703, B3704, B3709, B3712, B3726, B3731, B3734, B3737, B3738, B3746, B3748, B3749, B3752, B3757, B3758, B3768, B3793, B3809, C3845, C3846, C3862, C3865, C3901, C3917, C3938

Associates 1st Year, 42, 177, 209, 301, 392, 413, 414, 418, 424, 429, 433, 437, 439, 473, 512, 562, 564, 566, 588, 656, 701, 712, 713, 759, 775, 832, 991, 1037, 1102, 1247, 1265, 1267, 1275, 1279, 1300, 1324, 1331, 1382, 1389, 1404, 1420, 1429, 1451, 1471, 1560, 1563, 1594, 1597, 1788, 1933, 2045, 2051, 2053, 2072, 2162, 2300, 2345, 2489, 2541, 2575, 2737, 2833, 2834, 2887, 2927, 2965, 3040, 3071, 3117, 3250, 3280, 3587, 3595, B3653

Associates 2nd Year, 38, 66, 143, 209, 316, 355, 416, 419, 420, 422, 423, 431, 432, 436, 438, 469, 564, 566, 633, 710, 712, 713, 719, 742, 784, 804, 883, 900, 905, 943, 985, 1231, 1248, 1265, 1267, 1274, 1275, 1276, 1304, 1327, 1348, 1393, 1404, 1455, 1519, 1539, 1597, 1606, 1647, 1724, 1847, 1848, 1852, 1854, 1855, 1856, 1857, 1867, 1933, 1964, 2052, 2112, 2162, 2185, 2251, 2270, 2303, 2344, 2466, 2566, 2694, 2737, 2845, 2980, 3290, 3338, 3560, 3587

Associates 3rd Year, 38, 39, 49, 66, 98, 118, 139, 142, 143, 182, 192, 228, 316, 318, 355, 419, 420, 421, 423, 425, 426, 428, 430, 431, 435, 436, 467, 469, 524, 564, 566, 572, 601, 633, 653, 680, 703, 710, 719, 720, 742, 778, 779, 781, 782, 784, 785, 790, 804, 882, 883, 900, 905, 985, 1001, 1231, 1248, 1269, 1272, 1274, 1275, 1304, 1327, 1329, 1345, 1348,

1349, 1357, 1362, 1393, 1396, 1402, 1404, 1438, 1440, 1455, 1519, 1522, 1526, 1536, 1539, 1540, 1568, 1574, 1606, 1607, 1645, 1647, 1724, 1847, 1848, 1852, 1854, 1855, 1856, 1857, 1892, 1914, 2043, 2052, 2094, 2104, 2112, 2113, 2114, 2115, 2120, 2127, 2203, 2229, 2251, 2270, 2296, 2325, 2342, 2352, 2380, 2383, 2566, 2694, 2737, 2794, 2845, 2980, 3290, 3560

Transfer Student, 160, 275, 382, 392, 403, 635, 755, 912, 985, 1148, 1158, 1215, 1284, 1509, 1636, 2171, 2191, 2336, 2397, 2686, 2689, 2765, 2821, 3030, 3204, 3205, 3206, 3329, 3331, 3411, 3516, 3548

Bachelors, 6, 7, 9, 10, 12, 13, 14, 15, 16, 17, 18, 20, 21, 23, 24, 25, 26, 27, 28, 29, 30, 31, 32, 33, 34, 35, 36, 37, 41, 43, 44, 45, 46, 47, 51, 53, 54, 55, 56, 58, 60, 63, 65, 67, 69, 70, 71, 75, 76, 77, 79, 80, 81, 83, 85, 87, 88, 90, 91, 93, 94, 96, 99, 100, 101, 103, 106, 107, 108, 110, 111, 112, 113, 114, 115, 117, 120, 121, 122, 123, 124, 125, 126, 131, 132, 133, 134, 135, 136, 137, 138, 140, 141, 144, 147, 148, 149, 156, 157, 158, 164, 167, 168, 169, 170, 171, 172, 173, 174, 175, 178, 179, 180, 183, 184, 185, 186, 191, 195, 196, 197, 199, 200, 201, 202, 203, 208, 212, 213, 215, 216, 218, 221, 222, 223, 224, 225, 226, 230, 234, 235, 236, 237, 243, 244, 254, 255, 258, 259, 261, 263, 265, 266, 267, 268, 270, 271, 272, 275, 278, 279, 280, 282, 283, 284, 285, 287, 291, 293, 294, 296, 298, 299, 300, 303, 305, 307, 308, 310, 311, 313, 321, 322, 323, 327, 329, 331, 332, 335, 337, 338, 339, 340, 342, 343, 345, 347, 348, 349, 350, 351, 353, 354, 356, 357, 358, 362, 363, 370, 378, 386, 411, 412, 415, 417, 434, 445, 446, 447, 448, 449, 450, 451, 452, 453, 454, 455, 456, 457, 458, 461, 464, 470, 471, 472, 474, 476, 477, 481, 483, 484, 486, 487, 488, 489, 495, 499, 500, 502, 505, 506, 514, 517, 518, 521, 522, 527, 532, 533, 534, 536, 537, 539, 540, 541, 542, 543, 546, 550, 551, 552, 553, 555, 556, 560, 561, 565, 570, 575, 577, 578, 579, 580, 582, 585, 586, 587, 589, 590, 591, 592, 595, 597, 598, 603, 606, 607, 609, 610, 612, 613, 614, 615, 616, 617, 618, 619, 620, 621, 625, 626, 627, 628, 629, 630, 631, 637, 638, 639, 640, 641, 642, 643, 644, 645, 646, 647, 648, 649, 650, 652, 654, 655, 657, 658, 659, 660, 661, 662, 663, 664, 665, 666, 667, 668, 669, 670, 671, 672, 673, 676, 678, 683, 684, 685, 686, 689, 691, 695, 696, 698, 699, 700, 702, 706, 707, 708, 709, 714, 715, 716, 721, 726, 727, 729, 730, 731, 732, 733, 734, 735, 740, 741, 743, 744, 745, 746, 749, 757, 758, 762, 764, 765, 767, 769, 770, 772, 773, 774, 776,

777, 780, 786, 787, 792, 794, 796, 797,
798, 800, 805, 806, 809, 810, 811, 814,
815, 817, 819, 821, 822, 823, 827, 828,
829, 830, 831, 835, 837, 838, 840, 841,
843, 845, 847, 851, 852, 853, 856, 857,
858, 859, 860, 862, 865, 866, 869, 870,
871, 874, 875, 878, 884, 885, 886, 887,
888, 889, 891, 892, 897, 903, 904, 907,
912, 913, 916, 919, 920, 921, 923, 926,
927, 928, 929, 931, 932, 933, 934, 935,
937, 939, 940, 941, 942, 944, 946, 947,
949, 950, 952, 953, 954, 956, 961, 966,
969, 970, 973, 974, 980, 981, 989, 992,
997, 1004, 1005, 1006, 1007, 1019, 1020,
1021, 1022, 1028, 1031, 1032, 1033,
1041, 1042, 1043, 1044, 1045, 1047,
1048, 1049, 1050, 1053, 1054, 1055,
1056, 1057, 1059, 1060, 1061, 1064,
1065, 1066, 1073, 1074, 1075, 1077,
1078, 1079, 1081, 1083, 1088, 1092,
1093, 1096, 1100, 1101, 1103, 1104,
1107, 1108, 1113, 1121, 1122, 1124,
1129, 1134, 1135, 1136, 1137, 1138,
1143, 1147, 1148, 1152, 1154, 1158,
1160, 1162, 1166, 1167, 1168, 1171,
1172, 1176, 1177, 1179, 1180, 1181,
1182, 1184, 1186, 1187, 1188, 1189,
1190, 1192, 1193, 1194, 1195, 1196,
1197, 1198, 1199, 1201, 1202, 1203,
1204, 1205, 1206, 1207, 1209, 1211,
1212, 1213, 1215, 1216, 1218, 1219,
1220, 1221, 1221, 1222, 1225, 1226,
1227, 1229, 1230, 1232, 1234, 1235,
1239, 1240, 1243, 1244, 1245, 1249,
1252, 1258, 1266, 1271, 1273, 1277,
1278, 1280, 1281, 1282, 1284, 1285,
1288, 1289, 1291, 1294, 1297, 1301,
1303, 1306, 1307, 1308, 1309, 1310,
1311, 1312, 1313, 1314, 1315, 1316,
1317, 1318, 1319, 1320, 1321, 1322,
1323, 1326, 1333, 1334, 1337, 1338,
1340, 1341, 1342, 1343, 1344, 1350,
1351, 1352, 1353, 1354, 1356, 1360,
1361, 1364, 1365, 1366, 1369, 1371,
1372, 1376, 1378, 1379, 1380, 1383,
1384, 1387, 1390, 1395, 1398, 1400,
1401, 1406, 1407, 1408, 1409, 1412,
1415, 1416, 1417, 1418, 1419, 1421,
1423, 1427, 1430, 1431, 1432, 1434,
1435, 1436, 1437, 1442, 1445, 1447,
1452, 1453, 1457, 1459, 1461, 1462,
1463, 1464, 1465, 1466, 1467, 1470,
1474, 1475, 1477, 1478, 1480, 1482,
1483, 1486, 1488, 1492, 1493, 1495,
1498, 1499, 1500, 1504, 1507, 1508,
1511, 1517, 1521, 1523, 1524, 1525,
1530, 1531, 1532, 1534, 1538, 1543,
1545, 1548, 1549, 1550, 1554, 1555,
1556, 1558, 1561, 1564, 1565, 1566,
1569, 1570, 1572, 1576, 1577, 1578,
1580, 1583, 1585, 1586, 1591, 1598,
1601, 1603, 1613, 1614, 1617, 1618,
1622, 1624, 1625, 1626, 1630, 1633,
1635, 1639, 1648, 1649, 1651, 1652,

1653, 1654, 1655, 1656, 1659, 1660,
1661, 1662, 1663, 1664, 1665, 1666,
1667, 1668, 1669, 1672, 1674, 1675,
1676, 1677, 1681, 1682, 1683, 1684,
1685, 1686, 1690, 1691, 1692, 1693,
1698, 1699, 1700, 1701, 1702, 1706,
1708, 1709, 1710, 1711, 1712, 1713,
1714, 1716, 1719, 1720, 1722, 1725,
1729, 1734, 1735, 1736, 1737, 1739,
1740, 1741, 1745, 1746, 1747, 1748,
1749, 1750, 1751, 1753, 1755, 1756,
1757, 1758, 1761, 1763, 1764, 1765,
1769, 1770, 1771, 1772, 1773, 1774,
1775, 1778, 1784, 1785, 1786, 1791,
1792, 1793, 1794, 1796, 1797, 1798,
1802, 1803, 1804, 1806, 1809, 1810,
1811, 1812, 1813, 1815, 1817, 1819,
1820, 1823, 1824, 1827, 1828, 1829,
1832, 1833, 1835, 1837, 1838, 1839,
1841, 1842, 1843, 1844, 1858, 1859,
1860, 1861, 1862, 1863, 1864, 1865,
1871, 1872, 1873, 1877, 1878, 1879,
1880, 1882, 1884, 1885, 1887, 1889,
1890, 1893, 1894, 1895, 1896, 1897,
1898, 1899, 1900, 1903, 1905, 1907,
1908, 1909, 1915, 1916, 1917, 1918,
1919, 1920, 1921, 1922, 1923, 1924,
1926, 1927, 1928, 1930, 1931, 1934,
1935, 1936, 1938, 1939, 1940, 1941,
1942, 1945, 1946, 1947, 1948, 1950,
1951, 1952, 1953, 1954, 1955, 1957,
1958, 1959, 1965, 1966, 1967, 1968,
1969, 1970, 1971, 1972, 1973, 1974,
1975, 1976, 1977, 1980, 1982, 1983,
1985, 1986, 1987, 1989, 1991, 1996,
1997, 1998, 1999, 2000, 2001, 2002,
2003, 2004, 2005, 2006, 2007, 2008,
2009, 2012, 2013, 2014, 2015, 2016,
2017, 2018, 2019, 2020, 2021, 2022,
2023, 2024, 2025, 2026, 2027, 2028,
2031, 2033, 2034, 2036, 2037, 2038,
2039, 2040, 2041, 2042, 2044, 2046,
2047, 2048, 2049, 2050, 2054, 2055,
2056, 2057, 2058, 2059, 2060, 2062,
2067, 2070, 2075, 2079, 2081, 2085,
2086, 2087, 2088, 2091, 2093, 2095,
2096, 2097, 2098, 2100, 2103, 2106,
2110, 2111, 2121, 2123, 2124, 2126,
2130, 2132, 2135, 2136, 2142, 2143,
2144, 2145, 2146, 2148, 2150, 2152,
2155, 2160, 2161, 2163, 2164, 2165,
2166, 2168, 2171, 2176, 2179, 2180,
2181, 2183, 2184, 2186, 2187, 2188,
2189, 2190, 2199, 2201, 2202, 2204,
2205, 2209, 2211, 2214, 2216, 2218,
2220, 2223, 2224, 2227, 2228, 2231,
2232, 2233, 2234, 2235, 2236, 2237,
2238, 2241, 2243, 2245, 2248, 2249,
2250, 2252, 2255, 2259, 2260, 2261,
2264, 2265, 2267, 2268, 2271, 2273,
2274, 2275, 2276, 2277, 2281, 2282,
2283, 2284, 2285, 2286, 2287, 2288,
2289, 2290, 2292, 2293, 2294, 2295,
2298, 2299, 2301, 2305, 2309, 2310,

2311, 2313, 2315, 2316, 2317, 2320,
2321, 2324, 2328, 2331, 2332, 2333,
2334, 2335, 2338, 2340, 2343, 2347,
2349, 2351, 2353, 2357, 2358, 2361,
2362, 2363, 2364, 2365, 2366, 2367,
2369, 2371, 2372, 2373, 2375, 2379,
2381, 2384, 2385, 2387, 2389, 2394,
2397, 2399, 2400, 2401, 2403, 2403,
2404, 2405, 2407, 2408, 2409, 2410,
2411, 2412, 2413, 2417, 2418, 2419,
2420, 2425, 2426, 2428, 2431, 2433,
2436, 2437, 2438, 2439, 2440, 2441,
2442, 2444, 2445, 2446, 2447, 2448,
2450, 2455, 2458, 2459, 2460, 2464,
2475, 2476, 2477, 2479, 2480, 2481,
2482, 2484, 2485, 2487, 2490, 2491,
2492, 2493, 2494, 2495, 2496, 2497,
2499, 2500, 2502, 2504, 2505, 2507,
2514, 2516, 2517, 2518, 2519, 2522,
2525, 2527, 2528, 2529, 2530, 2531,
2532, 2533, 2538, 2540, 2542, 2543,
2544, 2546, 2547, 2548, 2549, 2550,
2551, 2552, 2553, 2554, 2556, 2557,
2558, 2559, 2560, 2562, 2564, 2565,
2567, 2568, 2569, 2572, 2573, 2574,
2576, 2577, 2579, 2581, 2582, 2583,
2587, 2588, 2590, 2591, 2592, 2594,
2595, 2598, 2599, 2600, 2602, 2603,
2606, 2607, 2608, 2609, 2610, 2611,
2612, 2615, 2616, 2617, 2618, 2620,
2621, 2622, 2623, 2624, 2626, 2627,
2628, 2629, 2630, 2631, 2633, 2635,
2636, 2637, 2638, 2640, 2641, 2642,
2643, 2649, 2652, 2658, 2660, 2661,
2662, 2664, 2665, 2666, 2668, 2670,
2672, 2674, 2675, 2676, 2677, 2678,
2679, 2682, 2683, 2684, 2685, 2686,
2687, 2688, 2689, 2692, 2695, 2696,
2697, 2699, 2700, 2701, 2702, 2703,
2704, 2705, 2706, 2708, 2709, 2710,
2711, 2712, 2713, 2714, 2716, 2717,
2718, 2719, 2720, 2721, 2722, 2724,
2725, 2726, 2727, 2728, 2729, 2732,
2733, 2734, 2735, 2736, 2738, 2739,
2740, 2741, 2742, 2743, 2744, 2747,
2748, 2749, 2750, 2751, 2752, 2753,
2757, 2758, 2760, 2761, 2762, 2764,
2765, 2766, 2767, 2768, 2772, 2774,
2775, 2776, 2780, 2784, 2785, 2786,
2788, 2790, 2791, 2793, 2798, 2800,
2801, 2803, 2804, 2805, 2807, 2808,
2811, 2813, 2814, 2815, 2816, 2818,
2819, 2821, 2823, 2825, 2827, 2829,
2830, 2832, 2835, 2836, 2837, 2838,
2841, 2843, 2844, 2848, 2850, 2851,
2852, 2853, 2854, 2856, 2858, 2859,
2860, 2861, 2863, 2865, 2869, 2871,
2872, 2873, 2876, 2877, 2879, 2880,
2882, 2883, 2884, 2885, 2886, 2888,
2889, 2890, 2891, 2896, 2897, 2898,
2899, 2904, 2905, 2908, 2911, 2914,
2915, 2917, 2919, 2920, 2926, 2928,
2929, 2931, 2932, 2933, 2936, 2940,
2942, 2943, 2944, 2945, 2946, 2948,

2952, 2953, 2954, 2955, 2956, 2961, 2962, 2963, 2964, 2966, 2967, 2968, 2969, 2970, 2971, 2973, 2974, 2976, 2977, 2981, 2982, 2983, 2984, 2988, 2989, 2991, 2992, 2993, 2995, 2996, 3000, 3001, 3002, 3004, 3005, 3006, 3007, 3010, 3013, 3015, 3018, 3019, 3020, 3021, 3022, 3023, 3025, 3026, 3027, 3028, 3032, 3033, 3034, 3035, 3036, 3037, 3041, 3043, 3044, 3046, 3048, 3049, 3050, 3051, 3052, 3053, 3054, 3055, 3057, 3058, 3059, 3060, 3062, 3063, 3064, 3065, 3066, 3067, 3068, 3070, 3073, 3074, 3077, 3078, 3079, 3080, 3082, 3083, 3084, 3085, 3086, 3087, 3088, 3090, 3095, 3096, 3097, 3098, 3099, 3100, 3102, 3104, 3105, 3106, 3109, 3112, 3114, 3115, 3116, 3122, 3124, 3126, 3127, 3128, 3129, 3130, 3131, 3132, 3133, 3134, 3135, 3136, 3139, 3140, 3141, 3143, 3144, 3145, 3147, 3148, 3150, 3152, 3153, 3154, 3155, 3156, 3157, 3158, 3159, 3160, 3161, 3162, 3165, 3169, 3173, 3174, 3175, 3178, 3179, 3180, 3181, 3182, 3183, 3184, 3185, 3186, 3187, 3189, 3190, 3191, 3192, 3193, 3195, 3196, 3197, 3198, 3199, 3200, 3202, 3203, 3205, 3206, 3207, 3208, 3210, 3211, 3212, 3214, 3215, 3216, 3219, 3220, 3222, 3225, 3226, 3229, 3231, 3232, 3234, 3235, 3238, 3241, 3243, 3244, 3246, 3247, 3248, 3252, 3257, 3258, 3259, 3261, 3263, 3266, 3268, 3274, 3276, 3277, 3281, 3282, 3283, 3284, 3285, 3286, 3287, 3292, 3293, 3294, 3295, 3296, 3301, 3302, 3303, 3304, 3305, 3308, 3313, 3315, 3316, 3317, 3323, 3325, 3327, 3328, 3334, 3335, 3336, 3337, 3339, 3340, 3341, 3342, 3344, 3345, 3346, 3347, 3348, 3349, 3350, 3352, 3355, 3356, 3357, 3360, 3361, 3365, 3366, 3367, 3368, 3369, 3370, 3371, 3372, 3373, 3375, 3376, 3377, 3378, 3381, 3382, 3383, 3384, 3387, 3389, 3390, 3392, 3393, 3394, 3395, 3396, 3397, 3398, 3400, 3406, 3407, 3409, 3410, 3411, 3413, 3414, 3415, 3417, 3418, 3420, 3424, 3427, 3434, 3435, 3438, 3440, 3441, 3444, 3445, 3446, 3448, 3452, 3453, 3454, 3455, 3456, 3457, 3458, 3459, 3460, 3461, 3462, 3463, 3464, 3465, 3467, 3469, 3472, 3474, 3477, 3479, 3480, 3483, 3485, 3487, 3488, 3489, 3491, 3495, 3496, 3498, 3500, 3502, 3503, 3506, 3507, 3510, 3511, 3512, 3513, 3516, 3519, 3521, 3523, 3526, 3527, 3530, 3532, 3534, 3535, 3538, 3542, 3543, 3545, 3546, 3548, 3550, 3553, 3555, 3558, 3563, 3565, 3568, 3569, 3570, 3571, 3573, 3575, 3579, 3580, 3581, 3588, 3590, 3591, 3593, 3594, 3596, 3598, 3607, B3608,

B3615, B3618, B3623, B3626, B3638, B3639, B3640, B3641, B3642, B3643, B3645, B3648, B3654, B3655, B3656, B3658, B3661, B3666, B3669, B3671, B3674, B3677, B3679, B3681, B3688, B3692, B3695, B3703, B3704, B3709, B3711, B3712, B3717, B3726, B3731, B3734, B3737, B3738, B3739, B3741, B3746, B3747, B3749, B3750, B3752, B3755, B3757, B3768, B3777, B3782, B3785, B3793, B3794, B3809, C3830, C3845, C3846, C3863, C3864, C3865, C3901, C3917, C3938, C3974, C3976, C3983

Bachelors Freshman, 6, 42, 80, 177, 209, 225, 301, 321, 366, 367, 368, 369, 371, 373, 374, 375, 376, 377, 379, 380, 381, 382, 383, 384, 385, 387, 388, 391, 392, 393, 394, 395, 397, 398, 399, 400, 401, 402, 404, 405, 406, 407, 408, 409, 413, 414, 418, 424, 429, 433, 437, 439, 462, 463, 473, 512, 562, 564, 566, 569, 588, 603, 632, 656, 701, 711, 712, 739, 751, 752, 754, 755, 756, 759, 768, 775, 802, 824, 832, 855, 873, 877, 959, 991, 1037, 1062, 1102, 1232, 1247, 1262, 1275, 1279, 1290, 1299, 1300, 1324, 1331, 1382, 1389, 1404, 1420, 1429, 1451, 1471, 1473, 1482, 1502, 1516, 1551, 1560, 1563, 1587, 1594, 1597, 1627, 1687, 1776, 1788, 1825, 1933, 1957, 2045, 2051, 2053, 2072, 2162, 2175, 2246, 2300, 2322, 2345, 2480, 2489, 2535, 2539, 2541, 2575, 2625, 2652, 2657, 2664, 2737, 2763, 2833, 2834, 2878, 2887, 2902, 2927, 2930, 2950, 2959, 2960, 2965, 2987, 3008, 3009, 3011, 3030, 3040, 3041, 3071, 3117, 3142, 3146, 3151, 3204, 3250, 3307, 3404, 3408, 3414, 3429, 3501, 3517, 3528, 3547, 3587, 3595, B3653, B3748

Bachelors Sophomore, 3, 4, 6, 38, 57, 61, 66, 72, 73, 74, 80, 82, 128, 130, 143, 146, 154, 155, 157, 166, 209, 225, 229, 241, 242, 256, 276, 316, 321, 355, 416, 419, 420, 422, 423, 431, 432, 436, 438, 443, 444, 469, 479, 485, 497, 498, 520, 545, 564, 566, 567, 569, 581, 593, 594, 603, 623, 624, 633, 674, 675, 693, 694, 704, 710, 711, 712, 719, 738, 742, 784, 801, 804, 812, 836, 861, 883, 900, 905, 943, 951, 985, 1038, 1051, 1052, 1231, 1232, 1248, 1253, 1255, 1256, 1257, 1259, 1261, 1263, 1274, 1275, 1298, 1304, 1327, 1348, 1393, 1397, 1404, 1411, 1455, 1482, 1502, 1519, 1528, 1529, 1539, 1551, 1587, 1596, 1597, 1599, 1600, 1606, 1619, 1620, 1621, 1627, 1647, 1678, 1680, 1687, 1718, 1724, 1733, 1767, 1768, 1776, 1782, 1783, 1822, 1825, 1845, 1846, 1849, 1850, 1851, 1853, 1854, 1855, 1888, 1912, 1933, 1956, 1957, 1994, 2052, 2060, 2074, 2101, 2112, 2147, 2156, 2157,

2159, 2162, 2173, 2175, 2185, 2196, 2246, 2247, 2251, 2270, 2302, 2303, 2327, 2337, 2344, 2346, 2350, 2374, 2382, 2393, 2415, 2421, 2454, 2456, 2466, 2483, 2489, 2535, 2539, 2566, 2580, 2586, 2594, 2646, 2652, 2694, 2737, 2756, 2763, 2783, 2797, 2839, 2845, 2950, 2959, 2979, 2980, 3213, 3290, 3297, 3338, 3433, 3449, 3490, 3494, 3525, 3528, 3529, 3560, 3587, 3606

Bachelors Junior, 3, 4, 5, 6, 11, 22, 38, 39, 48, 49, 50, 57, 61, 62, 64, 66, 72, 73, 74, 78, 80, 82, 98, 104, 109, 116, 118, 127, 128, 130, 139, 142, 143, 146, 154, 155, 157, 161, 162, 166, 176, 182, 190, 192, 193, 210, 217, 220, 225, 228, 229, 231, 239, 241, 242, 245, 252, 253, 256, 260, 269, 276, 281, 286, 289, 290, 295, 302, 315, 316, 318, 319, 320, 321, 325, 326, 333, 334, 336, 352, 355, 361, 419, 420, 421, 423, 425, 426, 428, 430, 431, 435, 436, 440, 444, 465, 466, 467, 469, 478, 479, 480, 485, 497, 501, 508, 509, 513, 515, 520, 524, 528, 531, 535, 538, 545, 547, 559, 564, 566, 567, 569, 572, 574, 581, 593, 594, 600, 601, 602, 603, 611, 623, 624, 633, 636, 651, 653, 674, 675, 679, 680, 687, 688, 693, 694, 703, 710, 711, 718, 719, 720, 728, 738, 742, 750, 763, 771, 778, 779, 781, 782, 783, 784, 785, 789, 790, 793, 804, 808, 812, 813, 818, 836, 848, 854, 856, 861, 883, 893, 900, 905, 908, 910, 943, 951, 985, 988, 993, 996, 1001, 1038, 1051, 1052, 1105, 1114, 1118, 1128, 1208, 1217, 1231, 1232, 1237, 1238, 1248, 1253, 1254, 1255, 1256, 1257, 1259, 1260, 1261, 1263, 1264, 1268, 1269, 1272, 1274, 1275, 1276, 1286, 1287, 1298, 1304, 1327, 1329, 1330, 1336, 1339, 1345, 1348, 1349, 1357, 1359, 1362, 1367, 1388, 1391, 1393, 1396, 1397, 1402, 1404, 1411, 1424, 1428, 1438, 1440, 1448, 1450, 1454, 1455, 1481, 1482, 1490, 1497, 1502, 1515, 1519, 1522, 1526, 1528, 1529, 1536, 1537, 1539, 1540, 1544, 1551, 1559, 1568, 1574, 1579, 1581, 1587, 1590, 1593, 1596, 1599, 1600, 1605, 1606, 1607, 1608, 1615, 1616, 1619, 1620, 1621, 1627, 1637, 1643, 1644, 1645, 1647, 1658, 1670, 1671, 1673, 1678, 1679, 1687, 1695, 1697, 1702, 1703, 1715, 1718, 1724, 1733, 1743, 1744, 1759, 1760, 1762, 1766, 1768, 1776, 1780, 1781, 1786, 1787, 1790, 1816, 1818, 1821, 1825, 1830, 1836, 1845, 1846, 1849, 1850, 1851, 1853, 1854, 1855, 1866, 1883, 1888, 1892, 1901, 1902, 1904, 1910, 1911, 1913, 1914, 1929, 1937, 1943, 1956, 1957, 1963, 1964, 1979, 1981, 1984, 1992, 1993, 2011, 2029, 2043, 2052, 2060, 2071, 2074,

2077, 2080, 2094, 2099, 2101, 2102, 2104, 2112, 2113, 2114, 2115, 2120, 2125, 2127, 2133, 2134, 2137, 2138, 2139, 2140, 2147, 2149, 2156, 2157, 2158, 2159, 2169, 2173, 2175, 2177, 2185, 2192, 2196, 2203, 2206, 2207, 2212, 2226, 2229, 2247, 2251, 2254, 2262, 2263, 2269, 2270, 2272, 2291, 2296, 2302, 2312, 2314, 2323, 2325, 2327, 2337, 2342, 2346, 2350, 2352, 2354, 2356, 2374, 2380, 2382, 2383, 2386, 2390, 2391, 2393, 2406, 2415, 2421, 2423, 2443, 2453, 2454, 2456, 2466, 469, 2483, 2515, 2561, 2566, 2580, 2586, 2594, 2646, 2669, 2694, 2737, 2756, 2783, 2792, 2794, 2795, 2797, 2806, 2839, 2845, 2846, 2867, 2950, 2979, 2980, 2990, 3012, 3014, 3213, 3227, 3249, 3289, 3290, 3297, 3309, 3311, 3433, 3437, 3449, 3482, 3490, 3494, 3525, 3544, 3554, 3560, 3606, B3718

Bachelors Senior, 3, 4, 5, 6, 11, 22, 38, 39, 48, 49, 50, 57, 61, 62, 64, 66, 72, 73, 74, 78, 80, 82, 98, 102, 104, 105, 109, 116, 118, 119, 127, 128, 139, 142, 145, 146, 154, 155, 157, 161, 162, 176, 182, 190, 192, 193, 194, 205, 206, 207, 210, 217, 220, 225, 228, 229, 231, 239, 241, 242, 245, 251, 252, 253, 256, 260, 262, 276, 281, 286, 289, 290, 295, 302, 309, 318, 319, 320, 321, 325, 326, 333, 334, 336, 352, 361, 389, 410, 419, 426, 427, 428, 431, 436, 440, 441, 444, 467, 469, 478, 479, 480, 485, 498, 501, 508, 509, 513, 516, 520, 524, 528, 530, 531, 535, 538, 544, 545, 547, 548, 549, 559, 563, 567, 568, 569, 572, 574, 581, 583, 601, 602, 603, 611, 623, 624, 633, 636, 651, 653, 680, 687, 688, 690, 693, 694, 697, 703, 710, 720, 728, 738, 747, 750, 763, 771, 778, 779, 781, 782, 783, 784, 785, 790, 793, 799, 804, 808, 813, 818, 825, 826, 844, 846, 848, 850, 854, 856, 861, 864, 882, 883, 893, 900, 905, 908, 910, 930, 938, 943, 951, 971, 972, 985, 986, 988, 993, 996, 1001, 1025, 1038, 1051, 1052, 1105, 1114, 1118, 1128, 1208, 1214, 1217, 1232, 1237, 1238, 1241, 1248, 1253, 1254, 1255, 1256, 1257, 1259, 1260, 1261, 1263, 1264, 1268, 1269, 1272, 1274, 1286, 1287, 1292, 1302, 1304, 1327, 1329, 1330, 1339, 1345, 1346, 1349, 1357, 1359, 1362, 1367, 1374, 1385, 1391, 1393, 1396, 1397, 1402, 1405, 1411, 1413, 1422, 1424, 1438, 1440, 1444, 1448, 1454, 1455, 1481, 1482, 1490, 1497, 1519, 1522, 1526, 1536, 1537, 1539, 1540, 1542, 1544, 1552, 1568, 1574, 1575, 1579, 1581, 1588, 1590, 1596, 1607, 1608, 1615, 1616, 1619, 1620, 1621, 1628, 1637, 1645, 1647, 1658, 1670, 1671, 1673, 1678, 1679, 1688, 1695, 1697,

1702, 1703, 1704, 1715, 1717, 1718, 1724, 1726, 1727, 1728, 1730, 1731, 1732, 1733, 1743, 1744, 1752, 1759, 1760, 1762, 1766, 1768, 1780, 1781, 1786, 1787, 1790, 1799, 1800, 1801, 1807, 1808, 1814, 1816, 1818, 1821, 1830, 1834, 1836, 1845, 1846, 1849, 1850, 1851, 1853, 1854, 1855, 1866, 1868, 1869, 1870, 1874, 1875, 1876, 1883, 1888, 1892, 1901, 1902, 1904, 1910, 1911, 1913, 1914, 1929, 1937, 1943, 1956, 1957, 1963, 1964, 1979, 1981, 1984, 1992, 1993, 2011, 2029, 2043, 2071, 2077, 2080, 2084, 2089, 2094, 2099, 2104, 2108, 2113, 2114, 2115, 2120, 2122, 2125, 2127, 2133, 2134, 2137, 2138, 2139, 2140, 2147, 2149, 2156, 2157, 2158, 2159, 2169, 2173, 2177, 2185, 2203, 2206, 2207, 2212, 2222, 2225, 2226, 2229, 2251, 2254, 2258, 2262, 2263, 2269, 2270, 2272, 2278, 2291, 2296, 2304, 2314, 2318, 2319, 2323, 2325, 2326, 2327, 2329, 2342, 2350, 2352, 2354, 2356, 2359, 2368, 2377, 2380, 2382, 2383, 2386, 2388, 2390, 2391, 2392, 2393, 2395, 2396, 2402, 2406, 2415, 2421, 2423, 2443, 2453, 2456, 2466, 2469, 2483, 2515, 2561, 2566, 2580, 2586, 2594, 2646, 2756, 2783, 2792, 2794, 2797, 2806, 2839, 2845, 2846, 2895, 2979, 2980, 2990, 3012, 3014, 3103, 3125, 3213, 3227, 3236, 3249, 3289, 3297, 3300, 3309, 3311, 3449, 3468, 3478, 3482, 3490, 3494, 3525, 3544, 3554, 3560, 3562, B3718, B3719

Non-Degree Course, 53, 64, 184, 298, 472, 477, 487, 499, 1171, 1172, 1667, 1753, 1815, 1898, 1940, 1976, 2214, 2372, 2385, 2407, 2408, 2426, 2427, 2458, 2465, 3293, 3349, 3576, 3580, 3581, B3615, C3845, C3917

Part-Time, 1854, 3535

Teaching Credential, 208, 210, 222, 223, 224

DEGREES RECEIVED

High School Graduate, 77, 163, 177, 211, 554, 584, 760, 1027, 1159, 1221, 1247, 1249, 1305, 1324, 1386, 1389, 1426, 1429, 1449, 1451, 1468, 1557, 1560, 1712, 1788, 1844, 2039, 2072, 2242, 2403, 2427, 2467, 2520, 2544, 2604, 2605, 2614, 2754, 2817, 2835, 2836, 2858, 2940, 2948, 3029, 3051, 3128, 3212, 3269, 3293, 3309, 3316, 3343, 3347, 3444, 3492, 3515, 3519, 3523, 3544, 3559, 3576

Associates (AA/AS), 2821

Registered Nurse (RN), 1705, 1975, 1982, 1992, 2009, 2030

ETHNIC BACKGROUND

African American, 48, 49, 56, 57, 61, 81, 86, 88, 104, 184, 205, 207, 209, 210, 224, 242, 283, 289, 290, 298, 343, 347, 351, 354, 463, 470, 471, 495, 500, 520, 528, 537, 542, 560, 561, 575, 580, 586, 587, 620, 623, 626, 654, 655, 691, 693, 695, 699, 700, 702, 705, 706, 735, 741, 768, 773, 774, 794, 797, 810, 811, 812, 836, 873, 1035, 1073, 1171, 1172, 1195, 1343, 1347, 1388, 1397, 1428, 1435, 1450, 1499, 1515, 1516, 1525, 1559, 1564, 1566, 1593, 1597, 1617, 1620, 1624, 1644, 1680, 1730, 1732, 1767, 1775, 1782, 1799, 1801, 1822, 1848, 1852, 1874, 1876, 1912, 1940, 1994, 2074, 2109, 2112, 2116, 2136, 2146, 2147, 2154, 2177, 2200, 2213, 2214, 2247, 2258, 2302, 2344, 2346, 2372, 2374, 2407, 2530, 2532, 2694, 2700, 2730, 2743, 2823, 2847, 2848, 2902, 2996, 3039, 3073, 3103, 3164, 3188, 3229, 3267, 3291, 3316, 3409, 3508, 3525, 3547, 3580, 3601, B3746

American Indian/Eskimo, 2, 20, 22, 48, 49, 56, 57, 61, 81, 86, 88, 104, 161, 175, 176, 189, 192, 196, 204, 205, 207, 209, 210, 224, 228, 242, 266, 281, 290, 305, 306, 329, 343, 347, 354, 356, 440, 470, 471, 495, 520, 528, 537, 560, 561, 575, 586, 587, 620, 623, 627, 651, 654, 655, 691, 693, 699, 700, 702, 703, 705, 706, 735, 773, 774, 794, 810, 811, 812, 836, 842, 866, 903, 1101, 1230, 1343, 1344, 1345, 1347, 1395, 1396, 1397, 1424, 1435, 1436, 1475, 1476, 1488, 1499, 1500, 1522, 1525, 1564, 1566, 1568, 1597, 1617, 1620, 1624, 1625, 1651, 1655, 1697, 1701, 1702, 1703, 1722, 1723, 1730, 1732, 1740, 1781, 1782, 1785, 1786, 1787, 1798, 1799, 1801, 1803, 1830, 1835, 1836, 1848, 1852, 1862, 1874, 1876, 1879, 1929, 1936, 1937, 1947, 1953, 2001, 2011, 2028, 2029, 2070, 2071, 2074, 2078, 2109, 2112, 2116, 2117, 2136, 2154, 2163, 2177, 2200, 2219, 2247, 2302, 2308, 2344, 2346, 2374, 2378, 2380, 2405, 2406, 2471, 2532, 2587, 2588, 2608, 2610, 2694, 2743, 2753, 2760, 2797, 2829, 2847, 2848, 2854, 2863, 2907, 2908, 2916, 2986, 2996, 3039, 3079, 3087, 3101, 3103, 3225, 3229, 3287, 3291, 3345, 3431, 3495, 3496, 3547, 3553, 3601, B3746

Arab, 224, 2743, 3601

Asian, 48, 49, 56, 86, 88, 205, 207, 209, 210, 224, 242, 290, 470, 471, 560, 561, 586, 587, 654, 655, 699, 700, 705, 706, 773, 774, 810, 811, 1525, 1730, 1732, 1799, 1801, 1848, 1852, 1874, 1876, 2095, 2096, 2097, 2109, 2112, 2116, 2136,

2154, 2177, 2200, 2532, 2669, 2743, 2847, 2848, 2996, 3039, 3049, 3103, 3229, 3250, 3251, 3271, 3291, 3547, 3601, B3746

Hispanic, 6, 48, 49, 51, 56, 57, 80, 81, 86, 88, 104, 108, 128, 209, 210, 224, 225, 242, 290, 321, 343, 354, 411, 470, 471, 495, 527, 537, 560, 561, 575, 586, 587, 603, 609, 620, 623, 654, 655, 686, 691, 693, 699, 700, 702, 705, 706, 726, 735, 773, 774, 794, 810, 811, 1232, 1343, 1347, 1435, 1482, 1499, 1508, 1525, 1564, 1566, 1597, 1617, 1620, 1624, 1656, 1741, 1757, 1758, 1782, 1804, 1848, 1852, 1880, 1899, 1900, 1955, 1957, 1978, 1995, 2109, 2112, 2116, 2123, 2136, 2142, 2154, 2177, 2200, 2344, 2353, 2528, 2529, 2532, 2595, 2604, 2605, 2723, 2737, 2743, 2820, 2847, 2848, 2905, 2996, 3034, 3035, 3039, 3072, 3078, 3103, 3229, 3291, 3527, 3547, 3601, B3746

Minority Affiliation, 40, 56, 90, 143, 147, 209, 210, 219, 242, 262, 285, 315, 354, 355, 357, 419, 435, 469, 514, 528, 534, 546, 600, 679, 705, 706, 718, 732, 742, 789, 812, 836, 865, 942, 1009, 1223, 1248, 1328, 1380, 1393, 1418, 1455, 1467, 1499, 1519, 1528, 1538, 1555, 1605, 1624, 1647, 1686, 1729, 1765, 1772, 1833, 1842, 1864, 1871, 1920, 2005, 2074, 2100, 2105, 2128, 2139, 2198, 2203, 2238, 2247, 2274, 2277, 2302, 2309, 2346, 2358, 2374, 2394, 2599, 3443, 3502, 3601, B3631, B3663, B3682, B3746, B3771

EXTRACURRICULAR ACTIVITIES

General, 2563

Athlete-College, 98, 162, 199, 636, 1637, 1892, 2120, 2352, 2383, 2580, 3584, B3646, B3757

Athlete-High School, 199, 211, 227, 1085, 1358, 1439, 1484, 1886, 2538, 2580, 2632, 2831, 3119, 3149, 3335, 3428, 3583, 3584, B3646, B3713, B3743, B3757

Athlete-NCAA, 3124, 3125, 3584, B3646, B3743

Aviation, 96, 488, 2431

Baseball-American Legion, 2535

Bowling, 2831, 3295, 3596, 3597, 3598

Caddie or Golf, 2831, 2838, 2871, 3200, 3564, 3585, B3760

Caddy at Golf Assn of Phil., 2831, 2952

College Newspaper Cartoonist, 937

Community Service, 96, 108, 119, 143, 153, 162, 355, 374, 404, 488, 527, 609, 636, 686, 726, 742, 846, 862, 1138, 1637, 2096, 2122, 2123, 2252, 2279, 2312,

2318, 2330, 2353, 2388, 2398, 2431, 2478, 2503, 2536, 2580, 2601, 2680, 2723, 2737, 2771, 2847, 2848, 2867, 2875, 2902, 2903, 2913, 2943, 2974, 2975, 2978, 3016, 3037, 3039, 3047, 3049, 3071, 3072, 3119, 3120, 3127, 3139, 3142, 3155, 3156, 3268, 3290, 3334, 3353, 3364, 3400, 3426, 3428, 3453, 3454, 3455, 3456, 3457, 3458, 3459, 3460, 3461, 3462, 3463, 3464, 3465, 3475, 3491, 3540, 3556

Dog Shows, 2775

Employment, 143, 355, 374, 742, 3071

Harness Racing, 2831, 2891

Horsemanship, 2544, 3582

Horseshoe Pitching, 2831, 3138

Inv w/Asian/Pacif/Am commty, 2095, 2096, 2585

Licensed Radio Amateur, 307, 590, 657, 658, 659, 660, 661, 662, 663, 664, 665, 666, 667, 668, 669, 670, 671, 1477, 2093, 2546, 2547, 2548, 2549, 2550, 2551, 2552, 2553, 2554, 2555, 2556, 2557, 2558, 2559, 2832

Licensed Radio Amateur-D-DEC, 590, 667, 2093

Musical Instrument, 1170, 1171

SCUBA Diving, 1445

School Clubs, 96, 143, 162, 355, 369, 374, 404, 425, 488, 636, 742, 1637, 2252, 2431, 2580, 2601, 2680, 2771, 2847, 2848, 2875, 2902, 2974, 3037, 3119, 3120, 3475

Sewing, 3163

Soccer, 3017

Student Government, 143, 162, 355, 425, 636, 742, 846, 1637, 2122, 2580, 2680, 2771, 2867, 2974, 3119, 3120, 3142, 3428, 3475, 3556, 3574

Swim Team H.S., 2715, 2831, 3119

FAMILY ANCESTRIES

African, 1775, 2147, 2200, 3525

American Indian, 866, 1655, 1740, 1803, 1879, 1953, 2587, 2588, 2829, 3345

Arapaho Tribe (Northern), 3356

Arapaho Tribe of Oklahoma, 2668

Armenian, 1652, 2249, 2579, 2580, 2800, 2853, 3013, B3664

Blackfeet, 2610

Cambodian, 2750, 3250, 3251

Canadian, 2830

Cherokee, 2666

Cheyenne Tribe of Oklahoma, 2668

Chinese, 2096, 2669, 2670, 2671, 3250, 3251, 3416

Choctaw Nation of Oklahoma, 2672

Cuban, 7, 93, 108, 327, 527, 609, 686, 726, 2110, 2123, 2310, 2353, 2746

Cypriot, 3045, 3425

Danish, 2561, 3228

Filipino, 2096, 3250, 3251

Finnish, 2561

French, 2830

Greek, 2752, 3045, 3425

Hawaiian, 1343, 1435, 1566, 2200

Hopi, 11, 109, 193, 239, 333, 574, 687, 728, 793, 1237, 1670, 1759, 1816, 1901, 1979, 2262, 2608, 2907, 2908

Hualapai Tribe, 2916

Huguenot, 3048

India, 308, 521, 591, 672, 776, 1351, 1398, 2663

Italian, 18, 19, 133, 134, 135, 136, 137, 138, 211, 350, 541, 822, 823, 860, 861, 862, 919, 920, 921, 1048, 1049, 1134, 1135, 1136, 1137, 1138, 1240, 1289, 1495, 2061, 2199, 2228, 2276, 2324, 2950, 2951, 3139, 3140, 3141, 3142, 3143, 3144, 3145, 3146, 3147, 3148, 3149, 3150, 3151, 3152, 3153, 3154, 3155, 3156, 3157, 3158, 3159, 3160, 3161, 3162, 3360, 3417, 3453, 3454, 3455, 3456, 3457, 3458, 3459, 3460, 3461, 3462, 3463, 3464, 3465, 3500

Japanese, 851, 907, 991, 1045, 1113, 1278, 1279, 1280, 2096, 2132, 2268, 2320, 2321, 2389, 2964, 2965, 2966, 3250, 3251

Jewish, 869, 2805, 2979, 3445

Korean, 342, 1239, 1493, 1675, 2096, 3446, 3449

Laotian, 2750

Lithuanian, 1307, 1558, 1698, 1784, 1832, 1935, 2013

Mexican/Hispanic, 51, 61, 108, 128, 205, 207, 283, 347, 411, 520, 527, 609, 686, 726, 812, 836, 1397, 1508, 1730, 1732, 1799, 1801, 1874, 1876, 1978, 1995, 2074, 2123, 2142, 2247, 2302, 2346, 2353, 2374, 2528, 2595, 2628, 2694, 2820, 3034, 3035, 3077, 3078, 3110, 3409, 3527, 3538

Miccosukee, 2827

Mongolian, 3100

Native Hawaiian, 1525

Navajo, 22, 161, 281, 440, 1424, 1697, 1781, 1830, 1929, 2011

Norwegian, 867, 2561

Oneida Tribe of Wisconsin, 3241

Pacific Islander, 57, 86, 88, 205, 207, 290, 470, 471, 560, 561, 586, 587, 654, 655, 699, 700, 773, 774, 810, 811, 1343, 1435, 1525, 1566, 1730, 1732, 1799, 1801, 1874, 1876, 2096, 2097, 2112, 2116, 2136, 2200, 2532, 2996, 3229, 3250, 3251, B3746

Polish, 58, 2091, 2589, 3014, 3474

Portuguese, 1046, 2626

Puerto Rican, 108, 347, 527, 609, 686, 726, 812, 836, 2074, 2123, 2247, 2302, 2346, 2353, 2374, 2694

Scandinavian, 867, 2561
Scottish, 3338, 3433
Seminole, 2827, 3345
Seneca, 3346
Serbian, 3347, 3388
Shoshone Tribe (Wind River), 3350
Singaporean, 3250, 3251
Spanish (from Spain), 2820
Swedish, 2561
Swiss, 3394
Thai, 2096, 3250, 3251
Vietnamese, 2096, 2750, 3250, 3251
Welsh, 2747, 3174, 3375

FOREIGN LANGUAGES SPOKEN

Chinese, 859
English, 507, 583, 747, 799, 825, 957, 983,
    1241, 1292, 1374, 1381, 1413, 1444,
    1542, 1552, 1575, 1588, 1592, 1628,
    1634, 1752, 1814, 2239, 2266, 2395,
    2562
French, 834, 1039, 2266, 2562
German, 1040, 2562
Italian, 835, 1041
Japanese, 2562
Russian, 2562
Spanish, 2266, 2562, 2746
Swahili, 2562

HONORS/AWARDS/CONTESTS

Eagle Scout/Explorer, 14, 122, 338, 616,
    2056, 2445, 2536, 2615, 2943, 2987,
    3172, 3376
Giftd Vis/Performing Artist, 329, 903, 910,
    1101, 1118, 1130, 1140, 1153, 1488
HS Valedictorian/Salutatorian, 2707, 2731
Kansas Scholar, 2996, 2998
National Honor Society, 3118
National Merit Scholarship, 2571, 2884,
    2996
National Merit Semi-Finalist, 2812
Religious Award of Faith, 2987

LEGAL CITY OF RESIDENCE

Agawan MA, 2912
Albertville AL, 24, 445, 637, 1309, 2014
Amherst MA, 2709
Ashland AL, 24, 445, 637, 1309, 2014
Atlanta GA, 2100, 2837
Aurora IL, 2592
Baltimore MD, 2655, 3448
Beloit WI, 2855
Blountsville AL, 24, 445, 637, 1309, 2014
Boston MA, 2790, 2874, 3126

Broken Bow OK, 33, 454, 646, 1318, 2023
Brooklyn NY, 318, 572, 601, 680, 720, 790,
    1357, 1438, 1536, 1574, 1607
Buena Vista GA, 27, 448, 640, 1312, 2017
Byfield MA, 2815
Carthage TX, 36, 457, 649, 1321, 2026
Center TX, 36, 457, 649, 1321, 2026
Chicago IL, 28, 252, 336, 449, 641, 1238,
    1313, 1490, 1544, 1579, 1615, 1616,
    1673, 1762, 1818, 1904, 1984, 2018,
    2133, 2269, 2390
Chicopee MA, 2710, 2716, 2912
Cleveland MS, 30, 451, 643, 1315, 2020
Corpus Christi TX, 3265
Corydon IN, 29, 450, 642, 1314, 2019
Cresswell NC, 32, 453, 645, 1317, 2022
Crete IL, 2257
Cumming GA, 27, 448, 640, 1312, 2017
Dawson GA, 27, 448, 640, 1312, 2017
Delano MN, 1197, 1659
Detroit MI, 2800, 2887
Dexter MO, 31, 452, 644, 1316, 2021
Dublin CA, 2515
E Longmeadow MA, 2780, 2912
East Palo Alto CA, 1007, 3267
Eliot ME, 1667, 1753, 1815, 1898, 1976,
    2385
Enfield CT, 2717, 2963
Forest MS, 30, 451, 643, 1315, 2020
Gadsen AL, 24, 445, 637, 1309, 2014
Georgetown MA, 2815
Glen Allen VA, 37, 458, 650, 1322, 2027
Glendale CA, 2869
Granby MA, 2721
Greenfield MA, 2699, 2704
Greenland NH, 1667, 1753, 1815, 1898,
    1976, 2385
Hadley MA, 573, 2709
Harrisonburg VA, 37, 458, 650, 1322, 2027
Heflin AL, 24, 445, 637, 1309, 2014
Holyoke MA, 2710, 2723, 2727
Houston TX, 2094, 2671, 3276
Ilion NY, 3053
Jackson MS, 30, 451, 643, 1315, 2020
Jacksonville FL, 26, 447, 639, 1311, 2016,
    3386
Jamestown NY, 2665
Kansas City KS, 2653
Kansas City MO, 2653
Kittery ME, 1667, 1753, 1815, 1898, 1976,
    2385
La Canada/Flintridge CA, 2869
La Crescenta CA, 2869
Laredo TX, 2748
Livermore CA, 2515
Lodi CA, 2583
Long Island NY, 1122, 3071, 3073
Longmeadow MA, 2912
Los Angeles CA, 77, 150, 504, 2462

Lubbock TX, 3032
Ludlow MA, 2912
Merced CA, 3544
Merrimack NH, 2480
Milwaukee WI, 3076, 3264
Monett MO, 31, 452, 644, 1316, 2021
Monroe NC, 32, 453, 645, 1317, 2022
Montrose CA, 2869
Mountain View CA, 1007, 3267
N Hampton NH, 1667, 1753, 1815, 1898,
    1976, 2385
Neosho MO, 31, 452, 644, 1316, 2021
New Bedford MA, 3193
New Castle NH, 1667, 1753, 1815, 1898,
    1976, 2385
New Holland PA, 34, 455, 647, 1319, 2024
New London CT, 3020
New York NY, 518, 1122, 2527, 2616,
    2962, 3071, 3073, 3504
Newbury MA, 2815
Newburyport MA, 2815
Newington NH, 1667, 1753, 1815, 1898,
    1976, 2385
Newton MA, 2980
Noel MO, 31, 452, 644, 1316, 2021
Norfolk VA, 3231
Northampton MA, 2709
Oxford AL, 24, 445, 637, 1309, 2014
Palo Alto CA, 1007, 1242, 1293, 1375,
    1414, 1446, 1460, 1503, 1553, 1589,
    1629, 1689, 1777, 1826, 1925, 2010,
    2066, 3267
Parkersburg WV, 3467
Philadelphia PA, 2747, 3433, 3492
Pleasanton CA, 2515
Portland IN, 29, 450, 642, 1314, 2019
Portsmouth NH, 1667, 1753, 1815, 1898,
    1976, 2385, 3283
Rowley MA, 2815
Rye NH, 1667, 1753, 1815, 1898, 1976,
    2385
Salisbury MA, 2815
Sanford NC, 32, 453, 645, 1317, 2022
Santa Cruz CA, 2875
Sedalia MO, 31, 452, 644, 1316, 2021
Seguin TX, 36, 457, 649, 1321, 2026
Shelbyville TN, 35, 456, 648, 1320, 2025
South Bend IN, 2841
Spokane WA, 2836
Springfield MA, 2702, 2710, 2730, 2734,
    2880, 2912
St. Louis MO, 2849, 3107, 3149
Stillwell OK, 33, 454, 646, 1318, 2023
Suffield CT, 2717, 2963
Sunol CA, 2515
Temperanceville VA, 37, 458, 650, 1322,
    2027
Turtle WI, 2855
Union City TN, 35, 456, 648, 1320, 2025
Verdugo City CA, 2869

Vicksburg MS, 30, 451, 643, 1315, 2020
Vienna GA, 27, 448, 640, 1312, 2017
Vina CA, 3023
W Springfield MA, 2912
Wakefield MA, 2679
Washington DC, 99, 896, 897, 978, 1091, 1289, 2772, 2975, 2976, 2977, 2978, 3453, 3557
West Newbury MA, 2815
Wheatland WY, 3569
Wilbraham MA, 2912
Wilkesboro NC, 32, 453, 645, 1317, 2022
Winona MN, 3576
York ME, 1667, 1753, 1815, 1898, 1976, 2385

LEGAL CONTINENT OF CITIZENSHIP

North America, 410, 778, 781, 1075, 1526

LEGAL COUNTRY OF CITIZENSHIP

Canada, 44, 63, 105, 140, 141, 151, 169, 245, 274, 289, 290, 410, 516, 715, 777, 786, 835, 888, 1041, 1075, 1133, 1145, 1188, 1189, 1256, 1258, 1265, 1294, 1530, 1671, 1739, 1760, 1902, 1981, 2047, 2417, 2418, 2878, 2938, 2982, 3008, 3168, 3333, 3364, 3365, 3509

Mexico, 170, 410, 777, 786, 835, 1041, 1075, 1530, 2047, 2418, 3364, 3365

United States, 5, 8, 9, 16, 20, 23, 24, 25, 26, 27, 28, 29, 30, 31, 32, 33, 34, 35, 36, 37, 39, 42, 44, 48, 49, 51, 57, 58, 61, 63, 66, 67, 69, 77, 78, 81, 83, 89, 94, 95, 97, 104, 105, 108, 115, 124, 128, 131, 139, 140, 141, 143, 145, 147, 148, 150, 151, 153, 162, 163, 175, 176, 177, 182, 183, 186, 190, 192, 194, 196, 200, 202, 203, 207, 207, 211, 217, 220, 221, 227, 228, 230, 236, 237, 241, 242, 243, 245, 251, 254, 259, 260, 266, 272, 274, 282, 286, 289, 290, 291, 292, 299, 301, 302, 303, 309, 310, 312, 313, 315, 316, 319, 320, 323, 324, 325, 326, 331, 335, 340, 342, 345, 347, 352, 353, 355, 356, 357, 359, 361, 390, 399, 402, 403, 410, 413, 416, 421, 422, 424, 432, 438, 439, 444, 445, 446, 447, 448, 449, 450, 451, 452, 453, 454, 455, 456, 457, 458, 459, 460, 462, 465, 467, 470, 471, 473, 474, 475, 478, 479, 480, 482, 485, 498, 501, 502, 504, 512, 516, 518, 519, 520, 523, 527, 534, 538, 544, 546, 547, 554, 556, 557, 558, 560, 561, 562, 567, 568, 569, 571, 573, 578, 584, 586, 587, 588, 589, 596, 598, 600, 602, 605, 609, 614, 618, 623, 627, 636, 637, 638, 639, 640, 641, 642, 643, 644, 645, 646, 647, 648, 649, 650, 651, 652, 653, 654, 655, 656, 677, 679, 681, 682, 686, 693, 699, 700, 701, 702, 709, 710, 715, 717, 718, 719, 721, 722, 723, 726, 738, 740, 742, 743, 744, 745, 760, 765, 767, 769, 773, 774, 775, 777, 780, 783, 786, 788, 789, 791, 792, 796, 807, 810, 811, 812, 813, 817, 826, 829, 832, 835, 836, 838, 849, 850, 851, 856, 861, 863, 867, 869, 871, 886, 888, 892, 894, 898, 907, 909, 915, 917, 923, 924, 930, 935, 936, 946, 947, 948, 950, 952, 954, 955, 960, 961, 962, 966, 968, 975, 976, 981, 991, 995, 998, 1008, 1011, 1012, 1014, 1017, 1018, 1022, 1023, 1027, 1029, 1032, 1034, 1037, 1040, 1041, 1044, 1045, 1057, 1058, 1065, 1066, 1067, 1068, 1069, 1070, 1073, 1075, 1076, 1082, 1084, 1085, 1109, 1113, 1116, 1117, 1122, 1125, 1132, 1133, 1145, 1149, 1150, 1151, 1155, 1159, 1161, 1163, 1164, 1165, 1166, 1167, 1171, 1172, 1173, 1177, 1179, 1185, 1188, 1189, 1190, 1200, 1204, 1205, 1209, 1210, 1214, 1216, 1217, 1220, 1227, 1229, 1231, 1233, 1234, 1235, 1239, 1247, 1251, 1256, 1258, 1265, 1278, 1279, 1280, 1286, 1294, 1305, 1309, 1310, 1311, 1312, 1313, 1314, 1315, 1316, 1317, 1318, 1319, 1320, 1321, 1322, 1324, 1331, 1342, 1343, 1346, 1347, 1348, 1349, 1350, 1353, 1354, 1358, 1359, 1365, 1373, 1386, 1387, 1388, 1389, 1397, 1407, 1426, 1427, 1428, 1429, 1434, 1435, 1439, 1443, 1449, 1450, 1451, 1457, 1463, 1468, 1471, 1474, 1479, 1481, 1484, 1485, 1486, 1493, 1496, 1497, 1498, 1500, 1501, 1511, 1512, 1513, 1514, 1515, 1517, 1521, 1525, 1527, 1528, 1529, 1530, 1531, 1533, 1534, 1537, 1542, 1548, 1557, 1559, 1560, 1563, 1564, 1565, 1566, 1569, 1571, 1572, 1575, 1576, 1581, 1583, 1585, 1590, 1593, 1594, 1596, 1597, 1602, 1603, 1605, 1606, 1608, 1610, 1611, 1614, 1619, 1620, 1622, 1625, 1637, 1639, 1640, 1641, 1642, 1643, 1644, 1645, 1648, 1649, 1653, 1658, 1661, 1663, 1667, 1668, 1671, 1672, 1675, 1678, 1682, 1683, 1685, 1686, 1688, 1693, 1695, 1699, 1701, 1702, 1703, 1710, 1713, 1717, 1718, 1719, 1720, 1721, 1726, 1727, 1728, 1729, 1732, 1732, 1733, 1735, 1737, 1739, 1743, 1744, 1748, 1749, 1752, 1753, 1755, 1760, 1771, 1772, 1780, 1782, 1783, 1785, 1786, 1787, 1788, 1793, 1797, 1801, 1801, 1814, 1815, 1817, 1821, 1833, 1834, 1835, 1836, 1838, 1858, 1859, 1860, 1861, 1864, 1865, 1866, 1867, 1868, 1869, 1870, 1871, 1872, 1876, 1876, 1885, 1886, 1889, 1889, 1891, 1898, 1902, 1903, 1913, 1914, 1915, 1916, 1918, 1920, 1930, 1931, 1932, 1933, 1936, 1937, 1939, 1942, 1943, 1946, 1960, 1962, 1964, 1965, 1968, 1969, 1969, 1976, 1977, 1978, 1981, 1983, 1995, 1998, 2000, 2001, 2005, 2007, 2008, 2012, 2014, 2015, 2016, 2017, 2018, 2019, 2020, 2021, 2022, 2023, 2024, 2025, 2026, 2027, 2028, 2029, 2034, 2035, 2036, 2043, 2044, 2045, 2047, 2058, 2062, 2063, 2064, 2065, 2070, 2071, 2072, 2074, 2075, 2077, 2084, 2088, 2090, 2091, 2095, 2096, 2097, 2100, 2109, 2118, 2119, 2123, 2132, 2134, 2136, 2141, 2150, 2165, 2174, 2175, 2176, 2177, 2178, 2181, 2202, 2208, 2216, 2224, 2225, 2229, 2230, 2231, 2237, 2242, 2243, 2247, 2248, 2250, 2251, 2254, 2258, 2260, 2268, 2274, 2277, 2279, 2286, 2289, 2296, 2300, 2302, 2304, 2305, 2312, 2317, 2319, 2320, 2321, 2325, 2326, 2328, 2330, 2333, 2338, 2341, 2342, 2343, 2345, 2346, 2347, 2349, 2353, 2358, 2367, 2374, 2375, 2377, 2379, 2380, 2385, 2389, 2392, 2394, 2398, 2401, 2405, 2406, 2410, 2411, 2412, 2413, 2415, 2417, 2418, 2421, 2423, 2424, 2428, 2430, 2432, 2434, 2447, 2448, 2449, 2456, 2457, 2459, 2460, 2462, 2467, 2470, 2477, 2478, 2481, 2483, 2489, 2490, 2491, 2493, 2513, 2517, 2518, 2521, 2531, 2532, 2533, 2537, 2557, 2558, 2560, 2563, 2564, 2574, 2581, 2582, 2585, 2589, 2591, 2595, 2603, 2609, 2611, 2612, 2613, 2616, 2617, 2625, 2626, 2627, 2632, 2634, 2635, 2636, 2637, 2638, 2639, 2640, 2646, 2648, 2651, 2654, 2666, 2676, 2680, 2683, 2685, 2687, 2689, 2695, 2698, 2699, 2700, 2701, 2703, 2704, 2705, 2706, 2708, 2709, 2710, 2711, 2712, 2713, 2714, 2715, 2717, 2718, 2719, 2720, 2721, 2722, 2723, 2724, 2725, 2726, 2727, 2728, 2729, 2730, 2732, 2733, 2734, 2735, 2736, 2737, 2738, 2739, 2743, 2747, 2748, 2753, 2756, 2757, 2758, 2759, 2768, 2770, 2771, 2772, 2776, 2779, 2782, 2783, 2786, 2788, 2789, 2791, 2795, 2797, 2806, 2813, 2818, 2820, 2823, 2831, 2833, 2834, 2837, 2839, 2841, 2844, 2846, 2847, 2848, 2853, 2856, 2858, 2864, 2867, 2876, 2878, 2895, 2896, 2902, 2904, 2905, 2913, 2916, 2918, 2919, 2920, 2922, 2923, 2924, 2925, 2926, 2927, 2928, 2929, 2930, 2931, 2932, 2933, 2938, 2939, 2945, 2946, 2947, 2951, 2954, 2955, 2964, 2965, 2966, 2967, 2968, 2969, 2971, 2976, 2979, 2981, 2982, 2987, 2988, 2993, 2996, 2997, 2998, 2999, 3004, 3005, 3014, 3017, 3021, 3026, 3027, 3028, 3035, 3041, 3048, 3049, 3050, 3060, 3071, 3072, 3073, 3074, 3081, 3082, 3084, 3086, 3088, 3089, 3090,

3091, 3093, 3094, 3097, 3104, 3105,
3107, 3110, 3111, 3112, 3113, 3114,
3117, 3118, 3119, 3120, 3122, 3137,
3164, 3167, 3168, 3170, 3172, 3174,
3175, 3188, 3189, 3195, 3202, 3204,
3205, 3206, 3209, 3212, 3213, 3221,
3225, 3226, 3230, 3239, 3242, 3243,
3245, 3246, 3247, 3250, 3251, 3252,
3263, 3268, 3270, 3271, 3272, 3273,
3275, 3281, 3284, 3286, 3287, 3288,
3290, 3291, 3292, 3294, 3298, 3301,
3304, 3311, 3312, 3313, 3316, 3320,
3321, 3330, 3331, 3332, 3334, 3341,
3344, 3345, 3346, 3354, 3355, 3359,
3360, 3362, 3364, 3365, 3366, 3367,
3368, 3369, 3378, 3383, 3384, 3385,
3390, 3393, 3397, 3398, 3401, 3408,
3409, 3410, 3411, 3412, 3414, 3419,
3421, 3425, 3426, 3428, 3430, 3432,
3433, 3436, 3437, 3438, 3439, 3443,
3447, 3449, 3466, 3470, 3471, 3472,
3474, 3478, 3489, 3493, 3494, 3495,
3496, 3497, 3498, 3500, 3503, 3507,
3509, 3510, 3516, 3517, 3518, 3521,
3522, 3526, 3530, 3531, 3549, 3550,
3551, 3552, 3553, 3560, 3563, 3571,
3573, 3579, 3580, 3581, 3585, 3599,
3600, 3601, 3602, 3603, 3605, B3721,
B3745, C3974, C3975

LEGAL COUNTY OF RESIDENCE

Adams PA, 3351
Alameda CA, 2182, 2195, 3441
Allegheny NC, 2960
Allegheny PA, 3188
Allen OH, 2896
Anne Arundel MD, 3448
Armstrong PA, 3188
Armstrong TX, 2512
Ashe NC, 2960
Athol MA, 2729
Atlantic NJ, 3351, 3391
Auglaize OH, 2896
Avery NC, 2960
Baldwin AL, 2135
Baltimore MD, 3448
Barnstable MA, 908, 1114, 1664, 1750,
 1809, 1890, 1970, 2443
Barton KS, 2953
Beaver PA, 3188
Bergen NJ, 1122, 1517, 3071, 3073
Berks PA, 3351, 3391
Berkshire MA, 2717, 2963, 3094
Big Horn MT, 2774
Bonner ID, 2835
Brazoria TX, 214
Brevard FL, 159, 160, 634, 635, 1509, 1636,
 2191, 2336, 2646, 3017
Briscoe TX, 2512
Bucks PA, 2105, 2478, 3391

Buncombe NC, 2960
Bureau IL, 2170
Burke NC, 2960
Butler PA, 3188
Caldwell NC, 2960
Calhoun AL, 2961
Calhoun MI, 3070, 3109
Campbell WY, 2774
Cape May NJ, 3351
Carroll MD, 3448
Carson TX, 2512
Castro TX, 2512
Cecil MD, 3351
Charlotte FL, 2697
Chautauqua NY, 1399
Cherokee NC, 2960
Chester PA, 3351, 3391
Childress TX, 2512
Clark NV, 3417
Clarke AL, 2135
Clay NC, 2960
Collingsworth TX, 2512
Columbiana OH, 1660, 1747, 1806, 1884,
 1959
Conecuh AL, 2135
Contra Costa CA, 2182, 2195, 3434, 3441
Converse WY, 2740
Cook IL, 252, 336, 341, 1238, 1490, 1491,
 1544, 1579, 1615, 1616, 1673, 1762,
 1818, 1904, 1984, 2133, 2269, 2390,
 2950
Crawford IA, 1165
Cumberland NJ, 3351, 3391
Cumberland PA, 3351
Cuyahoga OH, 1661, 1748, 1965, 2008
Dade FL, 2143
Dallam TX, 2512
Dauphin PA, 3351, 3391
Dayton OH, 2759
Deaf Smith TX, 2512
Delaware PA, 3351, 3391
Donley TX, 2512
Dupage IL, 2950
Dutchess NY, 1122, 3071, 3073
El Dorado CA, 3274
El Paso TX, 361, 547, 1217, 1590, 1695,
 1780, 2791
Ellis KS, 2953
Erving MA, 2729
Escambia AL, 2135
Escambia FL, 1209, 1672, 1893, 1903,
 1972, 1983, 2135
Essex NJ, 1122, 1517, 3071, 3073
Fairfield CT, 1122, 3071, 3073
Fairfield OH, 3239
Flagler FL, 159, 160, 634, 635, 1509, 1636,
 2191, 2336
Franklin MA, 2700, 2717, 2722, 2729,
 2732, 2963

Frederick MD, 3448
Fremont WY, 2614
Fulton IL, 2170
Geauga OH, 2008
George MS, 2135
Gloucester NJ, 3351, 3391
Goshen WY, 3040
Graham NC, 2960
Gray TX, 2512
Guernsey OH, 2678
Hall TX, 2512
Hampden MA, 2700, 2717, 2718, 2722,
 2732, 2911, 2963
Hampshire MA, 2700, 2708, 2717, 2719,
 2722, 2732, 2963
Hansford TX, 2512
Harford MD, 3448
Harris TX, 2671
Harrisburg PA, 3391
Hartley TX, 2512
Haywood NC, 2960
Hemphill TX, 2512
Henderson IL, 2170
Henderson NC, 2960
Herkimer NY, 3053
Hershey PA, 3391
Highland OH, 2651
Howard MD, 3448
Hudson NJ, 1122, 1517, 3071, 3073
Humboldt CA, 2917
Hunterdon NJ, 1122, 3071, 3073, 3391
Hutchinson TX, 2512
Imperial CA, 6, 80, 104, 225, 317, 321, 603,
 1134, 1232, 1482, 1657, 1742, 1805,
 1881, 1957, 2253, 2307, 2669
Indian River FL, 159, 160, 634, 635, 827,
 933, 1020, 1218, 1461, 1509, 1636, 2086,
 2179, 2191, 2235, 2331, 2336, 2365,
 2399
Isle of Wight VA, 2643
Jackson MS, 2135
Jackson NC, 2960
Jefferson MO, 3571
Jefferson-Davis LA, 2842
Johnson WY, 2774
Kanabec MN, 3480
Kane IL, 2950
Kendall IL, 2592
Kent MI, 23, 946, 947, 1167, 3436, 3438
Kern CA, 6, 80, 104, 225, 321, 603, 1232,
 1308, 1482, 1957, 2669, 2914
King WA, 1986
Knox IL, 2170
LaSalle IL, 2170
Lake IL, 2950
Lake OH, 2008
Lancaster PA, 3351, 3391
Laramie WY, 2270
Lawrence PA, 2915

Lebanon PA, 3351, 3391

Lee VA, 2624

Limestone TX, 1683, 3175

Lipscomb TX, 2512

Lorain OH, 2008, 2696

Los Angeles CA, 6, 77, 80, 104, 150, 225, 317, 321, 504, 603, 657, 1134, 1232, 1482, 1657, 1742, 1805, 1881, 1957, 2138, 2139, 2140, 2141, 2253, 2307, 2462, 2669, 2746, 2783, 2979, 3077

Lubbock TX, 3032

Macon NC, 2960

Madison NC, 2960

Manatee FL, 2697, 3344

Marin CA, 2182, 2195, 2620, 2969, 2970, 2971, 2972, 2973, 2974, 3049, 3050, 3262, 3441

Marshall-Putnam IL, 2170

Mason IL, 2170

McDonough IL, 2170

McDowell NC, 2960

McHenry IL, 2950

Mendocino CA, 1094, 1095

Mercer NJ, 3391

Middlesex NJ, 1122, 3071, 3073, 3586

Mitchell NC, 2960

Mobile AL, 2135

Monmouth NJ, 1122, 3071, 3073

Monroe AL, 2135

Monterey CA, 2136

Montgomery MD, 2060

Montgomery NY, 2757

Montgomery OH, 2759

Montgomery PA, 3391

Moore TX, 2512

Morris NJ, 1122, 3071, 3073

Napa CA, 1094, 1095, 2195, 3262, 3434, 3441

Nassau NY, 318, 572, 601, 680, 720, 790, 1357, 1438, 1536, 1574, 1607

Natrona WY, 3177

Ness KS, 2953

Nevada CA, 2865

New Castle DE, 3391

New London CT, 3573

New Salem MA, 2729

Ocean NJ, 1122, 3071, 3073

Ochiltree TX, 2512

Okalossa FL, 1209, 1672, 1893, 1903, 1972, 1983

Oldham TX, 2512

Orange CA, 6, 80, 104, 225, 317, 321, 603, 657, 1134, 1232, 1482, 1657, 1742, 1805, 1881, 1957, 2138, 2139, 2140, 2141, 2253, 2307, 2669

Orange FL, 3017

Orange MA, 2729

Orange NY, 1122, 3071, 3073

Osceola FL, 3017

Ottawa MI, 23

Palm Beach FL, 3016

Parmer TX, 2512

Passaic NJ, 1122, 3071, 3073

Pawnee KS, 2953

Peoria IL, 2170

Philadelphia PA, 2747, 3433

Pine MN, 3480

Polk NC, 2960

Posey IN, 2509

Potter TX, 2512

Powder River MT, 2774

Prince Georges MD, 3294

Putnam NY, 1122, 3071, 3073

Queens NY, 318, 572, 601, 680, 720, 790, 1357, 1438, 1536, 1574, 1607

Randall TX, 2512

Richmond NY, 1122, 3071, 3073

Riverside CA, 6, 80, 104, 225, 317, 321, 603, 1134, 1232, 1482, 1657, 1742, 1805, 1881, 1957, 2253, 2307, 2669

Roberts TX, 2512

Rock WI, 2855

Rockland NY, 1122, 3071, 3073

Rosebud MT, 2774

Ross OH, 3275

Rush KS, 2953

Rutherford NC, 2960

Sacramento CA, 3434

Salem NJ, 3351, 3391

San Benito CA, 2136

San Bernardino CA, 2, 6, 80, 104, 189, 204, 225, 306, 321, 603, 1134, 1232, 1476, 1482, 1723, 1957, 2669, 3035

San Diego CA, 6, 80, 104, 225, 317, 321, 363, 506, 603, 657, 1134, 1232, 1244, 1297, 1298, 1379, 1417, 1447, 1464, 1482, 1504, 1554, 1591, 1630, 1656, 1657, 1741, 1742, 1804, 1805, 1880, 1881, 1955, 1957, 2253, 2307, 2604, 2605, 2669

San Francisco CA, 2182, 2195, 2567, 2969, 2970, 2971, 2972, 2973, 2974, 3324, 3441, 3586

San Joaquin CA, 3434

San Mateo CA, 324, 1007, 1233, 1485, 1610, 1688, 1840, 2182, 2195, 2503, 2969, 2970, 2971, 2972, 2973, 2974, 3260, 3267, 3268, 3269, 3270, 3271, 3441

Santa Barbara CA, 6, 80, 104, 225, 321, 603, 657, 1134, 1155, 1156, 1232, 1482, 1957, 2669

Santa Clara CA, 324, 1233, 1485, 1610, 1688, 2136, 2195, 2969, 2970, 2971, 2972, 2973, 2974, 3260, 3268, 3441

Santa Cruz CA, 2136, 2182, 2875

Santa Rosa FL, 1209, 1672, 1893, 1903, 1972, 1983, 2135

Sarasota FL, 2697, 3344

Schenectady NY, 307, 668, 1477

Schuykill PA, 2892

Schuyler IL, 2170

Seminole FL, 3017

Shasta CA, 2856

Sheridan WY, 2774

Sherman TX, 2512

Shutesbury MA, 2729

Solano CA, 2195, 3434, 3441

Somerset NJ, 1122, 3071, 3073

Sonoma CA, 1094, 1095, 1146, 1949, 2182, 2195, 2969, 2970, 2971, 2972, 2973, 2974, 3049, 3262, 3441

Southhampton VA, 2643

Spokane WA, 3560

St Louis MO, 3107, 3336

Stanislaus CA, 2198

Stark IL, 2170

Suffolk NY, 318, 572, 601, 680, 720, 790, 1357, 1438, 1536, 1574, 1607

Sullivan NY, 1122, 3071, 3073

Sussex NJ, 1122, 3071, 3073

Sutter CA, 3057

Swain NC, 2960

Sweetwater WY, 2614

Swisher TX, 2512

Tazewell IL, 2170

Transylvania NC, 2960

Travis TX, 2593

Troup GA, 2843

Tulare CA, 191, 1746

Ulster NY, 1122, 3071, 3073

Union NJ, 1122, 3071, 3073

Ventura CA, 6, 80, 104, 225, 321, 603, 1134, 1232, 1482, 1957, 2138, 2139, 2140, 2617, 2669

Volusia FL, 159, 160, 634, 635, 1509, 1636, 2191, 2336, 3017

Walla Walla WA, 2858

Walton FL, 1209, 1672, 1893, 1903, 1972, 1983

Warren IL, 2170

Warren NJ, 1122, 3071, 3073

Washington AL, 2135

Washington MN, 3480

Washington PA, 3188

Watauga NC, 2960

Wayne MI, 296

Wendell MA, 2729

Westchester NY, 1122, 3071, 3073

Westmoreland PA, 3188

Wheeler TX, 2512

Will IL, 2950

Windham VT, 3575

Wise VA, 2624

Wood WV, 3467

Woodford IL, 2170

Yancey NC, 2960

Yolo CA, 3434

York PA, 3351, 3391

LEGAL STATE/PROV OF RESIDENCE

Alabama, 1221, 2135, 2403, 2479, 2497, 2498, 2542, 2549, 2961, 3281, 3463

Alaska, 46, 200, 928, 1338, 1361, 1400, 2499, 2500, 3293, 3460, B3668

American Samoa, 194, 251, 850, 2225, 2312, 2319, 2560

Arizona, 2, 189, 204, 306, 534, 657, 801, 1225, 1338, 1476, 1723, 2598, 3035, 3072, 3387, 3393, 3432, 3464

Arkansas, 25, 208, 209, 210, 446, 638, 662, 1310, 2015, 2130, 2550, 2570, 2571, 2572, 2573, 2574, 2575, 2576, 2812, 3390, 3456

British Columbia CANADA, 2870

California, 6, 18, 79, 80, 103, 104, 136, 220, 221, 225, 321, 363, 506, 603, 893, 936, 972, 1024, 1046, 1134, 1146, 1225, 1232, 1244, 1297, 1338, 1379, 1417, 1425, 1447, 1464, 1482, 1504, 1554, 1591, 1630, 1957, 2049, 2195, 2241, 2424, 2515, 2561, 2567, 2617, 2623, 2626, 2627, 2628, 2629, 2631, 2632, 2634, 2635, 2636, 2637, 2638, 2639, 2785, 2800, 2869, 2871, 2917, 2951, 2971, 2973, 2979, 2985, 2986, 3013, 3018, 3023, 3039, 3049, 3072, 3123, 3146, 3176, 3243, 3260, 3317, 3325, 3393, 3395, 3416, 3434, 3446, 3457, 3464, 3496, 3538, 3567, 3586, 3602, B3721, C3822

Colorado, 2, 84, 86, 189, 204, 306, 801, 1225, 1338, 1476, 1723, 2511, 2613, 2661, 2690, 2692, 3002, 3035, 3072, 3316, 3387, 3422, 3456, B3721

Connecticut, 330, 472, 608, 658, 1076, 1236, 1276, 1329, 1453, 1489, 1612, 1963, 1964, 2408, 2551, 2738, 2739, 2984, 3054, 3072, 3123, 3194, 3458, B3721

Delaware, 331, 332, 1076, 1207, 1289, 1576, 1577, 1668, 1669, 1755, 1756, 2260, 2261, 3072, 3351, 3391, 3455

District of Columbia, 144, 197, 267, 896, 926, 978, 1076, 1091, 1207, 1459, 2232, 2312, 2772, 2975, 2976, 2977, 2978, 3072, 3557, B3721

Florida, 100, 159, 160, 231, 524, 525, 634, 635, 659, 827, 899, 933, 979, 1020, 1097, 1218, 1221, 1269, 1270, 1362, 1363, 1402, 1403, 1440, 1441, 1461, 1509, 1540, 1541, 1636, 1893, 1895, 1896, 1897, 1972, 2086, 2135, 2179, 2191, 2235, 2331, 2336, 2365, 2399, 2403, 2813, 2816, 2817, 2818, 2819, 2820, 2821, 2822, 2825, 2826, 2827, 2828, 3017, 3072, 3216, 3281, 3345, 3462, 3602, B3690, C3877

Georgia, 1221, 1734, 1877, 1951, 2121, 2403, 2549, 2559, 2860, 2861, 2983, 3123, 3261, 3281, 3389, 3462, 3490, 3572

Guam, 2312, 3457

Hawaii, 101, 477, 531, 928, 1225, 1338, 2516, 2627, 2675, 2898, 3406, 3444, 3457, B3721

Idaho, 928, 1338, 2550, 2835, 2918, 2919, 2920, 3293, 3460, 3482, 3561

Illinois, 240, 241, 242, 243, 336, 489, 659, 660, 906, 987, 1048, 1106, 1203, 1238, 1307, 1490, 1558, 1615, 1662, 1698, 1784, 1832, 1935, 1967, 1980, 1989, 2013, 2050, 2438, 2556, 2557, 2558, 2592, 2876, 2921, 2922, 2923, 2924, 2925, 2926, 2927, 2928, 2929, 2930, 2931, 2951, 3072, 3388, 3394, 3459

Indiana, 282, 283, 659, 660, 669, 1048, 1930, 2012, 2509, 2517, 2556, 2557, 2558, 3072, 3123, 3384, 3385, 3388, 3459, B3721

Iowa, 229, 590, 665, 667, 1048, 1164, 1200, 1761, 1888, 2093, 2131, 2350, 2382, 2652, 2781, 2793, 2901, 2943, 2944, 2945, 2946, 2947, 2948, 2949, 3103, 3388, 3456, 3540

Kansas, 2, 189, 204, 254, 306, 590, 663, 665, 667, 1070, 1476, 1654, 1723, 1736, 1802, 1878, 1948, 1952, 2093, 2448, 2535, 2537, 2538, 2539, 2958, 2995, 2996, 2997, 2998, 2999, 3035, 3085, 3456, B3721

Kentucky, 1048, 3003, 3004, 3005, 3281, 3286, 3459, 3539

Louisiana, 195, 255, 662, 1221, 1366, 1409, 1442, 1545, 1580, 1618, 2130, 2403, 2487, 2600, 3025, 3026, 3027, 3028, 3029, 3259, 3428, 3463, B3721

Maine, 230, 472, 658, 890, 1076, 1276, 1329, 2408, 2551, 2622, 2984, 3041, 3042, 3043, 3044, 3194, 3414, 3458

Maryland, 127, 256, 344, 496, 576, 622, 692, 736, 795, 1076, 1207, 1221, 1289, 1494, 1511, 1546, 1582, 1639, 1906, 1907, 1987, 2060, 2403, 2449, 3058, 3059, 3060, 3061, 3062, 3072, 3448, 3453, B3721

Massachusetts, 238, 323, 472, 658, 721, 890, 901, 902, 1076, 1078, 1099, 1100, 1112, 1198, 1276, 1289, 1329, 1885, 1887, 1966, 2311, 2381, 2408, 2428, 2551, 2607, 2659, 2714, 2720, 2735, 2790, 2838, 2984, 3024, 3063, 3064, 3065, 3067, 3072, 3193, 3194, 3352, 3392, 3458, 3602, B3721

Michigan, 19, 102, 405, 659, 877, 959, 1048, 1062, 1166, 1282, 1473, 2517, 2598, 3079, 3080, 3081, 3082, 3083, 3084, 3085, 3388, 3436, 3437, 3459, 3513, 3602, B3721

Minnesota, 2, 189, 204, 306, 737, 852, 914, 994, 1009, 1010, 1012, 1048, 1126, 1202, 1284, 1476, 1677, 1723, 1725, 1847, 1909, 1991, 2452, 2540, 2652, 2829, 3035, 3085, 3087, 3088, 3089, 3090, 3091, 3092, 3388, 3459, 3540, 3576, 3602, B3721

Mississippi, 258, 662, 671, 1221, 1764, 1765, 1910, 1992, 2130, 2135, 2356, 2357, 2403, 2649, 2806, 3095, 3281, 3463

Missouri, 590, 665, 667, 1678, 2093, 3019, 3085, 3104, 3105, 3106, 3456

Montana, 2, 189, 204, 306, 801, 928, 1338, 1476, 1723, 2550, 2774, 3035, 3101, 3102, 3293, 3460, 3482, B3617

Nebraska, 590, 665, 667, 2093, 3085, 3420, 3456, 3515

Nevada, 1024, 1338, 2951, 3191, 3192, 3253, 3457, 3464, 3496

New Hampshire, 459, 472, 658, 890, 1076, 1249, 1276, 1329, 1513, 1641, 1712, 2039, 2048, 2408, 2433, 2460, 2482, 2551, 2830, 2984, 3194, 3195, 3418, 3458, 3475

New Jersey, 131, 464, 578, 740, 796, 823, 921, 1076, 1137, 1289, 1291, 1548, 1549, 1585, 2150, 2603, 2800, 3072, 3123, 3196, 3197, 3198, 3199, 3200, 3201, 3380, 3381, 3382, 3383, 3391, 3455, 3465, 3492, 3521, 3586, B3721

New Mexico, 2, 189, 204, 306, 662, 801, 1338, 1476, 1723, 2504, 2548, 3035, 3072, 3202, 3203, 3204, 3207, 3464

New York, 137, 147, 148, 357, 546, 658, 823, 921, 1076, 1137, 1289, 1686, 1772, 1919, 1920, 2004, 2005, 2165, 2277, 2328, 2358, 2394, 2601, 2757, 2800, 3053, 3069, 3072, 3141, 3208, 3209, 3210, 3211, 3212, 3213, 3230, 3298, 3319, 3346, 3465, B3721

North Carolina, 269, 270, 271, 664, 1005, 1006, 1207, 1221, 1773, 1774, 1921, 1922, 1923, 2403, 2618, 2682, 2683, 2684, 2685, 2794, 2811, 2960, 3123, 3217, 3218, 3219, 3220, 3221, 3223, 3281, 3286, 3462, B3721

North Dakota, 2, 189, 204, 306, 801, 1048, 1476, 1723, 1847, 2652, 2845, 2846, 3035, 3225, 3226, 3459, 3482, 3540

Ohio, 1048, 1211, 2007, 2111, 2678, 3140, 3233, 3234, 3235, 3236, 3237, 3238, 3257, 3427, 3459, 3487, B3721

Oklahoma, 2, 189, 204, 306, 662, 1476, 1502, 1551, 1587, 1627, 1687, 1723, 1776, 1825, 2130, 2554, 2555, 2666, 2769, 2807, 2872, 3035, 3068, 3072, 3456

Oregon, 2, 152, 189, 204, 272, 306, 893, 928, 1213, 1338, 1476, 1723, 2095, 2505, 2550, 2650, 2840, 3035, 3228, 3245, 3246, 3247, 3248, 3293, 3460, 3602

Pennsylvania, 483, 557, 955, 1034, 1076, 1124, 1185, 1289, 1699, 1700, 1889, 1969, 2105, 2169, 2419, 2478, 2483, 2546, 2603, 2667, 2784, 2992, 3072, 3108, 3123, 3188, 3272, 3273, 3391, 3433, 3433, 3440, 3455, B3721

Pennsylvania (Western), 2483

Puerto Rico, 2312, 2595, 3072

Rhode Island, 472, 658, 890, 1076, 1276, 1329, 2408, 2551, 2853, 2984, 3055, 3072, 3151, 3194, 3266, 3304, 3305, 3458, B3721

South Carolina, 664, 829, 935, 1022, 1220, 1221, 1463, 2088, 2181, 2237, 2333, 2367, 2401, 2403, 2612, 2625, 2662, 2955, 2959, 3007, 3281, 3366, 3367, 3368, 3415, 3462, B3721

South Dakota, 2, 189, 204, 306, 1048, 1476, 1723, 1847, 2652, 2786, 3035, 3369, 3370, 3371, 3372, 3459, 3482, 3540

Tennessee, 285, 286, 912, 1207, 1221, 2403, 3281, 3286, 3404, 3405, 3463, B3721

Texas, 172, 215, 442, 662, 801, 1083, 1192, 1246, 1430, 1469, 1510, 1638, 2079, 2220, 2481, 2554, 2555, 2593, 2671, 2748, 2791, 2897, 3072, 3190, 3412, 3413, 3463, 3538, B3698, B3721

Utah, 295, 801, 1338, 1789, 3457, 3530

Vermont, 472, 658, 890, 1076, 1276, 1329, 2408, 2551, 2658, 2850, 2984, 3194, 3458, 3534, 3535

Virgin Islands, 194, 251, 850, 1183, 1707, 2032, 2225, 2312, 2319, 3541, 3542

Virginia, 510, 511, 664, 954, 1076, 1221, 1226, 1289, 1958, 2403, 2473, 2643, 2741, 2787, 2798, 2993, 3033, 3072, 3123, 3281, 3286, 3453, 3545, 3546, 3547, 3548, B3721

Washington, 2, 189, 204, 306, 310, 928, 1225, 1338, 1353, 1476, 1531, 1569, 1653, 1708, 1709, 1721, 1723, 1735, 1775, 1791, 1792, 1837, 1938, 2033, 2212, 2550, 3035, 3123, 3228, 3293, 3429, 3460, 3553, 3554, 3555, 3556, 3558, 3559, 3560, 3561, 3602, B3721

West Virginia, 559, 664, 1221, 2403, 2798, 2904, 3072, 3162, 3281, 3286, 3378, 3453, 3563, B3721

Wisconsin, 297, 660, 1048, 1847, 2034, 2035, 2556, 2557, 2558, 2652, 2855, 3072, 3264, 3388, 3394, 3459, 3540, 3577, 3578, 3579

Wyoming, 185, 294, 772, 801, 804, 1330, 1338, 1432, 2037, 2475, 2647, 2758, 2774, 2877, 2994, 3072, 3338, 3460, 3510, 3589, 3590, 3592, 3595, B3780

MARITAL STATUS

Divorced, 3365

Married Parent, 68, 314, 599, 839, 881, 963, 967, 1071, 1191, 1355, 1458, 1535, 1573, 1604, 1738, 2076, 2217, 2306, 2348, 2376, 2862

Single, 1980, 2489, 2492, 2495, 2513, 2562, 2581, 2607, 2634, 2776, 2814, 2921, 3343, 3365, 3469, 3493, 3523, 3577, C3974, C3975

Single Parent/1 minor child, 2576, 3365

Unmarried Parent, 68, 314, 492, 599, 839, 881, 963, 967, 1071, 1191, 1355, 1458, 1535, 1573, 1604, 1738, 1859, 2076, 2217, 2306, 2348, 2376, 2576, 2588, 2862, 3365

Widowed, 3365, 3577

OCCUPATIONAL GOALS

Aeronautics/Astronautics, 43, 352, 353, 474, 476, 487, 499, 501, 502, 507, 1381, 1497, 1498, 1592, 1634, 2231, 2239, 2409, 2426, 2458, 2459, B3615, B3691, C3825, C3844, C3847

Armed Forces, 42, 301, 473, 512, 562, 588, 656, 701, 775, 832, 872, 1030, 1037, 1331, 1471, 1563, 1594, 2244, 2246, 2300, 2339, 2345, 3493, 3543, C3829, C3830, C3973, C3974, C3976, C3977

Artist, 910, 1118

Author/Writer, 507, 976, 983, 1018, 1381, 1592, 1634, 2116, 2239, C3871, C3984

Automotive Industry, 425, 737, 2452, 2594, B3638

Builder/Contractor, 567, 579

Christian Service, 275, 1148, 1206, 1215, 1401, 1666, 1710, 1751, 1793, 1813, 1838, 1894, 1939, 1973, 2036, 2171, 2384, 2397, B3709

Curator, 144, 197, 267, 913, 926, 944, 1033, 1459, 1470, 2232, 2245

Flight Engineer, 43, 476, 493, 499, 2409, 2458, B3615, C3825, C3844, C3847

Government Service, 2312, 2341, 3297, C3895

Historian, 144, 197, 267, 507, 926, 1033, 1381, 1459, 1470, 1592, 1634, 2232, 2239, 2245, B3703

Journalism, 2095, 2096, 2097, 2100, 2101, 2108, 2109, 2112, 2113, 2114, 2115, 2116, 2117, 2128, 2137, 2139, 2140, 2144, 2146, 2147, 2148, 2149, 2152, 2153, 2154, 2195, 2207, 2628, B3726, B3746

Law Enforcement, 2243, 2251, 2255, 2257, 2270, 2273, 2286, 2288, 2294, 2295, 2297, 2298, 2299, 2338, C3887

Librarian/Archivist, 144, 197, 219, 267, 926, 944, 1033, 1459, 1470, 2232, 2245

Ministry, 215, 236, 275, 1148, 1192, 1193, 1194, 1195, 1196, 1199, 1200, 1202, 1204, 1206, 1207, 1211, 1215, 1216, 1221, 1222, 1226, 1401, 1666, 1751, 1813, 1894, 1973, 2171, 2384, 2397, 2403, 3396, B3709

Missionary, 215, 236, 275, 1148, 1192, 1204, 1215, 1221, 1222, 1227, 1710, 1793, 1838, 1939, 2036, 2171, 2397, 2403, B3709

Music, 75, 165, 216, 227, 761, 840, 889, 908, 910, 945, 961, 969, 1065, 1066, 1077, 1081, 1085, 1086, 1114, 1118, 1121, 1122, 1128, 1131, 1160, 1171, 1182, 1358, 1439, 1484, 1679, 1766, 1886, 1911, 1993, 2068, 2103, 2193, 2413, 2443, 2453, 2468, B3614, B3679, B3698, B3742

Newspaper Industry, 2109, 2116, 2152, 2628

Pilot, 43, 70, 96, 130, 476, 477, 484, 488, 490, 491, 492, 494, 497, 503, 510, 2409, 2420, 2431, 2454, 2461, B3615, B3691, B3693, B3803, B3804, C3825, C3831, C3832, C3844, C3845, C3846, C3847, C3917, C3982

Police Administration, 2243, 2251, 2286, 2338

Priest or Nun, 211, 1203, B3709

Rabbi, 852, 857, 858, 1213, B3709

Radio/TV, 75, 118, 216, 840, 889, 969, 1077, 2094, 2096, 2103, 2127, 2152, 2175, 2176, 2177

Real Estate, 155

Research Scientist, 227, 507, 583, 747, 799, 825, 864, 1085, 1241, 1292, 1358, 1374, 1381, 1413, 1439, 1444, 1484, 1552, 1556, 1588, 1592, 1628, 1634, 1696, 1817, 1886, 2239, 2278, 2329, 2359, 2395, 2396

Sports Writer, 2208

Teacher, 194, 195, 209, 215, 220, 223, 224, 230, 231, 234, 235, 236, 238, 241, 242, 243, 251, 255, 256, 269, 270, 273, 274, 283, 286, 287, 289, 290, 291, 294, 295, 297, 850, 870, 1005, 1055, 1056, 1160, 1192, 1204, 1401, 1580, 1618, 1666, 1751, 1773, 1813, 1817, 1850, 1894, 1921, 1973, 2225, 2319, 2384, 2562, C3881, C3922, C3964

Transportation/Traffic Manager, 167, 168, 169, 170, 171, 172

Travel Industry, 63

OCCUPATIONS

Adult Professional, 198, 353, 502, 583, 747, 799, 825, 864, 1171, 1172, 1241, 1292, 1374, 1413, 1444, 1498, 1552, 1588, 1628, 2064, 2210, 2231, 2278, 2329, 2359, 2395, 2396, 2459, 3039, 3127, 3309, 3576, B3615, B3639, B3747, B3777

Agriculture, 2640

Agriculture-D, 1288, 1306, 2640, 2648, 2882, 3393

Air Traffic Controller-D, 2493, B3615, C3844, C3847

Amer Foreign Serv-D, 2525, 2526

Architect, 516, 518, 519, 526

Artist, 890, 895, 896, 899, 906, 914, 915, 918, 924, 936, 954, 977, 978, 979, 987, 994, 1087, 1091, 1097, 1106, 1126, 2210, 2662

Author/Writer, 181, 246, 247, 353, 502, 507, 895, 896, 899, 906, 914, 964, 975, 976, 977, 978, 979, 980, 984, 987, 994, 995, 1003, 1008, 1010, 1011, 1012, 1018, 1023, 1024, 1087, 1091, 1097, 1106, 1126, 1188, 1381, 1498, 1592, 1634, 2124, 2135, 2221, 2231, 2239, 2360, 2459, 2662, B3702

Calif Youth Authority-D-DEC, 2638

Calif Youth Authority-D-DIS, 2638

Calif Youth Authority-S-DEC, 2638

Calif Youth Authority-S-DIS, 2638

Cinematographer, 895, 899, 906, 954, 977, 979, 987, 1087, 1097, 1106

Composer, 895, 896, 899, 906, 977, 978, 979, 987, 1063, 1087, 1091, 1097, 1106, 2662

Conservatn of Natrl Resources, 583, 747, 799, 825, 1241, 1292, 1301, 1301, 1374, 1413, 1421, 1421, 1444, 1552, 1588, 1628, 2395

Dept Corrections-D-DEC, 2572, 2638, 2926, 3063, 3197

Dept Corrections-D-DIS, 2572, 2638, 2926

Dept Corrections-S-DEC, 2572, 2638

Dept Corrections-S-DIS, 2572, 2638

East Orth Priest/Deacon-D, 828, 934, 1021, 1219, 1462, 2087, 2180, 2236, 2332, 2366, 2400

Engineer, 415, 583, 747, 799, 825, 1241, 1292, 1374, 1413, 1444, 1552, 1588, 1628, 2395

Firefighter, 117, 1908, 2387, 2440, 2450, 3136

Firefighter-D, 3123

Firefighter-D-DEC, 2572, 2638, 2926, 2936, 3010, 3060, 3063, 3095, 3128, 3136, 3197, 3210

Firefighter-D-DIS, 2572, 2638, 2926, 3010, 3060, 3095, 3136

Firefighter-S-DEC, 2572, 2638, 3128, 3128

Firefighter-S-DIS, 2572, 2638

Foodservice/Hospitality, 2062, 2064, C3849

Footwear/Leather Industry, 487, 2426, 3489

Footwear/Leather Industry-D, 3489

Forester-D/S-DEC/DIS, 2572

Harness Racing, 2891

Harness Racing-D, 2891

Hwy/Transptn Dept-D/S-DEC/DIS, 2572

Journalist, 1121, 2092, 2107, 2124, 2128, 2129, 2135, 2152, 2163, 2167, 2172, 2178, 2187, 2194, 2197, 2210, 2893, B3702

Law Enforcement Officer in WY, 2298

Librarian, 250

MD/DO Family Medicine, 1677, 1909, 1991

MD/DO Gen Internal Medicine, 1677, 1909, 1991

MD/DO General Pediatrics, 1677, 1909, 1991

MD/DO Obstetrics/Gynecology, 1677, 1909, 1991

Merchant Seafarer, 1453

Merchant Seafarer-D, 1453

Migrant Farmworker, 2640

Migrant Farmworker-D, 2640

Musician, 1086

Non-Profit Faculty/Staff, 1795

Nurse-Midwife (Certified), 1677, 1909, 1991

Peace Officer in CA, 2297

Performer, 895, 896, 899, 906, 914, 977, 978, 979, 987, 994, 1087, 1091, 1097, 1106, 1126, 1141, 1142, 1147, 2662

Photographer, 895, 896, 899, 906, 911, 914, 936, 954, 977, 978, 979, 987, 994, 1087, 1091, 1097, 1106, 1126, 2662

Physician Assist-Primary Care, 1677, 1909, 1991

Pilot, 150, 503, 504, 2461, 2462

Pilot-Commercial, 70, 130, 484, 490, 491, 494, 497, 2420, 2454, 2474, B3615, B3691, B3693, C3832, C3844, C3845, C3846, C3847, C3917

Pilot-Helicopter, 70, 130, 484, 497, 2420, 2454, 2474, B3615, B3691, B3693, C3832, C3844, C3845, C3846, C3847, C3917

Police-D, 3123

Police-D-DEC, 2572, 2638, 2926, 3010, 3060, 3063, 3095, 3197, 3210

Police-D-DIS, 2572, 2638, 2926, 3010, 3095

Police-S-DEC, 2572, 2638

Police-S-DIS, 2572, 2638

Railroad Worker-D-DEC, 2981

Realtor, 3298

Realtor-D, 3298

Registered Nurse (RN), 1677, 1909, 1943, 1950, 1975, 1991, 1992, 2009

Rescue Squad Member, 1908, 2450

Research Scholar or Scientist, 181, 246, 247, 248, 312, 353, 482, 502, 523, 571, 596, 677, 717, 788, 1188, 1479, 1498, 1533, 1556, 1571, 1602, 1720, 2231, 2459, 2662, B3669, B3677, B3785, B3794

School Business Management, 1496, 3401, B3675

School Principal/Head, 3401, B3675

Sculptor, 895, 899, 977, 979, 1087, 1097, 2662

Seaman, 3342

Seaman-D, 3343

Small Business Owner-D, 3256

Teacher's Assistant, 271, 1006, 1774, 1922

Teacher-College, 63, 149, 188, 230, 248, 249, 268, 927, 1002, 1004, 1143, 1160, 1370, 1496, 1527, 2065, 2082, 2166, 2523, 3310, B3616, B3777

Teacher-College-D, 2909, 3566

Teacher-Non College, 149, 187, 194, 230, 232, 233, 248, 249, 250, 251, 256, 264, 268, 277, 287, 292, 468, 850, 870, 895, 927, 948, 977, 1004, 1029, 1055, 1058, 1080, 1087, 1143, 1160, 1173, 1370, 1392, 1496, 1512, 1518, 1640, 1646, 2065, 2082, 2083, 2090, 2166, 2225, 2319, 2470, 2523, 2584, 3401, B3616, B3675, B3777

Teacher-Non College-D, 2909, 3566

US Federal Employee, 2803

US Federal Employee-D, 2803

ORGANIZATIONS

4-H Club, 2740, 2992

Aid Assn for Lutherans, 2488

Air Force Sgt's Assn-D, 2492

Am Art Therapy Assn, 1843

Am Assn Critical Care Nurses, 1943

Am Assn Nurse Anesthetists, 1944

Am Assn of Bioanalysts, 2514

Am Bowling Congress, 3597, 3598

Am Coll Nurse-Midwives Fdn, 1945

Am Fed of Grain Millers, 2520

Am Fed of Grain Millers-D/M, 2520

Am Health Info Mgmt Assn, 1859, 1861

Am Historical Assn, 2215

Am Inst of Chem Engineers, 704, 706, 707, 708

Am Jr Brahman Assn, 1251, 2534

Am Legion, 1725, 3415

Am Legion-D, 2536, 2539, 2922, 3041, 3232, 3415

Am Radio Relay League, 659, 660, 2546

Am School Food Svc Assn, 2067

Am School Food Svc Assn-D, 2067

Am Soc for Microbiology, 1527

Ancient Order United Workmen, 2566

Appaloosa Horse Club, 2568

Appaloosa Horse Club-D, 2568

Appaloosa Youth Foundation, 2568

Arctic Slope Regional Corp, 2569

Arctic Slope Regional Corp-D, 2569

Assn Operating Room Nurses, 1954

Blackfeet Tribe Member, 2610

Boy Scouts, 2536, 2616, 2782, 2923, 2943

CA Grange, 2633

CA Grange-D, 2633

CA Hazardous Matls Invgtrs Assn, 2255

CA Teachers' Assn, 222, 224

CA Teachers' Assn-D, 224, 2641

Catholic Aid Assn, 2652

Catholic Library Assn, 973

Children American Revolution, 1999

Civil Air Patrol, 226, 322, 486, 487, 815, 1196, 1483, 2425, 2426, 2427
Coast Guard Mutual Assistance, 3520
Columbian Squires, 3009, 3011
Congress of MN Resorts-D, 2736
Coast Guard Mutual Assist-D, 3520
Danish Sisterhood of Amer, 2749
Daughters American Revolution, 1999
Daughters Amer Revolution-D, 1999, 3170
Daughters of Penelope, 2752
Daughters of Penelope-D, 2752
DeKalb Cnty (IL) Farm Bureau-D, 1662, 1967
DeMolay, 2758, 2763, 3317
Disabled Amer Vets Aux-D, 2770
Distrib Education Clubs Amer, 94
East Ohio Conference, 1199
Explorer Scout, 2288, 2616, 2923
First Cath Slovak Ladies Assn, 2808, 2809
First Untd Meth Ch St Cloud MN, 1401, 1666, 1751, 1813, 1894, 1973, 2384
Fond du Lac Reservation, 2829
Future Farmers Amer, 1288, 2992
Future Homemakers Amer, 3603
Future Homemakers Amer TX, 3412
Future Homemakers Amer WY, 3587
GCSAA-D (golf course group), 2873
Girl Scout, 2782
Harness Horsemen Intl Assn-D, 2890
Intl Assn Arson Invstigatrs, 2267, 2439
Intl Assn Arson Invstigatrs-D, 2267, 2439
Intl Assn of Fire Fighters-D, 2936
Intl Soc Clinical Lab Tech, 2940
Intl Soc Clinical Lab Tech-D, 2940
Jap Amer Citizens Leag, 851, 907, 991, 1045, 1113, 1278, 1279, 1280, 2132, 2268, 2320, 2321, 2389, 2964, 2965, 2966
Jap Amer Citizens Leag-D, 851, 907, 991, 1045, 1113, 1278, 1279, 1280, 2132, 2268, 2320, 2321, 2389, 2964, 2965, 2966
Job's Daughters, 2758
Kansas Grange, 3074
Knights of Columbus, 3009
Knights of Columbus-D, 3008, 3009, 3010
Laramie County WY Farm Bureu-D, 3015
Luso-Amer Fraternal Fed, 1046
Lutheran Brotherhood, 3036, 3037
Maids of Athena, 2752
Marine Corps Tanker Assn, 3052, 3052
Marine Corps Tanker Assn-D, 3052, 3052
Masonic Lodge CA-D, 3317
Milit Order Prpl Heart-DESC, 3086
Military Order Purple Heart-D, 3086
Minnesota United Methdst Conf, 1401, 1666, 1751, 1813, 1894, 1973, 2384
Modern Woodmen of America, 3099

NAACP, 259, 345, 346, 1410, 1583, 1584, 1622, 1623, 3112, 3113
Nat Assn Exec Secs, 2455
Nat Assn Exec Secs-D, 2455
Nat Assn Retired Federal Emp-D, 2804
Nat Athletic Trainer Assn, 1914
Nat Custms Bkrs & Fwkrs Assn, 132
Nat Fed Press Women Inc, 2152
Nat Jr Classical League, 999
Nat Slovak Society, 3169
Nat Soc Accountants-D-any rel, 141
Nat Twenty & Four, 3173
Nat Twenty & Four-D, 3173
Nat Urban League (NULITE), 2162
Natrona County WY Ed Assn-D, 3177
New Mexico Farm/Lvstk Bureau, 3203
New Mexico Farm/Lvstk Bureau-D, 3203
Non Commissioned Officers Assn, 3215
Order of Ahepa-D, 2752
Oregon Credit Union (any), 3244
Parents Without Partners-D, 3258
Portuguese Continental Union, 3284
Professional Horsemens Assn, 3296
Professional Horsemens Assn-D, 3296
Red River Valley FP Assn-D, 3301
Reserve Officers Assn of US-D, 3302
Reserve Officers Assn of US, 3303
Retired Officers Assn-D, 3469
Royal Neighbors America, 3312, 3313
Ruritan, 3315
San Mateo County Farm Bureau, 3328
San Mateo County Farm Bureau-D, 3328
Soc of Automotive Engineers, 389
Soc of Bio Psychiatry, 1696
Soc of Physics Students, 1635
Soc of Women Engineers, 427, 432
Soil Conservation Society, 1302, 1385, 1422
Sons American Revolution, 1999
Sons American Revolution-D, 1999
Sons of Norway, 3361
Sons of Norway-D, 3361
Sons of Poland, 2589
Space Coast Credit Union, 159, 160, 634, 635, 1509, 1636, 2191, 2336
Springfield Nwspr 25 yr Club-D, 2713
Stanhome Inc-D, 3377
Student Calif Teachers Assn, 223, 224
Transportation Clubs, 167
Transportation Clubs-D, 167
United Daughters Confederacy-D, 3503
Veterans Foreign Wars Lds Ax-D, 3536
Veterans Foreign Wars-D, 3536
Western Society Criminology, 2294
Western Sunbathing Assn, 3565
Western Sunbathing Assn-D, 3565
Wisconsin Farm Bureau, 1327
Wisconsin Farm Bureau-D, 1327
Wom Int Bowling Congress, 3596, 3597

Women Peace Officers Assn, 2297
Women Peace Officers Assn-D, 2297
World History Assn, 2234
Wyoming Farm Bureau, 3591
Wyoming Farm Bureau-D, 3591
Wyoming Fed Women's Clubs-D, 3593
YMCA Staff, 186, 299
YMCA-Sidney/Shelby County OH, 3353
Young Amer Bowling Alliance, 3596, 3597, 3598

PHYSICAL HANDICAPS

General, 206, 1731, 1800, 1875, 3098
Amputee, 2627, 3115
Any Handicap, 206, 682, 723, 791, 1538, 1611, 1731, 1800, 1875, 2119, 2632, 2657, 2687, 2781, 2833, 2834, 2836, 3080, 3098, 3533, 3541, B3667, B3683, B3767, B3770
Asthma, 3335
Attention Deficit Disorder, B3655
Blind, 202, 203, 212, 263, 303, 348, 349, 539, 540, 589, 625, 821, 916, 961, 997, 1047, 1065, 1066, 1212, 1229, 1342, 1371, 1434, 1474, 1521, 1565, 1649, 1681, 1719, 1769, 1797, 1823, 1858, 1946, 1996, 2227, 2275, 2412, 2413, 2518, 2527, 2627, 2674, 3129, 3130, 3131, 3132, 3133, 3134, 3135, 3219, 3300, 3558, B3723
Cooley's Anemia, 3144
Deaf/Speech/Impaired, 92, 604, 2429, 2506, 2507, 2508, 2627, 3093, 3244, 3348
Dyslexia, 3476, 3484, B3655
Epilepsy, 2627, 2796, 3263
Hemophilia/Bleeding Disorder, 3452
Learning Disability, 2661, 2833, 2834, 3171, 3299, 3476, 3484, B3655, B3800, C3918
Paraplegic, 2627
Visually Impaired, 303, 589, 1229, 1342, 1434, 1474, 1521, 1565, 1649, 1719, 1797, 1858, 1946, 2412, 2674, 2742
Wheelchair Confined, 2657

PRESENT/CURRENT/FUTURE

Academy of Vocal Arts PA/USA, 1060
Adelphi Univ NY/USA, 199, 875, 1061, 2484
Agawam HS MA/USA, 89, 894
Alabama A&M Univ AL/USA, 177, 1247, 1324, 1389, 1429, 1451, 1560, 1788, 2072
Alcorn State Univ MS/USA, 177, 1247, 1324, 1389, 1429, 1451, 1560, 1788, 2072
Amador Valley HS CA/USA, 2515

Amanda HS OH/USA, 3239
Amer River College CA/USA, 157
Amherst College MA/USA, 2709, 2726
Analy HS CA/USA, 2879
Arizona State Univ AZ/USA, 534
Arkansas Tech Univ AR/USA, 2577
Art Inst of Boston MA/USA, 901
Art Inst of So Calif CA/USA, 886
Arvin HS CA/USA, 1308
Auburn Univ AL/USA, 1356
Bakersfield HS CA/USA, 1308
Ball State Univ IN/USA, 2102, 2252
Barry Univ FL/USA, 3158
Berne Union HS OH/USA, 3239
Bethune-Cook Coll FL/USA, 2822
Bishop Rosecrans HS OH/USA, 2678
Bloom Carroll HS OH/USA, 3239
Boron HS CA/USA, 1308
Buckeye Trail HS OH/USA, 2678
Burroughs HS CA/USA, 1308
Cal Coll Arts/Crafts CA/USA, 892
Cal Poly-Pomona CA/USA, 532, 1281
Cal Poly-San Lus Obspo CA/USA, 532, 1281
Cal State-Sacramento CA/USA, 157
Cal State-San Francisco CA/USA, 3325
Cal State-San Jose CA/USA, 3327
Calvin College MI/USA, 366
Cambridge HS OH/USA, 2678
Cardinal Newman HS CA/USA, 2879
Casa Grande HS CA/USA, 2879
Catholic School-any, 3448
Cedarville College OH/USA, 367
Centennial HS CA/USA, 1308
Central HS Sprngfld/MA/USA, 2698, 2712
Chatham College PA/USA, 1081
Chautauqua Institution NY/USA, 814
Chicopee HS MA/USA, 2701
Chinook HS MT/USA, 3022
City Univ of New York NY/USA, 2590, 3519
Clarkson Univ NY/USA, 666
Clemson Univ SC/USA, 541
Cloverdale HS CA/USA, 2879
College of Insurance NY/USA, 83
College of Marin CA/USA, 2687
College of San Mateo CA/USA, 1840, 2503
College of St Elizabeth NJ/USA, 2688
College of St Francis IL/USA, 2689
Colorado State Univ CO/USA, 1268, 1578, 2692
Commerce HS MA/USA, 2703, 2725
Community Christian HS CA/USA, 1308
Cornell Univ NY/USA, 368
Dean Tech HS MA/USA, 1961
Del Valle HS CA/USA, 2515
Delano HS CA/USA, 1308

Delaware State Univ DE/USA, 177, 1247, 1324, 1389, 1429, 1451, 1560, 1788, 2072
Desert HS CA/USA, 1308
Dowling College NY/USA, 2425
Dublin HS CA/USA, 2515
East Bakersfield HS CA/USA, 1308
East Longmeadow HS MA/USA, 2733
Edward Waters Coll FL/USA, 2822
El Camino HS CA/USA, 2879
El Dorado HS CA/USA, 3274
El Molino HS CA/USA, 2879
Embry-Riddle Aero U FL & AZ/USA, 369, 486
Empire College CA/USA, 8, 97, 1891, 2432, 2879
Fairfield Union HS OH/USA, 3239
Fashion Inst of Tech NY/USA, 898
Fisher College MA/USA, 2852
Florida A&M Univ FL/USA, 177, 1247, 1324, 1389, 1429, 1451, 1560, 1788, 2072, 2822
Florida Memorial Coll FL/USA, 2822
Florida State Univ FL/USA, 2828
Foothill HS CA/USA, 1308, 2515
Fort Valley State College GA/USA, 177, 1247, 1324, 1389, 1429, 1451, 1560, 1788, 2072
Frontier Regional HS MA/USA, 2728
Gannon Univ PA/USA, 370
Garces HS CA/USA, 1308
Gateway Regional HS MA/USA, 227, 1085, 1358, 1439, 1484, 1886
Geneva College PA/USA, 371
George Washington Univ DC/USA, 985
Georgetown Univ DC/USA, 2726
Geyserville HS CA/USA, 2777, 2879
Granada HS CA/USA, 2515
Grand Valley State Univ MI/USA, 372
Greenfield HS MA/USA, 2711
Guernsey Co ABLE/GED OH/USA, 2678
Guernsey-Noble CC HS OH/USA, 2678
Hampshire College MA/USA, 2709
Hampton Univ VA/USA, 2795
Harvard Univ MA/USA, 2894
Harvey Mudd College CA/USA, 3146
Haystack Mountain ME/USA, 904, 2436
Healdsburg HS CA/USA, 1128, 1679, 1766, 1911, 1993, 2453, 2777, 2879
Highland HS CA/USA, 1308
Hillsdale College MI/USA, 10, 107, 2223, 2313
Holyoke Catholic HS MA/USA, 2379, 2726
Howard Univ DC/USA, 2795
Hutchinson HS KS/USA, 2958
Illinois Inst Tech IL/USA, 374
Indiana Univ IN/USA, 2694
IndianaU/PurduU-Indnpls IN/USA, 373

Iowa State Univ IA/USA, 375, 1268, 1299, 1578
Jacksonville St Univ AL/USA, 2956
Jacksonville Univ FL/USA, 2957
John Glenn HS OH/USA, 2678
Johnson & Wales Univ RI/USA, 13, 14, 15, 16, 121, 122, 123, 124, 337, 338, 339, 340, 615, 616, 617, 618, 2055, 2056, 2057, 2058, 2444, 2445, 2446, 2447, 2987, 3151
Juniata College PA/USA, 17, 619, 855, 1492, 1674, 1763, 1819, 1905, 1985, 2322, 2989, 2990, 2991, 2992
Kansas State Univ KS/USA, 376, 1268
Kate Duncan Smith DAR AL/USA, 2754
Kentucky State Univ KY/USA, 177, 1247, 1324, 1389, 1429, 1451, 1560, 1788, 2072
Kern Valley HS CA/USA, 1308
Kettering Univ MI/USA, 377
King's College PA/USA, 3150
Lafayette College PA/USA, 378
Laguna HS CA/USA, 2879
Lancaster HS OH/USA, 3239
Langston Univ OK/USA, 177, 1247, 1324, 1389, 1429, 1451, 1560, 1788, 2072
Liberty Union HS OH/USA, 3239
Lincoln Univ MO/USA, 177, 1247, 1324, 1389, 1429, 1451, 1560, 1788, 2072
Lincoln-Sudbury HS MA/USA, 3392
Livermore HS CA/USA, 2515
Longmeadow HS MA/USA, 2715
Louisiana State-Shrvprt LA/USA, 126, 621, 992, 993, 1367, 1581, 1619, 1676, 2226, 2271, 2272, 2323, 3029, 3030, 3031
Mankato State Univ MN/USA, 751
Maria Carillo HS CA/USA, 2879
Maricopa HS CA/USA, 1308
McFarland HS CA/USA, 1308
Meadowbrook HS OH/USA, 2678
Mercer Univ GA/USA, 379
Mercyhurst College PA/USA, 1124
Miami Univ OH/USA, 753
Michigan State Univ MI/USA, 752, 2694
Middletown HS CA/USA, 2879
Midway College KY/USA, 129, 257, 820, 1283, 1547, 1990, 2355, 2451
Millersport HS OH/USA, 3239
Milwaukee Schl Enginrg WI/USA, 802
Minnechaug Regional HS MA/USA, 1960
Minnesota SW State Univ MN/USA, 1268
Minnesota State U-Mnkto MN/USA, 2273
Mohawk Regional HS MA/USA, 2735
Mojave HS CA/USA, 1308
Monson HS MA/USA, 2705
Montana State Univ MT/USA, 1268
Montgomery HS CA/USA, 2879
Mountain View HS CA/USA, 2879
Mt Ida College MA/USA, 2851

Murray State Univ KY/USA, 754
Muskingum-Perry CC HS OH/USA, 2678
NOVA Univ FL/USA, 3157
NY Inst Tech NY/USA, 380
NY Univ NY/USA, 3147
New Mexico Tech NM/USA, 3204, 3205, 3206
New Vista Adult Sch CA/USA, 2879
Newcomerstown HS OH/USA, 2678
Newton North HS MA/USA, 2980
Newton South HS MA/USA, 2980
No Carolina A&T Univ NC/USA, 177, 1247, 1324, 1389, 1429, 1451, 1560, 1788, 2072
No Carolina State Univ NC/USA, 824, 1290
No Dakota State Univ ND/USA, 1268
Nonsuch School CA/USA, 2879
North HS CA/USA, 1308
Northwestern Univ IL/USA, 2694
Oakland Univ MI/USA, 381
Oberlin College OH/USA, 830
Ohio State Univ OH/USA, 382, 2694
Ohio Univ OH/USA, 3239
Oklahoma State Univ OK/USA, 383
Oregon State Univ OR/USA, 1268
Parks College St Luis U MO/USA, 384
Penn State Univ PA/USA, 386, 1376, 1415, 2694
Penn State-Erie/Behrend PA/USA, 385
Pepperdine Univ CA/USA, 18, 136, 861
Petaluma HS CA/USA, 2879
Pickerington HS OH/USA, 3239
Pine Bluffs HS WY/USA, 3282
Piner HS CA/USA, 2879
Pittsburgh State Univ PA/USA, 755
Portsmouth HS NH/USA, 3283
Prairie View A&M Univ TX/USA, 177, 1247, 1324, 1389, 1429, 1451, 1560, 1788, 2072
Purdue Univ IN/USA, 387, 1295, 1377, 2694
Putnam Voc-Tech HS MA/USA, 2725
Rancho Cotate HS CA/USA, 2879
Rawlins HS WY/USA, 3038
Ridgeview HS CA/USA, 1308
Ridgway HS CA/USA, 2879
Ripon College WI/USA, 932, 1019, 1152, 3307
Rochester Inst Tech NY/USA, 388
Rosamond HS CA/USA, 1308
SUNY-Alfred NY/USA, 392
SUNY-New Paltz NY/USA, 393
SUNY-Stony Brook NY/USA, 391
Sacramento City Coll CA/USA, 157
San Antonio HS CA/USA, 2879
Santa Rosa Chrstn Schl CA/USA, 2879
Santa Rosa HS CA/USA, 2879

Santa Rosa Jr College CA/USA, 2190, 3329, 3330, 3331
Shafter HS CA/USA, 1308
So Carolina State U SC/USA, 177, 1247, 1324, 1389, 1429, 1451, 1560, 1788, 2072
So Dakota State Univ SD/USA, 1268
So Hadley HS MA/USA, 573
Sonoma State Univ CA/USA, 2190, 3359
Sonoma Valley HS CA/USA, 2879
South HS CA/USA, 1308
Southern Univ LA/USA, 177, 1247, 1324, 1389, 1429, 1451, 1560, 1788, 2072
Springfield Central HS MA/USA, 1609, 2734
Springfield HS Sci & Tech MA/USA, 1609, 2734
St Mary's HS Westfield/MA/USA, 1962
St Thomas Aquinas HS NH/USA, 3283
St Vincent HS CA/USA, 2879
Stanford Univ CA/USA, 3376
Stevens Inst Tech NJ/USA, 394
Stockdale HS CA/USA, 1308
Summit HS CA/USA, 1308
Taft HS CA/USA, 1308
Tamassee DAR School SC/USA, 2754
Taunton HS MA/USA, 2578
Tehachapi HS CA/USA, 1308
Tennessee State Univ TN/USA, 177, 1247, 1324, 1389, 1429, 1451, 1560, 1788, 2072
Texas A&M Univ TX/USA, 3407, 3408, 3409, 3410, 3411
Towson State Univ MD/USA, 3479
Tulane Univ LA/USA, 3488
Tuskegee Institute AL/USA, 177, 1247, 1324, 1389, 1429, 1451, 1560, 1788, 2072
US Air Force Acd CO/USA, 2489
United Negro Colleges USA, 2795, 3073, 3508
Univ Alabama-Brmnghm AL/USA, 1178
Univ Alaska-Fairbanks AK/USA, 395
Univ Arkansas AR/USA, 396
Univ Arkansas-Pine Bluff AR/USA, 177, 1247, 1324, 1389, 1429, 1451, 1560, 1788, 2072
Univ Bridgeport CT/USA, 3511
Univ CA-Berkeley CA/USA, 3512
Univ CA-Davis CA/USA, 532, 1281, 1561
Univ CA-Irvine CA/USA, 532, 1281
Univ CA-Irvine Ext CA/USA, 532, 1281
Univ CA-Los Angeles Ext CA/USA, 532, 1281
Univ CA-Los Angeles CA/USA, 532, 841, 974, 1281, 2218
Univ Chicago IL/USA, 2694
Univ Connecticut CT/USA, 462
Univ Evansville IN/USA, 397
Univ Florida FL/USA, 398, 1271

Univ Idaho ID/USA, 1268
Univ Illinois IL/USA, 556, 952, 1179, 1325, 2073, 2694
Univ Illinois-Chicago IL/USA, 756
Univ Iowa IA/USA, 2694
Univ Maine-Orono ME/USA, 767
Univ Maryland MD/USA, 177, 463, 768, 873, 1247, 1324, 1389, 1429, 1451, 1516, 1560, 1788, 2072, 2204
Univ Massachusetts MA/USA, 2709, 2727
Univ Michigan MI/USA, 877, 959, 1062, 1473, 2694, 3437
Univ Minnesota MN/USA, 1268, 1326, 2694
Univ Missouri-Rolla MO/USA, 3514
Univ Nebraska NE/USA, 1268
Univ Nebraska-Omaha NE/USA, 2291
Univ Nevada-Reno NV/USA, 2184
Univ New Mexico NM/USA, 2201, 3516, 3517
Univ Oklahoma OK/USA, 179, 2205
Univ Ozarks AR/US, 3171
Univ Pittsburgh PA/USA, 399
Univ Rochester NY/USA, 1059, 2183
Univ S California CA/USA, 400, 2585
Univ S Dakota SD/USA, 2292, 2340
Univ Texas-Arlington TX/USA, 180, 1182, 2206, 2207, 2246, 2293, 3525, 3526, 3527, 3528, 3529
Univ Texas-Austin TX/USA, 401, 2175
Univ Toledo OH/USA, 402
Univ Utah UT/USA, 1789, 1790
Univ Washington WA/USA, 769
Univ Windsor CAN, 3519
Univ Wiscnsn-Pltvl/RvFl WI/USA, 1268
Univ Wisconsin-Madison WI/USA, 1268, 2694
Univ Wisconsin-Milwaukee WI/USA, 803, 3076
Univ Wyoming WY/USA, 1268, 1578
Ursuline HS CA/USA, 2879
Utah State Univ UT/USA, 1268
Valley Christian HS CA/USA, 2515
Vanderbilt Univ TN/USA, 2208
Village HS CA/USA, 2515
Virginia Military Inst VA/USA, 3543
Virginia Polytech Inst VA/USA, 350
Virginia State Univ VA/USA, 177, 1247, 1324, 1389, 1429, 1451, 1560, 1788, 2072
Vista HS CA/USA, 1308
Wasco HS CA/USA, 1308
Washington State Univ WA/USA, 1268
Washington Univ MO/USA, 404
Wayne State MI/USA, 403
Webb Inst Naval Arch NY/USA, 558, 807
Wellesley Coll Alumni MA/USA, 3562
Wellesley College MA/USA, 3562
West HS CA/USA, 1308
West Virginia Univ WV/USA, 406

Western Michigan Univ MI/USA, 405
Western New Englnd Coll MA/USA, 2724
Westfield HS MA/USA, 2707, 2731
Wheatland HS WY/USA, 3568
Whittier College CA/USA, 956, 1186, 3570
Wichita State Univ KS/USA, 407
Widener Univ PA/USA, 408
Wilkes University PA/USA, 2747
William Fischer Cath HS OH/USA, 3239
Wright State Univ OH/USA, 409

RELIGIOUS AFFILIATION

Atheist/Agnostic, 237, 817, 981, 1205, 1235, 1486, 2591
Baha'i Faith, 2720
Baptist, 236, 1204, 1226, 2599, 3122
Brethren, 2989
Catholic, 211, 1188, 1189, 1203, 2652, 2688, 2830, 2906, 2951, 3009, 3011, 3108, 3319, 3448, 3539
Christian, 360, 826, 1206, 1211, 1214, 1225, 1296, 1694, 1779, 2084, 2203, 2280, 2479, 2785, 3353, B3706
Christian Science, 2502
Christn Church-Disc of Chrst, 1193, 1194, 1195
Eastern Orthodox, 2782
Episcopal, 2607
Jewish, 252, 253, 336, 843, 846, 852, 853, 854, 857, 858, 1238, 1490, 1544, 1579, 1615, 1616, 1673, 1762, 1818, 1904, 1984, 2122, 2133, 2269, 2377, 2390, 2391, 2511, 2533, 2567, 2899, 2969, 2970, 2971, 2972, 2973, 2974, 2975, 2976, 2977, 2978, 3126, 3323, 3445
Lutheran, 183, 215, 1192, 1227, 1710, 1793, 1838, 1939, 2036, 2488, 3036, 3037, 3580, 3581
Muslim, 3424
Presbyterian, 1207, 1210, 1216, 1693, 3286, 3287, 3288, 3289, 3290, 3291, 3292, 3396
Protestant, 1211, 2708, 2793
Sikh, 3355
Unitarian, 831, 949, 1031, 1176, 2290
United Church of Christ, 3502
United Methodist Church, 1096, 1199, 1201, 1202, 1222, 1223, 1224, 1401, 1666, 1751, 1813, 1894, 1973, 2384, 2813, 3507

SEX

Female, 5, 17, 39, 64, 67, 68, 77, 78, 90, 125, 129, 182, 183, 184, 190, 198, 217, 257, 262, 298, 313, 314, 315, 318, 319, 320, 354, 413, 414, 415, 416, 417, 418, 419, 420, 421, 422, 423, 424, 425, 426, 427, 428, 429, 430, 431, 432, 433, 434, 435, 436, 437, 438, 439, 467, 477, 490, 491, 492, 493, 494, 503, 530, 572, 598, 599, 600, 601, 602, 623, 632, 633, 653, 679, 680, 693, 718, 720, 732, 734, 759, 789, 790, 813, 820, 830, 837, 838, 839, 881, 922, 961, 963, 966, 967, 1000, 1018, 1035, 1065, 1066, 1071, 1076, 1078, 1081, 1139, 1190, 1191, 1193, 1227, 1242, 1283, 1293, 1338, 1341, 1354, 1355, 1357, 1375, 1414, 1438, 1446, 1457, 1458, 1460, 1481, 1499, 1503, 1534, 1535, 1536, 1537, 1547, 1553, 1572, 1573, 1574, 1589, 1603, 1604, 1605, 1607, 1608, 1620, 1624, 1629, 1645, 1658, 1689, 1710, 1711, 1715, 1737, 1738, 1743, 1744, 1777, 1793, 1794, 1826, 1833, 1838, 1839, 1925, 1939, 1940, 1941, 1990, 2010, 2036, 2038, 2066, 2075, 2076, 2077, 2142, 2152, 2153, 2213, 2214, 2216, 2217, 2254, 2296, 2305, 2306, 2309, 2342, 2347, 2348, 2355, 2372, 2375, 2376, 2407, 2413, 2423, 2451, 2461, 2474, 2487, 2501, 2513, 2515, 2516, 2565, 2595, 2634, 2664, 2688, 2693, 2752, 2755, 2762, 2805, 2837, 2851, 2852, 2862, 2867, 2871, 2880, 2937, 2968, 2981, 2993, 3075, 3078, 3094, 3108, 3126, 3131, 3139, 3154, 3250, 3269, 3306, 3322, 3357, 3365, 3374, 3389, 3398, 3402, 3419, 3437, 3450, 3496, 3526, 3566, 3567, 3572, 3580, 3581, 3582, 3583, 3584, 3585, 3593, 3596, B3609, B3610, B3611, B3612, B3619, B3627, B3628, B3629, B3630, B3632, B3633, B3635, B3637, B3639, B3644, B3646, B3647, B3649, B3650, B3651, B3652, B3657, B3659, B3660, B3662, B3665, B3672, B3678, B3689, B3692, B3694, B3696, B3697, B3705, B3714, B3715, B3716, B3721, B3727, B3729, B3730, B3732, B3733, B3736, B3743, B3747, B3749, B3762, B3766, B3767, B3774, B3775, B3776, B3781, B3786, B3787, B3790, B3791, B3795, B3796, B3797, B3798, B3801, B3802, B3807, B3808, B3813, C3834, C3840, C3982, C3983
Male, 317, 345, 360, 734, 1200, 1221, 1296, 1583, 1622, 1657, 1694, 1742, 1779, 1805, 1833, 1848, 1852, 1881, 2253, 2280, 2307, 2403, 2667, 2793, 2841, 2862, 2937, 2943, 3001, 3277, 3283, 3306, 3486, 3496, 3560, 3592, 3598, B3609, B3610, B3611, B3612, B3619, B3627, B3628, B3629, B3630, B3633, B3635, B3637, B3639, B3644, B3647, B3649, B3650, B3651, B3652, B3657, B3659, B3660, B3662, B3672, B3678, B3689, B3692, B3694, B3696, B3697, B3705, B3714, B3715, B3716, B3727, B3729, B3730, B3732, B3733, B3736,

B3743, B3747, B3749, B3762, B3766, B3767, B3781, B3786, B3787, B3790, B3791, B3795, B3796, B3797, B3798, B3801, B3802, B3807, B3808, B3813, C3986

SORORITY/FRATERNAL

Alpha Epsilon Rho, 2151
Alpha Mu Gamma, 1038
Delta Gamma, 2761
Delta Gamma-D, 2761
Delta Phi Epsilon, 2762
Gamma Theta Upsilon, 1364
Kappa Omicron Nu, 2059
Kappa Sigma, 3001
Phi Alpha Theta, 2233, 2234
Phi Kappa Theta, 3277
Phi Theta Kappa Intl Honor Soc, 3278
Tau Beta Pi, 441

STATE/PROVINCE INTENDED STUDY

Alabama, 1291, 1549, 2496, 2497, 2498, 2542, 2549, 2956, 3281
Alaska, 46, 1361, 1400, B3668
Arizona, 95, 605, 681, 722, 2118, 2430, 2598, 3432
Arkansas, 208, 209, 210, 662, 2130, 2570, 2571, 2572, 2573, 2574, 2575, 2812, 3043, 3171, 3390
British Columbia CANADA, 2870
California, 95, 104, 198, 219, 220, 221, 223, 324, 325, 334, 532, 605, 681, 722, 784, 956, 971, 972, 1007, 1094, 1095, 1186, 1233, 1266, 1281, 1485, 1610, 1840, 2098, 2118, 2136, 2241, 2424, 2430, 2503, 2583, 2585, 2628, 2629, 2631, 2636, 2637, 2640, 2644, 2669, 2745, 2974, 2985, 2986, 3018, 3039, 3057, 3243, 3267, 3324, 3326, 3395, 3473, 3544, 3567, C3822, C3862, C3863, C3864, C3865
Colorado, 84, 85, 86, 87, 88, 1267, 2613, 2690, 2691, 2692, 2906, 3002, 3423
Connecticut, 472, 658, 1291, 1329, 1453, 1549, 1963, 1964, 2408, 2670, 3043, 3121, 3148, 3155, 3194, 3318, 3566
Delaware, 1291, 1549, 3043
District of Columbia, 99, 144, 197, 267, 897, 926, 1291, 1459, 1549, 2145, 2232, 2586, 3043, 3557
Florida, 100, 159, 160, 231, 524, 525, 634, 635, 659, 899, 918, 979, 1097, 1269, 1270, 1291, 1362, 1363, 1402, 1403, 1440, 1441, 1509, 1540, 1541, 1549, 1636, 1897, 1974, 2191, 2336, 2510, 2817, 2818, 2819, 2820, 2821, 2822, 2823, 2824, 2825, 2827, 2828, 3017,

3157, 3158, 3281, 3345, 3532, B3690, C3877

Georgia, 95, 605, 681, 722, 1207, 1291, 1549, 2100, 2101, 2118, 2121, 2430, 2549, 2860, 3261, 3281, 3389

Hawaii, 784, 845, 2516, 3406

Idaho, 1267, 3561

Illinois, 95, 241, 242, 243, 489, 605, 659, 660, 681, 685, 722, 1158, 1203, 1207, 1980, 2118, 2430, 2438, 2556, 2689, 2926, 2927, 2928, 2929, 2930, 2931

Indiana, 282, 283, 659, 660, 669, 685, 1107, 1108, 1184, 1291, 1549, 1930, 2012, 2517, 2556, 3384

Iowa, 665, 1184, 1200, 1267, 1299, 2131, 2793, 2943, 2944, 2946, 2947, 2948, 3103, 3540

Kansas, 254, 665, 822, 1240, 1267, 1495, 1948, 2448, 2535, 2538, 2539, 2541, 2653, 2995, 2996, 2997, 2998, 3000, 3085

Kentucky, 1093, 1207, 1291, 1549, 3004, 3281, 3539

Louisiana, 195, 255, 662, 1291, 1366, 1409, 1442, 1545, 1549, 1580, 1618, 2130, 3025, 3026, 3027, 3028

Maine, 472, 658, 904, 1291, 1329, 1549, 2006, 2408, 2436, 2622, 2900, 3006, 3043, 3044, 3121, 3148, 3194

Manitoba CANADA, 1184

Maryland, 127, 256, 344, 463, 496, 576, 622, 692, 736, 768, 795, 822, 873, 1240, 1291, 1494, 1495, 1516, 1546, 1549, 1582, 1906, 1907, 1908, 1987, 2060, 2449, 2450, 2586, 3043, 3058, 3059, 3061, 3062, 3111, 3240, 3240, 3419

Massachusetts, 472, 658, 1078, 1112, 1291, 1329, 1549, 2408, 2732, 3043, 3063, 3064, 3066, 3067, 3094, 3121, 3126, 3148, 3194, 3321, 3421

Michigan, 102, 296, 685, 947, 1282, 2517, 2598, 3079, 3082, 3083, 3084, 3085, 3437, 3438

Minnesota, 119, 659, 685, 737, 1103, 1104, 1184, 1267, 1284, 1650, 1677, 1725, 1909, 1991, 2318, 2388, 2452, 2540, 2882, 2883, 2884, 2885, 2886, 3085, 3087, 3089, 3090, 3091, 3092, 3320, 3474, 3540, 3576

Mississippi, 258, 662, 671, 1291, 1549, 1764, 1765, 1910, 2130, 2356, 2357, 2649, 3095, 3096, 3281

Missouri, 95, 605, 665, 681, 722, 1051, 1052, 1053, 1184, 2118, 2430, 2653, 3056, 3085, 3104, 3105, 3106

Montana, 1267, 3101, 3102, B3617

Nebraska, 665, 1184, 1267, 3085

Nevada, 334, 784, 2098, 3192

New Hampshire, 472, 658, 1291, 1329, 1549, 2408, 3043, 3121, 3148, 3194, 3195, 3280, 3461

New Jersey, 95, 131, 326, 464, 578, 605, 681, 722, 740, 796, 1049, 1207, 1291, 1359, 1548, 1549, 1585, 2118, 2150, 2430, 2670, 2688, 2866, 3196, 3197, 3199, 3380, 3381, 3382, 3383, 3442, 3521

New Mexico, 662, 3202, 3204, 3205, 3206

New York, 95, 147, 148, 149, 199, 268, 357, 518, 546, 558, 605, 658, 666, 681, 685, 722, 807, 875, 898, 927, 1004, 1061, 1143, 1157, 1245, 1291, 1507, 1549, 1633, 1686, 1772, 1920, 2005, 2118, 2145, 2165, 2166, 2277, 2328, 2358, 2394, 2425, 2430, 2484, 2501, 2590, 2601, 2670, 2799, 2910, 3210, 3211, 3212, 3213, 3230, 3319, 3439, 3486

North Carolina, 269, 664, 744, 1207, 1291, 1549, 2645, 2673, 2682, 2683, 2684, 2685, 3219, 3220, 3222, 3281

North Dakota, 581, 1184, 1267, 3225, 3226, 3540

Ohio, 95, 605, 681, 685, 722, 727, 830, 1187, 1291, 1549, 2007, 2111, 2118, 2430, 2437, 2693, 2764, 2765, 2766, 3233, 3234, 3235, 3236, 3237, 3238, 3470, 3487

Oklahoma, 662, 1502, 1551, 1587, 1627, 1687, 1776, 1825, 2130, 2769, 3068

Ontario CANADA, 685, 1184

Oregon, 272, 334, 1267, 3245, 3246, 3247, 3248

Pennsylvania, 275, 360, 685, 816, 1081, 1124, 1148, 1215, 1291, 1296, 1549, 1694, 1779, 1889, 1969, 2105, 2169, 2171, 2256, 2280, 2397, 2664, 2686, 2784, 2857, 2991, 3043, 3108, 3150, 3234, 3272, 3374, 3378, 3447

Quebec CANADA, 685

Rhode Island, 13, 14, 15, 16, 121, 122, 123, 124, 337, 338, 339, 340, 472, 615, 616, 617, 618, 658, 1291, 1329, 1549, 1699, 2055, 2056, 2057, 2058, 2408, 2444, 2445, 2446, 2447, 2853, 3043, 3121, 3148, 3194, 3304

South Carolina, 541, 664, 829, 935, 1022, 1220, 1291, 1463, 1549, 2088, 2181, 2237, 2333, 2367, 2401, 2625, 2662, 3007, 3281, 3366, 3368, 3484

South Dakota, 1184, 1267, 3370, 3371, 3540

Tennessee, 285, 286, 912, 1291, 1549, 2208, 3281, 3322, 3404

Texas, 95, 154, 178, 215, 293, 442, 605, 662, 681, 722, 953, 1083, 1180, 1181, 1192, 1246, 1469, 1510, 1638, 1683, 1757, 1899, 1977, 1978, 2079, 2118, 2173, 2220, 2430, 2463, 2481, 2642, 2839, 3175, 3373, 3407, 3408, 3409, 3410, 3411, 3413, 3476, 3485, B3698

Utah, 295, 1092, 1267, 1789, 1790, 3530

Vermont, 472, 658, 1291, 1329, 1549, 2408, 3043, 3121, 3148, 3194

Virginia, 664, 1207, 1291, 1549, 1958, 2586, 2695, 3033, 3224, 3281, 3450, 3451, 3543, 3545, 3546, 3547, 3548

Washington, 334, 1267, 2212, 2566, 2801, 2836, 3466, 3554, 3555, 3556, 3561

West Virginia, 664, 1291, 1549, 1704, 2904, 3281, 3378, 3563

Wisconsin, 660, 685, 1184, 1267, 2034, 2035, 2556, 3579

Wyoming, 185, 294, 772, 809, 1267, 1432, 1724, 2037, 2270, 2298, 2299, 2475, 3350, 3356, 3569, 3587, 3589, 3591, 3592, 3593, 3594, 3595, B3780

UNIONS

AFL/CIO, B3620

AFL/CIO-D, B3620

Airline Pilots Assn-D, 2494

Am Fed St/County/Muni Emp-D, 2303, 2521, 2522

Am Fed St/County/Muni Emp, 2522

Am Fed of Teachers, 2523

Amal Clothing/Textile Wkrs-D, 3501

Cal Correctional Peace Off, 2630

Cal Correctional Peace Off-D, 2630

Glass/Molders/Pottery Wkrs-D, 2868

Graphic Communications Intl-D, 2878

IA Bridge/Struct/Iron Wkrs-D, 2935

IA Theatre/Moving Pic Oper, 2934

IU Bricklyrs/Allied Crftsmn-D, 2941

IUE-Elec/Sal/Mach/Furn Wkrs-D, 2942

Intl Brotherhood/Teamsters-D, 2938

Intl Ladies Garment Workers, 2939

Intl Ladies Garment Workers-D, 2939, 3492

MN Teamsters Jnt Cncl #32, 3092

Operating Engineers Local 3-D, 3242

Screen Actors Guild, 3340

Screen Actors Guild-D, 3340

Service Employees Internat'l, 3349

Service Employees Internat'l-D, 3349

Transport Workers of Amer-D, 3481

Unit Food/Comml Wkrs-Loc 555-D, 3506

Unit Food/Comml Wkrs-Loc 555-S, 3506

Unit Food/Comml Wkrs-Loc 555, 3506

Unit Paprwrkrs Internat'l -D, 3509

United Food/Comml Wkrs IU, 3505

United Food/Comml Wkrs IU-D, 3505

Utility Workers of Amer-D, 3531

Wyoming Peace Off Assn-WPOA-D, 2299, 2299

UNUSUAL CHARACTERISTICS

1st Generation College Student, 3528

1st Generation US Citizen, 2820, 3468, 3589

1st Generation US Citizen-D, 2820, 3468

Cancer Survivor, 2517, 2954, 2955, 3387
Child of Unmarried Parent, 2981, 3406
Daughter-Crnt/Frmr US Army Off, 3357
Deceased Parents, 2603, 2959, 3137, 3253
Descendant-Decl of Indep Signer, 2768
Descendants-Confederate Soldier, 3503
Descendants-Seafarer, 3193, 3343
Descendants-Union Soldier, 2756
Economic/Cultural Disadvantage, 6, 80,
    92, 147, 225, 321, 332, 357, 514, 546,
    603, 604, 709, 1170, 1232, 1277, 1406,
    1425, 1482, 1538, 1543, 1577, 1669,
    1686, 1756, 1772, 1920, 1956, 1957,
    2005, 2141, 2156, 2157, 2158, 2261,
    2277, 2358, 2394, 2429, 2482, 2527,
    2588, 2593, 2600, 2601, 2621, 2637,
    2653, 2657, 2675, 2764, 2769, 2797,
    2811, 2845, 2850, 2964, 3033, 3039,
    3190, 3196, 3250, 3253, 3264, 3267,
    3268, 3269, 3270, 3311, 3386, 3406,
    3420, 3428, 3440, 3443, 3444, 3446,
    3474, 3554, 3555, 3559, 3606
English as a Second Language, 3201
Foster Child, 3137

Foster Parent, 3137
Foster Parent-D, 3137
From Former Soviet Union, 858, 3100
GED, 77, 2544, 2575, 3497
Gay or Lesbian, 499, 2458, 2565, 2590,
    2837, 3257, 3259, 3260, 3261, 3262,
    3271, 3276, 3293
Gay or Lesbian-D, 3260, 3262, 3441
Greencard Holder, 3468
Homeschooled, 829, 935, 1022, 1220, 1463,
    2088, 2181, 2237, 2333, 2367, 2401,
    B3706
Left-Hander attndg Juniata Col, 2990
Male Non-Regstrnt Selective Ser, 2844
Native-Born Californian, 936, 1023
Non-Drinker, 2660
Oklahoma City Bomb Victim-D, 2802
Orphan, 2959, 3137, 3253, 3406
Overweight, 3121
Parent Deaf/Hear Imp Child under 6,
    2508, 2508
Re-Entry Student after 2 yrs, 68, 198, 278,
    314, 318, 415, 417, 434, 572, 599, 601,

680, 720, 790, 839, 967, 1191, 1227,
    1355, 1357, 1438, 1458, 1535, 1536,
    1573, 1574, 1604, 1607, 1690, 1738,
    1827, 1926, 2076, 2217, 2306, 2348,
    2362, 2376, 3398, 3580, 3581
Re-Entry Student after 5 yrs, 68, 198, 278,
    314, 415, 417, 434, 599, 839, 967, 1191,
    1227, 1258, 1355, 1458, 1535, 1573,
    1604, 1690, 1738, 1827, 1926, 2076,
    2217, 2306, 2348, 2362, 2376, 3398,
    3580, 3581
Re-Entry to Workforce 2+ yrs, 415
Refugee/Asylee, 2750, 2899
Resident of Rural Community, 200, 1271,
    2882, 3166
Short Stature/Under 4'10", 2609
Tall (5'10" women/6'2" men), 3399
Unadopted Orphan, 2603, 2836, 2959,
    3137, 3252, 3406
Undergrad Named Gatlin/Gatling, 3222
Varsity Tennis Letter, 2831
Welfare/Public Assistance Pgm, 77

Field of Study Index

SCHOOL OF BUSINESS

General, 1, 2, 3, 4, 5, 6, 7, 8, 10, 11, 12, 13, 14, 15, 16, 17, 18, 19, 20, 21, 22, 23, 24, 25, 26, 27, 28, 29, 30, 31, 32, 33, 34, 35, 36, 37, 39, 40, 52, 73, 74, 77, 78, 80, 93, 97, 100, 101, 107, 109, 120, 121, 122, 123, 124, 126, 136, 161, 182, 189, 190, 193, 196, 204, 217, 225, 239, 266, 281, 304, 306, 319, 321, 327, 333, 337, 338, 339, 340, 356, 440, 445, 446, 447, 448, 449, 450, 451, 452, 453, 454, 455, 456, 457, 458, 467, 574, 602, 603, 615, 616, 617, 618, 627, 637, 638, 639, 640, 641, 642, 643, 644, 645, 646, 647, 648, 649, 650, 653, 687, 728, 758, 793, 805, 813, 1232, 1237, 1259, 1263, 1309, 1310, 1311, 1312, 1313, 1314, 1315, 1316, 1317, 1318, 1319, 1320, 1321, 1322, 1328, 1384, 1424, 1476, 1481, 1482, 1500, 1537, 1567, 1608, 1625, 1645, 1658, 1670, 1697, 1723, 1743, 1759, 1781, 1816, 1830, 1891, 1901, 1929, 1957, 1979, 2011, 2014, 2015, 2016, 2017, 2018, 2019, 2020, 2021, 2022, 2023, 2024, 2025, 2026, 2027, 2055, 2056, 2057, 2058, 2077, 2110, 2112, 2188, 2223, 2254, 2262, 2283, 2296, 2310, 2313, 2334, 2342, 2423, 2432, 2444, 2445, 2446, 2447, B3662

BUSINESS ADMINISTRATION

General, 1, 5, 6, 8, 11, 13, 14, 15, 16, 17, 18, 19, 22, 42, 52, 59, 71, 77, 78, 80, 95, 97, 100, 101, 104, 108, 109, 117, 119, 121, 122, 123, 124, 126, 129, 131, 135, 136, 137, 138, 143, 156, 159, 161, 162, 166, 183, 186, 190, 193, 198, 217, 225, 239, 257, 281, 299, 301, 304, 319, 321, 333, 337, 338, 339, 340, 355, 440, 473, 512, 527, 562, 574, 578, 588, 602, 603, 605, 609, 615, 616, 617, 618, 630, 634, 636, 656, 681, 686, 687, 696, 701, 722, 726, 728, 740, 742, 775, 793, 796, 813, 820, 832, 879, 1037, 1232, 1237, 1283, 1331, 1424, 1471, 1481, 1482, 1537, 1547, 1548, 1563, 1567, 1585, 1594, 1608, 1637, 1658, 1670, 1697, 1743, 1759, 1781, 1816, 1830, 1891, 1901, 1929, 1957, 1979, 1990, 2011, 2055, 2056, 2057, 2058, 2077, 2112, 2118, 2123, 2150, 2196, 2254, 2262, 2282, 2300, 2318, 2337, 2345, 2353, 2355, 2387, 2388, 2423, 2430, 2432, 2440, 2444, 2445, 2446, 2447, 2451, B3662

Accounting, 8, 41, 51, 57, 64, 69, 77, 84, 85, 86, 87, 88, 95, 97, 105, 110, 111, 116, 127, 140, 141, 147, 162, 164, 175, 176, 357, 546, 605, 636, 651, 681, 722, 1637,

1686, 1701, 1703, 1772, 1785, 1787, 1835, 1836, 1891, 1920, 1936, 1937, 2005, 2028, 2029, 2070, 2071, 2118, 2250, 2277, 2284, 2358, 2394, 2405, 2406, 2430, 2432, C3815, C3816, C3817, C3818

Actuarial Science, 81, 162, 636, 1637, C3819, C3913

Advertising, 48, 49, 89, 118, 179, 894, 2127, 2152, 2205, C3823

Art Administration/Management, 75, 76, 91, 149, 151, 216, 268, 840, 889, 891, 927, 969, 970, 1004, 1077, 1079, 1143, 1145, 2103, 2106, 2166

Aviation/Airport Management, 43, 44, 45, 50, 70, 96, 130, 150, 173, 476, 484, 488, 497, 504, 2409, 2420, 2431, 2454, 2462, B3615, C3844, C3845, C3846, C3847, C3917, C3983

Banking, 105

Business Ethics, 100

Club Management, 82, 178

Data Processing, 92, 604, 2429, C3873

Economics, 7, 10, 19, 39, 67, 68, 93, 101, 104, 106, 107, 112, 115, 125, 139, 156, 159, 160, 162, 166, 182, 313, 314, 327, 335, 467, 598, 599, 614, 630, 634, 635, 636, 653, 696, 838, 839, 966, 967, 1190, 1191, 1354, 1355, 1365, 1407, 1457, 1458, 1509, 1534, 1535, 1572, 1573, 1603, 1604, 1614, 1636, 1637, 1645, 1737, 1738, 2075, 2076, 2110, 2191, 2196, 2216, 2217, 2223, 2224, 2229, 2264, 2282, 2296, 2305, 2306, 2310, 2313, 2315, 2317, 2325, 2336, 2337, 2342, 2347, 2348, 2375, 2376

Finance, 4, 19, 74, 83, 102, 105, 116, 125, 143, 156, 159, 162, 355, 630, 634, 636, 696, 742, 1263, 1637, 2282, C3836

Garden Center Management, 4, 74, 1263

Golf Course Management, 82, 1273, 1274, 1275

Grocery Industry, 38

Hotel Administration, 13, 14, 15, 16, 46, 53, 54, 55, 56, 63, 103, 110, 121, 122, 123, 124, 142, 173, 178, 337, 338, 339, 340, 615, 616, 617, 618, 2049, 2055, 2056, 2057, 2058, 2444, 2445, 2446, 2447, C3911

Industrial & Labor Relations, 159, 181, 634

Information Systems, 12, 77, 120

Insurance, 83, 104, 162, 636, 1637, C3913

Integrated Resource Management., 65

International Business, 7, 72, 93, 132, 133, 134, 327, 860, 861, 1257, 2110, 2276, 2310, 2311, 2324

Labor Studies/Human Resources, 143, 159, 181, 355, 634, 742

Management, 12, 60, 91, 94, 114, 120, 162, 613, 636, 689, 729, 1613, 1637, C3919, C3938

Manufacturing, 125, 425

Marketing, 3, 48, 49, 73, 76, 94, 118, 143, 149, 158, 159, 160, 162, 178, 180, 268, 355, 553, 634, 635, 636, 742, 891, 927, 970, 1004, 1079, 1143, 1259, 1303, 1423, 1509, 1636, 1637, 2106, 2127, 2152, 2166, 2170, 2189, 2191, 2335, 2336

Merchandising, 12, 120

Operations Research, 114, 613, 689, 729, 1613, C3938

Production/Operations Management, 65, 143, 355, 742

Public Administration, 61, 90, 104, 113, 117, 119, 145, 146, 153, 163, 183, 244, 520, 544, 545, 554, 584, 760, 819, 989, 1027, 1159, 1305, 1386, 1397, 1426, 1449, 1468, 1557, 2081, 2126, 2242, 2265, 2279, 2309, 2316, 2318, 2326, 2327, 2330, 2387, 2388, 2392, 2393, 2398, 2440, 2467, C3854, C3957

Public Relations, 48, 49, 58, 76, 144, 148, 149, 154, 158, 197, 267, 268, 553, 891, 926, 927, 970, 1004, 1079, 1143, 1423, 1459, 2091, 2106, 2165, 2166, 2173, 2189, 2212, 2232, 2328, 2335, B3765

Real Estate, 66, 79, 155, 157, C3836

Real Estate Appraising, 66, C3836

Recreation/Resource Managemnt, 47, 163, 177, 201, 554, 584, 760, 1027, 1064, 1159, 1247, 1305, 1324, 1386, 1389, 1426, 1429, 1449, 1451, 1468, 1557, 1560, 1788, 1841, 2072, 2242, 2467

Restaurant Management, 38, 110, 142, 165, 178, 761, 945, 2062, 2063, 2064, 2065, 2068, 2193, 2468, C3849, C3894

Retail Management, 12, 82, 99, 120, 178, 897

Sports Management, 47, 98, 184, 201, 262, 298, 1064, 1841, 1892, 1940, 2120, 2214, 2352, 2372, 2383, 2407

Traffic Management, 61, 62, 167, 168, 169, 170, 171, 172, 174, 461, 520, 555, 585, 698, 764, 806, 1397, 2371, 2404

Transportation, 9, 61, 62, 167, 168, 169, 170, 171, 172, 174, 185, 410, 461, 520, 555, 585, 698, 764, 772, 806, 1397, 1432, 2371, 2404, 2475, C3831

Travel & Tourism, 8, 46, 63, 97, 142, 163, 173, 178, 554, 584, 760, 1027, 1159, 1305, 1386, 1426, 1449, 1468, 1557, 1891, 2242, 2432, 2467

Youth/Human Svc Agcy Adm, 119, 2318, 2388

SCHOOL OF EDUCATION

General, 2, 5, 11, 20, 78, 109, 144, 189, 190, 191, 192, 193, 194, 195, 196, 197, 204, 217, 222, 223, 224, 228, 239, 240, 251, 255, 266, 267, 269, 294, 295, 306, 319, 333, 356, 574, 602, 627, 687, 728, 793, 813, 850, 926, 1237, 1459, 1476, 1481, 1500, 1537, 1580, 1608, 1618, 1625, 1658, 1670, 1723, 1743, 1746, 1759, 1816, 1901, 1979, 2077, 2225, 2232, 2254, 2262, 2319, 2380, 2423, 2562, C3881

EDUCATION

General, 2, 5, 6, 11, 20, 22, 78, 80, 109, 113, 129, 144, 149, 161, 189, 190, 192, 193, 194, 195, 196, 197, 204, 209, 217, 222, 223, 224, 225, 226, 228, 230, 231, 236, 237, 238, 239, 240, 241, 242, 244, 251, 252, 255, 256, 257, 259, 266, 267, 268, 269, 270, 271, 274, 281, 283, 294, 295, 297, 306, 319, 321, 322, 333, 356, 440, 574, 602, 603, 627, 687, 728, 793, 813, 815, 817, 819, 820, 850, 926, 927, 981, 989, 1004, 1005, 1006, 1051, 1143, 1204, 1205, 1232, 1235, 1237, 1283, 1424, 1459, 1476, 1481, 1482, 1483, 1486, 1500, 1537, 1544, 1547, 1579, 1580, 1608, 1616, 1618, 1625, 1658, 1670, 1673, 1697, 1723, 1743, 1759, 1762, 1773, 1774, 1781, 1816, 1818, 1830, 1901, 1904, 1921, 1922, 1929, 1957, 1979, 1984, 1990, 2011, 2077, 2081, 2126, 2133, 2166, 2225, 2232, 2254, 2262, 2265, 2269, 2316, 2319, 2355, 2380, 2390, 2423, 2451, 2562, 3223, C3881, C3964

Administration/Management, C3963

Blind/Visually Impaired Education, 202, 203, 212, 213, 232, 245, 278, 279, 280, 1690, 1691, 1692, 1827, 1828, 1829, 1926, 1927, 1928, 2362, 2363, 2364, B3735, C3879

Child Care, 221, 2060

Christian Leadership Education, 215, 236, 275, 291, 1148, 1192, 1204, 1215, 2171, 2397

Deaf/Hearing Impaired Education, 205, 206, 207, 218, 232, 245, 260, 261, 270, 271, 278, 279, 280, 1005, 1006, 1690, 1691, 1692, 1730, 1731, 1732, 1745, 1773, 1774, 1799, 1800, 1801, 1827, 1828, 1829, 1874, 1875, 1876, 1882, 1913, 1921, 1922, 1926, 1927, 1928, 2362, 2363, 2364, B3735, C3879

Early Childhood Education, 210, 221, 253, 270, 271, 276, 291, 292, 293, 854, 948, 1005, 1006, 1029, 1058, 1173, 1512, 1640, 1773, 1774, 1921, 1922, 2090, 2391, 2470

Elementary Education, 200, 210, 211, 220, 238, 254, 258, 263, 270, 271, 272, 273, 276, 284, 285, 286, 287, 291, 292, 293, 296, 300, 870, 948, 1005, 1006, 1029, 1055, 1056, 1058, 1173, 1496, 1512, 1640, 1773, 1774, 1921, 1922, 2090, 2470, 3223

English as Second Language, 247, 250, 292, 948, 1029, 1058, 1173, 1512, 1640, 2090, 2470

Gifted/Talented Education, 232

Health Education, 47, 201, 253, 292, 854, 948, 1029, 1058, 1064, 1173, 1512, 1640, 1841, 2090, 2391, 2470

Learning Disabled Education, 232, 243, 245, 246, 247, 250, 260, 261, 270, 271, 278, 279, 280, 288, 289, 290, 1005, 1006, 1690, 1691, 1692, 1773, 1774, 1827, 1828, 1829, 1831, 1913, 1921, 1922, 1926, 1927, 1928, 2362, 2363, 2364, 2370, B3735, C3879

Music Education, 75, 149, 216, 268, 275, 840, 889, 927, 969, 1004, 1077, 1099, 1143, 1148, 1160, 1215, 2103, 2166, 2171, 2397, B3614

Orientation/Mobility, 202, 203, 212, 232

Physical Education, 47, 184, 199, 201, 227, 253, 262, 265, 270, 271, 292, 298, 854, 948, 1005, 1006, 1029, 1058, 1064, 1085, 1173, 1358, 1439, 1484, 1512, 1640, 1770, 1773, 1774, 1841, 1886, 1917, 1921, 1922, 1940, 2090, 2214, 2372, 2391, 2407, 2470

Post-Secondary Education, 253, 263, 854, 1496, 2391

Reading Education, 270, 271, 293, 1005, 1006, 1773, 1774, 1921, 1922

Reading Education-G, 246, 247, 248, 249, 250, 293

School Library/Media, 219

Secondary Education, 200, 208, 210, 220, 238, 254, 258, 263, 270, 271, 272, 273, 276, 284, 285, 286, 287, 291, 293, 296, 300, 870, 1005, 1006, 1055, 1056, 1496, 1773, 1774, 1921, 1922, 3223

Special Education, 208, 211, 212, 214, 229, 232, 243, 245, 246, 254, 261, 270, 271, 273, 276, 278, 279, 280, 282, 288, 289, 290, 1005, 1006, 1690, 1691, 1692, 1773, 1774, 1827, 1828, 1829, 1831, 1888, 1921, 1922, 1926, 1927, 1928, 1930, 2350, 2362, 2363, 2364, 2370, 2382, B3667, B3686, B3735, B3770, B3771, B3772, B3773, B3779, C3879, C3969

Technology Education, 233, 234, 235, 284, 292, 948, 1029, 1058, 1173, 1512, 1640, 2090, 2470

Youth Leadership, 186, 291, 299, C3985, C3986

SCHOOL OF ENGINEERING

General, 1, 2, 5, 6, 7, 11, 13, 14, 15, 16, 20, 22, 24, 25, 26, 27, 28, 29, 30, 31, 32, 33, 34, 35, 36, 37, 39, 42, 52, 67, 68, 78, 80, 93, 109, 115, 121, 122, 123, 124, 143, 147, 161, 174, 182, 189, 190, 193, 196, 204, 217, 225, 226, 239, 266, 281, 284, 301, 302, 303, 304, 305, 306, 307, 308, 310, 311, 312, 313, 314, 315, 316, 317, 318, 319, 320, 321, 322, 323, 324, 325, 326, 327, 328, 329, 330, 331, 332, 333, 335, 336, 337, 338, 339, 340, 341, 342, 343, 344, 345, 346, 347, 348, 349, 350, 351, 352, 353, 354, 355, 356, 357, 358, 359, 360, 361, 362, 363, 364, 365, 366, 367, 368, 369, 370, 371, 372, 373, 374, 375, 376, 377, 378, 379, 380, 381, 382, 384, 386, 387, 388, 389, 390, 391, 392, 393, 394, 395, 397, 398, 399, 400, 401, 402, 403, 404, 405, 406, 407, 408, 409, 410, 411, 414, 415, 417, 418, 419, 421, 422, 424, 426, 428, 429, 431, 432, 433, 434, 435, 436, 437, 439, 440, 441, 442, 444, 445, 446, 447, 448, 449, 450, 451, 452, 453, 454, 455, 456, 457, 458, 459, 460, 461, 462, 463, 464, 465, 466, 467, 468, 469, 470, 471, 473, 481, 482, 495, 496, 500, 501, 502, 505, 506, 512, 521, 522, 523, 537, 539, 540, 542, 546, 547, 555, 560, 561, 562, 570, 571, 572, 574, 575, 576, 580, 582, 585, 586, 587, 588, 589, 591, 595, 596, 598, 599, 600, 601, 602, 603, 608, 614, 615, 616, 617, 618, 620, 622, 626, 627, 628, 629, 637, 638, 639, 640, 641, 642, 643, 644, 645, 646, 647, 648, 649, 650, 653, 654, 655, 656, 668, 672, 676, 677, 679, 680, 687, 691, 692, 695, 698, 699, 700, 701, 716, 717, 718, 719, 720, 721, 724, 728, 735, 736, 741, 742, 746, 749, 764, 768, 773, 774, 775, 776, 787, 788, 789, 790, 793, 794, 795, 797, 800, 806, 810, 811, 813, 815, 832, 838, 839, 873, 903, 966, 967, 982, 1037, 1101, 1190, 1191, 1217, 1229, 1230, 1231, 1232, 1233, 1236, 1237, 1238, 1239, 1244, 1246, 1248, 1296, 1297, 1309, 1310, 1311, 1312, 1313, 1314, 1315, 1316, 1317, 1318, 1319, 1320, 1321, 1322, 1331, 1342, 1344, 1351, 1353, 1354, 1355, 1357, 1359, 1365, 1371, 1372, 1373, 1379, 1392, 1393, 1395, 1398, 1407, 1410, 1412, 1417, 1424, 1434, 1436, 1438, 1443, 1447, 1454, 1455, 1457, 1458, 1464, 1469, 1471, 1474, 1475, 1476, 1477, 1478, 1479, 1481, 1482, 1483, 1485, 1487, 1488, 1489, 1490, 1491, 1493, 1494, 1497, 1498, 1499, 1500, 1501, 1504, 1505, 1506, 1508, 1510, 1513, 1514, 1516, 1518, 1519, 1521, 1531, 1532, 1533, 1534, 1535, 1536, 1537, 1546, 1550, 1554, 1563, 1565, 1567, 1569, 1570, 1571, 1572, 1573, 1574,

1576, 1577, 1582, 1583, 1584, 1586,
1590, 1591, 1594, 1601, 1602, 1603,
1604, 1605, 1606, 1607, 1608, 1610,
1612, 1614, 1615, 1617, 1622, 1623,
1624, 1625, 1626, 1630, 1631, 1632,
1638, 1641, 1642, 1645, 1646, 1647,
1649, 1651, 1653, 1657, 1658, 1668,
1669, 1670, 1675, 1681, 1686, 1694,
1695, 1697, 1719, 1722, 1723, 1735,
1737, 1738, 1742, 1743, 1755, 1756,
1759, 1769, 1772, 1779, 1780, 1781,
1797, 1798, 1805, 1816, 1823, 1824,
1830, 1858, 1862, 1881, 1885, 1901,
1906, 1920, 1924, 1929, 1946, 1947,
1957, 1979, 1996, 2005, 2011, 2014,
2015, 2016, 2017, 2018, 2019, 2020,
2021, 2022, 2023, 2024, 2025, 2026,
2027, 2055, 2056, 2057, 2058, 2075,
2076, 2077, 2110, 2216, 2217, 2224,
2231, 2253, 2254, 2260, 2261, 2262,
2275, 2277, 2280, 2296, 2300, 2305,
2306, 2307, 2310, 2317, 2342, 2345,
2347, 2348, 2358, 2371, 2375, 2376,
2394, 2404, 2412, 2423, 2428, 2444,
2445, 2446, 2447, 2459, 3114, C3826,
C3883, C3884

AERONAUTICS

General, 43, 96, 150, 311, 312, 343, 344,
351, 352, 353, 358, 363, 427, 472, 474,
475, 476, 479, 481, 482, 485, 486, 487,
488, 495, 496, 498, 499, 500, 501, 502,
504, 505, 506, 507, 522, 523, 537, 542,
570, 571, 575, 576, 580, 582, 595, 596,
620, 622, 626, 628, 676, 677, 691, 692,
695, 716, 717, 735, 736, 741, 746, 787,
788, 794, 795, 797, 1244, 1297, 1372,
1379, 1381, 1412, 1417, 1447, 1464,
1478, 1479, 1494, 1497, 1498, 1504,
1532, 1533, 1546, 1550, 1554, 1570,
1571, 1582, 1586, 1591, 1592, 1596,
1601, 1602, 1617, 1626, 1630, 1634,
1824, 1906, 1924, 2231, 2239, 2408,
2409, 2415, 2421, 2426, 2431, 2456,
2458, 2459, 2462, B3615, B3691, B3803,
B3804, C3824, C3825, C3830, C3831,
C3844, C3846, C3847

Aerodynamics, 369, B3691

Aeronautical Engineering, 42, 96, 150,
301, 309, 352, 353, 369, 390, 427, 473,
478, 488, 501, 502, 504, 508, 512, 562,
588, 656, 701, 775, 832, 1037, 1331,
1471, 1497, 1498, 1563, 1594, 2231,
2300, 2345, 2431, 2459, 2462, 2469,
B3691

Aerospace History, 353, 502, 507, 1381,
1498, 1592, 1634, 2231, 2239, 2459,
B3691

Aerospace Technology, 42, 150, 301, 352,
353, 369, 473, 474, 475, 501, 502, 504,
512, 562, 588, 656, 701, 775, 832, 1037,

1331, 1471, 1497, 1498, 1563, 1594,
2231, 2300, 2345, 2459, 2462, B3691

Astronautics, 352, 353, 427, 478, 479, 501,
502, 1497, 1498, 1596, 2231, 2415, 2459,
B3691, C3824, C3901

Aviation, 43, 70, 96, 130, 150, 474, 475,
476, 477, 479, 480, 483, 484, 485, 488,
489, 490, 491, 492, 493, 494, 497, 498,
503, 504, 508, 510, 511, 1596, 2409,
2415, 2419, 2420, 2421, 2431, 2438,
2454, 2456, 2461, 2462, 2469, 2473,
B3691, B3693, B3803, B3804, C3831,
C3832, C3845, C3917

Aviation Electronics, 43, 70, 96, 130, 150,
369, 476, 479, 483, 484, 488, 489, 497,
498, 504, 511, 1596, 2409, 2415, 2419,
2420, 2431, 2438, 2454, 2456, 2462,
2473, B3691, B3693, B3804, C3831,
C3832, C3845, C3917

Aviation Writing, 96, 353, 488, 502, 1498,
2231, 2431, 2459, B3691, B3804

Aviation/Aerospace History, 507, 1381,
1592, 1634, 2239

Space Science, 352, 353, 478, 479, 501, 502,
1497, 1498, 1596, 2231, 2415, 2459,
B3691

Vertical Flight, 509

ARCHITECTURE

General, 42, 108, 147, 301, 308, 311, 312,
334, 343, 348, 349, 351, 357, 361, 470,
471, 473, 481, 482, 495, 500, 512, 513,
514, 515, 517, 521, 522, 523, 526, 527,
537, 539, 540, 541, 542, 546, 547, 548,
549, 550, 556, 557, 559, 560, 561, 562,
570, 571, 575, 580, 586, 587, 588, 591,
595, 596, 609, 620, 626, 654, 655, 656,
672, 676, 677, 686, 691, 695, 699, 700,
701, 716, 717, 726, 735, 741, 773, 774,
775, 776, 787, 788, 794, 797, 810, 811,
832, 878, 938, 939, 952, 955, 1034, 1037,
1179, 1185, 1217, 1331, 1351, 1371,
1398, 1465, 1471, 1478, 1479, 1532,
1533, 1563, 1570, 1571, 1590, 1594,
1601, 1602, 1617, 1681, 1686, 1695,
1769, 1772, 1780, 1823, 1920, 1996,
2005, 2123, 2275, 2277, 2300, 2345,
2353, 2358, 2394, B3621, C3839, C3912

Architectural Engineering, 42, 174, 301,
390, 461, 470, 471, 473, 512, 541, 549,
555, 560, 561, 562, 585, 586, 587, 588,
654, 655, 656, 698, 699, 700, 701, 764,
773, 774, 775, 806, 810, 811, 832, 938,
1037, 1331, 1471, 1563, 1594, 2300,
2345, 2371, 2404

Architectural History, 517, 550, 551, 552,
878, 939, 940, 941, 1465, 1466

Design Arts, 517, 549, 552, 878, 938, 941

Environmental Design, 163, 334, 443, 517,
524, 525, 538, 549, 552, 554, 584, 760,
878, 938, 941, 1027, 1159, 1269, 1270,
1286, 1305, 1362, 1363, 1386, 1402,

1403, 1426, 1440, 1441, 1449, 1468,
1540, 1541, 1557, 2242, 2467

Health Facilities, 516

Landscape Architecture, 147, 158, 163,
357, 517, 524, 525, 528, 529, 530, 531,
532, 533, 534, 535, 536, 538, 543, 546,
553, 554, 556, 584, 760, 878, 952, 1027,
1159, 1179, 1262, 1269, 1270, 1281,
1286, 1303, 1305, 1362, 1363, 1386,
1402, 1403, 1423, 1426, 1440, 1441,
1449, 1468, 1540, 1541, 1557, 1686,
1772, 1920, 2005, 2189, 2242, 2277,
2335, 2358, 2394, 2467

Naval Architecture, 309, 558, 807, C3932

Urban Planning, 61, 145, 146, 174, 461,
517, 520, 524, 525, 538, 544, 545, 549,
555, 556, 585, 698, 764, 806, 878, 938,
952, 1179, 1269, 1270, 1286, 1362, 1363,
1397, 1402, 1403, 1440, 1441, 1540,
1541, 2326, 2327, 2371, 2392, 2393,
2404, C3978

CIVIL ENGINEERING

General, 11, 42, 109, 131, 163, 174, 193,
239, 301, 309, 311, 312, 318, 325, 333,
334, 343, 344, 351, 358, 366, 367, 368,
369, 370, 371, 373, 374, 375, 376, 377,
378, 379, 386, 387, 388, 389, 390, 394,
395, 397, 398, 399, 400, 401, 402, 403,
404, 405, 406, 407, 408, 410, 414, 415,
417, 418, 419, 420, 421, 422, 424, 426,
428, 429, 431, 432, 433, 434, 435, 436,
437, 439, 443, 461, 470, 471, 473, 481,
482, 495, 496, 500, 505, 512, 522, 523,
537, 542, 554, 555, 560, 561, 562, 563,
564, 566, 568, 569, 570, 571, 572, 573,
574, 575, 576, 578, 579, 580, 581, 582,
583, 584, 585, 586, 587, 588, 595, 596,
601, 620, 622, 626, 628, 654, 655, 656,
676, 677, 680, 687, 691, 692, 695, 698,
699, 700, 701, 716, 717, 720, 728, 735,
736, 740, 741, 746, 747, 760, 764, 773,
774, 775, 787, 788, 790, 793, 794, 795,
796, 797, 799, 806, 810, 811, 825, 832,
1027, 1037, 1159, 1237, 1241, 1292,
1305, 1331, 1357, 1372, 1374, 1386,
1412, 1413, 1426, 1438, 1444, 1449,
1468, 1471, 1478, 1479, 1494, 1532,
1533, 1536, 1546, 1548, 1550, 1552,
1557, 1563, 1570, 1571, 1574, 1582,
1585, 1586, 1588, 1594, 1601, 1602,
1607, 1617, 1626, 1628, 1670, 1759,
1816, 1824, 1901, 1906, 1924, 1979,
2150, 2242, 2262, 2300, 2345, 2371,
2395, 2404, 2467, C3860

Construction, 410, 443, 565, 567, 568, 569,
577, 579, C3868

Public Works Administration, 174, 461,
555, 585, 698, 764, 806, 2371, 2404

Structural Engineering, 565, 579

COMPUTER SCIENCE

General, 5, 6, 13, 14, 15, 16, 20, 24, 25, 26, 27, 28, 29, 30, 31, 32, 33, 34, 35, 36, 37, 39, 42, 67, 68, 77, 78, 80, 92, 95, 108, 114, 115, 121, 122, 123, 124, 156, 159, 160, 162, 176, 182, 190, 196, 217, 225, 266, 301, 303, 308, 311, 312, 313, 314, 315, 318, 319, 321, 330, 335, 337, 338, 339, 340, 343, 344, 351, 356, 358, 362, 373, 375, 376, 377, 381, 384, 386, 387, 388, 390, 391, 393, 394, 397, 398, 399, 400, 401, 402, 403, 404, 405, 406, 407, 408, 409, 415, 416, 417, 418, 419, 421, 422, 423, 426, 428, 431, 433, 434, 435, 436, 444, 445, 446, 447, 448, 449, 450, 451, 452, 453, 454, 455, 456, 457, 458, 467, 470, 471, 473, 481, 482, 495, 496, 500, 505, 512, 521, 522, 523, 527, 537, 542, 560, 561, 562, 570, 571, 572, 575, 576, 580, 582, 586, 587, 588, 589, 590, 591, 592, 593, 594, 595, 596, 597, 598, 599, 600, 601, 602, 603, 604, 605, 606, 607, 608, 609, 610, 611, 612, 613, 614, 615, 616, 617, 618, 619, 620, 621, 622, 623, 624, 625, 626, 627, 628, 629, 630, 631, 632, 633, 634, 635, 636, 637, 638, 639, 640, 641, 642, 643, 644, 645, 646, 647, 648, 649, 650, 651, 652, 653, 654, 655, 656, 667, 672, 673, 674, 675, 676, 677, 678, 679, 680, 681, 683, 684, 686, 688, 689, 691, 692, 693, 694, 695, 696, 699, 700, 701, 716, 717, 718, 720, 722, 726, 729, 735, 736, 741, 746, 749, 765, 773, 774, 775, 776, 787, 788, 789, 790, 794, 795, 797, 800, 810, 811, 813, 832, 838, 839, 966, 967, 1037, 1190, 1191, 1229, 1232, 1236, 1309, 1310, 1311, 1312, 1313, 1314, 1315, 1316, 1317, 1318, 1319, 1320, 1321, 1322, 1331, 1342, 1351, 1354, 1355, 1357, 1365, 1372, 1387, 1398, 1407, 1412, 1419, 1427, 1434, 1438, 1457, 1458, 1471, 1474, 1478, 1479, 1481, 1482, 1489, 1494, 1500, 1509, 1521, 1532, 1533, 1534, 1535, 1536, 1537, 1546, 1550, 1563, 1565, 1570, 1571, 1572, 1573, 1574, 1582, 1586, 1594, 1598, 1599, 1600, 1601, 1602, 1603, 1604, 1605, 1607, 1608, 1612, 1613, 1614, 1617, 1620, 1621, 1625, 1626, 1636, 1637, 1645, 1649, 1658, 1703, 1719, 1737, 1738, 1743, 1787, 1797, 1824, 1836, 1858, 1906, 1924, 1937, 1946, 1957, 2014, 2015, 2016, 2017, 2018, 2019, 2020, 2021, 2022, 2023, 2024, 2025, 2026, 2027, 2029, 2055, 2056, 2057, 2058, 2071, 2075, 2076, 2077, 2093, 2118, 2123, 2191, 2202, 2216, 2217, 2224, 2254, 2282, 2289, 2296, 2300, 2305, 2306, 2317, 2336, 2342, 2345, 2347, 2348, 2353, 2375, 2376, 2406, 2412, 2423, 2429, 2430, 2444, 2445, 2446, 2447, B3734, C3866, C3867, C3873, C3938
Artificial Intelligence, 611, 688
Computer Graphics, 606, 607, 683, 684, 923, B3670

ELECTRICAL ENGINEERING

General, 11, 42, 95, 108, 109, 174, 193, 239, 301, 307, 308, 309, 311, 312, 315, 318, 333, 334, 343, 344, 351, 366, 367, 368, 369, 370, 371, 372, 373, 374, 375, 376, 377, 378, 379, 380, 381, 383, 384, 385, 386, 387, 388, 389, 390, 391, 392, 393, 394, 395, 397, 398, 399, 400, 401, 402, 403, 404, 405, 406, 407, 408, 409, 410, 413, 414, 415, 416, 417, 418, 419, 421, 422, 423, 424, 425, 426, 428, 429, 430, 431, 432, 433, 434, 435, 436, 437, 438, 439, 443, 461, 470, 471, 473, 481, 482, 495, 496, 500, 512, 521, 522, 523, 527, 537, 542, 555, 560, 561, 562, 570, 571, 572, 574, 575, 576, 580, 585, 586, 587, 588, 590, 591, 592, 593, 594, 595, 596, 597, 600, 601, 605, 606, 607, 609, 611, 620, 622, 623, 624, 626, 654, 655, 656, 657, 658, 659, 660, 661, 662, 663, 664, 665, 666, 667, 668, 669, 670, 671, 672, 673, 674, 675, 676, 677, 678, 679, 680, 681, 682, 683, 684, 686, 687, 688, 690, 691, 692, 693, 694, 695, 697, 698, 699, 700, 701, 716, 717, 718, 720, 722, 723, 726, 728, 735, 736, 738, 741, 764, 773, 774, 775, 776, 787, 788, 789, 790, 791, 793, 794, 795, 797, 806, 810, 811, 832, 1037, 1237, 1331, 1351, 1357, 1360, 1398, 1438, 1471, 1477, 1478, 1479, 1494, 1532, 1533, 1536, 1546, 1563, 1570, 1571, 1574, 1582, 1594, 1598, 1599, 1600, 1601, 1602, 1605, 1607, 1611, 1617, 1620, 1621, 1670, 1759, 1816, 1901, 1906, 1979, 2093, 2118, 2119, 2123, 2262, 2300, 2345, 2353, 2371, 2404, 2430, B3734, C3867, C3882, C3912
Communications, 95, 114, 156, 605, 613, 630, 657, 658, 659, 661, 662, 663, 664, 665, 669, 670, 671, 681, 685, 689, 696, 697, 722, 729, 1613, 2118, 2282, 2430, C3938
Electronics, 95, 590, 605, 657, 658, 661, 662, 663, 664, 665, 666, 667, 669, 670, 671, 681, 682, 685, 722, 723, 791, 1611, 2093, 2118, 2119, 2430
Microelectronics, 697, B3734
Vacuum Science, 697

TECHNICAL ENGINEERING

General, 11, 95, 109, 131, 193, 239, 311, 312, 316, 318, 320, 323, 328, 333, 343, 344, 351, 358, 362, 366, 367, 368, 370, 371, 373, 374, 375, 376, 377, 378, 379, 381, 382, 384, 385, 386, 387, 388, 389, 390, 391, 392, 393, 394, 395, 397, 398, 399, 400, 401, 402, 403, 404, 405, 406, 407, 408, 409, 410, 414, 415, 417, 418, 419, 421, 422, 424, 425, 426, 428, 429, 431, 432, 433, 434, 435, 436, 437, 439, 463, 481, 482, 495, 496, 500, 505, 522, 523, 537, 542, 570, 571, 572, 574, 575, 576, 578, 580, 582, 583, 595, 596, 601, 605, 620, 622, 626, 628, 629, 676, 677, 680, 681, 682, 687, 691, 692, 695, 716, 717, 719, 720, 721, 722, 723, 724, 728, 735, 736, 740, 741, 746, 747, 749, 750, 754, 757, 763, 768, 787, 788, 790, 791, 793, 794, 795, 796, 797, 799, 800, 825, 873, 982, 1231, 1237, 1241, 1292, 1357, 1372, 1374, 1412, 1413, 1438, 1444, 1478, 1479, 1487, 1494, 1516, 1532, 1533, 1536, 1546, 1548, 1550, 1552, 1570, 1571, 1574, 1582, 1585, 1586, 1588, 1601, 1602, 1606, 1607, 1611, 1617, 1626, 1628, 1670, 1759, 1816, 1824, 1885, 1901, 1906, 1924, 1979, 2118, 2119, 2150, 2262, 2395, 2428, 2430, C3954
Arc Welding Technology, 715, 727, 733, 766, 2417, 2437, 2442, 2472, C3981
Audio Production, 165, 761, 945, 2068, 2193, 2468
Automotive Technology, 185, 382, 410, 425, 725, 737, 751, 752, 755, 756, 766, 772, 1432, 2435, 2452, 2472, 2475, B3638, C3843
Chemical Engineering, 42, 301, 315, 413, 420, 425, 443, 470, 471, 473, 512, 560, 561, 562, 586, 587, 588, 600, 654, 655, 656, 679, 699, 700, 701, 702, 703, 705, 706, 707, 708, 718, 738, 759, 773, 774, 775, 789, 810, 811, 832, 1037, 1331, 1345, 1396, 1419, 1471, 1522, 1563, 1564, 1568, 1594, 1605, 2300, 2345, C3857
Die Casting Technology, 745
Environmental Engineering, 42, 163, 301, 410, 473, 512, 554, 562, 584, 588, 652, 656, 701, 703, 714, 760, 765, 770, 771, 775, 808, 832, 1027, 1037, 1159, 1305, 1331, 1345, 1352, 1360, 1386, 1387, 1390, 1391, 1396, 1419, 1426, 1427, 1431, 1437, 1449, 1452, 1468, 1471, 1522, 1557, 1563, 1568, 1594, 2202, 2242, 2289, 2300, 2345, 2467, C3828, C3962, C3980
Heating; Refrgeratn & Air-Cond, 711, 712, 713, 739, 748, 766, 2472, C3906
Industrial Engineering, 42, 108, 114, 301, 383, 413, 425, 473, 512, 527, 562, 588, 609, 613, 656, 682, 686, 689, 701, 723, 726, 729, 730, 731, 732, 757, 775, 791, 832, 1037, 1331, 1471, 1563, 1594, 1611, 1613, 2119, 2123, 2300, 2345, 2353, C3938, C3962

Industrial Hygiene, 174, 461, 555, 585, 682, 698, 723, 743, 764, 791, 806, 1611, 1685, 1771, 1918, 2119, 2371, 2404

Lubrication/Tribology Eng, 763

Manufacturing Engineering, 143, 355, 372, 425, 682, 723, 725, 742, 753, 757, 766, 791, 1611, 2119, 2435, 2472

Nuclear Engineering, 42, 301, 473, 512, 562, 588, 656, 701, 709, 710, 734, 738, 775, 832, 1037, 1331, 1471, 1563, 1594, 2300, 2345

Optical Engineering, 470, 471, 560, 561, 586, 587, 654, 655, 699, 700, 762, 773, 774, 810, 811

Photographic/Imaging Science, 750

Plumbing, 739

Power Generation, 410

Pulp & Paper Technology, 744, 767, 769

Radar, 21, 758, 805, 1384, 2188, 2283, 2334

Remote Sensing, 21, 758, 805, 1384, 2188, 2283, 2334

Robotics, 362, 629, 749, 757, 800

Satellites, 21, 758, 805, 1384, 2188, 2283, 2334

MECHANICAL ENGINEERING

General, 11, 42, 109, 131, 193, 239, 301, 309, 311, 312, 315, 318, 333, 343, 344, 351, 362, 366, 367, 368, 370, 371, 372, 373, 374, 375, 376, 377, 378, 379, 380, 381, 382, 383, 384, 385, 386, 387, 388, 389, 390, 391, 392, 394, 395, 396, 397, 398, 399, 400, 401, 402, 403, 404, 405, 406, 407, 408, 409, 410, 413, 414, 415, 417, 418, 419, 421, 422, 424, 425, 426, 428, 429, 430, 431, 432, 433, 434, 435, 436, 437, 438, 439, 443, 473, 481, 482, 495, 496, 500, 512, 522, 523, 537, 542, 562, 570, 571, 572, 574, 575, 576, 578, 580, 583, 588, 595, 596, 600, 601, 620, 622, 626, 629, 656, 676, 677, 679, 680, 682, 687, 691, 692, 695, 701, 716, 717, 718, 720, 723, 728, 735, 736, 738, 740, 741, 747, 749, 775, 777, 778, 779, 780, 781, 782, 783, 784, 785, 787, 788, 789, 790, 791, 793, 794, 795, 796, 797, 799, 800, 802, 803, 825, 832, 1037, 1237, 1241, 1292, 1331, 1357, 1374, 1413, 1438, 1444, 1471, 1478, 1479, 1494, 1532, 1533, 1536, 1546, 1548, 1552, 1563, 1570, 1571, 1574, 1582, 1585, 1588, 1594, 1601, 1602, 1605, 1607, 1611, 1617, 1628, 1670, 1759, 1816, 1901, 1906, 1979, 2119, 2150, 2262, 2300, 2345, 2395, C3923

Mat'ls Science/Metallurgy, 174, 308, 406, 425, 461, 470, 471, 521, 555, 560, 561, 585, 586, 587, 591, 654, 655, 672, 698, 699, 700, 764, 771, 773, 774, 776, 786, 792, 806, 808, 810, 811, 1351, 1391, 1398, 2371, 2404, C3927

Mining Engineering, 406, 771, 798, 801, 804, 808, 809, 1391, C3901

Naval Science, 309, C3973, C3977

Naval/Marine Engineering, 309, 558, 807, 1448, C3901, C3933

Navigation, 21, 758, 805, 1384, 2188, 2283, 2334

Petroleum Engineering, 412, 420, 771, 808, 1391, C3901, C3945

SCHOOL OF HUMANITIES

General, 5, 78, 113, 129, 190, 217, 226, 237, 244, 257, 319, 322, 583, 602, 747, 799, 812, 813, 815, 816, 817, 818, 819, 820, 821, 822, 823, 824, 825, 826, 827, 828, 829, 836, 848, 916, 921, 933, 934, 935, 981, 988, 989, 997, 1020, 1021, 1022, 1047, 1137, 1205, 1208, 1212, 1214, 1218, 1219, 1220, 1235, 1240, 1241, 1283, 1290, 1292, 1374, 1413, 1444, 1461, 1462, 1463, 1481, 1483, 1486, 1495, 1537, 1547, 1552, 1588, 1608, 1628, 1658, 1743, 1990, 2074, 2077, 2080, 2081, 2084, 2086, 2087, 2088, 2125, 2126, 2179, 2180, 2181, 2227, 2235, 2236, 2237, 2247, 2254, 2256, 2263, 2265, 2302, 2314, 2316, 2331, 2332, 2333, 2346, 2354, 2355, 2365, 2366, 2367, 2374, 2386, 2395, 2399, 2400, 2401, 2423, 2451, 2779, B3681

AREA STUDIES

General, 42, 194, 251, 301, 473, 512, 562, 588, 656, 701, 775, 812, 818, 832, 833, 836, 848, 850, 988, 1037, 1208, 1228, 1250, 1331, 1332, 1394, 1433, 1456, 1471, 1520, 1563, 1594, 2074, 2080, 2125, 2225, 2247, 2263, 2300, 2302, 2314, 2319, 2345, 2346, 2354, 2374, 2386, 2562

Afro-American Studies, 75, 216, 463, 768, 840, 873, 889, 969, 1077, 1516, 2103

American Indian Studies, 842, 865, 866, 942, 1380, 1418, 1467, 1555, 2078, 2219, 2238, 2308, 2378

Asian-American Studies, 2095

Australian Studies, 964

British Studies, 841, 974, 2218, 2619

Byzantine Studies, 844

Chinese Studies, 859

Civil Rights, 864, 2278, 2329, 2359, 2396

Classical Studies, 287, 870, 1055

Demography, 67, 68, 313, 314, 598, 599, 838, 839, 966, 967, 1190, 1191, 1354, 1355, 1457, 1458, 1534, 1535, 1572, 1573, 1603, 1604, 1737, 1738, 2075, 2076, 2216, 2217, 2305, 2306, 2347, 2348, 2375, 2376

French Studies, 834, 847, 1039, 1043

German Studies, 1040

Human Rights, 864, 2278, 2329, 2359, 2396

International Studies, 855, 861, 864, 2278, 2322, 2329, 2359, 2396

Irish Studies, 849

Israel Studies, 869, 2301

Italian Studies, 835, 1041

Italian/American Studies, 134, 860, 862

Japanese Studies, 851, 1045, 2321

Jewish Studies, 253, 843, 846, 852, 853, 854, 857, 858, 869, 2122, 2391

Norwegian Studies, 863, 867

Polish Studies, 856

Scandinavian Studies, 867, 2561

Sikh Studies, 3355

Spanish Studies, 871, 1057

United States Studies, 865, 868, 872, 942, 1030, 1380, 1418, 1467, 1555, 2238, 2244, 2339

Welsh Studies, 3174, 3375

Women's Issues, 837

ART

General, 89, 165, 292, 329, 556, 761, 814, 821, 823, 827, 828, 829, 831, 865, 875, 876, 877, 881, 886, 892, 894, 895, 896, 899, 901, 902, 903, 906, 907, 908, 910, 914, 916, 918, 920, 921, 922, 932, 933, 934, 935, 942, 945, 947, 948, 949, 952, 954, 956, 958, 959, 963, 977, 978, 979, 987, 994, 997, 1000, 1019, 1020, 1021, 1022, 1029, 1031, 1047, 1058, 1061, 1062, 1071, 1087, 1091, 1097, 1101, 1106, 1114, 1118, 1126, 1137, 1139, 1152, 1173, 1176, 1179, 1186, 1212, 1218, 1219, 1220, 1380, 1418, 1461, 1462, 1463, 1467, 1473, 1488, 1512, 1555, 1640, 2068, 2086, 2087, 2088, 2090, 2179, 2180, 2181, 2193, 2227, 2235, 2236, 2237, 2238, 2331, 2332, 2333, 2365, 2366, 2367, 2399, 2400, 2401, 2443, 2468, 2470, 3114, B3624, B3768

Animation, 874, 887, 929, 931, B3622, C3834

Art Administration/Mngmnt, 75, 76, 149, 216, 268, 551, 552, 840, 889, 891, 913, 927, 940, 941, 944, 969, 970, 1004, 1077, 1079, 1143, 1466, 2103, 2106, 2166

Art Conservation, 888, 913, 944

Art History, 144, 197, 267, 517, 551, 552, 865, 878, 913, 926, 940, 941, 942, 944, 954, 1380, 1418, 1459, 1466, 1467, 1555, 2232, 2238, 3152

Cartooning, 165, 761, 887, 888, 945, 2068, 2153, 2193, 2468, B3814, C3855, C3856

Ceramic Arts, 893, 904, 917, 998, 1132, 2436, 2457

Commercial Art, 59, 89, 556, 879, 880, 894, 918, 952, 1179, B3768, C3905

Crafts, 865, 888, 899, 904, 915, 942, 954, 979, 1097, 1380, 1418, 1467, 1555, 2238, 2436, C3870

Design, 89, 144, 197, 267, 551, 886, 894, 899, 926, 940, 979, 1097, 1459, 1466, 2232

Drawing, 899, 909, 917, 954, 979, 998, 1097, 1132, 2457

Fashion Design, 59, 99, 149, 165, 268, 761, 879, 880, 888, 897, 898, 917, 919, 927, 945, 998, 1004, 1132, 1143, 2068, 2166, 2193, 2457, 2468, C3889

Film & Video, 59, 75, 76, 149, 165, 216, 268, 761, 840, 874, 879, 880, 888, 889, 891, 899, 915, 917, 918, 927, 930, 936, 945, 950, 951, 954, 969, 970, 979, 998, 1004, 1032, 1077, 1079, 1097, 1132, 1143, 1177, 2068, 2094, 2103, 2106, 2166, 2193, 2457, 2468, B3768, C3929

Fine Arts, 556, 557, 888, 912, 915, 918, 946, 947, 952, 954, 955, 1034, 1179, 1185, B3768

Graphic Arts, 144, 165, 197, 267, 552, 556, 761, 888, 899, 900, 904, 917, 918, 923, 926, 928, 931, 941, 943, 945, 952, 979, 998, 1097, 1132, 1179, 1459, 2068, 2170, 2185, 2193, 2232, 2436, 2457, 2466, 2468, B3670, B3768, C3904, C3905

Interior Design, 59, 165, 517, 549, 556, 761, 878, 879, 880, 882, 883, 884, 885, 888, 938, 945, 952, 1179, 2068, 2193, 2468

Multimedia, 165, 556, 761, 895, 931, 943, 945, 952, 977, 1087, 1179, 2068, 2185, 2193, 2466, 2468

Museum Education, 550, 551, 552, 913, 939, 940, 941, 1465, 1466

Numismatics, 888

Painting, 556, 557, 888, 899, 909, 915, 917, 918, 946, 952, 954, 955, 979, 998, 1034, 1097, 1132, 1179, 1185, 2457, B3768

Photography, 165, 556, 557, 761, 888, 899, 911, 912, 915, 917, 918, 936, 945, 952, 954, 955, 979, 998, 1034, 1097, 1132, 1179, 1185, 1445, 2068, 2160, 2170, 2193, 2457, 2468, B3768

Printing, 888, 900, 923, 928, B3670, C3905

Printmaking, 888, 900, 915, 917, 923, 936, 954, 998, 1132, 2457, B3670, C3905

Sculpture, 556, 557, 888, 899, 915, 917, 924, 925, 952, 954, 955, 979, 998, 1034, 1097, 1132, 1179, 1185, 2457

Textile Design, 99, 897, 904, 905, 917, 998, 1132, 2436, 2457

Visual Arts, 556, 888, 895, 899, 908, 910, 912, 914, 915, 917, 918, 952, 953, 977, 979, 994, 998, 1087, 1097, 1114, 1118, 1126, 1132, 1179, 2443, 2457, B3768

ENGLISH LANGUAGE/ LITERATURE

General, 113, 237, 244, 292, 817, 818, 819, 821, 827, 828, 829, 848, 877, 896, 899, 906, 916, 933, 934, 935, 948, 959, 978, 979, 981, 985, 987, 988, 989, 992, 993, 997, 1020, 1021, 1022, 1029, 1035, 1047, 1058, 1062, 1091, 1097, 1106, 1173, 1205, 1208, 1212, 1218, 1219, 1220, 1235, 1461, 1462, 1463, 1473, 1486, 1512, 1640, 2080, 2081, 2086, 2087, 2088, 2090, 2125, 2126, 2179, 2180, 2181, 2213, 2226, 2227, 2235, 2236, 2237, 2263, 2265, 2272, 2314, 2316, 2323, 2331, 2332, 2333, 2354, 2365, 2366, 2367, 2386, 2399, 2400, 2401, 2470, 2562

British Literature, 841, 974, 2218, 2619

Classics, 999

Creative Writing, 328, 557, 724, 872, 876, 881, 895, 917, 922, 955, 958, 960, 961, 963, 964, 976, 977, 982, 983, 990, 995, 998, 1000, 1007, 1018, 1030, 1034, 1035, 1066, 1071, 1087, 1132, 1139, 1185, 1487, 2116, 2168, 2213, 2244, 2339, 2413, 2457, B3768, C3871

Debate-Forensics, 932, 991, 1019, 1152

Folklore, 75, 216, 840, 889, 969, 1077, 2103

Library Science-Law, C3916

Library Science, 163, 270, 271, 554, 584, 760, 965, 971, 972, 973, 986, 1005, 1006, 1025, 1027, 1033, 1159, 1305, 1386, 1426, 1449, 1468, 1470, 1557, 1773, 1774, 1921, 1922, 2242, 2245, 2467, B3687

Linguistics, 67, 68, 313, 314, 598, 599, 838, 839, 966, 967, 1190, 1191, 1354, 1355, 1457, 1458, 1534, 1535, 1572, 1573, 1603, 1604, 1737, 1738, 2075, 2076, 2216, 2217, 2305, 2306, 2347, 2348, 2375, 2376

Literature, 557, 899, 914, 955, 960, 961, 979, 994, 995, 1023, 1024, 1034, 1066, 1097, 1126, 1185, 2413

Oratory, 899, 962, 979, 991, 1001, 1002, 1097, 2206

Playwriting, 899, 950, 964, 968, 979, 980, 1008, 1009, 1010, 1011, 1012, 1017, 1026, 1028, 1032, 1035, 1097, 1168, 1177, 2213, B3751, B3768

Poetry, 557, 899, 917, 949, 955, 979, 983, 996, 998, 1013, 1014, 1015, 1016, 1031, 1034, 1035, 1097, 1132, 1176, 1185, 2213, 2457, B3768

Reading/Literacy Research-G, 246, 247, 248, 249, 250

Screenwriting, 76, 149, 268, 891, 899, 917, 927, 950, 957, 970, 979, 998, 1004, 1032, 1035, 1079, 1097, 1132, 1143, 1177, 2106, 2166, 2213, 2457, B3751, B3768

FOREIGN LANGUAGE

General, 42, 208, 292, 301, 473, 512, 562, 588, 656, 701, 775, 821, 832, 916, 948, 997, 1029, 1037, 1038, 1044, 1047, 1058, 1059, 1173, 1212, 1331, 1471, 1512, 1563, 1594, 1640, 2090, 2227, 2300, 2345, 2470, 2562

Arabic, 1054

Esperanto, 1050

French, 834, 847, 1039, 1043, 1051

German, 1040, 1052

Greek-G, 287, 870, 1055

Italian, 835, 1041, 1048, 1049

Japanese, 851, 1045, 2321

Latin, 287, 870, 1036, 1055, 1056

Portuguese, 1046

Spanish, 871, 1042, 1053, 1057, B3777

PERFORMING ARTS

General, 75, 216, 292, 329, 823, 840, 875, 877, 889, 896, 899, 903, 906, 921, 948, 956, 959, 969, 978, 979, 987, 1029, 1058, 1061, 1062, 1074, 1077, 1091, 1097, 1099, 1101, 1106, 1109, 1113, 1127, 1137, 1173, 1186, 1473, 1488, 1512, 1640, 2090, 2103, 2470, 3114, B3679, B3751, B3768, B3788

Accordion, 1063

Choral Conducting, 830, 1108

Choreography, 556, 814, 899, 952, 979, 1097, 1179

Conducting, 830

Dance, 47, 201, 556, 557, 814, 895, 899, 910, 914, 917, 952, 955, 977, 979, 994, 998, 1034, 1064, 1087, 1097, 1103, 1105, 1112, 1118, 1126, 1132, 1150, 1163, 1164, 1165, 1179, 1185, 1841, 2457, B3768

Drama, 76, 149, 163, 268, 554, 556, 557, 584, 760, 814, 891, 895, 899, 908, 910, 914, 917, 927, 932, 950, 952, 955, 970, 977, 979, 994, 998, 1004, 1019, 1027, 1028, 1032, 1034, 1079, 1087, 1097, 1103, 1105, 1114, 1118, 1126, 1132, 1138, 1143, 1151, 1152, 1159, 1163, 1164, 1165, 1166, 1168, 1177, 1178, 1179, 1185, 1305, 1386, 1426, 1449, 1468, 1557, 2106, 2166, 2242, 2443, 2457, 2467, B3751, B3768, C3880

Instrumental, 275, 895, 917, 977, 998, 1074, 1080, 1087, 1088, 1092, 1093, 1099, 1102, 1104, 1107, 1108, 1124, 1132, 1148, 1153, 1154, 1156, 1157, 1160, 1163, 1164, 1165, 1170, 1171, 1180, 1182, 1187, 1215, 2171, 2397, 2457, B3768

Jazz, 917, 998, 1132, 1174, 1175, 2457

Music Composition, 227, 814, 914, 917, 922, 932, 949, 994, 998, 1000, 1019, 1026, 1031, 1063, 1070, 1078, 1084, 1085, 1086, 1088, 1089, 1090, 1096, 1108, 1110, 1124, 1126, 1131, 1132, 1133, 1135, 1139, 1144, 1149, 1152, 1154, 1155, 1156, 1158, 1161, 1162, 1167, 1169, 1172, 1175, 1176, 1181, 1183, 1201, 1358, 1439, 1484, 1886, 2457, B3614, B3679, B3742, B3768

Music Performance, 75, 216, 227, 275, 814, 840, 889, 908, 910, 914, 917, 932, 949, 961, 969, 994, 998, 1019, 1031, 1065, 1066, 1070, 1074, 1077, 1078, 1080, 1085, 1088, 1092, 1096, 1099, 1102, 1104, 1108, 1114, 1118, 1124, 1126, 1128, 1131, 1132, 1134, 1135, 1146, 1148, 1152, 1154, 1155, 1156, 1158, 1162, 1167, 1169, 1171, 1176, 1180, 1181, 1182, 1183, 1187, 1201, 1215, 1358, 1439, 1484, 1679, 1766, 1886, 1911, 1993, 2103, 2171, 2397, 2413, 2443, 2453, 2457, B3614, B3679, B3742, B3768

Opera & Music Management, 151, 1060, 1075, 1088, 1099, 1120, 1125, 1145, 1167, B3614, B3679, B3742

Orchestra, 1073, 1078, 1080, 1094, 1098, 1099, 1121, 1140, 1167, 1184, B3614, B3679, B3742

Organ, 1067, 1068, 1069, 1147

Piano, 1078, 1082, 1089, 1094, 1098, 1099, 1116, 1123, 1135, 1153, 1167, 1169, 1184, B3614, B3679, B3742, B3768

Religious Music, 275, 1065, 1129, 1148, 1215, 2171, 2397

Singing, 275, 814, 881, 917, 963, 998, 1060, 1071, 1074, 1075, 1076, 1078, 1081, 1088, 1093, 1095, 1100, 1102, 1104, 1105, 1107, 1108, 1117, 1119, 1120, 1123, 1125, 1130, 1131, 1132, 1134, 1136, 1141, 1142, 1148, 1153, 1157, 1158, 1163, 1164, 1165, 1167, 1169, 1171, 1172, 1180, 1181, 1182, 1187, 1215, 2171, 2397, 2457, B3614, B3636, B3679, B3742, B3753, B3754, B3768

String Instruments, 1072, 1078, 1080, 1083, 1099, 1115, 1121, 1123, 1167, 1169, B3614, B3679, B3742

Trumpet, 1111, 1174

PHILOSOPHY

General, 67, 68, 237, 313, 314, 598, 599, 817, 818, 821, 826, 827, 828, 829, 838, 839, 848, 916, 933, 934, 935, 966, 967, 981, 988, 997, 1020, 1021, 1022, 1047, 1190, 1191, 1205, 1208, 1212, 1214, 1218, 1219, 1220, 1235, 1354, 1355, 1457, 1458, 1461, 1462, 1463, 1486, 1534, 1535, 1572, 1573, 1603, 1604, 1737, 1738, 2075, 2076, 2080, 2084,

2086, 2087, 2088, 2125, 2179, 2180, 2181, 2216, 2217, 2227, 2235, 2236, 2237, 2263, 2305, 2306, 2314, 2331, 2332, 2333, 2347, 2348, 2354, 2365, 2366, 2367, 2375, 2376, 2386, 2399, 2400, 2401

Theology, 215, 236, 275, 361, 547, 821, 916, 997, 1047, 1096, 1148, 1188, 1189, 1192, 1196, 1197, 1198, 1200, 1201, 1203, 1204, 1209, 1210, 1212, 1213, 1215, 1216, 1217, 1221, 1222, 1225, 1590, 1659, 1672, 1695, 1780, 1887, 1903, 1966, 1983, 2171, 2227, 2381, 2397, 2403, B3709

SCHOOL OF NATURAL RESOURCES

General, 6, 11, 80, 109, 177, 193, 225, 237, 239, 303, 305, 316, 321, 324, 330, 333, 336, 342, 363, 442, 469, 506, 574, 583, 589, 603, 608, 687, 719, 728, 747, 793, 799, 817, 822, 825, 833, 981, 1205, 1228, 1229, 1230, 1231, 1232, 1233, 1234, 1235, 1236, 1237, 1238, 1239, 1240, 1241, 1242, 1243, 1244, 1245, 1246, 1247, 1248, 1250, 1292, 1293, 1297, 1324, 1332, 1342, 1344, 1374, 1375, 1378, 1379, 1389, 1393, 1394, 1395, 1408, 1413, 1414, 1416, 1417, 1429, 1433, 1434, 1436, 1444, 1446, 1447, 1451, 1455, 1456, 1460, 1464, 1469, 1474, 1475, 1482, 1485, 1486, 1489, 1490, 1493, 1495, 1503, 1504, 1507, 1510, 1519, 1520, 1521, 1552, 1553, 1554, 1560, 1565, 1588, 1589, 1591, 1606, 1610, 1612, 1615, 1628, 1629, 1630, 1633, 1638, 1647, 1649, 1651, 1670, 1675, 1689, 1719, 1722, 1759, 1777, 1788, 1797, 1798, 1816, 1826, 1858, 1862, 1901, 1925, 1946, 1947, 1957, 1979, 2010, 2066, 2072, 2085, 2262, 2395, 2412, B3722, C3840, C3964

AGRICULTURE

General, 24, 25, 26, 27, 28, 29, 30, 31, 32, 33, 34, 35, 36, 37, 40, 163, 177, 360, 363, 445, 446, 447, 448, 449, 450, 451, 452, 453, 454, 455, 456, 457, 458, 506, 524, 525, 554, 583, 584, 637, 638, 639, 640, 641, 642, 643, 644, 645, 646, 647, 648, 649, 650, 747, 760, 799, 824, 825, 833, 1027, 1159, 1228, 1234, 1241, 1242, 1244, 1247, 1249, 1250, 1251, 1266, 1267, 1268, 1269, 1270, 1271, 1272, 1277, 1278, 1279, 1280, 1284, 1285, 1289, 1290, 1292, 1293, 1295, 1296, 1297, 1299, 1302, 1304, 1305, 1306, 1307, 1308, 1309, 1310, 1311, 1312, 1313, 1314, 1315, 1316, 1317, 1318, 1319, 1320, 1321, 1322, 1323, 1324,

1325, 1326, 1327, 1328, 1332, 1362, 1363, 1374, 1375, 1377, 1379, 1385, 1386, 1389, 1394, 1402, 1403, 1406, 1413, 1414, 1417, 1422, 1426, 1429, 1433, 1440, 1441, 1444, 1446, 1447, 1449, 1451, 1456, 1460, 1464, 1468, 1503, 1504, 1520, 1540, 1541, 1543, 1552, 1553, 1554, 1557, 1558, 1560, 1588, 1589, 1591, 1628, 1629, 1630, 1689, 1694, 1698, 1712, 1777, 1779, 1784, 1788, 1826, 1832, 1925, 1935, 2010, 2013, 2014, 2015, 2016, 2017, 2018, 2019, 2020, 2021, 2022, 2023, 2024, 2025, 2026, 2027, 2039, 2066, 2072, 2073, 2132, 2242, 2280, 2395, 2467, B3640, C3826, C3827

Agribusiness, 177, 1247, 1261, 1276, 1282, 1285, 1307, 1323, 1324, 1389, 1429, 1451, 1558, 1560, 1698, 1784, 1788, 1832, 1935, 2013, 2072

Agricultural Economics, 177, 1247, 1324, 1389, 1429, 1451, 1560, 1788, 2072

Agricultural Engineering/Mech, 177, 410, 1247, 1324, 1389, 1429, 1451, 1560, 1788, 2072

Agricultural Marketing, 1261, 1276, 1282

Agricultural Production/Tech, 177, 1247, 1324, 1389, 1429, 1451, 1560, 1788, 2072

Agronomy/Crop Sciences, 177, 1247, 1273, 1275, 1324, 1330, 1389, 1429, 1451, 1560, 1788, 2072, C3828

Animal Science, 177, 1247, 1298, 1324, 1389, 1429, 1451, 1560, 1788, 2072, C3833

Dairy Science, 1287

Equine Studies, 129, 257, 820, 1283, 1547, 1990, 2355, 2451

Farm Management, 177, 1247, 1276, 1306, 1324, 1389, 1429, 1451, 1560, 1788, 2072

Floriculture, 524, 525, 538, 1254, 1258, 1260, 1261, 1265, 1269, 1270, 1275, 1286, 1307, 1362, 1363, 1402, 1403, 1440, 1441, 1540, 1541, 1558, 1698, 1784, 1832, 1935, 2013, C3892

Golf Grounds Mngmnt, 1273, 1274, 1275

Green Industry, 1275

Herb Studies, 1275

Horticulture, 3, 4, 72, 73, 74, 177, 524, 525, 532, 538, 1247, 1252, 1253, 1255, 1256, 1257, 1258, 1259, 1260, 1262, 1263, 1264, 1265, 1269, 1270, 1272, 1275, 1276, 1281, 1286, 1291, 1307, 1324, 1329, 1362, 1363, 1389, 1402, 1403, 1429, 1440, 1441, 1451, 1540, 1541, 1549, 1558, 1560, 1698, 1784, 1788, 1832, 1935, 2013, 2072, C3892, C3909

Pomology, 1252, 1275

Poultry Science, 1277, 1406, 1543

Soil Science, 158, 163, 177, 553, 554, 584, 760, 1027, 1159, 1247, 1275, 1276, 1301,

1303, 1305, 1324, 1386, 1389, 1421,
1423, 1426, 1429, 1449, 1451, 1468,
1557, 1560, 1788, 2072, 2189, 2242,
2335, 2467, C3828, C3901, C3968

Turf/Grounds/Range Management, 158,
163, 177, 538, 553, 554, 584, 760, 1027,
1159, 1247, 1275, 1286, 1294, 1300,
1301, 1303, 1305, 1324, 1382, 1386,
1389, 1420, 1421, 1423, 1426, 1429,
1449, 1451, 1468, 1557, 1560, 1788,
2072, 2189, 2242, 2335, 2467, C3959

Turfgrass Science, 1273, 1275

EARTH SCIENCE

General, 67, 68, 115, 227, 303, 305, 310,
313, 314, 318, 335, 349, 358, 359, 363,
468, 469, 505, 506, 507, 540, 572, 582,
583, 589, 598, 599, 601, 614, 628, 680,
720, 746, 747, 771, 790, 799, 808, 825,
833, 838, 839, 865, 942, 966, 967, 1085,
1190, 1191, 1228, 1229, 1230, 1234,
1241, 1242, 1244, 1248, 1250, 1292,
1293, 1297, 1332, 1342, 1343, 1344,
1353, 1354, 1355, 1357, 1358, 1361,
1364, 1365, 1371, 1372, 1373, 1374,
1375, 1376, 1379, 1380, 1381, 1388,
1391, 1392, 1393, 1394, 1395, 1400,
1407, 1412, 1413, 1414, 1415, 1417,
1418, 1428, 1433, 1434, 1435, 1436,
1438, 1439, 1443, 1444, 1446, 1447,
1450, 1455, 1456, 1457, 1458, 1460,
1464, 1467, 1474, 1475, 1484, 1501,
1503, 1504, 1515, 1518, 1519, 1520,
1521, 1531, 1534, 1535, 1536, 1550,
1552, 1553, 1554, 1555, 1559, 1565,
1566, 1569, 1572, 1573, 1574, 1586,
1588, 1589, 1591, 1592, 1593, 1603,
1604, 1607, 1614, 1626, 1628, 1629,
1630, 1634, 1644, 1646, 1647, 1649,
1651, 1653, 1681, 1689, 1719, 1722,
1735, 1737, 1738, 1769, 1777, 1797,
1798, 1823, 1824, 1826, 1858, 1862,
1886, 1924, 1925, 1946, 1947, 1996,
2010, 2066, 2075, 2076, 2216, 2217,
2224, 2238, 2239, 2275, 2305, 2306,
2317, 2347, 2348, 2375, 2376, 2395,
2412, 2779, C3964

Astronomy, 67, 68, 313, 314, 598, 599, 833,
838, 839, 865, 942, 966, 967, 1190, 1191,
1228, 1250, 1332, 1343, 1348, 1349,
1354, 1355, 1380, 1394, 1418, 1433,
1435, 1456, 1457, 1458, 1467, 1520,
1534, 1535, 1555, 1566, 1572, 1573,
1603, 1604, 1737, 1738, 2075, 2076,
2216, 2217, 2238, 2305, 2306, 2347,
2348, 2375, 2376, C3840, C3841, C3901

Astrophysics, C3840, C3903

Cartography/Geodetic Surveying, 163,
554, 584, 760, 1027, 1159, 1305, 1333,
1334, 1336, 1337, 1338, 1339, 1340,
1341, 1343, 1386, 1426, 1435, 1449,
1468, 1557, 1566, 2242, 2467, C3901

Cave Research, 163, 554, 584, 760, 1027,
1159, 1305, 1386, 1426, 1449, 1468,
1557, 2242, 2467, C3901

Energy, 21, 410, 758, 805, 1243, 1360,
1376, 1378, 1384, 1415, 1416, 2085,
2188, 2283, 2334

Environmental Education, 163, 554, 584,
652, 760, 765, 770, 1027, 1159, 1305,
1386, 1387, 1390, 1426, 1427, 1431,
1449, 1452, 1468, 1557, 2202, 2242,
2289, 2467, C3980

Fish/Game/Wildlife Management, 177,
1247, 1324, 1389, 1429, 1451, 1560,
1788, 2072

Forestry/Forest Science, 163, 177, 524,
525, 554, 584, 760, 1027, 1159, 1247,
1269, 1270, 1275, 1295, 1300, 1302,
1305, 1324, 1356, 1362, 1363, 1366,
1377, 1382, 1385, 1386, 1389, 1402,
1403, 1409, 1420, 1422, 1426, 1429,
1440, 1441, 1442, 1449, 1451, 1468,
1540, 1541, 1545, 1557, 1560, 1788,
2072, 2242, 2467, B3722, C3896, C3897,
C3959

Geography, 42, 67, 68, 301, 313, 314, 473,
512, 562, 588, 598, 599, 656, 701, 775,
832, 838, 839, 966, 967, 1037, 1190,
1191, 1331, 1354, 1355, 1364, 1367,
1370, 1376, 1415, 1457, 1458, 1471,
1534, 1535, 1563, 1572, 1573, 1594,
1603, 1604, 1737, 1738, 1833, 2075,
2076, 2082, 2216, 2217, 2300, 2305,
2306, 2345, 2347, 2348, 2375, 2376,
C3900, C3901

Geology, 163, 554, 584, 760, 771, 808,
1027, 1159, 1305, 1343, 1368, 1369,
1383, 1386, 1391, 1426, 1435, 1449,
1454, 1468, 1557, 1566, 1833, 2242,
2467, C3901, C3902, C3903

Geophysics, 308, 521, 591, 672, 776, 1343,
1351, 1383, 1398, 1435, 1454, 1566,
1833, C3901, C3903

Geoscience, 67, 68, 308, 313, 314, 521, 591,
598, 599, 672, 776, 838, 839, 966, 967,
1190, 1191, 1351, 1354, 1355, 1368,
1369, 1376, 1398, 1415, 1457, 1458,
1534, 1535, 1572, 1573, 1603, 1604,
1737, 1738, 2075, 2076, 2216, 2217,
2305, 2306, 2347, 2348, 2375, 2376,
C3901

Hydrology, 163, 554, 584, 703, 714, 760,
770, 1027, 1159, 1302, 1305, 1343, 1345,
1346, 1347, 1348, 1349, 1352, 1385,
1386, 1390, 1396, 1422, 1426, 1431,
1435, 1437, 1449, 1452, 1468, 1522,
1557, 1566, 1568, 2242, 2467, C3901,
C3903, C3980

Limnology, 714, 770, 1352, 1390, 1431,
1437, 1452, C3980

Materials Sci & Engineering, 406, 1376,
1415, C3901

Meteorology, 21, 42, 301, 473, 512, 562,
588, 656, 701, 758, 775, 805, 832, 1037,

1331, 1343, 1346, 1347, 1348, 1349,
1350, 1376, 1384, 1415, 1435, 1454,
1471, 1563, 1566, 1594, 2188, 2283,
2300, 2334, 2345, C3901

Mineral Economics, 1376, 1415

Mineral Engineering, 1368, 1369, 1376,
1415, C3901

Riparian Area Management, 163, 554,
584, 714, 760, 770, 1027, 1159, 1305,
1352, 1386, 1390, 1426, 1431, 1437,
1449, 1452, 1468, 1557, 2242, 2467,
C3980

Surveying Technology, 163, 325, 326, 554,
584, 760, 1027, 1159, 1305, 1335, 1359,
1386, 1426, 1449, 1468, 1557, 2242,
2467, C3901

Trail Maintenance/Construction, 163, 554,
584, 760, 1027, 1159, 1305, 1386, 1426,
1449, 1468, 1557, 2242, 2467

Water Resources Policies, 163, 554, 584,
714, 760, 770, 1027, 1159, 1305, 1352,
1386, 1390, 1426, 1431, 1437, 1449,
1452, 1468, 1557, 2242, 2467, C3901,
C3980

ENVIRONMENTAL STUDIES

General, 22, 61, 115, 158, 161, 163, 281,
305, 335, 346, 358, 363, 440, 505, 506,
520, 524, 525, 553, 554, 582, 583, 584,
614, 628, 652, 703, 746, 747, 760, 765,
770, 799, 825, 833, 1027, 1159, 1228,
1230, 1234, 1241, 1242, 1243, 1244,
1250, 1269, 1270, 1277, 1292, 1293,
1297, 1301, 1302, 1303, 1305, 1332,
1344, 1345, 1360, 1361, 1362, 1363,
1365, 1372, 1374, 1375, 1378, 1379,
1385, 1386, 1387, 1388, 1390, 1394,
1395, 1396, 1397, 1400, 1401, 1402,
1403, 1404, 1406, 1407, 1408, 1410,
1412, 1413, 1414, 1416, 1417, 1419,
1421, 1422, 1423, 1424, 1425, 1426,
1427, 1428, 1430, 1431, 1433, 1436,
1440, 1441, 1444, 1446, 1447, 1449,
1450, 1452, 1456, 1460, 1464, 1468,
1475, 1503, 1504, 1515, 1520, 1522,
1540, 1541, 1543, 1550, 1552, 1553,
1554, 1557, 1559, 1568, 1584, 1586,
1588, 1589, 1591, 1593, 1614, 1623,
1626, 1628, 1629, 1630, 1644, 1651,
1666, 1689, 1697, 1722, 1751, 1777,
1781, 1798, 1813, 1824, 1826, 1830,
1862, 1894, 1924, 1925, 1929, 1947,
1973, 2010, 2011, 2066, 2085, 2189,
2202, 2224, 2242, 2255, 2289, 2317,
2335, 2384, 2395, 2467, 2629, 2779,
C3828, C3886, C3968, C3980

Conservation, 158, 163, 177, 524, 525, 553,
554, 584, 760, 1027, 1159, 1247, 1269,
1270, 1301, 1303, 1305, 1324, 1362,
1363, 1386, 1389, 1399, 1402, 1403,
1404, 1408, 1421, 1423, 1426, 1429,
1440, 1441, 1449, 1451, 1468, 1540,

1541, 1557, 1560, 1788, 2072, 2189, 2242, 2335, 2467

Ecology, 158, 163, 524, 525, 553, 554, 584, 760, 865, 942, 1027, 1159, 1269, 1270, 1275, 1301, 1303, 1305, 1362, 1363, 1380, 1386, 1399, 1402, 1403, 1404, 1408, 1418, 1421, 1423, 1426, 1440, 1441, 1449, 1467, 1468, 1540, 1541, 1555, 1557, 2189, 2238, 2242, 2335, 2467

Environmental Economics, 158, 553, 652, 703, 765, 1303, 1345, 1376, 1387, 1396, 1415, 1423, 1427, 1522, 1568, 2189, 2202, 2289, 2335

Environmental Health, 158, 163, 524, 525, 553, 554, 584, 760, 770, 1027, 1159, 1269, 1270, 1303, 1305, 1362, 1363, 1386, 1390, 1399, 1402, 1403, 1404, 1408, 1411, 1423, 1426, 1430, 1431, 1440, 1441, 1449, 1452, 1468, 1540, 1541, 1557, 1768, 2189, 2242, 2335, 2467

Environmental Science, 158, 163, 185, 308, 521, 524, 525, 553, 554, 584, 591, 652, 672, 703, 760, 765, 770, 772, 776, 865, 942, 1027, 1159, 1269, 1270, 1303, 1305, 1345, 1351, 1361, 1362, 1363, 1380, 1386, 1387, 1390, 1396, 1398, 1400, 1402, 1403, 1411, 1418, 1423, 1426, 1427, 1431, 1432, 1440, 1441, 1449, 1452, 1467, 1468, 1522, 1540, 1541, 1555, 1557, 1568, 1768, 2189, 2202, 2238, 2242, 2289, 2335, 2467, 2475

Pollution, 770, 1390, 1399, 1404, 1431, 1452, C3901, C3980

Range Management, 177, 524, 525, 1247, 1269, 1270, 1300, 1324, 1362, 1363, 1382, 1389, 1402, 1403, 1420, 1429, 1440, 1441, 1451, 1540, 1541, 1560, 1788, 2072, C3959

Wildlife Studies, 163, 177, 554, 584, 760, 865, 942, 1027, 1159, 1247, 1305, 1324, 1366, 1380, 1386, 1389, 1399, 1405, 1409, 1418, 1426, 1429, 1442, 1449, 1451, 1467, 1468, 1545, 1555, 1557, 1560, 1788, 2072, 2238, 2242, 2467

MARINE SCIENCE

General, 227, 303, 305, 318, 359, 363, 469, 506, 524, 525, 572, 583, 589, 601, 680, 714, 720, 747, 770, 790, 799, 825, 833, 1085, 1228, 1229, 1230, 1234, 1241, 1242, 1244, 1248, 1250, 1269, 1270, 1292, 1293, 1297, 1332, 1342, 1344, 1352, 1357, 1358, 1362, 1363, 1366, 1373, 1374, 1375, 1379, 1388, 1390, 1393, 1394, 1395, 1402, 1403, 1409, 1413, 1414, 1417, 1419, 1428, 1431, 1433, 1434, 1436, 1437, 1438, 1439, 1440, 1441, 1442, 1443, 1444, 1445, 1446, 1447, 1448, 1450, 1452, 1453, 1454, 1455, 1456, 1460, 1464, 1474,

1475, 1484, 1501, 1503, 1504, 1515, 1519, 1520, 1521, 1536, 1540, 1541, 1545, 1552, 1553, 1554, 1556, 1559, 1565, 1574, 1588, 1589, 1591, 1593, 1607, 1628, 1629, 1630, 1644, 1647, 1649, 1651, 1689, 1719, 1722, 1777, 1797, 1798, 1826, 1858, 1862, 1886, 1925, 1946, 1947, 2010, 2066, 2395, 2412, 2779, 3193, C3980

Fisheries, 163, 177, 554, 584, 760, 1027, 1159, 1247, 1305, 1324, 1386, 1389, 1426, 1429, 1445, 1448, 1449, 1451, 1468, 1557, 1560, 1788, 2072, 2242, 2467, B3674, C3891

Marine Biology-G, 524, 525, 1269, 1270, 1362, 1363, 1402, 1403, 1440, 1441, 1448, 1540, 1541, B3674

Marine Technology, 469, 1248, 1393, 1445, 1448, 1454, 1455, 1519, 1647, B3674, C3937

Oceanography, 469, 1248, 1343, 1346, 1347, 1348, 1349, 1393, 1435, 1445, 1448, 1454, 1455, 1519, 1566, 1647, B3674, C3901, C3937

Rivers/Lakes, 163, 554, 584, 760, 1027, 1159, 1305, 1386, 1426, 1449, 1468, 1557, 2242, 2467

NATURAL HISTORY

General, 363, 442, 506, 827, 828, 829, 933, 934, 935, 1020, 1021, 1022, 1218, 1219, 1220, 1234, 1242, 1244, 1246, 1293, 1297, 1375, 1379, 1414, 1417, 1446, 1447, 1460, 1461, 1462, 1463, 1464, 1469, 1503, 1504, 1510, 1553, 1554, 1589, 1591, 1629, 1630, 1638, 1689, 1777, 1826, 1925, 2010, 2066, 2086, 2087, 2088, 2179, 2180, 2181, 2235, 2236, 2237, 2331, 2332, 2333, 2365, 2366, 2367, 2399, 2400, 2401

Anthropology, 67, 68, 163, 313, 314, 554, 584, 598, 599, 760, 833, 838, 839, 865, 942, 966, 967, 1027, 1159, 1190, 1191, 1228, 1250, 1305, 1332, 1354, 1355, 1380, 1386, 1394, 1418, 1426, 1433, 1449, 1456, 1457, 1458, 1467, 1468, 1520, 1523, 1534, 1535, 1555, 1557, 1572, 1573, 1603, 1604, 1737, 1738, 2075, 2076, 2216, 2217, 2238, 2242, 2305, 2306, 2347, 2348, 2375, 2376, 2467, C3835

Archaeology, 67, 68, 163, 313, 314, 554, 584, 598, 599, 760, 838, 839, 865, 942, 966, 967, 1027, 1159, 1190, 1191, 1305, 1354, 1355, 1380, 1386, 1418, 1426, 1449, 1457, 1458, 1467, 1468, 1534, 1535, 1555, 1557, 1572, 1573, 1603, 1604, 1737, 1738, 2075, 2076, 2216, 2217, 2238, 2242, 2305, 2306, 2347, 2348, 2375, 2376, 2467, C3838, C3901

Backcountry, 163, 554, 584, 760, 1027, 1159, 1305, 1386, 1426, 1449, 1468, 1557, 2242, 2467

Museum Studies, 144, 163, 197, 267, 550, 551, 554, 584, 760, 865, 926, 939, 940, 942, 944, 1027, 1033, 1159, 1305, 1380, 1386, 1418, 1426, 1449, 1459, 1465, 1466, 1467, 1468, 1470, 1555, 1557, 2232, 2238, 2242, 2245, 2467

Paleontology, 163, 554, 584, 760, 865, 942, 1027, 1159, 1305, 1380, 1386, 1418, 1426, 1449, 1467, 1468, 1555, 1557, 2238, 2242, 2467, C3901, C3942

SCHOOL OF SCIENCE

General, 2, 5, 6, 20, 42, 78, 80, 160, 189, 190, 196, 204, 208, 217, 225, 226, 227, 237, 266, 284, 292, 301, 303, 305, 306, 307, 311, 312, 319, 321, 322, 324, 328, 329, 330, 336, 341, 342, 344, 352, 353, 354, 356, 359, 363, 364, 365, 411, 442, 459, 460, 463, 468, 469, 473, 481, 482, 496, 501, 502, 506, 512, 522, 523, 562, 570, 571, 576, 588, 589, 595, 596, 602, 603, 608, 622, 627, 635, 656, 668, 676, 677, 692, 701, 716, 717, 724, 736, 768, 775, 787, 788, 795, 813, 815, 817, 822, 832, 873, 877, 903, 948, 959, 981, 982, 1029, 1037, 1058, 1062, 1085, 1101, 1173, 1205, 1229, 1230, 1232, 1233, 1235, 1236, 1238, 1239, 1240, 1242, 1244, 1245, 1246, 1248, 1293, 1297, 1331, 1342, 1344, 1358, 1373, 1375, 1379, 1388, 1392, 1393, 1395, 1414, 1417, 1428, 1434, 1436, 1439, 1443, 1446, 1447, 1450, 1454, 1455, 1460, 1464, 1469, 1471, 1472, 1473, 1474, 1475, 1476, 1477, 1478, 1479, 1480, 1481, 1482, 1483, 1484, 1485, 1486, 1487, 1488, 1489, 1490, 1491, 1492, 1493, 1494, 1495, 1496, 1497, 1498, 1499, 1500, 1501, 1502, 1503, 1504, 1505, 1506, 1507, 1508, 1509, 1510, 1511, 1512, 1513, 1514, 1515, 1516, 1518, 1519, 1521, 1532, 1533, 1537, 1546, 1551, 1553, 1554, 1559, 1563, 1565, 1570, 1571, 1582, 1587, 1589, 1591, 1593, 1594, 1595, 1601, 1602, 1608, 1610, 1612, 1615, 1624, 1625, 1627, 1629, 1630, 1631, 1632, 1633, 1636, 1638, 1639, 1640, 1641, 1642, 1644, 1646, 1647, 1649, 1651, 1658, 1674, 1675, 1687, 1689, 1719, 1722, 1723, 1743, 1763, 1776, 1777, 1797, 1798, 1819, 1825, 1826, 1858, 1862, 1886, 1905, 1906, 1925, 1946, 1947, 1957, 1985, 2010, 2066, 2077, 2090, 2191, 2231, 2254, 2300, 2336, 2345, 2412, 2423, 2459, 2470, 2779, C3840, C3964

BIOLOGY

General, 5, 67, 68, 78, 129, 131, 177, 190, 217, 252, 257, 303, 310, 311, 312, 313, 314, 318, 319, 344, 358, 363, 481, 482, 496, 505, 506, 522, 523, 570, 571, 572, 576, 578, 582, 583, 589, 595, 596, 598, 599, 601, 602, 622, 628, 676, 677, 680, 692, 703, 716, 717, 720, 736, 740, 746, 747, 787, 788, 790, 795, 796, 799, 813, 820, 825, 833, 838, 839, 865, 942, 966, 967, 1190, 1191, 1228, 1229, 1241, 1242, 1244, 1247, 1250, 1277, 1283, 1292, 1293, 1297, 1307, 1324, 1332, 1342, 1345, 1353, 1354, 1355, 1357, 1372, 1374, 1375, 1379, 1380, 1388, 1389, 1394, 1396, 1406, 1412, 1413, 1414, 1417, 1418, 1428, 1429, 1433, 1434, 1438, 1444, 1446, 1447, 1450, 1451, 1454, 1456, 1457, 1458, 1460, 1464, 1467, 1474, 1478, 1479, 1481, 1494, 1502, 1503, 1504, 1515, 1520, 1521, 1522, 1531, 1532, 1533, 1534, 1535, 1536, 1537, 1539, 1542, 1543, 1544, 1546, 1547, 1548, 1550, 1551, 1552, 1553, 1554, 1555, 1558, 1559, 1560, 1565, 1568, 1569, 1570, 1571, 1572, 1573, 1574, 1575, 1579, 1582, 1585, 1586, 1587, 1588, 1589, 1591, 1593, 1601, 1602, 1603, 1604, 1607, 1608, 1616, 1626, 1627, 1628, 1629, 1630, 1644, 1649, 1653, 1658, 1673, 1687, 1689, 1698, 1719, 1735, 1737, 1738, 1743, 1752, 1762, 1776, 1777, 1784, 1788, 1797, 1814, 1818, 1824, 1825, 1826, 1832, 1858, 1904, 1906, 1924, 1925, 1935, 1946, 1984, 1990, 2010, 2013, 2066, 2072, 2075, 2076, 2077, 2133, 2150, 2216, 2217, 2238, 2254, 2269, 2305, 2306, 2347, 2348, 2355, 2375, 2376, 2390, 2395, 2412, 2423, 2451, C3826, C3850, C3851, C3964

Botany, 67, 68, 163, 177, 313, 314, 524, 525, 554, 584, 598, 599, 760, 838, 839, 966, 967, 1027, 1159, 1190, 1191, 1247, 1269, 1270, 1291, 1305, 1324, 1330, 1354, 1355, 1362, 1363, 1386, 1389, 1402, 1403, 1426, 1429, 1440, 1441, 1449, 1451, 1457, 1458, 1468, 1534, 1535, 1540, 1541, 1549, 1557, 1560, 1572, 1573, 1603, 1604, 1737, 1738, 1788, 2072, 2075, 2076, 2216, 2217, 2242, 2305, 2306, 2347, 2348, 2375, 2376, 2467

Enology/Viticulture, 1526, 1530, 1561, 2047, 2418

Entomology, 703, 1345, 1396, 1522, 1538, 1539, 1568, C3885

Evolutionary Biology, 1523

Health Physics, 1542, 1575, 1752, 1814

Herpetology, 163, 554, 584, 760, 1027, 1159, 1305, 1386, 1426, 1449, 1468, 1557, 2242, 2467

Microbiology, 1527, 1528, 1529, 1542, 1575, 1752, 1814, C3928

Molecular Biology-G, 1542, 1575, 1752, 1814

Neurobiology, 1542, 1575, 1752, 1814

Ornithology, 1405, 1419, 1524, 1562

Physiology, 1525, 1542, 1575, 1752, 1814

Virology-G, 1542, 1575, 1752, 1814

Zoology, 1307, 1366, 1409, 1442, 1539, 1545, 1558, 1698, 1784, 1832, 1935, 2013

CHEMISTRY

General, 1, 42, 52, 67, 68, 131, 195, 252, 255, 301, 303, 304, 310, 311, 312, 313, 314, 318, 331, 332, 344, 345, 346, 358, 361, 363, 473, 481, 482, 496, 505, 506, 512, 522, 523, 547, 562, 570, 571, 572, 576, 578, 582, 583, 588, 589, 595, 596, 598, 599, 601, 622, 628, 656, 676, 677, 680, 692, 701, 702, 703, 716, 717, 720, 736, 740, 746, 747, 775, 787, 788, 790, 795, 796, 799, 825, 832, 838, 839, 966, 967, 1037, 1190, 1191, 1217, 1229, 1241, 1242, 1244, 1292, 1293, 1297, 1331, 1342, 1345, 1353, 1354, 1355, 1357, 1372, 1374, 1375, 1379, 1388, 1396, 1410, 1412, 1413, 1414, 1417, 1419, 1428, 1434, 1438, 1444, 1446, 1447, 1450, 1454, 1457, 1458, 1460, 1464, 1471, 1474, 1478, 1479, 1494, 1502, 1503, 1504, 1515, 1521, 1522, 1531, 1532, 1533, 1534, 1535, 1536, 1544, 1546, 1548, 1550, 1551, 1552, 1553, 1554, 1559, 1563, 1564, 1565, 1567, 1568, 1569, 1570, 1571, 1572, 1573, 1574, 1576, 1577, 1578, 1579, 1580, 1581, 1582, 1583, 1584, 1585, 1586, 1587, 1588, 1589, 1590, 1591, 1593, 1594, 1601, 1602, 1603, 1604, 1607, 1616, 1618, 1622, 1623, 1626, 1627, 1628, 1629, 1630, 1644, 1649, 1653, 1668, 1669, 1673, 1687, 1689, 1695, 1719, 1735, 1737, 1738, 1755, 1756, 1762, 1776, 1777, 1780, 1797, 1818, 1824, 1825, 1826, 1858, 1904, 1906, 1924, 1925, 1946, 1984, 2010, 2066, 2075, 2076, 2133, 2150, 2216, 2217, 2260, 2261, 2269, 2300, 2305, 2306, 2345, 2347, 2348, 2375, 2376, 2390, 2395, 2412, C3861, C3964

Atmosphere Chemistry, 507, 1346, 1347, 1350, 1381, 1592, 1634, 2239, C3903

Biochemistry, 67, 68, 313, 314, 598, 599, 702, 703, 838, 839, 966, 967, 1190, 1191, 1345, 1354, 1355, 1396, 1457, 1458, 1522, 1534, 1535, 1542, 1564, 1568, 1572, 1573, 1575, 1603, 1604, 1737, 1738, 1752, 1814, 2075, 2076, 2216, 2217, 2305, 2306, 2347, 2348, 2375, 2376

Chemical Technology, 702, 1564

Geochemistry, 1343, 1435, 1566, C3903

MATHEMATICS

General, 5, 20, 39, 42, 67, 68, 78, 114, 115, 160, 162, 182, 190, 195, 196, 208, 217, 252, 255, 266, 292, 301, 311, 312, 313, 314, 315, 316, 318, 319, 324, 330, 335, 336, 343, 345, 346, 354, 356, 363, 364, 365, 442, 459, 460, 467, 468, 469, 473, 481, 482, 495, 506, 512, 522, 523, 537, 562, 570, 571, 572, 575, 583, 588, 592, 593, 594, 595, 596, 598, 599, 600, 601, 602, 608, 613, 614, 620, 623, 624, 627, 635, 636, 653, 656, 673, 674, 675, 676, 677, 679, 680, 689, 691, 693, 694, 701, 716, 717, 718, 719, 720, 729, 735, 747, 775, 787, 788, 789, 790, 794, 799, 813, 825, 832, 838, 839, 948, 966, 967, 1029, 1037, 1058, 1173, 1190, 1191, 1231, 1233, 1236, 1238, 1241, 1242, 1244, 1245, 1246, 1248, 1292, 1293, 1297, 1331, 1354, 1355, 1357, 1365, 1374, 1375, 1379, 1392, 1393, 1407, 1410, 1413, 1414, 1417, 1419, 1438, 1444, 1446, 1447, 1454, 1455, 1457, 1458, 1460, 1464, 1469, 1471, 1472, 1478, 1479, 1481, 1485, 1489, 1490, 1499, 1500, 1502, 1503, 1504, 1505, 1506, 1507, 1509, 1510, 1511, 1512, 1513, 1514, 1518, 1519, 1532, 1533, 1534, 1535, 1536, 1537, 1544, 1551, 1552, 1553, 1554, 1563, 1570, 1571, 1572, 1573, 1574, 1579, 1580, 1583, 1584, 1587, 1588, 1589, 1591, 1594, 1595, 1598, 1599, 1600, 1601, 1602, 1603, 1604, 1605, 1606, 1607, 1608, 1610, 1612, 1613, 1614, 1615, 1616, 1617, 1618, 1620, 1621, 1622, 1623, 1624, 1625, 1627, 1628, 1629, 1630, 1631, 1632, 1633, 1636, 1637, 1638, 1639, 1640, 1641, 1642, 1643, 1645, 1646, 1647, 1658, 1673, 1687, 1689, 1737, 1738, 1743, 1762, 1776, 1777, 1818, 1825, 1826, 1904, 1925, 1984, 2010, 2066, 2075, 2076, 2077, 2090, 2133, 2191, 2216, 2217, 2224, 2254, 2269, 2296, 2300, 2305, 2306, 2317, 2336, 2342, 2345, 2347, 2348, 2375, 2376, 2390, 2395, 2423, 2470, C3921, C3922, C3938

Physics, 39, 42, 67, 68, 182, 301, 313, 314, 345, 358, 363, 467, 473, 479, 505, 506, 507, 512, 562, 582, 588, 592, 593, 594, 598, 599, 623, 624, 628, 653, 656, 673, 674, 675, 682, 693, 694, 701, 723, 746, 775, 791, 832, 838, 839, 966, 967, 1037, 1190, 1191, 1244, 1297, 1331, 1354, 1355, 1372, 1379, 1381, 1388, 1412, 1417, 1428, 1447, 1450, 1454, 1457, 1458, 1464, 1471, 1504, 1515, 1534, 1535, 1550, 1554, 1559, 1563, 1572,

1573, 1583, 1586, 1591, 1592, 1593, 1594, 1596, 1597, 1598, 1599, 1600, 1603, 1604, 1609, 1611, 1619, 1620, 1621, 1622, 1626, 1630, 1634, 1635, 1644, 1645, 1737, 1738, 1824, 1924, 2075, 2076, 2119, 2216, 2217, 2239, 2296, 2300, 2305, 2306, 2342, 2345, 2347, 2348, 2375, 2376, 2415, C3903, C3952

Statistics, 162, 636, 1637

MEDICAL DOCTOR

General, 5, 11, 22, 78, 109, 147, 161, 175, 176, 190, 193, 217, 239, 252, 281, 303, 305, 310, 317, 319, 331, 332, 333, 342, 349, 357, 360, 361, 440, 540, 546, 547, 574, 589, 602, 651, 687, 728, 743, 793, 813, 1128, 1197, 1209, 1217, 1229, 1230, 1237, 1239, 1242, 1293, 1296, 1307, 1342, 1344, 1353, 1371, 1375, 1395, 1401, 1414, 1424, 1434, 1436, 1446, 1460, 1474, 1475, 1481, 1492, 1493, 1502, 1503, 1517, 1521, 1531, 1537, 1544, 1551, 1553, 1558, 1565, 1569, 1576, 1577, 1579, 1587, 1589, 1590, 1608, 1616, 1627, 1629, 1648, 1649, 1650, 1651, 1652, 1653, 1654, 1655, 1656, 1657, 1658, 1659, 1660, 1661, 1662, 1663, 1664, 1666, 1667, 1668, 1669, 1670, 1671, 1672, 1673, 1674, 1675, 1676, 1677, 1678, 1679, 1680, 1681, 1685, 1686, 1687, 1688, 1689, 1693, 1694, 1695, 1697, 1698, 1699, 1700, 1701, 1702, 1703, 1704, 1705, 1707, 1708, 1710, 1711, 1713, 1719, 1722, 1724, 1725, 1735, 1736, 1740, 1741, 1742, 1743, 1744, 1747, 1748, 1749, 1750, 1751, 1753, 1755, 1756, 1759, 1760, 1762, 1763, 1766, 1767, 1769, 1771, 1772, 1776, 1777, 1779, 1780, 1781, 1784, 1785, 1786, 1787, 1791, 1793, 1794, 1797, 1798, 1802, 1803, 1804, 1805, 1806, 1809, 1813, 1815, 1816, 1817, 1818, 1819, 1822, 1823, 1825, 1826, 1830, 1832, 1835, 1836, 1837, 1838, 1839, 1858, 1862, 1878, 1879, 1880, 1881, 1884, 1890, 1894, 1898, 1901, 1902, 1903, 1904, 1905, 1909, 1911, 1912, 1918, 1920, 1925, 1929, 1935, 1936, 1937, 1938, 1939, 1941, 1942, 1946, 1947, 1952, 1953, 1955, 1959, 1965, 1967, 1968, 1970, 1973, 1976, 1979, 1981, 1983, 1984, 1985, 1991, 1993, 1994, 1996, 2005, 2010, 2011, 2013, 2028, 2029, 2030, 2032, 2033, 2036, 2038, 2066, 2070, 2071, 2077, 2133, 2249, 2253, 2254, 2260, 2261, 2262, 2269, 2275, 2277, 2280, 2307, 2349, 2358, 2384, 2385, 2390, 2394, 2405, 2406, 2412, 2423, 2453, 2583, 2763, B3613, B3718, B3739, B3740, C3926

Anesthesiology-G, 1684, 1706, 2003, 2031
Family Practice-G, 1677, 1682, 1704, 1705, 1909, 1915, 1991, 1998, 2030
Gynecology-G, 1677, 1682, 1704, 1909, 1915, 1991, 1998
Naturopathy, C3931
Neurology-G, 1705, 2030
Obstetrics-G, 1677, 1682, 1704, 1909, 1915, 1991, 1998
Orthopedics-G, 1705, 2030
Osteopathy, 175, 176, 651, 1661, 1663, 1682, 1701, 1702, 1703, 1704, 1709, 1748, 1749, 1785, 1786, 1787, 1792, 1835, 1836, 1915, 1936, 1937, 1965, 1968, 1998, 2028, 2029, 2070, 2071, 2349, 2405, 2406, C3941
Pathology, C3943
Pediatrics, 1677, 1682, 1704, 1909, 1915, 1991, 1998, C3944
Psychiatry, 278, 279, 280, 1665, 1682, 1690, 1691, 1692, 1704, 1810, 1827, 1828, 1829, 1915, 1926, 1927, 1928, 1971, 1998, 2351, 2362, 2363, 2364, C3955
Surgery-G, 1677, 1684, 1705, 1706, 1909, 1991, 2003, 2030, 2031
Urology-G, 1705, 2030

MEDICAL-RELATED DISCIPLINES

General, 11, 22, 77, 109, 161, 175, 176, 193, 239, 252, 281, 303, 305, 317, 332, 333, 349, 360, 440, 540, 574, 589, 651, 687, 728, 793, 1128, 1229, 1230, 1237, 1242, 1293, 1296, 1307, 1342, 1344, 1371, 1375, 1395, 1401, 1414, 1424, 1434, 1436, 1446, 1460, 1474, 1475, 1492, 1502, 1503, 1521, 1544, 1551, 1553, 1558, 1565, 1577, 1579, 1587, 1589, 1616, 1627, 1629, 1648, 1649, 1651, 1654, 1655, 1656, 1657, 1664, 1666, 1667, 1669, 1670, 1673, 1674, 1679, 1680, 1681, 1687, 1689, 1693, 1694, 1697, 1698, 1701, 1703, 1708, 1710, 1711, 1713, 1719, 1722, 1724, 1725, 1734, 1736, 1740, 1741, 1742, 1744, 1750, 1751, 1753, 1756, 1759, 1762, 1763, 1766, 1767, 1769, 1776, 1777, 1779, 1781, 1784, 1785, 1787, 1791, 1793, 1794, 1797, 1798, 1802, 1803, 1804, 1805, 1809, 1813, 1815, 1816, 1818, 1819, 1822, 1823, 1825, 1826, 1830, 1832, 1835, 1836, 1837, 1838, 1839, 1858, 1862, 1877, 1878, 1879, 1880, 1881, 1890, 1894, 1898, 1901, 1904, 1905, 1911, 1912, 1925, 1929, 1935, 1936, 1937, 1938, 1939, 1941, 1942, 1946, 1947, 1951, 1952, 1953, 1955, 1970, 1973, 1976, 1979, 1984, 1985, 1993, 1994, 1996, 2010, 2011, 2013, 2028, 2029, 2033, 2036, 2038, 2066, 2070, 2071, 2133, 2253, 2261, 2262, 2269, 2275, 2280, 2307, 2384, 2385, 2390, 2405, 2406, 2412, 2453, 2583, B3613
Acupuncture/Oriental Medicine, C3820, C3821, C3822
Chiropractics, 147, 357, 546, 1686, 1754, 1772, 1920, 2005, 2277, 2358, 2394, C3858, C3859
Dentistry, 5, 78, 147, 175, 190, 191, 217, 310, 319, 331, 332, 357, 360, 546, 602, 743, 813, 1296, 1353, 1481, 1531, 1537, 1569, 1576, 1577, 1608, 1653, 1658, 1661, 1663, 1668, 1669, 1671, 1685, 1686, 1694, 1701, 1702, 1715, 1735, 1743, 1746, 1748, 1749, 1755, 1756, 1757, 1758, 1760, 1764, 1771, 1772, 1779, 1782, 1783, 1785, 1786, 1835, 1899, 1900, 1902, 1918, 1920, 1936, 1965, 1968, 1981, 2005, 2028, 2070, 2077, 2254, 2260, 2261, 2277, 2280, 2349, 2358, 2394, 2405, 2423, 2763, B3761, C3876, C3877
Health Care Administration, 2, 77, 189, 204, 306, 743, 1476, 1667, 1685, 1716, 1723, 1725, 1753, 1771, 1815, 1898, 1918, 1976, 2385, C3910
Homeopathy, C3907, C3908
Lab/Clinical Science, 1726, 1727, 1728, 1729, 1734, 1868, 1869, 1870, 1871, 1877, 1923, 1951
Optometry, 147, 175, 357, 546, 743, 1663, 1685, 1686, 1701, 1709, 1720, 1721, 1749, 1771, 1772, 1785, 1792, 1835, 1918, 1920, 1936, 1968, 2005, 2028, 2070, 2277, 2349, 2358, 2394, 2405, C3939, C3940
Pharmacology, 67, 68, 313, 314, 598, 599, 743, 838, 839, 966, 967, 1190, 1191, 1354, 1355, 1457, 1458, 1534, 1535, 1542, 1572, 1573, 1575, 1603, 1604, 1660, 1667, 1685, 1718, 1737, 1738, 1747, 1752, 1753, 1761, 1771, 1775, 1789, 1790, 1806, 1814, 1815, 1884, 1898, 1918, 1959, 1976, 2075, 2076, 2216, 2217, 2305, 2306, 2347, 2348, 2375, 2376, 2385, B3759, C3946, C3947, C3948, C3949
Pharmacy, 147, 357, 546, 743, 1542, 1575, 1660, 1661, 1671, 1685, 1686, 1714, 1717, 1718, 1734, 1747, 1748, 1752, 1760, 1771, 1772, 1775, 1789, 1790, 1806, 1814, 1877, 1884, 1902, 1918, 1920, 1951, 1959, 1965, 1981, 2005, 2277, 2358, 2394, B3759, C3946, C3947, C3948, C3949
Podiatry, 147, 357, 546, 1686, 1772, 1920, 2005, 2277, 2358, 2394, C3953
Public Health-G, 1411, 1667, 1753, 1768, 1815, 1898, 1976, 2385
Speech Pathology, 147, 205, 206, 207, 218, 270, 271, 357, 546, 1005, 1006, 1686, 1730, 1731, 1732, 1745, 1772, 1773, 1774, 1799, 1800, 1801, 1874, 1875,
2262, 2269, 2275, 2280, 2307, 2384, 2385, 2390, 2405, 2406, 2412, 2453, 2583, B3613

1876, 1882, 1920, 1921, 1922, 2005, 2277, 2358, 2394, C3842

Sports Medicine-G, 262, 265, 1770, 1917

Veterinary Medicine, 147, 177, 357, 361, 546, 547, 1217, 1247, 1249, 1324, 1389, 1429, 1451, 1560, 1590, 1663, 1686, 1695, 1712, 1733, 1739, 1749, 1765, 1772, 1780, 1788, 1920, 1968, 2005, 2039, 2072, 2277, 2349, 2358, 2394, C3979

Veterinary Medicine-G, 1663, 1749, 1968, 2349, C3979

MEDICAL RESEARCH

General, 11, 22, 109, 161, 175, 176, 193, 239, 252, 281, 303, 305, 317, 333, 349, 358, 440, 505, 540, 574, 582, 589, 628, 651, 687, 728, 746, 793, 1229, 1230, 1237, 1242, 1293, 1307, 1342, 1344, 1371, 1372, 1375, 1395, 1401, 1412, 1414, 1424, 1434, 1436, 1446, 1460, 1474, 1475, 1492, 1502, 1503, 1521, 1544, 1550, 1551, 1553, 1558, 1565, 1579, 1586, 1587, 1589, 1616, 1626, 1627, 1629, 1649, 1651, 1654, 1655, 1656, 1657, 1664, 1666, 1667, 1670, 1673, 1674, 1680, 1681, 1687, 1689, 1693, 1697, 1698, 1701, 1703, 1708, 1710, 1711, 1719, 1722, 1736, 1740, 1741, 1742, 1744, 1750, 1751, 1753, 1759, 1762, 1763, 1767, 1769, 1776, 1777, 1781, 1784, 1785, 1787, 1791, 1793, 1794, 1797, 1798, 1802, 1803, 1804, 1805, 1809, 1813, 1815, 1816, 1818, 1819, 1820, 1822, 1823, 1824, 1825, 1826, 1830, 1832, 1833, 1835, 1836, 1837, 1838, 1839, 1858, 1862, 1878, 1879, 1880, 1881, 1890, 1894, 1898, 1901, 1904, 1905, 1912, 1924, 1925, 1929, 1935, 1936, 1937, 1938, 1939, 1941, 1946, 1947, 1952, 1953, 1955, 1970, 1973, 1976, 1979, 1984, 1985, 1994, 1996, 2010, 2011, 2013, 2028, 2029, 2033, 2036, 2038, 2066, 2070, 2071, 2133, 2253, 2262, 2269, 2275, 2307, 2384, 2385, 2390, 2405, 2406, 2412, 2583

Alcohol/Drug Abuse-G, 1795

Alzheimer's Disease-G, 278, 279, 1690, 1691, 1796, 1827, 1828, 1926, 1927, 2362, 2363

Audiology, 205, 206, 1730, 1731, 1799, 1800, 1874, 1875

Biological Psychiatry-G, 1696

Biomedical Sciences, 1667, 1753, 1815, 1817, 1834, 1898, 1976, 2385

Birth Defects, B3735, C3879

Cancer, 1796

Cystic Fibrosis, 1807, 1808

Dental-G, C3877

Epidemiology-G, 1542, 1575, 1752, 1814

Epilepsy, 1665, 1810, 1811, 1971, 2351

Genetics, 1542, 1575, 1752, 1814

Gerontology/Aging, 1796

Immunology-G, 1542, 1575, 1752, 1796, 1814

Lupus Erythematosus, 1820

Mental Health Services, 278, 279, 280, 1690, 1691, 1692, 1827, 1828, 1829, 1926, 1927, 1928, 2362, 2363, 2364, B3735, C3879

Mental Retardation, 278, 279, 280, 288, 1690, 1691, 1692, 1827, 1828, 1829, 1831, 1926, 1927, 1928, 2362, 2363, 2364, 2370

Microscopy/Microanalysis, 1821

Neuroscience, 1542, 1575, 1752, 1796, 1814, 1817

Ophthalmology, 1812

Respiratory Disease-G, 1660, 1747, 1806, 1884, 1959

Speech-Language Pathology, 205, 206, 207, 1667, 1730, 1731, 1732, 1753, 1799, 1800, 1801, 1815, 1874, 1875, 1876, 1898, 1976, 2385

Strokes-G, 278, 279, 1690, 1691, 1827, 1828, 1926, 1927, 2362, 2363

MEDICAL TECHNOLOGIES

General, 11, 22, 109, 161, 175, 176, 193, 239, 252, 281, 303, 305, 317, 333, 344, 358, 440, 496, 505, 574, 576, 582, 589, 622, 628, 651, 687, 692, 728, 736, 746, 793, 795, 1128, 1198, 1209, 1229, 1230, 1237, 1242, 1293, 1307, 1342, 1344, 1372, 1375, 1395, 1401, 1412, 1414, 1424, 1434, 1436, 1446, 1460, 1474, 1475, 1492, 1494, 1503, 1521, 1544, 1546, 1550, 1553, 1558, 1565, 1579, 1582, 1586, 1589, 1616, 1626, 1629, 1649, 1651, 1654, 1655, 1656, 1657, 1660, 1664, 1666, 1670, 1671, 1672, 1673, 1674, 1679, 1680, 1689, 1693, 1697, 1698, 1701, 1703, 1708, 1710, 1711, 1719, 1722, 1724, 1734, 1736, 1740, 1741, 1742, 1744, 1747, 1750, 1751, 1759, 1760, 1762, 1763, 1766, 1767, 1777, 1781, 1784, 1785, 1787, 1791, 1793, 1794, 1797, 1798, 1802, 1803, 1804, 1805, 1806, 1809, 1813, 1816, 1818, 1819, 1822, 1824, 1826, 1830, 1832, 1835, 1836, 1837, 1838, 1839, 1858, 1862, 1877, 1878, 1879, 1880, 1881, 1884, 1887, 1889, 1890, 1893, 1894, 1901, 1902, 1903, 1904, 1905, 1906, 1911, 1912, 1924, 1925, 1929, 1935, 1936, 1937, 1938, 1939, 1941, 1946, 1947, 1951, 1952, 1953, 1955, 1959, 1966, 1969, 1970, 1972, 1973, 1979, 1981, 1983, 1984, 1985, 1993, 1994, 2010, 2011, 2013, 2028, 2029, 2033, 2036, 2038, 2066, 2070, 2071, 2133, 2253, 2262, 2269, 2307,

2381, 2384, 2390, 2405, 2406, 2412, 2453, 2583, B3613

Art Therapy, 1842, 1843, 1916

Athletic Trainer, 98, 184, 227, 262, 265, 298, 1085, 1358, 1439, 1484, 1770, 1886, 1892, 1914, 1917, 1940, 2120, 2214, 2352, 2372, 2383, 2407

Audiology, 147, 205, 206, 207, 218, 260, 270, 271, 357, 546, 1005, 1006, 1686, 1730, 1731, 1732, 1745, 1772, 1773, 1774, 1799, 1800, 1801, 1874, 1875, 1876, 1882, 1913, 1920, 1921, 1922, 2005, 2277, 2358, 2394, C3842, C3970

Clinical Chemistry, C3861

Cytotechnology, 1728, 1870, 1872

Dental Assistant, 8, 97, 1656, 1741, 1758, 1804, 1840, 1863, 1880, 1891, 1895, 1900, 1932, 1955, 2432, C3874, C3877

Dental Hygiene, 147, 357, 546, 1660, 1686, 1747, 1757, 1758, 1772, 1806, 1845, 1846, 1847, 1848, 1849, 1850, 1851, 1852, 1853, 1854, 1855, 1856, 1857, 1884, 1896, 1899, 1900, 1920, 1931, 1959, 2005, 2277, 2358, 2394, C3877

Dental Hygiene Education, 1758, 1850, 1900, C3877

Dental Hygiene-G, 1845, 1846, 1850, 1853, 1854, C3877

Dental Lab Tech, 1758, 1900, 1933, C3875, C3877

Dietetic Technician, 2043, 2044, 2045, C3878

Education Medical Tech, 8, 97, 1891, 1923, 2432

Emergency Medical Tech (EMT), 1908, 1934, 2450

Exercise Physiology, 47, 201, 265, 1064, 1770, 1841, 1917

Health Information Management, 77, 1859, 1860, 1861

Health Information Technology, 1859, 1860, 1861

Histologic Technology, 1728, 1870, 1872

Kinesiotherapy, 265, 1770, 1917

Massage Therapy, C3920

Medical Assistant, 8, 97, 1656, 1741, 1804, 1844, 1863, 1880, 1891, 1955, 2432

Medical Laboratory Technology, 8, 97, 1728, 1729, 1863, 1870, 1871, 1872, 1891, 2432

Medical Records, 8, 97, 1859, 1860, 1861, 1891, 2432, C3925

Medical Technology, 323, 721, 1660, 1667, 1726, 1727, 1728, 1729, 1747, 1753, 1806, 1815, 1863, 1868, 1869, 1870, 1871, 1872, 1884, 1885, 1898, 1923, 1959, 1976, 2385, 2428, C3924

Music Therapy, 260, 1099, 1913, 1916, C3930

Occupational Health, 278, 279, 280, 1690, 1691, 1692, 1827, 1828, 1829, 1926, 1927, 1928, 2362, 2363, 2364

Occupational Therapy, 147, 260, 282, 357, 546, 1660, 1671, 1686, 1747, 1760, 1772, 1806, 1884, 1897, 1902, 1907, 1910, 1913, 1916, 1920, 1930, 1959, 1981, 2005, 2277, 2356, 2358, 2394, B3686, B3770, B3771, B3772, B3773, B3779

Phlebotomy, 1863

Physical Therapy, 147, 260, 265, 282, 357, 546, 743, 1656, 1660, 1671, 1685, 1686, 1734, 1741, 1747, 1760, 1770, 1771, 1772, 1804, 1806, 1877, 1880, 1883, 1884, 1897, 1902, 1907, 1910, 1913, 1916, 1917, 1918, 1920, 1930, 1951, 1955, 1959, 1981, 2005, 2277, 2356, 2358, 2394, B3686, B3770, B3771, B3772, B3773, B3779, C3950

Physician Assistant, 147, 357, 546, 743, 1677, 1682, 1685, 1686, 1704, 1771, 1772, 1778, 1909, 1915, 1918, 1919, 1920, 1991, 1998, 2004, 2005, 2277, 2358, 2394, B3685, B3720, B3763, C3951

Radiology Tech, 1873, 1893, 1972, C3958

Recreation Therapy, 260, 265, 1770, 1913, 1917

Rehabilitation, 229, 260, 265, 1770, 1888, 1913, 1917, 2350, 2382, B3667

Respiratory Therapy, 1660, 1747, 1806, 1864, 1865, 1866, 1867, 1884, 1959, C3961

Speech Therapy, 147, 205, 206, 207, 278, 279, 280, 357, 546, 1686, 1690, 1691, 1692, 1730, 1731, 1732, 1772, 1799, 1800, 1801, 1827, 1828, 1829, 1874, 1875, 1876, 1920, 1926, 1927, 1928, 2005, 2206, 2277, 2358, 2362, 2363, 2364, 2394, B3667, C3970

Speech-Language Pathology, 205, 206, 207, 260, 278, 279, 280, 1667, 1690, 1691, 1692, 1730, 1731, 1732, 1753, 1799, 1800, 1801, 1815, 1827, 1828, 1829, 1874, 1875, 1876, 1898, 1910, 1913, 1926, 1927, 1928, 1976, 2206, 2356, 2362, 2363, 2364, 2385, B3686, B3770, B3771, B3772, B3773, B3779

NURSING

General, 6, 11, 22, 24, 25, 26, 27, 28, 29, 30, 31, 32, 33, 34, 35, 36, 37, 80, 109, 129, 147, 161, 175, 176, 193, 225, 239, 252, 257, 281, 303, 305, 321, 333, 349, 357, 440, 445, 446, 447, 448, 449, 450, 451, 452, 453, 454, 455, 456, 457, 458, 540, 546, 574, 589, 603, 637, 638, 639, 640, 641, 642, 643, 644, 645, 646, 647, 648, 649, 650, 651, 687, 728, 793, 820, 1128, 1198, 1209, 1229, 1230, 1232, 1237, 1242, 1283, 1293, 1307, 1309, 1310, 1311, 1312, 1313, 1314, 1315, 1316, 1317, 1318, 1319, 1320, 1321, 1322, 1342, 1344, 1371, 1375, 1395,

1401, 1414, 1424, 1434, 1436, 1446, 1460, 1474, 1475, 1482, 1492, 1503, 1517, 1521, 1544, 1547, 1553, 1558, 1565, 1579, 1589, 1616, 1629, 1648, 1649, 1651, 1654, 1655, 1656, 1660, 1661, 1662, 1664, 1666, 1667, 1670, 1671, 1672, 1673, 1674, 1677, 1679, 1680, 1681, 1684, 1686, 1689, 1693, 1697, 1698, 1701, 1703, 1706, 1707, 1708, 1710, 1711, 1713, 1719, 1722, 1724, 1725, 1734, 1736, 1740, 1741, 1744, 1747, 1748, 1750, 1751, 1753, 1759, 1760, 1762, 1763, 1766, 1767, 1769, 1772, 1777, 1781, 1784, 1785, 1787, 1791, 1793, 1794, 1797, 1798, 1802, 1803, 1804, 1806, 1809, 1813, 1815, 1816, 1818, 1819, 1822, 1823, 1826, 1830, 1832, 1835, 1836, 1837, 1838, 1839, 1858, 1862, 1877, 1878, 1879, 1880, 1884, 1887, 1889, 1890, 1893, 1894, 1898, 1901, 1902, 1903, 1904, 1905, 1909, 1911, 1912, 1920, 1925, 1929, 1935, 1936, 1937, 1938, 1939, 1941, 1942, 1943, 1946, 1947, 1951, 1952, 1953, 1954, 1955, 1956, 1957, 1958, 1959, 1960, 1961, 1962, 1963, 1964, 1965, 1966, 1967, 1969, 1970, 1972, 1973, 1974, 1976, 1977, 1978, 1979, 1980, 1981, 1982, 1983, 1984, 1985, 1986, 1987, 1989, 1990, 1991, 1992, 1993, 1994, 1995, 1996, 1999, 2000, 2001, 2002, 2003, 2005, 2006, 2007, 2008, 2010, 2011, 2012, 2013, 2014, 2015, 2016, 2017, 2018, 2019, 2020, 2021, 2022, 2023, 2024, 2025, 2026, 2027, 2028, 2029, 2031, 2032, 2033, 2034, 2035, 2036, 2037, 2038, 2066, 2070, 2071, 2133, 2262, 2269, 2275, 2277, 2355, 2358, 2381, 2384, 2385, 2390, 2394, 2405, 2406, 2412, 2451, 2453, 2583, 2677, B3613, B3769, C3936

Anesthetist, 1663, 1677, 1684, 1706, 1749, 1893, 1909, 1950, 1968, 1972, 1991, 2003, 2031, 2349, C3935

Behavioral Sciences-G, 1665, 1810, 1971, 2351

Cancer Nursing, 2009

Gynecology, 1682, 1915, 1998

Licensed Practical Nurse (LPN), 1677, 1909, 1948, 1958, 1991, 1997, 2007

Medical-Surgical Nursing, 1677, 1684, 1705, 1706, 1893, 1909, 1972, 1991, 2003, 2030, 2031

Nurse Assistant, 1949

Nurse Practitioner, 1677, 1682, 1704, 1909, 1915, 1919, 1958, 1974, 1991, 1997, 1998, 2004, 2006, 2007

Nurse/Midwifery, 1677, 1682, 1704, 1909, 1915, 1919, 1945, 1958, 1988, 1991, 1998, 2004

Obstetrics, 1677, 1682, 1909, 1915, 1991, 1998

Operating Room Nursing, 1677, 1684, 1705, 1706, 1909, 1950, 1991, 2003, 2030, 2031

Pediatric, 1682, 1915, 1998

NUTRITION

General, 177, 1242, 1247, 1293, 1324, 1325, 1375, 1389, 1414, 1429, 1446, 1451, 1460, 1503, 1553, 1560, 1589, 1629, 1689, 1777, 1788, 1826, 1925, 2010, 2040, 2059, 2066, 2067, 2072, 2073, C3893

Cereal Science/Technology, 2041

Culinary Arts, 13, 14, 15, 16, 103, 121, 122, 123, 124, 165, 337, 338, 339, 340, 615, 616, 617, 618, 761, 945, 1530, 2042, 2047, 2048, 2049, 2050, 2054, 2055, 2056, 2057, 2058, 2061, 2062, 2063, 2064, 2065, 2068, 2069, 2193, 2418, 2433, 2444, 2445, 2446, 2447, 2468, B3658, C3872, C3894

Dietetics, 175, 176, 651, 1701, 1703, 1785, 1787, 1835, 1836, 1936, 1937, 2028, 2029, 2043, 2044, 2045, 2046, 2070, 2071, 2405, 2406, C3878

Food Management/Science/Tech, 38, 103, 177, 1247, 1324, 1389, 1429, 1451, 1560, 1788, 2041, 2046, 2048, 2049, 2050, 2051, 2052, 2053, 2062, 2063, 2064, 2065, 2067, 2072, 2433, C3894

Home Econ/Fam & Consumer Sci, 177, 1247, 1249, 1324, 1389, 1429, 1451, 1560, 1712, 1788, 2039, 2059, 2072, C3888

Human Development, 177, 1247, 1324, 1389, 1429, 1451, 1560, 1788, 2072

SCHOOL OF SOCIAL SCIENCE

General, 5, 67, 68, 78, 113, 190, 217, 244, 292, 313, 314, 319, 598, 599, 602, 812, 813, 818, 819, 826, 827, 828, 829, 836, 838, 839, 842, 848, 933, 934, 935, 948, 966, 967, 988, 989, 1020, 1021, 1022, 1029, 1058, 1173, 1190, 1191, 1208, 1214, 1218, 1219, 1220, 1243, 1354, 1355, 1370, 1378, 1416, 1457, 1458, 1461, 1462, 1463, 1481, 1512, 1534, 1535, 1537, 1572, 1573, 1603, 1604, 1608, 1640, 1658, 1737, 1738, 1743, 2074, 2075, 2076, 2077, 2078, 2079, 2080, 2081, 2082, 2083, 2084, 2085, 2086, 2087, 2088, 2089, 2090, 2125, 2126, 2179, 2180, 2181, 2216, 2217, 2219, 2220, 2235, 2236, 2237, 2247, 2254, 2263, 2265, 2302, 2305, 2306, 2308, 2314, 2316, 2331, 2332, 2333, 2346, 2347, 2348, 2354, 2365, 2366, 2367, 2368, 2374, 2375, 2376, 2378, 2386, 2399, 2400, 2401, 2402, 2423, 2470, B3681

COMMUNICATIONS

General, 7, 21, 58, 93, 98, 108, 118, 131, 252, 327, 527, 578, 609, 652, 686, 726, 740, 758, 765, 796, 805, 818, 827, 828, 829, 848, 933, 934, 935, 988, 1020, 1021, 1022, 1035, 1208, 1218, 1219, 1220, 1384, 1387, 1427, 1461, 1462, 1463, 1544, 1548, 1579, 1585, 1616, 1673, 1762, 1818, 1892, 1904, 1984, 2080, 2086, 2087, 2088, 2091, 2110, 2120, 2123, 2125, 2127, 2133, 2143, 2150, 2154, 2162, 2179, 2180, 2181, 2188, 2199, 2202, 2206, 2212, 2213, 2235, 2236, 2237, 2263, 2269, 2283, 2289, 2310, 2314, 2331, 2332, 2333, 2334, 2352, 2353, 2354, 2365, 2366, 2367, 2383, 2386, 2390, 2399, 2400, 2401, B3673, B3724, B3725

Broadcasting, 21, 75, 118, 165, 179, 216, 758, 761, 805, 840, 889, 945, 969, 1077, 1384, 2068, 2094, 2096, 2098, 2103, 2104, 2105, 2127, 2128, 2130, 2131, 2134, 2136, 2138, 2141, 2142, 2146, 2147, 2148, 2149, 2151, 2152, 2154, 2162, 2175, 2176, 2177, 2178, 2182, 2186, 2188, 2190, 2193, 2195, 2201, 2205, 2211, 2212, 2283, 2334, 2468, 2628, C3852, C3853

Electronic Media, 165, 179, 761, 943, 945, 2068, 2096, 2104, 2117, 2152, 2175, 2176, 2177, 2178, 2185, 2193, 2205, 2466, 2468, C3852

Financial/Business Journalism, 2115, 2135, 2141, 2146, 2147, 2164, 2212, C3914

Home Workshop Writing, 2209

Journalism, 7, 21, 58, 75, 93, 113, 148, 154, 158, 160, 166, 179, 216, 244, 327, 553, 590, 635, 667, 758, 805, 818, 819, 840, 848, 889, 969, 988, 989, 1035, 1077, 1208, 1278, 1303, 1384, 1423, 1509, 1636, 2080, 2081, 2091, 2093, 2095, 2096, 2097, 2099, 2100, 2101, 2103, 2105, 2108, 2109, 2110, 2116, 2117, 2124, 2125, 2126, 2128, 2130, 2132, 2135, 2137, 2139, 2140, 2141, 2142, 2143, 2144, 2145, 2146, 2147, 2148, 2149, 2152, 2153, 2154, 2161, 2162, 2163, 2165, 2168, 2169, 2170, 2173, 2174, 2182, 2184, 2188, 2189, 2190, 2191, 2192, 2195, 2196, 2198, 2199, 2201, 2204, 2205, 2208, 2209, 2211, 2212, 2213, 2263, 2265, 2283, 2310, 2314, 2316, 2328, 2334, 2335, 2336, 2337, 2354, 2386, 2628, B3726, B3746, C3914, C3934

News Editing, 2099, 2170

News Graphics, 2096, 2152, 2153

Newspaper Business, 154, 179, 1035, 2100, 2105, 2142, 2152, 2154, 2173, 2183, 2199, 2205, 2213, 2628

Photojournalism, 2096, 2109, 2111, 2117, 2135, 2141, 2146, 2147, 2148, 2149, 2152, 2153, 2155, 2156, 2157, 2158, 2159, 2160, 2170, 2174, 2210, 2211, 2212, B3768, C3914

Print Journalism/Print Media, 154, 179, 1035, 2092, 2096, 2100, 2105, 2117, 2121, 2128, 2130, 2141, 2142, 2152, 2153, 2154, 2169, 2172, 2173, 2192, 2201, 2205, 2213, 2628

Public Relations, 48, 58, 76, 98, 148, 149, 154, 179, 268, 652, 765, 846, 891, 927, 970, 1004, 1079, 1143, 1387, 1427, 1892, 2091, 2106, 2120, 2122, 2142, 2152, 2162, 2165, 2166, 2173, 2200, 2202, 2205, 2289, 2328, 2352, 2383, B3765

Public Sector Communications, 113, 154, 244, 819, 989, 2081, 2126, 2173, 2199, 2265, 2316

Publishing, 923, 2142, 2145, 2162, B3670, C3905, C3914

Religious Journalism/Com, 275, 1148, 1215, 2135, 2141, 2146, 2147, 2171, 2203, 2397

Sports Reporting, 98, 184, 298, 1892, 1940, 2117, 2120, 2142, 2192, 2214, 2352, 2372, 2383, 2407

Technical Communication, 21, 95, 605, 681, 722, 758, 805, 943, 1384, 2118, 2185, 2188, 2283, 2334, 2430, 2466

Telecommunications, 682, 723, 791, 1611, 2102, 2119

Television Industry, 75, 98, 216, 840, 889, 969, 1077, 1892, 2094, 2096, 2103, 2120, 2136, 2142, 2146, 2147, 2152, 2154, 2175, 2176, 2177, 2178, 2352, 2383, C3853

Video Journalism, 2155, 2156, 2157, 2158, 2159

HISTORY

General, 10, 107, 115, 139, 144, 163, 187, 188, 197, 267, 335, 554, 584, 614, 760, 821, 827, 828, 829, 916, 926, 933, 934, 935, 993, 997, 1020, 1021, 1022, 1027, 1047, 1159, 1212, 1218, 1219, 1220, 1305, 1365, 1386, 1407, 1426, 1449, 1459, 1461, 1462, 1463, 1468, 1557, 1614, 2079, 2086, 2087, 2088, 2179, 2180, 2181, 2220, 2223, 2224, 2226, 2227, 2229, 2232, 2233, 2235, 2236, 2237, 2242, 2243, 2272, 2286, 2313, 2317, 2323, 2325, 2331, 2332, 2333, 2338, 2365, 2366, 2367, 2399, 2400, 2401, 2467, B3703

American Colonial History, 2215

American History, 194, 251, 850, 872, 1030, 1033, 1470, 2221, 2222, 2225, 2228, 2230, 2241, 2244, 2245, 2319, 2339

American Indian History-G, 842, 2078, 2219, 2308, 2378

Aviation/Aerospace History, 353, 502, 507, 1381, 1498, 1592, 1634, 2231, 2239, 2459

British History, 841, 974, 2218, 2619

Historical Writing, 1033, 1470, 2221, 2245

Military Science, 2246

Science/Medical History, 67, 68, 313, 314, 598, 599, 838, 839, 865, 942, 966, 967, 1190, 1191, 1354, 1355, 1380, 1418, 1457, 1458, 1467, 1534, 1535, 1555, 1572, 1573, 1603, 1604, 1737, 1738, 2075, 2076, 2216, 2217, 2238, 2305, 2306, 2347, 2348, 2375, 2376

Texas History, 2079, 2220, 2240

US Marine Corps History, 1033, 1470, 2245

US Military History, 144, 197, 267, 926, 1033, 1459, 1470, 2232, 2245

US Naval History, 144, 197, 267, 926, 1459, 2232

World History, 2234

LAW

General, 5, 11, 21, 39, 78, 109, 112, 113, 147, 153, 156, 164, 182, 190, 193, 217, 239, 244, 252, 317, 319, 331, 332, 333, 349, 357, 360, 467, 540, 546, 574, 602, 630, 653, 687, 696, 728, 758, 793, 805, 812, 813, 816, 818, 819, 836, 848, 864, 988, 989, 993, 1208, 1237, 1296, 1371, 1384, 1481, 1537, 1544, 1576, 1577, 1579, 1608, 1616, 1645, 1652, 1657, 1658, 1668, 1669, 1670, 1673, 1681, 1686, 1694, 1742, 1743, 1755, 1756, 1759, 1762, 1769, 1772, 1779, 1805, 1816, 1818, 1823, 1881, 1901, 1904, 1920, 1979, 1984, 1996, 2005, 2074, 2077, 2080, 2081, 2125, 2126, 2133, 2188, 2226, 2247, 2249, 2253, 2254, 2256, 2258, 2259, 2260, 2261, 2262, 2263, 2264, 2265, 2266, 2268, 2269, 2272, 2275, 2277, 2278, 2279, 2280, 2281, 2282, 2283, 2284, 2285, 2287, 2290, 2296, 2302, 2307, 2314, 2315, 2316, 2323, 2329, 2330, 2334, 2342, 2346, 2354, 2358, 2359, 2374, 2386, 2390, 2394, 2396, 2398, 2423, B3625, B3812, C3915

Business Law, 2248

Criminal Justice, 69, 2248, 2250, 2252, 2270, 2271, 2291, 2292, 2293, 2294, 2295, 2340

Environmental Law-G, 652, 765, 1387, 1427, 2202, 2281, 2289

International Law, 133, 2276, 2324

Law Enforcement, 69, 2243, 2248, 2250, 2251, 2255, 2257, 2267, 2267, 2270, 2273, 2274, 2286, 2288, 2294, 2295, 2297, 2298, 2299, 2338, 2439, 2439, C3887

POLITICAL SCIENCE

General, 10, 21, 39, 42, 67, 68, 107, 112, 115, 139, 148, 160, 166, 182, 301, 313, 314, 317, 335, 467, 473, 512, 562, 588, 598, 599, 614, 635, 653, 656, 701, 758, 775, 805, 812, 818, 827, 828, 829, 832, 836, 838, 839, 848, 864, 872, 933, 934, 935, 966, 967, 988, 993, 1020, 1021, 1022, 1030, 1037, 1190, 1191, 1208, 1218, 1219, 1220, 1331, 1354, 1355, 1365, 1384, 1407, 1457, 1458, 1461, 1462, 1463, 1471, 1509, 1534, 1535, 1563, 1572, 1573, 1594, 1603, 1604, 1614, 1636, 1645, 1657, 1737, 1738, 1742, 1805, 1881, 2074, 2075, 2076, 2080, 2086, 2087, 2088, 2125, 2165, 2179, 2180, 2181, 2188, 2191, 2196, 2216, 2217, 2223, 2224, 2226, 2229, 2235, 2236, 2237, 2243, 2244, 2247, 2253, 2263, 2264, 2272, 2278, 2283, 2286, 2292, 2296, 2300, 2302, 2303, 2304, 2305, 2306, 2307, 2313, 2314, 2315, 2317, 2323, 2325, 2328, 2329, 2331, 2332, 2333, 2334, 2336, 2337, 2338, 2339, 2340, 2342, 2345, 2346, 2347, 2348, 2354, 2359, 2365, 2366, 2367, 2374, 2375, 2376, 2386, 2396, 2399, 2400, 2401, 2629, 3494, B3671

Arms Control-G, 39, 182, 467, 653, 1645, 2296, 2342

Foreign Policy, 855, 872, 1030, 2244, 2322, 2339, 2343, 2344

Government, 21, 112, 139, 145, 146, 148, 153, 194, 251, 544, 545, 758, 805, 842, 850, 1384, 2078, 2165, 2188, 2219, 2225, 2229, 2264, 2279, 2283, 2308, 2312, 2315, 2319, 2325, 2326, 2327, 2328, 2330, 2334, 2341, 2378, 2392, 2393, 2398

International Relations, 7, 39, 93, 133, 182, 327, 467, 653, 851, 855, 872, 1030, 1045, 1645, 2110, 2244, 2276, 2296, 2310, 2311, 2321, 2322, 2324, 2339, 2342, 2343, 2344

International Peace & Security-G, 39, 182, 467, 653, 1645, 2296, 2342

National Security/Defense, 39, 182, 467, 653, 1645, 2296, 2342

Public Policy, 90, 112, 119, 158, 181, 553, 1303, 1423, 2189, 2264, 2309, 2315, 2318, 2335, 2388, C3854

Public Service, 90, 113, 145, 146, 148, 153, 244, 544, 545, 819, 842, 989, 2078, 2081, 2126, 2165, 2219, 2265, 2279, 2292, 2308, 2309, 2312, 2316, 2320, 2326, 2327, 2328, 2330, 2340, 2341, 2378, 2389, 2392, 2393, 2398, C3854

US-Israel Issues, 2301

PSYCHOLOGY

General, 42, 67, 68, 108, 129, 147, 257, 301, 313, 314, 357, 473, 512, 527, 546, 562, 588, 598, 599, 609, 656, 686, 701, 726, 775, 812, 818, 820, 827, 828, 829, 832, 836, 837, 838, 839, 848, 864, 933, 934, 935, 966, 967, 988, 1020, 1021, 1022, 1037, 1190, 1191, 1208, 1218, 1219, 1220, 1283, 1331, 1354, 1355, 1457, 1458, 1461, 1462, 1463, 1471, 1534, 1535, 1547, 1563, 1572, 1573, 1594, 1603, 1604, 1663, 1665, 1686, 1737, 1738, 1749, 1772, 1810, 1910, 1920, 1968, 1971, 1990, 2005, 2074, 2075, 2076, 2080, 2086, 2087, 2088, 2089, 2123, 2125, 2179, 2180, 2181, 2216, 2217, 2235, 2236, 2237, 2247, 2263, 2277, 2278, 2300, 2302, 2305, 2306, 2314, 2329, 2331, 2332, 2333, 2345, 2346, 2347, 2348, 2349, 2351, 2353, 2354, 2355, 2356, 2357, 2358, 2359, 2365, 2366, 2367, 2368, 2374, 2375, 2376, 2386, 2394, 2396, 2399, 2400, 2401, 2402, 2451, C3956

Behavioral Science-G, 174, 461, 555, 585, 698, 764, 806, 1665, 1810, 1971, 2351, 2371, 2404

Clinical Psychology, 278, 279, 280, 1690, 1691, 1692, 1827, 1828, 1829, 1926, 1927, 1928, 2362, 2363, 2364

Counseling, 2373

Counseling Psychology-G, 2373

Developmental Disabilities-G, 278, 279, 288, 1690, 1691, 1827, 1828, 1831, 1926, 1927, 2362, 2363, 2370, B3735, C3879

Human Sexuality, 2369

Mental Health, 278, 279, 280, 1690, 1691, 1692, 1827, 1828, 1829, 1926, 1927, 1928, 2362, 2363, 2364

Parapsychology, 2360, 2361, B3707

Rehabilitation Counseling, 212, 229, 278, 279, 280, 1665, 1690, 1691, 1692, 1810, 1827, 1828, 1829, 1888, 1926, 1927, 1928, 1971, 2350, 2351, 2362, 2363, 2364, 2382, B3667, C3960

Sports Psychology, 98, 184, 298, 1892, 1940, 2120, 2214, 2352, 2372, 2383, 2407

SOCIOLOGY

General, 67, 68, 275, 313, 314, 583, 598, 599, 747, 799, 812, 818, 825, 827, 828, 829, 836, 838, 839, 848, 864, 933, 934, 935, 966, 967, 988, 1020, 1021, 1022, 1148, 1190, 1191, 1208, 1215, 1218, 1219, 1220, 1241, 1292, 1354, 1355, 1374, 1413, 1444, 1457, 1458, 1461, 1462, 1463, 1534, 1535, 1552, 1572, 1573, 1588, 1603, 1604, 1628, 1737, 1738, 2074, 2075, 2076, 2080, 2086, 2087, 2088, 2089, 2125, 2171, 2179, 2180, 2181, 2216, 2217, 2235, 2236, 2237, 2247, 2263, 2278, 2302, 2305, 2306, 2314, 2329, 2331, 2332, 2333, 2346, 2347, 2348, 2354, 2359, 2365, 2366, 2367, 2368, 2374, 2375, 2376, 2386, 2395, 2396, 2397, 2399, 2400, 2401, 2402, C3967

Social Service, 119, 147, 192, 228, 253, 357, 546, 842, 854, 1401, 1666, 1686, 1751, 1772, 1813, 1894, 1920, 1973, 2005, 2078, 2219, 2277, 2308, 2318, 2320, 2358, 2378, 2380, 2384, 2388, 2389, 2391, 2394

Social Work, 147, 175, 176, 192, 228, 229, 252, 253, 357, 546, 651, 842, 854, 1198, 1221, 1401, 1544, 1579, 1616, 1666, 1667, 1673, 1686, 1701, 1703, 1751, 1753, 1762, 1772, 1785, 1787, 1813, 1815, 1818, 1835, 1836, 1887, 1888, 1894, 1898, 1904, 1920, 1936, 1937, 1966, 1973, 1976, 1984, 2005, 2028, 2029, 2070, 2071, 2078, 2133, 2219, 2269, 2277, 2308, 2350, 2358, 2377, 2378, 2379, 2380, 2381, 2382, 2384, 2385, 2390, 2391, 2394, 2403, 2405, 2406, C3966

Sports Sociology, 98, 184, 298, 1892, 1940, 2120, 2214, 2352, 2372, 2383, 2407

Urban Affairs, 117, 145, 146, 153, 174, 461, 544, 545, 555, 585, 698, 764, 806, 2279, 2293, 2326, 2327, 2330, 2371, 2387, 2392, 2393, 2398, 2404, 2440

SCHOOL OF VOCATIONAL ED

General, 292, 323, 721, 948, 1029, 1058, 1128, 1173, 1267, 1512, 1640, 1679, 1766, 1885, 1911, 1993, 2090, 2424, 2428, 2448, 2449, 2453, 2470, 2471, 2491, 2610, 2677, 2684, 2685, 2968, 3252, 3489, 3506, C3837

Aerospace Studies, 353, 479, 499, 502, 1498, 1596, 2231, 2415, 2425, 2427, 2458, 2459, B3615, B3691, C3844, C3847

Auto Mechanics, 185, 725, 772, 1432, 2435, 2475, B3638

Aviation Maintenance Technology, 43, 70, 96, 130, 150, 472, 476, 483, 484, 488, 489, 497, 498, 499, 504, 508, 511, 766, 2408, 2409, 2419, 2420, 2422, 2425, 2427, 2431, 2438, 2454, 2456, 2458, 2462, 2464, 2465, 2469, 2472, 2473, B3615, B3691, B3693, B3804, C3832, C3844, C3845, C3846, C3847, C3917

Baking Science, 2041, 2416

Bartending, B3634, B3764, C3848, C3849

Blacksmithing, 904, 2436

Computer Technology, 8, 77, 92, 95, 97, 165, 303, 589, 604, 605, 681, 722, 761, 943, 945, 1229, 1342, 1434, 1474, 1521, 1565, 1649, 1719, 1797, 1858, 1891, 1946, 2068, 2118, 2185, 2193, 2412, 2429, 2430, 2432, 2466, 2468, B3734, C3866

Cosmetology/Barber, 2410, 2414, 2463, C3869

Electrician, 2460

Fire Service, 117, 1908, 2267, 2267, 2387, 2439, 2439, 2440, 2450, C3890

Flight Attendants, B3693, C3832

Food Service, 13, 14, 15, 16, 38, 121, 122, 123, 124, 337, 338, 339, 340, 615, 616, 617, 618, 1530, 2047, 2048, 2055, 2056, 2057, 2058, 2062, 2063, 2064, 2065, 2067, 2418, 2433, 2441, 2444, 2445, 2446, 2447, C3849, C3894

Funeral Service, 2411, C3898

Gemology, 904, 917, 998, 1132, 2434, 2436, 2457, C3836, C3899

Guide, 163, 554, 584, 760, 1027, 1159, 1305, 1386, 1426, 1449, 1468, 1557, 2242, 2467

Maintenance Engineering, 766, 2416, 2472

Musical Instruments, 908, 961, 1065, 1066, 1102, 1114, 1128, 1155, 1182, 1679, 1766, 1911, 1993, 2413, 2443, 2453

Paralegal, 5, 8, 78, 97, 129, 190, 217, 257, 319, 602, 813, 820, 1283, 1481, 1537, 1547, 1608, 1658, 1743, 1891, 1990, 2077, 2254, 2355, 2423, 2432, 2451, B3752

Pilot Training, 43, 70, 96, 130, 150, 476, 477, 483, 484, 485, 487, 488, 489, 497, 499, 503, 504, 508, 511, 737, 2409, 2419, 2420, 2421, 2425, 2426, 2427, 2431, 2438, 2452, 2454, 2458, 2461, 2462, 2469, 2473, B3615, B3691, B3803, B3804, C3844, C3845, C3847, C3917

Secretarial School, 8, 97, 1891, 2432, 2455, C3965

Truckdriving, 185, 766, 772, 1432, 2472, 2475, C3971, C3972

Vertical Flight, 70, 130, 484, 497, 498, 499, 509, 2420, 2454, 2456, 2458, 2474, B3691, C3845, C3846, C3917

Welding, 715, 727, 733, 2417, 2437, 2442, C3981

Scholarships and Award Listings

SCHOOL OF BUSINESS

1—AMERICAN HEALTH AND BEAUTY AIDS INSTITUTE (Fred Luster, Sr. Education Foundation Scholarships for College-Bound High School Seniors)

401 North Michigan Ave.
Chicago IL 60611-4267
312/644-6610

AMOUNT: $250 and $500
DEADLINE(S): APR 15
FIELD(S): Chemistry, Business, or
    Engineering

For college-bound high school seniors who will be enrolled as a college freshman in a four-year college majoring in chemistry, business, or engineering. 3.0 GPA required.

Send two letters of recommendation (one from a school official) and high school transcript. Scholastic record, school activities, and extracurricular activities considered.

2—AMERICAN INDIAN SCIENCE AND ENGINEERING SOCIETY (Burlington Northern Santa Fe Pacific Foundation Scholarships)

P.O. Box 9828
Albuquerque NM 87119-9828
505/765-1052
FAX: 505/765-5608
E-mail: scholarships@aises.org
Internet: www.aises.org/scholarships

AMOUNT: $2,500/yr.
DEADLINE(S): MAR 31
FIELD(S): Business, Education, Science,
    Engineering, Health Administration

Open to high school seniors who are at least 1/4 American Indian. Must reside in KS, OK, CO, AZ, NM, MN, ND, OR, SD, WA, MT, or San Bernardino County, CA (Burlington Northern and Santa Fe Pacific service areas). Must demonstrate financial need.

5 awards annually. Renewable up to 4 years. See website or contact Patricia Browne for an application.

3—BEDDING PLANTS FOUNDATION, INC. (Harold Bettinger Memorial Scholarship)

P.O. Box 280
East Lansing MI 48826-0280
517/333-4617
FAX: 517/333-4494
E-mail: BPFI@aol.com
Internet: www.bpfi.org

AMOUNT: $1,000
DEADLINE(S): MAY 15
FIELD(S): Horticulture AND
    Business/Marketing

Open to graduate and undergraduate students already attending a four-year college/university who have either a horticulture major with business/marketing emphasis OR a business/marketing major with horticulture emphasis. Cash award, with checks issued jointly in name of recipient and college/institution he or she will attend for current year. Must submit references & transcripts.

1 award annually. See website or send printed self-addressed mailing label (or self-addressed, stamped envelope) to BPFI after January 1st for an application. Recipient will be notified.

4—BEDDING PLANTS FOUNDATION, INC. (Jerry Wilmot Scholarship)

P.O. Box 280
East Lansing MI 48826-0280
517/333-4617
FAX: 517/333-4494
E-mail: BPFI@aol.com
Internet: www.bpfi.org

AMOUNT: $2,000
DEADLINE(S): MAY 15
FIELD(S): Horticulture AND
    Business/Finance; Garden Center
    Management

Open to undergraduate students already attending a four-year college/university who have either a major in horticulture with business/finance emphasis OR have a major in business/finance with horticulture emphasis. Should wish to pursue a career in garden center management. Cash award, with checks issued jointly in name of recipient and college/institution he or she will attend for current year. Must submit references & transcripts.

1 award annually. See website or send printed self-addressed mailing label (or self-addressed, stamped envelope) to BPFI after January 1st for an application. Recipient will be notified.

5—BUSINESS & PROFESSIONAL WOMEN'S FOUNDATION (BPW Career Advancement Scholarship Program)

2012 Massachusetts Ave. NW
Washington DC 20036-1070
202/293-1200, ext. 169
FAX: 202/861-0298
Internet: www.bpwusa.org

AMOUNT: $500-$1,000
DEADLINE(S): APR 15
FIELD(S): Biology, Science, Education,
    Engineering, Social Science, Paralegal,
    Humanities, Business, Math,
    Computers, Law, MD, DD

For women (US citizens) aged 25+ accepted into accredited program at US institution (+Puerto Rico & Virgin Islands). Must graduate within 12 to 24 months from the date of grant and demonstrate critical financial need. Must have a plan to upgrade skills, train for a new career field, or to enter/re-enter the job market.

Full- or part-time study. For info see website or send business-sized, self-addressed, double-stamped envelope.

6—CAREER OPPORTUNITIES FOR YOUTH, INC. (Collegiate Scholarship Program)

P.O. Box 996
Manhattan Beach CA 90266
310/535-4838

AMOUNT: $250 to $1,000
DEADLINE(S): SEP 30
FIELD(S): Engineering, Science,
    Mathematics, Computer Science,
    Business Administration, Education,
    Nursing

For students of Latino/Hispanic background residing in the Southern California area who have completed at least one semester/quarter of study at an accredited four-year university. Must have a comulative GPA of 2.5 or higher.

Priority will be given to students who demonstrate financial need. Send SASE to above location for details.

7—CUBAN AMERICAN NATIONAL FOUNDATION (The Mas Family Scholarships)

7300 NW 35 Terrace
Miami FL 33122
305/592-7768
FAX: 305/592-7889
E-mail: canfnet.org
Internet: www.canfnet.org

AMOUNT: Individually negotiated
DEADLINE(S): MAR 15
FIELD(S): Engineering, Business,

International Relations, Economics, Communications, Journalism

For Cuban-American students, graduates, and undergraduates, born in Cuba or direct descendants of those who left Cuba. Must be in top 10% of high school class or maintain a 3.5 GPA in college.

10,000 awards/year. Recipients may re-apply for subsequent years. Financial need considered along with academic success, SAT and GRE scores, and leadership potential. Essays and proof of Cuban descent required.

8—EMPIRE COLLEGE (Dean's Scholarship)

3035 Cleveland Ave.
Santa Rosa CA 95403
707/546-4000
FAX: 707/546-4058

AMOUNT: $250-$1,500
DEADLINE(S): APR 15
FIELD(S): Accounting, Secretarial, Legal, Medical (Clinical & Administrative), Travel & Tourism, General Businessm, Computer Assembly, Network Assembly/Administration

Open to high school seniors who plan to attend Empire College. Must be US citizen.

10 awards annually. Contact Ms. Mary Farha for an application.

9—FEDERAL HIGHWAY ADMINISTRATION, DEPT OF TRANSPORTATION (Grants for Research Fellowships)

6300 Georgetown Pike
McLean VA 22101-2296
703/285-2781

AMOUNT: Tuition + stipend (depends on academic level) plus round-trip travel expenses
DEADLINE(S): FEB 1
FIELD(S): Highway transportation and related disciplines

Open to undergraduate and graduate students at accredited schools. Legal residency, citizenship, or verified intent to become citizen is required.

Students applying for awards must submit applications through their faculty advisors and be nominated for awards by their respective universities.

10—HILLSDALE COLLEGE (Freedom as Vocation Scholarship)

33 E. College Street
Hillsdale MI 49242-1298
517/437-7341
Internet: www.hillsdale.edu

AMOUNT: Varies
DEADLINE(S): None
FIELD(S): Business, History, Political Science, Economics

Open to Hillsdale College undergraduates who maintain a minimum 3.0 GPA and commit to a series of courses in the above fields. Student must rank in top 20% of class and top 10% of test scores. Must possess excellent communications, public speaking, and leadership skills and demonstrate outstanding character and citizenship. Financial need NOT a factor.

Renewable. No application process; students are selected. See website for details.

11—HOPI TRIBE (Priority Scholarships)

P.O. Box 123
Kykotsmovi AZ 86039
520/734-2441, ext. 520
800/762-9630
FAX: 520/734-2435

AMOUNT: Varies
DEADLINE(S): JUL 31
FIELD(S): Law, Natural Resources, Education, Medicine/Health, Engineering, Business

Open to enrolled members of the Hopi Tribe studying in one of the fields listed above, which are considered to be areas of priority interest to the Hopis. Available to college juniors, seniors, and graduate students. Program is to encourage graduates to apply their degrees to Hopi Tribal Goals and Objectives.

Contact Hopi Tribe for an application.

12—JC PENNEY (Scholarship Program)

Corporate Headquarters
Plano TX 75023
972/431-1347
Internet: www.jcpenneyinc.com

AMOUNT: $1,500
DEADLINE(S): Varies
FIELD(S): Business, Merchandising, Retail Studies, Information Systems

For undergraduates in above fields. Must be dependent children of or associates who are employed at JC Penney both at the time of applying for the scholarships and at the time of awarding the scholarships—or can be dependents of deceased/retired associates having three continuous years of service.

128 one-time awards. Current recipients may reapply as long as the scholarship program is offered at their school. The campuses which offer this scholarship are the 32 colleges where JC Penney recruits new management trainees—campuses

reevaluted each year. Contact your (participating) school for an application or visit your local JC Penney store.

13—JOHNSON AND WALES UNIVERSITY (Annual Johnson & Wales University National High School Recipe Contest)

8 Abbott Place
Providence RI 02903
401/598-2345

AMOUNT: $1,000 to $5,000
DEADLINE(S): JAN 31
FIELD(S): Business, Hospitality, Technology, Culinary Arts

For students planning to attend Johnson & Wales University, Providence, Rhode Island.

Write to above address for detailed description.

14—JOHNSON AND WALES UNIVERSITY (Gilbane Building Company Eagle Scout Scholarship)

8 Abbott Place
Providence RI 02903
401/598-2345

AMOUNT: $1,200
DEADLINE(S): None
FIELD(S): Business, Hospitality, Technology, Culinary Arts

For students attending Johnson & Wales University, Providence, Rhode Island. Must be Eagle Scouts.

Send letter of recommendation and transcript to above address.

15—JOHNSON AND WALES UNIVERSITY (National High School Entrepreneur of the Year Contest)

8 Abbott Place
Providence RI 02903
401/598-2345

AMOUNT: $1,000 to $10,000
DEADLINE(S): DEC 27
FIELD(S): Business, Hospitality, Technology, Culinary Arts

For students attending Johnson & Wales University, Providence, Rhode Island.

Send for detailed description to above address.

16—JOHNSON AND WALES UNIVERSITY (Scholarships)

8 Abbott Place
Providence RI 02903
401/598-2345

AMOUNT: $200 to $10,000
DEADLINE(S): None
FIELD(S): Business, Hospitality,
   Technology, Culinary Arts

For students attending Johnson &
Wales University, Providence, Rhode
Island.

Renewable for four years. Write for
complete information.

17—JUNIATA COLLEGE (Anna Groninger Smith Memorial Scholarship)

Financial Aid Office
Huntingdon PA 16652
814/641-3603
FAX: 814/641-3355
E-mail: clarkec@juniata.edu

AMOUNT: $4,000 (max.)
DEADLINE(S): APR 1
FIELD(S): Business

Open to females in business studies
applying to Juniata College. Must demonstrate financial need and fill out government FAFSA form.

Contact Cynthia G. Clarke, Research
Specialist, for an application or enrollment
information. See your financial aid office
for FAFSA.

18—NATIONAL ITALIAN AMERICAN FOUNDATION (George L. Graziado Fellowship for Business)

1860 19th Street NW
Washington DC 20009
202/530-5315

AMOUNT: $2,500 and $5,000
DEADLINE(S): MAY 30
FIELD(S): Business and Management

Open to undergraduate American stu-
dents of Italian ancestry studying at the
George L. Graziado School of Business and
Management at Pepperdine University,
California.

2 awards given. Academic merit, financial need, and community service are considered. Contact organization for application and details.

19—NATIONAL ITALIAN AMERICAN FOUNDATION (Norman R. Peterson Scholarship)

1860 19th Street NW
Washington DC 20009
202/530-5315

AMOUNT: One is $5,000; one is $2,500
DEADLINE(S): MAY 31
FIELD(S): Business/finance/economics

For undergraduate American students
from the mid-west (Michigan-based) of
Italian ancestry for study at John Cabot
University in Rome.

For info contact: Francesca Gleason,
Director of Admissions at 011-39-6-687-
8881.

20—NATIVE AMERICAN SCHOLARSHIP FUND, INC. (Scholarships)

8200 Mountain Rd., NE, Suite 203
Albuquerque NM 87110
505/262-2351
FAX: 505/262-0543
E-mail: NScholarsh@aol.com

AMOUNT: Varies
DEADLINE(S): MAR 15; APR 15; SEP 15
FIELD(S): Math, Engineering, Science,
   Business, Education, Computer Science

Open to American Indians or Alaskan
Natives (1/4 degree or more) enrolled as
members of a federally recognized, state
recognized, or terminated tribe. For graduate or undergraduate study at an accredited four-year college or university.

208 awards annually. Contact Lucille
Kelley, Director of Recruitment, for an
application.

21—SOCIETY OF SATELLITE PROFESSIONALS INTERNATIONAL (SSPI Scholarships)

225 Reinekers Lane, Suite 600
Alexandria VA 22314
703/857-3717
FAX: 703/857-6335
E-mail: neworbit@aol.com
Internet: www.sspi.org

AMOUNT: $1,500 to $4,000
DEADLINE(S): DEC 1
FIELD(S): Satellites as related to
   communications, domestic and
   international telecommunications
   policy, remote sensing, journalism, law,
   meteorology, energy, navigation,
   business, government, and
   broadcasting services.

Various scholarships for students
studying in the above fields.

Access website for details and applications or send a self-addressed, stamped
envelope (SASE) for a complete listing.

22—SRP/NAVAJO GENERATING STATION (Navajo Scholarship)

P.O. Box 850
Page AZ 86040

520/645-6539
FAX: 520/645-7295
E-mail: ljdawave@srp.gov

AMOUNT: Based on need
DEADLINE(S): APR 30
FIELD(S): Engineering, Environmental
   Studies, Business, Business
   Management, Health, Education

Scholarships for full-time students who
hold membership in the Navajo Tribe and
who are pursuing a degree in a field of
study recognized as significant to the
Navajo Nation, Salt River Project, or the
Navajo Generating Station, such as those
listed above. Must be junior or senior, have
and maintain a GPA of 3.0.

Average of 15 awards per year. Inquire
of Linda Dawavendewa at above location.

23—THE GRAND RAPIDS FOUNDATION (Economic Club of Grand Rapids Scholarship)

209-C Waters Bldg.
161 Ottawa Ave. NW
Grand Rapids MI 49503-2703
616/454-1751; 616/454-6455

AMOUNT: Varies
DEADLINE(S): APR 3
FIELD(S): Business

Open to full-time undergraduate students pursuing a degree in business at an
accredited college. Must have been a resident of Kent or Ottawa Counties in
Michigan for a minimum of 3 years and
have at least a 3.0 GPA.

Send SASE to above address for complete information.

24—TYSON FOUNDATION, INC. (Alabama Scholarship Program)

2210 W. Oaklawn
Springdale AR 72762-6999
501/290-4995

AMOUNT: Varies (according to need)
DEADLINE(S): FEB 28
FIELD(S): Business, Agriculture,
   Engineering, Computer Science,
   Nursing

Open to residents of the general areas
of Albertville, Ashland, Blountsville,
Gadsden, Heflin, or Oxford, Alabama,
who are US citizens and live in the vicinity
of a Tyson facility. Must be pursuing full-
time undergraduate study at an accredited
US institution and demonstrate financial
need. Must also be employed part-time
and/or summers to help fund education.

Renewable up to 8 semesters or 12
trimesters as long as student meets criteria.

Contact Tyson Foundation for an application no later than last day of February; deadline to return application is April 20th.

25—TYSON FOUNDATION, INC. (Arkansas Scholarship Program)

2210 W. Oaklawn
Springdale AR 72762-6999
501/290-4955

AMOUNT: Varies (according to need)
DEADLINE(S): FEB 28
FIELD(S): Business, Agriculture,
Engineering, Computer Science,
Nursing

Open to Arkansas residents who are US citizens pursuing full-time undergraduate study at an accredited US institution. Must demonstrate financial need and be employed part-time and/or summers to help fund education.

Renewable up to 8 semesters or 12 trimesters as long as student meets criteria. Contact Tyson Foundation for an application no later than last day of February; deadline to return application is April 20th.

26—TYSON FOUNDATION, INC. (Florida Scholarship Program)

2210 W. Oaklawn
Springdale AR 72762-6999
501/290-4995

AMOUNT: Varies (according to need)
DEADLINE(S): FEB 28
FIELD(S): Business, Agriculture,
Engineering, Computer Science,
Nursing

Open to residents of the general area of Jacksonville, Florida, who are US citizens and live in the vicinity of a Tyson facility. Must be pursuing full-time undergraduate study in an accredited US institution and demonstrate financial need. Must also be employed part-time and/or summers to help fund education.

Renewable up to 8 semesters or 12 trimesters as long as student meets criteria. Contact Tyson Foundation for an application no later than last day of February; deadline to return application is April 20th.

27—TYSON FOUNDATION, INC. (Georgia Scholarship Program)

2210 W. Oaklawn
Springdale AR 72762-6999
501/290-4995

AMOUNT: Varies (according to need)

DEADLINE(S): FEB 28
FIELD(S): Business, Agriculture,
Engineering, Computer Science,
Nursing

Open to residents of the general areas of Cumming, Buena Vista, Dawson, or Vienna, Georgia, who are US citizens and live in the vicinity of a Tyson facility. Must be pursuing full-time undergraduate study in an accredited US institution and demonstrate financial need. Must also be employed part-time and/or summers to help fund education.

Renewable up to 8 semesters or 12 trimesters as long as student meets criteria. Contact Tyson Foundation for an application no later than last day of February; deadline to return application is April 20th.

28—TYSON FOUNDATION, INC. (Illinois Scholarship Program)

2210 W. Oaklawn
Springdale AR 72762-6999
501/290-4995

AMOUNT: Varies (according to need)
DEADLINE(S): FEB 28
FIELD(S): Business, Agriculture,
Engineering, Computer Science,
Nursing

Open to residents of the general area of Chicago, Illinois, who are US citizens and live in the vicinity of a Tyson facility. Must be pursuing full-time undergraduate study in an accredited US institution and demonstrate financial need. Must also be employed part-time and/or summers to help fund education.

Renewable up to 8 semesters or 12 trimesters as long as student meets criteria. Contact Tyson Foundation for an application no later than last day of February; deadline to return application is April 20th.

29—TYSON FOUNDATION, INC. (Indiana Scholarship Program)

2210 W. Oaklawn
Springdale AR 72762-6999
501/290-4995

AMOUNT: Varies (according to need)
DEADLINE(S): FEB 28
FIELD(S): Business, Agriculture,
Engineering, Computer Science,
Nursing

Open to residents of the general areas of Portland or Corydon, Indiana, who are US citizens and live in the vicinity of a Tyson facility. Must be pursuing full-time undergraduate study at an accredited US

institution and demonstrate financial need. Must also be employed part-time and/or summers to help fund education.

Renewable up to 8 semesters or 12 trimesters as long as student meets criteria. Contact Tyson Foundation for an application no later than last day of February; deadline to return application is April 20th.

30—TYSON FOUNDATION, INC. (Mississippi Scholarship Program)

2210 W. Oaklawn
Springdale AR 72762-6999
501/290-4995

AMOUNT: Varies (according to need)
DEADLINE(S): FEB 28
FIELD(S): Business, Agriculture,
Engineering, Computer Science,
Nursing

Open to residents of the general areas of Cleveland, Jackson, Forest, or Vicksburg, Mississippi, who are US citizens and live in the vicinity of a Tyson facility. Must be pursuing full-time undergraduate study in an accredited US institution and demonstrate financial need. Must also be employed part-time and/or summers to help fund education.

Renewable up to 8 semesters or 12 trimesters as long as student meets criteria. Contact Tyson Foundation for an application no later than last day of February; deadline to return application is April 20th.

31—TYSON FOUNDATION, INC. (Missouri Scholarship Program)

2210 W. Oaklawn
Springdale AR 72762-6999
501/290-4995

AMOUNT: Varies (according to need)
DEADLINE(S): FEB 28
FIELD(S): Business, Agriculture,
Engineering, Computer Science,
Nursing

Open to residents of the general areas of Dexter, Monett, Neosho, Noel, or Sedalia, Missouri, who are US citizens and live in the vicinity of a Tyson facility. Must be pursuing full-time undergraduate study in an accredited US institution and demonstrate financial need. Must also be employed part-time and/or summers to help fund education.

Renewable up to 8 semesters or 12 trimesters as long as student meets criteria. Contact Tyson Foundation for an application no later than last day of February; deadline to return application is April 20th.

32—TYSON FOUNDATION, INC. (North Carolina Scholarship Program)

2210 W. Oaklawn
Springdale AR 72762-6999
501/290-4995

AMOUNT: Varies (according to need)
DEADLINE(S): FEB 28
FIELD(S): Business, Agriculture, Engineering, Computer Science, Nursing

Open to residents of the general areas of Creswell, Monroe, Sanford, or Wilkesboro, North Carolina, who are US citizens and live in the vicinity of a Tyson facility. Must be pursuing full-time undergraduate study in an accredited US institution and demonstrate financial need. Must also be employed part-time and/or summers to help fund education.

Renewable up to 8 semesters or 12 trimesters as long as student meets criteria. Contact Tyson Foundation for an application no later than the last day of February; deadline to return application is April 20th.

33—TYSON FOUNDATION, INC. (Oklahoma Scholarship Program)

2210 W. Oaklawn
Springdale AR 72762-6999
501/290-4995

AMOUNT: Varies (according to need)
DEADLINE(S): FEB 28
FIELD(S): Business, Agriculture, Engineering, Computer Science, Nursing

Open to residents of the general areas of Broken Bow or Stillwell, Oklahoma, who are US citizens and live in the vicinity of a Tyson facility. Must be pursuing full-time undergraduate study in an accredited US institution and demonstrate financial need. Must also be employed part-time and/or summers to help fund education.

Renewable up to 8 semesters or 12 trimesters as long as student meets criteria. Contact Tyson Foundation for an application no later than last day of February; deadline to return application is April 20th.

34—TYSON FOUNDATION, INC. (Pennsylvania Scholarship Program)

2210 W. Oaklawn
Springdale AR 72762-6999
501/290-4995

AMOUNT: Varies (according to need)
DEADLINE(S): FEB 28
FIELD(S): Business, Agriculture, Engineering, Computer Science, Nursing

Open to residents of the general area of New Holland, Pennsylvania, who are US citizens and live in the vicinity of a Tyson facility. Must be pursuing full-time undergraduate study in an accredited US institution and demonstrate financial need. Must also be employed part-time and/or summers to help fund education.

Renewable up to 8 semesters or 12 trimesters as long as student meets criteria. Contact Tyson Foundation for an application no later than last day of February; deadline to return application is April 20th.

35—TYSON FOUNDATION, INC. (Tennessee Scholarship Program)

2210 W. Oaklawn
Springdale AR 72762-6999
501/290-4995

AMOUNT: Varies (according to need)
DEADLINE(S): FEB 28
FIELD(S): Business, Agriculture, Engineering, Computer Science, Nursing

Open to residents of the general areas of Shelbyville or Union City, Tennessee, who are US citizens and live in the vicinity of a Tyson facility. Must be pursuing full-time undergraduate study in an accredited US institution and demonstrate financial need. Must also be employed part-time and/or summers to help fund education.

Renewable up to 8 semesters or 12 trimesters as long as student meets criteria. Contact Tyson Foundation for an application no later than last day of February; deadline to return application is April 20th.

36—TYSON FOUNDATION, INC. (Texas Scholarship Program)

2210 W. Oaklawn
Springdale AR 72762-6999
501/290-4995

AMOUNT: Varies (according to need)
DEADLINE(S): FEB 28
FIELD(S): Business, Agriculture, Engineering, Computer Science, Nursing

Open to residents of the general areas of Carthage, Center, or Seguin, Texas, who are US citizens and live in the vicinity of a Tyson facility. Must be pursuing full-time undergraduate study in an accredited US institution and demonstrate financial need. Must also be employed part-time and/or summers to help fund education.

Renewable up to 8 semesters or 12 trimesters as long as student meets criteria. Contact Tyson Foundation for an application no later than last day of February; deadline to return application is April 20th.

37—TYSON FOUNDATION, INC. (Virginia Scholarship Program)

2210 W. Oaklawn
Springdale AR 72762-6999
501/290-4995

AMOUNT: Varies (according to need)
DEADLINE(S): FEB 28
FIELD(S): Business, Agriculture, Engineering, Computer Science, Nursing

Open to residents of the general areas of Glen Allen, Harrisonburg, or Temperanceville, Virginia, who are US citizens and live in the vicinity of a Tyson facility. Must be pursuing full-time undergraduate study in an accredited US institution and demonstrate financial need. Must also be employed part-time and/or summers to help fund education.

Renewable up to 8 semesters or 12 trimesters as long as student meets criteria. Contact Tyson Foundation for an application no later than last day of February; deadline to return application is April 20th.

38—WOMEN GROCERS OF AMERICA (Mary Macey Scholarships)

1825 Samuel Morse Drive
Reston VA 20190-5317
703/437-5300
FAX: 703/437-7768
E-mail: wga@nationalgrocers.org
Internet: www.nationalgrocers.org

AMOUNT: $1,000 (minimum)
DEADLINE(S): JUN 1
FIELD(S): Food Marketing/Management, Food Service Technology, Business Administration as related to the Grocery Industry

For students with a minimum 2.0 GPA attending a US college/university. Must be entering sophomores or continuing students in good standing in a 2-year associate degree or 4-year degree granting institution or a graduate program, planning a career in the grocery industry. Financial need NOT considered.

2+ awards annually. Renewable. See website or contact Anne Wintersteen at above address for an application.

39—WOMEN IN DEFENSE (HORIZONS Scholarship Foundation)

NDIA; 2111 Wilson Blvd., Suite 400
Arlington VA 22201-3061
703/247-2552
FAX: 703/522-1885
E-mail: dnwlee@moon.jic.com
Internet: www.adpa.org/wid/
horizon/Scholar.htm

AMOUNT: $500+
DEADLINE(S): NOV 1; JUL 1
FIELD(S): Engineering, Computer
Science, Physics, Mathematics,
Business, Law, International Relations,
Political Science, Operations Research,
Economics, and fields relevant to a
career in the areas of national security
and defense

For women who are US citizens, have minimum GPA of 3.25, demonstrate financial need, are currently enrolled at an accredited university/college (full- or part-time—both grads and undergrad juniors/seniors are eligible), and demonstrate interest in pursuing a career related to national security.

Application is online or send SASE, #10 envelope, to Woody Lee, HORIZONS Scholarship Director.

40—WOODROW WILSON NATIONAL FELLOWSHIP FOUNDATION/U.S. DEPARTMENTS OF COMMERCE AND AGRICULTURE (Fellowships)

CN 5329
Princeton NJ 08543-5329
609/452-7007
FAX: 609/452-0066
E-mail: richard@woodrow.org
Internet: www.woodrow.org

AMOUNT: Varies
DEADLINE(S): Varies
FIELD(S): Commerce, Agriculture

Open to minority students in the US who are interested in careers in commerce or agriculture.

See website or contact WWNFF for an application.

BUSINESS ADMINISTRATION

41—ACCOUNTING/NET (Account for Your Future Scholarship Program)

600 Stewart Street, Suite 1101
Seattle WA 98101
206/441-8285
FAX: 206/441-8385
E-mail: money@accountingstudents.com
Internet: www.accountingstudents.com

AMOUNT: $1,000
DEADLINE(S): JUN 1
FIELD(S): Accounting

Scholarships for outstanding accounting students, undergraduate and graduate, sponsored by AccountingNet, John Wiley & Sons, and KPMG. Applications are accepted ONLY online.

3 awards annually. See website for details.

42—AIR FORCE RESERVE OFFICER TRAINING CORPS (AFROTC Scholarships)

551 E. Maxwell Blvd.
Maxwell AFB AL 36112-6106
334/953-7783

AMOUNT: Full tuition, books, & fees for
all 4 years of college
DEADLINE(S): DEC 1
FIELD(S): Science, Engineering,
Business, Political Science, Psychology,
Geography, Foreign Studies, Foreign
Language

Competitive scholarships based on individual merit to high school seniors and graduates who have not completed any full-time college work. Must be a US citizen between the ages of 17-27. Must also have GPA of 2.5 or above, be in top 40% of class, and complete Applicant Fitness Test. Cannot be a single parent. Your college/university must offer AFROTC.

2,300 awards annually. Contact above address for application packet.

43—AIRCRAFT ELECTRONICS ASSOCIATION EDUCATIONAL FOUNDATION (Scholarships)

P.O. Box 1963
Independence MO 64055
816/373-6565
FAX: 816/478-3100
Internet: aeaavnews.org

AMOUNT: $1,000-$16,000
DEADLINE(S): Varies
FIELD(S): Avionics, Aircraft Repair

Various scholarships for high school and college students attending post-secondary institutions, including technical schools. Some are for study in Canada or Europe as well as the US.

25 programs. See website or contact AEA for specific details and applications.

44—AIRPORTS COUNCIL INTERNATIONAL (Scholarships)

Southern Illinois. Univ. at Carbondale
Carbondale IL 62901
618/453-8898

AMOUNT: $2,500
DEADLINE(S): NOV 1
FIELD(S): Airport management or
airport administration

Scholarships for undergraduates enrolled in an accredited college or university focusing on a career in airport management. Must have at least a 3.0 GPA. Must reside and attend school in either the US, Canada, Saipan, Bermuda, US Virgin Islands, or Guam.

4 awards yearly. Write ATTN: Aviation Management and Flight Dept., College of Technical Careers, at above address.

45—AIRPORTS COUNCIL INTERNATIONAL-NORTH AMERICA (Commissioners Roundtable Scholarship Program)

1775 K Street NW, Suite 500
Washington DC 20006
202/293-8500
FAX: 202/331-1362

AMOUNT: Up to $2,500
DEADLINE(S): Varies
FIELD(S): Airport management or
airport administration

Scholarships for undergraduates enrolled in an accredited college or university focusing on a career in airport management. Must have at least a 3.0 GPA.

Contact above organization for details.

46—ALASKA VISITORS ASSOCIATION (Various Scholarships)

3201 C Street, Suite 403
Anchorage AK 99503
907/561-5733
FAX: 907/561-5727
E-mail: ava@alaskanet.com
Internet: www.visitalaska.org:/
visitalaska/about/
scholarships.html

AMOUNT: Varies: $500 and up
DEADLINE(S): MAR 31
FIELD(S): Travel and tourism, Hotel
Management

Several scholarship programs available through the Alaska Visitors Association for residents of Alaska pursuing careers in the above fields. Preference given to those studying in Alaska institutions. Must have GPA of at least 3.0.

Access website for details or contact organization.

47—AMERICAN ALLIANCE FOR HEALTH, PHYSICAL EDUCATION, RECREATION & DANCE

1900 Association Drive
Reston VA 20191
703/476-3400 or 800/213-7193
E-mail: webmaster@aahperd.org
Internet: www.aahperd.org

AMOUNT: Varies
DEADLINE(S): Varies
FIELD(S): Health Education, Leisure and Recreation, Girls and Women in Sports, Sport and Physical Education, Dance

This organization has six national sub-organizations specializing in the above fields. Some have grants and fellowships for both individuals and group projects. The website has the details for each group.

Visit website for details or write to above address for details.

48—AMERICAN ASSOCIATION OF ADVERTISING AGENCIES, INC. (Multicultural Advertising Internship Program)

405 Lexington Ave., 8th Fl.
New York NY 10174-1801
212/682-2500 or 1-800/676-9333
FAX: 212/573-8968
E-mail: rhonda@aaaa.org
Internet: www.commercepark.com/AAAA/maip/

AMOUNT: $350/wk. + partial expenses and travel
DEADLINE(S): JAN 30
FIELD(S): Advertising, Marketing, Public Relations

A ten-week summer internship for minorities (African-American, Native American, Hispanic, or Asian) working in the advertising business. Must be US citizen or permanent resident.

Write, call, or access website for application and information.

49—AMERICAN ASSOCIATION OF ADVERTISING AGENCIES, INC. (Multicultural Advertising Internship Program)

405 Lexington Ave., 18th Fl.
New York NY 10174-1801
212/682-2500 or 800/676-9333
FAX: 212/573-8968
E-mail: tiffany@aaaa.org
Internet: www.aaaa.org

AMOUNT: $350/wk. + partial expenses and travel
DEADLINE(S): JAN 22
FIELD(S): Advertising, Marketing, Public Relations

Ten-week summer internship in the US is open to African-Americans, Native Americans, Hispanics, or Asians interested in a career in advertising. Must be US citizen/permanent resident, have a minimum 3.0 GPA, and be a college junior, senior, or graduate student. Internships help students gain practical work experience and prepare them for entry-level positions. Scholarship program is also available for selected creative finishing schools.

75-100 awards annually. See website or contact AAAA for an application.

50—AMERICAN ASSOCIATION OF AIRPORT EXECUTIVES (Scholarships)

4212 King Street
Alexandria VA 22302
703/824-0500
FAX: 703/820-1395
Internet: www.airportnet.org

AMOUNT: $1,000
DEADLINE(S): MAY 15
FIELD(S): Airport management or airport administration

Scholarships for undergraduates who have reached junior standing or higher through graduate school. Selection based on scholastic achievement, financial need, and extracurricular/community activities. Must be focusing on a career in airport management and have at least a 3.0 GPA.

10 awards yearly. Each university may submit one student's application only. APPLY THROUGH YOUR UNIVERSITY.

51—AMERICAN ASSOCIATION OF HISPANIC CERTIFIED PUBLIC ACCOUNTANTS (Scholarships)

100 N. Main Street, Suite 406
San Antonio TX 78205
203/255-7003
FAX: 203/259-2872
E-mail: AAHCPA@netscape.net
Internet: www.aahcpa.org

AMOUNT: Varies
DEADLINE(S): SEP 15
FIELD(S): Accounting

Undergraduates must be of Hispanic descent and have completed or be enrolled in an intermediate-level accounting course. Graduate students must be of Hispanic descent and be enrolled in a program with an accounting emphasis or be in the last year of a 5-year accounting program. All applicants must have a minimum overall 3.0 GPA and be US citizens. Must submit offical transcripts, a letter of recommendation, copy of class schedule, and an essay along with application.

10-40 awards annually. Contact the AAHCPA Scholarship Committee for an application packet.

52—AMERICAN HEALTH AND BEAUTY AIDS INSTITUTE (Fred Luster, Sr. Education Foundation Scholarships for College-Bound High School Seniors)

401 North Michigan Ave.
Chicago IL 60611-4267
312/644-6610

AMOUNT: $250 and $500
DEADLINE(S): APR 15
FIELD(S): Chemistry, Business, or Engineering

For college-bound high school seniors who will be enrolled as a college freshman in a four-year college majoring in chemistry, business, or engineering. 3.0 GPA required.

Send two letters of recommendation (one from a school official) and high school transcript. Scholastic record, school activities, and extracurricular activities considered.

53—AMERICAN HOTEL FOUNDATION (American Express Card Scholarship Program)

1201 New York Ave. NW, Suite 600
Washington DC 20005-3931
202/289-3181
FAX: 202/289-3199
E-mail: ahf@ahma.com
Internet: www.ei-ahma.org

AMOUNT: Up to $2,000
DEADLINE(S): MAR 1
FIELD(S): Hospitality/Hotel Management

For full-time (20 hrs./wk. min.) American Hotel & Motel Association (AH&MA)-member property employees and their dependents enrolled in academic classes to enhance their professional development in the hospitatlity management field. For use at specified schools, either two-year or four-year, or for tuition assistance for distance learning courses and professional certification programs offered through the Educational Institute of AH&MA.

Check website for list of eligible schools. Applications (document #620) available via Fax-on-Demand: 1-800-701-7725. Input document number(s) you are requesting and your fax number.

54—AMERICAN HOTEL FOUNDATION (Arthur J. Packard Memorial Scholarship Competition)

1201 New York Ave. NW, Suite 600
Washington DC 20005-3931
202/289-3181
FAX: 202/289-3199
E-mail: ahf@ahma.com
Internet: www.ei-ahma.org

AMOUNT: $5,000 (1st); $2,000 (2nd); $3,000 (3rd)
DEADLINE(S): None
FIELD(S): Hospitality/Hotel Management

For students pursuing an undergraduate degree in hospitality or hotel management on a full-time basis (minimum 12 hours). For use at specified schools. Recipients are nominated by their colleges. Criteria are academic performance, hospitality work experience, extracurricular involvement, career goals, and financial needs.

Check website for list of eligible schools. Inquire at your dean's office for consideration of the nomination.

55—AMERICAN HOTEL FOUNDATION (Ecolab Scholarship Program)

1201 New York Ave. NW, Suite 600
Washington DC 20005-3931
202/289-3181
FAX: 202/289-3199
E-mail: ahf@ahma.com
Internet: www.ei-ahma.org

AMOUNT: $1,000
DEADLINE(S): JUN 1
FIELD(S): Hospitality/Hotel Management

For students pursuing an A.A. or B.A. degree in hospitality or hotel management on a full-time basis (minimum 12 hours).

12 annual awards. Applications (document #630) are available through Fax-on-Demand at 1-800-701-7725. The requested information will be faxed to you momentarily.

56—AMERICAN HOTEL FOUNDATION (Hyatt Hotel Fund for Minority Lodging Management Students)

1201 New York Ave. NW, Suite 600
Washington DC 20005-3931

202/289-3181
FAX: 202/289-3199
E-mail: ahf@ahma.com
Internet: www.ei-ahma.org

AMOUNT: $2,000
DEADLINE(S): None
FIELD(S): Hospitality/Hotel Management

For minority students pursuing an undergraduate degree in hospitality or hotel management on a full-time basis (minimum 12 hours). For use at specified schools. Recipients are nominated by their colleges. Criteria are academic performance, hospitality work experience, extracurricular involvement, career goals, and financial needs.

Check website for list of eligible schools. Inquire at your dean's office for consideration of the nomination.

57—AMERICAN INSTITUTE OF CERTIFIED PUBLIC ACCOUNTANTS (Undergraduate Minority Scholarships Program)

1211 Avenue of the Americas
New York NY 10036-8775
212/596-6270
FAX: 201/938-3787 (Select document #652)
Internet: www.aicpa.org

AMOUNT: Up to $5,000
DEADLINE(S): JUL 1
FIELD(S): Accounting

Open to full-time undergraduate students (US citizens) whose backgrounds are of African-American, Native American/Alaskan Native, Pacific Islander, or Hispanic origin. Must have declared accounting major, be going to four-year school. have a GPA of at least 3.0, and have completed at least 30 semester hours or equivalent (6 of which must be in accounting). Awards based primarily on merit (from offical transcript); financial need secondary.

Renewable; must reapply each year. Awards sent directly to school. FAFSA must be filled out (800-433-3243) to apply. CPAs not eligible. May be enrolled part-time ONLY IF it's your last semester.

58—AMERICAN INSTITUTE OF POLISH CULTURE (Scholarships)

1440 79th Street Causeway
Suite 117
Miami FL 33141
305/864-2349
FAX: 305/865-5150
E-mail: info@ampolinstitute.org
Internet: www.ampolinstitute.org

AMOUNT: $1,000
DEADLINE(S): FEB 15
FIELD(S): Journalism, Public Relations, Communications

Awards are to encourage young Americans of Polish descent to pursue the above professions. Can be used for full-time study at any accredited American college. Criteria for selection include achievement, talent, and involvement in public life.

$25 processing fee. Renewable. Send self-addressed, stamped envelope to Mrs. Harriet Irsay for an application.

59—AMERICAN INTERCONTINENTAL UNIVERSITY (Emilio Pucci Scholarships)

Admissions Committee
3330 Peachtree Rd. NE
Atlanta GA 30326
404/812-8192 or 1-888/248-7392

AMOUNT: $1,800 (deducted from tuition over 6 quarters)
DEADLINE(S): None
FIELD(S): Fashion Design, Fashion Marketing, Interior Design, Commercial Art, Business Administration, Video Production

Scholarships are for high school seniors who are interested in either a 2-year or 4-year program at one of the campuses of the American Intercontinental University: Atlanta, GA; Los Angeles, CA; London, UK; or Dubai, United Arab Emirates. Scholarship is applied toward tuition.

Write for applications and complete information.

60—AMERICAN MANAGEMENT ASSOCIATION INTERNATIONAL (Operation Enterprise—Business Leadership Training for Young Adults)

1601 Broadway
New York NY 10019
315/824-2000
FAX: 315/824-6710

AMOUNT: Varies
DEADLINE(S): DEC 1; MAR 1
FIELD(S): Management Seminars

Full and partial scholarships are available to high school and college students to attend 6-day Operation Enterprise business training seminars on practical leadership and management skills. Prominent executives serve as guest faculty. Must be over 16 years of age.

Write for complete information. Application procedures include writing an essay and providing transcripts and letters of recommendation.

61—AMERICAN PLANNING ASSOCIATION (Minority Scholarship and Fellowship Programs)

122 South Michigan Ave., Suite 1600
Chicago IL 60605
312/431-9100
FAX: 312/431-9985

AMOUNT: $2,000-$5,000 (grads); $2,500 (undergrads)
DEADLINE(S): MAY 14
FIELD(S): Urban Planning, Community Development, Environmental Sciences, Public Administration, Transportation, or Urban Studies

Scholarships for African-Americans, Hispanics, or Native American students pursing undergraduate degrees in the U.S. in the above fields. Must have completed first year. Fellowships for graduate students. Programs must be approved by the Planning Accreditation Board. US citizenship.

Call or write for complete information.

62—AMERICAN PUBLIC TRANSIT ASSOCIATION (Transit Hall of Fame Scholarships)

1201 New York Ave.
Washington DC 20005
FAX: 202/898-4029
E-mail: dfoth@apta.com
Internet: www.apta.com

AMOUNT: $2,500 or more
DEADLINE(S): None
FIELD(S): Transit-related fields of study

For college juniors, seniors, or graduate students enrolled in a degree program in a fully accredited institution who demonstrate an interest in entering the transit industry. Criteria include interest in the transit field, financial need, leadership characteristics, scholastic ashievement, citizenship, extracurricular activities, and essay, and a brief in-person or telephone interview. Must be nominated by an APTF representative who can oversee an internship program.

Write to above address to inquire about how to be nominated and other information.

63—AMERICAN SOCIETY OF TRAVEL AGENTS (ASTA) FOUNDATION (Student Scholarships)

1101 King Street
Alexandria VA 22314
703/739-2782
FAX: 703/684-8319

E-mail: myriaml@astahq.com
Internet: www.astanet.com

AMOUNT: $200-$3,000
DEADLINE(S): JUN; JUL; DEC
FIELD(S): Travel, Tourism, Hospitality

Various undergraduate and graduate scholarships are available to US and Canadian citizens, permanent residents, and legal aliens. Must have a minimum 2.5 GPA and submit proof of enrollment in travel and tourism courses. Must also submit official statement of tuition amount, letter of recommendation, transcripts, and other specific requirements for individual awards. Financial need usually NOT considered.

30-50 awards annually. Renewable. See website or contact Myriam Lechuga, Manager, for an application and specific award details. Research funds also available to individuals researching travel & tourism topic.

64—AMERICAN SOCIETY OF WOMEN ACCOUNTANTS (Scholarships)

60 Revere Drive, Suite 500
Northbrook IL 60062
800/326-2163 or 847/205-1029
FAX: 847/480-9282
Internet: www.aswa.org/scholarship.html

AMOUNT: $4,000 (1); $3,000 (2); $2,000 (4)
DEADLINE(S): Varies
FIELD(S): Accounting

Scholarships for female accounting majors who are either full- or part-time students. Must have completed a minimum of 60 semester hours or 90 quarter hours and be enrolled in an accredited college, university, or professional school of accounting (which is designated to award a post-baccalaureate Certificate of Accounting). Membership in ASWA not required.

Applications must be made through the local chapter. Call ASWA for the name of a local chapter.

65—APICS EDUCATION AND RESEARCH FOUNDATION (Donald W. Fogarty International Student Paper Competition)

5301 Shawnee Road
Alexandria VA 22312
800/444-2742
FAX: 703/354-8794
E-mail: h_kather@apics.org
Internet: www.apics.org

AMOUNT: $100-$1,700+
DEADLINE(S): MAY 15 (submit papers to a local APICS chapter)
FIELD(S): Production/Operations Management, Resource Management

Awards offered for winning papers on the subject of production and operations management or resource management, including inventory issues. Open to full-time or part-time undergraduate or graduate students; NOT for high school students. Financial need is NOT a factor.

Up to 180 awards annually. For complete information, please call APICS customer service at the above 800 number to request a D.W.F. International Student Paper Competition Manual (item #01002) and the name of a local APICS chapter.

66—APPRAISAL INSTITUTE EDUCATION TRUST (Scholarships)

875 N. Michigan Ave., Suite 2400
Chicago IL 60611-1980
312/335-4100
FAX 312/335-4400
E-mail: ocarreon@appraisalinstitute.org
Internet: www.appraisalinstitute.org

AMOUNT: $3,000 (graduate); $2,000 (undergrad)
DEADLINE(S): MAR 15
FIELD(S): Real Estate Appraisal; Land Economics; Real Estate

Scholarships are for graduate students and undergraduate sophomores, juniors, and seniors attending a college or university full-time. Must be US citizen. Selection is based on academic excellence.

50 awards annually. Contact Olivia Carreon, Project Coordinator, for an application (available in November).

67—ASSOCIATION FOR WOMEN IN SCIENCE EDUCATIONAL FOUNDATION (Dr. Vicki L. Schechtman Scholarship)

1200 New York Ave. NW, Suite 650
Washington DC 20005
202/326-8940 or 800/886-AWIS
E-mail: awis@awis.org
Internet: www.awis.org

AMOUNT: $1,000
DEADLINE(S): JAN 16
FIELD(S): Various Sciences and Social Sciences

For female undergraduate students who are US citizens and have a minimum GPA of 3.0. Summary page, essay describing career aspirations, transcripts, proof of matriculation (if available), and two reference letters required with application.

Scholarships may be used for tuition, books, housing, research, eqipment, etc.

See website or write to above address for an application and more information.

68—ASSOCIATION FOR WOMEN IN SCIENCE EDUCATIONAL FOUNDATION (Ruth Satter Memorial Award)

1200 New York Ave. NW, Suite 650
Washington DC 20005
202/326-8940 or 800/886-AWIS
E-mail: awis@awis.org
Internet: www.awis.org

AMOUNT: $1,000
DEADLINE(S): JAN 16
FIELD(S): Various Sciences and Social
 Sciences

Scholarships for female doctoral students who have interrupted their education three years or more to raise a family. Summary page, description of research project, resume, references, transcripts, biographical sketch, and proof of eligibility from department head required. US citizens may attend any graduate institution; non-citizens must be enrolled in US institutions.

See website or write to above address for more information or an application.

69—ASSOCIATION OF CERTIFIED FRAUD EXAMINERS (Scholarships)

The Gregor Building
716 West Ave.
Austin TX 78701
800/245-3321 or 512/478-9070
FAX: 512/478-9297
E-mail: acfe@tpoint.net
Internet: www.cfenet.com

AMOUNT: $500
DEADLINE(S): MAY 15
FIELD(S): Accounting and/or Criminal
 Justice

Scholarships for full-time graduate or undergraduate students majoring in accounting or criminal justice degree programs. Awards are based on overall academic achievement, three letters of recommendation, and an original 250-word essay explaining why the applicant deserves the award and how fraud awareness will affect his or her professional career development. Also required is a letter of recommendation from a Certified Fraud Examiner or a local CFE Chapter.

Contact organization for applications and further details.

70—AVIATION DISTRIBUTORS AND MANUFACTURERS ASSOCIATION INTERNATIONAL (ADMA International Scholarship Fund)

1900 Arch Street
Philadelphia PA 19103-1498
215/564-3484
FAX: 215/564-2175
E-mail: assnhqt@netaxs.com

AMOUNT: Varies
DEADLINE(S): MAR 15
FIELD(S): Aviation Management,
 Professional Pilot

Open to students seeking a career in aviation management or as a professional pilot. Emphasis may be in general aviation, airway science management, aviation maintenance, flight engineering, or airway a/c systems management.

Applicants must be studying in the aviation field in a four-year school having an aviation program. Write for complete information.

71—AYN RAND INSTITUTE (*Atlas Shrugged* Essay Contest for Undergraduate Business Students)

4640 Admiralty Way, Suite 406
Marina del Rey CA 90292
310/306-9232
FAX: 310/306-4925
E-mail: essay@aynrand.org
Internet: www.aynrand.org/contests

AMOUNT: $5,000-1st prize; $3,000-2nd
 prize; $1,000-3rd prize
DEADLINE(S): FEB 15
FIELD(S): Business

Essay competition for students enrolled in an undergraduate business program. Essays are judged on both style and content. Winning essays must demonstrate an outstanding grasp of the philosophical meaning of Ayn Rand's novel, *Atlas Shrugged*. Length: 1,000 to 1,200 words.

For information, contact your Business Ethics professor or visit the website.

72—BEDDING PLANTS FOUNDATION, INC. (Ed Markham International Scholarship)

P.O. Box 280
East Lansing MI 48826-0280
517/333-4617
FAX: 517/333-4494
E-mail: BPFI@aol.com
Internet: www.bpfi.org

AMOUNT: $1,000
DEADLINE(S): MAY 15

FIELD(S): Horticulture AND
 International Business

Open to graduate and undergraduate students already attending a four-year college/university who are majoring in horticultre or related field. Should wish to further understanding of domestic and international marketing through international horticulturally related study, work, or travel. Cash award, with checks issued jointly in name of recipient and college/institution he or she will attend for current year. Must submit references and transcripts.

1 award annually. See website or send printed self-addressed mailing label (or self-addressed, stamped envelope) to BPFI after January 1st for an application. Recipient will be notified.

73—BEDDING PLANTS FOUNDATION, INC. (Harold Bettinger Memorial Scholarship)

P.O. Box 280
East Lansing MI 48826-0280
517/333-4617
FAX: 517/333-4494
E-mail: BPFI@aol.com
Internet: www.bpfi.org

AMOUNT: $1,000
DEADLINE(S): MAY 15
FIELD(S): Horticulture AND
 Business/Marketing

Open to graduate and undergraduate students already attending a four-year college/university who have either a horticulture major with business/marketing emphasis OR a business/marketing major with horticulture emphasis. Cash award, with checks issued jointly in name of recipient and college/institution he or she will attend for current year. Must submit references and transcripts.

1 award annually. See website or send printed self-addressed mailing label (or self-addressed, stamped envelope) to BPFI after January 1st for an application. Recipient will be notified.

74—BEDDING PLANTS FOUNDATION, INC. (Jerry Wilmot Scholarship)

P.O. Box 280
East Lansing MI 48826-0280
517/333-4617
FAX: 517/333-4494
E-mail: BPFI@aol.com
Internet: www.bpfi.org

AMOUNT: $2,000
DEADLINE(S): MAY 15

FIELD(S): Horticulture AND
Business/Finance, Garden Center
Management

Open to undergraduate students already attending a four-year college/university who have either a major in horticulture with business/finance emphasis OR have a major in business/finance with horticulture emphasis. Should wish to pursue a career in garden center management. Cash award, with checks issued jointly in name of recipient and college/institution he or she will attend for current year. Must submit references and transcripts.

1 award annually. See website or send printed self-addressed mailing label (or self-addressed, stamped envelope) to BPFI after January 1st for an application. Recipient will be notified.

75—BLUES HEAVEN FOUNDATION, INC. (Muddy Waters Scholarship)

2120 S. Michigan Ave.
Chicago IL 60616
312/808-1286

AMOUNT: $2,000
DEADLINE(S): APR 30
FIELD(S): Music, Music Education,
African-American Studies, Folklore,
Performing Arts, Arts Management,
Journalism, Radio/TV/Film

Scholarship is made on a competitive basis with consideration given to scholastic achievement, concentration of studies, and financial need. Applicant must have full-time enrollment status in a Chicago area college/university in at least their first year of undergraduate studies or a graduate program. Scholastic aptitude, extracurricular involvement, grade point average, and financial need are all considered.

Contact Blues Heaven Foundation, Inc. to receive an application between February and April.

76—BUENA VISTA COLLEGE NETWORK (Internships in Film Marketing)

3900 W. Alameda Ave.
Burbank CA 91505-4316
818/567-5000
E-mail: College_Network@studio.
disney.com
AMOUNT: Varies
DEADLINE(S): None
FIELD(S): Fields of study related to the
motion picture industry, including
marketing and promotion

Internships for full-time college students age 18 and up interested in a career in a facet of the motion picture industry.

Must have unlimited access to computer with modem and transportation, be able to work 4-6 hours per week and 2-3 weekends per month. Attend film openings and sneak previews. Evaluate various aspects via an interactive computer system. Compensation ranges from $30 to $60/month. Possible school credit.

Access website by writing "Buena Vista College Network" from Yahoo. Available in most states and parts of Canada. Details, an interactive application, and e-mail access are located on website.

77—BUSINESS & PROFESSIONAL WOMEN'S FOUNDATION (AVON Products Foundation Career Empowerment Scholarship Program)

2012 Massachusetts Ave. NW
Washington DC 20036-1070
202/293-1200, ext. 169
FAX: 202/861-0298
Internet: www.bpwusa.org
AMOUNT: $1,000-$1,500
DEADLINE(S): APR 15
FIELD(S): Business, Accounting,
Computers, Health

For women age 25+ (US citizens) accepted into an accredited program at a Los Angeles County, CA institution or who are residents of Los Angeles County. Must graduate within 12 to 24 months from the date of grant and be currently receiving welfare/public assistance benefits or have stopped receiving benefits within 24 months prior to applying. Must plan to enter/re-enter the workforce or move out of a low wage/obsolete job.

Approx. 40 awards annually. Full- or part-time study. For info see website or send a #10 self-addressed, double-stamped envelope.

78—BUSINESS & PROFESSIONAL WOMEN'S FOUNDATION (BPW Career Advancement Scholarship Program)

2012 Massachusetts Ave. NW
Washington DC 20036-1070
202/293-1200, ext. 169
FAX: 202/861-0298
Internet: www.bpwusa.org
AMOUNT: $500-$1,000
DEADLINE(S): APR 15
FIELD(S): Biology, Science, Education,
Engineering, Social Science, Paralegal,
Humanities, Business, Math,
Computers, Law, MD, DD

For women (US citizens) aged 25+ accepted into accredited program at US

institution (+Puerto Rico and Virgin Islands). Must graduate within 12 to 24 months from the date of grant and demonstrate critical financial need. Must have a plan to upgrade skills, train for a new career field, or to enter/re-enter the job market.

Full- or part-time study. For info see website or send business-sized, self-addressed, double-stamped envelope.

79—CALIFORNIA ASSOCIATION OF REALTORS (CAR Scholarship Foundation)

525 S. Virgil Ave.
Los Angeles CA 90020
213/739-8200
FAX: 213/480-7724
Internet: www.CAR.ORG
AMOUNT: $1,000 (2-year colleges);
$2,000 (4-year colleges)
DEADLINE(S): Varies (three times per
year)
FIELD(S): Real Estate

Open to students who have been legal residents of California for at least one year prior to date of application and have a valid CA driver's license or CA I.D. card. Must have completed at least 12 units prior to submitting applications and be currently enrolled in a minimum of 6 units. Minimum of 2.6 GPA required.

Renewable. Preference to students who show financial need. Contact Cindy O'Toole, CAR Scholarship Coordinator, for an application.

80—CAREER OPPORTUNITIES FOR YOUTH, INC. (Collegiate Scholarship Program)

P.O. Box 996
Manhattan Beach CA 90266
310/535-4838
AMOUNT: $250 to $1,000
DEADLINE(S): SEP 30
FIELD(S): Engineering, Science,
Mathematics, Computer Science,
Business Administration, Education,
Nursing

For students of Latino/Hispanic background residing in the Southern California area who have completed at least one semester/quarter of study at an accredited four-year university. Must have a cumulative GPA of 2.5 or higher.

Priority will be given to students who demonstrate financial need. Send SASE to above location for details.

81—CAS/SOCIETY OF ACTUARIES (Minority Recruiting Program)

475 N. Martingale Road, Suite 800
Schaumburg IL 60173-2226
847/706-3509
FAX: 847/706-3599

AMOUNT: Varies (according to student's needs/credentials)
DEADLINE(S): MAY 1
FIELD(S): Actuarial science

Open to students enrolled in or accepted to accredited colleges/universities and who are members of ethnic minorities that are underrepresented in the actuarial profession, i.e., African Americans, Hispanics, and Native North Americans. Must be a US citizen or legal resident and demonstrate financial need.

Approximately 40 awards annually. Contact above address for an application.

82—CLUB MANAGERS ASSOCIATION OF AMERICA

1733 King Street
Alexandria VA 22314
703/739-9500

AMOUNT: $1,000-$2,000
DEADLINE(S): MAY 1
FIELD(S): Management of clubs

Grants for sophomores, juniors, and seniors specializing in club management at an accredited college or university. Should have 2.5 or better GPA. Awards are not based solely on need.

Send SASE to above location for details.

83—COLLEGE OF INSURANCE (Scholars Award Program)

Financial Aid Office
101 Murray Street
New York NY 10007
212/815-9222
FAX: 212/964-3381
E-mail: FinancialAid@tci.edu
Internet: www.tci.edu

AMOUNT: 40%-100% tuition + room/board in dormitory
DEADLINE(S): MAY
FIELD(S): Insurance, Finance

Awards tenable at the College of Insurance ONLY. Open to US citizens who will be full-time students in a bachelor's degree program. Freshmen awards are based on SAT scores (min. 900) and high school averages; awards for transfer students are based on GPA (2.75+), and number of credits attempted. Financial need is NOT a factor.

43 awards annually. Renewable, depending on grades. Contact Marjorie Melikian at above address for an application.

84—COLORADO SOCIETY OF CPAs EDUCATIONAL FOUNDATION (Scholarships for High School Seniors)

7979 E. Tufts Ave., #500
Denver CO 80237-2843
303/773-2877 or 800/523-9082
Internet: www.cocpa.org

AMOUNT: $1,000
DEADLINE(S): MAR 1
FIELD(S): Accounting

Open to high school seniors in Colorado schools with at least a 3.75 GPA who intend to major in accounting at Colorado colleges/universities which offer accredited accounting programs. Must submit an official transcript, including SAT or ACT scores, and class rank at end of 1st semester, senior year.

See website or contact Gena Mantz at above location for an application.

85—COLORADO SOCIETY OF CPAs EDUCATIONAL FOUNDATION (Gordon Scheer Scholarship)

7979 E. Tufts Ave., #500
Denver CO 80237-2843
303/773-2877 or 800/523-9082
Internet: www.cocpa.org

AMOUNT: $1,250
DEADLINE(S): JUN 30
FIELD(S): Accounting

For undergraduates who have completed intermediate accounting, have a 3.5 or better GPA, and are majoring in accounting at a Colorado college or university offering accredited accounting majors.

Renewable with reapplication. See website or contact Gena Mantz at above location for an application.

86—COLORADO SOCIETY OF CPAs EDUCATIONAL FOUNDATION (Scholarships for Ethnically Diverse High School Seniors)

7979 E. Tufts Ave., #500
Denver CO 80237-2843
303/773-2877 or 800/523-9082
Internet: www.cocpa.org

AMOUNT: $1,000
DEADLINE(S): MAR 1
FIELD(S): Accounting

Open to ethnically diverse high school seniors in Colorado schools who intend to major in accounting at Colorado colleges/universities which offer accredited accounting programs. Must have at least a 3.0 GPA and be African-American, Hispanic, Asian-American, American Indian, or Pacific Islander.

See website or contact Gena Mantz at above location for an application.

87—COLORADO SOCIETY OF CPAs EDUCATIONAL FOUNDATION (Scholarships for Undergraduates and Graduates)

7979 E. Tufts Ave., #500
Denver CO 80237-2843
303/773-2877 or 800/523-9082
Internet: www.cocpa.org

AMOUNT: $1,000
DEADLINE(S): JUN 30; NOV 30
FIELD(S): Accounting

For undergraduates and graduates who have completed intermediate accounting, have a 3.0 or better GPA, and are majoring in accounting at a Colorado college/university offering accredited accounting majors. Financial need considered.

Scholarships are renewable with reapplication. See website or contact Gena Mantz at above location for an application.

88—COLORADO SOCIETY OF CPAs EDUCATIONAL FOUNDATION (Scholarships for Ethnically Diverse Undergraduates and Graduates)

7979 E. Tufts Ave., #500
Denver CO 80237-2843
303/773-2877 or 800/523-9082
Internet: www.cocpa.org

AMOUNT: $1,000
DEADLINE(S): JUN 30
FIELD(S): Accounting

For ethnically diverse undergraduates and graduates who have completed intermediate accounting, have 3.0 or better GPA, and are majoring in accounting at a Colorado college/university offering accredited accounting majors. Must be African American, Hispanic, Asian-American-American Indian, or Pacific Islander. Financial need considered.

Renewable with reapplication. See website or contact Gena Mantz at above location for an application.

89—COMMUNITY FOUNDATION OF WEST-ERN MASSACHUSETTS (Joseph Bonfitto Scholarship)

1500 Main Street, P.O. Box 15769
Springfield MA 01115
413/732-2858

AMOUNT: $2,000
DEADLINE(S): APR 15
FIELD(S): Creative Design, Advertising, Art

Open to graduating seniors of Agawam High School in Massachusetts who are pursuing a career through higher education in one of the above areas of study. Based on financial need, academic merit, and extracurricular activities. Must submit transcripts and fill out government FAFSA form.

1 award annually. Renewable with reapplication. Send self-addressed, stamped envelope to Community Foundation for an application and contact your financial aid office for FAFSA. Notification is in June.

90—CONFERENCE OF MINORITY PUBLIC ADMINISTRATORS (Scholarships and Travel Grants)

P.O. Box 3010
Fort Worth TX 76113
817/871-8325
Internet: www.compa.org

AMOUNT: $400 (travel grants); up to $1,500 (academic year)
DEADLINE(S): Varies
FIELD(S): Public administration/public affairs

COMPA offers two academic scholarships, at least five travel grants, and a $1,000 gift to the college that has the largest number of student registrants at its annual conference. Travel grants are for attending the conference. For minorities and women pursuing full-time education in the above fields and committed to excellence in public service and administration in city, county, state, and federal governments.

Contact Edwin Cook at above location for details.

91—CONTRACT MANAGEMENT INSTITUTE (Scholarships)

1912 Woodford Road
Vienna VA 22182
703/448-9231
E-mail: info@ncmahq.org
Internet: www.ncmahq.org/cmi/scholar.html

AMOUNT: Varies
DEADLINE(S): Varies
FIELD(S): Business: Contract Management specialty

Scholarships for undergraduate and graduate students enrolled in a business-oriented curriculum who intend to enter into the Contract Management field. Available from each of the eight NMCA regions. One program, the Martin L. Kaufman Memorial Scholarship, is for business students who intend to enter the military service of the US upon graduation.

Inquire of organization for details.

92—COOPERATIVE ASSOCIATION OF STATES FOR SCHOLARSHIPS (CASS) (Scholarships)

c/o Commonwealth Liaison
Unit 310 The Garrison
St. Michael BARBADOS
809/436-8754

AMOUNT: Varies
DEADLINE(S): None
FIELD(S): Business application/computer science

Scholarships for economically disadvantaged deaf youth, ages 17-25, with strong leadership potential and an interest in computer science/business applications. Must be from Barbados, Street Kitts/Nevis, Grenada, Street Vincent, Antigua/ Barbuda, Street Lucia, Dominica, or Jamaica.

Write to E. Caribbean Regional Coordinator (CASS) at above address.

93—CUBAN AMERICAN NATIONAL FOUN-DATION (The Mas Family Scholarships)

7300 NW 35 Terrace
Miami FL 33122
305/592-7768
FAX: 305/592-7889
E-mail: canfnet.org
Internet: www.canfnet.org

AMOUNT: Individually negotiated
DEADLINE(S): MAR 15
FIELD(S): Engineering, Business, International Relations, Economics, Communications, Journalism

For Cuban-American students, graduates and undergraduates, born in Cuba or direct descendants of those who left Cuba. Must be in top 10% of high school class or maintain a 3.5 GPA in college.

10,000 awards/year. Recipients may re-apply for subsequent years. Financial need considered along with academic success, SAT and GRE scores, and leadership potential. Essays and proof of Cuban descent required.

94—DECA (Harry A. Applegate Scholarships)

1908 Association Drive
Reston VA 22091-1594
703/860-5000
FAX: 703/860-4013
E-mail: decainc@aol.com
Internet: www.deca.org

AMOUNT: $500-$1,000
DEADLINE(S): MAR (2nd Monday)
FIELD(S): Marketing, Management, Entrepreneurship, Merchandising

Open to high school seniors or graduates who are members of DECA (Distributive Education Clubs of America). Scholarships are for undergraduate study at accredited colleges or universities.

Renewable. Write for complete information.

95—DeVRY INC. (Dean's & Presidential Scholarships)

One Tower Lane
Oakbrook Terrace IL 60181-4624
800/733-3879, ext. 1935 or
630/571-7700
E-mail: outreach@devry.edu
Internet: www.devry.edu

AMOUNT: $1,000/term (Dean's); full tuition (Presidential)
DEADLINE(S): DEC 18; FEB 19; MAR 15
FIELD(S): Accounting, Business Admin, Computers, Electronics Engineering, Telecommunications Management, Electronics Technician

High school seniors who apply to any DeVry Institute are automatically considered for scholarships based on ACT/SAT scores. Presidential scholarships also consider community service, scholastic achievement, extracurricular activities, and essay. Must be US citizen or permanent resident.

Renewable if maintain 3.0 GPA. Number of Dean's Scholarships varies; 2 full-time Presidential awards annually. Contact Brenda Allen, Scholarship Coordinator, for an application.

96—EAA AVIATION FOUNDATION (Scholarship Program)

P.O. Box 3065
Oshkosh WI 54903-3065
920/426-6815 or 888/EAA-EAA9
or 888/322-3229
E-mail: education@eaa.org
Internet: www.eaa.org

AMOUNT: $500-$5,000
DEADLINE(S): MAY 1
FIELD(S): Aviation

Six different scholarship programs open to well-rounded individuals involved in school and community activities as well as aviation. Applicant's academic records should verify his/her ability to complete educational activity for which scholarship is requested. For all but one scholarship, students must major in aviation. Financial need considered in some programs. One scholarship includes tuition, books, fees, etc. at the Fox Valley Technical College in Wisconsin.

Renewable. $5 application fee. Contact EAA for an application (one application covers all of the scholarship programs).

97—EMPIRE COLLEGE (Dean's Scholarship)

3035 Cleveland Ave.
Santa Rosa CA 95403
707/546-4000
FAX: 707/546-4058

AMOUNT: $250-$1,500
DEADLINE(S): APR 15
FIELD(S): Accounting, Secretarial, Legal, Medical (Clinical & Administrative), Travel & Tourism, General Business, Computer Assembly, Network Assembly/Administration

Open to high school seniors who plan to attend Empire College. Must be US citizen.

10 awards annually. Contact Ms. Mary Farha for an application.

98—ESPN (Internship Programs)

Human Resources Dept.
ESPN, Inc., ESPN Plaza
Bristol CT 06010
No phone calls.
Internet: espnet.sportszone.com/editors/studios/97faq.html

AMOUNT: Paid internships
DEADLINE(S): OCT 1; MAR 1; JUN 1
FIELD(S): Television Industry, Public Relations, Sports

12-week internships in the spring, summer, and fall for undergraduate juniors/seniors and graduate students. Some areas require weekend/evening hours and a strong knowledge of sports. Interns receive hourly wages and take part in many company-sponsored activities. ESPN does not provide housing for students, but we do try to assist in finding suitable living arrangements once selected.

To apply for internship programs, please send cover letter and resume to the above address. If applying to the Communications Dept., please also enclose writing samples and send attention of Diane Lamb.

99—FASHION GROUP INTERNATIONAL OF GREATER WASHINGTON DC (Scholarships)

P.O. Box 71055
Chevy Chase MD 20813-1055
212/593-1715 (in New York)
Internet: fgi.org/washington.htm

AMOUNT: Up to $2,500
DEADLINE(S): APR 1
FIELD(S): Fashion-related areas

Scholarshps for students majoring in fashion-related fields. Must be permanent residents of the Greater Metropolitan Washington DC area. Must either graduate from high school in June and/or have been admitted to an accredited institution or be enrolled in a university or college as an undergraduate or graduate student.

Application form and details are available on website or contact organization for further information.

100—FLORIDA DEPT. OF EDUCATION (Ethics In Business Scholarship Program)

Student Financial Assist
255 Collins
Tallahassee FL 32399-0400
850/487-0049 or 888/827-2004
E-mail: OSFABF@mail.doe.state.fl.us
Internet: www.firn.edu/doe

AMOUNT: Varies
DEADLINE(S): Varies
FIELD(S): Business

Provides assistance to undergraduate students who enroll at community colleges and eligible private Florida colleges and universities. Applications and award procedures are determined by each sector representative.

Contact your school's financial aid office or Florida Department of Education for more information.

101—FUKUNAGA SCHOLARSHIP FOUN-DATION (Scholarships)

P.O. Box 2788
Honolulu HI 96803
808/521-6511
FAX: 808/523-3937

AMOUNT: $2,000/yr.
DEADLINE(S): FEB 15
FIELD(S): Business Administration

Scholarships to residents of Hawaii to study business administration at the University of Hawaii or other accredited 4-year universities. Must demonstrate academic ability (GPA above 3.0), leadership qualities, interest in business in the Pacific Basin area, and financial need. Must plan to return to Hawaii or the Pacific Island region to work and live. Transcripts, SAT/ACT scores, letters of recommendation, and copies of your household's prior year tax return required.

60 awards annually. Renewable for 4 years for entering freshmen; for those already in college, award will cover only the remainder of the student's originally approved undergraduate program. Contact the Scholarship Selection Committee for an application.

102—GEORGE HARDING SCHOLARSHIP FUND

22344 Long Blvd.
Dearborn MI 48124
313/225-2798

AMOUNT: $750
DEADLINE(S): Ongoing
FIELD(S): Business Administration/Finance

Scholarships for Michigan residents who are full-time students enrolled in four-year Michigan colleges or universities and pursuing finance-related degrees. To be used only for the senior year of college or first year of graduate school.

Write to Richard E. Gardner, Trustee, at above address for details.

103—GOLDEN GATE RESTAURANT ASSO-CIATION (David Rubenstein Memorial Scholarship Foundation Awards)

720 Market Street, Suite 200
San Francisco CA 94102
415/781-5348

AMOUNT: $500-$2,500
DEADLINE(S): MAR 31
FIELD(S): Hotel & Restaurant Management/Food Science

Open to students who have completed the first semester of college as a food service major and have a 2.75 or better GPA (4.0 scale) in hotel and restaurant courses.

Seven awards per year. Write for complete information.

104—GOLDEN STATE MINORITY FOUN-DATION (College Scholarships)

1055 Wilshire Blvd., Suite 1115
Los Angeles CA 90017

213/482-6300
FAX: 213/482-6305
E-mail: gsmf@earthlink.net
Internet: http://home.earthlink.net/~gsmf/
AMOUNT: $2,000
DEADLINE(S): APR 1 (Applications available Feb. 1)
FIELD(S): Business Administration, Economics, Public Administration, Life Insurance, or related fields

Open to minority students attending an accredited four-year school in Southern California or who are Southern California residents attending school elsewhere. Awards support full-time study at the undergrad college junior/senior or graduate levels. Must maintain a 3.0 GPA or better.

May not work more than 28 hours a week. Income must be insufficient to cover expenses. Approx 75 awards per year. Write for complete information.

105—GOVERNMENT FINANCE OFFICERS ASSOCIATION (Frank L. Greathouse Government Accounting Scholarship)

180 N. Michigan Ave., Suite 800
Chicago IL 60601-7476
312/977-9700
AMOUNT: $2,000
DEADLINE(S): FEB 12
FIELD(S): Finance

Scholarships for senior, full-time undergraduates preparing for a career in state or local government finance. Must be a citizen or permanent resident of the US or Canada. Criteria includes career/educational goals, GPA, and letters of recommendation.

Winner is invited to attend Annual Conference (at Government Finance Officers Association's expense) where award is presented. Contact John Wiley at above address for an application/more information.

106—GRASS VALLEY GROUP, INC. SCHOLARSHIP FOUNDATION

P.O. Box 1114, MIS 8N
Grass Valley CA 95945-1114
916/478-3136
AMOUNT: Varies
DEADLINE(S): APR 30
FIELD(S): Economics

Scholarships for dependents of Tektronix employees who are studying economics.

Contact Max Palmer, Scholarship Coordinator, at above address for an application.

107—HILLSDALE COLLEGE (Freedom as Vocation Scholarship)

33 E. College Street
Hillsdale MI 49242-1298
517/437-7341
Internet: www.hillsdale.edu
AMOUNT: Varies
DEADLINE(S): None
FIELD(S): Business, History, Political Science, Economics

Open to Hillsdale College undergraduates who maintain a minimum 3.0 GPA and commit to a series of courses in the above fields. Student must rank in top 20% of class and top 10% of test scores. Must possess excellent communications, public speaking, and leadership skills and demonstrate outstanding character and citizenship. Financial need NOT a factor.

Renewable. No application process; students are selected. See website for details.

108—HISPANIC COLLEGE FUND (Scholarships for Hispanic Students)

One Thomas Circle NW, Suite 375
Washington DC 20005
202/296-5400
FAX: 202/296-3774
E-mail: Hispanic.Fund@Internet MCl.com
Internet: http://hispanicfund.org
AMOUNT: Varies
DEADLINE(S): APR 15
FIELD(S): Most college majors leading to a career in business

Scholarships for deserving Hispanic college students pursuing a higher education in a major leading to a business career and who are full-time students at accredited institutions. US citizenship. Must demonstrate financial need.

Contact above organization for details or visit website for application.

109—HOPI TRIBE (Priority Scholarships)

P.O. Box 123
Kykotsmovi AZ 86039
520/734-2441, ext. 520
800/762-9630
FAX: 520/734-2435
AMOUNT: Varies
DEADLINE(S): JUL 31

FIELD(S): Law, Natural Resources, Education, Medicine/Health, Engineering, Business

Open to enrolled members of the Hopi Tribe studying in one of the fields listed above, which are considered to be areas of priority interest to the Hopis. Available to college juniors, seniors, and graduate students. Program is to encourage graduates to apply their degrees to Hopi Tribal Goals and Objectives.

Contact Hopi Tribe for an application.

110—HOSPITALITY FINANCIAL AND TECHNOLOGY PROFESSIONALS (Scholarships)

11709 Boulder Lane, Suite 110
Austin TX 78726
800/646-4387
Internet: www.hftp.org
AMOUNT: $1,000-$1,500
DEADLINE(S): JUL 15
FIELD(S): Accounting or Hospitality Management

For students majoring in either accounting or hospitality management at an accredited college or university.

Applications must come through an IAHA local chapter president. Send SASE for details.

111—INDEPENDENT ACCOUNTANTS INTERNATIONAL EDUCATIONAL FOUNDATION, INC. (Robert Kaufman Memorial Scholarship Award)

9200 S. Dadeland Blvd., Suite 510
Miami FL 33156
305/670-0580
Internet: www.accountants.org
AMOUNT: $250-$2,500
DEADLINE(S): FEB 28
FIELD(S): Accounting

Open to students who are pursuing or planning to pursue an education in accounting at recognized academic institutions throughout the world. Must demonstrate financial need for larger sums; not required for $250 honorary textbook award.

Up to 20 awards annually. See website ONLY for complete information.

112—INSTITUTE FOR HUMANE STUDIES (Koch Summer Fellow Program)

4084 University Drive, Suite 101
Fairfax VA 22030-6812
703/934-6920 or 800/697-8799

FAX: 703/352-7535
E-mail: ihs@gmu.edu
Internet: www.theihs.org
AMOUNT: $1,500 + airfare & housing
DEADLINE(S): MAR 1
FIELD(S): Economics, Politics, Law,
Government, Public Policy

For undergraduates and graduates to build skills and gain experience by participating in an 8-week summer internship program. Includes 2 week-long seminars, the internship, and research & writing projects with professionals. College transcripts, essays, and application required. Financial need NOT a factor.

32 awards annually. Not renewable. Apply online or contact IHS for an application.

113—INSTITUTE FOR HUMANE STUDIES (Summer Residential Program)

4084 University Drive, Suite 101
Fairfax VA 22030-6812
703/934-6920 or 800/697-8799
FAX: 703/352-7535
E-mail: ihs@gmu.edu
Internet: www.theihs.org
AMOUNT: All seminar fees: program
cost, room/board, materials, and books
DEADLINE(S): MAR 1
FIELD(S): Social Sciences, Humanities,
Law, Journalism, Public Policy,
Education, Writing

For college students, recent graduates, and graduate students who share an interest in learning and exchanging ideas about the scope of individual rights. One-week and weekend seminars at various campus locations across the US.

Apply online or contact IHS for an application.

114—INSTITUTE FOR OPERATIONS RESEARCH AND THE MANAGEMENT SCIENCES (INFORMS Summer Internship Directory)

P.O. Box 64794
Baltimore MD 21264-4794
800/4INFORMS
FAX: 410/684-2963
E-mail: jps@informs.org
Internet: www.informs.org/INTERN/
AMOUNT: Varies
DEADLINE(S): Varies
FIELD(S): Fields related to information
management: business management,
engineering, mathematics

A website listing of summer internships in the field of operations research and management sciences. Both applicants and employers can register online.

Access website for list.

115—INSTITUTE OF INTERNATIONAL EDUCATION (National Security Education Program—Undergraduate Scholarships)

1400 K Street NW, 6th Fl.
Washington DC 20005-2403
202/326-7697 or
800/618-NSEP (6737)
E-mail: nsep@iie.org
Internet: http://www.iie.org/nsep/
AMOUNT: Varies: up to $8,000/semester
DEADLINE(S): FEB 8
FIELD(S): Open to all majors; preference
to Applied Sciences, Engineering,
Business, Economics, Math, Computer
Science, International Affairs, Political
Science, History, and the Policy
Sciences

For study abroad OUTSIDE the US, Canada, Australia, New Zealand, and Western Europe. For study in areas deemed critical to US national security. Applications available on US campuses from August through early December. Or contact organization for details.

Inquire at above location for details.

116—INSTITUTE OF MANAGEMENT ACCOUNTANTS (National Scholarship Program)

10 Paragon Drive
Montvale NJ 07645-1760
800/638-4427 or 201/573-9000
FAX: 201/573-0559
E-mail: imastmbr@imanet.org OR
students@imanet.org
AMOUNT: $2,000, $3,000, or $5,000
DEADLINE(S): FEB 15
FIELD(S): Management
Accounting/Financial Management

Various scholarships for students pursuing undergraduate or graduate degrees in the above fields. Must be member of an IMA student chapter.

Write for application details or access website, where there is a printable application. Submit applications to your Chapter or student Chapter President between Jan. 1 and Feb. 1. For nearest IMA Chapter, call or e-mail organization.

117—INTERNATIONAL ASSOCIATION OF FIRE CHIEFS FOUNDATION (Scholarship Program)

1257 Wiltshire Road
York PA 17403
717/854-9083
AMOUNT: $250-$4,000
DEADLINE(S): AUG 15
FIELD(S): Business and Urban
Administration, Fire Science

Open to members of a fire service of a state, county, provincial, municipal, community, industrial, or federal fire department.

Renewable. Write for complete information.

118—INTERNATIONAL RADIO AND TELEVISION SOCIETY FOUNDATION (Summer Fellowship Program)

420 Lexington Ave., Suite 1714
New York NY 10170
212/867-6650
FAX: 212/867-6653
Internet: www.irts.org
AMOUNT: Housing, stipend, and travel
DEADLINE(S): NOV 12
FIELD(S): Broadcasting,
Communications, Sales, Marketing

Nine-week summer fellowship program in New York City is open to outstanding full-time undergraduate juniors and seniors with a demonstrated interest in a career in communications. Financial need NOT a factor.

20-25 awards annually. Not renewable. See website or contact Maria DeLeon-Fisher at IRTS for an application.

119—JAMES FORD BELL FOUNDATION (Summer Internship Program)

2925 Dean Parkway, Suite 811
Minneapolis MN 55416
612/285-5435
FAX: 612/285-5437
E-mail: famphiladv@uswest.net
AMOUNT: $4,000 for 3 months
DEADLINE(S): APR 30
FIELD(S): Business/Public
Administration, Public Policy,
Organization Leadership, Nonprofit
Management

Interns spend the summer with organizations selected by the Foundation; the organizations select interns from masters degree programs in above or related fields and college seniors with strong interest in nonprofit work. Internships normally in the Twin Cities area.

Contact Foundation for a list of internship opportunities in February and March ONLY; students should request position list, not an application for the program itself (only organizations apply for the program).

120—JC PENNEY (Scholarship Program)

Corporate Headquarters
Plano TX 75023
972/431-1347
Internet: www.jcpenneyinc.com

AMOUNT: $1,500
DEADLINE(S): Varies
FIELD(S): Business, Merchandising,
   Retail Studies, Information Systems

For undergraduates in above fields. Must be dependent children of or associates who are employed at JC Penney both at the time of applying for the scholarships and at the time of awarding the scholarships—or can be dependents of deceased/retired associates having three continuous years of service.

128 one-time awards. Current recipients may reapply as long as the scholarship program is offered at their school. The campuses which offer this scholarship are the 32 colleges where JC Penney recruits new management trainees—campuses reevaluted each year. Contact your (participating) school for an application or visit your local JC Penney store.

121—JOHNSON AND WALES UNIVERSITY (Annual Johnson & Wales University National High School Recipe Contest)

8 Abbott Place
Providence RI 02903
401/598-2345

AMOUNT: $1,000 to $5,000
DEADLINE(S): JAN 31
FIELD(S): Business, Hospitality,
   Technology, Culinary Arts

For students planning to attend Johnson & Wales University, Providence, Rhode Island.

Write to above address for detailed description.

122—JOHNSON AND WALES UNIVERSITY (Gilbane Building Company Eagle Scout Scholarship)

8 Abbott Place
Providence RI 02903
401/598-2345

AMOUNT: $1,200
DEADLINE(S): None
FIELD(S): Business, Hospitality,
   Technology, Culinary Arts

For students attending Johnson & Wales University, Providence, Rhode Island. Must be Eagle Scouts.

Send letter of recommendation and transcript to above address.

123—JOHNSON AND WALES UNIVERSITY (National High School Entrepreneur of the Year Contest)

8 Abbott Place
Providence RI 02903
401/598-2345

AMOUNT: $1,000 to $10,000
DEADLINE(S): DEC 27
FIELD(S): Business, Hospitality,
   Technology, Culinary Arts

For students attending Johnson & Wales University, Providence, Rhode Island.

Send for detailed description to above address.

124—JOHNSON AND WALES UNIVERSITY (Scholarships)

8 Abbott Place
Providence RI 02903
401/598-2345

AMOUNT: $200 to $10,000
DEADLINE(S): None
FIELD(S): Business, Hospitality,
   Technology, Culinary Arts

For students attending Johnson & Wales University, Providence, Rhode Island.

Renewable for four years. Write for complete information.

125—KARLA SCHERER FOUNDATION (Scholarships)

737 N. Michigan Ave., Suite 2330
Chicago IL 60611
312/943-9191

AMOUNT: Varies
DEADLINE(S): MAR 1
FIELD(S): Finance, Economics

Open to women who plan to pursue careers in finance and/or economics in the private manufacturing-based sector. For undergraduate or graduate study at any accredited institution. Send letter stating what school you attend or plan to attend, the courses you plan to take, and how you will use your education in your chosen career.

Renewable. With application request, please include above information as well as a self-addressed, stamped envelope to assure a prompt response.

126—LOUISIANA STATE UNIVERSITY AT SHREVEPORT (College of Business Administration Scholarships)

Dean's Office
One University Place
Shreveport LA 71115-2399
318/797-5363
FAX: 318/797-5366
E-mail: finaid@pilot.lsus.edu
Internet: www.lsus.edu

AMOUNT: Varies
DEADLINE(S): Varies
FIELD(S): Business Administration

A number of scholarships are funded for business students enrolled at various levels at LSUS.

Contact the Dean's Office in the College of Business Administration at LSUS for details on specific scholarships.

127—MARYLAND ASSOCIATION OF CERTIFIED PUBLIC ACCOUNTANTS EDUCATIONAL FOUNDATION (Scholarship Program)

P.O. Box 4417
Lutherville MD 21094-4417
410/296-6250 or 800/782-2036
FAX: 410/296-8713
Internet: www.macpa.org

AMOUNT: $1,000/yr.
DEADLINE(S): APR 15
FIELD(S): Accounting

For Maryland residents attending Maryland colleges/universities and pursuing careers as a CPA. Must be a full-time student with a cumulative GPA of at least 3.0 and maintain a 3.0 GPA throughout 150-hour requirement and eligibility for sitting for the CPA exam in Maryland. Must have completed at least 60 total credit hours by the time of the award, of which at least 6 hours of credit are accounting courses. Financial need must be demonstrated.

Renewable. Contact MACPA for an application.

128—MEXICAN AMERICAN GROCERS ASSOCIATION (Scholarships)

405 N. San Fernando Road
Los Angeles CA 90031
213/227-1565
FAX: 213/227-6935

AMOUNT: Varies
DEADLINE(S): JUL 31
FIELD(S): Business

Scholarships for Hispanic college students who are at least college sophomores. Must have 2.5 GPA or above, be U.S. citizen or permanent resident, and demonstrate financial need.

Send a self-addressed, stamped envelope to Jackie Solis at above address for further information.

129—MIDWAY COLLEGE (Institutional Aid Program—Scholarships & Grants)

Financial Aid Office
Midway KY 40347
606/846-4421

AMOUNT: Varies
DEADLINE(S): MAR 1
FIELD(S): Nursing, Paralegal, Education, Psychology, Biology, Equine Studies, Liberal Studies, Business Administration

Scholarships and grants open to women who are accepted for enrollment at Midway College. Awards support undergraduate study in the above areas.

Approx 80 awards per year. Write for complete information.

130—NATIONAL AIR TRANSPORTATION ASSOCIATION FOUNDATION (The Pioneers of Flight Scholarship)

4226 King Street
Alexandria VA 22302
703/845-9000
FAX: 703/845-8176

AMOUNT: $2,500
DEADLINE(S): None
FIELD(S): General aviation

Scholarship for college students who are in the sophomore or junior year at the time of application intending to pursue full-time study at an accredited four-year college or university and can demonstrate an interest in pursuing a career in general aviation.

Must be nominated by an NATA Regular or Associate Member company.

131—NATIONAL ASSOCIATION OF WATER COMPANIES—NEW JERSEY CHAPTER (Scholarship)

Elizabethtown Water Co.
600 South Ave.
Westfield NJ 07090
908/654-1234
FAX: 908/232-2719

AMOUNT: $2,500
DEADLINE(S): APR 1
FIELD(S): Business Administration, Biology, Chemistry, Engineering, Communications

For US citizens who have lived in NJ at least 5 years and plan a career in the investor-owned water utility industry in disciplines such as those above. Must be undergrad or graduate student in a 2- or 4-year NJ college or university.

GPA of 3.0 or better required. Contact Gail P. Brady for complete information.

132—NATIONAL CUSTOMS BROKERS & FORWARDERS ASSN OF AMERICA INC (NCBFAA Scholarship)

1200 18th Street NW, Suite 901
Washington DC 20036
202/466-0222

AMOUNT: $5,000
DEADLINE(S): FEB 1
FIELD(S): International Business— Customs Brokerage or Freight Forwarding

Open to family members and employees of regular NCBFAA members who are interested in a career in customs brokerage or freight forwarding. Applicants must have a 2.0 or better GPA and submit a 1,000- to 1,500-word essay.

Write for complete information.

133—NATIONAL ITALIAN AMERICAN FOUNDATION (Assunta Luchetti Martino Scholarship for International Studies)

1860 19th Street NW
Washington DC 20009-5315
202/530-5315

AMOUNT: $1,000
DEADLINE(S): MAY 31
FIELD(S): International studies

For undergraduates of Italian ancestry who are pursuing degrees in international studies.

Considerations are academic merit, financial need, and community service. Write for application and further information.

134—NATIONAL ITALIAN AMERICAN FOUNDATION (Bolla Wines Scholarship)

1860 19th Street NW
Washington DC 20009-5599
202/530-5315

AMOUNT: $1,000
DEADLINE(S): MAY 31

FIELD(S): International studies— emphasis on Italian business or Italian-American history

For undergraduate or graduate students of Italian heritage with a GPA of 3.0+ and a background in international studies. Must write an essay on "The Importance of Italy in Today's Business World" (3-pages, double-spaced, typed)

Community service and financial need considered. Write for application and details.

135—NATIONAL ITALIAN AMERICAN FOUNDATION (F.D. Stella Scholarship)

1860 19th Street NW
Washington DC 20009-5599
202/530-5315

AMOUNT: $1,000
DEADLINE(S): MAY 31
FIELD(S): For undergraduate and graduate business majors

Open to undergraduate or graduate business majors of Italian heritage.

Also considered are academic merit, financial need, and community service.

136—NATIONAL ITALIAN AMERICAN FOUNDATION (George L. Graziado Fellowship for Business)

1860 19th Street NW
Washington DC 20009
202/530-5315

AMOUNT: $2,500 and $5,000
DEADLINE(S): MAY 30
FIELD(S): Business and Management

Open to undergraduate American students of Italian ancestry studying at the George L. Graziado School of Business and Management at Pepperdine University, California.

2 awards given. Academic merit, financial need, and community service are considered. Contact organization for application and details.

137—NATIONAL ITALIAN AMERICAN FOUNDATION (Merrill Lynch Scholarship)

1860 19th Street NW
Washington DC 20009-5599
202/530-5315

AMOUNT: $1,000
DEADLINE(S): MAY 31
FIELD(S): Business

For undergraduates of Italian ancestry who are pursuing degrees in business and are residents of the state of New York.

Considerations are academic merit, financial need, and community service. Write for application and further information.

138—NATIONAL ITALIAN AMERICAN FOUNDATION (The Vennera Noto Scholarship)

1860 19th Street NW
Washington DC 20009-5599
202/530-5315

AMOUNT: $2,000
DEADLINE(S): MAY 31
FIELD(S): Business Administration

For undergraduates of Italian ancestry who are business majors.

Considerations are academic merit, financial need, and community service. Write for application and further information.

139—NATIONAL SOCIETY DAUGHTERS OF THE AMERICAN REVOLUTION (Enid Hall Griswold Memorial Scholarship)

1776 D Street NW
Washington DC 20006-5392
202/628-1776
Internet: www.dar.org

AMOUNT: $1,000
DEADLINE(S): FEB 15
FIELD(S): History, Political Science, Government, Economics

Open to undergraduate juniors and seniors (US citizens) attending an accredited US college or university. Awards are placed on deposit with school. Awards are judged on academic excellence, commitment to field of study, and need. Affiliation with DAR not required.

Not renewable. See website or send a self-addressed, stamped envelope for an application or more informtion.

140—NATIONAL SOCIETY OF ACCOUNTANTS SCHOLARSHIP FOUNDATION (NSA Annual Awards)

1010 North Fairfax Street
Alexandria VA 22314-1574
703/549-6400
FAX: 703/549-2984
E-mail: snoell@mindspring.com
Internet: www.nsacct.org

AMOUNT: $500-$1,000
DEADLINE(S): MAR 10
FIELD(S): Accounting

Open to undergraduate accounting students in an accredited two- or four-year

college in the US who are US or Canadian citizens. Must maintain an overall GPA of 3.0. Selection based on academic attainment, leadership ability, and financial need. Payment by Foundation is made directly to your college/university.

30 awards annually. See website or contact Susan Noell, Foundation Director, for an application.

141—NATIONAL SOCIETY OF ACCOUNTANTS SCHOLARSHIP FOUNDATION (Stanley H. Stearman Scholarship Award)

1010 North Fairfax Street
Alexandria VA 22314-1574
703/549-6400
FAX: 703/549-2984
E-mail: snoell@mindspring.com
Internet: www.nsacct.org

AMOUNT: $2,000/yr.
DEADLINE(S): MAR 10
FIELD(S): Accounting

For US or Canadian citizens in undergraduate or graduate programs in the US who have a minimum 3.0 GPA. Must be the spouse, child, grandchild, niece, nephew, or son/daughter-in-law of an active or deceased NSA member who has held membership for at least one year. Must include letter of intent, outlining reasons for seeking award, intended career objective, and how this award would be used to accomplish that objective.

1 award annually. Renewable up to 3 years. See website or contact Susan Noell, Foundation Director, for an application.

142—NATIONAL TOURISM FOUNDATION (NTF Scholarships)

P.O. Box 3071
Lexington KY 40596-3071
800/682-8886
FAX: 606/226-4414
Internet: www.ntaonline.com

AMOUNT: $500-$5,000
DEADLINE(S): APR 15
FIELD(S): Travel & Tourism

Various scholarships for full-time students at two- or four-year colleges/universities in North America who are entering their junior or senior year of study. Must be a strong academic performer and have at least a 3.0 GPA. Degree emphasis must be in a travel & tourism-related field, such as hotel management, restaurant management, or tourism. Letters of recommendation, resume, college transcript, and an essay are required.

See website for additional requirements of each individual scholarship. Students may apply for more than one award, but may only receive one. Send a self-addressed, stamped envelope to above address for an application.

143—NATIONAL URBAN LEAGUE, INC. (Duracell/NUL Scholarship/Intern Program for Minority Students)

120 Wall Street
New York NY 10005
212/558-5373
Internet: www.nul.org

AMOUNT: $10,000 + paid summer internship
DEADLINE(S): APR 15
FIELD(S): Engineering, Marketing, Manufacturing, Finance, Business, Human Resource, etc.

For undergraduate college/university students who will be juniors/3rd-year students at time scholarship commences. Must rank within top 25% of class and major in one of above fields. Other requirements include work experience in related field(s), extracurricular activities, leadership skills, and volunteer work. Must be US citizen/permanent resident.

For tuition, room/board, and required education materials/books. Internship with one of the Gillette companies takes place between junior and senior year. Send self-addressed, stamped envelope for application.

144—NAVAL HISTORICAL CENTER (Internship Program)

Washington Navy Yard
901 M Street SE
Washington DC 20374-5060
202/433-6901
FAX: 202/433-8200
E-mail: efurgol@nhc.navy.mil
Internet: www.history.navy.mil

AMOUNT: $400 possible honoraria; otherwise, unpaid
DEADLINE(S): None
FIELD(S): Education, History, Public Relations, Design

Registered students of colleges/universities and graduates thereof are eligible for this program, which must be a minimum of 3 weeks, full or part-time. Four specialities available: Curator, Education, Public Relations, and Design. Interns receive orientation and assist in their departments, and must complete individual project which contributes to Center. Must submit a letter of recommendation, unofficial transcript, and writing sample of not less than 1,000 words.

Contact Dr. Edward M. Furgol, Curator, for an application.

145—NEW YORK CITY DEPT. CITYWIDE ADMINISTRATIVE SERVICES (Urban Fellows Program)

1 Centre Street, 24th Fl.
New York NY 10007
212/487-5600
FAX: 212/487-5720

AMOUNT: $18,000 stipend
DEADLINE(S): JAN 20
FIELD(S): Public Administration, Urban Planning, Government, Public Service, Urban Affairs

Fellowship program provides one academic year (9 months) of full-time work experience in urban government. Open to graduating college seniors and recent college graduates. US citizenship required.

Write for complete information.

146—NEW YORK CITY DEPT. OF CITY-WIDE ADMINISTRATIVE SERVICES (Government Scholars Internship Program)

1 Centre Street, 24th Fl.
New York NY 10007
212/487-5600
FAX: 212/487-5720

AMOUNT: $3,000 stipend
DEADLINE(S): JAN 13
FIELD(S): Public Administration, Urban Planning, Government, Public Service, Urban Affairs

10-week summer intern program open to undergraduate sophomores, juniors, and seniors. Program provides students with unique opportunity to learn about NY City government. Internships available in virtually every city agency and mayoral office.

Write to New York City Fellowship Programs at above address for complete information.

147—NEW YORK STATE HIGHER EDUCATION SERVICES CORPORATION (N.Y. State Regents Professional/Health Care Opportunity Scholarships)

Cultural Education Center, Rm. 5C64
Albany NY 12230
518/486-1319
Internet: www.hesc.com

AMOUNT: $1,000-$10,000/yr.

DEADLINE(S): Varies
FIELD(S): Medicine and Dentistry and related fields, Architecture, Nursing, Psychology, Audiology, Landscape Architecture, Social Work, Chiropractic, Law, Pharmacy, Accounting, Speech Language Pathology

For NY state residents who are economically disadvantaged and members of a minority group underrepresented in the chosen profession and attending school in NY state. Some programs carry a service obligation in New York for each year of support. For US citizens or qualifying noncitizens.

Medical/dental scholarships require one year of professional work in NY.

148—NEW YORK STATE SENATE (Legislative Fellows Program; R. J. Roth Journalism Fellowship; R. A. Wiebe Public Service Fellowship)

NYS Senate Student Programs Office
90 South Swan Street, Room 401
Albany NY 12247
518/455-2611
FAX: 518/432-5470
E-mail: students@senate.state.ny.us

AMOUNT: $25,000 stipend (not a scholarship)
DEADLINE(S): MAY (first Friday)
FIELD(S): Political Science, Government, Public Service, Journalism, Public Relations

One-year programs for US citizens who are grad students and residents of New York state or enrolled in accredited programs in New York state. Fellows work as regular legislative staff members of the office to which they are assigned. The Roth Fellowship is for communications/journalism majors, and undergrads may be considered for this program.

14 fellowships per year. Fellowships take place at the New York State Legislative Office. Write for complete information.

149—NEW YORK STATE THEATRE INSTITUTE (Internships in Theatrical Production)

155 River Street
Troy NY 12180
518/274-3573
E-mail: nysti@crisny.org
Internet: www.crisny.org/not-for-profit/nysti/int.htm

AMOUNT: None
DEADLINE(S): None

FIELD(S): Fields of study related to theatrical production, including box office and PR

Internships for college students, high school seniors, and educators-in-residence interested in developing skills in above fields. Unpaid, but college credit is earned. Located at Russell Sage College in Troy, NY. Gain experience in box office, costumes, education, electrics, music, stage management, scenery, properties, performance, and public relations. Interns come from all over the world.

Must be associated with an accredited institution. See website for more information. Call Ms. Arlene Leff, Intern Director, at above location. Include your postal mailing address.

150—NINETY-NINES, SAN FERNANDO VALLEY CHAPTER/VAN NUYS AIRPORT (Aviation Career Scholarships)

P.O. Box 8160
Van Nuys CA 91409
818/989-0081

AMOUNT: $3,000
DEADLINE(S): MAY 1
FIELD(S): Aviation Careers

For men and women of the greater Los Angeles area pursuing careers as professional pilots, flight instructors, mechanics, or other aviation career specialists. Applicants must be at least 21 years of age and US citizens.

3 awards annually. Send self-addressed, stamped, business-sized envelope to above address for application.

151—OPERA AMERICA (Fellowship Program)

1156 15th Street NW, Suite 810
Washington DC 20005
202/293-4466
FAX: 202/393-0735

AMOUNT: $1,200/month + transportation and housing
DEADLINE(S): MAY 7
FIELD(S): General or Artistic Administration, Technical Direction, or Production Management

Open to opera personnel, individuals entering opera administration from other disciplines, and graduates of arts administration or technical/production training programs who are committed to a career in opera in North America.

Must be US or Canadian citizen or legal resident lawfully eligible to receive stipend.

152—OREGON AFL-CIO (Scholarship Contest)

2110 State Street
Salem OR 97301
503/585-6320
FAX: 503/585-1668
E-mail: askbeany@compuserve.com

AMOUNT: $750; $800; $1,000; $1,200
DEADLINE(S): MAR 1
FIELD(S): All fields of study

Open to graduating seniors from any accredited high school in Oregon for undergraduate study at any accredited US college or university or at an Oregon community college or trade school.

Candidates must take a written exam on labor history and labor issues. Finalists will be chosen on exam score, financial need, and high school GPA. Write to Arthur Kunis-Beany at above address for complete information.

153—PRESIDENT'S COMMISSION ON WHITE HOUSE FELLOWSHIPS

712 Jackson Place NW
Washington DC 20503
202/395-4522
FAX: 202/395-6179
E-mail: almanac@ace.esusda.gov

AMOUNT: Wage (up to GS-14 Step 3; approximately $65,000)
DEADLINE(S): DEC 1
FIELD(S): Public Service, Government, Community Involvement, Leadership

Mid-career professionals spend one year as special assistants to senior executive branch officials in Washington. Highly competitive. Non-partisan; no age or educational requirements. Fellowship year runs September 1 through August 31.

1,200 candidates applying for 11 to 19 fellowships each year. Write for complete information.

154—PRESS CLUB OF DALLAS FOUNDATION (Scholarship)

400 N. Olive
Dallas TX 75201
214/740-9988

AMOUNT: $1,000-$3,000
DEADLINE(S): APR 15
FIELD(S): Journalism and Public Relations

Open to students who are at least sophomore level in undergraduate studies or working towards a masters degree in the above fields in a Texas college or universi-

ty. This scholarship is renewable by re-application.

Write to Carol Wortham at the above address for complete information.

155—REAL ESTATE EDUCATORS ASSN. (REEA—Harwood Scholarship Program)

740 Florida Central Pkwy., Suite 1020
Longwood FL 32750
407/834-6688

AMOUNT: $250-$500
DEADLINE(S): DEC 31
FIELD(S): Real Estate

Open to undergrads (who have completed at least 2 semesters) and graduate students who are studying full-time at an accredited US school, have a 3.1 minimum GPA, and intend to pursue a career in real estate.

10 scholarships per year. Write for complete information.

156—ROYAL THAI EMBASSY, OFFICE OF EDUCATIONAL AFFAIRS (Revenue Dept. Scholarships for Thai Students)

1906 23rd Street NW
Washington DC 20008
202/667-9111 or 202/667-8010
FAX: 202/265-7239

AMOUNT: Varies
DEADLINE(S): APR
FIELD(S): Computer Science (Telecommunications), Law, Economics, Finance, Business Administration

Scholarships for students under age 35 from Thailand who have been accepted to study in the US or UK for the needs of the Revenue Dept., Ministry of Finance. Must pursue any level degree in one of the above fields.

Selections are based on academic records, employment history, and advisor recommendations.

157—SACRAMENTO ASSOCIATION OF REALTORS (Scholarship)

2003 Howe Ave.
Sacramento CA 95825
916/922-7711
FAX: 916/922-1221

AMOUNT: $1,500 (or based on available funds)
DEADLINE(S): FEB
FIELD(S): Real Estate and related fields

Open to students of not less than sophomore standing at Sacramento City

College, CSU Sacramento, or American River College. All applicants are interviewed and must submit a statement of why they are planning a real estate career.

Write for complete information.

158—SOIL AND WATER CONSERVATION SOCIETY (SWCS Internships)

7515 NE Ankeny Road
Ankeny IA 50021-9764
515/289-2331 or 1-800/THE-SOIL
FAX: 515/289-1227
E-mail: charliep@swcs.org
Internet: www.swcs.org

AMOUNT: Varies—most are uncompensated
DEADLINE(S): Varies
FIELD(S): Journalism, Marketing, Database Management, Meeting Planning, Public Policy Research, Environmental Education, Landscape Architecture

Internships for undergraduates and graduates to gain experience in the above fields as they relate to soil and water conservation issues. Internship openings vary through the year in duration, compensation, and objective. SWCS will coordinate particulars with your academic advisor.

Contact SWCS for internship availability at any time during the year or see website for jobs page.

159—SPACE COAST CREDIT UNION (Four-Year Scholarships)

Marketing Dept.
P.O. Box 2470
Melbourne FL 32902
Internet: www.sccu.com/scholarship/

AMOUNT: $1,250/year
DEADLINE(S): APR 15
FIELD(S): Computer Science, Business (Finance, Economics, Human Resources, Industrial Relations, Marketing)

Must be graduating from a high school in Brevard, Volusia, Flagler, or Indian River counties, Florida, be a member of SCCU, have a minimum GPA of 3.0, be planning to attend a four-year Florida institution of higher education, and write a 200-word essay on the topic "Why credit unions are valuable to society."

2 annual awards. For membership information or an application, see our web page or write to the above address.

160—SPACE COAST CREDIT UNION (Two-Year Scholarships)

Marketing Dept.
P.O. Box 2470
Melbourne FL 32902
Internet: www.sccu.com/
scholarship/

AMOUNT: $750/year, two years; $1,000 bonus if go on for Bachelors
DEADLINE(S): APR 15
FIELD(S): Math, Economics, Science, Computer Science, Marketing, Journalism, Political Science

Must be graduating from a high school in Brevard, Volusia, Flagler, or Indian River counties, Florida, be a member of SCCU, have a minimum 3.0 GPA, planning to attend a two-year Florida institution of higher education for an associates degree, and be willing to write a 200-word essay on the topic "Why credit unions are valuable to society."

4 annual awards. Students going on to complete a four-year degree could be eligible for a bonus scholarship of $1,000 for the next two years. For membership information or an application, see our web page or write to the above address.

161—SRP/NAVAJO GENERATING STATION (Navajo Scholarship)

P.O. Box 850
Page AZ 86040
520/645-6539
FAX: 520/645-7295
E-mail: ljdawave@srp.gov

AMOUNT: Based on need
DEADLINE(S): APR 30
FIELD(S): Engineering, Environmental Studies, Business, Business Management, Health, Education

Scholarships for full-time students who hold membership in the Navajo Tribe and who are pursuing a degree in a field of study recognized as significant to the Navajo Nation, Salt River Project, or the Navajo Generating Station, such as those listed above. Must be junior or senior, have and maintain a GPA of 3.0.

Average of 15 awards per year. Inquire of Linda Dawavendewa at above location.

162—STATE FARM COMPANIES FOUNDATION (Exceptional Student Fellowship)

One State Farm Plaza, SC-3
Bloomington IL 61710-0001
309/766-2039/2161

E-mail: Nancy.Lynn.gr3o
@statefarm.com
Internet: www.statefarm.com

AMOUNT: $3,000 (nominating institution receives $250)
DEADLINE(S): FEB 15
FIELD(S): Accounting, Business Administration, Actuarial Science, Computer Science, Economics, Finance, Insurance/Risk Management, Investments, Management, Marketing, Mathematics, Statistics

For US citizens who are full-time juniors or seniors when they apply. Must demonstrate significant leadership in extracurricular activities, have minimum 3.6 GPA, & attend accredited US college/university. Must be nominated by dean, department head, professor, or academic advisor.

50 awards annually. Not renewable. See website, visit your financial aid office, or write to above address for an application.

163—STUDENT CONSERVATION ASSOCIATION (SCA Resource Assistant Program)

P.O. Box 550
Charlestown NH 03603
603/543-1700
FAX: 603/543-1828
E-mail: internships@sca-inc.org
Internet: www.sca-inc.org

AMOUNT: $1,180-$4,725
DEADLINE(S): Varies
FIELD(S): Environment & related fields

Must be 18 & US citizen; need not be student. Fields: Agriculture, archaeology, anthropology, botany, caves, civil/environmental engineering, environmental education, fisheries, forests, herpetology, history, living history/roleplaying, visitor services, landscape architecture/environmental design, paleontology, recreation/resource /range management, trail maintenance/ construction, wildlife management, geology, hydrology, library/museums, surveying.

900 positions in US & Canada. Send $1 for postage for application; outside US/Canada, send $20.

164—THE AMERICAN ASSOCIATION OF ATTORNEY-CERTIFIED PUBLIC ACCOUNTANTS FOUNDATION (Student Writing Competition)

24196 Alicia Parkway, Suite K
Mission Viejo CA 92691
800/CPA-ATTY
FAX: 714/768-7062

AMOUNT: $250-$1,500
DEADLINE(S): APR 1
FIELD(S): Accounting, Law

Essay contest for accounting and/or law students.

Contact organization for current topics and rules.

165—THE ART INSTITUTES INTERNATIONAL (Evelyn Keedy Memorial Scholarship)

300 Sixth Ave., Suite 800
Pittsburgh PA 15222-2598
412/562-9800
FAX: 412/562-9802
E-mail: webadmin@aii.edu
Internet: www.aii.edu

AMOUNT: 2 years full tuition
DEADLINE(S): MAY 1
FIELD(S): Various fields in the creative and applied arts: video production, broadcasting, culinary arts, fashion design, website administration, etc.

Scholarships at 12 different locations nationwide in various fields described above. For graduating high school seniors admitted to an Arts Institutes International School, the New York Restaurant School, or NCPT. Transcripts, letters of recommendation, and resume must be submitted with application.

See website or contact AII for more information.

166—THE FUND FOR AMERICAN STUDIES (Institutes on Political Journalism; Business & Government Affairs & Comparative Political & Economic Systems)

1526 18th Street NW
Washington, DC 20036
202/986-0384; 800/741-6964
Internet: http://www.dcinternships.com

AMOUNT: Up to $2,975
DEADLINE(S): JAN 31 (early decision); MAR 15 (general application deadline)
FIELD(S): Political Science, Economics, Journalism, Business Administration

The Fund for American Studies, in conjunction with Georgetown University, sponsors summer institutes that include internships, courses for credit, site briefings, and dialogues with policy leaders. Scholarships are available to sophomores and juniors to cover the cost of the program.

Approx 100 awards per year. For Fund's programs only. Call, check website, or write for complete information.

167—TRANSPORTATION CLUBS INTERNATIONAL (Charlotte Woods Memorial Scholarship)

P.O. Box 1072
Glen Alpine NC 28628
206/549-2251

AMOUNT: $1,000
DEADLINE(S): MAY 31
FIELD(S): Transportation Logistics,
Traffic Management

Open to TCI members or their dependents enrolled at an accredited college or university in a program in transportation, traffic management, or related area and considering a career in transportation.

Type an essay of not more than 200 words on why you have chosen transportation or an allied field as a career path. Include your objectives. Financial need is also considered. Send SASE (business size) for complete information and application.

168—TRANSPORTATION CLUBS INTERNATIONAL (Denny Lydic Scholarship)

P.O. Box 1072
Glen Alpine NC 28628
206/549-2251

AMOUNT: $500
DEADLINE(S): MAY 31
FIELD(S): Transportation Logistics,
Traffic Management

For students enrolled in an accredited institution of higher learning in a degree or vocational program in the above areas.

Type an essay of not more than 200 words on why you have chosen transportation or an allied field as a career path. Include your objectives. Send an SASE for details.

169—TRANSPORTATION CLUBS INTERNATIONAL (Ginger & Fred Deines Canada Scholarships)

P.O. Box 1072
Glen Alpine NC 28628
206/549-2251

AMOUNT: $500 and/or $1,000
DEADLINE(S): MAY 31
FIELD(S): Transportation Logistics,
Traffic Management

For a student of Canadian nationality and enrolled in a school in Canada or US in a degree or vocational program in the above or related areas.

Type an essay of not more than 200 words on why you have chosen transportation or an allied field as a career path.

Include your objectives. Send an SASE for further details.

170—TRANSPORTATION CLUBS INTERNATIONAL (Ginger & Fred Deines Mexico Scholarships)

P.O. Box 1072
Glen Alpine NC 28688
206/549-2251

AMOUNT: $500 and/or $1,000
DEADLINE(S): May 31
FIELD(S): Transportation, Traffic
Management

Open to students of Mexican nationality who are enrolled in a Mexican or US institution of higher learning in a degree or vocational program in the above or related areas.

Type an essay of not more than 200 words on why you have chosen transportation or an allied field as a career path. Include your objectives. Send SASE for complete information.

171—TRANSPORTATION CLUBS INTERNATIONAL (Hooper Memorial Scholarships)

P.O. Box 1072
Glen Alpine NC 28628
206/549-2251

AMOUNT: $1,500
DEADLINE(S): MAY 31
FIELD(S): Transportation Logistics,
Traffic Management

For students enrolled in an accredited college or university in a degree or vocational program in transportation logistics, traffic management, or related fields and preparing for a career in transportation.

Type an essay of not more than 200 words on why you have chosen transportation or an allied field as a career. Include your objectives. Financial need is considered. Send SASE (business size) for complete information.

172—TRANSPORTATION CLUBS INTERNATIONAL (Texas Transportation Scholarship)

1275 Kamus Drive, Suite 101
Fox Island WA 98333
206/549-2251

AMOUNT: $1,000
DEADLINE(S): MAY 31
FIELD(S): Transporation, Traffic
Management

Open to students who have been enrolled in a school in Texas during elementary, secondary, or high school and enrolled in an accredited college or university in a degree or vocational program relating to transportation.

Type an essay of not more than 200 words on why you have chosen transportation or an allied field as a career path. Include your objectives. Financial need is considered. Send SASE (business size) for complete information.

173—TRAVEL AND TOURISM RESEARCH ASSOCIATION (Awards for Projects)

546 East Main Street
Lexington KY 40508
606/226-4344
FAX: 606/226-4355
Internet: www.ttra.com

AMOUNT: $700-$1,000
DEADLINE(S): MAR 1
FIELD(S): Travel and Tourism and
related fields

Three awards for undergraduate, graduate, and doctoral students in the area of travel and tourism research. Awards for outstanding papers and dissertations.

Visit website and/or send SASE to above location for details.

174—U.S. DEPARTMENT OF TRANSPORTATION (Dwight D. Eisenhower Transportation Fellowships)

U.S. Dept. of Transportation
Fed. Hwy. Admin.
6300 Georgetown Pike, HHI-20
McLean VA 22101-2296
703/235-0538

AMOUNT: Varies
DEADLINE(S): FEB
FIELD(S): Transportation—such majors
as chemistry; materials science;
corrosion; civil, chemical, & electronics
engineering; structures; human factors;
computer science; psychology

Research fellowships for undergrads and grad students at any Dept. of Transportation facility or selected IHE. For three to twelve months. Research must focus on transportation-related research and development in the above fields.

Contact Ilene Payne, Director, Universities and Grants Programs at above location for details.

175—U.S. DEPT. OF HEALTH & HUMAN SERVICES (Indian Health Service Preparatory Scholarship Program)

Twinbrook Metro Plaza, Suite 100
12300 Twinbrook Pkwy.
Rockville MD 20852

301/443-0234
FAX: 301/443-4815
Internet: www:ihs.gov/Recruitment/
DHPS/SP/SBTOC3.asp
AMOUNT: Tuition + fees & monthly
stipend of $938
DEADLINE(S): APR 1
FIELD(S): Health professions, Social
Work, or Accounting

Open to Native Americans or Alaska natives who enroll in courses leading to a baccalaureate degree and are preparing for acceptance into programs in the above fields. US citizenship required. Renewable annually with reapplication.

Scholarship recipients must intend to serve the Indian people. They incur a one-year service obligation to the IHS for each year of support for a minimum of two years. Write for complete information.

176—U.S. DEPT. OF HEALTH & HUMAN SERVICES (Indian Health Service Health Professions Scholarship Program)

Twinbrook Metro Plaza, Suite 100
12300 Twinbrook Pkwy.
Rockville MD 20852
301/443-0234
FAX: 301/443-4815
Internet: www:ihs.gov/Recruitment/
DHPS/SP/SBTOC3.asp
AMOUNT: Tuition + fees & monthly
stipend of $938
DEADLINE(S): APR 1
FIELD(S): Health professions,
Accounting, Social Work

Open to Native Americans or Alaska natives who are graduate students or college juniors or seniors in a program leading to a career in a field listed above. US citizenship required. Renewable annually with reapplication.

Scholarship recipients must intend to serve the Indian people. They incur a one-year service obligation to the IHS for each year of support for a minimum of two years. Write for complete information.

177—U.S. DEPARTMENT OF AGRICULTURE (1890 National Scholars Program)

14th & Independence Ave, SW
Room 301-W, Whitten Bldg.
Washington, DC 20250-9600
202/720-6905
E-mail: usda-m@fie.com
Internet: web.fie.com/htdoc/fed/
agr/ars/edu/prog/mti/
arpgaak.htm

AMOUNT: Tuition,
employment/benefits, use of
PC/software, fees, books, room/board
DEADLINE(S): JAN 15
FIELD(S): Agriculture, Food, or Natural
Resource sciences

For US citizens, high school grad/GED, GPA 3.0+, verbal/math SAT 1,000+, composite score 21+ ACT, 1st yr college student, and attend participating school.

34+ scholarships/yr/4 years. Send applications to USDA Liaison Officer at the 1890 Institution of your choice (see web page for complete list).

178—UNIVERSITY OF NORTH TEXAS (Merchandising and Hospitality Scholarships)

Dean, School of Merchandising/
Hospitality Management
P.O. Box 311100
Denton TX 76203-1100
817/565-2436
Internet: www.unt.edu/scholarships/
smhm.htm

AMOUNT: Varies
DEADLINE(S): Varies
FIELD(S): Business: Merchandising and
Hospitality Management

Several scholarships for students in the above fields are offered at the University of North Texas. Specialties and eligibility requirements vary.

See website for more information. Contact school for details.

179—UNIVERSITY OF OKLAHOMA—H.H. HERBERT SCHOOL OF JOURNALISM AND MASS COMMUNICATION (Undergraduate Scholarships)

860 Van Fleet Oval, Room 101
Norman OK 73019
405/325-2721

AMOUNT: $5,000/yr.
DEADLINE(S): FEB
FIELD(S): Journalism: Print or broadcast,
advertising, electronic media, news
communication, professional writing,
public relations

For undergraduate students studying in the above fields who plan to attend the University of Oklahoma. Interview is part of acceptance process.

Contact David Dary at above location for details.

180—UTA ALUMNI ASSOCIATION (Daniel Kauth Scholarship)

University of Texas at Arlington
Box 19457
Arlington TX 76019
Internet: www.uta.edu/alumni/
scholar.htm

AMOUNT: $250
DEADLINE(S): Varies
FIELD(S): Marketing

For full-time students at the University of Texas at Arlington who are majoring in marketing. Must submit transcript and letter stating career goals, future commitment to UTA, and financial need.

1 award annually. Contact UTA Alumni Association for an application.

181—W.E. UPJOHN INSTITUTE FOR EMPLOYMENT RESEARCH (Grant)

300 South Westnedge Ave.
Kalamazoo MI 49007-4686
616/343-5541
FAX: 616/343-7310
E-mail: webmaster
@we.upjohninst.org
Internet: www.upjohninst.org

AMOUNT: up to $45,000 + $25,000 to
conduct surveys/assemble data
DEADLINE(S): JAN 26
FIELD(S): Employment Relationships,
Low Wages/Public Policy, Social
Insurance

Grants are for proposals that will lead to a book that contributes to the Institute's research program. Proposals evaluated on contribution to important policy issues/professional literature, technical merit, professional qualifications, likelihood of timely completion of project, cost effectiveness, and consistency with Institute's interests. Must submit 8 copies of both a 3-page summary and curriculum vitae. Subset of applicants will then submit 15-page proposal.

Fax and e-mail submissions will not be accepted. See website for details or write to above address.

182—WOMEN IN DEFENSE (HORIZONS Scholarship Foundation)

NDIA; 2111 Wilson Blvd., Suite 400
Arlington VA 22201-3061
703/247-2552
FAX: 703/522-1885
E-mail: dnwlee@moon.jic.com
Internet: www.adpa.org/wid/
horizon/Scholar.htm

AMOUNT: $500+
DEADLINE(S): NOV 1; JUL 1
FIELD(S): Engineering, Computer
Science, Physics, Mathematics,
Business, Law, International Relations,
Political Science, Operations Research,
Economics, and fields relevant to a
career in the areas of national security
and defense

For women who are US citizens, have minimum GPA of 3.25, demonstrate financial need, are currently enrolled at an accredited university/college (full- or part-time—both grads and undergrad juniors/seniors are eligible), and demonstrate interest in pursuing a career related to national security.

Application is online or send SASE, #10 envelope, to Woody Lee, HORIZONS Scholarship Director.

183—WOMEN OF THE EVANGELICAL LUTHERAN CHURCH IN AMERICA (The Arne Administrative Leadership Scholarship)

8765 West Higgins Road
Chicago IL 60631-4189
800/638-3522, ext. 2747
FAX: 773/380-2419
E-mail: womnelca@elca.org

AMOUNT: Varies
DEADLINE(S): MAR 1
FIELD(S): Administration

For women who are ELCA members preparing for administrative positions. Coursework may be for an administrative degree, for certification, or for continuing education. Must be a US citizen and have a bachelor's degree. Must provide records of academic and professional courses taken since being awarded a bachelor's, and must provide proof of admission to educational institution. Funds must be used within year following award.

Renewable for an additional year. Contact Faith Fretheim, Program Director, for an application.

184—WOMEN'S SPORTS FOUNDATION (Jackie Joyner-Kersee & Zina Garrison Minority Internships)

Eisenhower Park
East Meadow NY 11554
800/227-3988
FAX: 516/542-4716
E-mail: WoSport@aol.com
Internet: www.lifetimetv.com/WoSport

AMOUNT: $4,000-$5,000
DEADLINE(S): Ongoing
FIELD(S): Sports-related fields

Provides women of color an opportunity to gain experience in a sports-related career and interact in the sports community. May be undergraduates, college graduates, graduate students, or women in a career change. Internships are located at the Women's Sports Foundation in East Meadow, New York.

4-6 awards annually. See website or write to above address for details.

185—WYOMING TRUCKING ASSOCIATION (Scholarships)

P.O. Box 1909
Casper WY 82602
Written inquiry

AMOUNT: $250-$300
DEADLINE(S): MAR 1
FIELD(S): Transportation Industry

For Wyoming high school graduates enrolled in a Wyoming college, approved trade school, or the University of Wyoming. Must be pursuing a course of study which will result in a career in the transportation industry in Wyoming, including but not limited to: safety, environmental science, diesel mechanics, truck driving, vocational trades, business management, sales management, computer skills, accounting, office procedures, and management.

1-10 awards annually. Write to WYTA for an application.

186—Y'S MEN INTERNATIONAL—US AREA (Alexander Scholarship Loan Fund)

12405 W. Lewis Ave.
Avondale AZ 85323-6518
Written Inquiry

AMOUNT: $1,000-$1,500/yr.
DEADLINE(S): MAY 30; OCT 30
FIELD(S): Business Administration, Youth Leadership

Open to US citizens/permanent residents with a strong desire to pursue professional YMCA service. Must be YMCA staff pursuing undergraduate or graduate study and demonstrate financial need. Repayment of loan is waived if recipient enters YMCA employment after graduation.

Send self-addressed, business-sized envelope plus $1 for postage & handling to above address for an application.

SCHOOL OF EDUCATION

187—AMERICAN HISTORICAL ASSOCIATION (Beveridge Family Teaching Prize for K-12 Teaching)

400 A Street SE
Washington DC 20003
202/544-2422
FAX: 202/544-8307
E-mail: aha@theaha.org
Internet: www.theaha.org

AMOUNT: Varies
DEADLINE(S): MAR 15
FIELD(S): History

To recognize excellence and innovation in elementary, middle school, and secondary history teaching. Awarded on a two-year cycle rotation: individual and group. In 1997, the prize was awarded to a group.

Letters of nomination deadline is March 15. See website or contact AHA for details.

188—AMERICAN HISTORICAL ASSOCIATION (Eugene Asher Distinguished Teaching Award for Postsecondary Teaching)

400 A Street SE
Washington DC 20003
202/544-2422
FAX: 202/544-8307
E-mail: aha@theaha.org
Internet: www.theaha.org

AMOUNT: Varies
DEADLINE(S): APR 15
FIELD(S): History

This prize is awarded annually for excellence in teaching techniques and knowledge of the subject of history at the postsecondary level.

Letters of nomination deadline is April 15. See website or contact AHA for details.

189—AMERICAN INDIAN SCIENCE AND ENGINEERING SOCIETY (Burlington Northern Santa Fe Pacific Foundation Scholarships)

P.O. Box 9828
Albuquerque NM 87119-9828
505/765-1052
FAX: 505/765-5608
E-mail: scholarships@aises.org
Internet: www.aises.org/scholarships

AMOUNT: $2,500/yr.

DEADLINE(S): MAR 31
FIELD(S): Business, Education, Science, Engineering, Health Administration

Open to high school seniors who are at least 1/4 American Indian. Must reside in KS, OK, CO, AZ, NM, MN, ND, OR, SD, WA, MT, or San Bernardino County, CA (Burlington Northern and Santa Fe Pacific service areas). Must demonstrate financial need.

5 awards annually. Renewable up to 4 years. See website or contact Patricia Browne for an application.

190—BUSINESS & PROFESSIONAL WOMEN'S FOUNDATION (BPW Career Advancement Scholarship Program)

2012 Massachusetts Ave. NW
Washington DC 20036-1070
202/293-1200, ext. 169
FAX: 202/861-0298
Internet: www.bpwusa.org

AMOUNT: $500-$1,000
DEADLINE(S): APR 15
FIELD(S): Biology, Science, Education, Engineering, Social Science, Paralegal, Humanities, Business, Math, Computers, Law, MD, DD

For women (US citizens) aged 25+ accepted into accredited program at US institution (+Puerto Rico & Virgin Islands). Must graduate within 12 to 24 months from the date of grant and demonstrate critical financial need. Must have a plan to upgrade skills, train for a new career field, or to enter/re-enter the job market.

Full- or part-time study. For info see website or send business-sized, self-addressed, double-stamped envelope.

191—CHARLES E. SAAK TRUST (Educational Grants)

Wells Fargo Bank
8405 N. Fresno Street, Suite 210
Fresno CA 93720
Written inquiry only

AMOUNT: Varies
DEADLINE(S): MAR 31
FIELD(S): Education, Dentistry

Undergraduate grants for residents of the Porterville-Poplar area of Tulare County, California. Must carry a minimum of 12 units, have at least a 2.0 GPA, be under age 21, and demonstrate financial need.

Approximately 100 awards per year. Renewable with reapplication. Write for complete information.

192—CONTINENTAL SOCIETY DAUGHTERS OF INDIAN WARS (Scholarship)

Rte. 2, Box 184
Locust Grove OK 74352
918/479-5670

AMOUNT: $1,000
DEADLINE(S): JUN 15
FIELD(S): Education, Social Work, Social Service

Open to Native American, certified tribal members with plans to work on a reservation. Must be an undergraduate junior or senior accepted to or already attending an accredited college/university, be carrying at least eight semester hours, and have a minimum 3.0 GPA. Must be US citizen and demonstrate financial need.

1 award annually. Renewable. Contact Mrs. Ronald Jacobs for an application.

193—HOPI TRIBE (Priority Scholarships)

P.O. Box 123
Kykotsmovi AZ 86039
520/734-2441, ext. 520
800/762-9630
FAX: 520/734-2435

AMOUNT: Varies
DEADLINE(S): JUL 31
FIELD(S): Law, Natural Resources, Education, Medicine/Health, Engineering, Business

Open to enrolled members of the Hopi Tribe studying in one of the fields listed above, which are considered to be areas of priority interest to the Hopis. Available to college juniors, seniors, and graduate students. Program is to encourage graduates to apply their degrees to Hopi Tribal Goals and Objectives.

Contact Hopi Tribe for an application.

194—JAMES MADISON MEMORIAL FELLOWSHIP (Fellowship for Teachers)

2000 K Street NW
Washington DC 20006
202/653-8700 or
800/525-6928
FAX: 202/653-6045
Internet: www.jamesmadison.com

AMOUNT: $24,000 prorated over study period
DEADLINE(S): MAR 1
FIELD(S): Teaching American History/government, or social studies—concentration on the US Constitution

Fellowships for teachers (senior fellows) in grades 7-12 in the above fields to pursue an M.A. degree. Also for full-time college seniors and grad students (junior fellows). US citizens or US nationals. Fellows are selected from each state and from DC, Puerto Rico, Guam, Virgin Islands, American Samoa, Northern Mariana Islands, and Palau. Program designed to enhance teaching about the US Constitution.

Application is on website or contact: American College Testing, P.O. Box 4030, Iowa City, IA 52243-4030; 800/525-6928
E-mail: Recogprog@ACT-ACT4-PO.act.org

195—LOUISIANA OFFICE OF STUDENT FINANCIAL ASSISTANCE (Tuition Opportunity Program for Students-Teachers Award)

P.O. Box 91202
Baton Rouge LA 70821-9202
800/259-5626, ext. 1012
FAX: 504/922-0790
Internet: www.osfa.state.la.us

AMOUNT: $4,000/yr. (education majors); $6,000/yr. (math/chemistry majors)
DEADLINE(S): JUN 1
FIELD(S): Education, Math, Chemistry

Open to Louisiana residents pursuing undergraduate or graduate study at Louisiana colleges/universities and majoring in one of the above fields leading to teacher certification. Loans are forgiven by working as a certified teacher in Louisiana one year for each year loan is received.

Apply by completing the Free Application for Federal Student Aid (FAFSA). See your school's financial aid office or contact LOSFA for FAFSA form.

196—NATIVE AMERICAN SCHOLARSHIP FUND, INC. (Scholarships)

8200 Mountain Road NE, Suite 203
Albuquerque NM 87110
505/262-2351
FAX: 505/262-0543
E-mail: NScholarsh@aol.com

AMOUNT: Varies
DEADLINE(S): MAR 15; APR 15; SEP 15
FIELD(S): Math, Engineering,. Science, Business, Education, Computer Science

Open to American Indians or Alaskan Natives (1/4 degree or more) enrolled as members of a federally recognized, state recognized, or terminated tribe. For graduate or undergraduate study at an accredited four-year college or university.

208 awards annually. Contact Lucille Kelley, Director of Recruitment, for an application.

197—NAVAL HISTORICAL CENTER (Internship Program)

Washington Navy Yard
901 M Street SE
Washington DC 20374-5060
202/433-6901
FAX: 202/433-8200
E-mail: efurgol@nhc.navy.mil
Internet: www.history.navy.mil

AMOUNT: $400 possible honoraria; otherwise, unpaid
DEADLINE(S): None
FIELD(S): Education, History, Public Relations, Design

Registered students of colleges/universities and graduates thereof are eligible for this program, which must be a minimum of 3 weeks, full or part-time. Four specialities available: Curator, Education, Public Relations, and Design. Interns receive orientation & assist in their departments, and must complete individual project which contributes to Center. Must submit a letter of recommendation, unofficial transcript, and writing sample of not less than 1,000 words.

Contact Dr. Edward M. Furgol, Curator, for an application.

198—UNIVERSITY OF SAN FRANCISCO McLAREN SCHOOL OF BUSINESS (Laura D. Sypin Memorial Scholarship)

2130 Fulton Street
San Francisco CA 94117-1080
415/422-2513

AMOUNT: Varies
DEADLINE(S): Varies
FIELD(S): Business Administration

A scholarship for women pursuing a degree in business. Earmarked for women who are currently employed or wishing to re-enter the workplace by earning a business degree.

Contact McLaren's Office of External Affairs at above location for details.

EDUCATION

199—ADELPHI UNIVERSITY (Athletic Grants)

1 South Ave.
Garden City NY 11530

516/877-3080
Internet: www.adelphi.edu/finaid/awards.html

AMOUNT: $2,000-$13,000
DEADLINE(S): FEB 15
FIELD(S): Any major, but must demonstrate exceptional ability in athletics

Various scholarships for full-time students at Adelphi University who demonstrate excellence in athletics. Must continue to participate in the University's athletic teams and maintain 2.0 GPA overall to maintain scholarship.

See website for further information; contact school to apply.

200—ALASKA COMMISSION ON POST-SECONDARY EDUCATION (Alaska Teacher Scholarship Loan Program)

3030 Vintage Blvd.
Juneau AK 99801
907/465-6741
FAX: 907/465-5316
E-mail: ftolbert@educ.state.ak.us

AMOUNT: Up to $7,500/yr., with $37,500 lifetime maximum
DEADLINE(S): MAY 1 (nominations from school superintendents)
FIELD(S): Elementary or Secondary Education

Loans for Alaska high school graduates from rural areas who intend to teach in rural areas. Students are nominated by their rural schools. Employment as a teacher in a rural area in Alaska can result in up to 100% forgiveness of the loan. For use in both Alaska and elsewhere.

75-100 awards per year. Contact ACPE for details and the qualifications of a "rural" resident.

201—AMERICAN ALLIANCE FOR HEALTH, PHYSICAL EDUCATION, RECREATION & DANCE

1900 Association Drive
Reston VA 20191
703/476-3400 or 800/213-7193
E-mail: webmaster@aahperd.org
Internet: www.aahperd.org

AMOUNT: Varies
DEADLINE(S): Varies
FIELD(S): Health Education, Leisure and Recreation, Girls and Women in Sports, Sport and Physical Education, Dance

This organization has six national sub-organizations specializing in the above fields. Some have grants and fellowships

for both individuals and group projects. The website has the details for each group.

Visit website for details or write to above address for details.

202—AMERICAN FOUNDATION FOR THE BLIND (Delta Gamma Foundation Memorial Scholarship)

11 Penn Plaza, Suite 300
New York NY 10001
212/502-7661
FAX: 212/502-7771
E-mail: juliet@afb.org
Internet: www.afb.org

AMOUNT: $1,000
DEADLINE(S): APR 30
FIELD(S): Rehabilitation/Education of Visually Impaired/Blind

Open to legally blind undergraduate and graduate students of good character who have exhibited academic excellence and are studying in field of rehabilitation/education of persons who are blind or visually impaired. Must be US citizen. Must submit evidence of legal blindness; official transcripts; proof of college/university acceptance; three letters of recommendation; and typewritten statement describing goals, work experience, activities, and how money will be used.

1 award annually. See website or contact Julie Tucker at AFB for an application.

203—AMERICAN FOUNDATION FOR THE BLIND (Rudolph Dillman Memorial Scholarships)

11 Penn Plaza, Suite 300
New York NY 10001
212/502-7661
FAX: 212/502-7771
E-mail: juliet@afb.org
Internet: www.afb.org

AMOUNT: $2,500
DEADLINE(S): APR 30
FIELD(S): Rehabilitation/Education of Visually Impaired/Blind

Open to legally blind undergraduate and graduate students studying in field of rehabilitation/education of persons who are blind or visually impaired. Must be US citizen studying in the US. Must submit evidence of legal blindness; official transcripts; proof of college/university acceptance; three letters of recommendation; and typewritten statement describing goals, work experience, extracurricular activities, how monies will be used, and economic need (if applicable).

4 awards annually, one of which requires evidence of economic need. Not renewable. See website or contact Julie Tucker at AFB for an application.

204—AMERICAN INDIAN SCIENCE AND ENGINEERING SOCIETY (Burlington Northern Santa Fe Pacific Foundation Scholarships)

P.O. Box 9828
Albuquerque NM 87119-9828
505/765-1052
FAX: 505/765-5608
E-mail: scholarships@aises.org
Internet: www.aises.org/scholarships

AMOUNT: $2,500/yr.
DEADLINE(S): MAR 31
FIELD(S): Business, Education, Science, Engineering, Health Administration

Open to high school seniors who are at least 1/4 American Indian. Must reside in KS, OK, CO, AZ, NM, MN, ND, OR, SD, WA, MT, or San Bernardino County, CA (Burlington Northern and Santa Fe Pacific service areas). Must demonstrate financial need.

5 awards annually. Renewable up to 4 years. See website or contact Patricia Browne for an application.

205—AMERICAN SPEECH-LANGUAGE-HEARING FOUNDATION (Kala Singh Memorial Fund-International/Minority Student Scholarship)

10801 Rockville Pike
RRockville MD 20852
301/897-5700
FAX: 301/571-0457

AMOUNT: $2,000
DEADLINE(S): JUN 6
FIELD(S): Communication Sciences and Disorders, Speech/Language Pathology, Audiology

Applicants must be international/ethnic minority graduate student studying communication sciences and disorders in the US and demonstrating outstanding academic achievement.

Applications available in February.

206—AMERICAN SPEECH-LANGUAGE-HEARING FOUNDATION (Leslie Isenberg Fund for Student With Disability)

10801 Rockville Pike
Rockville MD 20852
301/897-5700
FAX: 301/571-0457

AMOUNT: $2,000
DEADLINE(S): JUN 6
FIELD(S): Communication Sciences & Disorders

Open to full-time graduate student with disability enrolled in a communication sciences and disorders program and demonstrating outstanding academic achievement.

Applications available in February.

207—AMERICAN SPEECH-LANGUAGE-HEARING FOUNDATION (Young Scholars Award for Minority Student)

10801 Rockville Pike
Rockville MD 20852
301/897-5700
FAX: 301/571-0457

AMOUNT: $2,000
DEADLINE(S): JUN 6
FIELD(S): Speech/Language Pathology; Audiology

Open to ethnic minorities who are full-time college seniors accepted for graduate study in speech-language pathology or audiology. Applicants must be US citizens.

Applications available in February.

208—ARKANSAS DEPARTMENT OF HIGHER EDUCATION (Emergency Secondary Education Loan)

114 East Capitol
Little Rock AR 72201-3818
501/371-2050 or 800/54-STUDY
FAX: 501/371-2001
E-mail: finaid@adhe.arknet.edu
Internet: www.arscholarships.com

AMOUNT: $2,500
DEADLINE(S): APR 1
FIELD(S): Secondary Education: Math, Science, Foreign Language, or Special Education

For Arkansas residents who are full-time undergraduate or graduate students pursuing secondary education teaching certification in above fields at approved Arkansas public or private colleges/universities. Repayment of loan is forgiven at the rate of 20% per year for each year taught in approved subject shortage area in an Arkansas secondary school after graduation.

See website or contact ADHE for an application.

209—ARKANSAS DEPARTMENT OF HIGHER EDUCATION (Minority Grant Program)

114 East Capitol
Little Rock AR 72201-3818

501/371-2050 or 800/54-STUDY
FAX: 501/371-2001
E-mail: finaid@adhe.arknet.edu
Internet: www.arscholarships.com

AMOUNT: $1,000
DEADLINE(S): Varies
FIELD(S): Education

For minority students who are full-time freshmen or sophomores in college and interested in teacher education programs. Must be Arkansas residents attending approved Arkansas public or private colleges/universities. Students must perform pre-service internships in public school settings and sign a statement of interest in teaching.

Contact the College of Education Office or Dean of Students on the campus you plan to attend.

210—ARKANSAS DEPARTMENT OF HIGHER EDUCATION (Minority Teachers Scholarship)

114 East Capitol
Little Rock AR 72201-3818
501/371-2050 or 800/54-STUDY
FAX: 501/371-2001
E-mail: finaid@adhe.arknet.edu
Internet: www.arscholarships.com

AMOUNT: $5,000
DEADLINE(S): JUN 1
FIELD(S): Education

For Arkansas residents who are minority college students enrolled full-time at approved Arkansas public or private colleges/universities. Must have completed 60 semester credit hours, have been admitted to approved program for teacher certification, and have a minimum 2.5 GPA. After graduation, must teach full-time in Arkansas public school to receive full loan forgiveness. Financial need is NOT a factor.

100+ awards annually. See website or contact ADHE for an application.

211—AROMANDO FAMILY EDUCATIONAL FOUNDATION (Aromando & Mauriello Memorial Awards)

207 Route 541, R.D.#7
Medford NJ 08055
609/654-2397
E-mail: jha0227@netzero.net

AMOUNT: $200 (min.)
DEADLINE(S): DEC 1
FIELD(S): Elementary/Special Education; Theology (Priest/Nun)

Open to high school seniors/grads accepted to or attending any college/university full-time and majoring in teaching (elementary or special education) or for religious service (to become priest or nun). Must be an American of Italian heritage and a practicing Roman Catholic with a minimum 3.0 GPA. Must have received at least two varsity letters in one or more high school-sanctioned athletic or extracurricular programs. Financial need NOT a factor.

Send self-addressed, stamped, legal-size envelope for an application.

212—ASSOCIATION FOR EDUCATION AND REHABILITATION OF THE BLIND AND VISUALLY IMPAIRED (William and Dorothy Ferrell Scholarship)

4600 Duke Street, #430
P.O. Box 22397
Alexandria VA 22304
703/823-9690
FAX: 703/823-9695
E-mail: aer@aerbvi.org
Internet: www.aerbvi.org

AMOUNT: $500
DEADLINE(S): APR 15 (of even-numbered years)
FIELD(S): Fields of study related to the blind/visually impaired

Scholarships for students who are legally blind, pursuing postsecondary education in a field related to services for the blind or visually impaired. Financial need NOT a factor.

2 awards annually. See website or contact Carolyn Sharp at above address for details.

213—ASSOCIATION FOR EDUCATION AND REHABILITATION OF THE BLIND AND VISUALLY IMPAIRED (Telesensory Scholarship)

4600 Duke Street, #430
P.O. Box 22397
Alexandria VA 22304
703/823-9690
FAX: 703/823-9695
E-mail: aer@aerbvi.org
Internet: www.aerbvi.org

AMOUNT: $1,000
DEADLINE(S): APR 15 (of even-numbered years)
FIELD(S): Fields of study related to the blind/visually impaired

Scholarships for students who are members of AER pursuing postsecondary education in a field related to services for the blind or visually impaired. Must become an AER member before applying. Financial need NOT a factor.

1 award annually. For membership information or an application, see website or contact Carolyn Sharp at above address.

214—ASSOCIATION FOR RETARDED CITIZENS (Brazoria County Scholarships)

Highway 2004 & 332
Lake Jackson TX 77566
Internet: www.window.state.tx.us/scholars/aid/scholarship/scarcbc.html

AMOUNT: $250
DEADLINE(S): None specified
FIELD(S): Special Education

For two graduating high school seniors from Brazoria County area. Scholarship to be used toward degree in special education.

Apply to above address, giving information concerning your schooling and plans for the future.

215—B.M. WOLTMAN FOUNDATION (Lutheran Scholarships for Students of the Ministry and Teaching)

7900 U.S. 290 E.
Austin TX 78724
512/926-4272

AMOUNT: $500-$2,500
DEADLINE(S): Varies
FIELD(S): Theology (Lutheran Ministry); Teacher Education (Lutheran Schools)

Scholarships for undergrads and graduate students studying for careers in the Lutheran ministry or for teaching in a Lutheran school. For Texas residents attending, or planning to attend, any college in Texas.

45 awards. Renewable. Send for details.

216—BLUES HEAVEN FOUNDATION, INC. (Muddy Waters Scholarship)

2120 S. Michigan Ave.
Chicago IL 60616
312/808-1286

AMOUNT: $2,000
DEADLINE(S): APR 30
FIELD(S): Music, Music Education, African-American Studies, Folklore, Performing Arts, Arts Management, Journalism, Radio/TV/Film

Scholarship is made on a competitive basis with consideration given to scholastic achievement, concentration of studies, and financial need. Applicant must have full-time enrollment status in a Chicago area college/university in at least their first year of undergraduate studies or a graduate program. Scholastic aptitude, extracurricu-

lar involvement, grade point average, and financial need are all considered.

Contact Blues Heaven Foundation, Inc. to receive an application between February and April.

217—BUSINESS & PROFESSIONAL WOMEN'S FOUNDATION (BPW Career Advancement Scholarship Program)

2012 Massachusetts Ave. NW
Washington DC 20036-1070
202/293-1200, ext. 169
FAX: 202/861-0298
Internet: www.bpwusa.org

AMOUNT: $500-$1,000
DEADLINE(S): APR 15
FIELD(S): Biology, Science, Education, Engineering, Social Science, Paralegal, Humanities, Business, Math, Computers, Law, MD, DD

For women (US citizens) aged 25+ accepted into accredited program at US institution (+Puerto Rico & Virgin Islands). Must graduate within 12 to 24 months from the date of grant and demonstrate critical financial need. Must have a plan to upgrade skills, train for a new career field, or to enter/re-enter the job market.

Full- or part-time study. For info see website or send business-sized, self-addressed, double-stamped envelope.

218—CALIFORNIA GRANGE FOUNDATION (Deaf Activities Scholarships)

Pat Avila
2101 Stockton Blvd.
Sacramento CA 95817
Written inquiry

AMOUNT: Varies
DEADLINE(S): APR 1
FIELD(S): Course work that will be of benefit to the deaf community

Scholarships for students entering, continuing, or returning to college to pursue studies that will benefit the deaf community.

Write for information after Feb. 1 of each year.

219—CALIFORNIA SCHOOL LIBRARY ASSOCIATION (Leadership for Diversity Scholarship)

CSLA Office
1499 Old Bayshore Hwy., Suite 142
Burlingame CA 94010
415/692-2350
FAX: 415/692-4956

AMOUNT: $1,000
DEADLINE(S): JUN 1
FIELD(S): School librarian/media teacher

Scholarship for a member of a traditionally underrepresented group enrolled in a California accredited library media teacher credential program. Must intend to work as a library media teacher in a California school library media center for a minimum of three years.

Financial need considered. Send SASE for details to above organization.

220—CALIFORNIA STUDENT AID COMMISSION (Assumption Program of Loans for Education—APLE)

P.O. Box 419026
Rancho Cordova CA 95741-9026
916/526-7590
FAX: 916/526-8002
E-mail: custsvcs@csac.ca.gov
Internet: www.csac.ca.gov

AMOUNT: up to $11,000
DEADLINE(S): JUN 30
FIELD(S): Elementary/Secondary Education

Assumes loan debt for students pursuing K-12 teaching career, in exchange for teaching service. For California resident attending school in California, having completed 60 semester units undergrad study & continuing to be enrolled for at least 10 semester units/equivalent through end of each term. Must provide four consecutive years teaching in CA K-12 public school in designated-subject shortage area, or in school serving many low-income students.

Up to 4,500 awards annually. Must be nominated by participating colleges or school districts with approved teacher preparation programs. Contact the APLE Coordinator at your school or above address.

221—CALIFORNIA STUDENT AID COMMISSION (Child Development Teacher Grants)

P.O. Box 419026
Rancho Cordova CA 95741-9026
916/526-7590 or
TDD 916/526-7542
FAX: 916/526-8002
E-mail: custsvcs@csac.ca.gov
Internet: www.csac.ca.gov

AMOUNT: $1,000 (2-year colleges); $2,000 (4-year colleges)
DEADLINE(S): None given
FIELD(S): Early Childhood Education

For California residents attending California public/private 2- or 4-year institutions who plan to teach/supervise at a licensed children's center. Must have financial need and at least "C" average. Must be pursuing child development permit at the teacher, site supervisor, or program director level. In return, students must teach full-time in licensed CA children's center for one year for each year of assistance.

Up to 100 grants annually. Renewable for an additional year. For more information, contact your financial aid or early childhood education office, or the California Student Aid Commission.

222—CALIFORNIA TEACHERS ASSOCIATION (CTA Scholarships for Members)

P.O. Box 921
Burlingame CA 94011-0921
650/697-1400
E-mail: scholarships@cta.org
Internet: www.cta.org

AMOUNT: $2,000
DEADLINE(S): FEB 15
FIELD(S): Education

For active members of the California Teachers Association for undergraduate or graduate study. Financial need is NOT considered.

5 awards annually. Renewable with re-application. Contact the Human Rights Department at above address between October and February for an application.

223—CALIFORNIA TEACHERS ASSOCIATION (L. Gordon Bittle Memorial Scholarships)

P.O. Box 921
Burlingame CA 94011-0921
650/697-1400
E-mail: scholarships@cta.org
Internet: www.cta.org

AMOUNT: $2,000
DEADLINE(S): FEB 15
FIELD(S): Education

For members of SCTA (Student California Teachers Association) for undergraduate or graduate study in a teacher preparatory program in California. Financial need is NOT considered.

3 awards annually. Renewable with re-application. Contact Human Rights Department at above address between October and February for an application.

224—CALIFORNIA TEACHERS ASSOCIATION (Martin Luther King, Jr. Memorial Scholarship)

P.O. Box 921
Burlingame CA 94011-0921
650/697-1400
E-mail: scholarships@cta.org
Internet: www.cta.org

AMOUNT: $1,000-$2,000
DEADLINE(S): MAR 15
FIELD(S): Education

Open to ethnic minorities who are CTA members, dependents of CTA members, or Student CTA members. Awards are for undergraduate or graduate study and are to be used in pursuit of degrees or credentials for teaching-related careers in public education. Financial need considered.

20-30 awards annually. Renewable with reapplication. Contact Human Rights Department at above address between January and March for an application.

225—CAREER OPPORTUNITIES FOR YOUTH, INC. (Collegiate Scholarship Program)

P.O. Box 996
Manhattan Beach CA 90266
310/535-4838

AMOUNT: $250 to $1,000
DEADLINE(S): SEP 30
FIELD(S): Engineering, Science, Mathematics, Computer Science, Business Administration, Education, Nursing

For students of Latino/Hispanic background residing in the Southern California area who have completed at least one semester/quarter of study at an accredited four-year university. Must have a cumulative GPA of 2.5 or higher.

Priority will be given to students who demonstrate financial need. Send SASE to above location for details.

226—CIVIL AIR PATROL (CAP Undergraduate Scholarships)

Civil Air Patrol
National Headquarters
Maxwell AFB AL 36112-6332
334/953-5315

AMOUNT: $750
DEADLINE(S): JAN 31
FIELD(S): Humanities, Science, Engineering, Education

Open to CAP members who have received the Billy Mitchell Award or the senior rating in Level II of the senior training program. For undergraduate study in the above areas.

Write for complete information.

227—COMMUNITY FOUNDATION OF WESTERN MASSACHUSETTS (Nate McKinney Memorial Scholarship)

1500 Main Street, P.O. Box 15769
Springfield MA 01115
413/732-2858
AMOUNT: $1,000
DEADLINE(S): APR 15
FIELD(S): Music, Athletics, Science

Open to graduating seniors of Gateway Regional High School in Huntington, Massachusetts. Recipient must excel academically, demonstrate good citizenship, and have a strong interest in at least two of the following areas: music, science, and athletics. Based on financial need, academic merit, and extracurricular activities. Must submit transcripts and fill out government FAFSA form.

1 award annually. Renewable up to 4 years with reapplication. Contact Community Foundation for an application and your financial aid office for FAFSA. Notification is in June.

228—CONTINENTAL SOCIETY DAUGHTERS OF INDIAN WARS (Scholarship)

Route 2, Box 184
Locust Grove OK 74352
918/479-5670
AMOUNT: $1,000
DEADLINE(S): JUN 15
FIELD(S): Education, Social Work, Social Service

Open to Native American, certified tribal members with plans to work on a reservation. Must be an undergraduate junior or senior accepted to or already attending an accredited college/university, be carrying at least eight semester hours, and have a minimum 3.0 GPA. Must be US citizen and demonstrate financial need.

1 award annually. Renewable. Contact Mrs. Ronald Jacobs for an application.

229—EASTER SEAL SOCIETY OF IOWA, INC. (Scholarships & Awards)

P.O. Box 4002
Des Moines IA 50333-4002
515/289-1933
AMOUNT: $400-$600
DEADLINE(S): APR 15

FIELD(S): Physical Rehabilitation, Mental Rehabilitation, and related areas

Open ONLY to Iowa residents who are full-time undergraduate sophomores, juniors, seniors, or graduate students at accredited institutions planning a career in the broad field of rehabilitation. Must indicate financial need and be in top 40% of their class.

6 scholarships per year. Must reapply each year.

230—FINANCE AUTHORITY OF MAINE (Teachers for Maine)

119 State House Station
Augusta ME 04333
207/287-2183
(in state 800/228-3734)
FAX: 207/626-8208
Internet: www.famemaine.com
AMOUNT: $3,000
DEADLINE(S): APR 1
FIELD(S): Education-teacher preparation

For Maine residents. High school seniors, college students, and teachers are eligible to apply for interest-free loans. Loans are competitive and based on academic merit, relevance of field of study, etc.

400 new awards per year. Renewable. Write for complete information.

231—FLORIDA DEPT. OF EDUCATION (Florida Teacher Scholarship & Forgivable Loan Program)

Student Financial Assistance
255 Collins
Tallahassee FL 32399-0400
850/487-0049 or 888/827-2004
E-mail: OSFABF@mail.doe.state.fl.us
Internet: www.firn.edu/doe
AMOUNT: $1,500/yr (scholarship); $4,000/yr (undergrad loan); $8,000/yr (graduate loan)
DEADLINE(S): MAR 1
FIELD(S): Teaching

Undergraduate scholarships are for nominated high school seniors in top 25% of class for freshman & sophomore years. Two-year Critical Teacher Shortage Loans are for upper division undergrads & graduates who intend to teach in CTS areas in Florida. Undergrads must have 40th percentile on SAT/ACT & have minimum 2.5 GPA. Grads must have undergrad 3.0 GPA or at least 1000 on Graduate Record Exam.

438 scholarships, 300 loans annually. Loans must be repaid by teaching in a

Florida public school or in cash. Request applications from above address.

232—FOUNDATION FOR EXCEPTIONAL CHILDREN (Minigrant Awards for Teachers)

1920 Association Drive
Reston VA 22091
703/620-1054
AMOUNT: Up to $500
DEADLINE(S): MAR 1
FIELD(S): Education projects for gifted children or for those with disabilities

Minigrant awards for innovative education-related projects benefiting gifted children or children or youth with disabilities. Only for teachers employed by public or nonprofit institutions.

Apply to Minigrant Committee at above location.

233—FOUNDATION FOR TECHNOLOGY EDUCATION (Hearlihy/FTE Grant)

1914 Association Drive, Suite 201
Reston VA 20191-1539
Phone/Fax: 804/559-4226
E-mail: thughes@pen.k12.va.us
Internet: www.iteawww.org
AMOUNT: $2,000
DEADLINE(S): DEC 1
FIELD(S): Technology education

Grant for a technology teacher (K-12). Purpose is to recognize and encourage the integration of a quality technology education program within the school curriculum.

Access website or contact above organization for details.

234—FOUNDATION FOR TECHNOLOGY EDUCATION (Litherland/FTE Scholarship)

1914 Association Drive, Suite 201
Reston VA 20191-1539
Phone/Fax: 804/559-4226
E-mail: thughes@pen.k12.va.us
Internet: www.iteawww.org
AMOUNT: $1,000
DEADLINE(S): DEC 1
FIELD(S): Technology education teacher preparation

Scholarship for an undergraduate student majoring in the above field. Based upon interest in teaching, academic ability, need, and faculty recommendation. Must not be a senior by application deadline and must be a current, full-time undergraduate. Min. GPA of 2.5 required.

Must be a member of the International Technology Education Association. Membership may be enclosed with scholarship application.

235—FOUNDATION FOR TECHNOLOGY EDUCATION (Undergraduate Scholarship)

1914 Association Drive, Suite 201
Reston VA 20191-1539
Phone/Fax: 804/559-4226
E-mail: thughes@pen.k12.va.us
Internet: www.iteawww.org

AMOUNT: $1,000
DEADLINE(S): DEC 1
FIELD(S): Technology education teacher preparation

Scholarship for an undergraduate student majoring in the above field. Based upon interest in teaching, academic ability, need, and faculty recommendation. Must not be a senior by application deadline and must be a current, full-time undergraduate. Min. GPA of 2.5 required.

Must be a member of the International Technology Education Association. Membership may be enclosed with scholarship application.

236—FRANCIS NATHANIEL AND KATHERYN PADGETT KENNEDY FOUNDATION (Scholarships for Southern Baptists)

933 Sunset Drive
Greenwood SC 29646
803/942-1400

AMOUNT: $400-$1,000
DEADLINE(S): MAY 15
FIELD(S): Theology (in preparation for the ministry or missionary work) or Christian education

Scholarships for college-bound high school seniors and undergraduates who are active members of the church of the National Baptist Convention. Must be planning a career as a Southern Baptist minister, foreign missionary, or in Christian education.

Send SASE for details.

237—FREEDOM FROM RELIGION FOUNDATION (Student Essay Contest)

P.O. Box 750
Madison WI 53701
608/256-5800
Internet: www.infidels.org/org/ffrf

AMOUNT: $1,000; $500; $250
DEADLINE(S): JUL 15
FIELD(S): Humanities, English, Education, Philosophy, Science

Essay contest on topics related to church–state entanglement in public schools or growing up a "freethinker" in religious-oriented society. Topics change yearly, but all are on general theme of maintaining separation of church and state. New topics available in February. For high school seniors and currently enrolled college/technical students. Must be US citizen.

Send SASE to address above for complete information. Please indicate whether wanting information for college competition or high school. Information will be sent when new topics are announced each February. See website for details.

238—GENERAL FEDERATION OF WOMEN'S CLUBS OF MASSACHUSETTS (Newtonville Woman's Club Scholarship)

245 Dutton Road, Box 679
Sudbury MA 01776-0679
508/229-2023

AMOUNT: $600
DEADLINE(S): MAR 1
FIELD(S): Education/Teaching

For high school seniors in Massachusetts who will enroll in a four-year accredited college or university in a teacher training program that leads to certification to teach. Letter of endorsement from sponsoring GFWC of MA club, personal letter stating need and pertinent information, letter of recommendation from a high school department head or career counselor, transcripts, and personal interview required with application.

At least one scholarship annually. For more information or an application, send a self-addressed, stamped envelope to Marilyn Perry, Scholarship Chairman, at above address.

239—HOPI TRIBE (Priority Scholarships)

P.O. Box 123
Kykotsmovi AZ 86039
520/734-2441, ext. 520
800/762-9630
FAX: 520/734-2435

AMOUNT: Varies
DEADLINE(S): JUL 31
FIELD(S): Law, Natural Resources, Education, Medicine/Health, Engineering, Business

Open to enrolled members of the Hopi Tribe studying in one of the fields listed above, which are considered to be areas of priority interest to the Hopis. Available to college juniors, seniors, and graduate students. Program is to encourage graduates to apply their degrees to Hopi Tribal Goals and Objectives.

Contact Hopi Tribe for an application.

240—ILLINOIS CONGRESS OF PARENTS AND TEACHERS (Illinois PTA Scholarships)

901 S. Spring Street
Springfield IL 62704
217/528-9617

AMOUNT: $500-$1,000
DEADLINE(S): MAR 1
FIELD(S): Education

For Illinois residents who are graduating public high school seniors who plan to major in education at an accredited US college or university. Must be in the upper 25% of class.

44 awards annually (2 per PTA district). Applications available after January 1st at public high schools.

241—ILLINOIS STUDENT ASSISTANCE COMMISSION (David A. DeBolt Teacher Shortage Scholarship Program)

1755 Lake Cook Road
Deerfield IL 60015-5209
800/899-ISAC
Internet: www.isac1.org

AMOUNT: Tuition, fees, room/board or $5,000
DEADLINE(S): MAY 1
FIELD(S): Education—Teacher training

Scholarships and loans for Illinois students planning to teach at approved Illinois preschools, elementary schools, or secondary schools in a designated teacher shortage discipline.

300 annual awards. Illinois residency and US citizenship required. Access website or write for complete information.

242—ILLINOIS STUDENT ASSISTANCE COMMISSION (Minority Teachers of Illinois Scholarship Program)

1755 Lake Cook Road
Deerfield IL 60015-5209
800/899-ISAC
Internet: www.isac1.org

AMOUNT: Tuition, fees, room/board or $5,000
DEADLINE(S): MAY 1
FIELD(S): Education—Teacher training

Scholarships and loans for Illinois students planning to teach at approved Illinois preschools, elementary schools, or secondary schools.

400 annual awards. Illinois residency and US citizenship required. Access website or write for complete information.

243—ILLINOIS STUDENT ASSISTANCE COMMISSION (Special Education Teacher Tuition Waiver Program)

1755 Lake Cook Road
Deerfield IL 60015-5209
800/899-ISAC
Internet: www.isac1.org
AMOUNT: Tuition and fees
DEADLINE(S): FEB 15
FIELD(S): Special Education Teacher Training

Waiver of tuition and fees for Illinois students seeking initial certification in special education and who attend Illinois public universities.

300 annual awards. Illinois residency and US citizenship required. Access website or write for complete information.

244—INSTITUTE FOR HUMANE STUDIES (Summer Residential Program)

4084 University Drive, Suite 101
Fairfax VA 22030-6812
703/934-6920 or 800/697-8799
FAX: 703/352-7535
E-mail: ihs@gmu.edu
Internet: www.theihs.org
AMOUNT: All seminar fees: program cost, room/board, materials, and books
DEADLINE(S): MAR 1
FIELD(S): Social Sciences, Humanities, Law, Journalism, Public Policy, Education, Writing

For college students, recent graduates, and graduate students who share an interest in learning and exchanging ideas about the scope of individual rights. One-week and weekend seminars at various campus locations across the US.

Apply online or contact IHS for an application.

245—INTERNATIONAL ORDER OF THE ALHAMBRA (Undergraduate Scholarship Grant)

4200 Leeds Ave.
Baltimore MD 21229-5496
410/242-0660
FAX: 410/536-5729
AMOUNT: $400
DEADLINE(S): JAN 1; JUL 1
FIELD(S): Special Education

Open to undergraduate students who will be entering their junior or senior year in an accredited program for teaching the mentally challenged and the handicapped. Tenable in the United States and Canada.

US or Canadian citizenship required. Write for complete information.

246—INTERNATIONAL READING ASSOCI-ATION (Albert J. Harris Award)

800 Barksdale Road
P.O. Box 8139
Newark DE 19714-8139
302/731-1600, ext. 226
FAX: 302/731-1057
E-mail: gkeating@reading.org
AMOUNT: $500
DEADLINE(S): SEP 15
FIELD(S): Reading Disabilities

This prize recognizes outstanding published works (single- or joint-authored research-based articles) on the topics of reading disabilities and the prevention, assessment, or instruction of learners experiencing difficulty learning to read. Publications that have appeared in a refereed professional journal or monograph from June of the previous year to June of the current year are eligible, and may be submitted by the author or anyone else. IRA membership NOT required.

1 award annually. Contact Gail Keating, Projects Manager, Division of Research and Policy, at above address for guidelines.

247—INTERNATIONAL READING ASSOCI-ATION (Dina Feitelson Research Award)

800 Barksdale Road
P.O. Box 8139
Newark DE 19714-8139
302/731-1600, ext. 226
FAX: 302/731-1057
E-mail: gkeating@reading.org
AMOUNT: $500
DEADLINE(S): SEP 15
FIELD(S): Beginning Reading

This prize is to recognize an outstanding empirical study, or a literacy or reading related topic published in a refereed journal. Article must have been published between June of the previous year and June of the current year, and may be submitted by the author or anyone else. IRA membership is NOT required.

1 award annually. Contact Gail Keating, Projects Manager, Division of Research and Policy, at above address for guidelines.

248—INTERNATIONAL READING ASSOCI-ATION (Elva Knight Research Grant)

800 Barksdale Road
P.O. Box 8139
Newark DE 19714-8139
302/731-1600, ext. 226
FAX: 302/731-1057
E-mail: gkeating@reading.org
AMOUNT: $5,000 max.
DEADLINE(S): OCT 15
FIELD(S): Reading/Literacy Research

Grant is to assist researcher in a reading and literacy project. Research is defined as inquiry that addresses significant questions about literacy instruction and practice. Open to IRA members worldwide. Projects should be completed within two years.

1 award annually to researcher outside the US/Canada, 1 to a teacher-initiated research project, & up to 5 additional grants. For membership information, use extension 267. For guidelines, contact Gail Keating, Projects Manager, Division of Research and Policy, at above address.

249—INTERNATIONAL READING ASSOCI-ATION (Nila Banton Smith Research Dissemination Support Grant)

800 Barksdale Road
P.O. Box 8139
Newark DE 19714-8139
302/731-1600, ext. 226
FAX: 302/731-1057
E-mail: gkeating@reading.org
AMOUNT: $5,000
DEADLINE(S): OCT 15
FIELD(S): Reading/Literacy Research

Purpose of this award is to facilitate the dissemination of literacy research to the educational community. Open to all IRA members worldwide.

1 award annually. For membership information, use extension 267. For guidelines, contact Gail Keating, Projects Manager, Division of Research and Policy, at above address.

250—INTERNATIONAL READING ASSOCI-ATION (Teacher as Researcher Grant)

800 Barksdale Road
P.O. Box 8139
Newark DE 19714-8139
302/731-1600, ext. 226
FAX: 302/731-1057
E-mail: gkeating@reading.org
AMOUNT: $1,000-$5,000

DEADLINE(S): OCT 15
FIELD(S): Reading/Literacy Instruction

Award is to support teachers in their inquiries about literacy learning and instruction. IRA members who are practicing K-12 teachers with full-time teaching responsibilities (includes librarians, Title 1 teachers, classroom, and resource teachers) may apply.

Several awards annually. For membership information, use extension 267. For guidelines, contact Gail Keating, Projects Manager, Division of Research and Policy, at above address.

251—JAMES MADISON MEMORIAL FELLOWSHIP (Fellowship for Teachers)

2000 K Street NW
Washington DC 20006
202/653-8700 or 1-800/525-6928
FAX: 202/653-6045
Internet: www.jamesmadison.com

AMOUNT: $24,000 prorated over study period
DEADLINE(S): MAR 1
FIELD(S): Teaching American History/government, or social studies—concentration on the US Constitution

Fellowships for teachers (senior fellows) in grades 7-12 in the above fields to pursue an M.A. degree. Also for full-time college seniors and grad students (junior fellows). US citizens or US nationals. Fellows are selected from each state and from DC, Puerto Rico, Guam, Virgin Islands, American Samoa, Northern Mariana Islands, and Palau. Program designed to enhance teaching about the US Constitution.

Application is on website or contact: American College Testing, P.O. Box 4030, Iowa City, IA 52243-4030; 800/525-6928
E-mail: Recogprog@ACT-ACT4-PO.ct.org

252—JEWISH VOCATIONAL SERVICE (Academic Scholarship Program)

One S. Franklin Street
Chicago IL 60606
312/357-4500
FAX: 312/855-3282
TTY: 312/855-3282
E-mail: jvschicago@jon.cjfny.org

AMOUNT: $5,000 (max.)
DEADLINE(S): MAR 1
FIELD(S): "Helping" Professions, Mathematics, Engineering, Sciences, Communications (at Univ IL only), Law (certain schools in IL only)

Open to Jewish men and women legally domiciled in the greater Chicago metropolitan area, who are identified as having promise for significant contributions in their chosen careers, and are in need of financial assistance for full-time academic programs in above areas. Must have entered undergraduate junior year in career programs requiring no postgrad education, be in graduate/professional school, or be in a voc-tech training program. Interview required.

Renewable. Contact JVS for an application between December 1st and February 15th.

253—JEWISH WELFARE BOARD (Scholarships)

15 E. 26th Street
New York NY 10010
212/532-4949

AMOUNT: $1,000-$4,000
DEADLINE(S): FEB 1
FIELD(S): Social Work, Adult Education, Early Childhood Educaiton, Health Education, Physical Education, Cultural Studies, Jewish Education

Scholarships for Jewish college juniors or seniors pursuing careers in the above fields. Must be committed to the work of the YMHA, YWHA, or Jewish community centers. Must do a year of field work in a Jewish community center.

Renewable. Contact organization for details.

254—KANSAS BOARD OF REGENTS (Kansas Teacher Scholarship)

700 SW Harrison Street, Suite 1410
Topeka KS 66603-3760
785/296-3518

AMOUNT: $5,000/yr.
DEADLINE(S): APR 1
FIELD(S): Education

For Kansas residents committed to teaching in Kansas. Preference given to students who will teach in special education, secondary science, and vocational/practical arts. May change annually. Graduate work can be funded if it is required for initial certification. If recipient does not teach in Kansas, the scholarship converts to a loan with 15% interest. Must complete the FAFSA.

$10 application fee. Renewable for 4 years (or 5 if a 5-yr. program). Contact Kansas Board of Regents for an application. See your financial aid office for the FAFSA.

255—LOUISIANA OFFICE OF STUDENT FINANCIAL ASSISTANCE (Tuition Opportunity Program for Students-Teachers Award)

P.O. Box 91202
Baton Rouge LA 70821-9202
800/259-5626, ext. 1012
FAX: 504/922-0790
Internet: www.osfa.state.la.us

AMOUNT: $4,000/yr. (education majors); $6,000/yr. (math/chemistry majors)
DEADLINE(S): JUN 1
FIELD(S): Education, Math, Chemistry

Open to Louisiana residents pursuing undergraduate or graduate study at Louisiana colleges/universities and majoring in one of the above fields leading to teacher certification. Loans are forgiven by working as a certified teacher in Louisiana one year for each year loan is received.

Apply by completing the Free Application for Federal Student Aid (FAFSA). See your school's financial aid office or contact LOSFA for FAFSA form.

256—MARYLAND HIGHER EDUCATION COMMISSION (Sharon Christa McAuliffe Critical Shortage Teacher Program)

State Scholarship Administration
16 Francis Street
Annapolis MD 21401-1781
410/974-5370
TTY: 800/735-2258

AMOUNT: Up to $9,600 for tuition, fees, and room & board
DEADLINE(S): DEC 31
FIELD(S): Education (critical shortages determined annually)

For Maryland residents who agree to teach in critical shortage area in Maryland for one year for each year of funding. Open to full or part-time undergraduates or graduates studying at a Maryland degree-granting institution.

Minimum of 60 credits of undergraduate course work & GPA of 3.0 or better required. Renewable if 3.0 GPA is maintained. Write for complete information.

257—MIDWAY COLLEGE (Institutional Aid Program—Scholarships & Grants)

Financial Aid Office
Midway KY 40347
606/846-4421

AMOUNT: Varies
DEADLINE(S): MAR 1

FIELD(S): Nursing, Paralegal, Education, Psychology, Biology, Equine Studies, Liberal Studies, Business Administration

Scholarships and grants open to women who are accepted for enrollment at Midway College. Awards support undergraduate study in the above areas.

Approx 80 awards per year. Write for complete information.

258—MISSISSIPPI OFFICE OF STATE STUDENT FINANCIAL AID (William Winter Teacher Education Program)

3825 Ridgewood Road
Jackson MS 39211-6453
601/982-6527 or 800-327-2980

AMOUNT: up to $3,000/yr.
DEADLINE(S): APR 30
FIELD(S): Teaching (public schools)

For full-time undergraduate students in a Mississippi college or university who are in a teacher education program which will lead to "Class A" certification. Entering freshmen must have a cumulative high school GPA of 3.0 & an ACT score of 21; must maintain GPA of 2.5 or higher in college. Financial need is NOT considered.

Call or write for an application.

259—NAACP NATIONAL OFFICE (Sutton Education Scholarship)

4805 Mount Hope Drive
Baltimore MD 21215-3297
410/486-9133

AMOUNT: $1,000 undergrads; $2,000 grads.
DEADLINE(S): APR 30
FIELD(S): Teacher education

Open to undergrads with a GPA of at least 2.5 and to grads with a GPA of at least 3.0 who are majoring in the field of education. Must be a full-time student and a member of the NAACP.

Renewable if GPA is maintained. Write for complete information; enclose self-addressed 9 x 12 envelope.

260—NATIONAL ASSOCIATION OF AMERICAN BUSINESS CLUBS (AMBUCS Scholarships for Therapists)

P.O. Box 5127
High Point NC 27262
910/869-2166
FAX: 910/887-8451
E-mail: ambucs@ambucs.com
Internet: www.ambucs.com

AMOUNT: $500-$6,000
DEADLINE(S): APR 15
FIELD(S): Physical Therapy, Music Therapy, Occupational Therapy, Speech-Language Pathology, Audiology, Rehabilitation, Recreation Therapy, and related areas

Open to undergraduate juniors and seniors or graduate students who have good scholastic standing and plan to enter the fields listed above. GPA of 3.0 or better (4.0 scale) and US citizenship required. Must demonstrate financial need.

Renewable. Please include a self-addressed stamped envelope (SASE); applications are mailed in December; incomplete applications will not be considered.

261—NATIONAL CLEARINGHOUSE FOR PROFESSIONS IN SPECIAL EDUCATION (Various Financial Aid Sources)

NCPSE, 1920 Association Drive
Reston VA 20191-1589
800/641-7824
783/264-9476
TTY: 703/264-9480
E-mail: ncpse@cec.sped.org
Internet: www.cec.sped.org/ncpse.htm

AMOUNT: Varies
DEADLINE(S): Varies
FIELD(S): Special Education

A listing of financial aid resources through the U.S. Dept. of Education, Office of Special Education Programs for training professionals in the field of special education. Funds are available through certain colleges and universities. Applicants may be eligible to have all or part of their college tuition paid and receive an annual stipend.

For listing of colleges and universities who have received these funds, contact NCPSE for information. State your level in college, the states in which you are interested, and the specialty areas in which you would like to concentrate.

262—NATIONAL COLLEGIATE ATHLETIC ASSOCIATION (NCAA Ethnic Minority and Women's Enhancement Program)

6201 College Blvd.
Overland Park KS 66211
913/339-1906

AMOUNT: $6,000
DEADLINE(S): FEB 15
FIELD(S): Sports Administration, Coaching, Sports Medicine, Officiating

Scholarships for women and ethnic minorities entering the first semester of initial postgraduate studies in the above or related fields. Internships of approximately one year at the NCAA national office.

Write for complete information.

263—NATIONAL FEDERATION OF THE BLIND (Educator of Tomorrow Award)

805 Fifth Ave.
Grinnell IA 50112
515/236-3366

AMOUNT: $3,000
DEADLINE(S): MAR 31
FIELD(S): Education: Elementary, Secondary, & Postsecondary

For legally blind students pursuing or planning to pursue a full-time postsecondary course of study in the US. Based on academic excellence, service to the community, and financial need. Membership NOT required.

1 award annually. Renewable. Contact Mrs. Peggy Elliot, Scholarship Committee Chairman, for an application.

264—NATIONAL SCHOOL SUPPLY AND EQUIPMENT ASSOCIATION-EDUCATION EXCELLENCE FOUNDATION (Be Your Best! Teacher Scholarships)

8300 Colesville Rd., Suite 250
Silver Spring MD 20910
301/495-0240 or 800/395-5550
FAX: 301/495-3330
Internet: http://www.nssea.org

AMOUNT: $500
DEADLINE(S): JUN 30
FIELD(S): Teacher education

Scholarships for teachers who can demonstrate a need for professional development.

20 awards to be made.

265—NATIONAL STRENGTH & CONDITIONING ASSN. (Challenge Scholarships)

P.O. Box 38909
Colorado Springs CO 80937-8909
719/632-6722
FAX: 719/632-6722
E-mail: nsca@usa.net
Internet: www.colosoft.com/nsca

AMOUNT: $1,000
DEADLINE(S): MAR 1
FIELD(S): Fields related to body strength & conditioning

Open to National Strength & Conditioning Association members. Awards are for undergraduate or graduate study.

For membership information or an application, write to the above address.

266—NATIVE AMERICAN SCHOLARSHIP FUND, INC. (Scholarships)

8200 Mountain Road NE, Suite 203
Albuquerque NM 87110
505/262-2351
FAX: 505/262-0543
E-mail: NScholarsh@aol.com

AMOUNT: Varies
DEADLINE(S): MAR 15; APR 15; SEP 15
FIELD(S): Math, Engineering, Science, Business, Education, Computer Science

Open to American Indians or Alaskan Natives (1/4 degree or more) enrolled as members of a federally recognized, state recognized, or terminated tribe. For graduate or undergraduate study at an accredited four-year college or university.

208 awards annually. Contact Lucille Kelley, Director of Recruitment, for an application.

267—NAVAL HISTORICAL CENTER (Internship Program)

Washington Navy Yard
901 M Street SE
Washington DC 20374-5060
202/433-6901
FAX: 202/433-8200
E-mail: efurgol@nhc.navy.mil
Internet: www.history.navy.mil

AMOUNT: $400 possible honoraria; otherwise, unpaid
DEADLINE(S): None
FIELD(S): Education, History, Public Relations, Design

Registered students of colleges/universities and graduates thereof are eligible for this program, which must be a minimum of 3 weeks, full or part-time. Four specialities available: Curator, Education, Public Relations, and Design. Interns receive orientation & assist in their departments, and must complete individual project which contributes to Center. Must submit a letter of recommendation, unofficial transcript, and writing sample of not less than 1,000 words.

Contact Dr. Edward M. Furgol, Curator, for an application.

268—NEW YORK STATE THEATRE INSTITUTE (Internships in Theatrical Production)

155 River Street
Troy NY 12180
518/274-3573
nysti@crisny.org

Internet: www.crisny.org/not-for-profit/nysti/int.htm

AMOUNT: None
DEADLINE(S): None
FIELD(S): Fields of study related to theatrical production, including box office and PR

Internships for college students, high school seniors, and educators-in-residence interested in developing skills in above fields. Unpaid, but college credit is earned. Located at Russell Sage College in Troy, NY. Gain experience in box office, costumes, education, electrics, music, stage management, scenery, properties, performance, and public relations. Interns come from all over the world.

Must be associated with an accredited institution. See website for more information. Call Ms. Arlene Leff, Intern Director, at above location. Include your postal mailing address.

269—NORTH CAROLINA ASSOCIATION OF EDUCATORS (Mary Morrow Scholarships)

P.O. Box 27347
700 S. Salisbury Street
Raleigh NC 27611
919/832-3000

AMOUNT: $1,000
DEADLINE(S): JAN
FIELD(S): Education/Teaching

Awards given in junior year to students in an accredited North Carolina undergraduate institution for use in their senior year. Recipients must live in North Carolina and agree to teach in the state for at least two years after graduation. Financial need is considered.

4-7 awards annually. Deadline is the second Monday in January. Contact NCAE for an application.

270—NORTH CAROLINA DEPARTMENT OF PUBLIC INSTRUCTION (Scholarship Loan Program for Prospective Teachers)

301 N. Wilmington Street
Raleigh NC 27601-2825
919/715-1120

AMOUNT: Up to $2,500/yr.
DEADLINE(S): FEB
FIELD(S): Education: Teaching, school psychology and counseling, speech/language impaired, audiology, library/media services

For NC residents planning to teach in NC public schools. At least 3.0 high school GPA required; must maintain 2.5 GPA during freshman year and 3.0 cumulative thereafter. Recipients are obligated to teach one year in an NC public school for each year of assistance. Those who do not fulfill their teaching obligation are required to repay the loan plus interest.

200 awards per year. For full-time students. Applications available in Dec. from high school counselors and college and university departments of education.

271—NORTH CAROLINA DEPT. OF PUBLIC INSTRUCTION (Teacher Assistant Scholarship Loan)

301 N. Wilmington Street
Raleigh NC 27601-2825
919/715-1120

AMOUNT: Up to $1,200/yr
DEADLINE(S): JAN
FIELD(S): Education: Teaching, school psychology or counseling, speech/language impaired, audiology, library/media services

For NC residents employed as K-12 teaching assistants in public schools who wish to pursue teacher licensure. Must either hold a B.A. degree or have completed general college courses prerequisite to admission to degree program and be admitted to an approved teacher education program at a four-year instititution. Two-year community college early childhood education program is acceptable.

Must remain employed as teaching assistant while pursuing licensure and teach one year in an NC public school for each year of assistance received. Applications available in Sept. from local school superintendent.

272—OREGON PTA (Teacher Education Scholarships)

531 SE 14th Ave., #205
Portland OR 97214
503/234-3928

AMOUNT: $500
DEADLINE(S): MAR 1
FIELD(S): Education

Open to outstanding students who are Oregon residents and are preparing to teach in Oregon at the elementary or secondary school level. The scholarships may be used for any Oregon public university or college where credits transfer for an education major. Must be a US citizen.

Nonrenewable. Scholarships are based on scholastic record, leadership, and need. Preference given to students with PTA connection. Send a self-addressed, stamped envelope for an application (available January 1st).

273—PHI DELTA KAPPA (Scholarship Grants for Prospective Educators)

408 N. Union
P.O. Box 789
Bloomington IN 47402-0789
812/339-1156
FAX: 812/339-0018
E-mail: headquarters@PDKintl.org
Internet: www.PDKintl.org

AMOUNT: $1,000-$5,000
DEADLINE(S): JAN 31
FIELD(S): Education/Teaching Career

Undergraduate scholarships for high school seniors who plan to pursue a college major in education and to become teachers.

51 annual awards.

274—PHI DELTA KAPPA, INC. (Scholarship Grants for Prospective Educators)

408 N. Union
P.O. Box 789
Bloomington IN 47402-0789
812/339-1156
FAX: 812/339-0018
E-mail: headquarters@PDkimtl.org
Internet: www.PDKimtl.org

AMOUNT: $1,000 (45); $2,000 (1); $5,000 (1); $4,000 (1)
DEADLINE(S): JAN 15
FIELD(S): Education/Teacher Training

Open to high school seniors who plan to pursue careers as teachers or educators. Based on scholastic achievement, school/community activities, recommendations, and an essay. Must be US or Canadian citizen or legal resident. Financial need NOT considered.

53 awards annually. See website or send self-addressed, stamped envelope to Shari Bradley at above address for an application.

275—PHILADELPHIA COLLEGE OF BIBLE (Scholarships, Grants, and Loans)

Financial Aid Dept.
200 Manor Ave.
Langhorne PA 19047
800/366-0049
Internet: www.pcb.edu

AMOUNT: Varies
DEADLINE(S): Varies
FIELD(S): Fields of study relating to Christian education

Various scholarships, loans, and grants are available to students attending this undergraduate Bible college in Philadelphia, PA. High school seniors, transfer students, and others may apply. Some programs are for students with outstanding academic achievement, musical talent, or leadership skills. Some are for dependents of Christian workers, missionaries, or alumni. Some are based on financial need.

Access website for details and/or send SASE to school for further information.

276—PI LAMBDA THETA (Distinguished Student Scholar Award for Education Majors)

P.O. Box 6626
Bloomington IN 47401-5599
812/339-3411
FAX: 812/339-3462
E-mail: pam@pilambda.org
Internet: http://www.pilambda.org

AMOUNT: $500
DEADLINE(S): NOV 1
FIELD(S): Education

Award for an outstanding undergraduate student who is an education major and is at least a second-semester sophomore. Membership in Pi Lambda Theta not required. GPA of 3.5 required. Must demonstrate leadership potential and a strong dedication to the field of education. Nomination must be made by a college/university instructor, professor, or supervisor.

Contact above location for details.

277—PI LAMBDA THETA (Thelma Jean Brown Classroom Teacher Award)

P.O. Box 6626
Bloomington IN 47401-5599
812/339-3411
FAX: 812/339-3462
E-mail: pam@pilambda.org
Internet: http://www.pilambda.org

AMOUNT: $500
DEADLINE(S): FEB 10
FIELD(S): Classroom Teacher, K-12

Award for an outstanding classroom teacher in grades K-12 in a public or parochial school which is not exceptionally well supported financially. Must demonstrate ability to build supportive and effective relationships with students, parents, and co-workers and an exceptional commitment to teaching. Nomination must be made by a Pi Lambda Theta member in good standing.

Contact above location for details.

278—PILOT INTERNATIONAL FOUNDATION (PIF/Lifeline Scholarship)

P.O. Box 5600
Macon GA 31208-5600
Written inquiries

AMOUNT: Varies
DEADLINE(S): MAR 1
FIELD(S): Disabilities/Brain-related Disorders

This program assists ADULT students re-entering the job market, preparing for a second career, or improving their professional skills for an established career. Applicants must be preparing for, or already involved in, careers working with people with disabilities/brain-related disorders. GPA of 3.5 or more is required.

Must be sponsored by a Pilot Club in your home town, or in the city in which your college or university is located. Send a self-addressed, stamped envelope for complete information.

279—PILOT INTERNATIONAL FOUNDATION (Ruby Newhall Memorial Scholarship)

P.O. Box 5600
Macon GA 31208-5600
Written inquiries

AMOUNT: Varies
DEADLINE(S): MAR 15
FIELD(S): Disabilities/Brain-related Disorders

For international students who have studied in the US for at least one year, and who intend to return to their home country six months after graduation. Applicants must be full-time students majoring in a field related to human health and welfare, and have a GPA of 3.5 or more.

Applicants must be sponsored by a Pilot Club in their home town, or in the city in which their college or university is located. Send a self-addressed, stamped envelope for complete information.

280—PILOT INTERNATIONAL FOUNDATION (The Pilot International Scholarship Program)

P.O. Box 5600
Macon GA 31208-5600
Written inquiries

AMOUNT: Varies
DEADLINE(S): MAR 1
FIELD(S): Disabilities/Brain-related Disorders

This program provides assistance to undergraduate students preparing for careers working directly with people with disabilities or training those who will. GPA of 3.5 or greater required.

Applicants must be sponsored by a Pilot Club in their home town, or in the city in which their college or university is located. Send a self-addressed, stamped envelope for complete information.

281—SRP/NAVAJO GENERATING STATION (Navajo Scholarship)

P.O. Box 850
Page AZ 86040
520/645-6539
FAX: 520/645-7295
E-mail: ljdawave@srp.gov

AMOUNT: Based on need
DEADLINE(S): APR 30
FIELD(S): Engineering, Environmental Studies, Business, Business Management, Health, Education

Scholarships for full-time students who hold membership in the Navajo Tribe and who are pursuing a degree in a field of study recognized as significant to the Navajo Nation, Salt River Project, or the Navajo Generating Station, such as those listed above. Must be junior or senior, have and maintain a GPA of 3.0.

Average of 15 awards per year. Inquire of Linda Dawavendewa at above location.

282—STATE STUDENT ASSISTANCE COMMISSION OF INDIANA (Scholarships for Special Education Teachers & Physical/Occupational Therapists)

150 W. Market Street, 5th Fl.
Indianapolis IN 46204
317/232-2350
FAX: 317/232-3260
E-mail: grants@ssaci.in.us
Internet: www.ai.org/ssaci/

AMOUNT: $1,000
DEADLINE(S): Varies (with college)
FIELD(S): Special Education, Physical & Occupational Therapy

Open to Indiana residents pursuing full-time undergraduate or graduate study in special education or physical or occupational therapy at an Indiana college/university. Must be US citizen, have a minimum 2.0 GPA, and demonstrate financial need.

See website or contact SSACI for an application.

283—STATE STUDENT ASSISTANCE COMMISSION OF INDIANA (Minority Teacher & Special Education Teacher Scholarship Program)

150 W. Market Street, 5th Fl.
Indianapolis IN 46204
317/232-2350
FAX: 317/232-3260
E-mail: grants@ssaci.in.us
Internet: www.ai.org/ssaci/

AMOUNT: $1,000
DEADLINE(S): Varies (with college)
FIELD(S): Education

For black or Hispanic Indiana residents working toward a teaching certificate and who plan to enter the teaching field. For full-time undergraduate or graduate study at an Indiana college. GPA of 2.0 or better (4.0 scale) is required. US citizenship.

Must demonstrate financial need (FAF). Indiana residency required. Must agree to teach 3 out of 5 years in the state of Indiana.

284—TECHNOLOGY STUDENT ASSOCIATION (Scholarships for Future Teachers)

1914 Association Dr.
Reston VA 20191
703/860-9000
FAX: 703/860-9000
E-mail: tsa@iris.org
Internet: www.tsawww.org

AMOUNT: $500
DEADLINE(S): MAY 1
FIELD(S): Technology Education

Open to student members of the Technology Student Association who can demonstrate financial need and are pursuing a career as a teacher in a technology field. Grade point average is NOT a consideration but applicants must be accepted to a post-secondary program or university.

Funds are sent to and administered by the recipient's college or university. Write for complete information.

285—TENNESSEE STUDENT ASSISTANCE CORPORATION (TSAC Minority Teaching Fellows Program)

Suite 1950, Parkway Towers
404 James Robertson Parkway
Nashville TN 37243-0820
615/532-3499 or 800/447-1523
FAX: 615/741-5555

AMOUNT: $5,000/yr. (max. $20,000)
DEADLINE(S): APR 15
FIELD(S): Education

For minority Tennessee residents who are attending Tennessee institutions and studying to be teachers. Entering freshmen must have at least a 2.75 high school GPA, and continuing college students must have a minimum 2.5 college GPA. Must also be in top 25% of class or have at least 18 ACT or 850 SAT. Recipients must agree to teach at a K-12 level Tennessee public school one year for each year the award is received.

Apply at your high school guidance office, college financial aid office, or contact Michael C. Roberts, Student Aid Compliance Administrator, at above address.

286—TENNESSEE STUDENT ASSISTANCE CORPORATION (Tennessee Teaching Scholars Program)

Suite 1950, Parkway Towers
404 James Robertson Parkway
Nashville TN 37243-0820
615/ 741-1346 or 800/342-1663

AMOUNT: $3,000 forgivable loan
DEADLINE(S): APR 15
FIELD(S): Education

A $3,000 forgivable loan to college seniors, juniors, and post-baccalaureate students admitted to state-approved teacher education programs at a Tennessee institution of higher education. Applicants must pledge to teach at the public preschool, elementary, or secondary level one year for each year the award is received.

Contact the school financial aid office, teacher education program or write to the above address for complete information.

287—THE AMERICAN CLASSICAL LEAGUE (Ed Phinney Commemorative Scholarship)

Miami University
Oxford OH 45056
513/529-7741
FAX: 513/529-7742
E-mail: AmericanClassicalLeague @muohio.edu OR a.c.l@mich.edu
Internet: www.umich.edu/~acleague/phinney.html

AMOUNT: Up to $500
DEADLINE(S): JAN 15
FIELD(S): Teachers or teacher candidates in the classics (Latin and/or Greek)

Scholarships of up to $500 to apply to first-time attendance at the League's institute OR up to $500 to cover cost of other activities that serve to enhance a teacher's skills in the classroom in the classics OR up to $150 for purchase of materials from the ACL Teaching and Materials Resource Center. Memberships required except for first-time attendance at institute.

Send request for information to above address.

288—THE ARC (Research Grants Program in Mental Retardation)

500 E. Border Street, Suite 300
Arlington TX 76010
817/261-6003
FAX: 817/277-3491
E-mail: thearc@metronet.com
Internet: http://www.theArc.org/welcome.html

AMOUNT: Up to $25,000
DEADLINE(S): APR 1
FIELD(S): Prevention, amelioration, or cure of mental retardation

The ARC invites applications from researchers from diverse sources—individuals and universities, hospitals, and professional organizations with research interests.

Contact Dr. Michael Wehmeyer, Assistant Director, Department of Research and Program Services, The ARC, at above address, or Ann Balson.

289—THE COUNCIL FOR EXCEPTIONAL CHILDREN (Black Caucus Scholarship)

1920 Association Drive
Reston VA 20191-1589
Internet: www.cec.sped.org

AMOUNT: $500
DEADLINE(S): DEC 2
FIELD(S): Special Education

Scholarship for a student pursuing a degree in Special Education and who is of African American background. Must be US or Canadian citizen. Must be a student member of the Council for Exceptional Children. Min. GPA of 2.5 required.

Write to Coordinator of Student Activities at above address or visit website for further information. Application is on website.

290—THE COUNCIL FOR EXCEPTIONAL CHILDREN (Ethnic Diversity Scholarship)

1920 Association Drive
Reston VA 20191-1589
Internet: www.cec.sped.org

AMOUNT: $500
DEADLINE(S): DEC 2

FIELD(S): Special Education

Scholarship for a student pursuing a degree in Special Education and who is a member of one of these groups: African American, American Indian, Alaska Native, Native Canadian, Hispanic, Asian, or Pacific Islander. Must be US or Canadian citizen. Must be a student member of the Council for Exceptional Children. Min. GPA of 2.5 required.

Write to Coordinator of Student Activities at above address or visit website for further information. Application is on website.

291—THE ROOTHBERT FUND, INC. (Scholarships and Grants)

475 Riverside Drive, Rm. 252
New York NY 10115
212/870-3116

AMOUNT: $500-$2,000
DEADLINE(S): FEB 1
FIELD(S): Education—teacher training

Scholarships for undergraduates and graduate students pursuing teaching as a vocation, who are primarily motivated by spiritual values, and who need financial aid to further their education. Must be able to attend an interview in March in New York City, Washington DC, New Haven, or Philadelphia. Recipients are called Roothbert Fellows and may receive grants for projects after their education is completed. High scholastic achievement required. For study in the US.

20 awards yearly. Renewable. Send SASE (#10 envelope) to above address for application.

292—THE WALT DISNEY COMPANY (American Teacher Awards)

P.O. Box 9805
Calabasas CA 91372

AMOUNT: $2,500 (36 awards); $25,000 (Outstanding Teacher of the Year)
DEADLINE(S): FEB 15
FIELD(S): Teachers: athletic coach, early childhood, English, foreign language/ESL, general elementary, mathematics, performing arts, physical education/health, science, social studies, visual arts, voc-tech education

Awards for K-12 teachers in the above fields.

Teachers, or anyone who knows a great teacher, can write for applications at the above address.

293—UNIVERSITY OF NORTH TEXAS (Scholarships for Elementary and Secondary Education Majors)

P.O. Box 311337
Denton TX 76203-1337
940/565-2992 (Elem.) or
940/565-2826 (Secondary)
Internet: www.unt.edu/scholarships/gelem.htm AND
www.unt.edu/scholarships/teacher.htm

AMOUNT: Varies
DEADLINE(S): Varies
FIELD(S): Education: Elementary and Secondary Teaching

Several scholarships for students in the teacher education departments at the University of North Texas. Eligibility requirements vary.

See website for more information. Write to either Dept. of Elementary, Early Childhood, and Reading Education OR Dept. of Teacher Education and Administration/Secondary Education for details.

294—UNIVERSITY OF WYOMING (Superior Students in Education Scholarship)

College of Education
Undergraduate Studies Office
Room 100
McWhinnie Hall
P.O. Box 3374
Laramie WY 82071-3374
307/766-2533

AMOUNT: Varies
DEADLINE(S): OCT
FIELD(S): Education

For Wyoming high school graduates who have demonstrated high scholastic achievement and qualities of leadership and who plan to teach in Wyoming public schools. May attend the University of Wyoming or any community college in the state and major in education. Based on residency, ACT scores, grades, courses taken, school activities, letters of recommendation, and student responses to prepared questions. Must maintain a 2.5 GPA to remain in program.

16 awards annually. Renewable up to ten semesters (no more than five may be at a community college). Contact the University of Wyoming's College of Education Undergraduate Studies Office for an application.

295—UTAH STATE OFFICE OF EDUCATION (T.H. Bell Teaching Incentive Loan Program)

Office of Certification
250 E. 500 So.
Salt Lake City UT 84111
801/538-7741
FAX: 801/538-7969

AMOUNT: Full tuition
DEADLINE(S): MAR 30
FIELD(S): Education/Teacher Training

Student loans for outstanding seniors at a Utah high school who plan to attend a Utah college. Also for college-level juniors and seniors studying to become teachers.

Approx 150 awards annually. High school seniors should get an application from their high school counselors after January 15th.

296—WAYNE RESA (Scholarships)

33500 Van Born Road
Wayne MI 48184-2497
E-mail: Robinsp@resa.net
Internet: www.resa.net/scholarship

AMOUNT: $2,500/yr.
DEADLINE(S): FEB 18
FIELD(S): Elementary & Secondary Education

Open to Wayne County, Michigan, high school graduates, college students, and career-changing adults to pursue K-12 teaching careers at accredited four-year Michigan colleges/universities. Must have minimum "B" average.

See website or contact Dr. Phyllis Robinson, Scholarship Administrator, for an application.

297—WISCONSIN CONGRESS OF PARENTS AND TEACHERS INC. (Brookmire-Hastings Scholarships)

4797 Hayes Road, Suite 2
Madison WI 53704-3256
608/244-1455

AMOUNT: $1,000
DEADLINE(S): FEB 15
FIELD(S): Education, Teaching

Open to Wisconsin residents who are seniors in public high schools. Awarded to outstanding high school graduates who intend to pursue a career in the field of child care/education.

See your high school principal or counselor after Dec. 1 for application.

298—WOMEN'S SPORTS FOUNDATION (Jackie Joyner-Kersee & Zina Garrison Minority Internships)

Eisenhower Park
East Meadow NY 11554
800/227-3988
FAX: 516/542-4716
E-mail: WoSport@aol.com
Internet: www.lifetimetv.com/WoSport

AMOUNT: $4,000-$5,000
DEADLINE(S): Ongoing
FIELD(S): Sports-related fields

Provides women of color an opportunity to gain experience in a sports-related career and interact in the sports community. May be undergraduates, college graduates, graduate students, or women in a career change. Internships are located at the Women's Sports Foundation in East Meadow, New York.

4-6 awards annually. See website or write to above address for details.

299—Y'S MEN INTERNATIONAL—US AREA (Alexander Scholarship Loan Fund)

12405 W. Lewis Ave.
Avondale AZ 85323-6518
Written inquiry

AMOUNT: $1,000-$1,500/yr.
DEADLINE(S): MAY 30; OCT 30
FIELD(S): Business Administration, Youth Leadership

Open to US citizens/permanent residents with a strong desire to pursue professional YMCA service. Must be YMCA staff pursuing undergraduate or graduate study and demonstrate financial need. Repayment of loan is waived if recipient enters YMCA employment after graduation.

Send self-addressed, business-sized envelope plus $1 for postage & handling to above address for an application.

300—ZETA PHI BETA SORORITY EDUCATIONAL FOUNDATION (Isabel M. Herson Scholarship in Education)

1734 New Hampshire Ave. NW
Washington DC 20009
Internet: www.zpb1920.org/nefforms.htm

AMOUNT: $500-$1,000
DEADLINE(S): FEB 1
FIELD(S): Elementary & Secondary Education

Open to graduate and undergraduate level students enrolled in a degree program in either elementary or secondary education. Award is for full-time study for one academic year (Fall-Spring). Must submit proof of enrollment.

Send self-addressed, stamped envelope to above address between September 1st and December 15th for an application.

SCHOOL OF ENGINEERING

301—AIR FORCE RESERVE OFFICER TRAINING CORPS (AFROTC Scholarships)

551 E. Maxwell Blvd.
Maxwell AFB AL 36112-6106
334/953-7783

AMOUNT: Full tuition, books, & fees for all 4 years of college
DEADLINE(S): DEC 1
FIELD(S): Science, Engineering, Business, Political Science, Psychology, Geography, Foreign Studies, Foreign Language

Competitive scholarships based on individual merit to high school seniors and graduates who have not completed any full-time college work. Must be a US citizen between the ages of 17-27. Must also have GPA of 2.5 or above, be in top 40% of class, and complete Applicant Fitness Test. Cannot be a single parent. Your college/university must offer AFROTC.

2,300 awards annually. Contact above address for application packet.

302—AMERICAN CONSULTING ENGINEERS COUNCIL (Scholarships)

1015 15th Street NW, Suite 802
Washington DC 20005
202/347-7474
FAX: 202/898-0068
E-mail: acec@acec.org
Internet: www.acec.org

AMOUNT: $2,500-$5,000
DEADLINE(S): None given
FIELD(S): All engineering fields

For engineering students who are junior and senior undergraduates or graduates.

Contact Francis George at above address.

303—AMERICAN FOUNDATION FOR THE BLIND (Paul W. Ruckes Scholarship)

11 Penn Plaza, Suite 300
New York NY 10001
212/502-7661
FAX: 212/502-7771

E-mail: juliet@afb.org
Internet: www.afb.org

AMOUNT: $1,000
DEADLINE(S): APR 30
FIELD(S): Engineering;
    Computer/Physical/Life Sciences

Open to legally blind and visually impaired undergraduate and graduate students pursuing a degree in one of above fields. Must be US citizen. Must submit written documentation of visual impairment from ophthalmologist or optometrist (need not be legally blind); official transcripts; proof of college/university acceptance; three letters of recommendation; and typewritten statement describing goals, work experience, extracurricular activities, and how monies will be used.

1 award annually. See website or contact Julie Tucker at AFB for an application.

304—AMERICAN HEALTH AND BEAUTY AIDS INSTITUTE (Fred Luster, Sr. Education Foundation Scholarships for College-Bound High School Seniors)

401 North Michigan Ave.
Chicago IL 60611-4267
312/644-6610

AMOUNT: $250 and $500
DEADLINE(S): APR 15
FIELD(S): Chemistry, Business, or
    Engineering

For college-bound high school seniors who will be enrolled as a college freshman in a four-year college majoring in chemistry, business, or engineering. 3.0 GPA required.

Send two letters of recommendation (one from a school official) and high school transcript. Scholastic record, school activities, and extracurricular activities considered.

305—AMERICAN INDIAN SCIENCE AND ENGINEERING SOCIETY (A.T. Anderson Memorial Scholarship)

P.O. Box 9828
Albuquerque NM 87119-9828
505/765-1052
FAX: 505/765-5608
E-mail: scholarships@aises.org
Internet: www.aises.org/scholarships

AMOUNT: $1,000-$2,000
DEADLINE(S): JUN 15
FIELD(S): Medicine, Natural Resources,
    Science, Engineering

Open to undergraduate and graduate students who are at least 1/4 American Indian or recognized as member of a tribe.

Must be member of AISES ($10 fee), enrolled full-time at an accredited institution, and demonstrate financial need.

Renewable. See website or contact Patricia Browne for an application and/or membership information.

306—AMERICAN INDIAN SCIENCE AND ENGINEERING SOCIETY (Burlington Northern Santa Fe Pacific Foundation Scholarships)

P.O. Box 9828
Albuquerque NM 87119-9828
505/765-1052
FAX: 505/765-5608
E-mail: scholarships@aises.org
Internet: www.aises.org/scholarships

AMOUNT: $2,500/yr.
DEADLINE(S): MAR 31
FIELD(S): Business, Education, Science,
    Engineering, Health Administration

Open to high school seniors who are at least 1/4 American Indian. Must reside in KS, OK, CO, AZ, NM, MN, ND, OR, SD, WA, MT, or San Bernardino County, CA (Burlington Northern and Santa Fe Pacific service areas). Must demonstrate financial need.

5 awards annually. Renewable up to 4 years. See website or contact Patricia Browne for an application.

307—AMERICAN RADIO RELAY LEAGUE FOUNDATION (The Henry Broughton, K2AE Memorial Scholarship)

225 Main Street
Newington CT 06111
860/594-0200
FAX: 860/594-0259
Internet: www.arrl.org/

AMOUNT: $1,000
DEADLINE(S): FEB 1
FIELD(S): Engineering, Science

For radio amateurs with a general class license whose home residence is within 70 miles of Schenectady, New York. For study leading to a bachelor's degree at an accredited four-year college/university.

1+ awards annually. Contact ARRL for an application.

308—AMERICAN SOCIETY OF ENGINEERS OF INDIAN ORIGIN (Undergraduate Scholarship Programs)

P.O. Box 49494
Atlanta GA 30359-1494

770/451-2299
Internet: www.iasf.org/asei.htm

AMOUNT: Up to $1,000
DEADLINE(S): AUG 15
FIELD(S): Engineering fields:
    architecture, computer technology,
    geotechnical or geoenvironmental
    engineering, and allied sciences

Several scholarships for undergraduate engineering students in the above fields who were born in India or who are Indian by ancestry or relation. For study in the US. Some programs have residency requirements in certain states.

Contact Dr. Narsi Narasimhan at above location for applications and details.

309—AMERICAN SOCIETY OF NAVAL ENGINEERS (ASNE Scholarships)

1452 Duke Street
Alexandria VA 22314-3458
703/836-6727
FAX: 703/836-7491
E-mail: scholarships
@navalengineering.org
Internet: www.jhuapl.edu/ASNE

AMOUNT: $2,500 (undergrad); $3,500
    (graduate)
DEADLINE(S): FEB 15
FIELD(S): Naval Engineering & related
    fields

For the last year of a full-time undergraduate program or for one year of full-time graduate study leading to a designated engineering or physical science degree in an accredited college/university. Must be US citizen and have expressed genuine interest in naval engineering. Based on academic record, work history, professional promise, extracurricular activities, letters of recommendation, and possibly financial need. Graduate students must be members of ASNE or SNAME.

19-20 awards annually. Not renewable. Awards announced in May. For an application, send a self-addressed, stamped envelope to Dennis Pignotti at above address.

310—ARTHUR & DOREEN PARRETT SCHOLARSHIP TRUST FUND (Scholarships)

c/o U.S. Bank of Washington
P.O. Box 720; Trust Dept., 8th Fl.
Seattle WA 98111-0720
206/344-4653

AMOUNT: Up to $3,500
DEADLINE(S): JUL 31
FIELD(S): Engineering, Science,
    Medicine, Dentistry

Washington state resident who has completed her/his first year of college by July 31. Open to students enrolled in above schools. Awards tenable at any accredited undergrad college or university.

Approximately 15 awards per year. Write for complete information.

311—ASSOCIATED WESTERN UNIVERSITIES, INC. (AWU Undergraduate Student Fellowships)

4190 S. Highland Drive, Suite 211
Salt Lake City UT 84124-2600
801/273-8911
FAX: 801/277-5632
Internet: www.awu.org

AMOUNT: $300/week stipend + travel allowance
DEADLINE(S): FEB 1
FIELD(S): Mathematics, Engineering, Technology, Science

Eight- to- sixteen-week fellowships for undergraduate students enrolled in accredited institutions and who have completed at least one year of college by the start of the fellowship. Applicants reviewed on the basis of academic performance/class standing, career goals, recommendations, and compatibility of scientific interests and abilities with the needs and resources of the host facility. Citizenship restrictions may apply for some facilities.

500+ awards annually. Renewable (competitively with new application). Contact above address for an application.

312—ASSOCIATED WESTERN UNIVERSITIES, INC. (AWU Visiting Scientist Fellowships)

4190 S. Highland Drive, Suite 211
Salt Lake City UT 84124-2600
801/273-8900

AMOUNT: Varies
DEADLINE(S): Varies (Two months prior to starting date)
FIELD(S): Engineering, Science, Mathematics, and Technology

Research fellowships for professionals with continued commitment to science and engineering. For use at one of 62 participating universities. US citizenship or permanent residency required.

For detailed information and list of cooperating facilities contact above location.

313—ASSOCIATION FOR WOMEN IN SCIENCE EDUCATIONAL FOUNDATION (Dr. Vicki L. Schechtman Scholarship)

1200 New York Ave. NW, Suite 650
Washington DC 20005
202/326-8940 or 800/886-AWIS
E-mail: awis@awis.org
Internet: www.awis.org

AMOUNT: $1,000
DEADLINE(S): JAN 16
FIELD(S): Various Sciences and Social Sciences

For female undergraduate students who are US citizens and have a minimum GPA of 3.0. Summary page, essay describing career aspirations, transcripts, proof of matriculation (if available), and two reference letters required with application. Scholarships may be used for tuition, books, housing, research, equipment, etc.

See website or write to above address for an application and more information.

314—ASSOCIATION FOR WOMEN IN SCIENCE EDUCATIONAL FOUNDATION (Ruth Satter Memorial Award)

1200 New York Ave. NW, Suite 650
Washington DC 20005
202/326-8940 or 800/886-AWIS
E-mail: awis@awis.org
Internet: www.awis.org

AMOUNT: $1,000
DEADLINE(S): JAN 16
FIELD(S): Various Sciences and Social Sciences

Scholarships for female doctoral students who have interrupted their education three years or more to raise a family. Summary page, description of research project, resume, references, transcripts, biographical sketch, and proof of eligibility from department head required. US citizens may attend any graduate institution; non-citizens must be enrolled in US institutions.

See website or write to above address for more information or an application.

315—AT&T BELL LABORATORIES (Summer Research Program for Minorities & Women)

101 Crawfords Corner Road
Holmdel NJ 07733-3030
Written inquiry

AMOUNT: Salary + travel & living expenses for summer
DEADLINE(S): DEC 1
FIELD(S): Engineering, Math, Sciences, Computer Science

Program offers minority students and women students technical employment experience at Bell Laboratories. Students should have completed their third year of study at an accredited college or university. US citizen or permanent resident.

Selection is based partially on academic achievement and personal motivation. Write special programs manager—SRP for complete information.

316—BARRY GOLDWATER SCHOLARSHIP AND EXCELLENCE IN EDUCATION FOUNDATION (Scholarships)

6225 Brandon Ave., Suite 315
Springfield VA 22150-2519
703/756-6012
FAX: 703/756-6015
E-mail: GOLDH2o@EROLS.COM
Internet: www.act.org/goldwater

AMOUNT: $7,500/yr. (max.)
DEADLINE(S): FEB 1
FIELD(S): Math, Natural Sciences, Engineering

Open to college sophomores and juniors with a minimum 3.0 GPA. Must be US citizen, resident alien, or American national pursuing a degree at an accredited institution in math, natural sciences, or engineering disciplines that contribute to technological advances.

300 awards annually. See website or contact your Goldwater Faculty Representative on campus. Students must be nominated by their institution and cannot apply on their own.

317—BOYS AND GIRLS CLUBS OF SAN DIEGO (Spence Reese Scholarship Fund)

1761 Hotel Circle So., Suite 123
San Diego CA 92108
619/298-3520

AMOUNT: $2,000/yr.
DEADLINE(S): MAY 15
FIELD(S): Medicine, Law, Engineering, Political Science

Open to male high school seniors planning a career in one of the above fields. Must be residents of Imperial, Riverside, Orange, San Diego, or Los Angeles counties in California. Boys & Girls Club affiliation NOT required.

$10 application fee. Renewable up to 4 years. Send a self-addressed, stamped envelope to Boys & Girls Club for an application after January 1st.

318—BROOKHAVEN WOMEN IN SCIENCE (Renate W. Chasman Scholarship)

P.O. Box 183
Upton NY 11973-5000
E-mail: pam@bnl.gov

AMOUNT: $2,000
DEADLINE(S): APR 1
FIELD(S): Natural Sciences, Engineering, Mathematics

Open ONLY to women who are residents of the boroughs of Brooklyn or Queens or the counties of Nassau or Suffolk in New York who are re-entering school after a period of study. For juniors, seniors, or first-year graduate students.

1 award annually. Not renewable. Contact Pam Mansfield at above location for an application. Phone calls are NOT accepted.

319—BUSINESS & PROFESSIONAL WOMEN'S FOUNDATION (BPW Career Advancement Scholarship Program)

2012 Massachusetts Ave. NW
Washington DC 20036-1070
202/293-1200, ext. 169
FAX: 202/861-0298
Internet: www.bpwusa.org

AMOUNT: $500-$1,000
DEADLINE(S): APR 15
FIELD(S): Biology, Science, Education, Engineering, Social Science, Paralegal, Humanities, Business, Math, Computers, Law, MD, DD

For women (US citizens) aged 25+ accepted into accredited program at US institution (+Puerto Rico & Virgin Islands). Must graduate within 12 to 24 months from the date of grant and demonstrate critical financial need. Must have a plan to upgrade skills, train for a new career field, or to enter/re-enter the job market.

Full- or part-time study. For info see website or send business-sized, self-addressed, double-stamped envelope.

320—BUSINESS & PROFESSIONAL WOMEN'S FOUNDATION (BPW Loans for Women in Engineering Studies)

2012 Massachusetts Ave. NW
Washington DC 20036-1070
202/293-1200, ext. 169
FAX: 202/861-0298
Internet: www.bpwusa.org

AMOUNT: Up to $5,000/year
DEADLINE(S): APR 15
FIELD(S): Engineering

Open to women accepted for undergraduate or graduate study in a program accredited by the Accrediting Board for Engineering and Technology. For last two years of study. US citizenship required. Must demonstrate financial need.

Renewable. Interest of 7% per annum begins immediately after graduation. Repaid in 20 equal quarterly installments commencing 12 months after graduation. For more info, see website or send double-stamped, self-addressed, business-sized envelope.

321—CAREER OPPORTUNITIES FOR YOUTH, INC. (Collegiate Scholarship Program)

P.O. Box 996
Manhattan Beach CA 90266
310/535-4838

AMOUNT: $250 to $1,000
DEADLINE(S): SEP 30
FIELD(S): Engineering, Science, Mathematics, Computer Science, Business Administration, Education, Nursing

For students of Latino/Hispanic background residing in the Southern California area who have completed at least one semester/quarter of study at an accredited four-year university. Must have a cumulative GPA of 2.5 or higher.

Priority will be given to students who demonstrate financial need. Send SASE to above location for details.

322—CIVIL AIR PATROL (CAP Undergraduate Scholarships)

Civil Air Patrol
National Headquarters
Maxwell AFB AL 36112-6332
334/953-5315

AMOUNT: $750
DEADLINE(S): JAN 31
FIELD(S): Humanities, Science, Engineering, Education

Open to CAP members who have received the Billy Mitchell Award or the senior rating in Level II of the senior training program. For undergraduate study in the above areas.

Write for complete information.

323—COMMUNITY FOUNDATION OF WESTERN MASSACHUSETTS (James L. Shriver Scholarship)

1500 Main Street
P.O. Box 15769
Springfield MA 01115
413/732-2858

AMOUNT: $750
DEADLINE(S): APR 15
FIELD(S): Technical Fields

Open to residents of Western Massachusetts to pursue technical careers through college, trade, or technical school. Based on financial need, academic merit, and extracurricular activities. Must submit transcripts and fill out government FAFSA form.

1 award annually. Renewable with reapplication. Contact Community Foundation for an application and your financial aid office for FAFSA. Notification is in June.

324—COMMUNITY FOUNDATION SILICON VALLEY (Valley Scholars Program)

111 W. Saint John Street, Suite 230
San Jose CA 95113
408/278-0270
FAX: 408/278-0280
Internet: www.cfsv.org

AMOUNT: $20,000 (over 4 years of college)
DEADLINE(S): Varies (early spring)
FIELD(S): Science and/or math

A scholarship program for public high school students in the Silicon Valley (San Mateo and Santa Clara counties and Fremont Union High school District, California) who have demonstrated enthusiasm and aptitude for science and math. Must be US citizen or permanent resident.

Up to 20 students are selected each year. Each Valley Scholar receives financial support, guidance through the college admission process, and a mentor whose interests match their own. Students may apply during their sophomore year of high school and must be academically outstanding.

325—CONSULTING ENGINEERS AND LAND SURVEYORS OF CALIFORNIA (CEL-SOC Undergraduate Scholarships)

1303 J Street, Suite 370
Sacramento CA 95814

916/441-7991
FAX: 916/441-6312
E-mail: callen@celsoc.org
Internet: www.celsoc.org
AMOUNT: $1,000-$7,500
DEADLINE(S): FEB
FIELD(S): Engineering, Land Surveying

For US citizens working toward a bachelor's degree in an accredited Board for Engineering and Technology-approved engineering program or in an accredited land surveying program in California. Must be entering their junior, senior, or fifth year in a five-year program. Must have a minimum 3.5 GPA in engineering courses and a minimum 3.2 GPA overall.

Contact Cindy Allen at above address for a list of eligible colleges/universities and application information.

326—CONSULTING ENGINEERS COUNCIL OF NEW JERSEY (Louis Goldberg Scholarship Fund)

66 Morris Ave.
Springfield NJ 07081
973/564-5848
FAX: 973/564-7480
AMOUNT: $1,000
DEADLINE(S): JAN 1
FIELD(S): Engineering or Land
Surveying

Open to undergraduate students who have completed at least two years of study (or fifth year in a five-year program) at an ABET-accredited college or university in New Jersey, are in top half of their class, and are considering a career as a consulting engineer or land surveyor. Must be US citizen.

Recipients will be eligible for American Consulting Engineers Council national scholarships of $2,000 to $5,000. Write for complete information.

327—CUBAN AMERICAN NATIONAL FOUNDATION (The Mas Family Scholarships)

7300 NW 35 Terrace
Miami FL 33122
305/592-7768
FAX: 305/592-7889
E-mail canfnet.org
Internet: www.canfnet.org
AMOUNT: Individually negotiated
DEADLINE(S): MAR 15
FIELD(S): Engineering, Business,
International Relations, Economics,
Communications, Journalism

For Cuban-American students, graduates and undergraduates, born in Cuba or direct descendants of those who left Cuba. Must be in top 10% of high school class or maintain a 3.5 GPA in college.

10,000 awards/year. Recipients may reapply for subsequent years. Financial need considered along with academic success, SAT and GRE scores, and leadership potential. Essays and proof of Cuban descent required.

328—GENERAL LEARNING COMMUNICA-TIONS (DuPont Challenge Science Essay Awards Program)

900 Skokie Blvd., Suite 200
Northbrook IL 60062-4028
847/205-3000
FAX: 847/564-8197
Internet: www.glcomm.com/dupont
AMOUNT: $1,500 (max.)
DEADLINE(S): JAN 28
FIELD(S): Science & Technology

Annual essay competition open to students in grades 7-12 in the US and Canada. Cash awards for 1st, 2nd, and honorable mention. 1st-place essayists in each of two divisions, their science teacher, and a parent of each receive a trip to the Space Center Houston/NASA at the end of April.

102 awards annually. See website or contact your science teacher or GLC for official entry blank.

329—GEORGE BIRD GRINNELL AMERI-CAN INDIAN CHILDREN'S FUND (Al Qoyawayma Award)

11602 Montague Ct.
Potomac MD 20854
301/424-2440
FAX: 301/424-8281
E-mail: Grinnell_Fund@MSN.com
AMOUNT: $1,000
DEADLINE(S): JUN 1
FIELD(S): Science, Engineering

Open to Native American undergraduate and graduate students majoring in science or engineering and who have demonstrated an outstanding interest and skill in any one of the arts. Must be American Indian/Alaska Native (documented with Certified Degree of Indian Blood), be enrolled in college/university, be able to demonstrate commitment to serving community or other tribal nations, and document financial need.

Contact Dr. Paula M. Mintzies, President, for an application after January 1st.

330—GERBER SCIENTIFIC, INC. (H. Joseph Gerber Vision Scholarship Program)

83 Gerber Road West
South Windsor CT 06074
860/648-8027
Internet: www.gerberscientific.com
AMOUNT: Varies
DEADLINE(S): MAR 15
FIELD(S): Engineering, Mathematics,
Computer Science, Natural Sciences

Scholarship program for high school seniors in Connecticut.

50 scholarships to be awarded.

331—H. FLETCHER BROWN FUND (Scholarships)

c/o PNC Bank, Trust Dept.
P.O. Box 791
Wilmington DE 19899
302/429-1186
AMOUNT: Varies
DEADLINE(S): APR 15
FIELD(S): Medicine, Dentistry, Law,
Engineering, Chemistry

Open to US citizens born in Delaware and still residing in Delaware. For 4 years of study (undergrad or grad) leading to a degree that enables applicant to practice in chosen field.

Scholarships are based on need, scholastic achievement, and good moral character. Applications available in February. Write for complete information.

332—H. FLETCHER BROWN TRUST (Scholarships)

222 Delaware Ave., 16th Fl.
Wilmington DE 19899
302/429-1338
AMOUNT: Varies
DEADLINE(S): APR 9
FIELD(S): Chemistry, Engineering, Law,
Medicine, Dentistry

Open to financially needy native-born Delaware residents ONLY who are pursuing an undergraduate degree. Must have minimum 1,000 SAT score and rank in upper 20% of class. Interview required.

Send self-addressed, stamped envelope to Donald Drois, Account Administrator, PNC Bank, at above address for an application.

333—HOPI TRIBE (Priority Scholarships)

P.O. Box 123
Kykotsmovi AZ 86039
520/734-2441, ext. 520
800/762-9630
FAX: 520/734-2435

AMOUNT: Varies
DEADLINE(S): JUL 31
FIELD(S): Law, Natural Resources,
  Education, Medicine/Health,
  Engineering, Business

Open to enrolled members of the Hopi Tribe studying in one of the fields listed above, which are considered to be areas of priority interest to the Hopis. Available to college juniors, seniors, and graduate students. Program is to encourage graduates to apply their degrees to Hopi Tribal Goals and Objectives.

Contact Hopi Tribe for an application.

334—ILLUMINATING ENGINEERING SOCIETY OF NORTH AMERICA (Robert W. Thunen Memorial Scholarships)

IES Golden Gate Section
460 Brannen Street
P.O. Box 77527
San Francisco CA 94107-1527
Written inquiry

AMOUNT: $2,500
DEADLINE(S): MAR 1
FIELD(S): Illumination (Architectural;
  Commercial; Residential; Airport;
  Navigational; Theatrical or TV; Vision;
  etc.)

Open to junior and senior undergrads or grad students who are studying illumination full-time at an accredited 4-year college or university in Northern California or Nevada, Oregon, or Washington.

This scholarship is intended to cover any and all fields of lighting. Write for complete information.

335—INSTITUTE OF INTERNATIONAL EDUCATION (National Security Education Program-Undergraduate Scholarships)

1400 K Street NW, 6th Fl.
Washington DC 20005-2403
202/326-7697
800/618-NSEP (6737)
E-mail: nsep@iie.org
Internet: http://www.iie.org/nsep/

AMOUNT: Varies: up to $8,000/semester
DEADLINE(S): FEB 8

FIELD(S): Open to all majors; preference to applied sciences, engineering, business, economics, math, computer science, international affairs, political science, history, and the policy sciences

For study abroad OUTSIDE the US, Canada, Australia, New Zealand, and Western Europe. For study in areas deemed critical to US national security. Applications available on US campuses from August through early December. Or contact organization for details.

Inquire at above location for details.

336—JEWISH FEDERATION OF METROPOLITAN CHICAGO (Academic Scholarship Program for Studies in the Sciences)

One South Franklin Street
Chicago IL 60606
Written inquiry

AMOUNT: Varies
DEADLINE(S): MAR 1
FIELD(S): Mathematics, Engineering, or
  Science

Scholarships for college juniors, seniors, and graduate students who are Jewish and are residents of Chicago, IL and Cook County.

Academic achievement and financial need are considered. Applications accepted after Dec. 1.

337—JOHNSON AND WALES UNIVERSITY (Annual Johnson & Wales University National High School Recipe Contest)

8 Abbott Place
Providence RI 02903
401/598-2345

AMOUNT: $1,000 to $5,000
DEADLINE(S): JAN 31
FIELD(S): Business, Hospitality,
  Technology, Culinary Arts

For students planning to attend Johnson & Wales University, Providence, Rhode Island.

Write to above address for detailed description.

338—JOHNSON AND WALES UNIVERSITY (Gilbane Building Company Eagle Scout Scholarship)

8 Abbott Place
Providence RI 02903
401/598-2345

AMOUNT: $1,200
DEADLINE(S): None

FIELD(S): Business, Hospitality,
  Technology, Culinary Arts

For students attending Johnson & Wales University, Providence, Rhode Island. Must be Eagle Scouts.

Send letter of recommendation and transcript to above address.

339—JOHNSON AND WALES UNIVERSITY (National High School Entrepreneur of the Year Contest)

8 Abbott Place
Providence RI 02903
401/598-2345

AMOUNT: $1,000 to $10,000
DEADLINE(S): DEC 27
FIELD(S): Business, Hospitality,
  Technology, Culinary Arts

For students attending Johnson & Wales University, Providence, Rhode Island.

Send for detailed description to above address.

340—JOHNSON AND WALES UNIVERSITY (Scholarships)

8 Abbott Place
Providence RI 02903
401/598-2345

AMOUNT: $200 to $10,000
DEADLINE(S): None
FIELD(S): Business, Hospitality,
  Technology, Culinary Arts

For students attending Johnson & Wales University, Providence, Rhode Island.

Renewable for four years. Write for complete information.

341—JOSEPH BLAZEK FOUNDATION (Scholarships)

8 South Michigan Ave.
Chicago IL 60603
312/372-3880

AMOUNT: $750 per year for 4 years
DEADLINE(S): FEB 1
FIELD(S): Science, Chemistry,
  Engineering, Mathematics, Physics

Open to residents of Cook County (Illinois) who are high school seniors planning to study in the above fields at a four-year college or university.

20 scholarships per year. Renewable. Write for complete information.

342—KOREAN-AMERICAN SCIENTISTS AND ENGINEERS ASSOCIATION (KSEA Scholarships)

1952 Gallows Road, Suite 300
Vienna VA 22182
703/748-1221
FAX: 703/748-1331
E-mail: admin@ksea.org
Internet: www.ksea.org

AMOUNT: $1,000
DEADLINE(S): FEB 28
FIELD(S): Science, Engineering, or Medicine

Scholarships to encourage Korean-American students to study in a science, engineering, or pre-med discipline and to recognize high-performing students. Must have graduated from a high school in the US.

5 to 8 awards yearly. Must be a student member of KSEA or a child of a member.

343—LOS ANGELES COUNCIL OF BLACK PROFESSIONAL ENGINEERS (Al-Ben Scholarship)

P.O. Box 881029
Los Angeles CA 90009
310/635-7734
E-mail: secy1@lablackengineers.org
Internet: www.lablackengineers.org/scholarships.html

AMOUNT: Varies
DEADLINE(S): Varies
FIELD(S): Engineering, Mathematics, Computer Studies, or Applied Scientific Studies

This organization provides scholarships for technically inclined pre-college and undergraduate students enrolled in one of the above fields. Must be of African American, Native American, or Hispanic ancestry. Although preference is given to students attending college in Southern California or who are Southern California residents, the awards are open to all qualified students attending college in the United States.

See website for more information. Application for the coming year will be on the website during November.

344—MARYLAND HIGHER EDUCATION COMMISSION (Maryland Science and Technology Scholarship Program)

16 Francis Street
Annapolis Park MD 21401
410/974-5370
800/974-1024
E-mail: ssamail@mhec.state.md.us
Internet: http://www.mhec.state.md.us/SSA/stech_qa.htm

AMOUNT: $3,000/yr. (B.A.); $1,000/yr. (A.A.)
DEADLINE(S): None
FIELD(S): Computer Science, Engineering, Technology

Scholarships for college-bound Maryland high school seniors who will major in one of the above fields and who are accepted to an eligible associate or bachelor's degree program in Maryland. Students in the class of 1999 were eligible for the first awards. The deadline was not known at this writing, so check for deadline date. Must agree to work in the state after graduation in a related field, one year for each year of assistance received. Must maintain a 3.0 GPA.

345—NAACP NATIONAL OFFICE (NAACP Willems Scholarship)

4805 Mount Hope Drive
Baltimore MD 21215
401/358-8900

AMOUNT: $2,000 undergrads; $3,000 grads
DEADLINE(S): APR 30
FIELD(S): Engineering, Chemistry, Physics, Mathematics

Open to NAACP male members majoring in one of the above areas. Undergrads must have GPA of 2.5+; graduates' GPAs must be 3.0+. Renewable if the required GPA is maintained.

Financial need must be established. Two letters of recommendation typed on letterhead from teachers or professors in the major field of specialization. Write for complete information. Include a legal size, self-addressed, stamped envelope.

346—NAACP NATIONAL OFFICE (NAACP/Department of Energy Scholarship)

4805 Mount Hope Drive
Baltimore MD 21215-3297
410/486-9133

AMOUNT: $10,000/year tuition/stipend
DEADLINE(S): APR 30
FIELD(S): Engineering, Science, Computer Science, Mathematics, Environmental Studies

Open to high school seniors who are NAACP members with a minimum 3.0 GPA. Applicants must participate in 120 hours of community service; at least 1 summer internship at a DOE facility and be employed by DOE or DOE contractor for 2 years.

Write for complete information; enclose a self-addressed 9 x 12 envelope.

347—NATIONAL ACTION COUNCIL FOR MINORITIES IN ENGINEERING—NACME, INC. (Scholarships)

The Empire State Bldg.
350 Fifth Ave., Suite 2212
New York NY 10118-2299
212/279-2626
FAX: 212/629-5178
E-mail: scholarships @www.nacme.org
Internet: www.nacme.org

AMOUNT: Up to $10,000/yr.
DEADLINE(S): Varies (set by colleges)
FIELD(S): Engineering

Various scholarships for Native American, African American, and Hispanic/Latino students. For college-bound high school seniors and undergraduates in engineering. For full-time enrollment in one of the participating colleges (see list on website). GPA of 3.0 required. U.S. citizen or permanent resident.

Apply through participating colleges. See website or write for complete information and list of participating colleges.

348—NATIONAL FEDERATION OF THE BLIND (Frank Walton Horn Memorial Scholarship)

805 Fifth Ave.
Grinnell IA 50112
515/236-3366

AMOUNT: $3,000
DEADLINE(S): MAR 31
FIELD(S): Architecture, Engineering

Open to legally blind students pursuing or planning to pursue a full-time postsecondary course of study in the US. Based on academic excellence, service to the community, and financial need. Membership NOT required.

1 award annually. Renewable. Contact Mrs. Peggy Elliot, Scholarship Committee Chairman, for an application.

349—NATIONAL FEDERATION OF THE BLIND (Howard Brown Rickard Scholarship)

805 Fifth Ave.
Grinnell IA 50112
515/236-3366

AMOUNT: $3,000
DEADLINE(S): MAR 31

FIELD(S): Law, Medicine, Engineering, Architecture, Natural Sciences

For legally blind students pursuing or planning to pursue a full-time postsecondary course of study in the US. Based on academic excellence, service to the community, and financial need. Membership NOT required.

1 award annually. Renewable. Contact Mrs. Peggy Elliot, Scholarship Committee Chairman, for an application.

350—NATIONAL ITALIAN AMERICAN FOUNDATION (Alexander Defilippis Scholarship)

1860 19th Street NW
Washington DC 20009
202/530-5315
AMOUNT: $1,000
DEADLINE(S): MAY 31
FIELD(S): Engineering

For undergraduate engineering students of Italian ancestry attending Virginia Polytechnic Institute.

Scholastic merit, financial need, and community service are considered.

351—NATIONAL SOCIETY OF BLACK ENGINEERS (Scholarships)

1454 Duke Street
Alexandria VA 22314
703/549-2207
FAX: 703/683-5312
E-mail: nsbehq@nsbe.org
Internet: www.nsbe.org
AMOUNT: Varies
DEADLINE(S): Varies
FIELD(S): Engineering and engineering technologies

Programs for black and other ethnic minorities in the fields of engineering and the engineering technologies. Organization offers pre-college programs, scholarships, career fairs, a journal, a newsletter, etc.

Contact organization for details.

352—NATIONAL SPACE CLUB (Dr. Robert H. Goddard Scholarship)

2000 L Street NW, Suite 710
Washington DC 20036-4907
202/973-8661
AMOUNT: $10,000
DEADLINE(S): JAN 8
FIELD(S): Science & Engineering

Open to undergraduate juniors and seniors and graduate students who have scholastic plans leading to future participation in the aerospace sciences and technology. Must be US citizen. Award based on transcript, letters of recommendation, accomplishments, scholastic plans, and proven past research and participation in space-related science and engineering. Personal need is considered, but is not controlling.

Renewable. Send a self-addressed, stamped envelope for more information.

353—NATIONAL SPACE CLUB (Dr. Robert H. Goddard Historical Essay Award)

2000 L Street NW, Suite 710
Washington DC 20036-4907
202/973-8661
AMOUNT: $1,000 + plaque
DEADLINE(S): DEC 4
FIELD(S): Aerospace History

Essay competition open to any US citizen on a topic dealing with any significant aspect of the historical development of rocketry and astronautics. Essays should not exceed 5,000 words and should be fully documented. Will be judged on originality and scholarship.

Previous winners not eligible. Send self-addressed, stamped envelope for complete information.

354—NATIONAL TECHNICAL ASSOCIATION, INC. (Scholarship Competitions for Minorities and Women in Science and Engineering)

6919 North 19th Street
Philadelphia PA 19126-1506
215/549-5743
FAX: 215/549-6509
E-mail: ntamfj1@aol.com
Internet: www.huenet.com/nta
AMOUNT: $500-$5,000
DEADLINE(S): Varies
FIELD(S): Science, Mathematics, Engineering, and Applied Technology

Scholarships competitions for minorities and women pursuing degrees in the above fields. Additional scholarships are available through local chapters of NTA.

Check website or write to above address for details and for locations of local chapters.

355—NATIONAL URBAN LEAGUE, INC. (Duracell/NUL Scholarship/Intern Program for Minority Students)

120 Wall Street
New York NY 10005
212/558-5373
Internet: www.nul.org
AMOUNT: $10,000 + paid summer internship
DEADLINE(S): APR 15
FIELD(S): Engineering, Marketing, Manufacturing, Finance, Business, Human Resource, etc.

For undergraduate college/university students who will be juniors/3rd-year students at time scholarship commences. Must rank within top 25% of class and major in one of above fields. Other requirements include work experience in related field(s), extracurricular activities, leadership skills, and volunteer work. Must be US citizen/permanent resident.

For tuition, room/board, and required education materials/books. Internship with one of the Gillette companies takes place between junior and senior year. Send self-addressed, stamped envelope for application.

356—NATIVE AMERICAN SCHOLARSHIP FUND, INC. (Scholarships)

8200 Mountain Rd., NE, Suite 203
Albuquerque NM 87110
505/262-2351
FAX: 505/262-0543
E-mail: NScholarsh@aol.com
AMOUNT: Varies
DEADLINE(S): MAR 15; APR 15; SEP 15
FIELD(S): Math, Engineering, Science, Business, Education, Computer Science

Open to American Indians or Alaskan Natives (1/4 degree or more) enrolled as members of a federally recognized, state recognized, or terminated tribe. For graduate or undergraduate study at an accredited four-year college or university.

208 awards annually. Contact Lucille Kelley, Director of Recruitment, for an application.

357—NEW YORK STATE HIGHER EDUCATION SERVICES CORPORATION (N.Y. State Regents Professional/Health Care Opportunity Scholarships)

Cultural Education Center, Room 5C64
Albany NY 12230

518/486-1319
Internet: www.hesc.com
AMOUNT: $1,000-$10,000/yr.
DEADLINE(S): Varies
FIELD(S): Medicine and Dentistry and
related fields; Architecture, Nursing,
Psychology, Audiology, Landscape
Architecture, Social Work, Chiropractic,
Law, Pharmacy, Accounting, Speech
Language Pathology

For NY state residents who are economically disadvantaged and members of a
minority group underrepresented in the
chosen profession and attending school in
NY state. Some programs carry a service
obligation in New York for each year of
support. For US citizens or qualifying
noncitizens.

Medical/dental scholarships require
one year of professional work in NY.

358—OAK RIDGE INSTITUTE FOR SCI-ENCE AND EDUCATION (ORISE Education & Training Programs)

P.O. Box 117
Oak Ridge TN 37831-0117
Internet: www.orau.gov/orise/
educ.htm
AMOUNT: Varies
DEADLINE(S): Varies
FIELD(S): Engineering, Aeronautics,
Computer Science, Technology, Earth
Science, Environmental Studies,
Biology, Chemistry, Physics, Medical
Research

Numerous programs funded by the US
Department of Energy are offered for
undergraduate students through postgraduate researchers. Includes fellowship and
internship opportunities throughout the
US. Some have citizenship restrictions.
Travel may be included.

See website or write for a catalog of
specific programs and requirements.

359—OFFICE OF NAVAL RESEARCH (NSAP—Naval Science Awards Program)

ONR 353; 800 N. Quincy Street
Arlington VA 22217-5660
800/422-6727 or 703/696-5787
E-mail: thurmab@onrhq.onr.navy.mil
Internet: www.onr.navy.mil or
www.jshs.org
AMOUNT: $2,000-$20,000
DEADLINE(S): Varies (established by
individual regional, state, and district
science fairs)
FIELD(S): Science, Engineering

For high school students (grades 9-12)
who participate in a regional/district/state
science fair. Winners can participate in
Junior Science & Humanities Symposia
(JSHS) Program. Awards also offered in
each of 14 categories at International
Science & Engineering Fair (ISEF), sponsored by Science Service, Inc. Must be US
citizen or permanent resident.

24 awards annually. Renewable. See
website or contact Mrs. Barbara M.
Thurman (Project Officer) at address
above for complete information on NSAP,
ISEF, and JSHS.

360—RAYMOND J. HARRIS EDUCATION TRUST

P.O. Box 7899
Philadelphia PA 19101-7899
Written inquiry
AMOUNT: Varies
DEADLINE(S): FEB 1
FIELD(S): Medicine, Law, Engineering,
Dentistry, or Agriculture

Scholarships for Christian men to
obtain a professional education in medicine, law, engineering, dentistry, or agriculture at nine Philadelphia area colleges.

Contact Mellon Bank, N.A. at above
location for details and the names of the
nine colleges.

361—ROBERT SCHRECK MEMORIAL FUND (Grants)

c/o Texas Commerce Bank
Trust Dept., P.O. Drawer 140
El Paso TX 79980
915/546-6515
AMOUNT: $500-$1500
DEADLINE(S): JUL 15; NOV 15
FIELD(S): Medicine, Veterinary
Medicine, Physics, Chemistry,
Architecture, Engineering, Episcopal
Clergy

Grants to undergraduate juniors or
seniors or graduate students who have
been residents of El Paso County for at
least two years. Must be US citizen or legal
resident and have a high grade point average. Financial need is a consideration.

Write for complete information.

362—ROBOTIC INDUSTRIES ASSOCIA-TION (RIA Robotics Scholarship Competition)

900 Victors Way
P.O. Box 3724
Ann Arbor MI 48106

734/994-6088
FAX: 734/994-3338
E-mail: mlehtinen@robotics.org
Internet: www.robotics.org
AMOUNT: $1,000
DEADLINE(S): DEC 10
FIELD(S): Robotics

Competition is for undergraduate students attending school in North America.
Students must submit a paper that poses a
technical problem and offers a solution
that involves robotics. Team entries are
allowed. Financial need NOT a factor.

3 awards annually. Not renewable. See
website or contact Marcy Lehtinen at RIA
for full guidelines and past winners.

363—SAN DIEGO AEROSPACE MUSEUM (Bill Gibbs Scholarship)

Education Dept.
2001 Pan American Plaza
San Diego CA 92101
619/234-8291, ext. 19
FAX: 619/233-4526
Internet: aerospacemuseum.org/
scholastic.html
AMOUNT: Varies
DEADLINE(S): Varies
FIELD(S): Aerospace: math, physics,
science, or engineering

For students who are residents of San
Diego County, California, who have an
aerospace career interest and who have
been accepted to a four-year college or
university in a degree program relating to
math, physics, science, or engineering.

Call or write museum for further information.

364—SCIENCE SERVICE (Intel International Science & Engineering Fair)

1719 N Street NW
Washington DC 20036
202/785-2255
FAX: 202/785-1243
E-mail: jkim@sciserv.org
Internet: www.sciserv.org
AMOUNT: Varies (totaling $2 million)
DEADLINE(S): DEC 1
FIELD(S): Science, Math, Engineering

Open to high school students (grades
9-12) who participate in this worldwide
science competition. Scholarships, internships with noted scientists, and travel &
equipment grants are awarded.

Contact Jinny Kim at Science Service
for official ISEF entry book. Sponsored by
the Intel Corporation.

365—SCIENCE SERVICE (Intel Science Talent Search)

1719 N Street NW
Washington DC 20036
202/785-2255
FAX: 202/785-1243
E-mail: cmdroms@sciserv.org
Internet: www.sciserv.org

AMOUNT: $100,000 (1st place); $75,000 (2nd); $50,000 (3rd); $25,000 (4th-6th); $20,000 (7th-10th); 30 at $5,000; 300 at $1,000; 40 laptops
DEADLINE(S): DEC 1
FIELD(S): Science, Math, Engineering

Open to high school seniors who submit a report of an independent research project in science, math, or engineering. Must include transcripts, SAT scores, and official entry form. Forty finalists are invited to Washington, DC, to participate in competition. Purpose is to encourage students to pursue careers in science and engineering.

40 awards annually. Contact Courtney Droms at Science Service for official STS entry book. Sponsored by the Intel Corporation.

366—SOCIETY OF AUTOMOTIVE ENGINEERS (Calvin College/James Bosscher/SAE Scholarship)

400 Commonwealth Drive
Warrendale PA 15096-0001
724/772-4047
E-mail: connie@sae.org
Internet: www.sae.org/students/schlrshp.htm

AMOUNT: $1,500
DEADLINE(S): DEC 1
FIELD(S): Engineering

Scholarships are awarded to incoming freshmen enrolled in the engineering program at Calvin College in Grand Rapids, Michigan. Must demonstrate outstanding academic achievement and potential.

$5 application fee. 1 award annually. Renewable for sophomore year. See website or contact Connie Harnish, SAE Educational Relations Division, for an application. Notification is in June.

367—SOCIETY OF AUTOMOTIVE ENGINEERS (Cedarville College/SAE Scholarship)

400 Commonwealth Drive
Warrendale PA 15096-0001
724/772-4047 or 800/233-2784
E-mail: connie@sae.org OR admissions@cedarville.edu
Internet: www.sae.org/students/schlrshp.htm

AMOUNT: $500
DEADLINE(S): DEC 1
FIELD(S): Engineering

Scholarships are awarded based on academic achievement to incoming freshmen pursuing a degree in engineering at Cedarville College in southwestern Ohio. Criteria include ACT/SAT scores and high school GPA. Financial need is considered.

$5 application fee. 2 awards annually. See website or contact Connie Harnish, SAE Educational Relations Division, for an application. Or write to Admissions, Cedarville College, P.O. Box 601, Cedarville, OH 45314-0601. Notification is in June.

368—SOCIETY OF AUTOMOTIVE ENGINEERS (Cornell Univ/McMullin Dean's Scholar/SAE Scholarship)

400 Commonwealth Drive
Warrendale PA 15096-0001
724/772-4047
E-mail: connie@sae.org
Internet: www.sae.org/students/schlrshp.htm

AMOUNT: $500-$2,500
DEADLINE(S): DEC 1
FIELD(S): Engineering

For incoming first-year students who have been accepted to the College of Engineering at Cornell University in New York. Amount will be based on academic achievement, leadership potential, involvement in extracurricular activities, and interest in engineering.

$5 application fee. 1 or more awards annually. Renewable up to 3 years. See website or contact Connie Harnish, SAE Educational Relations Division, for an application. Notification is in June.

369—SOCIETY OF AUTOMOTIVE ENGINEERS (Embry-Riddle Aeronautical Univ/SAE Scholarship)

400 Commonwealth Drive
Warrendale PA 15096-0001
724/772-4047
E-mail: connie@sae.org
Internet: www.sae.org/students/schlrshp.htm

AMOUNT: $3,000/yr. for 4 years
DEADLINE(S): DEC 1
FIELD(S): Engineering

Incoming freshmen pursuing a degree in the College of Engineering at Embry-Riddle Aeronautical University in Florida or Arizona are eligible. Requirements include a 1300 SAT or 30 ACT score, a 3.5 high school GPA, and involvement in high school activities. For yearly renewal, must maintain 3.0 GPA.

$5 application fee. 1 award annually. See website or contact Connie Harnish, SAE Educational Relations Division, for an application. Notification is in June.

370—SOCIETY OF AUTOMOTIVE ENGINEERS (Gannon Univ/SAE Scholarship)

400 Commonwealth Drive
Warrendale PA 15096-0001
724/772-4047
E-mail: connie@sae.org
Internet: www.sae.org/students/schlrshp.htm

AMOUNT: $1,000
DEADLINE(S): DEC 1
FIELD(S): Engineering

Students must be accepted to one of the Engineering programs at Gannon University in northwestern Pennsylvania. Awards based on SAT/ACT scores, rank in class, and GPA. Must maintain 3.0 GPA for renewal.

$5 application fee. 1 award annually. Renewable up to 3 years. See website or contact Connie Harnish, SAE Educational Relations Division, for an application. Notification is in June.

371—SOCIETY OF AUTOMOTIVE ENGINEERS (Geneva College/SAE Scholarship)

400 Commonwealth Drive
Warrendale PA 15096-0001
724/772-4047 or 724/847-6530
E-mail: connie@sae.org
Internet: www.sae.org/students/schlrshp.htm

AMOUNT: $2,000/yr.
DEADLINE(S): DEC 1
FIELD(S): Engineering

Prospective student must be an incoming freshman who will major in engineering at Geneva College in Pennsylvania. Scholarship based on merit and financial need. Must file a Free Application for Federal Student Aid (FAFSA) by March 1st. Must maintain 3.0 GPA for renewal.

$5 application fee. 1 award annually. Renewable up to 3 years. See website or contact Connie Harnish, SAE Educational Relations Division, for an application. Or write to Director of Financial Aid, Geneva College, Beaver Falls, PA 15010. See your school for a FAFSA form. Notification is in June.

372—SOCIETY OF AUTOMOTIVE ENGINEERS (Grand Valley State Univ/Padnos/SAE Scholarship)

400 Commonwealth Drive
Warrendale PA 15096-0001
724/772-4047
E-mail: connie@sae.org
Internet: www.sae.org/students/
schlrshp.htm

AMOUNT: $1,000
DEADLINE(S): DEC 1
FIELD(S): Engineering

Applicants must be high school seniors intending to pursue a degree in engineering on a full-time basis and must have been admitted to Grand State University in western Michigan.

$5 application fee. 1 award annually. Renewable for sophomore year. See website or contact Connie Harnish, SAE Educational Relations Division, for an application. Notification is in June.

373—SOCIETY OF AUTOMOTIVE ENGINEERS (IUPUI/SAE Scholarship)

400 Commonwealth Drive
Warrendale PA 15096-0001
724/772-4047
E-mail: connie@sae.org
Internet: www.sae.org/students/
schlrshp.htm

AMOUNT: $1,000 (minimum)
DEADLINE(S): DEC 1
FIELD(S): Engineering

Applicants should be incoming freshmen with direct admission to The Purdue School of Engineering and Technology at Indiana University Purdue University, Indianapolis (IUPUI). Awards based on scholarship, leadership, and academic achievement.

$5 application fee. Various awards; some renewable, some nonrenewable. See website or contact Connie Harnish, SAE Educational Relations Division, for an application. Notification is in June.

374—SOCIETY OF AUTOMOTIVE ENGINEERS (Illinois Institute of Technology/SAE Scholarship)

400 Commonwealth Drive
Warrendale PA 15096-0001
724/772-4047
E-mail: connie@sae.org
Internet: www.sae.org/students/
schlrshp.htm

AMOUNT: 1/2 tuition
DEADLINE(S): DEC 1
FIELD(S): Engineering

Applicants must be incoming freshmen planning to major in engineering at the Illinois Institute of Technology. Selection will be based on test scores, GPA, activities, community service, and work experience. Must maintain satisfactory academic performance for renewal.

$5 application fee. 5 awards annually. Renewable for total of 4 years. See website or contact Connie Harnish, SAE Educational Relations Division, for an application. Notification is in June.

375—SOCIETY OF AUTOMOTIVE ENGINEERS (Iowa State Univ/SAE Scholarship)

400 Commonwealth Drive
Warrendale PA 15096-0001
724/772-4047
E-mail: connie@sae.org
Internet: www.sae.org/students/
schlrshp.htm

AMOUNT: $1,000
DEADLINE(S): DEC 1
FIELD(S): Engineering

Applicants must be incoming freshmen who have been offered admission in the College of Engineering at Iowa State University. Typically, students have ACT scores 30 or above (or equivalent SAT scores).

$5 application fee. 1 award annually. See website or contact Connie Harnish, SAE Educational Relations Division, for an application. Notification is in June.

376—SOCIETY OF AUTOMOTIVE ENGINEERS (Kansas State Univ/SAE Scholarship)

400 Commonwealth Drive
Warrendale PA 15096-0001
724/772-4047
E-mail: connie@sae.org
Internet: www.sae.org/students/
schlrshp.htm

AMOUNT: $1,000/yr.
DEADLINE(S): DEC 1
FIELD(S): Engineering

Incoming freshmen pursuing a degree in the College of Engineering at Kansas State University are eligible. Applicants must meet the following requirements: 30

ACT composite, a 3.5 GPA, upper 10% graduating class. Must maintain 3.5 GPA.

$5 application fee. 1 four-year award annually. See website or contact Connie Harnish, SAE Educational Relations Division, for an application. Notification is in June.

377—SOCIETY OF AUTOMOTIVE ENGINEERS (Kettering Univ/SAE Scholarship)

400 Commonwealth Drive
Warrendale PA 15096-0001
724/772-4047
E-mail: connie@sae.org
Internet: www.sae.org/students/
schlrshp.htm

AMOUNT: $1,000/yr.
DEADLINE(S): DEC 1
FIELD(S): Engineering

High school juniors and seniors, as well as high school graduates entering college for the first time, may apply. Must be planning to attend Kettering University in Flint, Michigan.

$5 application fee. 4 awards annually. Not renewable. See website or contact Connie Harnish, SAE Educational Relations Division, for an application. Notification is in June.

378—SOCIETY OF AUTOMOTIVE ENGINEERS (LaFayette College/SAE Scholarship)

400 Commonwealth Drive
Warrendale PA 15096-0001
724/772-4047
E-mail: connie@sae.org
Internet: www.sae.org/students/
schlrshp.htm

AMOUNT: up to $5,000/yr.
DEADLINE(S): DEC 1
FIELD(S): Engineering

Scholarship is based on need and academic achievement. Must enroll in the B.S. engineering program at LaFayette College in Pennsylvania, and must maintain minimum 2.5 GPA. The scholarship will be supplemented with other grant and self-help to meet student's demonstrated need.

$5 application fee. 1 award annually. Renewable if need is demonstrated. See website or contact Connie Harnish, SAE Educational Relations Division, for an application. Notification is in June.

379—SOCIETY OF AUTOMOTIVE ENGINEERS (Mercer Univ/SAE Scholarship)

400 Commonwealth Drive
Warrendale PA 15096-0001
724/772-4047
E-mail: connie@sae.org
Internet: www.sae.org/students/
schlrshp.htm
AMOUNT: $2,500
DEADLINE(S): DEC 1
FIELD(S): Engineering

Awarded to an incoming freshman at Mercer University in Georgia.

$5 application fee. 1 award annually. Renewable up to 3 years. See website or contact Connie Harnish, SAE Educational Relations Division, for an application. Notification is in June.

380—SOCIETY OF AUTOMOTIVE ENGINEERS (New York Institute of Technology/SAE Scholarship)

400 Commonwealth Drive
Warrendale PA 15096-0001
724/772-4047
E-mail: connie@sae.org
Internet: www.sae.org/students/
schlrshp.htm
AMOUNT: $4,700
DEADLINE(S): DEC 1
FIELD(S): Engineering

Student must be an incoming freshman at the New York Institute of Technology. Awards based on academic credentials.

$5 application fee. 4 awards annually. Renewable for 4 years. See website or contact Connie Harnish, SAE Educational Relations Division, for an application. Notification is in June.

381—SOCIETY OF AUTOMOTIVE ENGINEERS (Oakland Univ/SAE Scholarship)

400 Commonwealth Drive
Warrendale PA 15096-0001
724/772-4047
E-mail: connie@sae.org
Internet: www.sae.org/students/
schlrshp.htm
AMOUNT: $1,000
DEADLINE(S): DEC 1
FIELD(S): Engineering, Computer Science

Applicant must be an incoming freshman at Oakland University near Detroit, Michigan.

$5 application fee. 1 award annually. See website or contact Connie Harnish,

SAE Educational Relations Division, for an application. Notification is in June.

382—SOCIETY OF AUTOMOTIVE ENGINEERS (Ohio State Univ/Motorsports Team/SAE Scholarship)

400 Commonwealth Drive
Warrendale PA 15096-0001
724/772-4047
E-mail: connie@sae.org
Internet: www.sae.org/students/
schlrshp.htm
AMOUNT: $500
DEADLINE(S): DEC 1
FIELD(S): Engineering

For incoming (first year or transfer) students at Ohio State University; two students for engineering, one unrestricted as to major. Selection based on demonstrated potential to contribute to the success of Ohio State's motorsports teams. Prior participation in successful team efforts, technical aptitude, leadership potential, and a solid record are all important elements in the selection process.

$5 application fee. 3 awards annually. See website or contact Connie Harnish, SAE Educational Relations Division, for an application. Notification is in June.

383—SOCIETY OF AUTOMOTIVE ENGINEERS (Oklahoma State Univ [CEAT]/SAE Scholarship)

400 Commonwealth Drive
Warrendale PA 15096-0001
724/772-4047
E-mail: connie@sae.org
Internet: www.sae.org/students/
schlrshp.htm
AMOUNT: $1,000
DEADLINE(S): DEC 1
FIELD(S): Engineering: Mechanical, Electrical, & Industrial

For high school graduates in the upper 10% of the graduating class who plan to attend Oklahoma State University.

$5 application fee. 1 award annually. Renewable for 3 years. See website or contact Connie Harnish, SAE Educational Relations Division, for an application. Notification is in June.

384—SOCIETY OF AUTOMOTIVE ENGINEERS (Parks College of Street Louis Univ/SAE Scholarship)

400 Commonwealth Drive
Warrendale PA 15096-0001

724/772-4047
E-mail: connie@sae.org
Internet: www.sae.org/students/
schlrshp.htm OR www.slu.edu
AMOUNT: $1,000
DEADLINE(S): DEC 1
FIELD(S): Engineering, Computer Science

For an entering freshman at Parks College of Saint Louis University in Missouri. Award based on academic achievement and financial need.

$5 application fee. 1 award annually. Not renewable. See website or contact Connie Harnish, SAE Educational Relations Division, for an application. Notification is in June.

385—SOCIETY OF AUTOMOTIVE ENGINEERS (Penn State Erie-Behrend College/SAE Scholarship)

400 Commonwealth Drive
Warrendale PA 15096-0001
724/772-4047
E-mail: connie@sae.org
Internet: www.sae.org/students/
schlrshp.htm
AMOUNT: $500-$1,000
DEADLINE(S): DEC 1
FIELD(S): Engineering

Applicants must be incoming freshmen accepted into a Penn State-Behrend engineering or engineering technology program.

$5 application fee. 1 award annually. See website or contact Connie Harnish, SAE Educational Relations Division, for an application. Notification is in June.

386—SOCIETY OF AUTOMOTIVE ENGINEERS (Penn State Univ [PSES]/SAE Scholarship)

400 Commonwealth Drive
Warrendale PA 15096-0001
724/772-4047
E-mail: connie@sae.org
Internet: www.sae.org/students/
schlrshp.htm
AMOUNT: $2,500
DEADLINE(S): DEC 1
FIELD(S): Engineering, Computer Science

Applicants must be accepted at the University Park Campus of Penn State University and pursue a major in the College of Engineering.

$5 application fee. 1 award annually. Renewable for 3 years. See website or contact Connie Harnish, SAE Educational Relations Division, for an application. Notification is in June.

387—SOCIETY OF AUTOMOTIVE ENGINEERS (Purdue Univ/Dean's Engineering Scholar/SAE Scholarship)

400 Commonwealth Drive
Warrendale PA 15096-0001
724/772-4047
E-mail: connie@sae.org
Internet: www.sae.org/students/
schlrshp.htm

AMOUNT: $1,250
DEADLINE(S): DEC 1
FIELD(S): Engineering, Computer
Science

Applicants must be accepted at Purdue's West Lafayette Campus in Indiana. Most winners have an SAT score above 1300 and are in the top 5% of their high school class. Excellent applicants will automatically be considered for other Dean's Engineering Scholar Awards.

$5 application fee. 1 award annually. See website or contact Connie Harnish, SAE Educational Relations Division, for an application. Notification is in June.

388—SOCIETY OF AUTOMOTIVE ENGINEERS (Rochester Institute of Technology/SAE Scholarship)

400 Commonwealth Drive
Warrendale PA 15096-0001
724/772-4047
E-mail: connie@sae.org
Internet: www.sae.org/students/
schlrshp.htm

AMOUNT: $5,000
DEADLINE(S): DEC 1
FIELD(S): Engineering, Computer
Science

Applicants must be incoming freshmen and enrolled at the Rochester Institute of Technology in New York. Awards based on academic credentials and leadership potential. A personal interview is recommended. Must maintain 3.0 GPA for renewal.

$5 application fee. 25 awards annually. Renewable up to 3 years. See website or contact Connie Harnish, SAE Educational Relations Division, for an application. Notification is in June.

389—SOCIETY OF AUTOMOTIVE ENGINEERS (SAE Long-Term Member Sponsored Scholarships)

400 Commonwealth Drive
Warrendale PA 15096-0001

724/772-4047
E-mail: connie@sae.org
Internet: www.sae.org/students/
schlrshp.htm

AMOUNT: $1,000
DEADLINE(S): DEC 1
FIELD(S): Engineering

Applicant must be in their senior year of undergraduate engineering, student member of SAE, and nominated by the SAE Faculty Advisor, Section Chair, or Vice Chair for Student Activities. Must show demonstration of leadership and support of SAE, the SAE collegiate chapter on campus, and the local SAE section.

2-3 awards annually. See website or contact Connie Harnish, SAE Educational Relations Division, for nomination information. Notification is in June.

390—SOCIETY OF AUTOMOTIVE ENGINEERS (SAE Undesignated Engineering Scholarships)

400 Commonwealth Drive
Warrendale PA 15096-0001
724/772-4047
E-mail: connie@sae.org
Internet: www.sae.org/students/
schlrshp.htm

AMOUNT: $1,000-$6,000
DEADLINE(S): DEC 1
FIELD(S): Engineering & Related
Sciences

For high school seniors who are US citizens, have a minimum 3.5 GPA, and are in the 90th percentile for SAT/ACT scores. To be used freshmen year of an ABET accredited 4-year engineering or related science program. Based on scholastic performance, extracurricular activities, essay, & specific criteria established by each scholarship sponsor. One award is for high school juniors.

$5 application fee. Up to 120 awards annually. See website or contact Connie Harnish, SAE Educational Relations Division, for an application. Notification is in June.

391—SOCIETY OF AUTOMOTIVE ENGINEERS (SUNY-Stony Brook/SAE Scholarship)

400 Commonwealth Drive
Warrendale PA 15096-0001
724/772-4047
E-mail: connie@sae.org
Internet: www.sae.org/students/
schlrshp.htm

AMOUNT: $1,000
DEADLINE(S): DEC 1
FIELD(S): Engineering, Computer
Science

Incoming freshmen admitted directly to SUNY-Stony Brook may apply. Based on academic achievement and demonstrated motivation for a career as a professional engineer. Must maintain a 3.0 GPA for renewal.

$5 application fee. 4 awards annually. Renewable up to 4 years. See website or contact Connie Harnish, SAE Educational Relations Division, for an application. Notification is in June.

392—SOCIETY OF AUTOMOTIVE ENGINEERS (SUNY-Alfred/Vernon Gleasman/SAE Scholarship)

400 Commonwealth Drive
Warrendale PA 15096-0001
724/772-4047
E-mail: connie@sae.org
Internet: www.sae.org/students/
schlrshp.htm

AMOUNT: $500
DEADLINE(S): DEC 1
FIELD(S): Engineering

For incoming freshmen and transfer students academically prepared to pursue an Associate in Applied Science and/or Bachelor's in Engineering Technologies at SUNY-Alfred. Preference given to students enrolling in Mechanical Engineering Technology.

$5 application fee. 1 award annually. See website or contact Connie Harnish, SAE Educational Relations Division, for an application. Notification is in June.

393—SOCIETY OF AUTOMOTIVE ENGINEERS (SUNY-New Paltz/SAE Scholarship)

400 Commonwealth Drive
Warrendale PA 15096-0001
724/772-4047
E-mail: connie@sae.org
Internet: www.sae.org/students/
schlrshp.htm

AMOUNT: $1,500
DEADLINE(S): DEC 1
FIELD(S): Engineering, Computer
Science

Applicants must be incoming freshmen accepted for study at SUNY-New Paltz. Minimum high school average of 90 (100 point scale) in a college preparatory program and a 1300 SAT combined score (30 ACT composite) are required. Must maintain 3.0 GPA for renewal.

$5 application fee. 1 award annually. Renewable for 5 years. See website or contact Connie Harnish, SAE Educational Relations Division, for an application. Notification is in June.

394—SOCIETY OF AUTOMOTIVE ENGINEERS (Stevens Institute of Technology/SAE Scholarship)

400 Commonwealth Drive
Warrendale PA 15096-0001
724/772-4047 or 201/216-5194
E-mail: connie@sae.org
Internet: www.sae.org/students/ schlrshp.htm

AMOUNT: $6,000+/yr.
DEADLINE(S): DEC 1
FIELD(S): Engineering, Computer Science

For incoming freshmen at Stevens Institute of Technology in New Jersey. Recipients must maintain a "B" average for this scholarship to continue past freshman year. Additional financial aid, up to $12,000/year, awarded on the basis of need as indicated by the Free Application for Federal Student Aid (FAFSA) and the Stevens Financial Aid Application (file both by March 1st).

$5 application fee. 2 four-year awards annually. See website or contact Connie Harnish, SAE Educational Relations Division, for an application. Notification is in June.

395—SOCIETY OF AUTOMOTIVE ENGINEERS (Univ Alaska-Fairbanks/SAE Scholarship)

400 Commonwealth Drive
Warrendale PA 15096-0001
724/772-4047
E-mail: connie@sae.org
Internet: www.sae.org/students/ schlrshp.htm

AMOUNT: Full tuition for 1 year
DEADLINE(S): DEC 1
FIELD(S): Engineering

High school seniors as well as high school graduates entering college for the first time may apply. Must have minimum 3.6 GPA, 1270 SAT or 28 ACT, and be fully admitted to a UAF engineering program.

$5 application fee. 1 award annually. See website or contact Connie Harnish, SAE Educational Relations Division, for an application. Notification is in June.

396—SOCIETY OF AUTOMOTIVE ENGINEERS (Univ Arkansas/SAE Scholarship)

400 Commonwealth Drive
Warrendale PA 15096-0001
724/772-4047
E-mail: connie@sae.org
Internet: www.sae.org/students/ schlrshp.htm

AMOUNT: $1,500/yr. or Tuition + $1,000/yr.
DEADLINE(S): DEC 1
FIELD(S): Mechanical Engineering

Applicants must be high school seniors intending to pursue studies in mechanical engineering at the University of Arkansas. Based on SAT/ACT scores, GPA, and extracurricular activities.

$5 application fee. 1 award annually. Renewable. See website or contact Connie Harnish, SAE Educational Relations Division, for an application. Notification is in June.

397—SOCIETY OF AUTOMOTIVE ENGINEERS (Univ Evansville/John R. Tooley/SAE Scholarship)

400 Commonwealth Drive
Warrendale PA 15096-0001
724/772-4047
E-mail: connie@sae.org
Internet: www.sae.org/students/ schlrshp.htm

AMOUNT: $1,000
DEADLINE(S): DEC 1
FIELD(S): Engineering, Computer Science

Scholarships are awarded to incoming freshmen accepted into the School of Engineering at the University of Evansville in Indiana. Awarded on the basis of academic achievement and involvement in extracurricular activities. A minimum 1300 SAT, 30 ACT, and 3.5 high school GPA are required. Must maintain 3.0 GPA for renewal.

$5 application fee. 3 awards annually. Renewable up to 3 years. See website or contact Connie Harnish, SAE Educational Relations Division, for an application. Notification is in June.

398—SOCIETY OF AUTOMOTIVE ENGINEERS (Univ Florida/Dean's Engineering Scholar/SAE Scholarship)

400 Commonwealth Drive
Warrendale PA 15096-0001
724/772-4047
E-mail: connie@sae.org
Internet: www.sae.org/students/ schlrshp.htm

AMOUNT: $1,000
DEADLINE(S): DEC 1
FIELD(S): Engineering

Applicants must be incoming freshmen who plan to major in any program in the College of Engineering at the University of Florida.

$5 application fee. 1 award annually. See website or contact Connie Harnish, SAE Educational Relations Division, for an application. Notification is in June.

399—SOCIETY OF AUTOMOTIVE ENGINEERS (Univ Pittsburgh/SAE Scholarship)

400 Commonwealth Drive
Warrendale PA 15096-0001
724/772-4047
E-mail: connie@sae.org
Internet: www.sae.org/students/ schlrshp.htm

AMOUNT: $1,000/yr.
DEADLINE(S): DEC 1
FIELD(S): Engineering, Computer Science

Must be a freshman applicant at the University of Pittsburgh with a 1250 SAT score and high school class rank in the top 10%. Must be US citizen or permanent resident. Must maintain 3.0 GPA for renewal.

$5 application fee. 1 award annually. Renewable for 3 years. See website or contact Connie Harnish, SAE Educational Relations Division, for an application. Notification is in June.

400—SOCIETY OF AUTOMOTIVE ENGINEERS (Univ Southern California/SAE Scholarship)

400 Commonwealth Drive
Warrendale PA 15096-0001
724/772-4047
E-mail: connie@sae.org
Internet: www.sae.org/students/ schlrshp.htm

AMOUNT: $4,000
DEADLINE(S): DEC 1
FIELD(S): Engineering, Computer Science

Applicants must be incoming freshmen who have been admitted to the University of Southern California in Los Angeles. Awarded based on the academic merit of the student. Must maintain 3.0 GPA for renewal.

$5 application fee. 2 awards annually. Renewable up to 4 years. See website or contact Connie Harnish, SAE Educational Relations Division, for an application. Notification is in June.

401—SOCIETY OF AUTOMOTIVE ENGINEERS (Univ Texas-Austin/SAE Scholarship)

400 Commonwealth Drive
Warrendale PA 15096-0001
724/772-4047
E-mail: connie@sae.org
Internet: www.sae.org/students/schlrshp.htm

AMOUNT: $3,000
DEADLINE(S): DEC 1
FIELD(S): Engineering, Computer Science

For incoming freshmen at the University of Texas at Austin. Selection is based on high school grades and SAT (1350 minimum) or ACT (31 minimum) scores. Recipients must not accept other scholarships from UT (except National Merit). Must maintain GPA of 3.25 for renewal.

$5 application fee. 2 awards annually. Renewable 3 more years. See website or contact Connie Harnish, SAE Educational Relations Division, for an application. SAT/ACT scores must be sent to UT by Febrary 1st. Notification is in June.

402—SOCIETY OF AUTOMOTIVE ENGINEERS (Univ Toledo/SAE Scholarship)

400 Commonwealth Drive
Warrendale PA 15096-0001
724/772-4047 or 800/5-TOLEDO
E-mail: connie@sae.org
Internet: www.sae.org/students/schlrshp.htm

AMOUNT: $1,000
DEADLINE(S): DEC 1
FIELD(S): Engineering, Computer Science

Applicants must be US citizens who are incoming freshmen at the University of Toledo in Ohio. Must maintain 3.0 GPA for renewal.

$5 application fee. 1 award annually. Renewable 3 more years. See website or contact Connie Harnish, SAE Educational Relations Division, for an application. Notification is in June. For admissions info, write to University of Toledo, Office of Admissions, 2801 West Bancroft, Toledo, OH 43606.

403—SOCIETY OF AUTOMOTIVE ENGINEERS (Wayne State Univ/College of Engineering/Dean's/SAE Scholarship)

400 Commonwealth Drive
Warrendale PA 15096-0001
724/772-4047 or 313/577-3780
E-mail: connie@sae.org
Internet: www.sae.org/students/schlrshp.htm

AMOUNT: $1,500
DEADLINE(S): DEC 1
FIELD(S): Engineering, Computer Science

For high school seniors and/or transfer students planning to attend Wayne State University in Michigan. Must have 3.5 GPA, be a US citizen, and maintain full-time enrollment status. Selection also based on ACT/SAT scores. Award is based solely on merit, NOT financial need. Must maintain minimum 3.0 GPA for renewal.

1 four-year award annually. See website or contact Connie Harnish, SAE Educational Relations Division, for an application. Or write to Dr. Gerald Thompkins, Assistant Dean of Student Affairs, Wayne State University, College of Engineering, 5050 Anthony Wayne Drive, Detroit, MI 48202. Notification is in June.

404—SOCIETY OF AUTOMOTIVE ENGINEERS (Washington Univ/SAE Scholarship)

400 Commonwealth Drive
Warrendale PA 15096-0001
724/772-4047
E-mail: connie@sae.org
Internet: www.sae.org/students/schlrshp.htm

AMOUNT: $3,000
DEADLINE(S): DEC 1
FIELD(S): Engineering, Computer Science

Applicants must be incoming freshmen to the School of Engineering and Applied Science at Washington University in Street Louis, Missouri. Selection based on demonstrated academic achievement and leadership ability, contribution to school and community, and potential for professional achievement.

$5 application fee. Several awards annually. Renewable up to 4 years. See website or contact Connie Harnish, SAE Educational Relations Division, for an application. Notification is in June.

405—SOCIETY OF AUTOMOTIVE ENGINEERS (Western Michigan Univ/SAE Scholarship)

400 Commonwealth Drive
Warrendale PA 15096-0001
724/772-4047
E-mail: connie@sae.org
Internet: www.sae.org/students/schlrshp.htm

AMOUNT: $5,000-$10,000 (over a 4-yr. period)
DEADLINE(S): DEC 1
FIELD(S): Engineering, Computer Science

Applicants must be residents of Michigan who are incoming freshmen at Western Michigan University. Award based on appropriateness of high school courses to preparation for engineering technology education, admission GPA, and ACT scores. Must maintain 2.5 GPA for renewal.

$5 application fee. 2 four-year awards annually. See website or contact Connie Harnish, SAE Educational Relations Division, for an application. Notification is in June.

406—SOCIETY OF AUTOMOTIVE ENGINEERS (West Virginia Univ/SAE Scholarship)

400 Commonwealth Drive
Warrendale PA 15096-0001
724/772-4047
E-mail: connie@sae.org
Internet: www.sae.org/students/schlrshp.htm

AMOUNT: $1,000
DEADLINE(S): DEC 1
FIELD(S): Engineering, Computer Science

Applicants must be incoming freshmen pursuing a degree in the College of Engineering and Mineral Resources at West Virginia University.

$5 application fee. 1 award annually. See website or contact Connie Harnish, SAE Educational Relations Division, for an application. Notification is in June.

407—SOCIETY OF AUTOMOTIVE ENGINEERS (Wichita State Univ/SAE Scholarship)

400 Commonwealth Drive
Warrendale PA 15096-0001
724/772-4047

E-mail: connie@sae.org
Internet: www.sae.org/students/
schlrshp.htm

AMOUNT: $1,500
DEADLINE(S): DEC 1
FIELD(S): Engineering, Computer
Science

Applicants must be incoming freshmen at Wichita State University in Kansas. Selection based on academic and leadership achievement. Must maintain 3.0 GPA for renewal.

$5 application fee. 1 award annually. Renewable for 3 years. See website or contact Connie Harnish, SAE Educational Relations Division, for an application. Notification is in June.

408—SOCIETY OF AUTOMOTIVE ENGINEERS (Widener Univ/SAE Scholarship)

400 Commonwealth Drive
Warrendale PA 15096-0001
724/772-4047
E-mail: connie@sae.org
Internet: www.sae.org/students/
schlrshp.htm

AMOUNT: $5,000
DEADLINE(S): DEC 1
FIELD(S): Engineering, Computer
Science

Applicants must be new freshmen at Widener University near Philadelphia, Pennsylvania. Must maintain 3.0 GPA for renewal.

$5 application fee. 2 four-year awards annually. See website or contact Connie Harnish, SAE Educational Relations Division, for an application. Notification is in June.

409—SOCIETY OF AUTOMOTIVE ENGINEERS (Wright State Univ/SAE Scholarship)

400 Commonwealth Drive
Warrendale PA 15096-0001
724/772-4047
E-mail: connie@sae.org
Internet: www.sae.org/students/
schlrshp.htm

AMOUNT: $1,000
DEADLINE(S): DEC 1
FIELD(S): Engineering, Computer
Science

Applicants must be freshmen at Wright State University in Dayton, Ohio. Award based on scholarship and achievement. Applicant may also be considered for other university scholarships based on merit and achievement.

$5 application fee. 1 award annually. Not renewable. See website or contact Connie Harnish, SAE Educational Relations Division, for an application. Notification is in June.

410—SOCIETY OF AUTOMOTIVE ENGINEERS (Yanmar/SAE Scholarship)

400 Commonwealth Drive
Warrendale PA 15096-0001
724/772-4047
E-mail: connie@sae.org
Internet: www.sae.org/students/
schlrshp.htm

AMOUNT: $2,000 ($1,000/year)
DEADLINE(S): APR 1
FIELD(S): Engineering, as related to the
Conservation of Energy in
Transportation, Agriculture &
Construction, and Power Generation

For graduate students and undergraduates in their senior year who are citizens of North America (US/Canada/Mexico). Based on previous scholastic performance with additional consideration given for special study or honors in the field of award, and for leadership achievement related to engineering or science. Emphasis will be placed on research or study related to the internal combustion engine.

1 award annually. See website or contact Connie Harnish, SAE Educational Relations Division, for an application. Notification is in June.

411—SOCIETY OF HISPANIC PROFESSIONAL ENGINEERS FOUNDATION (SHPE Scholarships)

5400 E. Olympic Blvd., Suite 210
Los Angeles CA 90022
323/888-2080

AMOUNT: $500-$3,000
DEADLINE(S): APR 15
FIELD(S): Engineering, Science

Open to deserving students of Hispanic descent who are seeking careers in engineering or science. For full-time undergraduate or graduate study at a college or university. Based on academic achievement and financial need.

Send self-addressed, stamped envelope to above address for an application.

412—SOCIETY OF PETROLEUM ENGINEERS (Gus Archie Memorial Scholarship)

P.O. Box 833836
Richardson, TX 75083-3836

972/952-9315
FAX: 972/952-9435
E-mail: twhipple@spelink.spe.org
Internet: www.spe.org

AMOUNT: $4,000/year
DEADLINE(S): MAY
FIELD(S): Petroleum Engineering

For students who are pursuing an undergraduate degree in petroleum engineering.

1 to 2 awards per year. Renewable. Financial need a factor but not primary. Contact Tom Whipple at above address for an application.

413—SOCIETY OF WOMEN ENGINEERS (3M Company Scholarships)

120 Wall Street, 11th Fl.
New York NY 10005-3902
800/666-ISWE or 212/509-9577
FAX: 212/509-0224
E-mail: hq@swe.org
Internet: www.swe.org

AMOUNT: $1,050
DEADLINE(S): MAY 15
FIELD(S): Engineering

Open to women who are entering freshmen in a college/university with an ABET-accredited program or in a SWE-approved school. Must be US citizen. Preference is given to chemical, electrical, industrial, and mechanical engineering majors.

3 awards annually. Send a self-addressed, stamped envelope to SWE for an application. Recipients are notified in September.

414—SOCIETY OF WOMEN ENGINEERS (Anne Maureen Whitney Barrow Memorial Scholarship)

120 Wall Street, 11th Fl.
New York NY 10005-3902
800/666-ISWE or 212/509-9577
FAX: 212/509-0224
E-mail: hq@swe.org
Internet: www.swe.org

AMOUNT: $5,000
DEADLINE(S): MAY 15
FIELD(S): Engineering

Open to women who are incoming freshmen in a college/university with an ABET-accredited program or in a SWE-approved school.

1 award every 4 years. Renewable for 3 years. Send a self-addressed, stamped envelope to SWE for an application. Recipient is notified in September.

415—SOCIETY OF WOMEN ENGINEERS (B.K. Krenzer Memorial Re-entry Scholarship)

120 Wall Street, 11th Fl.
New York NY 10005-3902
800/666-ISWE or 212/509-9577
FAX: 212/509-0224
E-mail: hq@swe.org
Internet: www.swe.org

AMOUNT: $1,000
DEADLINE(S): MAY 15
FIELD(S): Engineering, Computer
   Science

For women who have been out of the engineering job market as well as out of school for a minimum of two years. For any year undergraduate or graduate study, full- or part-time, at a college/university with an ABET-accredited program or in a SWE-approved school. Must have a minimum 3.5 GPA. Preference is given to degreed engineers desiring to return to the workforce following a period of temporary retirement.

1 award annually. Send a self-addressed, stamped envelope to SWE for an application. Recipient is notified in September.

416—SOCIETY OF WOMEN ENGINEERS (Central Intelligence Agency Scholarship)

120 Wall Street, 11th Fl.
New York NY 10005-3902
800/666-ISWE or 212/509-9577
FAX: 212/509-0224
E-mail: hq@swe.org
Internet: www.swe.org

AMOUNT: $1,000
DEADLINE(S): FEB 1
FIELD(S): Electrical Engineering,
   Computer Science

Open to entering sophomores at a college/university with an ABET-accredited program or in a SWE-approved school. Must have a minimum 3.5 GPA and be a US citizen.

1 award annually. Send a self-addressed, stamped envelope to SWE for an application. Recipient is notified in May.

417—SOCIETY OF WOMEN ENGINEERS (Chrysler Corporation Re-entry Scholarship)

120 Wall Street, 11th Fl.
New York NY 10005-3902

800/666-ISWE or 212/509-9577
FAX: 212/509-0224
E-mail: hq@swe.org
Internet: www.swe.org

AMOUNT: $2,000
DEADLINE(S): MAY 15
FIELD(S): Engineering, Computer
   Science

For women who have been out of the engineering job market as well as out of school for a minimum of two years. For any level of study at a college/university with an ABET-accredited program or in a SWE-approved school. Must have a minimum 3.5 GPA.

1 award annually. Send a self-addressed, stamped envelope to SWE for an application. Recipient is notified in September.

418—SOCIETY OF WOMEN ENGINEERS (Chrysler Corporation Scholarships)

120 Wall Street, 11th Fl.
New York NY 10005-3902
800/666-ISWE or 212/509-9577
FAX: 212/509-0224
E-mail: hq@swe.org
Internet: www.swe.org

AMOUNT: $1,500
DEADLINE(S): MAY 15
FIELD(S): Engineering, Computer
   Science

Open to women who are entering freshmen in a college/university with an ABET-accredited program or in a SWE-approved school.

2 awards annually. Send a self-addressed, stamped envelope to SWE for an application. Recipients are notified in September.

419—SOCIETY OF WOMEN ENGINEERS (Chrysler Corporation Scholarship)

120 Wall Street, 11th Fl.
New York NY 10005-3902
800/666-ISWE or 212/509-9577
FAX: 212/509-0224
E-mail: hq@swe.org
Internet: www.swe.org

AMOUNT: $1,750
DEADLINE(S): FEB 1
FIELD(S): Engineering, Computer
   Science

Open to women who are entering sophomores, juniors, or seniors in a college/university with an ABET-accredited program or in a SWE-approved school. Must be a member of an underrepresented group in the engineering or computer science field. Must have a minimum 3.5 GPA.

1 award annually. Send a self-addressed, stamped envelope to SWE for an application. Recipient is notified in May.

420—SOCIETY OF WOMEN ENGINEERS (Chevron Scholarships)

120 Wall Street, 11th Fl.
New York NY 10005-3902
800/666-ISWE or 212/509-9577
FAX: 212/509-0224
E-mail: hq@swe.org
Internet: www.swe.org

AMOUNT: $2,000
DEADLINE(S): FEB 1
FIELD(S): Chemical, Civil, & Petroleum
   Engineering

Open to entering sophomores and juniors at a college/university with an ABET-accredited program or in a SWE-approved school. Must have a minimum 3.5 GPA and be majoring in one of the above fields.

2 awards annually. Send a self-addressed, stamped envelope to SWE for an application. Recipients are notified in May.

421—SOCIETY OF WOMEN ENGINEERS (David Sarnoff Research Center Scholarship)

120 Wall Street, 11th Fl.
New York NY 10005-3902
800/666-ISWE or 212/509-9577
FAX: 212/509-0224
E-mail: hq@swe.org
Internet: www.swe.org

AMOUNT: $1,500
DEADLINE(S): FEB 1
FIELD(S): Engineering, Computer
   Science

Open to women who are entering juniors at a college/university with an ABET-accredited program or in a SWE-approved school. Must have a minimum 3.5 GPA and be a US citizen.

1 award annually. Send a self-addressed, stamped envelope to SWE for an application. Recipient is notified in May.

422—SOCIETY OF WOMEN ENGINEERS (Dorothy Lemke Howarth Scholarships)

120 Wall Street, 11th Fl.
New York NY 10005-3902
800/666-ISWE or 212/509-9577
FAX: 212/509-0224

E-mail: hq@swe.org
Internet: www.swe.org
AMOUNT: $2,000
DEADLINE(S): FEB 1
FIELD(S): Engineering, Computer Science

Open to women who are entering sophomores at a college/university with an ABET-accredited program or in a SWE-approved school. Must have a minimum 3.5 GPA and be a US citizen.

5 awards annually. Send a self-addressed, stamped envelope to SWE for an application. Recipients are notified in May.

423—SOCIETY OF WOMEN ENGINEERS (GTE Foundation Scholarships)

120 Wall Street, 11th Fl.
New York NY 10005-3902
800/666-ISWE or 212/509-9577
FAX: 212/509-0224
E-mail: hq@swe.org
Internet: www.swe.org
AMOUNT: $1,000
DEADLINE(S): FEB 1
FIELD(S): Electrical Engineering, Computer Science

Open to women who are entering sophomores or juniors at a college/university with an ABET-accredited program or in a SWE-approved school. Must have a minimum 3.5 GPA.

9 awards annually. Send a self-addressed, stamped envelope to SWE for an application. Recipients are notified in May.

424—SOCIETY OF WOMEN ENGINEERS (General Electric Fund Scholarships)

120 Wall Street, 11th Fl.
New York NY 10005-3902
800/666-ISWE or 212/509-9577
FAX: 212/509-0224
E-mail: hq@swe.org
Internet: www.swe.org
AMOUNT: $1,000 + $500 travel grant
DEADLINE(S): MAY 15
FIELD(S): Engineering

Open to outstanding women engineering students who are incoming freshmen at a college/university with an ABET-accredited program or in a SWE-approved school. Must be US citizen. Travel grants also available for each recipient to attend the SWE National Convention and Student Conference.

3 awards annually. Renewable 3 years. Send a self-addressed, stamped envelope to SWE for an application. Recipients are notified in September.

425—SOCIETY OF WOMEN ENGINEERS (General Motors Foundation Scholarships)

120 Wall Street, 11th Fl.
New York NY 10005-3902
800/666-ISWE or 212/509-9577
FAX: 212/509-0224
E-mail: hq@swe.org
Internet: www.swe.org
AMOUNT: $1,500 + $500 travel grant
DEADLINE(S): FEB 1
FIELD(S): Engineering: Mechanical, Electrical, Chemical, Industrial, Materials, Automotive, Manufacturing, Technology

For women entering as juniors at a college/university with ABET-accredited program or in SWE-approved school. Must exhibit career interest in automotive industry or manufacturing environment. Must have minimum 3.5 GPA and demonstrate leadership by holding position of responsibility in student organization. Travel grant available to recipients to attend SWE National Convention & Student Conference.

2 awards annually. Renewable senior year. Send self-addressed, stamped envelope to SWE for application. Recipients notified in May.

426—SOCIETY OF WOMEN ENGINEERS (Ivy Parker Memorial Scholarship)

120 Wall Street, 11th Fl.
New York NY 10005-3902
800/666-ISWE or 212/509-9577
FAX: 212/509-0224
E-mail: hq@swe.org
Internet: www.swe.org
AMOUNT: $2,000
DEADLINE(S): FEB 1
FIELD(S): Engineering, Computer Science

Open to women who are entering sophomores or juniors at a college/university with an ABET-accredited program or in a SWE-approved school. Must have a minimum 3.5 GPA and demonstrate financial need.

1 award annually. Send a self-addressed, stamped envelope to SWE for an application. Recipient is notified in May.

427—SOCIETY OF WOMEN ENGINEERS (Judith Resnick Memorial Scholarship)

120 Wall Street, 11th Fl.
New York NY 10005-3902
800/666-ISWE or 212/509-9577
FAX: 212/509-0224

E-mail: hq@swe.org
Internet: www.swe.org
AMOUNT: $2,000
DEADLINE(S): FEB 1
FIELD(S): Aerospace; Aeronautical/Astronautical Engineering

Open to women who are entering seniors at a college/university with an ABET-accredited program or in a SWE-approved school. Must have a minimum 3.5 GPA and be an active SWE Student Member. This award is in memory of astronaut Judith Resnik, who lost her life aboard the space shuttle Challenger.

1 award annually. Send a self-addressed, stamped envelope to SWE for an application. Recipient is notified in May.

428—SOCIETY OF WOMEN ENGINEERS (Lillian Moller Gilbreth Scholarship)

120 Wall Street, 11th Fl.
New York NY 10005-3902
800/666-ISWE or 212/509-9577
FAX: 212/509-0224
E-mail: hq@swe.org
Internet: www.swe.org
AMOUNT: $5,000
DEADLINE(S): FEB 1
FIELD(S): Engineering, Computer Science

Open to women who are entering juniors or seniors at a college/university with an ABET-accredited program or in a SWE-approved school. Must have a minimum 3.5 GPA and demonstrate oustanding achievement and potential.

1 award annually. Send a self-addressed, stamped envelope to SWE for an application. Recipient is notified in May.

429—SOCIETY OF WOMEN ENGINEERS (Lockheed-Martin Corporation Scholarships)

120 Wall Street, 11th Fl.
New York NY 10005-3902
800/666-ISWE or 212/509-9577
FAX: 212/509-0224
E-mail: hq@swe.org
Internet: www.swe.org
AMOUNT: $3,000
DEADLINE(S): MAY 15
FIELD(S): Engineering

Open to women who are entering freshmen in a college/university with an ABET-accredited program or in a SWE-approved school.

2 awards annually. Send a self-addressed, stamped envelope to SWE for an application. Recipients are notified in September.

430—SOCIETY OF WOMEN ENGINEERS (Lockheed-Martin Fort Worth Scholarships)

120 Wall Street, 11th Fl.
New York NY 10005-3902
800/666-ISWE or 212/509-9577
FAX: 212/509-0224
E-mail: hq@swe.org
Internet: www.swe.org

AMOUNT: $1,000
DEADLINE(S): FEB 1
FIELD(S): Electrical & Mechanical Engineering

Open to women who are entering juniors at a college/university with an ABET-accredited program or in a SWE-approved school. Must have a minimum 3.5 GPA.

2 awards annually. Send a self-addressed, stamped envelope to SWE for an application. Recipients are notified in May.

431—SOCIETY OF WOMEN ENGINEERS (MASWE Memorial Scholarships)

120 Wall Street, 11th Fl.
New York NY 10005-3902
800/666-ISWE or 212/509-9577
FAX: 212/509-0224
E-mail: hq@swe.org
Internet: www.swe.org

AMOUNT: $1,000-$2,000
DEADLINE(S): FEB 1
FIELD(S): Engineering, Computer Science

Open to women who are entering sophomores, juniors, or seniors at a college/university with an ABET-accredited program or in a SWE-approved school. Must have a minimum 3.5 GPA, show outstanding scholarship, and demonstrate financial need.

3 awards annually. Send a self-addressed, stamped envelope to SWE for an application. Recipients are notified in May.

432—SOCIETY OF WOMEN ENGINEERS (Northrop Corporation Founders Scholarship)

120 Wall Street, 11th Fl.
New York NY 10005-3902
800/666-ISWE or 212/509-9577
FAX: 212/509-0224

E-mail: hq@swe.org
Internet: www.swe.org

AMOUNT: $1,000
DEADLINE(S): FEB 1
FIELD(S): Engineering

Open to women who are entering sophomores at a college/university with an ABET-accredited program or in a SWE-approved school. Must have a minimum 3.5 GPA, be a US citizen, and be a current SWE Student Member.

1 award annually. Send a self-addressed, stamped envelope to SWE for an application. Recipient is notified in May.

433—SOCIETY OF WOMEN ENGINEERS (Northrop Grumman Scholarships)

120 Wall Street, 11th Fl.
New York NY 10005-3902
800/666-ISWE or 212/509-9577
FAX: 212/509-0224
E-mail: hq@swe.org
Internet: www.swe.org

AMOUNT: $1,000-$1,500
DEADLINE(S): MAY 15
FIELD(S): Engineering, Computer Science

Open to women who are entering freshmen in a college/university with an ABET-accredited program or in a SWE-approved school.

3 awards annually. Send a self-addressed, stamped envelope to SWE for an application. Recipients are notified in September.

434—SOCIETY OF WOMEN ENGINEERS (Olive Lynn Salembier Scholarship)

120 Wall Street, 11th Fl.
New York NY 10005-3902
800/666-ISWE or 212/509-9577
FAX: 212/509-0224
E-mail: hq@swe.org
Internet: www.swe.org

AMOUNT: $2,000
DEADLINE(S): MAY 15
FIELD(S): Engineering, Computer Science

For women who have been out of the engineering job market as well as out of school for a minimum of two years. For any year undergraduate or graduate study, full- or part-time, at a college/university with an ABET-accredited program or in a SWE-approved school. Must have a minimum 3.5 GPA.

1 award annually. Send a self-addressed, stamped envelope to SWE for

an application. Recipient is notified in September.

435—SOCIETY OF WOMEN ENGINEERS (Rockwell Corporation Scholarships)

120 Wall Street, 11th Fl.
New York NY 10005-3902
800/666-ISWE or 212/509-9577
FAX: 212/509-0224
E-mail: hq@swe.org
Internet: www.swe.org

AMOUNT: $3,000
DEADLINE(S): FEB 1
FIELD(S): Engineering, Computer Science

Open to minority women who are entering juniors at a college/university with an ABET-accredited program or in a SWE-approved school. Must demonstrate leadership ability and have a minimum 3.5 GPA.

2 awards annually. Send a self-addressed, stamped envelope to SWE for an application. Recipients are notified in May.

436—SOCIETY OF WOMEN ENGINEERS (Stone & Webster Scholarships)

120 Wall Street, 11th Fl.
New York NY 10005-3902
800/666-ISWE or 212/509-9577
FAX: 212/509-0224
E-mail: hq@swe.org
Internet: www.swe.org

AMOUNT: $1,000-$1,500
DEADLINE(S): FEB 1
FIELD(S): Engineering, Computer Science

Open to women who are entering sophomores, juniors, or seniors at a college/university with an ABET-accredited program or in a SWE-approved school. Must have a minimum 3.5 GPA.

4 awards annually. Send a self-addressed, stamped envelope to SWE for an application. Recipients are notified in May.

437—SOCIETY OF WOMEN ENGINEERS (TRW Foundation Scholarships)

120 Wall Street, 11th Fl.
New York NY 10005-3902
800/666-ISWE or 212/509-9577
FAX: 212/509-0224
E-mail: hq@swe.org
Internet: www.swe.org

AMOUNT: $200-$500
DEADLINE(S): MAY 15

FIELD(S): Engineering

Open to women who are incoming freshmen at a college/university with an ABET-accredited program or in a SWE-approved school. These scholarships are administered on a local level by SWE's Best National, Regional, and New Student Sections.

11 awards annually. Send a self-addressed, stamped envelope to SWE for an application. Recipients are notified in September.

438—SOCIETY OF WOMEN ENGINEERS (United Technologies Corporation Scholarships)

120 Wall Street, 11th Fl.
New York NY 10005-3902
800/666-ISWE or 212/509-9577
FAX: 212/509-0224
E-mail: hq@swe.org
Internet: www.swe.org
AMOUNT: $1,000
DEADLINE(S): FEB 1
FIELD(S): Electrical & Mechanical Engineering

Open to women who are entering sophomores at a college/university with an ABET-accredited program or in a SWE-approved school. Must have a minimum 3.5 GPA and be a US citizen.

2 awards annually. Renewable 2 years. Send a self-addressed, stamped envelope to SWE for an application. Recipients are notified in May.

439—SOCIETY OF WOMEN ENGINEERS (Westinghouse/Bertha Lamme Scholarships)

120 Wall Street, 11th Fl.
New York NY 10005-3902
800/666-ISWE or 212/509-9577
FAX: 212/509-0224
E-mail: hq@swe.org
Internet: www.swe.org
AMOUNT: $1,000
DEADLINE(S): MAY 15
FIELD(S): Engineering

Open to women who are incoming freshmen at a college/university with an ABET-accredited program or in a SWE-approved school. Must be US citizen.

3 awards annually. Send a self-addressed, stamped envelope to SWE for an application. Recipients are notified in September.

440—SRP/NAVAJO GENERATING STATION (Navajo Scholarship)

P.O. Box 850
Page AZ 86040
520/645-6539
FAX: 520/645-7295
E-mail: ljdawave@srp.gov
AMOUNT: Based on need
DEADLINE(S): APR 30
FIELD(S): Engineering, Environmental Studies, Business, Business Management, Health, Education

Scholarships for full-time students who hold membership in the Navajo Tribe and who are pursuing a degree in a field of study recognized as significant to the Navajo Nation, Salt River Project, or the Navajo Generating Station, such as those listed above. Must be junior or senior, have and maintain a GPA of 3.0.

Average of 15 awards per year. Inquire of Linda Dawavendewa at above location.

441—TAU BETA PI ASSOCIATION, INC. (Undergraduate Scholarships)

P.O. Box 2697
Knoxville TN 37901-2697
423/546-4578
AMOUNT: $2,000
DEADLINE(S): JAN 15
FIELD(S): Engineering

For members of Tau Beta Pi to use for their senior year of full-time undergraduate study. Membership is not by application—only by collegiate chapter invitation and initiation. Reference letters are required to apply for scholarship.

9 awards annually. Not renewable. Write for complete information.

442—TEXAS SOCIETY OF PROFESSIONAL ENGINEERS (Scholarships)

P.O. Box 2145
Austin TX 78768
512/472-9286 or 1-800/580-8973
Internet: www.tspe.org
AMOUNT: Varies
DEADLINE(S): JAN 30
FIELD(S): Engineering (math, sciences)

Scholarships for graduating high school seniors who are Texas residents planning to attend Texas engineering colleges

Contact organization for details. Application is on website.

443—THE FLUOR FOUNDATION (Fluor Daniel Engineering Scholarship Program)

3333 Michelson Drive
Irvine CA 92730
Written inquiry
AMOUNT: $400
DEADLINE(S): MAR 15
FIELD(S): Chemical, Civil, Electrical, Mechanical, and Environmental Engineering or Building Construction

Open to sophomores enrolled in a full-time undergraduate program in one of the above areas of study. Students must be selected by the dean of engineering or an appropriate selection committee to receive an application.

Contact the dean of engineering at the school you are enrolled to determine whether your school is designated as a participant in the Fluor Daniel Engineering Scholarship Program.

444—THE JOHNS HOPKINS UNIVERSITY APPLIED PHYSICS LAB (APL Summer Employment Program)

Johns Hopkins Road
Laurel MD 20723
301/953-5000
FAX: 301/953-5274
E-mail: jill.clevernger@juhapl.edu
Internet: www.jhuapl.edu
AMOUNT: Varies
DEADLINE(S): MAR 1
FIELD(S): Engineering or Computer Science

Paid internship for undergraduates who preferably have completed their sophomore year and graduate students studying engineering and/or computer science. Most positions require strong computer skills and US citizenship.

50-100 awards per year. Program can be combined/alternated with programs in many other universities in the US.

445—TYSON FOUNDATION, INC. (Alabama Scholarship Program)

2210 W. Oaklawn
Springdale AR 72762-6999
501/290-4995
AMOUNT: Varies (according to need)
DEADLINE(S): FEB 28
FIELD(S): Business, Agriculture, Engineering, Computer Science, Nursing

Open to residents of the general areas of Albertville, Ashland, Blountsville,

Gadsden, Heflin, or Oxford, Alabama, who are US citizens and live in the vicinity of a Tyson facility. Must be pursuing full-time undergraduate study at an accredited US institution and demonstrate financial need. Must also be employed part-time and/or summers to help fund education.

Renewable up to 8 semesters or 12 trimesters as long as student meets criteria. Contact Tyson Foundation for an application no later than last day of February; deadline to return application is April 20th.

446—TYSON FOUNDATION, INC. (Arkansas Scholarship Program)

2210 W. Oaklawn
Springdale AR 72762-6999
501/290-4955

AMOUNT: Varies (according to need)
DEADLINE(S): FEB 28
FIELD(S): Business, Agriculture, Engineering, Computer Science, Nursing

Open to Arkansas residents who are US citizens pursuing full-time undergraduate study at an accredited US institution. Must demonstrate financial need and be employed part-time and/or summers to help fund education.

Renewable up to 8 semesters or 12 trimesters as long as student meets criteria. Contact Tyson Foundation for an application no later than last day of February; deadline to return application is April 20th.

447—TYSON FOUNDATION, INC. (Florida Scholarship Program)

2210 W. Oaklawn
Springdale AR 72762-6999
501/290-4995

AMOUNT: Varies (according to need)
DEADLINE(S): FEB 28
FIELD(S): Business, Agriculture, Engineering, Computer Science, Nursing

Open to residents of the general area of Jacksonville, Florida, who are US citizens and live in the vicinity of a Tyson facility. Must be pursuing full-time undergraduate study in an accredited US institution and demonstrate financial need. Must also be employed part-time and/or summers to help fund education.

Renewable up to 8 semesters or 12 trimesters as long as student meets criteria. Contact Tyson Foundation for an application no later than last day of February; deadline to return application is April 20th.

448—TYSON FOUNDATION, INC. (Georgia Scholarship Program)

2210 W. Oaklawn
Springdale AR 72762-6999
501/290-4995

AMOUNT: Varies (according to need)
DEADLINE(S): FEB 28
FIELD(S): Business, Agriculture, Engineering, Computer Science, Nursing

Open to residents of the general areas of Cumming, Buena Vista, Dawson, or Vienna, Georgia, who are US citizens and live in the vicinity of a Tyson facility. Must be pursuing full-time undergraduate study in an accredited US institution and demonstrate financial need. Must also be employed part-time and/or summers to help fund education.

Renewable up to 8 semesters or 12 trimesters as long as student meets criteria. Contact Tyson Foundation for an application no later than last day of February; deadline to return application is April 20th.

449—TYSON FOUNDATION, INC. (Illinois Scholarship Program)

2210 W. Oaklawn
Springdale AR 72762-6999
501/290-4995

AMOUNT: Varies (according to need)
DEADLINE(S): FEB 28
FIELD(S): Business, Agriculture, Engineering, Computer Science, Nursing

Open to residents of the general area of Chicago, Illinois, who are US citizens and live in the vicinity of a Tyson facility. Must be pursuing full-time undergraduate study in an accredited US institution and demonstrate financial need. Must also be employed part-time and/or summers to help fund education.

Renewable up to 8 semesters or 12 trimesters as long as student meets criteria. Contact Tyson Foundation for an application no later than last day of February; deadline to return application is April 20th.

450—TYSON FOUNDATION, INC. (Indiana Scholarship Program)

2210 W. Oaklawn
Springdale AR 72762-6999
501/290-4995

AMOUNT: Varies (according to need)
DEADLINE(S): FEB 28

FIELD(S): Business, Agriculture, Engineering, Computer Science, Nursing

Open to residents of the general areas of Portland or Corydon, Indiana, who are US citizens and live in the vicinity of a Tyson facility. Must be pursuing full-time undergraduate study at an accredited US institution and demonstrate financial need. Must also be employed part-time and/or summers to help fund education.

Renewable up to 8 semesters or 12 trimesters as long as student meets criteria. Contact Tyson Foundation for an application no later than last day of February; deadline to return application is April 20th.

451—TYSON FOUNDATION, INC. (Mississippi Scholarship Program)

2210 W. Oaklawn
Springdale AR 72762-6999
501/290-4995

AMOUNT: Varies (according to need)
DEADLINE(S): FEB 28
FIELD(S): Business, Agriculture, Engineering, Computer Science, Nursing

Open to residents of the general areas of Cleveland, Jackson, Forest, or Vicksburg, Mississippi, who are US citizens and live in the vicinity of a Tyson facility. Must be pursuing full-time undergraduate study in an accredited US institution and demonstrate financial need. Must also be employed part-time and/or summers to help fund education.

Renewable up to 8 semesters or 12 trimesters as long as student meets criteria. Contact Tyson Foundation for an application no later than last day of February; deadline to return application is April 20th.

452—TYSON FOUNDATION, INC. (Missouri Scholarship Program)

2210 W. Oaklawn
Springdale AR 72762-6999
501/290-4995

AMOUNT: Varies (according to need)
DEADLINE(S): FEB 28
FIELD(S): Business, Agriculture, Engineering, Computer Science, Nursing

Open to residents of the general areas of Dexter, Monett, Neosho, Noel, or Sedalia, Missouri, who are US citizens and live in the vicinity of a Tyson facility. Must be pursuing full-time undergraduate study in an accredited US institution and demonstrate financial need. Must also be employed part-time and/or summers to help fund education.

Renewable up to 8 semesters or 12 trimesters as long as student meets criteria. Contact Tyson Foundation for an application no later than last day of February; deadline to return application is April 20th.

453—TYSON FOUNDATION, INC. (North Carolina Scholarship Program)

2210 W. Oaklawn
Springdale AR 72762-6999
501/290-4995

AMOUNT: Varies (according to need)
DEADLINE(S): FEB 28
FIELD(S): Business, Agriculture, Engineering, Computer Science, Nursing

Open to residents of the general areas of Creswell, Monroe, Sanford, or Wilkesboro, North Carolina, who are US citizens and live in the vicinity of a Tyson facility. Must be pursuing full-time undergraduate study in an accredited US institution and demonstrate financial need. Must also be employed part-time and/or summers to help fund education.

Renewable up to 8 semesters or 12 trimesters as long as student meets criteria. Contact Tyson Foundation for an application no later than the last day of February; deadline to return application is April 20th.

454—TYSON FOUNDATION, INC. (Oklahoma Scholarship Program)

2210 W. Oaklawn
Springdale AR 72762-6999
501/290-4995

AMOUNT: Varies (according to need)
DEADLINE(S): FEB 28
FIELD(S): Business, Agriculture, Engineering, Computer Science, Nursing

Open to residents of the general areas of Broken Bow or Stillwell, Oklahoma, who are US citizens and live in the vicinity of a Tyson facility. Must be pursuing full-time undergraduate study in an accredited US institution and demonstrate financial need. Must also be employed part-time and/or summers to help fund education.

Renewable up to 8 semesters or 12 trimesters as long as student meets criteria. Contact Tyson Foundation for an application no later than last day of February; deadline to return application is April 20th.

455—TYSON FOUNDATION, INC. (Pennsylvania Scholarship Program)

2210 W. Oaklawn
Springdale AR 72762-6999
501/290-4995

AMOUNT: Varies (according to need)
DEADLINE(S): FEB 28
FIELD(S): Business, Agriculture, Engineering, Computer Science, Nursing

Open to residents of the general area of New Holland, Pennsylvania, who are US citizens and live in the vicinity of a Tyson facility. Must be pursuing full-time undergraduate study in an accredited US institution and demonstrate financial need. Must also be employed part-time and/or summers to help fund education.

Renewable up to 8 semesters or 12 trimesters as long as student meets criteria. Contact Tyson Foundation for an application no later than last day of February; deadline to return application is April 20th.

456—TYSON FOUNDATION, INC. (Tennessee Scholarship Program)

2210 W. Oaklawn
Springdale AR 72762-6999
501/290-4995

AMOUNT: Varies (according to need)
DEADLINE(S): FEB 28
FIELD(S): Business, Agriculture, Engineering, Computer Science, Nursing

Open to residents of the general areas of Shelbyville or Union City, Tennessee, who are US citizens and live in the vicinity of a Tyson facility. Must be pursuing full-time undergraduate study in an accredited US institution and demonstrate financial need. Must also be employed part-time and/or summers to help fund education.

Renewable up to 8 semesters or 12 trimesters as long as student meets criteria. Contact Tyson Foundation for an application no later than last day of February; deadline to return application is April 20th.

457—TYSON FOUNDATION, INC. (Texas Scholarship Program)

2210 W. Oaklawn
Springdale AR 72762-6999
501/290-4995

AMOUNT: Varies (according to need)
DEADLINE(S): FEB 28

FIELD(S): Business, Agriculture, Engineering, Computer Science, Nursing

Open to residents of the general areas of Carthage, Center, or Seguin, Texas, who are US citizens and live in the vicinity of a Tyson facility. Must be pursuing full-time undergraduate study in an accredited US institution and demonstrate financial need. Must also be employed part-time and/or summers to help fund education.

Renewable up to 8 semesters or 12 trimesters as long as student meets criteria. Contact Tyson Foundation for an application no later than last day of February; deadline to return application is April 20th.

458—TYSON FOUNDATION, INC. (Virginia Scholarship Program)

2210 W. Oaklawn
Springdale AR 72762-6999
501/290-4995

AMOUNT: Varies (according to need)
DEADLINE(S): FEB 28
FIELD(S): Business, Agriculture, Engineering, Computer Science, Nursing

Open to residents of the general areas of Glen Allen, Harrisonburg, or Temperanceville, Virginia, who are US citizens and live in the vicinity of a Tyson facility. Must be pursuing full-time undergraduate study in an accredited US institution and demonstrate financial need. Must also be employed part-time and/or summers to help fund education.

Renewable up to 8 semesters or 12 trimesters as long as student meets criteria. Contact Tyson Foundation for an application no later than last day of February; deadline to return application is April 20th.

459—U.S. DEPARTMENT OF DEFENSE (High School Apprenticeship Program)

US Army Cold Regions Research
and Engineering Laboratory
72 Lyme Road
Hanover NH 03755
603/646-4500
DSN: 220-4500
FAX: 603/646-4693
Internet: www.acq.osd.mil/ddre/
edugate/s-aindx.html

AMOUNT: Internship
DEADLINE(S): None specified
FIELD(S): Sciences and Engineering

A teacher must recommend student for these three competitive high school apprenticeships with Laboratory. High school students from New Hampshire who are at least 16 and who have completed their junior year in high school are eligible. Should have interest and ability in science, engineering, or mathematics.

Applications are available from participating local high school guidance counselors. Contact Susan Koh at the above address for more information.

460—U.S. DEPARTMENT OF DEFENSE (SEAP Science & Engineering Apprenticeship Program)

707 22nd Street NW
Washington DC 20052
202/994-2234
FAX: 202/994-2459
Internet: www.acq.osd.mil/ddre/
edugate/ceeindx.htm/#A010

AMOUNT: $1,400 (min.)
DEADLINE(S): JAN 26
FIELD(S): Science, Engineering

Eight-week summer apprenticeships throughout the US are available to high school students who are US citizens planning careers in science or engineering. Based on grades, science/math courses taken, scores on standardized tests, areas of interest, teacher recommendations, and personal student statement. Students responsible for transportation to and from site.

See website or contact M. Phillips for an application. Refer to Code #A010.

461—U.S. DEPARTMENT OF TRANS-PORTATION (Dwight D. Eisenhower Transportation Fellowships)

U.S. Dept. of Transportation
Fed. Hwy. Admin.
6300 Georgetown Pike, HHI-20
McLean VA 22101-2296
703/235-0538

AMOUNT: Varies
DEADLINE(S): FEB
FIELD(S): Transportation—such majors as chemistry; materials science; corrosion; civil, chemical, & electronics engineering; structures; human factors; computer science; psychology.

Research fellowships for undergrads and grad students at any Dept. of Transportation facility or selected IHE. For three to twelve months. Research must focus on transportation-related research and development in the above fields.

Contact Ilene Payne, Director, Universities and Grants Programs at above location for details.

462—UNIVERSITY OF CONNECTICUT (BRIDGE Pratt & Whitney Scholarships)

Engineering II Bldg., Room 320
191 Auditorium Rd., U-187
Storrs CT 06269-3187
860/486-5536
FAX: 860/486-2295
E-mail: boyd@eng2.uconn.edu

AMOUNT: $2,000-$3,000
DEADLINE(S): JUN
FIELD(S): Engineering

For rising college freshmen enrolling in the school of engineering at the University of Connecticut who participate in the summer BRIDGE program. Must be US citizen and permanent resident. Financial need NOT a factor.

10 awards annually. Renewable. Contact Teresa E. Boyd, Director, for more information.

463—UNIVERSITY OF MARYLAND (John B. & Ida Slaughter Endowed Scholarship in Science, Technology, & the Black Community)

2169 Lefrak Hall
College Park MD 20742-7225
301/405-1158
FAX: 301/314-9867
Internet: www.bsos.umd.edu/aasp/
scholarship.html

AMOUNT: Varies (in-state tuition costs)
DEADLINE(S): MAR
FIELD(S): Science & Technology AND African-American Studies

Open to African-Americans who are US residents with a minimum 2.8 GPA. Must be accepted to or enrolled at UMCP for freshman year and must submit letter of recommendation from high school counselor or UMCP faculty member. Should have an interest in applying science and technology to the problems of the black community. Essay required.

Renewable. Contact the Center for Minorities in Science & Engineering at UMCP for an application.

464—U.S. DEPARTMENT OF DEFENSE (CO-OP Program-CECOM Research, Development, & Engineering Center-ADO)

US Army CECOM; RD&E Center
ATTN: AMSEL-RD-ADO-MS-PD

Fort Monmouth NJ 07703-5201
908/427-4889; DSN: 987-4889
FAX: 908/427-3425
Internet: www.acq.osd.mil/ddre/
edugate/s-aindx.html

AMOUNT: Salary + college/university credit
DEADLINE(S): None specified
FIELD(S): Engineering

Students presently attending local colleges/universities work with engineers and scientists on specified projects for six-month periods. Open to all high-caliber college students majoring in engineering. Purpose is to stimulate interest in SME careers. Upon graduation, students often become candidates for recruitment and placement as engineer and scientist interns.

For more information, contact Connie Zimmerman at the above address.

465—WASHINGTON INTERNSHIPS FOR STUDENTS OF ENGINEERING (Summer Internships)

400 Commonwealth Drive
Warrendale PA 15096-0001
724/776-4841, ext. 7476
FAX: 724/776-2103
E-mail: anne@sae.org
Internet: www.ieee.org/wise

AMOUNT: $1,800
DEADLINE(S): DEC 4
FIELD(S): Engineering

For engineering majors who are US citizens who have completed their junior year at the time of the 10-week summer internship in Washington DC. Students learn how engineers contribute to public policy decisions on complex technological matters. If seeking sponsorship by ANS, ASCE, ASME, IEEE, or NSPE, applicant must be a member of that society. AIChE and SAE will consider non-members of their societies.

16 internships per summer. Write for complete information.

466—WASHINGTON INTERNSHIPS FOR STUDENTS OF ENGINEERING (WISE Program)

400 Commonwealth Drive
Warrendale PA 15096-0001
412/776-4841
FAX: 412/776-2103
E-mail: anne@sae.org
Internet: www.wise-intern.org

AMOUNT: $1,800 stipend + travel allowance & housing
DEADLINE(S): DEC
FIELD(S): Engineering

Many engineering societies sponsor this program. Third-year students are selected in a nationwide competition to spend 10 weeks in Washington DC learning about the interaction between the engineering community and the government.

15 awards annually. Not renewable. Contact Anne Hickox at above address for an application.

467—WOMEN IN DEFENSE (HORIZONS Scholarship Foundation)

NDIA
2111 Wilson Blvd., Suite 400
Arlington VA 22201-3061
703/247-2552
FAX: 703/522-1885
E-mail: dnwlee@moon.jic.com
Internet: www.adpa.org/wid/horizon/Scholar.htm

AMOUNT: $500+
DEADLINE(S): NOV 1; JUL 1
FIELD(S): Engineering, Computer Science, Physics, Mathematics, Business, Law, International Relations, Political Science, Operations Research, Economics, and fields relevant to a career in the areas of national security and defense

For women who are US citizens, have minimum GPA of 3.25, demonstrate financial need, are currently enrolled at an accredited university/college (full- or part-time—both grads and undergrad juniors/seniors are eligible), and demonstrate interest in pursuing a career related to national security.

Application is online or send SASE, #10 envelope, to Woody Lee, HORIZONS Scholarship Director.

468—WOODROW WILSON NATIONAL FELLOWSHIP FOUNDATION (Leadership Program for Teachers)

CN 5281
Princeton NJ 08543-5281
609/452-7007
FAX: 609/452-0066
E-mail: marchioni@woodrow.org OR irish@woodrow.org
Internet: www.woodrow.org

AMOUNT: Varies
DEADLINE(S): Varies
FIELD(S): Science, Mathematics

WWLPT offers summer institutes for middle and high school teachers in science and mathematics. One- and two-week teacher outreach, TORCH Institutes, are held in the summer throughout the US.

See website or contact WWNFF for an application.

469—WOODS HOLE OCEANOGRAPHIC INSTITUTION (Traineeships in Oceanography for Minority Group Undergraduates)

360 Woods Hole Road
Woods Hole MA 02543-1541
508/289-2219
FAX: 508/457-2188
E-mail: mgately@whoi.edu
Internet: www.whoi.edu

AMOUNT: Varies
DEADLINE(S): FEB 16
FIELD(S): Physical/Natural Sciences, Mathematics, Engineering

For minority undergraduates enrolled in US colleges/universities who have completed at least two semesters. These awards provide training and research experience for students with interests in the above fields. Traineeships may be awarded for a ten- to twelve-week period in the summer or for a semester during the academic year.

Renewable. For an application/more information, contact the Education Office, Clark Laboratory 223, MS #31, at above address.

470—XEROX TECHNICAL MINORITY SCHOLARSHIP (School-Year Tuition)

907 Culver Road
Rochester NY 14609
Internet: www.xerox.com/employment

AMOUNT: Up to $5,000 (varies according to tuition and academic excellence)
DEADLINE(S): SEP 15
FIELD(S): Various engineering and science disciplines

Scholarships for minorities enrolled full-time in a technical degree program at the bachelor level or above. Must be African-American, Native American, Hispanic, or Asian. Recipient may not have tuition or related expenses covered by other scholarships or grants.

If above requirements are met, obtain application from website or address above. Your financial aid office must fill out the bottom half of the form. Send completed application, your resume, and a cover let-ter to Xerox Technical Minority Scholarship Program at above address.

471—XEROX TECHNICAL MINORITY SCHOLARSHIP (Summer Employment Program)

Xerox Square
Rochester NY 14644
Written inquiry

AMOUNT: Up to $5,000 (varies according to tuition and academic excellence)
DEADLINE(S): SEP 15
FIELD(S): Various engineering and science disciplines

Scholarships for minorities enrolled in a technical degree program at the bachelor level or above. Must be African-American, Native American, Hispanic, or Asian. Xerox will match your skills with a sponsoring organization that will offer a meaningful summer work experience complimenting your academic learning.

If above requirements are met, send your resume and a cover letter to Xerox Corporation Corporate Employment and College Relations Technical Mfinority Scholarship Program at above address.

AERONAUTICS

472—AERO CLUB OF NEW ENGLAND (Aviation Scholarships)

4 Emerson Drive
Acton MA 01720
978/263-7793
E-mail: pattis22@aol.com
Internet: www.acone.org

AMOUNT: $500-$2,000
DEADLINE(S): MAR 31
FIELD(S): Aviation and related fields

Several scholarships with varying specifications for eligibility for New England residents to be used at FAA-approved flight schools in New England states.

Information and applications are on website above.

473—AIR FORCE RESERVE OFFICER TRAINING CORPS (AFROTC Scholarships)

551 E. Maxwell Blvd.
Maxwell AFB AL 36112-6106
334/953-7783

AMOUNT: Full tuition, books, & fees for all 4 years of college
DEADLINE(S): DEC 1

FIELD(S): Science, Engineering, Business, Political Science, Psychology, Geography, Foreign Studies, Foreign Language

Competitive scholarships based on individual merit to high school seniors and graduates who have not completed any full-time college work. Must be a US citizen between the ages of 17-27. Must also have GPA of 2.5 or above, be in top 40% of class, and complete Applicant Fitness Test. Cannot be a single parent. Your college/university must offer AFROTC.

2,300 awards annually. Contact above address for application packet.

474—AIR TRAFFIC CONTROL ASSOCIATION INC (Scholarship Awards Program)

2300 Clarendon Blvd., #711
Arlington VA 22201
703/522-5717
FAX: 703/527-7251
E-mail: atca@worldnit.att.net
Internet: www.atca.org

AMOUNT: $1,500 to $2,500
DEADLINE(S): MAY 1
FIELD(S): Aeronautics, Aviation, Aerospace, and related areas

Open to undergraduate and graduate students enrolled in aviation-related course of study, aviation career employees doing part-time study to enhance job skills, and children of air traffic control specialists enrolled in a college program. Must demonstrate financial need.

Write for complete information.

475—AIR TRAFFIC CONTROL ASSOCIATION INC (Scholarships for Full-time Employees)

2300 Clarendon Blvd., #711
Arlington VA 22201
703/522-5717
FAX: 703/527-7251
E-mail: atca@worldnit.att.net
Internet: www.atca.org

AMOUNT: $600
DEADLINE(S): MAY 1
FIELD(S): Aeronautics, Aviation, Aerospace, and related Areas

For full-time employees in aviation-related fields in government, US military, or industry who wish to pursue coursework designed to enhance skills in an ATC or aviation discipline. Must demonstrate financial need.

Write for complete information.

476—AIRCRAFT ELECTRONICS ASSOCIATION EDUCATIONAL FOUNDATION (Scholarships)

P.O. Box 1963
Independence MO 64055
816/373-6565
FAX: 816/478-3100
Internet: aeaavnews.org

AMOUNT: $1,000-$16,000
DEADLINE(S): Varies
FIELD(S): Avionics, Aircraft Repair

Various scholarships for high school and college students attending post-secondary institutions, including technical schools. Some are for study in Canada or Europe as well as the US.

25 programs. See website or contact AEA for specific details and applications.

477—AMERICAN ASSOCIATION OF UNIVERSITY WOMEN—HONOLULU BRANCH (Tweet Coleman Aviation Scholarship)

1802 Keeaumoku Street
Honolulu HI 96822
808/537-4702

AMOUNT: $240-$3,000
DEADLINE(S): DEC 1
FIELD(S): Aviation/Pilot Training

Open to female residents of Hawaii who are seeking a pilot's license. Must be able to pass a first-class Federal Aviation Administration Medical Examination and demonstrate financial need.

Write for complete information.

478—AMERICAN ASTRONAUTICAL SOCIETY (Donald K. "Deke" Slayton Memorial Scholarship)

6352 Rolling Mill Place, Suite 102
Springfield VA 22152
703/866-0020
FAX: 703/866-3526
E-mail: info@astronautical.org
Internet: www.astronautical.org

AMOUNT: $5,000
DEADLINE(S): FEB 17
FIELD(S): Engineering/Astronautics

Scholarship to engineering student enrolled in an accredited college or university pursuing a career in astronautics. For undergrads who have completed at least the junior year or graduates. Must be US citizen or resident. Min. 3.5 GPA required. Financial need considered as well as college and community activities, offices, awards, work experience, etc.

Access website or contact organization for application package. DO NOT FAX COMPLETED APPLICATION.

479—AMERICAN INSTITUTE OF AERONAUTICS AND ASTRONAUTICS (Undergraduate Scholarships)

1801 Alexander Bell Drive, Suite 500
Reston VA 20191-4344
800/639-AIAA, 703/264-7500
FAX: 703/264-7551
E-mail: custserv@aiaa.org
Internet: www.aiaa.org

AMOUNT: $2,000
DEADLINE(S): JAN 31
FIELD(S): Science, Engineering, Aeronautics, Astronautics

For students who have completed at least one academic semester or quarter of full-time college work in the area of science or engineering encompassed by the technical activities of the AIAA. Must have GPA of at least 3.0, be currently enrolled in accredited college or university. Membership in AIAA not required to apply but must become one before receiving a scholarship award.

Students who receive these awards are eligible for yearly continuation until completion of senior year upon submission of application, career essay, transcripts, and 2 letters of recommendation from college professor.

480—AOPA AIR SAFETY FOUNDATION (Mcallister & Burnside Scholarships)

421 Aviation Way
Frederick MD 21701-4798
301/695-2170

AMOUNT: $1,000
DEADLINE(S): MAR 31
FIELD(S): Aviation

Scholarships for undergraduate juniors and seniors who are enrolled in an accredited aviation degree program with a GPA of 3.25 or better. Must be US citizen.

Send a business-sized, self-addressed, stamped envelope to above address for an application.

481—ASSOCIATED WESTERN UNIVERSITIES, INC. (AWU Undergraduate Student Fellowships)

4190 S. Highland Drive, Suite 211
Salt Lake City UT 84124-2600
801/273-8911
FAX: 801/277-5632
Internet: www.awu.org

AMOUNT: $300/week stipend + travel allowance
DEADLINE(S): FEB 1
FIELD(S): Mathematics, Engineering, Technology, Science

Eight- to- sixteen-week fellowships for undergraduate students enrolled in accredited institutions and who have completed at least one year of college by the start of the fellowship. Applicants reviewed on the basis of academic performance/class standing, career goals, recommendations, and compatibility of scientific interests and abilities with the needs and resources of the host facility. Citizenship restrictions may apply for some facilities.

500+ awards annually. Renewable (competitively with new application). Contact above address for an application.

482—ASSOCIATED WESTERN UNIVERSITIES, INC. (AWU Visiting Scientist Fellowships)

4190 S. Highland Drive, Suite 211
Salt Lake City UT 84124-2600
801/273-8900
AMOUNT: Varies
DEADLINE(S): Varies (Two months prior to starting date)
FIELD(S): Engineering, Science, Mathematics, and Technology

Research fellowships for professionals with continued commitment to science and engineering. For use at one of 62 participating universities. US citizenship or permanent residency required.

For detailed information and list of cooperating facitilies contact above location.

483—AVIATION COUNCIL OF PENNSYLVANIA (Scholarships)

3111 Arcadia Ave.
Allentown PA 18103
215/797-1133
AMOUNT: $1,000
DEADLINE(S): JUL 31
FIELD(S): Aviation Maintenance, Aviaiton Management, or Pilot Training

Scholarships for individuals in the above fields who are residents of Pennsylvania but can attend school outside Pennsylvania.

3 awards yearly.

484—AVIATION DISTRIBUTORS AND MANUFACTURERS ASSOCIATION INTERNATIONAL (ADMA International Scholarship Fund)

1900 Arch Street
Philadelphia PA 19103-1498
215/564-3484
FAX: 215/564-2175
E-mail: assnhqt@netaxs.com
AMOUNT: Varies
DEADLINE(S): MAR 15
FIELD(S): Aviation Management, Professional Pilot

Open to students seeking a career in aviation management or as a professional pilot. Emphasis may be in general aviation, airway science management, aviation maintenance, flight engineering, or airway a/c systems management.

Applicants must be studying in the aviation field in a four-year school having an aviation program. Write for complete information.

485—AVIATION INSURANCE ASSOCIATION (Scholarship)

Aviation Technology Department
1 Purdue Airport
West Lafayette IN 47906-3398
954/986-8080
AMOUNT: $1,000
DEADLINE(S): FEB
FIELD(S): Aviation

Scholarships for aviation students who have completed at least 30 college credits, 15 of which are in aviation. Must have GPA of at least 2.5 and be a US citizen.

Write to Professor Bernard Wuile at Purdue University at above address for application and details.

486—CIVIL AIR PATROL (Col. Louisa Spruance Morse CAP Scholarship)

105 S. Hansell Street
Maxwell AFB AL 36112-6332
334/953-5315
AMOUNT: $1,000
DEADLINE(S): JAN 31
FIELD(S): Aeronautics

Scholarship for members (or former members) of the Civil Air Patrol who are enrolled in the AFROTC program at Embry-Riddle Aeronautical University in either Daytona Beach, Florida, or Prescott, Arizona.

Contact CAP for applicationa details.

487—CIVIL AIR PATROL (Major Gen. Lucas V. Beau Flight Scholarship)

Civil Air Patrol National HQ
Maxwell AFB AL 36112-6332
334/953-5315
AMOUNT: $2,100
DEADLINE(S): MAR 31
FIELD(S): Ground and Air Training for FAA private pilot licensing

Open to CAP cadets pursuing studies in the above field. Undergraduate study in the above areas.

Write for complete information.

488—EAA AVIATION FOUNDATION (Scholarship Program)

P.O. Box 3065
Oshkosh WI 54903-3065
920/426-6815 or 888/EAA-EAA9 or 888/322-3229
E-mail: education@eaa.org
Internet: www.eaa.org
AMOUNT: $500-$5,000
DEADLINE(S): MAY 1
FIELD(S): Aviation

Six different scholarship programs open to well-rounded individuals involved in school and community activities as well as aviation. Applicant's academic records should verify his/her ability to complete educational activity for which scholarship is requested. For all but one scholarship, students must major in aviation. Financial need considered in some programs. One scholarship includes tuition, books, fees, etc., at the Fox Valley Technical College in Wisconsin.

Renewable. $5 application fee. Contact EAA for an application (one application covers all of the scholarship programs).

489—ILLINOIS PILOTS ASSOCIATION (Scholarships)

46 Apache Lane
Huntley IL 60142
Written request
AMOUNT: $500
DEADLINE(S): APR 1
FIELD(S): Aviation

Scholarships for individuals in aviation who are residents of Illinois and attending a college or university in Illinois.

Write for details.

490—INTERNATIONAL SOCIETY OF WOMEN AIRLINE PILOTS (ISA International Career Scholarship)

2250 E. Tropicana Ave., Suite 19-395
Las Vegas NV 89119-6594
Written inquiry
AMOUNT: Varies
DEADLINE(S): None specified
FIELD(S): Airline Pilot Advanced Ratings

Open to women whose goals are to fly the world's airlines. For advanced pilot ratings, such as the US FAA ATP certificate or equivalent.

Applicants must have a US FAA Commercial Pilot Certificate with an Instrument Rating and a First Class medical (or equivalent). Also must have a minimum of 750 flight hours. Personal interview is required. Write for complete information.

491—INTERNATIONAL SOCIETY OF WOMEN AIRLINE PILOTS (Fiorenze De Bernardi Merit Award.)

2250 E. Tropicana Ave., Suite 19-395
Las Vegas NV 89119-6541
Internet: www.aswap.org

AMOUNT: Varies
DEADLINE(S): Varies
FIELD(S): Airline Pilot Training

A merit scholarship for women throughout the world who are pursuing airline pilot careers. Selection based on need, demonstrated dedication to career goal, work history, experience, and recommendations.

To aid pilots with CFI, CFII, MEI, or any equivalents. Must have a US FAA Commercial Pilot Certificate with an Instrument Rating and a First Class medical (or equivalent). Candidates must have a minimum of 350 flight hours. Personal interview required. Contact Gail Redden-Jones at above address.

492—INTERNATIONAL SOCIETY OF WOMEN AIRLINE PILOTS (Holly Mullins Memorial Scholarship)

2250 E. Tropicana Ave., Suite 19-395
Las Vegas NV 89119-6594
Internet: www.aswap.org

AMOUNT: Varies
DEADLINE(S): Varies
FIELD(S): Airline Pilot Training

A merit scholarship for women who are single mothers and pursuing airline pilot careers. Selection is based on need, demonstrated dedication to career goal, work history experience, and recommendations.

To aid pilots with CFI, CRII, MEI, or any equivalents. Must have a US FAA Commercial Pilot Certificate with an Instrument Rating and a First Class medical (or equivalent). Additionally, candidates must have a minimum of 750 flight hours.

493—INTERNATIONAL SOCIETY OF WOMEN AIRLINE PILOTS (The International Airline Scholarship)

2250 E. Tropicana Ave., Suite 19-395
Las Vegas NV 89119-6594
Internet: www.aswap.org

AMOUNT: Varies
DEADLINE(S): None given
FIELD(S): Flight Engineering and Type Ratings

For women seeking careers in aviation and need Flight Engineer Certificates and Type Ratings on 727, 737, 747, 757, and DC-10 aircraft. For Flight Engineers, 1,000 hours flight time and a current FE written required. For Type Rating scholarship, an ATP Certificate and a current FE written.

Contact Gail Redden-Jones at above address.

494—INTERNATIONAL SOCIETY OF WOMEN AIRLINE PILOTS-ISA+21 (ISA Scholarship Fund)

2250 E. Tropicana Ave., Suite 19-395
Las Vegas NV 89118-6594
847/599-9886
Internet: www.iswap.org

AMOUNT: Varies-$1,000-$3,000
DEADLINE(S): APR 1
FIELD(S): Aviation

For women pilots needing advanced ratings and certificates.

Must have a minimum of 750 flight hours and a Commercial Pilot's License.

495—LOS ANGELES COUNCIL OF BLACK PROFESSIONAL ENGINEERS (Al-Ben Scholarship)

P.O. Box 881029
Los Angeles CA 90009
310/635-7734
E-mail: secy1@lablackengineers.org
Internet: www.lablackengineers.org/scholarships.html

AMOUNT: Varies
DEADLINE(S): Varies
FIELD(S): Engineering, Mathematics, Computer Studies, or Applied Scientific Studies

This organization provides scholarships for technically inclined pre-college and undergraduate students enrolled in one of the above fields. Must be of African American, Native American, or Hispanic ancestry. Although preference is given to students attending college in Southern California or who are Southern California

residents, the awards are open to all qualified students attending college in the United States.

See website for more information. Application for the coming year will be on the website during November.

496—MARYLAND HIGHER EDUCATION COMMISSION (Maryland Science and Technology Scholarship Program)

16 Francis Street
Annapolis Park MD 21401
410/974-5370 or 800/974-1024
E-mail: ssamail@mhec.state.md.us
Internet:
http://www.mhec.state.md.us/SSA/stech_qa.htm

AMOUNT: $3,000/yr. (B.A.); $1,000/yr. (A.A.)
DEADLINE(S): None
FIELD(S): Computer Science, Engineering, Technology

Scholarships for college-bound Maryland high school seniors who will major in one of the above fields and who are accepted to an eligible associate or bachelor's degree program in Maryland. Students in the class of 1999 were eligible for the first awards. The deadline was not known at this writing, so check for deadline date. Must agree to work in the state after graduation in a related field, one year for each year of assistance received.

Must maintain a 3.0 GPA.

497—NATIONAL AIR TRANSPORTATION ASSOCIATION FOUNDATION (The Pioneers of Flight Scholarship)

4226 King Street
Alexandria VA 22302
703/845-9000
FAX: 703/845-8176

AMOUNT: $2,500
DEADLINE(S): None
FIELD(S): General Aviation

Scholarship for college students who are in the sophomore or junior year at the time of application intending to pursue full-time study at an accredited four-year college or university and can demonstrate an interest in pursuing a career in general aviation.

Must be nominated by an NATA Regular or Associate Member company.

498—NATIONAL BUSINESS AIRCRAFT ASSOCIATION (Scholarships)

1200 Eighteenth Street NW, 2nd Fl
.Washington DC 20036-2598

202/783-9000
FAX: 202/331-8364
E-mail: info@nbaa.org
Internet: lifeofluxury.com/nbaa.html

AMOUNT: $500
DEADLINE(S): OCT 15
FIELD(S): Aviation-related curricula

Valid only for students enrolled at institutions that are NBAA and University Aviation Association (UAA) members. Open to college sophomores, juniors, or seniors who will be continuing in school the following academic year in an aviation-related baccalaureate or graduate program at these specific member institutions. Must be US citizen and have 3.0 or better GPA.

5 awards per year. Write for complete information.

499—NATIONAL GAY PILOTS ASSOCIA-TION (Pilot Scholarships)

NGPA-EF
P.O. Box 2010-324
South Burlington VT 05407-2010
703/660-3852
24-hr. voice mail: 703/660-3852
Internet: www.ngpa.org

AMOUNT: $1,500
DEADLINE(S): JUL 31
FIELD(S): Pilot training and related
fields in aerospace, aerodynamics,
engineering, airport management, etc.

Scholarships for tuition or flight training costs for student pilots enrolled at a college or university offering an accredited aviation curriculum in the above fields. Also for flight training costs in a professional pilot training program at any training facility certified by the FAA. Not for training for a Private Pilot license. Send SASE for application or visit website for further instructions.

For gay/lesbian applicants or others who can provide evidence of volunteering in an AIDS organization or in any group that supports the gay/lesbian community and their rights.

500—NATIONAL SOCIETY OF BLACK ENGINEERS (Scholarships)

1454 Duke Street
Alexandria VA 22314
703/549-2207
FAX: 703/683-5312
E-mail: nsbehq@nsbe.org
Internet: www.nsbe.org

AMOUNT: Varies
DEADLINE(S): Varies
FIELD(S): Engineering and engineering
technologies

Programs for black and other ethnic minorities in the fields of engineering and the engineering technologies. Organization offers pre-college programs, scholarships, career fairs, a journal, a newsletter, etc.

Contact organization for details.

501—NATIONAL SPACE CLUB (Dr. Robert H. Goddard Scholarship)

2000 L Street NW, Suite 710
Washington DC 20036-4907
202/973-8661

AMOUNT: $10,000
DEADLINE(S): JAN 8
FIELD(S): Science, Engineering

Open to undergraduate juniors and seniors and graduate students who have scholastic plans leading to future participation in the aerospace sciences and technology. Must be US citizen. Award based on transcript, letters of recommendation, accomplishments, scholastic plans, and proven past research and participation in space-related science and engineering. Personal need is considered, but is not controlling.

Renewable. Send a self-addressed, stamped envelope for more information.

502—NATIONAL SPACE CLUB (Dr. Robert H. Goddard Historical Essay Award)

2000 L Street NW, Suite 710
Washington DC 20036-4907
202/973-8661

AMOUNT: $1,000 + plaque
DEADLINE(S): DEC 4
FIELD(S): Aerospace History

Essay competition open to any US citizen on a topic dealing with any significant aspect of the historical development of rocketry and astronautics. Essays should not exceed 5,000 words and should be fully documented. Will be judged on originality and scholarship.

Previous winners not eligible. Send self-addressed, stamped envelope for complete information.

503—NINETY-NINES, INC. (Amelia Earhart Memorial Scholarships)

Box 965, 7100 Terminal Drive
Oklahoma City OK 73159-0965
800/994-1929 or 405/685-7969
FAX: 405/685-7985
E-mail: 10476.406@compuserve.com
Internet: ninety-nines.org

AMOUNT: Varies
DEADLINE(S): Varies
FIELD(S): Advanced Aviation Ratings

Scholarships for female licensed pilots who are members of the 99s, Inc.

15-20 awards annually. Financial need considered. Contact Lu Hollander at above address for application and/or membership information.

504—NINETY-NINES, SAN FERNANDO VALLEY CHAPTER/VAN NUYS AIRPORT (Aviation Career Scholarships)

P.O. Box 8160
Van Nuys CA 91409
818/989-0081

AMOUNT: $3,000
DEADLINE(S): MAY 1
FIELD(S): Aviation Careers

For men and women of the greater Los Angeles area pursuing careers as professional pilots, flight instructors, mechanics, or other aviation career specialists. Applicants must be at least 21 years of age and US citizens.

3 awards annually. Send self-addressed, stamped, business-sized envelope to above address for application.

505—OAK RIDGE INSTITUTE FOR SCIENCE AND EDUCATION (ORISE Education & Training Programs)

P.O. Box 117
Oak Ridge TN 37831-0117
Internet: www.orau.gov/orise/
educ.htm

AMOUNT: Varies
DEADLINE(S): Varies
FIELD(S): Engineering, Aeronautics,
Computer Science, Technology, Earth
Science, Environmental Studies,
Biology, Chemistry, Physics, Medical
Research

Numerous programs funded by the US Department of Energy are offered for undergraduate students through postgraduate researchers. Includes fellowship and internship opportunities throughout the US. Some have citizenship restrictions. Travel may be included.

See website or write for a catalog of specific programs and requirements.

506—SAN DIEGO AEROSPACE MUSEUM (Bill Gibbs Scholarship)

Education Dept.
2001 Pan American Plaza
San Diego CA 92101

619/234-8291, ext. 19
FAX: 619/233-4526
Internet: aerospacemuseum.org/
Scholastic.HTML

AMOUNT: Varies
DEADLINE(S): Varies
FIELD(S): Aerospace: math, physics,
science, or engineering

For students who are residents of San Diego County, California, who have an aerospace career interest, and who have been accepted to a four-year college or university in a degree program relating to math, physics, science, or engineering.

Call or write museum for further information.

507—SMITHSONIAN INSTITUTION (National Air & Space Museum Verville Fellowship)

National Air and Space Museum
MRC 312
Washington DC 20560
Written inquiry

AMOUNT: $30,000 stipend for 12 months
+ travel and misc. expenses
DEADLINE(S): JAN 15
FIELD(S): Analysis of major trends,
developments, and accomplishments in
the history of aviation or space studies

A competitive nine- to twelve-month in-residence fellowship in the above field of study. Advanced degree is NOT a requirement. Contact Fellowship Coordinator at above location.

Open to all nationalities. Fluency in English required.

508—THE FRASCA FAMILY/UNIVERSITY AVIATION ASSOCIATION (The Joseph Frasca Excellence in Aviation Scholarship)

c/o College of Technical Careers
Southern Illinois University
Carbondale IL 62901-6621
618/453-8898

AMOUNT: $500
DEADLINE(S): APR 1 (varies)
FIELD(S): Aviation maintenance or
flight training

Scholarships for college juniors or seniors currently enrolled in a University Aviation Association (UAA)-affiliated institution and pursuing a career in one of the above fields. Minimum GPA of 3.0. Must show membership in a flight-related organization.

2 pilot and 2 mechanic awards yearly.

509—VERTICAL FLIGHT FOUNDATION (Scholarships)

217 N. Washington Street
Alexandria VA 22314-2538
703/684-6777
FAX: 703/739-9279
E-mail: ahs703@aol.com
Internet: www.vtol.org

AMOUNT: $2,000-$4,000
DEADLINE(S): FEB 1
FIELD(S): Vertical Flight

These merit-based awards are open to undergraduate juniors and seniors and graduate students pursuing full-time studies in vertical flight at accredited schools of engineering. Must submit transcripts and references. Scholarships awarded to student once as an undergraduate senior, once as a master's student, and once as a Ph.D. student. Financial need NOT a factor.

See website or contact VFF for an application. Recipients notified by April 15th.

510—VIRGINIA AIRPORT OPERATORS COUNCIL (VAOC Aviation Scholarship Award)

201 Bowen Loop
Charlottesville VA 22911
804/973-8342

AMOUNT: $2,000
DEADLINE(S): Varies (in the Spring)
FIELD(S): Aviation

Open to Virginia high school seniors who have been accepted into an accredited postsecondary aviation education program. Applicants need a 3.0 or better GPA and should be planning a career in aviation.

1 award annually. Financial need NOT necessary. Contact Barbara Hutchinson, Charlottesville-Aebemaile Airport, at above address for more information.

511—VIRGINIA AVIATION AND SPACE EDUCATION FORUM (Scholarships)

5701 Huntsman Road
Sandston VA 23150
800/292-1034
Internet: www.doav.state.va.us/
vaocship.htm

AMOUNT: $2,000
DEADLINE(S): FEB 16
FIELD(S): Aviation-related programs

Scholarships for high school seniors planning a career in aviation who are residents of Virginia and who have been accepted and are enrolled in an accredited college. Must have at least a 3.75 GPA.

Contact Betty Wilson at above location or access website for application and details of eligibility requirements.

ARCHITECTURE

512—AIR FORCE RESERVE OFFICER TRAINING CORPS (AFROTC Scholarships)

551 E. Maxwell Blvd.
Maxwell AFB AL 36112-6106
334/953-7783

AMOUNT: Full tuition, books, & fees for
all 4 years of college
DEADLINE(S): DEC 1
FIELD(S): Science, Engineering,
Business, Political Science, Psychology,
Geography, Foreign Studies, Foreign
Language

Competitive scholarships based on individual merit to high school seniors and graduates who have not completed any full-time college work. Must be a US citizen between the ages of 17-27. Must also have GPA of 2.5 or above, be in top 40% of class, and complete Applicant Fitness Test. Cannot be a single parent. Your college/university must offer AFROTC.

2,300 awards annually. Contact above address for application packet.

513—AMERICAN INSTITUTE OF ARCHITECTS/AMERICAN ARCHITECTURAL FOUNDATION (Scholarship Program)

1735 New York Ave., NW
Washington DC 20006-5292
202/626-7511
FAX: 202/626-7420
E-mail: felberm@aiamail.aia.org

AMOUNT: $500-$2,500
DEADLINE(S): JAN 31
FIELD(S): Architecture

Open to undergraduate students in their final two years or graduate students pursuing their master's degree in architecture. Awards tenable at accredited institutions in the US and Canada.

Applications available ONLY through the office of the dean or department head at an NAAB or RAIC school of architecture. Contact Mary Felber at AIA/AAF for more information.

514—AMERICAN INSTITUTE OF ARCHITECTS/AMERICAN ARCHITECTURAL FOUNDATION (Minority/Disadvantaged Scholarship Program)

1735 New York Ave. NW
Washington DC 20006-5292
202/626-7511
FAX: 202/626-7420
E-mail: felberm@aiamail.aia.org

AMOUNT: $500-$2,500
DEADLINE(S): DEC (nomination);
   JAN 15 (application)
FIELD(S): Architecture

Open to minority and/or disadvantaged students who are entering a program leading to a B.A. or M.A. of architecture. High school seniors, junior college students, and college students may apply.

25 awards annually. Renewable for three years. Nomination by an individual familiar with student's interest and potential to be an architect is required. Contact Mary Felber at AIA/AAF for more information.

515—AMERICAN INSTITUTE OF ARCHITECTS/AMERICAN ARCHITECTURAL FOUNDATION (RTKL Traveling Fellowship)

1735 New York Ave. NW
Washington DC 20006
202/626-7511
FAX: 202/626-7420
E-mail: felberm@aiamail.aia.org

AMOUNT: $2,500
DEADLINE(S): FEB 14
FIELD(S): Architecture

Fellowship to encourage and support foreign travel undertaken to further education toward a degree in architecture. Must be in second-to-last year of bachelor or master's program and planning to travel outside the US or accepted in a professional degree program.

Forms are sent to all NAAB-accredited schools of architecture.

516—AMERICAN INSTITUTE OF ARCHITECTS/AMERICAN HOSPITAL ASSOCIATION (AIA/AHA Fellowships in Health Facilities Planning and Design)

1735 New York Ave. NW
Washington DC 20006
202/626-7511
FAX: 202/626-7420
E-mail: felberm@aiamail.aia.org

AMOUNT: $22,000
DEADLINE(S): JAN 15

FIELD(S): Architecture—Health
   Facilities

For architects, graduate students, and those in last year of undergraduate work in architecture who are US or Canadian citizens for coursework or independent study. Funds provided by The American Sterilizer Company.

For one year. Write for complete information.

517—AMERICAN INSTITUTE OF ARCHITECTS, NEW YORK CHAPTER (Haskell Awards for Student Architectural Journalism)

200 Lexington Ave., 6th Fl.
New York NY 10016
212/683-0023, ext. 14

AMOUNT: Varies
DEADLINE(S): FEB 13
FIELD(S): Architectural Writing

Awards to encourage fine writing on architecture and related design subjects and to foster regard for intelligent criticism among future professionals. For students enrolled in a professional architecture or related program, such as art history, interior design, urban studies, and landscape architecture. Submit a news story, an essay or feature article, book review, or journal accompanied by a 100-word statement describing the purpose of the piece.

Write to above location for complete information.

518—AMERICAN INSTITUTE OF ARCHITECTS, NEW YORK CHAPTER (Women's Architectural Auxiliary, Eleanor Allwork Scholarships)

200 Lexington Ave., 6th Fl.
New York NY 10016
212/683-0023, ext. 14
FAX: 212/696-5022

AMOUNT: $5,000 (Honor Grants);
   $2,500 (Citation Grants)
DEADLINE(S): MAR 6
FIELD(S): Architecture

Scholarship grants for students seeking their first professional degree in architecture. Must be New York City resident or a NYC resident attending an upstate school. High level of academic achievement and legitimate financial need required as determined by the Financial Aid Officer at the school.

Write or call for complete information.

519—AMERICAN INSTITUTE OF ARCHITECTS, NEW YORK CHAPTER (Stewardson, Keefe, and LeBrun Travel Grants)

200 Lexington Ave., 6th Fl.
New York NY 10016
212/683-0023, ext. 14

AMOUNT: $3,000
DEADLINE(S): FEB 13
FIELD(S): Architecture Research

Travel grants for architectural education and professional development. Submit a statement of purpose regarding travel plans—a brief, 500-word description of where travel will take place, why it is important to professional development, etc. For professional architects who are US citizens.

Write for complete information.

520—AMERICAN PLANNING ASSOCIATION (Minority Scholarship and Fellowship Programs)

122 South Michigan Ave., Ste. 1600
Chicago IL 60605
312/431-9100
FAX: 312/431-9985

AMOUNT: $2,000-$5,000 (grads); $2,500
   (undergrads)
DEADLINE(S): MAY 14
FIELD(S): Urban Planning, Community
   Development, Environmental
   Sciences, Public Administration,
   Transportation, or Urban Studies

Scholarships for African-Americans, Hispanics, or Native American students pursuing undergraduate degrees in the U.S. in the above fields. Must have completed first year. Fellowships for graduate students. Programs must be approved by the Planning Accreditation Board. US citizenship.

Call or write for complete information.

521—AMERICAN SOCIETY OF ENGINEERS OF INDIAN ORIGIN (Undergraduate Scholarship Programs)

P.O. Box 49494
Atlanta GA 30359-1494
770/451-2299
Internet: www.iasf.org/asei.htm

AMOUNT: Up to $1,000
DEADLINE(S): AUG 15
FIELD(S): Engineering fields:
   architecture, computer technology,
   geotechnical or geoenvironmental
   engineering, and allied sciences

Several scholarships for undergraduate engineering students in the above fields who were born in India or who are Indian by ancestry or relation. For study in the US Some programs have residency requirements in certain states.

Contact Dr. Narsi Narasimhan at above location for applications and details.

522—ASSOCIATED WESTERN UNIVERSITIES, INC. (AWU Undergraduate Student Fellowships)

4190 S. Highland Drive, Suite 211
Salt Lake City UT 84124-2600
801/273-8911
FAX: 801/277-5632
Internet: www.awu.org

AMOUNT: $300/week stipend + travel allowance
DEADLINE(S): FEB 1
FIELD(S): Mathematics, Engineering, Technology, Science

Eight- to- sixteen-week fellowships for undergraduate students enrolled in accredited institutions and who have completed at least one year of college by the start of the fellowship. Applicants reviewed on the basis of academic performance/class standing, career goals, recommendations, and compatibility of scientific interests and abilities with the needs and resources of the host facility. Citizenship restrictions may apply for some facilities.

500+ awards annually. Renewable (competitively with new application). Contact above address for an application.

523—ASSOCIATED WESTERN UNIVERSITIES, INC. (AWU Visiting Scientist Fellowships)

4190 S. Highland Drive, Suite 211
Salt Lake City UT 84124-2600
801/273-8900

AMOUNT: Varies
DEADLINE(S): Varies (Two months prior to starting date)
FIELD(S): Engineering, Science, Mathematics, and Technology

Research fellowships for professionals with continued commitment to science and engineering. For use at one of 62 participating universities. US citizenship or permanent residency required.

For detailed information and list of cooperating facitilies contact above location.

524—FLORIDA FEDERATION OF GARDEN CLUBS, INC. (FFGC Scholarships for College Students)

6065 21st Street SW
Vero Beach FL 32968-9427
561/778-1023
Internet: www.ffgc.org

AMOUNT: $1,500-$3,500
DEADLINE(S): MAY 1
FIELD(S): Ecology, Environmental Issues, Land Management, City Planning, Environmental Control, Horticulture, Landscape Design, Conservation, Botany, Forestry, Marine Biology, Floriculture, Agriculture

Various scholarships for Florida residents with a "B" average or better enrolled full-time as a junior, senior, or graduate student at a Florida college or university.

See website or contact Melba Campbell at FFGC for an application.

525—FLORIDA FEDERATION OF GARDEN CLUBS, INC. (FFGC Scholarships for High School Students)

6065 21st Street SW
Vero Beach FL 32968-9427
561/778-1023
Internet: www.ffgc.org

AMOUNT: $1,500
DEADLINE(S): MAY 1
FIELD(S): Ecology, Environmental Issues, Land Management, City Planning, Environmental Control, Horticulture, Landscape Design, Conservation, Botany, Forestry, Marine Biology, Floriculture, Agriculture

Scholarships for Florida residents with a "B" average or better who will be incoming freshmen at a Florida college or university.

See website or contact Melba Campbell at FFGC for an application.

526—GRAHAM FOUNDATION FOR ADVANCED STUDIES IN THE FINE ARTS (Research Grants)

Four West Burton Place
Chicago IL 60610
312/787-4071
Internet: www.grahamfoundation.org

AMOUNT: Up to $10,000
DEADLINE(S): JAN 15; JUL 15
FIELD(S): Architecture

Research grants open to individuals and institutions for specific projects relating to contemporary architecture planning. Grants do not support study or research in pursuit of an academic degree. No scholarships available.

100+ awards per year. Write for more information.

527—HISPANIC COLLEGE FUND (Scholarships for Hispanic Students)

One Thomas Circle NW, Suite 375
Washington DC 20005
202/296-5400
FAX: 202/296-3774
E-mail: Hispanic.Fund@Internet MCI.com
Internet: http://hispanicfund.org

AMOUNT: Varies
DEADLINE(S): APR 15
FIELD(S): Most college majors leading to a career in business

Scholarships for deserving Hispanic college students pursuing a higher education in a major leading to a business career and who are full-time students at accredited institutions. US citizenship. Must demonstrate financial need.

Contact above organization for details or visit website for application.

528—LANDSCAPE ARCHITECTURE FOUNDATION (Edward D. Stone Jr. & Associates Minority Scholarship)

Use website below
202/216-2356
E-mail: tpadian@asla.org
Internet: www.asla.org

AMOUNT: $1,000
DEADLINE(S): MAR 31
FIELD(S): Landscape Architecture

Open to African-American, Hispanic, Native American, and minority students of other cultural and ethnic backgrounds entering their final two years of undergrad study in landscape architecture.

Access website for details and for application.

529—LANDSCAPE ARCHITECTURE FOUNDATION (Edith H. Henderson Scholarship)

636 Eye Street NW
Washington DC 20001-3736
202/898-2444
FAX: 202/898-1185
E-mail: tpadian@asla.org
Internet: www.asla.org

AMOUNT: $1,000
DEADLINE(S): MAR 31
FIELD(S): Landscape Architecture

Scholarship available to any landscape architecture student who has in the past or is participating in a class in public speaking or creative writing. Must write a 200- to 400-word typed review of Edith H. Henderson's book *Edith Henderson's Home Landscape Companion.*

Locate the book in a library or call 800-787-2665 or 800-241-0113 to order. Be sure and state that you are a landscape architect student applying for the Henderson scholarship.

530—LANDSCAPE ARCHITECTURE FOUNDATION (Harriett Barnhart Wimmer Scholarship)

Use website below
202/216-2356
E-mail: tpadian@asla.org
Internet: www.asla.org

AMOUNT: $1,000
DEADLINE(S): MAR 31
FIELD(S): Landscape Architecture

Open to women going into their final year of undergraduate study at a U.S. university who have demonstrated excellence in their design ability and sensitivity to the environment.

Access website for details and application information.

531—LANDSCAPE ARCHITECTURE FOUNDATION (Hawaii Chapter/The David T. Woolsey Scholarship)

Use website below
202/216-2356
E-mail: tpadian@asla.org
Internet: www.asla.org

AMOUNT: $1,000
DEADLINE(S): MAR 31
FIELD(S): Landscape Architecture

Scholarship open to third-, fourth-, and fifth-year or graduate students of landscape architecture who are residents of Hawaii.

Access website for application information.

532—LANDSCAPE ARCHITECTURE FOUNDATION (LAF/CLASS Fund Scholarships)

Use website below
202/216-2356

E-mail: tpadian@asla.org
Internet: www.asla.org

AMOUNT: $500-$2,000
DEADLINE(S): MAR 31
FIELD(S): Landscape Architecture or Ornamental Horticulture

Scholarships and internships for students enrolled in certain California colleges: California Polytechnic Institute (Pomona or San Luis Obispo), UCLA, UC-Irvine, and UC-Davis who show promise and a commitment to landscape architecture as a profession.

Access website for complete information.

533—LANDSCAPE ARCHITECTURE FOUNDATION (Raymond E. Page Scholarship)

636 Eye Street NW
Washington DC 20001-3736
202/898-2444
FAX: 202/898-1185
E-mail: tpadian@asla.org
Internet: www.asla.org

AMOUNT: $1,000
DEADLINE(S): MAR 31
FIELD(S): Landscape Architecture

Scholarships for undergraduate or graduate students pursuing studies in landscape architecture.

Access website for complete application information.

534—LANDSCAPE ARCHITECTURE FOUNDATION (Thomas P. Papandrew Scholarship)

Use website below
202/216-2356
E-mail: tpadian@asla.org
Internet: www.asla.org

AMOUNT: $1,000
DEADLINE(S): MAR 31
FIELD(S): Landscape Architecture

Open to minority students enrolled full-time in the Landscape Architecture program at Arizona State University. Students must be legal residents of Arizona and US citizens. Must demonstrate financial need.

Access website for complete application information.

535—LANDSCAPE ARCHITECTURE FOUNDATION (The Rain Bird Company Scholarship)

636 Eye Street NW
Washington DC 20001-3736
202/898-2444
FAX: 202/898-1185
E-mail: tpadian@asla.org
Internet: www.asla.org

AMOUNT: $1,000
DEADLINE(S): MAR 31
FIELD(S): Landscape Architecture

For landscape architecture students in their final two years of undergraduate study who have demonstrated commitment to the profession through participation in extracurricular activities and exemplary scholastic achievements.

Access website for complete information.

536—LANDSCAPE ARCHITECTURE FOUNDATION (William J. Locklin Scholarship)

636 Eye Street NW
Washington DC 20001-3736
202/898-2444
FAX: 202/898-1185
E-mail: tpadian@asla.org
Internet: www.asla.org

AMOUNT: $1,000
DEADLINE(S): MAR 31
FIELD(S): Landscape Architecture

Scholarships open to undergraduate and graduate students pursuing a program in lighting design. Purpose is to stress the importance of 24-hour lighting in landscape design.

Access website for complete application information.

537—LOS ANGELES COUNCIL OF BLACK PROFESSIONAL ENGINEERS (Al-Ben Scholarship)

P.O. Box 881029
Los Angeles CA 90009
310/635-7734
E-mail: secy1@lablackengineers.org
Internet: www.lablackengineers.org/scholarships.html

AMOUNT: Varies
DEADLINE(S): Varies

FIELD(S): Engineering, Mathematics, Computer Studies, or Applied Scientific Studies

This organization provides scholarships for technically inclined pre-college and undergraduate students enrolled in one of the above fields. Must be of African American, Native American, or Hispanic ancestry. Although preference is given to students attending college in Southern California or who are Southern California residents, the awards are open to all qualified students attending college in the United States.

See website for more information. Application for the coming year will be on the website during November.

538—NATIONAL COUNCIL OF STATE GARDEN CLUBS, INC. (Scholarships)

4401 Magnolia Ave.
St. Louis MO 63110-3492
314/776-7574
FAX: 314/776-5108
E-mail: scsgc.franm@worldnet.att.net
Internet: www.gardenclub.org

AMOUNT: $3,500
DEADLINE(S): MAR 1
FIELD(S): Horticulture, Floriculture, Landscape Design, City Planning, Land Management, and allied subjects

Open to junior, seniors, and graduate students who are US citizens and are studying any of the above or related subjects. Student must have the endorsement of the state in which he/she resides permanently. Applications will be forwarded to the National State Chairman and judged on a national level.

32 scholarships are awarded. Write to the above address for complete information.

539—NATIONAL FEDERATION OF THE BLIND (Frank Walton Horn Memorial Scholarship)

805 Fifth Ave.
Grinnell IA 50112
515/236-3366

AMOUNT: $3,000
DEADLINE(S): MAR 31
FIELD(S): Architecture, Engineering

Open to legally blind students pursuing or planning to pursue a full-time postsecondary course of study in the US. Based on academic excellence, service to the community, and financial need. Membership NOT required.

1 award annually. Renewable. Contact Mrs. Peggy Elliot, Scholarship Committee Chairman, for an application.

540—NATIONAL FEDERATION OF THE BLIND (Howard Brown Rickard Scholarship)

805 Fifth Ave.
Grinnell IA 50112
515/236-3366

AMOUNT: $3,000
DEADLINE(S): MAR 31
FIELD(S): Law, Medicine, Engineering, Architecture, Natural Sciences

For legally blind students pursuing or planning to pursue a full-time postsecondary course of study in the US. Based on academic excellence, service to the community, and financial need. Membership NOT required.

1 award annually. Renewable. Contact Mrs. Peggy Elliot, Scholarship Committee Chairman, for an application.

541—NATIONAL ITALIAN AMERICAN FOUNDATION (Cesare Fera/NIAF Memorial Matching Scholarship)

1860 19th Street
Washington DC 20009-5599
202/530-5315

AMOUNT: $2,000
DEADLINE(S): MAY 31
FIELD(S): Architecture

For graduate and undergraduate students of Italian ancestry majoring in architecture at Clemson University in South Carolina.

Write for application and details. Financial need, academic merit, and community service are considered.

542—NATIONAL SOCIETY OF BLACK ENGINEERS (Scholarships)

1454 Duke Street
Alexandria VA 22314
703/549-2207
FAX: 703/683-5312
E-mail: nsbehq@nsbe.org
Internet: www.nsbe.org

AMOUNT: Varies
DEADLINE(S): Varies
FIELD(S): Engineering and engineering technologies

Programs for black and other ethnic minorities in the fields of engineering and the engineering technologies. Organization offers pre-college programs, scholarships, career fairs, a journal, a newsletter, etc.

Contact organization for details.

543—NATIONAL STONE ASSN./AMERICAN SOCIETY OF LANDSCAPE ARCHITECTS (Student Competition)

1415 Elliot Place NW
Washington DC 20007
202/342-1100

AMOUNT: $1,000; $500; $300
DEADLINE(S): MAY 1
FIELD(S): Landscape Architecture

Contest in which undergraduate landscape architecture students work with a local rock quarry to produce a reclamation proposal.

Write for complete information.

544—NEW YORK CITY DEPT. CITYWIDE ADMINISTRATIVE SERVICES (Urban Fellows Program)

1 Centre Street, 24th Fl.
New York NY 10007
212/487-5600
FAX: 212/487-5720

AMOUNT: $18,000 stipend
DEADLINE(S): JAN 20
FIELD(S): Public Administration, Urban Planning, Government, Public Service, Urban Affairs

Fellowship program provides one academic year (9 months) of full-time work experience in urban government. Open to graduating college seniors and recent college graduates. US citizenship required.

Write for complete information.

545—NEW YORK CITY DEPT. OF CITYWIDE ADMINISTRATIVE SERVICES (Government Scholars Internship Program)

1 Centre Street, 24th Fl.
New York NY 10007
212/487-5600
FAX: 212/487-5720

AMOUNT: $3,000 stipend
DEADLINE(S): JAN 13
FIELD(S): Public Administration, Urban Planning, Government, Public Service, Urban Affairs

10-week summer intern program open to undergraduate sophomores, juniors, and seniors. Program provides students with unique opportunity to learn about NY City government. Internships available in virtually every city agency and mayoral office.

Write to New York City Fellowship Programs at above address for complete information.

546—NEW YORK STATE HIGHER EDUCATION SERVICES CORPORATION (N.Y. State Regents Professional/Health Care Opportunity Scholarships)

Cultural Education Center, Rm. 5C64
Albany NY 12230
518/486-1319
Internet: www.hesc.com

AMOUNT: $1,000-$10,000/yr.
DEADLINE(S): Varies
FIELD(S): Medicine and Dentistry and related fields, Architecture, Nursing, Psychology, Audiology, Landscape Architecture, Social Work, Chiropractic, Law, Pharmacy, Accounting, Speech Language Pathology

For NY state residents who are economically disadvantaged and members of a minority group underrepresented in the chosen profession and attending school in NY state. Some programs carry a service obligation in New York for each year of support. For US citizens or qualifying noncitizens.

Medical/dental scholarships require one year of professional work in NY.

547—ROBERT SCHRECK MEMORIAL FUND (Grants)

c/o Texas Commerce Bank
Trust Dept.
P.O. Drawer 140
El Paso TX 79980
915/546-6515

AMOUNT: $500—$1500
DEADLINE(S): JUL 15; NOV 15
FIELD(S): Medicine, Veterinary Medicine, Physics, Chemistry, Architecture, Engineering, Episcopal Clergy

Grants to undergraduate juniors or seniors or graduate students who have been residents of El Paso County for at least two years. Must be US citizen or legal resident and have a high grade point average. Financial need is a consideration.

Write for complete information.

548—SKIDMORE, OWINGS & MERRILL FOUNDATION (Architecture Traveling Fellowship Program)

224 S. Michigan Ave., Suite 1000
Chicago IL 60604
312/554-9090

FAX: 312/360-4545
AMOUNT: $10,000
DEADLINE(S): Varies (contact school)
FIELD(S): Architecture

For students graduating with a B.Arch. or M.Arch. degree from a US accredited architectural school to help broaden their education and take an enlightened view of society's need to improve the built and natural environments.

3 awards annually. Must submit portfolio and a proposed travel itinerary. Write for complete information.

549—SKIDMORE, OWINGS & MERRILL FOUNDATION (Interior Architecture Traveling Fellowship Program)

224 S. Michigan Ave., Suite 1000
Chicago IL 60604
312/554-9090
FAX: 312/360-4545

AMOUNT: $7,500
DEADLINE(S): Varies (consult with school)
FIELD(S): Architecture or Interior Design

For a student graduating with a B.A. or M.A. degree from an accredited US architectural or FIDER school. It will allow the Fellow to visit buildings and settings that are central to his or her area of interest and study.

Must submit portfolio and a proposed travel itinerary, etc. Write for complete information.

550—SMITHSONIAN INSTITUTION (Cooper-Hewitt, National Design Museum-Mark Kaminski Summer Internship)

2 East 91st Street
New York NY 10128
212/860-6868
FAX: 212/860-6909

AMOUNT: $2,500 for 10-week period
DEADLINE(S): MAR 31
FIELD(S): Architecture, Architectural History, Design and Criticism, Museum Education, Museum Studies

These internships are open to college students considering a career in one of the above areas of study. Also open to graduate students who have not yet completed their M.A. degree. This ten-week program is designed to acquaint participants with the programs, policies, procedures, and operations of Cooper-Hewitt Museum and of museums in general.

1 award each summer. Internship commences in June and ends in August.

Housing is not provided. Write to Linda Herd at the above address for complete information.

551—SMITHSONIAN INSTITUTION (Cooper-Hewitt, National Design Museum-Peter Krueger Summer Internship Program)

2 East 91st Street
New York NY 10128
212/860-6868
FAX: 212/860-6909

AMOUNT: $2,500
DEADLINE(S): MAR 31
FIELD(S): Art History, Design, Museum Studies, and Museum Education, or Architectural History

Ten-week summer internships open to graduate and undergraduate students considering a career in the museum profession. Interns will assist on special research or exhibition projects and participate in daily museum activities.

6 awards each summer. Internship commences in June and ends in August. Housing is not provided. Write for complete information.

552—SMITHSONIAN INSTITUTION (Cooper-Hewitt, National Design Museum-The Lippincott & Margulies Summer Internship)

2 East 91st Street
New York NY 10128
212/860-6868
FAX: 212/860-6909

AMOUNT: $2,500
DEADLINE(S): MAR 31
FIELD(S): Graphic, environmental, and industrial design

Ten-week summer internships open to graduate and undergraduate students considering a career in the fields listed above.

1 award each summer. Internship commences in June and ends in August. Housing is not provided. Write for complete information.

553—SOIL AND WATER CONSERVATION SOCIETY (SWCS Internships)

7515 NE Ankeny Road
Ankeny IA 50021-9764
515/289-2331 or 1-800/THE-SOIL
FAX: 515/289-1227
E-mail: charliep@swcs.org
Internet: www.swcs.org

AMOUNT: Varies—most are uncompensated

DEADLINE(S): Varies

FIELD(S): Journalism, Marketing, Database Management, Meeting Planning, Public Policy Research, Environmental Education, Landscape Architecture

Internships for undergraduates and graduates to gain experience in the above fields as they relate to soil and water conservation issues. Internship openings vary through the year in duration, compensation, and objective. SWCS will coordinate particulars with your academic advisor.

Contact SWCS for internship availability at any time during the year or see website for jobs page.

554—STUDENT CONSERVATION ASSOCIATION (SCA Resource Assistant Program)

P.O. Box 550
Charlestown NH 03603
603/543-1700
FAX: 603/543-1828
E-mail: internships@sca-inc.org
Internet: www.sca-inc.org

AMOUNT: $1,180-$4,725

DEADLINE(S): Varies

FIELD(S): Environment & related fields

Must be 18 and US citizen; need not be student. Fields: Agricultural, archaeology, anthropology, botany, caves, civil/environmental engineering, environmental education, fisheries, forests, herpetology, history, living history/roleplaying, visitor services, landscape architectural/environmental design, paleontology, recreation/resource/range management, trail maintenance/construction, wildlife management, geology, hydrology, library/museums, surveying.

900 positions in US and Canada. Send $1 for postage for application; outside US/Canada, send $20.

555—U.S. DEPARTMENT OF TRANSPORTATION (Dwight D. Eisenhower Transportation Fellowships)

U.S. Dept. of Transportation
Fed. Hwy. Admin.
6300 Georgetown Pike, HHI-20
McLean VA 22101-2296
703/235-0538

AMOUNT: Varies

DEADLINE(S): FEB

FIELD(S): Transportation—such majors as chemistry; materials science; corrosion; civil, chemical, & electronics engineering; structures; human factors; computer science; psychology

Research fellowships for undergrads and grad students at any Dept. of Transportation facility or selected IHE. For three to twelve months. Research must focus on transportation-related research and development in the above fields.

Contact Ilene Payne, Director, Universities and Grants Programs at above location for details.

556—UNIVERSITY OF ILLINOIS AT URBANA-CHAMPAIGN (Lydia E. Parker Bates Scholarship)

Turner Student Services Bldg.
MC-306, 610 East John Street
Champaign IL 61820
217/333-0100

AMOUNT: Varies

DEADLINE(S): MAR 15

FIELD(S): Art, Architecture, Landscape Architecture, Urban Planning, Dance, Theater, and all related subjects except Music

Open to undergraduate students in the College of Fine & Applied Arts who are attending the University of Illinois at Urbana-Champaign. Must demonstrate financial need and have 3.85 GPA. Complete the Free Application for Federal Student Aid.

175 awards per year. Recipients must carry at least 12 credit hours per semester. Contact office of student financial aid.

557—WAVERLY COMMUNITY HOUSE INC. (F. Lammot Belin Arts Scholarships)

Scholarships Selection Committee
P.O. Box 142
Waverly PA 18471
717/586-8191

AMOUNT: $10,000

DEADLINE(S): DEC 15

FIELD(S): Painting, Sculpture, Music, Drama, Dance, Literature, Architecture, Photography

Applicants must have resided in the Abington or Pocono regions of Northeastern Pennsylvania. They must furnish proof of exceptional ability in their chosen field but no formal training in any academic or professional program.

US citizenship required. Finalists must appear in person before the selection committee. Write for complete information.

558—WEBB INSTITUTE (Naval Architecture Scholarships)

Crescent Beach Road
Glen Cove NY 11542-1398
516/671-2213

AMOUNT: Full tuition for 4 years

DEADLINE(S): FEB 15

FIELD(S): Naval Architecture, Marine Engineering

Open to high school students aged 16-24 who are in the top 10% of their class and have a minimum 3.2 GPA. Based on college boards, SAT scores, demonstrated interest in above areas, and an interview. Must be US citizen. Tenable at the Webb Institute.

20-25 awards annually. Contact Webb Institute for an application.

559—WEST VIRGINIA SOCIETY OF ARCHITECTS/AMERICAN INSTITUTE OF ARCHITECTS (Scholarships)

P.O. Box 813
Charleston WV 25323
304/344-9872
FAX: 304/343-0205

AMOUNT: $2,500

DEADLINE(S): MAY 30

FIELD(S): Architecture

Open to West Virginia residents enrolled in an accredited architectural program who have completed six semesters or its equivalent by May 30th. Candidates must submit letter stating need, qualifications, and desire.

Request applications after January 30th each year. Contact Roberta J. Guffey, Hon. AIA, Executive Director, at above address.

560—XEROX TECHNICAL MINORITY SCHOLARSHIP (School-Year Tuition)

907 Culver Road
Rochester NY 14609
Internet: www.xerox.com/employment

AMOUNT: Up to $5,000 (varies according to tuition and academic excellence)

DEADLINE(S): SEP 15

FIELD(S): Various engineering and science disciplines

Scholarships for minorities enrolled full-time in a technical degree program at the bachelor level or above. Must be African-American, Native American, Hispanic, or Asian. Recipient may not have tuition or related expenses covered by other scholarships or grants.

If above requirements are met, obtain application from website or address above. Your financial aid office must fill out the bottom half of the form. Send completed application, your resume, and a cover letter to Xerox Technical Minority Scholarship Program at above address.

561—XEROX TECHNICAL MINORITY SCHOLARSHIP (Summer Employment Program)

Xerox Square
Rochester NY 14644
Written inquiry

AMOUNT: Up to $5,000 (varies according to tuition and academic excellence)
DEADLINE(S): SEP 15
FIELD(S): Various engineering and science disciplines

Scholarships for minorities enrolled in a technical degree program at the bachelor level or above. Must be African-American, Native American, Hispanic, or Asian. Xerox will match your skills with a sponsoring organization that will offer a meaningful summer work experience complimenting your academic learning.

If above requirements are met, send your resume and a cover letter to Xerox Corporation Corporate Employment and College Relations Technical Mfinority Scholarship Program at above address.

CIVIL ENGINEERING

562—AIR FORCE RESERVE OFFICER TRAINING CORPS (AFROTC Scholarships)

551 E. Maxwell Blvd.
Maxwell AFB AL 36112-6106
334/953-7783

AMOUNT: Full tuition, books, & fees for all 4 years of college
DEADLINE(S): DEC 1
FIELD(S): Science, Engineering, Business, Political Science, Psychology, Geography, Foreign Studies, Foreign Language

Competitive scholarships based on individual merit to high school seniors and graduates who have not completed any full-time college work. Must be a US citizen between the ages of 17-27. Must also have GPA of 2.5 or above, be in top 40% of class, and complete Applicant Fitness Test. Cannot be a single parent. Your college/university must offer AFROTC.

2,300 awards annually. Contact above address for application packet.

563—AMERICAN SOCIETY OF CIVIL ENGINEERS (Arthur S. Tuttle Memorial Scholarship)

1801 Alexander Bell Drive
Reston VA 20191-4400
800/548-ASCE or 703/295-6000
FAX: 703/295-6333
E-mail: student@asce.org
Internet: www.asce.org

AMOUNT: $3,000-$5,000
DEADLINE(S): FEB 20
FIELD(S): Civil Engineering

Award is for the first year of formal graduate tuition; undergraduates should apply during their senior year. Must be a member of ASCE. (Membership applications may be submitted along with scholarship applications.)

See website or contact ASCE for an application between October and February.

564—AMERICAN SOCIETY OF CIVIL ENGINEERS (B. Charles Tiney Memorial Student Chapter Scholarship)

1801 Alexander Bell Drive
Reston VA 20191-4400
800/548-ASCE or 703/295-6000
FAX: 703/295-6333
E-mail: student@asce.org
Internet: www.asce.org

AMOUNT: $2,000
DEADLINE(S): FEB 20
FIELD(S): Civil Engineering

Open to undergraduate freshmen, sophomores, and juniors who are ASCE National Student Members. (NSM applications may be submitted along with scholarship applications.) To be used towards tuition.

1 award annually. See website or contact ASCE for an application between October and February.

565—AMERICAN SOCIETY OF CIVIL ENGINEERS (O.H. Ammann Research Fellowship in Structural Engineering)

1801 Alexander Bell Drive
Reston VA 20191-4400
800/548-ASCE or 703/295-6000
FAX: 703/295-6333
E-mail: student@asce.org
Internet: www.asce.org

AMOUNT: $5,000
DEADLINE(S): FEB 20
FIELD(S): Structural Engineering

For ASCE members in any grade to create new knowledge in the field of structural design and construction. Membership application may be submitted along with fellowship application.

1 award annually. See website or contact ASCE for an application between October and February.

566—AMERICAN SOCIETY OF CIVIL ENGINEERS (Samuel Fletcher Tapman Student Chapter/Club Scholarships)

1801 Alexander Bell Drive
Reston VA 20191-4400
800/548-ASCE or 703/295-6000
FAX: 703/295-6333
E-mail: student@asce.org
Internet: www.asce.org

AMOUNT: $1,500
DEADLINE(S): FEB 20
FIELD(S): Civil Engineering

Open to undergraduate freshmen, sophomores, and juniors who are ASCE National Student Members. (NSM applications may be submitted along with scholarship applications.) To be used towards tuition.

12 awards annually. See website or contact ASCE for an application between October and February.

567—ASSOCIATED BUILDERS AND CONTRACTORS SCHOLARSHIP PROGRAM

1300 N. 17th Street
Rosslyn VA 22209
703/812-2025
FAX: 703/812-8235
E-mail: cmoore@abc.org

AMOUNT: $500 to $2,000
DEADLINE(S): JUNE 1
FIELD(S): Construction

Open to undergrads enrolled in an accredited 4-year degree program who have completed at least 1 year of study in construction (other than a design discipline). Must have at least 1 full year remaining subsequent to application deadline. If an ABC student chapter exists at the college or institution, student must be a member.

Approximately 20 scholarships per year. Applications available April 1 each year. Write for complete information.

568—ASSOCIATED GENERAL CONTRACTOR'S EDUCATION AND RESEARCH FOUNDATION (Horowitz/Heffner Scholarships for Graduate Students)

1957 E. Street NW
Washington DC 20006
202/393-2040
FAX: 202/347-4004
E-mail: agcf@agc.org

AMOUNT: $7,500/yr.
DEADLINE(S): NOV 1

FIELD(S): Construction, Civil
Engineering

Open to college seniors enrolled in a ABET or ACCE-accredited construction or civil engineering program or students possessing an undergraduate construction or civil engineering degree from such a program. Applicants must have at least one full year of academic training remaining and be a US citizen or a documented permanent resident of the US.

$7,500 will be used for the duration of the student's graduate degree and paid in two installments of $3,750. For complete information, write to the above address.

569—ASSOCIATED GENERAL CONTRACTOR'S EDUCATION AND RESEARCH FOUNDATION (Undergraduate Scholarship Program)

1957 E. Street NW
Washington DC 20006
202/393-2040
FAX: 202/347-4004
E-mail: agcf@agc.org

AMOUNT: $1,500/yr. up to 4 years
DEADLINE(S): NOV 1 (applications
available Sept. 1)
FIELD(S): Construction, Civil
Engineering

Open to college freshmen, sophomores, juniors, or a beginning senior in a five-year program. Junior and senior applicants must have one full academic year of coursework. Must pursue a career in construction. Student must be a US citizen or documented permanent resident of the US.

Award is renewable for up to four years of undergraduate study in construction, civil engineering or combination. Maximum award: $6,000.

570—ASSOCIATED WESTERN UNIVERSITIES, INC. (AWU Undergraduate Student Fellowships)

4190 S. Highland Drive, Suite 211
Salt Lake City UT 84124-2600
801/273-8911
FAX: 801/277-5632
Internet: www.awu.org

AMOUNT: $300/week stipend + travel
allowance
DEADLINE(S): FEB 1
FIELD(S): Mathematics, Engineering,
Technology, Science

Eight- to- sixteen-week fellowships for undergraduate students enrolled in accredited institutions and who have completed

at least one year of college by the start of the fellowship. Applicants reviewed on the basis of academic performance/class standing, career goals, recommendations, and compatibility of scientific interests and abilities with the needs and resources of the host facility. Citizenship restrictions may apply for some facilities.

500+ awards annually. Renewable (competitively with new application). Contact above address for an application.

571—ASSOCIATED WESTERN UNIVERSITIES, INC. (AWU Visiting Scientist Fellowships)

4190 S. Highland Drive, Suite 211
Salt Lake City UT 84124-2600
801/273-8900

AMOUNT: Varies
DEADLINE(S): Varies (Two months
prior to starting date)
FIELD(S): Engineering, Science,
Mathematics, and Technology

Research fellowships for professionals with continued commitment to science and engineering. For use at one of 62 participating universities. US citizenship or permanent residency required.

For detailed information and list of cooperating facitilies contact above location.

572—BROOKHAVEN WOMEN IN SCIENCE (Renate W. Chasman Scholarship)

P.O. Box 183
Upton NY 11973-5000
E-mail: pam@bnl.gov

AMOUNT: $2,000
DEADLINE(S): APR 1
FIELD(S): Natural Sciences, Engineering,
Mathematics

Open ONLY to women who are residents of the boroughs of Brooklyn or Queens or the counties of Nassau or Suffolk in New York who are re-entering school after a period of study. For juniors, seniors, or first-year graduate students.

1 award annually. Not renewable. Contact Pam Mansfield at above location for an application. Phone calls are NOT accepted.

573—COMMUNITY FOUNDATION OF WESTERN MASSACHUSETTS (George H. McDonell Scholarship)

1500 Main Street
P.O. Box 15769
Springfield MA 01115
413/732-2858

AMOUNT: $2,500
DEADLINE(S): APR 15
FIELD(S): Civil Engineering

Open to graduating seniors from South Hadley High School in Massachusetts, who are also town residents and will attend a four-year college with a major in civil engineering or related field. Based on financial need, academic merit, and extracurricular activities. Must submit transcripts and government FAFSA form.

1 award annually. Contact Community Foundation for an application and your financial aid office for FAFSA. Notification is in June.

574—HOPI TRIBE (Priority Scholarships)

P.O. Box 123
Kykotsmovi AZ 86039
520/734-2441, ext. 520
800/762-9630
FAX: 520/734-2435

AMOUNT: Varies
DEADLINE(S): JUL 31
FIELD(S): Law, Natural Resources,
Education, Medicine/Health,
Engineering, Business

Open to enrolled members of the Hopi Tribe studying in one of the fields listed above, which are considered to be areas of priority interest to the Hopis. Available to college juniors, seniors, and graduate students. Program is to encourage graduates to apply their degrees to Hopi Tribal Goals and Objectives.

Contact Hopi Tribe for an application.

575—LOS ANGELES COUNCIL OF BLACK PROFESSIONAL ENGINEERS (Al-Ben Scholarship)

P.O. Box 881029
Los Angeles CA 90009
310/635-7734
E-mail: secy1@lablackengineers.org
Internet: www.lablackengineers.org/
scholarships.html

AMOUNT: Varies
DEADLINE(S): Varies
FIELD(S): Engineering, Mathematics,
Computer Studies, or Applied
Scientific Studies

This organization provides scholarships for technically inclined pre-college and undergraduate students enrolled in one of the above fields. Must be of African American, Native American, or Hispanic ancestry. Although preference is given to students attending college in Southern California or who are Southern California residents, the awards are open to all qualified students attending college in the United States.

See website for more information. Application for the coming year will be on the website during November.

576—MARYLAND HIGHER EDUCATION COMMISSION (Maryland Science and Technology Scholarship Program)

16 Francis Street
Annapolis Park MD 21401
410/974-5370 or 1-800/974-1024
E-mail: ssamail@mhec.state.md.us
Internet: http://www.mhec.state.md.us/SSA/stech_qa.htm

AMOUNT: $3,000/yr. (B.A.); $1,000/yr. (A.A.)
DEADLINE(S): None
FIELD(S): Computer Science, Engineering, Technology

Scholarships for college-bound Maryland high school seniors who will major in one of the above fields and who are accepted to an eligible associate or bachelor's degree program in Maryland. Students in the class of 1999 were eligible for the first awards. The deadline was not known at this writing, so check for deadline date. Must agree to work in the state after graduation in a related field, one year for each year of assistance received.

Must maintain a 3.0 GPA.

577—MIDWEST ROOFING CONTRACTORS ASSOCIATION (Construction Industry Scholarships)

4840 West 15th Street, Suite 1000
Lawrence KS 66049-3876
800/497-6722
E-mail: mrca@mrca.org
Internet: www.mrca.org

AMOUNT: Varies
DEADLINE(S): JUN 20
FIELD(S): Construction

Applicants must be pursuing or planning to pursue a curriculum at an accredited university, college, community college, vocational, or trade school that will lead to a career in the construction industry. Three letters of recommendation required.

Contact MRCA for an application. Award is presented at Annual Convention and Trade Show.

578—NATIONAL ASSOCIATION OF WATER COMPANIES—NEW JERSEY CHAPTER (Scholarship)

Elizabethtown Water Co.
600 South Ave.
Westfield NJ 07090

908/654-1234
FAX: 908/232-2719
AMOUNT: $2,500
DEADLINE(S): APR 1
FIELD(S): Business Administration, Biology, Chemistry, Engineering, Communications

For US citizens who have lived in NJ at least 5 years and plan a career in the investor-owned water utility industry in disciplines such as those above. Must be undergrad or graduate student in a 2- or 4-year NJ college or university.

GPA of 3.0 or better required. Contact Gail P. Brady for complete information.

579—NATIONAL ASSOCIATION OF WOMEN IN CONSTRUCTION (Founders' Scholarship Foundation Awards)

327 South Adams
Fort Worth TX 76104
817/877-5551 or 1-800/552-3506
FAX: 817/877-0324
Internet: www.nawic.org

AMOUNT: $500-$2,000
DEADLINE(S): FEB 1
FIELD(S): Construction-related fields

Open to full-time students (men or women) enrolled in a construction-related program leading to an associate's or bachelor's degree. Applicants should be in at least their 1st year of college and have at least 1 year remaining.

Awards committee considers grades, interest in construction, extracurricular activities, employment experience, financial need, and evaluation by academic advisor. Applications available after Oct. 15. Write or access website for further information.

580—NATIONAL SOCIETY OF BLACK ENGINEERS (Scholarships)

1454 Duke Street
Alexandria VA 22314
703/549-2207
FAX: 703/683-5312
E-mail: nsbehq@nsbe.org
Internet: www.nsbe.org

AMOUNT: Varies
DEADLINE(S): Varies
FIELD(S): Engineering and engineering technologies

Programs for black and other ethnic minorities in the fields of engineering and the engineering technologies. Organization offers pre-college programs, scholarships, career fairs, a journal, a newsletter, etc.

Contact organization for details.

581—NORTH DAKOTA DEPARTMENT OF TRANSPORTATION (Grants)

Human Resources Division
608 East Blvd. Ave.
Bismarck ND 58505
701/328-2574

AMOUNT: $1,000 per year
DEADLINE(S): FEB 15
FIELD(S): Civil Engineering, Survey Technology, or Construction Engineering

Financial aid grants open to undergraduate students at recognized colleges & universities in North Dakota who have completed at least one year of study in the above fields.

2 to 4 grants per year. Renewable. Write for complete information.

582—OAK RIDGE INSTITUTE FOR SCIENCE AND EDUCATION (ORISE Education & Training Programs)

P.O. Box 117
Oak Ridge TN 37831-0117
Internet: www.orau.gov/orise/educ.htm

AMOUNT: Varies
DEADLINE(S): Varies
FIELD(S): Engineering, Aeronautics, Computer Science, Technology, Earth Science, Environmental Studies, Biology, Chemistry, Physics, Medical Research

Numerous programs funded by the US Department of Energy are offered for undergraduate students through postgraduate researchers. Includes fellowship and internship opportunities throughout the US. Some have citizenship restrictions. Travel may be included.

See website or write for a catalog of specific programs and requirements.

583—OPEN SOCIETY INSTITUTE (Environmental Management Fellowships)

400 West 59th Street
New York NY 10019
212/548-0600 or 212/757-2323
FAX: 212/548-4679 or 212/548-4600
Internet: www.soros.org/efp.html

AMOUNT: Fees, room, board, living stipend, textbooks, international transportation, health insurance
DEADLINE(S): NOV 15
FIELD(S): Earth Sciences, Natural Sciences, Humanities (exc. language), Anthropology, Sociology, Mathematics, or Engineering

Two-year fellowships for use in selected universities in the US for international students. For students/professionals in fields related to environmental policy, legislation, and remediation techniques applicable to their home countries.

To apply, contact your local Soros Foundation or Open Society Institute. Further details on website.

584—STUDENT CONSERVATION ASSOCIATION (SCA Resource Assistant Program)

P.O. Box 550
Charlestown NH 03603
603/543-1700
FAX: 603/543-1828
E-mail: internships@sca-inc.org
Internet: www.sca-inc.org

AMOUNT: $1,180-$4,725
DEADLINE(S): Varies
FIELD(S): Environment & related fields

Must be 18 and US citizen; need not be student. Fields: Agricultural, archaeology, anthropology, botany, caves, civil/environmental engineering, environmental education, fisheries, forests, herpetology, history, living history/roleplaying, visitor services, landscape architectural/environmental design, paleontology, recreation/resource/range management, trail maintenance/construction, wildlife management, geology, hydrology, library/museums, surveying.

900 positions in US and Canada. Send $1 for postage for application; outside US/Canada, send $20.

585—U.S. DEPARTMENT OF TRANSPORTATION (Dwight D. Eisenhower Transportation Fellowships)

U.S. Dept. of Transportation
Fed. Hwy. Admin.
6300 Georgetown Pike, HHI-20
McLean VA 22101-2296
703/235-0538

AMOUNT: Varies
DEADLINE(S): FEB
FIELD(S): Transportation—such majors
  as chemistry; materials science;
  corrosion; civil, chemical, & electronics
  engineering; structures; human factors;
  computer science; psychology

Research fellowships for undergrads and grad students at any Dept. of Transportation facility or selected IHE. For three to twelve months. Research must focus on transportation-related research and development in the above fields.

Contact Ilene Payne, Director, Universities and Grants Programs at above location for details.

586—XEROX TECHNICAL MINORITY SCHOLARSHIP (School-Year Tuition)

907 Culver Road
Rochester NY 14609
Internet: www.xerox.com/employment

AMOUNT: Up to $5,000 (varies
  according to tuition and academic
  excellence)
DEADLINE(S): SEP 15
FIELD(S): Various engineering and
  science disciplines

Scholarships for minorities enrolled full-time in a technical degree program at the bachelor level or above. Must be African-American, Native American, Hispanic, or Asian. Recipient may not have tuition or related expenses covered by other scholarships or grants.

If above requirements are met, obtain application from website or address above. Your financial aid office must fill out the bottom half of the form. Send completed application, your resume, and a cover letter to Xerox Technical Minority Scholarship Program at above address.

587—XEROX TECHNICAL MINORITY SCHOLARSHIP (Summer Employment Program)

Xerox Square
Rochester NY 14644
Written inquiry

AMOUNT: Up to $5,000 (varies according
  to tuition and academic excellence)
DEADLINE(S): SEP 15
FIELD(S): Various engineering and
  science disciplines

Scholarships for minorities enrolled in a technical degree program at the bachelor level or above. Must be African-American, Native American, Hispanic, or Asian. Xerox will match your skills with a sponsoring organization that will offer a meaningful summer work experience complimenting your academic learning.

If above requirements are met, send your resume and a cover letter to Xerox Corporation Corporate Employment and College Relations Technical Mfinority Scholarship Program at above address.

COMPUTER SCIENCE

588—AIR FORCE RESERVE OFFICER TRAINING CORPS (AFROTC Scholarships)

551 E. Maxwell Blvd.
Maxwell AFB AL 36112-6106
334/953-7783

AMOUNT: Full tuition, books, & fees for
  all 4 years of college
DEADLINE(S): DEC 1
FIELD(S): Science, Engineering,
  Business, Political Science, Psychology,
  Geography, Foreign Studies, Foreign
  Language

Competitive scholarships based on individual merit to high school seniors and graduates who have not completed any full-time college work. Must be a US citizen between the ages of 17-27. Must also have GPA of 2.5 or above, be in top 40% of class, and complete Applicant Fitness Test. Cannot be a single parent. Your college/university must offer AFROTC.

2,300 awards annually. Contact above address for application packet.

589—AMERICAN FOUNDATION FOR THE BLIND (Paul W. Ruckes Scholarship)

11 Penn Plaza, Suite 300
New York NY 10001
212/502-7661
FAX: 212/502-7771
E-mail: juliet@afb.org
Internet: www.afb.org

AMOUNT: $1,000
DEADLINE(S): APR 30
FIELD(S): Engineering,
  Computer/Physical/Life Sciences

Open to legally blind and visually impaired undergraduate and graduate students pursuing a degree in one of above fields. Must be US citizen. Must submit written documentation of visual impairment from ophthalmologist or optometrist (need not be legally blind); official transcripts; proof of college/university acceptance; three letters of recommendation; and typewritten statement describing goals, work experience, extracurricular activities, and how monies will be used.

1 award annually. See website or contact Julie Tucker at AFB for an application.

590—AMERICAN RADIO RELAY LEAGUE FOUNDATION (The PHD ARA Scholarship)

225 Main Street
Newington CT 06111
860/594-0200
FAX: 860/594-0259
Internet: www.arrl.org/

AMOUNT: $1,000
DEADLINE(S): FEB 1
FIELD(S): Journalism, Computer
  Science, Electronic Engineering

For undergraduate or graduate students who are residents of the ARRL

Midwest Division (IA, KS, MO, NE) who hold any class of radio amateur license—or student may be the child of a deceased radio amateur.

1 award annually. Contact ARRL for an application.

591—AMERICAN SOCIETY OF ENGINEERS OF INDIAN ORIGIN (Undergraduate Scholarship Programs)

P.O. Box 49494
Atlanta GA 30359-1494
770/451-2299
Internet: www.iasf.org/asei.htm

AMOUNT: Up to $1,000
DEADLINE(S): AUG 15
FIELD(S): Engineering fields: architecture, computer technology, geotechnical or geoenvironmental engineering, and allied sciences

Several scholarships for undergraduate engineering students in the above fields who were born in India or who are Indian by ancestry or relation. For study in the US. Some programs have residency requirements in certain states.

Contact Dr. Narsi Narasimhan at above location for applications and details.

592—ARMED FORCES COMMUNICATIONS AND ELECTRONICS ASSOCIATION (General Emmett Paige Scholarships for Military Personnel, Veterans, and Their Dependents)

4400 Fair Lakes Ct.
Fairfax VA 22033-3899
800/336-4583, ext. 6147
703/631-6100
Internet: www.afcea.org/awards/scholarships.htm

AMOUNT: $1,500
DEADLINE(S): MAR 1
FIELD(S): Electrical Engineering, Electronics, Computer Science, Computer Engineering, Physics, Mathematics

Scholarships in the above fields for persons on active duty in a military service or veterans and to their spouses or dependents who are working toward a degree in an accredited four-year college or university in the U.S. Must have GPA of 3.4 or more.

Send a self-addressed, stamped envelope with information on the name of your school, field of study, GPA, and year in school to AFCEA Educational Foundation at above address. Applications available November through Feb. 1.

593—ARMED FORCES COMMUNICATIONS AND ELECTRONICS ASSOCIATION (AFCEA ROTC Scholarships)

4400 Fair Lakes Ct.
Fairfax VA 22033-3899
800/336-4583, ext. 6147
703/631-6100
Internet: www.afcea.org/awards/scholarships.htm

AMOUNT: $1,500
DEADLINE(S): APR 1
FIELD(S): Electrical Engineering, Electronics, Computer Science, Computer Engineering, Physics, Mathematics

Scholarships in the above fields for ROTC students working toward a degree in an accredited four-year college or university in the US.

Must be nominated by Professors of Military Science, Naval Science, or Aerospace Studies. Contact the commander of each ROTC unit at your school.

594—ARMED FORCES COMMUNICATIONS AND ELECTRONICS ASSOCIATION (General John A. Wickham Scholarships)

4400 Fair Lakes Ct.
Fairfax VA 22033-3899
800/336-4583, ext. 6149
703/631-6149
Internet: www.afcea.org/awards/scholarships.htm

AMOUNT: $1,500
DEADLINE(S): MAY 1
FIELD(S): Electrical Engineering, Electronics, Computer Science, Computer Engineering, Physics, Mathematics

Scholarships in the above fields for persons working toward degrees in accredited four-year colleges or universities in the US. Must have GPA of 3.4 or more.

Send a self-addressed, stamped envelope with information on the name of your school, field of study, GPA, and year in school to AFCEA Educational Foundation at above address. Applications available November through Feb. 1.

595—ASSOCIATED WESTERN UNIVERSITIES, INC. (AWU Undergraduate Student Fellowships)

4190 S. Highland Drive, Suite 211
Salt Lake City UT 84124-2600
801/273-8911

FAX: 801/277-5632
Internet: www.awu.org
AMOUNT: $300/week stipend + travel allowance
DEADLINE(S): FEB 1
FIELD(S): Mathematics, Engineering, Technology, Science

Eight- to- sixteen-week fellowships for undergraduate students enrolled in accredited institutions and who have completed at least one year of college by the start of the fellowship. Applicants reviewed on the basis of academic performance/class standing, career goals, recommendations, and compatibility of scientific interests and abilities with the needs and resources of the host facility. Citizenship restrictions may apply for some facilities.

500+ awards annually. Renewable (competitively with new application). Contact above address for an application.

596—ASSOCIATED WESTERN UNIVERSITIES, INC. (AWU Visiting Scientist Fellowships)

4190 S. Highland Drive, Suite 211
Salt Lake City UT 84124-2600
801/273-8900

AMOUNT: Varies
DEADLINE(S): Varies (Two months prior to starting date)
FIELD(S): Engineering, Science, Mathematics, and Technology

Research fellowships for professionals with continued commitment to science and engineering. For use at one of 62 participating universities. US citizenship or permanent residency required.

For detailed information and list of cooperating facilities contact above location.

597—ASSOCIATION FOR COMPUTING MACHINERY (Listing of Internships & Summer Jobs)

1515 Broadway, 17th Fl.
New York NY 10036
800/342-6626
212/626-0500 (global)
FAX: 212/944-1318
Internet: www.acm.org/student/internships.html

AMOUNT: Varies
DEADLINE(S): Varies
FIELD(S): Computer Science

A listing on the Internet of several internships and summer employment in the field of computer science at various companies and colleges in the US, Canada, and elsewhere. Each one has its own requirements.

Access website for details.

598—ASSOCIATION FOR WOMEN IN SCIENCE EDUCATIONAL FOUNDATION (Dr. Vicki L. Schechtman Scholarship)

1200 New York Ave. NW, Suite 650
Washington DC 20005
202/326-8940 or 800/886-AWIS
E-mail: awis@awis.org
Internet: www.awis.org

AMOUNT: $1,000
DEADLINE(S): JAN 16
FIELD(S): Various Sciences and Social Sciences

For female undergraduate students who are US citizens and have a minimum GPA of 3.0. Summary page, essay describing career aspirations, transcripts, proof of matriculation (if available), and two reference letters required with application. Scholarships may be used for tuition, books, housing, research, equipment, etc.

See website or write to above address for an application and more information.

599—ASSOCIATION FOR WOMEN IN SCIENCE EDUCATIONAL FOUNDATION (Ruth Satter Memorial Award)

1200 New York Ave. NW, Suite 650
Washington DC 20005
202/326-8940 or 800/886-AWIS
E-mail: awis@awis.org
Internet: www.awis.org

AMOUNT: $1,000
DEADLINE(S): JAN 16
FIELD(S): Various Sciences and Social Sciences

Scholarships for female doctoral students who have interrupted their education three years or more to raise a family. Summary page, description of research project, resume, references, transcripts, biographical sketch, and proof of eligibility from department head required. US citizens may attend any graduate institution; noncitizens must be enrolled in US institutions.

See website or write to above address for more information or an application.

600—AT&T BELL LABORATORIES (Summer Research Program for Minorities & Women)

101 Crawfords Corner Road
Holmdel, NJ 07733-3030
Written inquiry

AMOUNT: Salary + travel & living expenses for summer
DEADLINE(S): DEC 1
FIELD(S): Engineering, Math, Sciences, Computer Science

Program offers minority students and women students technical employment experience at Bell Laboratories. Students should have completed their third year of study at an accredited college or university. US citizen or permanent resident.

Selection is based partially on academic achievement and personal motivation. Write special programs manager–SRP for complete information.

601—BROOKHAVEN WOMEN IN SCIENCE (Renate W. Chasman Scholarship)

P.O. Box 183
Upton NY 11973-5000
E-mail: pam@bnl.gov

AMOUNT: $2,000
DEADLINE(S): APR 1
FIELD(S): Natural Sciences, Engineering, Mathematics

Open ONLY to women who are residents of the boroughs of Brooklyn or Queens or the counties of Nassau or Suffolk in New York who are re-entering school after a period of study. For juniors, seniors, or first-year graduate students.

1 award annually. Not renewable. Contact Pam Mansfield at above location for an application. Phone calls are NOT accepted.

602—BUSINESS & PROFESSIONAL WOMEN'S FOUNDATION (BPW Career Advancement Scholarship Program)

2012 Massachusetts Ave. NW
Washington DC 20036-1070
202/293-1200, ext. 169
FAX: 202/861-0298
Internet: www.bpwusa.org

AMOUNT: $500-$1,000
DEADLINE(S): APR 15
FIELD(S): Biology, Science, Education, Engineering, Social Science, Paralegal, Humanities, Business, Math, Computers, Law, MD, DD

For women (US citizens) aged 25+ accepted into accredited program at US institution (+Puerto Rico & Virgin Islands). Must graduate within 12 to 24 months from the date of grant and demonstrate critical financial need. Must have a plan to upgrade skills, train for a new career field, or to enter/re-enter the job market.

Full- or part-time study. For info see website or send business-sized, self-addressed, double-stamped envelope.

603—CAREER OPPORTUNITIES FOR YOUTH, INC. (Collegiate Scholarship Program)

P.O. Box 996
Manhattan Beach CA 90266
310/535-4838

AMOUNT: $250 to $1,000
DEADLINE(S): SEP 30
FIELD(S): Engineering, Science, Mathematics, Computer Science, Business Administration, Education, Nursing

For students of Latino/Hispanic background residing in the Southern California area who have completed at least one semester/quarter of study at an accredited four-year university. Must have a cumulative GPA of 2.5 or higher.

Priority will be given to students who demonstrate financial need. Send SASE to above location for details.

604—COOPERATIVE ASSOCIATION OF STATES FOR SCHOLARSHIPS (CASS) (Scholarships)

c/o Commonwealth Liaison
Unit 310, The Garrison
St. Michael BARBADOS
809/436-8754

AMOUNT: Varies
DEADLINE(S): None
FIELD(S): Business Application/ Computer Science

Scholarships for economically disadvanted deaf youth, ages 17-25, with strong leadership potential and an interest in computer science/business applications. Must be from Barbados, Street Kitts/Nevis, Grenada, Street Vincent, Antigua/Barbuda, Street Lucia, Dominica, or Jamaica.

Write to E. Caribbean Reg. Coordinator (CASS) at above address.

605—DeVRY INC. (Dean's & Presidential Scholarships)

One Tower Lane
Oakbrook Terrace IL 60181-4624
800/733-3879, ext. 1935
630/571-7700
E-mail: outreach@devry.edu
Internet: www.devry.edu

AMOUNT: $1,000/term (Dean's); Full Tuition (Presidential)

DEADLINE(S): DEC 18; FEB 19; MAR 15
FIELD(S): Accounting, Business Admin, Computers, Electronics Engineering, Telecommunications Management, Electronics Technician

High school seniors who apply to any DeVry Institute are automatically considered for scholarships based on ACT/SAT scores. Presidential scholarships also consider community service, scholastic achievement, extracurricular activities, and essay. Must be US citizen or permanent resident.

Renewable if maintain 3.0 GPA. Number of Dean's Scholarships varies; 2 full-time Presidential awards annually. Contact Brenda Allen, Scholarship Coordinator, for an application.

606—FRAUNHOFER CENTER FOR RESEARCH IN COMPUTER GRAPHICS (Student & Scholar Exchange Programs)

321 S. Main Street
Providence RI 02903
401/453-6363
FAX: 401/453-0444
E-mail: info@crcg.edu
Internet: www.crcg.edu/Education/exchange.html

AMOUNT: Stipend for living expenses; transportation costs reimbursed
DEADLINE(S): None
FIELD(S): Computer Graphics

Educational exchanges between US and Europe for participants to become involved in the new information society. In the US, sites are in Rhode Island. In Europe, the Technical University of Darmstadt in Germany is the main site. Students conducting thesis research or practicums can stay for up to six months. Summer students normally stay for ten to twelve weeks.

Europeans apply to Dr. Joachim Rix, Dept. of Industrial Applications at above company, Rundeturmstr. 6, D-64283 Darmstadt, Germany. Phone: (+49) 6151 155 220. FAX: (+49) 6151 155 299. US students apply to Bert Scholz at above address.

607—FRAUNHOFER CENTER FOR RESEARCH IN COMPUTER GRAPHICS (Student & Scholar Exchange Programs)

321 S. Main Street
Providence RI 02903
401/453-6363
FAX: 401/453-0444
E-mail: info@crcg.edu
Internet: www.crcg.edu/Education/exchange.html

AMOUNT: Stipend for living expenses; transportation costs reimbursed
DEADLINE(S): None
FIELD(S): Computer Graphics

Educational exchanges between US and Europe for participants to become involved in the new information society. In the US, sites are in Rhode Island. In Europe, the Technical University of Darmstadt in Germany is the main site. Students conducting thesis research or practicums can stay for up to six months. Summer students normally stay for ten to twelve weeks.

Europeans apply to Dr. Joachim Rix, Dept. of Industrial Applications at above company, Rundeturmstr. 6, D-64283 Darmstadt, Germany. Phone: (+49) 6151 155 220. FAX: (+49) 6151 155 299. US students apply to Bert Scholz at above address.

608—GERBER SCIENTIFIC, INC. (H. Joseph Gerber Vision Scholarship Program)

83 Gerber Road West
South Windsor CT 06074
860/648-8027
Internet: www.gerberscientific.com

AMOUNT: Varies
DEADLINE(S): MAR 15
FIELD(S): Engineering, Mathematics, Computer Science, Natural Sciences

Scholarship program for high school seniors in Connecticut.

50 scholarships to be awarded.

609—HISPANIC COLLEGE FUND (Scholarships for Hispanic Students)

One Thomas Circle NW, Suite 375
Washington DC 20005
202/296-5400
FAX: 202/296-3774
E-mail: Hispanic.Fund@InternetMCI.com
Internet: http://hispanicfund.org

AMOUNT: Varies
DEADLINE(S): APR 15
FIELD(S): Most college majors leading to a career in business

Scholarships for deserving Hispanic college students pursuing a higher education in a major leading to a business career and who are full-time students at accredited institutions. US citizenship. Must demonstrate financial need.

Contact above organization for details or visit website for application.

610—IEEE COMPUTER SOCIETY (Lance Stafford Larson Student Scholarship)

1730 Massachusetts Ave. NW
Washington DC 20036-1992
202/371-1013
FAX: 202/778-0884
Internet: www.computer.org

AMOUNT: $500
DEADLINE(S): OCT 31
FIELD(S): Computer Science

Scholarships for undergraduate members of the IEEE Computer Society who write a winning essay on a computer-related subject. Minimum GPA of 3.0 required.

Contact organization for details.

611—IEEE COMPUTER SOCIETY (Richard Merwin Student Scholarship)

1730 Massachusetts Ave. NW
Washington DC 20036-1992
202/371-1013
FAX: 202/778-0884
Internet: www.computer.org

AMOUNT: $3,000
DEADLINE(S): MAY 31
FIELD(S): Computer Science, Computer Engineering, or Electrical Engineering

Scholarships for active leaders in student branch chapters of the IEEE Computer Society who show promise in their academic and professional efforts.

4 awards. Contact above address or website for details.

612—IEEE COMPUTER SOCIETY (Upsilon Pi Epsilon Student Award)

1730 Massachusetts Ave. NW
Washington DC 20036-1992
202/371-1013
FAX: 202/778-0884
Internet: www.computer.org

AMOUNT: $500
DEADLINE(S): OCT 31
FIELD(S): Computer Science

Scholarships for undergraduate members of the IEEE Computer Society who are full-time students at an academic institution. Minimum GPA of 3.0 required.

Contact organization for details.

613—INSTITUTE FOR OPERATIONS RESEARCH AND THE MANAGEMENT SCIENCES (INFORMS Summer Internship Directory)

P.O. Box 64794
Baltimore MD 21264-4794

800/4INFORMS
FAX: 410/684-2963
E-mail: jps@informs.org
Internet: www.informs.org/INTERN/
AMOUNT: Varies
DEADLINE(S): Varies
FIELD(S): Fields related to information
management: business management,
engineering, mathematics
A website listing of summer internships
in the field of operations research and
management sciences. Both applicants and
employers can register online.
Access website for list.

614—INSTITUTE OF INTERNATIONAL EDUCATION (National Security Education Program-Undergraduate Scholarships)

1400 K Street NW, 6th Fl.
Washington DC 20005-2403
202/326-7697
800/618-NSEP (6737)
E-mail: nsep@iie.org
Internet: http://www.iie.org/nsep/
AMOUNT: Varies: up to $8,000/semester
DEADLINE(S): FEB 8
FIELD(S): Open to all majors, preference
to Applied Sciences, Engineering,
Business, Economics, Math, Computer
Science, International Affairs, Political
Science, History, and the Policy
Sciences
For study abroad OUTSIDE the US,
Canada, Australia, New Zealand, and
Western Europe. For study in areas
deemed critical to US national security.
Applications available on US campuses
from August through early December. Or
contact organization for details.
Inquire at above location for details.

615—JOHNSON AND WALES UNIVERSITY (Annual Johnson & Wales University National High School Recipe Contest)

8 Abbott Place
Providence RI 02903
401/598-2345
AMOUNT: $1,000 to $5,000
DEADLINE(S): JAN 31
FIELD(S): Business, Hospitality,
Technology, Culinary Arts
For students planning to attend
Johnson & Wales University, Providence,
Rhode Island.
Write to above address for detailed
description.

616—JOHNSON AND WALES UNIVERSITY (Gilbane Building Company Eagle Scout Scholarship)

8 Abbott Place
Providence RI 02903
401/598-2345
AMOUNT: $1,200
DEADLINE(S): None
FIELD(S): Business, Hospitality,
Technology, Culinary Arts
For students attending Johnson &
Wales University, Providence, Rhode
Island. Must be Eagle Scouts.
Send letter of recommendation and
transcript to above address.

617—JOHNSON AND WALES UNIVERSITY (National High School Entrepreneur of the Year Contest)

8 Abbott Place
Providence RI 02903
401/598-2345
AMOUNT: $1,000 to $10,000
DEADLINE(S): DEC 27
FIELD(S): Business, Hospitality,
Technology, Culinary Arts
For students attending Johnson &
Wales University, Providence, Rhode
Island.
Send for detailed description to above
address.

618—JOHNSON AND WALES UNIVERSITY (Scholarships)

8 Abbott Place
Providence RI 02903
401/598-2345
AMOUNT: $200 to $10,000
DEADLINE(S): None
FIELD(S): Business, Hospitality,
Technology, Culinary Arts
For students attending Johnson &
Wales University, Providence, Rhode
Island.
Renewable for four years. Write for
complete information.

619—JUNIATA COLLEGE (Information Technology Scholarships)

Financial Aid Office
Huntingdon PA 16652
814/641-3603
FAX: 814/641-3355
E-mail: clarkec@juniata.edu
AMOUNT: $3,000 (max.)
DEADLINE(S): APR 1
FIELD(S): Information Technology
Open to students applying to Juniata
College with a major of information tech-
nology.
Contact Cynthia G. Clarke, Research
Specialist, for an application or enrollment
information.

620—LOS ANGELES COUNCIL OF BLACK PROFESSIONAL ENGINEERS (Al-Ben Scholarship)

P.O. Box 881029
Los Angeles CA 90009
310/635-7734
E-mail: secy1@lablackengineers.org
Internet: www.lablackengineers.org/
scholarships.html
AMOUNT: Varies
DEADLINE(S): Varies
FIELD(S): Engineering, Mathematics,
Computer Studies, or Applied
Scientific Studies
This organization provides scholarships
for technically inclined pre-college and
undergraduate students enrolled in one of
the above fields. Must be of African
American, Native American, or Hispanic
ancestry. Although preference is given to
students attending college in Southern
California or who are Southern California
residents, the awards are open to all quali-
fied students attending college in the
United States.
See website for more information.
Application for the coming year will be on
the website during November.

621—LOUISIANA STATE UNIVERSITY AT SHREVEPORT (Association for Information and Technical Professionals Scholarship and The Northwest Louisiana PC Users Group Scholarship)

Financial Aid Office
One University Place
Shreveport LA 71115-2399
318/797-5363
FAX: 318/797-5366
E-mail: finaid@pilot.lsus.edu
Internet: www.lsus.edu
AMOUNT: $910; $500
DEADLINE(S): Varies
FIELD(S): Computer Science
The one-year AITP Scholarship is
awarded annually by the Shreveport
Chapter of the AITP to a student majoring
in computer science at LSUS. Recipient is
chosen on the basis of academic achieve-
ment. A committee of computer science
faculty evaluates all the computer science

majors in selecting the recipient. The NW Louisiana PC Users Group Scholarship has the same criteria.

Contact the Student Financial Aid Office at LSUS for applications.

622—MARYLAND HIGHER EDUCATION COMMISSION (Maryland Science and Technology Scholarship Program)

16 Francis Street
Annapolis Park MD 21401
410/974-5370 or 800/974-1024
E-mail: ssamail@mhec.state.md.us
Internet: http://www.mhec.state.md.us/SSA/stech_qa.htm

AMOUNT: $3,000/yr. (B.A.); $1,000/yr. (A.A.)
DEADLINE(S): None
FIELD(S): Computer Science, Engineering, Technology

Scholarships for college-bound Maryland high school seniors who will major in one of the above fields and who are accepted to an eligible associate or bachelor's degree program in Maryland. Students in the class of 1999 were eligible for the first awards. The deadline was not known at this writing, so check for deadline date. Must agree to work in the state after graduation in a related field, one year for each year of assistance received.

Must maintain a 3.0 GPA.

623—MICROSOFT CORPORATION (National Minority and/or Women's Technical Scholarships)

One Microsoft Way
Redmond WA 98052-8303
E-mail: scholar@microsoft.com
Internet: microsoft.com/college/scholarship.htm

AMOUNT: $1,000
DEADLINE(S): FEB 27
FIELD(S): Computer Science, Computer Engineering, or a related technical discipline, such as Math or Physics

Scholarships for women and minorities (African Americans, Hispanics, or Native Americans) enrolled full-time in the above fields with a demonstrated interest in computers and making satisfactory progress towards a degree. Must be in sophomore or junior year (or fourth year in a five-year program). Awards are made through designated schools and are not transferable to other institutions.

10 awards—five for women and five for people of color listed above. For US citizens or permanent residents. See website above for details.

624—MICROSOFT CORPORATION (Summer Internships)

One Microsoft Way
Redmond WA 98052-8303
425/882-8080 (recruiting)
800/892-3181 (jobline)
E-mail: scholar@microsoft.com
Internet: microsoft.com/college/scholarship.htm

AMOUNT: Varies
DEADLINE(S): None
FIELD(S): Computer Science, Computer Engineering, or a related technical discipline, such as Math or Physics

Summer internships for individuals with a deep passion for technological advancement. Must commit to a 12-week minimum. Includes transportation, shipping costs, and shared cost of housing. Competitive compensation offered.

Check website above for details.

625—NATIONAL FEDERATION OF THE BLIND (Computer Science Scholarship)

805 Fifth Ave.
Grinnell IA 50112
515/236-3366

AMOUNT: $3,000
DEADLINE(S): MAR 31
FIELD(S): Computer Science

For legally blind students pursuing or planning to pursue a full-time postsecondary course of study in the US. Based on academic excellence, service to the community, and financial need. Membership NOT required.

1 award annually. Renewable. Contact Mrs. Peggy Elliot, Scholarship Committee Chairman, for an application.

626—NATIONAL SOCIETY OF BLACK ENGINEERS (Scholarships)

1454 Duke Street
Alexandria VA 22314
703/549-2207
FAX: 703/683-5312
E-mail: nsbehq@nsbe.org
Internet: www.nsbe.org

AMOUNT: Varies
DEADLINE(S): Varies
FIELD(S): Engineering and engineering technologies

Programs for black and other ethnic minorities in the fields of engineering and the engineering technologies. Organization offers pre-college programs, scholarships, career fairs, a journal, a newsletter, etc.

Contact organization for details.

627—NATIVE AMERICAN SCHOLARSHIP FUND, INC. (Scholarships)

8200 Mountain Road, NE, Ste. 203
Albuquerque NM 87110
505/262-2351
FAX: 505/262-0543
E-mail: NScholarsh@aol.com

AMOUNT: Varies
DEADLINE(S): MAR 15; APR 15; SEP 15
FIELD(S): Math, Engineering, Science, Business, Education, Computer Science

Open to American Indians or Alaskan Natives (1/4 degree or more) enrolled as members of a federally recognized, state recognized, or terminated tribe. For graduate or undergraduate study at an accredited four-year college or university.

208 awards annually. Contact Lucille Kelley, Director of Recruitment, for an application.

628—OAK RIDGE INSTITUTE FOR SCIENCE AND EDUCATION (ORISE Education & Training Programs)

P.O. Box 117
Oak Ridge TN 37831-0117
Internet: www.orau.gov/orise/educ.htm

AMOUNT: Varies
DEADLINE(S): Varies
FIELD(S): Engineering, Aeronautics, Computer Science, Technology, Earth Science, Environmental Studies, Biology, Chemistry, Physics, Medical Research

Numerous programs funded by the US Department of Energy are offered for undergraduate students through postgraduate researchers. Includes fellowship and internship opportunities throughout the US. Some have citizenship restrictions. Travel may be included.

See website or write for a catalog of specific programs and requirements.

629—ROBOTIC INDUSTRIES ASSOCIATION (RIA Robotics Scholarship Competition)

900 Victors Way, P.O. Box 3724
Ann Arbor MI 48106
734/994-6088
FAX: 734/994-3338

E-mail: mlehtinen@robotics.org

Internet: www.robotics.org

AMOUNT: $1,000

DEADLINE(S): DEC 10

FIELD(S): Robotics

Competition is for undergraduate students attending school in North America. Students must submit a paper that poses a technical problem and offers a solution that involves robotics. Team entries are allowed. Financial need NOT a factor.

3 awards annually. Not renewable. See website or contact Marcy Lehtinen at RIA for full guidelines and past winners.

630—ROYAL THAI EMBASSY, OFFICE OF EDUCATIONAL AFFAIRS (Revenue Dept. Scholarships for Thai Students)

1906 23rd Street NW

Washington DC 20008

202/667-9111 or 202/667-8010

FAX: 202/265-7239

AMOUNT: Varies

DEADLINE(S): APR

FIELD(S): Computer Science
(Telecommunications), Law,
Economics, Finance, Business
Administration

Scholarships for students under age 35 from Thailand who have been accepted to study in the US or UK for the needs of the Revenue Dept., Ministry of Finance. Must pursue any level degree in one of the above fields.

Selections are based on academic records, employment history, and advisor recommendations.

631—SOCIETY FOR SOFTWARE QUALITY (Grant-In-Aid Essay Contest)

Scholarship Committee Chair

P.O. Box 86958

San Diego CA 92138-6958

619/646-9214

E-mail: kozak@hctg.saic.com

AMOUNT: $500

DEADLINE(S): Varies

FIELD(S): Computer Software

Annual essay contest on a general computer software subject. One contest is open to high school seniors, college freshmen, and college sophomores. Another is open to college juniors, college seniors, and graduate students.

Contact the Society for Software Quality for more information.

632—SOCIETY OF WOMEN ENGINEERS (Admiral Grace Murray Hopper Scholarships)

120 Wall Street, 11th Fl.

New York NY 10005-3902

800/666-ISWE or 212/509-9577

FAX: 212/509-0224

E-mail: hq@swe.org

Internet: www.swe.org

AMOUNT: $1,000

DEADLINE(S): MAY 15

FIELD(S): Computer Science, Computer
Engineering

Open to women who are entering freshmen at a college/university with an ABET-accredited program or in a SWE-approved school. Must be studying computer engineering or computer science in any form of a four-year program.

5 awards annually. Send a self-addressed, stamped envelope to SWE for an application. Recipients are notified in September.

633—SOCIETY OF WOMEN ENGINEERS (Microsoft Corporation Scholarships)

120 Wall Street, 11th Fl.

New York NY 10005-3902

800/666-ISWE or 212/509-9577

FAX: 212/509-0224

E-mail: hq@swe.org

Internet: www.swe.org

AMOUNT: $1,000

DEADLINE(S): FEB 1

FIELD(S): Computer Science, Computer
Engineering

Open to women who are entering sophomores, juniors, or seniors at a college/university with an ABET-accredited program or in a SWE-approved school. Must have a minimum 3.5 GPA.

10 awards annually. Send a self-addressed, stamped envelope to SWE for an application. Recipients are notified in May.

634—SPACE COAST CREDIT UNION (Four-Year Scholarships)

Marketing Dept.

P.O. Box 2470

Melbourne FL 32902

Internet: www.sccu.com/scholarship/

AMOUNT: $1,250/year

DEADLINE(S): APR 15

FIELD(S): Computer Science, Business
(Finance, Economics, Human

Resources, Industrial Relations, Marketing)

Must be graduating from a high school in Brevard, Volusia, Flagler, or Indian River counties, be a member of SCCU, have a minimum GPA of 3.0, be planning to attend a four-year Florida institution of higher education, and write a 200-word essay on the topic "Why credit unions are valuable to society."

2 annual awards. For membership information or an application, see our web page or write to the above address.

635—SPACE COAST CREDIT UNION (Two-Year Scholarships)

Marketing Dept.

P.O. Box 2470

Melbourne FL 32902

Internet: www.sccu.com/scholarship/

AMOUNT: $750/year, two years; $1,000
bonus if go on for Bachelors

DEADLINE(S): APR 15

FIELD(S): Math, Economics, Science,
Computer Science, Marketing,
Journalism, Political Science

Must be graduating from a high school in Brevard, Volusia, Flagler, or Indian River counties, be a member of SCCU, have a minimum 3.0 GPA, planning to attend a two-year Florida institution of higher education for an associates degree, and be willing to write a 200-word essay on the topic "Why credit unions are valuable to society."

4 annual awards. Students going on to complete a four-year degree could be eligible for a bonus scholarship of $1,000 for the next two years. For membership information or an application, see our web page or write to the above address.

636—STATE FARM COMPANIES FOUNDATION (Exceptional Student Fellowship)

One State Farm Plaza, SC-3

Bloomington IL 61710-0001

309/766-2039/2161

E-mail: Nancy.Lynn.gr3o
@statefarm.com

Internet: www.statefarm.com

AMOUNT: $3,000 (nominating institution
receives $250)

DEADLINE(S): FEB 15

FIELD(S): Accounting, Business
Administration, Actuarial Science,
Computer Science, Economics,
Finance, Insurance/Risk Management,
Investments, Management, Marketing,
Mathematics, Statistics

For US citizens who are full-time juniors or seniors when they apply. Must demonstrate significant leadership in extracurricular activities, have minimum 3.6 GPA, and attend accredited US college/university. Must be nominated by dean, department head, professor, or academic advisor.

50 awards annually. Not renewable. See website, visit your financial aid office, or write to above address for an application.

637—TYSON FOUNDATION, INC. (Alabama Scholarship Program)

2210 W. Oaklawn
Springdale AR 72762-6999
501/290-4995

AMOUNT: Varies (according to need)
DEADLINE(S): FEB 28
FIELD(S): Business, Agriculture, Engineering, Computer Science, Nursing

Open to residents of the general areas of Albertville, Ashland, Blountsville, Gadsden, Heflin, or Oxford, Alabama, who are US citizens and live in the vicinity of a Tyson facility. Must be pursuing full-time undergraduate study at an accredited US institution and demonstrate financial need. Must also be employed part-time and/or summers to help fund education.

Renewable up to 8 semesters or 12 trimesters as long as student meets criteria. Contact Tyson Foundation for an application no later than last day of February; deadline to return application is April 20th.

638—TYSON FOUNDATION, INC. (Arkansas Scholarship Program)

2210 W. Oaklawn
Springdale AR 72762-6999
501/290-4955

AMOUNT: Varies (according to need)
DEADLINE(S): FEB 28
FIELD(S): Business, Agriculture, Engineering, Computer Science, Nursing

Open to Arkansas residents who are US citizens pursuing full-time undergraduate study at an accredited US institution. Must demonstrate financial need and be employed part-time and/or summers to help fund education.

Renewable up to 8 semesters or 12 trimesters as long as student meets criteria. Contact Tyson Foundation for an application no later than last day of February; deadline to return application is April 20th.

639—TYSON FOUNDATION, INC. (Florida Scholarship Program)

2210 W. Oaklawn
Springdale AR 72762-6999
501/290-4995

AMOUNT: Varies (according to need)
DEADLINE(S): FEB 28
FIELD(S): Business, Agriculture, Engineering, Computer Science, Nursing

Open to residents of the general area of Jacksonville, Florida, who are US citizens and live in the vicinity of a Tyson facility. Must be pursuing full-time undergraduate study in an accredited US institution and demonstrate financial need. Must also be employed part-time and/or summers to help fund education.

Renewable up to 8 semesters or 12 trimesters as long as student meets criteria. Contact Tyson Foundation for an application no later than last day of February; deadline to return application is April 20th.

640—TYSON FOUNDATION, INC. (Georgia Scholarship Program)

2210 W. Oaklawn
Springdale AR 72762-6999
501/290-4995

AMOUNT: Varies (according to need)
DEADLINE(S): FEB 28
FIELD(S): Business, Agriculture, Engineering, Computer Science, Nursing

Open to residents of the general areas of Cumming, Buena Vista, Dawson, or Vienna, Georgia, who are US citizens and live in the vicinity of a Tyson facility. Must be pursuing full-time undergraduate study in an accredited US institution and demonstrate financial need. Must also be employed part-time and/or summers to help fund education.

Renewable up to 8 semesters or 12 trimesters as long as student meets criteria. Contact Tyson Foundation for an application no later than last day of February; deadline to return application is April 20th.

641—TYSON FOUNDATION, INC. (Illinois Scholarship Program)

2210 W. Oaklawn
Springdale AR 72762-6999
501/290-4995

AMOUNT: Varies (according to need)
DEADLINE(S): FEB 28

FIELD(S): Business, Agriculture, Engineering, Computer Science, Nursing

Open to residents of the general area of Chicago, Illinois, who are US citizens and live in the vicinity of a Tyson facility. Must be pursuing full-time undergraduate study in an accredited US institution and demonstrate financial need. Must also be employed part-time and/or summers to help fund education.

Renewable up to 8 semesters or 12 trimesters as long as student meets criteria. Contact Tyson Foundation for an application no later than last day of February; deadline to return application is April 20th.

642—TYSON FOUNDATION, INC. (Indiana Scholarship Program)

2210 W. Oaklawn
Springdale AR 72762-6999
501/290-4995

AMOUNT: Varies (according to need)
DEADLINE(S): FEB 28
FIELD(S): Business, Agriculture, Engineering, Computer Science, Nursing

Open to residents of the general areas of Portland or Corydon, Indiana, who are US citizens and live in the vicinity of a Tyson facility. Must be pursuing full-time undergraduate study at an accredited US institution and demonstrate financial need. Must also be employed part-time and/or summers to help fund education.

Renewable up to 8 semesters or 12 trimesters as long as student meets criteria. Contact Tyson Foundation for an application no later than last day of February; deadline to return application is April 20th.

643—TYSON FOUNDATION, INC. (Mississippi Scholarship Program)

2210 W. Oaklawn
Springdale AR 72762-6999
501/290-4995

AMOUNT: Varies (according to need)
DEADLINE(S): FEB 28
FIELD(S): Business, Agriculture, Engineering, Computer Science, Nursing

Open to residents of the general areas of Cleveland, Jackson, Forest, or Vicksburg, Mississippi, who are US citizens and live in the vicinity of a Tyson facility. Must be pursuing full-time undergraduate study in an accredited US institution and demonstrate financial need. Must also be employed part-time and/or summers to help fund education.

Renewable up to 8 semesters or 12 trimesters as long as student meets criteria. Contact Tyson Foundation for an application no later than last day of February; deadline to return application is April 20th.

644—TYSON FOUNDATION, INC. (Missouri Scholarship Program)

2210 W. Oaklawn
Springdale AR 72762-6999
501/290-4995

AMOUNT: Varies (according to need)
DEADLINE(S): FEB 28
FIELD(S): Business, Agriculture, Engineering, Computer Science, Nursing

Open to residents of the general areas of Dexter, Monett, Neosho, Noel, or Sedalia, Missouri, who are US citizens and live in the vicinity of a Tyson facility. Must be pursuing full-time undergraduate study in an accredited US institution and demonstrate financial need. Must also be employed part-time and/or summers to help fund education.

Renewable up to 8 semesters or 12 trimesters as long as student meets criteria. Contact Tyson Foundation for an application no later than last day of February; deadline to return application is April 20th.

645—TYSON FOUNDATION, INC. (North Carolina Scholarship Program)

2210 W. Oaklawn
Springdale AR 72762-6999
501/290-4995

AMOUNT: Varies (according to need)
DEADLINE(S): FEB 28
FIELD(S): Business, Agriculture, Engineering, Computer Science, Nursing

Open to residents of the general areas of Creswell, Monroe, Sanford, or Wilkesboro, North Carolina, who are US citizens and live in the vicinity of a Tyson facility. Must be pursuing full-time undergraduate study in an accredited US institution and demonstrate financial need. Must also be employed part-time and/or summers to help fund education.

Renewable up to 8 semesters or 12 trimesters as long as student meets criteria. Contact Tyson Foundation for an application no later than the last day of February; deadline to return application is April 20th.

646—TYSON FOUNDATION, INC. (Oklahoma Scholarship Program)

2210 W. Oaklawn
Springdale AR 72762-6999
501/290-4995

AMOUNT: Varies (according to need)
DEADLINE(S): FEB 28
FIELD(S): Business, Agriculture, Engineering, Computer Science, Nursing

Open to residents of the general areas of Broken Bow or Stillwell, Oklahoma, who are US citizens and live in the vicinity of a Tyson facility. Must be pursuing full-time undergraduate study in an accredited US institution and demonstrate financial need. Must also be employed part-time and/or summers to help fund education.

Renewable up to 8 semesters or 12 trimesters as long as student meets criteria. Contact Tyson Foundation for an application no later than last day of February; deadline to return application is April 20th.

647—TYSON FOUNDATION, INC. (Pennsylvania Scholarship Program)

2210 W. Oaklawn
Springdale AR 72762-6999
501/290-4995

AMOUNT: Varies (according to need)
DEADLINE(S): FEB 28
FIELD(S): Business, Agriculture, Engineering, Computer Science, Nursing

Open to residents of the general area of New Holland, Pennsylvania, who are US citizens and live in the vicinity of a Tyson facility. Must be pursuing full-time undergraduate study in an accredited US institution and demonstrate financial need. Must also be employed part-time and/or summers to help fund education.

Renewable up to 8 semesters or 12 trimesters as long as student meets criteria. Contact Tyson Foundation for an application no later than last day of February; deadline to return application is April 20th.

648—TYSON FOUNDATION, INC. (Tennessee Scholarship Program)

2210 W. Oaklawn
Springdale AR 72762-6999
501/290-4995

AMOUNT: Varies (according to need)
DEADLINE(S): FEB 28

FIELD(S): Business, Agriculture, Engineering, Computer Science, Nursing

Open to residents of the general areas of Shelbyville or Union City, Tennessee, who are US citizens and live in the vicinity of a Tyson facility. Must be pursuing full-time undergraduate study in an accredited US institution and demonstrate financial need. Must also be employed part-time and/or summers to help fund education.

Renewable up to 8 semesters or 12 trimesters as long as student meets criteria. Contact Tyson Foundation for an application no later than last day of February; deadline to return application is April 20th.

649—TYSON FOUNDATION, INC. (Texas Scholarship Program)

2210 W. Oaklawn
Springdale AR 72762-6999
501/290-4995

AMOUNT: Varies (according to need)
DEADLINE(S): FEB 28
FIELD(S): Business, Agriculture, Engineering, Computer Science, Nursing

Open to residents of the general areas of Carthage, Center, or Seguin, Texas, who are US citizens and live in the vicinity of a Tyson facility. Must be pursuing full-time undergraduate study in an accredited US institution and demonstrate financial need. Must also be employed part-time and/or summers to help fund education.

Renewable up to 8 semesters or 12 trimesters as long as student meets criteria. Contact Tyson Foundation for an application no later than last day of February; deadline to return application is April 20th.

650—TYSON FOUNDATION, INC. (Virginia Scholarship Program)

2210 W. Oaklawn
Springdale AR 72762-6999
501/290-4995

AMOUNT: Varies (according to need)
DEADLINE(S): FEB 28
FIELD(S): Business, Agriculture, Engineering, Computer Science, Nursing

Open to residents of the general areas of Glen Allen, Harrisonburg, or Temperanceville, Virginia, who are US citizens and live in the vicinity of a Tyson facility. Must be pursuing full-time undergraduate study in an accredited US institution and demonstrate financial need. Must also be employed part-time and/or summers to help fund education.

Renewable up to 8 semesters or 12 trimesters as long as student meets criteria. Contact Tyson Foundation for an application no later than last day of February; deadline to return application is April 20th.

651—U.S. DEPT. OF HEALTH & HUMAN SERVICES (Indian Health Service Health Professions Scholarship Program)

Twinbrook Metro Plaza, Suite 100
12300 Twinbrook Pkwy.
Rockville MD 20852
301/443-0234
FAX: 301/443-4815
Internet: www:IHS.gov/Recruitment/DHPS/SP/SBTOC3.asp

AMOUNT: Tuition + fees & monthly stipend of $938
DEADLINE(S): APR 1
FIELD(S): Health professions, Accounting, Social Work

Open to Native Americans or Alaska natives who are graduate students or college juniors or seniors in a program leading to a career in a field listed above. US citizenship required. Renewable annually with reapplication.

Scholarship recipients must intend to serve the Indian people. They incur a one-year service obligation to the IHS for each year of support for a minimum of two years. Write for complete information.

652—U.S. ENVIRONMENTAL PROTECTION AGENCY—NATIONAL NETWORK FOR ENVIRONMENTAL MANAGEMENT STUDIES (Fellowships)

401 M Street SW, Mailcode 1704
Washington DC 20460
202/260-5283
FAX: 202/260-4095
E-mail: jojokian.sheri@epa.gov
Internet: www.epa.gov/enviroed/students.html

AMOUNT: Varies
DEADLINE(S): DEC
FIELD(S): Environmental Policies, Regulations, & Law; Environmental Management & Administration; Environmental Science; Public Relations & Communications; Computer Programming & Development

Fellowships are open to undergraduate and graduate students working on research

projects in the above fields, either full-time during the summer or part-time during the school year. Must be US citizen or legal resident. Financial need NOT a factor.

85-95 awards annually. Not renewable. See website or contact the Career Service Center of participating universities for an application.

653—WOMEN IN DEFENSE (HORIZONS Scholarship Foundation)

NDIA; 2111 Wilson Blvd., Ste. 400
Arlington VA 22201-3061
703/247-2552
FAX: 703/522-1885
E-mail: dnwlee@moon.jic.com
Internet: www.adpa.org/wid/horizon/Scholar.htm

AMOUNT: $500+
DEADLINE(S): NOV 1; JUL 1
FIELD(S): Engineering, Computer Science, Physics, Mathematics, Business, Law, International Relations, Political Science, Operations Research, Economics, and fields relevant to a career in the areas of national security and defense

For women who are US citizens, have minimum GPA of 3.25, demonstrate financial need, are currently enrolled at an accredited university/college (full- or part-time—both grads and undergrad juniors/seniors are eligible), and demonstrate interest in pursuing a career related to national security.

Application is online or send SASE, #10 envelope, to Woody Lee, HORIZONS Scholarship Director.

654—XEROX TECHNICAL MINORITY SCHOLARSHIP (School-Year Tuition)

907 Culver Road
Rochester NY 14609
Internet: www.xerox.com/employment

AMOUNT: Up to $5,000 (varies according to tuition and academic excellence)
DEADLINE(S): SEP 15
FIELD(S): Various engineering and science disciplines

Scholarships for minorities enrolled full-time in a technical degree program at the bachelor level or above. Must be African-American, Native American, Hispanic, or Asian. Recipient may not have tuition or related expenses covered by other scholarships or grants.

If above requirements are met, obtain application from website or address above.

Your financial aid office must fill out the bottom half of the form. Send completed application, your resume, and a cover letter to Xerox Technical Minority Scholarship Program at above address.

655—XEROX TECHNICAL MINORITY SCHOLARSHIP (Summer Employment Program)

Xerox Square
Rochester NY 14644
Written inquiry

AMOUNT: Up to $5,000 (varies according to tuition and academic excellence)
DEADLINE(S): SEP 15
FIELD(S): Various engineering and science disciplines

Scholarships for minorities enrolled in a technical degree program at the bachelor level or above. Must be African-American, Native American, Hispanic, or Asian. Xerox will match your skills with a sponsoring organization that will offer a meaningful summer work experience complimenting your academic learning.

If above requirements are met, send your resume and a cover letter to Xerox Corporation Corporate Employment and College Relations Technical Mfinority Scholarship Program at above address.

ELECTRICAL ENGINEERING

656—AIR FORCE RESERVE OFFICER TRAINING CORPS (AFROTC Scholarships)

551 E. Maxwell Blvd.
Maxwell AFB AL 36112-6106
334/953-7783

AMOUNT: Full tuition, books, & fees for all 4 years of college
DEADLINE(S): DEC 1
FIELD(S): Science, Engineering, Business, Political Science, Psychology, Geography, Foreign Studies, Foreign Language

Competitive scholarships based on individual merit to high school seniors and graduates who have not completed any full-time college work. Must be a US citizen between the ages of 17-27. Must also have GPA of 2.5 or above, be in top 40% of class, and complete Applicant Fitness Test. Cannot be a single parent. Your college/university must offer AFROTC.

2,300 awards annually. Contact above address for application packet.

657—AMERICAN RADIO RELAY LEAGUE FOUNDATION (Charles N. Fisher Memorial Scholarship)

225 Main Street
Newington CT 06111
860/594-0200
FAX: 860/594-0259
Internet: www.arrl.org/

AMOUNT: $1,000
DEADLINE(S): FEB 1
FIELD(S): Electronics, Communications, & related fields

Open to residents of the ARRL Southwestern Division (Arizona and the California counties of Los Angeles, Orange, San Diego, and Santa Barbara) who hold any class radio amateur license. For any level of study at a regionally accredited institution.

1 award annually. Contact ARRL for an application.

658—AMERICAN RADIO RELAY LEAGUE FOUNDATION (Dr. James L. Lawson Memorial Scholarship)

225 Main Street
Newington CT 06111
860/594-0200
FAX: 860/594-0259
Internet: www.arrl.org/

AMOUNT: $500
DEADLINE(S): FEB 1
FIELD(S): Electronics, Communications, & related fields

For radio amateurs holding a general license who are residents of the New England states (ME, NH, VT, MA, CT, RI) or New York State. Must be studying for a bachelor's degree or higher course of study at an institution in New England or New York State.

1 award annually. Contact ARRL for an application.

659—AMERICAN RADIO RELAY LEAGUE FOUNDATION (Earl I. Anderson Scholarship)

225 Main Street
Newington CT 06111
860/594-0200
FAX: 860/594-0259
Internet: www.arrl.org/

AMOUNT: $1,250
DEADLINE(S): FEB 1
FIELD(S): Electrical Engineering & related technical fields

For ARRL members with any class of license who are residents attending classes in Illinois, Indiana, Michigan, or Florida.

3 awards annually. Contact ARRL for an application.

660—AMERICAN RADIO RELAY LEAGUE FOUNDATION (Edmund A. Metzger Scholarship)

225 Main Street
Newington CT 06111
860/594-0200
FAX: 860/594-0259
Internet: www.arrl.org

AMOUNT: $500
DEADLINE(S): FEB 1
FIELD(S): Electrical Engineering

For ARRL members who are residents attending school in ARRL's Central Division (IL, IN, WI). Must be studying for a bachelor's degree or higher course of study.

1 award annually. Contact ARRL for an application.

661—AMERICAN RADIO RELAY LEAGUE FOUNDATION (F. Charles Ruling, N6FR Memorial Scholarship)

225 Main Street
Newington CT 06111
860/594-0200
FAX: 860/594-0259
Internet: www.arrl.org/

AMOUNT: $1,000
DEADLINE(S): FEB 1
FIELD(S): Electronics, Communications, & related fields

For undergraduate or graduate students who hold a general class amateur radio license.

1 award annually. Contact ARRL for an application.

662—AMERICAN RADIO RELAY LEAGUE FOUNDATION (Fred R. McDaniel Memorial Scholarship)

225 Main Street
Newington CT 06111
860/594-0200
FAX: 860/594-0259
Internet: www.arrl.org/

AMOUNT: $500
DEADLINE(S): FEB 1
FIELD(S): Electronics, Communications, & related fields

Open to radio amateurs holding a general license and who are residents of the

FCC Fifth Call District (TX, OK, AK, LA, MI, NM). Must be studying for a bachelor's degree or higher course of study at an institution in the FCC Fifth Call District. Preference is given to a student with a minimum 3.0 GPA.

1 award annually. Contact ARRL for an application.

663—AMERICAN RADIO RELAY LEAGUE FOUNDATION (Irving W. Cook, WAOCGS Scholarship)

225 Main Street
Newington CT 06111
860/594-0200
FAX: 860/594-0259
Internet: www.arrl.org/

AMOUNT: $1,000
DEADLINE(S): FEB 1
FIELD(S): Electronics, Communications, & related fields

Open to residents of Kansas who hold any class amateur radio license and are studying for a bachelor's degree or higher course of study.

1 award annually. Contact ARRL for an application.

664—AMERICAN RADIO RELAY LEAGUE FOUNDATION (L. Phil Wicker Scholarship)

225 Main Street
Newington CT 06111
860/594-0200
FAX: 860/594-0259
Internet: www.arrl.org/

AMOUNT: $1,000
DEADLINE(S): FEB 1
FIELD(S): Electronics, Communications, & related fields

For radio amateurs who have a general radio license and are residents attending school in the ARRL Roanoke Division: North Carolina, South Carolina, Virginia, or West Virginia. For study leading to a bachelor's degree or higher course of study.

1 award annually. Contact ARRL for an application.

665—AMERICAN RADIO RELAY LEAGUE FOUNDATION (Paul and Helen L. Grauer Scholarship)

225 Main Street
Newington CT 06111
860/594-0200
FAX: 860/594-0259
Internet: www.arrl.org/

AMOUNT: $1,000
DEADLINE(S): FEB 1
FIELD(S): Electronics, Communications, & related fields

For licensed radio amateurs at the novice level who are residents attending school in the ARRL Midwest Division: Iowa, Kansas, Missouri, or Nebraska. Must be studying for a bachelor's degree or higher course of study.

1 award annually. Contact ARRL for an application.

666—AMERICAN RADIO RELAY LEAGUE FOUNDATION (Perry F. Hadlock Memorial Scholarship)

225 Main Street
Newington CT 06111
860/594-0200
FAX: 860/594-0259
Internet: www.arrl.org/

AMOUNT: $1,000
DEADLINE(S): FEB 1
FIELD(S): Electronic Engineering

Open to students who are radio amateurs with a general license. Must be enrolled full-time as an undergraduate or graduate student at Clarkson University in Potsdam, New York.

1 award annually. Contact ARRL for an application.

667—AMERICAN RADIO RELAY LEAGUE FOUNDATION (The PHD ARA Scholarship)

225 Main Street
Newington CT 06111
860/594-0200
FAX: 860/594-0259
Internet: www.arrl.org/

AMOUNT: $1,000
DEADLINE(S): FEB 1
FIELD(S): Journalism, Computer Science, Electronic Engineering

For undergraduate or graduate students who are residents of the ARRL Midwest Division (IA, KS, MO, NE) who hold any class of radio amateur license—or student may be the child of a deceased radio amateur.

1 award annually. Contact ARRL for an application.

668—AMERICAN RADIO RELAY LEAGUE FOUNDATION (The Henry Broughton, K2AE Memorial Scholarship)

225 Main Street
Newington CT 06111
860/594-0200

FAX: 860/594-0259
Internet: www.arrl.org/

AMOUNT: $1,000
DEADLINE(S): FEB 1
FIELD(S): Engineering, Science

For radio amateurs with a general class license whose home residence is within 70 miles of Schenectady, New York. For study leading to a bachelor's degree at an accredited four-year college/university.

1+ awards annually. Contact ARRL for an application.

669—AMERICAN RADIO RELAY LEAGUE FOUNDATION (The IDEA Scholarship)

225 Main Street
Newington CT 06111
860/594-0200
FAX: 860/594-0259
Internet: www.arrl.org/

AMOUNT: $500
DEADLINE(S): FEB 1
FIELD(S): Electronics, Communications

Open to radio amateurs holding a technician license and who are residents of Indiana. For high school graduates attending college at any accredited Indiana college or institution.

1 award annually. Contact ARRL for an application.

670—AMERICAN RADIO RELAY LEAGUE FOUNDATION (The Nemal Electronics Scholarship)

225 Main Street
Newington CT 06111
860/594-0200
FAX: 860/594-0259
Internet: www.arrl.org/

AMOUNT: $500
DEADLINE(S): FEB 1
FIELD(S): Electronics, Communications, & related fields

For radio amateurs with a general license who are studying for a bachelor's degree or higher course of study. Preference is given to students with a minimum 3.0 GPA. Student must write a brief letter explaining background and future plans.

1 award annually. Contact ARRL for an application.

671—AMERICAN RADIO RELAY LEAGUE FOUNDATION (The Mississippi Scholarship)

225 Main Street
Newington CT 06111
860/594-0200

FAX: 860/594-0259
Internet: www.arrl.org/

AMOUNT: $500
DEADLINE(S): FEB 1
FIELD(S): Electronics, Communications, & related fields

Open to radio amateurs under age 30 holding any class of license. Must be resident of Mississippi, studying for a bachelor's degree or higher course of study at a school in Mississippi.

1 award annually. Contact ARRL for an application.

672—AMERICAN SOCIETY OF ENGINEERS OF INDIAN ORIGIN (Undergraduate Scholarship Programs)

P.O. Box 49494
Atlanta GA 30359-1494
770/451-2299
Internet: www.iasf.org/asei.htm

AMOUNT: Up to $1,000
DEADLINE(S): AUG 15
FIELD(S): Engineering fields: architecture, computer technology, geotechnical or geoenvironmental engineering, and allied sciences

Several scholarships for undergraduate engineering students in the above fields who were born in India or who are Indian by ancestry or relation. For study in the US. Some programs have residency requirements in certain states.

Contact Dr. Narsi Narasimhan at above location for applications and details.

673—ARMED FORCES COMMUNICATIONS AND ELECTRONICS ASSOCIATION (General Emmett Paige Scholarships for Military Personnel, Veterans, and Their Dependents)

4400 Fair Lakes Ct.
Fairfax VA 22033-3899
800/336-4583, ext. 6147
703/631-6100
Internet: www.afcea.org/awards/scholarships.htm

AMOUNT: $1,500
DEADLINE(S): MAR 1
FIELD(S): Electrical Engineering, Electronics, Computer Science, Computer Engineering, Physics, Mathematics

Scholarships in the above fields for persons on active duty in a military service or veterans and to their spouses or dependents who are working toward a degree in an accredited four-year college or university in the U.S. Must have GPA of 3.4 or more.

Send a self-addressed, stamped envelope with information on the name of your school, field of study, GPA, and year in school to AFCEA Educational Foundation at above address. Applications available November through Feb. 1.

674—ARMED FORCES COMMUNICATIONS AND ELECTRONICS ASSOCIATION (AFCEA ROTC Scholarships)

4400 Fair Lakes Ct.
Fairfax VA 22033-3899
800/336-4583, ext. 6147
703/631-6100
Internet: www.afcea.org/awards/
scholarships.htm

AMOUNT: $1,500
DEADLINE(S): APR 1
FIELD(S): Electrical Engineering,
Electronics, Computer Science,
Computer Engineering, Physics,
Mathematics

Scholarships in the above fields for ROTC students working toward a degree in an accredited four-year college or university in the US.

Must be nominated by Professors of Military Science, Naval Science, or Aerospace Studies. Contact the commander of each ROTC unit at your school.

675—ARMED FORCES COMMUNICATIONS AND ELECTRONICS ASSOCIATION (General John A. Wickham Scholarships)

4400 Fair Lakes Ct.
Fairfax VA 22033-3899
800/336-4583, ext. 6149
703/631-6149
Internet: www.afcea.org/awards/
scholarships.htm

AMOUNT: $1,500
DEADLINE(S): MAY 1
FIELD(S): Electrical Engineering,
Electronics, Computer Science,
Computer Engineering, Physics,
Mathematics

Scholarships in the above fields for persons working toward degrees in accredited four-year colleges or universities in the US. Must have GPA of 3.4 or more.

Send a self-addressed, stamped envelope with information on the name of your school, field of study, GPA, and year in school to AFCEA Educational Foundation at above address. Applications available November through Feb. 1.

676—ASSOCIATED WESTERN UNIVERSITIES, INC. (AWU Undergraduate Student Fellowships)

4190 S. Highland Drive, Suite 211
Salt Lake City UT 84124-2600
801/273-8911
FAX: 801/277-5632
Internet: www.awu.org

AMOUNT: $300/week stipend + travel
allowance
DEADLINE(S): FEB 1
FIELD(S): Mathematics, Engineering,
Technology, Science

Eight- to- sixteen-week fellowships for undergraduate students enrolled in accredited institutions and who have completed at least one year of college by the start of the fellowship. Applicants reviewed on the basis of academic performance/class standing, career goals, recommendations, and compatibility of scientific interests and abilities with the needs and resources of the host facility. Citizenship restrictions may apply for some facilities.

500+ awards annually. Renewable (competitively with new application). Contact above address for an application.

677—ASSOCIATED WESTERN UNIVERSITIES, INC. (AWU Visiting Scientist Fellowships)

4190 S. Highland Drive, Suite 211
Salt Lake City UT 84124-2600
801/273-8900

AMOUNT: Varies
DEADLINE(S): Varies (Two months
prior to starting date)
FIELD(S): Engineering, Science,
Mathematics, and Technology

Research fellowships for professionals with continued commitment to science and engineering. For use at one of 62 participating universities. US citizenship or permanent residency required.

For detailed information and list of cooperating facitilies contact above location.

678—ASSOCIATION FOR COMPUTING MACHINERY (Listing of Internships & Summer Jobs)

1515 Broadway, 17th Fl.
New York NY 10036
800/342-6626
212/626-0500 (global)

FAX: 212/944-1318
Internet: www.acm.org/student/
internships.html

AMOUNT: Varies
DEADLINE(S): Varies
FIELD(S): Computer Science

A listing on the Internet of several internships and summer employment in the field of computer science at various companies and colleges in the US, Canada, and elsewhere. Each one has its own requirements.

Access website for details.

679—AT&T BELL LABORATORIES (Summer Research Program for Minorities & Women)

101 Crawfords Corner Road
Holmdel NJ 07733-3030
Written inquiry

AMOUNT: Salary + travel & living
expenses for summer
DEADLINE(S): DEC 1
FIELD(S): Engineering, Math, Sciences,
Computer Science

Program offers minority students and women students technical employment experience at Bell Laboratories. Students should have completed their third year of study at an accredited college or university. US citizen or permanent resident.

Selection is based partially on academic achievement and personal motivation. Write special programs manager—SRP for complete information.

680—BROOKHAVEN WOMEN IN SCIENCE (Renate W. Chasman Scholarship)

P.O. Box 183
Upton NY 11973-5000
E-mail: pam@bnl.gov

AMOUNT: $2,000
DEADLINE(S): APR 1
FIELD(S): Natural Sciences, Engineering,
Mathematics

Open ONLY to women who are residents of the boroughs of Brooklyn or Queens or the counties of Nassau or Suffolk in New York who are re-entering school after a period of study. For juniors, seniors, or first-year graduate students.

1 award annually. Not renewable. Contact Pam Mansfield at above location for an application. Phone calls are NOT accepted.

681—DeVRY INC. (Dean's & Presidential Scholarships)

One Tower Lane
Oakbrook Terrace IL 60181-4624
800/733-3879, ext. 1935
630/571-7700
E-mail: outreach@devry.edu
Internet: www.devry.edu

AMOUNT: $1,000/term (Dean's); Full Tuition (Presidential)
DEADLINE(S): DEC 18; FEB 19; MAR 15
FIELD(S): Accounting, Business Admin, Computers, Electronics Engineering, Telecommunications Management, Electronics Technician

High school seniors who apply to any DeVry Institute are automatically considered for scholarships based on ACT/SAT scores. Presidential scholarships also consider community service, scholastic achievement, extracurricular activities, and essay. Must be US citizen or permanent resident.

Renewable if maintain 3.0 GPA. Number of Dean's Scholarships varies; 2 full-time Presidential awards annually. Contact Brenda Allen, Scholarship Coordinator, for an application.

682—ELECTRONIC INDUSTRIES FOUNDATION (Scholarship Program)

2500 Wilson Blvd., Suite 210
Arlington VA 22201-3834
703/907-7408
E-mail: mvorac@eia.org

AMOUNT: $5,000
DEADLINE(S): FEB 1
FIELD(S): Electronics, Telecommunications, Electrical Engineering, Industrial Manufacturing, Industrial Engineering, Physics, Electromechanical Technology, Mechanical Applied Sciences

Open to students with disabilities (as defined by Americans w/ Disabilities Act) who are high school seniors accepted at an accredited four-year college/university. Must be US citizen pursuing studies that lead to career in design, manufacture, or provision of materials, components, products, and services for US high tech, electronics, and communications industries. Based on GPA, goals, activities, need, essay, and letters of recommendation.

Send self-addressed, stamped envelope to EIA for an application. Recipients notified by May 1st; awards paid directly to school.

683—FRAUNHOFER CENTER FOR RESEARCH IN COMPUTER GRAPHICS (Student & Scholar Exchange Programs)

321 S. Main Street
Providence RI 02903
401/453-6363
FAX: 401/453-0444
E-mail: info@crcg.edu
Internet: www.crcg.edu/Education/exchange.html

AMOUNT: Stipend for living expenses; transportation costs reimbursed
DEADLINE(S): None
FIELD(S): Computer Graphics

Educational exchanges between US and Europe for participants to become involved in the new information society. In the US, sites are in Rhode Island. In Europe, the Technical University of Darmstadt in Germany is the main site. Students conducting thesis research or practicums can stay for up to six months. Summer students normally stay for ten to twelve weeks.

Europeans apply to Dr. Joachim Rix, Dept. of Industrial Applications at above company, Rundeturmstr. 6, D-64283 Darmstadt, Germany. Phone: (+49) 6151 155 220. FAX: (+49) 6151 155 299. US students apply to Bert Scholz at above address.

684—FRAUNHOFER CENTER FOR RESEARCH IN COMPUTER GRAPHICS (Student & Scholar Exchange Programs)

321 S. Main Street
Providence RI 02903
401/453-6363
FAX: 401/453-0444
E-mail: info@crcg.edu
Internet: www.crcg.edu/Education/exchange.html

AMOUNT: Stipend for living expenses; transportation costs reimbursed
DEADLINE(S): None
FIELD(S): Computer Graphics

Educational exchanges between US and Europe for participants to become involved in the new information society. In the US, sites are in Rhode Island. In Europe, the Technical University of Darmstadt in Germany is the main site. Students conducting thesis research or practicums can stay for up to six months. Summer students normally stay for ten to twelve weeks.

Europeans apply to Dr. Joachim Rix, Dept. of Industrial Applications at above company, Rundeturmstr. 6, D-64283 Darmstadt, Germany. Phone: (+49) 6151 155 220. FAX: (+49) 6151 155 299. US students apply to Bert Scholz at above address.

685—GREAT LAKES COMMISSION (Carol A. Ratza Memorial Scholarship)

400 Fourth Street
Ann Arbor MI 48103-4816
734/665-9135
FAX: 734/665-4370
E-mail: glc@great-lakes.net
Internet: www.glc.org

AMOUNT: $500
DEADLINE(S): MAR 31
FIELD(S): Electronic Communications Technology

Open to high school seniors and full-time undergrads attending school in IL, IN, MI, MN, NY, OH, PA, WI, Ontario CAN, or Quebec CAN. Must have demonstrated interest in environmental or economic applications of electronic communications technology, show academic excellence, and have sincere appreciation for Great Lakes and their protection. Must submit resume, transcripts, letters of recommendation, and essay/original webpage on Great Lakes issue. Financial need NOT a factor.

1 award annually. Renewable. Contact Christine Manninen for an application. Award announced by May 1st.

686—HISPANIC COLLEGE FUND (Scholarships for Hispanic Students)

One Thomas Circle NW, Suite 375
Washington DC 20005
202/296-5400
FAX: 202/296-3774
E-mail: Hispanic.Fund@Internet MCI.com
Internet: http://hispanicfund.org

AMOUNT: Varies
DEADLINE(S): APR 15
FIELD(S): Most college majors leading to a career in business

Scholarships for deserving Hispanic college students pursuing a higher education in a major leading to a business career and who are full-time students at accredited institutions. US citizenship. Must demonstrate financial need.

Contact above organization for details or visit website for application.

687—HOPI TRIBE (Priority Scholarships)

P.O. Box 123
Kykotsmovi AZ 86039
520/734-2441, ext. 520
800/762-9630
FAX: 520/734-2435

AMOUNT: Varies

DEADLINE(S): JUL 31
FIELD(S): Law, Natural Resources, Education, Medicine/Health, Engineering, Business

Open to enrolled members of the Hopi Tribe studying in one of the fields listed above, which are considered to be areas of priority interest to the Hopis. Available to college juniors, seniors, and graduate students. Program is to encourage graduates to apply their degrees to Hopi Tribal Goals and Objectives.

Contact Hopi Tribe for an application.

688—IEEE COMPUTER SOCIETY (Richard Merwin Student Scholarship)

1730 Massachusetts Ave. NW
Washington DC 20036-1992
202/371-1013
FAX: 202/778-0884
Internet: www.computer.org
AMOUNT: $3,000
DEADLINE(S): MAY 31
FIELD(S): Computer Science, Computer Engineering, or Electrical Engineering

Scholarships for active leaders in student branch chapters of the IEEE Computer Society who show promise in their academic and professional efforts.

4 awards. Contact above address or website for details.

689—INSTITUTE FOR OPERATIONS RESEARCH AND THE MANAGEMENT SCIENCES (INFORMS Summer Internship Directory)

P.O. Box 64794
Baltimore MD 21264-4794
800/4INFORMS
FAX: 410/684-2963
E-mail: jps@informs.org
Internet: www.informs.org/INTERN/
AMOUNT: Varies
DEADLINE(S): Varies
FIELD(S): Fields related to information management: business management, engineering, mathematics

A website listing of summer internships in the field of operations research and management sciences. Both applicants and employers can register online.

Access website for list.

690—INSTITUTE OF ELECTRICAL & ELECTRONICS ENGINEERS (Charles Le Geyt Fortescue Fellowship)

445 Hoes Lane
Piscataway NJ 08855-1331
908/562-3840
AMOUNT: $24,000

DEADLINE(S): JAN 15 (of odd-numbered years)
FIELD(S): Electrical Engineering

Fellowship is open to first-year graduate students at recognized engineering schools in the US or Canada. Awards support full-time study for one academic year.

Awards granted every other year. Contact above location for details.

691—LOS ANGELES COUNCIL OF BLACK PROFESSIONAL ENGINEERS (Al-Ben Scholarship)

P.O. Box 881029
Los Angeles CA 90009
310/635-7734
E-mail: secy1@lablackengineers.org
Internet: www.lablackengineers.org/scholarships.html
AMOUNT: Varies
DEADLINE(S): Varies
FIELD(S): Engineering, Mathematics, Computer Studies, or Applied Scientific Studies

This organization provides scholarships for technically inclined pre-college and undergraduate students enrolled in one of the above fields. Must be of African American, Native American, or Hispanic ancestry. Although preference is given to students attending college in Southern California or who are Southern California residents, the awards are open to all qualified students attending college in the United States.

See website for more information. Application for the coming year will be on the website during November.

692—MARYLAND HIGHER EDUCATION COMMISSION (Maryland Science and Technology Scholarship Program)

16 Francis Street
Annapolis Park MD 21401
410/974-5370 or 800/974-1024
E-mail: ssamail@mhec.state.md.us
Internet: http://www.mhec.state.md.us/SSA/stech_qa.htm
AMOUNT: $3,000/yr. (B.A.); $1,000/yr. (A.A.)
DEADLINE(S): None
FIELD(S): Computer Science; Engineering; Technology

Scholarships for college-bound Maryland high school seniors who will major in one of the above fields and who are accepted to an eligible associate or bachelor's degree program in Maryland. Students in the class of 1999 were eligible for the first awards. The deadline was not known at this writing, so check for deadline date. Must agree to

work in the state after graduation in a related field, one year for each year of assistance received.

Must maintain a 3.0 GPA.

693—MICROSOFT CORPORATION (National Minority and/or Women's Technical Scholarships)

One Microsoft Way
Redmond WA 98052-8303
E-mail: scholar@microsoft.com
Internet: microsoft.com/college/scholarship.htm
AMOUNT: $1,000
DEADLINE(S): FEB 27
FIELD(S): Computer Science, Computer Engineering, or a related technical discipline, such as Math or Physics

Scholarships for women and minorities (African Americans, Hispanics, or Native Americans) enrolled full-time in the above fields with a demonstrated interest in computers and making satisfactory progress towards a degree. Must be in sophomore or junior year (or fourth year in a five-year program). Awards are made through designated schools and are not transferable to other institutions.

10 awards—five for women and five for people of color listed above. For US citizens or permanent residents. See website above for details.

694—MICROSOFT CORPORATION (Summer Internships)

One Microsoft Way
Redmond WA 98052-8303
425/882-8080 (recruiting)
800/892-3181 (jobline)
E-mail: scholar@microsoft.com
Internet: microsoft.com/college/scholarship.htm
AMOUNT: Varies
DEADLINE(S): None
FIELD(S): Computer Science, Computer Engineering, or a related technical discipline, such as Math or Physics

Summer internships for individuals with a deep passion for technological advancement. Must commit to a 12-week minimum. Includes transportation, shipping costs, and shared cost of housing. Competitive compensation offered.

Check website above for details.

695—NATIONAL SOCIETY OF BLACK ENGINEERS (Scholarships)

1454 Duke Street
Alexandria VA 22314

703/549-2207
FAX: 703/683-5312
E-mail: nsbehq@nsbe.org
Internet: www.nsbe.org

AMOUNT: Varies
DEADLINE(S): Varies
FIELD(S): Engineering and engineering
technologies

Programs for black and other ethnic minorities in the fields of engineering and the engineering technologies. Organization offers pre-college programs, scholarships, career fairs, a journal, a newsletter, etc.

Contact organization for details.

696—ROYAL THAI EMBASSY, OFFICE OF EDUCATIONAL AFFAIRS (Revenue Dept. Scholarships for Thai Students)

1906 23rd Street NW
Washington DC 20008
202/667-9111 or 202/667-8010
FAX: 202/265-7239

AMOUNT: Varies
DEADLINE(S): APR
FIELD(S): Computer Science
(Telecommunications), Law,
Economics, Finance, Business
Administration

Scholarships for students under age 35 from Thailand who have been accepted to study in the US or UK for the needs of the Revenue Dept., Ministry of Finance. Must pursue any level degree in one of the above fields.

Selections are based on academic records, employment history, and advisor recommendations.

697—THE ELECTRICAL WOMEN'S ROUND TABLE INC. (Julia Kiene & Lyle Mamer Fellowships)

P.O. Box 335
White's Creek TN 37189
615/876-5444

AMOUNT: $1,000 to $2,000
DEADLINE(S): MAR 1
FIELD(S): Electrical energy and related
fields listed below

Open to graduate students (or graduating seniors) pursuing an advanced degree in any phase of electrical energy, incl. communications, education, elec. util., elec. eng., elec. home appliances/equip. mfg., marketing research, etc.

The college or university selected by applicant must be accredited and approved by the EWRT Fellowship Committee. Send SASE to above location for complete information.

698—U.S. DEPARTMENT OF TRANSPORTATION (Dwight D. Eisenhower Transportation Fellowships)

U.S. Dept. of Transportation
Fed. Hwy. Admin.
6300 Georgetown Pike, HHI-20
McLean VA 22101-2296
703/235-0538

AMOUNT: Varies
DEADLINE(S): FEB
FIELD(S): Transportation—such majors
as chemistry; materials science;
corrosion; civil, chemical, & electronics
engineering; structures; human factors;
computer science; psychology

Research fellowships for undergrads and grad students at any Dept. of Transportation facility or selected IHE. For three to twelve months. Research must focus on transportation-related research and development in the above fields.

Contact Ilene Payne, Director, Universities and Grants Programs at above location for details.

699—XEROX TECHNICAL MINORITY SCHOLARSHIP (School-Year Tuition)

907 Culver Road
Rochester NY 14609
Internet: www.xerox.com/employment

AMOUNT: Up to $5,000 (varies
according to tuition and academic
excellence)
DEADLINE(S): SEP 15
FIELD(S): Various engineering and
science disciplines

Scholarships for minorities enrolled full-time in a technical degree program at the bachelor level or above. Must be African-American, Native American, Hispanic, or Asian. Recipient may not have tuition or related expenses covered by other scholarships or grants.

If above requirements are met, obtain application from website or address above. Your financial aid office must fill out the bottom half of the form. Send completed application, your resume, and a cover letter to Xerox Technical Minority Scholarship Program at above address.

700—XEROX TECHNICAL MINORITY SCHOLARSHIP (Summer Employment Program)

Xerox Square
Rochester NY 14644
Written inquiry

AMOUNT: Up to $5,000 (varies
according to tuition and academic
excellence)
DEADLINE(S): SEP 15
FIELD(S): Various engineering and
science disciplines

Scholarships for minorities enrolled in a technical degree program at the bachelor level or above. Must be African-American, Native American, Hispanic, or Asian. Xerox will match your skills with a sponsoring organization that will offer a meaningful summer work experience complimenting your academic learning.

If above requirements are met, send your resume and a cover letter to Xerox Corporation Corporate Employment and College Relations Technical Minority Scholarship Program at above address.

ENGINEERING TECHNOLOGY

701—AIR FORCE RESERVE OFFICER TRAINING CORPS (AFROTC Scholarships)

551 E. Maxwell Blvd.
Maxwell AFB AL 36112-6106
334/953-7783

AMOUNT: Full tuition, books, & fees for
all 4 years of college
DEADLINE(S): DEC 1
FIELD(S): Science, Engineering,
Business, Political Science, Psychology,
Geography, Foreign Studies, Foreign
Language

Competitive scholarships based on individual merit to high school seniors and graduates who have not completed any full-time college work. Must be a US citizen between the ages of 17-27. Must also have GPA of 2.5 or above, be in top 40% of class, and complete Applicant Fitness Test. Cannot be a single parent. Your college/university must offer AFROTC.

2,300 awards annually. Contact above address for application packet.

702—AMERICAN CHEMICAL SOCIETY (Minority Scholars Program)

1155 Sixteenth Street, NW
Washington DC 20036
202/872-6250 or 800/227-5558
FAX: 202/776-8003
E-mail: rjh91@acs.org
Internet: www.acs.org

AMOUNT: up to $2,500
DEADLINE(S): FEB 15

FIELD(S): Chemistry, Biochemistry, Chemical Engineering, Chemical Technology

Open to a) high school seniors who will enter college in the coming year, b) college students currently/planning to pursue full time study, c) community college graduates/transfer students pursuing a bachelor's, and d) community college freshmen. Awarded on the basis of merit and financial need to African American, Hispanic, and American Indian students with outstanding academic records combined with strong interest in chemistry. Must be US citizen/permanent resident.

75 awards annually. Contact ACS for an application.

703—AMERICAN INDIAN SCIENCE AND ENGINEERING SOCIETY (EPA Tribal Lands Environmental Science Scholarship)

P.O. Box 9828
Albuquerque NM 87119-9828
505/765-1052
FAX: 505/765-5608
E-mail: scholarships@aises.org
Internet: www.aises.org/scholarships
AMOUNT: $4,000
DEADLINE(S): JUN 15
FIELD(S): Biochemistry, Biology, Chemical Engineering, Chemistry, Entomology, Environmental Economics/Science, Hydrology, Environmental Studies

Open to American Indian college juniors, seniors, and graduate students enrolled full-time at an accredited institution. Must demonstrate financial need. Certificate of Indian blood NOT required.

Renewable. See website or contact Patricia Browne for an application.

704—AMERICAN INSTITUTE OF CHEMICAL ENGINEERS (Donald F. Othmer Sophomore Academic Excellence Award)

345 E. 47th Street
New York NY 10017
212/705-7478
FAX: 212/752-3294
E-mail: awards@aiche.org
AMOUNT: One year's subscription to *AIChE Journal* or a copy of Perry's *Chemical Engineers' Handbook*
DEADLINE(S): Varies
FIELD(S): Chemical Engineering

Presented to an AIChE member in each student chapter who has attained the highest scholastic GPA during his/her freshman and sophomore years.

Based on recommendaiton of the Student Chapter Advisor.

705—AMERICAN INSTITUTE OF CHEMICAL ENGINEERS (Minority Scholarship Award for High School Students)

345 E. 47th Street
New York NY 10017
212/705-7478
FAX: 212/752-3294
E-mail: awards@aiche.org
AMOUNT: $1,000
DEADLINE(S): APR 15
FIELD(S): Chemical Engineering

For minority high school students planning to study chemical engineering. Students must be nominated by a local section of AIChE. Call to find out the contact in your area.

Academic record and financial need considered.

706—AMERICAN INSTITUTE OF CHEMICAL ENGINEERS (Minority Scholarship Award for College Students)

345 E. 47th Street
New York NY 10017
212/705-7478
FAX: 212/752-3294
E-mail: awards@aiche.org
AMOUNT: $1,000
DEADLINE(S): APR 15
FIELD(S): Chemical Engineering

Award for minority national student members of AIChE. Based on academic record, participation in AIChE activities, career objectives, and financial need.

6 awards.

707—AMERICAN INSTITUTE OF CHEMICAL ENGINEERS (National Scholarship Award)

345 E. 47th Street
New York NY 10017
212/705-7478
FAX: 212/752-3294
E-mail: awards@aiche.org
AMOUNT: $1,000
DEADLINE(S): APR
FIELD(S): Chemical Engineering

Award for national student members of AIChE. Based on academic performance and activity in their AIChE Student Chapter.

15 awards.

708—AMERICAN INSTITUTE OF CHEMICAL ENGINEERS (National Student Design Competition)

345 E. 47th Street
New York NY 10017
212/705-7478
FAX: 212/752-3294
E-mail: awards@aiche.org
AMOUNT: $600, $300, $200, and $100
DEADLINE(S): JUNE 7
FIELD(S): Chemical Engineering

Chemical engineers from a designated company devise and judge a student contest problem that typifies a real, working, chemical engineering design situation. Students must be AIChE national members and have a faculty advisor's permission.

Runners-up receive Honorable Mention.

709—AMERICAN NUCLEAR SOCIETY (John & Muriel Landis Scholarships)

555 North Kensington Ave.
La Grange Park IL 60526-5592
312/352-6611
AMOUNT: $3,500
DEADLINE(S): MAR 1
FIELD(S): Nuclear Engineering

Open to any undergraduate or graduate student who has a greater-than-average financial need and is planning a career in nuclear engineering or a nuclear-related field. Awards tenable at accredited institutions in the US. Must be US citizen or legal resident.

8 awards annually. Send a self-addressed, stamped envelope to above address for an application.

710—AMERICAN NUCLEAR SOCIETY (Undergraduate Scholarships)

555 North Kensington Ave.
La Grange Park IL 60526-5592
312/352-6611
AMOUNT: Varies
DEADLINE(S): MAR 1
FIELD(S): Nuclear Engineering

Scholarships open to undergraduate students who have completed at least one year of study in an accredited nuclear engineering (or nuclear-related area) program at a college or university in the US. Must be US citizen or legal resident.

Send a self-addressed, stamped envelope to above address for an application.

711—AMERICAN SOCIETY OF HEATING, REFRIGERATION, AND AIR-CONDITIONING ENGINEERS (ASHRAE Scholarship Program)

1791 Tullie Circle, NE
Atlanta GA 30329-2305
404/636-8400
FAX: 404/321-5478
Internet: www.ashrae.org

AMOUNT: $3,000
DEADLINE(S): DEC 1
FIELD(S): Heating, Refrigeration, Air-Conditioning, & Ventilation (HVAC&R)

Open to engineering undergraduate students planning a career in HVAC&R. Must have completed a full semester or quarter of college study and be currently enrolled full-time in an ABET-accredited program with at least one full year of undergraduate study remaining. Minimum 3.0 GPA, letters of recommendation, transcripts, and financial need are required. Awards tenable at accredited institutions.

6 awards annually. Not renewable. Contact Lois Benedict at above address for an application.

712—AMERICAN SOCIETY OF HEATING, REFRIGERATION, AND AIR-CONDITIONING ENGINEERS (Reuben Trane Scholarships)

1791 Tullie Circle, NE
Atlanta GA 30329-2305
404/636-8400
FAX: 404/321-5478
Internet: www.ashrae.org

AMOUNT: $5,000
DEADLINE(S): DEC 1
FIELD(S): Heating, Refrigeration, Air-Conditioning, & Ventilation (HVAC&R)

Open to engineering undergraduate students planning a career in HVAC&R. Must have completed a full semester or quarter of college, be currently enrolled full-time in an ABET-accredited program with at least two full years of undergraduate study remaining. Minimum 3.0 GPA required. Must demonstrate financial need and leadership abilities. For eligibility in second year, student must remain full-time with GPA of 3.0 or higher. Awards tenable at accredited institutions.

4 two-year awards annually. Contact Lois Benedict at above address for an application.

713—AMERICAN SOCIETY OF HEATING, REFRIGERATION, AND AIR-CONDITIONING ENGINEERS (ASHRAE Engineering Technology Scholarships)

1791 Tullie Circle, NE
Atlanta GA 30329-2305
404/636-8400
FAX: 404/321-5478
Internet: www.ashrae.org

AMOUNT: $3,000
DEADLINE(S): MAY 1
FIELD(S): Engineering Technology

For full-time students in a two-year associates degree engineering technology program with one full-year of study remaining. Must have GPA of 3.0 or higher and demonstrate financial need. Letters of recommendation and transcripts are required.

1 award annually. Not renewable. Contact Lois K. Benedict at above address for an application.

714—AMERICAN WATER RESOURCES ASSOCIATION (Richard A. Herbert Memorial Scholarships)

101 Comer Hall
Auburn Univ AL 36849-5431
715/355-3684
FAX: 715/355-3648
E-mail: stdi@ltus.com
Internet: www.uwin.siu.ed/~awra

AMOUNT: $1,000 + complimentary AWRA membership
DEADLINE(S): APR 30
FIELD(S): Water Resources & related fields

For full-time undergraduates working towards 1st degree and for graduates. Based on academic performance, including cumulative GPA, relevance of curriculum to water resources, and leadership in extracurricular activities related to water resources. Quality and relevance of research is also considered from graduate students. Transcripts, letters of reference, and summary of academic interests/achievements, extracurricular interests, and career goals required (2-page limit).

2 awards annually: 1 undergrad and 1 graduate. Recipients announced in the summer. Contact Stephen Dickman, AWRA Student Activities Committee, for an application.

715—AMERICAN WELDING SOCIETY (Scholarships)

550 NW LeJeune Road
Miami FL 33126

800/443-9353, ext. 461
305/445-6628
FAX: 305/443-7559

AMOUNT: $2,500-$3,000
DEADLINE(S): JAN 15
FIELD(S): Welding Engineering & Technology

AWS has eight different scholarship programs for US citizens pursuing undergraduate study at an accredited US institution. One program is also for Canadian citizens studying at Canadian institutions. Must be at least 18 years of age with a high school diploma or equivalent and a minimum 2.0 GPA. Some programs require financial need. Must submit two letters of reference, brief autobiography, transcript, proposed curriculum, and verification of enrollment/employment.

Renewable up to 4 years. Contact AWS for details on specific scholarships. Awards announced in February.

716—ASSOCIATED WESTERN UNIVERSITIES, INC. (AWU Undergraduate Student Fellowships)

4190 S. Highland Drive, Suite 211
Salt Lake City UT 84124-2600
801/273-8911
FAX: 801/277-5632
Internet: www.awu.org

AMOUNT: $300/week stipend + travel allowance
DEADLINE(S): FEB 1
FIELD(S): Mathematics, Engineering, Technology, Science

Eight- to- sixteen-week fellowships for undergraduate students enrolled in accredited institutions and who have completed at least one year of college by the start of the fellowship. Applicants reviewed on the basis of academic performance/class standing, career goals, recommendations, and compatibility of scientific interests and abilities with the needs and resources of the host facility. Citizenship restrictions may apply for some facilities.

500+ awards annually. Renewable (competitively with new application). Contact above address for an application.

717—ASSOCIATED WESTERN UNIVERSITIES, INC. (AWU Visiting Scientist Fellowships)

4190 S. Highland Drive, Suite 211
Salt Lake City UT 84124-2600
801/273-8900

AMOUNT: Varies
DEADLINE(S): Varies (Two months prior to starting date)

FIELD(S): Engineering, Science, Mathematics, and Technology

Research fellowships for professionals with continued commitment to science and engineering. For use at one of 62 participating universities. US citizenship or permanent residency required.

For detailed information and list of cooperating facilities contact above location.

718—AT&T BELL LABORATORIES (Summer Research Program for Minorities & Women)

101 Crawfords Corner Road
Holmdel NJ 07733-3030
Written inquiry

AMOUNT: Salary + travel & living expences for summer
DEADLINE(S): DEC 1
FIELD(S): Engineering, Math, Sciences, Computer Science

Program offers minority students and women students technical employment experience at Bell Laboratories. Students should have completed their third year of study at an accredited college or university. US citizen or permanent resident.

Selection is based partially on academic achievement and personal motivation. Write special programs manager—SRP for complete information.

719—BARRY GOLDWATER SCHOLARSHIP AND EXCELLENCE IN EDUCATION FOUNDATION (Scholarships)

6225 Brandon Ave., Suite 315
Springfield VA 22150-2519
703/756-6012
FAX: 703/756-6015
E-mail: GOLDH2o@EROLS.COM
Internet: www.act.org/goldwater

AMOUNT: $7,500/yr. (max.)
DEADLINE(S): FEB 1
FIELD(S): Math, Natural Sciences, Engineering

Open to college sophomores and juniors with a minimum 3.0 GPA. Must be US citizen, resident alien, or American national pursuing a degree at an accredited institution in math, natural sciences, or engineering disciplines that contribute to technological advances.

300 awards annually. See website or contact your Goldwater Faculty Representative on campus. Students must be nominated by their institution and cannot apply on their own.

720—BROOKHAVEN WOMEN IN SCIENCE (Renate W. Chasman Scholarship)

P.O. Box 183
Upton NY 11973-5000
E-mail: pam@bnl.gov

AMOUNT: $2,000
DEADLINE(S): APR 1
FIELD(S): Natural Sciences, Engineering, Mathematics

Open ONLY to women who are residents of the boroughs of Brooklyn or Queens or the counties of Nassau or Suffolk in New York who are re-entering school after a period of study. For juniors, seniors, or first-year graduate students.

1 award annually. Not renewable. Contact Pam Mansfield at above location for an application. Phone calls are NOT accepted.

721—COMMUNITY FOUNDATION OF WESTERN MASSACHUSETTS (James L. Shriver Scholarship)

1500 Main Street
P.O. Box 15769
Springfield MA 01115
413/732-2858

AMOUNT: $750
DEADLINE(S): APR 15
FIELD(S): Technical Fields

Open to residents of Western Massachusetts to pursue technical careers through college, trade, or technical school. Based on financial need, academic merit, and extracurricular activities. Must submit transcripts and fill out government FAFSA form.

1 award annually. Renewable with reapplication. Contact Community Foundation for an application and your financial aid office for FAFSA. Notification is in June.

722—DeVRY INC. (Dean's & Presidential Scholarships)

One Tower Lane
Oakbrook Terrace IL 60181-4624
800/733-3879, ext. 1935
630/571-7700
E-mail: outreach@devry.edu
Internet: www.devry.edu

AMOUNT: $1,000/term (Dean's); Full Tuition (Presidential)
DEADLINE(S): DEC 18; FEB 19; MAR 15
FIELD(S): Accounting, Business Admin, Computers, Electronics Engineering,

Telecommunications Management, Electronics Technician

High school seniors who apply to any DeVry Institute are automatically considered for scholarships based on ACT/SAT scores. Presidential scholarships also consider community service, scholastic achievement, extracurricular activities, and essay. Must be US citizen or permanent resident.

Renewable if maintain 3.0 GPA. Number of Dean's Scholarships varies; 2 full-time Presidential awards annually. Contact Brenda Allen, Scholarship Coordinator, for an application.

723—ELECTRONIC INDUSTRIES FOUNDATION (Scholarship Program)

2500 Wilson Blvd., Suite 210
Arlington VA 22201-3834
703/907-7408
E-mail: mvorac@eia.org

AMOUNT: $5,000
DEADLINE(S): FEB 1
FIELD(S): Electronics, Telecommunications, Electrical Engineering, Industrial Manufacturing, Industrial Engineering, Physics, Electromechanical Technology, Mechanical Applied Sciences

Open to students with disabilities (as defined by Americans w/ Disabilities Act) who are high school seniors accepted at an accredited four-year college/university. Must be US citizen pursuing studies that lead to career in design, manufacture, or provision of materials, components, products, and services for US high tech, electronics, and communications industries. Based on GPA, goals, activities, need, essay, and letters of recommendation.

Send self-addressed, stamped envelope to EIA for an application. Recipients notified by May 1st; awards paid directly to school.

724—GENERAL LEARNING COMMUNICATIONS (DuPont Challenge Science Essay Awards Program)

900 Skokie Blvd., Suite 200
Northbrook IL 60062-4028
847/205-3000
FAX: 847/564-8197
Internet: www.glcomm.com/dupont

AMOUNT: $1,500 (max.)
DEADLINE(S): JAN 28
FIELD(S): Science & Technology

Annual essay competition open to students in grades 7-12 in the US and Canada. Cash awards for 1st, 2nd, and honorable mention. 1st-place essayists in each of two divisions, their science teacher, and a parent of each receive a trip to the Space Center Houston/NASA at the end of April.

102 awards annually. See website or contact your science teacher or GLC for official entry blank.

725—GLOBAL AUTOMOTIVE AFTERMARKET SYMPOSIUM (Scholarship)

9140 Ward Parkway, Suite 200
Kansas City MO 64114
Internet: www.aftmkt.com/associations/AWDA/gass/scholarshipap

AMOUNT: Varies
DEADLINE(S): MAY 15
FIELD(S): Automotive aftermarket: various aspects

Scholarship for students pursuing careers in the automotive aftermarket. Must be a graduating senior or have graduated from high school within the past three years. Must be enrolled on a college-level program or a NATEF-accredited automotive technician program.

Application is accessible at above website.

726—HISPANIC COLLEGE FUND (Scholarships for Hispanic Students)

One Thomas Circle NW, Suite 375
Washington DC 20005
202/296-5400
FAX: 202/296-3774
E-mail: Hispanic.Fund@Internet MCI.com
Internet: http://hispanicfund.org

AMOUNT: Varies
DEADLINE(S): APR 15
FIELD(S): Most college majors leading to a career in business

Scholarships for deserving Hispanic college students pursuing a higher education in a major leading to a business career and who are full-time students at accredited institutions. US citizenship. Must demonstrate financial need.

Contact above organization for details or visit website for application.

727—HOBART INSTITUTE OF WELDING TECHNOLOGY (Scholarships)

400 Trade Square East
Troy OH 45373
800/332-9448
FAX: 937/332-5200

E-mail: hiwt@welding.org
Internet: www.welding.org

AMOUNT: $4,998
DEADLINE(S): APR 1; AUG 1; DEC 1
FIELD(S): Structural Welding

Open to undergraduates and technical school students in a structural welding program at the Hobart Institute of Welding Technology. Must have graduated from high school within the past seven years, or have obtained a GED equivalent during that time. Based on an essay, grades, and references; financial need NOT a factor.

3 awards annually. Send self-addressed, stamped envelope to Terre Baily for an application.

728—HOPI TRIBE (Priority Scholarships)

P.O. Box 123
Kykotsmovi AZ 86039
520/734-2441, ext. 520
800/762-9630
FAX: 520/734-2435

AMOUNT: Varies
DEADLINE(S): JUL 31
FIELD(S): Law, Natural Resources, Education, Medicine/Health, Engineering, Business

Open to enrolled members of the Hopi Tribe studying in one of the fields listed above, which are considered to be areas of priority interest to the Hopis. Available to college juniors, seniors, and graduate students. Program is to encourage graduates to apply their degrees to Hopi Tribal Goals and Objectives.

Contact Hopi Tribe for an application.

729—INSTITUTE FOR OPERATIONS RESEARCH AND THE MANAGEMENT SCIENCES (INFORMS Summer Internship Directory)

P.O. Box 64794
Baltimore MD 21264-4794
800/4INFORMS
FAX: 410/684-2963
E-mail: jps@informs.org
Internet: www.informs.org/INTERN/

AMOUNT: Varies
DEADLINE(S): Varies
FIELD(S): Fields related to information management: business management, engineering, mathematics

A website listing of summer internships in the field of operations research and management sciences. Both applicants and employers can register online.

Access website for list.

730—INSTITUTE OF INDUSTRIAL ENGINEERS (Dwight D. Gardner Scholarship and A.O. Putnam Scholarship)

25 Technology Park/Atlanta
Norcross GA 30092-2988
770/449-0461 or 800/263-8532
FAX: 770/441-3295
Internet: www.iienet.org

AMOUNT: $2,000 (Gardner); $500 (Putnam)
DEADLINE(S): NOV 15
FIELD(S): Industrial Engineering

Undergraduate scholarships for active IIE members with at least three semester (5 quarters) of study remaining at an accredited college or university in the US and its territories, Canada, or Mexico. A GPA of 3.4 or better is required. The Putnam Scholarship is for students pursuing an interest in management consulting within the field of industrial engineering.

Do not apply directly for these scholarships. Student must be nominated by their department head or faculty advisor. Nomination forms are sent to each school at the beginning of the fall term.

731—INSTITUTE OF INDUSTRIAL ENGINEERS (IIE Council of Fellows Undergraduate Scholarships)

25 Technology Park/Atlanta
Norcross GA 30092-2988
770/449-0461 or 800/263-8532
FAX: 770/441-3295
Internet: www.iienet.org

AMOUNT: $500
DEADLINE(S): NOV 15
FIELD(S): Industrial Engineering

Undergraduate scholarships for active IIE members with at least three semester (5 quarters) of study remaining at an accredited college or university in the US and its territories, Canada, or Mexico. A GPA of 3.4 or better is required. Scholarship is intended to reward outstanding academic scholarship and leadership.

Send to organization and address above to receive application.

732—INSTITUTE OF INDUSTRIAL ENGINEERS (United Parcel Service Scholarships for Female and Minority Students)

25 Technology Park/Atlanta
Norcross GA 30092-2988
770/449-0461 or 800/263-8532
FAX: 770/441-3295
Internet: www.iienet.org

AMOUNT: $4,000
DEADLINE(S): NOV 15
FIELD(S): Industrial Engineering

Graduate and undergraduate scholarships for active IIE members with at least three semester (5 quarters) of study remaining at an accredited college or university in the US and its territories, Canada, or Mexico. A GPA of 3.4 or better is required. One for a minority student, and one is for a female.

Do not apply directly for these scholarships. Student must be nominated by their department head or faculty advisor. Nomination forms are sent to each school at the beginning of the fall term.

733—JAMES F. LINCOLN ARC WELDING FOUNDATION (Scholarships)

22801 Clair Ave.
Cleveland OH 44117-1199
216/481-4300

AMOUNT: Varies
DEADLINE(S): MAY 1 (through JUN 15, depending on program)
FIELD(S): Arc Welding and Engineering Design

Open to high school students, college undergraduates, and graduate students, and to professionals working in the fields of arc welding and engineering design. Various programs are available.

Send self-addressed, stamped envelope to Richard S. Sabo, Executive Director, at above address.

734—LADIES OF NORTHANTS (Scholarship)

P.O. Box 6694
Coddingtown CA 95406-0694
Written inquiry

AMOUNT: $250
DEADLINE(S): FEB 8
FIELD(S): Nuclear Engineering

The Ladies of Northants offers a scholarship to a woman over 40 who migrates to the United States from Northamptonshire, England and is committed to a career in nuclear engineering. For undergraduate or graduate study.

Preference to natives of the village of Podington who have a 3.75 or better grade point average (4.0 scale) and can demonstrate financial need. Write for complete information.

735—LOS ANGELES COUNCIL OF BLACK PROFESSIONAL ENGINEERS (Al-Ben Scholarship)

P.O. Box 881029
Los Angeles CA 90009
310/635-7734
E-mail: secy1@lablackengineers.org
Internet: www.lablackengineers.org/scholarships.html

AMOUNT: Varies
DEADLINE(S): Varies
FIELD(S): Engineering, Mathematics, Computer Studies, or Applied Scientific Studies

This organization provides scholarships for technically inclined pre-college and undergraduate students enrolled in one of the above fields. Must be of African American, Native American, or Hispanic ancestry. Although preference is given to students attending college in Southern California or who are Southern California residents, the awards are open to all qualified students attending college in the United States.

See website for more information. Application for the coming year will be on the website during November.

736—MARYLAND HIGHER EDUCATION COMMISSION (Maryland Science and Technology Scholarship Program)

16 Francis Street
Annapolis Park MD 21401
410/974-5370 or 800/974-1024
E-mail: ssamail@mhec.state.md.us
Internet: http://www.mhec.state.md.us/SSA/stech_qa.htm

AMOUNT: $3,000/yr. (B.A.); $1,000/yr. (A.A.)
DEADLINE(S): None
FIELD(S): Computer Science, Engineering, Technology

Scholarships for college-bound Maryland high school seniors who will major in one of the above fields and who are accepted to an eligible associate or bachelor's degree program in Maryland. Students in the class of 1999 were eligible for the first awards. The deadline was not known at this writing, so check for deadline date. Must agree to work in the state after graduation in a related field, one year for each year of assistance received.

Must maintain a 3.0 GPA.

737—MINNESOTA AUTOMOBILE DEALERS ASSOCIATION (MADA Scholarships)

277 University Ave., W.
St. Paul MN 55103-2085
612/291-2400
Internet: www.mada.org

AMOUNT: Tuition for one quarter at an accredited Minnesota technical institution
DEADLINE(S): Varies
FIELD(S): Automotive Mechanics, Automotive Body Repair, Parts and Service Management, Automotive Machinist, Automotive Diagnostic Technician

Tuition reimbursement in the above fields of study for students currently enrolled in a Minnesota technical school. Must have completed two quarters of study in the field, be planning to enroll in further study, have maintained an above-average GPA, and be nominated by an instructor or class advisor at a Minnesota technical institution.

Contact instructor, guidance counselor, or check website above for more information.

738—NATIONAL ACADEMY FOR NUCLEAR TRAINING (Undergraduate Scholarships and Graduate Fellowships)

Scott B. Law
700 Galleria Parkway
Atlanta GA 30339-5957
800/828-5489

AMOUNT: $2,500 (scholarship); $13,000 (fellowship)
DEADLINE(S): FEB 1; NOV 11
FIELD(S): Nuclear Engineering, Chemical Engineering, Mechanical Engineering, Electrical Engineering

Open to full-time undergrads and graduates studying in the above fields. Must be US citizen and have a 3.0 or better GPA.

Write for complete information.

739—NATIONAL ASSOCIATION OF PLUMBING-HEATING-COOLING CONTRACTORS (NAPHCC Educational Foundation Scholarship Program)

P.O. Box 6808
Falls Church VA 22046
703/237-8100 or 800/533-7694
FAX: 703/237-7442

AMOUNT: $2,500
DEADLINE(S): APR 1

FIELD(S): Plumbing, Heating, Cooling

For NAPHCC members in good standing OR family members/friends/employees sponsored by NAPHCC member. Must be high school senior or college freshman planning to attend a four-year accredited college in the US to study in the above fields.

Scholarships renewable for four years; maintaining a C average or better needed for renewal. Write for complete information.

740—NATIONAL ASSOCIATION OF WATER COMPANIES—NEW JERSEY CHAPTER (Scholarship)

Elizabethtown Water Co.
600 South Ave.
Westfield NJ 07090
908/654-1234
FAX: 908/232-2719

AMOUNT: $2,500
DEADLINE(S): APR 1
FIELD(S): Business Administration, Biology, Chemistry, Engineering, Communications

For US citizens who have lived in NJ at least 5 years and plan a career in the investor-owned water utility industry in disciplines such as those above. Must be undergrad or graduate student in a 2- or 4-year NJ college or university.

GPA of 3.0 or better required. Contact Gail P. Brady for complete information.

741—NATIONAL SOCIETY OF BLACK ENGINEERS (Scholarships)

1454 Duke Street
Alexandria VA 22314
703/549-2207
FAX: 703/683-5312
E-mail: nsbehq@nsbe.org
Internet: www.nsbe.org

AMOUNT: Varies
DEADLINE(S): Varies
FIELD(S): Engineering and engineering technologies

Programs for black and other ethnic minorities in the fields of engineering and the engineering technologies. Organization offers pre-college programs, scholarships, career fairs, a journal, a newsletter, etc.

Contact organization for details.

742—NATIONAL URBAN LEAGUE, INC. (Duracell/NUL Scholarship/Intern Program for Minority Students)

120 Wall Street
New York NY 10005
212/558-5373
Internet: www.nul.org

AMOUNT: $10,000 + paid summer internship
DEADLINE(S): APR 15
FIELD(S): Engineering, Marketing, Manufacturing, Finance, Business, Human Resource, etc.

For undergraduate college/university students who will be juniors/3rd-year students at time scholarship commences. Must rank within top 25% of class and major in one of above fields. Other requirements include work experience in related field(s), extracurricular activities, leadership skills, and volunteer work. Must be US citizen/permanent resident.

For tuition, room/board, and required education materials/books. Internship with one of the Gillette companies takes place between junior and senior year. Send self-addressed, stamped envelope for application.

743—NAVY RECRUITING COMMAND (Armed Forces Health Professions Scholarships)

Commander
801 N. Randolph Street, Code 325
Arlington VA 22203-1991
800/USA-NAVY or 703/696-4926
E-mail: omegahouse@erols.com
Internet: www.navyjobs.com

AMOUNT: $938/month stipend + tuition, fees, books, lab fees, etc.
DEADLINE(S): APR 28
FIELD(S): Medicine, Dentistry, Optometry, Physical Therapy, Pharmacology, Health Care Administration, Industrial Hygiene, etc.

Open to US citizens enrolled or accepted for enrollment in any of the above fields at an accredited institution in the US or Puerto Rico. Must qualify for appointment as a Navy officer and sign a contractual agreement. Must be between the ages of 18 and 36 and have a GPA of at least 3.0.

See website, contact local Navy Recruiting Office, or contact Lieutenant Roger A. House, MPA, CAAMA, Medical Service Corps at above address.

744—NCSU PULP & PAPER FOUNDATION (Scholarships)

Attn: J. Ben Chilton, Exec. Dir.
P.O. Box 8005
Raleigh NC 27695-8005
919/515-5661

AMOUNT: $2,000-$4,050
DEADLINE(S): JAN 15
FIELD(S): Pulp & Paper Science & Technology

Open to undergraduate students enrolled in North Carolina State University who are majoring in pulp and paper science technology. US citizenship.

North Carolina residents receive $2,000; out-of-state students receive $4,050. Awards renewable annually. Write for complete information.

745—NORTH AMERICAN DIE CASTING ASSOCIATION (David Laine Memorial Scholarships)

9701 W Higgins Road, Suite 880
Rosemont IL 60018
708/292-3600

AMOUNT: Varies
DEADLINE(S): MAY 1
FIELD(S): Die Casting Technology

Open to students enrolled at an engineering college affiliated with The Foundry Educational Foundation (FEF) and registered with FEF for the current year. US citizen.

For undergraduate or graduate study. Write for complete information.

746—OAK RIDGE INSTITUTE FOR SCIENCE AND EDUCATION (ORISE Education & Training Programs)

P.O. Box 117
Oak Ridge TN 37831-0117
Internet: www.orau.gov/orise/educ.htm

AMOUNT: Varies
DEADLINE(S): Varies
FIELD(S): Engineering, Aeronautics, Computer Science, Technology, Earth Science, Environmental Studies, Biology, Chemistry, Physics, Medical Research

Numerous programs funded by the US Department of Energy are offered for undergraduate students through postgraduate researchers. Includes fellowship and internship opportunities throughout the US. Some have citizenship restrictions. Travel may be included.

See website or write for a catalog of specific programs and requirements.

747—OPEN SOCIETY INSTITUTE (Environmental Management Fellowships)

400 West 59th Street
New York NY 10019

212/548-0600 or 212/757-2323
FAX: 212/548-4679 or
212/548-4600
Internet: www.soros.org/efp.html
AMOUNT: Fees, room, board, living
stipend, textbooks, international
transportation, health insurance
DEADLINE(S): NOV 15
FIELD(S): Earth Sciences, Natural
Sciences, Humanities (exc. language),
Anthropology, Sociology,
Mathematics, or Engineering

Two-year fellowships for use in selected universities in the US for international students. For students/professionals in fields related to environmental policy, legislation, and remediation techniques applicable to their home countries.

To apply, contact your local Soros Foundation or Open Society Institute. Further details on website.

748—REFRIGERATION SERVICE ENGINEERS SOCIETY EDUCATIONAL FOUNDATION (J.W. Harris Company Scholarship)

Scholarship Committee
1666 Rand Road
Des Plaines IL 60016-3552
847/297-6464
FAX: 847/297-5038
E-mail: rses@starnetinc.com
Internet: www.rses.org
AMOUNT: Year's tuition
DEADLINE(S): JUN 1
FIELD(S): Heating, Ventilating, Air
Conditioning, and Refrigeration

A year's tuition for an RSES training course in refrigeration/air conditioning, heating, controls, heat pump, and electricity. Includes a one-year membership in RSES.

Contact Jane Hissong at above location.

749—ROBOTIC INDUSTRIES ASSOCIATION (RIA Robotics Scholarship Competition)

900 Victors Way
P.O. Box 3724
Ann Arbor MI 48106
734/994-6088
FAX: 734/994-3338
E-mail: mlehtinen@robotics.org
Internet: www.robotics.org
AMOUNT: $1,000
DEADLINE(S): DEC 10
FIELD(S): Robotics

Competition is for undergraduate students attending school in North America. Students must submit a paper that poses a technical problem and offers a solution that involves robotics. Team entries are allowed. Financial need NOT a factor.

3 awards annually. Not renewable. See website or contact Marcy Lehtinen at RIA for full guidelines and past winners.

750—SOCIETY FOR IMAGING SCIENCE AND TECHNOLOGY (Raymond Davis Scholarship)

7003 Kilworth Lane
Springfield VA 22151
703/642-9090
FAX: 703/642-9094
E-mail: info@imaging.org
Internet: www.imaging.org
AMOUNT: $1,000
DEADLINE(S): DEC 15
FIELD(S): Photographic/Imaging Science
or Engineering

Scholarships for undergraduate juniors or seniors or graduate students for full-time continuing studies in the theory or practice of photographic or imaging science or engineering, including research in the theory or practice of image formation by radiant energy.

Write for complete information.

751—SOCIETY OF AUTOMOTIVE ENGINEERS (Mankato State Univ/SAE Scholarship)

400 Commonwealth Drive
Warrendale PA 15096-0001
724/772-4047
E-mail: connie@sae.org
Internet: www.sae.org/students/
schlrshp.htm
AMOUNT: $600
DEADLINE(S): DEC 1
FIELD(S): Automotive Engineering
Technology

Incoming freshmen planning on a major in Automotive Engineering Technology at Mankato State University in Minnesota may apply. Scholarship is based on merit.

$5 application fee. 2 awards annually. See website or contact Connie Harnish, SAE Educational Relations Division, for an application. Notification is in June.

752—SOCIETY OF AUTOMOTIVE ENGINEERS (Michigan State Univ/SAE Scholarship)

400 Commonwealth Drive
Warrendale PA 15096-0001
724/772-4047
E-mail: connie@sae.org
Internet: www.sae.org/students/
schlrshp.htm

AMOUNT: $1,000
DEADLINE(S): DEC 1
FIELD(S): Automotive Engineering

Applicants must be incoming freshmen with a strong interest in the automotive industry who will be pursuing a degree in the College of Engineering at Michigan State University. Selection based on high school grades and ACT/SAT scores.

$5 application fee. 1 award annually. See website or contact Connie Harnish, SAE Educational Relations Division, for an application. Notification is in June.

753—SOCIETY OF AUTOMOTIVE ENGINEERS (Miami Univ/Ken Shinn/SAE Scholarship)

400 Commonwealth Drive
Warrendale PA 15096-0001
724/772-4047
E-mail: connie@sae.org
Internet: www.sae.org/students/
schlrshp.htm
AMOUNT: $1,000
DEADLINE(S): DEC 1
FIELD(S): Manufacturing Engineering

Applicants must be high school seniors intending to pursue studies at Miami University in Oxford, Ohio. Awards based on SAT/ACT scores, high school GPA, and extracurricular activities.

$5 application fee. 1 award annually. Not renewable. See website or contact Connie Harnish, SAE Educational Relations Division, for an application. Notification is in June.

754—SOCIETY OF AUTOMOTIVE ENGINEERS (Murray State Univ/SAE Scholarship)

400 Commonwealth Drive
Warrendale PA 15096-0001
724/772-4047
E-mail: connie@sae.org
Internet: www.sae.org/students/
schlrshp.htm
AMOUNT: $500
DEADLINE(S): DEC 1
FIELD(S): Engineering Physics

Applicants must be incoming freshmen at Murray State University in western Kentucky. Selection based on high school grades and ACT/SAT scores.

$5 application fee. 3 awards annually. See website or contact Connie Harnish, SAE Educational Relations Division, for an application. Notification is in June.

755—SOCIETY OF AUTOMOTIVE ENGI-NEERS (Pittsburgh State Univ/SAE Scholarship)

400 Commonwealth Drive
Warrendale PA 15096-0001
724/772-4047
E-mail: connie@sae.org
Internet: www.sae.org/students/
schlrshp.htm

AMOUNT: $1,500
DEADLINE(S): DEC 1
FIELD(S): Automotive Technology

For students accepted to Pittsburgh State University. Zero-hour freshmen must be in upper 20% of high school graduating class. College transfers must have a 3.5 GPA. Must maintain 3.5 GPA and complete minimum 30 hours/year for renewal.

$5 application fee. 1 award annually. Renewable for 3 years. See website or contact Connie Harnish, SAE Educational Relations Division, for an application. Notification is in June.

756—SOCIETY OF AUTOMOTIVE ENGI-NEERS (Univ Illinois-Chicago/SAE Scholarship)

400 Commonwealth Drive
Warrendale PA 15096-0001
724/772-4047
E-mail: connie@sae.org
Internet: www.sae.org/students/
schlrshp.htm

AMOUNT: $1,000/yr.
DEADLINE(S): DEC 1
FIELD(S): Automotive Engineering

Applicants must be incoming freshmen who will be pursuing a degree in the UIC College of Engineering with an interest in the automotive engineering applications. Selection based on ACT scores, high school rank, application essay, outside activities, and experiences. Must maintain 4.0 GPA on 5.0 scale for renewal.

$5 application fee. 2 awards annually. Renewable for 4 years. See website or contact Connie Harnish, SAE Educational Relations Division, for an application. Notification is in June.

757—SOCIETY OF MANUFACTURING ENGINEERING EDUCATION FOUNDATION (Scholarships & Fellowship)

One SME Drive, P.O. Box 930
Dearborn MI 48121-0930
313/271-1500
FAX: 313/240-6095

E-mail: murrdor@sme.org
Internet: www.sme.org/foundation

AMOUNT: $500-$5,000
DEADLINE(S): FEB 1
FIELD(S): Manufacturing Engineering/
Technology, Industrial Engineering,
Robotics

Twelve scholarship programs and one fellowship are available annually to high school, undergraduate, and graduate students. Minimum GPA varies with each scholarship. Financial need NOT a factor.

61 awards annually. Renewable. Contact Dora Murray at SME for an application.

758—SOCIETY OF SATELLITE PROFES-SIONALS INTERNATIONAL (SSPI Scholarships)

225 Reinekers Lane, Suite 600
Alexandria VA 22314
703/857-3717
FAX: 703/857-6335
E-mail: neworbit@aol.com
Internet: www.sspi.org

AMOUNT: $1,500 to $4,000
DEADLINE(S): DEC 1
FIELD(S): Satellites as related to
Communications, Domestic and
International Telecommunications
Policy, Remote Sensing, Journalism,
Law, Meteorology, Energy,
Navigation, Business, Government,
and Broadcasting Services.

Various scholarships for students studying in the above fields.

Access website for details and applications or send a self-addressed, stamped envelope (SASE) for a complete listing.

759—SOCIETY OF WOMEN ENGINEERS (Nalco Foundation Scholarship)

120 Wall Street, 11th Fl.
New York NY 10005-3902
800/666-ISWE or 212/509-9577
FAX: 212/509-0224
E-mail: hq@swe.org
Internet: www.swe.org

AMOUNT: $1,050
DEADLINE(S): MAY 15
FIELD(S): Chemical Engineering

Open to women who are entering freshmen in a college/university with an ABET-accredited program or in a SWE-approved school. Must plan to major in chemical engineering.

1 award every 4 years. Renewable 3 years. Send a self-addressed, stamped envelope to SWE for an application. Recipient is notified in September.

760—STUDENT CONSERVATION ASSOCIA-TION (SCA Resource Assistant Program)

P.O. Box 550
Charlestown NH 03603
603/543-1700
FAX: 603/543-1828
E-mail: internships@sca-inc.org
Internet: www.sca-inc.org

AMOUNT: $1,180-$4,725
DEADLINE(S): Varies
FIELD(S): Environment & related fields

Must be 18 and US citizen; need not be student. Fields: Agriculture, archaeology, anthropology, botany, caves, civil/environmental engineering, environmental education, fisheries, forests, herpetology, history, living history/roleplaying, visitor services, landscape architectural/environmental design, paleontology, recreation/resource/range management, trail maintenance/construction, wildlife management, geology, hydrology, library/museums, surveying.

900 positions in US & Canada. Send $1 for postage for application; outside US/Canada, send $20.

761—THE ART INSTITUTES INTERNATION-AL (Evelyn Keedy Memorial Scholarship)

300 Sixth Ave., Suite 800
Pittsburgh PA 15222-2598
412/562-9800
FAX: 412/562-9802
E-mail: webadmin@aii.edu
Internet: www.aii.edu

AMOUNT: 2 years full tuition
DEADLINE(S): MAY 1
FIELD(S): Various fields in the creative
and applied arts: Video Production,
Broadcasting, Culinary Arts, Fashion
Design, Website Administration, etc.

Scholarships at 12 different locations nationwide in various fields described above. For graduating high school seniors admitted to an Arts Institutes International School, the New York Restaurant School, or NCPT. Transcripts, letters of recommendation, and resume must be submitted with application.

See website or contact AII for more information.

762—THE INTERNATIONAL SOCIETY FOR OPTICAL ENGINEERING (Scholarships and Grants)

P.O. Box 10
Bellingham WA 98225

360/676-3290
FAX: 360/647-1445
E-mail: spie@spie.org
Internet: http://www.spie.org
AMOUNT: $500-$7,000
DEADLINE(S): APR 6
FIELD(S): Optics and Optical Engineering
Open to college students at all levels for study of optical or optoelectronic applied science and engineering. May be awarded to students in community colleges or technical institutes and to undergraduate and graduate students at colleges and universities.
Write to the SPIE Scholarship Committee Chair or visit website (address above) for complete information.

763—THE SOCIETY OF TRIBOLOGISTS AND LUBRICATION ENGINEERS (Scholarships and Fellowships)

840 Busse Highway
Park Ridge IL 60068-2376
847/825-5536
FAX: 847/825-1456
Internet: www.stle.org
AMOUNT: $4,000 (undergrads); $5,000 (grads); plus $500 to the department where research will be conducted
DEADLINE(S): JAN 30
FIELD(S): Engineering Technology, especially the study of lubrication/tribology
Scholarships for undergrads and grads to study in the fields of lubrication, friction, wear, and related technologies.
Contact organization for details.

764—U.S. DEPARTMENT OF TRANSPORTATION (Dwight D. Eisenhower Transportation Fellowships)

U.S. Dept. of Transportation
Fed. Hwy. Admin.
6300 Georgetown Pike, HHI-20
McLean VA 22101-2296
703/235-0538
AMOUNT: Varies
DEADLINE(S): FEB
FIELD(S): Transportation—such majors as chemistry; materials science; corrosion; civil, chemical, & electronics engineering; structures; human factors; computer science; psychology
Research fellowships for undergrads and grad students at any Dept. of Transportation facility or selected IHE. For three to twelve months. Research must focus on transportation-related research and development in the above fields.

Contact Ilene Payne, Director, Universities and Grants Programs at above location for details.

765—U.S. ENVIRONMENTAL PROTECTION AGENCY—NATIONAL NETWORK FOR ENVIRONMENTAL MANAGEMENT STUDIES (Fellowships)

401 M Street SW; Mailcode 1704
Washington DC 20460
202/260-5283
FAX: 202/260-4095
E-mail: jojokian.sheri@epa.gov
Internet: www.epa.gov/enviroed/students.html
AMOUNT: Varies
DEADLINE(S): DEC
FIELD(S): Environmental Policies, Regulations, & Law; Environmental Management & Administration; Environmental Science; Public Relations & Communications; Computer Programming & Development
Fellowships are open to undergraduate and graduate students working on research projects in the above fields, either full-time during the summer or part-time during the school year. Must be US citizen or legal resident. Financial need NOT a factor.
85-95 awards annually. Not renewable. See website or contact the Career Service Center of participating universities for an application.

766—UNIVERSAL TECHNICAL INSTITUTE (Al Unser National High School Competition)

3002 N. 27th Ave.
Phoenix AZ 85017
800/859-1201
Internet: www.utiedu.com
AMOUNT: Up to $5,000
DEADLINE(S): APR; MAR
FIELD(S): Technical areas, such as auto/truck mechanics or HVAC (heating, ventilation, air conditioning)
Competition for high school seniors pursuing careers as technicians in the above areas. Winners will receive scholarships valued from $1,000 to $5,000 for use at UTI, which has campuses in Arizona, Illinois, and Texas. Awards are based on a written test of technical skills to be taken at various sites in the US Awards also are given to schools by students finishing in the top 10%.
Nearly $400,000 will be awarded in the Auto/Truck competition, and over $100,000

in the HVAC/R competition. Call, check website, or write for details.

767—UNIVERSITY OF MAINE PULP & PAPER FOUNDATION (Pulp & Paper Foundation Scholarships)

5737 Jenness Hall
Orono ME 04469-5737
207/581-2297
AMOUNT: $1,000
DEADLINE(S): FEB 1
FIELD(S): Engineering
Open to undergraduate students accepted to or enrolled in the University of Maine at Orono who have demonstrated an interest in a paper-related career. US citizenship.
25 $1,000 scholarships plus 100 tuition scholarships awarded.

768—UNIVERSITY OF MARYLAND (John B. & Ida Slaughter Endowed Scholarship in Science, Technology, & the Black Community)

2169 Lefrak Hall
College Park MD 20742-7225
301/405-1158
FAX: 301/314-9867
Internet: www.bsos.umd.edu/aasp/scholarship.html
AMOUNT: Varies (in-state tuition costs)
DEADLINE(S): MAR
FIELD(S): Science & Technology AND African-American Studies
Open to African-Americans who are US residents with a minimum 2.8 GPA. Must be accepted to or enrolled at UMCP for freshman year and must submit letter of recommendation from high school counselor or UMCP faculty member. Should have an interest in applying science and technology to the problems of the black community. Essay required.
Renewable. Contact the Center for Minorities in Science & Engineering at UMCP for an application.

769—WASHINGTON PULP & PAPER FOUNDATION (Scholarship Program)

c/o Univ. of Washington
Box 352100
Seattle WA 98195-2100
206/543-2763
AMOUNT: Varies-approx. 2/3 tuition
DEADLINE(S): FEB 1
FIELD(S): Paper Science & Engineering

Undergraduate tuition scholarships at the Univ. of Washington. Open to students who are accepted to or enrolled in the paper science & engineering curriculum at the university. For high school seniors or college transfer students ranking in the top 25% of class or otherwise recommended by principal. US citizenship required.

Approximately 20 new awards per year (45 total). Renewable for up to 12 quarters. GPA 3.0 college or 3.5 high school. Write for complete information.

770—WATER ENVIRONMENT FEDERATION (Student Paper Competition)

Access website
Internet: www.wef.org
AMOUNT: $1,000 (1st prize); $500 (2nd); $250 (3rd)
DEADLINE(S): FEB 1
FIELD(S): Water pollution control and related fields

Awards for 500 1,000-word abstracts dealing with water pollution control, water quality problems, water-related concerns, or hazardous wastes. Open to undergrad (A.A. and B.A.) and grad students.

Also open to recently graduated students (within 1 calendar year of Feb. 1 deadline). See website for details—go to "Member Programs" then to "Student Paper Competition." Organization will not mail this information.

771—WOMEN'S AUXILIARY TO THE AMERICAN INSTITUTE OF MINING METAL-LURGICAL & PETROLEUM ENGINEERS (WAAIME Scholarship Loan Fund)

345 E. 47th Street, 14th Fl.
New York NY 10017-2304
212/705-7692
AMOUNT: Varies
DEADLINE(S): MAR 15
FIELD(S): Earth Sciences, as related to the Minerals Industry

Open to undergraduate juniors and seniors and grad students, whose majors relate to an interest in the minerals industry. Eligible applicants receive a scholarship loan for all or part of their education. Recipients repay only 50%, with no interest charges.

Repayment to begin by 6 months after graduation and be completed within 6 years. Write to WAAIME Scholarship Loan Fund (address above) for complete information.

772—WYOMING TRUCKING ASSOCIATION (Scholarships)

P.O. Box 1909
Casper WY 82602
Written inquiry
AMOUNT: $250-$300
DEADLINE(S): MAR 1
FIELD(S): Transportation Industry

For Wyoming high school graduates enrolled in a Wyoming college, approved trade school, or the University of Wyoming. Must be pursuing a course of study that will result in a career in the transportation industry in Wyoming, including but not limited to: safety, environmental science, diesel mechanics, truck driving, vocational trades, business management, sales management, computer skills, accounting, office procedures, and management.

1-10 awards annually. Write to WYTA for an application.

773—XEROX TECHNICAL MINORITY SCHOLARSHIP (School-Year Tuition)

907 Culver Road
Rochester NY 14609
Internet: www.xerox.com/employment
AMOUNT: Up to $5,000 (varies according to tuition and academic excellence)
DEADLINE(S): SEP 15
FIELD(S): Various engineering and science disciplines

Scholarships for minorities enrolled full-time in a technical degree program at the bachelor level or above. Must be African-American, Native American, Hispanic, or Asian. Recipient may not have tuition or related expenses covered by other scholarships or grants.

If above requirements are met, obtain application from website or address above. Your financial aid office must fill out the bottom half of the form. Send completed application, your resume, and a cover letter to Xerox Technical Minority Scholarship Program at above address.

774—XEROX TECHNICAL MINORITY SCHOLARSHIP (Summer Employment Program)

Xerox Square
Rochester NY 14644
Written inquiry
AMOUNT: Up to $5,000 (varies according to tuition and academic excellence)
DEADLINE(S): SEP 15
FIELD(S): Various engineering and science disciplines

Scholarships for minorities enrolled in a technical degree program at the bachelor level or above. Must be African-American, Native American, Hispanic, or Asian. Xerox will match your skills with a sponsoring organization that will offer a meaningful summer work experience complimenting your academic learning.

If above requirements are met, send your resume and a cover letter to Xerox Corporation Corporate Employment and College Relations Technical Minority Scholarship Program at above address.

MECHANICAL ENGINEERING

775—AIR FORCE RESERVE OFFICER TRAINING CORPS (AFROTC Scholarships)

551 E. Maxwell Blvd.
Maxwell AFB AL 36112-6106
334/953-7783
AMOUNT: Full tuition, books, & fees for all 4 years of college
DEADLINE(S): DEC 1
FIELD(S): Science, Engineering, Business, Political Science, Psychology, Geography, Foreign Studies, Foreign Language

Competitive scholarships based on individual merit to high school seniors and graduates who have not completed any full-time college work. Must be a US citizen between the ages of 17-27. Must also have GPA of 2.5 or above, be in top 40% of class, and complete Applicant Fitness Test. Cannot be a single parent. Your college/university must offer AFROTC.

2,300 awards annually. Contact above address for application packet.

776—AMERICAN SOCIETY OF ENGINEERS OF INDIAN ORIGIN (Undergraduate Scholarship Programs)

P.O. Box 49494
Atlanta GA 30359-1494
770/451-2299
Internet: www.iasf.org/asei.htm
AMOUNT: Up to $1,000
DEADLINE(S): AUG 15
FIELD(S): Engineering fields: architecture, computer technology, geotechnical or geoenvironmental engineering, and allied sciences

Several scholarships for undergraduate engineering students in the above fields who were born in India or who are Indian by ancestry or relation. For study in the US. Some programs have residency requirements in certain states.

Contact Dr. Narsi Narasimhan at above location for applications and details.

777—AMERICAN SOCIETY OF MECHANICAL ENGINEERS (ASME Student Loans)

3 Park Avenue
New York NY 10016-5990
212/591-8131
FAX: 212/591-7143
E-mail: malaven@asme.org
Internet: www.asme.org
AMOUNT: $3,000
DEADLINE(S): APR 15; OCT 15
FIELD(S): Mechanical Engineering

Loans for ASME student members who are undergraduate or graduate students in a mechanical engineering or related program. Must be citizens or residents of the US, Canada, or Mexico. Loans are 1% below the Stafford loan rate. Financial need is considered.

100 awards annually. Not renewable. Contact Nellie Malave at above address for an application or membership information.

778—AMERICAN SOCIETY OF MECHANICAL ENGINEERS (Frank William and Dorothy Given Miller Scholarship)

3 Park Avenue
New York NY 10016-5990
212/591-8131
FAX: 212/591-7143
E-mail: malaven@asme.org
Internet: www.asme.org
AMOUNT: $1,500
DEADLINE(S): MAR 15
FIELD(S): Mechanical Engineering

For ASME student members in their junior or senior undergraduate year in mechanical engineering or related program. Must be US citizen or North American resident. Financial need NOT considered.

2 awards annually. Not renewable. Contact Nellie Malave at above address for an application or membership information.

779—AMERICAN SOCIETY OF MECHANICAL ENGINEERS (Garland Duncan Scholarship)

3 Park Avenue
New York NY 10016-5990
212/705-8131
FAX: 212/705-7143
E-mail: malaven@asme.org
Internet: www.asme.org
AMOUNT: $3,000
DEADLINE(S): MAR 15

FIELD(S): Mechanical Engineering

For ASME student members in their junior or senior undergraduate years studying mechanical engineering or a related program. Must demonstrate financial need.

2 awards annually. Not renewable. Contact Nellie Malave at above address for an application or membership information.

780—AMERICAN SOCIETY OF MECHANICAL ENGINEERS (John and Elsa Gracik Scholarship)

3 Park Avenue
New York NY 10016-5990
212/591-8131
FAX: 212/591-7143
E-mail: malaven@asme.org
Internet: www.asme.org
AMOUNT: $1,500
DEADLINE(S): MAR 15
FIELD(S): Mechanical Engineering

Open to ASME student members who are undergraduates in a mechanical engineering program or in related programs. Must be US citizen and demonstrate financial need.

16 awards annually. Not renewable. Contact Nellie Malave at above address for an application or membership information.

781—AMERICAN SOCIETY OF MECHANICAL ENGINEERS (Kenneth Andrew Roe Scholarship)

3 Park Avenue
New York NY 10016-5990
212/591-8131
FAX: 212/591-7143
E-mail: malaven@asme.org
Internet: www.asme.org
AMOUNT: $7,000
DEADLINE(S): MAR 15
FIELD(S): Mechanical Engineering

Open to ASME student members in their junior or senior undergraduate years studying mechanical engineering or related program. Must be US citizen or North American resident. Financial need considered.

1 award annually. Not renewable. Contact Nellie Malave at above address for an application or membership information.

782—AMERICAN SOCIETY OF MECHANICAL ENGINEERS (Melvin R. Green Scholarship)

3 Park Avenue
New York NY 10016-5990
212/591-8131

FAX: 212/591-7143
E-mail: malaven@asme.org
Internet: www.asme.org
AMOUNT: $3,000
DEADLINE(S): MAR 15
FIELD(S): Mechanical Engineering

For ASME student members who are in their junior or senior undergraduate years studying mechanical engineering or a related program. Financial need NOT considered.

2 awards annually. Not renewable. Contact Nellie Malave at above address for an application or membership information.

783—AMERICAN SOCIETY OF MECHANICAL ENGINEERS (Sylvia W. Farny Scholarship)

3 Park Avenue
New York NY 10016-5990
212/591-7733
E-mail: Horvathb@asme.org
Internet: www.asme.org
AMOUNT: $1,500
DEADLINE(S): FEB 15
FIELD(S): Mechanical Engineering

Open to US citizens enrolled in their junior year of undergraduate study in a US school with accredited mechanical engineering curricula. Award is for their senior year of study. Must be a student member of ASME.

6-12 awards annually. Not renewable. Contact Barbara Horvath at above address for an application or membership information.

784—AMERICAN SOCIETY OF MECHANICAL ENGINEERS (William J. & Marijane E. Adams, Jr. Scholarship)

3 Park Avenue
New York NY 10016-5990
212/591-8131
FAX: 212/591-7143
E-mail: malaven@asme.org
Internet: www.asme.org
AMOUNT: $1,500
DEADLINE(S): MAR 15
FIELD(S): Mechanical Engineering

For ASME student members studying mechanical engineering with a special interest in product development and design. Must be at least at the sophomore level and attending a college/university in California, Hawaii, or Nevada. Must also demonstrate financial need.

1 award annually. Not renewable. Contact Nellie Malave at above address for an application or membership information.

785—AMERICAN SOCIETY OF MECHANI-CAL ENGINEERS AUXILIARY INC. (F.W. Beichley Scholarship)

3 Park Avenue
New York NY 10016-5990
212/591-8131
FAX: 212/591-7143
E-mail: malaven@asme.org
Internet: www.asme.org

AMOUNT: $1,500
DEADLINE(S): MAR 15
FIELD(S): Mechanical Engineering

For junior and senior undergraduate students who are student members of ASME, studying mechanical engineering or a related program. Must demonstrate financial need.

1 award annually. Not renewable. Contact Nellie Malave at above address for an application or membership information.

786—ASM INTERNATIONAL FOUNDATION (Undergraduate Scholarships)

Scholarship Program
Materials Park OH 44073-0002
440/338-5151
FAX: 440/338-4643
E-mail: ASMIF@po.ASM~intl.org
Internet: www.asm~intl.org

AMOUNT: $500 to full tuition
DEADLINE(S): MAY 1
FIELD(S): Metallurgy, Materials Science

For undergraduate students majoring in metallurgy/materials. For citizens of the US, Canada, or Mexico who are enrolled in a recognized college or university in one of those countries. Must be a student member of ASM. Some awards have more specific requirements.

See website or write to ASM for membership information or more details on their scholarship program.

787—ASSOCIATED WESTERN UNIVERSI-TIES, INC. (AWU Undergraduate Student Fellowships)

4190 S. Highland Drive, Suite 211
Salt Lake City UT 84124-2600
801/273-8911
FAX: 801/277-5632
Internet: www.awu.org

AMOUNT: $300/week stipend + travel allowance
DEADLINE(S): FEB 1
FIELD(S): Mathematics, Engineering, Technology, Science

Eight- to- sixteen-week fellowships for undergraduate students enrolled in accredited institutions and who have completed at least one year of college by the start of the fellowship. Applicants reviewed on the basis of academic performance/class standing, career goals, recommendations, and compatibility of scientific interests and abilities with the needs and resources of the host facility. Citizenship restrictions may apply for some facilities.

500+ awards annually. Renewable (competitively with new application). Contact above address for an application.

788—ASSOCIATED WESTERN UNIVERSI-TIES, INC. (AWU Visiting Scientist Fellowships)

4190 S. Highland Drive, Suite 211
Salt Lake City UT 84124-2600
801/273-8900

AMOUNT: Varies
DEADLINE(S): Varies (Two months prior to starting date)
FIELD(S): Engineering, Science, Mathematics, and Technology

Research fellowships for professionals with continued commitment to science and engineering. For use at one of 62 participating universities. US citizenship or permanent residency required.

For detailed information and list of cooperating faciities contact above location.

789—AT&T BELL LABORATORIES (Summer Research Program for Minorities & Women)

101 Crawfords Corner Road
Holmdel NJ 07733-3030
Written inquiry

AMOUNT: Salary + travel & living expences for summer
DEADLINE(S): DEC 1
FIELD(S): Engineering, Math, Sciences, Computer Science

Program offers minority students and women students technical employment experience at Bell Laboratories. Students should have completed their third year of study at an accredited college or university. US citizen or permanent resident.

Selection is based partially on academic achievement and personal motivation. Write special programs manager—SRP for complete information.

790—BROOKHAVEN WOMEN IN SCIENCE (Renate W. Chasman Scholarship)

P.O. Box 183
Upton NY 11973-5000
E-mail: pam@bnl.gov

AMOUNT: $2,000
DEADLINE(S): APR 1
FIELD(S): Natural Sciences, Engineering, Mathematics

Open ONLY to women who are residents of the boroughs of Brooklyn or Queens or the counties of Nassau or Suffolk in New York who are re-entering school after a period of study. For juniors, seniors, or first-year graduate students.

1 award annually. Not renewable. Contact Pam Mansfield at above location for an application. Phone calls are NOT accepted.

791—ELECTRONIC INDUSTRIES FOUNDA-TION (Scholarship Program)

2500 Wilson Blvd., Suite 210
Arlington VA 22201-3834
703/907-7408
E-mail: mvorac@eia.org

AMOUNT: $5,000
DEADLINE(S): FEB 1
FIELD(S): Electronics, Telecommunications, Electrical Engineering, Industrial Manufacturing, Industrial Engineering, Physics, Electromechanical Technology, Mechanical Applied Sciences

Open to students with disabilities (as defined by Americans w/ Disabilities Act) who are high school seniors accepted at an accredited four-year college/university. Must be US citizen pursuing studies that lead to career in design, manufacture, or provision of materials, components, products, and services for US high tech, electronics, and communications industries. Based on GPA, goals, activities, need, essay, and letters of recommendation.

Send self-addressed, stamped envelope to EIA for an application. Recipients notified by May 1st; awards paid directly to school.

792—H.H. HARRIS FOUNDATION

One North Franklin Street, Suite 1200
Chicago IL 60606-3401
Written inquiry

AMOUNT: Varies
DEADLINE(S): JUN 15
FIELD(S): Metallurgical and metal casting fields

Scholarships and other forms of educational aid to students and professionals who are US citizens studying in the fields listed above.

Write to John Hough, Mgr., at above address for detailed information.

793—HOPI TRIBE (Priority Scholarships)

P.O. Box 123
Kykotsmovi AZ 86039
520/734-2441, ext. 520
800/762-9630
FAX: 520/734-2435

AMOUNT: Varies
DEADLINE(S): JUL 31
FIELD(S): Law, Natural Resources, Education, Medicine/Health, Engineering, Business

Open to enrolled members of the Hopi Tribe studying in one of the fields listed above, which are considered to be areas of priority interest to the Hopis. Available to college juniors, seniors, and graduate students. Program is to encourage graduates to apply their degrees to Hopi Tribal Goals and Objectives.

Contact Hopi Tribe for an application.

794—LOS ANGELES COUNCIL OF BLACK PROFESSIONAL ENGINEERS (Al-Ben Scholarship)

P.O. Box 881029
Los Angeles CA 90009
310/635-7734
E-mail: secy1@lablackengineers.org
Internet: www.lablackengineers.org/scholarships.html

AMOUNT: Varies
DEADLINE(S): Varies
FIELD(S): Engineering, Mathematics, Computer Studies, or Applied Scientific Studies

This organization provides scholarships for technically inclined pre-college and undergraduate students enrolled in one of the above fields. Must be of African American, Native American, or Hispanic ancestry. Although preference is given to students attending college in Southern California or who are Southern California residents, the awards are open to all qualified students attending college in the United States.

See website for more information. Application for the coming year will be on the website during November.

795—MARYLAND HIGHER EDUCATION COMMISSION (Maryland Science and Technology Scholarship Program)

16 Francis Street
Annapolis Park MD 21401
410/974-5370 or 800/974-1024
E-mail: ssamail@mhec.state.md.us
Internet: http://www.mhec.state.md.us/SSA/stech_qa.htm

AMOUNT: $3,000/yr. (B.A.); $1,000/yr. (A.A.)
DEADLINE(S): None
FIELD(S): Computer Science, Engineering, Technology

Scholarships for college-bound Maryland high school seniors who will major in one of the above fields and who are accepted to an eligible associate or bachelor's degree program in Maryland. Students in the class of 1999 were eligible for the first awards. The deadline was not known at this writing, so check for deadline date. Must agree to work in the state after graduation in a related field, one year for each year of assistance received.

Must maintain a 3.0 GPA.

796—NATIONAL ASSOCIATION OF WATER COMPANIES—NEW JERSEY CHAPTER (Scholarship)

Elizabethtown Water Co.
600 South Ave.
Westfield NJ 07090
908/654-1234
FAX: 908/232-2719

AMOUNT: $2,500
DEADLINE(S): APR 1
FIELD(S): Business Administration, Biology, Chemistry, Engineering, Communications

For US citizens who have lived in NJ at least 5 years and plan a career in the investor-owned water utility industry in disciplines such as those above. Must be undergrad or graduate student in a 2- or 4-year NJ college or university.

GPA of 3.0 or better required. Contact Gail P. Brady for complete information.

797—NATIONAL SOCIETY OF BLACK ENGINEERS (Scholarships)

1454 Duke Street
Alexandria VA 22314
703/549-2207
FAX: 703/683-5312
E-mail: nsbehq@nsbe.org
Internet: www.nsbe.org

AMOUNT: Varies
DEADLINE(S): Varies
FIELD(S): Engineering and engineering technologies

Programs for black and other ethnic minorities in the fields of engineering and the engineering technologies. Organization offers pre-college programs, scholarships, career fairs, a journal, a newsletter, etc.

Contact organization for details.

798—NATIONAL STONE ASSOCIATION (NSA Quarry Engineering Scholarships)

1415 Elliot Place NW
Washington DC 20007
Written inquiry only

AMOUNT: $2,500
DEADLINE(S): MAY 1
FIELD(S): Quarry Engineering

Open to students intending to pursue a career in the aggregate industry and who are enrolled in an undergraduate program working toward this objective.

Employment in industry a plus; write for complete information.

799—OPEN SOCIETY INSTITUTE (Environmental Management Fellowships)

400 West 59th Street
New York NY 10019
212/548-0600 or 212/757-2323
FAX: 212/548-4679 or 212/548-4600
Internet: www.soros.org/efp.html

AMOUNT: Fees, room, board, living stipend, textbooks, international transportation, health insurance
DEADLINE(S): NOV 15
FIELD(S): Earth Sciences, Natural Sciences, Humanities (exc. language), Anthropology, Sociology, Mathematics, or Engineering

Two-year fellowships for use in selected universities in the U.S. for international students. For students/professionals in fields related to environmental policy, legislation, and remediation techniques applicable to their home countries.

To apply, contact your local Soros Foundation or Open Society Institute. Further details on website.

800—ROBOTIC INDUSTRIES ASSOCIATION (RIA Robotics Scholarship Competition)

900 Victors Way
P.O. Box 3724
Ann Arbor MI 48106

734/994-6088
FAX: 734/994-3338
E-mail: mlehtinen@robotics.org
Internet: www.robotics.org
AMOUNT: $1,000
DEADLINE(S): DEC 10
FIELD(S): Robotics

Competition is for undergraduate students attending school in North America. Students must submit a paper that poses a technical problem and offers a solution that involves robotics. Team entries are allowed. Financial need NOT a factor.

3 awards annually. Not renewable. See website or contact Marcy Lehtinen at RIA for full guidelines and past winners.

801—ROCKY MOUNTAIN COAL MINING INSTITUTE (Scholarships)

3000 Youngfield Street, Suite 324
Lakewood CO 80215-6553
303/238-9099
FAX: 303/238-0509
E-mail: RMCoalMine@aol.com
AMOUNT: $1,500/yr.
DEADLINE(S): FEB 1
FIELD(S): Engineering as related to Coal

College sophomores ONLY may apply for this award for their junior year at an accredited school. Must be residents of Arizona, Colorado, Montana, New Mexico, North Dakota, Texas, Utah, or Wyoming. Financial need NOT a factor.

16 awards annually (8 new, 8 renewed). Renewable for senior year. Contact Karen L. Inzano at above address for an application.

802—SOCIETY OF AUTOMOTIVE ENGINEERS (Milwaukee School of Engineering/SAE Scholarship)

400 Commonwealth Drive
Warrendale PA 15096-0001
724/772-4047
E-mail: connie@sae.org
Internet: www.sae.org/students/schlrshp.htm
AMOUNT: $1,000
DEADLINE(S): DEC 1
FIELD(S): Mechanical Engineering

Applicants should be incoming freshmen accepted into either the Mechanical Engineering or Mechanical Engineering Technology program at Milwaukee School of Engineering in Wisconsin. Must maintain 3.0 GPA for renewal.

$5 application fee. 1 award annually. Renewable for 3 years. See website or contact Connie Harnish, SAE Educational

Relations Division, for an application. Notification is in June.

803—SOCIETY OF AUTOMOTIVE ENGINEERS (Univ Wisconsin-Milwaukee/Sundstrand/SAE Scholarship)

400 Commonwealth Drive
Warrendale PA 15096-0001
724/772-4047
E-mail: connie@sae.org
Internet: www.sae.org/students/schlrshp.htm
AMOUNT: $1,000
DEADLINE(S): DEC 1
FIELD(S): Mechanical Engineering

Must be high school seniors planning to attend the University of Wisconsin-Milwaukee. Award based on merit; must have minimum 1100 SAT or 26 ACT and 3.3 high school GPA. Must maintain 3.0 GPA for renewal. Applicants must be accepted into the College of Engineering & Science by Jan 1st, and must write "Mech. Eng. SAE Scholarship" in space for Intended Major on admission application.

$5 application fee. 1 award annually. Renewable for $500 junior year. See website or contact Connie Harnish, SAE Educational Relations Division, for an application. Notification is in June. For admissions info, write to UWM Office of Admissions, P.O. Box 749, Milwaukee, WI 53201.

804—SOCIETY OF MECHANICAL ENGINEERS-WYOMING SECTION (Coates-Wolff-Russell Memorial Mining Industry Scholarships)

800 Werner Ct., Suite 352
Casper WY 82601
Written inquiry
AMOUNT: $1,000
DEADLINE(S): Varies
FIELD(S): Mining

Available to sophomores, juniors, and seniors in mining or mining-related programs who are Wyoming residents.

1-3 awards annually. Write to R.L. Thurman at SME for details.

805—SOCIETY OF SATELLITE PROFESSIONALS INTERNATIONAL (SSPI Scholarships)

225 Reinekers Lane, Suite 600
Alexandria VA 22314
703/857-3717
FAX: 703/857-6335

E-mail: neworbit@aol.com
Internet: www.sspi.org
AMOUNT: $1,500 to $4,000
DEADLINE(S): DEC 1
FIELD(S): Satellites as related to communications, domestic and international telecommunications policy, remote sensing, journalism, law, meteorology, energy, navigation, business, government, and broadcasting services

Various scholarships for students studying in the above fields.

Access website for details and applications or send a self-addressed, stamped envelope (SASE) for a complete listing.

806—U.S. DEPARTMENT OF TRANSPORTATION (Dwight D. Eisenhower Transportation Fellowships)

U.S. Dept. of Transportation
Fed. Hwy. Admin.
6300 Georgetown Pike, HHI-20
McLean VA 22101-2296
703/235-0538
AMOUNT: Varies
DEADLINE(S): FEB
FIELD(S): Transportation—such majors as chemistry; materials science; corrosion; civil, chemical, & electronics engineering; structures; human factors; computer science; psychology

Research fellowships for undergrads and grad students at any Dept. of Transportation facility or selected IHE. For three to twelve months. Research must focus on transportation-related research and development in the above fields.

Contact Ilene Payne, Director, Universities and Grants Programs at above location for details.

807—WEBB INSTITUTE (Naval Architecture Scholarships)

Crescent Beach Rd.
Glen Cove NY 11542-1398
516/671-2213
AMOUNT: Full tuition for 4 years
DEADLINE(S): FEB 15
FIELD(S): Naval Architecture, Marine Engineering

Open to high school students aged 16-24 who are in the top 10% of their class and have a minimum 3.2 GPA. Based on college boards, SAT scores, demonstrated interest in above areas, and an interview. Must be US citizen. Tenable at the Webb Institute.

20-25 awards annually. Contact Webb Institute for an application.

808—WOMEN'S AUXILIARY TO THE AMERICAN INSTITUTE OF MINING METAL-LURGICAL & PETROLEUM ENGINEERS (WAAIME Scholarship Loan Fund)

345 E. 47th Street, 14th Fl.
New York NY 10017-2304
212/705-7692

AMOUNT: Varies
DEADLINE(S): MAR 15
FIELD(S): Earth Sciences, as related to the Minerals Industry

Open to undergraduate juniors and seniors and grad students, whose majors relate to an interest in the minerals industry. Eligible applicants receive a scholarship loan for all or part of their education. Recipients repay only 50%, with no interest charges.

Repayment to begin by 6 months after graduation and be completed within 6 years. Write to WAAIME Scholarship Loan Fund (address above) for complete information.

809—WYOMING MINING ASSOCIATION (Scholarships)

P.O. Box 866
Cheyenne WY 82003
Written inquiry

AMOUNT: $500+
DEADLINE(S): JUN 1
FIELD(S): Mining

For students enrolled in a Wyoming college and pursuing a career related to mining. Submit official transcripts and a letter of application, outlining goals and need for scholarship.

Send above materials to the Executive Vice President at above address.

810—XEROX TECHNICAL MINORITY SCHOLARSHIP (School-Year Tuition)

907 Culver Road
Rochester NY 14609
Internet: www.xerox.com/employment

AMOUNT: Up to $5,000 (varies according to tuition and academic excellence)
DEADLINE(S): SEP 15
FIELD(S): Various engineering and science disciplines

Scholarships for minorities enrolled full-time in a technical degree program at the bachelor level or above. Must be African-American, Native American, Hispanic, or Asian. Recipient may not have tuition or related expenses covered by other scholarships or grants.

If above requirements are met, obtain application from website or address above. Your financial aid office must fill out the bottom half of the form. Send completed application, your resume, and a cover letter to Xerox Technical Minority Scholarship Program at above address.

811—XEROX TECHNICAL MINORITY SCHOLARSHIP (Summer Employment Program)

Xerox Square
Rochester NY 14644
Written inquiry

AMOUNT: Up to $5,000 (varies according to tuition and academic excellence)
DEADLINE(S): SEP 15
FIELD(S): Various engineering and science disciplines

Scholarships for minorities enrolled in a technical degree program at the bachelor level or above. Must be African-American, Native American, Hispanic, or Asian. Xerox will match your skills with a sponsoring organization that will offer a meaningful summer work experience complimenting your academic learning.

If above requirements are met, send your resume and a cover letter to Xerox Corporation Corporate Employment and College Relations Technical Minority Scholarship Program at above address.

SCHOOL OF HUMANITIES

812—AMERICAN BAR FOUNDATION (Summer Research Fellowships in Law and Social Science for Minority Undergraduate Students)

750 N. Lake Shore Drive
Chicago IL 60611
312/988-6500
Internet: www.abf-sociolegal.org

AMOUNT: $3,500 stipend
DEADLINE(S): MAR 1
FIELD(S): Social Sciences, Humanities, Law

Summer research opportunity open to sophomore and junior undergraduates who are Native American, African American, Mexican, Puerto Rican, or other minority. Must be US citizen or permanent resident and have at least a 3.0 GPA. Students are assigned a mentor and participate in seminars; must also work at the Foundation's office in Chicago for 35 hours per week for 10 weeks. Essay, transcripts, and letter of recommendation required.

4 awards annually; announced in April. See website or contact ABF for an application.

813—BUSINESS & PROFESSIONAL WOMEN'S FOUNDATION (BPW Career Advancement Scholarship Program)

2012 Massachusetts Ave. NW
Washington DC 20036-1070
202/293-1200, ext. 169
FAX: 202/861-0298
Internet: www.bpwusa.org

AMOUNT: $500-$1,000
DEADLINE(S): APR 15
FIELD(S): Biology, Science, Education, Engineering, Social Science, Paralegal, Humanities, Business, Math, Computers, Law, MD, DD

For women (US citizens) aged 25+ accepted into accredited program at US institution (+Puerto Rico & Virgin Islands). Must graduate within 12 to 24 months from the date of grant and demonstrate critical financial need. Must have a plan to upgrade skills, train for a new career field, or to enter/re-enter the job market.

Full- or part-time study. For info see website or send business-sized, self-addressed, double-stamped envelope.

814—CHAUTAUQUA INSTITUTION (Scholarships)

Schools Office
Box 1098, Dept. 6
Chautauqua NY 14722
716/357-6233
FAX: 716/357-6200

AMOUNT: Varies
DEADLINE(S): APR 1
FIELD(S): Art, Music, Dance, Theater

Scholarships for summer school only. Awards are based on auditions (portfolio in art) indicating proficiency. Financial need is a consideration. Some auditions are required in person, but taped auditions are also acceptable.

250 awards annually. Contact Chautauqua Institution for an application.

815—CIVIL AIR PATROL (CAP Undergraduate Scholarships)

Civil Air Patrol
National Headquarters
Maxwell AFB AL 36112-6332
334/953-5315

AMOUNT: $750
DEADLINE(S): JAN 31

FIELD(S): Humanities, Science,
Engineering, Education

Open to CAP members who have
received the Billy Mitchell Award or the
senior rating in Level II of the senior training program. For undergraduate study in
the above areas.

Write for complete information.

816—COLLEGE MISERICORDIA (Presidential Scholarships)

301 Lake Street
Dallas PA 18612-1098
800/852-7675
Internet: http://miseri.edu/scholar.htm

AMOUNT: Full or part tuition
DEADLINE(S): MAR 1
FIELD(S): Prelaw or the humanities

Scholarships for incoming freshmen to
this co-educational Catholic college in
Pennsylvania. High school senior applicants must rank in the upper 20% of their
classes and have achieved SAT or ACT
scores in the 8th percentile or better.

Obtain applications from the
Admissions Office.

817—FREEDOM FROM RELIGION FOUN-DATION (Student Essay Contest)

P.O. Box 750
Madison WI 53701
608/256-5800
Internet: www.infidels.org/org/ffrf

AMOUNT: $1,000; $500; $250
DEADLINE(S): JUL 15
FIELD(S): Humanities, English,
Education, Philosophy, Science

Essay contest on topics related to
church–state entanglement in public
schools or growing up a "freethinker" in
religious-oriented society. Topics change
yearly, but all are on general theme of
maintaining separation of church and state.
New topics available in February. For high
school seniors and currently enrolled col-
lege/technical students. Must be US citizen.

Send SASE to address above for complete information. Please indicate whether
wanting information for college competition or high school. Information will be
sent when new topics are announced each
February. See website for details.

818—INSTITUTE FOR HUMANE STUDIES (Humane Studies Fellowship)

4084 University Drive, Suite 101
Fairfax VA 22030-6812
703/934-6920 or 800/697-8799

FAX: 703/352-7535
E-mail: ihs@gmu.edu
Internet: www.theihs.org

AMOUNT: up to $12,000
DEADLINE(S): DEC 31
FIELD(S): Social Sciences, Law,
Humanities, Jurisprudence, Journalism

Awards are for graduate and advanced
undergraduate students pursuing degrees
at any accredited domestic or foreign
school. Based on academic performance,
demonstrated interest in classical liberal
ideas, and potential to contribute to the
advancement of a free society.

90 awards annually. Apply online or
contact IHS for an application.

819—INSTITUTE FOR HUMANE STUDIES (Summer Residential Program)

4084 University Drive, Suite 101
Fairfax VA 22030-6812
703/934-6920 or 800/697-8799
FAX: 703/352-7535
E-mail: ihs@gmu.edu
Internet: www.theihs.org

AMOUNT: All seminar fees: program
cost, room/board, materials, and books
DEADLINE(S): MAR 1
FIELD(S): Social Sciences, Humanities,
Law, Journalism, Public Policy,
Education, Writing

For college students, recent graduates,
and graduate students who share an interest in learning and exchanging ideas about
the scope of individual rights. One-week
and weekend seminars at various campus
locations across the US.

Apply online or contact IHS for an
application.

820—MIDWAY COLLEGE (Institutional Aid Program—Scholarships & Grants)

Financial Aid Office
Midway KY 40347
606/846-4421

AMOUNT: Varies
DEADLINE(S): MAR 1
FIELD(S): Nursing, Paralegal, Education,
Psychology, Biology, Equine Studies,
Liberal Studies, Business
Administration

Scholarships and grants open to women
who are accepted for enrollment at
Midway College. Awards support undergraduate study in the above areas.

Approx 80 awards per year. Write for
complete information.

821—NATIONAL FEDERATION OF THE BLIND (Humanities Scholarship)

805 5th Ave.
Grinnell IA 50112
515/236-3366

AMOUNT: $3,000
DEADLINE(S): MAR 31
FIELD(S): Humanities (Art, English,
Foreign Languages, History,
Philosophy, Religion)

Open to legally blind students pursuing
or planning to pursue a full-time postsecondary education in the US. Scholarships
are awarded on basis of academic excellence, service to the community, and financial need. Must include transcripts and two
letters of recommendation. Membership
NOT required.

1 award annually. Renewable. Contact
Mrs. Peggy Elliot, Scholarship Committee
Chairman, for an application.

822—NATIONAL ITALIAN AMERICAN FOUNDATION (Italian Cultural Society and NIAF Matching Scholarship)

1860 19th Street NW
Washington DC 20009-5599
202/530-5315

AMOUNT: $2,000
DEADLINE(S): MAR 31
FIELD(S): Science or Humanities

Open to undergraduate students of
Italian descent majoring in science or the
humanities in the Washington DC,
Maryland, and Virginia areas. Financial
need must be demonstrated.

Write for application and details.

823—NATIONAL ITALIAN AMERICAN FOUNDATION (Thomas Joseph "Willie" Ambrosole Scholarship)

1860 19th Street NW
Washington DC 20009
202/530-5315

AMOUNT: $1,000
DEADLINE(S): MAY 31
FIELD(S): Arts or Humanities

Open to undergraduate American students of Italian ancestry majoring in the
arts or humanities from the New York-
New Jersey area.

Academic merit, financial need, and
community service are considered. Contact
organization for application and details.

824—NORTH CAROLINA STATE UNIVERSITY (Thomas Jefferson Scholarship in Agriculture & Humanities)

115 Patterson Hall, Box 7642
Raleigh NC 27695-7642
Written inquiry

AMOUNT: $1,000
DEADLINE(S): MAR 1
FIELD(S): Agriculture AND Humanities

Open to first-year undergraduate students with a double major in agriculture and humanities who attend or plan to attend North Carolina State University.

Contact George Barthalmus for an application.

825—OPEN SOCIETY INSTITUTE (Environmental Management Fellowships)

400 West 59th Street
New York NY 10019
212/548-0600 or 212/757-2323
FAX: 212/548-4679 or
212/548-4600
Internet: www.soros.org/efp.html

AMOUNT: Fees, room, board, living
stipend, textbooks, international
transportation, health insurance
DEADLINE(S): NOV 15
FIELD(S): Earth Sciences, Natural
Sciences, Humanities (exc. language),
Anthropology, Sociology,
Mathematics, or Engineering

Two-year fellowships for use in selected universities in the US for international students. For students/professionals in fields related to environmental policy, legislation, and remediation techniques applicable to their home countries.

To apply, contact your local Soros Foundation or Open Society Institute. Further details on website.

826—PEW YOUNGER SCHOLARS PROGRAM (Graduate Fellowships)

G-123 Hesburgh Library
University of Notre Dame
Notre Dame IN 46556
219/631-4531
FAX: 219/631-8721
E-mail: Karen.M.Heinig.2@nd.edu
Internet: www.nd.edu/~pesp/pew/
PYSPHistory.html

AMOUNT: $13,000
DEADLINE(S): NOV 30
FIELD(S): Social Sciences, Humanities,
Theology

Program is for use at any Christian undergraduate school and most seminaries. Check with organization to see if your school qualifies. Apply during senior year. Recipients may enter a competition in which ten students will be awarded a $39,000 ($13,000/yr.) fellowship for three years of dissertation study. For use at top-ranked Ph.D. programs at outstanding universities.

NOT for study in medicine, law, business, performing arts, fine arts, or the pastorate. Check website and/or organization for details.

827—ROSE HILL COLLEGE (Louella Robinson Memorial Scholarship)

P.O. Box 3126
Aiken SC 29802-3126
800/684-3769
FAX: 803/641-0240
E-mail: rosehill@.edu
Internet: www.rosehill.edu

AMOUNT: $10,000/yr. for four years
DEADLINE(S): Varies
FIELD(S): Liberal Arts and Humanities
curricula

For undergraduate residents of Indian River County, Florida, to attend Rose Hill College in Aiken, South Carolina. The school offers a liberal arts education and follows the Great Books curriculum, a program of reading and seminars.

1 annual award. Applicants must meet entry requirements of RHC. Contact above location for details.

828—ROSE HILL COLLEGE (Scholarships for Children of Eastern Orthodox Priests/Deacons)

P.O. Box 3126
Aiken SC 29802-3126
800/684-3769
FAX: 803/641-0240
E-mail: rosehill@edu
Internet: www.rosehill.edu

AMOUNT: Full scholarship: $10,000/yr.
for four years
DEADLINE(S): Varies
FIELD(S): Liberal Arts and Humanities
curricula

For undergraduates who are children of Eastern Orthodox Christian priests or deacons to attend Rose Hill College in Aiken, South Carolina. The school offers a liberal arts education and follows the Great Books curriculum, a program of reading and seminars.

6-10 annual awards. Applicants must meet entry requirements of RHC. Contact above location for details.

829—ROSE HILL COLLEGE (Scholarships for the Homeschooled)

P.O. Box 3126
Aiken SC 29802-3126
800/684-3769
FAX: 803/641-0240
E-mail: rosehill@rosehill.edu
Internet: www.resehill.edu

AMOUNT: Full scholarship: $10,000/yr.
for four years
DEADLINE(S): Varies
FIELD(S): Liberal Arts and Humanities
curricula

For undergraduates who have been homeschooled for three of the last five years of their high school education. For use at Rose Hill College in Aiken, South Carolina. The school offers a liberal arts education and follows the Great Books curriculum, a program of reading and seminars. Scholarships will be awarded primarily on the basis of an essay which the student will be asked to write.

4 annual awards. Applicants must meet entry requirements of RHC. Contact above location for details.

830—SOPHIA SCHNITMAN EDUCATIONAL FOUNDATION (Scholarship)

c/o Oberlin College
101 N. Professor
Oberlin OH 44074
440/775-8569
E-mail: Laura.Stockwell@oberlin.edu

AMOUNT: $1,000
DEADLINE(S): Varies
FIELD(S): Conducting

An endowed scholarship fund that can only be used for needy and worthy women conservatory students at Oberlin College who are interested in conducting.

Contact Laura Stockwell, Director of Scholarship, Oberlin College, for more information.

831—UNITARIAN UNIVERSALIST ASSN. (Marion Barr Stanfield Art Scholarship)

25 Beacon Street
Boston MA 02108
617/742-2100

AMOUNT: Varies
DEADLINE(S): FEB 15
FIELD(S): Art

Art scholarships for undergraduate art students. Applicants must be Unitarian Universalists.

No phone calls please.

AREA STUDIES

832—AIR FORCE RESERVE OFFICER TRAINING CORPS (AFROTC Scholarships)

551 E. Maxwell Blvd.
Maxwell AFB AL 36112-6106
334/953-7783

AMOUNT: Full tuition, books, & fees for all 4 years of college
DEADLINE(S): DEC 1
FIELD(S): Science, Engineering, Business, Political Science, Psychology, Geography, Foreign Studies, Foreign Language

Competitive scholarships based on individual merit to high school seniors and graduates who have not completed any full-time college work. Must be a US citizen between the ages of 17-27. Must also have GPA of 2.5 or above, be in top 40% of class, and complete Applicant Fitness Test. Cannot be a single parent. Your college/university must offer AFROTC.

2,300 awards annually. Contact above address for application packet.

833—ALLIANCE FOR YOUNG ARTISTS AND WRITERS, INC./AMERICAN MUSEUM OF NATURAL HISTORY (Young Naturalist Awards)

Scholastic, Inc.
555 Broadway
New York NY 10012-3999
212/343-6582
800-SCHOLASTIC
FAX: 212/343-4885
E-mail: mjohnson@scholastic.com
Internet: www.amnh.org/youngnaturalistawards

AMOUNT: up to $2,500 + trip to New York to visit AMNH
DEADLINE(S): JAN 3
FIELD(S): Natural Sciences

For all students in grades 7-12 currently enrolled in a public or non-public school in the US, Canada, US territories, or US-sponsored schools abroad. Program focuses on finding and rewarding excellence in biology, earth science, astronomy, and cultural studies. Students are encouraged to perform observation-based projects that require creativity, inquiry, and critical analysis. Specific topics vary annually.

48 awards annually. See website or contact Mike Johnson, Program Manager, for an application.

834—AMERICAN ASSOCIATION OF TEACHERS OF FRENCH (National French Contest)

Sidney L. Teitelbaum
Box 32030
Sarasota FL 34278
FAX: 941/364-9820

AMOUNT: Varies
DEADLINE(S): FEB 4
FIELD(S): French Language, French Studies

National French contest is an examination taken throughout the country. Students are ranked regionally and nationally and are eligible for both local and national awards.

Not a scholarship. Winners receive trips, medals, and books. Write for complete information or ask your French teacher.

835—AMERICAN ASSOCIATION OF TEACHERS OF ITALIAN (College Essay in Italian)

Cal. State Univ.—Chico
Foreign Language Dept.
Chico CA 95929
Written inquiries

AMOUNT: $100-$300
DEADLINE(S): JUN 15
FIELD(S): Italian Language, Italian Studies

Contest open to undergraduate students at accredited colleges and universities in North America. Essay in Italian language on topic pertaining to literature or culture.

Write to Prof. Eugenio Frongia at address above for complete information.

836—AMERICAN BAR FOUNDATION (Summer Research Fellowships in Law and Social Science for Minority Undergraduate Students)

750 N. Lake Shore Drive
Chicago IL 60611
312/988-6500
Internet: www.abf-sociolegal.org

AMOUNT: $3,500 stipend
DEADLINE(S): MAR 1
FIELD(S): Social Sciences, Humanities, Law

Summer research opportunity open to sophomore and junior undergraduates who are Native American, African American, Mexican, Puerto Rican, or other minority. Must be US citizen or permanent resident and have at least a 3.0 GPA. Students are assigned a mentor and

participate in seminars; must also work at the Foundation's office in Chicago for 35 hours per week for 10 weeks. Essay, transcripts, and letter of recommendation required.

4 awards annually; announced in April. See website or contact ABF for an application.

837—ASSOCIATION FOR WOMEN IN PSYCHOLOGY/AMERICAN PSYCHOLOGICAL ASSOCIATION DIVISION 35 (Annual Student Research Prize)

Connecticut College
Box 548
270 Mohegan Ave.
New London CT 06320
860/439-2325
FAX: 860/439-5300

AMOUNT: $200
DEADLINE(S): APR 1
FIELD(S): Women's Issues

Undergraduate and graduate students may submit research papers relevant in some way to women's lives. Research can be either basic or applied. Entries should be of approximately journal length and written in APA style.

Send four copies of the paper and a self-addressed, stamped, postcard and business-sized envelope to Ingrid Johnston-Robledo, Ph.D., Department of Psychology, at the above address.

838—ASSOCIATION FOR WOMEN IN SCIENCE EDUCATIONAL FOUNDATION (Dr. Vicki L. Schechtman Scholarship)

1200 New York Ave. NW
Suite 650
Washington DC 20005
202/326-8940 or 800/886-AWIS
E-mail: awis@awis.org
Internet: www.awis.org

AMOUNT: $1,000
DEADLINE(S): JAN 16
FIELD(S): Various Sciences and Social Sciences

For female undergraduate students who are US citizens and have a minimum GPA of 3.0. Summary page, essay describing career aspirations, transcripts, proof of matriculation (if available), and two reference letters required with application. Scholarships may be used for tuition, books, housing, research, equipment, etc.

See website or write to above address for an application and more information.

839—ASSOCIATION FOR WOMEN IN SCI- ENCE EDUCATIONAL FOUNDATION (Ruth Satter Memorial Award)

1200 New York Ave. NW
Suite 650
Washington DC 20005
202/326-8940 or 800/886-AWIS
E-mail: awis@awis.org
Internet: www.awis.org

AMOUNT: $1,000
DEADLINE(S): JAN 16
FIELD(S): Various Sciences and Social
Sciences

Scholarships for female doctoral students who have interrupted their education three years or more to raise a family. Summary page, description of research project, resume, references, transcripts, biographical sketch, and proof of eligibility from department head required. US citizens may attend any graduate institution; noncitizens must be enrolled in US institutions.

See website or write to above address for more information or an application.

840—BLUES HEAVEN FOUNDATION, INC. (Muddy Waters Scholarship)

2120 S. Michigan Ave.
Chicago IL 60616
312/808-1286

AMOUNT: $2,000
DEADLINE(S): APR 30
FIELD(S): Music, Music Education,
African-American Studies, Folklore,
Performing Arts, Arts Management,
Journalism, Radio/TV/Film

Scholarship is made on a competitive basis with consideration given to scholastic achievement, concentration of studies, and financial need. Applicant must have full-time enrollment status in a Chicago area college/university in at least their first year of undergraduate studies or a graduate program. Scholastic aptitude, extracurricular involvement, grade point average, and financial need are all considered.

Contact Blues Heaven Foundation, Inc. to receive an application between February and April.

841—CENTER FOR 17TH- AND 18TH- CENTURY STUDIES (Fellowships)

UCLA
310 Reyce Hall
Los Angeles CA 90095-1404
310/206-8522
FAX: 310/206-8577
E-mail: c1718cs@humnet.ucla.edu

AMOUNT: $1,000-$18,400
DEADLINE(S): MAR 15
FIELD(S): British Literature/History
(17th & 18th Centuries)

Undergraduate stipends, graduate assistantships, and Ahmanson & Getty postdoctoral fellowships are for advanced study and research regarding British literature and history of the 17th and 18th centuries. Tenable at the William Andrews Clark Memorial Library at the University of California, Los Angeles.

Contact the Center for current year's theme and an application.

842—CHRISTIAN A. JOHNSON ENDEAV- OR FOUNDATION (Native American Fellows)

Harvard Univ.
79 John F. Kennedy Street
Cambridge MA 02138
617/495-1152
FAX: 617/496-3900
Internet: www.ksg.harvard.edu/
hpaied/cjohn.htm

AMOUNT: Varies
DEADLINE(S): MAY 1
FIELD(S): Social Sciences, Government,
or program related to Native
American studies

Fellowships for students of Native American ancestry who attend a John F. Kennedy School of Government degree program. Applicant, parent, or grandparent must hold membership in a federally or state-recognized tribe, band, or other organized group of Native Americans. Must be committed to a career in American Indian affairs. Awards based on merit and need.

Renewable, based on renomination and availability of funds. To apply, contact John F. Kennedy School of Government at above address.

843—COALITION FOR THE ADVANCE- MENT OF JEWISH EDUCATION (Abraham A. Spack Fellowship)

261 W. 35th Street, Fl. 12A
New York NY 10001
212/268-4210
FAX: 212/268-4214

AMOUNT: Up to $1,000
DEADLINE(S): APR 30
FIELD(S): Jewish Studies/Education

Scholarships for Jewish undergraduates pursuing education in Jewish Studies. For use at a four-year college.

Not renewable. Write for information.

844—DUMBARTON OAKS (The Bliss Prize Fellowship in Byzantine Studies)

1703 32nd Street, NW
Washington DC 20007-2961
202/339-6410

AMOUNT: Varies (estimated by the
graduate school in which successful
candidate enrolls for two academic
years)
DEADLINE(S): NOV 1 (nominations
due OCT 15)
FIELD(S): Byzantine Studies

Open to outstanding college seniors who plan to enter the field of Byzantine studies. Must be in last year of studies or already hold B.A. and have completed at least one year of Greek by January of senior year. Restricted to candidates currently enrolled or recent graduates of US or Canadian universities/colleges. Students must be nominated by their advisors.

Contact Dumbarton Oaks for complete information.

845—EAST-WEST CENTER (Undergraduate and Graduate Fellowships for Pacific Islanders)

1601 East-West Rd., Room 2066
Honolulu HI 96848-1601
808/944-7735
FAX: 808/944-7730

AMOUNT: Varies
DEADLINE(S): None given
FIELD(S): Asian Pacific Studies

Open to Pacific Islanders who wish to pursue studies relevant to development needs in the Pacific Islands region. Applicants should have a strong academic record and a desire to broaden their knowledge of the Pacific, Asia, and the US.

Write for complete information.

846—HILLEL FOUNDATION FOR JEWISH CAMPUS LIFE (Steinhardt Jewish Campus Service Corps)

900 Hilgard Ave.
Los Angeles CA 20036
310/208-5561
E-mail: rweisman@hillel.org
Internet: www.hillel.org

AMOUNT: $19,000
DEADLINE(S): MAR 6
FIELD(S): Student Leadership

Open to college seniors and recent college graduates with leadership skills and ability to create dynamic and innovative engagement strategies designed to reach

Jewish college students. Must possess commitment to service; willingness to use time, abilities, and talents to enhance lives of others; and dedication to strengthening Jewish identity among students with whom they work. Corps fellows get to know interests and concerns of students and build programs and activities to match.

100 awards annually. Renewable. See website or contact Rhonda Weisman for an application.

847—INSTITUT D'ETUDES FRANCAISES D'AVIGNON/BRYN MAWR COLLEGE (Scholarships for Summer Study in Avignon, France)

Institut d'etudes francaises d'Avignon
Bryn Mawr College
Bryn Mawr PA 19010-2899
610/526-5083
FAX: 610/526-7479
Internet: www.brynmawr.edu/
Adm/academic/special/avignon/
details.html

AMOUNT: Varies
DEADLINE(S): MAR 15
FIELD(S): French-related studies

Scholarships based on academic excellence and financial need for a six-week summer study program in Avignon, France. Program is offered to male and female students from other colleges as well as Bryn Mawr. For graduates and undergraduates who have completed three years of college-level French or equivalent.

Contact the Director of the Institute for application information.

848—INSTITUTE FOR HUMANE STUDIES (Humane Studies Fellowship)

4084 University Drive, Suite 101
Fairfax VA 22030-6812
703/934-6920 or 800/697-8799
FAX: 703/352-7535
E-mail: ihs@gmu.edu
Internet: www.theihs.org

AMOUNT: up to $12,000
DEADLINE(S): DEC 31
FIELD(S): Social Sciences, Law,
   Humanities, Jurisprudence, Journalism

Awards are for graduate and advanced undergraduate students pursuing degrees at any accredited domestic or foreign school. Based on academic performance, demonstrated interest in classical liberal ideas, and potential to contribute to the advancement of a free society.

90 awards annually. Apply online or contact IHS for an application.

849—IRISH AMERICAN CULTURAL INSTITUTE (Irish Way Scholarships)

1 Lackawanna Place
Morristown NJ 07960
973/605-1991

AMOUNT: $250-$1,000
DEADLINE(S): APR 1
FIELD(S): Irish Studies

A summer study and recreation program in Ireland. Open to 9th-12th grade high school students who have an interest in Irish culture and are US citizens. This is not a scholarship.

30-40 awards per year. Write for complete information.

850—JAMES MADISON MEMORIAL FELLOWSHIP (Fellowship for Teachers)

2000 K Street NW
Washington DC 20006
202/653-8700 or 800/525-6928
FAX: 202/653-6045
Internet: www.jamesmadison.com

AMOUNT: $24,000 prorated over study
   period
DEADLINE(S): MAR 1
FIELD(S): Teaching American
   History/Government, or Social
   Studies—concentration on the US
   Constitution

Fellowships for teachers (senior fellows) in grades 7-12 in the above fields to pursue an M.A. degree. Also for full-time college seniors and grad students (junior fellows). US citizens or US nationals. Fellows are selected from each state and from D.C., Puerto Rico, Guam, Virgin Islands, American Samoa, Northern Mariana Islands, and Palau. Program designed to enhance teaching about the US Constitution.

Application is on website or contact: American College Testing, P.O. Box 4030, Iowa City, IA 52243-4030; 800/525-6928

   E-mail: Recogprog@ACT-ACT4-PO. act.org

851—JAPANESE AMERICAN CITIZENS LEAGUE (Yoshiko Tanaka Memorial Scholarship)

1765 Sutter Street
San Francisco CA 94115
415/921-5225
FAX: 415/931-4671
E-mail: jacl@jacl.org
Internet: www.jacl.org

AMOUNT: $1,000-$5,000
DEADLINE(S): APR 1

FIELD(S): Japanese Language/Culture;
   U.S.-Japan Relations

Open to JACL members and their children only. For undergraduate students with an interest in Japanese language, culture, or the enhancement of US-Japan relations and who are planning to attend a college, university, trade school, business school, or any other institution of higher learning. Must submit personal statement, letters of recommendation, and transcripts. Financial need NOT a factor.

For membership information or an application, send a self-addressed, stamped envelope to above address, stating your level of study. Applications available October 1st through March 20th; recipients notified in July.

852—JEWISH VOCATIONAL SERVICE (E.E. Grosmann/I.S. Joseph Scholarship Program)

13100 Wayzata Blvd.
Minnetonka MN 55305
E-mail: jvs@jvsmn.org

AMOUNT: up to $2,500
DEADLINE(S): APR 1
FIELD(S): Jewish Studies/Communal
   Service

For Jewish undergraduate and graduate students who are Minnesota residents and show academic achievement and financial need.

10 awards annually. Renewable. Write to Leah Temkin at above address for an application.

853—JEWISH VOCATIONAL SERVICE (Recruitment Scholarship)

1500 S. Lilac Drive, Suite 311
Minneapolis MN 55416
Written inquiry

AMOUNT: To $2,500
DEADLINE(S): APR 1
FIELD(S): Jewish education

For Jewish undergraduates studying in the field of Jewish education. High school seniors may apply.

Must show scholastic achievement and financial need. Renewable. Must be sponsored by a Jewish community agency or institution. Write for complete information.

854—JEWISH WELFARE BOARD (Scholarships)

15 E. 26th Street
New York NY 10010
212/532-4949

AMOUNT: $1,000-$4,000
DEADLINE(S): FEB 1
FIELD(S): Social Work, Adult
   Education, Early Childhood
   Educaiton, Health Educaiton, Physical
   Education, Cultural Studies, Jewish
   Education

Scholarships for Jewish college juniors or seniors pursuing careers in the above fields. Must be committed to the work of the YMHA, YWHA, or Jewish community centers. Must do a year of field work in a Jewish community center.

Renewable. Contact organization for details.

855—JUNIATA COLLEGE (Baker Peace Scholarship)

Baker Institute
Peace & Conflict Studies
Huntingdon PA 16652-2119
814/641-3265

AMOUNT: $1,000-$2,000
DEADLINE(S): FEB 1
FIELD(S): Peace & Conflict Studies,
   International Affairs

Open to incoming freshmen at Juniata College who rank in the upper 20% of their high school class, have above-average SAT scores, and demonstrate an interest in peace-related issues. Must submit 1,000-word essay on designated topic, two letters of recommendation, and maintain a minimum 3.0 GPA.

Renewable up to 4 years. Contact Baker Institute for an application.

856—KOSCIUSZKO FOUNDATION (Study/Research Programs for Americans in Poland)

15 East 65th Street
New York NY 10021-6595
212/734-2130
FAX 212/628-4552
Internet: www.kosciuszkofoundation.
org/grants/poland.htm

AMOUNT: Varies
DEADLINE(S): JAN 15
FIELD(S): Polish Language, Literature,
   History, and/or Culture

Open to American students entering their junior or senior college year and graduate students enrolled in an M.A. or Ph.D program with the exception of Ph.D candidates at the dissertation level. For study at universities in Poland.

$50 nonrefundable application fee. Application is at website. Contact organization or visit website for complete information.

857—MEMORIAL FOUNDATION FOR JEWISH CULTURE (International Scholarship Program for Community Service)

15 East 26th Street, Room 1703
New York NY 10010
212/679-4074

AMOUNT: Varies
DEADLINE(S): NOV 30
FIELD(S): Jewish Studies

Open to any individual regardless of country of origin for undergrad study that leads to careers in the Rabbinate, Jewish education, social work, or as religious functionaries in Diaspora Jewish communities outside the US, Israel, and Canada.

Must commit to serve in a community of need for 3 years. Those planning to serve in the US, Canada, or Israel are excluded from this program. Write for complete information.

858—MEMORIAL FOUNDATION FOR JEWISH CULTURE (Soviet Jewry Community Service Scholarship Program)

15 East 26th Street, Room 1703
New York NY 10010
212/679-4074

AMOUNT: Not specified
DEADLINE(S): NOV 30
FIELD(S): Jewish studies

Open to Jews from the former Soviet Union enrolled or planning to enroll in recognized institutions of higher Jewish learning. Must agree to serve a community of Soviet Jews anywhere in the world for a minimum of three years.

Grants are to help prepare well qualified Soviet Jews to serve in the FSU. Write for complete information.

859—MINISTRY OF EDUCATION OF THE REPUBLIC OF CHINA (Scholarships for Foreign Students)

5 South Chung-Shan Road
Taipei, Taiwan
REPUBLIC OF CHINA
(86) (02) 356-5696
FAX: (86) (02) 397-6778

AMOUNT: NT$10,000 (per month)
DEADLINE(S): Varies (inquire of
   school)
FIELD(S): Chinese studies or language

Undergraduate and graduate scholarships are available to foreign students wishing to study in Taiwan. Must have already studied in R.O.C. for at least one term. Must study full time.

Scholarships are renewable. 300 awards per year. Write for complete information or please contact colleges directly.

860—NATIONAL ITALIAN AMERICAN FOUNDATION (Bolla Wines Scholarship)

1860 19th Street NW
Washington DC 20009-5599
202/530-5315

AMOUNT: $1,000
DEADLINE(S): MAY 31
FIELD(S): International studies—
   emphasis on Italian business or Italian-
   American history

For undergraduate or graduate students of Italian heritage with a GPA of 3.0+ and a background in international studies. Must write an essay on "The Importance of Italy in Today's Business World" (3-pages, double spaced, typed).

Community service and financial need considered. Write for appliacation and details.

861—NATIONAL ITALIAN AMERICAN FOUNDATION (NIAF/Pepperdine University Scholarship)

1860 19th Street NW
Washington DC 20009-5599
202/530-5315

AMOUNT: $2,000
DEADLINE(S): MAY 31
FIELD(S): International Program at
   Pepperdine University

For sophomore, junior, and senior students of Italian ancestry at Pepperdine University accepted into the International Program. Academic merit, community service, and financial need considered.

Call William B. Phillips at 310/456-4532.

862—NATIONAL ITALIAN AMERICAN FOUNDATION (Rose Basile Green Scholarship)

1860 19th Street NW
Washington DC 20009-5599
202/530-5315

AMOUNT: $1,000
DEADLINE(S): MAY 31
FIELD(S): Italian-American Studies

Open to undergraduates of Italian heritage whose emphasis is on Italian-American studies. Write a 2- to 3-page typed essay on a family member or a personality you consider: "An Italian American Hero."

Write for complete application information.

863—NORWEGIAN INFORMATION SERVICE (Norwegian Emigration Fund of 1975)

825 Third Ave, 38th Fl.
New York NY 10022-7584
212/421-7333

AMOUNT: Varies (NOK 5,000 to NOK 70,000)
DEADLINE(S): FEB 1
FIELD(S): History of Norwegian emigration and relations between the US and Norway

Purpose of the fund is to award scholarships to Americans for advanced or specialized studies in Norway of subjects dealing with emigration history and relations between Norway and the US.

Must be US citizen or resident. US institutions may also be eligible. Write for complete information.

864—OPEN SOCIETY INSTITUTE (Individual Project Fellowships)

400 West 59th Street
New York NY 10019
212/548-0600 or 212/757-2323
FAX: 212/548-4679 or 212/548-4600
Internet: www.soros.org/fellow/individual.html

AMOUNT: Varies
DEADLINE(S): Varies
FIELD(S): Any field of study related to creating an open society: reliance on the rule of law, the existence of a democratically elected government, a diverse and vigorous civil society, and respect for minorities and minority opinions

Two-year fellowships for use in selected universities in the US for international students. For students/professionals in fields related to environmental policy, legislation, and remediation techniques applicable to their home countries.

To apply, contact the Soros Foundation/Open Society Institute. Further details on website.

865—SMITHSONIAN INSTITUTION (Minority Student Internship Program)

Fellowships & Grants
955 L'Enfant Plaza, Suite 7000
MRC 902
Washington DC 20560
202/287-3271
FAX: 202/287-3691

E-mail: siofg@ofg.si.edu
Internet: www.si.edu/research+study

AMOUNT: $300/week + possible travel expenses
DEADLINE(S): FEB 15
FIELD(S): Humanities, Environmental Studies, Cultural Studies, Natural History, Earth Science, Art History, Biology, & related fields

Ten-week internships in residence at the Smithsonian for US minority students to participate in research or museum-related activities in above fields. For undergrads or grads with at least a 3.0 GPA. Essay, resume, transcripts, and references required with application. Internships are full-time and are offered for Summer, Fall, or Spring tenures.

Write for application.

866—SMITHSONIAN INSTITUTION (Native American Internship Program)

955 L'Enfant Plaza, Suite 7000
Washington DC 20560
202/287-3271
E-mail: http://www.si.edu/research+study
Internet: siofg@sivm.si.edu

AMOUNT: $250/wk. for undergrads; $300/wk. for grads.
DEADLINE(S): MAR 1; JUL 1; NOV 1
FIELD(S): Native American Studies

10-week internships for undergraduate and graduate Native American students to participate in research or museum activities related to Native American studies.

Travel allowance may be provided.

867—SONS OF NORWAY FOUNDATION (King Olav V Norwegian-American Heritage Fund)

1455 West Lake Street
Minneapolis MN 55408
612/827-3611

AMOUNT: $250-$3,000
DEADLINE(S): MAR 1
FIELD(S): Norwegian Studies

For US citizens 18 or older who have demonstrated a keen and sincere interest in the Norwegian heritage. Must be enrolled in a recognized educational institution and be studying such topics as arts, crafts, literature, history, music, folklore, etc., of Norway.

Financial need is a consideration but it is secondary to scholarship. 12 awards per year.

868—SONS OF NORWAY FOUNDATION (King Olav V Norwegian-American Heritage Fund)

1455 West Lake Street
Minneapolis MN 55408
Written inquiry

AMOUNT: $250-$3,000
DEADLINE(S): MAR 1
FIELD(S): American Studies

For Norwegian citizens 18 or older who have demonstrated a keen and sincere interest in the heritage of the United States. Must be enrolled in a recognized educational institution and be studying such topics as arts, crafts, literature, history, music, folklore, etc., of the US.

Financial need is a consideration but it is secondary to scholarship. 12 awards per year.

869—THE ALISA FLATOW MEMORIAL FUND (Scholarships for the Study of the Jewish Religion in Israel)

901 Route 10
Whippany NJ 07981
973/884-4800, ext. 195
Internet: www.ou.org/alisa/

AMOUNT: Varies
DEADLINE(S): Varies
FIELD(S): Jewish religion

Scholarships for students to study their Jewish religion in Israel. Established in honor of Alisa Flatow, a 20-year-old student from the US who was killed in a terrorist attack near the settlement of Kfar darom on April 9, 1995.

Contact the organization and/or website for details.

870—THE AMERICAN CLASSICAL LEAGUE (Ed Phinney Commemorative Scholarship)

Miami University
Oxford OH 45056
513/529-7741
FAX: 513/529-7742
E-mail: AmericanClassicalLeague@muohio.edu OR a.c.l@mich.edu
Internet: www.umich.edu/~acleague/phinney.html

AMOUNT: Up to $500
DEADLINE(S): JAN 15
FIELD(S): Teachers or teacher candidates in the classics (Latin and/or Greek)

Scholarships of up to $500 to apply to first-time attendance at the League's institute OR up to $500 to cover cost of other activities that serve to enhance a teacher's skills in the classroom in the classics OR up to $150 for purchase of materials from the ACL Teaching and Materials Resource Center. Memberships required except for first-time attendance at institute.

Send request for information to above address.

871—THE CENTER FOR CROSS-CULTURAL STUDY (Tuition Awards for Study in Seville, Spain)

446 Main Street
Amherst MA 01002-2314
413/256-0011 or 800/377-2621
FAX: 413/256-1968
E-mail: cccs@crocker.com
Internet: www.cccs.com

AMOUNT: $500
DEADLINE(S): Varies
FIELD(S): Study of Spanish and Spanish Culture

Partial tuition assistance is available at this facility in Spain. Applicants must submit an original essay in Spanish, between 2 or 3 double-spaced, typed pages. Also required are a short description in English of your experience with the Spanish language and culture and a faculty recommendation.

Awards are for one semester or academic year programs in Seville. Contact organization for specific details regarding the essays.

872—U.S. INSTITUTE OF PEACE (National Peace Essay Contest)

1200 17th Street NW, Suite 200
Washington DC 20036
202/429-3834
FAX 202/429-6063
E-mail: essay_contest@usip.org
Internet: www.usip.org

AMOUNT: $1,000-$10,000
DEADLINE(S): JAN 26
FIELD(S): Political Science, US History

1,500-word essay contest for high school students on the US response to international conflict. No restrictions as to citizenship/residency.

53 awards annually. Not renewable. See website or contact USIP for specific guidelines.

873—UNIVERSITY OF MARYLAND (John B. & Ida Slaughter Endowed Scholarship in Science, Technology, & the Black Community)

2169 Lefrak Hall
College Park MD 20742-7225
301/405-1158
FAX: 301/314-9867
Internet: www.bsos.umd.edu/aasp/scholarship.html

AMOUNT: Varies (in-state tuition costs)
DEADLINE(S): MAR
FIELD(S): Science & Technology AND African-American Studies

Open to African-Americans who are US residents with a minimum 2.8 GPA. Must be accepted to or enrolled at UMCP for freshman year and must submit letter of recommendation from high school counselor or UMCP faculty member. Should have an interest in applying science and technology to the problems of the black community. Essay required.

Renewable. Contact the Center for Minorities in Science & Engineering at UMCP for an application.

ART

874—ACADEMY OF MOTION PICTURE ARTS AND SCIENCES (Student Academy Awards)

8949 Wilshire Blvd.
Beverly Hills CA 90211-1972
310/247-3059, ext. 130
E-mail: ampas@ampas.org
Internet: www.ampas.org

AMOUNT: $1,000, $1,500, and $2,000
DEADLINE(S): APR 1
FIELD(S): Film production: alternative, animation, documentary, or dramatic

Student academy awards competition is open to students enrolled at a US college, university, film school, or art school. The film must have been made in a teacher-student relationship. No professional may be involved in the production.

Up to 5 awards each year. Award may not be used for educational purposes. Contact Richard Miller at above location or access website for complete information.

875—ADELPHI UNIVERSITY (Talent Awards)

1 South Ave.
Garden City NY 11530
516/877-3080

Internet: www.adelphi.edu/finaid/awards.html

AMOUNT: Up to $6,000
DEADLINE(S): FEB 15
FIELD(S): Theater, Dance, Art, or Music

Various scholarships for full-time students at Adelphi University in the above fields. Must document financial need—fill out a FAFSA form. Must maintain 3.0 GPA in major and 2.5 overall to maintain scholarship.

See website for further information; contact school to apply.

876—ALLIANCE FOR YOUNG ARTISTS AND WRITERS, INC. (Scholastic Art & Writing Awards)

Scholastic, Inc.
555 Broadway
New York NY 10012-3999
212/343-6582 or 800-SCHOLASTIC
FAX: 212/343-4885
E-mail: mjohnson@scholastic.com
Internet: www.scholastic.com/artandwriting/about.htm

AMOUNT: Varies
DEADLINE(S): Varies (upon location)
FIELD(S): Art, Writing

For all students in grades 7-12 currently enrolled in a public or non-public school in the US, Canada, US territories, or US-sponsored schools abroad. Awards are available in 10 writing categories and 16 art categories. Publishing opportunities may be available for winning students in both art and writing categories.

1,000+ awards annually. See website or contact Mike Johnson, Program Manager, for details and entry forms.

877—ALVIN M. BENTLEY FOUNDATION (Scholarship Program)

P.O. Box 1516
Owosso MI 48867
517/729-9040
FAX: 517/723-2454

AMOUNT: $40,000 (4-year); $1,000/yr. (freshman)
DEADLINE(S): None
FIELD(S): Literature, Science, Arts

Open to Michigan residents applying as freshmen to the University of Michigan's College of Literature, Science, and the Arts. Based on academic excellence and extracurricular activities. Must be nominated; there are no separate applications. Candidates are chosen from U of M applications received from Michigan resident freshmen.

4 four-year awards and 8 freshman awards annually. Contact University of Michigan for details.

878—AMERICAN INSTITUTE OF ARCHITECTS, NEW YORK CHAPTER (Haskell Awards for Student Architectural Journalism)

200 Lexington Ave., 6th Fl.
New York NY 10016
212/683-0023, ext. 14
AMOUNT: Varies
DEADLINE(S): FEB 13
FIELD(S): Architectural Writing

Awards to encourage fine writing on architecture and related design subjects and to foster regard for intelligent criticism among future professionals. For students enrolled in a professional architecture or related program, such as art history, interior design, urban studies, and landscape architecture. Submit a news story, an essay or feature article, book review, or journal accompanied by a 100-word statement describing the purpose of the piece.

Write to above location for complete information.

879—AMERICAN INTERCONTINENTAL UNIVERSITY (Emilio Pucci Scholarships)

Admissions Committee
3330 Peachtree Rd., NE
Atlanta GA 30326
404/812-8192 or 888/248-7392
AMOUNT: $1,800 (deducted from tuition over 6 quarters)
DEADLINE(S): None
FIELD(S): Fashion Design, Fashion Marketing, Interior Design, Commercial Art, Business Administration, Video Production

Scholarships are for high school seniors who are interested in either a 2-year or 4-year program at one of the campuses of the American Intercontinental University: Atlanta, GA; Los Angeles, CA; London, UK; or Dubai, United Arab Emirates. Scholarship is applied toward tuition.

Write for applications and complete information.

880—AMERICAN INTERCONTINENTAL UNIVERSITY (One-Year Tuition Scholarship)

Admissions Committee
3330 Peachtree Rd., NE
Atlanta GA 30326
404/812-8192 or 888/248-7392
AMOUNT: Tuition for one academic year
DEADLINE(S): MAR 15
FIELD(S): Fashion Design, Fashion Marketing, Interior Design, Commercial Art, Video Production

Scholarships are for high school juniors or seniors who are interested in studying in the above fields at one of the campuses of the American Intercontinental University: Atlanta, GA; Los Angeles, CA; London, UK; or Dubai, United Arab Emirates.

Write or call for applications and complete information.

881—AMERICAN MOTHERS, INC. (Gertrude Fogelson Cultural and Creative Arts Awards)

1296 E. 21st Street
Brooklyn NY 11201
718/253-5676
AMOUNT: Up to $1,000
DEADLINE(S): JAN 1 (annually)
FIELD(S): Visual Arts, Creative Writing, and Vocal Music

An award to encourage and honor mothers in artistic pursuits.

Write to Alice Miller at above address for details.

882—AMERICAN SOCIETY OF INTERIOR DESIGNERS EDUCATIONAL FOUNDATION (Yale R. Burge Competition)

608 Massachusetts Ave. NE
Washington DC 20002-6006
202/546-3480
FAX: 202/546-3240
E-mail: education@asid.org
Internet: www.asid.org
AMOUNT: $250-$500
DEADLINE(S): FEB 12
FIELD(S): Interior Design

Competition designed to encourage students to seriously plan their portfolios. Open to students in their final year of undergrad study who are enrolled in at least a three-year program of interior design. Portfolio components, submitted on slides, may be as few as eight, but are not to exceed twelve. Judged on presentation skills, design/planning competency, and conceptual creativity.

1 award of $500; 1 reserve award of $250; and up to 5 certificates of excellence. A $10 entry fee is required with registration by February 12th; actual entries must be postmarked by March 12th. Send self-addressed, stamped, legal-sized envelope to ASID for an application.

883—AMERICAN SOCIETY OF INTERIOR DESIGNERS EDUCATIONAL FOUNDATION (S. Harris Memorial Scholarship)

608 Massachussetts Ave. NE
Washington DC 20002-6006
202/546-3480
FAX: 202/546-3240
E-mail: education@asid.org
Internet: www.asid.org
AMOUNT: $1,500
DEADLINE(S): MAR 5
FIELD(S): Interior Design

To assist talented undergraduate students of interior design enrolled at degree-granting academic institutions. A student must be in at least his/her second year of studies to be eligible. Awards based on financial need and academic/creative accomplishment, as demonstrated by transcripts and letters of recommendation from faculty.

1 award annually. Send self-addressed, stamped, legal-sized envelope to ASID for an application.

884—AMERICAN SOCIETY OF INTERIOR DESIGNERS EDUCATIONAL FOUNDATION (Joe Polsky-Fixtures Furniture Prize)

608 Massachusetts Ave. NE
Washington DC 20002-6006
202/546-3480
FAX: 202/546-3240
E-mail: education@asid.org
Internet: www.asid.org
AMOUNT: $1,000
DEADLINE(S): MAR 15
FIELD(S): Interior Design

This award is given to recognize outstanding academic contribution to the discipline of interior design through literature or visual communication. Material will be judged on innovative subject matter, comprehensive coverage of topic, organization, graphic presentation, bibliography, and references.

1 award annually. Send self-addressed, stamped, legal-sized envelope to ASID for an application.

885—AMERICAN SOCIETY OF INTERIOR DESIGNERS EDUCATIONAL FOUNDATION (Joel Polsky-Fixtures Furniture Academic Achievement Award)

608 Massachusetts Ave., NE
Washington DC 20002-6006
202/546-3480
FAX: 202/546-3240
E-mail: education@asid.org

Internet: www.asid.org

AMOUNT: $1,000

DEADLINE(S): MAR 15

FIELD(S): Interior Design

For an outstanding undergraduate or graduate student's interior design research or thesis project related to interior design topics. Entries judged on content, breadth of material, comprehensive coverage of topic, innovative subject matter, and bibliography/references.

1 award annually. Send self-addressed, stamped, legal-sized envelope to ASID for an application.

886—ART INSTITUTE OF SOUTHERN CALIFORNIA (Scholarships)

2222 Laguna Canyon Road
Laguna Beach CA 92651
714/376-6000
FAX: 714/376-6009

AMOUNT: $500-$2,000

DEADLINE(S): MAY 1

FIELD(S): Art, Design

Open to undergraduate art students at the Art Institute of Southern California. Merit scholarships are based on the strength of the student's portfolio. Students must be US citizens and have a GPA of at least 2.5. Some applicants may be asked to fill out a Free Application for Federal Student Aid (FAFSA).

Contact the Art Institute for an application and/or FAFSA form.

887—ASIFA (Helen Victoria Haynes World Peace Storyboard & Animation Contest)

3400 W. 111th Street, Box 324
Chicago IL 60655
E-mail: morgPk@aol.com
Internet: www.swcp.com/~asifa/whatsnew.htm

AMOUNT: $500 + software & ASIFA conference registration

DEADLINE(S): APR 30

FIELD(S): Animation, Cartooning

For high school and college students to design, draw, and mount a storyboard for an animated short for the Annual ASIFA/Central Conference & Retreat. The storyboard should depict your vision of how to achieve World Peace.

2 prize packages: 1 for high school students and 1 for college students. See website for official rules or contact Mary Lou Haynes at above address for more information.

888—BINNEY & SMITH INC.-LIQUITEX (Liquitex Student Paint Exchange)

1100 Church Lane
P.O. Box 431
Easton PA 18044-0431
610/253-6272*4233

AMOUNT: Free Paint & Mediums awarded

DEADLINE(S): Varies (25th of each month)

FIELD(S): Art

Open to undergraduate or graduate students who are US or Canadian citizens. Students must be enrolled in an accredited program.

Send an SASE to the above address for application.

889—BLUES HEAVEN FOUNDATION, INC. (Muddy Waters Scholarship)

2120 S. Michigan Ave.
Chicago IL 60616
312/808-1286

AMOUNT: $2,000

DEADLINE(S): APR 30

FIELD(S): Music, Music Education, African-American Studies, Folklore, Performing Arts, Arts Management, Journalism, Radio/TV/Film

Scholarship is made on a competitive basis with consideration given to scholastic achievement, concentration of studies, and financial need. Applicant must have full-time enrollment status in a Chicago area college/university in at least their first year of undergraduate studies or a graduate program. Scholastic aptitude, extracurricular involvement, grade point average, and financial need are all considered.

Contact Blues Heaven Foundation, Inc. to receive an application between February and April.

890—BOSTON SAFE DEPOSIT & TRUST CO. (Blanche E. Colman Awards)

One Boston Place
Boston MA 02108
617/722-7340

AMOUNT: $500 to $5,000

DEADLINE(S): MAR 1

FIELD(S): Art (career support—NOT for students)

Open to mature artists age 21 and over who are perm. residents of New England (MA, NH, RI, VT, ME) and who have completed academic education. Recommendations from art professionals are required.

Must provide copy of U.S. tax return to show need.

Award is for career support. It is NOT a scholarship. Students are ineligible. Write for complete information.

891—BUENA VISTA COLLEGE NETWORK (Internships in Film Marketing)

3900 W. Alameda Ave.
Burbank CA 91505-4316
818/567-5000
E-mail: College_Network@studio.disney.com

AMOUNT: Varies

DEADLINE(S): None

FIELD(S): Fields of study related to the motion picture industry, including marketing and promotion

Internships for full-time college students age 18 and up interested in a career in a facet of the motion picture industry. Must have unlimited access to computer with modem and transportation, be able to work 4-6 hours per week and 2-3 weekends per month. Attend film openings and sneak previews. Evaluate various aspects via an interactive computer system. Compensation ranges from $30 to $60/month. Possible school credit.

Access website by writing "Buena Vista College Network" from Yahoo. Available in most states and parts of Canada. Details, an interactive application, and e-mail access are located on website.

892—CALIFORNIA COLLEGE OF ARTS & CRAFTS (Scholarships)

450 Irwin Street
San Francisco CA 94107-2207
415/703-9500 or 800/447-1278

AMOUNT: Varies

DEADLINE(S): MAR 1

FIELD(S): Art

Open to undergraduate and graduate students accepted to or enrolled in a degree program at the California College of Arts and Crafts. Must be a US citizen or legal resident and demonstrate financial need.

600 awards annually. Renewable. Contact the Office of Enrollment Services for an application.

893—CLAYFOLK (Ellice T. Johnston Scholarship)

P.O. Box 274
Talent OR 97540
Written inquiry

AMOUNT: $1,000
DEADLINE(S): JUN 15
FIELD(S): Ceramic Arts

Scholarship for upper division students of ceramic arts who reside either in Oregon or Northern California. Must be enrolled in an accredited college, university, or art school.

Submit FAFSA form or 1040 tax form from previous year.

894—COMMUNITY FOUNDATION OF WESTERN MASSACHUSETTS (Joseph Bonfitto Scholarship)

1500 Main Street
P.O. Box 15769
Springfield MA 01115
413/732-2858

AMOUNT: $2,000
DEADLINE(S): APR 15
FIELD(S): Creative Design, Advertising, Art

Open to graduating seniors of Agawam High School in Massachusetts who are pursuing a career through higher education in one of the above areas of study. Based on financial need, academic merit, and extracurricular activities. Must submit transcripts and fill out government FAFSA form.

1 award annually. Renewable with reapplication. Send self-addressed, stamped envelope to Community Foundation for an application and contact your financial aid office for FAFSA. Notification is in June.

895—COUNCIL FOR BASIC EDUCATION (Arts Education Fellowships)

2506 Buckelew Drive
Falls Church VA 22046
703/876-5782

AMOUNT: $2,800 stipend + $200 grant to school
DEADLINE(S): JAN
FIELD(S): Teaching of the arts (visual arts, creative writing, dance, media, music, theatre)

Fellowships for K-12 teachers in the above fields, artist-teachers, or professional artists who teach at least 20 hours per week. Funding from the National Endowment for the Arts and the Getty Center for Education in the Arts, and others.

Contact organization for details.

896—DISTRICT OF COLUMBIA COMMISSION ON THE ARTS & HUMANITIES (Grants)

410 Eighth Street NW, 5th Fl.
Washington DC 20004
202/724-5613
TDD: 202/727-3148

FAX: 202/727-4135
AMOUNT: $2,500
DEADLINE(S): MAR 1
FIELD(S): Performing Arts, Literature, Visual Arts

Applicants for grants must be professional artists and residents of Washington DC for at least one year prior to submitting application. Awards intended to generate art endeavors within the Washington DC community.

Open also to art organizations that train, exhibit, or perform within DC. 150 grants per year. Write for complete information.

897—FASHION GROUP INTERNATIONAL OF GREATER WASHINGTON DC (Scholarships)

P.O. Box 71055
Chevy Chase MD 20813-1055
212/593-1715 (in New York)
Internet: fgi.org/washington.htm

AMOUNT: Up to $2,500
DEADLINE(S): APR 1
FIELD(S): Fashion-related areas

Scholarshps for students majoring in fashion-related fields. Must be permanent residents of the Greater Metropolitan Washington DC area. Must either graduate from high school in June and/or have been admitted to an accredited institution or be enrolled in a university or college as an undergraduate or graduate student.

Application form and details are available on website or contact organization for further information.

898—FASHION INSTITUTE OF TECHNOLO-GY (Scholarships)

Financial Aid Office
Seventh Ave. @ 27th Street
New York NY 10001-5992
212/217-7684 or 800/GO-TO-FIT
E-mail: FITinfo@sfitva.cc.fitsuny.edu
Internet: www.fitnyc.suny.edu

AMOUNT: Varies
DEADLINE(S): MAR 1
FIELD(S): Fashion Design

The institute provides scholarships, loans, grants, and college work-study jobs for eligible applicants who wish to attend F.I.T. US citizenship or permanent residency required. Financial need considered.

Write for complete information.

899—FLORIDA DEPARTMENT OF STATE—ARTS COUNCIL (Individual Artists' Fellowships)

Division of Cultural Affairs
The Capitol
Tallahassee FL 32399-0250
850/487-2980
TDD: 850/488-5779
FAX: 850/922-5259
Internet: www.dos.state.fl.us

AMOUNT: $5,000
DEADLINE(S): JAN 15
FIELD(S): Dance, Choreography, Poetry, Literature, Music, Music Composition, Theatre, Visual Arts, Film, Crafts, Fiction, Interdisciplinary

Open to legal residents of Florida who are professional creative artists of at least 18 years of age. May NOT be enrolled in any undergraduate or graduate degree-seeking program during fellowship period.

38 awards annually. Renewable with reapplication after four years since date of previous award. Contact Florida Arts Council for information packet. Notification during summer.

900—FOUNDATION OF FLEXOGRAPHIC TECHNICAL ASSOCIATION (Flexographic Scholarship)

900 Marconi Ave.
Ronkonkoma NY 11779
516/737-6020
FAX: 516/737-6813
E-mail: srubin@vax.ftafftta.org
Internet: www.fta-ffta.org

AMOUNT: $2,000
DEADLINE(S): MAR 19
FIELD(S): Graphic Communication—Flexography

Must have a GPA of at least 3.0 and be going to a school offering flexography as a course of study. Must be a high school senior going to college (proof required), or a college sophomore, junior, or senior.

19 awards per year. Renewable. Contact Shelley Rubin at above address for an application.

901—GENERAL FEDERATION OF WOMEN'S CLUBS OF MASSACHUSETTS (Scholarship to attend the Art Institute of Boston)

245 Dutton Road, Box 679
Sudbury MA 01776-0679
508/229-2023

AMOUNT: $1,000
DEADLINE(S): MAR 1
FIELD(S): Art

For a Massachusetts high school senior to attend the Art Institute of Boston their freshman year. Must have completed admissions application, submitted the school's application for financial aid, completed financial aid form to College Scholarship Service, and completed application form in duplicate to chairman in order to apply.

1 scholarship annually. For more information or an application, send a self-addressed, stamped envelope to Marilyn Perry, Scholarship Chairman, at above address. For more info on the Institute, call 617/262-1223. Or write to 700 Beacon Street, Boston, MA 02215.

902—GENERAL FEDERATION OF WOMEN'S CLUBS OF MASSACHUSETTS (Pennies for Art)

P.O. Box 679
Sudbury MA 01776-0679
508/283-4040

AMOUNT: $500
DEADLINE(S): FEB 1
FIELD(S): Art

Scholarship for a senior in a Massachusetts high school who will major in art in a college or university. Letter of endorsement from sponsoring GFWC of MA, personal letter stating goals, letter of recommendation from a high school art instructor, and portfolio of three examples of original work are required with application.

For more information or an application, send a self-addressed, stamped envelope to Betty Porter, Chairman, Arts & Crafts Division, at above address.

903—GEORGE BIRD GRINNELL AMERICAN INDIAN CHILDREN'S FUND (Al Qoyawayma Award)

11602 Montague Ct.
Potomac MD 20854
301/424-2440
FAX: 301/424-8281
E-mail: Grinnell_Fund@MSN.com

AMOUNT: $1,000
DEADLINE(S): JUN 1
FIELD(S): Science, Engineering

Open to Native American undergraduate and graduate students majoring in science or engineering and who have demonstrated an outstanding interest and skill in any one of the arts. Must be American Indian/Alaska Native (documented with Certified Degree of Indian Blood), be enrolled in college/university, be able to

demonstrate commitment to serving community or other tribal nations, and document financial need.

Contact Dr. Paula M. Mintzies, President, for an application after January 1st.

904—HAYSTACK MOUNTAIN SCHOOL OF CRAFTS (Scholarship Program)

Admissions Office
P.O. Box 518
Deer Isle ME 04627
207/348-2306

AMOUNT: $500-$1,000
DEADLINE(S): MAR 25
FIELD(S): Crafts

Open to technical assistants and work-study students in graphics, ceramics, weaving, jewelry, glass, blacksmithing, fabric, or wood. Tenable for one of the six two- to three-week summer sessions at Haystack Mountain School. One year of graduate study or equivalent experience is required for TA applicants.

Contact Candy Haskell for an application.

905—HOME FASHION PRODUCTS ASSN. (Home Textile Surface Design Competition)

355 Lexington Ave.
New York NY 10017
212/661-4261

AMOUNT: $1,000
DEADLINE(S): OCT 30
FIELD(S): Home textile surface design

Annual home furnishings textile design competition open to undergraduate students enrolled in an accredited 2-year or 4-year school of art or design. Must have completed one year of college level study in this field. Not for interior design students.

Applications accepted from department chairman only—NOT individuals. Write for complete information.

906—ILLINOIS ARTS COUNCIL (Artists Fellowship Awards)

100 W. Randolph, Suite 10-500
Chicago IL 60601-3298
312/814-6750

AMOUNT: $500; $5,000; $10,000
DEADLINE(S): SEP 1
FIELD(S): Choreography, Visual Arts, Poetry Prose, Film, Video, Playwriting, Music Composition, Crafts, Ethnic &

Folk Arts, Performance Art, Photography, Audio Art.

Open to professional artists who are Illinois residents. Awards are in recognition of work in the above areas; they are not for continuing study. Students are NOT eligible.

Write to address above for application form.

907—JAPANESE AMERICAN CITIZENS LEAGUE (Henry & Chiyo Kuwahara Creative Arts Award)

1765 Sutter Street
San Francisco CA 94115
415/921-5225
FAX: 415/931-4671
E-mail: jacl@jacl.org
Internet: www.jacl.org

AMOUNT: $1,000-$5,000
DEADLINE(S): APR 1
FIELD(S): Creative Arts

Open to JACL members and their children only. For undergraduate and graduate students planning to attend a college, university, trade school, or any other institution of higher learning. Purpose is to encourage creative projects that reflect the Japanese-American experience and culture. All techinical work of the applicant should be university level. Professional artists NOT eligible.

For membership information or an application, send a self-addressed, stamped envelope to above address, stating your level of study. Applications available October 1st through March 20th; recipients notified in July.

908—JOHN K. & THIRZA F. DAVENPORT FOUNDATION (Scholarships in the Arts)

20 North Main Street
South Yarmouth MA 02664-3143
508/398-2293
FAX: 508/394-6765

AMOUNT: Varies
DEADLINE(S): JUL 15
FIELD(S): Theatre, Music, Art

For Barnstable County, Massachusetts residents in their last two years of undergraduate or graduate (preferred) study in visual or performing arts. Must demonstrate financial need.

6-8 awards annually. Renewable. Contact Mrs. Chris M. Walsh for more information.

909—LADIES AUXILIARY TO THE VETERANS OF FOREIGN WARS OF THE UNITED STATES (Young American Creative Patriotic Art Awards)

406 West 34th Street
Kansas City MO 64111
816/561-8655
FAX: 816/931-4753

AMOUNT: $3,000 (1st prize); $2,000 (2nd); $1,500 (3rd); $1,000 (4th); $500 (5th)
DEADLINE(S): JAN 1
FIELD(S): Art

An opportunity for high school students to display their artistic talents and to demonstrate their American patriotism while at the same time be eligible to compete for educational funds. Art must be on paper or canvas. Watercolor, pencil, pastel, charcoal, tempera, crayon, acrylic, pen-and-ink, or oil may be used.

Contact local VFW auxiliary office or Judy Millick, Administrator of Programs, at above address for details.

910—LIBERACE FOUNDATION FOR THE PERFORMING AND CREATIVE ARTS (Scholarship Fund)

1775 East Tropicana Avenue
Las Vegas NV 89119-6529
Internet: www.liberace.org

AMOUNT: Varies
DEADLINE(S): MAR 15
FIELD(S): Music, Theatre, Dance, Visual Arts

Provides grants to accredited INSTITUTIONS that offer training in above fields. Grants are to be used exclusively for scholarship assistance to talented and deserving students. Recipients should be promising and deserving upperclassmen (Jr., Sr., Graduate) enrolled in a course of study leading up to a career in the arts.

NO DIRECT-TO-STUDENT GRANTS ARE MADE. Student's school must apply on their behalf. See website or write to above address for details.

911—LIGHT WORK (Artist-in-Residence Program)

316 Waverly Avenue
Syracuse NY 13244
315/443-1300
FAX: 315/443-9516
E-mail: cdlight@syr.edu

AMOUNT: $2,000 stipend
DEADLINE(S): None
FIELD(S): Photography

Career support for mid-career professional artists from around the world working with photography or digital imaging. Residency is for one month, and financial need is NOT considered.

12-15 awards annually. Not renewable. Contact Jeffrey Hoone, Director, at above address for an application.

912—MEMPHIS COLLEGE OF ART (Portfolio Awards)

Overton Park
1930 Poplar Ave.
Memphis TN 38104-2764
901/726-4085

AMOUNT: $500-$11,450 (full tuition) per year
DEADLINE(S): Varies (NOV 15 through JUL 31)
FIELD(S): Visual Arts

Awards are given to excellent visual art portfolios submitted by either high school students or transfer students. Awards to be used for full-time enrollment at Memphis College of Art. International students are welcome.

Awards are renewable for four years. Write for complete information.

913—METROPOLITAN MUSEUM OF ART (Internships)

1000 Fifth Ave.
New York NY 10028-0198
212/570-3710
Internet: www.metmuseum.org

AMOUNT: $2,750 (grads); $2,500 (juniors & seniors); up to $12,000 for certain longer programs
DEADLINE(S): JAN; FEB
FIELD(S): Art History

Internships for undergraduates and graduates who intend to pursue careers in art museums. Programs vary in length and requirements. Interns work in curatorial, education, conservation, administration, or library department of museum. Some require demonstration of economic need. Duration ranges from nine weeks to ten months. Volunteer positions also available.

Contact Marcie Karp for details.

914—MINNESOTA STATE ARTS BOARD (Grants Program)

Park Square Ct.
400 Sibley Street, Suite 200
St. Paul MN 55101-1928
651/215-1600

AMOUNT: $8,000 (fellowships); $500-$1,500 (grants)
DEADLINE(S): AUG (Visual Arts); SEP (Music & Dance); OCT (Literature & Theatre)
FIELD(S): Literature, Music, Theater, Dance, Visual Arts

Fellowships and career opportunity grants are open to professional artists who are residents of Minnesota. Grants may NOT be used for support of tuition or work toward any degree.

Contact MSAB for an application.

915—NATIONAL ENDOWMENT FOR THE ARTS (Visual Artists Fellowships)

1100 Pennsylvania Ave. NW
Washington DC 20506
202/682-5448

AMOUNT: $15,000-$20,000
DEADLINE(S): JAN; FEB; MAR
FIELD(S): Visual Arts

Fellowships open to practicing professional artists of exceptional talent in all areas of the visual arts. Awards are to assist creative development. They will not support academic study. US citizen or legal resident.

Students are NOT eligible to apply. Write for complete information.

916—NATIONAL FEDERATION OF THE BLIND (Humanities Scholarship)

805 5th Ave.
Grinnell IA 50112
515/236-3366

AMOUNT: $3,000
DEADLINE(S): MAR 31
FIELD(S): Humanities (Art, English, Foreign Languages, History, Philosophy, Religion)

Open to legally blind students pursuing or planning to pursue a full-time postsecondary education in the US. Scholarships are awarded on basis of academic excellence, service to the community, and financial need. Must include transcripts and two letters of recommendation. Membership NOT required.

1 award annually. Renewable. Contact Mrs. Peggy Elliot, Scholarship Committee Chairman, for an application.

917—NATIONAL FOUNDATION FOR ADVANCEMENT IN THE ARTS (Arts Recognition and Talent Search)

800 Brickell Ave.
Miami FL 33131

800/970-ARTS or 305/377-1140
FAX: 305/377-1149
Internet: www.nfaa.org

AMOUNT: $100-$3,000
DEADLINE(S): OCT 1
FIELD(S): Creative & Performing Arts

Talent contest for high school seniors and 17- and 18-year-olds in dance, jazz, music, photography, theatre, visual arts, voice, and writing. Except for those applying in Music/Jazz, applicants must be US citizens or permanent residents. May apply in more than one category, but only one financial award will be given to any individual, and a fee is required for each category in which student applies.

$35 application fee ($25 if apply by June 1st); fee may be waived if you are unable to meet this requirement. 400 awards annually. Not renewable. Contact NFAA for an application packet.

918—NATIONAL FOUNDATION FOR ADVANCEMENT IN THE ARTS (Fellowships in the Visual Arts)

800 Brickell Ave., Suite 500
Miami FL 33131
800/970-ARTS or 305/377-1147
FAX: 305/377-1149
E-mail: nfaa@nfaa.org
Internet: www.nfaa.org

AMOUNT: $1,000/mo. + housing, studio space, and funds for supplies
DEADLINE(S): Varies
FIELD(S): Visual Arts

Fellowships for emerging visual artists to work in a supportive through the Career Advancement in Visual Arts (CAVA) residency program in Miami Beach, Florida. Work will be exhibited at the Corcoran Gallery of Art in Washington DC.

Contact organization for details. Can apply online at above website.

919—NATIONAL ITALIAN AMERICAN FOUNDATION (Gianni Versace Scholarship in Fashion Design)

1860 19th Street NW
Washington DC 20009-5599
202/530-5315

AMOUNT: $1,000
DEADLINE(S): MAY 31
FIELD(S): Fashion Design

For undergraduates of Italian ancestry who are pursuing degrees and careers in fashion design.

Considerations are academic merit, financial need, and commmunity service. Write for application and further information.

920—NATIONAL ITALIAN AMERICAN FOUNDATION (Nerone/NIAF Matching Art Scholarship)

1860 19th Street NW
Washington DC 20009-5599
202/530-5315

AMOUNT: $1,000
DEADLINE(S): MAY 31
FIELD(S): Art

For students of Italian ancestry who are art majors.

Financial need, community service, and academic merit are considered.

921—NATIONAL ITALIAN AMERICAN FOUNDATION (Thomas Joseph "Willie" Ambrosole Scholarship)

1860 19th Street NW
Washington DC 20009
202/530-5315

AMOUNT: $1,000
DEADLINE(S): MAY 31
FIELD(S): Arts or Humanities

Open to undergraduate American students of Italian ancestry majoring in the arts or humanities from the New York-New Jersey area.

Academic merit, financial need, and community service are considered. Contact organization for application and details.

922—NATIONAL LEAGUE OF AMERICAN PEN WOMEN, INC. (Scholarships for Mature Women)

1300 17th Street NW
Washington DC 20036
717/225-3023

AMOUNT: $1,000
DEADLINE(S): JAN 15 (even-numbered years)
FIELD(S): Art, Music, Creative Writing

The National League of American Pen Women gives three $1,000 grants in even-numbered years to women aged 35 and over. Should submit three 4 x 6 or bigger color prints, manuscripts, or musical compositions suited to the criteria for the year.

Send SASE for details at the above address.

923—NATIONAL SCHOLARSHIP TRUST FUND OF THE GRAPHIC ARTS (Scholarships & Fellowships)

200 Deer Run Road
Sewickley PA 15143-2600
412/741-6860

FAX: 412/741-2311
E-mail: nstf@gatf.org
Internet: www.gatf.org

AMOUNT: $1,000-$1,500
DEADLINE(S): MAR 1 (high school seniors); APR 1 (undergraduates); JAN 10 (graduate students)
FIELD(S): Printing, Publishing, Graphic Technology

Scholarships for high school seniors and college undergraduates, and fellowships for graduate students. Must be US citizen, have a minimum 3.0 cumulative GPA, and be pursuing a career in the printing and/or graphic technology industry. Financial need NOT a factor.

350 awards annually. Renewable. Contact Kristin Winkowski at NSTF for an application.

924—NATIONAL SCULPTURE SOCIETY (Alex J. Ettl Grant)

1177 Ave. of the Americas
New York NY 10036
212/764-5645
FAX: 212/764-5651
E-mail: NSS1893@aol.com
Internet: www.sculptor.org

AMOUNT: $5,000
DEADLINE(S): OCT 31
FIELD(S): Sculpture

Open to US citizens or residents who are realist or figurative sculptors and have demonstrated a commitment to sculpting with outstanding ability. Applicants must submit at least ten 8 x 10 photos of work and a brief autobiography. May not be sculptor members of the National Sculpture Society.

Send a self-addressed, stamped envelope to above address for an application.

925—NATIONAL SCULPTURE SOCIETY (Young Sculptor Awards Competition)

1177 Ave. of the Americas
New York NY 10036
212/764-5645
FAX: 212/764-5651
E-mail: NSS1893@aol.com
Internet: www.sculptor.org

AMOUNT: $1,000 (1st place); $750 (2nd); $500 (3rd); $250 (4th)
DEADLINE(S): MAY 31
FIELD(S): Sculpture

Competition is open to sculptors at the beginning of their careers who are residents of the US. A jury of professional sculptors will make their selections based upon 5-10 black & white 8 x 10 photos of each entrant's works. In addition to cash awards and prizes, photos of winners' works will be published in *Sculpture Review* magazine.

Send a self-addressed, stamped envelope to above address for an application.

926—NAVAL HISTORICAL CENTER (Internship Program)

Washington Navy Yard
901 M Street SE
Washington DC 20374-5060
202/433-6901
FAX: 202/433-8200
E-mail: efurgol@nhc.navy.mil
Internet: www.history.navy.mil

AMOUNT: $400 possible honoraria; otherwise, unpaid
DEADLINE(S): None
FIELD(S): Education, History, Public Relations, Design

Registered students of colleges/universities and graduates thereof are eligible for this program, which must be a minimum of 3 weeks, full or part-time. Four specialities available: Curator, Education, Public Relations, and Design. Interns receive orientation and assist in their departments, and must complete individual project which contributes to Center. Must submit a letter of recommendation, unofficial transcript, and writing sample of not less than 1,000 words.

Contact Dr. Edward M. Furgol, Curator, for an application.

927—NEW YORK STATE THEATRE INSTITUTE (Internships in Theatrical Production)

155 River Street
Troy NY 12180
518/274-3573
E-mail: nysti@crisny.org
Internet: www.crisny.org/not-for-profit/nysti/int.htm

AMOUNT: None
DEADLINE(S): None
FIELD(S): Fields of study related to theatrical production, including box office and PR

Internships for college students, high school seniors, and educators-in-residence interested in developing skills in above fields. Unpaid, but college credit is earned. Located at Russell Sage College in Troy, NY. Gain experience in box office, costumes, education, electrics, music, stage management, scenery, properties, performance, and public relations. Interns come from all over the world.

Must be associated with an accredited institution. See website for more information. Call Ms. Arlene Leff, Intern Director at above location. Include your postal mailing address.

928—PACIFIC PRINTING AND IMAGING ASSOCIATION (Scholarships)

5319 SW Westgate Drive, Suite 117
Portland OR 97221
800/762-7328 or 887/762-7328
Internet: www.ppi-assoc.org/student.html

AMOUNT: $500 to $2,500
DEADLINE(S): APR 1
FIELD(S): Printing/Printing Management

Scholarships for students in the above field who are residents of Alaska, Hawaii, Idaho, Montana, Oregon, or Washington. Considered are academic and social achievements and an essay stating the reason why the student should be chosen for the scholarship. Recipients are assigned mentors who are members of PPI to counsel and advise the student during his/her academic career.

See website for more information. Call Laura Ellis at above number for application information.

929—PIXAR ANIMATION STUDIOS (Summer Internships)

1001 W. Cutting Blvd.
Richmond CA 94804
510/412-6017
FAX: 510/236-0388
E-mail: hr@pixar.com
Internet: www.pixar.com

AMOUNT: Varies
DEADLINE(S): MAR
FIELD(S): Animation

Summer internships offer "hands on" experience for currently enrolled college/university students, based on departmental needs. Send a resume with name/address/phone, position, work experience/education, internships, and hardware/software experience. Must also submit reels: VHS (NTSC or PAL) or 3/4″ (NTSC), 5 minutes in length starting with most recent work, music optional—visual skills nicer, and credit list explaining your reel and software used.

Call the job hotline for details/available positions.

930—PRINCESS GRACE FOUNDATION-USA (Scholarships for Senior and Graduate Thesis Film Productions)

150 East 58th Street, 21st Fl.
New York NY 10155
212/317-1470 or 212/317-1473
E-mail: pgfusa@pgfusa.com
Internet: www.pgfusa.com

AMOUNT: Varies
DEADLINE(S): JUN 1
FIELD(S): Film production

Scholarships for undergrad seniors and graduate students for thesis film productions. Must be nominated by deans or department chairman of established US colleges and universities that have been invited to apply. Nominees must have already completed one film and be age 30 or younger. Contact Foundation to see if your school is eligible to apply.

Do not apply directly to the Foundation. US citizenship or permanent residency required.

931—RHYTHM & HUES STUDIOS (Computer Graphics Scholarship)

5404 Jandy Place
Los Angeles CA 90066
310/448-7619
E-mail: scholarship@rhythm.com
Internet: www.iwc.pair.com/scholarshipage/subjects/arts/companimat.html

AMOUNT: $1,000/category
DEADLINE(S): JUN 1
FIELD(S): Computer Modeling, Computer Character Animation, Digital Cinematography

Open to all students enrolled full-time in an accredited undergraduate or graduate degree program within six months of the deadline. Entries should include cover sheet stating name, address, phone, SSN, school, major, faculty advisor name/address/phone, and category under which entry is being submitted. Also include photocopy of current student ID and typewritten description of entry, including hardware/software used.

1 award in modeling, 1 in animation, and 3 in cinematography; 1 $4,000 grant also goes to each winner's academic department. Contact Rhythm & Hues Studios for more information.

932—RIPON COLLEGE (Performance/Recognition Tuition Scholarships)

Admissions Office
300 Seward Street
P.O. Box 248
Ripon WI 54971
920/748-8102 or 800/94-RIPON
E-mail: adminfo@ripon.edu
Internet: www.ripon.edu

AMOUNT: $5,000-$10,000/yr.
DEADLINE(S): MAR 1
FIELD(S): Music, Forensics, Art, Theatre

Open to undergraduate and graduate students attending or planning to attend Ripon College. Purpose is to recognize and encourage academic potential and accomplishment in above fields. Interview, audition, or nomination may be required.

Renewable. Contact Office of Admission for an application.

933—ROSE HILL COLLEGE (Louella Robinson Memorial Scholarship)

P.O. Box 3126
Aiken SC 29802-3126
800/684-3769
FAX: 803/641-0240
E-mail: rosehill@.edu
Internet: www.rosehill.edu

AMOUNT: $10,000/yr. for four years
DEADLINE(S): Varies
FIELD(S): Liberal Arts and Humanities curricula

For undergraduate residents of Indian River County, Florida, to attend Rose Hill College in Aiken, South Carolina. The school offers a liberal arts education and follows the Great Books curriculum, a program of reading and seminars.

1 annual awaRoad Applicants must meet entry requirements of RHC. Contact above location for details.

934—ROSE HILL COLLEGE (Scholarships for Children of Eastern Orthodox Priests/Deacons)

P.O. Box 3126
Aiken SC 29802-3126
800/684-3769
FAX: 803/641-0240
E-mail: rosehill@edu
Internet: www.rosehill.edu

AMOUNT: Full scholarship: $10,000/yr. for four years
DEADLINE(S): Varies

FIELD(S): Liberal Arts and Humanities curricula

For undergraduates who are children of Eastern Orthodox Christian priests or deacons to attend Rose Hill College in Aiken, South Carolina. The school offers a liberal arts education and follows the Great Books curriculum, a program of reading and seminars.

6-10 annual awards. Applicants must meet entry requirements of RHC. Contact above location for details.

935—ROSE HILL COLLEGE (Scholarships for the Homeschooled)

P.O. Box 3126
Aiken SC 29802-3126
800/684-3769
FAX: 803/641-0240
E-mail: rosehill@rosehill.edu
Internet: www.resehill.edu

AMOUNT: Full scholarship: $10,000/yr. for four years
DEADLINE(S): Varies
FIELD(S): Liberal Arts and Humanities curricula

For undergraduates who have been homeschooled for three of the last five years of their high school education. For use at Rose Hill College in Aiken, South Carolina. The school offers a liberal arts education and follows the Great Books curriculum, a program of reading and seminars. Scholarships will be awarded primarily on the basis of an essay which the student will be asked to write.

4 annual awards. Applicants must meet entry requirements of RHC. Contact above location for details.

936—SAN FRANCISCO FOUNDATION (James D. Phelan Art Awards)

225 Bush Street, Suite 500
San Francisco CA 94104-4224
415/733-8500
FAX: 415/477-2783
Internet: www.sff.org

AMOUNT: $2,500-$7,500
DEADLINE(S): JUL (film, even yr.); OCT (video, even yr.); JUN (printmaking, odd yr.); SEP (photography, odd yr.)
FIELD(S): Printmaking, Photography, Film, and Video

Open to California residents who are California-born artists in the above areas. Printmaking and photography awards in odd-numbered years, and film and video awards in even-numbered years. US citizenship required.

6 annual awards, 3 in each eligible discipline. Awards will be presented at a public reception and screening of winners' works. Write for complete information.

937—SCRIPPS HOWARD FOUNDATION (Charles M. Schulz Award)

312 Walnut Street
P.O. Box 5380
Cincinnati OH 45201-5380
513/977-3035
E-mail: Cottingham@scripps.com
Internet: www.scripps.com/ foundation

AMOUNT: $2,500
DEADLINE(S): JAN 8
FIELD(S): College Cartoonist

Award to honor an outstanding college cartoonist. Open to any student cartoonist at a college newspaper or magazine in the US or its territories. Student must attend same college.

See website for official rules and entry form.

938—SKIDMORE, OWINGS & MERRILL FOUNDATION (Interior Architecture Traveling Fellowship Program)

224 S. Michigan Ave., Suite 1000
Chicago IL 60604
312/554-9090
FAX: 312/360-4545

AMOUNT: $7,500
DEADLINE(S): Varies (consult with school)
FIELD(S): Architecture or Interior Design

For a student graduating with a B.A. or M.A. degree from an accredited US architectural or FIDER school. It will allow the Fellow to visit buildings and settings that are central to his or her area of interest and study.

Must submit portfolio and a proposed travel itinerary, etc. Write for complete information.

939—SMITHSONIAN INSTITUTION (Cooper-Hewitt, National Design Museum- Mark Kaminski Summer Internship)

2 East 91st Street
New York NY 10128
212/860-6868
FAX: 212/860-6909

AMOUNT: $2,500 for 10-week period
DEADLINE(S): MAR 31

FIELD(S): Architecture, Architectural History, Design and Criticism, Museum Education, Museum Studies

These internships are open to college students considering a career in one of the above areas of study. Also open to graduate students who have not yet completed their M.A. degree. This ten-week program is designed to acquaint participants with the programs, policies, procedures, and operations of Cooper-Hewitt Museum and of museums in general.

1 award each summer. Internship commences in June and ends in August. Housing is not provided. Write to Linda Herd at the above address for complete information.

940—SMITHSONIAN INSTITUTION (Cooper-Hewitt, National Design Museum-Peter Krueger Summer Internship Program)

Cooper-Hewitt
National Design Museum
2 East 91st Street
New York NY 10128
212/860-6868
FAX: 212/860-6909

AMOUNT: $2,500
DEADLINE(S): MAR 31
FIELD(S): Art History, Design, Museum Studies, and Museum Education, or Architectural History

Ten-week summer internships open to graduate and undergraduate students considering a career in the museum profession. Interns will assist on special research or exhibition projects and participate in daily museum activities.

6 awards each summer. Internship commences in June and ends in August. Housing is not provided. Write for complete information.

941—SMITHSONIAN INSTITUTION (Cooper-Hewitt, National Design Museum-The Lippincott & Margulies Summer Internship)

Cooper-Hewitt
National Design Museum
2 East 91st Street
New York NY 10128
212/860-6868
FAX 212/860-6909

AMOUNT: $2,500
DEADLINE(S): MAR 31
FIELD(S): Graphic, environmental, and industrial design

Ten-week summer internships open to graduate and undergraduate students considering a career in the fields listed above.

1 award each summer. Internship commences in June and ends in August. Housing is not provided. Write for complete information.

942—SMITHSONIAN INSTITUTION (Minority Student Internship Program)

Fellowships & Grants
955 L'Enfant Plaza, Suite 7000
MRC 902
Washington DC 20560
202/287-3271
FAX: 202/287-3691
E-mail: siofg@ofg.si.edu
Internet: www.si.edu/research+study

AMOUNT: $300/week + possible travel expenses
DEADLINE(S): FEB 15
FIELD(S): Humanities, Environmental Studies, Cultural Studies, Natural History, Earth Science, Art History, Biology, & related fields

Ten-week internships in residence at the Smithsonian for US minority students to participate in research or museum-related activities in above fields. For undergrads or grads with at least a 3.0 GPA. Essay, resume, transcripts, and references required with application. Internships are full-time and are offered for Summer, Fall, or Spring tenures.

Write for application.

943—SOCIETY FOR TECHNICAL COMMUNICATION (Undergraduate Scholarships)

901 N. Stuart Street, Suite 904
Arlington VA 22203-1854
703/522-4114
FAX: 703/522-2075
E-mail: stc@stc-va.org
Internet: www.stc-va.org/scholarships.html

AMOUNT: $2,500
DEADLINE(S): FEB 15
FIELD(S): Technical Communication

Open to full-time undergraduate students who have completed at least one year of study and are enrolled in an accredited 2- or 4-year degree program for career in any area of technical communication: technical writing, editing, graphic design, multimedia art, etc.

Awards tenable at recognized colleges and universities in US and Canada. 14 awards per year—7 undergraduate and 7 graduate. See website and/or write for complete information.

944—SOLOMON R. GUGGENHEIM MUSEUM (Internship Programs)

1071 Fifth Ave.
New York NY 10128-0173
212/423-3526
FAX: 212/423-3650
E-mail: aderusha@guggenheim.org

AMOUNT: Varies (some positions non-paid)
DEADLINE(S): FEB 15 (Summer); JUL 15 (Fall); NOV 15 (Spring)
FIELD(S): Art Administration, Art History

Various internships, which offer practical museum training experience, are available for undergraduates, recent graduates, and graduate students in art history, administration, conservation, education, and related fields. Location varies, including New York, Italy, and Spain. Housing NOT included. Cover letter, resume, transcripts, letters of recommendation, list of foreign languages/relevant coursework, and essay (less than 500 words, describing interest) required.

Contact the Internship Coordinator, Education Department, at the Museum for details of each internship and application procedures.

945—THE ART INSTITUTES INTERNATIONAL (Evelyn Keedy Memorial Scholarship)

300 Sixth Ave., Suite 800
Pittsburgh PA 15222-2598
412/562-9800
FAX: 412/562-9802
E-mail: webadmin@aii.edu
Internet: www.aii.edu

AMOUNT: 2 years full tuition
DEADLINE(S): MAY 1
FIELD(S): Various fields in the creative and applied arts: video production, broadcasting, culinary arts, fashion design, website administration, etc.

Scholarships at 12 different locations nationwide in various fields described above. For graduating high school seniors admitted to an Arts Institutes International School, the New York Restaurant School, or NCPT. Transcripts, letters of recommendation, and resume must be submitted with application.

See website or contact AII for more information.

946—THE GRAND RAPIDS FOUNDATION (Mathilda Gallmeyer Scholarship)

209-C Waters Bldg.
161 Ottawa Ave. NW
Grand Rapids MI 49503-2703

616/454-1751 or 616/454-6455

AMOUNT: Varies
DEADLINE(S): APR 3
FIELD(S): Painting, Fine Arts

Open to full-time undergrads studying painting or fine arts at an accredited institution. Must be a Kent County resident (for a minimum of 5 years), have a minimum 2.75 GPA, and demonstrate artistic talent.

Send SASE to above address for complete information.

947—THE GRAND RAPIDS FOUNDATION (Paul Collins Scholarship)

209-C Waters Bldg.
161 Ottawa Ave. NW
Grand Rapids MI 49503-2703
616/454-1751
FAX: 616/454-6455

AMOUNT: Varies
DEADLINE(S): APR 3
FIELD(S): Fine Arts, Applied Arts

Open to Kent County residents who are full-time undergrads at Aquinas or Calvin Colleges, Grand Valley State Univ., Grand Rapids Community College, or Kendall College of Art & Design. GPA of 2.5 or better. Must demonstrate artistic talent.

Awards based on academic achievement, extracurricular activities, personal aspirations/educational goals, and financial need. Write for complete information.

948—THE WALT DISNEY COMPANY (American Teacher Awards)

P.O. Box 9805
Calabasas CA 91372

AMOUNT: $2,500 (36 awards); $25,000 (Outstanding Teacher of the Year)
DEADLINE(S): FEB 15
FIELD(S): Teachers: athletic coach, early childhood, English, foreign language/ESL, general elementary, mathematics, performing arts, physical education/health, science, social studies, visual arts, voc-tech education

Awards for K-12 teachers in the above fields.

Teachers, or anyone who knows a great teacher, can write for applications at the above address.

949—UNITARIAN UNIVERSALIST ASSOCIATION (Musicians' Network Scholarships)

4190 Front Street
San Diego CA 92103

Written inquiry

AMOUNT: $100-$700
DEADLINE(S): MAR 1
FIELD(S): Art, Poetry, Music

Financial aid to undergraduate students in the above fields. Must be active with the Unitarian Universalist Association.

Renewable. Write for complete information.

950—UNIVERSITY FILM & VIDEO ASSOCIATION (Carole Fielding Student Grants)

University of Baltimore
School of Comm.
1420 N. Charles Street
Baltimore MD 21201
410/837-6061

AMOUNT: $1,000 to $4,000
DEADLINE(S): MAR 31
FIELD(S): Film, Video, Multi-media Production

Open to undergraduate/graduate students. Categories are narrative, experimental, animation, documentary, multimedia/installation and research. Applicant must be sponsored by a faculty member who is an active member of the University Film and Video Association.

Write to the above address for application and complete details.

951—UNIVERSITY FILM AND VIDEO FOUNDATION (Eastman Scholarship Program)

RTVF, P.O. 13138
Denton TX 76203-3138
Internet: www.kodak.com

AMOUNT: Up to $5,000
DEADLINE(S): Varies (spring)
FIELD(S): Cinematography

Scholarships for tuition and fees for one scholastic year or for use as a production grant.

Applications are NOT accepted from students. Applications must be requested by the deans and chairpersons of US universities and colleges offering B.A., B.F.A., M.A. or M.F.A. degree in this field. Each school may nominate up to two candidates. See website for details. Faculty or administration can write to above address for applications.

952—UNIVERSITY OF ILLINOIS AT URBANA-CHAMPAIGN (Lydia E. Parker Bates Scholarship)

Turner Student Services Bldg.
MC-306, 610 East John Street
Champaign IL 61820

217/333-0100

AMOUNT: Varies
DEADLINE(S): MAR 15
FIELD(S): Art, Architecture, Landscape Architecture, Urban Planning, Dance, Theater, and all related subjects except Music

Open to undergraduate students in the College of Fine & Applied Arts who are attending the University of Illinois at Urbana-Champaign. Must demonstrate financial need and have 3.85 GPA. Complete the Free Application for Federal Student Aid.

175 awards per year. Recipients must carry at least 12 credit hours per semester. Contact office of student financial aid.

953—UNIVERSITY OF NORTH TEXAS (Scholarships for Visual Arts Students)

P.O. Box 305100
Denton TX 76203-5100
940/565-2216
Internet: www.unt.edu/scholarships/

AMOUNT: Varies
DEADLINE(S): Varies
FIELD(S): Visual Arts

Several scholarships for students in Department of Visual Arts at the University of North Texas. Eligibility requirements, specialties, and amounts of funding vary.

See website or contact department for details.

954—VIRGINIA MUSEUM OF FINE ARTS (Fellowships)

2800 Grove Ave.
Richmond VA 23221-2466
804/204-2661
FAX: 804/204-2675
Internet: vmfa.state.va.us

AMOUNT: $4,000 (undergrads-max.); $6,000 (grads); $8,000 (professionals)
DEADLINE(S): MAR 1
FIELD(S): Art, Fine Arts, Crafts, Drawing, Filmmaking, Painting, Photography, Printmaking, Sculpture, Video, Art History (graduate only)

Open to Virginia residents of at least one year who are US citizens or legal residents. Fellowships are available to undergraduates, graduates, and professional artists. Financial need is considered.

Contact VMFA for an application.

955—WAVERLY COMMUNITY HOUSE INC. (F. Lammot Belin Arts Scholarships)

Scholarships Selection Committee
P.O. Box 142
Waverly PA 18471
717/586-8191

AMOUNT: $10,000
DEADLINE(S): DEC 15
FIELD(S): Painting, Sculpture, Music, Drama, Dance, Literature, Architecture, Photography

Applicants must have resided in the Abington or Pocono regions of Northeastern Pennsylvania. They must furnish proof of exceptional ability in their chosen field but no formal training in any academic or professional program.

US citizenship required. Finalists must appear in person before the selection committee. Write for complete information.

956—WHITTIER COLLEGE (Talent Scholarship)

13406 E. Philadelphia Street
Whittier CA 90608
562/907-4238
FAX: 562/907-4870
E-mail: admission@whittier.edu
Internet: www.whittier.edu

AMOUNT: $2,000-$10,000
DEADLINE(S): FEB 1
FIELD(S): Art, Music, Theater

Eligibility based on portfolio or audition submissions judged by music, art, or theater department.

Write above address for complete information.

ENGLISH LANGUAGE & LITERATURE

957—ACADEMY OF MOTION PICTURE ARTS AND SCIENCES (Nicholl Fellowships in Screenwriting)

8949 Wilshire Blvd.
Beverly Hills CA 90211-1972
310/247-3000
E-mail: gbeal@oscars.org
Internet: www.oscars.org/nicholl

AMOUNT: $25,000
DEADLINE(S): MAY 1
FIELD(S): Screenwriting

Academy awards competition is open to any screenwriter who has not sold any form of a screenplay for more than $5,000. Screenplays must be originally written in English. Award may not be used for educational purposes.

Up to 5 awards annually. Send self-addressed, stamped, business-sized envelope after January 1st to AMPAS for an application.

958—ALLIANCE FOR YOUNG ARTISTS AND WRITERS, INC. (Scholastic Art & Writing Awards)

Scholastic, Inc.
555 Broadway
New York NY 10012-3999
212/343-6582 or 800-SCHOLASTIC
FAX: 212/343-4885
E-mail: mjohnson@scholastic.com
Internet: www.scholastic.com/
artandwriting/about.htm

AMOUNT: Varies
DEADLINE(S): Varies (upon location)
FIELD(S): Art, Writing

For all students in grades 7-12 currently enrolled in a public or non-public school in the US, Canada, US territories, or US-sponsored schools abroad. Awards are available in 10 writing categories and 16 art categories. Publishing opportunities may be available for winning students in both art and writing categories.

1,000+ awards annually. See website or contact Mike Johnson, Program Manager, for details and entry forms.

959—ALVIN M. BENTLEY FOUNDATION (Scholarship Program)

P.O. Box 1516
Owosso MI 48867
517/729-9040
FAX: 517/723-2454

AMOUNT: $40,000 (4-year); $1,000/yr. (freshman)
DEADLINE(S): None
FIELD(S): Literature, Science, Arts

Open to Michigan residents applying as freshmen to the University of Michigan's College of Literature, Science, and the Arts. Based on academic excellence and extracurricular activities. Must be nominated; there are no separate applications. Candidates are chosen from U of M applications received from Michigan resident freshmen.

4 four-year awards and 8 freshmen awards annually. Contact University of Michigan for details.

960—AMELIA MAGAZINE (Creative Writing Contest)

329 "E" Street
Bakersfield CA 93304
805/323-4064

AMOUNT: $200
DEADLINE(S): MAY 15
FIELD(S): Literature

This creative writing contest is for US high school students only. Winner is selected from best entries. There is no entry fee; however, if complete guideline and sample of past winners is desired, a $3 handling fee is required with request.

Write to Frederick A. Raborg, Jr. at the above address for complete information. Always include a self-addressed, stamped envelope.

961—AMERICAN FOUNDATION FOR THE BLIND (R.L. Gillette Scholarships)

11 Penn Plaza, Suite 300
New York NY 10001
212/502-7661
FAX: 212/502-7771
E-mail: juliet@afb.org
Internet: www.afb.org

AMOUNT: $1,000
DEADLINE(S): APR 30
FIELD(S): Literature, Music

Open to legally blind women enrolled in a four-year undergraduate degree program in literature or music. Must be US citizen. Must submit evidence of legal blindness; official transcripts; proof of college/university acceptance; three letters of recommendation; performance tape (30 minutes max.) or creative writing sample; and typewritten statement describing educational and personal goals, work experience, extracurricular activities, and how monies will be used.

2 awards annually. See website or contact Julie Tucker at AFB for an application.

962—AMERICAN LEGION (National High School Oratorical Contest)

P.O. Box 1055
Indianapolis IN 46206
317/635-8411 or 317/630-1200
Internet: www.legion.org/
orarules.htm

AMOUNT: $14,000 to $18,000 (national); $1,500 (quarter finalist); $1,500 additional to semi-finalists who do not advance to the National Finals contest
DEADLINE(S): Varies according to state/region
FIELD(S): Oratory

Competition open to high school students (gr. 9-12). Undergraduate scholarship awards go to the winners. US citizenship or lawful permanent resident.

Write to the American Legion headquarters in your state of residence for contest procedures or visit website above for details.

963—AMERICAN MOTHERS, INC. (Gertrude Fogelson Cultural and Creative Arts Awards)

1296 E. 21st Street
Brooklyn NY 11201
718/253-5676

AMOUNT: Up to $1,000
DEADLINE(S): JAN 1 (annually)
FIELD(S): Visual Arts, Creative Writing, and Vocal Music

An award to encourage and honor mothers in artistic pursuits.

Write to Alice Miller at above address for details.

964—ARTS MANAGEMENT P/L (Miles Franklin Literary Award)

Station House, Rawson Place
790 George Street
Sydney NSW 2000 AUSTRALIA
(612) 9212 5066
FAX: (612) 9211 7762
E-mail: vbraden@ozemail.com.au

AMOUNT: Aus. $27,000
DEADLINE(S): JAN 31
FIELD(S): Novel/Playwriting

Annual award for the best book on some aspect of Australian life published in the 12-month period prior to the award deadline each year. If no novel is worthy of the award, a play will be chosen. More than one entry may be submitted by each author; a novel/play written by two or more authors in collaboration is also eligible.

Winner announced in May or June. Contact Claudia Crosariol, Projects Administrator, for complete information/entry form.

965—ASSOCIATION FOR LIBRARY & INFORMATION SCIENCE EDUCATION (Alise Research Grants Program)

P.O. Box 7640
Arlington VA 22207
703/243-8040

AMOUNT: $5,000
DEADLINE(S): SEP 15
FIELD(S): Library Science

Grants are to help support research costs. Open to members of the Association for Library & Information Science.

For membership information or an application, write to above address.

966—ASSOCIATION FOR WOMEN IN SCIENCE EDUCATIONAL FOUNDATION (Dr. Vicki L. Schechtman Scholarship)

1200 New York Ave. NW, Suite 650
Washington DC 20005
202/326-8940 or 800/886-AWIS
E-mail: awis@awis.org
Internet: www.awis.org

AMOUNT: $1,000
DEADLINE(S): JAN 16
FIELD(S): Various Sciences and Social Sciences

For female undergraduate students who are US citizens and have a minimum GPA of 3.0. Summary page, essay describing career aspirations, transcripts, proof of matriculation (if available), and two reference letters required with application. Scholarships may be used for tuition, books, housing, research, equipment, etc.

See website or write to above address for an application and more information.

967—ASSOCIATION FOR WOMEN IN SCIENCE EDUCATIONAL FOUNDATION (Ruth Satter Memorial Award)

1200 New York Ave. NW, Suite 650
Washington DC 20005
202/326-8940 or 800/886-AWIS
E-mail: awis@awis.org
Internet: www.awis.org

AMOUNT: $1,000
DEADLINE(S): JAN 16
FIELD(S): Various Sciences and Social Sciences

Scholarships for female doctoral students who have interrupted their education three years or more to raise a family. Summary page, description of research project, resume, references, transcripts, biographical sketch, and proof of eligibility from department head required. US citizens may attend any graduate institution; non-citizens must be enrolled in US institutions.

See website or write to above address for more information or an application.

968—BEVERLY HILLS THEATRE GUILD (Julie Harris Playwright Award Competition)

2815 N. Beachwood Drive
Los Angeles CA 90068-1923
323/465-2703

AMOUNT: $5,000 (1st prize); $2,000 (2nd); $1,000 (3rd)
DEADLINE(S): NOV 1
FIELD(S): Playwriting

Annual competition of full-length (90 minutes) unproduced, unpublished plays. Must be US citizen. Co-authorship is allowed. Musicals, short one-act plays, adaptations, translations, and plays having won other competitions or entered in previous BHTG competitions are not eligible.

Send a self-addressed, stamped envelope for an application. Entries accepted August 1st to November 1st.

969—BLUES HEAVEN FOUNDATION, INC. (Muddy Waters Scholarship)

2120 S. Michigan Ave.
Chicago IL 60616
312/808-1286

AMOUNT: $2,000
DEADLINE(S): APR 30
FIELD(S): Music, Music Education, African-American Studies, Folklore, Performing Arts, Arts Management, Journalism, Radio/TV/Film

Scholarship is made on a competitive basis with consideration given to scholastic achievement, concentration of studies, and financial need. Applicant must have full-time enrollment status in a Chicago area college/university in at least their first year of undergraduate studies or a graduate program. Scholastic aptitude, extracurricular involvement, grade point average, and financial need are all considered.

Contact Blues Heaven Foundation, Inc. to receive an application between February and April.

970—BUENA VISTA COLLEGE NETWORK (Internships in Film Marketing)

3900 W. Alameda Ave.
Burbank CA 91505-4316
818/567-5000
E-mail: College_Network @studio.disney.com

AMOUNT: Varies
DEADLINE(S): None
FIELD(S): Fields of study related to the motion picture industry, including marketing and promotion

Internships for full-time college students age 18 and up interested in a career in a facet of the motion picture industry. Must have unlimited access to computer with modem and transportation, be able to work 4-6 hours per week and 2-3 weekends per month. Attend film openings and sneak previews. Evaluate various aspects via an interactive computer system. Compensation ranges from $30 to $60/month. Possible school credit.

Access website by writing "Buena Vista College Network" from Yahoo. Available in most states and parts of Canada. Details, an interactive application, and e-mail access are located on website.

971—CALIFORNIA LIBRARY ASSOCIATION (Reference Service Press Fellowship)

717 K Street, Suite 300
Sacramento CA 95814-3477
916/447-8541

AMOUNT: $2,000
DEADLINE(S): MAY 31
FIELD(S): Reference/informaiton service librarianship

Open to college seniors or graduates who have been accepted in an accredited MLS program. For residents of any state pursuing an MLS at a school in California.

Students pursuing an MLS on a part-time or full-time basis are equally eligible. Write for complete information.

972—CALIFORNIA LIBRARY ASSOCIATION (Reference Service Press Fellowship)

717 K Street, Suite 300
Sacramento CA 95814-3477
916/447-8541

AMOUNT: $2,000
DEADLINE(S): MAY 31
FIELD(S): Library Science

Open to college seniors or graduates who have been accepted to an accredited Master's of Library or Information Science program. For California residents attending library school in any state OR for residents of any state attending a library school in California. Students pursuing an MLS on a part-time or full-time basis are equally eligible.

Contact CLA for an application.

973—CATHOLIC LIBRARY ASSOCIATION (World Book, Inc., Award)

100 North Street, Suite 224
Pittsfield MA 01201-5109
413/443-2CLA
FAX: 413/442-2CLA
E-mail: cla@vgernet.net
Internet: www.cathla.org

AMOUNT: $1,500
DEADLINE(S): MAR 15
FIELD(S): Library Science

Open to members of the National Catholic Library Association who are interested in gaining added proficiency in school or children's librarianship. Must submit report describing program of study (workshops, seminars, summer sessions, sabbaticals, etc.), including statement of expenses (tuition, room/board, and travel) relative to program of study. Grant is NOT given for library science degree.

1-3 awards annually. See website or send self-addressed, stamped envelope for an application. Awards announced at annual convention during Easter Week.

974—CENTER FOR 17TH- AND 18TH-CENTURY STUDIES (Fellowships)

UCLA
310 Reyce Hall
Los Angeles CA 90095-1404
310/206-8522
FAX: 310/206-8577
E-mail: c1718cs@humnet.ucla.edu

AMOUNT: $1,000-$18,400
DEADLINE(S): MAR 15
FIELD(S): British Literature/History
(17th & 18th Centuries)

Undergraduate stipends, graduate assistantships, and Ahmanson & Getty postdoctoral fellowships are for advanced study and research regarding British literature and history of the 17th and 18th centuries. Tenable at the William Andrews Clark Memorial Library at the University of California, Los Angeles.

Contact the Center for current year's theme and an application.

975—CHICAGO TRIBUNE (Heartland Prizes)

Editorial Dept.
435 N. Michigan Ave.
Chicago IL 60611-4041
Written inquiry

AMOUNT: $5,000
DEADLINE(S): JUL 31
FIELD(S): Creative Writing

Two annual prizes honor a novel and a book of nonfiction embodying the spirit of the nation's Heartland. Established to recognize works that reinforce and perpetuate the values of heartland America; however, awards are not limited to Midwestern writers or regional subjects.

Books must be submitted by publishers. Notification in August. NO scholarships are offered. Contact *Chicago Tribune* in writing for further details.

976—CHICAGO TRIBUNE (Nelson Algren Awards)

Editorial Dept.
435 N. Michigan Ave.
Chicago IL 60611-4041
Written inquiry

AMOUNT: $5,000 (1st prize); $1,000 (3 runners-up)
DEADLINE(S): JUL 31
FIELD(S): Fiction Writing

Open to Americans who submit unpublished short fiction. Stories must be typed and double-spaced, between 2,500 and 10,000 words. Manuscripts will not be returned. Author's names should not appear on the manuscript. Author should enclose a cover sheet with name, address, phone, and title of entry.

Notification in August. Winning stories are published in the *Tribune*. NO scholarships are offered. Contact *Chicago Tribune* in writing for further details.

977—COUNCIL FOR BASIC EDUCATION (Arts Education Fellowships)

2506 Buckelew Drive
Falls Church VA 22046
703/876-5782

AMOUNT: $2,800 stipend + $200 grant to school
DEADLINE(S): JAN
FIELD(S): Teaching of the arts (visual arts, creative writing, dance, media, music, theatre)

Fellowships for K-12 teachers in the above fields, artist-teachers, or professional artists who teach at least 20 hours per week. Funding from the National Endowment for the Arts and the Getty Center for Education in the Arts, and others.

Contact organization for details.

978—DISTRICT OF COLUMBIA COMMISSION ON THE ARTS & HUMANITIES (Grants)

410 Eighth Street NW, 5th Fl.
Washington DC 20004
202/724-5613
TDD: 202/727-3148
FAX: 202/727-4135

AMOUNT: $2,500
DEADLINE(S): MAR 1
FIELD(S): Performing Arts, Literature, Visual Arts

Applicants for grants must be professional artists and residents of Washington DC for at least one year prior to submitting application. Awards intended to generate art endeavors within the Washington DC community.

Open also to art organizations that train, exhibit, or perform within DC. 150 grants per year. Write for complete information.

979—FLORIDA DEPARTMENT OF STATE—ARTS COUNCIL (Individual Artists' Fellowships)

Division of Cultural Affairs
The Capitol
Tallahassee FL 32399-0250
850/487-2980
TDD: 850/488-5779
FAX: 850/922-5259
Internet: www.dos.state.fl.us

AMOUNT: $5,000
DEADLINE(S): JAN 15
FIELD(S): Dance, Choreography, Poetry, Literature, Music, Music Composition, Theatre, Visual Arts, Film, Crafts, Fiction, Interdisciplinary

Open to legal residents of Florida who are professional creative artists of at least 18 years of age. May NOT be enrolled in any undergraduate or graduate degree-seeking program during fellowship period.

38 awards annually. Renewable with reapplication after four years since date of previous awaRoad Contact Florida Arts Council for information packet. Notification during summer.

980—FOREST ROBERTS THEATRE (Mildred & Albert Panowski Playwriting Award)

Northern Michigan Univ.
1401 Presque Isle Ave.
Marquette MI 49855-5364
906/227-2553
FAX: 906/227-2567
Internet: www.nmu.edu/theatre

AMOUNT: $2,000
DEADLINE(S): Varies
FIELD(S): Playwriting

This competition is open to any playwright, but only one play per playwright may be entered. Entries must be original, full-length plays not previously produced or published. May be co-authored, based upon factual material, or an adaptation. Scripts must be typewritten or word processed and securely bound within a cover or folder and clearly identified.

1 award annually. Not renewable. Contact James Panowski at above address for contest rules and entry blank.

981—FREEDOM FROM RELIGION FOUNDATION (Student Essay Contest)

P.O. Box 750
Madison WI 53701
608/256-5800
Internet: www.infidels.org/org/ffrf

AMOUNT: $1,000; $500; $250
DEADLINE(S): JUL 15
FIELD(S): Humanities, English, Education, Philosophy, Science

Essay contest on topics related to church-state entanglement in public schools or growing up a "freethinker" in religious-oriented society. Topics change yearly, but all are on general theme of maintaining separation of church and state. New topics available in February. For high school seniors and currently enrolled college/technical students. Must be US citizen.

Send SASE to address above for complete information. Please indicate whether wanting information for college competition or high school. Information will be sent when new topics are announced each February. See website for details.

982—GENERAL LEARNING COMMUNICATIONS (DuPont Challenge Science Essay Awards Program)

900 Skokie Blvd., Suite 200
Northbrook IL 60062-4028
847/205-3000
FAX: 847/564-8197
Internet: www.glcomm.com/dupont

AMOUNT: $1,500 (max.)
DEADLINE(S): JAN 28
FIELD(S): Science & Technology

Annual essay competition open to students in grades 7-12 in the US and Canada. Cash awards for 1st, 2nd, and honorable mention. 1st-place essayists in each of two divisions, their science teacher, and a parent of each receive a trip to the Space Center Houston/NASA at the end of April.

102 awards annually. See website or contact your science teacher or GLC for official entry blank.

983—GEORGE MASON UNIVERSITY (Associated Writing Programs Award Series; St. Martin's Press Award)

Tallwood House
Mail Stop 1E3
Fairfax VA 22030
703/934-6920
FAX: 703/352-7535
E-mail: awp@gmu.edu
Internet: http://web.gmu.edu/departments/awp/

AMOUNT: $2,000 honorarium (AWP); $10,000 advance against royalties (St. Martin's Press)
DEADLINE(S): JAN 1 (through FEB 28—postmark)

FIELD(S): Writing: poetry, short fiction, creative nonfiction and novels

AWP competition is for book-length manuscripts in poetry, short fiction, and creative nonfiction; St. Martin's Press Young Writers Award is for a novel whose author is 32 years of age or younger. Open to authors writing in English, regardless of their nationality or residence.

Novel manuscripts will be judged and published by St. Martin's Press. All genres require a handling fee of $10 for AWP members and $15 for nonmembers. Contact above address or website for details.

984—GEORGE MASON UNIVERSITY (Mary Roberts Rinehart Awards)

English Dept.
MSN 3E4
4400 University Drive
Fairfax VA 22030-4444
703/993-1180
FAX: 703/993-1161

AMOUNT: $2,000-$2,500
DEADLINE(S): NOV 30
FIELD(S): Creative Writing

Grants are given to unpublished writers to complete previously unpublished works of fiction, poetry, biography, autobiography, or history with a strong narrative quality. Need not be US citizen, but works must be in English, and awards are in US dollars. Submitted samples of a nominee's writing may be up to 30 pages in length for all categories. Financial need NOT considered.

3 awards annually. Candidates must be nominated by writing program faculty member or a sponsoring writer, agent, or editor. Contact William Miller at address above for complete information.

985—GEORGE WASHINGTON UNIVERSITY (Maud E. McPherson Scholarship)

Office of Student Financial Assistance
Washington DC 20052
202/994-6620 or 800/222-6242
TTY: 202/994-8250
FAX: 202/994-0906

AMOUNT: Partial Tuition
DEADLINE(S): APR 22
FIELD(S): English

Need-based scholarships at George Washington University in DC for continuing or transfer students majoring in English. GPA of 3.0 or better (4.0 scale) is required, and must have completed at least 3 semester hours of English. Continuing students should have a minimum of 15 semester hours total; transfer students should have a minimum of 30 semester hours total. Must demonstrate financial need.

Renewable through senior year with reapplication. Contact GWU's Financial Aid Office for an application.

986—GEORGIA LIBRARY ASSOCIATION ADMINISTRATIVE SERVICES (Hubbard Scholarship Fund)

SOLINET
1438 W. Peachtree Street, NW
Atlanta GA 30309-2955
Written inquiry

AMOUNT: $3,000
DEADLINE(S): MAY 1
FIELD(S): Library Science

For graduating seniors and graduates of accredited colleges who have been accepted into an ALA-accredited degree program. Must be ready to begin study in fall term of award year and intend to complete degree requirements within two years. Recipients agree to work (following graduation) for one year in a library or library-related capacity in Georgia OR to pay back a prorated amount of the award within two years (with interest).

Contact GLA for an application.

987—ILLINOIS ARTS COUNCIL (Artists Fellowship Awards)

100 W. Randolph, Suite 10-500
Chicago IL 60601-3298
312/814-6750

AMOUNT: $500; $5,000; $10,000
DEADLINE(S): SEP 1
FIELD(S): Choreography, Visual Arts, Poetry Prose, Film, Video, Playwriting, Music Composition, Crafts, Ethnic & Folk Arts, Performance Art, Photography, Audio Art.

Open to professional artists who are Illinois residents. Awards are in recognition of work in the above areas; they are not for continuing study. Students are NOT eligible.

Write to address above for application form.

988—INSTITUTE FOR HUMANE STUDIES (Humane Studies Fellowship)

4084 University Drive, Suite 101
Fairfax VA 22030-6812
703/934-6920 or 800/697-8799
FAX: 703/352-7535
E-mail: ihs@gmu.edu
Internet: www.theihs.org

AMOUNT: up to $12,000
DEADLINE(S): DEC 31
FIELD(S): Social Sciences, Law, Humanities, Jurisprudence, Journalism

Awards are for graduate and advanced undergraduate students pursuing degrees at any accredited domestic or foreign school. Based on academic performance, demonstrated interest in classical liberal ideas, and potential to contribute to the advancement of a free society.

90 awards annually. Apply online or contact IHS for an application.

989—INSTITUTE FOR HUMANE STUDIES (Summer Residential Program)

4084 University Drive, Suite 101
Fairfax VA 22030-6812
703/934-6920 or 800/697-8799
FAX: 703/352-7535
E-mail: ihs@gmu.edu
Internet: www.theihs.org

AMOUNT: All seminar fees: program cost, room/board, materials, and books
DEADLINE(S): MAR 1
FIELD(S): Social Sciences, Humanities, Law, Journalism, Public Policy, Education, Writing

For college students, recent graduates, and graduate students who share an interest in learning and exchanging ideas about the scope of individual rights. One-week and weekend seminars at various campus locations across the US.

Apply online or contact IHS for an application.

990—IOWA SCHOOL OF LETTERS (The John Simmons Short Fiction Award)

Univ. of Iowa
102 Dey House
507 N. Clinton Street
Iowa City IA 52242-1000
319/335-0416

AMOUNT: Winners' manuscripts will be published by University of Iowa under standard press contract
DEADLINE(S): Varies (AUG 1-SEP 30)
FIELD(S): Creative Writing: Fiction

Any writer who has not previously published a volume of prose fiction is eligible to enter the competition. The manuscript must be a collection of short stories of at least 150 typewritten pages. Writers who have published a volume of poetry are eligible. Revised manuscripts that have been previously entered may be resubmitted.

Send a self-addressed, stamped envelope to Connie Brothers at above address for guidelines.

991—JAPANESE AMERICAN CITIZENS LEAGUE (Gongoro Nakamura Memorial Scholarship)

1765 Sutter Street
San Francisco CA 94115
415/921-5225
FAX: 415/931-4671
E-mail: jacl@jacl.org
Internet: www.jacl.org

AMOUNT: $1,000-$5,000
DEADLINE(S): MAR 1
FIELD(S): Public Speaking, Debate

Open to JACL members and their children only. For entering freshmen with an interest in public speaking or debate, who are planning to attend a college, university, trade school, business school, or any other institution of higher learning. Must submit personal statement, letters of recommendation, and transcript. Financial need NOT a factor.

For membership information or an application, send a self-addressed, stamped envelope to above address, stating your level of study. Applications available October 1st through February 20th; recipients notified in July.

992—LOUISIANA STATE UNIVERSITY AT SHREVEPORT (H.J. Sachs English Scholarship)

Dean of Liberal Arts
One University Place
Shreveport LA 71115-2399
318/797-5363 or 318/797-5371
FAX: 318/797-5366
E-mail: finaid@pilot.lsus.edu
Internet: www.lsus.edu

AMOUNT: $600
DEADLINE(S): Varies
FIELD(S): English

This stipend is awarded for one academic year to either an English major or an English education major at LSUS. The recipient is chosen on the basis of academic merit, character, and need.

Contact the Dean's Office in the College of Liberal Arts at LSUS for an application.

993—LOUISIANA STATE UNIVERSITY AT SHREVEPORT (Walter O. Bigby Scholarship)

Dean of Liberal Arts
One University Place
Shreveport LA 71115-2399
318/797-5363 or 318/797-5371
FAX: 318/797-5366
E-mail: finaid@pilot.lsus.edu
Internet: www.lsus.edu

AMOUNT: up to $500/semester
DEADLINE(S): Varies
FIELD(S): Political Science, English, History, Law

Recipient must be entering the junior or senior year at LSUS with a major in political science, English, or history; may also be enrolled in some other Liberal Arts degree program if preparing to enter law school.

Contact the Dean's Office in the College of Liberal Arts at LSUS for an application.

994—MINNESOTA STATE ARTS BOARD (Grants Program)

Park Square Ct.
400 Sibley Street, Suite 200
St. Paul MN 55101-1928
651/215-1600

AMOUNT: $8,000 (fellowships); $500-$1,500 (grants)
DEADLINE(S): AUG (Visual Arts); SEP (Music & Dance); OCT (Literature & Theatre)
FIELD(S): Literature, Music, Theater, Dance, Visual Arts

Fellowships and career opportunity grants are open to professional artists who are residents of Minnesota. Grants may NOT be used for support of tuition or work toward any degree.

Contact MSAB for an application.

995—NATIONAL ENDOWMENT FOR THE ARTS (Literature Fellowships)

1100 Pennsylvania Ave. NW
Washington DC 20506
202/682-5428

AMOUNT: Varies
DEADLINE(S): MAR (poetry); JAN (prose)
FIELD(S): Literature/creative writing

Fellowships open to writer of exceptional talent. Awards are not to support academic study. US citizen or legal resident.

Students are NOT eligible to apply. Write for complete information.

996—NATIONAL FEDERATION OF STATE POETRY SOCIETIES (Edna Meudt Memorial Scholarship Fund)

c/o P.J. Doyle
4242 Stevens
Minneapolis MN 55409-2004
612/824-1964
FAX: 612/872-3200
E-mail: pjdoyle@mplsredcross.org

AMOUNT: $500
DEADLINE(S): FEB 1
FIELD(S): Poetry

Any junior or senior of an accredited university or college will be eligible for consideration based on the following: 1) submission of a completed application; 2) submission of 10 original poems, single-spaced, 1-page limit, 50-character-per-line limit, 40-line-per-poem limit; and 3) the 10-poem manuscript must be titled. Financial need NOT a factor. Winning manuscripts are published by NFSPS, and each recipient will receive 75 copies & can read at annual convention.

2 awards annually. Send a self-addressed, stamped, business-sized envelope to NFSPS for an application. Award recipients announced after April 1st.

997—NATIONAL FEDERATION OF THE BLIND (Humanities Scholarship)

805 5th Ave.
Grinnell IA 50112
515/236-3366

AMOUNT: $3,000
DEADLINE(S): MAR 31
FIELD(S): Humanities (Art, English, Foreign Languages, History, Philosophy, Religion)

Open to legally blind students pursuing or planning to pursue a full-time postsecondary education in the US. Scholarships are awarded on basis of academic excellence, service to the community, and financial need. Must include transcripts and two letters of recommendation. Membership NOT required.

1 award annually. Renewable. Contact Mrs. Peggy Elliot, Scholarship Committee Chairman, for an application.

998—NATIONAL FOUNDATION FOR ADVANCEMENT IN THE ARTS (Arts Recognition and Talent Search)

800 Brickell Ave.
Miami FL 33131

800/970-ARTS or 305/377-1140
FAX: 305/377-1149
Internet: www.nfaa.org

AMOUNT: $100-$3,000
DEADLINE(S): OCT 1
FIELD(S): Creative & Performing Arts

Talent contest for high school seniors and 17- to 18-year-olds in dance, jazz, music, photography, theatre, visual arts, voice, and writing. Except for those applying in Music/Jazz, applicants must be US citizens or permanent residents. May apply in more than one category, but only one financial award will be given to any individual, and a fee is required for each category in which student applies.

$35 application fee ($25 if apply by June 1st); fee may be waived if you are unable to meet this requirement. 400 awards annually. Not renewable. Contact NFAA for an application packet.

999—NATIONAL JUNIOR CLASSICAL LEAGUE (Scholarships)

Miami University
Oxford OH 45056
513/529-7741

AMOUNT: $500 to $1,000
DEADLINE(S): MAY 1
FIELD(S): Classics

Open to NJCL members who are high school seniors and plan to study Classics (though Classics major is not required). Preference will be given to a student who plans to pursue a teaching career in the Classics (also not a requirement).

Must be a member of a National Junior Classical League club. Write for complete information.

1000—NATIONAL LEAGUE OF AMERICAN PEN WOMEN, INC. (Scholarships for Mature Women)

1300 17th Street NW
Washington DC 20036
717/225-3023

AMOUNT: $1,000
DEADLINE(S): JAN 15 (even-numbered years)
FIELD(S): Art, Music, Creative Writing

The National League of American Pen Women gives three $1,000 grants in even-numbered years to women aged 35 and over. Should submit three 4 x 6 or bigger color prints, manuscripts, or musical compositions suited to the criteria for the year.

Send SASE for details at the above address.

1001—NATIONAL SPEAKERS ASSOCIATION (NSA Scholarship)

1500 S. Priest Drive
Tempe AZ 85281
602/968-2552
FAX: 602/968-0911
E-mail: information@nsaspeaker.org
Internet: www.nsaspeaker.org

AMOUNT: $3,000
DEADLINE(S): JUN 1
FIELD(S): Speech

For college juniors, seniors, and graduate students who are majoring or minoring in speech. Must be full-time student with above-average academic record. Applicant should be a well-rounded student, capable of leadership, with the potential to make an impact using oral communication skills. Must submit official transcript, 500-word essay on career objectives, and letter of recommendation from speech teacher/department head along with application (7 copies each).

4 awards annually. Financial need NOT a factor. See website or contact Melanie Stroud at above address for an application/more information.

1002—NATIONAL SPEAKERS ASSOCIATION (Outstanding Professor Awards)

1500 S. Priest Drive
Tempe AZ 85281
602/968-2552
FAX: 602/968-0911
E-mail: information@nsaspeaker.org
Internet: www.nsaspeaker.org

AMOUNT: $2,000
DEADLINE(S): JUN 1
FIELD(S): Speech/Communications

Open to full-time faculty members in the Department of Speech Communication of accredited US colleges or universities. Nominations to be forwarded through department head and should include vitae and two letters of recommendation from students. Must show commitment through effective teaching courses in public speaking, presentations, etc., and/or through research in same areas.

2 awards annually. No nominations will be accepted prior to May 1st. See website or contact Melanie Stroud at above address for more information.

1003—NATIONAL WRITERS ASSOCIATION FOUNDATION (Scholarship)

3140 S. Peoria, PMB 295
Aurora CO 80014

303/841-0246
FAX: 303/751-8593
E-mail: sandywrter@aol.com
Internet: www.nationalwriters.com

AMOUNT: $1,000
DEADLINE(S): DEC 31
FIELD(S): Writing

Scholarship for career support. Financial need must be demonstrated.

1 award annually. See website or contact Sandy Whelchel for an application.

1004—NEW YORK STATE THEATRE INSTITUTE (Internships in Theatrical Production)

155 River Street
Troy NY 12180
518/274-3573
nysti@crisny.org
Internet: www.crisny.org/not-for-profit/nysti/int.htm

AMOUNT: None
DEADLINE(S): None
FIELD(S): Fields of study related to theatrical production, including box office and PR

Internships for college students, high school seniors, and educators-in-residence interested in developing skills in above fields. Unpaid, but college credit is earned. Located at Russell Sage College in Troy, NY. Gain experience in box office, costumes, education, electrics, music, stage management, scenery, properties, performance, and public relations. Interns come from all over the world.

Must be associated with an accredited institution. See website for more information. Call Ms. Arlene Leff, Intern Director, at above location. Include your postal mailing address.

1005—NORTH CAROLINA DEPARTMENT OF PUBLIC INSTRUCTION (Scholarship Loan Program for Prospective Teachers)

301 N. Wilmington Street
Raleigh NC 27601-2825
919/715-1120

AMOUNT: Up to $2,500/yr.
DEADLINE(S): FEB
FIELD(S): Education: Teaching, School Psychology and Counseling, Speech/Language Impaired, Audiology, Library/Media Services

For NC residents planning to teach in NC public schools. At least 3.0 high school GPA required; must maintain 2.5 GPA during freshman year and 3.0 cumulative thereafter. Recipients are obligated to teach one year in an NC public school for each year of assistance. Those who do not fulfill their teaching obligation are required to repay the loan plus interest.

200 awards per year. For full-time students. Applications available in Dec. from high school counselors and college and university departments of education.

1006—NORTH CAROLINA DEPT. OF PUBLIC INSTRUCTION (Teacher Assistant Scholarship Loan)

301 N. Wilmington Street
Raleigh NC 27601-2825
919/715-1120

AMOUNT: Up to $1,200/yr
DEADLINE(S): JAN
FIELD(S): Education: Teaching, School Psychology or Counseling, Speech/Language Impaired, Audiology, Library/Media Services

For NC residents employed as K-12 teaching assistants in public schools who wish to pursue teacher licensure. Must either hold a B.A. degree or have completed general college courses prerequisite to admission to degree program and be admitted to an approved teacher education program at a four-year instituition. Two-year community college early childhood education program is acceptable.

Must remain employed as teaching assistant while pursuing licensure and teach one year in an NC public school for each year of assistance received. Applications available in Sept. from local school superintendent.

1007—PENINSULA COMMUNITY FOUNDATION (Bobette Bibo Gugliotta Memorial Scholarship for Creative Writing)

1700 S. El Camino Real, #300
San Mateo CA 94402
650/358-9369
FAX: 650/358-9817

AMOUNT: $2,000 (college students); up to $500 (high school students)
DEADLINE(S): MAR 27 (5 P.M.)
FIELD(S): Creative writing

Scholarships for high school, undergraduate, or graduate students seeking higher education focused on the field of creative writing. Must be attending or be graduates of a high school in San Mateo County or Northern Santa Clara County (Daly City to Mountain View), California. High school students will be judged separately from college students. Must submit evidence of writing skills and commitment to creative writing.

Program was established in honor of Bobette Bibo Gugliotta, author of several books, and creator of a story (when she was 11 years old), about a mouse who later became Mickey.

1008—PLAYWRIGHTS' CENTER (Jerome Fellowships)

2301 East Franklin Ave.
Minneapolis MN 55406-1099
612/332-7481
FAX: 612/332-6037
E-mail: pwcenter@mtn.org
Internet: www.pwcenter.org
AMOUNT: $7,200
DEADLINE(S): SEP 15
FIELD(S): Playwriting

For emerging playwrights who are US citizens/permanent residents who have not had more than two productions of their work fully staged by professional theaters. Fellows spend 12 months as core members of the Playwrights' Center. Purpose is to provide playwrights with funds and services to aid them in the development of their craft.

Send a self-addressed, stamped envelope to above address for an application.

1009—PLAYWRIGHTS' CENTER (Many Voices Residency & Collaboration Grants Programs)

2301 East Franklin Ave.
Minneapolis MN 55406-1099
612/332-7481
FAX: 612/332-6037
E-mail: pwcenter@mtn.org
Internet: www.pwcenter.org
AMOUNT: $750 stipend + tuition to a
Center class
DEADLINE(S): JUL 1
FIELD(S): Playwriting

Residencies for minority individuals interested in becoming playwrights who live in Minnesota or within a 110-mile radius of the Twin Cities at the time of application whose work demonstrates exceptional artistic merit and potential. Award recipients will spend an 8- to 9-month residency at the Center, have a one-on-one mentorship with a playwright, and other opportunities to develop their craft.

Collaboration grants are for culturally diverse teams of 2 or more writers to create new theater pieces. Awards range from $200 to $2,000. Send a self-addressed, stamped envelope to above address for an application.

1010—PLAYWRIGHTS' CENTER (McKnight Advancement Grant)

2301 East Franklin Ave.
Minneapolis MN 55406-1099
612/332-7481
FAX: 612/332-6037
E-mail: pwcenter@mtn.org
Internet: www.pwcenter.org
AMOUNT: $8,500
DEADLINE(S): FEB 1
FIELD(S): Playwriting

Open to playwrights whose primary residence is Minnesota and whose work demonstrates exceptional artistic merit and potential. Two works by applicant must have been fully produced by professional theatres. Recipients must designate two months of the grant year for active participation in Center programs.

Send a self-addressed, stamped envelope to above address for an application.

1011—PLAYWRIGHTS' CENTER (McKnight Fellowships)

2301 East Franklin Ave.
Minneapolis MN 55406-1099
612/332-7481
FAX: 612/332-6037
E-mail: pwcenter@mtn.org
Internet: www.pwcenter.org
AMOUNT: $10,000
DEADLINE(S): JAN 15
FIELD(S): Playwriting

For US playwrights whose work has had a significant impact on the contemporary theatre. Two works must have been fully produced by professional theatres. Eligible playwrights must be nominated by a theatre professional.

2 awards annually. Professionals wishing to nominate a playwright should contact the Center in early Fall, attention Megan Monaghan.

1012—PLAYWRIGHTS' CENTER (PlayLabs)

2301 East Franklin Ave.
Minneapolis MN 55406-1099
612/332-7481
FAX: 612/332-6037
E-mail: pwcenter@mtn.org
Internet: www.pwcenter.org
AMOUNT: Honoraria + travel expenses
+ room & board
DEADLINE(S): DEC 15
FIELD(S): Playwriting

Two-week workshop open to US citizens who are authors of unproduced, unpublished full-length plays (no one-acts). Each play receives a public reading followed by audience discussion of the work. Must live within a 110-mile radius of the Twin Cities. Conference is intended to allow playwrights to take risks free of artistic restraint.

4 to 6 playwrights chosen by open script competition. Send a self-addressed, stamped envelope to above address for an application.

1013—POETRY SOCIETY OF AMERICA (George Bogin Memorial Award)

15 Gramercy Park
New York NY 10003
212/254-9628
FAX: 212/673-2352
Internet: www.poetrysociety.org
AMOUNT: $500
DEADLINE(S): DEC 21
FIELD(S): Poetry

Prizes for the best selections of four or five poems that reflect the encounter of the ordinary and the extraordinary, use language in an original way, and take a stand against oppression in any of its forms.

$5 entry fee for non-members. Contact PSA for submission guidelines.

1014—POETRY SOCIETY OF AMERICA (Louise Louis/Emily F. Bourne Student Poetry Award)

15 Gramercy Park
New York NY 10003
212/254-9628
FAX: 212/673-2352
Internet: www.poetrysociety.org
AMOUNT: $250
DEADLINE(S): DEC 21
FIELD(S): Poetry

Prizes for the best unpublished poems by high school or preparatory school students (grades 9-12) from the United States. High schools may submit an unlimited number of their students' poems for $10 in one submission (one poem per student); individual entry fee is $1.

Contact PSA for submission guidelines.

1015—POETRY SOCIETY OF AMERICA (Robert H. Winner Memorial Award)

15 Gramercy Park
New York NY 10003
212/254-9628

FAX: 212/673-2352

Internet: www.poetrysociety.org

AMOUNT: $2,500

DEADLINE(S): DEC 21

FIELD(S): Poetry

For poets over 50 years of age who have not published or who have no more than one book. This award acknowledges original work done in midlife by someone who has not had substantial recognition. Send a brief but cohesive manuscript of up to 10 poems or 20 pages. Poems entered here may be submitted to other contests as well. Please include date of birth on cover page.

$5 entry fee for non-members. Contact PSA for submission guidelines.

1016—POETRY SOCIETY OF AMERICA (Shelley Memorial Award)

15 Gramercy Park
New York NY 10003
212/254-9628
FAX: 212/673-2352
Internet: www.poetrysociety.org

AMOUNT: $250-$1,000

DEADLINE(S): DEC 21

FIELD(S): Poetry

This contest (NOT scholarship) is open to both PSA members and non-members. All submissions must be unpublished on the date of entry and not scheduled for publication by the date of the PSA awards ceremony held in the spring.

$5 entry fee for non-members. Contact PSA for submission guidelines.

1017—PRINCESS GRACE FOUNDATION-USA (Grants for Young Playwrights)

150 East 58th Street, 21st Fl.
New York NY 10155
212/317-1470
FAX: 212/317-1473
E-mail: pgfusa@pgfusa.com
Internet: www.pgfusa.com

AMOUNT: $7,500 + 10-week residency at New Dramatists, Inc., New York City & other benefits

DEADLINE(S): MAR 31

FIELD(S): Playwriting

Grants for young playwrights up to age 30 who are US citizens or permanent residents. Awards based primarily on artistic quality of submitted play, appropriateness of activities to individual's artistic growth, and potential future excellence. Script will be included in New Dramatists' lending library, be distributed to catalogue subscribers for one year, and possibly be published through the Dramatists' Play Service.

1 award annually. See website or contact Ms. Toby E. Boshak, Executive Director, for an application.

1018—RAGDALE FOUNDATION (Frances Shaw Fellowship)

1260 N. Green Bay Road
Lake Forest IL 60045-1106
847/234-1063
FAX: 847/234-1075
E-mail: ragdale1@aol.com
Internet: nsn.nslsilus.org/ifkhome/ragdale

AMOUNT: 2-month residency

DEADLINE(S): FEB 1

FIELD(S): Creative Writing

Writing residency for women who have begun to write seriously after the age of 55. US citizenship required, and financial need must be demonstrated.

1 award annually. Not renewable. Contact Sylvia Brown at above address for details.

1019—RIPON COLLEGE (Performance/Recognition Tuition Scholarships)

Admissions Office
300 Seward Street
P.O. Box 248
Ripon WI 54971
920/748-8102 or 800/94-RIPON
E-mail: adminfo@ripon.edu
Internet: www.ripon.edu

AMOUNT: $5,000-$10,000/yr.

DEADLINE(S): MAR 1

FIELD(S): Music, Forensics, Art, Theatre

Open to undergraduate and graduate students attending or planning to attend Ripon College. Purpose is to recognize and encourage academic potential and accomplishment in above fields. Interview, audition, or nomination may be required.

Renewable. Contact Office of Admission for an application.

1020—ROSE HILL COLLEGE (Louella Robinson Memorial Scholarship)

P.O. Box 3126
Aiken SC 29802-3126
800/684-3769
FAX: 803/641-0240
E-mail: rosehill@.edu
Internet: www.rosehill.edu

AMOUNT: $10,000/yr. for four years

DEADLINE(S): Varies

FIELD(S): Liberal Arts and Humanities curricula

For undergraduate residents of Indian River County, Florida, to attend Rose Hill College in Aiken, South Carolina. The school offers a liberal arts education and follows the Great Books curriculum, a program of reading and seminars.

1 annual award. Applicants must meet entry requirements of RHC. Contact above location for details.

1021—ROSE HILL COLLEGE (Scholarships for Children of Eastern Orthodox Priests/Deacons)

P.O. Box 3126
Aiken SC 29802-3126
800/684-3769
FAX: 803/641-0240
E-mail: rosehill@edu
Internet: www.rosehill.edu

AMOUNT: Full scholarship: $10,000/yr. for four years

DEADLINE(S): Varies

FIELD(S): Liberal Arts and Humanities curricula

For undergraduates who are children of Eastern Orthodox Christian priests or deacons to attend Rose Hill College in Aiken, South Carolina. The school offers a liberal arts education and follows the Great Books curriculum, a program of reading and seminars.

6-10 annual awards. Applicants must meet entry requirements of RHC. Contact above location for details.

1022—ROSE HILL COLLEGE (Scholarships for the Homeschooled)

P.O. Box 3126
Aiken SC 29802-3126
800/684-3769
FAX: 803/641-0240
E-mail: rosehill@rosehill.edu
Internet: www.resehill.edu

AMOUNT: Full scholarship: $10,000/yr. for four years

DEADLINE(S): Varies

FIELD(S): Liberal Arts and Humanities curricula

For undergraduates who have been homeschooled for three of the last five years of their high school education. For use at Rose Hill College in Aiken, South Carolina. The school offers a liberal arts education and follows the Great Books curriculum, a program of reading and seminars. Scholarships will be awarded primarily on the basis of an essay which the student will be asked to write.

4 annual awards. Applicants must meet entry requirements of RHC. Contact above location for details.

1023—SAN FRANCISCO FOUNDATION (James D. Phelan Literary Award)

225 Bush Street, Suite 500
San Francisco CA 94104-4224
415/733-8500
FAX: 415/477-2783
Internet: www.sff.org

AMOUNT: $2,000
DEADLINE(S): JAN 31
FIELD(S): Writing: Fiction, nonfiction, poetry, prose, or drama

Open to California-born authors of unpublished works-in-progress who are between the ages of 20 and 35, and are US citizens.

Writers of nonfiction are also eligible for the $1,000 "Special Award in Non-Fictional Prose." Write to the above address for complete information.

1024—SAN FRANCISCO FOUNDATION (Joseph Henry Jackson Literary Award)

225 Bush Street, Suite 500
San Francisco CA 94104-4224
415/733-8500
FAX: 415/477-2783
Internet: sff.org

AMOUNT: $2,000
DEADLINE(S): JAN 31
FIELD(S): Literature/Creative Writing

Open to Northern California or Nevada residents (for 3 consecutive years immediately prior to closing date of the competition) who are authors of unpublished work-in-progress (fiction, nonfiction, poetry) and between 20-35 years of age.

Writers of nonfiction are also eligible for the $1,000 "Special Award in Non-Fictional Prose." Write for complete information.

1025—SPECIAL LIBRARIES ASSOCIATION (SLA Scholarship Program)

1700 18th Street NW
Washington DC 20009-2508
202/234-4700
FAX: 202/265-9317
E-mail: sla@sla.org
Internet: www.sla.org

AMOUNT: $6,000
DEADLINE(S): OCT 31

FIELD(S): Library Science

Open to college graduates or college seniors with an interest in special librarianship. Scholarship is for graduate study in librarianship leading to a master's degree at a recognized school of library or information science.

Applicants must submit evidence of financial need. Write for complete information.

1026—STANLEY DRAMA AWARD (Playwriting/Musical Awards Competition)

Dept. of Theatre
Wagner College
One Campus Road
Staten Island NY 10301
718/390-3325

AMOUNT: $2,000
DEADLINE(S): OCT 1
FIELD(S): Playwriting, Music Composition

Annual award for an original full-length play or musical that has not been professionally produced or received tradebook publication. Must submit musical works on cassette tape with book and lyrics. A series of 2-3 thematically related one-act plays will also be considered. When submitting scripts, send self-addressed, stamped envelope large enough to accommodate the script.

Contact the Department of Theatre at Wagner College for complete information.

1027—STUDENT CONSERVATION ASSOCIATION (SCA Resource Assistant Program)

P.O. Box 550
Charlestown NH 03603
603/543-1700
FAX: 603/543-1828
E-mail: internships@sca-inc.org
Internet: www.sca-inc.org

AMOUNT: $1,180-$4,725
DEADLINE(S): Varies
FIELD(S): Environment & related fields

Must be 18 and US citizen; need not be student. Fields: Agriculture, archaeology, anthropology, botany, caves, civil/environmental engineering, environmental education, fisheries, forests, herpetology, history, living history/roleplaying, visitor services, landscape architectural/environmental design, paleontology, recreation/resource/range management, trail maintenance/construction, wildlife management, geology, hydrology, library/museums, surveying.

900 positions in US and Canada. Send $1 for postage for application; outside US/Canada, send $20.

1028—THE JOHN F. KENNEDY CENTER FOR THE PERFORMING ARTS (Awards, Fellowships, and Scholarships)

The Kennedy Center
Washington DC 20566-0001
202/416-8857
FAX: 202/416-8802
E-mail: skshaffer@mail.kennedy-center.org
Internet: www.kennedy-center.org/education/actf

AMOUNT: Varies
DEADLINE(S): Varies
FIELD(S): Playwriting, Stage Design, and Acting

Various scholarships and awards in the above fields.

Contact organization for a booklet: "The Kennedy Center American College Theater Festival" for details and/or visit website.

1029—THE WALT DISNEY COMPANY (American Teacher Awards)

P.O. Box 9805
Calabasas CA 91372

AMOUNT: $2,500 (36 awards); $25,000 (Outstanding Teacher of the Year)
DEADLINE(S): FEB 15
FIELD(S): Teachers: athletic coach, early childhood, English, foreign language/ESL, general elementary, mathematics, performing arts, physical education/health, science, social studies, visual arts, voc-tech education

Awards for K-12 teachers in the above fields.

Teachers, or anyone who knows a great teacher, can write for applications at the above address.

1030—U.S. INSTITUTE OF PEACE (National Peace Essay Contest)

1200 17th Street NW, Suite 200
Washington DC 20036
202/429-3834
FAX 202/429-6063
E-mail: essay_contest@usip.org
Internet: www.usip.org

AMOUNT: $1,000-$10,000
DEADLINE(S): JAN 26
FIELD(S): Political Science, US History

1,500-word essay contest for high school students on the US response to international conflict. No restrictions as to citizenship/residency.

53 awards annually. Not renewable. See website or contact USIP for specific guidelines.

1031—UNITARIAN UNIVERSALIST ASSO-CIATION (Musicians' Network Scholarships)

4190 Front Street
San Diego CA 92103
Written inquiry

AMOUNT: $100-$700
DEADLINE(S): MAR 1
FIELD(S): Art, Poetry, Music

Financial aid to undergraduate students in the above fields. Must be active with the Unitarian Universalist Association.

Renewable. Write for complete information.

1032—UNIVERSITY FILM & VIDEO ASSO-CIATION (Carole Fielding Student Grants)

University of Baltimore
School of Communication
1420 N. Charles Street
Baltimore MD 21201
410/837-6061

AMOUNT: $1,000 to $4,000
DEADLINE(S): MAR 31
FIELD(S): Film, Video, Multi-media Production

Open to undergraduate/graduate students. Categories are narrative, experimental, animation, documentary, multimedia/installation and research. Applicant must be sponsored by a faculty member who is an active member of the University Film and Video Association.

Write to the above address for application and complete details.

1033—U.S. MARINE CORPS HISTORICAL CENTER (College Internships)

Building 58
Washington Navy Yard
Washington DC 20374
202/433-3839

AMOUNT: Stipend to cover daily expenses
DEADLINE(S): None specified
FIELD(S): US Military History, Library Science, History, Museum Studies

Open to undergraduate students at a college or university which will grant academic credit for work experience as interns at the address above or at the Marine Corps Air-Ground Museum in Quantico, Virginia.

All internships are regarded as beginning professional-level historian, curator, librarian, or archivist positions. Write for complete information.

1034—WAVERLY COMMUNITY HOUSE INC. (F. Lammot Belin Arts Scholarships)

Scholarships Selection Committee
P.O. Box 142
Waverly PA 18471
717/586-8191

AMOUNT: $10,000
DEADLINE(S): DEC 15
FIELD(S): Painting, Sculpture, Music, Drama, Dance, Literature, Architecture, Photography

Applicants must have resided in the Abington or Pocono regions of Northeastern Pennsylvania. They must furnish proof of exceptional ability in their chosen field but no formal training in any academic or professional program.

US citizenship required. Finalists must appear in person before the selection committee. Write for complete information.

1035—WOMEN ON BOOKS (Scholarships for African-American Women)

879 Rainier Ave. N., Suite A105
Renton WA 98055
206/626-2323

AMOUNT: $1,000
DEADLINE(S): JUN (Mid-month)
FIELD(S): English or Journalism, with intention to pursue a writing career

Scholarships for African-American women pursuing careers in writing. Must major in English or journalism in a four-year university, have a min. GPA of 2.5, and demonstrate financial need.

Write for details.

FOREIGN LANGUAGE

1036—ACL/NJCL NATIONAL LATIN EXAM (Scholarships)

P.O. Box 95
Mount Vernon VA 22121
800/459-9847 or 888/378-7721
Internet: acs.rhodes.edu/~nle

AMOUNT: $1,000
DEADLINE(S): JAN 10
FIELD(S): Latin Language

Applications for the scholarship will be mailed to gold medal winners in Latin III-IV Prose, III-IV Poetry, or Latin V-VI who are high school seniors. Applicants must agree to take at least one year of Latin or classical Greek in college. Exams are taken in March at your high school.

$3 application fee for exam. 20 awards annually. Renewable. Contact Jane Hall, National Latin Exam Committee, for an exam order form, or tell your teacher/principal that you would like to take the test.

1037—AIR FORCE RESERVE OFFICER TRAINING CORPS (AFROTC Scholarships)

551 E. Maxwell Blvd.
Maxwell AFB AL 36112-6106
334/953-7783

AMOUNT: Full tuition, books, & fees for all 4 years of college
DEADLINE(S): DEC 1
FIELD(S): Science, Engineering, Business, Political Science, Psychology, Geography, Foreign Studies, Foreign Language

Competitive scholarships based on individual merit to high school seniors and graduates who have not completed any full-time college work. Must be a US citizen between the ages of 17-27. Must also have GPA of 2.5 or above, be in top 40% of class, and complete Applicant Fitness Test. Cannot be a single parent. Your college/university must offer AFROTC.

2,300 awards annually. Contact above address for application packet.

1038—ALPHA MU GAMMA NATIONAL OFFICE (Goddard/Indovina/Krakowski Scholarships)

c/o Los Angeles City College
855 N. Vermont Ave.
Los Angeles CA 90029
213/664-8742

AMOUNT: $200-$500
DEADLINE(S): JAN 10
FIELD(S): Foreign Language

Scholarships open to college or university students who are MEMBERS OF ALPHA MU GAMMA CHAPTERS. Students must have completed at least 1-1/2 semesters of college work and have two "A" grades in a foreign language. Applicants must participate in a national scholarship competition.

5 awards annually. Applications available ONLY from local AMG chapter advisors (in mid-October). The National Office will NOT reply to any inquiries concerning these scholarships.

1039—AMERICAN ASSOCIATION OF TEACHERS OF FRENCH (National French Contest)

Sidney L. Teitelbaum
Box 32030
Sarasota FL 34278
FAX: 941/364-9820

AMOUNT: Varies
DEADLINE(S): FEB 4
FIELD(S): French Language, French Studies

National French contest is an examination taken throughout the country. Students are ranked regionally and nationally and are eligible for both local and national awards.

Not a scholarship. Winners receive trips, medals, and books. Write for complete information or ask your French teacher.

1040—AMERICAN ASSOCIATION OF TEACHERS OF GERMAN (National AATG/PAD Awards)

112 Haddontowne Ct., #104
Cherry Hill NJ 08034
609/795-5553

AMOUNT: Costs of study trip
DEADLINE(S): DEC 1 (deadline for teachers to order test)
FIELD(S): German Language

This summer-study trip award to Germany is open to high school students aged 16 or older who score at or above the 90 percentile on the AATG National German Test. US citizenship or permanent residency is required.

Up to 47 travel-study awards per year. Tests are administered by high school German teachers. Write to address above for complete information or inquire of your German teacher. FINANCIAL AID FOR POSTSECONDARY EDUCATION IS NOT AVAILABLE.

1041—AMERICAN ASSOCIATION OF TEACHERS OF ITALIAN (College Essay in Italian)

Cal State Univ.—Chico
Foreign Language Dept.
Chico CA 95929
Written inquiries

AMOUNT: $100-$300
DEADLINE(S): JUN 15
FIELD(S): Italian Language, Italian Studies

Contest open to undergraduate students at accredited colleges and universities in North America. Essay in Italian language on topic pertaining to literature or culture.

Write to Prof. Eugenio Frongia at address above for complete information.

1042—BAJA CALIFORNIA LANGUAGE COLLEGE (Spanish Language Immersion Contest)

Barcelona #191
Ensenada BC MEXICO
619/758-9711
E-mail: college@bajacal.com
Internet: www.bajacal.com

AMOUNT: $1,000
DEADLINE(S): APR 30
FIELD(S): Spanish Language

For all levels of study. Must compete in contest offered weekly by bi-lingual newspaper *La Presna de Minnesota* (www.laprensa-mn.com). Contest runs from February to April.

2 awards annually. See website or contact Keith Rolle for more information. US address: P.O. Box 7556, San Diego, CA 92167.

1043—INSTITUT D'ETUDES FRANCAISES D'AVIGNON/BRYN MAWR COLLEGE (Scholarships for Summer Study in Avignon, France)

Institut d'etudes francaises d'Avignon
Bryn Mawr College
Bryn Mawr PA 1901000-2899
610/526-5083
FAX: 610/526-7479
Internet: www.brynmawr.edu/Adm/academic/special/avignon/details.html

AMOUNT: Varies
DEADLINE(S): MAR 15
FIELD(S): French-related studies

Scholarships based on academic excellence and financial need for a six-week summer study program in Avignon, France. Program is offered to male and female students from other colleges as well as Bryn Mawr. For graduates and undergraduates who have completed three years of college-level French or equivalent.

Contact the Director of the Institute for application information.

1044—INSTITUTE OF INTERNATIONAL EDUCATION (National Security Education Program Undergraduate Scholarship)

1400 K Street NW
Washington DC 20005-2403
202/326-7697 or 800/618-NSEP
FAX: 202/326-7698
E-mail: nsep@iie.org
Internet: http://www.iie.org/nsep/

AMOUNT: Varies: up to $8,000
DEADLINE(S): Varies
FIELD(S): Foreign Language

Scholarships are available to enable recipients to pursue serious study abroad in critical world areas that do NOT include Western Europe, Canada, Australia, or New Zealand.

A foreign language component must be included in every applicant's study abroad proposal. Check with NSEP respresentative at your local campus or write or call above location for complete information.

1045—JAPANESE AMERICAN CITIZENS LEAGUE (Yoshiko Tanaka Memorial Scholarship)

1765 Sutter Street
San Francisco CA 94115
415/921-5225
FAX: 415/931-4671
E-mail: jacl@jacl.org
Internet: www.jacl.org

AMOUNT: $1,000-$5,000
DEADLINE(S): APR 1
FIELD(S): Japanese Language/Culture, U.S.-Japan Relations

Open to JACL members and their children only. For undergraduate students with an interest in Japanese language, culture, or the enhancement of US-Japan relations and who are planning to attend a college, university, trade school, business school, or any other institution of higher learning. Must submit personal statement, letters of recommendation, and transcripts. Financial need NOT a factor.

For membership information or an application, send a self-addressed, stamped envelope to above address, stating your level of study. Applications available October 1st through March 20th; recipients notified in July.

1046—LUSO-AMERICAN EDUCATION FOUNDATION (General Scholarships)

P.O. Box 2967
Dublin CA 94568

510/828-3883
AMOUNT: Varies
DEADLINE(S): MAR 1
FIELD(S): Portuguese Language or
Portuguese Descent-related fields

Open to Calif. high school seniors (under 21) of Portuguese descent who will enroll full-time in a 4-year program that includes Portuguese language classes. Also open to members of Luso-American Fraternal Federation.

Write for complete information.

1047—NATIONAL FEDERATION OF THE BLIND (Humanities Scholarship)

805 5th Ave.
Grinnell IA 50112
515/236-3366

AMOUNT: $3,000
DEADLINE(S): MAR 31
FIELD(S): Humanities (Art, English,
Foreign Languages, History,
Philosophy, Religion)

Open to legally blind students pursuing or planning to pursue a full-time postsecondary education in the US. Scholarships are awarded on basis of academic excellence, service to the community, and financial need. Must include transcripts and two letters of recommendation. Membership NOT required.

1 award annually. Renewable. Contact Mrs. Peggy Elliot, Scholarship Committee Chairman, for an application.

1048—NATIONAL ITALIAN AMERICAN FOUNDATION (Mola Foundation of Chicago Scholarships)

1860 19th Street NW
Washington DC 20009-5599
202/530-5315

AMOUNT: $1,000
DEADLINE(S): MAY 31
FIELD(S): Italian major

Open to undergraduates majoring in Italian and who are of Italian ancestry. Must be from Illinois, Indiana, Michigan, Wisconsin, Ohio, Iowa, Minnesota, Kentucky, South Dakota, or North Dakota.
9 awards.

1049—NATIONAL ITALIAN AMERICAN FOUNDATION (Paragano Scholarship)

1860 19th Street NW
Washington DC 20009-5599
202/530-5315

AMOUNT: $2,000

DEADLINE(S): MAY 31
FIELD(S): Italian majors

For undergraduate Italian majors of Italian ancestry who reside in New Jersey.
2 awards. Financial need, community service, and academic merit are considered.

1050—NORWICH JUBILEE ESPERANTO FOUNDATION (Travel Grants)

37 Granville Court
Oxford OX3 0HS ENGLAND
01865-245509

AMOUNT: 1,000 pounds sterling (max.)
DEADLINE(S): None
FIELD(S): Esperanto

Travel grants open to those who speak Esperanto and wish to improve their use of the language through travel in the UK. Candidates must be under the age of 26 and be able to lecture in Esperanto.

Up to 25 awards annually. Renewable. Inquiries MUST include fluency and interest in Esperanto. Contact Kathleen M. Hall, Secretary to the Foundation, for an application.

1051—SOUTHEAST MISSOURI STATE UNIVERSITY (Constance Rowe French Scholarship)

One University Plaza
Cape Girardeau MO 63701
573/651-2000
Internet: www.2.semo.edu/
foreignlang/SCH-FR.HTML

AMOUNT: Up to full tuition and fees
DEADLINE(S): Varies
FIELD(S): French or Education with a
French minor

Scholarships for French majors or Education majors with a French minor at Southeast Missouri State University. Awarded for study in a French-speaking country for the summer after the sophomore year, either semester of the junior year, or for the summer after the junior year. Financial need may be considered.

Contact Dr. Daniel A. MacLeay at the University for more information. His e-mail contact point is accessible at the website listed.

1052—SOUTHEAST MISSOURI STATE UNIVERSITY (German Scholarship)

One University Plaza
Cape Girardeau MO 63701

573/651-2000
Internet: www2.semo.edu/
foreignlang/SCH-GN.HTML

AMOUNT: Varies
DEADLINE(S): Varies
FIELD(S): German language

Scholarships for full-time students who are German majors at Southeast Missouri State University. Awarded for overseas study purposes. Must have a 2.5 or higher GPA.

Contact Dr. Dieter Jedan at the University for more information. His e-mail contact point is accessible at the website listed.

1053—SOUTHEAST MISSOURI STATE UNIVERSITY (The Frances and Cornelius Crowley Spanish Club Scholarship)

One University Plaza
Cape Girardeau MO 63701
573/651-2000
Internet: www.2.semo.edu/
foreignlang/SCH-SN.HTML

AMOUNT: Varies
DEADLINE(S): Varies
FIELD(S): Spanish

Scholarships for Spanish Club members at Southeast Missouri State University. Must have a 2.8 overall GPA; must have a 3.0 Spanish GPA.

Contact Dr. Will Derusha at the University for more information.

1054—THE AMERICAN ASSOCIATION OF TEACHERS OF ARABIC (Translation Contest)

Princeton University, Dept. of NES
110 Jones Hall
Princeton NJ 08544
609/258-4280
Internet: humanities.byu.edu/AATA/
contest.html

AMOUNT: $600 (1st); $400 (2nd)
DEADLINE(S): OCT 1
FIELD(S): Arabic

A contest for students of Arabic who translate certain types of works from Arabic to English. Only individuals who are non-native speaker students of Arabic enrolled in Arabic as a Foreign Language classes or programs at any level or who have done so during the past two years are eligible.

Contact Professor Margaret Larkin, Contest Chair, at above location or check website for details.

1055—THE AMERICAN CLASSICAL LEAGUE (Ed Phinney Commemorative Scholarship)

Miami University
Oxford OH 45056
513/529-7741
FAX: 513/529-7742
E-mail: AmericanClassicalLeague@muohio.edu OR a.c.l@mich.edu
Internet: www.umich.edu/~acleague/phinney.html

AMOUNT: Up to $500
DEADLINE(S): JAN 15
FIELD(S): Teachers or teacher candidates in the classics (Latin and/or Greek)

Scholarships of up to $500 to apply to first-time attendance at the League's institute OR up to $500 to cover cost of other activities that serve to enhance a teacher's skills in the classroom in the classics OR up to $150 for purchase of materials from the ACL Teaching and Materials Resource Center. Memberships required except for first-time attendance at institute.

Send request for information to above address.

1056—THE AMERICAN CLASSICAL LEAGUE (Maureen V. O'Donnell Memorial Teacher Training Scholarship)

Miami University
Oxford OH 45056
513/529-7741
FAX: 513/529-7742
E-mail: AmericanClassicalLeague@muohio.edu OR a.c.l@mich.edu
Internet: www.umich.edu/~acleague/O'Donnell.html

AMOUNT: Up to $500
DEADLINE(S): MAR 1; DEC 1
FIELD(S): Teacher education for Latin

Scholarships for candidates in training for certification to teach Latin. Must have completed a substantial part of course work. At time of application, must be members of ACL.

Funds may be used for tuition costs or other expenses, such as travel, childcare, income replacement, etc. Send request for information to above address.

1057—THE CENTER FOR CROSS-CULTURAL STUDY (Tuition Awards for Study in Seville, Spain)

446 Main Street
Amherst MA 01002-2314
413/256-0011 or 1-800/377-2621
FAX: 413/256-1968
E-mail: cccs@crocker.com
Internet: www.cccs.com

AMOUNT: $500
DEADLINE(S): Varies
FIELD(S): Study of Spanish and Spanish Culture

Partial tuition assistance is available at this facility in Spain. Applicants must submit an original essay in Spanish, between 2 or 3 double-spaced, typed pages. Also required as a short description in English of your experience with the Spanish language and culture and a faculty recommendation.

Awards are for one semester or academic year programs in Seville. Contact organization for specific details regarding the essays.

1058—THE WALT DISNEY COMPANY (American Teacher Awards)

P.O. Box 9805
Calabasas CA 91372

AMOUNT: $2,500 (36 awards); $25,000 (Outstanding Teacher of the Year)
DEADLINE(S): FEB 15
FIELD(S): Teachers: athletic coach, early childhood, English, foreign language/ESL, general elementary, mathematics, performing arts, physical education/health, science, social studies, visual arts, voc-tech education

Awards for K-12 teachers in the above fields.

Teachers, or anyone who knows a great teacher, can write for applications at the above address.

1059—UNIVERSITY OF ROCHESTER (Mildred R. Burton Summer Study Grants/Scholarships for Summer Language Study)

Box 270251
Rochester NY 14627-0251
716/275-3221 or 888/822-2256
Internet: www.rochester.edu/College/MLC/burton.html

AMOUNT: Varies
DEADLINE(S): MAR 17
FIELD(S): Foreign language

Scholarships for undergraduate students to complete an approved course of summer language study in a country where that language is spoken. Preference will be given to Univ. of Rochester students who intend to study in a program run by the University if such a program is available in the language the student wishes to study.

Must have completed at least one year of foreign language study at U.R. and graduate students in the Dept. of Modern Languages & Cultures.

Based on merit and need. Applications are available from the Dept. of Modern Languages & Cultures.

PERFORMING ARTS

1060—ACADEMY OF VOCAL ARTS (Scholarships)

1920 Spruce Street
Philadelphia PA 19103-6685
215/735-1685

AMOUNT: Full Tuition
DEADLINE(S): Varies (2 weeks prior to auditions in Spring)
FIELD(S): Vocal Music, Operatic Acting

Tenable only at the Academy of Vocal Arts. Open to unusually gifted singers with at least two years college vocal training or equivalent. College degree recommended. Award includes full tuition scholarships and complete training in voice, operatic acting, and repertoire. Winners are selected in Spring competitive auditions. Total student enrollment limited to 30.

Contact the Academy of Vocal Arts for an application.

1061—ADELPHI UNIVERSITY (Talent Awards)

1 South Ave.
Garden City NY 11530
516/877-3080
Internet: www.adelphi.edu/finaid/awards.html

AMOUNT: Up to $6,000
DEADLINE(S): FEB 15
FIELD(S): Theater, Dance, Art, or Music

Various scholarships for full-time students at Adelphi University in the above fields. Must document financial need—fill out a FAFSA form. Must maintain 3.0 GPA in major and 2.5 overall to maintain scholarship.

See website for further information; contact school to apply.

1062—ALVIN M. BENTLEY FOUNDATION (Scholarship Program)

P.O. Box 1516
Owosso MI 48867
517/729-9040
FAX: 517/723-2454

AMOUNT: $40,000 (4-year); $1,000/yr. (freshman)

DEADLINE(S): None
FIELD(S): Literature, Science, Arts

Open to Michigan residents applying as freshmen to the University of Michigan's College of Literature, Science, and the Arts. Based on academic excellence and extracurricular activities. Must be nominated; there are no separate applications. Candidates are chosen from U of M applications received from Michigan resident freshmen.

4 four-year awards and 8 freshmen awards annually. Contact University of Michigan for details.

1063—AMERICAN ACCORDION MUSICO-LOGICAL SOCIETY (Contest)

334 South Broadway
Pitman NJ 08071
609/854-6628

AMOUNT: $100-$250
DEADLINE(S): SEP 10
FIELD(S): Music Composition for Accordion

Annual competition open to amateur or professional music composers who write a serious piece music (of six minutes or more) for the accordion.

Write for complete information.

1064—AMERICAN ALLIANCE FOR HEALTH, PHYSICAL EDUCATION, RECREATION & DANCE

1900 Association Drive
Reston VA 20191
703/476-3400 or 800/213-7193
E-mail: webmaster@aahpeRoadorg
Internet: www.aahpeRoadorg

AMOUNT: Varies
DEADLINE(S): Varies
FIELD(S): Health Education, Leisure and Recreation, Girls and Women in Sports, Sport and Physical Education, Dance

This organization has six national sub-organizations specializing in the above fields. Some have grants and fellowships for both individuals and group projects. The website has the details for each group.

Visit website for details or write to above address for details.

1065—AMERICAN FOUNDATION FOR THE BLIND (Gladys C. Anderson Memorial Scholarship)

11 Penn Plaza, Suite 300
New York NY 10001
212/502-7661
FAX: 212/502-7771

E-mail: juliet@afb.org
Internet: www.afb.org

AMOUNT: $1,000
DEADLINE(S): APR 30
FIELD(S): Religious/Classical Music

Open to legally blind women studying religious or classical music at the college level. Must be US citizen. Must submit evidence of legal blindness; official transcripts; proof of college/university acceptance; three letters of recommendation; performance tape of voice/instrumental selection (30 minutes max.); and typewritten statement describing educational and personal goals, work experience, extracurricular activities, and how scholarship monies will be used.

1 award annually. See website or contact Julie Tucker at AFB for an application.

1066—AMERICAN FOUNDATION FOR THE BLIND (R.L. Gillette Scholarships)

11 Penn Plaza, Suite 300
New York NY 10001
212/502-7661
FAX: 212/502-7771
E-mail: juliet@afb.org
Internet: www.afb.org

AMOUNT: $1,000
DEADLINE(S): APR 30
FIELD(S): Literature, Music

Open to legally blind women enrolled in a four-year undergraduate degree program in literature or music. Must be US citizen. Must submit evidence of legal blindness; official transcripts; proof of college/university acceptance; three letters of recommendation; performance tape (30 minutes max.) or creative writing sample; and typewritten statement describing educational and personal goals, work experience, extracurricular activities, and how monies will be used.

2 awards annually. See website or contact Julie Tucker at AFB for an application.

1067—AMERICAN GUILD OF ORGANISTS (National Competition in Organ Improvisation)

475 Riverside Drive, Suite 1260
New York NY 10115
212/870-2310
FAX: 212/870-2163

AMOUNT: $2,000 (1st prize); $1,000 (2nd); $500 (3rd)
DEADLINE(S): JAN 1
FIELD(S): Organ Performance

Competition seeks to further the art of improvisation in organ performance by recognizing and rewarding superior performers in the field. Membership in AGO required. Open to all members, including student members.

$35 registration fee. Contact AGO for membership information or an application.

1068—AMERICAN GUILD OF ORGANISTS (National Young Artists Competition)

475 Riverside Drive, Suite 1260
New York NY 10115
212/870-2310
FAX: 212/870-2163

AMOUNT: $2,000 (1st prize); $1,500 (2nd); $750 (3rd)
DEADLINE(S): Varies
FIELD(S): Organ Performance

Competition for organists between the ages of 22 and 32. Must be members of AGO.

Contact AGO for membership information or an application.

1069—AMERICAN GUILD OF ORGANISTS (Regional Competitions for Young Organists)

475 Riverside Drive, Suite 1260
New York NY 10115
212/870-2310
FAX: 212/870-2163

AMOUNT: $1,000 (1st prize); $500 (2nd)
DEADLINE(S): JAN 31
FIELD(S): Organ Performance

Competition for young people up to age 23 in nine different regions of the US. Membership NOT required.

$25 registration fee. Contact AGO for an application.

1070—AMERICAN LEGION-KANSAS (Music Committee Scholarship)

1314 SW Topeka Blvd.
Topeka KS 66612-1886
913/232-9315

AMOUNT: $1,000
DEADLINE(S): FEB 15
FIELD(S): Music

Scholarship for Kansas high school seniors who have distinguished themselves in the field of music and/or will major or minor in music at an approved Kansas junior college, college, or university.

For complete information write to the above address.

1071—AMERICAN MOTHERS, INC. (Gertrude Fogelson Cultural and Creative Arts Awards)

1296 E. 21st Street
Brooklyn NY 11201
718/253-5676

AMOUNT: Up to $1,000
DEADLINE(S): JAN 1 (annually)
FIELD(S): Visual Arts, Creative Writing, and Vocal Music

An award to encourage and honor mothers in artistic pursuits.

Write to Alice Miller at above address for details.

1072—AMERICAN STRING TEACHERS ASSOCIATION (ASTA) (Solo Competitions)

Univ. of Michigan, School of Music
1100 Baits Drive
Ann Arbor MI 48109-2085
313/764-6518
FAX: 313/763-5097
E-mail: sbshipps@u.mich.edu
Internet: www.astaweb.com

AMOUNT: Up to $4,000
DEADLINE(S): Varies
FIELD(S): Music (strings): violin, viola, cello, double bass, classical guitar, and harp

Participants must be ASTA members or current students of ASTA members. Involves state competitions which lead to national competition. Two age groups: Junior Division—under 19 and Senior Division—19-25. Application fees required. For US and Canadian citizens/ legal residents.

Details of rules and various deadlines are on website above. List of state solo competition chairpersons is on website. Address questions to Professor Stephen B. Shipps, ASTA Solo Competition Chair, at above address/e-mail.

1073—AMERICAN SYMPHONY ORCHESTRA LEAGUE (Music Assistance Fund)

1156 15th St NW, Suite 800
Washington DC 20005-1704
202/776-0212
FAX: 202/776-0223

AMOUNT: $500; $3,500
DEADLINE(S): DEC 15
FIELD(S): Music

Open to US citizens of African descent studying and performing an orchestra instrument, and intending to pursue a career in symphony orchestras. Voice, piano, composition, and conducting not included.

Scholarships to be applied towards summer music program, academic tuition, or any performance-related study. Must apply each year.

1074—ASSOCIATED MALE CHORUSES OF AMERICA (Scholarships)

43 Freemont Ave.
Etobicoke Ontario M9P 2W4
CANADA
416/241-2028
E-mail: trayner@istar.ca
Internet: www.tc
umn.edu/nlhome/m042/
thoma075/scholar.html

AMOUNT: $500 or more
DEADLINE(S): MAR 1
FIELD(S): Music: Voice/Choral or Instrumental

6 awards/year. Scholarships for music majors, both male and female, enrolled as full-time college students in Bachelor's Degree programs. Student must be sponsored by a member chorus of the AMCA. List of member choruses available online. May reapply.

Applications and details are online at above website OR send self-addressed, stamped envelope (at rate appropriate for Canada) to Tom Rayner, AMCA Scholarship Chair, at above e-mail or postal address for detailed information and application. However, applications will not be available until Oct. 1. Include your regular mail address.

1075—BALTIMORE OPERA STUDIO (Apprenticeship)

110 W. Mount Royal Ave.
Suite 306
Baltimore MD 21201
410/625-1600
FAX: 410/625-6474
E-mail: hstevens@
baltimoreopera.com
Internet: www.baltimoreopera.com

AMOUNT: $300/wk. + housing & health insurance
DEADLINE(S): APR 1
FIELD(S): Singing

12-week training program for young undergraduate students to prepare for a career in opera. Studio artists receive instruction in vocal interpretation, diction and language, theatre arts, movement and stage combat, and professional development. Performance opportunities include education and outreach programs and possible mainstage assignments. Must be AGMA member and between the ages of 21-35. Must be North American citizen or have current US employment authorization.

$40 application fee. 4-6 awards annually. Not renewable. See website or contact Helen Stevens, Education Coordinator, for an application and/or membership information. No phone calls.

1076—BARNUM FESTIVAL (Jenny Lind Competition for Sopranos)

1070 Main Street, Room 208
Bridgeport CT 06604
203/366-3300

AMOUNT: $2,000 1st prize + summer concert tour of Sweden; runner-up wins $500
DEADLINE(S): APR 23
FIELD(S): Singing

For sopranos aged 20-30 who are US citizens and residents of the Northeast (ME, VT, NH, NY, MA, CT, RI, NJ, PA, DE, MD, DC, VA). With application, must send 8x10 glossy, proof of age, resume (training, etc.), repertoire of pieces you will sing (3 contrasting arias in original language, 4 art songs in at least 2 languages, 2 selections from Operetta & Musical Theatre), standard cassette tape (w/ 2 contrasting arias and 1 art song), and letter of recommendation.

Application fee of $25 is required. Competition held in May. Contact Mary Dardanis at above number for details.

1077—BLUES HEAVEN FOUNDATION, INC. (Muddy Waters Scholarship)

2120 S. Michigan Ave.
Chicago IL 60616
312/808-1286

AMOUNT: $2,000
DEADLINE(S): APR 30
FIELD(S): Music, Music Education, African-American Studies, Folklore, Performing Arts, Arts Management, Journalism, Radio/TV/Film

Scholarship is made on a competitive basis with consideration given to scholastic achievement, concentration of studies, and financial need. Applicant must have full-time enrollment status in a Chicago area college/university in at least their first year of undergraduate studies or a graduate program. Scholastic aptitude, extracurricular involvement, grade point average, and financial need are all considered.

Contact Blues Heaven Foundation, Inc. to receive an application between February and April.

1078—BOSTON SAFE DEPOSIT & TRUST COMPANY (Madeline H. Soren Trust; Susan Glover Hitchcock Music Scholarship)

One Boston Place
Boston MA 02108
617/722-7340

AMOUNT: $500-$1,000
DEADLINE(S): MAY 1
FIELD(S): Music

For women who are Massachusetts residents and are graduates of Massachusetts high schools for undergraduate study at Massachusetts colleges or universities.

Recommendation of music department and financial aid office of a Boston area university or college is required. Write for complete information.

1079—BUENA VISTA COLLEGE NETWORK (Internships in Film Marketing)

3900 W. Alameda Ave.
Burbank CA 91505-4316
818/567-5000
E-mail: College_Network@
studio.disney.com

AMOUNT: Varies
DEADLINE(S): None
FIELD(S): Fields of study related to the motion picture industry, including marketing and promotion

Internships for full-time college students age 18 and up interested in a career in a facet of the motion picture industry. Must have unlimited access to computer with modem and transportation, be able to work 4-6 hours per week and 2-3 weekends per month. Attend film openings and sneak previews. Evaluate various aspects via an interactive computer system. Compensation ranges from $30 to $60/month. Possible school credit.

Access website by writing "Buena Vista College Network" from Yahoo. Available in most states and parts of Canada. Details, an interactive application, and e-mail access are located on website.

1080—CHAMBER MUSIC AMERICA (Gruber Foundation Award/Heidi Castleman Award for Excellence in Chamber Music Teaching)

305 Seventh Ave.
New York NY 10001

212/242-2022
E-mail: info@chamber-music.org
Internet: www.chamber-music.org

AMOUNT: $1,000
DEADLINE(S): DEC
FIELD(S): Chamber Music

Awards to honor teachers' efforts to involve students ages 6 to 18 in performing chamber music. Must be a music educator responsible for a chamber music program in elementary or high school.

Contact CMA for an application after August 1st.

1081—CHATHAM COLLEGE (Minna Kaufmann Ruud Fund)

Office of Admissions
Woodland Road
Pittsburgh PA 15232
412/365-1290

AMOUNT: $3,500/yr. (average) + fees & private accompanist
DEADLINE(S): MAR 31
FIELD(S): Vocal Music

Awards for full-time undergraduate women at Chatham College in Pennsylvania. Scholarships are open to promising young female vocalists who are accepted for admission, pass an audition, and plan to major in music.

Renewable. Contact the Office of Admissions for an application.

1082—CHOPIN FOUNDATION OF THE UNITED STATES, INC. (Scholarship Program for Young Pianists)

1440 79th Street Causeway
Suite 117
Miami FL 33141
305/868-0624
FAX: 305/865-5150
E-mail: info@choin.org
Internet: www.chopin.org

AMOUNT: $1,000/yr. up to 4 yrs.
DEADLINE(S): FEB 15
FIELD(S): Music: Piano

Scholarship program for pianists 15 to 20 years old who demonstrate an affinity for the interpretation of Chopin's music. The pianist is supported and encouraged throughout four years of preparation to qualify for the American Naitonal Chopin Piano Competition held in Miami, FL, every 5 years. The winners of this competition are sent to the International Chopin Piano Competition in Warsaw, Poland.

For US citizens or legal residents whose field of study is music and whose

major is piano. $25 registration fee. Must be a full-time student. Submit references, audio tape, and formal application which is available at the above website or write for details.

1083—COLBURN-PLEDGE MUSIC SCHOLARSHIP FOUNDATION (Scholarships for Texas String Instrument Students)

101 Cardinal Ave.
San Antonio TX 78209
Written inquiry

AMOUNT: Varies
DEADLINE(S): APR 23
FIELD(S): Music: String instruments

Awards for Texas residents studying a string instrument—violin, viola, cello, bass—in classical music with the intention of becoming a professional musician and in need of financial aid. Applicants can be in junior high, high school, or college. Texas residents may attend out-of-state music schools and/or music camps. Auditions of selected applicants are held in San Antonio around June 1.

Write for detailed information.

1084—COLUMBIA UNIVERSITY (Joseph H. Bearns Prize in Music)

Dept. of Music
621 Dodge Hall, MC 1813
New York NY 10027
212/854-3825
FAX: 212/854-8191

AMOUNT: $2,000-$3,000
DEADLINE(S): MAR 15
FIELD(S): Musical Composition

Competition open to young composers aged 18-25. There are two categories for music composition: 1 award of $3,000 for larger forms and 1 award of $2,000 for smaller forms. No more than one entry should be sent. US citizenship required.

Write to Attn: Bearns Prize Committee at address above for an application.

1085—COMMUNITY FOUNDATION OF WESTERN MASSACHUSETTS (Nate McKinney Memorial Scholarship)

1500 Main Street
P.O. Box 15769
Springfield MA 01115
413/732-2858

AMOUNT: $1,000
DEADLINE(S): APR 15
FIELD(S): Music, Athletics, Science

Open to graduating seniors of Gateway Regional High School in Huntington, Massachusetts. Recipient must excel academically, demonstrate good citizenship, and have a strong interest in at least two of the following areas: music, science, and athletics. Based on financial need, academic merit, and extracurricular activities. Must submit transcripts and fill out government FAFSA form.

1 award annually. Renewable up to 4 years with reapplication. Contact Community Foundation for an application and your financial aid office for FAFSA. Notification is in June.

1086—CONTEMPORARY RECORD SOCIETY (CRS Competitions)

724 Winchester Road
Broomall PA 19008
610/544-5920
FAX: 610/544-5921
E-mail: crsnews@erols.com
Internet: www.erols.com/crsnews

AMOUNT: up to $2,500
DEADLINE(S): DEC 1
FIELD(S): Music

All musicians are accepted for consideration.

3 awards annually. Renewable. Contact Caroline Hunt at CRS for an application.

1087—COUNCIL FOR BASIC EDUCATION (Arts Education Fellowships)

2506 Buckelew Drive
Falls Church VA 22046
703/876-5782

AMOUNT: $2,800 stipend + $200 grant to school
DEADLINE(S): JAN
FIELD(S): Teaching of the arts (visual arts, creative writing, dance, media, music, theatre)

Fellowships for K-12 teachers in the above fields, artist-teachers, or professional artists who teach at least 20 hours per week. Funding from the National Endowment for the Arts and the Getty Center for Education in the Arts, and others.

Contact organization for details.

1088—CURTIS INSTITUTE OF MUSIC (Tuition Scholarships)

Admissions Office
1726 Locust Street
Philadelphia PA 19103-6187
215/893-5262

FAX: 215/893-7900
Internet: www.curtis.edu

AMOUNT: Full tuition
DEADLINE(S): JAN 15
FIELD(S): Music, Voice, Opera

Full-tuition scholarships open to students in the above areas who are accepted for full-time study at the Curtis Institute of Music. (Opera is for master of music only.)

Scholarships are renewable. Write or see website for complete information.

1089—DELTA OMICRON (Triennial Composition Competition for Solo Piano)

12297 W. Tennessee Place
Lakewood CO 80228-3325
606/266-1215

AMOUNT: $500 + premiere performance at Conference
DEADLINE(S): MAR 18
FIELD(S): Music composition competition

Award for solo piano composition with a time length from seven to ten minutes. No music fraternity affiliation required.

Prior publication or performance not allowed. Entry fee of $10 is required. Contact Judith Eidson at above address for details.

1090—DELTA OMICRON INTERNATIONAL MUSIC FRATERNITY (Triennial Composition Competition for Sacred Choral Anthem for Three- or Four-Part Voices)

12297 W. Tennessee Place
Lakewood CO 80228-3325
606/266-1215

AMOUNT: $500 and premiere
DEADLINE(S): MAR 20
FIELD(S): Music Composition

Sacred choral anthem for 3- or 4-part voices; SSA, SAB, or SATB with keyboard accompaniment or a capella with optional obligato. Competition open to composers of college age or over. No music fraternity affiliation required.

Prior publication or public performance of entry is NOT allowed. Entry fee of $10 is required. Contact Judith Eidson at above address for complete information.

1091—DISTRICT OF COLUMBIA COMMISSION ON THE ARTS & HUMANITIES (Grants)

410 Eighth Street NW, 5th Fl.
Washington DC 20004
202/724-5613
TDD: 202/727-3148
FAX: 202/727-4135

AMOUNT: $2,500

DEADLINE(S): MAR 1
FIELD(S): Performing Arts, Literature, Visual Arts

Applicants for grants must be professional artists and residents of Washington DC for at least one year prior to submitting application. Awards intended to generate art endeavors within the Washington DC community.

Open also to art organizations that train, exhibit, or perform within DC. 150 grants per year. Write for complete information.

1092—DIXIE COLLEGE (Music Scholarships)

225 South 700 East
St. George UT 84770
435/652-7802 (vocal)
435/652-7996 (strings)
435/652-7997 (brass, woodwinds, percussion)
435/652-7803 (flute, piano)
E-mail: kim@cc.dixie.edu
Internet: http://faserver.fa.dixie.edu/music/Schol.html

AMOUNT: Varies
DEADLINE(S): MAR 1
FIELD(S): Music

Scholarships at Dixie College in St. George, Utah, for music students. Available for music majors and minors, and some are for non-majors/minors who participate in ensembles. Available for both vocal and instrumental. Auditions required.

See website for audition details. Request scholarship forms from your high school counselor or from the Dixie College Financial Aid Office at 435/652-7575.

1093—EASTERN KENTUCKY UNIVERSITY (Music Scholarships)

Dr. John Roberts, Chair
Dept. of Music
Foster 101
Richmond KY 40475-3116
E-mail: musruber@acs.eku.edu/sch.htm

AMOUNT: Varies
DEADLINE(S): Varies
FIELD(S): Music

Scholarships for talented young instrument or voice musicians preparing themselves for careers in music or music education. Must audition for scholarship. Audition day is mid-February; however, where distance is a problem, a taped audition may be substituted. Application (on website) is due at least two weeks prior to the desired audition date.

Scholarshiip recipients are required to participate in performing ensembles and maintain a GPA of 2.5 to retain scholarship.

1094—ETUDE MUSIC CLUB OF SANTA ROSA (Music Competition for Instrumentalists)

P.O. Box 823
Santa Rosa CA 95402
707/538-1370

AMOUNT: Varies
DEADLINE(S): MAR 1
FIELD(S): Classical Instrumental Music

Competition is open to any high school student (grades 9-12) who is a resident of Sonoma, Napa, or Mendocino county and is studying music with a private teacher of music or is recommended by his/her school's music department.

Write for complete information.

1095—ETUDE MUSIC CLUB OF SANTA ROSA (Music Competition for Vocalists)

P.O. Box 823
Santa Rosa CA 95402
707/538-1370

AMOUNT: Varies
DEADLINE(S): MAR 2 (competition is MAR 16)
FIELD(S): Classical Vocalists

Competition is open to high school vocalists in grades 9-12 who are residents of Sonoma, Napa, or Mendocino county and are studying music with a private teacher of music or are recommended by their school's music department.

Write for complete information.

1096—FELLOWSHIP OF UNITED METHODISTS IN MUSIC AND WORSHIP ARTS (Scholarships)

P.O. Box 840
Nashville TN 37202
615/340-7453

AMOUNT: $500
DEADLINE(S): JUN 15
FIELD(S): Music or Theology

Scholarship for college-bound high school seniors and undergraduates who are active members of the United Methodist church. Based on talent, leadershp ability, and potential for success.

Renewable. Contact organization for details.

1097—FLORIDA DEPARTMENT OF STATE—ARTS COUNCIL (Individual Artists' Fellowships)

Division Cultural Affairs
The Capitol
Tallahassee FL 32399-0250
850/487-2980
TT: 850/488-5779
FAX: 850/922-5259
Internet: www.dos.state.fl.us

AMOUNT: $5,000
DEADLINE(S): JAN 15
FIELD(S): Dance, Choreography, Poetry, Literature, Music, Music Composition, Theatre, Visual Arts, Film, Crafts, Fiction, Interdisciplinary

Open to legal residents of Florida who are professional creative artists of at least 18 years of age. May NOT be enrolled in any undergraduate or graduate degree-seeking program during fellowship period.

38 awards annually. Renewable with reapplication after four years since date of previous award. Contact Florida Arts Council for information packet. Notification during summer.

1098—FORT COLLINS SYMPHONY ASSOCIATION (National Young Artist Competition)

P.O. Box 1963
Fort Collins CO 80522-1963
970/482-4823 or 970/482-4858
E-mail: Leehill@fcsymphony.org
Internet: www.fcsymphony.org

AMOUNT: 2 Divisions: Sr.—up to $3,000; Jr.—up to $250
DEADLINE(S): JAN 20
FIELD(S): Music

A competition for orchestral instruments/piano. Applicants must be ages 12 to 18 for the junior division and between 18 and 25 for the senior division. Cassette tape of work to be performed, completed application form, fee of $35, and proof of age must be received by Jan 20th. In March, semi-finalists compete. Finalists will be flown (within 48 states) to Fort Collins at FCSO expense for final competition in April.

Not renewable (if first place—junior competition winners may re-enter in senior division). See website or send self-addressed, stamped envelope to the above address for complete information.

1099—GENERAL FEDERATION OF WOMEN'S CLUBS OF MASSACHUSETTS (Music Scholarship)

245 Dutton Road, Box 679
Sudbury MA 01776-0679
508/283-8665

AMOUNT: $500
DEADLINE(S): FEB 1
FIELD(S): Piano, Instrument, Music Education, or Music Therapy

Competitive scholarships for seniors in Massachusetts high schools. Letter of endorsement from sponsoring GFWC of MA club, letter of recommendation from either a high school principal or music teacher, transcripts, and personal audition (two short pieces contrasting in nature) required with application.

For more information or an application, send a self-addressed, stamped envelope to Alyce Burke, Coordinator, Arts Department, at above address.

1100—GENERAL FEDERATION OF WOMEN'S CLUBS OF MASSACHUSETTS (Dorchester Women's Club Scholarship)

245 Dutton Road, Box 679
Sudbury MA 01776-0679
508/283-8665

AMOUNT: $500
DEADLINE(S): FEB 1
FIELD(S): Voice

For undergraduates enrolled in a four-year accredited college, university, or school of music. Letter of endorsement from sponsoring GFWC of MA club, personal letter stating your need and other pertinent information, letter of recommendation from college department head or music professor, and transcripts required with application.

At least one scholarship annually. For more information or an application, send self-addressed, stamped envelope to Alyce Burke, Coordinator, Arts Department, at above address.

1101—GEORGE BIRD GRINNELL AMERICAN INDIAN CHILDREN'S FUND (Al Qoyawayma Award)

11602 Montague Ct.
Potomac MD 20854
301/424-2440
FAX: 301/424-8281
E-mail: Grinnell_Fund@MSN.com

AMOUNT: $1,000
DEADLINE(S): JUN 1

FIELD(S): Science, Engineering

Open to Native American undergraduate and graduate students majoring in science or engineering and who have demonstrated an outstanding interest and skill in any one of the arts. Must be American Indian/Alaska Native (documented with Certified Degree of Indian Blood), be enrolled in college/university, be able to demonstrate commitment to serving community or other tribal nations, and document financial need.

Contact Dr. Paula M. Mintzies, President, for an application after January 1st.

1102—GLENN MILLER BIRTHPLACE SOCI-ETY (Scholarship Program)

107 E. Main
Clarinda IA 51632
712/542-4439

AMOUNT: $750-$1,750
DEADLINE(S): MAR 15
FIELD(S): Music Performance
(Instrumental & Vocal)

Competitions open to high school seniors and undergraduate freshmen who intend to make music a central part of their future life (music major NOT required). Audition tape and refundable $25 appearance fee required with application. Finalists perform at Clarinda's Glenn Miller Festival in June, where checks are presented to the winners.

4 awards annually. Send self-addressed, stamped envelope for an application. Notification by May 15th.

1103—GUSTAVUS ADOLPHUS COLLEGE (Anderson Theatre and Dance Scholarships)

Office of Admission
800 West College Ave.
St. Peter MN 56082
507/933-7676
800/GUSTAVUS
E-mail: admission@gustavus.edu
Internet: www.gustavus.edu/

AMOUNT: $500-$2,000
DEADLINE(S): APR 15
FIELD(S): Theatre and/or Dance

Scholarships tenable at Gustavus Adolphus College, St. Peter, Minnesota, for students pursuing studies in theatre and/or dance. Students may be enrolled in any major. For renewal, recipient must participate in a departmental project and maintain a 3.0 GPA.

Contact college for details.

1104—GUSTAVUS ADOLPHUS COLLEGE (The Jussi Bjorling Music Scholarships)

Office of Admission
800 West College Ave.
St. Peter MN 56082
507/933-7676
800/GUSTAVUS
E-mail: admission@gustavus.edu
Internet: www.gustavus.edu/

AMOUNT: Up to $2,000
DEADLINE(S): JAN 15
FIELD(S): Music

Scholarships tenable at Gustavus Adolphus College, St. Peter, Minnesota, for students pursuing studies and participation in music. Recipients may be of any major, but are required to participate in a performing ensemble and take private lessons.

25-30 awards per year. Renewable. Contact college for details.

1105—HOWARD UNIVERSITY (Debbie Allen & Phylicia Rashad's Dr. Andrew Allen Creative Arts Scholarship)

College of Fine Arts
Dept. of Theatre Arts
6th & Fairmont NW
Washington DC 20059
202/806-7050

AMOUNT: $5,000
DEADLINE(S): APR 1
FIELD(S): Drama, Singing, Dancing

Scholarship open only to students of senior status who are in the Department of Theatre Arts at Howard University in Washington DC. For singing, dancing, and acting.

Write for complete information.

1106—ILLINOIS ARTS COUNCIL (Artists Fellowship Awards)

100 W. Randolph, Suite 10-500
Chicago IL 60601-3298
312/814-6750

AMOUNT: $500; $5,000; $10,000
DEADLINE(S): SEP 1
FIELD(S): Choreography, Visual Arts,
Poetry Prose, Film, Video, Playwriting,
Music Composition, Crafts, Ethnic &
Folk Arts, Performance Art,
Photography, Audio Art

Open to professional artists who are Illinois residents. Awards are in recognition of work in the above areas; they are not for continuing study. Students are NOT eligible.

Write to address above for application form.

1107—INDIANA STATE UNIVERSITY (Music Scholarships)

Department of Music
Terre Haute IN 47809
812/237-2768
Internet: www.indstate.edu/music/
scholar.html

AMOUNT: Varies
DEADLINE(S): Varies
FIELD(S): Music

Various scholarships for music students at Indiana State University. Requirements and specialties vary. See website for details.

On website, send e-mail to Dr. James O'Donnell for details, or call or write for further information. Dates for auditions are available from the office of the Dept. of Music. Some scholarships are through the University, and several are from private donors.

1108—INDIANA UNIVERSITY SCHOOL OF MUSIC (Music Scholarships)

School of Music
Admissions MU101
300 North Jordan Ave.
Bloomington IN 47405
812/855-7998
E-mail: musicadm@indiana.edu
Internet: www.music.indiana.edu/
admissions/GenInfo.html

AMOUNT: Varies
DEADLINE(S): Varies
FIELD(S): Music

Several scholarships are available in the Indiana University Dept. of Music. All undergraduate music majors must audition prior to admission and study a classical instrument. Music minors need not audition.

A listing of the scholarships is on the website as well as the various deadline dates for the university as well as for the audition dates for the music department. Deadlines begin as early as Nov. 11 for applying to the department, and auditions occur as early as December.

1109—INSTITUTE OF INTERNATIONAL EDUCATION (Arts International Fund for Performing Arts)

809 United Nations Plaza
New York NY 10017

212/984-5370
Internet: www.iie.org/ai
AMOUNT: $500-$2,000
DEADLINE(S): SEP; JAN; MAY
FIELD(S): Performing Arts

Grants to support US artists at international festivals and exhibitions. The festival must take place outside the US and be international in scope with representation from at least two countries outside the host country or have a US theme with representation from at least three US performing artists or groups.

Must be open to the general public. Call for details.

1110—INTERNATIONAL COMPETITION FOR SYMPHONIC COMPOSITION (Premio Citta Di Trieste)

Piazza Dell'unita D'Italia 4
Palazzo municipale
34121 Trieste ITALY
040-366030
AMOUNT: 10 mil. lira (1st)
DEADLINE(S): APR 30
FIELD(S): Music Composition

Open to anyone who submits an original composition for full orchestra (normal symphonic instrumentation). Composition must never have been performed and be unpublished.

Previous first-prize winners are excluded from competition. Write to secretariat of the music award at address above for complete information.

1111—INTERNATIONAL TRUMPET GUILD (Conference Scholarships)

241 East Main Street, #247
Westfield MA 01086-1633
413/564-0337
FAX: 413/568-1913
E-mail: treasurer@trumpetguild.org
Internet: www.dana.edu/~itg or
www.trumpetguild.org
AMOUNT: $200 + waive Conference registration fee
DEADLINE(S): FEB 15
FIELD(S): Trumpet

Music competition for trumpet players under age 25 to enable them to attend ITG's annual conference. Must be a student member of the International Trumpet Guild by the deadline. Must submit the appropriate taped audition to the current scholarship competition chair. Generally, the student's trumpet playing must be at a relatively advanced level in order to play the repertoire.

See website for membership information and audition requirements.

1112—JACOB'S PILLOW DANCE FESTIVAL (Scholarships)

P.O. Box 287
Lee MA 02138
413/637-1322
FAX: 413/243-4744
Internet: www.jacobspillow.org
AMOUNT: Varies
DEADLINE(S): APR 5
FIELD(S): Dance

Pre-professional dance training for 16-year-old dancers at the School at Jacob's Pillow. Must demonstrate financial need.

Not renewable. Contact J.R. Glover for an application.

1113—JAPANESE AMERICAN CITIZENS LEAGUE (Aiko Susanna Tashiro Hiratsuka Memorial Scholarship)

1765 Sutter Street
San Francisco CA 94115
415/921-5225
FAX: 415/931-4671
E-mail: jacl@jacl.org
Internet: www.jacl.org
AMOUNT: $1,000-$5,000
DEADLINE(S): APR 1
FIELD(S): Performing Arts

Open to JACL members and their children only. For undergraduate and graduate students in the performing arts who are planning to attend a college, university, trade school, or any other institution of higher learning. Must submit personal statement, letters of recommendation, and transcripts. Professional artists NOT eligible to apply.

For membership information or an application, send a self-addressed, stamped envelope to above address, stating your level of study. Applications available October 1st through March 20th; recipients notified in July.

1114—JOHN K. & THIRZA F. DAVENPORT FOUNDATION (Scholarships in the Arts)

20 North Main Street
South Yarmouth MA 02664-3143
508/398-2293
FAX: 508/394-6765
AMOUNT: Varies
DEADLINE(S): JUL 15
FIELD(S): Theatre, Music, Art

For Barnstable County, Massachusetts residents in their last two years of undergraduate or graduate (preferred) study in visual or performing arts. Must demonstrate financial need.

6-8 awards annually. Renewable. Contact Mrs. Chris M. Walsh for more information.

1115—JULIUS AND ESTHER STULBERG COMPETITION, INC. (International String Competition)

P.O. Box 50107
Kalamazoo MI 49005
616/372-6237
FAX: 616/372-7513
AMOUNT: $3,000 (1st prize); $2,000 (2nd); $1,000 (3rd)
DEADLINE(S): JAN 10
FIELD(S): Stringed Instruments (Violin, Viola, Cello, Double Bass)

Contest is open to talented musicians aged 19 or younger who perform on violin, viola, cello, or double bass.

Application fee of $30. Send self-addressed, stamped envelope to above location for complete information.

1116—KOSCIUSZKO FOUNDATION (Chopin Piano Competition)

15 E. 65th Street
New York NY 10021
212/734-2130
FAX: 212/628-4552
E-mail: thekf@aol.com
Internet: www.kosciuszkofoundation.
org/grants/chopin.htm
AMOUNT: $2,500 (1st place)
DEADLINE(S): MAR
FIELD(S): Piano

Open to US citizens/permanent residents and international full-time students with valid student visas. Must be between the ages of 16 and 22 as of April in contest year. Preliminaries are held in the spring in Chicago, Houston, and New York City, with finals in New York City. Must have ready a program of 60-75 minutes, including Chopin and other required composers. Must also submit biography/curriculum vitae, letters of recommendation, proof of age, and photo.

$35 application fee required. Contact Kosciuszko Foundation for entry details.

1117—KOSCIUSZKO FOUNDATION (Marcella Sembrich Voice Competition)

15 East 65th Street
New York NY 10021-6595

212/734-2130 or 800/287-9956
FAX: 212/628-4552
E-mail: thekf@pagasusnet.com
Internet: www.kosciuszkofoundation.
org/grants/sembrich.htm
AMOUNT: Up to $1,000 + travel to
various domestic and international
recitals
DEADLINE(S): DEC 15
FIELD(S): Music: Voice

A voice competition open to citizens
and permanent residents of the US and
international students with valid student
visas. Must be at least age 18. An entry fee
of $35 is required.

For details of required repertoire and
exact dates, check website and/or contact
organization.

1118—LIBERACE FOUNDATION FOR THE PERFORMING AND CREATIVE ARTS (Scholarship Fund)

1775 East Tropicana Ave.
Las Vegas NV 89119-6529
Internet: www.liberace.org

AMOUNT: Varies
DEADLINE(S): MAR 15
FIELD(S): Music, Theatre, Dance, Visual
Arts

Provides grants to accredited INSTI-
TUTIONS that offer training in above
fields. Grants are to be used exclusively for
scholarship assistance to talented and
deserving students. Recipients should be
promising and deserving upperclassmen
(Jr., Sr., Graduate) enrolled in a course of
study leading up to a career in the arts.

NO DIRECT-TO-STUDENT GRANTS
ARE MADE. Student's school must apply
on their behalf. See website or write to
above address for details.

1119—LIEDERKRANZ FOUNDATION, INC. (Scholarship Awards)

6 East 87th Street
New York NY 10128
212/534-0880

AMOUNT: $1,000-$5,000
DEADLINE(S): DEC 1
FIELD(S): Vocal Music

Awards can be used anywhere. Age
limit for General Voice is 20-35 years old,
and limit for Wagnerian Voice is 25-45
years. There is a $35 application fee.

14-18 scholarships annually. NOT
renewable. Contact competition director
John Balme at address above for application regulations, audition schedules, and
other details.

1120—LOREN L. ZACHARY SOCIETY FOR THE PERFORMING ARTS (National Vocal Competition for Young Opera Singers)

2250 Gloaming Way
Beverly Hills CA 90210
310/276-2731
FAX: 310/275-8245

AMOUNT: $10,000 (1st prize); $1,000
(finalists)
DEADLINE(S): JAN (NY); MAR (LA);
MAY (final competition)
FIELD(S): Opera Singing

Annual vocal competition open to
young (aged 21-33 females; 21-35 males)
Opera singers. The competition is geared
toward finding employment for them in
European Opera houses. Financial assistance is only possible through participation
in the audition program. Financial need
NOT considered.

$35 application fee. 10 awards annually.
Send self-addressed, stamped envelope to
Mrs. Nedra Zachary at address above for
an application.

1121—MARTIN MUSICAL SCHOLARSHIP FUND (Scholarships)

Lawn Cottage
23a Brackley Road
Beckenham, Kent BR3 1RB
ENGLAND
PHONE/FAX: 0181-658-9432

AMOUNT: Up to 2,000 pounds sterling
DEADLINE(S): DEC 1
FIELD(S): Instrumental Music

Scholarships are administered by the
London Philharmonic Orchestra. For
applicants of exceptional talent under age
25. Awards are for study at any approved
institution in England for non-UK citizens;
citizens of the UK may study anywhere.
Candidates must be studying for a career
as either soloist, chamber musician, or
orchestral player. Additional programs are
for viola players, violinists, and woodwind
performers.

Not open to organists, singers, composers, or for academic studies. Awards
are valid for two years. Auditions are held
in London the January following the
December deadline date. Write for complete information.

1122—McDONALD'S (GospelFest Music Scholarships)

See your local McDonald's
Tri-State restaurant

Internet: www.archingintoeducation.
com/
AMOUNT: $1,000; $5,000
DEADLINE(S): MAR 31
FIELD(S): Music

New York Tri-State residents (NYC,
Long Island and specific counties in CT and
NJ) planning to major in music are eligible.

10 $1,000 awards annually; 1 $5,000
award for a student demonstrating outstanding academic merit. Not renewable. Pick up
an application in your local New York, New
Jersey, or Connecticut McDonald's.

1123—MERCYHURST COLLEGE D'ANGE-LO SCHOOL OF MUSIC (Young Artists Competition)

501 E. 38th Street
Erie PA 16546
814/824-2394
FAX: 814/824-2438
E-mail: kwok@mercyhurst.edu

AMOUNT: $10,000 (1st prize); $5,000
(2nd); $3,000 (3rd)
DEADLINE(S): FEB 1
FIELD(S): Voice, Strings, Piano

For musicians aged 18-30 (voice—age
35). There is a rotating cycle of areas
(strings 2000, piano 2001, voice 2002). As
well as dollar awards, there are performance contracts.

Contact Glen Kwok at above address
for an application and repertoire requirements in the Fall of the year preceding
competition.

1124—MERCYHURST COLLEGE D'ANGE-LO SCHOOL OF MUSIC (Scholarships)

501 E. 38th Street
Erie PA 16546
814/824-2394
FAX: 814/824-2438
E-mail: kwok@mercyhurst.edu

AMOUNT: up to $10,000
DEADLINE(S): None
FIELD(S): Music

For music students who wish to attend
the D'Angelo School of Music at Mercyhurst
College in Erie, Pennsylvania. Audition
required.

Renewable for four years. Contact
Glen Kwok for an application.

1125—METROPOLITAN OPERA ASSOCIA-TION (National Council Auditions)

Lincoln Center
New York NY 10023

148

212/799-3100
AMOUNT: $800 (1st place); $600 (2nd); $400 (3rd)
DEADLINE(S): Varies
FIELD(S): Operatic Singing

The National Opera Council Auditions are for SERIOUS musicians with talent in the operatic style of singing. Student must be prepared to sing five operatic arias. Once a person has become a National Finalist or Winner, he/she is eligible for additional educational funding. Females must be aged 19-33, and males must be aged 20-33. Must be US citizen.

Contact Jill Kuntz at MET for details.

1126—MINNESOTA STATE ARTS BOARD (Grants Program)

Park Square Ct.
400 Sibley Street, Suite 200
St. Paul MN 55101-1928
651/215-1600
AMOUNT: $8,000 (fellowships); $500-$1,500 (grants)
DEADLINE(S): AUG (Visual Arts); SEP (Music & Dance); OCT (Literature & Theatre)
FIELD(S): Literature, Music, Theater, Dance, Visual Arts

Fellowships and career opportunity grants are open to professional artists who are residents of Minnesota. Grants may NOT be used for support of tuition or work toward any degree.

Contact MSAB for an application.

1127—MUSIC ACADEMY OF THE WEST (Scholarships)

1070 Fairway Road
Santa Barbara CA 93108-2899
805/969-4726
FAX: 805/969-0686
E-mail: catalog@musicacademy.org
Internet: www.musicacademy.org
AMOUNT: Tuition, room & board
DEADLINE(S): Varies
FIELD(S): Music

Scholarships for this eight-week summer session for musicians age 16 and up. Maximum age for vocalists is 32. Student must pay transportation and limited fees. Deadlines run from January 9 through March 15, depending on instrument. Audition dates are set up throughout the US.

Access website for details and application, or write for information.

1128—McCORD CAREER CENTER (Level II McCord Medical/Music Scholarship)

Healdsburg High School
1024 Prince Street
Healdsburg CA 95448
707/431-3473
AMOUNT: Varies
DEADLINE(S): APR 30
FIELD(S): Medicine, Music

For graduates of Healdsburg High School who are planning a career in music or medicine. Must be enrolled full-time at a college/university as an undergraduate junior or senior in the fall, or earning an advanced degree in graduate or medical school, or entering into a vocational/certificate program. Transcripts, proof of attendance, and an essay are required.

Contact the McCord Career Center at Healdsburg High School for an application.

1129—NATIONAL ASSOCIATION OF PASTORAL MUSICIANS (Scholarships)

225 Sheridan Street NW
Washington DC 20011
202/723-5800
FAX: 202/723-2262
E-mail: NPSMing@aol.com
Internet: www.npm.org
AMOUNT: Up to $3,000
DEADLINE(S): FEB 27
FIELD(S): Pastoral music

Various scholarships for students in the field of pastoral (religious) music. Membership in the above association required. Must demonstrate financial need and commitment to a career in the field.

Extensive information can be found on the website or write to above address for membership and scholarship details.

1130—NATIONAL ASSOCIATION OF TEACHERS OF SINGING (Artist Awards Competition)

2800 University Blvd. North
Jacksonville FL 32211
904/744-9022
FAX: 904/744-9033
E-mail: WmVessels@aol.com
Internet: www.nats.org
AMOUNT: Varies
DEADLINE(S): Varies
FIELD(S): Singing

Purpose of the program is to select young singers who are ready for professional careers and to encourage them to carry on the tradition of fine singing. Selection based on present accomplishments rather than future potential. Applicants should be between 21 and 35 years old and have studied with a NATS teacher or a member of NATS.

Contact NATS for an application.

1131—NATIONAL FEDERATION OF MUSIC CLUBS COMPETITIVE AWARDS PROGRAM (Student Awards)

1336 N. Delaware Street
Indianapolis IN 46202
317/638-4003
FAX: 317/638-0503
AMOUNT: $100-$5,000
DEADLINE(S): Varies
FIELD(S): Music Performance, Music Composition

Numerous award programs open to young musicians aged 16-35 who are either group or individual members of the Nat'l. Fed. of Music Clubs. The programs provide opportunities for students interested in professional music careers.

Send self-addressed, stamped envelope (SASE) to address above for membership information and/or award details. Include check for $1 to cover costs.

1132—NATIONAL FOUNDATION FOR ADVANCEMENT IN THE ARTS (Arts Recognition and Talent Search)

800 Brickell Ave.
Miami FL 33131
800/970-ARTS or 305/377-1140
FAX: 305/377-1149
Internet: www.nfaa.org
AMOUNT: $100-$3,000
DEADLINE(S): OCT 1
FIELD(S): Creative & Performing Arts

Talent contest for high school seniors and 17- to 18-year-olds in dance, jazz, music, photography, theatre, visual arts, voice, and writing. Except for those applying in Music/Jazz, applicants must be US citizens or permanent residents. May apply in more than one category, but only one financial award will be given to any individual, and a fee is required for each category in which student applies.

$35 application fee ($25 if apply by June 1st); fee may be waived if you are unable to meet this requirement. 400 awards annually. Not renewable. Contact NFAA for an application packet.

1133—NATIONAL GUILD OF COMMUNITY SCHOOLS OF THE ARTS (Young Composers Awards)

40 N. Van Brunt Street, Suite 32
Englewood NJ 07631
201/871-3337
FAX: 201/871-7639

AMOUNT: $1,000 (1st place); $500 (2nd)
DEADLINE(S): MAY 1
FIELD(S): Music Composition

Competition open to students aged 13-18 (as of June 30th of award year) who are enrolled in a public or private secondary school, recognized musical school, or engaged in private study of music with an established teacher in the US or Canada. Must be US or Canadian citizen/legal resident.

Contact Lolita Mayadas, Executive Director, for an application.

1134—NATIONAL ITALIAN AMERICAN FOUNDATION (NIAF-Pavarotti Scholarship)

1860 19th Street NW
Washington DC 20009-5599
202/530-5315

AMOUNT: $1,000
DEADLINE(S): MAY 31
FIELD(S): Vocal Music

Open to undergraduate or graduate music students of Italian heritage from Southern California. Must send a cassette tape of your voice in performance.

Academic merit, financial need, and community service also considered.

1135—NATIONAL ITALIAN AMERICAN FOUNDATION (Nina Santavicca Scholarship)

1860 19th Street NW
Washington DC 20009-5599
202/530-5315

AMOUNT: $1,000
DEADLINE(S): MAY 31
FIELD(S): Music major—piano

Open to undergraduate or graduate music students, preferably piano, of Italian heritage.

Academic merit, financial need, and community service considered.

1136—NATIONAL ITALIAN AMERICAN FOUNDATION (Sergio Franchi Music Scholarship in Voice Performance)

1860 19th Street NW
Washington DC 20009-5599
202/530-5315

AMOUNT: Varies
DEADLINE(S): MAY 31
FIELD(S): Vocal Music (tenors)

Open to undergraduate or graduate vocal music students (tenors) of Italian heritage. Send cassette tape of your voice in performance.

Academic merit, financial need, and community service are considered.

1137—NATIONAL ITALIAN AMERICAN FOUNDATION (Thomas Joseph "Willie" Ambrosole Scholarship)

1860 19th Street NW
Washington DC 20009
202/530-5315

AMOUNT: $1,000
DEADLINE(S): MAY 31
FIELD(S): Arts or Humanities

Open to undergraduate American students of Italian ancestry majoring in the arts or humanities from the New York-New Jersey area.

Academic merit, financial need, and community service are considered. Contact organization for application and details.

1138—NATIONAL ITALIAN AMERICAN FOUNDATION (Vincente Minelli Scholarship)

1860 19th Street NW
Washington DC 20009-5599
202/530-5315

AMOUNT: $1,000
DEADLINE(S): MAY 31
FIELD(S): Drama majors

For undergraduates of Italian ancestry majoring in drama. Write a 2- to 3-page essay on a family member or a personality you consider: "An Italian American Hero."

Also considered are academic merit, financial need, and community service.

1139—NATIONAL LEAGUE OF AMERICAN PEN WOMEN, INC. (Scholarships for Mature Women)

1300 17th Street NW
Washington DC 20036
717/225-3023

AMOUNT: $1,000
DEADLINE(S): JAN 15 (even-numbered years)
FIELD(S): Art, Music, Creative Writing

The National League of American Pen Women gives three $1,000 grants in even-numbered years to women aged 35 and over. Should submit three 4 x 6 or bigger color prints, manuscripts, or musical compositions suited to the criteria for the year.

Send SASE for details at the above address.

1140—NATIONAL ORCHESTRAL INSTITUTE (School of Music Scholarship)

Univ. of Maryland
2114 Tawes, Fine Arts Bldg.
College Park MD 20742-1211
301/405-2317
FAX: 301/314-9504
E-mail: noi@umdacc.umd.edu

AMOUNT: Tuition
DEADLINE(S): JAN
FIELD(S): Orchestra

This full scholarship institute offers intensive professional-level orchestral training to only the most advanced music students ages 18-28. Program is offered at the University of Maryland, College Park, for three weeks each June. Students must submit an application, application fee, resume, and letter of recommendation. Applicants must audition at one of the audition centers in 20 cities across the US during February and March.

Contact Donald Reinhold, Director, for an application.

1141—NEW JERSEY STATE OPERA (Cash Awards)

Robert Treat Center
50 Park Place, 10th Fl.
Newark NJ 07102
201/623-5757

AMOUNT: Awards total $10,000
DEADLINE(S): Varies
FIELD(S): Opera

Professional singers between the ages of 22 and 34 can apply for this competition. Singers competing should have been represented by an artist's management firm for no more than one year. Management representation not required for entry.

Contact address above for complete information.

1142—NEW JERSEY STATE OPERA (International Vocal Competition)

Robert Treat Center
50 Park Place, 10th Fl.
Newark NJ 07102
201/623-5757
FAX: 201/623-5761

AMOUNT: $10,000 total
DEADLINE(S): Varies
FIELD(S): Opera singing

Professional opera singers between the ages of 22 and 34 can apply for this international competition.

Renewable yearly. Contact Mrs. Wanda Anderton at above address for information.

1143—NEW YORK STATE THEATRE INSTITUTE (Internships in Theatrical Production)

155 River Street
Troy NY 12180
518/274-3573
E-mail: nysti@crisny.org
Internet: www.crisny.org/not-for-profit/nysti/int.htm
AMOUNT: None
DEADLINE(S): None
FIELD(S): Fields of study related to theatrical production, including box office and PR

Internships for college students, high school seniors, and educators-in-residence interested in developing skills in above fields. Unpaid, but college credit is earned. Located at Russell Sage College in Troy, NY. Gain experience in box office, costumes, education, electrics, music, stage management, scenery, properties, performance, and public relations. Interns come from all over the world.

Must be associated with an accredited institution. See website for more information. Call Ms. Arlene Leff, Intern Director, at above location. Include your postal mailing address.

1144—OMAHA SYMPHONY GUILD (International New Music Competition)

1605 Howard Street
Omaha NE 68102
402/342-3836
FAX: 402/342-3819
E-mail: bravo@omahasymphony.org
Internet: www.omahasymphony.org
AMOUNT: $3,000
DEADLINE(S): APR 15
FIELD(S): Musical Composition

For composers aged 25 or above to enter a composition of 20 minutes in length or less. Composition is scored for chamber orchestra or ensemble. Work must be previously unpublished and not performed by a professional orchestra.

$30 entry fee. 1 award annually. Not renewable. Contact Kimberly Mettenbrink for application procedures.

1145—OPERA AMERICA (Fellowship Program)

1156 15th Street NW, Suite 810
Washington DC 20005
202/293-4466
FAX: 202/393-0735
AMOUNT: $1,200/month + transportation & housing
DEADLINE(S): MAY 7
FIELD(S): General or Artistic Administration, Technical Direction, or Production Management

Open to opera personnel, individuals entering opera administration from other disciplines, and graduates of arts administration or technical/production training programs who are committed to a career in opera in North America.

Must be US or Canadian citizen or legal resident lawfully eligible to receive stipend.

1146—ORCHESTRA SONOMA GUILD (Scholarship)

6040 Della Court
Rohnert Park CA 94928
Written inquiry
E-mail: RubyCh@ap.net
AMOUNT: $350 (1st); $100 (2nd)
DEADLINE(S): MAY
FIELD(S): Music

Scholarships for youth in grades 5 through 12 and who excel in music. Applicants not selected may reapply until they win first place.

Send self-addressed, stamped envelope to Ruby Chroninger, Secretary, at above address for application and details. Recommendations from private or school music teacher and audition tape with two contrasting pieces required.

1147—ORGAN HISTORICAL SOCIETY (E. Power Biggs Fellowship)

P.O. Box 26811
Richmond VA 23261
804/353-9226
AMOUNT: Funding for attendance at Annual Convention
DEADLINE(S): DEC 31
FIELD(S): Historic Pipe Organs

Fellowships are to encourage students and others to become involved in the appreciation of historic pipe organs by funding their attendance at the OHS Annual Convention.

3-4 awards annually. Contact Robert Zanca, Biggs Committee Chair, for an application.

1148—PHILADELPHIA COLLEGE OF BIBLE (Scholarships, Grants, and Loans)

Financial Aid Dept.
200 Manor Ave.
Langhorne PA 19047
800/366-0049
Internet: www.pcb.edu
AMOUNT: Varies
DEADLINE(S): Varies
FIELD(S): Fields of study relating to Christian education

Various scholarships, loans, and grants are available to students attending this undergraduate Bible college in Philadelphia, PA. High school seniors, transfer students, and others may apply. Some programs are for students with outstanding academic achievement, musical talent, or leaderships skills. Some are for dependents of Christian workers, missionaries, or alumni. Some are based on financial need.

Access website for details and/or send SASE to school for further information.

1149—PITTSBURGH NEW MUSIC ENSEMBLE (Harvey Gaul Composition Contest)

Duquesne University
School of Music
Pittsburgh PA 15282
412/261-0554
AMOUNT: $3,000
DEADLINE(S): APR 15
FIELD(S): Music Composition

Contest for US citizens to compose for chamber ensembles of five players or more or orchestras. Must submit score, cassette, and current biography. Winning composition will be performed by the Pittsburgh New Music Ensemble. Composers may enter more than one composition, but separate entry fee is required for each.

$20 entry fee. Contact Michelle Kruggel, Executive Director, or Gil Rose, Music Director & Conductor, for entry rules.

1150—PRINCESS GRACE FOUNDATION-USA (Dance Scholarships)

150 East 58th Street, 21st Fl.
New York NY 10155
212/317-1470
FAX: 212/317-1473
E-mail: pgfusa@pgfusa.com

Internet: www.pgfusa.com

AMOUNT: Varies

DEADLINE(S): APR 30

FIELD(S): Dance: all categories

Scholarships for dancers in their last year of professional training at a nonprofit school in the US. Also fellowships for salary assistance for an apprentice or new member in a dance company. New members must have joined the company within the past five years. Ballet dancers must be age 21 or under, and all others 25 and under. Must be nominated by the dean or department chairman of a professional school in dance. Do not apply directly to the Foundation.

US citizenship or legal residency required. Write or access website for further information.

1151—PRINCESS GRACE FOUNDATION-USA (Drama Scholarships and Fellowships)

150 East 58th Street, 21st Fl.
New York NY 10155
212/317-1470
FAX: 212/317-1473
E-mail: pgfusa@pgfusa.com
Internet: www.pgfusa.com

AMOUNT: Varies

DEADLINE(S): MAR 31

FIELD(S): Theater/Drama

Scholarships for students age 25 or under in acting, directing, and design (scenic, lighting, and costume design) in their last year of professional training at a nonprofit school or organization in the US. Also fellowships for salary assistance for an apprentice or new member age 30 or younger in a theater company. New members must have joined the company within the past two years.

Must be nominated by the artistic director of a theater company or by the dean or department chair of a professional school in theater. Do not apply to Foundation. US citizenship or legal residency required. Write or access website for further information.

1152—RIPON COLLEGE (Performance/Recognition Tuition Scholarships)

Admissions Office
300 Seward Street
P.O. Box 248
Ripon WI 54971
920/748-8102 or 800/94-RIPON
E-mail: adminfo@ripon.edu
Internet: www.ripon.edu

AMOUNT: $5,000-$10,000/yr.

DEADLINE(S): MAR 1

FIELD(S): Music, Forensics, Art, Theatre

Open to undergraduate and graduate students attending or planning to attend Ripon College. Purpose is to recognize and encourage academic potential and accomplishment in above fields. Interview, audition, or nomination may be required.

Renewable. Contact Office of Admission for an application.

1153—SAN ANGELO SYMPHONY SOCIETY (Sorantin Young Artist Award)

P.O. Box 5922
San Angelo TX 76902
915/658-5877
FAX: 915/653-1045

AMOUNT: $3,000 (winner); $1,000 (3 others); $400 (runners-up)

DEADLINE(S): OCT 15

FIELD(S): Music: Voice, Instrumental, Piano

A competition open to instrumentalists who have not reached their 28th birthdays by November 22nd and to vocalists who have not reached their 31st birthdays by November 22nd. Provides opportunity for a cash award with the symphony orchestra.

Contact the San Angelo Symphony Society for an application.

1154—SAN FRANCISCO CONSERVATORY OF MUSIC (Various Scholarships)

1201 Ortega Street
San Francisco CA 94122
415/564-8086
Internet: www.sfcm.edu

AMOUNT: Varies

DEADLINE(S): Varies

FIELD(S): Music

A variety of scholarships for music students attending the San Francisco Conservatory of Music. Graduate assistantships are available for full-time candidates for Master of Music degree.

See website or write for detailed information.

1155—SANTA BARBARA FOUNDATION (Mary & Edith Pillsbury Foundation Scholarships)

15 E. Carrillo Street
Santa Barbara CA 93101
805/963-1873

AMOUNT: Varies

DEADLINE(S): MAY 15

FIELD(S): Music Performance, Music Composition

Open to talented music students who are Santa Barbara County residents or have strong Santa Barbara ties. Awards may be used for music lessons or college tuition. Must be US citizen. Financial need is a consideration.

30 awards annually. Renewable. Contact SBF for an application.

1156—SANTA BARBARA FOUNDATION (Pillsbury/Fahlman Music Scholarship Program)

15 E. Carrillo Street
Santa Barbara CA 93101-2780
805/963-1873
FAX: 805/966-2345
E-mail: kbruce@SBFoundation.org
Internet: www.sbfoundation.org

AMOUNT: Varies

DEADLINE(S): MAY 15

FIELD(S): Music

For students of music who have resided in Santa Barbara County for two years prior to application deadline or who have resided long-term in the county. Must be planning to attend a US accredited college or university.

Applications are available from April 1st to May 15th at the Foundation office.

1157—SKIDMORE COLLEGE (Filene Music Scholarships)

Office of Admissions
Saratoga Springs NY 12866-1632
Internet: www.skidmore.edu/academics/music/scholarships/Schlrshp.htm

AMOUNT: $6,000/yr.

DEADLINE(S): FEB 1

FIELD(S): Music

Scholarships for talented young instrument or voice musicians based on musical excellence as revealed by a competition. Must submit a cassette performance tape by Feb. 1. Filene scholars need not major in music; however, recipients are expected to continue to develop their skills through private instruction in the Music Department each semester and to participate in department ensembles. Final round of competitions is in April and is done in person.

4 scholarships per year. US citizens and permanent residents will receive additional assistance to meet financial need if it exceeds $6,000 in a given academic year. Renewable if student continues in good academic standing and receives the recommendation of the Dept. of Music.

1158—SOUTHERN ILLINOIS UNIVERSITY (Music Scholarships)

School of Music, Mailcode 4302
Carbondale IL 62901-4302
618/53-MUSIC (536-8742)
FAX: 618/453-5808
Internet: www.siu.edu/departments/
cola/music001/scholar.html

AMOUNT: Varies
DEADLINE(S): APR 15
FIELD(S): Music

Several music scholarships are available for freshmen and transfer students at Southern Illinois University. An audition is required, usually held in February and March. A taped audition can be arranged.

See website and/or contact Dr. Daniel Mellado for more information.

1159—STUDENT CONSERVATION ASSOCI-ATION (SCA Resource Assistant Program)

P.O. Box 550
Charlestown NH 03603
603/543-1700
FAX: 603/543-1828
E-mail: internships@sca-inc.org
Internet: www.sca-inc.org

AMOUNT: $1,180-$4,725
DEADLINE(S): Varies
FIELD(S): Environment & related fields

Must be 18 and US citizen; need not be student. Fields: Agriculture, archaeology, anthropology, botany, caves, civil/environmental engineering, environmental education, fisheries, forests, herpetology, history, living history/roleplaying, visitor services, landscape architectural/environmental design, paleontology, recreation/resource/range management, trail maintenance/construction, wildlife management, geology, hydrology, library/museums, surveying.

900 positions in US & Canada. Send $1 for postage for application; outside US/Canada, send $20.

1160—SUZUKI ASSOCIATION OF THE AMERICAS (Music Teacher Scholarships)

P.O. Box 17310
Boulder CO 80308
303/444-0948
FAX: 303/444-0984
E-mail: Suzuki@rmi.net
Internet: www.suzukiassociation.org/
scholar1.htm

AMOUNT: $150-$500
DEADLINE(S): FEB 15
FIELD(S): Teaching: Music

Scholarships for music teachers and prospective music teachers who are full-time college students. Membership in above organization for a minimum of six months prior to application required. Visit website for details.

Request membership information or application from above location.

1161—THE ASCAP FOUNDATION (Morton Gould Young Composer Awards)

One Lincoln Plaza
New York NY 10023
212/621-6219
Internet: www.ascap.org

AMOUNT: Varies
DEADLINE(S): MAR 15
FIELD(S): Music Composition

Competition is for American composers who are under 30 years of age as of March 15th of the year of application. Must be US citizen or permanent resident. Original music of any style will be considered. Along with application, must submit one reproduction of a manuscript or score, biographical information listing prior music studies, background and experience, and a list of compositions to date. Winning compositions selected by panel of music authorities.

Contact Frances Richard at The ASCAP Foundation for an application.

1162—THE BAGBY FOUNDATION FOR THE MUSICAL ARTS, INC. (Musical Study Grants)

501 Fifth Ave., Suite 1401
New York NY 10017
212/986-6094

AMOUNT: $2,000-$6,000
DEADLINE(S): Ongoing
FIELD(S): Music

Musical study grants based on talent and need.

Send a letter to above location outlining financial need.

1163—THE DONNA REED FOUNDATION (National Scholarships)

1305 Broadway
Denison IA 51442
712/263-3334
FAX: 712/263-8026
E-mail: dreedfpa@pionet.net
Internet: www.frii.com/donna_reed/
html

AMOUNT: $4,000
DEADLINE(S): MAR 16

FIELD(S): Performing Arts: acting, vocal, instrumental, or dance

Scholarships for high school seniors in the performing arts listed above. May be used at an accredited university or an approved program of instruction. Involves a competition.

4 awards. Contact Foundation or access website for application details.

1164—THE DONNA REED FOUNDATION (Performing Arts Scholarships for Iowa High School Seniors)

1305 Broadway
Denison IA 51442
712/263-3334
FAX: 712/263-8026
E-mail: dreedfpa@pionet.net
Internet: www.frii.com/donna_reed/
html

AMOUNT: $1,000
DEADLINE(S): MAR 16
FIELD(S): Performing Arts: acting, vocal, instrumental, or dance

Scholarships for high school seniors who are residents of Iowa and pursuing an education in the performing arts listed above. May be used at an accredited university or an approved program of instruction. Involves a competition.

4 awards. Contact Foundation or access website for application details.

1165—THE DONNA REED FOUNDATION (Performing Arts Scholarships for Crawford County, Iowa, High School Seniors)

1305 Broadway
Denison IA 51442
712/263-3334
FAX: 712/263-8026
E-mail: dreedfpa@pionet.net
Internet: www.frii.com/donna_reed/
html

AMOUNT: $500
DEADLINE(S): MAR 16
FIELD(S): Performing Arts: acting, vocal, instrumental, or dance

Scholarships for high school seniors who are residents of Crawford County, Iowa, and pursuing an education in the performing arts listed above. May be used at an accredited university or an approved program of instruction. Involves a competition.

4 awards. Contact Foundation or access website for application details.

1166—THE GRAND RAPIDS FOUNDATION (Grand Rapids Combined Theatre Scholarship Fund)

209-C Waters Bldg.
161 Ottawa Ave. NW
Grand Rapids MI 49503-2703
616/454-1751 or 616/454-6455

AMOUNT: Varies
DEADLINE(S): APR 3
FIELD(S): Theatre Arts

Must be enrolled full-time in an accredited college or training program. Preference given to theatre arts majors. Must have worked in Grand Rapids, Michigan area community theatre. Must demonstrate talent, ability, dedication to the theatre arts.

Contact the Foundation, Actor's Theatre, Community Circle Theatre, Grand Rapids Civic Theatre, or Broadway Theatre Guild for more information.

1167—THE GRAND RAPIDS FOUNDATION (Mildred E. Troske Music Scholarship)

209-C Waters Bldg.
161 Ottawa Ave. NW
Grand Rapids MI 49503-2703
616/454-1751 or 616/454-6455

AMOUNT: Varies
DEADLINE(S): APR 3
FIELD(S): Music

Open to full-time undergrads attending an accredited institution with an educational emphasis on music. Must have been a Kent County, Michigan, resident at least 5 years, have 3.0 or better GPA, and demonstrate financial need.

Send SASE to above address for complete information.

1168—THE JOHN F. KENNEDY CENTER FOR THE PERFORMING ARTS (Awards, Fellowships, and Scholarships)

The Kennedy Center
Washington DC 20566-0001
202/416-8857
FAX: 202/416-8802
E-mail: skshaffer@mail.kennedy-center.org
Internet: www.kennedy-center.org/education/actf

AMOUNT: Varies
DEADLINE(S): Varies
FIELD(S): Playwriting, Stage Design, and Acting

Various scholarships and awards in the above fields.

Contact organization for a booklet: "The Kennedy Center American College Theater Festival" for details and/or visit website.

1169—THE KUN SHOULDER REST, INC. (Listing of Music Competitions)

200 MacLaren Street
Ottawa Ontario CANADA K2P 0L6
+1 (613) 232-1861
FAX: +1 (613) 232-9771
E-mail: kun@kunrest.com
Internet: www.kunrest.com

AMOUNT: Varies
DEADLINE(S): Varies
FIELD(S): Music: Various instruments and voice

This manufacturer of shoulder rests for violinists offers a listing of international competitions in various types of music, primarily (but not limited to) for players of stringed instruments.

The listing is available on the website above, or a list can be requested of the company.

1170—THE MR. HOLLAND'S OPUS FOUNDATION (Solo Program: Musical Instruments for Individuals)

900 Allen Ave.
Glendale CA 91201
818/242-9600
FAX: 818/242-9635
E-mail: mhopus@aol.com
Internet: www.mhopus.org

AMOUNT: A musical instrument
DEADLINE(S): None
FIELD(S): Instrumental music

Founded by actor Richard Dreyfuss; composer Michael Kamen; and director Stephen Herek, all of whom were involved in the film with the same name as this group, the program provides used and/or new instruments to schools and individuals who are financially limited. The students must have completed at least three years of continuous group or private study and must have performed with school and/or community ensembles or provided accompaniment for same.

Send SASE (self-addressed stamped envelope [55 cents postage]) for application or access website, which has an application as well as more details. Recommendations and cassette performance tape required.

1171—THE NATIONAL ASSOCIATION OF NEGRO MUSICIANS, INC. (Scholarship Competitions)

11551 S. Laflin Street
Chicago IL 60643-5029
773/779-1325
Internet: www.edtech.morehouse.edu/cgrimes/scholars.htm

AMOUNT: $1,500 (1st); $1,000 (2nd); $750 (3rd); $500 (4th); $250 (5th)
DEADLINE(S): Varies
FIELD(S): Music: organ, winds, piano, voice, or strings

An annual competition for African-Americans talented in music performance in the above areas. For ages 18-30. Contestants must be sponsored by a local branch in good standing. Competition involves local, regional, and national events. Winners proceed to next level. Contact organization for location of your nearest branch. Specialty rotates yearly. 1999-winds; 2000-piano; 2001-voice; 2002-strings; 2003-organ, etc. Not for professional musicians.

See website for further information. There is a $5 fee for the local competitions.

1172—THE NATIONAL ASSOCIATION OF NEGRO MUSICIANS, INC. (Brantley Choral Arranging Competition)

237 East 115th Street
P.O. Box S-011
Chicago IL 60628
773/779-1325
Internet: www.edtech.morehouse.edu/cgrimes/brantley.htm

AMOUNT: $500
DEADLINE(S): APR 30
FIELD(S): Music: choral arrangement

An annual competition for African-Americans talented in music arrangement. The work must be a choral arrangement of a Negro spiritual. Should be between 3-5 minutes in length. Arranger's name must not appear on the score—use a "nom de plume." See more information on website.

There is a $25 entrance fee. For specific details, contact organization.

1173—THE WALT DISNEY COMPANY (American Teacher Awards)

P.O. Box 9805
Calabasas CA 91372

AMOUNT: $2,500 (36 awards); $25,000 (Outstanding Teacher of the Year)
DEADLINE(S): FEB 15

FIELD(S): Teachers: athletic coach, early childhood, English, foreign language/ESL, general elementary, mathematics, performing arts, physical education/health, science, social studies, visual arts, voc-tech education

Awards for K-12 teachers in the above fields.

Teachers, or anyone who knows a great teacher, can write for applications at the above address.

1174—THELONIOUS MONK INSTITUTE OF JAZZ (International Jazz Trumpet Competition)

5225 Wisconsin Ave. NW
Washington DC 20001
202/364-7272
FAX: 202/364-0176
Internet: jazzcentralstation.com/jcs/station/musicexp/foundati/tmonk/ijtc.html

AMOUNT: $20,000 (1st); $10,000 (2nd); $5,000 (3rd); $1,000 (additional finalists)
DEADLINE(S): AUG 5
FIELD(S): Music: Jazz trumpet

Competition for the world's most promising young musicians to receive college-level training by America's jazz masters, world-wide recognition, and performance opportunities. Musicians under contract with a major label are not eligible. Decisions based on audiotape presentation and application.

Application is on website or contact above organization for current information regarding application. Instructions for audiotape selections are very specific.

1175—THELONIOUS MONK INSTITUTE OF JAZZ (International Jazz Composers Competition)

5225 Wisconsin Ave. NW
Washington DC 20001
202/364-7272
FAX: 202/364-0176
Internet: jazzcentralstation.com/jcs/station/musicexp/foundati/tmonk/ijtc.html

AMOUNT: $10,000 grand prize
DEADLINE(S): AUG 5
FIELD(S): Music: Composition for jazz trumpet

Competition presented by the Thelonious Monk Institute of Jazz and BMI to reward excellence in jazz composition. Composition to be written for trumpet. Can be written for up to five instruments with

trumpet being the featured instrument. Solos for trumpet okay. Composers must not have had their jazz compositions recorded on a major label or recorded by a major jazz artist.

Application is on website or contact above organization for current information regarding application. Instructions for audiotape selections are very specific.

1176—UNITARIAN UNIVERSALIST ASSOCIATION (Musicians' Network Scholarships)

4190 Front Street
San Diego CA 92103
Written inquiry
AMOUNT: $100-$700
DEADLINE(S): MAR 1
FIELD(S): Art, Poetry, Music

Financial aid to undergraduate students in the above fields. Must be active with the Unitarian Universalist Association.

Renewable. Write for complete information.

1177—UNIVERSITY FILM & VIDEO ASSOCIATION (Carole Fielding Student Grants)

University of Baltimore
School of Communications
1420 N. Charles Street
Baltimore MD 21201
410/837-6061
AMOUNT: $1,000 to $4,000
DEADLINE(S): MAR 31
FIELD(S): Film, Video, Multi-media Production

Open to undergraduate/graduate students. Categories are narrative, experimental, animation, documentary, multimedia/installation and research. Applicant must be sponsored by a faculty member who is an active member of the Univesity Film and Video Association.

Write to the above address for application and complete details.

1178—UNIVERSITY OF ALABAMA AT BIRMINGHAM (Theatre Scholarships)

UAB Station
School of Arts & Humanities
Dept. of Theatre
Birmingham AL 35294-3340
205/934-3236
AMOUNT: Varies
DEADLINE(S): JAN 15
FIELD(S): Theatre

Scholarships for high school seniors with above-average GPAs and theatre talent. For undergraduate study at the University of Alabama/Birmingham.

Contact the department chairman for an application.

1179—UNIVERSITY OF ILLINOIS AT URBANA-CHAMPAIGN (Lydia E. Parker Bates Scholarship)

Turner Student Services Bldg.
MC-306, 610 East John Street
Champaign IL 61820
217/333-0100
AMOUNT: Varies
DEADLINE(S): MAR 15
FIELD(S): Art, Architecture, Landscape Architecture, Urban Planning, Dance, Theater, and all related subjects except Music

Open to undergraduate students in the College of Fine & Applied Arts who are attending the University of Illinois at Urbana-Champaign. Must demonstrate financial need and have 3.85 GPA. Complete the Free Application for Federal Student Aid.

175 awards per year. Recipients must carry at least 12 credit hours per semester. Contact office of student financial aid.

1180—UNIVERSITY OF NORTH TEXAS (Music Scholarships)

College of Music Auditions
P.O. Box 311367
Denton TX 76203-6887
817/565-2791
Internet: www.unt.edu/scholarships/Musicgen.htm
AMOUNT: Varies
DEADLINE(S): Varies
FIELD(S): Music

Several scholarships for music students are offered at the University of North Texas. Specialties and eligibility requirements vary.

See website for more information. Contact school for details.

1181—UNIVERSITY OF TEXAS AT EL PASO (Music Scholarships)

Music Department
UTEP
El Paso TX 79968
915/747-5606
FAX: 915/747-5023
E-mail: music@utep.edu
Internet: www.utep.edu/~music1/
AMOUNT: Varies
DEADLINE(S): MAR
FIELD(S): Music

Several music scholarships are available at the University of Texas at El Paso. Virtually all members of large ensembles receive a service award of some type, while more serious students may audition for a music scholarship. Auditions are usually held in March or April.

See website and/or contact Dr. Ron Hufstader, chair, for more information.

1182—UTA ALUMNI ASSOCIATION (Sue & Art Mosby Scholarship Endowment in Music)

University of Texas at Arlington
Box 19457
Arlington TX 76019
Internet: www.uta.edu/alumni/
scholar.htm
AMOUNT: $500
DEADLINE(S): Varies
FIELD(S): Music

Must be a full-time student in good standing at the University of Texas at Arlington. Must demonstrate financial need and musical ability with potential to complete UTA degree. Audition required.

1 award annually. Contact UTA Alumni Association for an application.

1183—VIRGIN ISLANDS BOARD OF EDUCATION (Music Scholarships)

P.O. Box 11900
St. Thomas VI 00801
809/774-4546
AMOUNT: $2,000
DEADLINE(S): MAR 31
FIELD(S): Music

Open to bona fide residents of the Virgin Islands who are enrolled in an accredited music program at an institution of higher learning.

This scholarship is granted for the duration of the course provided the recipients maintain at least a 'C' average. Write for complete information.

1184—WAMSO (Young Artist Competition)

1111 Nicollet Mall
Minneapolis MN 55403
612/371-5654
AMOUNT: $3,000 1st prize + $2,250
WAMSO Achievement Award &
performance with MN Orchestra
DEADLINE(S): OCT 15
FIELD(S): Piano & Orchestral
Instruments

Competition offers 4 prizes and possible scholarships to high school and college

students in schools in IN, IA, MN, MO, NE, ND, SD, WI, and the Canadian provinces of Manitoba and Ontario. Entrants may not have passed their 26th birthday on date of competition (which is usually held in January).

For list of repertoires and complete information, specify your instrument and write to address above.

1185—WAVERLY COMMUNITY HOUSE INC. (F. Lammot Belin Arts Scholarships)

Scholarships Selection Committee
P.O. Box 142
Waverly PA 18471
717/586-8191
AMOUNT: $10,000
DEADLINE(S): DEC 15
FIELD(S): Painting, Sculpture, Music,
Drama, Dance, Literature,
Architecture, Photography

Applicants must have resided in the Abington or Pocono regions of Northeastern Pennsylvania. They must furnish proof of exceptional ability in their chosen field but no formal training in any academic or professional program.

US citizenship required. Finalists must appear in person before the selection committee. Write for complete information.

1186—WHITTIER COLLEGE (Talent Scholarship)

13406 E. Philadelphia Street
Whittier CA 90608
562/907-4238
FAX: 562/907-4870
E-mail: admission@whittier.edu
Internet: www.whittier.edu
AMOUNT: $2,000-$10,000
DEADLINE(S): FEB 1
FIELD(S): Art, Music, Theater

Eligibility based on portfolio or audition submissions judged by music, art, or theater department.

Write above address for complete information.

1187—WITTENBERG UNIVERSITY (Music Scholarship Funds)

P.O. Box 720
Springfield OH 45501-0720
937/327-7340 or 800/677-7347
FAX: 937/327-7347
E-mail: music@wittenberg.edu
Internet: www.wittenberg.edu/
academics/music/scholaid.shtml

AMOUNT: $600-$7,500
DEADLINE(S): MAR 19
FIELD(S): Music

Scholarships for music majors and minors and also for students who continue to study and participate in music ensembles while pursuing non-music degrees. Interested students must complete application to the University and be accepted and participate in an audition by March 19.

Request a Music Audition Packet for instructions. See website for more information, and write to: Dr. Joyce Wendel, Music Admission and Audition Coordinator, Dept. of Music, Wittenberg University, at above address.

PHILOSOPHY

1188—AMERICAN CATHOLIC HISTORICAL ASSOCIATION (John Gilmary Shea Prize)

c/o Catholic University of America
Washington DC 20064
202/319-5079
AMOUNT: $500
DEADLINE(S): AUG 1
FIELD(S): Catholic Church History

Prize for best book during the preceding twelve-month period on the history of the Catholic Church. US or Canadian citizen or legal resident.

Write for complete information.

1189—AMERICAN CATHOLIC HISTORICAL ASSOCIATION (Peter Guilday Prize)

c/o Catholic University of America
Washington DC 20064
202/319-5079
AMOUNT: $100
DEADLINE(S): OCT 1
FIELD(S): Catholic Church History

Prize for best article of 30 pages or less in manuscript form on the history of the Catholic church. Must not have had previous works published. Parts of doctoral dissertations accepted. US or Canadian citizen or legal resident.

Judges are the editors of *Catholic History Review*. Write for complete information.

1190—ASSOCIATION FOR WOMEN IN SCIENCE EDUCATIONAL FOUNDATION (Dr. Vicki L. Schechtman Scholarship)

1200 New York Ave. NW
Suite 650
Washington DC 20005
202/326-8940 or 800/886-AWIS

E-mail: awis@awis.org
Internet: www.awis.org
AMOUNT: $1,000
DEADLINE(S): JAN 16
FIELD(S): Various Sciences and Social Sciences

For female undergraduate students who are US citizens and have a minimum GPA of 3.0. Summary page, essay describing career aspirations, transcripts, proof of matriculation (if available), and two reference letters required with application. Scholarships may be used for tuition, books, housing, research, equipment, etc.

See website or write to above address for an application and more information.

1191—ASSOCIATION FOR WOMEN IN SCIENCE EDUCATIONAL FOUNDATION (Ruth Satter Memorial Award)

1200 New York Ave. NW
Suite 650
Washington DC 20005
202/326-8940 or 800/886-AWIS
E-mail: awis@awis.org
Internet: www.awis.org
AMOUNT: $1,000
DEADLINE(S): JAN 16
FIELD(S): Various Sciences and Social Sciences

Scholarships for female doctoral students who have interrupted their education three years or more to raise a family. Summary page, description of research project, resume, references, transcripts, biographical sketch, and proof of eligibility from department head required. US citizens may attend any graduate institution; non-citizens must be enrolled in US institutions.

See website or write to above address for more information or an application.

1192—B.M. WOLTMAN FOUNDATION (Lutheran Scholarships for Students of the Ministry and Teaching)

7900 U.S. 290 E.
Austin TX 78724
512/926-4272
AMOUNT: $500-$2,500
DEADLINE(S): Varies
FIELD(S): Theology (Lutheran Ministry); Teacher Education (Lutheran Schools)

Scholarships for undergrads and graduate students studying for careers in the Lutheran ministry or for teaching in a Lutheran school. For Texas residents attending, or planning to attend, any college in Texas.

45 awards. Renewable. Send for details.

1193—CHRISTIAN CHURCH—DISCIPLES OF CHRIST (Katherine J. Schutze Memorial/ Edwin G. & Lauretta M. Michael Scholarship)

P.O. Box 1986
Indianapolis IN 46206-1986
317/635-3100
FAX: 317/635-4426
E-mail: cwebb@dhm.disciples.org
AMOUNT: Varies
DEADLINE(S): MAR 15
FIELD(S): Theology

Open to Christian Church (Disciples of Christ) members who are female seminary students preparing for the ordained ministry. Must be enrolled as a full-time student in an accredited school or seminary, have an above-average GPA (minimum C+), and demonstrate financial need. Must submit transcripts and references. Schutze scholarship is open to all women who meet above criteria; Michael Scholarship is for ministers' wives only.

Renewable. Contact Division of Homeland Ministries at above address for an application.

1194—CHRISTIAN CHURCH—DISCIPLES OF CHRIST (Rowley/Ministerial Education Scholarship)

P.O. Box 1986
Indianapolis IN 46206-1986
317/635-3100
FAX 317/635-4426
E-mail: cwebb@dhm.disciples.org
AMOUNT: Varies
DEADLINE(S): MAR 15
FIELD(S): Theology

Open to Christian Church (Disciples of Christ) members who are seminary students preparing for the ordained ministry. Must be enrolled as a full-time student in an accredited school or seminary, have an above-average GPA (minimum C+), and demonstrate financial need. Must submit transcripts and references.

Renewable. Contact Division of Homeland Ministries at above address for an application.

1195—CHRISTIAN CHURCH—DISCIPLES OF CHRIST (Star Supporter Scholarship/ Loan)

P.O. Box 1986
Indianapolis IN 46206-1986
317/635-3100
FAX: 317/635-4426
E-mail: cwebb@dhm.disciples.org
AMOUNT: $2,000
DEADLINE(S): MAR 15
FIELD(S): Theology

Open to Christian Church (Disciples of Christ) members who are Black/Afro-American students preparing for the ordained ministry. Must be enrolled as a full-time student at an accredited school or seminary, have an above-average GPA (minimum C+), and demonstrate financial need. Must submit transcripts and references. Three years of service in a full-time professional ministry will repay the scholarship/loan.

100 awards annually. Renewable. Contact Division of Homeland Ministries at above address for an application.

1196—CIVIL AIR PATROL (Casaday-Elmore Ministerial Scholarship)

Civil Air Patrol
National Headquarters/ETTC
Maxwell AFB AL 36112-6332
334/293-5315
AMOUNT: $750
DEADLINE(S): JAN 31
FIELD(S): Ministry

Open to a CAP cadet who plans to enter the ministry and has been accepted into an accredited college. One-year scholarship for undergraduate study.

Write for complete information.

1197—CLEM JAUNICH EDUCATION TRUST (Scholarships)

7801 E. Bushlake Road, Suite 260
Bloomington MN 55439
612/546-1555
AMOUNT: $750-$3,000
DEADLINE(S): JUL 1
FIELD(S): Theology, Medicine

Open to students who have attended public or parochial school in the Delano (MN) school district or currently reside within 7 miles of the city of Delano, MN. Awards support undergraduate or graduate study in theology or medicine.

4-6 awards annually. Contact Joseph Abrahams for an application.

1198—CYNTHIA E. AND CLARA H. HOLLIS FOUNDATION

100 Summer Street
Boston MA 02110
Written inquiry

AMOUNT: Varies
DEADLINE(S): APR 1
FIELD(S): Nursing, Social Work, Dental or Medical Technology, and Religion

Scholarships for Massachusetts with preference given to students in the above fields. For undergraduates, graduates, voc-tech, and adult education. Must demonstrate financial need.

Send SASE to Walter E. Palmer, Esq., 35 Harvard Street, Brookline, MA 02146 for application details. Scholarship forms are also available from the rector of All Saints Church, Brookline High School, and St. Mary's High School, all in Brookline, Massachusetts.

1199—EAST OHIO CONFERENCE BOARD OF ORDAINED MINISTRY (Ministerial Student Grants)

Church of the Cross
236 Otterbein Drive
Lexington OH 44904
Written inquiry

AMOUNT: $750-$1,500
DEADLINE(S): APR 1
FIELD(S): Theology

Open to undergraduate and graduate students preparing for ordained ministry in East Ohio Conference of the United Methodist Church. Must demonstrate financial need and attend a college or seminary that is fully accredited by the University Senate. Transcripts and two letters of recommendation are required.

Contact Rev. Don Christensen, Scholarship Chairperson, for an application. Notification is in May.

1200—ELMER O. & IDA PRESTON EDUCATIONAL TRUST (Grants & Loans)

801 Grand Ave., Suite 3700
Des Moines IA 50309-2727
515/243-4191

AMOUNT: Varies
DEADLINE(S): JUN 30
FIELD(S): Christian Ministry

Open to male residents of Iowa who are pursuing theology studies at an Iowa college or university. Applicants must provide recommendation from a minister commenting on student's potential in his chosen church vocation.

Awards are one-half grant and one-half loan. The loan is repayable at 6% per annum. Write for complete information.

1201—FELLOWSHIP OF UNITED METHODISTS IN MUSIC AND WORSHIP ARTS (Scholarships)

P.O. Box 840
Nashville TN 37202
615/340-7453

AMOUNT: $500
DEADLINE(S): JUN 15
FIELD(S): Music or Theology

Scholarship for college-bound high school seniors and undergraduates who are active members of the United Methodist Church. Based on talent, leadership ability, and potential for success.

Renewable. Contact organization for details.

1202—FIRST UNITED METHODIST CHURCH (Grannis-Martin Educational Foundation Fund)

302 5th Ave., S.
St. Cloud MN 56301
FAX: 320/251-0878
E-mail: FUMCloud@aol.com

AMOUNT: $400-$1,200/yr.
DEADLINE(S): JUN 1
FIELD(S): Theology

Scholarship loans and grants are open to college or seminary students with a Minnesota connection who are entering or in seminary and who are planning to work in the United Methodist Church. Loan will be forgiven after three years of service to United Methodist Church; otherwise, repayment must commence within one year of program completion. Must submit transcripts and letters of reference.

Renewable. Contact Scholarship Committee for an application.

1203—FITZGERALD TRUST FUND (Scholarships)

NC Illinois Trust Company
C-PO2-77, P.O. Box 749
Peoria IL 61652-0749
309/655-5000

AMOUNT: Varies
DEADLINE(S): None
FIELD(S): Theology

For priesthood students attending a Catholic University for four years of college or university. Restricted to seminarians preparing for the priesthood for the Diocese of Peoria only.

Write for complete information.

1204—FRANCIS NATHANIEL AND KATHERYN PADGETT KENNEDY FOUNDATION (Scholarships for Southern Baptists)

933 Sunset Drive
Greenwood SC 29646
803/942-1400

AMOUNT: $400-$1,000
DEADLINE(S): MAY 15
FIELD(S): Theology (in preparation for the ministry or missionary work) or Christian education

Scholarships for college-bound high school seniors and undergraduates who are active members of a church of the National Baptist Convention. Must be planning a career as a Southern Baptist minister, foreign missionary, or in Christian education.

Send SASE for details.

1205—FREEDOM FROM RELIGION FOUNDATION (Student Essay Contest)

P.O. Box 750
Madison WI 53701
608/256-5800
Internet: www.infidels.org/org/ffrf

AMOUNT: $1,000; $500; $250
DEADLINE(S): JUL 15
FIELD(S): Humanities, English, Education, Philosophy, Science

Essay contest on topics related to church-state entanglement in public schools or growing up a "freethinker" in religious-oriented society. Topics change yearly, but all are on general theme of maintaining separation of church and state. New topics available in February. For high school seniors and currently enrolled college/technical students. Must be US citizen.

Send SASE to address above for complete information. Please indicate whether wanting information for college competition or high school. Information will be sent when new topics are announced each February. See website for details.

1206—GRAND AVE. PRESBYTERIAN CHURCH (Davis Foute Eagleton Memorial Student Loan Fund)

Secretary
1601 N. Travis Street
Sherman TX 75092-3761
903/893-7428

E-mail: Snyder@texoma.net

AMOUNT: Varies

DEADLINE(S): AUG 15 (fall); DEC 15 (spring)

FIELD(S): Theology, Christian Service

Open to full-time students of any Christian denomination in an accredited seminary, college, or university who desire to prepare for career in parish ministry, chaplain ministry, or other Christian service. Loans made in following priority: Members of Grand Ave. Presbyterian Church, current Austin College students/alumni, Presbyterians in Pres. schools, Presbyterians in other schools, non-Presbyterians in Pres. schools, and Presbyterians in graduate religion studies.

Contact Susan G. Snyder, Secretary, DFE Board, for an application.

1207—HENRY P. BRIDGES MINISTERS' TRUST (Scholarships)

First Presbyterian Church
105 S. Boone Street
Johnson City TN 37604
615/926-5108 (TN/NC)
301/678-5510 (MD/DC/DE)

AMOUNT: Varies (for living expenses, tuition, books, etc.)

DEADLINE(S): Varies

FIELD(S): Theology

For college/seminary students intending to go into Presbyterian ministry. Must reside in/be members of church in one of six presbyteries in TN or NC (E. Tennessee, Holston, W. North Carolina) or MD, DC, or DE (Baltimore, National Capital, New Castle). Must attend Davidson College (NC), Hampden-Sydney College (VA), or one of these seminaries: Columbia (GA), Louisville (KY), McCormick (IL), Princeton (NJ), or Union (VA). Based on achievement, need, and church involvement.

Residents of TN and NC should write to above address for an application; residents of MD, DC, and DE should write to Hancock Presbyterian Church, P.O. Box 156, 17 E. Main Street, Hancock, MD 21750.

1208—INSTITUTE FOR HUMANE STUDIES (Humane Studies Fellowship)

4084 University Drive, Suite 101
Fairfax VA 22030-6812
703/934-6920 or 800/697-8799
FAX: 703/352-7535
E-mail: ihs@gmu.edu

Internet: www.theihs.org

AMOUNT: up to $12,000

DEADLINE(S): DEC 31

FIELD(S): Social Sciences, Law, Humanities, Jurisprudence, Journalism

Awards are for graduate and advanced undergraduate students pursuing degrees at any accredited domestic or foreign school. Based on academic performance, demonstrated interest in classical liberal ideas, and potential to contribute to the advancement of a free society.

90 awards annually. Apply online or contact IHS for an application.

1209—J. HUGH & EARLE W. FELLOWS MEMORIAL FUND (Scholarship Loans)

Pensacola Junior College, President
1000 College Blvd.
Pensacola FL 32504-8998
904/484-1700

AMOUNT: Each is negotiated individually

DEADLINE(S): None

FIELD(S): Medicine, Nursing, Medical Technology, Theology (Episcopal)

Open to bona fide residents of the Florida counties of Escambia, Santa Rosa, Okaloosa, or Walton. For undergraduate study in the fields listed above. US citizenship required.

Loans are interest-free until graduation. Write for complete information.

1210—JIMMIE ULLERY CHARITABLE TRUST (Scholarship Grant)

709 S. Boston
Tulsa OK 74119
918/586-5594

AMOUNT: Varies

DEADLINE(S): JUN 1

FIELD(S): Theology

Open to Presbyterian students in full-time Christian service. Scholarships are usually (but not always) awarded for study at Presbyterian theological seminaries. US citizen or legal resident.

5-6 scholarships per year. Write for complete information.

1211—MARY GONTER AND SARA O'BRIEN SCHOLARSHIP FOUNDATION

P.O. Box 232
Dover OH 44622
Written inquiry

AMOUNT: $2,000 (approx.)

DEADLINE(S): Varies

FIELD(S): Protestant Christian Ministry

Scholarships for young Ohio residents studying to become ordained Protestant Christian ministers.

Contact Larry Markworth, V.P., Huntington Trust Company, at above location for an application.

1212—NATIONAL FEDERATION OF THE BLIND (Humanities Scholarship)

805 5th Ave.
Grinnell IA 50112
515/236-3366

AMOUNT: $3,000

DEADLINE(S): MAR 31

FIELD(S): Humanities (Art, English, Foreign Languages, History, Philosophy, Religion)

Open to legally blind students pursuing or planning to pursue a full-time postsecondary education in the US. Scholarships are awarded on basis of academic excellence, service to the community, and financial need. Must include transcripts and two letters of recommendation. Membership NOT required.

1 award annually. Renewable. Contact Mrs. Peggy Elliot, Scholarship Committee Chairman, for an application.

1213—OREGON STATE SCHOLARSHIP COMMISSION GRANTS DIVISION (Ben Selling Student Loan Fund)

1500 Valley River Drive, #100
Eugene OR 97401
Written request

AMOUNT: $2,000

DEADLINE(S): None

FIELD(S): Rabbinical studies

Open to students in Rabbinical studies for any college, university, normal school of the state of Oregon or any Rabbinical college in the United States on a full-time basis. Priority is given to Oregon residents. Loans are made on the basis of need. A co-signer is required

Write for details.

1214—PEW YOUNGER SCHOLARS PROGRAM (Graduate Fellowships)

G-123 Hesburgh Library
University of Notre Dame
Notre Dame IN 46556
219/631-4531
FAX: 219/631-8721
E-mail: Karen.M.Heinig.2@nd.edu
Internet: www.nd.edu/~pesp/pew/PYSPHistory.html

AMOUNT: $13,000

DEADLINE(S): NOV 30

FIELD(S): Social Sciences, Humanities, Theology

Program is for use at any Christian undergraduate school and most seminaries. Check with organization to see if your school qualifies. Apply during senior year. Recipients may enter a competition in which ten students will be awarded a $39,000 ($13,000/yr.) fellowship for three years of dissertation study. For use at top-ranked Ph.D. programs at outstanding universities.

NOT for study in medicine, law, business, performing arts, fine arts, or the pastorate. Check website and/or organization for details.

1215—PHILADELPHIA COLLEGE OF BIBLE (Scholarships, Grants, and Loans)

Financial Aid Dept.
200 Manor Ave.
Langhorne PA 19047
800/366-0049
Internet: www.pcb.edu

AMOUNT: Varies

DEADLINE(S): Varies

FIELD(S): Fields of study relating to Christian education

Various scholarships, loans, and grants are available to students attending this undergraduate Bible college in Philadelphia, PA. High school seniors, transfer students, and others may apply. Some programs are for students with outstanding academic achievement, musical talent, or leadership skills. Some are for dependents of Christian workers, missionaries, or alumni. Some are based on financial need.

Access website for details and/or send SASE to school for further information.

1216—PRESBYTERIAN CHURCH (U.S.A.) (Loan Program for Theological Studies)

100 Witherspoon Street
Louisville KY 40202-1396
502/567-5745
E-mail: FrancesC@ctr.pcusa.org
Internet: www.pcusa.org/highered

AMOUNT: $200-$10,000

DEADLINE(S): None

FIELD(S): Theology

All theological students who are preparing for professional church occupations must be US citizens/permanent residents, demonstrate financial need, be in good academic standing, be members of the Presbyterian Church (USA), be enrolled full-time, be studying in a PC (USA) seminary or in a theological institution approved by the students' Committee on Preparation for Ministry, and be recommended by financial aid advisor.

Renewable. Contact Frances Cook at above address for more information.

1217—ROBERT SCHRECK MEMORIAL FUND (Grants)

c/o Texas Commerce Bank
Trust Dept., P.O. Drawer 140
El Paso TX 79980
915/546-6515

AMOUNT: $500—$1500

DEADLINE(S): JUL 15; NOV 15

FIELD(S): Medicine, Veterinary Medicine, Physics, Chemistry, Architecture, Engineering, Episcopal Clergy

Grants to undergraduate juniors or seniors or graduate students who have been residents of El Paso County for at least two years. Must be US citizen or legal resident and have a high grade point average. Financial need is a consideration.

Write for complete information.

1218—ROSE HILL COLLEGE (Louella Robinson Memorial Scholarship)

P.O. Box 3126
Aiken SC 29802-3126
800/684-3769
FAX: 803/641-0240
E-mail: rosehill@.edu
Internet: www.rosehill.edu

AMOUNT: $10,000/yr. for four years

DEADLINE(S): Varies

FIELD(S): Liberal arts and humanities curricula

For undergraduate residents of Indian River County, Florida, to attend Rose Hill College in Aiken, South Carolina. The school offers a liberal arts education and follows the Great Books curriculum, a program of reading and seminars.

1 annual award. Applicants must meet entry requirements of RHC. Contact above location for details.

1219—ROSE HILL COLLEGE (Scholarships for Children of Eastern Orthodox Priests/Deacons)

P.O. Box 3126
Aiken SC 29802-3126
800/684-3769
FAX: 803/641-0240
E-mail: rosehill@edu
Internet: www.rosehill.edu

AMOUNT: Full scholarship: $10,000/yr. for four years

DEADLINE(S): Varies

FIELD(S): Liberal arts and humanities curricula

For undergraduates who are children of Eastern Orthodox Christian priests or deacons to attend Rose Hill College in Aiken, South Carolina. The school offers a liberal arts education and follows the Great Books curriculum, a program of reading and seminars.

6-10 annual awards. Applicants must meet entry requirements of RHC. Contact above location for details.

1220—ROSE HILL COLLEGE (Scholarships for the Homeschooled)

P.O. Box 3126
Aiken SC 29802-3126
800/684-3769
FAX: 803/641-0240
E-mail: rosehill@rosehill.edu
Internet: www.resehill.edu

AMOUNT: Full scholarship: $10,000/yr. for four years

DEADLINE(S): Varies

FIELD(S): Liberal arts and humanities curricula

For undergraduates who have been homeschooled for three of the last five years of their high school education. For use at Rose Hill College in Aiken, South Carolina. The school offers a liberal arts education and follows the Great Books curriculum, a program of reading and seminars. Scholarships will be awarded primarily on the basis of an essay that the student will be asked to write.

4 annual awards. Applicants must meet entry requirements of RHC. Contact above location for details.

1221—THE HEATH EDUCATION FUND (Scholarships for Ministers, Priests, and Missionaries)

Barnett Bank, N.A.
P.O. Box 40200
Jacksonville FL 32203-0200
904/464-2877

AMOUNT: $750-$1,000

DEADLINE(S): JUL 31

FIELD(S): Ministry, missionary work, or social work

Scholarships to high school graduates from the southeastern US who wish to study in the above fields. Eligible states of residence: Alabama, Florida, Georgia, Kentucky, Louisiana, Maryland, Mississippi, North & South Carolina, Tennessee, Virginia, and West Virginia.

Write to Barnett Bank's Trust Co., N.A., at above address for details and guidelines. Send SASE and letter with brief background of applicant, field of study, religious denomination, and reason for request. Preference to Methodists or Episcopalians.

1222—UNITED METHODIST CHURCH (Ernest and Eurice Miller Bass Scholarship Fund)

P.O. Box 871
Nashville TN 37202
615/327-2700

AMOUNT: $1,000
DEADLINE(S): JUN 1
FIELD(S): Theology, in preparation for the ministry

Scholarship for undergraduates who are members of the United Methodist Church and planning a career in the ministry or other religious full-time career.

Renewable. Contact organization for details.

1223—UNITED METHODIST CHURCH (Youth Ministry—Richard S. Smith Scholarship)

P.O. Box 480
Nashville TN 37202-0840
615/340-7184
FAX: 615/340-1702
E-mail: nymo@aol.com
Internet: www.umc.org/nymo/nymohome

AMOUNT: Up to $1,000
DEADLINE(S): JUN 1
FIELD(S): All fields of study

Open to United Methodist Church youth from ethnic minority backgrounds who have at least a 2.0 high school GPA, been active in a local church at least 1 year, and are entering college as freshmen.

Must be able to establish need. Obtain application between Nov. 1 and May 15.

1224—UNITED METHODIST CHURCH (Youth Ministry—David W. Self Scholarship)

P.O. Box 840
Nashville TN 37202-0840
615/340-7184
FAX: 615/340-1702

E-mail: nymo@aol.com
Internet: www.umc.org/nymo/nymohome

AMOUNT: Up to $1,000
DEADLINE(S): JUN 1
FIELD(S): All fields of study

Open to United Methodist Church youth who have at least a 2.0 high school GPA, been active in a local church at least 1 year, and are entering college as freshmen.

Must be able to establish need. Obtain application between November 1 and May 15. Write for complete information.

1225—VIOLET R. AND NADA V. BOHNETT MEMORIAL FOUNDATION

15600 Redmond Way, #200
Redmond WA 98052
FAX: 206/869-8195
E-mail: Here4dads@aol.com

AMOUNT: $475-$1,000
DEADLINE(S): Ongoing
FIELD(S): Christian ministry

Scholarships for individuals in western Washington, California, Arizona, Colorado, and Hawaii for the study of Christian ministry. Students from western Washington have priority.

Apply by sending a letter of no more than one page to Mr. Jamie Bohnett, Administrator, at above address.

1226—VIRGINIA BAPTIST MISSION BOARD (Virginia Baptist Ministerial Undergraduate Student Loans)

P.O. Box 8568
Richmond VA 23226-0568
Written inquiry

AMOUNT: Varies
DEADLINE(S): AUG 1
FIELD(S): Ministry

Open to Virginia residents enrolled full-time as undergraduate college students and studying to become Southern Baptist ministers. Must be a member of a church associated with the Baptist General Association of Virginia. Loans do not have to be repaid if recipient works for a Christian-related service for two years.

50 awards annually. Write for an application.

1227—WOMEN OF THE EVANGELICAL LUTHERAN CHURCH IN AMERICA (The Belmer-Flora Prince Scholarships)

8765 West Higgins Road
Chicago IL 60631-4189

800/638-3522, ext. 2747
FAX: 773/380-2419
E-mail: womnelca@elca.org

AMOUNT: $2,000 max.
DEADLINE(S): MAR 1
FIELD(S): Christian Service

Assists women who are members of the ELCA studying for ELCA service abroad that does not lead to a church-certified profession. Must be a US citizen at least 21 years of age who has experienced an interruption of two or more years since completion of high school. Academic records of any coursework completed in last five years as well as written confirmation of admission from educational institution are required.

Renewable for an additional year. Contact Faith Fretheim, Program Director, for an application.

SCHOOL OF NATURAL RESOURCES

1228—ALLIANCE FOR YOUNG ARTISTS AND WRITERS, INC./AMERICAN MUSEUM OF NATURAL HISTORY (Young Naturalist Awards)

Scholastic, Inc.
555 Broadway
New York NY 10012-3999
212/343-6582 or 800-SCHOLASTIC
FAX: 212/343-4885
E-mail: mjohnson@scholastic.com
Internet: www.amnh.org/youngnaturalistawards

AMOUNT: up to $2,500 + trip to New York to visit AMNH
DEADLINE(S): JAN 3
FIELD(S): Natural Sciences

For all students in grades 7-12 currently enrolled in a public or non-public school in the US, Canada, US territories, or US-sponsored schools abroad. Program focuses on finding and rewarding excellence in biology, earth science, astronomy, and cultural studies. Students are encouraged to perform observation-based projects that require creativity, inquiry, and critical analysis. Specific topics vary annually.

48 awards annually. See website or contact Mike Johnson, Program Manager, for an application.

1229—AMERICAN FOUNDATION FOR THE BLIND (Paul W. Ruckes Scholarship)

11 Penn Plaza, Suite 300
New York NY 10001
212/502-7661
FAX: 212/502-7771
E-mail: juliet@afb.org
Internet: www.afb.org
AMOUNT: $1,000
DEADLINE(S): APR 30
FIELD(S): Engineering,
    Computer/Physical/Life Sciences

Open to legally blind and visually impaired undergraduate and graduate students pursuing a degree in one of above fields. Must be US citizen. Must submit written documentation of visual impairment from ophthalmologist or optometrist (need not be legally blind); official transcripts; proof of college/university acceptance; three letters of recommendation; and typewritten statement describing goals, work experience, extracurricular activities, and how monies will be used.

1 award annually. See website or contact Julie Tucker at AFB for an application.

1230—AMERICAN INDIAN SCIENCE AND ENGINEERING SOCIETY (A.T. Anderson Memorial Scholarship)

P.O. Box 9828
Albuquerque NM 87119-9828
505/765-1052
FAX: 505/765-5608
E-mail: scholarships@aises.org
Internet: www.aises.org/scholarships
AMOUNT: $1,000-$2,000
DEADLINE(S): JUN 15
FIELD(S): Medicine, Natural Resources,
    Science, Engineering

Open to undergraduate and graduate students who are at least 1/4 American Indian or recognized as member of a tribe. Must be member of AISES ($10 fee), enrolled full-time at an accredited institution, and demonstrate financial need.

Renewable. See website or contact Patricia Browne for an application and/or membership information.

1231—BARRY GOLDWATER SCHOLARSHIP AND EXCELLENCE IN EDUCATION FOUNDATION (Scholarships)

6225 Brandon Ave., Suite 315
Springfield VA 22150-2519

703/756-6012
FAX: 703/756-6015
E-mail: goldh2o@erols.com
Internet: www.act.org/goldwater
AMOUNT: $7,500/yr. (max.)
DEADLINE(S): FEB 1
FIELD(S): Math, Natural Sciences,
    Engineering

Open to college sophomores and juniors with a minimum 3.0 GPA. Must be US citizen, resident alien, or American national pursuing a degree at an accredited institution in math, natural sciences, or engineering disciplines that contribute to technological advances.

300 awards annually. See website or contact your Goldwater Faculty Representative on campus. Students must be nominated by their institution and cannot apply on their own.

1232—CAREER OPPORTUNITIES FOR YOUTH, INC. (Collegiate Scholarship Program)

P.O. Box 996
Manhattan Beach CA 90266
310/535-4838
AMOUNT: $250 to $1,000
DEADLINE(S): SEP 30
FIELD(S): Engineering, Science,
    Mathematics, Computer Science,
    Business Administration, Education,
    Nursing

For students of Latino/Hispanic background residing in the Southern California area who have completed at least one semester/quarter of study at an accredited four-year university. Must have a cumulative GPA of 2.5 or higher.

Priority will be given to students who demonstrate financial need. Send SASE to above location for details.

1233—COMMUNITY FOUNDATION SILICON VALLEY (Valley Scholars Program)

111 W. Saint John Street, Suite 230
San Jose CA 95113
408/278-0270
FAX: 408/278-0280
Internet: www.cfsv.org
AMOUNT: $20,000 (over 4 years of
    college)
DEADLINE(S): Varies (early spring)
FIELD(S): Science and/or Math

A scholarship program for public high school students in the Silicon Valley (San Mateo and Santa Clara counties and Fremont Union High School District, California) who have demonstrated enthu-

siasm and aptitude for science and math. Must be US citizen or permanent resident.

Up to 20 students are selected each year. Each Valley Scholar receives financial support, guidance through the college admission process, and a mentor whose interests match their own. Students may apply during their sophomore year of high school and must be academically outstanding.

1234—EXPLORERS CLUB (Youth Activity Fund)

46 East 70th Street
New York NY 10021
212/628-8383
FAX: 212/288-4449
AMOUNT: $200-$1,000
DEADLINE(S): APR 1
FIELD(S): Natural Sciences

Open to high school and undergraduate college students to help them participate in field research in the natural sciences anywhere in the world under the supervision of a qualified scientist. Grants are to help with travel costs and expenses. Applicants must provide a brief but knowledgeable explanation of proposed project in own words, as well as two letters of recommendation. Joint funding is encouraged. Must be US citizen or permanent resident.

Applications available in February. Write to above address for details.

1235—FREEDOM FROM RELIGION FOUNDATION (Student Essay Contest)

P.O. Box 750
Madison WI 53701
608/256-5800
Internet: www.infidels.org/org/ffrf
AMOUNT: $1,000; $500; $250
DEADLINE(S): JUL 15
FIELD(S): Humanities, English,
    Education, Philosophy, Science

Essay contest on topics related to church-state entanglement in public schools or growing up a "freethinker" in religious-oriented society. Topics change yearly, but all are on general theme of maintaining separation of church and state. New topics available in February. For high school seniors and currently enrolled college/technical students. Must be US citizen.

Send SASE to address above for complete information. Please indicate whether wanting information for college competition or high school. Information will be sent when new topics are announced each February. See website for details.

1236—GERBER SCIENTIFIC, INC. (H. Joseph Gerber Vision Scholarship Program)

83 Gerber Road West
South Windsor CT 06074
860/648-8027
Internet: www.gerberscientific.com

AMOUNT: Varies
DEADLINE(S): MAR 15
FIELD(S): Engineering, Mathematics, Computer Science, Natural Sciences

Scholarship program for high school seniors in Connecticut.

50 scholarships to be awarded.

1237—HOPI TRIBE (Priority Scholarships)

P.O. Box 123
Kykotsmovi AZ 86039
520/734-2441, ext. 520
800/762-9630
FAX: 520/734-2435

AMOUNT: Varies
DEADLINE(S): JUL 31
FIELD(S): Law, Natural Resources, Education, Medicine/Health, Engineering, Business

Open to enrolled members of the Hopi Tribe studying in one of the fields listed above, which are considered to be areas of priority interest to the Hopis. Available to college juniors, seniors, and graduate students. Program is to encourage graduates to apply their degrees to Hopi Tribal Goals and Objectives.

Contact Hopi Tribe for an application.

1238—JEWISH FEDERATION OF METRO-POLITAN CHICAGO (Academic Scholarship Program for Studies in the Sciences)

One South Franklin Street
Chicago IL 60606
Written inquiry

AMOUNT: Varies
DEADLINE(S): MAR 1
FIELD(S): Mathematics, Engineering, or Science

Scholarships for college juniors, seniors, and graduate students who are Jewish and are residents of Chicago, IL and Cook County.

Academic achievement and financial need are considered. Applications accepted after Dec. 1.

1239—KOREAN-AMERICAN SCIENTISTS AND ENGINEERS ASSOCIATION (KSEA Scholarships)

1952 Gallows Road, Suite 300
Vienna VA 22182
703/748-1221
FAX: 703/748-1331
E-mail: admin@ksea.org
Internet: www.ksea.org

AMOUNT: $1,000
DEADLINE(S): FEB 28
FIELD(S): Science, Engineering, or Medicine

Scholarships to encourage Korean-American students to study in a science, engineering, or pre-med discipline and to recognize high-performing students. Must have graduated from a high school in the US.

5 to 8 awards yearly. Must be a student member of KSEA or a child of a member.

1240—NATIONAL ITALIAN AMERICAN FOUNDATION (Italian Cultural Society and NIAF Matching Scholarship)

1860 19th Street NW
Washington DC. 20009-5599
202/530-5315

AMOUNT: $2,000
DEADLINE(S): MAR 31
FIELD(S): Science or Humanities

Open to undergraduate students of Italian descent majoring in science or the humanities in the Washington DC, Maryland, and Virginia areas. Financial need must be demonstrated.

Write for application and details.

1241—OPEN SOCIETY INSTITUTE (Environmental Management Fellowships)

400 West 59th Street
New York NY 10019
212/548-0600 or 212/757-2323
FAX: 212/548-4679 or
212/548-4600
Internet: www.soros.org/efp.html

AMOUNT: Fees, room, board, living stipend, textbooks, international transportation, health insurance
DEADLINE(S): NOV 15
FIELD(S): Earth Sciences, Natural Sciences, Humanities (exc. language), Anthropology, Sociology, Mathematics, or Engineering

Two-year fellowships for use in selected universities in the US for international students. For students/professionals in fields related to environmental policy, legislation, and remediation techniques applicable to their home countries.

To apply, contact your local Soros Foundation or Open Society Institute. Further details on website.

1242—PENINSULA COMMUNITY FOUNDATION (Dr. Mary Finegold Scholarship)

1700 S. El Camino Real, #300
San Mateo CA 94402
650/358-9369
FAX: 650/358-9817

AMOUNT: $1,000
DEADLINE(S): MAR 27 (5 P.M.)
FIELD(S): Sciences

Scholarships for senior girls graduating from high school in Palo Alto, California, who intend to complete a four-year degree in the sciences. Special consideration will be given to girls who have demonstrated a "pioneering" spirit in that they have not been constrained by stereotypical female roles and to those facing financial hardship.

Award was established in the honor of Dr. Mary Finegold who, after completing her medical studies, elected to stay at home until her youngest child was in high school before beginning her medical practice. She was a school physician.

1243—RESOURCES FOR THE FUTURE (RFF Summer Internship Program)

1616 P Street NW
Washington DC 20036-1400
202/328-5000
E-mail: lewis@rff.org OR voigt@rff.org
Internet: www.rff.org

AMOUNT: $375/week
DEADLINE(S): MAR 12
FIELD(S): Social Sciences, Natural Resources, Energy, Environment

Resident-paid summer internships for undergraduate and graduate students for research in the above fields. Divisions are Center for Risk Management, Energy and Natural Resources, and Quality of the Environment. Candidates should have outstanding policy analysis and writing skills. For both US and non- US citizens.

All information is on website. Address inquiries and applications to Sue Lewis (Energy & Natural Resources and Quality of the Environment) or Marilyn Voigt (Center for Risk Management). NO fax submissions.

1244—SAN DIEGO AEROSPACE MUSEUM (Bill Gibbs Scholarship)

Education Dept.
2001 Pan American Plaza
San Diego CA 92101
619/234-8291, ext. 19
FAX: 619/233-4526
Internet: aerospacemuseum.org/
Scholastic.HTML

AMOUNT: Varies
DEADLINE(S): Varies
FIELD(S): Aerospace: math, physics,
science, or engineering

For students who are residents of San Diego County, California, who have an aerospace career interest, who have been accepted to a four-year college or university in a degree program relating to math, physics, science, or engineering.

Call or write museum for further information.

1245—SKIDMORE COLLEGE (Merit Scholarships in Math and Science)

Office of Admissions
Saratoga Springs NY 12866-1632
800/867-6007
E-mail: admissions@skidmore.edu
Internet: www.skidmore.edu/campus/
merit2.html

AMOUNT: $10,000/yr.
DEADLINE(S): FEB 1
FIELD(S): Math or Science

Scholarships for students excelling in the above fields. Awards are based on talent, not financial need. Recipients are not required to major in a scientific or mathematical discipline, but they will be expected to demonstrate serious research in one or more of these areas.

5 scholarships per year. For more information, visit website.

1246—TEXAS SOCIETY OF PROFESSIONAL ENGINEERS (Scholarships)

P.O. Box 2145
Austin TX 78768
512/472-9286 or 800/580-8973
Internet: www.tspe.org

AMOUNT: Varies
DEADLINE(S): JAN 30
FIELD(S): Engineering (math, sciences)

Scholarships for graduating high school seniors who are Texas residents planning to attend Texas engineering colleges

Contact organization for details. Application is on website.

1247—U.S. DEPARTMENT OF AGRICULTURE (1890 National Scholars Program)

14th & Independence Ave. SW
Room 301-W, Whitten Bldg.
Washington DC 20250-9600
202/720-6905
E-mail: usda-m@fie.com
Internet: web.fie.com/htdoc/fed/
agr/ars/edu/prog/mti/agrpgaak.htm

AMOUNT: Tuition,
employment/benefits, use of
PC/software, fees, books, room/board
DEADLINE(S): JAN 15
FIELD(S): Agriculture, Food, or Natural
Resource sciences

For US citizens, high school grad/GED, GPA 3.0+, verbal/math SAT 1,000+, composite score 21+ ACT, 1st-yr college student, and attend participating school.

34+ scholarships/yr/4 years. Send applications to USDA Liaison Officer at the 1890 Institution of your choice (see Web page for complete list).

1248—WOODS HOLE OCEANOGRAPHIC INSTITUTION (Traineeships in Oceanography for Minority Group Undergraduates)

360 Woods Hole Road
Woods Hole MA 02543-1541
508/289-2219
FAX: 508/457-2188
E-mail: mgately@whoi.edu
Internet: www.whoi.edu

AMOUNT: Varies
DEADLINE(S): FEB 16
FIELD(S): Physical/Natural Sciences,
Mathematics, Engineering

For minority undergraduates enrolled in US colleges/universities who have completed at least two semesters. These awards provide training and research experience for students with interests in the above fields. Traineeships may be awarded for a ten- to twelve-week period in the summer or for a semester during the academic year.

Renewable. For an application/more information, contact the Education Office, Clark Laboratory 223, MS #31, at above address.

AGRICULTURE

1249—ABBIE SARGENT MEMORIAL SCHOLARSHIP INC. (Scholarships)

295 Sheep Davis Road
Concord NH 03301

603/224-1934
FAX: 603/228-8432

AMOUNT: $400
DEADLINE(S): MAR 15
FIELD(S): Agriculture, Veterinary
Medicine, Home Economics

Open to New Hampshire residents who are high school graduates with good grades and character. For undergraduate or graduate study. Must be legal resident of US and demonstrate financial need.

3 annual awards. Renewable with reapplication. Write for complete information.

1250—ALLIANCE FOR YOUNG ARTISTS AND WRITERS, INC./AMERICAN MUSEUM OF NATURAL HISTORY (Young Naturalist Awards)

Scholastic, Inc.
555 Broadway
New York NY 10012-3999
212/343-6582 or 800-SCHOLASTIC
FAX: 212/343-4885
E-mail: mjohnson@scholastic.com
Internet: www.amnh.org/
youngnaturalistawards

AMOUNT: up to $2,500 + trip to New
York to visit AMNH
DEADLINE(S): JAN 3
FIELD(S): Natural Sciences

For all students in grades 7-12 currently enrolled in a public or non-public school in the US, Canada, US territories, or US-sponsored schools abroad. Program focuses on finding and rewarding excellence in biology, earth science, astronomy, and cultural studies. Students are encouraged to perform observation-based projects that require creativity, inquiry, and critical analysis. Specific topics vary annually.

48 awards annually. See website or contact Mike Johnson, Program Manager, for an application.

1251—AMERICAN JUNIOR BRAHMAN ASSOCIATION (Ladies of the ABBA Scholarship)

1313 La Concha Lane
Houston TX 77054-1890
Written inquiry

AMOUNT: $500 to $1,000
DEADLINE(S): APR 30
FIELD(S): Agriculture

Open to graduating high school seniors who are members of the Junior Brahman Association. For full-time undergraduate study. US citizenship required.

Up to 4 awards per year. Write for complete information.

1252—AMERICAN POMOLOGICAL SOCIETY (U.P. Hedrick Awards)

103 Tyson Bldg.
Penn State University
University Park PA 16802
814/863-6163

AMOUNT: $100 second place; $300 first place
DEADLINE(S): JUN 1
FIELD(S): Horticulture, particularly Pomology (fruit)

For best student papers on topics related to fruit/fruit cultivation. Two types of papers will be considered: one with content relating to cultivars of deciduous, tropical, or subtropical fruit as related to climate, soil, rootstocks, a specific experiment, a breeding project, history, and performance of new or old cultivars; another can be a library review paper pertinent to pomology—an M.S. or Ph.D. thesis or personal experience with a particular fruit cultivar.

Winning papers will be published in *Fruit Varieties Journal.* Write to Dr. Robert M. Crassweller, Dept. of Horticulture, at the above address for complete information.

1253—BEDDING PLANTS FOUNDATION, INC. (Barbara Carlson & Dosatron International, Inc. Scholarships)

P.O. Box 280
East Lansing MI 48826-0280
517/333-4617
FAX: 517/333-4494
E-mail: BPFI@aol.com
Internet: www.bpfi.org

AMOUNT: $1,000
DEADLINE(S): MAY 15
FIELD(S): Horticulture

Open to graduate and undergraduate students already attending a four-year college/university who are majoring in horticulture or related field. For Carlson Scholarship, should intend to intern or work for public gardens. Cash award, with checks issued jointly in name of recipient and college/institution he or she will attend for current year. Must submit references and transcripts.

2 awards annually. See website or send printed self-addressed mailing label (or self-addressed, stamped envelope) to BPFI after January 1st for an application. Recipients will be notified.

1254—BEDDING PLANTS FOUNDATION, INC. (Ball Horticultural Company & Paris Fracasso Production Floriculture Scholarships)

P.O. Box 280
East Lansing MI 48826-0280
517/333-4617
FAX: 517/333-4494
E-mail: BPFI@aol.com
Internet: www.bpfi.org

AMOUNT: $1,000-$2,000
DEADLINE(S): MAY 15
FIELD(S): Floriculture

Open to undergraduates entering junior or senior year at a four-year college/university. Ball Scholarship requires pursuit of career in commercial floriculture; Paris Scholarship requires pursuit of career in floriculture production. Cash award, with checks issued jointly in name of recipient and college/institution he or she will attend for current year. Must submit references and transcripts.

2 awards annually. See website or send printed self-addressed mailing label (or self-addressed, stamped envelope) to BPFI after January 1st for an application. Recipients will be notified.

1255—BEDDING PLANTS FOUNDATION, INC. (Carl F. Dietz Memorial Scholarship)

P.O. Box 280
East Lansing MI 48826-0280
517/333-4617
FAX: 517/333-4494
E-mail: BPFI@aol.com
Internet: www.bpfi.org

AMOUNT: $1,000
DEADLINE(S): MAY 15
FIELD(S): Horticulture

Open to undergraduate students already attending a four-year college/university who are majoring in horticulture or related field, with a specific interest in bedding plants. Cash awards, with checks issued jointly in name of recipient and college or institution he or she will attend for current year. Must submit references and transcripts.

1 award annually. See website or send printed self-addressed mailing label (or self-addressed, stamped envelope) to BPFI after January 1st for an application. Recipient will be notified.

1256—BEDDING PLANTS FOUNDATION, INC. (Earl J. Small Growers, Inc. Scholarships)

P.O. Box 280
East Lansing MI 48826-0280
517/333-4617
FAX: 517/333-4494
E-mail: BPFI@aol.com
Internet: www.bpfi.org

AMOUNT: $1,000
DEADLINE(S): MAY 15
FIELD(S): Horticulture

Open to undergraduate students already attending a four-year college/university who are majoring in horticulture or related field, with the intention of pursuing a career in greenhouse production. Must be US or Canadian citizen. Cash award, with checks issued jointly in name of recipient and college/institution he or she will attend for current year. Must submit references and transcripts.

2 awards annually. See website or send printed self-addressed mailing label (or self-addressed, stamped envelope) to BPFI after January 1st for an application. Recipients will be notified.

1257—BEDDING PLANTS FOUNDATION, INC. (Ed Markham International Scholarship)

P.O. Box 280
East Lansing MI 48826-0280
517/333-4617
FAX: 517/333-4494
E-mail: BPFI@aol.com
Internet: www.bpfi.org

AMOUNT: $1,000
DEADLINE(S): MAY 15
FIELD(S): Horticulture AND International Business

Open to graduate and undergraduate students already attending a four-year college/university who are majoring in horticulture or related field. Should wish to further understanding of domestic and international marketing through international horticulturally related study, work, or travel. Cash award, with checks issued jointly in name of recipient and college/institution he or she will attend for current year. Must submit references and transcripts.

1 award annually. See website or send printed self-addressed mailing label (or self-addressed, stamped envelope) to BPFI after January 1st for an application. Recipient will be notified.

1258—BEDDING PLANTS FOUNDATION, INC. (Fran Johnson Non-Traditional Scholarship)

P.O. Box 280
East Lansing MI 48826-0280
517/333-4617
FAX: 517/333-4494
E-mail: BPFI@aol.com
Internet: www.bpfi.org

AMOUNT: $500-$1,000
DEADLINE(S): MAY 15
FIELD(S): Horticulture, Floriculture

Open to undergraduate and graduate students at 2- or 4-year college/university in US or Canada. Must be US or Canadian citizen with major in horticulture or related field, specifically bedding plants or other floral crops. Must be reentering an academic program after an absence of at least 5 years. Cash award, with checks issued jointly in name of recipient and college/institution he or she will attend for current year. Must submit references and transcripts.

1 award annually. See website or send printed self-addressed mailing label (or self-addressed, stamped envelope) to BPFI after January 1st for an application. Recipient will be notified.

1259—BEDDING PLANTS FOUNDATION, INC. (Harold Bettinger Memorial Scholarship)

P.O. Box 280
East Lansing MI 48826-0280
517/333-4617
FAX: 517/333-4494
E-mail: BPFI@aol.com
Internet: www.bpfi.org

AMOUNT: $1,000
DEADLINE(S): MAY 15
FIELD(S): Horticulture AND
Business/Marketing

Open to graduate and undergraduate students already attending a four-year college/university who have either a horticulture major with business/marketing emphasis OR a business/marketing major with horticulture emphasis. Cash award, with checks issued jointly in name of recipient and college/institution he or she will attend for current year. Must submit references and transcripts.

1 award annually. See website or send printed self-addressed mailing label (or self-addressed, stamped envelope) to BPFI after January 1st for an application. Recipient will be notified.

1260—BEDDING PLANTS FOUNDATION, INC. (James K. Rathmell, Jr. Memorial Scholarship)

P.O. Box 280
East Lansing MI 48826-0280
517/333-4617
FAX: 517/333-4494
E-mail: BPFI@aol.com
Internet: www.bpfi.org

AMOUNT: $2,500 (max.)
DEADLINE(S): MAY 15
FIELD(S): Horticulture, Floriculture

Open to undergraduates entering junior or senior year at a four-year college/university, and graduate students. Must have plans to work/study outside of US in the field of floriculture or horticulture, with preference to those planning to work/study six months or longer. Cash award, with checks issued jointly in name of recipient and college/institution he or she will attend for current year. Must submit references and transcripts.

1 award annually. See website or send printed self-addressed mailing label (or self-addressed, stamped envelope) to BPFI after January 1st for an application. Recipient will be notified.

1261—BEDDING PLANTS FOUNDATION, INC. (Jacob Van Namen/Vans Marketing Scholarship)

P.O. Box 280
East Lansing MI 48826-0280
517/333-4617
FAX: 517/333-4494
E-mail: BPFI@aol.com
Internet: www.bpfi.org

AMOUNT: $1,250
DEADLINE(S): MAY 15
FIELD(S): Agribusiness AND
Floriculture

Open to undergraduate students already attending a four-year college/university who wish to be involved in agribusiness marketing and distribution of floral products. Cash award, with checks issued jointly in name of recipient and college/institution he or she will attend for current year. Must submit references and transcripts.

1 award annually. See website or send printed self-addressed mailing label (or self-addressed, stamped envelope) to BPFI after January 1st for an application. Recipients will be notified.

1262—BEDDING PLANTS FOUNDATION, INC. (Jerry Baker College Freshman Scholarships)

P.O. Box 280
East Lansing MI 48826-0280
517/333-4617
FAX: 517/333-4494
E-mail: BPFI@aol.com
Internet: www.bpfi.org

AMOUNT: $1,000
DEADLINE(S): MAY 15
FIELD(S): Horticulture, Landscaping,
Gardening

Open to undergraduates entering freshman year who are interested in careers in horticulture, landscaping, or gardening. Must be enrolled in an accredited four-year college/university program in the US or Canada during next year. Cash awards, with checks issued jointly in name of recipient and college/institution he or she will attend for current year. Must submit references and transcripts.

2 awards annually. See website or send printed self-addressed mailing label (or self-addressed, stamped envelope) to BPFI after January 1st for an application. Recipients will be notified.

1263—BEDDING PLANTS FOUNDATION, INC. (Jerry Wilmot Scholarship)

P.O. Box 280
East Lansing MI 48826-0280
517/333-4617
FAX: 517/333-4494
E-mail: BPFI@aol.com
Internet: www.bpfi.org

AMOUNT: $2,000
DEADLINE(S): MAY 15
FIELD(S): Horticulture AND
Business/Finance; Garden Center
Management

Open to undergraduate students already attending a four-year college/university who have either a major in horticulture with business/finance emphasis OR have a major in business/finance with horticulture emphasis. Should wish to pursue a career in garden center management. Cash award, with checks issued jointly in name of recipient and college/institution he or she will attend for current year. Must submit references and transcripts.

1 award annually. See website or send printed self-addressed mailing label (or self-addressed, stamped envelope) to BPFI after January 1st for an application. Recipient will be notified.

1264—BEDDING PLANTS FOUNDATION, INC. (Seed Companies Scholarship)

P.O. Box 280
East Lansing MI 48826-0280
517/333-4617
FAX: 517/333-4494
E-mail: BPFI@aol.com
Internet: www.bpfi.org

AMOUNT: $1,000
DEADLINE(S): MAY 15
FIELD(S): Horticulture

Open to undergraduate students entering junior or senior year at a four-year college/university—and graduate students—who are majoring in horticulture or related field, with the intention of pursuing a career in the seed industry. Cash award, with checks issued jointly in name of recipient and college/institution he or she will attend for current year. Must submit references and transcripts.

1 award annually. See website or send printed self-addressed mailing label (or self-addressed, stamped envelope) to BPFI after January 1st for an application. Recipient will be notified.

1265—BEDDING PLANTS FOUNDATION, INC. (Vocational Scholarships)

P.O. Box 280
East Lansing MI 48826-0280
517/333-4617
FAX: 517/333-4494
E-mail: BPFI@aol.com
Internet: www.bpfi.org

AMOUNT: $500-$1,000
DEADLINE(S): MAY 15
FIELD(S): Horticulture, Floriculture

Open to entering freshmen or 2nd-year students in a 1- or 2-year program who will be enrolled for entire next year. Must be US or Canadian citizen, have minimum 3.0 GPA, and have major interest in horticulture or related field with intentions of becoming floriculture plant producer and/or operations manager. Cash awards, with checks issued jointly in name of recipient and college/institution he or she will attend for current year. Must submit references and transcripts.

2-4 awards annually. See website or send printed self-addressed mailing label (or self-addressed, stamped envelope) to BPFI after January 1st for an application. Recipients will be notified.

1266—CALIFORNIA FARM BUREAU SCHOLARSHIP FOUNDATION (Scholarships)

2300 River Plaza Drive
Sacramento CA 95833
800/698-3276

AMOUNT: $1,250-$2,000
DEADLINE(S): MAR 1
FIELD(S): Agriculture

For any student entering or attending a four-year accredited college or university in California and pursuing a career in the agricultural industry. Membership in a county farm bureau is NOT required. Applications must include all transcripts and three current letters of recommendation. Junior college students are not eligible. Awards based on academic achievement, career goals, extracurricular activities, determination, and leadership skills.

30+ awards annually. Renewable. Write for complete information.

1267—CENEX FOUNDATION SCHOLARSHIP PROGRAM (Agricultural Studies)

5500 Cenex Drive
Inver Grove Heights MN 55077
651/451-5129

AMOUNT: $600
DEADLINE(S): FEB 15
FIELD(S): Agriculture

For students attending a participating vocational, technical, or community college in the first or second year of their school's two-year program. Participating schools are located in the Cenex Harvest States market area: Colorado, Idaho, Iowa, Kansas, Minnesota, Montana, Nebraska, North Dakota, Oregon, South Dakota, Utah, Washington, Wisconsin, and Wyoming. Selection is based on scholastic achievement rather than need. Schools must submit applications.

81 awards annually. Money is mailed to school at end of term for student's use. Contact Cenex Foundation or your participating school for an application.

1268—CENEX FOUNDATION SCHOLARSHIP PROGRAM (Cooperative Studies)

5500 Cenex Drive
Inver Grove Heights MN 55077
651/451-5129

AMOUNT: $750
DEADLINE(S): Varies
FIELD(S): Agriculture

For students attending agricultural college of participating university enrolled in courses on cooperative principles and cooperative business practices. Must be enrolled in junior or senior year. Selection based on scholastic achievement. Participating universites are within Cenex Harvest States market area: CO State, U ID, IA State, KS State, MN State, U MN, MT State, U NE, ND State, OR State, SD State, UT State, WA State, U WI, and U WY. Universities administer program.

79 awards annually. Renewable if apply in junior year. Contact Cenex Foundation or your participating school for an application. Recipients are selected in spring and receive award in fall.

1269—FLORIDA FEDERATION OF GARDEN CLUBS, INC. (FFGC Scholarships for College Students)

6065 21st Street, SW
Vero Beach FL 32968-9427
561/778-1023
Internet: www.ffgc.org

AMOUNT: $1,500-$3,500
DEADLINE(S): MAY 1
FIELD(S): Ecology, Environmental
Issues, Land Management, City
Planning, Environmental Control,
Horticulture, Landscape Design,
Conservation, Botany, Forestry,
Marine Biology, Floriculture,
Agriculture

Various scholarships for Florida residents with a "B" average or better enrolled full-time as a junior, senior, or graduate student at a Florida college or university.

See website or contact Melba Campbell at FFGC for an application.

1270—FLORIDA FEDERATION OF GARDEN CLUBS, INC. (FFGC Scholarships for High School Students)

6065 21st Street, SW
Vero Beach FL 32968-9427
561/778-1023
Internet: www.ffgc.org

AMOUNT: $1,500
DEADLINE(S): MAY 1
FIELD(S): Ecology, Environmental
Issues, Land Management, City
Planning, Environmental Control,
Horticulture, Landscape Design,
Conservation, Botany, Forestry,
Marine Biology, Floriculture,
Agriculture

Scholarships for Florida residents with a "B" average or better who will be incoming freshmen at a Florida college or university.

See website or contact Melba Campbell at FFGC for an application.

1271—FLORIDA RURAL REHABILITATION SCHOLARSHIP

P.O. Box 110270
Gainesville FL 32611
Written inquiry

AMOUNT: Up to $1,000
DEADLINE(S): JAN 15
FIELD(S): Agriculture

Scholarships for Florida students from rural areas who plan to study agriculture at the Institute of Food and Agricultural Sciences at the University of Florida. Financial need, leadership ability, and merit are considered.

Write to Institute of Food and Ag Sciences, University of Florida, at above address.

1272—GARDEN CLUB OF AMERICA (Katharine M. Grosscup Scholarships)

Cleveland Botanical Garden
11030 East Blvd.
Cleveland OH 44106
FAX: 216/721-2056
Internet: www.gcamerica.org

AMOUNT: up to $3,000
DEADLINE(S): FEB 15
FIELD(S): Horticulture & related fields

Financial assistance to college juniors, seniors, or graduate students, preferably from (though not restricted to) Ohio, Pennsylvania, West Virginia, Michigan, and Indiana. Purpose is to encourage the study of horticulture and related fields.

Funds several students annually. See website or contact Mrs. Nancy Stevenson at above address for more information/an application.

1273—GOLF COURSE SUPERINTENDENTS ASSOCIATION OF AMERICA (GCSAA Essay Contest)

1421 Research Park Drive
Lawrence KS 66049-3859
785/832-3678
FAX: 785/832-3665
E-mail: psmith@gcsaa.org
Internet: www.gcsaa.org

AMOUNT: $2,000 (total prizes)
DEADLINE(S): MAR 31
FIELD(S): Turfgrass Science, Agronomy, Golf Course Management

Contest open to undergraduate and graduate students pursuing degrees in one of the above fields. Essays should be 7-12 pages long and should focus on the golf course management profession.

See website or contact Pam Smith at GCSAA for details.

1274—GOLF COURSE SUPERINTENDENTS ASSOCIATION OF AMERICA (GCSAA Scholars Program)

1421 Research Park Drive
Lawrence KS 66049-3859
785/832-3678
FAX: 785/832-3665
E-mail: psmith@gcsaa.org
Internet: www.gcsaa.org

AMOUNT: $500-$3,500
DEADLINE(S): JUN 1
FIELD(S): Golf/Turf Management

Awards available to outstanding undergraduate students planning careers as golf course superintendents. Must be enrolled in a recognized major field related to golf/turf management. Must successfully have completed at least 24 credit hours or the equivalent of one year of full-time study in an appropriate major. Must be a member of GCSAA.

For membership information or an application, see website or contact Pam Smith at GCSAA.

1275—GOLF COURSE SUPERINTENDENTS ASSOCIATION OF AMERICA (The Scotts Company Scholars Program)

1421 Research Park Drive
Lawrence KS 66049-3859
785/832-3678
FAX: 785/832-3665
E-mail: psmith@gcsaa.org
Internet: www.gcsaa.org

AMOUNT: $500 award; $2,500 scholarship + internship
DEADLINE(S): MAR 1
FIELD(S): "Green Industry"

For graduating high school seniors and college freshmen, sophomores, and juniors accepted/currently enrolled in a 2 or more year accredited college. Applicants evaluated on cultural diversity, academic achievement, extracurricular activities, leadership, employment potential, essay responses, and letters of recommendation. Financial need is NOT a factor.

5 finalists receive award; scholarships awarded to 2 of finalists. Scholarship not renewable. Employees of Scotts Company and current members/family members of GCSAA Foundation Board of Trustees not eligible.

1276—HORTICULTURAL RESEARCH INSTITUTE (Timothy Bigelow Scholarship)

1250 I Street NW, Suite 500
Washington, DC 20005
202/789-2900
FAX: 202/789-1893

AMOUNT: Varies
DEADLINE(S): MAY 20
FIELD(S): Horticulture

Open to New England residents enrolled in a two- or four-year institution. Students must be seniors in a two-year program, juniors in a four-year program, or graduate students. Applicants must have at least a 2.25 GPA and be interested in horticulture.

Write to the above address for complete information.

1277—HUBBARD FARMS CHARITABLE FOUNDATION

P.O. Box 505
Walpole NH 03608-0505
603/756-3311

AMOUNT: Varies
DEADLINE(S): APR 1; OCT 1
FIELD(S): Poultry science, genetics, and other life sciences

Scholarships are for financially needy students at universities that the foundation trustees consider to be leaders in the field of progress in technology and efficiency of production of poultry products.

Send SASE to Jane F. Kelly, Clerk, at above address for current application guidelines.

1278—JAPANESE AMERICAN CITIZENS LEAGUE (Kyutaro & Yasuo Abiko Memorial Scholarship)

1765 Sutter Street
San Francisco CA 94115
415/921-5225
FAX: 415/931-4671
E-mail: jacl@jacl.org
Internet: www.jacl.org

AMOUNT: $1,000-$5,000
DEADLINE(S): APR 1
FIELD(S): Agriculture, Journalism

Open to JACL members and their children only. For undergraduate students with an interest in either journalism or agriculture and who are planning to attend a college, university, trade school, business school, or any other institution of higher learning. Must submit personal statement, letters of recommendation, and transcripts. Financial need NOT a factor.

For membership information or an application, send a self-addressed, stamped envelope to above address, stating your level of study. Applications available October 1st through March 20th; recipients notified in July.

1279—JAPANESE AMERICAN CITIZENS LEAGUE (Sam S. Kuwahara Memorial Scholarship for Entering Freshmen)

1765 Sutter Street
San Francisco CA 94115
415/921-5225
FAX: 415/931-4671
E-mail: jacl@jacl.org
Internet: www.jacl.org
AMOUNT: $1,000-$5,000
DEADLINE(S): MAR 1
FIELD(S): Agriculture

Open to JACL members and their children only. For entering freshmen with an interest in agriculture or related field who are planning to attend a college, university, trade school, business school, or any other institution of higher learning. Must submit personal statement, letters of recommendation, and transcript.

For membership information or an application, send a self-addressed, stamped envelope to above address, stating your level of study. Applications available October 1st through February 20th; recipients notified in July.

1280—JAPANESE AMERICAN CITIZENS LEAGUE (Sam S. Kuwahara Memorial Scholarship for Undergraduates)

1765 Sutter Street
San Francisco CA 94115
415/921-5225
FAX: 415/931-4671
E-mail: jacl@jacl.org
Internet: www.jacl.org
AMOUNT: $1,000-$5,000
DEADLINE(S): APR 1
FIELD(S): Agriculture

Open to JACL members and their children only. For undergraduate students with an interest in agriculture or related field who are planning to attend a college, university, trade school, business school, or any other institution of higher learning. Must submit personal statement, letters of recommendation, and transcripts.

For membership information or an application, send a self-addressed, stamped envelope to above address, stating your level of study. Applications available October 1st through March 20th; recipients notified in July.

1281—LANDSCAPE ARCHITECTURE FOUNDATION (LAF/CLASS Fund Scholarships)

Use website below
202/216-2356
E-mail: tpadian@asla.org
Internet: www.asla.org
AMOUNT: $500-$2,000
DEADLINE(S): MAR 31
FIELD(S): Landscape Architecture or Ornamental Horticulture

Scholarships and internships for students enrolled in certain California colleges: California Polytechnic Institute (Pomona or San Luis Obispo), UCLA, UC-Irvine, and UC-Davis, who show promise and a commitment to landscape architecture as a profession.

Access website for complete information.

1282—MICHIGAN AGRI-BUSINESS ASSO-CIATION EDUCATIONAL TRUST FUND

Ag. Hall, Room 120
East Lansing MI 48824
517/355-0190
AMOUNT: Varies
DEADLINE(S): Ongoing
FIELD(S): Agri-business or related field, such as grain elevator management

Scholarships for students in Michigan studying in the fields listed above. Selections based on grades, acceptance at an accredited college or university in an agri-business-related program, financial need, references, participation in student affairs, and personal character.

Send SASE to Dr. Clifford Jump, Michigan State University, at above address for details.

1283—MIDWAY COLLEGE (Institutional Aid Program—Scholarships & Grants)

Financial Aid Office
Midway KY 40347
606/846-4421
AMOUNT: Varies
DEADLINE(S): MAR 1
FIELD(S): Nursing, Paralegal, Education, Psychology, Biology, Equine Studies, Liberal Studies, Business Administration

Scholarships and grants open to women who are accepted for enrollment at Midway College. Awards support undergraduate study in the above areas.

Approx 80 awards per year. Write for complete information.

1284—MINNESOTA HIGHER EDUCATION SERVICES OFFICE (Assistance for Farm Families)

1450 Energy Park Drive, #350
St. Paul MN 55108-5265
612/296-3974
FAX: 612/297-8880
E-mail: info@heso.state.mn.us
Internet: www.heso.state.mn.us/
AMOUNT: Up to $4,000
DEADLINE(S): JAN 15
FIELD(S): Agriculture

For Minnesota agricultural students who are current students, new freshmen, and students transferring to the College of Agriculture. Must have graduated in the upper 10 percent of their high school class or have a GPA of 3.25 at a previous college.

Contact: Scholarships, College of Agricultureal, Food, and Environmental Sciences, University of Minnesota, 120 Biosystems & Agricultural Engineering, 1390 Eckles Ave., St. Paul, MN 55108. Also availabe at certain private colleges for farm families in rural areas. Financial need and academic merit considered.

1285—NATIONAL COUNCIL OF FARMER COOPERATIVES (Undergraduate Awards & Scholarships)

50 F Street NW, Suite 900
Washington DC 20001
202/626-8700
FAX: 202/626-8722
AMOUNT: $200-$1,000
DEADLINE(S): JUN 1
FIELD(S): Agricultural Cooperatives

Awards are open to undergraduate students who are writing term papers on the operations of American cooperatives. Scholarships are open to undergraduates with an expressed interest in agricultural cooperatives who are nominated by the Dean of Agricultural Economics at their college/university.

8 awards annually. Not renewable. Contact NCFC Education Foundation for registration forms and/or nomination procedures.

1286—NATIONAL COUNCIL OF STATE GARDEN CLUBS, INC. (Scholarships)

4401 Magnolia Ave.
St. Louis MO 63110-3492
314/776-7574
FAX: 314/776-5108
E-mail: scsgc.franm@worldnet.att.net
Internet: www.gardenclub.org

AMOUNT: $3,500
DEADLINE(S): MAR 1
FIELD(S): Horticulture, Floriculture,
Landscape Design, City Planning,
Land Management, and allied subjects

Open to juniors, seniors and graduate students who are US citizens and are studying any of the above or related subjects. Student must have the endorsement of the state in which he/she resides permanently. Applications will be forwarded to the National State Chairman and judged on a national level.

32 scholarships are awarded. Write to the above address for complete information.

1287—NATIONAL DAIRY SHRINE (Dairy Student Recognition Program Scholarship Awards)

Maurice E. Core, Exec. Dir.
1224 Alton Darby Creek Road
Columbus OH 43228-9792
614/878-5333
FAX: 614/870-2622

AMOUNT: $500 to $1,500
DEADLINE(S): MAR 15
FIELD(S): Dairy Science

Scholarships for college juniors and seniors majoring in dairy science and related fields who plan to work with dairy cattle and/or within the dairy industry after graduation. Must be nominated by college dairy science department.

5 or more awards per year. Contact your dairy science department or write for complete information.

1288—NATIONAL FFA FOUNDATION (College & Voc/Tech School Scholarship Program)

P.O. Box 68960
Indianapolis IN 46268-0960
317/802-4321
E-mail: mlindell@ffa.org
Internet: www.ffa.org

AMOUNT: Varies
DEADLINE(S): FEB 16
FIELD(S): All fields of study

Various scholarships for members and former members of Future Farmers of America. Many are for agriculture, but several are in other fields or for any field of study. One scholarship program is for non-members whose family's primary income is from farming.

More than $1 million available. See website for details of individual awards or contact Marti Lindell at above address for the Program Guide.

1289—NATIONAL ITALIAN AMERICAN FOUNDATION (Piancone Family Agricultural Scholarship)

1860 19th Street NW
Washington DC 20009-5599
202/530-5315

AMOUNT: $2,000
DEADLINE(S): MAY 31
FIELD(S): Study of agriculture

Open to undergraduate or graduate student of Italian ancestry from New Jersey, New York, Pennsylvania, Delaware, Virginia, Maryland, Washington, DC, and Massachusetts majoring in agriculture.

Evidence of financial need, academic merit, and community service also considered.

1290—NORTH CAROLINA STATE UNIVERSITY (Thomas Jefferson Scholarship in Agriculture & Humanities)

115 Patterson Hall, Box 7642
Raleigh NC 27695-7642
Written inquiry

AMOUNT: $1,000
DEADLINE(S): MAR 1
FIELD(S): Agriculture AND Humanities

Open to first-year undergraduate students with a double major in agriculture and humanities who attend or plan to attend North Carolina State University.

Contact George Barthalmus for an application.

1291—NORTHERN NEW JERSEY UNIT-HERB SOCIETY OF AMERICA (Scholarship)

2068 Dogwood Drive
Scotch Plains NJ 07076
908/233-2348

AMOUNT: $2,000
DEADLINE(S): FEB 15
FIELD(S): Horticulture, Botany

For New Jersey residents, undergraduate through postgraduate, who will attend colleges/universities east of the Mississippi River. Financial need is considered.

1 award annually. Renewable. Contact Mrs. Charlotte R. Baker at above address for an application.

1292—OPEN SOCIETY INSTITUTE (Environmental Management Fellowships)

400 West 59th Street
New York NY 10019
212/548-0600 or 212/757-2323
FAX: 212/548-4679 or
212/548-4600
Internet: www.soros.org/efp.html

AMOUNT: Fees, room, board, living stipend, textbooks, international transportation, health insurance
DEADLINE(S): NOV 15
FIELD(S): Earth Sciences, Natural Sciences, Humanities (exc. language), Anthropology, Sociology, Mathematics, or Engineering

Two-year fellowships for use in selected universities in the US for international students. For students/professionals in fields related to environmental policy, legislation, and remediation techniques applicable to their home countries.

To apply, contact your local Soros Foundation or Open Society Institute. Further details on website.

1293—PENINSULA COMMUNITY FOUNDATION (Dr. Mary Finegold Scholarship)

1700 S. El Camino Real, #300
San Mateo CA 94402
650/358-9369
FAX: 650/358-9817

AMOUNT: $1,000
DEADLINE(S): MAR 27 (5 P.M.)
FIELD(S): Sciences

Scholarships for senior girls graduating from high school in Palo Alto, California, who intend to complete a four-year degree in the sciences. Special consideration will be given to girls who have demonstrated a "pioneering" spirit in that they have not been constrained by stereotypical female roles and to those facing financial hardship.

Award was established in the honor of Dr. Mary Finegold who, after completing her medical studies, elected to stay at home until her youngest child was in high school before beginning her medical practice. She was a school physician.

1294—PROFESSIONAL GROUNDS MANAGEMENT SOCIETY (Anne Seaman Memorial Scholarships)

120 Cockeysville Road, Suite 104
Hunt Valley MD 21030
Written inquiry

AMOUNT: $250-$1,000
DEADLINE(S): JUL 5
FIELD(S): Grounds Management

Scholarships in grounds management or closely related field to be used toward a 2- or 4-year degree or graduate study. Applicants must be US or Canadian citizens.

1-4 awards annually. Contact PGMS for an application.

1295—PURDUE UNIVERSITY (Freshman Scholarship Awards of Excellence)

School of Agriculture
West Lafayette IN 47906
Written inquiry

AMOUNT: $1,500
DEADLINE(S): FEB
FIELD(S): Agriculture, Forestry

Various scholarships in agriculture and forestry are available to high school seniors who will be incoming freshmen at Purdue University.

Write to above address for an application.

1296—RAYMOND J. HARRIS EDUCATION TRUST

P.O. Box 7899
Philadelphia PA 19101-7899
Written inquiry

AMOUNT: Varies
DEADLINE(S): FEB 1
FIELD(S): Medicine, Law, Engineering, Dentistry, or Agriculture

Scholarships for Christian men to obtain a professional education in medicine, law, engineering, dentistry, or agriculture at nine Philadelphia area colleges.

Contact Mellon Bank, N.A. at above location for details and the names of the nine colleges.

1297—SAN DIEGO AEROSPACE MUSEUM (Bill Gibbs Scholarship)

Education Dept.
2001 Pan American Plaza
San Diego CA 92101
619/234-8291, ext. 19

FAX: 619/233-4526
Internet: aerospacemuseum.org/Scholastic.HTML
AMOUNT: Varies
DEADLINE(S): Varies
FIELD(S): Aerospace: math, physics, science, or engineering

For students who are residents of San Diego County, California, who have an aerospace career interest and who have been accepted to a four-year college or university in a degree program relating to math, physics, science, or engineering.

Call or write museum for further information.

1298—SAN DIEGO COUNTY COW-BELLES (Memorial Scholarship)

P.O. Box 570
Campo CA 91906
619/478-2364

AMOUNT: $700
DEADLINE(S): JUL 31
FIELD(S): Animal Science

Open to students with a beef industry-related career goal who have completed 1 year of a 4-year college or have been accepted by a 4-year college after 2 years in a community college. Must live in San Diego County and show financial need.

Need a 3.0 or better GPA. Write for complete details.

1299—SCHOLARSHIPS FOR EXCELLENCE IN AGRICULTURE

Iowa State University
Ames IA 50011
Written inquiry

AMOUNT: Full in-state tuition
DEADLINE(S): DEC 2
FIELD(S): Agriculture

Scholarships for Iowa State University freshmen studying agriculture.

15 annual awards. Renewable if recipients remain academically eligible. Based on scholarship, ACT, or SAT scores. Write to Associate Dean for Academic Programs, 124 Curtis Hall, at above location.

1300—SOCIETY FOR RANGE MANAGEMENT (Masonic Range Science Scholarship)

1839 York Street
Denver CO 80206
303/355-7070
FAX: 303/355-5059
E-mail: srmden@ix.netcom.com

Internet: srm.org
AMOUNT: $1,500
DEADLINE(S): JAN 15
FIELD(S): Range Science/Management

Open to high school seniors or college freshmen pursuing a major in range science/management. Must attend a college or university with a range science program.

1 award annually. Financial need NOT a factor. See website or contact Ann Harris at above address for an application/more information.

1301—SOIL AND WATER CONSERVATION SOCIETY (Donald A. Williams Soil Conservation Scholarship)

7515 NE Ankeny Road
Ankeny IA 50021-9764
515/289-2331 or 800-THE-SOIL
FAX: 515/289-1227
E-mail: cahrliep@swcs.rog
Internet: www.swcs.org

AMOUNT: $1,500
DEADLINE(S): FEB 13
FIELD(S): Conservation-related fields (technical or administrative course work)

For SWCS members currently employed in a related field and have completed at least 1 year of natural resource conservation work with a governmental agency or private organization. Need not be working toward a degree. Must show reasonable financial need.

For undergraduates. Write or visit website for complete information.

1302—SOIL AND WATER CONSERVATION SOCIETY (Melville H. Cohee Student Leader Conservation Scholarship)

7515 NE Ankeny Road
Ankeny IA 50021-9764
515/289-2331 or 800-THE-SOIL
FAX: 515/289-1227
E-mail: charliep@swcs.org
Internet: www.swcs.org

AMOUNT: $900
DEADLINE(S): FEB 113
FIELD(S): Conservation or Natural Resource-Related Field

Open to 1+ year member of SWCS having served as an officer in a student chapter with 15+ members. GPA of 3.0 or better. Final year F/T undergrad or graduate.

2 awards. Course load must be 50% or more at accredited college or university. Financial need is not a factor. Write or visit website for complete information.

1303—SOIL AND WATER CONSERVATION SOCIETY (SWCS Internships)

7515 NE Ankeny Road
Ankeny IA 50021-9764
515/289-2331 or 800/THE-SOIL
FAX: 515/289-1227
E-mail: charliep@swcs.org
Internet: www.swcs.org

AMOUNT: Varies—most are uncompensated
DEADLINE(S): Varies
FIELD(S): Journalism, Marketing, Database Management, Meeting Planning, Public Policy Research, Environmental Education, Landscape Architecture

Internships for undergraduates and graduates to gain experience in the above fields as they relate to soil and water conservation issues. Internship openings vary through the year in duration, compensation, and objective. SWCS will coordinate particulars with your academic advisor.

Contact SWCS for internship availability at any time during the year or see website for jobs page.

1304—SOUTH CAROLINA FARM BUREAU FOUNDATION (Scholarships)

P.O. Box 754
Columbia SC 29202-0754
803/936-4212
FAX: 800/421-6515
E-mail: scfbsaraha@aol.com
Internet: www.scfb.com

AMOUNT: $1,000
DEADLINE(S): APR 30
FIELD(S): Agriculture

Scholarships are awarded to sophomores, juniors, and seniors pursuing a degree in agriculture or an agricultural related major. Based on character, demonstrated leadership abilities, and dedication to agriculture or related fields. Must have minimum 2.3 GPA. Financial need NOT a factor.

Not renewable. Contact Benjie Rhoad at SCFB for an application.

1305—STUDENT CONSERVATION ASSOCI-ATION (SCA Resource Assistant Program)

P.O. Box 550
Charlestown NH 03603
603/543-1700
FAX: 603/543-1828
E-mail: internships@sca-inc.org
Internet: www.sca-inc.org

AMOUNT: $1,180-$4,725
DEADLINE(S): Varies
FIELD(S): Environment & related fields

Must be 18 and US citizen; need not be student. Fields: Agriculture, archaeology, anthropology, botany, caves, civil/environmental engineering, environmental education, fisheries, forests, herpetology, history, living history/roleplaying, visitor services, landscape architectural/environmental design, paleontology, recreation/resource/range management, trail maintenance/construction, wildlife management, geology, hydrology, library/museums, surveying.

900 positions in US and Canada. Send $1 for postage for application; outside US/Canada, send $20.

1306—SUCCESSFUL FARMING-BAYER CORPORATION (Crop Protection Scholarships)

1716 Locust Street, LN 424
Des Moines IA 50309-3023
515/284-2903
E-mail: devans@mdp.com
Internet: www.agriculture.com

AMOUNT: $500 (2-yr. schools); $1,000 (4-yr. schools)
DEADLINE(S): MAR 15
FIELD(S): Agriculture

For high school seniors entering 2- or 4-year colleges and for college seniors-to-be returning to farm after college. Parents/guardians must derive majority of their income from farming. Must rank in upper 50% of class and in national test scores, demonstrate leadership potential through extracurricular activities/work experience, and have financial need. Scholarships will be granted to the school of your choice in your name in two equal payments (one for each semester).

30 awards annually. Not renewable. Awards announced by May 1st. Applications available on website or write to above address.

1307—THE AUGIE J. ALTAR SCHOLARSHIP

7115 W. 91st Street
Bridgeview IL 60455-2048
Write for information

AMOUNT: $500
DEADLINE(S): MAY 31
FIELD(S): Medicine or agricultural fields

Scholarships for students enrolled or accepted to an accredited college, university, or community college who are of Lithuanian descent and are residents of Illinois. Must be studying in the areas of medicine or agriculture. Financial need

considered. Must have and maintain at least a 2.0 GPA.

Send application request to above address with a stamped, self-addressed envelope (SASE).

1308—THERESA CORTI FAMILY AGRICUL-TURAL TRUST (Scholarship Program)

Wells Fargo Bank, Trust Dept.
8405 N. Fresno Street, Suite 210
Fresno CA 93720-1538
209/437-3056

AMOUNT: Varies
DEADLINE(S): FEB
FIELD(S): Agriculture

Open to undergraduate students who are agriculture majors and graduates of Kern County high schools. Must carry at least 12 units at an accredited college/university, have a minimum 2.0 GPA, and demonstrate financial need.

Contact Trust Dept. for an application.

1309—TYSON FOUNDATION, INC. (Alabama Scholarship Program)

2210 W. Oaklawn
Springdale AR 72762-6999
501/290-4995

AMOUNT: Varies (according to need)
DEADLINE(S): FEB 28
FIELD(S): Business, Agriculture, Engineering, Computer Science, Nursing

Open to residents of the general areas of Albertville, Ashland, Blountsville, Gadsden, Heflin, or Oxford, Alabama, who are US citizens and live in the vicinity of a Tyson facility. Must be pursuing full-time undergraduate study at an accredited US institution and demonstrate financial need. Must also be employed part-time and/or summers to help fund education.

Renewable up to 8 semesters or 12 trimesters as long as student meets criteria. Contact Tyson Foundation for an application no later than last day of February; deadline to return application is April 20th.

1310—TYSON FOUNDATION, INC. (Arkansas Scholarship Program)

2210 W. Oaklawn
Springdale AR 72762-6999
501/290-4955

AMOUNT: Varies (according to need)
DEADLINE(S): FEB 28

FIELD(S): Business, Agriculture, Engineering, Computer Science, Nursing

Open to Arkansas residents who are US citizens pursuing full-time undergraduate study at an accredited US institution. Must demonstrate financial need and be employed part-time and/or summers to help fund education.

Renewable up to 8 semesters or 12 trimesters as long as student meets criteria. Contact Tyson Foundation for an application no later than last day of February; deadline to return application is April 20th.

1311—TYSON FOUNDATION, INC. (Florida Scholarship Program)

2210 W. Oaklawn
Springdale AR 72762-6999
501/290-4995

AMOUNT: Varies (according to need)
DEADLINE(S): FEB 28
FIELD(S): Business, Agriculture, Engineering, Computer Science, Nursing

Open to residents of the general area of Jacksonville, Florida, who are US citizens and live in the vicinity of a Tyson facility. Must be pursuing full-time undergraduate study in an accredited US institution and demonstrate financial need. Must also be employed part-time and/or summers to help fund education.

Renewable up to 8 semesters or 12 trimesters as long as student meets criteria. Contact Tyson Foundation for an application no later than last day of February; deadline to return application is April 20th.

1312—TYSON FOUNDATION, INC. (Georgia Scholarship Program)

2210 W. Oaklawn
Springdale AR 72762-6999
501/290-4995

AMOUNT: Varies (according to need)
DEADLINE(S): FEB 28
FIELD(S): Business, Agriculture, Engineering, Computer Science, Nursing

Open to residents of the general areas of Cumming, Buena Vista, Dawson, or Vienna, Georgia, who are US citizens and live in the vicinity of a Tyson facility. Must be pursuing full-time undergraduate study in an accredited US institution and demonstrate financial need. Must also be employed part-time and/or summers to help fund education.

Renewable up to 8 semesters or 12 trimesters as long as student meets criteria.

Contact Tyson Foundation for an application no later than last day of February; deadline to return application is April 20th.

1313—TYSON FOUNDATION, INC. (Illinois Scholarship Program)

2210 W. Oaklawn
Springdale AR 72762-6999
501/290-4995

AMOUNT: Varies (according to need)
DEADLINE(S): FEB 28
FIELD(S): Business, Agriculture, Engineering, Computer Science, Nursing

Open to residents of the general area of Chicago, Illinois, who are US citizens and live in the vicinity of a Tyson facility. Must be pursuing full-time undergraduate study in an accredited US institution and demonstrate financial need. Must also be employed part-time and/or summers to help fund education.

Renewable up to 8 semesters or 12 trimesters as long as student meets criteria. Contact Tyson Foundation for an application no later than last day of February; deadline to return application is April 20th.

1314—TYSON FOUNDATION, INC. (Indiana Scholarship Program)

2210 W. Oaklawn
Springdale AR 72762-6999
501/290-4995

AMOUNT: Varies (according to need)
DEADLINE(S): FEB 28
FIELD(S): Business, Agriculture, Engineering, Computer Science, Nursing

Open to residents of the general areas of Portland or Corydon, Indiana, who are US citizens and live in the vicinity of a Tyson facility. Must be pursuing full-time undergraduate study at an accredited US institution and demonstrate financial need. Must also be employed part-time and/or summers to help fund education.

Renewable up to 8 semesters or 12 trimesters as long as student meets criteria. Contact Tyson Foundation for an application no later than last day of February; deadline to return application is April 20th.

1315—TYSON FOUNDATION, INC. (Mississippi Scholarship Program)

2210 W. Oaklawn
Springdale AR 72762-6999
501/290-4995

AMOUNT: Varies (according to need)
DEADLINE(S): FEB 28
FIELD(S): Business, Agriculture, Engineering, Computer Science, Nursing

Open to residents of the general areas of Cleveland, Jackson, Forest, or Vicksburg, Mississippi, who are US citizens and live in the vicinity of a Tyson facility. Must be pursuing full-time undergraduate study in an accredited US institution and demonstrate financial need. Must also be employed part-time and/or summers to help fund education.

Renewable up to 8 semesters or 12 trimesters as long as student meets criteria. Contact Tyson Foundation for an application no later than last day of February; deadline to return application is April 20th.

1316—TYSON FOUNDATION, INC. (Missouri Scholarship Program)

2210 W. Oaklawn
Springdale AR 72762-6999
501/290-4995

AMOUNT: Varies (according to need)
DEADLINE(S): FEB 28
FIELD(S): Business, Agriculture, Engineering, Computer Science, Nursing

Open to residents of the general areas of Dexter, Monett, Neosho, Noel, or Sedalia, Missouri, who are US citizens and live in the vicinity of a Tyson facility. Must be pursuing full-time undergraduate study in an accredited US institution and demonstrate financial need. Must also be employed part-time and/or summers to help fund education.

Renewable up to 8 semesters or 12 trimesters as long as student meets criteria. Contact Tyson Foundation for an application no later than last day of February; deadline to return application is April 20th.

1317—TYSON FOUNDATION, INC. (North Carolina Scholarship Program)

2210 W. Oaklawn
Springdale AR 72762-6999
501/290-4995

AMOUNT: Varies (according to need)
DEADLINE(S): FEB 28
FIELD(S): Business, Agriculture, Engineering, Computer Science, Nursing

Open to residents of the general areas of Creswell, Monroe, Sanford, or Wilkesboro, North Carolina, who are US citizens and live in the vicinity of a Tyson facility. Must be pursuing full-time undergraduate study in an accredited US institution and demonstrate financial need. Must also be employed part-time and/or summers to help fund education.

Renewable up to 8 semesters or 12 trimesters as long as student meets criteria. Contact Tyson Foundation for an application no later than the last day of February; deadline to return application is April 20th.

1318—TYSON FOUNDATION, INC. (Oklahoma Scholarship Program)

2210 W. Oaklawn
Springdale AR 72762-6999
501/290-4995

AMOUNT: Varies (according to need)
DEADLINE(S): FEB 28
FIELD(S): Business, Agriculture, Engineering, Computer Science, Nursing

Open to residents of the general areas of Broken Bow or Stillwell, Oklahoma, who are US citizens and live in the vicinity of a Tyson facility. Must be pursuing full-time undergraduate study in an accredited US institution and demonstrate financial need. Must also be employed part-time and/or summers to help fund education.

Renewable up to 8 semesters or 12 trimesters as long as student meets criteria. Contact Tyson Foundation for an application no later than last day of February; deadline to return application is April 20th.

1319—TYSON FOUNDATION, INC. (Pennsylvania Scholarship Program)

2210 W. Oaklawn
Springdale AR 72762-6999
501/290-4995

AMOUNT: Varies (according to need)
DEADLINE(S): FEB 28
FIELD(S): Business, Agriculture, Engineering, Computer Science, Nursing

Open to residents of the general area of New Holland, Pennsylvania, who are US citizens and live in the vicinity of a Tyson facility. Must be pursuing full-time undergraduate study in an accredited US institution and demonstrate financial need. Must also be employed part-time and/or summers to help fund education.

Renewable up to 8 semesters or 12 trimesters as long as student meets criteria. Contact Tyson Foundation for an application no later than last day of February; deadline to return application is April 20th.

1320—TYSON FOUNDATION, INC. (Tennessee Scholarship Program)

2210 W. Oaklawn
Springdale AR 72762-6999
501/290-4995

AMOUNT: Varies (according to need)
DEADLINE(S): FEB 28
FIELD(S): Business, Agriculture, Engineering, Computer Science, Nursing

Open to residents of the general areas of Shelbyville or Union City, Tennessee, who are US citizens and live in the vicinity of a Tyson facility. Must be pursuing full-time undergraduate study in an accredited US institution and demonstrate financial need. Must also be employed part-time and/or summers to help fund education.

Renewable up to 8 semesters or 12 trimesters as long as student meets criteria. Contact Tyson Foundation for an application no later than last day of February; deadline to return application is April 20th.

1321—TYSON FOUNDATION, INC. (Texas Scholarship Program)

2210 W. Oaklawn
Springdale AR 72762-6999
501/290-4995

AMOUNT: Varies (according to need)
DEADLINE(S): FEB 28
FIELD(S): Business, Agriculture, Engineering, Computer Science, Nursing

Open to residents of the general areas of Carthage, Center, or Seguin, Texas, who are US citizens and live in the vicinity of a Tyson facility. Must be pursuing full-time undergraduate study in an accredited US institution and demonstrate financial need. Must also be employed part-time and/or summers to help fund education.

Renewable up to 8 semesters or 12 trimesters as long as student meets criteria. Contact Tyson Foundation for an application no later than last day of February; deadline to return application is April 20th.

1322—TYSON FOUNDATION, INC. (Virginia Scholarship Program)

2210 W. Oaklawn
Springdale AR 72762-6999
501/290-4995

AMOUNT: Varies (according to need)
DEADLINE(S): FEB 28
FIELD(S): Business, Agriculture, Engineering, Computer Science, Nursing

Open to residents of the general areas of Glen Allen, Harrisonburg, or Temperanceville, Virginia, who are US citizens and live in the vicinity of a Tyson facility. Must be pursuing full-time undergraduate study in an accredited US institution and demonstrate financial need. Must also be employed part-time and/or summers to help fund education.

Renewable up to 8 semesters or 12 trimesters as long as student meets criteria. Contact Tyson Foundation for an application no later than last day of February; deadline to return application is April 20th.

1323—UNITED AGRIBUSINESS LEAGUE (UAL Scholarship Program)

54 Corporate Park
Irvine CA 92606-5105
800/223-4590 or 949/975-1424
FAX: 949/975-1671
E-mail: ual@earthlink.net
Internet: www.ual.org

AMOUNT: Varies
DEADLINE(S): APR 16
FIELD(S): Agriculture, Agribusiness

Any ag student presently enrolled, or who will be enrolled any time during the year of application in any accredited college/university offering a degree in agriculture, may apply. Minimum GPA of 2.5 is required. With application, must submit essay on "My Future in Agribusiness," resume of education/work/community activities/etc., and three letters of recommendation. Financial need will not be considered unless you specifically request it and provide documentation.

Over $10,000 available annually. Renewable with new application. Contact Christine M. Steele, Executive Secretary, for more information.

1324—U.S. DEPARTMENT OF AGRICULTURE (1890 National Scholars Program)

14th & Independence Ave. SW
Room 301-W, Whitten Bldg.
Washington DC 20250-9600
202/720-6905
E-mail: usda-m@fie.com
Internet: web.fie.com/htdoc/fed/agr/ars/edu/prog/mti/agrpgaak.htm

AMOUNT: Tuition, employment/benefits, use of PC/software, fees, books, room/board
DEADLINE(S): JAN 15
FIELD(S): Agriculture, Food, or Natural Resource sciences

For US citizens, high school grad/GED, GPA 3.0+, verbal/math SAT 1,000+, composite score 21+ ACT, 1st-yr college student, and attend participating school.

34+ scholarships/yr/4 years. Send applications to USDA Liaison Officer at the 1890 Institution of your choice (see Web page for complete list).

1325—UNIVERSITY OF ILLINOIS COLLEGE OF ACES (Jonathan Baldwin Turner Agricultural Merit Scholarship Program)

101 Mumford Hall
1301 W. Gregory Drive
Urbana IL 61801
Written inquiry

AMOUNT: $4,000
DEADLINE(S): Varies (start of high school senior year)
FIELD(S): Agriculture, Nutritional Science

Scholarships in agricultural, food, and human nutritional sciences for outstanding incoming freshmen at the University of Illinois. Must have minimum ACT composite score of 27, equivalent SAT combined scores, or be in the 90th percentile of high school class rank at the end of junior year. Interview required.

60 awards annually. Contact Charles Olson, Assistant Dean, College of Agriculture, for an application.

1326—UNIVERSITY OF MINNESOTA COLLEGE OF AGRICULTURE (Scholarship Program)

277 Coffey Hall
1420 Eckles Ave.
St. Paul MN 55108
612/624-3009 or 800/866-2474

AMOUNT: Varies
DEADLINE(S): FEB 1
FIELD(S): Agriculture

Extensive scholarship program through the College of Agriculture for freshmen, transfer, and continuing students.

Write or call Annette Day, COA Scholarshp Program, University of Minnesota, at above location.

1327—WISCONSIN FARM BUREAU FOUNDATION (Scholarship Program)

1212 Deming Way
Madison WI 53717
608/828-5710, 608/828-5769
E-mail: bleege@wfbf.com
Internet: www.wfbf.com

AMOUNT: $500

DEADLINE(S): SEP 30
FIELD(S): Agriculture

For undergraduates, graduates, or postgraduates studying agriculture or related fields. Applicants must have completed two or more semesters in an accredited college, university, or technical school. A minimum GPA of 2.5 (4.0 scale) is required. Must be from a Wisconsin Farm Bureau member family; if 21 or older, applicant must have his/her own membership. Financial need is NOT a factor.

9 awards annually. Not renewable. Contact Bob Leege at WFBF for an application.

1328—WOODROW WILSON NATIONAL FELLOWSHIP FOUNDATION/U.S. DEPARTMENTS OF COMMERCE AND AGRICULTURE (Fellowships)

CN 5329
Princeton NJ 08543-5329
609/452-7007
FAX: 609/452-0066
E-mail: richard@woodrow.org
Internet: www.woodrow.org

AMOUNT: Varies
DEADLINE(S): Varies
FIELD(S): Commerce, Agriculture

Open to minority students in the US who are interested in careers in commerce or agriculture.

See website or contact WWNFF for an application.

1329—WORCESTER COUNTY HORTICULTURE SOCIETY (WCHS Scholarship)

11 French Drive
P.O. Box 598
Boylston MA 01505-0598
508/869-6111
FAX: 508/869-0314
E-mail: thbg@towerhillbg.org

AMOUNT: $500-$2,000
DEADLINE(S): MAY 1
FIELD(S): Horticulture

Open to residents of the New England states or students who are attending a college/university in New England. For junior or senior year of undergraduate or graduate studies in horticulture or related field. Award based on interest in horticulture, sincerity of purpose, academic performance, and financial need.

See website or contact Susanne M. Cayford, Administrative Assistant, Tower Hill Botanic Garden, at above address for an application.

1330—WYOMING CROP IMPROVEMENT ASSOCIATION (Scholarship)

Secretary
P.O. Box 983
Powell WY 82435
Written inquiry

AMOUNT: $500
DEADLINE(S): Varies
FIELD(S): Agronomy; Plant Science

Available to students majoring in the field of agronomy or related plant science fields who are entering their junior or senior year of study at a four-year college or university. Applicant must be a graduate of a Wyoming high school. No limitation will be placed upon which college or university recipient must attend.

1 award annually. Write to Mr. R. Denny Hall, Secretary, at above address for an application.

EARTH SCIENCE

1331—AIR FORCE RESERVE OFFICER TRAINING CORPS (AFROTC Scholarships)

551 E. Maxwell Blvd.
Maxwell AFB AL 36112-6106
334/953-7783

AMOUNT: Full tuition, books, & fees for all 4 years of college
DEADLINE(S): DEC 1
FIELD(S): Science, Engineering, Business, Political Science, Psychology, Geography, Foreign Studies, Foreign Language

Competitive scholarships based on individual merit to high school seniors and graduates who have not completed any full-time college work. Must be a US citizen between the ages of 17-27. Must also have GPA of 2.5 or above, be in top 40% of class, and complete Applicant Fitness Test. Cannot be a single parent. Your college/university must offer AFROTC.

2,300 awards annually. Contact above address for application packet.

1332—ALLIANCE FOR YOUNG ARTISTS AND WRITERS, INC./AMERICAN MUSEUM OF NATURAL HISTORY (Young Naturalist Awards)

Scholastic, Inc.
555 Broadway
New York NY 10012-3999
212/343-6582 or 800-SCHOLASTIC
FAX: 212/343-4885

E-mail: mjohnson@scholastic.com

Internet: www.amnh.org/youngnaturalistawards

AMOUNT: up to $2,500 + trip to New York to visit AMNH

DEADLINE(S): JAN 3

FIELD(S): Natural Sciences

For all students in grades 7-12 currently enrolled in a public or non-public school in the US, Canada, US territories, or US-sponsored schools abroad. Program focuses on finding and rewarding excellence in biology, earth science, astronomy, and cultural studies. Students are encouraged to perform observation-based projects that require creativity, inquiry, and critical analysis. Specific topics vary annually.

48 awards annually. See website or contact Mike Johnson, Program Manager, for an application.

1333—AMERICAN CONGRESS ON SURVEYING AND MAPPING (AAGS Joseph F. Dracup Scholarship Award, Nettie Dracup Memorial Scholarship, & Berntsen International Scholarship in Surveying)

5410 Grosvenor Lane, Suite 100
Bethesda MD 20814-2144
301/493-0200, ext. 102
FAX: 301/493-8245
E-mail: lillym@mindspring.com
Internet: www.survmap.org

AMOUNT: $2,000 (Joseph & Nettie); $1,500 (Berntsen)

DEADLINE(S): DEC 1

FIELD(S): Geodetic Surveying

Open to students enrolled in four-year degree programs in surveying or closely related degree programs, such as geomatics or surveying engineering. Must submit personal statement (including goals and financial need), letters of recommendation, and transcripts. Nettie Dracup applicants must be US citizens. Must join ACSM.

3 awards annually. Contact Lilly Matheson at ACSM for membership information and/or applications.

1334—AMERICAN CONGRESS ON SURVEYING AND MAPPING (Allen Chelf Scholarship)

5410 Grosvenor Lane, Suite 100
Bethesda MD 20814-2144
301/493-0200, ext. 102
FAX: 301/493-8245
E-mail: lillym@mindspring.com

Internet: www.survmap.org

AMOUNT: $500

DEADLINE(S): DEC 1

FIELD(S): Surveying

Open to students enrolled in a two-year or four-year surveying (or closely related fields) degree program, either full- or part-time, in the US. Must submit personal statement (including goals and financial need), letters of recommendation, and transcripts. Must join ACSM.

1 award annually. Contact Lilly Matheson at ACSM for membership information and/or an application.

1335—AMERICAN CONGRESS ON SURVEYING AND MAPPING (Bernsten International Scholarship in Surveying Technology)

5410 Grosvenor Lane, Suite 100
Bethesda MD 20814-2144
301/493-0200, ext. 102
FAX: 301/493-8245
E-mail: lillym@mindspring.com
Internet: www.survmap.org

AMOUNT: $500

DEADLINE(S): DEC 1

FIELD(S): Surveying Technology

Open to students enrolled in two-year degree programs in surveying technology. Must submit personal statement (including goals and financial need), letters of recommendation, and transcripts. Must join ACSM.

1 award annually. Contact Lilly Matheson at ACSM for membership information and/or an application.

1336—AMERICAN CONGRESS ON SURVEYING AND MAPPING (National Society of Professional Surveyors Board of Governor's Scholarship)

5410 Grosvenor Lane, Suite 100
Bethesda MD 20814-2144
301/493-0200, ext. 102
FAX: 301/493-8245
E-mail: lillym@mindspring.com
Internet: www.survmap.org

AMOUNT: $1,000

DEADLINE(S): DEC 1

FIELD(S): Surveying

Open to students enrolled in studies in surveying, entering their junior year of study in a four-year degree program of their choice, and who have maintained a minimum 3.0 GPA. Must submit personal statement (including goals and financial

need), letters of recommendation, and transcripts. Must join ACSM.

1 award annually. Contact Lilly Matheson at ACSM for membership information and/or an application.

1337—AMERICAN CONGRESS ON SURVEYING AND MAPPING (National Society of Professional Surveyors Scholarships)

5410 Grosvenor Lane, Suite 100
Bethesda MD 20814-2144
301/493-0200, ext. 102
FAX: 301/493-8245
E-mail: lillym@mindspring.com
Internet: www.survmap.org

AMOUNT: $1,000

DEADLINE(S): DEC 1

FIELD(S): Surveying

Open to students enrolled in four-year degree programs in surveying or closely related degree programs, such as geomatics or surveying engineering. Awards recognize outstanding students enrolled full-time. Must submit personal statement (including goals and financial need), letters of recommendation, and transcripts. Must join ACSM.

2 awards annually. Contact Lilly Matheson at ACSM for membership information and/or an application.

1338—AMERICAN CONGRESS ON SURVEYING AND MAPPING (Cady McDonnell Memorial Scholarship)

5410 Grosvenor Lane, Suite 100
Bethesda MD 20814-2144
301/493-0200, ext. 102
FAX: 301/493-8245
E-mail: lillym@mindspring.com
Internet: www.survmap.org

AMOUNT: $1,000

DEADLINE(S): DEC 1

FIELD(S): Surveying

Open to women enrolled in a two-year or four-year surveying (or closely related fields) degree program, either full- or part-time. Applicants must be residents of one of the following Western states: MT, ID, WA, OR, WY, CO, UT, NV, CA, AZ, NM, AK, or HI. Must submit personal statement (including goals and financial need), letters of recommendation, and transcripts. Must join ACSM.

1 award annually. Contact Lilly Matheson at ACSM for membership information and/or an application.

1339—AMERICAN CONGRESS ON SURVEYING AND MAPPING (Schonstedt Scholarships in Surveying)

5410 Grosvenor Lane, Suite 100
Bethesda MD 20814-2144
301/493-0200, ext. 102
FAX: 301/493-8245
E-mail: lillym@mindspring.com
Internet: www.survmap.org

AMOUNT: $1,500
DEADLINE(S): DEC 1
FIELD(S): Surveying

Open to students enrolled in four-year degree programs in surveying or closely related degree programs, such as geomatics or surveying engineering. Preference given to applicants with junior or senior standing. Must submit personal statement (including goals and financial need), letters of recommendation, and transcripts. Must join ACSM.

2 awards annually. Contact Lilly Matheson at ACSM for membership information and/or an application. Schonstedt also donates a magnetic locator to the surveying program at each recipient's school.

1340—AMERICAN CONGRESS ON SURVEYING AND MAPPPING (Cartography and Geographic Information Society Scholarship)

5410 Grosvenor Lane, Suite 100
Bethesda MD 20814-2144
301/493-0200, ext. 102
301/493-8245
E-mail: lillym@mindspring.com
Internet: www.survmap.org

AMOUNT: $1,000
DEADLINE(S): DEC 1
FIELD(S): Cartography, Geographic
    Information Science

Open to outstanding students enrolled full-time in a four-year or graduate degree program. Preference given to undergraduates with junior or senior standing, the purpose being to encourage completion of undergrad program and/or pursuit of graduate education in above fields. Must submit personal statement (including goals and financial need), letters of recommendation, and transcripts. Must join ACSM.

1 award annually. Contact Lilly Matheson at ACSM for membership information and/or an application.

1341—AMERICAN CONGRESS ON SURVEYING AND MAPPING (Mary Feindt Forum for Women in Surveying Scholarship)

5410 Grosvenor Lane, Suite 100
Bethesda MD 20814-2144
301/493-0200, ext. 102
FAX: 301/493-8245
E-mail: lillym@mindspring.com
Internet: www.survmap.org

AMOUNT: $1,000
DEADLINE(S): DEC 1
FIELD(S): Surveying

Open to women enrolled in a four-year degree program in a surveying and mapping curriculum within the US. Must submit personal statement (including goals and financial need), letters of recommendation, and transcripts. Must join ACSM.

1 award annually. Contact Lilly Matheson at ACSM for membership information and/or an application.

1342—AMERICAN FOUNDATION FOR THE BLIND (Paul W. Ruckes Scholarship)

11 Penn Plaza, Suite 300
New York NY 10001
212/502-7661
FAX: 212/502-7771
E-mail: juliet@afb.org
Internet: www.afb.org

AMOUNT: $1,000
DEADLINE(S): APR 30
FIELD(S): Engineering,
    Computer/Physical/Life Sciences

Open to legally blind and visually impaired undergraduate and graduate students pursuing a degree in one of above fields. Must be US citizen. Must submit written documentation of visual impairment from ophthalmologist or optometrist (need not be legally blind); official transcripts; proof of college/university acceptance; three letters of recommendation; and typewritten statement describing goals, work experience, extracurricular activities, and how monies will be used.

1 award annually. See website or contact Julie Tucker at AFB for an application.

1343—AMERICAN GEOLOGICAL INSTITUTE (AGI Minority Geoscience Scholarships)

4220 King Street
Alexandria VA 22302-1502

703/379-2480
FAX 703/379-7563
E-mail: ehr@agiweb.org
Internet: www.agiweb.org

AMOUNT: Varies
DEADLINE(S): FEB 1
FIELD(S): Geoscience

Open to full-time undergrads or grads majoring in geology, geophysics, geochemistry, hydrology, meteorology, physical oceanography, planetary geology, or earth science education. NOT for engineering, mathematics, or natural science majors.

Must be ethnic minority and US citizen. Financial need must be demonstrated. Must reapply for renewal. Contact Veronika Litvale at above location for details.

1344—AMERICAN INDIAN SCIENCE AND ENGINEERING SOCIETY (A.T. Anderson Memorial Scholarship)

P.O. Box 9828
Albuquerque NM 87119-9828
505/765-1052
FAX: 505/765-5608
E-mail: scholarships@aises.org
Internet: www.aises.org/scholarships

AMOUNT: $1,000-$2,000
DEADLINE(S): JUN 15
FIELD(S): Medicine, Natural Resources,
    Science, Engineering

Open to undergraduate and graduate students who are at least 1/4 American Indian or recognized as member of a tribe. Must be member of AISES ($10 fee), enrolled full-time at an accredited institution, and demonstrate financial need.

Renewable. See website or contact Patricia Browne for an application and/or membership information.

1345—AMERICAN INDIAN SCIENCE AND ENGINEERING SOCIETY (EPA Tribal Lands Environmental Science Scholarship)

P.O. Box 9828
Albuquerque NM 87119-9828
505/765-1052
FAX: 505/765-5608
E-mail: scholarships@aises.org
Internet: www.aises.org/scholarships

AMOUNT: $4,000
DEADLINE(S): JUN 15
FIELD(S): Biochemistry, Biology,
    Chemical Engineering, Chemistry,
    Entomology, Environmental
    Economics/Science, Hydrology,
    Environmental Studies

Open to American Indian college juniors, seniors, and graduate students enrolled full-time at an accredited institution. Must demonstrate financial need. Certificate of Indian blood NOT required.

Renewable. See website or contact Patricia Browne for an application.

1346—AMERICAN METEOROLOGICAL SOCIETY (AMS/Industry/Government Graduate Fellowships)

45 Beacon Street
Boston MA 02108-3693
617/227-2426, ext. 246
E-mail: dfernand@ametsoc.org
Internet: www.ametsoc.org/AMS

AMOUNT: $15,000 stipend
DEADLINE(S): FEB 18
FIELD(S): Atmospheric, Oceanic, & Hydrologic Sciences

Nine-month award is open to students who will be entering their first year of graduate study in the Fall. For candidates currently studying atmospheric sciences, oceanography, hydrology, chemistry, computer sciences, engineering, environmental sciences, mathematics, and physics who intend to pursue careers in the atmospheric or related oceanic or hydrologic sciences.

See website or send self-addressed, stamped envelope to Donna Fernandez or Stephanie Armstrong at AMS for an application.

1347—AMERICAN METEOROLOGICAL SOCIETY (AMS/Industry Minority Scholarships)

45 Beacon Street
Boston MA 02108-3693
617/227-2426, ext. 246
E-mail: dfernand@ametsoc.org
Internet: www.ametsoc.org/AMS

AMOUNT: $3,000/yr.
DEADLINE(S): FEB 11
FIELD(S): Atmospheric, Oceanic, & Hydrologic Sciences

Two-year awards are open to US citizens/permanent residents who are Hispanic, Native American, or African American students entering their freshman year of college in the Fall. Must plan to pursue careers in the atmospheric or related oceanic or hydrologic sciences.

See website or send self-addressed, stamped envelope to Donna Fernandez or Stephanie Armstrong at AMS for an application.

1348—AMERICAN METEOROLOGICAL SOCIETY (AMS/Industry Undergraduate Scholarships)

45 Beacon Street
Boston MA 02108-3693
617/227-2426, ext. 246
E-mail: dfernand@ametsoc.org
Internet: www.ametsoc.org/AMS

AMOUNT: $2,000/yr.
DEADLINE(S): FEB 25
FIELD(S): Atmospheric, Oceanic, & Hydrologic Sciences

Two-year awards are open to US citizens/permanent residents who will be college juniors in the Fall. For prospective candidates from the fields of atmospheric sciences, oceanography, hydrology, chemistry, computer sciences, mathematics, engineering, and physics who intend to pursue a career in the atmospheric or related oceanic or hydrologic sciences.

See website or send self-addressed, stamped envelope to Donna Fernandez or Stephanie Armstrong at AMS for an application.

1349—AMERICAN METEOROLOGICAL SOCIETY (AMS Undergraduate Scholarships)

45 Beacon Street
Boston MA 02108-3693
617/227-2426, ext. 246
E-mail: dfernand@ametsoc.org
Internet: www.ametsoc.org/AMS

AMOUNT: Varies
DEADLINE(S): MAR 3
FIELD(S): Atmospheric, Oceanic, & Hydrologic Sciences

Open to US citizens/permanent residents who will be entering their final year of undergraduate study in the Fall. Must be majoring in the atmospheric or related oceanic or hydrologic sciences and/or must show clear intent to make the atmospheric or related sciences their career.

See website or send self-addressed, stamped envelope to Donna Fernandez or Stephanie Armstrong at AMS for an application.

1350—AMERICAN METEOROLOGICAL SOCIETY (Father James B. Macelwane Award)

45 Beacon Street
Boston MA 02108-3693
617/227-2426, ext. 246
E-mail: dfernand@ametsoc.org
Internet: www.ametsoc.org/AMS

AMOUNT: $300
DEADLINE(S): JUN 16
FIELD(S): Meteorology, Atmosphere Science

Open to US citizens/permanent residents enrolled as undergraduates. Purpose of award is to stimulate interest in meteorology among college students through the encouragement of original student papers concerned with some phase of the atmospheric sciences. No more than two students from any one institution may enter papers in any one contest.

See website or send self-addressed, stamped envelope to Donna Fernandez or Stephanie Armstrong at AMS for an application.

1351—AMERICAN SOCIETY OF ENGINEERS OF INDIAN ORIGIN (Undergraduate Scholarship Programs)

P.O. Box 49494
Atlanta GA 30359-1494
770/451-2299
Internet: www.iasf.org/asei.htm

AMOUNT: Up to $1,000
DEADLINE(S): AUG 15
FIELD(S): Engineering fields: architecture, computer technology, geotechnical or geoenvironmental engineering, and allied sciences

Several scholarships for undergraduate engineering students in the above fields who were born in India or who are Indian by ancestry or relation. For study in the US. Some programs have residency requirements in certain states.

Contact Dr. Narsi Narasimhan at above location for applications and details.

1352—AMERICAN WATER RESOURCES ASSOCIATION (Richard A. Herbert Memorial Scholarships)

101 Comer Hall
Auburn Univ AL 36849-5431
715/355-3684
FAX: 715/355-3648
E-mail: stdi@ltus.com
Internet: www.uwin.siu.ed/~awra

AMOUNT: $1,000 + complimentary AWRA membership
DEADLINE(S): APR 30
FIELD(S): Water Resources & related fields

For full-time undergraduates working towards 1st degree and for graduates. Based on academic performance, including cumulative GPA, relevance of curriculum to water resources, and leadership in extracurricular activities related to water resources. Quality and relevance of research is also considered from graduate students. Transcripts, letters of reference, and summary of academic interests/achievements, extracurricular interests, and career goals required (2-page limit).

2 awards annually: 1 undergrad and 1 graduate. Recipients announced in the summer. Contact Stephen Dickman, AWRA Student Activities Committee, for an application.

1353—ARTHUR & DOREEN PARRETT SCHOLARSHIP TRUST FUND (Scholarships)

c/o U.S. Bank of Washington
Trust Dept., 8th Fl.
P.O. Box 720
Seattle WA 98111-0720
206/344-4653

AMOUNT: Up to $3,500
DEADLINE(S): JUL 31
FIELD(S): Engineering, Science,
Medicine, Dentistry

Washington state resident who has completed her/his first year of college by July 31. Open to students enrolled in above schools. Awards tenable at any accredited undergrad college or university.

Approximately 15 awards per year. Write for complete information.

1354—ASSOCIATION FOR WOMEN IN SCIENCE EDUCATIONAL FOUNDATION (Dr. Vicki L. Schechtman Scholarship)

1200 New York Ave. NW
Suite 650
Washington DC 20005
202/326-8940 or 800/886-AWIS
E-mail: awis@awis.org
Internet: www.awis.org

AMOUNT: $1,000
DEADLINE(S): JAN 16
FIELD(S): Various Sciences and Social
Sciences

For female undergraduate students who are US citizens and have a minimum GPA of 3.0. Summary page, essay describing career aspirations, transcripts, proof of matriculation (if available), and two reference letters required with application. Scholarships may be used for tuition, books, housing, research, equipment, etc.

See website or write to above address for an application and more information.

1355—ASSOCIATION FOR WOMEN IN SCIENCE EDUCATIONAL FOUNDATION (Ruth Satter Memorial Award)

1200 New York Ave. NW
Suite 650
Washington DC 20005
202/326-8940 or 800/886-AWIS
E-mail: awis@awis.org
Internet: www.awis.org

AMOUNT: $1,000
DEADLINE(S): JAN 16
FIELD(S): Various Sciences and Social
Sciences

Scholarships for female doctoral students who have interrupted their education three years or move to raise a family. Summary page, description of research project, resume, references, transcripts, biographical sketch, and proof of eligibility from department head required. US citizens may attend any graduate institution; non-citizens must be enrolled in US institutions.

See website or write to above address for more information or an application.

1356—AUBURN UNIVERSITY SCHOOL OF FORESTRY (Various Scholarships)

Chairman, Scholarship Committee
100 M. White Smith Hall
Auburn AL 36849-5418

AMOUNT: Varies
DEADLINE(S): Varies
FIELD(S): Forestry

Various scholarships for students attending Auburn University School of Forestry. Many give preference to Alabama or Georgia residents.

Write for a complete listing of scholarships.

1357—BROOKHAVEN WOMEN IN SCIENCE (Renate W. Chasman Scholarship)

P.O. Box 183
Upton NY 11973-5000
E-mail: pam@bnl.gov

AMOUNT: $2,000
DEADLINE(S): APR 1
FIELD(S): Natural Sciences, Engineering,
Mathematics

Open ONLY to women who are residents of the boroughs of Brooklyn or Queens or the counties of Nassau or Suffolk in New York who are re-entering school after a period of study. For juniors, seniors, or first-year graduate students.

1 award annually. Not renewable. Contact Pam Mansfield at above location for an application. Phone calls are NOT accepted.

1358—COMMUNITY FOUNDATION OF WESTERN MASSACHUSETTS (Nate McKinney Memorial Scholarship)

1500 Main Street
P.O. Box 15769
Springfield MA 01115
413/732-2858

AMOUNT: $1,000
DEADLINE(S): APR 15
FIELD(S): Music, Athletics, Science

Open to graduating seniors of Gateway Regional High School in Huntington, Massachusetts. Recipient must excel academically, demonstrate good citizenship, and have a strong interest in at least two of the following areas: music, science, and athletics. Based on financial need, academic merit, and extracurricular activities. Must submit transcripts and fill out government FAFSA form.

1 award annually. Renewable up to 4 years with reapplication. Contact Community Foundation for an application and your financial aid office for FAFSA. Notification is in June.

1359—CONSULTING ENGINEERS COUNCIL OF NEW JERSEY (Louis Goldberg Scholarship Fund)

66 Morris Ave.
Springfield NJ 07081
973/564-5848
FAX: 973/564-7480

AMOUNT: $1,000
DEADLINE(S): JAN 1
FIELD(S): Engineering or Land
Surveying

Open to undergraduate students who have completed at least two years of study (or fifth year in a five-year program) at an ABET-accredited college or university in New Jersey, are in top half of their class, and are considering a career as a consulting engineer or land surveyor. Must be US citizen.

Recipients will be eligible for American Consulting Engineers Council national scholarships of $2,000 to $5,000. Write for complete information.

1360—DEMONSTRATION OF ENERGY-EFFICIENT DEVELOPMENTS (DEED Scholarship Program)

2301 M Street NW
Washington DC 20037
202/467-2942
FAX: 202/467-2992
E-mail: ewatson@APPPAnet.org

Internet: APPAnet.org

AMOUNT: $3,000
DEADLINE(S): Varies
FIELD(S): Energy-related fields

Open for undergraduate, graduate, and postgraduate students enrolled at an accredited college or university studying in an energy-related field. Must propose and complete a project that can benefit public power utilities. Students must be sponsored by a DEED member utility.

10 annual awards. Application is online at website above. Call for information on potential sponsors.

1361—EDWARD AND ANNA RANGE SCHMIDT CHARITABLE TRUST (Grants & Emergency Financial Assistance)

P.O. Box 770982
Eagle River AK 99577
Written inquiry

AMOUNT: Varies
DEADLINE(S): None
FIELD(S): Earth & Environmental Sciences

Open to Alaska residents or students in Alaska programs. Grants are awarded for a variety of expenses incurred by students, such as internship support, travel, expenses related to workshops and science fairs, support needed to secure employment in earth science-related fields, or emergency needs. Alaska Natives and other minorities are urged to apply.

Not renewable. Requests are given immediate consideration. Application should be made by letter from a sponsor (teacher, advisor, or other adult familiar with applicant's situation). Both sponsor and applicant should send letter describing applicant, nature of financial need, and amount requested.

1362—FLORIDA FEDERATION OF GARDEN CLUBS, INC. (FFGC Scholarships for College Students)

6065 21st Street, SW
Vero Beach FL 32968-9427
561/778-1023
Internet: www.ffgc.org

AMOUNT: $1,500-$3,500
DEADLINE(S): MAY 1
FIELD(S): Ecology, Environmental Issues, Land Management, City Planning, Environmental Control, Horticulture, Landscape Design, Conservation, Botany, Forestry, Marine Biology, Floriculture, Agriculture

Various scholarships for Florida residents with a "B" average or better enrolled full-time as a junior, senior, or graduate student at a Florida college or university.

See website or contact Melba Campbell at FFGC for an application.

1363—FLORIDA FEDERATION OF GARDEN CLUBS, INC. (FFGC Scholarships for High School Students)

6065 21st Street, SW
Vero Beach FL 32968-9427
561/778-1023
Internet: www.ffgc.org

AMOUNT: $1,500
DEADLINE(S): MAY 1
FIELD(S): Ecology, Environmental Issues, Land Management, City Planning, Environmental Control, Horticulture, Landscape Design, Conservation, Botany, Forestry, Marine Biology, Floriculture, Agriculture

Scholarships for Florida residents with a "B" average or better who will be incoming freshmen at a Florida college or university.

See website or contact Melba Campbell at FFGC for an application.

1364—GAMMA THETA UPSILON INTERNATIONAL GEOGRAPHIC HONOR SOCIETY (Buzzard, Richason, & Maxfield Presidents Scholarships)

1725 State Street
La Crosse WI 54601
608/785-8355
FAX: 608/785-8332
E-mail: holdevh@mail.uwlax.edu

AMOUNT: $500
DEADLINE(S): JUN 1
FIELD(S): Geography

Undergraduate and graduate scholarships are open to Gamma Theta Upsilon members who maintain at least a "B" grade point average in any accredited geography program.

Contact Dr. Virgil Holder, Dept. of Geography, University of Wisconsin, at above address for an application.

1365—INSTITUTE OF INTERNATIONAL EDUCATION (National Security Education Program-Undergraduate Scholarships)

1400 K Street NW, 6th Fl.
Washington DC 20005-2403
202/326-7697 or
800/618-NSEP (6737)

E-mail: nsep@iie.org
Internet: http://www.iie.org/nsep/

AMOUNT: Varies: up to $8,000/semester
DEADLINE(S): FEB 8
FIELD(S): Open to all majors; preference to applied sciences, engineering, business, economics, math, computer science, international affairs, political science, history, and the policy sciences

For study abroad OUTSIDE the US, Canada, Australia, New Zealand, and Western Europe. For study in areas deemed critical to US national security. Applications available on US campuses from August through early December. Or contact organization for details.

Inquire at above location for details.

1366—LOUISIANA OFFICE OF STUDENT FINANCIAL ASSISTANCE (Rockefeller State Wildlife Scholarship)

P.O. Box 91202
Baton Rouge LA 70821-9202
800/259-5626, ext. 1012
FAX: 504/922-0790
Internet: www.osfa.state.la.us

AMOUNT: $1,000/yr.
DEADLINE(S): JUN 1
FIELD(S): Forestry, Wildlife, Marine Science

Open to Louisiana residents pursuing undergraduate or graduate study in a Louisiana college/university. Must have minimum 2.5 GPA. Recipients must attain a degree in one of the three eligible fields or repay the funds plus interest.

30 awards annually. Renewable up to 5 years undergraduate study and 2 years graduate study. Apply by completing the Free Application for Federal Student Aid (FAFSA). See your school's financial aid office or contact LOSFA for FAFSA form.

1367—LOUISIANA STATE UNIVERSITY AT SHREVEPORT (Neal Dlin Memorial Award)

Dean of Liberal Arts
One University Place
Shreveport LA 71115-2399
318/797-5363 or 318/797-5371
FAX: 318/797-5366
E-mail: finaid@pilot.lsus.edu
Internet: www.lsus.edu

AMOUNT: Varies
DEADLINE(S): Varies
FIELD(S): Geography

For a junior or senior student majoring in geography at LSUS. Award is based on scholarly achievement, and a minimum 3.0 GPA is required. Amount of award is determined by the faculty committee that selects the recipient each year. Candidates for the award are required to have a brief, informal interview with the faculty selection committee.

Contact the Dean's Office in the College of Liberal Arts at LSUS for an application.

1368—MINERALOGICAL SOCIETY OF AMERICA (MSA Grant for Research in Crystallography)

1015 18th Street NW, Suite 601
Washington DC 20036-5274
202/775-4344
FAX: 202/775-0018
E-mail: j_a_speer@minsocam.org
Internet: www.minsocam.org

AMOUNT: $3,500
DEADLINE(S): JUN 1
FIELD(S): Crystallography

Research grant based on qualifications of applicant; quality, innovativeness, and scientific significance of proposed research; and the likelihood of success of the project. Applicant must have reached his or her 25th birthday but not have reached his or her 36th birthday on the date the grant is awarded. There are no restrictions on how the grant funds may be spent, as long as they are used in support of research. MSA Counselors may not apply.

See website or contact Dr. J. Alex Speer at the MSA Business Office for an application.

1369—MINERALOGICAL SOCIETY OF AMERICA (MSA Grant for Student Research in Mineralogy and Petrology)

1015 18th Street, NW Suite 601
Washington DC 20036-5274
202/775-4344
FAX: 202/775-0018
E-mail: j_a_speer@minsocam.org
Internet: www.minsocam.org

AMOUNT: $3,500
DEADLINE(S): JUN 1
FIELD(S): Mineralogy, Petrology

Research grant for undergraduate or graduate students based on qualifications of applicant; the quality, innovativeness, and scientific significance of the proposed research; and the likelihood of success of the project. There are no restrictions on how the grant funds may be spent, as long as they are used in support of research.

See website or contact Dr. J. Alex Speer at the MSA Business Office for an application.

1370—NATIONAL COUNCIL FOR THE SOCIAL STUDIES (Grant for the Enhancement of Geographic Literacy)

3501 Newark Street NW
Washington DC 20016
202/966-7840
FAX: 202/966-2061
Internet: www.ncss.org/awards/grants.html

AMOUNT: $2,500
DEADLINE(S): JUL 3
FIELD(S): Social Studies

Grant is co-sponsored by the George F. Cram Company, map publishers. For teachers of any level who present a program to promote and enhance geography education in the schools. Must incorporate the National Geography Standards in "Geography for Life," the "Fundamental Themes in Geography," and appropriate sections of "Expectations of Excellence: Curriculum Standards for Social Studies."

Check website or contact organization for details.

1371—NATIONAL FEDERATION OF THE BLIND (Howard Brown Rickard Scholarship)

805 Fifth Ave.
Grinnell IA 50112
515/236-3366

AMOUNT: $3,000
DEADLINE(S): MAR 31
FIELD(S): Law, Medicine, Engineering, Architecture, Natural Sciences

For legally blind students pursuing or planning to pursue a full-time postsecondary course of study in the US. Based on academic excellence, service to the community, and financial need. Membership NOT required.

1 award annually. Renewable. Contact Mrs. Peggy Elliot, Scholarship Committee Chairman, for an application.

1372—OAK RIDGE INSTITUTE FOR SCIENCE AND EDUCATION (ORISE Education & Training Programs)

P.O. Box 117
Oak Ridge TN 37831-0117
Internet: www.orau.gov/orise/educ.htm

AMOUNT: Varies
DEADLINE(S): Varies
FIELD(S): Engineering, Aeronautics, Computer Science, Technology, Earth Science, Environmental Studies, Biology, Chemistry, Physics, Medical Research

Numerous programs funded by the US Department of Energy are offered for undergraduate students through postgraduate researchers. Includes fellowship and internship opportunities throughout the US. Some have citizenship restrictions. Travel may be included.

See website or write for a catalog of specific programs and requirements.

1373—OFFICE OF NAVAL RESEARCH (NSAP—Naval Science Awards Program)

ONR 353
800 N. Quincy Street
Arlington VA 22217-5660
800/422-6727 or 703/696-5787
E-mail: thurmab@onrhq.onr.navy.mil
Internet: www.onr.navy.mil or www.jshs.org

AMOUNT: $2,000-$20,000
DEADLINE(S): Varies (established by individual regional, state, and district science fairs)
FIELD(S): Science, Engineering

For high school students (grades 9-12) who participate in a regional/district/state science fair. Winners can participate in Junior Science & Humanities Symposia (JSHS) Program. Awards also offered in each of 14 categories at International Science & Engineering Fair (ISEF), sponsored by Science Service, Inc. Must be US citizen or permanent resident.

24 awards annually. Renewable. See website or contact Mrs. Barbara M. Thurman (Project Officer) at address above for complete information on NSAP, ISEF, and JSHS.

1374—OPEN SOCIETY INSTITUTE (Environmental Management Fellowships)

400 West 59th Street
New York NY 10019
212/548-0600 or 212/757-2323
FAX: 212/548-4679 or 212/548-4600
Internet: www.soros.org/efp.html

AMOUNT: Fees, room, board, living stipend, textbooks, international transportation, health insurance
DEADLINE(S): NOV 15
FIELD(S): Earth Sciences, Natural Sciences, Humanities (exc. language), Anthropology, Sociology, Mathematics, or Engineering

Two-year fellowships for use in selected universities in the US for international students. For students/professionals in fields related to environmental policy, legislation, and remediation techniques applicable to their home countries.

To apply, contact your local Soros Foundation or Open Society Institute. Further details on website.

1375—PENINSULA COMMUNITY FOUNDATION (Dr. Mary Finegold Scholarship)

1700 S. El Camino Real, #300
San Mateo CA 94402
650/358-9369
FAX: 650/358-9817

AMOUNT: $1,000
DEADLINE(S): MAR 27 (5 P.M.)
FIELD(S): Sciences

Scholarships for senior girls graduating from high school in Palo Alto, California, who intend to complete a four-year degree in the sciences. Special consideration will be given to girls who have demonstrated a "pioneering" spirit in that they have not been constrained by stereotypical female roles and to those facing financial hardship.

Award was established in the honor of Dr. Mary Finegold who, after completing her medical studies, elected to stay at home until her youngest child was in high school before beginning her medical practice. She was a school physician.

1376—PENN STATE UNIVERSITY—COLLEGE OF EARTH & MINERAL SCIENCES (Scholarships)

Committee on Scholarships & Awards
116 Deike Bldg.
University Park PA 16802
814/865-6546

AMOUNT: $500-$2,500
DEADLINE(S): None
FIELD(S): Geosciences; Meteorology; Energy, Environmental, and Mineral Economics; Materials Science and Engineering; Mineral Engineering; Geography

Scholarship program open to outstanding undergraduate students accepted to or enrolled in Penn State's College of Earth & Mineral Sciences. Minimum GPA of 3.15 on 4.0 scale.

Approximately 275 awards per year. Renewable. Contact Dean's office for complete information.

1377—PURDUE UNIVERSITY (Freshman Scholarship Awards of Excellence)

School of Agriculture
West Lafayette IN 47906
Written inquiry

AMOUNT: $1,500
DEADLINE(S): FEB
FIELD(S): Agriculture, Forestry

Various scholarships in agriculture and forestry are available to high school seniors who will be incoming freshmen at Purdue University.

Write to above address for an application.

1378—RESOURCES FOR THE FUTURE (RFF Summer Internship Program)

1616 P Street NW
Washington DC 20036-1400
202/328-5000
E-mail: lewis@rff.org OR voigt@rff.org
Internet: www.rff.org

AMOUNT: $375/week
DEADLINE(S): MAR 12
FIELD(S): Social Sciences, Natural Resources, Energy, Environment

Resident-paid summer internships for undergraduate and graduate students for research in the above fields. Divisions are Center for Risk Management, Energy and Natural Resources, and Quality of the Environment. Candidates should have outstanding policy analysis and writing skills. For both US and non-US citizens.

All information is on website. Address inquiries and applications to Sue Lewis (Energy & Natural Resources and Quality of the Environment) or Marilyn Voigt (Center for Risk Management). NO fax submissions.

1379—SAN DIEGO AEROSPACE MUSEUM (Bill Gibbs Scholarship)

Education Dept.
2001 Pan American Plaza
San Diego CA 92101
619/234-8291, ext. 19
FAX: 619/233-4526
Internet: aerospacemuseum.org/ Scholastic.HTML

AMOUNT: Varies
DEADLINE(S): Varies
FIELD(S): Aerospace: math, physics, science, or engineering

For students who are residents of San Diego County, California, who have an aerospace career interest and who have been accepted to a four-year college or university in a degree program relating to math, physics, science, or engineering.

Call or write museum for further information.

1380—SMITHSONIAN INSTITUTION (Minority Student Internship Program)

Fellowships & Grants
955 L'Enfant Plaza, Suite 7000
MRC 902
Washington DC 20560
202/287-3271
FAX: 202/287-3691
E-mail: siofg@ofg.si.edu
Internet: www.si.edu/research+study

AMOUNT: $300/week + possible travel expenses
DEADLINE(S): FEB 15
FIELD(S): Humanities, Environmental Studies, Cultural Studies, Natural History, Earth Science, Art History, Biology, and related fields

Ten-week internships in residence at the Smithsonian for US minority students to participate in research or museum-related activities in above fields. For undergrads or grads with at least a 3.0 GPA. Essay, resume, transcripts, and references required with application. Internships are full-time and are offered for Summer, Fall, or Spring tenures.

Write for application.

1381—SMITHSONIAN INSTITUTION (National Air & Space Museum Verville Fellowship)

National Air and Space Museum
MRC 312
Washington DC 20560
Written inquiry

AMOUNT: $30,000 stipend for 12 months + travel and misc. expenses
DEADLINE(S): JAN 15
FIELD(S): Analysis of major trends, developments, and accomplishments in the history of aviation or space studies

A competitive nine- to twelve-month in-residence fellowship in the above field of study. Advanced degree is NOT a requirement. Contact Fellowship Coordinator at above location.

Open to all nationalities. Fluency in English required.

1382—SOCIETY FOR RANGE MANAGEMENT (Masonic Range Science Scholarship)

1839 York Street
Denver CO 80206
303/355-7070
FAX: 303/355-5059
E-mail: srmden@ix.netcom.com
Internet: srm.org

AMOUNT: $1,500
DEADLINE(S): JAN 15
FIELD(S): Range Science/Management

Open to high school seniors or college freshmen pursuing a major in range science/management. Must attend a college or university with a range science program.

1 award annually. Financial need NOT a factor. See website or contact Ann Harris at above address for an application/more information.

1383—SOCIETY OF EXPLORATION GEOPHYSICISTS (SEG) FOUNDATION (Scholarships)

P.O. Box 702740
Tulsa OK 74170-2740
918/497-5530

AMOUNT: $500-$3,000
DEADLINE(S): MAR 1
FIELD(S): Geophysics

Open to a high school student with above-average grades planning to enter college the next fall term or an undergraduate college student whose grades are above average, or a graduate college student whose studies are directed toward a career in exploration geophysics in operations, teaching, or research.

Write to the above address for complete information.

1384—SOCIETY OF SATELLITE PROFESSIONALS INTERNATIONAL (SSPI Scholarships)

225 Reinekers Lane, Suite 600
Alexandria VA 22314
703/857-3717
FAX: 703/857-6335
E-mail: neworbit@aol.com
Internet: www.sspi.org

AMOUNT: $1,500 to $4,000
DEADLINE(S): DEC 1
FIELD(S): Satellites as related to Communications, Domestic and International Telecommunications Policy, Remote Sensing, Journalism, Law, Meteorology, Energy, Navigation, Business, Government, and Broadcasting Services

Various scholarships for students studying in the above fields.

Access website for details and applications or send a self-addressed, stamped envelope (SASE) for a complete listing.

1385—SOIL AND WATER CONSERVATION SOCIETY (Melville H. Cohee Student Leader Conservation Scholarship)

7515 NE Ankeny Road
Ankeny IA 50021-9764
515/289-2331 or 800-THE-SOIL
FAX 515/289-1227
E-mail: charliep@swcs.org
Internet: www.swcs.org

AMOUNT: $900
DEADLINE(S): FEB 113
FIELD(S): Conservation or Natural Resource-Related Field

Open to 1+ year member of SWCS having served as an officer in a student chapter with 15+ members. GPA of 3.0 or better. Final year F/T undergrad or graduate.

2 awards. Course load must be 50% or more at accredited college or university. Financial need is not a factor. Write or visit website for complete information.

1386—STUDENT CONSERVATION ASSOCIATION (SCA Resource Assistant Program)

P.O. Box 550
Charlestown NH 03603
603/543-1700
FAX: 603/543-1828
E-mail: internships@sca-inc.org
Internet: www.sca-inc.org

AMOUNT: $1,180-$4,725
DEADLINE(S): Varies
FIELD(S): Environment & related fields

Must be 18 and US citizen; need not be student. Fields: Agriculture, archaeology, anthropology, botany, caves, civil/environmental engineering, environmental education, fisheries, forests, herpetology, history, living history/roleplaying, visitor services, landscape architectural/environmental design, paleontology, recreation/resource/range management, trail maintenance/construction, wildlife management, geology, hydrology, library/museums, surveying.

900 positions in US and Canada. Send $1 for postage for application; outside US/Canada, send $20.

1387—U.S. ENVIRONMENTAL PROTECTION AGENCY—NATIONAL NETWORK FOR ENVIRONMENTAL MANAGEMENT STUDIES (Fellowships)

401 M Street SW
Mailcode 1704
Washington DC 20460
202/260-5283
FAX: 202/260-4095
E-mail: jojokian.sheri@epa.gov
Internet: www.epa.gov/enviroed/students.html

AMOUNT: Varies
DEADLINE(S): DEC
FIELD(S): Environmental Policies, Regulations, & Law; Environmental Management & Administration; Environmental Science; Public Relations & Communications; Computer Programming & Development

Fellowships are open to undergraduate and graduate students working on research projects in the above fields, either full-time during the summer or part-time during the school year. Must be US citizen or legal resident. Financial need NOT a factor.

85-95 awards annually. Not renewable. See website or contact the Career Service Center of participating universities for an application.

1388—UNCF/MERCK SCIENCE INITIATIVE (Undergraduate Science Research Scholarship Awards)

8260 Willow Oaks Corporate Dr.
P.O. Box 10444
Fairfax VA 22031-4511
703/205-3503
FAX: 703/205-3574
E-mail: uncfmerck@uncf.org
Internet: www.uncf.org/merck

AMOUNT: $25,000/yr. (max.)
DEADLINE(S): JAN 31
FIELD(S): Life & Physical Sciences

Open to African-Americans in their junior year of college who will receive a bachelor's degree in the following academic year. Must be enrolled full-time in any four-year college/university in the US and have a minimum 3.3 GPA. Must be US citizen/permanent resident. Financial need NOT a factor.

15 awards annually. Not renewable. Contact Jerry Bryant, Ph.D., for an application.

1389—U.S. DEPARTMENT OF AGRICULTURE (1890 National Scholars Program)

14th & Independence Ave. SW
Room 301-W, Whitten Bldg.
Washington DC 20250-9600
202/720-6905
E-mail: usda-m@fie.com
Internet: web.fie.com/htdoc/fed/
agr/ars/edu/prog/mti/agrpgaak.htm

AMOUNT: Tuition,
employment/benefits, use of
PC/software, fees, books, room/board
DEADLINE(S): JAN 15
FIELD(S): Agriculture, Food, or Natural
Resource sciences

For US citizens, high school grad/GED, GPA 3.0+, verbal/math SAT 1,000+, composite score 21+ ACT, 1st-yr college student, and attend participating school.

34+ scholarships/yr/4 years. Send applications to USDA Liaison Officer at the 1890 Institution of your choice (see Web page for complete list).

1390—WATER ENVIRONMENT FEDERATION (Student Paper Competition)

Access website
Internet: www.wef.org

AMOUNT: $1,000 (1st prize); $500 (2nd);
$250 (3rd)
DEADLINE(S): FEB 1
FIELD(S): Water pollution control and
related fields

Awards for 500 1,000-word abstracts dealing with water pollution control, water quality problems, water-related concerns, or hazardous wastes. Open to undergrad (A.A. and B.A.) and grad students.

Also open to recently graduated students (within 1 calendar year of Feb. 1 deadline). See website for details—go to "Member Programs" then to "Student Paper Competition." Organization will not mail this information.

1391—WOMEN'S AUXILIARY TO THE AMERICAN INSTITUTE OF MINING METALLURGICAL & PETROLEUM ENGINEERS (WAAIME Scholarship Loan Fund)

345 E. 47th Street, 14th Fl.
New York NY 10017-2304
212/705-7692

AMOUNT: Varies
DEADLINE(S): MAR 15
FIELD(S): Earth Sciences, as related to
the Minerals Industry

Open to undergraduate juniors and seniors and grad students, whose majors relate to an interest in the minerals industry. Eligible applicants receive a scholarship loan for all or part of their education. Recipients repay only 50%, with no interest charges.

Repayment to begin by 6 months after graduation and be completed within 6 years. Write to WAAIME Scholarship Loan Fund (address above) for complete information.

1392—WOODROW WILSON NATIONAL FELLOWSHIP FOUNDATION (Leadership Program for Teachers)

CN 5281
Princeton NJ 08543-5281
609/452-7007
FAX: 609/452-0066
E-mail: marchioni@woodrow.org OR
irish@woodrow.org
Internet: www.woodrow.org

AMOUNT: Varies
DEADLINE(S): Varies
FIELD(S): Science, Mathematics

WWLPT offers summer institutes for middle and high school teachers in science and mathematics. One- and two-week teacher outreach, TORCH Institutes, are held in the summer throughout the US.

See website or contact WWNFF for an application.

1393—WOODS HOLE OCEANOGRAPHIC INSTITUTION (Traineeships in Oceanography for Minority Group Undergraduates)

360 Woods Hole Road
Woods Hole MA 02543-1541
508/289-2219
FAX: 508/457-2188
E-mail: mgately@whoi.edu
Internet: www.whoi.edu

AMOUNT: Varies
DEADLINE(S): FEB 16
FIELD(S): Physical/Natural Sciences,
Mathematics, Engineering

For minority undergraduates enrolled in US colleges/universities who have completed at least two semesters. These awards provide training and research experience for students with interests in the above fields. Traineeships may be awarded for a ten- to twelve-week period in the summer or for a semester during the academic year.

Renewable. For an application/more information, contact the Education Office, Clark Laboratory 223, MS #31, at above address.

ENVIRONMENTAL STUDIES

1394—ALLIANCE FOR YOUNG ARTISTS AND WRITERS, INC./AMERICAN MUSEUM OF NATURAL HISTORY (Young Naturalist Awards)

Scholastic, Inc.
555 Broadway
New York NY 10012-3999
212/343-6582 or 800-SCHOLASTIC
FAX: 212/343-4885
E-mail: mjohnson@scholastic.com
Internet: www.amnh.org/
youngnaturalistawards

AMOUNT: up to $2,500 + trip to New
York to visit AMNH
DEADLINE(S): JAN 3
FIELD(S): Natural Sciences

For all students in grades 7-12 currently enrolled in a public or non-public school in the US, Canada, US territories, or US-sponsored schools abroad. Program focuses on finding and rewarding excellence in biology, earth science, astronomy, and cultural studies. Students are encouraged to perform observation-based projects that require creativity, inquiry, and critical analysis. Specific topics vary annually.

48 awards annually. See website or contact Mike Johnson, Program Manager, for an application.

1395—AMERICAN INDIAN SCIENCE AND ENGINEERING SOCIETY (A.T. Anderson Memorial Scholarship)

P.O. Box 9828
Albuquerque NM 87119-9828
505/765-1052
FAX: 505/765-5608
E-mail: scholarships@aises.org
Internet: www.aises.org/scholarships

AMOUNT: $1,000-$2,000
DEADLINE(S): JUN 15
FIELD(S): Medicine, Natural Resources,
Science, Engineering

Open to undergraduate and graduate students who are at least 1/4 American Indian or recognized as member of a tribe. Must be member of AISES ($10 fee), enrolled full-time at an accredited institution, and demonstrate financial need.

Renewable. See website or contact Patricia Browne for an application and/or membership information.

1396—AMERICAN INDIAN SCIENCE AND ENGINEERING SOCIETY (EPA Tribal Lands Environmental Science Scholarship)

P.O. Box 9828
Albuquerque NM 87119-9828
505/765-1052
FAX: 505/765-5608
E-mail: scholarships@aises.org
Internet: www.aises.org/scholarships

AMOUNT: $4,000
DEADLINE(S): JUN 15
FIELD(S): Biochemistry, Biology, Chemical Engineering, Chemistry, Entomology, Environmental Economics/Science, Hydrology, Environmental Studies

Open to American Indian college juniors, seniors, and graduate students enrolled full-time at an accredited institution. Must demonstrate financial need. Certificate of Indian blood NOT required.

Renewable. See website or contact Patricia Browne for an application.

1397—AMERICAN PLANNING ASSOCIA-TION (Minority Scholarship and Fellowship Programs)

122 South Michigan Ave., Suite 1600
Chicago IL 60605
312/431-9100
FAX: 312/431-9985

AMOUNT: $2,000-$5,000 (grads); $2,500 (undergrads)
DEADLINE(S): MAY 14
FIELD(S): Urban Planning, Community Development, Environmental Sciences, Public Administration, Transportation, or Urban Studies

Scholarships for African-Americans, Hispanics, or Native American students pursuing undergraduate degrees in the US in the above fields. Must have completed first year. Fellowships for graduate students. Programs must be approved by the Planning Accreditation BoaRoad US citizenship.

Call or write for complete information.

1398—AMERICAN SOCIETY OF ENGI-NEERS OF INDIAN ORIGIN (Undergraduate Scholarship Programs)

P.O. Box 49494
Atlanta GA 30359-1494
770/451-2299
Internet: www.iasf.org/asei.htm

AMOUNT: Up to $1,000
DEADLINE(S): AUG 15

FIELD(S): Engineering fields: architecture, computer technology, geotechnical or geoenvironmental engineering, and allied sciences

Several scholarships for undergraduate engineering students in the above fields who were born in India or who are Indian by ancestry or relation. For study in the U.S. Some programs have residency requirements in certain states.

Contact Dr. Narsi Narasimhan at above location for applications and details.

1399—CHAUTAUQUA LAKE FISHING ASSOCIATION (Scholarship)

P.O. Box 473
Celeron NY 14720
Written inquiry

AMOUNT: $500
DEADLINE(S): MAY 31
FIELD(S): Conservation or Environmental Studies

Open to graduating high school seniors from Chautauqua County, NY, who have been accepted at an accredited college and who are interested in conservation or other environment-related fields.

Write to the above address for complete information.

1400—EDWARD AND ANNA RANGE SCHMIDT CHARITABLE TRUST (Grants & Emergency Financial Assistance)

P.O. Box 770982
Eagle River AK 99577
Written inquiry

AMOUNT: Varies
DEADLINE(S): None
FIELD(S): Earth & Environmental Sciences

Open to Alaska residents or students in Alaska programs. Grants are awarded for a variety of expenses incurred by students, such as internship support, travel, expenses related to workshops and science fairs, support needed to secure employment in earth science-related fields, or emergency needs. Alaska Natives and other minorities are urged to apply.

Not renewable. Requests are given immediate consideration. Application should be made by letter from a sponsor (teacher, advisor, or other adult familiar with applicant's situation). Both sponsor and applicant should send letter describing applicant, nature of financial need, and amount requested.

1401—FIRST UNITED METHODIST CHURCH (Robert Stevenson & Doreene E. Cater Scholarships)

302 5th Ave., S.
St. Cloud MN 56301
FAX: 320/251-0878
E-mail: FUMCloud@aol.com

AMOUNT: $100-$300
DEADLINE(S): JUN 1
FIELD(S): Humanitarian & Christian Service: Teaching, Medicine, Social Work, Environmental Studies, etc.

Stevenson Scholarship is open to undergraduate members of the First United Methodist Church of St. Cloud. Cater Scholarship is open to members of the Minnesota United Methodist Conference who are entering the sophomore year or higher of college work. Both require two letters of reference, transcripts, and financial need.

5-6 awards annually. Contact Scholarship Committee for an application.

1402—FLORIDA FEDERATION OF GAR-DEN CLUBS, INC. (FFGC Scholarships for College Students)

6065 21st Street SW
Vero Beach FL 32968-9427
561/778-1023
Internet: www.ffgc.org

AMOUNT: $1,500-$3,500
DEADLINE(S): MAY 1
FIELD(S): Ecology, Environmental Issues, Land Management, City Planning, Environmental Control, Horticulture, Landscape Design, Conservation, Botany, Forestry, Marine Biology, Floriculture, Agriculture

Various scholarships for Florida residents with a "B" average or better enrolled full-time as a junior, senior, or graduate student at a Florida college or university.

See website or contact Melba Campbell at FFGC for an application.

1403—FLORIDA FEDERATION OF GAR-DEN CLUBS, INC. (FFGC Scholarships for High School Students)

6065 21st Street SW
Vero Beach FL 32968-9427
561/778-1023
Internet: www.ffgc.org

AMOUNT: $1,500
DEADLINE(S): MAY 1

FIELD(S): Ecology, Environmental Issues, Land Management, City Planning, Environmental Control, Horticulture, Landscape Design, Conservation, Botany, Forestry, Marine Biology, Floriculture, Agriculture

Scholarships for Florida residents with a "B" average or better who will be incoming freshmen at a Florida college or university.

See website or contact Melba Campbell at FFGC for an application.

1404—GARDEN CLUB OF AMERICA (CGA Awards for Summer Environmental Studies)

14 East 60th Street
New York NY 10022-1046
212/753-8287
FAX: 212/753-0134
Internet: www.gcamerica.org

AMOUNT: $1,500
DEADLINE(S): FEB 15
FIELD(S): Environmental Studies

Financial aid toward a SUMMER course in above field for college students following their freshman, sophomore, or junior year. Purpose of award is to encourage studies and careers in the environmental field.

2+ awards annually. Application available on website or send self-addressed, stamped envelope to Ms. Shelley Burch at above address.

1405—GARDEN CLUB OF AMERICA (Frances M. Peacock Scholarship)

Cornell Lab of Ornithology
159 Sapsucker Woods Road
Ithaca NY 14850
FAX: 607/254-2415
E-mail: 1h17@cornell.edu
Internet: www.gcamerica.org

AMOUNT: $4,000
DEADLINE(S): JAN 15
FIELD(S): Habitats of
    Threatened/Endangered Native Birds

To provide financial aid to "an advanced student (college senior or graduate student) to study areas in the US that provide winter or summer habitat for our threatened and endangered native birds." Proposals will be judged upon the significance of the research project, prior accomplishments of awardee, and appropriateness of research topic.

1 award annually. Not renewable. Funds can be used at the discretion of the awardee: for fees, expenses, or even tuition provided they are directly related to the project at hand. Contact Scott Sutcliffe, Associate Director, for more information.

1406—HUBBARD FARMS CHARITABLE FOUNDATION

P.O. Box 505
Walpole NH 03608-0505
603/756-3311

AMOUNT: Varies
DEADLINE(S): APR 1; OCT 1
FIELD(S): Poultry science, genetics, and other life sciences

Scholarships are for financially needy students at universities that the foundation trustees consider to be leaders in the field of progress in technology and efficiency of production of poultry products.

Send SASE to Jane F. Kelly, Clerk, at above address for current application guidelines.

1407—INSTITUTE OF INTERNATIONAL EDUCATION (National Security Education Program-Undergraduate Scholarships)

1400 K Street NW, 6th Fl.
Washington DC 20005-2403
202/326-7697 or
800/618-NSEP (6737)
E-mail: nsep@iie.org
Internet: http://www.iie.org/nsep/

AMOUNT: Varies: up to $8,000/semester
DEADLINE(S): FEB 8
FIELD(S): Open to all majors; preference to Applied Sciences, Engineering, Business, Economics, Math, Computer Science, International Affairs, Political Science, History, and the Policy Sciences

For study abroad OUTSIDE the US, Canada, Australia, New Zealand, and Western Europe. For study in areas deemed critical to US national security. Applications available on US campuses from August through early December. Or contact organization for details.

Inquire at above location for details.

1408—LAND IMPROVEMENT FOUNDATION FOR EDUCATION (Scholarship)

3060 Ogden Ave., Suite 304
Lisle IL 60532-1690
630/548-1984

AMOUNT: Varies
DEADLINE(S): MAR 15
FIELD(S): Natural
    Resources/Conservation

Open to students who are interested in land improvement. Applicants must send three letters of recommendation along with a photo when applying.

Send SASE to above address for complete information.

1409—LOUISIANA OFFICE OF STUDENT FINANCIAL ASSISTANCE (Rockefeller State Wildlife Scholarship)

P.O. Box 91202
Baton Rouge LA 70821-9202
800/259-5626, ext. 1012
FAX: 504/922-0790
Internet: www.osfa.state.la.us

AMOUNT: $1,000/yr.
DEADLINE(S): JUN 1
FIELD(S): Forestry, Wildlife, Marine Science

Open to Louisiana residents pursuing undergraduate or graduate study in a Louisiana college/university. Must have minimum 2.5 GPA. Recipients must attain a degree in one of the three eligible fields or repay the funds plus interest.

30 awards annually. Renewable up to 5 years undergraduate study and 2 years graduate study. Apply by completing the Free Application for Federal Student Aid (FAFSA). See your school's financial aid office or contact LOSFA for FAFSA form.

1410—NAACP NATIONAL OFFICE (NAACP/Department of Energy Scholarship)

4805 Mount Hope Drive
Baltimore MD 21215-3297
410/486-9133

AMOUNT: $10,000/year tuition/stipend
DEADLINE(S): APR 30
FIELD(S): Engineering, Science, Computer Science, Mathematics, Environmental Studies

Open to high school seniors who are NAACP members with a minimum 3.0 GPA. Applicants must participate in 120 hours of community service; at least 1 summer internship at a DOE facility and be employed by DOE or DOE contractor for 2 years.

Write for complete information; enclose a self-addressed 9 x 12 envelope.

1411—NATIONAL ENVIRONMENTAL HEALTH ASSOCIATION (NEHA/AAS Scholarship)

720 S. Colorado Blvd., Suite 970
South Tower
Denver CO 80246-1925

303/756-9090
E-mail: veronica.white@juno.com
Internet: www.neha.org
AMOUNT: Varies
DEADLINE(S): FEB 1
FIELD(S): Environmental
Health/Science, Public Health

Undergraduate scholarships to be used for tuition and fees during junior or senior year at an Environmental Health Accreditation Council accredited school or NEHA school. Graduate scholarships are for students or career professionals who are enrolled in a graduate program of studies in environmental health sciences and/or public health. Transcript, letters of recommendation, and financial need considered.

Renewable. Scholarships are paid directly to the college/university for the fall semester of the award Contact Veronica White, NEHA Liaison, for an application.

1412—OAK RIDGE INSTITUTE FOR SCIENCE AND EDUCATION (ORISE Education & Training Programs)

P.O. Box 117
Oak Ridge TN 37831-0117
Internet: www.orau.gov/orise/educ.htm
AMOUNT: Varies
DEADLINE(S): Varies
FIELD(S): Engineering, Aeronautics, Computer Science, Technology, Earth Science, Environmental Studies, Biology, Chemistry, Physics, Medical Research

Numerous programs funded by the US Department of Energy are offered for undergraduate students through postgraduate researchers. Includes fellowship and internship opportunities throughout the US. Some have citizenship restrictions. Travel may be included.

See website or write for a catalog of specific programs and requirements.

1413—OPEN SOCIETY INSTITUTE (Environmental Management Fellowships)

400 West 59th Street
New York NY 10019
212/548-0600 or 212/757-2323
FAX: 212/548-4679 or
212/548-4600
Internet: www.soros.org/efp.html
AMOUNT: Fees, room, board, living stipend, textbooks, international transportation, health insurance
DEADLINE(S): NOV 15

FIELD(S): Earth Sciences, Natural Sciences, Humanities (exc. language), Anthropology, Sociology, Mathematics, or Engineering

Two-year fellowships for use in selected universities in the US for international students. For students/professionals in fields related to environmental policy, legislation, and remediation techniques applicable to their home countries.

To apply, contact your local Soros Foundation or Open Society Institute. Further details on website.

1414—PENINSULA COMMUNITY FOUNDATION (Dr. Mary Finegold Scholarship)

1700 S. El Camino Real, #300
San Mateo CA 94402
650/358-9369
FAX: 650/358-9817
AMOUNT: $1,000
DEADLINE(S): MAR 27 (5 P.M.)
FIELD(S): Sciences

Scholarships for senior girls graduating from high school in Palo Alto, California, who intend to complete a four-year degree in the sciences. Special consideration will be given to girls who have demonstrated a "pioneering" spirit in that they have not been constrained by stereotypical female roles and to those facing financial hardship.

Award was established in the honor of Dr. Mary Finegold who, after completing her medical studies, elected to stay at home until her youngest child was in high school before beginning her medical practice. She was a school physician.

1415—PENN STATE UNIVERSITY—COLLEGE OF EARTH & MINERAL SCIENCES (Scholarships)

Committee on Scholarships & Awards
116 Deike Bldg.
University Park PA 16802
814/865-6546
AMOUNT: $500-$2,500
DEADLINE(S): None
FIELD(S): Geosciences; Meteorology; Energy, Environmental, and Mineral Economics; Materials Science and Engineering; Mineral Engineering; Geography

Scholarship program open to outstanding undergraduate students accepted to or enrolled in Penn State's College of Earth & Mineral Sciences. Minimum GPA of 3.15 on 4.0 scale.

Approximately 275 awards per year. Renewable. Contact Dean's office for complete information.

1416—RESOURCES FOR THE FUTURE (RFF Summer Internship Program)

1616 P Street NW
Washington DC 20036-1400
202/328-5000
E-mail: lewis@rff.org OR voigt@rff.org
Internet: www.rff.org
AMOUNT: $375/week
DEADLINE(S): MAR 12
FIELD(S): Social Sciences, Natural Resources, Energy, Environment

Resident-paid summer internships for undergraduate and graduate students for research in the above fields. Divisions are Center for Risk Management, Energy and Natural Resources, and Quality of the Environment. Candidates should have outstanding policy analysis and writing skills. For both US and non-US citizens.

All information is on website. Address inquiries and applications to Sue Lewis (Energy & Natural Resources and Quality of the Environment) or Marilyn Voigt (Center for Risk Management). NO fax submissions.

1417—SAN DIEGO AEROSPACE MUSEUM (Bill Gibbs Scholarship)

Education Dept.
2001 Pan American Plaza
San Diego CA 92101
619/234-8291, ext. 19
FAX: 619/233-4526
Internet: aerospacemuseum.org/Scholastic.HTML
AMOUNT: Varies
DEADLINE(S): Varies
FIELD(S): Aerospace: math, physics, science, or engineering

For students who are residents of San Diego County, California, and who have an aerospace career interest who have been accepted to a four-year college or university in a degree program relating to math, physics, science, or engineering.

Call or write museum for further information.

1418—SMITHSONIAN INSTITUTION (Minority Student Internship Program)

Fellowships & Grants
955 L'Enfant Plaza, Suite 7000
MRC 902
Washington DC 20560

202/287-3271
FAX: 202/287-3691
E-mail: siofg@ofg.si.edu
Internet: www.si.edu/research+study
AMOUNT: $300/week + possible travel expenses
DEADLINE(S): FEB 15
FIELD(S): Humanities, Environmental Studies, Cultural Studies, Natural History, Earth Science, Art History, Biology, and related fields

Ten-week internships in residence at the Smithsonian for US minority students to participate in research or museum-related activities in above fields. For undergrads or grads with at least a 3.0 GPA. Essay, resume, transcripts, and references required with application. Internships are full-time and are offered for Summer, Fall, or Spring tenures.

Write for application.

1419—SMITHSONIAN INSTITUTION ENVIRONMENTAL RESEARCH CENTER (Work/Learn Program in Environmental Studies)

P.O. Box 28
Edgewater MD 21037
301/261-4084
E-mail: education@serc.si.edu
AMOUNT: $190/week + dorm housing; minority graduate students receive $240/wk.
DEADLINE(S): MAR 1; NOV 1
FIELD(S): Environmental Studies, Ecology, Ornithology, Marine Life, Computer Science, Chemistry, Mathematics

Work/learn internships at the center open to undergraduate and graduate students. Competitive program which offers unique opportunity to gain exposure to and experience in environmental research. Selected students paid $240 per week when they live at the center in Edgewater. No academic credit.

Projects generally coincide with academic semesters and summer sessions and are normally 12-15 weeks in duration. Write for complete information. Can e-mail for application.

1420—SOCIETY FOR RANGE MANAGEMENT (Masonic Range Science Scholarship)

1839 York Street
Denver CO 80206
303/355-7070
FAX: 303/355-5059
E-mail: srmden@ix.netcom.com
Internet: srm.org
AMOUNT: $1,500
DEADLINE(S): JAN 15
FIELD(S): Range Science/Management

Open to high school seniors or college freshmen pursuing a major in range science/management. Must attend a college or university with a range science program.

1 award annually. Financial need NOT a factor. See website or contact Ann Harris at above address for an application/more information.

1421—SOIL AND WATER CONSERVATION SOCIETY (Donald A. Williams Soil Conservation Scholarship)

7515 NW Ankeny Road
Ankeny IA 50021-9764
515/289-2331 or 800-THE-SOIL
FAX 515/289-1227
E-mail: cahrliep@swcs.rog
Internet: www.swcs.org
AMOUNT: $1,500
DEADLINE(S): FEB 13
FIELD(S): Conservation-related fields (technical or administrative course work)

For SWCS members currently employed in a related field and have completed at least 1 year of natural resource conservation work with a governmental agency or private organization. Need not be working toward a degree. Must show reasonable financial need.

For undergraduates. Write or visit website for complete information.

1422—SOIL AND WATER CONSERVATION SOCIETY (Melville H. Cohee Student Leader Conservation Scholarship)

7515 NE Ankeny Road
Ankeny IA 50021-9764
515/289-2331 or 800-THE-SOIL
FAX 515/289-1227
E-mail: charliep@swcs.org
Internet: www.swcs.org
AMOUNT: $900
DEADLINE(S): FEB 113
FIELD(S): Conservation or Natural Resource-Related Field

Open to 1+ year member of SWCS having served as an officer in a student chapter with 15+ members. GPA of 3.0 or better. Final year F/T undergrad or graduate.

2 awards. Course load must be 50% or more at accredited college or university.

Financial need is not a factor. Write or visit website for complete information.

1423—SOIL AND WATER CONSERVATION SOCIETY (SWCS Internships)

7515 NE Ankeny Road
Ankeny IA 50021-9764
515/289-2331 or 800/THE-SOIL
FAX: 515/289-1227
E-mail: charliep@swcs.org
Internet: www.swcs.org
AMOUNT: Varies—most are uncompensated
DEADLINE(S): Varies
FIELD(S): Journalism, Marketing, Database Management, Meeting Planning, Public Policy Research, Environmental Education, Landscape Architecture

Internships for undergraduates and graduates to gain experience in the above fields as they relate to soil and water conservation issues. Internship openings vary through the year in duration, compensation, and objective. SWCS will coordinate particulars with your academic advisor.

Contact SWCS for internship availability at any time during the year or see website for jobs page.

1424—SRP/NAVAJO GENERATING STATION (Navajo Scholarship)

P.O. Box 850
Page AZ 86040
520/645-6539
FAX: 520/645-7295
E-mail: ljdawave@srp.gov
AMOUNT: Based on need
DEADLINE(S): APR 30
FIELD(S): Engineering, Environmental Studies, Business, Business Management, Health, Education

Scholarships for full-time students who hold membership in the Navajo Tribe and who are pursuing a degree in a field of study recognized as significant to the Navajo Nation, Salt River Project, or the Navajo Generating Station, such as those listed above. Must be junior or senior, have and maintain a GPA of 3.0.

Average of 15 awards per year. Inquire of Linda Dawavendewa at above location.

1425—STANFORD YOUTH ENVIRONMENTAL SCIENCE PROGRAM (SYESP Summer Residence Program)

P.O. Box 8453
Stanford, CA 94305

415/854-5220, ext. 2
Internet: www-
leland.stanfoRoadedu/
group/syesp/program/program.html
AMOUNT: Internship
DEADLINE(S): None specified
FIELD(S): Environmental Concerns

A summer residence program for exceptionally gifted, low-income, underserved, predominantly minority high school juniors and seniors who are concerned with the environment. SYESP hopes to foster future environmental leaders from this traditionally non-environmentally career oriented group, who could impact their neighborhoods and other disenfranchised communities.

300-600 applicants for 22 positions. California resident, preferably Northern California. Interest in professional/graduate school; demonstration of aptitude in math and science; and demonstration of maturity, initiative, and curiosity, as well as a concern for the environment.

1426—STUDENT CONSERVATION ASSOCIATION (SCA Resource Assistant Program)

P.O. Box 550
Charlestown NH 03603
603/543-1700
FAX: 603/543-1828
E-mail: internships@sca-inc.org
Internet: www.sca-inc.org

AMOUNT: $1,180-$4,725
DEADLINE(S): Varies
FIELD(S): Environment & related fields

Must be 18 and US citizen; need not be student. Fields: Agriculture, archaeology, anthropology, botany, caves, civil/environmental engineering, environmental education, fisheries, forests, herpetology, history, living history/roleplaying, visitor services, landscape architectural/environmental design, paleontology, recreation/resource/range management, trail maintenance/construction, wildlife management, geology, hydrology, library/museums, surveying.

900 positions in US and Canada. Send $1 for postage for application; outside US/Canada, send $20.

1427—U.S. ENVIRONMENTAL PROTECTION AGENCY—NATIONAL NETWORK FOR ENVIRONMENTAL MANAGEMENT STUDIES (Fellowships)

401 M Street SW
Mailcode 1704
Washington DC 20460
202/260-5283

FAX: 202/260-4095
E-mail: jojokian.sheri@epa.gov
Internet: www.epa.gov/enviroed/
students.html

AMOUNT: Varies
DEADLINE(S): DEC
FIELD(S): Environmental Policies, Regulations, & Law; Environmental Management & Administration; Environmental Science; Public Relations & Communications; Computer Programming & Development

Fellowships are open to undergraduate and graduate students working on research projects in the above fields, either full-time during the summer or part-time during the school year. Must be US citizen or legal resident. Financial need NOT a factor.

85-95 awards annually. Not renewable. See website or contact the Career Service Center of participating universities for an application.

1428—UNCF/MERCK SCIENCE INITIATIVE (Undergraduate Science Research Scholarship Awards)

8260 Willow Oaks Corporate Dr.
P.O. Box 10444
Fairfax VA 22031-4511
703/205-3503
FAX: 703/205-3574
E-mail: uncfmerck@uncf.org
Internet: www.uncf.org/merck

AMOUNT: $25,000/yr. (max.)
DEADLINE(S): JAN 31
FIELD(S): Life & Physical Sciences

Open to African-Americans in their junior year of college who will receive a bachelor's degree in the following academic year. Must be enrolled full-time in any four-year college/university in the US and have a minimum 3.3 GPA. Must be US citizen/permanent resident. Financial need NOT a factor.

15 awards annually. Not renewable. Contact Jerry Bryant, Ph.D., for an application.

1429—U.S. DEPARTMENT OF AGRICULTURE (1890 National Scholars Program)

14th & Independence Ave. SW
Room 301-W, Whitten Bldg.
Washington DC 20250-9600
202/720-6905
E-mail: usda-m@fie.com
Internet: web.fie.com/htdoc/fed/
agr/ars/edu/prog/mti/agrpgaak.htm

AMOUNT: Tuition, employment/benefits, use of PC/software, fees, books, room/board
DEADLINE(S): JAN 15
FIELD(S): Agriculture, Food, or Natural Resource sciences

For US citizens, high school grad/GED, GPA 3.0+, verbal/math SAT 1,000+, composite score 21+ ACT, 1st-yr college student, and attend participating school.

34+ scholarships/yr/4 years. Send applications to USDA Liaison Officer at the 1890 Institution of your choice (see Web page for complete list).

1430—V.M. EHLERS MEMORIAL FUND, INC.

6813 Comanche Trail
Austin TX 78732
512/266-2573

AMOUNT: Varies
DEADLINE(S): JUL 1
FIELD(S): Environmental health fields

Scholarships to Texas residents studying in environmental health fields.

Write to above address for application guidelines.

1431—WATER ENVIRONMENT FEDERATION (Student Paper Competition)

Access website
Internet: www.wef.org

AMOUNT: $1,000 (1st prize); $500 (2nd); $250 (3rd)
DEADLINE(S): FEB 1
FIELD(S): Water pollution control and related fields

Awards for 500 1,000-word abstracts dealing with water pollution control, water quality problems, water-related concerns, or hazardous wastes. Open to undergrad (A.A. and B.A.) and grad students.

Also open to recently graduated students (within 1 calendar year of Feb. 1 deadline). See website for details—go to "Member Programs" then to "Student Paper Competition." Organization will not mail this information.

1432—WYOMING TRUCKING ASSOCIATION (Scholarships)

P.O. Box 1909
Casper WY 82602
Written inquiry

AMOUNT: $250-$300
DEADLINE(S): MAR 1
FIELD(S): Transportation Industry

For Wyoming high school graduates enrolled in a Wyoming college, approved trade school, or the University of Wyoming. Must be pursuing a course of study which will result in a career in the transportation industry in Wyoming, including but not limited to: safety, environmental science, diesel mechanics, truck driving, vocational trades, business management, sales management, computer skills, accounting, office procedures, and management.

1-10 awards annually. Write to WYTA for an application.

MARINE SCIENCE

1433—ALLIANCE FOR YOUNG ARTISTS AND WRITERS, INC./AMERICAN MUSEUM OF NATURAL HISTORY (Young Naturalist Awards)

Scholastic, Inc.
555 Broadway
New York NY 10012-3999
212/343-6582 or 800-SCHOLASTIC
FAX: 212/343-4885
E-mail: mjohnson@scholastic.com
Internet: www.amnh.org/youngnaturalistawards

AMOUNT: up to $2,500 + trip to New York to visit AMNH
DEADLINE(S): JAN 3
FIELD(S): Natural Sciences

For all students in grades 7-12 currently enrolled in a public or non-public school in the US, Canada, US territories, or US-sponsored schools abroad. Program focuses on finding and rewarding excellence in biology, earth science, astronomy, and cultural studies. Students are encouraged to perform observation-based projects that require creativity, inquiry, and critical analysis. Specific topics vary annually.

48 awards annually. See website or contact Mike Johnson, Program Manager, for an application.

1434—AMERICAN FOUNDATION FOR THE BLIND (Paul W. Ruckes Scholarship)

11 Penn Plaza, Suite 300
New York NY 10001
212/502-7661
FAX: 212/502-7771
E-mail: juliet@afb.org
Internet: www.afb.org

AMOUNT: $1,000
DEADLINE(S): APR 30
FIELD(S): Engineering, Computer/Physical/Life Sciences

Open to legally blind and visually impaired undergraduate and graduate students pursuing a degree in one of above fields. Must be US citizen. Must submit written documentation of visual impairment from ophthalmologist or optometrist (need not be legally blind); official transcripts; proof of college/university acceptance; three letters of recommendation; and typewritten statement describing goals, work experience, extracurricular activities, and how monies will be used.

1 award annually. See website or contact Julie Tucker at AFB for an application.

1435—AMERICAN GEOLOGICAL INSTITUTE (AGI Minority Geoscience Scholarships)

4220 King Street
Alexandria VA 22302-1502
703/379-2480
FAX 703/379-7563
E-mail: ehr@agiweb.org
Internet: www.agiweb.org

AMOUNT: Varies
DEADLINE(S): FEB 1
FIELD(S): Geoscience

Open to full-time undergrads or grads majoring in geology, geophysics, geochemistry, hydrology, meteorology, physical oceanography, planetary geology, or earth science education. NOT for engineering, mathematics, or natural science majors.

Must be ethnic minority and US citizen. Financial need must be demonstrated. Must reapply for renewal. Contact Veronika Litvale at above location for details.

1436—AMERICAN INDIAN SCIENCE AND ENGINEERING SOCIETY (A.T. Anderson Memorial Scholarship)

P.O. Box 9828
Albuquerque NM 87119-9828
505/765-1052
FAX: 505/765-5608
E-mail: scholarships@aises.org
Internet: www.aises.org/scholarships

AMOUNT: $1,000-$2,000
DEADLINE(S): JUN 15
FIELD(S): Medicine, Natural Resources, Science, Engineering

Open to undergraduate and graduate students who are at least 1/4 American Indian or recognized as member of a tribe. Must be member of AISES ($10 fee), enrolled full-time at an accredited institution, and demonstrate financial need.

Renewable. See website or contact Patricia Browne for an application and/or membership information.

1437—AMERICAN WATER RESOURCES ASSOCIATION (Richard A. Herbert Memorial Scholarships)

101 Comer Hall
Auburn Univ AL 36849-5431
715/355-3684
FAX: 715/355-3648
E-mail: stdi@ltus.com
Internet: www.uwin.siu.ed/~awra

AMOUNT: $1,000 + complimentary AWRA membership
DEADLINE(S): APR 30
FIELD(S): Water Resources & related fields

For full-time undergraduates working towards 1st degree and for graduates. Based on academic performance, including cumulative GPA, relevance of curriculum to water resources, and leadership in extracurricular activities related to water resources. Quality and relevance of research is also considered from graduate students. Transcripts, letters of reference, and summary of academic interests/achievements, extracurricular interests, and career goals required (2 page limit).

2 awards annually: 1 undergrad and 1 graduate. Recipients announced in the summer. Contact Stephen Dickman, AWRA Student Activities Committee, for an application.

1438—BROOKHAVEN WOMEN IN SCIENCE (Renate W. Chasman Scholarship)

P.O. Box 183
Upton NY 11973-5000
E-mail: pam@bnl.gov

AMOUNT: $2,000
DEADLINE(S): APR 1
FIELD(S): Natural Sciences, Engineering, Mathematics

Open ONLY to women who are residents of the boroughs of Brooklyn or Queens or the counties of Nassau or Suffolk in New York who are re-entering school after a period of study. For juniors, seniors, or first-year graduate students.

1 award annually. Not renewable. Contact Pam Mansfield at above location for an application. Phone calls are NOT accepted.

1439—COMMUNITY FOUNDATION OF WESTERN MASSACHUSETTS (Nate McKinney Memorial Scholarship)

1500 Main Street
P.O. Box 15769
Springfield MA 01115
413/732-2858

AMOUNT: $1,000
DEADLINE(S): APR 15
FIELD(S): Music, Athletics, Science

Open to graduating seniors of Gateway Regional High School in Huntington, Massachusetts. Recipient must excel academically, demonstrate good citizenship, and have a strong interest in at least two of the following areas: music, science, and athletics. Based on financial need, academic merit, and extracurricular activities. Must submit transcripts and fill out government FAFSA form.

1 award annually. Renewable up to 4 years with reapplication. Contact Community Foundation for an application and your financial aid office for FAFSA. Notification is in June.

1440—FLORIDA FEDERATION OF GARDEN CLUBS, INC. (FFGC Scholarships for College Students)

6065 21st Street SW
Vero Beach FL 32968-9427
561/778-1023
Internet: www.ffgc.org

AMOUNT: $1,500-$3,500
DEADLINE(S): MAY 1
FIELD(S): Ecology, Environmental Issues, Land Management, City Planning, Environmental Control, Horticulture, Landscape Design, Conservation, Botany, Forestry, Marine Biology, Floriculture, Agriculture

Various scholarships for Florida residents with a "B" average or better enrolled full-time as a junior, senior, or graduate student at a Florida college or university.

See website or contact Melba Campbell at FFGC for an application.

1441—FLORIDA FEDERATION OF GARDEN CLUBS, INC. (FFGC Scholarships for High School Students)

6065 21st Street SW
Vero Beach FL 32968-9427
561/778-1023
Internet: www.ffgc.org

AMOUNT: $1,500

DEADLINE(S): MAY 1
FIELD(S): Ecology, Environmental Issues, Land Management, City Planning, Environmental Control, Horticulture, Landscape Design, Conservation, Botany, Forestry, Marine Biology, Floriculture, Agriculture

Scholarships for Florida residents with a "B" average or better who will be incoming freshmen at a Florida college or university.

See website or contact Melba Campbell at FFGC for an application.

1442—LOUISIANA OFFICE OF STUDENT FINANCIAL ASSISTANCE (Rockefeller State Wildlife Scholarship)

P.O. Box 91202
Baton Rouge LA 70821-9202
800/259-5626, ext. 1012
FAX: 504/922-0790
Internet: www.osfa.state.la.us

AMOUNT: $1,000/yr.
DEADLINE(S): JUN 1
FIELD(S): Forestry, Wildlife, Marine Science

Open to Louisiana residents pursuing undergraduate or graduate study in a Louisiana college/university. Must have minimum 2.5 GPA. Recipients must attain a degree in one of the three eligible fields or repay the funds plus interest.

30 awards annually. Renewable up to 5 years undergraduate study and 2 years graduate study. Apply by completing the Free Application for Federal Student Aid (FAFSA). See your school's financial aid office or contact LOSFA for FAFSA form.

1443—OFFICE OF NAVAL RESEARCH (NSAP—Naval Science Awards Program)

ONR 353
800 N. Quincy Street
Arlington VA 22217-5660
800/422-6727 or 703/696-5787
E-mail: thurmab@onrhq.onr.navy.mil
Internet: www.onr.navy.mil or www.jshs.org

AMOUNT: $2,000-$20,000
DEADLINE(S): Varies (established by individual regional, state, and district science fairs)
FIELD(S): Science, Engineering

For high school students (grades 9-12) who participate in a regional/district/state science fair. Winners can participate in Junior Science & Humanities Symposia (JSHS) Program. Awards also offered in

each of 14 categories at International Science & Engineering Fair (ISEF), sponsored by Science Service, Inc. Must be US citizen or permanent resident.

24 awards annually. Renewable. See website or contact Mrs. Barbara M. Thurman (Project Officer) at address above for complete information on NSAP, ISEF, & JSHS.

1444—OPEN SOCIETY INSTITUTE (Environmental Management Fellowships)

400 West 59th Street
New York NY 10019
212/548-0600 or 212/757-2323
FAX: 212/548-4679 or 212/548-4600
Internet: www.soros.org/efp.html

AMOUNT: Fees, room, board, living stipend, textbooks, international transportation, health insurance
DEADLINE(S): NOV 15
FIELD(S): Earth Sciences, Natural Sciences, Humanities (exc. language), Anthropology, Sociology, Mathematics, or Engineering

Two-year fellowships for use in selected universities in the US for international students. For students/professionals in fields related to environmental policy, legislation, and remediation techniques applicable to their home countries.

To apply, contact your local Soros Foundation or Open Society Institute. Further details on website.

1445—OUR WORLD-UNDERWATER SCHOLARSHIP SOCIETY (Scholarship & Internships)

P.O. Box 4428
Chicago IL 60680
312/666-6525
FAX: 312/666-6846
Internet: www.owuscholarship.org

AMOUNT: $20,000 (experience-based scholarship)
DEADLINE(S): NOV 30
FIELD(S): Marine & Aquatics related disciplines

Must be certified SCUBA divers no younger than 21 and no older than 24 on March 1st of the scholarship year. Cannot have yet received a postgraduate degree. Experiences include active participation in field studies, underwater research, scientific expeditions, laboratory assignments, equipment testing and design, and photographic instruction. Financial need NOT a factor. Funds are used for transportation and minimal living expenses, if necessary.

1 scholarship and several internships annually. Contact the Secretary for an application.

1446—PENINSULA COMMUNITY FOUNDATION (Dr. Mary Finegold Scholarship)

1700 S. El Camino Real, #300
San Mateo CA 94402
650/358-9369
FAX: 650/358-9817

AMOUNT: $1,000
DEADLINE(S): MAR 27 (5 P.M.)
FIELD(S): Sciences

Scholarships for senior girls graduating from high school in Palo Alto, California, who intend to complete a four-year degree in the sciences. Special consideration will be given to girls who have demonstrated a "pioneering" spirit in that they have not been constrained by stereotypical female roles and to those facing financial hardship.

Award was established in the honor of Dr. Mary Finegold who, after completing her medical studies, elected to stay at home until her youngest child was in high school before beginning her medical practice. She was a school physician.

1447—SAN DIEGO AEROSPACE MUSEUM (Bill Gibbs Scholarship)

Education Dept.
2001 Pan American Plaza
San Diego CA 92101
619/234-8291, ext. 19
FAX: 619/233-4526
Internet: aerospacemuseum.org/Scholastic.HTML

AMOUNT: Varies
DEADLINE(S): Varies
FIELD(S): Aerospace: math, physics, science, or engineering

For students who are residents of San Diego County, California, who have an aerospace career interest and who have been accepted to a four-year college or university in a degree program relating to math, physics, science, or engineering.

Call or write museum for further information.

1448—SEASPACE (Scholarships)

P.O. Box 3753
Houston TX 77253-3753

E-mail: captx@iname.com
Internet: www.seaspace.ycg.org/schship.htm

AMOUNT: $1,000-$4,000
DEADLINE(S): FEB 1
FIELD(S): Marine/Aquatic Sciences

Open to college juniors, seniors, and graduate students attending school in the US. Must have a 3.3/4.0 GPA and demonstrate financial need.

15-25 awards annually. Not renewable. See website or contact Carolyn Peterson for an application.

1449—STUDENT CONSERVATION ASSOCIATION (SCA Resource Assistant Program)

P.O. Box 550
Charlestown NH 03603
603/543-1700
FAX: 603/543-1828
E-mail: internships@sca-inc.org
Internet: www.sca-inc.org

AMOUNT: $1,180-$4,725
DEADLINE(S): Varies
FIELD(S): Environment & related fields

Must be 18 and US citizen; need not be student. Fields: Agriculture, archaeology, anthropology, botany, caves, civil/environmental engineering, environmental education, fisheries, forests, herpetology, history, living history/roleplaying, visitor services, landscape architectural/environmental design, paleontology, recreation/resource/range management, trail maintenance/construction, wildlife management, geology, hydrology, library/museums, surveying.

900 positions in US and Canada. Send $1 for postage for application; outside US/Canada, send $20.

1450—UNCF/MERCK SCIENCE INITIATIVE (Undergraduate Science Research Scholarship Awards)

8260 Willow Oaks Corporate Drive
P.O. Box 10444
Fairfax VA 22031-4511
703/205-3503
FAX: 703/205-3574
E-mail: uncfmerck@uncf.org
Internet: www.uncf.org/merck

AMOUNT: $25,000/yr. (max.)
DEADLINE(S): JAN 31
FIELD(S): Life & Physical Sciences

Open to African-Americans in their junior year of college who will receive a bachelor's degree in the following academ-

ic year. Must be enrolled full-time in any four-year college/university in the US and have a minimum 3.3 GPA. Must be US citizen/permanent resident. Financial need NOT a factor.

15 awards annually. Not renewable. Contact Jerry Bryant, Ph.D., for an application.

1451—U.S. DEPARTMENT OF AGRICULTURE (1890 National Scholars Program)

14th & Independence Ave. SW
Room 301-W, Whitten Bldg.
Washington DC 20250-9600
202/720-6905
E-mail: usda-m@fie.com
Internet: web.fie.com/htdoc/fed/agr/ars/edu/prog/mti/agrpgaak.htm

AMOUNT: Tuition, employment/benefits, use of PC/software, fees, books, room/board
DEADLINE(S): JAN 15
FIELD(S): Agriculture, Food, or Natural Resource sciences

For US citizens, high school grad/GED, GPA 3.0+, verbal/math SAT 1,000+, composite score 21+ ACT, 1st-yr college student, and attend participating school.

34+ scholarships/yr/4 years. Send applications to USDA Liaison Officer at the 1890 Institution of your choice (see Web page for complete list).

1452—WATER ENVIRONMENT FEDERATION (Student Paper Competition)

Access website
Internet: www.wef.org

AMOUNT: $1,000 (1st prize); $500 (2nd); $250 (3rd)
DEADLINE(S): FEB 1
FIELD(S): Water pollution control and related fields

Awards for 500 1,000-word abstracts dealing with water pollution control, water quality problems, water-related concerns, or hazardous wastes. Open to undergrad (A.A. and B.A.) and grad students.

Also open to recently graduated students (within 1 calendar year of Feb. 1 deadline). See website for details—go to "Member Programs" then to "Student Paper Competition." Organization will not mail this information.

1453—WOMAN'S SEAMEN'S FRIEND SOCIETY OF CONNECTICUT, INC. (Scholarships)

74 Forbes Ave.
New Haven CT 06512
203/467-3887

AMOUNT: Varies
DEADLINE(S): APR 1 (summer); MAY 15 (fall/spring)
FIELD(S): Marine Sciences, Merchant Seafarers

Open to Connecticut residents who are merchant seafarers and their dependents attending any institution of higher learning; CT residents studying at state maritime academies; CT residents majoring in marine science in-state or out-of-state; and residents of other states majoring in marine science in CT. Based on financial need, academic achievement, letters of recommendation, and proposed programs of study. Awards also available for graduate work in marine science.

Renewable. Contact Woman's Seamen's Friend Society for applications.

1454—WOODS HOLE OCEANOGRAPHIC INSTITUTION (Summer Student Fellowship)

360 Woods Hole Road
Woods Hole MA 02543-1541
508/289-2219
FAX: 508/457-2188
E-mail: education@whoi.edu
Internet: www.whoi.edu

AMOUNT: $335/week stipend for 10-12 weeks, housing, & possible travel allowance
DEADLINE(S): FEB 16
FIELD(S): Science/engineering with interest in ocean sciences

Summer fellowships to study oceanography at the Woods Hole Oceanographic Institution. Open to undergraduates who have completed their junior or senior years. Students with backgrounds in science, math, and engineering with interests in the marine sciences and oceanography are encouraged to apply.

For an application/more information, contact the Education Office, Clark Laboratory 223, MS #31, at above address.

1455—WOODS HOLE OCEANOGRAPHIC INSTITUTION (Traineeships in Oceanography for Minority Group Undergraduates)

360 Woods Hole Road
Woods Hole MA 02543-1541

508/289-2219
FAX: 508/457-2188
E-mail: mgately@whoi.edu
Internet: www.whoi.edu

AMOUNT: Varies
DEADLINE(S): FEB 16
FIELD(S): Physical/Natural Sciences, Mathematics, Engineering

For minority undergraduates enrolled in US colleges/universities who have completed at least two semesters. These awards provide training and research experience for students with interests in the above fields. Traineeships may be awarded for a ten- to twelve-week period in the summer or for a semester during the academic year.

Renewable. For an application/more information, contact the Education Office, Clark Laboratory 223, MS #31, at above address.

NATURAL HISTORY

1456—ALLIANCE FOR YOUNG ARTISTS AND WRITERS, INC./AMERICAN MUSEUM OF NATURAL HISTORY (Young Naturalist Awards)

Scholastic, Inc.
555 Broadway
New York NY 10012-3999
212/343-6582 or 800-SCHOLASTIC
FAX: 212/343-4885
E-mail: mjohnson@scholastic.com
Internet: www.amnh.org/youngnaturalistawards

AMOUNT: up to $2,500 + trip to New York to visit AMNH
DEADLINE(S): JAN 3
FIELD(S): Natural Sciences

For all students in grades 7-12 currently enrolled in a public or non-public school in the US, Canada, US territories, or US-sponsored schools abroad. Program focuses on finding and rewarding excellence in biology, earth science, astronomy, and cultural studies. Students are encouraged to perform observation-based projects that require creativity, inquiry, and critical analysis. Specific topics vary annually.

48 awards annually. See website or contact Mike Johnson, Program Manager, for an application.

1457—ASSOCIATION FOR WOMEN IN SCIENCE EDUCATIONAL FOUNDATION (Dr. Vicki L. Schechtman Scholarship)

1200 New York Ave. NW, Suite 650
Washington DC 20005

202/326-8940 or 800/886-AWIS
E-mail: awis@awis.org
Internet: www.awis.org

AMOUNT: $1,000
DEADLINE(S): JAN 16
FIELD(S): Various Sciences and Social Sciences

For female undergraduate students who are US citizens and have a minimum GPA of 3.0. Summary page, essay describing career aspirations, transcripts, proof of matriculation (if available), and two reference letters required with application. Scholarships may be used for tuition, books, housing, research, equipment, etc.

See website or write to above address for an application and more information.

1458—ASSOCIATION FOR WOMEN IN SCIENCE EDUCATIONAL FOUNDATION (Ruth Satter Memorial Award)

1200 New York Ave. NW, Suite 650
Washington DC 20005
202/326-8940 or 800/886-AWIS
E-mail: awis@awis.org
Internet: www.awis.org

AMOUNT: $1,000
DEADLINE(S): JAN 16
FIELD(S): Various Sciences and Social Sciences

Scholarships for female doctoral students who have interrupted their education three years or more to raise a family. Summary page, description of research project, resume, references, transcripts, biographical sketch, and proof of eligibility from department head required. US citizens may attend any graduate institution; noncitizens must be enrolled in US institutions.

See website or write to above address for more information or an application.

1459—NAVAL HISTORICAL CENTER (Internship Program)

Washington Navy Yard
901 M Street SE
Washington DC 20374-5060
202/433-6901
FAX: 202/433-8200
E-mail: efurgol@nhc.navy.mil
Internet: www.history.navy.mil

AMOUNT: $400 possible honoraria; otherwise, unpaid
DEADLINE(S): None
FIELD(S): Education, History, Public Relations, Design

Registered students of colleges/universities and graduates thereof are eligible for this program, which must be a minimum of

3 weeks, full or part-time. Four specialities available: Curator, Education, Public Relations, and Design. Interns receive orientation and assist in their departments, and must complete individual project which contributes to Center. Must submit a letter of recommendation, unofficial transcript, and writing sample of not less than 1,000 words.

Contact Dr. Edward M. Furgol, Curator, for an application.

1460—PENINSULA COMMUNITY FOUNDATION (Dr. Mary Finegold Scholarship)

1700 S. El Camino Real, #300
San Mateo CA 94402
650/358-9369
FAX: 650/358-9817

AMOUNT: $1,000
DEADLINE(S): MAR 27 (5 P.M.)
FIELD(S): Sciences

Scholarships for senior girls graduating from high school in Palo Alto, California, who intend to complete a four-year degree in the sciences. Special consideration will be given to girls who have demonstrated a "pioneering" spirit in that they have not been constrained by stereotypical female roles and to those facing financial hardship.

Award was established in the honor of Dr. Mary Finegold who, after completing her medical studies, elected to stay at home until her youngest child was in high school before beginning her medical practice. She was a school physician.

1461—ROSE HILL COLLEGE (Louella Robinson Memorial Scholarship)

P.O. Box 3126
Aiken SC 29802-3126
800/684-3769
FAX: 803/641-0240
E-mail: rosehill@.edu
Internet: www.rosehill.edu

AMOUNT: $10,000/yr. for four years
DEADLINE(S): Varies
FIELD(S): Liberal arts and humanities curricula

For undergraduate residents of Indian River County, Florida, to attend Rose Hill College in Aiken, South Carolina. The school offers a liberal arts education and follows the Great Books curriculum, a program of reading and seminars.

1 annual award. Applicants must meet entry requirements of RHC. Contact above location for details.

1462—ROSE HILL COLLEGE (Scholarships for Children of Eastern Orthodox Priests/Deacons)

P.O. Box 3126
Aiken SC 29802-3126
800/684-3769
FAX: 803/641-0240
E-mail: rosehill@edu
Internet: www.rosehill.edu

AMOUNT: Full scholarship: $10,000/yr. for four years
DEADLINE(S): Varies
FIELD(S): Liberal arts and humanities curricula

For undergraduates who are children of Eastern Orthodox Christian priests or deacons to attend Rose Hill College in Aiken, South Carolina. The school offers a liberal arts education and follows the Great Books curriculum, a program of reading and seminars.

6-10 annual awards. Applicants must meet entry requirements of RHC. Contact above location for details.

1463—ROSE HILL COLLEGE (Scholarships for the Homeschooled)

P.O. Box 3126
Aiken SC 29802-3126
800/684-3769
FAX: 803/641-0240
E-mail: rosehill@rosehill.edu
Internet: www.resehill.edu

AMOUNT: Full scholarship: $10,000/yr. for four years
DEADLINE(S): Varies
FIELD(S): Liberal arts and humanities curricula

For undergraduates who have been homeschooled for three of the last five years of their high school education. For use at Rose Hill College in Aiken, South Carolina. The school offers a liberal arts education and follows the Great Books curriculum, a program of reading and seminars. Scholarships will be awarded primarily on the basis of an essay which the student will be asked to write.

4 annual awards. Applicants must meet entry requirements of RHC. Contact above location for details.

1464—SAN DIEGO AEROSPACE MUSEUM (Bill Gibbs Scholarship)

Education Dept.
2001 Pan American Plaza
San Diego CA 92101
619/234-8291, ext. 19
FAX: 619/233-4526
Internet: aerospacemuseum.org/ Scholastic.HTML

AMOUNT: Varies
DEADLINE(S): Varies
FIELD(S): Aerospace: math, physics, science, or engineering

For students who are residents of San Diego County, California, who have an aerospace career interest and who have been accepted to a four-year college or university in a degree program relating to math, physics, science, or engineering.

Call or write museum for further information.

1465—SMITHSONIAN INSTITUTION (Cooper-Hewitt, National Design Museum-Mark Kaminski Summer Internship)

2 East 91st Street
New York NY 10128
212/860-6868
FAX: 212/860-6909

AMOUNT: $2,500 for 10-week period
DEADLINE(S): MAR 31
FIELD(S): Architecture, Architectural History, Design and Criticism, Museum Education, Museum Studies

These internships are open to college students considering a career in one of the above areas of study. Also open to graduate students who have not yet completed their M.A. degree. This ten-week program is designed to acquaint participants with the programs, policies, procedures, and operations of Cooper-Hewitt Museum and of museums in general.

1 award each summer. Internship commences in June and ends in August. Housing is not provided. Write to Linda Herd at the above address for complete information.

1466—SMITHSONIAN INSTITUTION (Cooper-Hewitt, National Design Museum-Peter Krueger Summer Internship Program)

Cooper-Hewitt National Design Museum
2 East 91st Street
New York NY 10128
212/860-6868
FAX: 212/860-6909

AMOUNT: $2,500
DEADLINE(S): MAR 31
FIELD(S): Art History, Design, Museum Studies, and Museum Education, or Architectural History

Ten-week summer internships open to graduate and undergraduate students considering a career in the museum profession. Interns will assist on special research or exhibition projects and participate in daily museum activities.

6 awards each summer. Internship commences in June and ends in August. Housing is not provided. Write for complete information.

1467—SMITHSONIAN INSTITUTION (Minority Student Internship Program)

Fellowships & Grants
955 L'Enfant Plaza, Suite 7000
MRC 902
Washington DC 20560
202/287-3271
FAX: 202/287-3691
E-mail: siofg@ofg.si.edu
Internet: www.si.edu/research+study

AMOUNT: $300/week + possible travel expenses
DEADLINE(S): FEB 15
FIELD(S): Humanities, Environmental Studies, Cultural Studies, Natural History, Earth Science, Art History, Biology, & related fields

Ten-week internships in residence at the Smithsonian for US minority students to participate in research or museum-related activities in above fields. For undergrads or grads with at least a 3.0 GPA. Essay, resume, transcripts, and references required with application. Internships are full-time and are offered for Summer, Fall, or Spring tenures. Write for application.

1468—STUDENT CONSERVATION ASSOCI-ATION (SCA Resource Assistant Program)

P.O. Box 550
Charlestown NH 03603
603/543-1700
FAX: 603/543-1828
E-mail: internships@sca-inc.org
Internet: www.sca-inc.org

AMOUNT: $1,180-$4,725
DEADLINE(S): Varies
FIELD(S): Environment & related fields

Must be 18 and US citizen; need not be student. Fields: Agriculture, archaeology, anthropology, botany, caves, civil/environmental engineering, environmental education, fisheries, forests, herpetology, history, living history/roleplaying, visitor services, landscape architectural/environmental design, paleontology, recreation/resource/range management, trail maintenance/construction, wildlife management, geology, hydrology, library/museums, surveying.

900 positions in US and Canada. Send $1 for postage for application; outside US/Canada, send $20.

1469—TEXAS SOCIETY OF PROFESSION-AL ENGINEERS (Scholarships)

P.O. Box 2145
Austin TX 78768
512/472-9286 or 800/580-8973
Internet: www.tspe.org

AMOUNT: Varies
DEADLINE(S): JAN 30
FIELD(S): Engineering (math, sciences)

Scholarships for graduating high school seniors who are Texas residents planning to attend Texas engineering colleges

Contact organization for details. Application is on website.

1470—U.S. MARINE CORPS HISTORICAL CENTER (College Internships)

Building 58
Washington Navy Yard
Washington DC 20374
202/433-3839

AMOUNT: Stipend to cover daily expenses
DEADLINE(S): None specified
FIELD(S): US Military History, Library Science, History, Museum Studies

Open to undergraduate students at a college or university which will grant academic credit for work experience as interns at the address above or at the Marine Corps Air-Ground Museum in Quantico, Virginia.

All internships are regarded as beginning professional-level historian, curator, librarian, or archivist positions. Write for complete information.

SCHOOL OF SCIENCE

1471—AIR FORCE RESERVE OFFICER TRAINING CORPS (AFROTC Scholarships)

551 E. Maxwell Blvd.
Maxwell AFB AL 36112-6106
334/953-7783

AMOUNT: Full tuition, books, & fees for all 4 years of college
DEADLINE(S): DEC 1
FIELD(S): Science, Engineering, Business, Political Science, Psychology, Geography, Foreign Studies, Foreign Language

Competitive scholarships based on individual merit to high school seniors and graduates who have not completed any full-time college work. Must be a US citizen between the ages of 17-27. Must also have GPA of 2.5 or above, be in top 40% of class, and complete Applicant Fitness Test. Cannot be a single parent. Your college/university must offer AFROTC.

2,300 awards annually. Contact above address for application packet.

1472—ALPHA KAPPA ALPHA SORORITY INC. (AKA/PIMS Summer Youth Mathematics & Science Camp)

5656 S. Stony Island Ave.
Chicago IL 60637
312/684-1282

AMOUNT: $1,000 value (for room; board & travel)
DEADLINE(S): MAY 1
FIELD(S): Mathematics, Science

Open to high school students grades 9-11 who have at least a 'B' average. Essay required for entry. This 2-week camp includes A.M. classes; P.M. activities and a minimum of 4 field trips.

30 awards. Write for complete information.

1473—ALVIN M. BENTLEY FOUNDATION (Scholarship Program)

P.O. Box 1516
Owosso MI 48867
517/729-9040
FAX: 517/723-2454

AMOUNT: $40,000 (4-year); $1,000/yr. (freshman)
DEADLINE(S): None
FIELD(S): Literature, Science, Arts

Open to Michigan residents applying as freshmen to the University of Michigan's College of Literature, Science, and the Arts. Based on academic excellence and extracurricular activities. Must be nominated; there are no separate applications. Candidates are chosen from U of M applications received from Michigan resident freshmen.

4 four-year awards and 8 freshman awards annually. Contact University of Michigan for details.

1474—AMERICAN FOUNDATION FOR THE BLIND (Paul W. Ruckes Scholarship)

11 Penn Plaza, Suite. 300
New York NY 10001
212/502-7661
FAX: 212/502-7771
E-mail: juliet@afb.org
Internet: www.afb.org

AMOUNT: $1,000
DEADLINE(S): APR 30

FIELD(S): Engineering, Computer/ Physical/Life Sciences

Open to legally blind and visually impaired undergraduate and graduate students pursuing a degree in one of above fields. Must be US citizen. Must submit written documentation of visual impairment from ophthalmologist or optometrist (need not be legally blind); official transcripts; proof of college/university acceptance; three letters of recommendation; and typewritten statement describing goals, work experience, extracurricular activities, and how monies will be used.

1 award annually. See website or contact Julie Tucker at AFB for an application.

1475—AMERICAN INDIAN SCIENCE AND ENGINEERING SOCIETY (A.T. Anderson Memorial Scholarship)

P.O. Box 9828
Albuquerque NM 87119-9828
505/765-1052
FAX: 505/765-5608
E-mail: scholarships@aises.org
Internet: www.aises.org/scholarships
AMOUNT: $1,000-$2,000
DEADLINE(S): JUN 15
FIELD(S): Medicine, Natural Resources, Science, Engineering

Open to undergraduate and graduate students who are at least 1/4 American Indian or recognized as member of a tribe. Must be member of AISES ($10 fee), enrolled full-time at an accredited institution, and demonstrate financial need.

Renewable. See website or contact Patricia Browne for an application and/or membership information.

1476—AMERICAN INDIAN SCIENCE AND ENGINEERING SOCIETY (Burlington Northern Santa Fe Pacific Foundation Scholarships)

P.O. Box 9828
Albuquerque NM 87119-9828
505/765-1052
FAX: 505/765-5608
E-mail: scholarships@aises.org
Internet: www.aises.org/scholarships
AMOUNT: $2,500/yr.
DEADLINE(S): MAR 31
FIELD(S): Business, Education, Science, Engineering, Health Administration

Open to high school seniors who are at least 1/4 American Indian. Must reside in KS, OK, CO, AZ, NM, MN, ND, OR, SD, WA, MT, or San Bernardino County, CA (Burlington Northern and Santa Fe Pacific service areas). Must demonstrate financial need.

5 awards annually. Renewable up to 4 years. See website or contact Patricia Browne for an application.

1477—AMERICAN RADIO RELAY LEAGUE FOUNDATION (The Henry Broughton, K2AE Memorial Scholarship)

225 Main Street
Newington CT 06111
860/594-0200
FAX: 860/594-0259
Internet: www.arrl.org/
AMOUNT: $1,000
DEADLINE(S): FEB 1
FIELD(S): Engineering, Science

For radio amateurs with a general class license whose home residence is within 70 miles of Schenectady, New York. For study leading to a bachelor's degree at an accredited four-year college/university.

1+ awards annually. Contact ARRL for an application.

1478—ASSOCIATED WESTERN UNIVERSITIES, INC. (AWU Undergraduate Student Fellowships)

4190 South Highland Drive
Suite 211
Salt Lake City UT 84124-2600
801/273-8911
FAX: 801/277-5632
Internet: www.awu.org
AMOUNT: $300/week stipend + travel allowance
DEADLINE(S): FEB 1
FIELD(S): Mathematics, Engineering, Technology, Science

Eight- to- sixteen-week fellowships for undergraduate students enrolled in accredited institutions and who have completed at least one year of college by the start of the fellowship. Applicants reviewed on the basis of academic performance/class standing, career goals, recommendations, and compatibility of scientific interests and abilities with the needs and resources of the host facility. Citizenship restrictions may apply for some facilities.

500+ awards annually. Renewable (competitively with new application). Contact above address for an application.

1479—ASSOCIATED WESTERN UNIVERSITIES, INC. (AWU Visiting Scientist Fellowships)

4190 South Highland Dr., Suite 211
Salt Lake City UT 84124-2600
801/273-8900
AMOUNT: Varies
DEADLINE(S): Varies (Two months prior to starting date)
FIELD(S): Engineering, Science, Mathematics, and Technology

Research fellowships for professionals with continued commitment to science and engineering. For use at one of 62 participating universities. US citizenship or permanent residency required.

For detailed information and list of cooperating facitilies contact above location.

1480—BFGOODRICH (Collegiate Inventors Program) (BFG-CIP)

c/o Inventure Place
221 S. Broadway Street
Akron OH 44308-1505
330/849-6887
E-mail: pkunce@invent.org
AMOUNT: Varies
DEADLINE(S): JUN 3
FIELD(S): Invention, Idea, or Process

National competition for college and university students across the country whose innovations, discoveries, and research are deemed the year's most outstanding. Must be an original idea and the work of a student or team with his/her university advisor. Should be reproducible; may not have been 1) available to public or 2) patented/published more than one year prior to submission.

Up to 3 entries. All-Collegiate category will receive $7,500 prize; their advisors $2,500 each. In addition, up to 3 undergrad entries receive $3,000; their advisors $1,000 each. Students may enter as teams. Contact Paul Kunce, Program Coordinator, for more information.

1481—BUSINESS & PROFESSIONAL WOMEN'S FOUNDATION (BPW Career Advancement Scholarship Program)

2012 Massachusetts Ave. NW
Washington DC 20036-1070
202/293-1200, ext. 169
FAX: 202/861-0298

Internet: www.bpwusa.org

AMOUNT: $500-$1,000

DEADLINE(S): APR 15

FIELD(S): Biology, Science, Education, Engineering, Social Science, Paralegal, Humanities, Business, Math, Computers, Law, MD, DD

For women (US citizens) aged 25+ accepted into accredited program at US institution (+Puerto Rico & Virgin Islands). Must graduate within 12 to 24 months from the date of grant and demonstrate critical financial need. Must have a plan to upgrade skills, train for a new career field, or to enter/re-enter the job market.

Full- or part-time study. For info see website or send business-sized, self-addressed, double-stamped envelope.

1482—CAREER OPPORTUNITIES FOR YOUTH, INC. (Collegiate Scholarship Program)

P.O. Box 996
Manhattan Beach CA 90266
310/535-4838

AMOUNT: $250 to $1,000

DEADLINE(S): SEP 30

FIELD(S): Engineering, Science, Mathematics, Computer Science, Business Administration, Education, Nursing

For students of Latino/Hispanic background residing in the Southern California area who have completed at least one semester/quarter of study at an accredited four-year university. Must have a cumulative GPA of 2.5 or higher.

Priority will be given to students who demonstrate financial need. Send SASE to above location for details.

1483—CIVIL AIR PATROL (CAP Undergraduate Scholarships)

Civil Air Patrol
National Headquarters
Maxwell AFB AL 36112-6332
334/953-5315

AMOUNT: $750

DEADLINE(S): JAN 31

FIELD(S): Humanities, Science, Engineering, Education

Open to CAP members who have received the Billy Mitchell Award or the senior rating in Level II of the senior training program. For undergraduate study in the above areas.

Write for complete information.

1484—COMMUNITY FOUNDATION OF WESTERN MASSACHUSETTS (Nate McKinney Memorial Scholarship)

1500 Main Street
P.O. Box 15769
Springfield MA 01115
413/732-2858

AMOUNT: $1,000

DEADLINE(S): APR 15

FIELD(S): Music; Athletics; Science

Open to graduating seniors of Gateway Regional High School in Huntington, Massachusetts. Recipient must excel academically, demonstrate good citizenship, and have a strong interest in at least two of the following areas: music, science, and athletics. Based on financial need, academic merit, and extracurricular activities. Must submit transcripts and fill out government FAFSA form.

1 award annually. Renewable up to 4 years with reapplication. Contact Community Foundation for an application and your financial aid office for FAFSA. Notification is in June.

1485—COMMUNITY FOUNDATION SILICON VALLEY (Valley Scholars Program)

111 W. Saint John Street, Suite 230
San Jose CA 95113
408/278-0270
FAX: 408/278-0280
Internet: www.cfsv.org

AMOUNT: $20,000 (over 4 years of college)

DEADLINE(S): Varies (early spring)

FIELD(S): Science and/or Math

A scholarship program for public high school students in the Silicon Valley (San Mateo and Santa Clara counties and Fremont Union High School District, California) who have demonstrated enthusiasm and aptitude for science and math. Must be US citizen or permanent resident.

Up to 20 students are selected each year. Each Valley Scholar receives financial support, guidance through the college admission process, and a mentor whose interests match their own. Students may apply during their sophomore year of high school and must be academically outstanding.

1486—FREEDOM FROM RELIGION FOUNDATION (Student Essay Contest)

P.O. Box 750
Madison WI 53701

608/256-5800
Internet: www.infidels.org/org/ffrf

AMOUNT: $1,000; $500; $250

DEADLINE(S): JUL 15

FIELD(S): Humanities, English, Education, Philosophy, Science

Essay contest on topics related to church-state entanglement in public schools or growing up a "freethinker" in religious-oriented society. Topics change yearly, but all are on general theme of maintaining separation of church and state. New topics available in February. For high school seniors and currently enrolled college/technical students. Must be US citizen.

Send SASE to address above for complete information. Please indicate whether wanting information for college competition or high school. Information will be sent when new topics are announced each February. See website for details.

1487—GENERAL LEARNING COMMUNICATIONS (DuPont Challenge Science Essay Awards Program)

900 Skokie Blvd., Suite 200
Northbrook IL 60062-4028
847/205-3000
FAX: 847/564-8197
Internet: www.glcomm.com/dupont

AMOUNT: $1,500 (max.)

DEADLINE(S): JAN 28

FIELD(S): Science & Technology

Annual essay competition open to students in grades 7-12 in the US and Canada. Cash awards for 1st, 2nd, and honorable mention. 1st-place essayists in each of two divisions, their science teacher, and a parent of each receive a trip to the Space Center Houston/NASA at the end of April.

102 awards annually. See website or contact your science teacher or GLC for official entry blank.

1488—GEORGE BIRD GRINNELL AMERICAN INDIAN CHILDREN'S FUND (Al Qoyawayma Award)

11602 Montague Ct.
Potomac MD 20854
301/424-2440
FAX: 301/424-8281
E-mail: Grinnell_Fund@MSN.com

AMOUNT: $1,000

DEADLINE(S): JUN 1

FIELD(S): Science, Engineering

Open to Native American undergraduate and graduate students majoring in science or engineering and who have demonstrated an outstanding interest and skill in any one of the arts. Must be American Indian/Alaska Native (documented with Certified Degree of Indian Blood), be enrolled in college/university, be able to demonstrate commitment to serving community or other tribal nations, and document financial need.

Contact Dr. Paula M. Mintzies, President, for an application after January 1st.

1489—GERBER SCIENTIFIC, INC. (H. Joseph Gerber Vision Scholarship Program)

83 Gerber Road West
South Windsor CT 06074
860/648-8027
Internet: www.gerberscientific.com

AMOUNT: Varies
DEADLINE(S): MAR 15
FIELD(S): Engineering, Mathematics, Computer Science, Natural Sciences

Scholarship program for high school seniors in Connecticut.

50 scholarships to be awarded.

1490—JEWISH FEDERATION OF METROPOLITAN CHICAGO (Academic Scholarship Program for Studies in the Sciences)

One South Franklin Street
Chicago IL 60606
Written inquiry

AMOUNT: Varies
DEADLINE(S): MAR 1
FIELD(S): Mathematics, Engineering, or Science

Scholarships for college juniors, seniors, and graduate students who are Jewish and are residents of Chicago, IL and Cook County.

Academic achievement and financial need are considered. Applications accepted after Dec. 1.

1491—JOSEPH BLAZEK FOUNDATION (Scholarships)

8 South Michigan Ave.
Chicago IL 60603
312/372-3880

AMOUNT: $750 per year for 4 years
DEADLINE(S): FEB 1
FIELD(S): Science, Chemistry, Engineering, Mathematics, Physics

Open to residents of Cook County (Illinois) who are high school seniors planning to study in the above fields at a four-year college or university.

20 scholarships per year. Renewable. Write for complete information.

1492—JUNIATA COLLEGE (Robert Steele Memorial Scholarship)

Financial Aid Office
Huntingdon PA 16652
814/641-3603
FAX: 814/641-3355
E-mail: clarkec@juniata.edu

AMOUNT: $4,000 (max.)
DEADLINE(S): APR 1
FIELD(S): Science, Medical Studies

Open to science/medical students applying to Juniata College. Must demonstrate financial need and fill out government FAFSA form.

Contact Cynthia G. Clarke, Research Specialist, for an application or enrollment information. See your financial aid office for FAFSA.

1493—KOREAN-AMERICAN SCIENTISTS AND ENGINEERS ASSOCIATION (KSEA Scholarships)

1952 Gallows Road, Suite 300
Vienna VA 22182
703/748-1221
FAX: 703/748-1331
E-mail: admin@ksea.org
Internet: www.ksea.org

AMOUNT: $1,000
DEADLINE(S): FEB 28
FIELD(S): Science, Engineering, or Medicine

Scholarships to encourage Korean-American students to study in a science, engineering, or pre-med discipline and to recognize high-performing students. Must have graduated from a high school in the US.

5 to 8 awards yearly. Must be a student member of KSEA or a child of a member.

1494—MARYLAND HIGHER EDUCATION COMMISSION (Maryland Science and Technology Scholarship Program)

16 Francis Street
Annapolis Park MD 21401
410/974-5370 or 800/974-1024
E-mail: ssamail@mhec.state.md.us
Internet: http://www.mhec.state.md.us/SSA/stech_qa.htm

AMOUNT: $3,000/yr. (B.A.); $1,000/yr. (A.A.)
DEADLINE(S): None
FIELD(S): Computer Science; Engineering; Technology

Scholarships for college-bound Maryland high school seniors who will major in one of the above fields and who are accepted to an eligible associate or bachelor's degree program in Maryland. Students in the class of 1999 were eligible for the first awards. The deadline was not known at this writing, so check for deadline date. Must agree to work in the state after graduation in a related field, one year for each year of assistance received.

Must maintain a 3.0 GPA.

1495—NATIONAL ITALIAN AMERICAN FOUNDATION (Italian Cultural Society and NIAF Matching Scholarship)

1860 19th Street NW
Washington DC 20009-5599
202/530-5315

AMOUNT: $2,000
DEADLINE(S): MAR 31
FIELD(S): Science or Humanities

Open to undergraduate students of Italian descent majoring in science or the humanities in the Washington DC, Maryland, and Virginia areas. Financial need must be demonstrated.

Write for application and details.

1496—NATIONAL SCIENCE TEACHERS ASSOCIATION (Teacher Award Programs)

1840 Wilson Blvd.
Arlington VA 22201-3000
703/243-7100
Internet: www.nsta.org

AMOUNT: $1,000-$10,000
DEADLINE(S): Varies
FIELD(S): Science

Awards and grants are for school teachers and administrators at all levels for excellence in science teaching. Some require membership in the National Science Teachers Association. Must be US citizen/permanent resident.

See website or contact NSTA for an application.

1497—NATIONAL SPACE CLUB (Dr. Robert H. Goddard Scholarship)

2000 L Street NW, Suite 710
Washington DC 20036-4907
202/973-8661

AMOUNT: $10,000

DEADLINE(S): JAN 8

FIELD(S): Science & Engineering

Open to undergraduate juniors and seniors and graduate students who have scholastic plans leading to future participation in the aerospace sciences and technology. Must be US citizen. Award based on transcript, letters of recommendation, accomplishments, scholastic plans, and proven past research and participation in space-related science and engineering. Personal need is considered, but is not controlling.

Renewable. Send a self-addressed, stamped envelope for more information.

1498—NATIONAL SPACE CLUB (Dr. Robert H. Goddard Historical Essay Award)

2000 L Street NW, Suite 710
Washington DC 20036-4907
202/973-8661

AMOUNT: $1,000 + plaque

DEADLINE(S): DEC 4

FIELD(S): Aerospace History

Essay competition open to any US citizen on a topic dealing with any significant aspect of the historical development of rocketry and astronautics. Essays should not exceed 5,000 words and should be fully documented. Will be judged on originality and scholarship.

Previous winners not eligible. Send self-addressed, stamped envelope for complete information.

1499—NATIONAL TECHNICAL ASSOCIATION, INC. (Scholarship Competitions for Minorities and Women in Science and Engineering)

6919 North 19th Street
Philadelphia PA 19126-1506
215/549-5743
FAX: 215/549-6509
E-mail: ntamfj1@aol.com
Internet: www.huenet.com/nta

AMOUNT: $500-$5,000

DEADLINE(S): Varies

FIELD(S): Science, Mathematics, Engineering, and Applied Technology

Scholarship competitions for minorities and women pursuing degrees in the above fields. Additional scholarships are available through local chapters of NTA.

Check website or write to above address for details and for locations of local chapters.

1500—NATIVE AMERICAN SCHOLARSHIP FUND, INC. (Scholarships)

8200 Mountain Road NE, Suite 203
Albuquerque NM 87110
505/262-2351
FAX: 505/262-0543
E-mail: NScholarsh@aol.com

AMOUNT: Varies

DEADLINE(S): MAR 15; APR 15; SEP 15

FIELD(S): Math, Engineering, Science, Business, Education, Computer Science

Open to American Indians or Alaskan Natives (1/4 degree or more) enrolled as members of a federally recognized, state recognized, or terminated tribe. For graduate or undergraduate study at an accredited four-year college or university.

208 awards annually. Contact Lucille Kelley, Director of Recruitment, for an application.

1501—OFFICE OF NAVAL RESEARCH (NSAP—Naval Science Awards Program)

ONR 353, 800 N. Quincy Street
Arlington VA 22217-5660
800/422-6727 or 703/696-5787
E-mail: thurmab@onrhq.onr.navy.mil
Internet: www.onr.navy.mil or www.jshs.org

AMOUNT: $2,000-$20,000

DEADLINE(S): Varies (established by individual regional, state, and district science fairs)

FIELD(S): Science, Engineering

For high school students (grades 9-12) who participate in a regional/district/state science fair. Winners can participate in Junior Science & Humanities Symposia (JSHS) Program. Awards also offered in each of 14 categories at International Science & Engineering Fair (ISEF), sponsored by Science Service, Inc. Must be US citizen or permanent resident.

24 awards annually. Renewable. See website or contact Mrs. Barbara M. Thurman (Project Officer) at address above for complete information on NSAP, ISEF, & JSHS.

1502—OKLAHOMA MEDICAL RESEARCH FOUNDATION (Sir Alexander Fleming Scholar Program)

825 Northeast 13th Street
Oklahoma City OK 73104
405/271-7218 or
800/522-0211 (in-state)

AMOUNT: $2,500 salary + housing

DEADLINE(S): MAR 1

FIELD(S): Sciences

Summer scholarship program (June and July) for Oklahoma students who have completed their junior year of high school through those in their junior year of college at time of application. Excellent academic standing and aptitude in science and math are essential. Students will work in the laboratories of the above organization. Research projects will be selected from: alcoholism/liver disease, arthritis/immunology, carcinogenesis, cardiovascular biology, and more.

Named for the scientist who discovered penicillin and dedicated OMRF in 1949. Contact organization for further information and application forms.

1503—PENINSULA COMMUNITY FOUNDATION (Dr. Mary Finegold Scholarship)

1700 S. El Camino Real, #300
San Mateo CA 94402
650/358-9369
FAX: 650/358-9817

AMOUNT: $1,000

DEADLINE(S): MAR 27 (5 P.M.)

FIELD(S): Sciences

Scholarships for senior girls graduating from high school in Palo Alto, California, who intend to complete a four-year degree in the sciences. Special consideration will be given to girls who have demonstrated a "pioneering" spirit in that they have not been constrained by stereotypical female roles and to those facing financial hardship.

Award was established in the honor of Dr. Mary Finegold who, after completing her medical studies, elected to stay at home until her youngest child was in high school before beginning her medical practice. She was a school physician.

1504—SAN DIEGO AEROSPACE MUSEUM (Bill Gibbs Scholarship)

Education Dept.
2001 Pan American Plaza
San Diego CA 92101
619/234-8291, ext. 19
FAX: 619/233-4526
Internet: aerospacemuseum.org/ Scholastic.HTML

AMOUNT: Varies

DEADLINE(S): Varies

FIELD(S): Aerospace: math, physics, science, or engineering

For students who are residents of San Diego County, California, who have an aerospace career interest and who have been accepted to a four-year college or university in a degree program relating to math, physics, science, or engineering.

Call or write museum for further information.

1505—SCIENCE SERVICE (Intel International Science & Engineering Fair)

1719 N Street NW
Washington DC 20036
202/785-2255
FAX: 202/785-1243
E-mail: jkim@sciserv.org
Internet: www.sciserv.org

AMOUNT: Varies (totaling $2 million)
DEADLINE(S): DEC 1
FIELD(S): Science, Math, Engineering

Open to high school students (grades 9-12) who participate in this worldwide science competition. Scholarships, internships with noted scientists, and travel and equipment grants are awarded.

Contact Jinny Kim at Science Service for official ISEF entry book. Sponsored by the Intel Corporation.

1506—SCIENCE SERVICE (Intel Science Talent Search)

1719 N Street NW
Washington DC 20036
202/785-2255
FAX: 202/785-1243
E-mail: cmdroms@sciserv.org
Internet: www.sciserv.org

AMOUNT: $100,000 (1st place); $75,000 (2nd); $50,000 (3rd); $25,000 (4th-6th); $20,000 (7th-10th); 30 at $5,000; 300 at $1,000; 40 laptops
DEADLINE(S): DEC 1
FIELD(S): Science, Math, Engineering

Open to high school seniors who submit a report of an independent research project in science, math, or engineering. Must include transcripts, SAT scores, and official entry form. Forty finalists are invited to Washington, DC, to participate in competition. Purpose is to encourage students to pursue careers in science and engineering.

40 awards annually. Contact Courtney Droms at Science Service for official STS entry book. Sponsored by the Intel Corporation.

1507—SKIDMORE COLLEGE (Merit Scholarships in Math and Science)

Office of Admissions
Saratoga Springs NY 12866-1632
1-800/867-6007
E-mail: admissions@skidmore.edu
Internet: www.skidmore.edu/campus/merit2.html

AMOUNT: $10,000/yr.
DEADLINE(S): FEB 1
FIELD(S): Math or Science

Scholarships for students excelling in the above fields. Awards are based on talent, not financial need. Recipients are not required to major in a scientific or mathematical discipline, but they will be expected to demonstrate serious research in one or more of these areas.

5 scholarships per year. For more information, visit website.

1508—SOCIETY OF HISPANIC PROFESSIONAL ENGINEERS FOUNDATION (SHPE Scholarships)

5400 E. Olympic Blvd., Suite 210
Los Angeles CA 90022
323/888-2080

AMOUNT: $500-$3,000
DEADLINE(S): APR 15
FIELD(S): Engineering, Science

Open to deserving students of Hispanic descent who are seeking careers in engineering or science. For full-time undergraduate or graduate study at a college or university. Based on academic achievement and financial need.

Send self-addressed, stamped envelope to above address for an application.

1509—SPACE COAST CREDIT UNION (Two-Year Scholarships)

Marketing Dept.
P.O. Box 2470
Melbourne FL 32902
Internet: www.sccu.com/scholarship/

AMOUNT: $750/year, two years; $1,000 bonus if go on for Bachelors
DEADLINE(S): APR 15
FIELD(S): Math, Economics, Science, Computer Science, Marketing, Journalism, Political Science

Must be graduating from a high school in Brevard, Volusia, Flagler, or Indian River counties, be a member of SCCU, have a minimum 3.0 GPA, planning to attend a two-year Florida institution of higher education for an associates degree,

and be willing to write a 200-word essay on the topic "Why credit unions are valuable to society."

4 annual awards. Students going on to complete a four-year degree could be eligible for a bonus scholarship of $1,000 for the next two years. For membership information or an application, see our web page or write to the above address.

1510—TEXAS SOCIETY OF PROFESSIONAL ENGINEERS (Scholarships)

P.O. Box 2145
Austin TX 78768
512/472-9286 or 800/580-8973
Internet: www.tspe.org

AMOUNT: Varies
DEADLINE(S): JAN 30
FIELD(S): Engineering (math, sciences)

Scholarships for graduating high school seniors who are Texas residents planning to attend Texas engineering colleges.

Contact organization for details. Application is on website.

1511—THE AMERICAN LEGION, DEPT. OF MARYLAND, INC. (Scholarship Program)

101 N. Gay Street
Baltimore MD 21202
410/752-3104
FAX: 410/752-3822
Internet: mdlegion@clark.net

AMOUNT: $500
DEADLINE(S): APR 1
FIELD(S): Math, Science

Open to the dependents of veterans who are residents of Maryland. Must not have attained their 20th birthday by January 1 of the year applying. Must intend to be a full-time student (at least 12 credits a semester).

5 awards annually. Send letter stating scholarship as well as financial need to Dept. Adjutant at above address.

1512—THE WALT DISNEY COMPANY (American Teacher Awards)

P.O. Box 9805
Calabasas CA 91372

AMOUNT: $2,500 (36 awards); $25,000 (Outstanding Teacher of the Year)
DEADLINE(S): FEB 15
FIELD(S): Teachers: athletic coach, early childhood, English, foreign language/ESL, general elementary, mathematics, performing arts, physical education/health, science, social studies, visual arts, voc-tech education

Awards for K-12 teachers in the above fields.

Teachers, or anyone who knows a great teacher, can write for applications at the above address.

1513—U.S. DEPARTMENT OF DEFENSE (High School Apprenticeship Program)

US Army Cold Regions Research
  and Engineering Laboratory
72 Lyme Road
Hanover NH 03755
603/646-4500
DSN: 220-4500
FAX: 603/646-4693
Internet: www.acq.osd.mil/ddre/
  edugate/s-aindx.html

AMOUNT: Internship
DEADLINE(S): None specified
FIELD(S): Sciences and Engineering

A teacher must recommend you for these three competitive high school apprenticeships with our Laboratory. High school students from New Hampshire who are at least 16 and who have completed their junior year in high school are eligible. Should have interest and ability in science, engineering, or mathematics.

Applications are available from participating local high school guidance counselors. Contact Susan Koh at the above address for more information.

1514—U.S. DEPARTMENT OF DEFENSE (SEAP—Science & Engineering Apprenticeship Program)

707 22nd Street NW
Washington DC 20052
202/994-2234
FAX: 202/994-2459
Internet: www.acq.osd.mil/ddre/
  edugate/ceeindx.htm/#A010

AMOUNT: $1,400 (min.)
DEADLINE(S): JAN 26
FIELD(S): Science, Engineering

Eight-week summer apprenticeships throughout the US are available to high school students who are US citizens planning careers in science or engineering. Based on grades, science/math courses taken, scores on standardized tests, areas of interest, teacher recommendations, and personal student statement. Students responsible for transportation to and from site.

See website or contact M. Phillips for an application. Refer to Code #A010.

1515—UNCF/MERCK SCIENCE INITIATIVE (Undergraduate Science Research Scholarship Awards)

8260 Willow Oaks Corporate Dr.
P.O. Box 10444
Fairfax VA 22031-4511
703/205-3503
FAX: 703/205-3574
E-mail: uncfmerck@uncf.org
Internet: www.uncf.org/merck

AMOUNT: $25,000/yr. (max.)
DEADLINE(S): JAN 31
FIELD(S): Life & Physical Sciences

Open to African-Americans in their junior year of college who will receive a bachelor's degree in the following academic year. Must be enrolled full-time in any four-year college/university in the US and have a minimum 3.3 GPA. Must be US citizen/permanent resident. Financial need NOT a factor.

15 awards annually. Not renewable. Contact Jerry Bryant, Ph.D., for an application.

1516—UNIVERSITY OF MARYLAND (John B. & Ida Slaughter Endowed Scholarship in Science, Technology, & the Black Community)

2169 Lefrak Hall
College Park MD 20742-7225
301/405-1158
FAX: 301/314-9867
Internet: www.bsos.umd.edu/aasp/
  scholarship.html

AMOUNT: Varies (in-state tuition costs)
DEADLINE(S): MAR
FIELD(S): Science & Technology AND
  African-American Studies

Open to African-Americans who are US residents with a minimum 2.8 GPA. Must be accepted to or enrolled at UMCP for freshmen year and must submit letter of recommendation from high school counselor or UMCP faculty member. Should have an interest in applying science and technology to the problems of the black community. Essay required.

Renewable. Contact the Center for Minorities in Science & Engineering at UMCP for an application.

1517—WILLIAM M. GRUPE FOUNDATION, INC. (Scholarships)

P.O. Box 775
Livingston NJ 07039
973/428-1190

AMOUNT: $2,000-$3,000
DEADLINE(S): MAR 1
FIELD(S): Medicine, Nursing

For residents of Bergen, Essex, or Hudson Counties in New Jersey. Awarded to good students in need of financial support to pursue undergraduate or graduate studies in medicine or nursing. Must be US citizen.

20-30 awards annually. Renewable. Contact William M. Grupe Foundation for an application.

1518—WOODROW WILSON NATIONAL FELLOWSHIP FOUNDATION (Leadership Program for Teachers)

CN 5281
Princeton NJ 08543-5281
609/452-7007
FAX: 609/452-0066
E-mail: marchioni@woodrow.org OR
  irish@woodrow.org
Internet: www.woodrow.org

AMOUNT: Varies
DEADLINE(S): Varies
FIELD(S): Science, Mathematics

WWLPT offers summer institutes for middle and high school teachers in science and mathematics. One- and two-week teacher outreach, TORCH Institutes, are held in the summer throughout the US.

See website or contact WWNFF for an application.

1519—WOODS HOLE OCEANOGRAPHIC INSTITUTION (Traineeships in Oceanography for Minority Group Undergraduates)

360 Woods Hole Road
Woods Hole MA 02543-1541
508/289-2219
FAX: 508/457-2188
E-mail: mgately@whoi.edu
Internet: www.whoi.edu

AMOUNT: Varies
DEADLINE(S): FEB 16
FIELD(S): Physical/Natural Sciences,
  Mathematics, Engineering

For minority undergraduates enrolled in US colleges/universities who have completed at least two semesters. These awards provide training and research experience for students with interests in the above fields. Traineeships may be awarded for a ten- to twelve-week period in the summer or for a semester during the academic year.

Renewable. For an application/more information, contact the Education Office, Clark Laboratory 223, MS #31, at above address.

BIOLOGY

1520—ALLIANCE FOR YOUNG ARTISTS AND WRITERS, INC./AMERICAN MUSEUM OF NATURAL HISTORY (Young Naturalist Awards)

Scholastic, Inc.
555 Broadway
New York NY 10012-3999
212/343-6582 or 800-SCHOLASTIC
FAX: 212/343-4885
E-mail: mjohnson@scholastic.com
Internet: www.amnh.org/youngnaturalistawards

AMOUNT: up to $2,500 + trip to New York to visit AMNH
DEADLINE(S): JAN 3
FIELD(S): Natural Sciences

For all students in grades 7-12 currently enrolled in a public or non-public school in the US, Canada, US territories, or US-sponsored schools abroad. Program focuses on finding and rewarding excellence in biology, earth science, astronomy, and cultural studies. Students are encouraged to perform observation-based projects that require creativity, inquiry, and critical analysis. Specific topics vary annually.

48 awards annually. See website or contact Mike Johnson, Program Manager, for an application.

1521—AMERICAN FOUNDATION FOR THE BLIND (Paul W. Ruckes Scholarship)

11 Penn Plaza, Suite 300
New York NY 10001
212/502-7661
FAX: 212/502-7771
E-mail: juliet@afb.org
Internet: www.afb.org

AMOUNT: $1,000
DEADLINE(S): APR 30
FIELD(S): Engineering, Computer/Physical/Life Sciences

Open to legally blind and visually impaired undergraduate and graduate students pursuing a degree in one of above fields. Must be US citizen. Must submit written documentation of visual impairment from ophthalmologist or optometrist (need not be legally blind); official transcripts; proof of college/university acceptance; three letters of recommendation; and typewritten statement describing goals,

work experience, extracurricular activities, and how monies will be used.

1 award annually. See website or contact Julie Tucker at AFB for an application.

1522—AMERICAN INDIAN SCIENCE AND ENGINEERING SOCIETY (EPA Tribal Lands Environmental Science Scholarship)

P.O. Box 9828
Albuquerque NM 87119-9828
505/765-1052
FAX: 505/765-5608
E-mail: scholarships@aises.org
Internet: www.aises.org/scholarships

AMOUNT: $4,000
DEADLINE(S): JUN 15
FIELD(S): Biochemistry, Biology, Chemical Engineering, Chemistry, Entomology, Environmental Economics/Science, Hydrology, Environmental Studies

Open to American Indian college juniors, seniors, and graduate students enrolled full-time at an accredited institution. Must demonstrate financial need. Certificate of Indian blood NOT required.

Renewable. See website or contact Patricia Browne for an application.

1523—AMERICAN MUSEUM OF NATURAL HISTORY (Research Experiences for Undergraduates)

Central Park West at 79th Street
New York NY 10024-5192
FAX: 212/769-5495
E-mail: bynum@amnh.org
Internet: research.amnh.org

AMOUNT: Stipend, research expenses, & possibly travel
DEADLINE(S): APR
FIELD(S): Evolutionary Biology

Ten-week summer internships for qualified undergraduates to pursue scientific projects in conjunction with Museum scientists. Must be enrolled in a degree program at a college/university, have a high GPA, and a strong science background. Included in program is orientation, bi-weekly meetings, and seminars. At conclusion, students deliver oral presentations of work and prepare research papers. Must submit list of courses, statement of interest, and recommendations.

See website or contact Office of Grants & Fellowships for an application.

1524—AMERICAN ORNITHOLOGISTS' UNION (AOU Student Research Awards)

National Museum of Natural History
MRC-116
Washington DC 20560-0116

202/357-2051
FAX: 202/633-8084
E-mail: aou@nmnh.si.edu
Internet: pica.wru.umt.edu/aou/aou.html

AMOUNT: $500-$1,500
DEADLINE(S): FEB
FIELD(S): Ornithology

Student research grants for undergraduates, graduates, and postgraduates; must not have received Ph.D. Must be a member of the American Ornithologists' Union. Financial need NOT a factor.

5-15 awards annually. Not renewable. For membership information or an application, contact James Dean at AOU.

1525—AMERICAN PHYSIOLOGICAL SOCIETY (Porter Physiology Development Program)

Education Office
9650 Rockville Pike
Bethesda MD 20814-3991
301/530-7132
E-mail: educatio@aps.faseb.org

AMOUNT: $15,000 stipend
DEADLINE(S): JUN 15; JAN 15
FIELD(S): Physiology

Open to underrepresented ethnic minority applicants (African Americans, Hispanics, Native Americans, Native Alaskans, and Native Pacific Islanders) who are citizens or permanent residents of the US or its territories. Must have been accepted into or currently in a graduate program; undergraduate summer research support also available. Awards based on ability as shown by academic records, proposed study and training goals, research plans, and letters of recommendation.

Renewable. Contact Dr. Pamela J. Gunter-Smith, Co-Chair, Development Committee, for an application.

1526—AMERICAN SOCIETY FOR ENOLOGY AND VITICULTURE (Scholarship)

P.O. Box 1855
Davis CA 95617
530/753-3142

AMOUNT: Varies (no predetermined amounts)
DEADLINE(S): MAR 1
FIELD(S): Enology (Wine Making) Viticulture (Grape Growing)

For college juniors, seniors, or graduate students enrolled in an accredited North American college or university in a science curriculum basic to the wine and grape industry. Must be resident of North

America, have a minimum 3.0 GPA (undergrad) or 3.2 GPA (grad), and demonstrate financial need.

Renewable. Contact ASEV for an application.

1527—AMERICAN SOCIETY FOR MICRO-BIOLOGY (ASM Faculty Fellowship Program)

1325 Massachusetts Ave. NW
Washington DC 20005
Written inquiry
E-mail: Fellowships-Careerinformation@asmusa.Org
Internet: http:www.asmusa.org/edusrc/edu23f.htm

AMOUNT: Up to $4,000 stipend
DEADLINE(S): FEB 1
FIELD(S): Microbiological Sciences

For minority full-time undergraduate faculty OR full-time undergraduate faculty at underserved institutions. Must be an ASM member.

Fellowship is for 1-2 months.

1528—AMERICAN SOCIETY FOR MICRO-BIOLOGY (Minority Undergraduate Research Fellowship [MURF])

1325 Massachusetts Ave. NW
Washington DC 20005
Written inquiry
E-mail: Fellowships-Careerinformation@asmusa.org
Internet: http:www.asmusa.org/edusrc/edu23b.htm

AMOUNT: $2,500 stipend; up to $1,000 for travel; up to $500 for housing.
DEADLINE(S): June 1
FIELD(S): Biological Sciences with emphasis in Microbiological Sciences

Fellowships for under-represented minority undergraduates in microbiological sciences. Must be planning to attend grad school.

Fellowship is for 2-3 months.

1529—AMERICAN SOCIETY FOR MICRO-BIOLOGY (Undergraduate Research Fellowship)

1325 Massachusetts Ave. NW
Washington DC 20005
Written inquiry
E-mail: Fellowships-Careerinformation@asmusa.org
Internet: http://www.asmusa.org/edusrc/edu23a.htm

AMOUNT: Up to $2,500 stipend; $800 for equipment; $700 for travel
DEADLINE(S): FEB 1
FIELD(S): Microbiological Sciences

Fellowship awarded to 2nd- or 3rd-year undergraduates in microbiology planning to attend grad school. Must be US citizen or legal resident.

Fellowship is for 3-6 months. Send for complete information and application.

1530—AMERICAN WINE SOCIETY EDUCATIONAL FOUNDATION (Scholarships and Grants)

1134 West Market Street
Bethlehem PA 18018-4910
610/865-2401 or 610/758-3845
FAX: 610/758-4344
E-mail: lhso@lehigh.edu

AMOUNT: $2,000
DEADLINE(S): MAR 31
FIELD(S): Wine industry professional study: enology, viticulture, health aspects of food and wine, and using and appreciating fine wines

To provide academic scholarships and research grants to students based on academic excellence. Must show financial need and genuine interest in pursuing careers in wine-related fields. For North American citizens, defined as US, Canada, Mexico, the Bahamas, and the West Indies at all levels of education.

Contact L.H. Sperling at above location for application.

1531—ARTHUR & DOREEN PARRETT SCHOLARSHIP TRUST FUND (Scholarships)

c/o U.S. Bank of Washington
P.O. Box 720
Trust Dept., 8th Floor
Seattle WA 98111-0720
206/344-4653

AMOUNT: Up to $3,500
DEADLINE(S): JUL 31
FIELD(S): Engineering, Science, Medicine, Dentistry

Washington state resident who has completed her/his first year of college by July 31. Open to students enrolled in above schools. Awards tenable at any accredited undergrad college or university.

Approximately 15 awards per year. Write for complete information.

1532—ASSOCIATED WESTERN UNIVERSITIES, INC. (AWU Undergraduate Student Fellowships)

4190 S. Highland Drive, Suite 211
Salt Lake City UT 84124-2600
801/273-8911
FAX: 801/277-5632
Internet: www.awu.org

AMOUNT: $300/week stipend + travel allowance
DEADLINE(S): FEB 1
FIELD(S): Mathematics, Engineering, Technology, Science

Eight- to- sixteen-week fellowships for undergraduate students enrolled in accredited institutions and who have completed at least one year of college by the start of the fellowship. Applicants reviewed on the basis of academic performance/class standing, career goals, recommendations, and compatibility of scientific interests and abilities with the needs and resources of the host facility. Citizenship restrictions may apply for some facilities.

500+ awards annually. Renewable (competitively with new application). Contact above address for an application.

1533—ASSOCIATED WESTERN UNIVERSITIES, INC. (AWU Visiting Scientist Fellowships)

4190 South Highland Dr., Suite 211
Salt Lake City UT 84124-2600
801/273-8900

AMOUNT: Varies
DEADLINE(S): Varies (Two months prior to starting date)
FIELD(S): Engineering, Science, Mathematics, and Technology

Research fellowships for professionals with continued commitment to science and engineering. For use at one of 62 participating universities. US citizenship or permanent residency required.

For detailed information and list of cooperating facitilies contact above location.

1534—ASSOCIATION FOR WOMEN IN SCIENCE EDUCATIONAL FOUNDATION (Dr. Vicki L. Schechtman Scholarship)

1200 New York Ave. NW, Suite 650
Washington DC 20005
202/326-8940 or 800/886-AWIS
E-mail: awis@awis.org

Internet: www.awis.org

AMOUNT: $1,000

DEADLINE(S): JAN 16

FIELD(S): Various Sciences and Social Sciences

For female undergraduate students who are US citizens and have a minimum GPA of 3.0. Summary page, essay describing career aspirations, transcripts, proof of matriculation (if available), and two reference letters required with application. Scholarships may be used for tuition, books, housing, research, equipment, etc.

See website or write to above address for an application and more information.

1535—ASSOCIATION FOR WOMEN IN SCIENCE EDUCATIONAL FOUNDATION (Ruth Satter Memorial Award)

1200 New York Ave. NW
Suite 650
Washington DC 20005
202/326-8940 or 800/886-AWIS
E-mail: awis@awis.org
Internet: www.awis.org

AMOUNT: $1,000

DEADLINE(S): JAN 16

FIELD(S): Various Sciences and Social Sciences

Scholarships for female doctoral students who have interrupted their education three years or more to raise a family. Summary page, description of research project, resume, references, transcripts, biographical sketch, and proof of eligibility from department head required. US citizens may attend any graduate institution; noncitizens must be enrolled in US institutions.

See website or write to above address for more information or an application.

1536—BROOKHAVEN WOMEN IN SCIENCE (Renate W. Chasman Scholarship)

P.O. Box 183
Upton NY 11973-5000
E-mail: pam@bnl.gov

AMOUNT: $2,000

DEADLINE(S): APR 1

FIELD(S): Natural Sciences, Engineering, Mathematics

Open ONLY to women who are residents of the boroughs of Brooklyn or Queens or the counties of Nassau or Suffolk in New York who are re-entering school after a period of study. For juniors, seniors, or first-year graduate students.

1 award annually. Not renewable. Contact Pam Mansfield at above location for an application. Phone calls are NOT accepted.

1537—BUSINESS & PROFESSIONAL WOMEN'S FOUNDATION (BPW Career Advancement Scholarship Program)

2012 Massachusetts Ave. NW
Washington DC 20036-1070
202/293-1200, ext. 169
FAX: 202/861-0298
Internet: www.bpwusa.org

AMOUNT: $500-$1,000

DEADLINE(S): APR 15

FIELD(S): Biology, Science, Education, Engineering, Social Science, Paralegal, Humanities, Business, Math, Computers, Law, MD, DD

For women (US citizens) aged 25+ accepted into accredited program at US institution (+Puerto Rico & Virgin Islands). Must graduate within 12 to 24 months from the date of grant and demonstrate critical financial need. Must have a plan to upgrade skills, train for a new career field, or to enter/re-enter the job market.

Full- or part-time study. For info see website or send business-sized, self-addressed, double-stamped envelope.

1538—ENTOMOLOGICAL SOCIETY OF AMERICA (Stan Beck Fellowship)

9301 Annapolis Road, Suite 300
Lanham MD 20706-3115
301/731-4535
FAX: 301/731-4538
E-mail: esa@entsoc.org
Internet: www.entsoc.org

AMOUNT: $4,000

DEADLINE(S): SEP 1

FIELD(S): Entomology

For undergraduate or graduate study in entomology. Must be enrolled in a recognized college or university in the US. To assist needy students whose need may be based on physical limitations or economic, minority, or environmental condition.

Secure a nomination from an ESA member. Send SASE for complete information.

1539—ENTOMOLOGICAL SOCIETY OF AMERICA (Undergraduate Scholarships)

9301 Annapolis Road, Suite. 300
Lanham MD 20706-3115
301/731-4535
FAX: 301/731-4538
E-mail: esa@entsoc.org
Internet: www.entsoc.org

AMOUNT: $1,500

DEADLINE(S): MAY 31

FIELD(S): Entomology, Biology, Zoology

For undergraduate study in the above or related fields. Must be enrolled in a recognized college or university in the US, Canada, or Mexico. Applicants must have accumulated at least 30 semester hours by the time award is presented and have completed at least one class or project on entomology. Financial need is NOT a factor.

4 awards annually. Send self-addressed, stamped envelope for an application.

1540—FLORIDA FEDERATION OF GARDEN CLUBS, INC. (FFGC Scholarships for College Students)

6065 21st Street SW
Vero Beach FL 32968-9427
561/778-1023
Internet: www.ffgc.org

AMOUNT: $1,500-$3,500

DEADLINE(S): MAY 1

FIELD(S): Ecology, Environmental Issues, Land Management, City Planning, Environmental Control, Horticulture, Landscape Design, Conservation, Botany, Forestry, Marine Biology, Floriculture, Agriculture

Various scholarships for Florida residents with a "B" average or better enrolled full-time as a junior, senior, or graduate student at a Florida college or university.

See website or contact Melba Campbell at FFGC for an application.

1541—FLORIDA FEDERATION OF GARDEN CLUBS, INC. (FFGC Scholarships for High School Students)

6065 21st Street SW
Vero Beach FL 32968-9427
561/778-1023
Internet: www.ffgc.org

AMOUNT: $1,500

DEADLINE(S): MAY 1

FIELD(S): Ecology, Environmental Issues, Land Management, City Planning, Environmental Control, Horticulture, Landscape Design, Conservation, Botany, Forestry, Marine Biology, Floriculture, Agriculture

Scholarships for Florida residents with a "B" average or better who will be incoming freshmen at a Florida college or university.

See website or contact Melba Campbell at FFGC for an application.

1542—FORD FOUNDATION/NATIONAL RESEARCH COUNCIL (Howard Hughes Medical Institute Predoctoral Fellowships in Biological Sciences)

2101 Constitution Ave.
Washington DC 20418
202/334-2872
FAX: 202/334-3419
E-mail: infofell@nas.edu
Internet: national-academics.org/osep.fo

AMOUNT: $16,000 stipend + tuition at US institution
DEADLINE(S): NOV 9
FIELD(S): Biochemistry, Biophysics, Epidemiology, Genetics, Immunology, Microbiology, Neuroscience, Pharmacology, Physiology, Virology

Five-year award is open to college seniors and first-year graduate students pursuing a Ph.D. or Sc.D. degree. US citizens/nationals may choose any institution in the US or abroad; foreign students must choose US institution. Based on ability, academic records, proposed study/research, previous experience, reference reports, and GRE scores.

80 awards annually. See website or contact NRC for an application.

1543—HUBBARD FARMS CHARITABLE FOUNDATION

P.O. Box 505
Walpole NH 03608-0505
603/756-3311

AMOUNT: Varies
DEADLINE(S): APR 1; OCT 1
FIELD(S): Poultry Science, Genetics, and other life sciences

Scholarships are for financially needy students at universities that the foundation trustees consider to be leaders in the field of progress in technology and efficiency of production of poultry products.

Send SASE to Jane F. Kelly, Clerk, at above address for current application guidelines.

1544—JEWISH VOCATIONAL SERVICE (Academic Scholarship Program)

One S. Franklin Street
Chicago IL 60606
312/357-4500
FAX: 312/855-328
TTY: 312/855-3282
E-mail: jvschicago@jon.cjfny.org

AMOUNT: $5,000 (max.)
DEADLINE(S): MAR 1
FIELD(S): "Helping" Professions, Mathematics, Engineering, Sciences, Communications (at Univ IL only), Law (certain schools in IL only)

Open to Jewish men and women legally domiciled in the greater Chicago metropolitan area, who are identified as having promise for significant contributions in their chosen careers, and are in need of financial assistance for full-time academic programs in above areas. Must have entered undergraduate junior year in career programs requiring no postgrad education, be in graduate/professional school, or be in a voc-tech training program. Interview required.

Renewable. Contact JVS for an application between December 1st and February 15th.

1545—LOUISIANA OFFICE OF STUDENT FINANCIAL ASSISTANCE (Rockefeller State Wildlife Scholarship)

P.O. Box 91202
Baton Rouge LA 70821-9202
800/259-5626, ext. 1012
FAX: 504/922-0790
Internet: www.osfa.state.la.us

AMOUNT: $1,000/yr.
DEADLINE(S): JUN 1
FIELD(S): Forestry, Wildlife, Marine Science

Open to Louisiana residents pursuing undergraduate or graduate study in a Louisiana college/university. Must have minimum 2.5 GPA. Recipients must attain a degree in one of the three eligible fields or repay the funds plus interest.

30 awards annually. Renewable up to 5 years undergraduate study and 2 years graduate study. Apply by completing the Free Application for Federal Student Aid (FAFSA). See your school's financial aid office or contact LOSFA for FAFSA form.

1546—MARYLAND HIGHER EDUCATION COMMISSION (Maryland Science and Technology Scholarship Program)

16 Francis Street
Annapolis Park MD 21401
410/974-5370 or 800/974-1024
E-mail: ssamail@mhec.state.md.us
Internet: http://www.mhec.state.md.us/SSA/stech_qa.htm

AMOUNT: $3,000/yr. (B.A.); $1,000/yr. (A.A.)
DEADLINE(S): None
FIELD(S): Computer Science, Engineering, Technology

Scholarships for college-bound Maryland high school seniors who will major in one of the above fields and who are accepted to an eligible associate or bachelor's degree program in Maryland. Students in the class of 1999 were eligible for the first awards. The deadline was not known at this writing, so check for deadline date. Must agree to work in the state after graduation in a related field, one year for each year of assistance received.

Must maintain a 3.0 GPA.

1547—MIDWAY COLLEGE (Institutional Aid Program—Scholarships & Grants)

Financial Aid Office
Midway KY 40347
606/846-4421

AMOUNT: Varies
DEADLINE(S): MAR 1
FIELD(S): Nursing, Paralegal, Education, Psychology, Biology, Equine Studies, Liberal Studies, Business Administration

Scholarships and grants open to women who are accepted for enrollment at Midway College. Awards support undergraduate study in the above areas.

Approx 80 awards per year. Write for complete information.

1548—NATIONAL ASSOCIATION OF WATER COMPANIES—NEW JERSEY CHAPTER (Scholarship)

Elizabethtown Water Co.
600 South Ave.
Westfield NJ 07090
908/654-1234
FAX: 908/232-2719

AMOUNT: $2,500
DEADLINE(S): APR 1
FIELD(S): Business Administration, Biology, Chemistry, Engineering, Communications

For US citizens who have lived in NJ at least 5 years and plan a career in the investor-owned water utility industry in disciplines such as those above. Must be undergrad or graduate student in a 2- or 4-year NJ college or university.

GPA of 3.0 or better required. Contact Gail P. Brady for complete information.

1549—NORTHERN NEW JERSEY UNIT-HERB SOCIETY OF AMERICA (Scholarship)

2068 Dogwood Drive
Scotch Plains NJ 07076
908/233-2348

AMOUNT: $2,000
DEADLINE(S): FEB 15
FIELD(S): Horticulture, Botany

For New Jersey residents, undergraduate through postgraduate, who will attend colleges/universities east of the Mississippi River. Financial need is considered.

1 award annually. Renewable. Contact Mrs. Charlotte R. Baker at above address for an application.

1550—OAK RIDGE INSTITUTE FOR SCIENCE AND EDUCATION (ORISE Education & Training Programs)

P.O. Box 117
Oak Ridge TN 37831-0117
Internet: www.orau.gov/orise/educ.htm

AMOUNT: Varies
DEADLINE(S): Varies
FIELD(S): Engineering, Aeronautics, Computer Science, Technology, Earth Science, Environmental Studies, Biology, Chemistry, Physics, Medical Research

Numerous programs funded by the US Department of Energy are offered for undergraduate students through postgraduate researchers. Includes fellowship and internship opportunities throughout the US. Some have citizenship restrictions. Travel may be included.

See website or write for a catalog of specific programs and requirements.

1551—OKLAHOMA MEDICAL RESEARCH FOUNDATION (Sir Alexander Fleming Scholar Program)

825 Northeast 13th Street
Oklahoma City OK 73104
405/271-7218
800/522-0211 (in-state)

AMOUNT: $2,500 salary + housing
DEADLINE(S): MAR 1
FIELD(S): Sciences

Summer scholarship program (June and July) for Oklahoma students who have completed their junior year of high school through those in their junior year of college at time of application. Excellent academic standing and aptitude in science and math are essential. Students will work in the laboratories of the above organization. Research projects will be selected from: alcoholism/liver disease, arthritis/immunology, carcinogenesis, cardiovascular biology, and more.

Named for the scientist who discovered penicillin and dedicated OMRF in 1949.

Contact organization for further information and application forms.

1552—OPEN SOCIETY INSTITUTE (Environmental Management Fellowships)

400 West 59th Street
New York NY 10019
212/548-0600 or 212/757-2323
FAX: 212/548-4679 or
212/548-4600
Internet: www.soros.org/efp.html

AMOUNT: Fees, room, board, living stipend, textbooks, international transportation, health insurance
DEADLINE(S): NOV 15
FIELD(S): Earth Sciences, Natural Sciences, Humanities (exc. language), Anthropology, Sociology, Mathematics, or Engineering

Two-year fellowships for use in selected universities in the US for international students. For students/professionals in fields related to environmental policy, legislation, and remediation techniques applicable to their home countries.

To apply, contact your local Soros Foundation or Open Society Institute. Further details on website.

1553—PENINSULA COMMUNITY FOUNDATION (Dr. Mary Finegold Scholarship)

1700 S. El Camino Real, #300
San Mateo CA 94402
650/358-9369
FAX: 650/358-9817

AMOUNT: $1,000
DEADLINE(S): MAR 27 (5 P.M.)
FIELD(S): Sciences

Scholarships for senior girls graduating from high school in Palo Alto, California, who intend to complete a four-year degree in the sciences. Special consideration will be given to girls who have demonstrated a "pioneering" spirit in that they have not been constrained by stereotypical female roles and to those facing financial hardship.

Award was established in the honor of Dr. Mary Finegold who, after completing her medical studies, elected to stay at home until her youngest child was in high school before beginning her medical practice. She was a school physician.

1554—SAN DIEGO AEROSPACE MUSEUM (Bill Gibbs Scholarship)

Education Dept.
2001 Pan American Plaza
San Diego CA 92101

619/234-8291, ext. 19
FAX: 619/233-4526
Internet: aerospacemuseum.org/Scholastic.HTML

AMOUNT: Varies
DEADLINE(S): Varies
FIELD(S): Aerospace: math, physics, science, or engineering

For students who are residents of San Diego County, California, who have an aerospace career interest and who have been accepted to a four-year college or university in a degree program relating to math, physics, science, or engineering.

Call or write museum for further information.

1555—SMITHSONIAN INSTITUTION (Minority Student Internship Program)

Fellowships & Grants
955 L'Enfant Plaza, Suite 7000
MRC 902
Washington DC 20560
202/287-3271
FAX: 202/287-3691
E-mail: siofg@ofg.si.edu
Internet: www.si.edu/research+study

AMOUNT: $300/week + possible travel expenses
DEADLINE(S): FEB 15
FIELD(S): Humanities, Environmental Studies, Cultural Studies, Natural History, Earth Science, Art History, Biology, & related fields

Ten-week internships in residence at the Smithsonian for US minority students to participate in research or museum-related activities in above fields. For undergrads or grads with at least a 3.0 GPA. Essay, resume, transcripts, and references required with application. Internships are full-time and are offered for Summer, Fall, or Spring tenures.

Write for application.

1556—SOCIETY FOR MARINE MAMMALOGY (The Emily B. Shane Award)

c/o Univ. of Calif., EMS Bldg.
Room A319
Santa Cruz CA 95064
Internet: http://pegasus.cc.ucf.efu/~smm/shane.htm

AMOUNT: Up to $10,000
DEADLINE(S): MAY 1
FIELD(S): Marine Mammalogy

Awards to support conservation-orientation, nonharmful research on free-ranging odontocetes (dolphins, orcas, and sperm whales) and sirenians (sea-cows, dugongs, manatees). The award may be divided if there is more than one equally deserving applicant. For students at all levels and other researchers. Requires formal research proposal to apply.

Visit website for application instructions. Mail application to Carol Fairfield, Chair, Awards/Scholarship Committee, at Santa Cruz address.

1557—STUDENT CONSERVATION ASSOCIATION (SCA Resource Assistant Program)

P.O. Box 550
Charlestown NH 03603
603/543-1700
FAX: 603/543-1828
E-mail: internships@sca-inc.org
Internet: www.sca-inc.org

AMOUNT: $1,180-$4,725
DEADLINE(S): Varies
FIELD(S): Environment & related fields

Must be 18 and US citizen; need not be student. Fields: Agriculture, archaeology, anthropology, botany, caves, civil/environmental engineering, environmental education, fisheries, forests, herpetology, history, living history/roleplaying, visitor services, landscape architectural/environmental design, paleontology, recreation/resource /range management, trail maintenance/construction, wildlife management, geology, hydrology, library/museums, surveying.

900 positions in US and Canada. Send $1 for postage for application; outside US/Canada, send $20.

1558—THE AUGIE J. ALTAR SCHOLARSHIP

7115 W. 91st Street
Bridgeview IL 60455-2048
Write for information

AMOUNT: $500
DEADLINE(S): MAY 31
FIELD(S): Medicine or Agricultural fields

Scholarships for students enrolled or accepted to an accredited college, university, or community college who are of Lithuanian descent and are residents of Illinois. Must be studying in the areas of medicine or agriculture. Financial need considered. Must have and maintain at least a 2.0 GPA.

Send application request to above address with a stamped, self-addressed envelope (SASE).

1559—UNCF/MERCK SCIENCE INITIATIVE (Undergraduate Science Research Scholarship Awards)

8260 Willow Oaks Corporate Drive
P.O. Box 10444
Fairfax VA 22031-4511

703/205-3503
FAX: 703/205-3574
E-mail: uncfmerck@uncf.org
Internet: www.uncf.org/merck

AMOUNT: $25,000/yr. (max.)
DEADLINE(S): JAN 31
FIELD(S): Life & Physical Sciences

Open to African-Americans in their junior year of college who will receive a bachelor's degree in the following academic year. Must be enrolled full-time in any four-year college/university in the US and have a minimum 3.3 GPA. Must be US citizen/permanent resident. Financial need NOT a factor.

15 awards annually. Not renewable. Contact Jerry Bryant, Ph.D., for an application.

1560—U.S. DEPARTMENT OF AGRICULTURE (1890 National Scholars Program)

14th & Independence Ave. SW
Room 301-W, Whitten Bldg.
Washington DC 20250-9600
202/720-6905
E-mail: usda-m@fie.com
Internet: web.fie.com/htdoc/fed/
agr/ars/edu/prog/mti/agrpgaak.htm

AMOUNT: Tuition,
employment/benefits, use of
PC/software, fees, books, room/board
DEADLINE(S): JAN 15
FIELD(S): Agriculture, Food, or Natural
Resource sciences

For US citizens, high school grad/GED, GPA 3.0+, verbal/math SAT 1,000+, composite score 21+ ACT, 1st-yr college student, and attend participating school.

34+ scholarships/yr/4 years. Send applications to USDA Liaison Officer at the 1890 Institution of your choice (see Web page for complete list).

1561—UNIVERSITY OF CALIFORNIA-DAVIS (Brad Webb Scholarship Fund)

Dept. Enology & Viticulture
Shield's Ave.
Davis CA 95616
530/752-2390 (undergrad)
530/752-9246 (graduate)
Internet: faoman.ucdavis.edu

AMOUNT: Varies
DEADLINE(S): Varies
FIELD(S): Enology/Viticulture

Open to students attending or planning to attend UC Davis. Award is made in memory of Brad Webb, friend of NSRS President, Dan Cassidy.

Contact the Department of Enology & Viticulture for an application.

1562—WILSON ORNITHOLOGICAL SOCIETY (Fuertes, Nice, & Stewart Grants)

Museum of Zoology
Univ. of Michigan
1109 Geddes Ave.
Ann Arbor MI 48109-1079
Internet: www.ummz.lsa.umich.edu/
birds/wos.html

AMOUNT: $600 (Fuertes); $200 (Nice & Stewart)
DEADLINE(S): JAN 15
FIELD(S): Ornithology

Grants to support research on birds only—NOT for general college funding. Open to anyone presenting a suitable research problem in ornithology. Research proposal required.

5-6 awards annually. Not renewable. See website for an application.

CHEMISTRY

1563—AIR FORCE RESERVE OFFICER TRAINING CORPS (AFROTC Scholarships)

551 E. Maxwell Blvd.
Maxwell AFB AL 36112-6106
334/953-7783

AMOUNT: Full tuition, books, & fees for all 4 years of college
DEADLINE(S): DEC 1
FIELD(S): Science, Engineering,
Business, Political Science, Psychology,
Geography, Foreign Studies, Foreign
Language

Competitive scholarships based on individual merit to high school seniors and graduates who have not completed any full-time college work. Must be a US citizen between the ages of 17-27. Must also have GPA of 2.5 or above, be in top 40% of class, and complete Applicant Fitness Test. Cannot be a single parent. Your college/university must offer AFROTC.

2,300 awards annually. Contact above address for application packet.

1564—AMERICAN CHEMICAL SOCIETY (Minority Scholars Program)

1155 Sixteenth Street NW
Washington DC 20036
202/872-6250 or 800/227-5558
FAX: 202/776-8003
E-mail: rjh91@acs.org
Internet: www.acs.org

AMOUNT: up to $2,500
DEADLINE(S): FEB 15
FIELD(S): Chemistry, Biochemistry,
Chemical Engineering, Chemical
Technology

Open to a) high school seniors who will enter college in the coming year, b) college students currently/planning to pursue full time study, c) community college graduates/transfer students pursuing a bachelor's, and d) community college freshmen. Awarded on the basis of merit and financial need to African American, Hispanic, and American Indian students with outstanding academic records combined with strong interest in chemistry. Must be US citizen/permanent resident.

75 awards annually. Contact ACS for an application.

1565—AMERICAN FOUNDATION FOR THE BLIND (Paul W. Ruckes Scholarship)

11 Penn Plaza, Suite 300
New York NY 10001
212/502-7661
FAX: 212/502-7771
E-mail: juliet@afb.org
Internet: www.afb.org

AMOUNT: $1,000
DEADLINE(S): APR 30
FIELD(S): Engineering, Computer/
Physical/Life Sciences

Open to legally blind and visually impaired undergraduate and graduate students pursuing a degree in one of above fields. Must be US citizen. Must submit written documentation of visual impairment from ophthalmologist or optometrist (need not be legally blind); official transcripts; proof of college/university acceptance; three letters of recommendation; and typewritten statement describing goals, work experience, extracurricular activities, and how monies will be used.

1 award annually. See website or contact Julie Tucker at AFB for an application.

1566—AMERICAN GEOLOGICAL INSTITUTE (AGI Minority Geoscience Scholarships)

4220 King Street
Alexandria VA 22302-1502
703/379-2480
FAX 703/379-7563
E-mail: ehr@agiweb.org
Internet: www.agiweb.org

AMOUNT: Varies
DEADLINE(S): FEB 1

FIELD(S): Geoscience

Open to full-time undergrads or grads majoring in geology, geophysics, geochemistry, hydrology, meteorology, physical oceanography, planetary geology, or earth science education. NOT for engineering, mathematics, or natural science majors.

Must be ethnic minority and US citizen. Financial need must be demonstrated. Must reapply for renewal. Contact Veronika Litvale at above location for details.

1567—AMERICAN HEALTH AND BEAUTY AIDS INSTITUTE (Fred Luster, Sr. Education Foundation Scholarships for College-Bound High School Seniors)

401 North Michigan Ave.
Chicago IL 60611-4267
312/644-6610

AMOUNT: $250 and $500
DEADLINE(S): APR 15
FIELD(S): Chemistry, Business, or
Engineering

For college-bound high school seniors who will be enrolled as a college freshman in a four-year college majoring in chemistry, business, or engineering. 3.0 GPA required.

Send two letters of recommendation (one from a school official) and high school transcript. Scholastic record, school activities, and extracurricular activities considered.

1568—AMERICAN INDIAN SCIENCE AND ENGINEERING SOCIETY (EPA Tribal Lands Environmental Science Scholarship)

P.O. Box 9828
Albuquerque NM 87119-9828
505/765-1052
FAX: 505/765-5608
E-mail: scholarships@aises.org
Internet: www.aises.org/scholarships

AMOUNT: $4,000
DEADLINE(S): JUN 15
FIELD(S): Biochemistry, Biology,
Chemical Engineering, Chemistry,
Entomology, Environmental
Economics/Science, Hydrology,
Environmental Studies

Open to American Indian college juniors, seniors, and graduate students enrolled full-time at an accredited institution. Must demonstrate financial need. Certificate of Indian blood NOT required.

Renewable. See website or contact Patricia Browne for an application.

1569—ARTHUR & DOREEN PARRETT SCHOLARSHIP TRUST FUND (Scholarships)

c/o U.S. Bank of Washington
P.O. Box 720
Trust Dept., 8th Floor
Seattle WA 98111-0720
206/344-4653

AMOUNT: Up to $3,500
DEADLINE(S): JUL 31
FIELD(S): Engineering, Science,
Medicine, Dentistry

Washington state resident who has completed her/his first year of college by July 31. Open to students enrolled in above schools. Awards tenable at any accredited undergrad college or university.

Approximately 15 awards per year. Write for complete information.

1570—ASSOCIATED WESTERN UNIVERSITIES, INC. (AWU Undergraduate Student Fellowships)

4190 S. Highland Drive, Suite 211
Salt Lake City UT 84124-2600
801/273-8911
FAX: 801/277-5632
Internet: www.awu.org

AMOUNT: $300/week stipend + travel
allowance
DEADLINE(S): FEB 1
FIELD(S): Mathematics, Engineering,
Technology, Science

Eight- to sixteen-week fellowships for undergraduate students enrolled in accredited institutions and who have completed at least one year of college by the start of the fellowship. Applicants reviewed on the basis of academic performance/class standing, career goals, recommendations, and compatibility of scientific interests and abilities with the needs and resources of the host facility. Citizenship restrictions may apply for some facilities.

500+ awards annually. Renewable (competitively with new application). Contact above address for an application.

1571—ASSOCIATED WESTERN UNIVERSITIES, INC. (AWU Visiting Scientist Fellowships)

4190 S. Highland Drive, Suite 211
Salt Lake City UT 84124-2600
801/273-8900

AMOUNT: Varies
DEADLINE(S): Varies (Two months
prior to starting date)

FIELD(S): Engineering, Science, Mathematics, and Technology

Research fellowships for professionals with continued commitment to science and engineering. For use at one of 62 participating universities. US citizenship or permanent residency required.

For detailed information and list of cooperating facitilies contact above location.

1572—ASSOCIATION FOR WOMEN IN SCIENCE EDUCATIONAL FOUNDATION (Dr. Vicki L. Schechtman Scholarship)

1200 New York Ave. NW
Suite 650
Washington DC 20005
202/326-8940 or 800/886-AWIS
E-mail: awis@awis.org
Internet: www.awis.org

AMOUNT: $1,000
DEADLINE(S): JAN 16
FIELD(S): Various Sciences and Social Sciences

For female undergraduate students who are US citizens and have a minimum GPA of 3.0. Summary page, essay describing career aspirations, transcripts, proof of matriculation (if available), and two reference letters required with application. Scholarships may be used for tuition, books, housing, research, eqipment, etc.

See website or write to above address for an application and more information.

1573—ASSOCIATION FOR WOMEN IN SCIENCE EDUCATIONAL FOUNDATION (Ruth Satter Memorial Award)

1200 New York Ave. NW
Suite 650
Washington DC 20005
202/326-8940 or 800/886-AWIS
E-mail: awis@awis.org
Internet: www.awis.org

AMOUNT: $1,000
DEADLINE(S): JAN 16
FIELD(S): Various Sciences and Social Sciences

Scholarships for female doctoral students who have interrupted their education three years or more to raise a family. Summary page, description of research project, resume, references, transcripts, biographical sketch, and proof of eligibility from department head required. US citizens may attend any graduate institution; non-citizens must be enrolled in US institutions.

See website or write to above address for more information or an application.

1574—BROOKHAVEN WOMEN IN SCIENCE (Renate W. Chasman Scholarship)

P.O. Box 183
Upton NY 11973-5000
E-mail: pam@bnl.gov

AMOUNT: $2,000
DEADLINE(S): APR 1
FIELD(S): Natural Sciences, Engineering, Mathematics

Open ONLY to women who are residents of the boroughs of Brooklyn or Queens or the counties of Nassau or Suffolk in New York who are re-entering school after a period of study. For juniors, seniors, or first-year graduate students.

1 award annually. Not renewable. Contact Pam Mansfield at above location for an application. Phone calls are NOT accepted.

1575—FORD FOUNDATION/NATIONAL RESEARCH COUNCIL (Howard Hughes Medical Institute Predoctoral Fellowships in Biological Sciences)

2101 Constitution Ave.
Washington DC 20418
202/334-2872
FAX: 202/334-3419
E-mail: infofell@nas.edu
Internet: national-academics.org/osep.fo

AMOUNT: $16,000 stipend + tuition at US institution
DEADLINE(S): NOV 9
FIELD(S): Biochemistry, Biophysics, Epidemiology, Genetics, Immunology, Microbiology, Neuroscience, Pharmacology, Physiology, Virology

Five-year award is open to college seniors and first-year graduate students pursuing a Ph.D. or Sc.D. degree. US citizens/nationals may choose any institution in the US or abroad; foreign students must choose US institution. Based on ability, academic records, proposed study/ research, previous experience, reference reports, and GRE scores.

80 awards annually. See website or contact NRC for an application.

1576—H. FLETCHER BROWN FUND (Scholarships)

Trust Dept.
c/o PNC Bank
P.O. Box 791
Wilmington DE 19899
302/429-1186

AMOUNT: Varies

DEADLINE(S): APR 15
FIELD(S): Medicine, Dentistry, Law, Engineering, Chemistry

Open to US citizens born in Delaware and still residing in Delaware. For 4 years of study (undergrad or grad) leading to a degree that enables applicant to practice in chosen field.

Scholarships are based on need, scholastic achievement, and good moral character. Applications available in February. Write for complete information.

1577—H. FLETCHER BROWN TRUST (Scholarships)

222 Delaware Ave., 16th Fl.
Wilmington DE 19899
302/429-1338

AMOUNT: Varies
DEADLINE(S): APR 9
FIELD(S): Chemistry, Engineering, Law, Medicine, Dentistry

Open to financially needy native-born Delaware residents only who are pursuing an undergraduate degree. Must have minimum 1,000 SAT score and rank in upper 20% of class. Interview required.

Send self-addressed, stamped envelope to Donald Drois, Account Administrator, PNC Bank, at above address for an application.

1578—HACH SCIENTIFIC FOUNDATION (Chemistry Scholarships)

1856 Piedras Circle
Alamo CA 94507
Written inquiry

AMOUNT: Varies
DEADLINE(S): Varies
FIELD(S): Chemistry

Open to undergraduate students majoring in chemistry at the University of Wyoming, Colorado State University, or Iowa State University.

Contact your Department Chair for an application: Univ. WY, Dept. of Chemistry, Scholarship Director, Laramie, WY 82071-3963; CO State, Dept. of Chemistry, Scholarship Director, Ft. Collins, CO 80523; Iowa State, Dept. of Chemistry, Scholarship Director, Ames, IA 50011.

1579—JEWISH VOCATIONAL SERVICE (Academic Scholarship Program)

One S. Franklin Street
Chicago IL 60606

312/357-4500
FAX: 312/855-3282
TTY: 312/855-3282
E-mail: jvschicago@jon.cjfny.org
AMOUNT: $5,000 (max.)
DEADLINE(S): MAR 1
FIELD(S): "Helping" Professions, Mathematics, Engineering, Sciences, Communications (at Univ IL only), Law (certain schools in IL only)

Open to Jewish men and women legally domiciled in the greater Chicago metropolitan area, who are identified as having promise for significant contributions in their chosen careers, and are in need of financial assistance for full-time academic programs in above areas. Must have entered undergraduate junior year in career programs requiring no postgrad education, be in graduate/professional school, or be in a voc-tech training program. Interview required.

Renewable. Contact JVS for an application between December 1st and February 15th.

1580—LOUISIANA OFFICE OF STUDENT FINANCIAL ASSISTANCE (Tuition Opportunity Program for Students-Teachers Award)

P.O. Box 91202
Baton Rouge LA 70821-9202
800/259-5626, ext. 1012
FAX: 504/922-0790
Internet: www.osfa.state.la.us

AMOUNT: $4,000/yr. (education majors); $6,000/yr. (math/chemistry majors)
DEADLINE(S): JUN 1
FIELD(S): Education, Math, Chemistry

Open to Louisiana residents pursuing undergraduate or graduate study at Louisiana colleges/universities and majoring in one of the above fields leading to teacher certification. Loans are forgiven by working as a certified teacher in Louisiana one year for each year loan is received.

Apply by completing the Free Application for Federal Student Aid (FAFSA). See your school's financial aid office or contact LOSFA for FAFSA form.

1581—LOUISIANA STATE UNIVERSITY AT SHREVEPORT (Gary Brashier Scholarship)

Dept. of Chemistry & Physics
One University Place
Shreveport LA 71115-2399
318/797-5363 or 318/797-5246
FAX: 318/797-5366

E-mail: finaid@pilot.lsus.edu
Internet: www.lsus.edu
AMOUNT: Varies (partial tuition)
DEADLINE(S): Varies
FIELD(S): Chemistry

Must be US citizen who is a junior or senior chemistry major at LSUS. Must have minimum 3.0 GPA, and preference is given to students with financial need who intend to pursue advanced study in chemistry.

Contact the Department of Chemistry & Physics at LSUS for an application.

1582—MARYLAND HIGHER EDUCATION COMMISSION (Maryland Science and Technology Scholarship Program)

16 Francis Street
Annapolis Park MD 21401
410/974-5370 or 800/974-1024
E-mail: ssamail@mhec.state.md.us
Internet: http://www.mhec.state.md.us/SSA/stech_qa.htm

AMOUNT: $3,000/yr. (B.A.); $1,000/yr. (A.A.)
DEADLINE(S): None
FIELD(S): Computer Science, Engineering, Technology

Scholarships for college-bound Maryland high school seniors who will major in one of the above fields and who are accepted to an eligible associate or bachelor's degree program in Maryland. Students in the class of 1999 were eligible for the first awards. The deadline was not known at this writing, so check for deadline date. Must agree to work in the state after graduation in a related field, one year for each year of assistance received.

Must maintain a 3.0 GPA.

1583—NAACP NATIONAL OFFICE (NAACP Willems Scholarship)

4805 Mount Hope Drive
Baltimore MD 21215
401/358-8900
AMOUNT: $2,000 undergrads; $3,000 grads
DEADLINE(S): APR 30
FIELD(S): Engineering, Chemistry, Physics, Mathematics

Open to NAACP male members majoring in one of the above areas. Undergrads must have GPA of 2.5+; graduates' GPAs must be 3.0+. Renewable if the required GPA is maintained.

Financial need must be established. Two letters of recommendation typed on letterhead from teachers or professors in

the major field of specialization. Write for complete information. Include a legal size, self-addressed, stamped envelope.

1584—NAACP NATIONAL OFFICE (NAACP/Department of Energy Scholarship)

4805 Mount Hope Drive
Baltimore MD 21215-3297
410/486-9133
AMOUNT: $10,000/year tuition/stipend
DEADLINE(S): APR 30
FIELD(S): Engineering, Science, Computer Science, Mathematics, Environmental Studies

Open to high school seniors who are NAACP members with a minimum 3.0 GPA. Applicants must participate in 120 hours of community service; at least 1 summer internship at a DOE facility and be employed by DOE or DOE contractor for 2 years.

Write for complete information; enclose a self-addressed 9 x 12 envelope.

1585—NATIONAL ASSOCIATION OF WATER COMPANIES—NEW JERSEY CHAPTER (Scholarship)

Elizabethtown Water Co.
600 South Ave.
Westfield NJ 07090
908/654-1234
FAX: 908/232-2719
AMOUNT: $2,500
DEADLINE(S): APR 1
FIELD(S): Business Administration, Biology, Chemistry, Engineering, Communications

For US citizens who have lived in NJ at least 5 years and plan a career in the investor-owned water utility industry in disciplines such as those above. Must be undergrad or graduate student in a 2- or 4-year NJ college or university.

GPA of 3.0 or better required. Contact Gail P. Brady for complete information.

1586—OAK RIDGE INSTITUTE FOR SCIENCE AND EDUCATION (ORISE Education & Training Programs)

P.O. Box 117
Oak Ridge TN 37831-0117
Internet: www.orau.gov/orise/educ.htm
AMOUNT: Varies
DEADLINE(S): Varies

FIELD(S): Engineering, Aeronautics, Computer Science, Technology, Earth Science, Environmental Studies, Biology, Chemistry, Physics, Medical Research

Numerous programs funded by the US Department of Energy are offered for undergraduate students through postgraduate researchers. Includes fellowship and internship opportunities throughout the US. Some have citizenship restrictions. Travel may be included.

See website or write for a catalog of specific programs and requirements.

1587—OKLAHOMA MEDICAL RESEARCH FOUNDATION (Sir Alexander Fleming Scholar Program)

825 Northeast 13th Street
Oklahoma City OK 73104
405/271-7218
800/522-0211 (in-state)

AMOUNT: $2,500 salary + housing
DEADLINE(S): MAR 1
FIELD(S): Sciences

Summer scholarship program (June and July) for Oklahoma students who have completed their junior year of high school through those in their junior year of college at time of application. Excellent academic standing and aptitude in science and math are essential. Students will work in the laboratories of the above organization. Research projects will be selected from: alcoholism/liver disease, arthritis/ immunology, carcinogenesis, cardiovascular biology, and more.

Named for the scientist who discovered penicillin and dedicated OMRF in 1949. Contact organization for further information and application forms.

1588—OPEN SOCIETY INSTITUTE (Environmental Management Fellowships)

400 West 59th Street
New York NY 10019
212/548-0600 or 212/757-2323
FAX: 212/548-4679 or
212/548-4600
Internet: www.soros.org/efp.html

AMOUNT: Fees, room, board, living stipend, textbooks, international transportation, health insurance
DEADLINE(S): NOV 15
FIELD(S): Earth Sciences, Natural Sciences, Humanities (exc. language), Anthropology, Sociology, Mathematics, or Engineering

Two-year fellowships for use in selected universities in the US for international students. For students/professionals in fields related to environmental policy, legislation, and remediation techniques applicable to their home countries.

To apply, contact your local Soros Foundation or Open Society Institute. Further details on website.

1589—PENINSULA COMMUNITY FOUNDATION (Dr. Mary Finegold Scholarship)

1700 S. El Camino Real, #300
San Mateo CA 94402
650/358-9369
FAX: 650/358-9817

AMOUNT: $1,000
DEADLINE(S): MAR 27 (5 P.M.)
FIELD(S): Sciences

Scholarships for senior girls graduating from high school in Palo Alto, California, who intend to complete a four-year degree in the sciences. Special consideration will be given to girls who have demonstrated a "pioneering" spirit in that they have not been constrained by stereotypical female roles and to those facing financial hardship.

Award was established in the honor of Dr. Mary Finegold who, after completing her medical studies, elected to stay at home until her youngest child was in high school before beginning her medical practice. She was a school physician.

1590—ROBERT SCHRECK MEMORIAL FUND (Grants)

c/o Texas Commerce Bank
Trust Dept., P.O. Drawer 140
El Paso TX 79980
915/546-6515

AMOUNT: $500-$1,500
DEADLINE(S): JUL 15; NOV 15
FIELD(S): Medicine, Veterinary Medicine, Physics, Chemistry, Architecture, Engineering, Episcopal Clergy

Grants to undergraduate juniors or seniors or graduate students who have been residents of El Paso County for at least two years. Must be US citizen or legal resident and have a high grade point average. Financial need is a consideration.

Write for complete information.

1591—SAN DIEGO AEROSPACE MUSEUM (Bill Gibbs Scholarship)

Education Dept.
2001 Pan American Plaza
San Diego CA 92101
619/234-8291, ext. 19

FAX: 619/233-4526
Internet: aerospacemuseum.org/Scholastic.HTML

AMOUNT: Varies
DEADLINE(S): Varies
FIELD(S): Aerospace: math, physics, science, or engineering

For students who are residents of San Diego County, California, who have an aerospace career interest and who have been accepted to a four-year college or university in a degree program relating to math, physics, science, or engineering.

Call or write museum for further information.

1592—SMITHSONIAN INSTITUTION (National Air & Space Museum Verville Fellowship)

National Air and Space Museum
MRC 312
Washington DC 20560
Written inquiry

AMOUNT: $30,000 stipend for 12 months + travel and misc. expenses
DEADLINE(S): JAN 15
FIELD(S): Analysis of major trends, developments, and accomplishments in the history of aviation or space studies

A competitive nine- to twelve-month in-residence fellowship in the above field of study. Advanced degree is NOT a requirement. Contact Fellowship Coordinator at above location.

Open to all nationalities. Fluency in English required.

1593—UNCF/MERCK SCIENCE INITIATIVE (Undergraduate Science Research Scholarship Awards)

8260 Willow Oaks Corporate Dr.
P.O. Box 10444
Fairfax VA 22031-4511
703/205-3503
FAX: 703/205-3574
E-mail: uncfmerck@uncf.org
Internet: www.uncf.org/merck

AMOUNT: $25,000/yr. (max.)
DEADLINE(S): JAN 31
FIELD(S): Life & Physical Sciences

Open to African-Americans in their junior year of college who will receive a bachelor's degree in the following academic year. Must be enrolled full-time in any four-year college/university in the US and have a minimum 3.3 GPA. Must be US citizen/permanent resident. Financial need NOT a factor.

15 awards annually. Not renewable. Contact Jerry Bryant, Ph.D., for an application.

MATHEMATICS

1594—AIR FORCE RESERVE OFFICER TRAINING CORPS (AFROTC Scholarships)

551 E. Maxwell Blvd.
Maxwell AFB AL 36112-6106
334/953-7783

AMOUNT: Full tuition, books, & fees for all 4 years of college
DEADLINE(S): DEC 1
FIELD(S): Science, Engineering, Business, Political Science, Psychology, Geography, Foreign Studies, Foreign Language

Competitive scholarships based on individual merit to high school seniors and graduates who have not completed any full-time college work. Must be a US citizen between the ages of 17-27. Must also have GPA of 2.5 or above, be in top 40% of class, and complete Applicant Fitness Test. Cannot be a single parent. Your college/university must offer AFROTC.

2,300 awards annually. Contact above address for application packet.

1595—ALPHA KAPPA ALPHA SORORITY INC. (AKA/PIMS Summer Youth Mathematics & Science Camp)

5656 S. Stony Island Ave.
Chicago IL 60637
312/684-1282

AMOUNT: $1,000 value (for room; board & travel)
DEADLINE(S): MAY 1
FIELD(S): Mathematics, Science

Open to high school students grades 9-11 who have at least a 'B' average. Essay required for entry. This 2-week camp includes A.M. classes, P.M. activities, and a minimum of 4 field trips.

30 awards. Write for complete information.

1596—AMERICAN INSTITUTE OF AERO-NAUTICS AND ASTRONAUTICS (Undergraduate Scholarships)

1801 Alexander Bell Drive, Suite 500
Reston VA 20191-4344
800/639-AIAA or 703/264-7500
FAX: 703/264-7551
E-mail: custserv@aiaa.org
Internet: www.aiaa.org

AMOUNT: $2,000
DEADLINE(S): JAN 31
FIELD(S): Science, Engineering, Aeronautics, Astronautics

For students who have completed at least one academic semester or quarter of full-time college work in the area of science or engineering encompassed by the technical activities of the AIAA. Must have GPA of at least 3.0, be currently enrolled in accredited college or university. Membership in AIAA not required to apply but must become one before receiving a scholarship award.

Students who receive these awards are eligible for yearly continuation until completion of senior year upon submission of application, career essay, transcripts, and 2 letters of recommendation from college professor.

1597—AMERICAN PHYSICAL SOCIETY (Scholarships for Minority Undergraduate Students in Physics)

One Physics Ellipse
College Park MD 20740-3844
301/209-3232
Internet: www.aps.org

AMOUNT: $2,000
DEADLINE(S): FEB (1st Friday)
FIELD(S): Physics

Open to African Americans, Hispanic Americans, and American Indians who are US citizens majoring or planning to major in physics. Must be high school senior, college freshman, or college sophomore. Must submit completed application, personal statement, reference forms, official transcripts, and academic aptitude test scores.

Renewable an additional year. Contact APS for an application.

1598—ARMED FORCES COMMUNICATIONS AND ELECTRONICS ASSOCIATION (General Emmett Paige Scholarships for Military Personnel, Veterans, and Their Dependents)

4400 Fair Lakes Ct.
Fairfax VA 22033-3899
800/336-4583, ext. 6147
703/631-6100
Internet: www.afcea.org/awards/scholarships.htm

AMOUNT: $1,500
DEADLINE(S): MAR 1
FIELD(S): Electrical Engineering, Electronics, Computer Science, Computer Engineering, Physics, Mathematics

Scholarships in the above fields for persons on active duty in a military service or veterans and to their spouses or dependents who are working toward a degree in an accredited four-year college or university in the US Must have GPA of 3.4 or more.

Send a self-addressed, stamped envelope with information on the name of your school, field of study, GPA, and year in school to AFCEA Educational Foundation at above address. Applications available November through Feb. 1.

1599—ARMED FORCES COMMUNICA-TIONS AND ELECTRONICS ASSOCIATION (AFCEA ROTC Scholarships)

4400 Fair Lakes Ct.
Fairfax VA 22033-3899
800/336-4583, ext. 6147
703/631-6100
Internet: www.afcea.org/awards/scholarships.htm

AMOUNT: $1,500
DEADLINE(S): APR 1
FIELD(S): Electrical Engineering, Electronics, Computer Science, Computer Engineering, Physics, Mathematics

Scholarships in the above fields for ROTC students working toward a degree in an accredited four-year college or university in the US.

Must be nominated by Professors of Military Science, Naval Science, or Aerospace Studies. Contact the commander of each ROTC unit at your school.

1600—ARMED FORCES COMMUNICA-TIONS AND ELECTRONICS ASSOCIATION (General John A. Wickham Scholarships)

4400 Fair Lakes Ct.
Fairfax VA 22033-3899
800/336-4583, ext. 6149
703/631-6149
Internet: www.afcea.org/awards/scholarships.htm

AMOUNT: $1,500
DEADLINE(S): MAY 1
FIELD(S): Electrical Engineering, Electronics, Computer Science, Computer Engineering, Physics, Mathematics

Scholarships in the above fields for persons working toward degrees in accredited four-year colleges or universities in the US. Must have GPA of 3.4 or more.

Send a self-addressed, stamped envelope with information on the name of your school, field of study, GPA, and year in school to AFCEA Educational Foundation at above address. Applications available November through Feb. 1.

1601—ASSOCIATED WESTERN UNIVERSITIES, INC. (AWU Undergraduate Student Fellowships)

4190 S. Highland Drive, Suite 211
Salt Lake City UT 84124-2600
801/273-8911
FAX: 801/277-5632
Internet: www.awu.org

AMOUNT: $300/week stipend + travel allowance
DEADLINE(S): FEB 1
FIELD(S): Mathematics, Engineering, Technology, Science

Eight- to sixteen-week fellowships for undergraduate students enrolled in accredited institutions and who have completed at least one year of college by the start of the fellowship. Applicants reviewed on the basis of academic performance/class standing, career goals, recommendations, and compatibility of scientific interests and abilities with the needs and resources of the host facility. Citizenship restrictions may apply for some facilities.

500+ awards annually. Renewable (competitively with new application). Contact above address for an application.

1602—ASSOCIATED WESTERN UNIVERSITIES, INC. (AWU Visiting Scientist Fellowships)

4190 S. Highland Drive, Suite 211
Salt Lake City UT 84124-2600
801/273-8900

AMOUNT: Varies
DEADLINE(S): Varies (Two months prior to starting date)
FIELD(S): Engineering, Science, Mathematics, and Technology

Research fellowships for professionals with continued commitment to science and engineering. For use at one of 62 participating universities. US citizenship or permanent residency required.

For detailed information and list of cooperating facilities contact above location.

1603—ASSOCIATION FOR WOMEN IN SCIENCE EDUCATIONAL FOUNDATION (Dr. Vicki L. Schechtman Scholarship)

1200 New York Ave. NW
Suite 650
Washington DC 20005
202/326-8940 or 800/886-AWIS
E-mail: awis@awis.org
Internet: www.awis.org

AMOUNT: $1,000
DEADLINE(S): JAN 16
FIELD(S): Various Sciences and Social Sciences

For female undergraduate students who are US citizens and have a minimum GPA of 3.0. Summary page, essay describing career aspirations, transcripts, proof of matriculation (if available), and two reference letters required with application. Scholarships may be used for tuition, books, housing, research, equipment, etc.

See website or write to above address for an application and more information.

1604—ASSOCIATION FOR WOMEN IN SCIENCE EDUCATIONAL FOUNDATION (Ruth Satter Memorial Award)

1200 New York Ave. NW
Suite 650
Washington DC 20005
202/326-8940 or 800/886-AWIS
E-mail: awis@awis.org
Internet: www.awis.org

AMOUNT: $1,000
DEADLINE(S): JAN 16
FIELD(S): Various Sciences and Social Sciences

Scholarships for female doctoral students who have interrupted their education three years or more to raise a family. Summary page, description of research project, resume, references, transcripts, biographical sketch, and proof of eligibility from department head required. US citizens may attend any graduate institution; non-citizens must be enrolled in US institutions.

See website or write to above address for more information or an application.

1605—AT&T BELL LABORATORIES (Summer Research Program for Minorities & Women)

101 Crawfords Corner Road
Holmdel NJ 07733-3030
Written inquiry

AMOUNT: Salary + travel & living expenses for summer
DEADLINE(S): DEC 1
FIELD(S): Engineering, Math, Sciences, Computer Science

Program offers minority students and women students technical employment experience at Bell Laboratories. Students should have completed their third year of study at an accredited college or university. US citizen or permanent resident.

Selection is based partially on academic achievement and personal motivation. Write special programs manager—SRP for complete information.

1606—BARRY GOLDWATER SCHOLARSHIP AND EXCELLENCE IN EDUCATION FOUNDATION (Scholarships)

6225 Brandon Ave., Suite 315
Springfield VA 22150-2519
703/756-6012
FAX: 703/756-6015
E-mail: goldh2o@erols.com
Internet: www.act.org/goldwater

AMOUNT: $7,500/yr. (max.)
DEADLINE(S): FEB 1
FIELD(S): Math, Natural Sciences, Engineering

Open to college sophomores and juniors with a minimum 3.0 GPA. Must be US citizen, resident alien, or American national pursuing a degree at an accredited institution in math, natural sciences, or engineering disciplines that contribute to technological advances.

300 awards annually. See website or contact your Goldwater Faculty Representative on campus. Students must be nominated by their institution and cannot apply on their own.

1607—BROOKHAVEN WOMEN IN SCIENCE (Renate W. Chasman Scholarship)

P.O. Box 183
Upton NY 11973-5000
E-mail: pam@bnl.gov

AMOUNT: $2,000
DEADLINE(S): APR 1
FIELD(S): Natural Sciences, Engineering, Mathematics

Open ONLY to women who are residents of the boroughs of Brooklyn or Queens or the counties of Nassau or Suffolk in New York who are re-entering school after a period of study. For juniors, seniors, or first-year graduate students.

1 award annually. Not renewable. Contact Pam Mansfield at above location for an application. Phone calls are NOT accepted.

1608—BUSINESS & PROFESSIONAL WOMEN'S FOUNDATION (BPW Career Advancement Scholarship Program)

2012 Massachusetts Ave. NW
Washington DC 20036-1070
202/293-1200, ext. 169

FAX: 202/861-0298
Internet: www.bpwusa.org
AMOUNT: $500-$1,000
DEADLINE(S): APR 15
FIELD(S): Biology, Science, Education, Engineering, Social Science, Paralegal, Humanities, Business, Math, Computers, Law, MD, DD

For women (US citizens) aged 25+ accepted into accredited program at US institution (+Puerto Rico & Virgin Islands). Must graduate within 12 to 24 months from the date of grant and demonstrate critical financial need. Must have a plan to upgrade skills, train for a new career field, or to enter/re-enter the job market.

Full- or part-time study. For info see website or send business-sized, self-addressed, double-stamped envelope.

1609—COMMUNITY FOUNDATION OF WESTERN MASSACHUSETTS (Charles R. Allan & Judith V. Carlson Scholarships)

1500 Main Street
P.O. Box 15769
Springfield MA 01115
413/732-2858
AMOUNT: $1,500
DEADLINE(S): APR 15
FIELD(S): Physics

Open to graduating seniors from Springfield Central High School and Springfield High School of Science and Technology to pursue full-time study at a four-year college. Based on financial need, academic merit, and extracurricular activities. Recipients will be chosen as the best scholars in physics by each high school.

2 awards annually. Contact Community Foundation or your financial aid office for details. Notification is in June.

1610—COMMUNITY FOUNDATION SILICON VALLEY (Valley Scholars Program)

111 W. Saint John Street, Suite 230
San Jose CA 95113
408/278-0270
FAX: 408/278-0280
Internet: www.cfsv.org
AMOUNT: $20,000 (over 4 years of college)
DEADLINE(S): Varies (early spring)
FIELD(S): Science and/or Math

A scholarship program for public high school students in the Silicon Valley (San Mateo and Santa Clara counties and Fremont Union High School District, California) who have demonstrated enthusiasm and aptitude for science and math. Must be US citizen or permanent resident.

Up to 20 students are selected each year. Each Valley Scholar receives financial support, guidance through the college admission process, and a mentor whose interests match their own. Students may apply during their sophomore year of high school and must be academically outstanding.

1611—ELECTRONIC INDUSTRIES FOUNDATION (Scholarship Program)

2500 Wilson Blvd., Suite 210
Arlington VA 22201-3834
703/907-7408
E-mail: mvorac@eia.org
AMOUNT: $5,000
DEADLINE(S): FEB 1
FIELD(S): Electronics, Telecommunications, Electrical Engineering, Industrial Manufacturing, Industrial Engineering, Physics, Electromechanical Technology, Mechanical Applied Sciences

Open to students with disabilities (as defined by Americans with Disabilities Act) who are high school seniors accepted at an accredited four-year college/university. Must be US citizen pursuing studies that lead to career in design, manufacture, or provision of materials, components, products, and services for US high tech, electronics, and communications industries. Based on GPA, goals, activities, need, essay, and letters of recommendation.

Send self-addressed, stamped envelope to EIA for an application. Recipients notified by May 1st; awards paid directly to school.

1612—GERBER SCIENTIFIC, INC. (H. Joseph Gerber Vision Scholarship Program)

83 Gerber Road West
South Windsor CT 06074
860/648-8027
Internet: www.gerberscientific.com
AMOUNT: Varies
DEADLINE(S): MAR 15
FIELD(S): Engineering, Mathematics, Computer Science, Natural Sciences

Scholarship program for high school seniors in Connecticut.

50 scholarships to be awarded.

1613—INSTITUTE FOR OPERATIONS RESEARCH AND THE MANAGEMENT SCIENCES (INFORMS Summer Internship Directory)

P.O. Box 64794
Baltimore MD 21264-4794
800/4INFORMS
FAX: 410/684-2963
E-mail: jps@informs.org
Internet: www.informs.org/INTERN/
AMOUNT: Varies
DEADLINE(S): Varies
FIELD(S): Fields related to information management: business management, engineering, mathematics

A website listing of summer internships in the field of operations research and management sciences. Both applicants and employers can register online.

Access website for list.

1614—INSTITUTE OF INTERNATIONAL EDUCATION (National Security Education Program-Undergraduate Scholarships)

1400 K Street NW, 6th Floor
Washington DC 20005-2403
202/326-7697
800/618-NSEP (6737)
E-mail: nsep@iie.org
Internet: http://www.iie.org/nsep/
AMOUNT: Varies: up to $8,000/semester
DEADLINE(S): FEB 8
FIELD(S): Open to all majors; preference to applied sciences, engineering, business, economics, math, computer science, international affairs, political science, history, and the policy sciences

For study abroad OUTSIDE the US, Canada, Australia, New Zealand, and Western Europe. For study in areas deemed critical to US national security. Applications available on US campuses from August through early December. Or contact organization for details.

Inquire at above location for details.

1615—JEWISH FEDERATION OF METROPOLITAN CHICAGO (Academic Scholarship Program for Studies in the Sciences)

One South Franklin Street
Chicago IL 60606
Written inquiry
AMOUNT: Varies
DEADLINE(S): MAR 1
FIELD(S): Mathematics, Engineering, or Science

Scholarships for college juniors, seniors, and graduate students who are Jewish and are residents of Chicago, IL and Cook County.

Academic achievement and financial need are considered. Applications accepted after Dec. 1.

1616—JEWISH VOCATIONAL SERVICE (Academic Scholarship Program)

One S. Franklin Street
Chicago IL 60606
312/357-4500
FAX: 312/855-3282
TTY: 312/855-3282
E-mail: jvschicago@jon.cjfny.org

AMOUNT: $5,000 (max.)
DEADLINE(S): MAR 1
FIELD(S): "Helping" Professions, Mathematics, Engineering, Sciences, Communications (at Univ IL only), Law (certain schools in IL only)

Open to Jewish men and women legally domiciled in the greater Chicago metropolitan area, who are identified as having promise for significant contributions in their chosen careers, and are in need of financial assistance for full-time academic programs in above areas. Must have entered undergraduate junior year in career programs requiring no postgrad education, be in graduate/professional school, or be in a voc-tech training program. Interview required.

Renewable. Contact JVS for an application between December 1st and February 15th.

1617—LOS ANGELES COUNCIL OF BLACK PROFESSIONAL ENGINEERS (Al-Ben Scholarship)

P.O. Box 881029
Los Angeles CA 90009
310/635-7734
E-mail: secy1@lablackengineers.org
Internet: www.lablackengineers.org/scholarships.html

AMOUNT: Varies
DEADLINE(S): Varies
FIELD(S): Engineering, Mathematics, Computer Studies, or Applied Scientific Studies

This organization provides scholarships for technically inclined pre-college and undergraduate students enrolled in one of the above fields. Must be of African American, Native American, or Hispanic ancestry. Although preference is given to students attending college in Southern

California or who are Southern California residents, the awards are open to all qualified students attending college in the United States.

See website for more information. Application for the coming year will be on the website during November.

1618—LOUISIANA OFFICE OF STUDENT FINANCIAL ASSISTANCE (Tuition Opportunity Program for Students-Teachers Award)

P.O. Box 91202
Baton Rouge LA 70821-9202
800/259-5626, ext. 1012
FAX: 504/922-0790
Internet: www.osfa.state.la.us

AMOUNT: $4,000/yr. (education majors); $6,000/yr. (math/chemistry majors)
DEADLINE(S): JUN 1
FIELD(S): Education, Math, Chemistry

Open to Louisiana residents pursuing undergraduate or graduate study at Louisiana colleges/universities and majoring in one of the above fields leading to teacher certification. Loans are forgiven by working as a certified teacher in Louisiana one year for each year loan is received.

Apply by completing the Free Application for Federal Student Aid (FAFSA). See your school's financial aid office or contact LOSFA for FAFSA form.

1619—LOUISIANA STATE UNIVERSITY AT SHREVEPORT (George Paul Bonner Physics Scholarship)

College of Sciences
One University Place
Shreveport LA 71115-2399
318/797-5363 or 318/797-5246
FAX: 318/797-5366
E-mail: finaid@pilot.lsus.edu
Internet: www.lsus.edu

AMOUNT: Varies
DEADLINE(S): Varies
FIELD(S): Physics

Must be US citizen who is a sophomore, junior, or senior physics major at LSUS. Must have minimum 3.0 GPA, and preference is given to students with financial need who are interested in applied physics, as determined by an interview. Recipient is selected by a committee appointed by the Dean of the College of Sciences.

Contact the Dean of the College of Sciences at LSUS for an application.

1620—MICROSOFT CORPORATION (National Minority and/or Women's Technical Scholarships)

One Microsoft Way
Redmond WA 98052-8303
E-mail: scholar@microsoft.com
Internet: microsoft.com/college/scholarship.htm

AMOUNT: $1,000
DEADLINE(S): FEB 27
FIELD(S): Computer Science, Computer Engineering, or a related technical discipline, such as Math or Physics

Scholarships for women and minorities (African Americans, Hispanics, or Native Americans) enrolled full-time in the above fields with a demonstrated interest in computers and making satisfactory progress towards a degree. Must be in sophomore or junior year (or fourth year in a five-year program). Awards are made through designated schools and are not transferable to other institutions.

10 awards—five for women and five for people of color listed above. For US citizens or permanent residents. See website above for details.

1621—MICROSOFT CORPORATION (Summer Internships)

One Microsoft Way
Redmond WA 98052-8303
425/882-8080 (recruiting)
800/892-3181 (jobline)
E-mail: scholar@microsoft.com
Internet: microsoft.com/college/scholarship.htm

AMOUNT: Varies
DEADLINE(S): None
FIELD(S): Computer Science, Computer Engineering, or a relatied technical discipline, such as Math or Physics

Summer internships for individuals with a deep passion for technological advancement. Must commit to a 12-week minimum. Includes transportation, shipping costs, and shared cost of housing. Competitive compensation offered.

Check website above for details.

1622—NAACP NATIONAL OFFICE (NAACP Willems Scholarship)

4805 Mount Hope Drive
Baltimore MD 21215
401/358-8900

AMOUNT: $2,000 undergrads; $3,000 grads

DEADLINE(S): APR 30

FIELD(S): Engineering, Chemistry, Physics, Mathematics

Open to NAACP male members majoring in one of the above areas. Undergrads must have GPA of 2.5+; graduates' GPAs must be 3.0+. Renewable if the required GPA is maintained.

Financial need must be established. Two letters of recommendation typed on letterhead from teachers or professors in the major field of specialization. Write for complete information. Include a legal size, self-addressed, stamped envelope.

1623—NAACP NATIONAL OFFICE (NAACP/Department of Energy Scholarship)

4805 Mount Hope Drive
Baltimore MD 21215-3297
410/486-9133

AMOUNT: $10,000/year tuition/stipend

DEADLINE(S): APR 30

FIELD(S): Engineering, Science, Computer Science, Mathematics, Environmental Studies

Open to high school seniors who are NAACP members with a minimum 3.0 GPA. Applicants must participate in 120 hours of community service; at least 1 summer internship at a DOE facility and be employed by DOE or DOE contractor for 2 years.

Write for complete information; enclose a self-addressed 9 x 12 envelope.

1624—NATIONAL TECHNICAL ASSOCIATION, INC. (Scholarship Competitions for Minorities and Women in Science and Engineering)

6919 North 19th Street
Philadelphia PA 19126-1506
215/549-5743
FAX: 215/549-6509
E-mail: ntamfj1@aol.com
Internet: www.huenet.com/nta

AMOUNT: $500-$5,000

DEADLINE(S): Varies

FIELD(S): Science, Mathematics, Engineering, and Applied Technology

Scholarships competitions for minorities and women pursuing degrees in the above fields. Additional scholarships are available through local chapters of NTA.

Check website or write to above address for details and for locations of local chapters.

1625—NATIVE AMERICAN SCHOLARSHIP FUND, INC. (Scholarships)

8200 Mountain Road NE, Suite 203
Albuquerque NM 87110
505/262-2351
FAX: 505/262-0543
E-mail: NScholarsh@aol.com

AMOUNT: Varies

DEADLINE(S): MAR 15; APR 15; SEP 15

FIELD(S): Math, Engineering, Science, Business, Education, Computer Science

Open to American Indians or Alaskan Natives (1/4 degree or more) enrolled as members of a federally recognized, state recognized, or terminated tribe. For graduate or undergraduate study at an accredited four-year college or university.

208 awards annually. Contact Lucille Kelley, Director of Recruitment, for an application.

1626—OAK RIDGE INSTITUTE FOR SCIENCE AND EDUCATION (ORISE Education & Training Programs)

P.O. Box 117
Oak Ridge TN 37831-0117
Internet: www.orau.gov/orise/educ.htm

AMOUNT: Varies

DEADLINE(S): Varies

FIELD(S): Engineering, Aeronautics, Computer Science, Technology, Earth Science, Environmental Studies, Biology, Chemistry, Physics, Medical Research

Numerous programs funded by the US Department of Energy are offered for undergraduate students through postgraduate researchers. Includes fellowship and internship opportunities throughout the US. Some have citizenship restrictions. Travel may be included.

See website or write for a catalog of specific programs and requirements.

1627—OKLAHOMA MEDICAL RESEARCH FOUNDATION (Sir Alexander Fleming Scholar Program)

825 Northeast 13th Street
Oklahoma City OK 73104
405/271-7218
800/522-0211 (in-state)

AMOUNT: $2,500 salary + housing

DEADLINE(S): MAR 1

FIELD(S): Sciences

Summer scholarship program (June and July) for Oklahoma students who have completed their junior year of high school through those in their junior year of college at time of application. Excellent academic standing and aptitude in science and math are essential. Students will work in the laboratories of the above organization. Research projects will be selected from: alcoholism/liver disease, arthritis/immunology, carcinogenesis, cardiovascular biology, and more.

Named for the scientist who discovered penicillin and dedicated OMRF in 1949. Contact organization for further information and application forms.

1628—OPEN SOCIETY INSTITUTE (Environmental Management Fellowships)

400 West 59th Street
New York NY 10019
212/548-0600 or 212/757-2323
FAX: 212/548-4679 or 212/548-4600
Internet: www.soros.org/efp.html

AMOUNT: Fees, room, board, living stipend, textbooks, international transportation, health insurance

DEADLINE(S): NOV 15

FIELD(S): Earth Sciences, Natural Sciences, Humanities (exc. language), Anthropology, Sociology, Mathematics, or Engineering

Two-year fellowships for use in selected universities in the US for international students. For students/professionals in fields related to environmental policy, legislation, and remediation techniques applicable to their home countries.

To apply, contact your local Soros Foundation or Open Society Institute. Further details on website.

1629—PENINSULA COMMUNITY FOUNDATION (Dr. Mary Finegold Scholarship)

1700 S. El Camino Real, #300
San Mateo CA 94402
650/358-9369
FAX: 650/358-9817

AMOUNT: $1,000

DEADLINE(S): MAR 27 (5 P.M.)

FIELD(S): Sciences

Scholarships for senior girls graduating from high school in Palo Alto, California, who intend to complete a four-year degree in the sciences. Special consideration will be given to girls who have demonstrated a "pioneering" spirit in that they have not been constrained by stereotypical female roles and to those facing financial hardship.

Award was established in the honor of Dr. Mary Finegold who, after completing her medical studies, elected to stay at home until her youngest child was in high school before beginning her medical practice. She was a school physician.

1630—SAN DIEGO AEROSPACE MUSEUM (Bill Gibbs Scholarship)

Education Dept.
2001 Pan American Plaza
San Diego CA 92101
619/234-8291, ext. 19
FAX: 619/233-4526
Internet: aerospacemuseum.org/ Scholastic.HTML

AMOUNT: Varies
DEADLINE(S): Varies
FIELD(S): Aerospace: math, physics, science, or engineering

For students who are residents of San Diego County, California, who have an aerospace career interest and who have been accepted to a four-year college or university in a degree program relating to math, physics, science, or engineering.

Call or write museum for further information.

1631—SCIENCE SERVICE (Intel International Science & Engineering Fair)

1719 N Street NW
Washington DC 20036
202/785-2255
FAX: 202/785-1243
E-mail: jkim@sciserv.org
Internet: www.sciserv.org

AMOUNT: Varies (totaling $2 million)
DEADLINE(S): DEC 1
FIELD(S): Science, Math, Engineering

Open to high school students (grades 9-12) who participate in this worldwide science competition. Scholarships, internships with noted scientists, and travel and equipment grants are awarded.

Contact Jinny Kim at Science Service for official ISEF entry book. Sponsored by the Intel Corporation.

1632—SCIENCE SERVICE (Intel Science Talent Search)

1719 N Street NW
Washington DC 20036
202/785-2255
FAX: 202/785-1243
E-mail: cmdroms@sciserv.org
Internet: www.sciserv.org

AMOUNT: $100,000 (1st place); $75,000 (2nd); $50,000 (3rd); $25,000 (4th-6th); $20,000 (7th-10th); 30 at $5,000; 300 at $1,000; 40 laptops
DEADLINE(S): DEC 1
FIELD(S): Science, Math, Engineering

Open to high school seniors who submit a report of an independent research project in science, math, or engineering. Must include transcripts, SAT scores, and official entry form. Forty finalists are invited to Washington, DC, to participate in competition. Purpose is to encourage students to pursue careers in science and engineering.

40 awards annually. Contact Courtney Droms at Science Service for official STS entry book. Sponsored by the Intel Corporation.

1633—SKIDMORE COLLEGE (Merit Scholarships in Math and Science)

Office of Admissions
Saratoga Springs NY 12866-1632
800/867-6007
E-mail: admissions@skidmore.edu
Internet: www.skidmore.edu/campus/ merit2.html

AMOUNT: $10,000/yr.
DEADLINE(S): FEB 1
FIELD(S): Math or Science

Scholarships for students excelling in the above fields. Awards are based on talent, not financial need. Recipients are not required to major in a scientific or mathematical discipline, but they will be expected to demonstrate serious research in one or more of these areas.

5 scholarships per year. For more information, visit website.

1634—SMITHSONIAN INSTITUTION (National Air & Space Museum Verville Fellowship)

National Air and Space Museum
MRC 312
Washington DC 20560
Written inquiry

AMOUNT: $30,000 stipend for 12 months + travel and misc. expenses
DEADLINE(S): JAN 15
FIELD(S): Analysis of major trends, developments, and accomplishments in the history of aviation or space studies

A competitive nine- to twelve-month in-residence fellowship in the above field of study. Advanced degree is NOT a requirement. Contact Fellowship Coordinator at above location.

Open to all nationalities. Fluency in English required.

1635—SOCIETY OF PHYSICS STUDENTS (SPS Scholarships)

National Office
One Physics Ellipse
College Park MD 20740-3843
301/209-3007

AMOUNT: $4,000 (1st place); $2,000 (second); $1,000 (all others)
DEADLINE(S): FEB 15
FIELD(S): Physics

SPS members. For final year of full-time study leading to a B.S. degree in physics. Consideration given to high scholastic performance, potential for continued scholastic development in physics, and active SPS participation.

Nonrenewable. 14 scholarships per year. Write for complete information.

1636—SPACE COAST CREDIT UNION (Two-Year Scholarships)

Marketing Dept.
P.O. Box 2470
Melbourne FL 32902
Internet: www.sccu.com/scholarship/

AMOUNT: $750/year, two years; $1,000 bonus if go on for Bachelors
DEADLINE(S): APR 15
FIELD(S): Math, Economics, Science, Computer Science, Marketing, Journalism, Political Science

Must be graduating from a high school in Brevard, Volusia, Flagler, or Indian River counties, be a member of SCCU, have a minimum 3.0 GPA, planning to attend a two-year Florida institution of higher education for an associates degree, and be willing to write a 200-word essay on the topic "Why credit unions are valuable to society."

4 annual awards. Students going on to complete a four-year degree could be eligible for a bonus scholarship of $1,000 for the next two years. For membership information or an application, see our web page or write to the above address.

1637—STATE FARM COMPANIES FOUNDATION (Exceptional Student Fellowship)

One State Farm Plaza, SC-3
Bloomington IL 61710-0001
309/766-2039/2161
E-mail: Nancy.Lynn.gr3o@ statefarm.com

Internet: www.statefarm.com

AMOUNT: $3,000 (nominating institution receives $250)

DEADLINE(S): FEB 15

FIELD(S): Accounting, Business Administration, Actuarial Science, Computer Science, Economics, Finance, Insurance/Risk Management, Investments, Management, Marketing, Mathematics, Statistics

For US citizens who are full-time juniors or seniors when they apply. Must demonstrate significant leadership in extracurricular activities, have minimum 3.6 GPA, and attend accredited US college/university. Must be nominated by dean, department head, professor, or academic advisor.

50 awards annually. Not renewable. See website, visit your financial aid office, or write to above address for an application.

1638—TEXAS SOCIETY OF PROFESSIONAL ENGINEERS (Scholarships)

P.O. Box 2145
Austin TX 78768
512/472-9286 or 800/580-8973
Internet: www.tspe.org

AMOUNT: Varies

DEADLINE(S): JAN 30

FIELD(S): Engineering (math, sciences)

Scholarships for graduating high school seniors who are Texas residents planning to attend Texas engineering colleges

Contact organization for details. Application is on website.

1639—THE AMERICAN LEGION, DEPT. OF MARYLAND, INC. (Scholarship Program)

101 N. Gay Street
Baltimore MD 21202
410/752-3104
FAX: 410/752-3822
Internet: mdlegion@clark.net

AMOUNT: $500

DEADLINE(S): APR 1

FIELD(S): Math, Science

Open to the dependents of veterans who are residents of Maryland. Must not have attained their 20th birthday by January 1 of the year applying. Must intend to be a full-time student (at least 12 credits a semester).

5 awards annually. Send letter stating scholarship as well as financial need to Dept. Adjutant at above address.

1640—THE WALT DISNEY COMPANY (American Teacher Awards)

P.O. Box 9805
Calabasas CA 91372

AMOUNT: $2,500 (36 awards); $25,000 (Outstanding Teacher of the Year)

DEADLINE(S): FEB 15

FIELD(S): Teachers: athletic coach, early childhood, English, foreign language/ESL, general elementary, mathematics, performing arts, physical education/health, science, social studies, visual arts, voc-tech education

Awards for K-12 teachers in the above fields.

Teachers, or anyone who knows a great teacher, can write for applications at the above address.

1641—U.S. DEPARTMENT OF DEFENSE (High School Apprenticeship Program)

US Army Cold Regions Research and Engineering Laboratory
72 Lyme Road
Hanover NH 03755
603/646-4500
DSN: 220-4500
FAX: 603/646-4693
Internet: www.acq.osd.mil/ddre/edugate/s-aindx.html

AMOUNT: Internship

DEADLINE(S): None specified

FIELD(S): Sciences and Engineering

A teacher must recommend you for these three competitive high school apprenticeships with our Laboratory. High school students from New Hampshire who are at least 16 and who have completed their junior year in high school are eligible. Should have interest and ability in science, engineering, or mathematics.

Applications are available from participating local high school guidance counselors. Contact Susan Koh at the above address for more information.

1642—U.S. DEPARTMENT OF DEFENSE (SEAP–Science & Engineering Apprenticeship Program)

707 22nd Street NW
Washington DC 20052
202/994-2234
FAX: 202/994-2459
Internet: www.acq.osd.mil/ddre/edugate/ceeindx.htm/#A010

AMOUNT: $1,400 (min.)

DEADLINE(S): JAN 26

FIELD(S): Science, Engineering

Eight-week summer apprenticeships throughout the US are available to high school students who are US citizens planning careers in science or engineering. Based on grades, science/math courses taken, scores on standardized tests, areas of interest, teacher recommendations, and personal student statement. Students responsible for transportation to and from site.

See website or contact M. Phillips for an application. Refer to Code #A010.

1643—U.S. DEPARTMENT OF DEFENSE-NATIONAL SECURITY AGENCY (Director's Summer Program)

9800 Savage Road
Ste. 6779—Summer (S234)
Fort Meade MD 20755-6779
800/669-0703
FAX: 410/854-4593
E-mail: cmoconn@ncsc.mil
Internet: www.nsa.gov

AMOUNT: Internship only

DEADLINE(S): OCT 15

FIELD(S): Mathematics

Twelve-week summer work experience between junior and senior year in college or grad school for math majors. Must be US citizen and be eligible for top security clearance. Financial need NOT a factor.

See website or contact C. O'Connor for more information on this program.

1644—UNCF/MERCK SCIENCE INITIATIVE (Undergraduate Science Research Scholarship Awards)

8260 Willow Oaks Corporate Dr.
P.O. Box 10444
Fairfax VA 22031-4511
703/205-3503
FAX: 703/205-3574
E-mail: uncfmerck@uncf.org
Internet: www.uncf.org/merck

AMOUNT: $25,000/yr. (max.)

DEADLINE(S): JAN 31

FIELD(S): Life & Physical Sciences

Open to African-Americans in their junior year of college who will receive a bachelor's degree in the following academic year. Must be enrolled full-time in any four-year college/university in the US and have a minimum 3.3 GPA. Must be US citizen/permanent resident. Financial need NOT a factor.

15 awards annually. Not renewable. Contact Jerry Bryant, Ph.D., for an application.

1645—WOMEN IN DEFENSE (HORIZONS Scholarship Foundation)

NDIA
2111 Wilson Blvd., Suite 400
Arlington VA 22201-3061
703/247-2552
FAX: 703/522-1885
E-mail: dnwlee@moon.jic.com
Internet: www.adpa.org/wid/
horizon/Scholar.htm

AMOUNT: $500+
DEADLINE(S): NOV 1; JUL 1
FIELD(S): Engineering, Computer Science, Physics, Mathematics, Business, Law, International Relations, Political Science, Operations Research, Economics, and fields relevant to a career in the areas of national security and defense

For women who are US citizens, have minimum GPA of 3.25, demonstrate financial need, are currently enrolled at an accredited university/college (full- or part-time—both grads and undergrad juniors/seniors are eligible), and demonstrate interest in pursuing a career related to national security.

Application is online or send SASE, #10 envelope, to Woody Lee, HORIZONS Scholarship Director.

1646—WOODROW WILSON NATIONAL FELLOWSHIP FOUNDATION (Leadership Program for Teachers)

CN 5281
Princeton NJ 08543-5281
609/452-7007
FAX: 609/452-0066
E-mail: marchioni@woodrow.org OR irish@woodrow.org
Internet: www.woodrow.org

AMOUNT: Varies
DEADLINE(S): Varies
FIELD(S): Science, Mathematics

WWLPT offers summer institutes for middle and high school teachers in science and mathematics. One- and two-week teacher outreach, TORCH Institutes, are held in the summer throughout the US.

See website or contact WWNFF for an application.

1647—WOODS HOLE OCEANOGRAPHIC INSTITUTION (Traineeships in Oceanography for Minority Group Undergraduates)

360 Woods Hole Road
Woods Hole MA 02543-1541

508/289-2219
FAX: 508/457-2188
E-mail: mgately@whoi.edu
Internet: www.whoi.edu

AMOUNT: Varies
DEADLINE(S): FEB 16
FIELD(S): Physical/Natural Sciences, Mathematics, Engineering

For minority undergraduates enrolled in US colleges/universities who have completed at least two semesters. These awards provide training and research experience for students with interests in the above fields. Traineeships may be awarded for a ten- to twelve-week period in the summer or for a semester during the academic year.

Renewable. For an application/more information, contact the Education Office, Clark Laboratory 223, MS #31, at above address.

MEDICAL DOCTOR

1648—AIR FORCE RESERVE OFFICER TRAINING CORPS (AFROTC Pre-Health Scholarships)

551 E. Maxwell Blvd.
Maxwell AFB AL 36112-6106
334/953-7783

AMOUNT: Full tuition, lab fees, books, + $150/month
DEADLINE(S): JUN 15
FIELD(S): Health Professions

For US citizens who are currently enrolled full-time college students, with at least a 3.5 GPA. Must provide personal statement of interest in a career in the medical profession in the uniformed services, as well as three letters of recommendation. Certain courses must be completed by end of junior year.

Contact above address for application packet. The AFHPSP continues your education by providing up to 4 years of medical school to eligible Air Force ROTC Pre-Health cadets.

1649—AMERICAN FOUNDATION FOR THE BLIND (Paul W. Ruckes Scholarship)

11 Penn Plaza, Suite 300
New York NY 10001
212/502-7661
FAX: 212/502-7771
E-mail: juliet@afb.org
Internet: www.afb.org

AMOUNT: $1,000
DEADLINE(S): APR 30

FIELD(S): Engineering, Computer/Physical/Life Sciences

Open to legally blind and visually impaired undergraduate and graduate students pursuing a degree in one of above fields. Must be US citizen. Must submit written documentation of visual impairment from ophthalmologist or optometrist (need not be legally blind); official transcripts; proof of college/university acceptance; three letters of recommendation; and typewritten statement describing goals, work experience, extracurricular activities, and how monies will be used.

1 award annually. See website or contact Julie Tucker at AFB for an application.

1650—AMERICAN HEART ASSOCIATION (Helen N. and Harold B. Shapira Scholarship)

4701 West 77th Street
Minneapolis MN 55435
612/835-3300

AMOUNT: $1,000
DEADLINE(S): APR 1
FIELD(S): Medicine

For pre-med undergraduate students and medical students who are accepted to or enrolled in an accredited Minnesota college or university. Medical students should be in a curriculum that is related to the heart and circulatory system.

May be renewed once. US citizenship or legal residency required. Write for complete information.

1651—AMERICAN INDIAN SCIENCE AND ENGINEERING SOCIETY (A.T. Anderson Memorial Scholarship)

P.O. Box 9828
Albuquerque NM 87119-9828
505/765-1052
FAX: 505/765-5608
E-mail: scholarships@aises.org
Internet: www.aises.org/scholarships

AMOUNT: $1,000-$2,000
DEADLINE(S): JUN 15
FIELD(S): Medicine, Natural Resources, Science, Engineering

Open to undergraduate and graduate students who are at least 1/4 American Indian or recognized as member of a tribe. Must be member of AISES ($10 fee), enrolled full-time at an accredited institution, and demonstrate financial need.

Renewable. See website or contact Patricia Browne for an application and/or membership information.

1652—ARMENIAN GENERAL BENEVO-LENT UNION (Educational Loan Program)

Education Dept.
31 W. 52nd Street
New York NY 10019-6118
212/765-8260
FAX: 212/765-8209/8209
E-mail: agbuny@aol.com

AMOUNT: $5,000 to $7,500/yr.
DEADLINE(S): APR 1
FIELD(S): Law (J.D.) and Medicine (M.D.)

Loans for full-time students of Armenian heritage pursuing their first professional degrees in law or medicine. Must be attending highly competitive institutions in the US GPA of 3.5 or more required.

Loan repayments begin within 12 months of completion of full-time study and extend 5 to 10 years, depending on the size of the loan. Interest is 3%. Write for complete information.

1653—ARTHUR & DOREEN PARRETT SCHOLARSHIP TRUST FUND (Scholarships)

c/o U.S. Bank of Washington
P.O. Box 720
Trust Dept., 8th Floor
Seattle WA 98111-0720
206/344-4653

AMOUNT: Up to $3,500
DEADLINE(S): JUL 31
FIELD(S): Engineering, Science, Medicine, Dentistry

Washington state resident who has completed her/his first year of college by July 31. Open to students enrolled in above schools. Awards tenable at any accredited undergrad college or university.

Approximately 15 awards per year. Write for complete information.

1654—ARTHUR M. MILLER FUND

P.O. Box 1122
Wichita KS 67201-0004
316/261-4609

AMOUNT: Varies
DEADLINE(S): MAR 31
FIELD(S): Medicine or related fields

Scholarships for Kansas residents for the study of medicine or related fields at accredited institutions.

Send SASE for formal application.

1655—ASSOCIATION ON AMERICAN INDIAN AFFAIRS, INC. (Emergency Aid and Health Professions Scholarships)

P.O. Box 268
Sisseton SD 57262
605/698-3998 or 605/698-3787
FAX: 605/698-3316

AMOUNT: $50-$300
DEADLINE(S): MAY 1
FIELD(S): Health professions

Emergency funding program for full-time undergraduates studying full-time in a health field. Based on financial need. Must be at least 1/4 Indian and write a one- to two-page essay on the nature of the emergency need.

Applications available Sept. 1. Send SASE to above location.

1656—BECA FOUNDATION (Alice Newell Joslyn Medical Fund)

310 Via Vera Cruz, Suite 101
San Marcos CA 92069
760/471-5465
FAX: 760/471-9175

AMOUNT: $500-$2,000
DEADLINE(S): MAR 1
FIELD(S): Medicine, Health Care, Nursing, Dental/Medical Assisting, Physical Therapy

Open to Latino students who live in or attend college in San Diego County, CA, at time of application. For high school seniors and those already in college pursuing undergraduate or graduate education. Based on financial need, scholastic determination, and community/cultural awareness. BECA also provides a mentor to each scholarship recipient.

Send self-addressed, stamped envelope to BECA for an application.

1657—BOYS AND GIRLS CLUBS OF SAN DIEGO (Spence Reese Scholarship Fund)

1761 Hotel Circle So., Suite 123
San Diego CA 92108
619/298-3520

AMOUNT: $2,000/yr.
DEADLINE(S): MAY 15
FIELD(S): Medicine, Law, Engineering, Political Science

Open to male high school seniors planning a career in one of the above fields. Must be residents of Imperial, Riverside, Orange, San Diego, or Los Angeles counties in California. Boys and Girls Club affiliation NOT required.

$10 application fee. Renewable up to 4 years. Send a self-addressed, stamped envelope to Boys and Girls Club for an application after January 1st.

1658—BUSINESS & PROFESSIONAL WOMEN'S FOUNDATION (BPW Career Advancement Scholarship Program)

2012 Massachusetts Ave. NW
Washington DC 20036-1070
202/293-1200, ext. 169
FAX: 202/861-0298
Internet: www.bpwusa.org

AMOUNT: $500-$1,000
DEADLINE(S): APR 15
FIELD(S): Biology, Science, Education, Engineering, Social Science, Paralegal, Humanities, Business, Math, Computers, Law, MD, DD

For women (US citizens) aged 25+ accepted into accredited program at US institution (+Puerto Rico & Virgin Islands). Must graduate within 12 to 24 months from the date of grant and demonstrate critical financial need. Must have a plan to upgrade skills, train for a new career field, or to enter/re-enter the job market.

Full- or part-time study. For info see website or send business-sized, self-addressed, double-stamped envelope.

1659—CLEM JAUNICH EDUCATION TRUST (Scholarships)

7801 E. Bushlake Road, Suite 260
Bloomington MN 55439
612/546-1555

AMOUNT: $750-$3,000
DEADLINE(S): JUL 1
FIELD(S): Theology, Medicine

Open to students who have attended public or parochial school in the Delano (MN) school district or currently reside within 7 miles of the city of Delano MN. Awards support undergraduate or graduate study in theology or medicine.

4-6 awards annually. Contact Joseph Abrahams for an application.

1660—COLUMBIANA COUNTY PUBLIC HEALTH LEAGUE TRUST FUND (Grants)

P.O. Box 1428
Steubenville OH 43952
740/283-8433
FAX: 740/282-4530

AMOUNT: Varies
DEADLINE(S): FEB 28

FIELD(S): Respiratory Illness, Medicine, Medical Research, Pharmacy, Medical Technology, Physical Therapy, Nursing, Dental Hygiene, Occupational Therapy

Open to undergraduate and graduate Columbiana County, Ohio, residents who are pursuing medical education or research in one of the above fields. Preference given to respiratory illness. Students of veterinary medicine NOT eligible.

Contact Sherrill Schmied for an application.

1661—CUYAHOGA COUNTY MEDICAL FOUNDATION (Scholarship Grant Program)

6000 Rockside Woods Blvd.
Suite 150
Cleveland OH 44131-2352
216/520-1000

AMOUNT: $600-$1,700
DEADLINE(S): JUN 1
FIELD(S): Medicine, Dentistry, Pharmacy, Nursing, Osteopathy

Grants open to residents of Cuyahoga County who are accepted to or enrolled in an accredited professional school in one of the above areas.

Approx 40 awards per year. Write for complete information.

1662—DEKALB COUNTY PRODUCERS SUPPLY & FARM BUREAU (Medical Scholarship)

1350 W. Prairie Drive
Sycamore IL 60178
815/756-6361

AMOUNT: Varies
DEADLINE(S): JUNE
FIELD(S): Medical Doctor, Nursing

Applicants (or their parents) must have been voting or associate members of Dekalb County Farm Bureau for at least 2 years prior to application; agree to practice in rural Illinois for 3 years upon completion of training and be a US citizen.

Must have been accepted to or be attending medical school or a nursing program. Write to Virginia Fleetwood at above address for complete information.

1663—DEPARTMENT OF THE ARMY (Armed Forces Health Professions Scholarships)

Attn: RC-HS
1307 Third Ave.
Fort Knox KY 40121

502/626-0367
FAX: 502/626-0923

AMOUNT: Tuition + monthly stipend
DEADLINE(S): None
FIELD(S): Medicine, Osteopathy, Nurse Anesthetist, Veterinary Medicine, Optometry, Psychology, Dentistry

Open to health professionals and students participating in a Reserve Service of the US Armed Forces, training in the specialties listed above. Varying lengths of service are required to pay back the stipend. Must be US citizen. Award is based on a competitive process, including GPA. Financial need NOT a factor.

400 awards annually. Contact Major Beecher at above address for an application.

1664—EDWARD BANGS KELLEY AND ELZA KELLEY FOUNDATION, INC. (Scholarship Program)

P.O. Drawer M
Hyannis MA 02601-1412
508/775-3117

AMOUNT: $4,000 (max.)
DEADLINE(S): APR 30
FIELD(S): Medicine, Nursing, Health Sciences

Open to residents of Barnstable County, Massachusetts. Scholarships are intended to benefit health and welfare of Barnstable County residents. Awards support study at recognized undergraduate, graduate, and professional institutions. Financial need is considered.

Contact Foundation for an application.

1665—EPILEPSY FOUNDATION OF AMER-ICA (Behavioral Sciences Student Fellowships)

4351 Garden City Drive
Landover MD 20785-2267
301/459-3700 or 800/EFA-1000
FAX: 301/577-2684
TDD: 800/332-2070
E-mail: postmaster@efa.org
Internet: www.efa.org

AMOUNT: $2,000
DEADLINE(S): FEB 1
FIELD(S): Epilepsy as related to Behavioral Sciences

Three-month fellowships awarded to students in the behavioral sciences for work on an epilepsy study project. For students of vocational rehabilitation counseling. Students propose an epilepsy-related study or training project to be carried out at a US institution of their choice. A pre-ceptor must accept responsibility for supervision of the student and the project.

Contact EFA for an application.

1666—FIRST UNITED METHODIST CHURCH (Robert Stevenson & Doreene E. Cater Scholarships)

302 5th Ave., S.
St. Cloud MN 56301
FAX: 320/251-0878
E-mail: FUMCloud@aol.com

AMOUNT: $100-$300
DEADLINE(S): JUN 1
FIELD(S): Humanitarian & Christian Service: Teaching, Medicine, Social Work, Environmental Studies, etc.

Stevenson Scholarship is open to undergraduate members of the First United Methodist Church of St. Cloud. Cater Scholarship is open to members of the Minnesota United Methodist Conference who are entering the sophomore year or higher of college work. Both require two letters of reference, transcripts, and financial need.

5-6 awards annually. Contact Scholarship Committee for an application.

1667—FOUNDATION FOR SEACOAST HEALTH (Scholarship Program)

P.O. Box 4606
Portsmouth NH 03802-4606
603/433-3008
FAX: 603/433-2036
E-mail: ffsh@nh.ultranet.com
Internet: www.nh.ultranet.com/~ffsh

AMOUNT: $1,000-10,000
DEADLINE(S): FEB 1
FIELD(S): Health-related fields

Open to undergraduate and graduate students pursuing health-related fields of study who are legal residents of the following cities in New Hampshire: Portsmouth, Newington, New Castle, Rye, Greenland, N. Hampton, or these cities in Maine: Kittery, Eliot, or York. Must have resided in the area for at least two years.

Write or check website for details. $150,000 awarded annually; 35 awards given.

1668—H. FLETCHER BROWN FUND (Scholarships)

c/o PNC Bank, Trust Dept.
P.O. Box 791
Wilmington DE 19899
302/429-1186

AMOUNT: Varies

DEADLINE(S): APR 15
FIELD(S): Medicine, Dentistry, Law,
Engineering, Chemistry

Open to US citizens born in Delaware and still residing in Delaware. For 4 years of study (undergrad or grad) leading to a degree that enables applicant to practice in chosen field.

Scholarships are based on need, scholastic achievement, and good moral character. Applications available in February. Write for complete information.

1669—H. FLETCHER BROWN TRUST (Scholarships)

222 Delaware Ave., 16th Fl.
Wilmington DE 19899
302/429-1338

AMOUNT: Varies
DEADLINE(S): APR 9
FIELD(S): Chemistry, Engineering, Law,
Medicine, Dentistry

Open to financially needy native-born Delaware residents only who are pursuing an undergraduate degree. Must have minimum 1,000 SAT score and rank in upper 20% of class. Interview required.

Send self-addressed, stamped envelope to Donald Drois, Account Administrator, PNC Bank, at above address for an application.

1670—HOPI TRIBE (Priority Scholarships)

P.O. Box 123
Kykotsmovi AZ 86039
520/734-2441, ext. 520
800/762-9630
FAX: 520/734-2435

AMOUNT: Varies
DEADLINE(S): JUL 31
FIELD(S): Law, Natural Resources,
Education, Medicine/Health,
Engineering, Business

Open to enrolled members of the Hopi Tribe studying in one of the fields listed above, which are considered to be areas of priority interest to the Hopis. Available to college juniors, seniors, and graduate students. Program is to encourage graduates to apply their degrees to Hopi Tribal Goals and Objectives.

Contact Hopi Tribe for an application.

1671—INTERNATIONAL ORDER OF THE KING'S DAUGHTERS AND SONS (Health Careers Scholarships)

c/o Mrs. Fred Cannon
Box 1310
Brookhaven MS 39602

Written inquiry
AMOUNT: $1,000 (max.)
DEADLINE(S): APR 1
FIELD(S): Medicine, Dentistry, Nursing,
Physical Therapy, Occupational
Therapy, Medical Technologies,
Pharmacy

Open to students accepted to/enrolled in an accredited US or Canadian four-year or graduate school. R.N. candidates must have completed first year of program; M.D. or D.D.S. candidates must be for at least the second year of medical or dental school; all others must be in at least third year of four-year program. Pre-med students NOT eligible. Must be US or Canadian citizen.

Send self-addressed, stamped envelope, along with a letter stating the field of study and present level, to the Director at above address for an application.

1672—J. HUGH & EARLE W. FELLOWS MEMORIAL FUND (Scholarship Loans)

President
Pensacola Junior College
1000 College Blvd.
Pensacola FL 32504-8998
904/484-1700

AMOUNT: Each is negotiated
individually
DEADLINE(S): None
FIELD(S): Medicine, Nursing, Medical
Technology, Theology (Episcopal)

Open to bona fide residents of the Florida counties of Escambia, Santa Rosa, Okaloosa, or Walton. For undergraduate study in the fields listed above. US citizenship required.

Loans are interest-free until graduation. Write for complete information.

1673—JEWISH VOCATIONAL SERVICE (Academic Scholarship Program)

One S. Franklin Street
Chicago IL 60606
312/357-4500
FAX: 312/855-3282
TTY: 312/855-3282
E-mail: jvschicago@jon.cjfny.org

AMOUNT: $5,000 (max.)
DEADLINE(S): MAR 1
FIELD(S): "Helping" Professions,
Mathematics, Engineering, Sciences,
Communications (at Univ IL only),
Law (certain schools in IL only)

Open to Jewish men and women legally domiciled in the greater Chicago metropolitan area, who are identified as having promise for significant contributions in their chosen careers, and are in need of

financial assistance for full-time academic programs in above areas. Must have entered undergraduate junior year in career programs requiring no postgrad education, be in graduate/professional school, or be in a vo-tech training program. Interview required.

Renewable. Contact JVS for an application between December 1st and February 15th.

1674—JUNIATA COLLEGE (Robert Steele Memorial Scholarship)

Financial Aid Office
Huntingdon PA 16652
814/641-3603
FAX: 814/641-3355
E-mail: clarkec@juniata.edu

AMOUNT: $4,000 (max.)
DEADLINE(S): APR 1
FIELD(S): Science, Medical Studies

Open to science/medical students applying to Juniata College. Must demonstrate financial need and fill out government FAFSA form.

Contact Cynthia G. Clarke, Research Specialist, for an application or enrollment information. See your financial aid office for FAFSA.

1675—KOREAN-AMERICAN SCIENTISTS AND ENGINEERS ASSOCIATION (KSEA Scholarships)

1952 Gallows Road, Suite 300
Vienna VA 22182
703/748-1221
FAX: 703/748-1331
E-mail: admin@ksea.org
Internet: www.ksea.org

AMOUNT: $1,000
DEADLINE(S): FEB 28
FIELD(S): Science, Engineering, or
Medicine

Scholarships to encourage Korean-American students to study in a science, engineering, or pre-med discipline and to recognize high-performing students. Must have graduated from a high school in the US.

5 to 8 awards yearly. Must be a student member of KSEA or a child of a member.

1676—LOUISIANA STATE UNIVERSITY AT SHREVEPORT (Manchandia Trust Fund Pre-Med Scholarship)

Financial Aid Office
One University Place
Shreveport LA 71115-2399

318/797-5363
FAX: 318/797-5366
E-mail: finaid@pilot.lsus.edu
Internet: www.lsus.edu

AMOUNT: $1,000
DEADLINE(S): Varies
FIELD(S): Pre-Medicine

Awarded to a student enrolled in the pre-med program at LSUS with a minimum 3.5 GPA. May be applied towards tuition in fall and spring. Preference is given to students with financial need and high ACT scores. Recipient is selected by the Financial Aid Selection Committee.

Renewable. Contact the Student Financial Aid Office at LSUS for an application.

1677—MINNESOTA HIGHER EDUCATION SERVICES OFFICE (Health Professions Loan Forgiveness)

1450 Energy Park Drive #350
St. Paul MN 55108-5265
612/296-3974
FAX: 612/297-8880
E-mail: info@heso.state.mn.us
Internet: www.heso.state.mn.us/

AMOUNT: Varies
DEADLINE(S): None
FIELD(S): Health Professions

Five loan repayment programs for health professionals who agree to serve in federally designated Health Professional Shortage Areas, in designated, underserved urban or rural areas, in licensed nursing homes, or in intermediate care facilities for persons with mental retardation or related conditions.

For details contact Office of Rural Health and Primary Care at 612/282-3838 or 800/366-5424 (Minnesota only).

1678—MISSOURI STATE MEDICAL FOUNDATION (Medical School Low-interest Loans)

P.O. Box 1028
113 Madison Street
Jefferson City MO 65102
573/636-5151

AMOUNT: $6,000
DEADLINE(S): APR 15
FIELD(S): Medicine

Open to US citizens who are Missouri residents and are registered as full-time students at an American Medical Association accredited school of medicine in the US. Applicants must have completed at least one year toward M.D. degree and become members of the Missouri State Medical Society (an $8 fee).

Approximately 100 loans per year. Write for complete information.

1679—McCORD CAREER CENTER (Level II McCord Medical/Music Scholarship)

Healdsburg High School
1024 Prince Street
Healdsburg CA 95448
707/431-3473

AMOUNT: Varies
DEADLINE(S): APR 30
FIELD(S): Medicine, Music

For graduates of Healdsburg High School who are planning a career in music or medicine. Must be enrolled full-time at a college/university as an undergraduate junior or senior in the fall, or earning an advanced degree in graduate or medical school, or entering into a vocational/certificate program. Transcripts, proof of attendance, and an essay are required.

Contact the McCord Career Center at Healdsburg High School for an application.

1680—McDONALD'S/UNITED NEGRO COLLEGE FUND (Scholarships for Medical and Healthcare Students)

312/443-8708

AMOUNT: Full tuition (10); $1,000 (50)
DEADLINE(S): None
FIELD(S): Medicine and healthcare fields

Scholarships for college sophomores attending any of the United Negro College Fund schools and pursuing a career in medicine or related healthcare areas. Must maintain 3.0 GPA and demonstrate participation in community and school activities and financial need.

10 two-year scholarships provide full tuition; 50 scholarships are for $1,000 each. Contact school counselor, UNCF office, or call Burrell Communications at above phone number.

1681—NATIONAL FEDERATION OF THE BLIND (Howard Brown Rickard Scholarship)

805 Fifth Ave.
Grinnell IA 50112
515/236-3366

AMOUNT: $3,000
DEADLINE(S): MAR 31
FIELD(S): Law, Medicine, Engineering, Architecture, Natural Sciences

For legally blind students pursuing or planning to pursue a full-time postsecondary course of study in the US. Based on academic excellence, service to the community, and financial need. Membership NOT required.

1 award annually. Renewable. Contact Mrs. Peggy Elliot, Scholarship Committee Chairman, for an application.

1682—NATIONAL HEALTH SERVICE CORPS (NHSC Scholarship Program)

2070 Chain Bridge Road, Suite 450
Vienna VA 22182-2536
800/221-9393
Internet: www.bphc.hrsa.dhhs.gov/nhsc

AMOUNT: Full tuition/books/fees/supplies + monthly stipend
DEADLINE(S): MAR
FIELD(S): Family Medicine, General Internal Medicine, General Pediatrics, Obstetrics/Gynecology, Family Nurse Practitioners, Primary Care Physician Assistants, Certified Nurse-Midwives

Must be US citizen attending or enrolled in fully accredited US allopathic/osteopathic medical school, nursing program, or physician assistant program. For each year of support received, you must serve one year in federally designated health professional shortage area of greatest need. Minimum two years service commitment begins upon completion of your residency and/or training.

300 awards annually. Renewable up to 4 years. Contact NHSC for an application.

1683—NATIONS BANK TRUST DEPT (Minne L. Maffett Scholarship Trust)

P.O. Box 831515
Dallas TX 75283
214/559-6476

AMOUNT: $50-$1,000
DEADLINE(S): APR 1
FIELD(S): All fields of study

Open to US citizens who graduated from Limestone County, Texas, high schools. Scholarships for full-time study at an accredited Texas institution.

30 scholarships per year. Write to Debra Hitzelberger, vice president and trust officer, at address above for complete information.

1684—NAVAL RESERVE RECRUITING COMMAND (Armed Forces Health Professions Scholarships)

Attn: Code 132
4400 Dauphine Street
New Orleans LA 70146
Written inquiry

AMOUNT: Varies
DEADLINE(S): None specified
FIELD(S): Physicians: Anesthesiology, surgical specialties; Nursing: Anesthesia, operating room, or medical surgical nursing

For health professionals and students participating in a Reserve Service of the US Armed Forces training in the specialties listed above and for undergraduate nursing students. A monthly stipend is paid, and varying lengths of service are required to pay back the stipend.

Navy: above address; OR Army: Headquarters, Dept. of the Army, 5109 Leesburg Pike, Falls Church, VA 22041-3258; OR US Air Force Reserve Personnel Center, ATTN: ARPC SGI, Denver, CO 80280-5000.

1685—NAVY RECRUITING COMMAND (Armed Forces Health Professions Scholarships)

Commander
801 N. Randolph Street, Code 325
Arlington VA 22203-1991
800/USA-NAVY or 703/696-4926
E-mail: omegahouse@erols.com
Internet: www.navyjobs.com

AMOUNT: $938/month stipend + tuition, fees, books, lab fees, etc.
DEADLINE(S): APR 28
FIELD(S): Medicine, Dentistry, Optometry, Physical Therapy, Pharmacology, Health Care Administration, Industrial Hygiene, etc.

Open to US citizens enrolled or accepted for enrollment in any of the above fields at an accredited institution in the US or Puerto Rico. Must qualify for appointment as a Navy officer and sign a contractual agreement. Must be between the ages of 18 and 36 and have a GPA of at least 3.0.

See website, contact local Navy Recruiting Office, or contact Lieutenant Roger A. House, MPA, CAAMA, Medical Service Corps at above address.

1686—NEW YORK STATE HIGHER EDUCATION SERVICES CORPORATION (N.Y. State Regents Professional/Health Care Opportunity Scholarships)

Cultural Education Center
Room 5C64
Albany NY 12230
518/486-1319
Internet: www.hesc.com

AMOUNT: $1,000-$10,000/yr.
DEADLINE(S): Varies
FIELD(S): Medicine and Dentistry and related fields, Architecture, Nursing, Psychology, Audiology, Landscape Architecture, Social Work, Chiropractic, Law, Pharmacy, Accounting, Speech Language Pathology

For NY state residents who are economically disadvantaged and members of a minority group underrepresented in the chosen profession and attending school in NY state. Some programs carry a service obligation in New York for each year of support. For US citizens or qualifying noncitizens.

Medical/dental scholarships require one year of professional work in NY.

1687—OKLAHOMA MEDICAL RESEARCH FOUNDATION (Sir Alexander Fleming Scholar Program)

825 Northeast 13th Street
Oklahoma City OK 73104
405/271-7218
800/522-0211 (in-state)

AMOUNT: $2,500 salary + housing
DEADLINE(S): MAR 1
FIELD(S): Sciences

Summer scholarship program (June & July) for Oklahoma students who have completed their junior year of high school through those in their junior year of college at time of application. Excellent academic standing and aptitude in science and math are essential. Students will work in the laboratories of the above organization. Research projects will be selected from: alcoholism/liver disease, arthritis/ immunology, carcinogenesis, cardiovascular biology, and more.

Named for the scientist who discovered penicillin and dedicated OMRF in 1949. Contact organization for further information and application forms.

1688—PENINSULA COMMUNITY FOUNDATION (Dr. James L. Hutchinson and Evelyn Ribbs Hutchinson Scholarship Fund)

1700 S. El Camino Real, #300
San Mateo CA 94402
650/358-9369
FAX: 650/358-9817

AMOUNT: Up to $2,000
DEADLINE(S): MAR 27 (5 P.M.)
FIELD(S): Medicine

Scholarships for graduates of a San Mateo County or Santa Clara County, California, high school. Must be US citizen in final year of college and accepted to a medical school or be currently enrolled full-time in an accredited medical school program.

Awards are for one year, but recipients may reapply.

1689—PENINSULA COMMUNITY FOUNDATION (Dr. Mary Finegold Scholarship)

1700 S. El Camino Real, #300
San Mateo CA 94402
650/358-9369
FAX: 650/358-9817

AMOUNT: $1,000
DEADLINE(S): MAR 27 (5 P.M.)
FIELD(S): Sciences

Scholarships for senior girls graduating from high school in Palo Alto, California, who intend to complete a four-year degree in the sciences. Special consideration will be given to girls who have demonstrated a "pioneering" spirit in that they have not been constrained by stereotypical female roles and to those facing financial hardship.

Award was established in the honor of Dr. Mary Finegold who, after completing her medical studies, elected to stay at home until her youngest child was in high school before beginning her medical practice. She was a school physician.

1690—PILOT INTERNATIONAL FOUNDATION (PIF/Lifeline Scholarship)

P.O. Box 5600
Macon GA 31208-5600
Written inquiries

AMOUNT: Varies
DEADLINE(S): MAR 1
FIELD(S): Disabilities/Brain-related Disorders

This program assists ADULT students re-entering the job market, preparing for a second career, or improving their professional skills for an established career. Applicants must be preparing for, or already involved in, careers working with people with disabilities/brain-related disorders. GPA of 3.5 or more is required.

Must be sponsored by a Pilot Club in your home town, or in the city in which your college or university is located. Send a self-addressed, stamped envelope for complete information.

1691—PILOT INTERNATIONAL FOUNDATION (Ruby Newhall Memorial Scholarship)

P.O. Box 5600
Macon GA 31208-5600
Written inquiries

AMOUNT: Varies
DEADLINE(S): MAR 15
FIELD(S): Disabilities/Brain-related Disorders

For international students who have studied in the US for at least one year, and who intend to return to their home country six months after graduation. Applicants must be full-time students majoring in a field related to human health and welfare, and have a GPA of 3.5 or more.

Applicants must be sponsored by a Pilot Club in their home town, or in the city in which their college or university is located. Send a self-addressed, stamped envelope for complete information.

1692—PILOT INTERNATIONAL FOUNDATION (The Pilot International Scholarship Program)

P.O. Box 5600
Macon GA 31208-5600
Written inquiries

AMOUNT: Varies
DEADLINE(S): MAR 1
FIELD(S): Disabilities/Brain-related Disorders

This program provides assistance to undergraduate students preparing for careers working directly with people with disabilities or training those who will. GPA of 3.5 or greater required.

Applicants must be sponsored by a Pilot Club in their home town, or in the city in which their college or university is located. Send a self-addressed, stamped envelope for complete information.

1693—PRESBYTERIAN CHURCH (U.S.A.) (Grant Program for Medical Studies)

100 Witherspoon Street
Louisville KY 40202-1396
502/567-5745
E-mail: FrancesC@ctr.pcusa.org
Internet: www.pcusa.org/highered

AMOUNT: $500-$1,500
DEADLINE(S): None specified
FIELD(S): Medicine

Provides funding to students enrolled full-time pursuing a medical profession. Applicants must be members of the Presbyterian Church (U.S.A.), be US citizens/permanent residents, demonstrate financial need, be recommended by academic advisor at institution, and be recommended by church pastor.

Renewable. Contact Frances Cook at above address for more information.

1694—RAYMOND J. HARRIS EDUCATION TRUST

P.O. Box 7899
Philadelphia PA 19101-7899
Written inquiry

AMOUNT: Varies
DEADLINE(S): FEB 1
FIELD(S): Medicine, Law, Engineering, Dentistry, or Agriculture

Scholarships for Christian men to obtain a professional education in medicine, law, engineering, dentistry, or agriculture at nine Philadelphia area colleges.

Contact Mellon Bank, N.A. at above location for details and the names of the nine colleges.

1695—ROBERT SCHRECK MEMORIAL FUND (Grants)

c/o Texas Commerce Bank
Trust Dept.
P.O. Drawer 140
El Paso TX 79980
915/546-6515

AMOUNT: $500-$1,500
DEADLINE(S): JUL 15; NOV 15
FIELD(S): Medicine, Veterinary Medicine, Physics, Chemistry, Architecture, Engineering, Episcopal Clergy

Grants to undergraduate juniors or seniors or graduate students who have been residents of El Paso County for at least two years. Must be US citizen or legal resident and have a high grade point average. Financial need is a consideration.

Write for complete information.

1696—SOCIETY OF BIOLOGICAL PSYCHIATRY (Ziskind-Somerfield Research Award)

Elliot Richelson, M.D.
Mayo Clinic
Jacksonville FL 32224
904/953-2842

AMOUNT: $2,500
DEADLINE(S): JAN 31
FIELD(S): Biological Psychiatry

Open to senior investigators who are members of the Society of Biological Psychiatry. Award is for basic or clinical research by senior investigators 35 or older.

Candidates must be members in good standing of the society of Biological Psychiatry. Write for complete information.

1697—SRP/NAVAJO GENERATING STATION (Navajo Scholarship)

P.O. Box 850
Page AZ 86040
520/645-6539
FAX: 520/645-7295
E-mail: ljdawave@srp.gov

AMOUNT: Based on need
DEADLINE(S): APR 30
FIELD(S): Engineering, Environmental Studies, Business, Business Management, Health, Education

Scholarships for full-time students who hold membership in the Navajo Tribe and who are pursuing a degree in a field of study recognized as significant to the Navajo Nation, Salt River Project, or the Navajo Generating Station, such as those listed above. Must be junior or senior, have and maintain a GPA of 3.0.

Average of 15 awards per year. Inquire of Linda Dawavendewa at above location.

1698—THE AUGIE J. ALTAR SCHOLARSHIP

7115 W. 91st Street
Bridgeview IL 60455-2048
Write for information

AMOUNT: $500
DEADLINE(S): MAY 31
FIELD(S): Medicine or Agricultural fields

Scholarships for students enrolled or accepted to an accredited college, university, or community college who are of Lithuanian descent and are residents of Illinois. Must be studying in the areas of medicine or agriculture. Financial need considered. Must have and maintain at least a 2.0 GPA.

Send application request to above address with a stamped, self-addressed envelope (SASE).

1699—THE EDUCATIONAL AND SCIENTIFIC TRUST OF THE PENNSYLVANIA MEDICAL SOCIETY (Loan Program for Pennsylvania Medical School Students)

777 East Park Drive
P.O. Box 8820
Harrisburg PA 17105-8820
717/558-7750, ext. 1257
FAX: 717/558-7818
E-mail: studentloans-trust@pamedsoc.org
Internet: www.pitt.edu/HOME/GHNet/PA_Trust

AMOUNT: Up to $3,000 for bona fide Pennsylvania residents
DEADLINE(S): JUN 1
FIELD(S): Medicine

Open to Pennsylvania residents with demonstrated financial need who are seeking a medical degree.

Approx. 200 loans per year. Must be US citizen. Contact above location for complete information.

1700—THE EDUCATIONAL AND SCIENTIFIC TRUST OF THE PENNSYLVANIA MEDICAL SOCIETY (Loan Program for Out-of-State Pennsylvania Medical School Students)

777 East Park Drive
P.O. Box 8820
Harrisburg PA 17105-8820
717/558-7750, ext. 1257
FAX: 717/558-7818
E-mail: studentloans-trust@pamedsoc.org
Internet: www.pitt.edu/HOME/GHNet/PA_Trust

AMOUNT: Up to $3,000 for bona fide Pennsylvania residents
DEADLINE(S): JUN 1
FIELD(S): Medicine

Open to Pennsylvania residents with demonstrated financial need who are seeking a medical degree and are attending an out-of-state school.

Approx. 200 loans per year. Must be US citizen. Contact above location for complete information.

1701—U.S. DEPT. OF HEALTH & HUMAN SERVICES (Indian Health Service Preparatory Scholarship Program)

Twinbrook Metro Plaza, Suite 100
12300 Twinbrook Pkwy.
Rockville MD 20852
301/443-0234
FAX: 301/443-4815
Internet: www.ihs.gov/Recruitment/DHPS/SP/SBTOC3.asp

AMOUNT: Tuition + fees & monthly stipend of $938
DEADLINE(S): APR 1
FIELD(S): Health Professions, Social Work, or Accounting

Open to Native Americans or Alaska natives who enroll in courses leading to a baccalaureate degree and are preparing for acceptance into programs in the above fields. US citizenship required. Renewable annually with reapplication.

Scholarship recipients must intend to serve the Indian people. They incur a one-year service obligation to the IHS for each year of support for a minimum of two years. Write for complete information.

1702—U.S. DEPT. OF HEALTH & HUMAN SERVICES (Indian Health Service Health Professions Pregraduate Scholarship Program)

Twinbrook Metro Plaza, Suite 100
12300 Twinbrook Pkwy.
Rockville MD 20852
301/443-0234
FAX: 301/443-4815
Internet: www.ihs.gov/Recruitment/DHPS/SP/SBTOC3.asp

AMOUNT: Tuition + fees & monthly stipend of $938
DEADLINE(S): APR 1
FIELD(S): Health professions: premedicine, predentistry

Open to Native Americans or Alaska natives who are college juniors and seniors in a baccalaureate degree program leading to a career in medicine or dentistry. US citizenship required. Renewable annually with reapplication.

Scholarship recipients must intend to serve the Indian people. They incur a one-year service obligation to the IHS for each year of support for a minimum of two years. Write for complete information.

1703—U.S. DEPT. OF HEALTH & HUMAN SERVICES (Indian Health Service Health Professions Scholarship Program)

Twinbrook Metro Plaza, Suite 100
12300 Twinbrook Pkwy.
Rockville MD 20852
301/443-0234
FAX: 301/443-4815
Internet: www.ihs.gov/Recruitment/DHPS/SP/SBTOC3.asp

AMOUNT: Tuition + fees & monthly stipend of $938
DEADLINE(S): APR 1
FIELD(S): Health Professions, Accounting, Social Work

Open to Native Americans or Alaska natives who are graduate students or college juniors or seniors in a program leading to a career in a field listed above. US citizenship required. Renewable annually with reapplication.

Scholarship recipients must intend to serve the Indian people. They incur a one-year service obligation to the IHS for each year of support for a minimum of two years. Write for complete information.

1704—UNIVERSITY SYSTEM OF WEST VIRGINIA (Health Sciences Scholarship Program)

1018 Kanawha Blvd. East, Suite 1101
Charleston WV 25301-2827
304/558-0530

AMOUNT: $10,000
DEADLINE(S): OCT 31
FIELD(S): Osteopathic Medicine, Family Medicine, Pediatric Medicine, Internal Medicine, Obstetrical/Gynecological Medicine, General Psychiatry, Nurse Practitioner, Physician Assistants, Nurse-Midwifery

Open to West Virginia undergraduate and graduate students. Students must make a commitment to practice primary care for two years in an underserved rural area of West Virginia upon completion of training.

Write to the above address for complete information.

1705—USAF RESERVE BONUS PROGRAM

6760 East Irvington Place, #7000
Denver CO 80280-7000
800-525-0102, ext. 231 or 237
DSN 926-6490 or 6484
Commercial: 303/676-6484 or 6490

FAX: 303/676-6164
FAX: DSN: 926-6164
E-mail: spresley@arpcmail.den.disa.mil
AMOUNT: $10,000/yr. for physicians;
$3,000/year for operating room nurses
DEADLINE(S): None
FIELD(S): Physicians and nurses in
critically needed specialties

A bonus pay program to recruit critically needed medical specialties into the Selected Reserve of the US Air Force.

Direct questions to: Medical Readiness & Incentives Division, SrA Sonja Presley, at above location.

1706—USAF RESERVE PERSONNEL CENTER (Armed Forces Health Professionals Scholarships)

6760 E. Irvington Place #7000
Denver CO 80280-7000
Written inquiry

AMOUNT: Varies
DEADLINE(S): None specified
FIELD(S): Physicians: Anesthesiology,
surgical specialties; Nursing:
Anesthesia, operating room, or
medical surgical nursing

For health professionals and students participating in a Reserve Service of the US Armed Forces training in the specialties listed above and for undergraduate nursing students. A monthly stipend is paid, and varying lengths of service are required to pay back the stipend.

Air Force: above address; Army: Headquarters, Dept. of the Army, 5109 Leesburg Pike, Falls Church, VA 22041-3258; Navy: Naval Reserve Recruiting Command, 4400 Dauphine Street, New Orleans, LA 70146.

1707—VIRGIN ISLANDS BOARD OF EDUCATION (Nursing & Other Health Scholarships)

P.O. Box 11900
St. Thomas VI 00801
809/774-4546

AMOUNT: Up to $1,800
DEADLINE(S): MAR 31
FIELD(S): Nursing, Medicine, Health-
related Areas

Open to bona fide residents of the Virgin Islands who are accepted by an accredited school of nursing or an accredited institution offering courses in one of the health-related fields.

This scholarship is granted for one academic year. Recipients may reapply with at least a 'C' average. Write for complete information.

1708—WASHINGTON STATE HIGHER EDUCATION COORDINATING BOARD (Health Professional Loan Repayment & Scholarship Program)

P.O. Box 43430
Olympia WA 98504-3430
360/753-7850
FAX: 360/753-7808
Internet: www.hecb.wa.gov

AMOUNT: Varies
DEADLINE(S): APR (scholarship); FEB
(loan repayment); JUL (loan
repayment)
FIELD(S): Health Care

Scholarships are open to students in accredited undergraduate or graduate health care programs leading to eligibility for licensure in Washington state. Must agree to work in designated shortage area for minimum of three years. Loan repayment recipients receive payment from program for purpose of repaying education loans secured while attending program of health care training leading to licensure in Washington state. Financial need NOT a factor.

Renewable up to 5 years. Contact Program Manager for a loan repayment application after November 15th and for scholarship application after January 15th.

1709—WASHINGTON STATE HIGHER EDUCATION COORDINATING BOARD (WICHE Professional Student Exchange)

P.O. Box 43430
Olympia WA 98504-3430
360/753-7850
FAX: 360/753-7808

AMOUNT: $8,000-$12,000
DEADLINE(S): OCT 15
FIELD(S): Optometry, Osteopathy

Program provides state support to Washington residents pursuing undergraduate or graduate study out-of-state.

12 awards annually (10 renewals, 2 new). Contact Program Manager for an application.

1710—WOMEN OF THE EVANGELICAL LUTHERAN CHURCH IN AMERICA (The Kahler-Vickers/Raup-Emma Wettstein Scholarships)

8765 West Higgins Road
Chicago IL 60631-4189
800/638-3522, ext. 2747
FAX: 773/380-2419
E-mail: womnelca@elca.org

AMOUNT: $2,000 max.
DEADLINE(S): MAR 1
FIELD(S): Health Professions &
Christian Service

Assists women who are members of the ELCA studying for service in health professions associated with ELCA projects abroad that do not lead to church-certified professions. Must be US citizen and have experienced an interruption of two or more years since completion of high school. Academic records of coursework completed in last five years as well as proof of admission from educational institution are required.

Renewable for an additional year. Contact Faith Fretheim, Program Director, for an application.

1711—ZETA PHI BETA SORORITY EDUCATIONAL FOUNDATION (S. Evelyn Lewis Memorial Scholarship in Medical Health Sciences)

1734 New Hampshire Ave. NW
Washington DC 20009
Internet: www.zpb1920.org/
nefforms.htm

AMOUNT: $500-$1,000
DEADLINE(S): FEB 1
FIELD(S): Medicine, Health Sciences

Open to graduate and undergraduate young women enrolled in a program leading to a degree in medicine or health sciences. Award is for full-time study for one academic year (Fall-Spring) and is paid directly to college/university. Must submit proof of enrollment.

Send self-addressed, stamped envelope to above address between September 1st and December 15th for an application.

MEDICAL-RELATED DISCIPLINES

1712—ABBIE SARGENT MEMORIAL SCHOLARSHIP INC. (Scholarships)

295 Sheep Davis Road
Concord NH 03301
603/224-1934
FAX: 603/228-8432

AMOUNT: $400
DEADLINE(S): MAR 15
FIELD(S): Agriculture, Veterinary
Medicine, Home Economics

Open to New Hampshire residents who are high school graduates with good grades and character. For undergraduate or graduate study. Must be legal resident of US and demonstrate financial need.

3 annual awards. Renewable with reapplication. Write for complete information.

1713—AIR FORCE RESERVE OFFICER TRAINING CORPS (AFROTC Pre-Health Scholarships)

551 E. Maxwell Blvd.
Maxwell AFB AL 36112-6106
334/953-7783

AMOUNT: Full tuition, lab fees, books, +
$150/month
DEADLINE(S): JUN 15
FIELD(S): Health Professions

For US citizens who are currently enrolled full-time college students, with at least a 3.5 GPA. Must provide personal statement of interest in a career in the medical profession in the uniformed services, as well as three letters of recommendation. Certain courses must be completed by end of junior year.

Contact above address for application packet. The AFHPSP continues your education by providing up to 4 years of medical school to eligible Air Force ROTC Pre-Health cadets.

1714—AMERICAN ASSOCIATION OF COLLEGES OF PHARMACY (PHARMLOAN Program)

Office of Student Affairs
1426 Prince Street
Alexandria VA 22314
703/739-2330
FAX: 703/836-8982
E-mail: markaacp@aol.com
Internet: www.aacp.org

AMOUNT: Up to $100,000
DEADLINE(S): None
FIELD(S): Pharmacy

Loans for undergraduate and graduate students in the field of pharmacy.

Contact organization for details.

1715—AMERICAN ASSOCIATION OF WOMEN DENTISTS (Gillette Hayden Memorial Foundation)

401 N. Michigan Ave.
Chicago IL 60611
800/920-2293
E-mail: aawd@sba.com

AMOUNT: $2,000
DEADLINE(S): AUG 1
FIELD(S): Dentistry

Loans available to women who are 3rd- and 4th-year pre-dental students or are graduate degree candidates. Academic achievement, need for assistance, and amount of debt currently accumulated are main points considered.

10 awards yearly. Write for complete information.

1716—AMERICAN COLLEGE OF MEDICAL PRACTICE EXECUTIVES (ACMPE Scholarships)

104 Inverness Terrace East
Englewood CO 80112-5306
303/643-9573, ext. 206

AMOUNT: $500 to $2,000
DEADLINE(S): JUN 1
FIELD(S): Health Care
Administration/Medical Practice
Management

Open to undergraduate or graduate students who are pursuing a degree relevant to medical practice management at an accredited university or college.

Send #10 SASE to receive application.

1717—AMERICAN FOUNDATION FOR PHARMACEUTICAL EDUCATION (First-Year Graduate Scholarship Program)

One Church Street, Suite 202
Rockville MD 20850
301/738-2160
FAX: 301/738-2161

AMOUNT: $5,000-$7,000
DEADLINE(S): JAN 1; MAY 1
FIELD(S): Pharmacy

Several scholarships for pharmacy students beginning their first graduate year and are seeking doctorates in pharmacy. Must be US citizens or legal residents. Some require membership in professional organizations, and deadline dates vary.

Students may apply during last year of B.A./B.S program. Write for complete information.

1718—AMERICAN FOUNDATION FOR PHARMACEUTICAL EDUCATION (Gateway Scholarship Program)

One Church Street, Suite 202
Rockville MD 20850
301/738-2160
FAX: 301/738-2161

AMOUNT: $9,250
DEADLINE(S): DEC 1
FIELD(S): Pharmacy

Open to undergraduates in the last three years of a bachelor's program in a college of pharmacy or Pharm.D graduate students. US citizen or permanent resident.

Purpose is to encourage undergraduates to pursue the Ph.D in a pharmacy college graduate program. Multiple scholarships available. Write for complete information.

1719—AMERICAN FOUNDATION FOR THE BLIND (Paul W. Ruckes Scholarship)

11 Penn Plaza, Suite 300
New York NY 10001
212/502-7661
FAX: 212/502-7771
E-mail: juliet@afb.org
Internet: www.afb.org

AMOUNT: $1,000
DEADLINE(S): APR 30
FIELD(S): Engineering, Computer/
Physical/Life Sciences

Open to legally blind and visually impaired undergraduate and graduate students pursuing a degree in one of above fields. Must be US citizen. Must submit written documentation of visual impairment from ophthalmologist or optometrist (need not be legally blind); official transcripts; proof of college/university acceptance; three letters of recommendation; and typewritten statement describing goals, work experience, extracurricular activities, and how monies will be used.

1 award annually. See website or contact Julie Tucker at AFB for an application.

1720—AMERICAN FOUNDATION FOR VISION AWARENESS (Education/Research Grants)

243 N. Lindbergh Blvd.
St. Louis MO 63141
800/927-AFVA (2382)
FAX: 314/991-4101

AMOUNT: $5,000 to $10,000 (research grants); $1,000 (scholarships)
DEADLINE(S): FEB 1
FIELD(S): Optometry

Scholarships open to US optometry students who have finished at least one semester and participated in vision-related public service. Research grants open to scientists doing research in the field of vision.

Write for complete information.

1721—AMERICAN FOUNDATION FOR VISION AWARENESS OF WASHINGTON (Scholarships)

c/o Mrs. Chris Cash
28923 15th Place South
Federal Way WA 98003

206/941-7554
AMOUNT: $700-$1,000
DEADLINE(S): DEC 15
FIELD(S): Optometry

Competitive awards open to Washington state residents accepted and enrolled in an accredited school of optometry. Winners cannot be related to a Washington state optometrist as an immediate family member.

Can win the award each year the student is enrolled in optometry school (on a competitive basis.) Write for complete information.

1722—AMERICAN INDIAN SCIENCE AND ENGINEERING SOCIETY (A.T. Anderson Memorial Scholarship)

P.O. Box 9828
Albuquerque NM 87119-9828
505/765-1052
FAX: 505/765-5608
E-mail: scholarships@aises.org
Internet: www.aises.org/scholarships
AMOUNT: $1,000-$2,000
DEADLINE(S): JUN 15
FIELD(S): Medicine, Natural Resources, Science, Engineering

Open to undergraduate and graduate students who are at least 1/4 American Indian or recognized as member of a tribe. Must be member of AISES ($10 fee), enrolled full-time at an accredited institution, and demonstrate financial need.

Renewable. See website or contact Patricia Browne for an application and/or membership information.

1723—AMERICAN INDIAN SCIENCE AND ENGINEERING SOCIETY (Burlington Northern Santa Fe Pacific Foundation Scholarships)

P.O. Box 9828
Albuquerque NM 87119-9828
505/765-1052
FAX: 505/765-5608
E-mail: scholarships@aises.org
Internet: www.aises.org/scholarships
AMOUNT: $2,500/yr.
DEADLINE(S): MAR 31
FIELD(S): Business, Education, Science, Engineering, Health Administration

Open to high school seniors who are at least 1/4 American Indian. Must reside in KS, OK, CO, AZ, NM, MN, ND, OR, SD, WA, MT, or San Bernardino County, CA (Burlington Northern and Santa Fe Pacific service areas). Must demonstrate financial need.

5 awards annually. Renewable up to 4 years. See website or contact Patricia Browne for an application.

1724—AMERICAN LEGION AUXILIARY (Healthcare Scholarships)

Department Secretary
118 Ridge Road
Torrington WY 82240
Written inquiry
AMOUNT: $300
DEADLINE(S): Varies
FIELD(S): Healthcare

Applicant must have completed at least two semesters of school, have a minimum 3.0 GPA, and submit transcripts as well as a letter stating need. Scholarships available for the University of Wyoming or any of the community colleges in Wyoming offering nursing programs. Preference to nursing students, but students in other health-related programs are also eligible. Preference also goes to a veteran or a veteran's child, but this is not mandatory.

Write to above address for an application.

1725—AMERICAN LEGION AUXILIARY (Past Presidents Parley Healthcare Scholarship)

State Veterans Service Building
St. Paul MN 55155
612/224-7634
AMOUNT: $750
DEADLINE(S): MAR 15
FIELD(S): Healthcare

For Minnesota residents who are members of the Department of Minnesota American Legion Auxiliary and have a minimum 2.0 GPA. Award is to help needy and deserving students or adults commence or further their education in healthcare at a Minnesota school.

Contact American Legion for an application.

1726—AMERICAN SOCIETY FOR CLINICAL LABORATORY SCIENCE (Dorothy Morrison Undergraduate Scholarship)

7910 Woodmont Ave., Suite 530
Bethesda MD 20814
301/657-2768
FAX: 301/657-2909
AMOUNT: $1,000
DEADLINE(S): MAR 1
FIELD(S): Clinical Laboratory Science or Medical Technology

Scholarships for students in the above field enrolled in an approved undergraduate program. Must be in last year of study. US citizenship or permanent US residency required.

CContact address above for complete information. Enclose self-addressed, stamped business-size envelope. Applications available after Nov. 1.

1727—AMERICAN SOCIETY FOR CLINICAL LABORATORY SCIENCE (Ruth M. French Graduate or Undergraduate Scholarship)

7910 Woodmont Ave., Suite 530
Bethesda MD 20814
301/657-2768
FAX: 301/657-2909
AMOUNT: $1,000
DEADLINE(S): MAR 1
FIELD(S): Clinical Laboratory Science or Medical Technology

Scholarships for students in the above field enrolled in an approved undergraduate or graduate program. Undergrads must be in last year of study. US citizenship or permanent US residency required.

Contact address above for complete information. Enclose self-addressed, stamped business-size envelope. Applications available after Nov. 1.

1728—AMERICAN SOCIETY FOR CLINICAL LABORATORY SCIENCE (Alpha Mu Tau Undergraduate Scholarship)

7910 Woodmont Ave., Suite 530
Bethesda MD 20814
301/657-2768
FAX: 301/657-2909
AMOUNT: Up to $1,000
DEADLINE(S): MAR 15
FIELD(S): Clinical Laboratory Science, Medical Technology, Clinical Laboratory Technician, Cytotechnology, Histotechnology

Scholarships for undergraduate students in their last year of study in the above fields enrolled in an approved NAACLS accredited program. US citizenship or permanent US residency required.

Contact address above for complete information. Enclose self-addressed, stamped business-size envelope. Applications available after Nov. 1.

1729—AMERICAN SOCIETY FOR CLINICAL LABORATORY SCIENCE (Forum for Concern of Minorities Scholarship)

7910 Woodmont Ave., Suite 530
Bethesda MD 20814
301/657-2768
FAX: 301/657-2909

AMOUNT: Varies
DEADLINE(S): FEB 15
FIELD(S): Clinical Laboratory Science, Medical Technology, Clinical Laboratory Technology

Scholarships for undergraduate minority students enrolled in an approved NAACLS accredited program in the above fields. Min. 2.5 GPA required. US citizenship or permanent US residency required. Must demonstrate financial need.

Contact address above for complete information. Enclose self-addressed, stamped business-size envelope. Applications available after Nov. 1.

1730—AMERICAN SPEECH-LANGUAGE-HEARING FOUNDATION (Kala Singh Memorial Fund-International/Minority Student Scholarship)

10801 Rockville Pike
Rockville MD 20852
301/897-5700
FAX: 301/571-0457

AMOUNT: $2,000
DEADLINE(S): JUN 6
FIELD(S): Communication Sciences and Disorders, Speech/Language Pathology, Audiology

Applicants must be international/ethnic minority graduate student studying communication sciences and disorders in the US and demonstrating outstanding academic achievement.

Applications available in February.

1731—AMERICAN SPEECH-LANGUAGE-HEARING FOUNDATION (Leslie Isenberg Fund for Student With Disability)

10801 Rockville Pike
Rockville MD 20852
301/897-5700
FAX: 301/571-0457

AMOUNT: $2,000
DEADLINE(S): JUN 6
FIELD(S): Communication Sciences & Disorders

Open to full-time graduate student with disability enrolled in a communication sciences and disorders program and demonstrating outstanding academic achievement.

Applications available in February.

1732—AMERICAN SPEECH-LANGUAGE-HEARING FOUNDATION (Young Scholars Award for Minority Student)

10801 Rockville Pike
Rockville MD 20852
301/897-5700
FAX 301/571-0457

AMOUNT: $2,000
DEADLINE(S): JUN 6
FIELD(S): Speech/Language Pathology, Audiology

Open to ethnic minorities who are full-time college seniors accepted for graduate study in speech-language pathology or audiology. Applicants must be US citizens.

Applications available in February.

1733—AMERICAN VETERINARY MEDICAL FOUNDATION (AVMA Auxiliary Student Loan Fund)

1931 N. Meacham Rd., Suite 100
Schaumburg IL 60173-4360
847/925-8070, ext. 208
E-mail: avmf@avma.org

AMOUNT: up to $4,000 (seniors); up to $8,000 (sophomores/juniors)
DEADLINE(S): MAR 31
FIELD(S): Veterinary Medicine

Loans are available to students in AVMA-accredited colleges of veterinary medicine who need financial aid to complete their schooling. Preference is to seniors, but sophomores and juniors may be considered. Must be US citizen and be a member of an AVMA student chapter.

Contact AVMA for membership information or an application.

1734—ARCHBOLD MEDICAL CENTER (Archbold Scholarship/Loan)

Dept. of Education
P.O. Box 1018
Thomasville GA 31799-1018
912/228-2795

AMOUNT: $4,000-$6,000; $500 for technical courses
DEADLINE(S): None specified
FIELD(S): Healthcare fields such as Registered Nurse, Medical Lab, Pharmacy, Physical Therapy, etc.

Open to undergrad and grad students accepted into an accredited healthcare school and within 2 years of completing course work. Student must agree to work at AMC for 3 years following graduation (1 year for tech school students).

Must be Georgia resident. Personal interview required. Repayment is required if recipient fails to work at Archbold for the designated period. Write for complete information.

1735—ARTHUR & DOREEN PARRETT SCHOLARSHIP TRUST FUND (Scholarships)

c/o U.S. Bank of Washington
P.O. Box 720
Trust Dept., 8th Floor
Seattle WA 98111-0720
206/344-4653

AMOUNT: Up to $3,500
DEADLINE(S): JUL 31
FIELD(S): Engineering, Science, Medicine, Dentistry

Washington state resident who has completed her/his first year of college by July 31. Open to students enrolled in above schools. Awards tenable at any accredited undergrad college or university.

Approximately 15 awards per year. Write for complete information.

1736—ARTHUR M. MILLER FUND

P.O. Box 1122
Wichita KS 67201-0004
316/261-4609

AMOUNT: Varies
DEADLINE(S): MAR 31
FIELD(S): Medicine or related fields

Scholarships for Kansas residents for the study of medicine or related fields at accredited institutions.

Send SASE for formal application.

1737—ASSOCIATION FOR WOMEN IN SCIENCE EDUCATIONAL FOUNDATION (Dr. Vicki L. Schechtman Scholarship)

1200 New York Ave. NW
Suite 650
Washington DC 20005
202/326-8940 or 800/886-AWIS
E-mail: awis@awis.org
Internet: www.awis.org

AMOUNT: $1,000
DEADLINE(S): JAN 16
FIELD(S): Various Sciences and Social Sciences

For female undergraduate students who are US citizens and have a minimum GPA of 3.0. Summary page, essay describing career aspirations, transcripts, proof of matriculation (if available), and two reference letters required with application. Scholarships may be used for tuition, books, housing, research, equipment, etc.

See website or write to above address for an application and more information.

1738—ASSOCIATION FOR WOMEN IN SCIENCE EDUCATIONAL FOUNDATION (Ruth Satter Memorial Award)

1200 New York Ave. NW
Suite 650
Washington DC 20005
202/326-8940 or 800/886-AWIS
E-mail: awis@awis.org
Internet: www.awis.org

AMOUNT: $1,000
DEADLINE(S): JAN 16
FIELD(S): Various Sciences and Social Sciences

Scholarships for female doctoral students who have interrupted their education three years or more to raise a family. Summary page, description of research project, resume, references, transcripts, biographical sketch, and proof of eligibility from department head required. US citizens may attend any graduate institution; non-citizens must be enrolled in US institutions.

See website or write to above address for more information or an application.

1739—ASSOCIATION FOR WOMEN VETERINARIANS (Student Scholarship)

6200 Jefferson Street, NE, #117
Albuquerque NM 87109-3434
Written inquiry

AMOUNT: $1,500
DEADLINE(S): FEB 18
FIELD(S): Veterinary Medicine

Open to second- or third-year veterinary medicine students in the US or Canada who are US or Canadian citizens. Both women and men are eligible. Essay is required.

Write for complete information or contact the Dean of your veterinary school.

1740—ASSOCIATION ON AMERICAN INDIAN AFFAIRS, INC. (Emergency Aid and Health Professions Scholarships)

P.O. Box 268
Sisseton SD 57262
605/698-3998 or 605/698-3787
FAX: 605/698-3316
AMOUNT: $50-$300

DEADLINE(S): MAY 1
FIELD(S): Health professions

Emergency funding program for full-time undergraduates studying full-time in a health field. Based on financial need. Must be at least 1/4 Indian and write a one- to two-page essay on the nature of the emergency need.

Applications available Sept. 1. Send SASE to above location.

1741—BECA FOUNDATION (Alice Newell Joslyn Medical Fund)

310 Via Vera Cruz, Suite 101
San Marcos CA 92069
760/471-5465
FAX: 760/471-9175

AMOUNT: $500-$2,000
DEADLINE(S): MAR 1
FIELD(S): Medicine, Health Care, Nursing, Dental/Medical Assisting, Physical Therapy

Open to Latino students who live in or attend college in San Diego County, CA, at time of application. For high school seniors and those already in college pursuing undergraduate or graduate education. Based on financial need, scholastic determination, and community/cultural awareness. BECA also provides a mentor to each scholarship recipient.

Send self-addressed, stamped envelope to BECA for an application.

1742—BOYS AND GIRLS CLUBS OF SAN DIEGO (Spence Reese Scholarship Fund)

1761 Hotel Circle S., Suite 123
San Diego CA 92108
619/298-3520

AMOUNT: $2,000/yr.
DEADLINE(S): MAY 15
FIELD(S): Medicine, Law, Engineering, Political Science

Open to male high school seniors planning a career in one of the above fields. Must be residents of Imperial, Riverside, Orange, San Diego, or Los Angeles counties in California. Boys and Girls Club affiliation NOT required.

$10 application fee. Renewable up to 4 years. Send a self-addressed, stamped envelope to Boys and Girls Club for an application after January 1st.

1743—BUSINESS & PROFESSIONAL WOMEN'S FOUNDATION (BPW Career Advancement Scholarship Program)

2012 Massachusetts Ave. NW
Washington DC 20036-1070

202/293-1200, ext. 169
FAX: 202/861-0298
Internet: www.bpwusa.org

AMOUNT: $500-$1,000
DEADLINE(S): APR 15
FIELD(S): Biology, Science, Education, Engineering, Social Science, Paralegal, Humanities, Business, Math, Computers, Law, MD, DD

For women (US citizens) aged 25+ accepted into accredited program at US institution (+Puerto Rico & Virgin Islands). Must graduate within 12 to 24 months from the date of grant and demonstrate critical financial need. Must have a plan to upgrade skills, train for a new career field, or to enter/re-enter the job market.

Full- or part-time study. For info see website or send business-sized, self-addressed, double-stamped envelope.

1744—BUSINESS & PROFESSIONAL WOMEN'S FOUNDATION (New York Life Foundation Scholarship Program for Women in the Health Professions)

2012 Massachusetts Ave. NW
Washington DC 20036-1070
202/293-1200, ext. 169
FAX: 202/861-0298
Internet: www.bpwusa.org

AMOUNT: $500-$1,000
DEADLINE(S): APR 15
FIELD(S): Healthcare fields

For women ages 25+ (US citizens) accepted into an accredited, undergraduate program at a US institution (+Puerto Rico & the Virgin Islands). Must graduate within 12 to 24 months from the date of grant and have financial need. Must have a plan to upgrade skills, train for a new career field, or to enter/re-enter job market.

50-100 awards annually. Full- or part-time study. For info see website or send a self-addressed, double-stamped, business-sized envelope.

1745—CALIFORNIA GRANGE FOUNDATION (Deaf Activities Scholarships)

Pat Avila
2101 Stockton Blvd.
Sacramento CA 95817
Written inquiry

AMOUNT: Varies
DEADLINE(S): APR 1
FIELD(S): Course work that will be of benefit to the deaf community

Scholarships for students entering, continuing, or returning to college to pursue studies that will benefit the deaf community.

Write for information after Feb. 1 of each year.

1746—CHARLES E. SAAK TRUST (Educational Grants)

Wells Fargo Bank
8405 N. Fresno Street, Suite 210
Fresno CA 93720
Written inquiry only

AMOUNT: Varies
DEADLINE(S): MAR 31
FIELD(S): Education, Dentistry

Undergraduate grants for residents of the Porterville-Poplar area of Tulare County, California. Must carry a minimum of 12 units, have at least a 2.0 GPA, be under age 21, and demonstrate financial need.

Approximately 100 awards per year. Renewable with reapplication. Write for complete information.

1747—COLUMBIANA COUNTY PUBLIC HEALTH LEAGUE TRUST FUND (Grants)

P.O. Box 1428
Steubenville OH 43952
740/283-8433
FAX: 740/282-4530

AMOUNT: Varies
DEADLINE(S): FEB 28
FIELD(S): Respiratory Illness, Medicine, Medical Research, Pharmacy, Medical Technology, Physical Therapy, Nursing, Dental Hygiene, Occupational Therapy

Open to undergraduate and graduate Columbiana County, Ohio, residents who are pursuing medical education or research in one of the above fields. Preference given to respiratory illness. Students of veterinary medicine NOT eligible.

Contact Sherrill Schmied for an application.

1748—CUYAHOGA COUNTY MEDICAL FOUNDATION (Scholarship Grant Program)

6000 Rockside Woods Blvd.
Suite 150
Cleveland OH 44131-2352
216/520-1000

AMOUNT: $600-$1,700
DEADLINE(S): JUN 1
FIELD(S): Medicine, Dentistry, Pharmacy, Nursing, Osteopathy

Grants open to residents of Cuyahoga County who are accepted to or enrolled in an accredited professional school in one of the above areas.

Approx 40 awards per year. Write for complete information.

1749—DEPARTMENT OF THE ARMY (Armed Forces Health Professions Scholarships)

Attn: RC-HS, 1307 Third Ave.
Fort Knox KY 40121
502/626-0367
FAX: 502/626-0923

AMOUNT: Tuition + monthly stipend
DEADLINE(S): None
FIELD(S): Medicine, Osteopathy, Nurse Anesthetist, Veterinary Medicine, Optometry, Psychology, Dentistry

Open to health professionals and students participating in a Reserve Service of the US Armed Forces, training in the specialties listed above. Varying lengths of service are required to pay back the stipend. Must be US citizen. Award is based on a competitive process, including GPA. Financial need NOT a factor.

400 awards annually. Contact Major Beecher at above address for an application.

1750—EDWARD BANGS KELLEY AND ELZA KELLEY FOUNDATION, INC. (Scholarship Program)

P.O. Drawer M
Hyannis MA 02601-1412
508/775-3117

AMOUNT: $4,000 (max.)
DEADLINE(S): APR 30
FIELD(S): Medicine, Nursing, Health Sciences

Open to residents of Barnstable County, Massachusetts. Scholarships are intended to benefit health and welfare of Barnstable County residents. Awards support study at recognized undergraduate, graduate, and professional institutions. Financial need is considered.

Contact Foundation for an application.

1751—FIRST UNITED METHODIST CHURCH (Robert Stevenson & Doreene E. Cater Scholarships)

302 5th Ave., S.
St. Cloud MN 56301
FAX: 320/251-0878
E-mail: FUMCloud@aol.com

AMOUNT: $100-$300

DEADLINE(S): JUN 1
FIELD(S): Humanitarian & Christian Service: Teaching, Medicine, Social Work, Environmental Studies, etc.

Stevenson Scholarship is open to undergraduate members of the First United Methodist Church of St. Cloud. Cater Scholarship is open to members of the Minnesota United Methodist Conference who are entering the sophomore year or higher of college work. Both require two letters of reference, transcripts, and financial need.

5-6 awards annually. Contact Scholarship Committee for an application.

1752—FORD FOUNDATION/NATIONAL RESEARCH COUNCIL (Howard Hughes Medical Institute Predoctoral Fellowships in Biological Sciences)

2101 Constitution Ave.
Washington DC 20418
202/334-2872
FAX: 202/334-3419
E-mail: infofell@nas.edu
Internet: national-academics.org/osep.fo

AMOUNT: $16,000 stipend + tuition at US institution
DEADLINE(S): NOV 9
FIELD(S): Biochemistry, Biophysics, Epidemiology, Genetics, Immunology, Microbiology, Neuroscience, Pharmacology, Physiology, Virology

Five-year award is open to college seniors and first-year graduate students pursuing a Ph.D. or Sc.D. degree. US citizens/nationals may choose any institution in the US or abroad; foreign students must choose US institution. Based on ability, academic records, proposed study/research, previous experience, reference reports, and GRE scores.

80 awards annually. See website or contact NRC for an application.

1753—FOUNDATION FOR SEACOAST HEALTH (Scholarship Program)

P.O. Box 4606
Portsmouth NH 03802-4606
603/433-3008
FAX: 603/433-2036
E-mail: ffsh@nh.ultranet.com
Internet: www.nh.ultranet.com/~ffsh

AMOUNT: $1,000-10,000
DEADLINE(S): FEB 1
FIELD(S): Health-related fields

Open to undergraduate and graduate students pursuing health-related fields of study who are legal residents of the following cities in New Hampshire: Portsmouth, Newington, New Castle, Rye, Greenland, N. Hampton, or these cities in Maine: Kittery, Eliot, or York. Must have resided in the area for at least two years.

Write or check website for details. $150,000 awarded annually; 35 awards given.

1754—GONSTEAD CHIROPRACTIC EDUCATIONAL TRUST

One West Main Street
Madison WI 53705
608/252-5958

AMOUNT: Varies
DEADLINE(S): Ongoing
FIELD(S): Chiropractic medicine

Scholarships for students who have maintained at least a 3.0 GPA for two years at a member college of the Council of Chiropractic Education.

Write to Oscar Seibel, Marshall & Illsley Trust Co., at above address, or obtain application forms from a member college.

1755—H. FLETCHER BROWN FUND (Scholarships)

c/o PNC Bank
Trust Dept.
P.O. Box 791
Wilmington DE 19899
302/429-1186

AMOUNT: Varies
DEADLINE(S): APR 15
FIELD(S): Medicine, Dentistry, Law, Engineering, Chemistry

Open to US citizens born in Delaware and still residing in Delaware. For 4 years of study (undergrad or grad) leading to a degree that enables applicant to practice in chosen field.

Scholarships are based on need, scholastic achievement, and good moral character. Applications available in February. Write for complete information.

1756—H. FLETCHER BROWN TRUST (Scholarships)

222 Delaware Ave., 16th Fl.
Wilmington DE 19899
302/429-1338

AMOUNT: Varies
DEADLINE(S): APR 9
FIELD(S): Chemistry, Engineering, Law, Medicine, Dentistry

Open to financially needy native-born Delaware residents only who are pursuing

an undergraduate degree. Must have minimum 1,000 SAT score and rank in upper 20% of class. Interview required.

Send self-addressed, stamped envelope to Donald Drois, Account Administrator, PNC Bank, at above address for an application.

1757—HISPANIC DENTAL ASSOCIATION AND DR. JUAN D. VILLARREAL FOUNDATION (Dental/Dental Hygienist Scholarships)

188 W. Randolph Street, Ste. 1811
Chicago IL 60601-3001
800/852-7921 or 312/577-4013
FAX: 312/577-4013
E-mail: hdassoc@aol.com
Internet: www.hdassoc.org

AMOUNT: $500-$1,000
DEADLINE(S): JUN 15
FIELD(S): Dentistry, Dental Hygiene

Open to Hispanic students pursuing undergraduate study in an accredited Texas dental school.

Contact HDA for an application.

1758—HISPANIC DENTAL ASSOCIATION AND PROCTER & GAMBLE ORAL CARE (Scholarships)

188 W. Randolph Street, Ste. 1811
Chicago IL 60606
800/852-7921 or 312/577-4013
FAX: 312/577-0052
E-mail: hdassoc@aol.com
Internet: www.hdassoc.org

AMOUNT: $500-$1,000
DEADLINE(S): JUN 15
FIELD(S): Dentistry, Dental Hygiene, Dental Assisting, Dental Technician

Open to Hispanic students for undergraduate study in above programs. Based on scholastic achievement, community service, leadership skills, and commitment to improving health in the Hispanic community.

Contact HDA for an application.

1759—HOPI TRIBE (Priority Scholarships)

P.O. Box 123
Kykotsmovi AZ 86039
520/734-2441, ext. 520
800/762-9630
FAX: 520/734-2435

AMOUNT: Varies
DEADLINE(S): JUL 31

FIELD(S): Law, Natural Resources, Education, Medicine/Health, Engineering, Business

Open to enrolled members of the Hopi Tribe studying in one of the fields listed above, which are considered to be areas of priority interest to the Hopis. Available to college juniors, seniors, and graduate students. Program is to encourage graduates to apply their degrees to Hopi Tribal Goals and Objectives.

Contact Hopi Tribe for an application.

1760—INTERNATIONAL ORDER OF THE KING'S DAUGHTERS AND SONS (Health Careers Scholarships)

c/o Mrs. Fred Cannon
Box 1310
Brookhaven MS 39602
Written inquiry

AMOUNT: $1,000 (max.)
DEADLINE(S): APR 1
FIELD(S): Medicine, Dentistry, Nursing, Physical Therapy, Occupational Therapy, Medical Technologies, Pharmacy

Open to students accepted to/enrolled in an accredited US or Canadian four-year or graduate school. RN candidates must have completed first year of program; M.D. or D.D.S. candidates must be for at least the second year of medical or dental school; all others must be in at least third year of four-year program. Pre-med students NOT eligible. Must be US or Canadian citizen.

Send self-addressed, stamped envelope, along with a letter stating the field of study and present level, to the Director at above address for an application.

1761—IOWA PHARMACY FOUNDATION

8515 Douglas Ave., Suite 16
Des Moines IA 50322
Written inquiry

AMOUNT: Varies
DEADLINE(S): Ongoing
FIELD(S): Pharmacology

Scholarships and research grants in pharmacology to residents of Iowa.

Write to Thomas R. Temple, Secretary-Treasurer, at above address for details.

1762—JEWISH VOCATIONAL SERVICE (Academic Scholarship Program)

One S. Franklin Street
Chicago IL 60606
312/357-4500

FAX: 312/855-3282
TTY: 312/855-3282
E-mail: jvschicago@jon.cjfny.org
AMOUNT: $5,000 (max.)
DEADLINE(S): MAR 1
FIELD(S): "Helping" Professions, Mathematics, Engineering, Sciences, Communications (at Univ IL only), Law (certain schools in IL only)

Open to Jewish men and women legally domiciled in the greater Chicago metropolitan area, who are identified as having promise for significant contributions in their chosen careers, and are in need of financial assistance for full-time academic programs in above areas. Must have entered undergraduate junior year in career programs requiring no postgrad education, be in graduate/professional school, or be in a voc-tech training program. Interview required.

Renewable. Contact JVS for an application between December 1st and February 15th.

1763—JUNIATA COLLEGE (Robert Steele Memorial Scholarship)

Financial Aid Office
Huntingdon PA 16652
814/641-3603
FAX: 814/641-3355
E-mail: clarkec@juniata.edu
AMOUNT: $4,000 (max.)
DEADLINE(S): APR 1
FIELD(S): Science, Medical Studies

Open to science/medical students applying to Juniata College. Must demonstrate financial need and fill out government FAFSA form.

Contact Cynthia G. Clarke, Research Specialist, for an application or enrollment information. See your financial aid office for FAFSA.

1764—MISSISSIPPI OFFICE OF STATE STUDENT FINANCIAL AID (Dental Education Loan/Scholarship Program)

3825 Ridgewood Road
Jackson MS 39211-6453
601/982-6663 or 800-327-2980
AMOUNT: $4,000/year up to 4 years
DEADLINE(S): JUL 1
FIELD(S): Dentistry

For Mississippi residents who have been accepted for admission to the University of Mississippi School of Dentistry. Post-graduate training must be taken at an accredited hospital in family medicine dentistry and shall not exceed one year.

In acceptance of this loan/scholarship, the student is obligated to practice full-time in a geographical area of critical need in Mississippi or enter full-time public health work at a state health institution or community health center. Obligation can be discharged on the basis of one year's service for one year's loan/scholarship.

1765—MISSISSIPPI OFFICE OF STATE STUDENT FINANCIAL AID (Veterinary Medicine Minority Loan/Scholarship Program)

3825 Ridgewood Road
Jackson MS 39211-6453
601/982-6663 or 800-327-2980
AMOUNT: $6,000/year up to 4 years
DEADLINE(S): MAY 16
FIELD(S): Veterinary Medicine

For full-time minority veterinary students who are Mississippi residents accepted to Mississippi State University College of Veterinary Medicine. The applicant must be classified as a minority student by the Registrar's Office at MSU.

The student is obligated to serve in the profession in Mississippi one year for each year's scholarship.

1766—McCORD CAREER CENTER (Level II McCord Medical/Music Scholarship)

Healdsburg High School
1024 Prince Street
Healdsburg CA 95448
707/431-3473
AMOUNT: Varies
DEADLINE(S): APR 30
FIELD(S): Medicine, Music

For graduates of Healdsburg High School who are planning a career in music or medicine. Must be enrolled full-time at a college/university as an undergraduate junior or senior in the fall, or earning an advanced degree in graduate or medical school, or entering into a vocational/certificate program. Transcripts, proof of attendance, and an essay are required.

Contact the McCord Career Center at Healdsburg High School for an application.

1767—McDONALD'S/UNITED NEGRO COLLEGE FUND (Scholarships for Medical and Healthcare Students)

312/443-8708
AMOUNT: Full tuition (10); $1,000 (50)
DEADLINE(S): None

FIELD(S): Medicine and healthcare fields

Scholarships for college sophomores attending any of the United Negro College Fund schools and pursuing a career in medicine or related healthcare areas. Must maintain 3.0 GPA and demonstrate participation in community and school activities and financial need.

10 two-year scholarships provide full tuition; 50 scholarships are for $1,000 each. Contact school counselor, UNCF office, or call Burrell Communications at above phone number.

1768—NATIONAL ENVIRONMENTAL HEALTH ASSOCIATION (NEHA/AAS Scholarship)

720 S. Colorado Blvd., Suite 970
South Tower
Denver CO 80246-1925
303/756-9090
E-mail: veronica.white@juno.com
Internet: www.neha.org
AMOUNT: Varies
DEADLINE(S): FEB 1
FIELD(S): Environmental Health/Science, Public Health

Undergraduate scholarships to be used for tuition and fees during junior or senior year at an Environmental Health Accreditation Council accredited school or NEHA school. Graduate scholarships are for students or career professionals who are enrolled in a graduate program of studies in environmental health sciences and/or public health. Transcript, letters of recommendation, and financial need considered.

Renewable. Scholarships are paid directly to the college/university for the fall semester of the award. Contact Veronica White, NEHA Liaison, for an application.

1769—NATIONAL FEDERATION OF THE BLIND (Howard Brown Rickard Scholarship)

805 Fifth Ave.
Grinnell IA 50112
515/236-3366
AMOUNT: $3,000
DEADLINE(S): MAR 31
FIELD(S): Law, Medicine, Engineering, Architecture, Natural Sciences

For legally blind students pursuing or planning to pursue a full-time postsecondary course of study in the US. Based on academic excellence, service to the community, and financial need. Membership NOT required.

1 award annually. Renewable. Contact Mrs. Peggy Elliot, Scholarship Committee Chairman, for an application.

1770—NATIONAL STRENGTH & CONDITIONING ASSN. (Challenge Scholarships)

P.O. Box 38909
Colorado Springs CO 80937-8909
719/632-6722
FAX: 719/632-6722
E-mail: nsca@usa.net
Internet: www.colosoft.com/nsca

AMOUNT: $1,000
DEADLINE(S): MAR 1
FIELD(S): Fields related to body strength & conditioning

Open to National Strength & Conditioning Association members. Awards are for undergraduate or graduate study.

For membership information or an application, write to the above address.

1771—NAVY RECRUITING COMMAND (Armed Forces Health Professions Scholarships)

Commander
801 N. Randolph Street, Code 325
Arlington VA 22203-1991
800/USA-NAVY or 703/696-4926
E-mail: omegahouse@erols.com
Internet: www.navyjobs.com

AMOUNT: $938/month stipend + tuition, fees, books, lab fees, etc.
DEADLINE(S): APR 28
FIELD(S): Medicine, Dentistry, Optometry, Physical Therapy, Pharmacology, Health Care Administration, Industrial Hygiene, etc.

Open to US citizens enrolled or accepted for enrollment in any of the above fields at an accredited institution in the US or Puerto Rico. Must qualify for appointment as a Navy officer and sign a contractual agreement. Must be between the ages of 18 and 36 and have a GPA of at least 3.0.

See website, contact local Navy Recruiting Office, or contact Lieutenant Roger A. House, MPA, CAAMA, Medical Service Corps at above address.

1772—NEW YORK STATE HIGHER EDUCATION SERVICES CORPORATION (N.Y. State Regents Professional/Health Care Opportunity Scholarships)

Cultural Education Center
Room 5C64
Albany NY 12230
518/486-1319
Internet: www.hesc.com

AMOUNT: $1,000-$10,000/yr.
DEADLINE(S): Varies
FIELD(S): Medicine and Dentistry and related fields, Architecture, Nursing, Psychology, Audiology, Landscape Architecture, Social Work, Chiropractic, Law, Pharmacy, Accounting, Speech Language Pathology

For NY state residents who are economically disadvantaged and members of a minority group underrepresented in the chosen profession and attending school in NY state. Some programs carry a service obligation in New York for each year of support. For US citizens or qualifying noncitizens.

Medical/dental scholarships require one year of professional work in NY.

1773—NORTH CAROLINA DEPARTMENT OF PUBLIC INSTRUCTION (Scholarship Loan Program for Prospective Teachers)

301 N. Wilmington Street
Raleigh NC 27601-2825
919/715-1120

AMOUNT: Up to $2,500/yr.
DEADLINE(S): FEB
FIELD(S): Education: Teaching, School Psychology and Counseling, Speech/Language Impaired, Audiology, Library/Media Services

For NC residents planning to teach in NC public schools. At least 3.0 high school GPA required; must maintain 2.5 GPA during freshman year and 3.0 cumulative thereafter. Recipients are obligated to teach one year in an NC public school for each year of assistance. Those who do not fulfill their teaching obligation are required to repay the loan plus interest.

200 awards per year. For full-time students. Applications available in Dec. from high school counselors and college and university departments of education.

1774—NORTH CAROLINA DEPT. OF PUBLIC INSTRUCTION (Teacher Assistant Scholarship Loan)

301 N. Wilmington Street
Raleigh NC 27601-2825
919/715-1120

AMOUNT: Up to $1,200/yr
DEADLINE(S): JAN
FIELD(S): Education: Teaching, School Psychology or Counseling, Speech/Language Impaired, Audiology, Library/Media Services

For NC residents employed as K-12 teaching assistants in public schools who wish to pursue teacher licensure. Must

either hold a B.A. degree or have completed general college courses prerequisite to admission to degree program and be admitted to an approved teacher education program at a four-year institution. Two-year community college early childhood education program is acceptable.

Must remain employed as teaching assistant while pursuing licensure and teach one year in an NC public school for each year of assistance received. Applications available in Sept. from local school superintendent.

1775—NORTHWEST PHARMACISTS COALITION (Prepharmacy Scholarships)

P.O. Box 22975
Seattle WA 98122
425/746-9618 or 206/329-0315

AMOUNT: $100-$1,000
DEADLINE(S): MAY 1
FIELD(S): Prepharmacy

Award for undergraduate residents of Washington state who are of black ethnic origin. Must submit transcripts and an essay on why you wish to become a pharmacist and why you feel you should receive the scholarship. Must have discussed the pharmacy profession with at least one practicing pharmacist and provide their name & phone number. Student must also be available for an in-person interview in the Seattle area. Financial need is NOT a factor.

1-3 awards annually. Renewable with reapplication. Write to N.P.C. representative for an application.

1776—OKLAHOMA MEDICAL RESEARCH FOUNDATION (Sir Alexander Fleming Scholar Program)

825 Northeast 13th Street
Oklahoma City OK 73104
405/271-7218
800/522-0211 (in-state)

AMOUNT: $2,500 salary + housing
DEADLINE(S): MAR 1
FIELD(S): Sciences

Summer scholarship program (June and July) for Oklahoma students who have completed their junior year of high school through those in their junior year of college at time of application. Excellent academic standing and aptitude in science and math are essential. Students will work in the laboratories of the above organization. Research projects will be selected from: alcoholism/liver disease, arthritis/

immunology, carcinogenesis, cardiovascular biology, and more.

Named for the scientist who discovered penicillin and dedicated OMRF in 1949. Contact organization for further information and application forms.

1777—PENINSULA COMMUNITY FOUNDATION (Dr. Mary Finegold Scholarship)

1700 S. El Camino Real, #300
San Mateo CA 94402
650/358-9369
FAX: 650/358-9817

AMOUNT: $1,000
DEADLINE(S): MAR 27 (5 P.M.)
FIELD(S): Sciences

Scholarships for senior girls graduating from high school in Palo Alto, California, who intend to complete a four-year degree in the sciences. Special consideration will be given to girls who have demonstrated a "pioneering" spirit in that they have not been constrained by stereotypical female roles and to those facing financial hardship.

Award was established in the honor of Dr. Mary Finegold who, after completing her medical studies, elected to stay at home until her youngest child was in high school before beginning her medical practice. She was a school physician.

1778—PHYSICIAN ASSISTANT FOUNDATION (Scholarships, Traineeships, & Grants)

950 N. Washington Street
Alexandria VA 22314-1552
703/519-5686
Internet: www.aapa.org

AMOUNT: Varies
DEADLINE(S): FEB 1
FIELD(S): Physician Assistant

Must be attending an accredited physician assistant program in order to qualify. Judging is based on financial need, academic standing, community involvement, and knowledge of physician assistant profession.

Contact Edna C. Scott, Administrative Manager, for an application.

1779—RAYMOND J. HARRIS EDUCATION TRUST

P.O. Box 7899
Philadelphia PA 19101-7899
Written inquiry

AMOUNT: Varies
DEADLINE(S): FEB 1

FIELD(S): Medicine, Law, Engineering, Dentistry, or Agriculture

Scholarships for Christian men to obtain a professional education in medicine, law, engineering, dentistry, or agriculture at nine Philadelphia area colleges.

Contact Mellon Bank, N.A. at above location for details and the names of the nine colleges.

1780—ROBERT SCHRECK MEMORIAL FUND (Grants)

c/o Texas Commerce Bank
Trust Dept., P.O. Drawer 140
El Paso TX 79980
915/546-6515

AMOUNT: $500-$1500
DEADLINE(S): JUL 15; NOV 15
FIELD(S): Medicine, Veterinary Medicine, Physics, Chemistry, Architecture, Engineering, Episcopal Clergy

Grants to undergraduate juniors or seniors or graduate students who have been residents of El Paso County for at least two years. Must be US citizen or legal resident and have a high grade point average. Financial need is a consideration.

Write for complete information.

1781—SRP/NAVAJO GENERATING STATION (Navajo Scholarship)

P.O. Box 850
Page AZ 86040
520/645-6539
FAX: 520/645-7295
E-mail: ljdawave@srp.gov

AMOUNT: Based on need
DEADLINE(S): APR 30
FIELD(S): Engineering, Environmental Studies, Business, Business Management, Health, Education

Scholarships for full-time students who hold membership in the Navajo Tribe and who are pursuing a degree in a field of study recognized as significant to the Navajo Nation, Salt River Project, or the Navajo Generating Station, such as those listed above. Must be junior or senior, have and maintain a GPA of 3.0.

Average of 15 awards per year. Inquire of Linda Dawavendewa at above location.

1782—THE ADA ENDOWMENT AND ASSISTANCE FUND, INC. (Minority Dental Student Scholarship)

211 East Chicago Ave.
Chicago IL 60611

312/440-2567
AMOUNT: Up to $2,000
DEADLINE(S): JUL 1
FIELD(S): Dentistry

Applicants must be US citizens and a member of one of the following groups: Black/African American, Native American Indian, Hispanic. For students entering second year at a dental school accredited by the Commisssion on Dental Accreditation. GPA 2.5 or higher. Must demonstrate financial need.

Application forms are available at the dental schools or write to the above address for complete information.

1783—THE ADA ENDOWMENT AND ASSISTANCE FUND INC. (Dental Student Scholarship)

211 East Chicago Ave.
Chicago IL 60611
312/440-2567

AMOUNT: Varies
DEADLINE(S): JUN 15
FIELD(S): Dentistry

Open to second-year students who are currently attending a dental school accredited by the Commission on Dental Accreditation. Applicants must have an accumulative grade point average of 3.0.

Write to above address for complete information or check with your school's financial aid office.

1784—THE AUGIE J. ALTAR SCHOLARSHIP

7115 W. 91st Street
Bridgeview IL 60455-2048
Write for information

AMOUNT: $500
DEADLINE(S): MAY 31
FIELD(S): Medicine or Agricultural fields

Scholarships for students enrolled or accepted to an accredited college, university, or community college who are of Lithuanian descent and are residents of Illinois. Must be studying in the areas of medicine or agriculture. Financial need considered. Must have and maintain at least a 2.0 GPA.

Send application request to above address with a stamped, self-addressed envelope (SASE).

1785—U.S. DEPT. OF HEALTH & HUMAN SERVICES (Indian Health Service Preparatory Scholarship Program)

Twinbrook Metro Plaza, Suite 100
12300 Twinbrook Pkwy.

Rockville MD 20852
301/443-0234
FAX: 301/443-4815
Internet: www.ihs.gov/Recruitment/
DHPS/SP/SBTOC3.asp

AMOUNT: Tuition + fees & monthly
stipend of $938
DEADLINE(S): APR 1
FIELD(S): Health Professions, Social
Work, or Accounting

Open to Native Americans or Alaska
natives who enroll in courses leading to a
baccalaureate degree and are preparing for
acceptance into programs in the above
fields. US citizenship required. Renewable
annually with reapplication.

Scholarship recipients must intend to
serve the Indian people. They incur a one-
year service obligation to the IHS for each
year of support for a minimum of two
years. Write for complete information.

1786—U.S. DEPT. OF HEALTH & HUMAN SERVICES (Indian Health Service Health Professions Pregraduate Scholarship Program)

Twinbrook Metro Plaza, Suite 100
12300 Twinbrook Pkwy.
Rockville MD 20852
301/443-0234
FAX: 301/443-4815
Internet: www.ihs.gov/Recruitment/
DHPS/SP/SBTOC3.asp

AMOUNT: Tuition + fees & monthly
stipend of $938
DEADLINE(S): APR 1
FIELD(S): Health Professions:
Premedicine, Predentistry

Open to Native Americans or Alaska
natives who are college juniors and seniors
in a baccalaureate degree program leading
to a career in medicine or dentistry. US citizenship required. Renewable annually
with reapplication.

Scholarship recipients must intend to
serve the Indian people. They incur a one-
year service obligation to the IHS for each
year of support for a minimum of two
years. Write for complete information.

1787—U.S. DEPT. OF HEALTH & HUMAN SERVICES (Indian Health Service Health Professions Scholarship Program)

Twinbrook Metro Plaza, Suite 100
12300 Twinbrook Pkwy.
Rockville MD 20852
301/443-0234
FAX: 301/443-4815

Internet: www.ihs.gov/Recruitment/
DHPS/SP/SBTOC3.asp

AMOUNT: Tuition + fees & monthly
stipend of $938
DEADLINE(S): APR 1
FIELD(S): Health Professions,
Accounting, Social Work

Open to Native Americans or Alaska
natives who are graduate students or college juniors or seniors in a program leading
to a career in a field listed above. US citizenship required. Renewable annually
with reapplication.

Scholarship recipients must intend to
serve the Indian people. They incur a one-
year service obligation to the IHS for each
year of support for a minimum of two
years. Write for complete information.

1788—U.S. DEPARTMENT OF AGRICULTURE (1890 National Scholars Program)

14th & Independence Ave. SW
Room 301-W, Whitten Bldg.
Washington, DC 20250-9600
202/720-6905
E-mail: usda-m@fie.com
Internet: web.fie.com/htdoc/fed/agr/
ars/edu/prog/mti/agrpgaak.htm

AMOUNT: Tuition,
employment/benefits, use of
PC/software, fees, books, room/board
DEADLINE(S): JAN 15
FIELD(S): Agriculture, Food, or Natural
Resource sciences

For US citizens, high school grad/GED,
GPA 3.0+, verbal/math SAT 1,000+, composite score 21+ ACT, 1st-yr college student, and attend participating school.

34+ scholarships/yr/4 years. Send applications to USDA Liaison Officer at the
1890 Institution of your choice (see Web
page for complete list).

1789—UNIVERSITY OF UTAH COLLEGE OF PHARMACY (Departmental Scholarships)

30 So. 2000 E., Room 203
Salt Lake City UT 84112-5820
801/581-4960
FAX: 801/581-3716
E-mail: ccoffman@
deans.pharm.utah.edu

AMOUNT: Full tuition
DEADLINE(S): MAR
FIELD(S): Pharmacy

Open to junior college students who are
Utah residents registering in pharmacy at
the University of Utah College of

Pharmacy. Must maintain minimum 3.5
GPA. Financial need NOT a factor.
2-3 awards annually. Renewable.
Contact Cathy Coffman for an application.

1790—UNIVERSITY OF UTAH COLLEGE OF PHARMACY (Pharmacy Scholarships)

30 So. 2000 E., Room 203
Salt Lake City UT 84112-5820
801/581-4960
FAX: 801/581-3716
E-mail: ccoffman@
deans.pharm.utah.edu

AMOUNT: $500-$2,500
DEADLINE(S): APR
FIELD(S): Pharmacy

Several scholarship programs for students enrolled in the professional pharmacy program at the University of Utah
College of Pharmacy. For juniors through
doctoral level. Some require financial
need; others are merit-based.

60 awards annually. Contact Cathy
Coffman for an application.

1791—WASHINGTON STATE HIGHER EDUCATION COORDINATING BOARD (Health Professional Loan Repayment & Scholarship Program)

P.O. Box 43430
Olympia WA 98504-3430
360/753-7850
FAX: 360/753-7808
Internet: www.hecb.wa.gov

AMOUNT: Varies
DEADLINE(S): APR (scholarship); FEB
(loan repayment); JUL (loan
repayment)
FIELD(S): Healthcare

Scholarships are open to students in
accredited undergraduate or graduate
healthcare programs leading to eligibility
for licensure in Washington state. Must
agree to work in designated shortage area
for minimum of three years. Loan repayment recipients receive payment from program for purpose of repaying education
loans secured while attending program of
healthcare training leading to licensure in
Washington state. Financial need NOT a
factor.

Renewable up to 5 years. Contact
Program Manager for a loan repayment
application after November 15th and for
scholarship application after January
15th.

1792—WASHINGTON STATE HIGHER EDUCATION COORDINATING BOARD (WICHE Professional Student Exchange)

P.O. Box 43430
Olympia WA 98504-3430
360/753-7850
FAX: 360/753-7808

AMOUNT: $8,000-$12,000
DEADLINE(S): OCT 15
FIELD(S): Optometry, Osteopathy

Program provides state support to Washington residents pursuing undergraduate or graduate study out-of-state.

12 awards annually (10 renewals, 2 new). Contact Program Manager for an application.

1793—WOMEN OF THE EVANGELICAL LUTHERAN CHURCH IN AMERICA (The Kahler-Vickers/Raup-Emma Wettstein Scholarships)

8765 West Higgins Road
Chicago IL 60631-4189
800/638-3522, ext. 2747
FAX: 773/380-2419
E-mail: womnelca@elca.org

AMOUNT: $2,000 max.
DEADLINE(S): MAR 1
FIELD(S): Health Professions & Christian Service

Assists women who are members of the ELCA studying for service in health professions associated with ELCA projects abroad that do not lead to church-certified professions. Must be US citizen and have experienced an interruption of two or more years since completion of high school. Academic records of coursework completed in last five years as well as proof of admission from educational institution are required.

Renewable for an additional year. Contact Faith Fretheim, Program Director, for an application.

1794—ZETA PHI BETA SORORITY EDUCA-TIONAL FOUNDATION (S. Evelyn Lewis Memorial Scholarship in Medical Health Sciences)

1734 New Hampshire Ave. NW
Washington DC 20009
Internet: www.zpb1920.org/
nefforms.htm

AMOUNT: $500-$1,000
DEADLINE(S): FEB 1
FIELD(S): Medicine, Health Sciences

Open to graduate and undergraduate young women enrolled in a program leading to a degree in medicine or health sciences. Award is for full-time study for one academic year (Fall-Spring) and is paid directly to college/university. Must submit proof of enrollment.

Send self-addressed, stamped envelope to above address between September 1st and December 15th for an application.

MEDICAL RESEARCH

1795—ALCOHOLIC BEVERAGE MEDICAL RESEARCH FOUNDATION (Grants for Alcohol Research)

1122 Kenilworth, Suite 407
Baltimore MD 21204-2189
410/821-7066
FAX: 410/821-7065
E-mail: info@abmrf.org

AMOUNT: $40,000/yr. (max.)
DEADLINE(S): FEB 1; SEP 1
FIELD(S): Biomedical & Psychosocial Research on Alcohol Effects

Open to the staff or faculty ONLY of public or private non-profit organizations in the US and Canada for research into the biomedical and psychosocial effects of alcoholic beverages. Graduate/medical students and postdoctoral fellows are NOT eligible; NO funding for thesis/dissertation research.

40 awards annually. Contact Research Foundation for an application ONLY if you fit criteria.

1796—AMERICAN FOUNDATION FOR AGING RESEARCH (Fellowship Program)

NC State Univ., Biochem Dept.
Box 7622
Raleigh NC 27695-7622
919/515-5679

AMOUNT: $500-$1,000
DEADLINE(S): None
FIELD(S): Aging (as related to molecular/celluar biology, immunobiology, cancer, neurobiology, biochemistry, and/or molecular biophysics)

Applicants in degree programs must be undergraduate, graduate, or pre-doctoral students at colleges/universities in the US. Individuals most often chosen utilize modern and innovative approaches and technologies. Letters of reference from research advisor and two instructors are required, as well as official transcripts.

Number of awards varies. $3 processing fee for pre-application; no fee for submission of full application. All interested student researchers should write directly to AFAR Headquarters to receive application forms—specify year in school and type of proposed research.

1797—AMERICAN FOUNDATION FOR THE BLIND (Paul W. Ruckes Scholarship)

11 Penn Plaza, Suite 300
New York NY 10001
212/502-7661
FAX: 212/502-7771
E-mail: juliet@afb.org
Internet: www.afb.org

AMOUNT: $1,000
DEADLINE(S): APR 30
FIELD(S): Engineering, Computer/ Physical/Life Sciences

Open to legally blind and visually impaired undergraduate and graduate students pursuing a degree in one of above fields. Must be US citizen. Must submit written documentation of visual impairment from ophthalmologist or optometrist (need not be legally blind); official transcripts; proof of college/university acceptance; three letters of recommendation; and typewritten statement describing goals, work experience, extracurricular activities, and how monies will be used.

1 award annually. See website or contact Julie Tucker at AFB for an application.

1798—AMERICAN INDIAN SCIENCE AND ENGINEERING SOCIETY (A.T. Anderson Memorial Scholarship)

P.O. Box 9828
Albuquerque NM 87119-9828
505/765-1052
FAX: 505/765-5608
E-mail: scholarships@aises.org
Internet: www.aises.org/scholarships

AMOUNT: $1,000-$2,000
DEADLINE(S): JUN 15
FIELD(S): Medicine, Natural Resources, Science, Engineering

Open to undergraduate and graduate students who are at least 1/4 American Indian or recognized as member of a tribe. Must be member of AISES ($10 fee), enrolled full-time at an accredited institution, and demonstrate financial need.

Renewable. See website or contact Patricia Browne for an application and/or membership information.

1799—AMERICAN SPEECH-LANGUAGE-HEARING FOUNDATION (Kala Singh Memorial Fund-International/Minority Student Scholarship)

10801 Rockville Pike
Rockville MD 20852
301/897-5700
FAX: 301/571-0457

AMOUNT: $2,000
DEADLINE(S): JUN 6
FIELD(S): Communication Sciences and Disorders, Speech/Language Pathology, Audiology

Applicants must be international/ethnic minority graduate student studying communication sciences and disorders in the US and demonstrating outstanding academic achievement.

Applications available in February.

1800—AMERICAN SPEECH-LANGUAGE-HEARING FOUNDATION (Leslie Isenberg Fund for Student With Disability)

10801 Rockville Pike
Rockville MD 20852
301/897-5700
FAX: 301/571-0457

AMOUNT: $2,000
DEADLINE(S): JUN 6
FIELD(S): Communication Sciences & Disorders

Open to full-time graduate student with disability enrolled in a communication sciences and disorders program and demonstrating outstanding academic achievement.

Applications available in February.

1801—AMERICAN SPEECH-LANGUAGE-HEARING FOUNDATION (Young Scholars Award for Minority Student)

10801 Rockville Pike
Rockville MD 20852
301/897-5700
FAX 301/571-0457

AMOUNT: $2,000
DEADLINE(S): JUN 6
FIELD(S): Speech/Language Pathology, Audiology

Open to ethnic minorities who are full-time college seniors accepted for graduate study in speech-language pathology or audiology. Applicants must be US citizens.

Applications available in February.

1802—ARTHUR M. MILLER FUND

P.O. Box 1122
Wichita KS 67201-0004
316/261-4609

AMOUNT: Varies
DEADLINE(S): MAR 31
FIELD(S): Medicine or related fields

Scholarships for Kansas residents for the study of medicine or related fields at accredited institutions.

Send SASE for formal application.

1803—ASSOCIATION ON AMERICAN INDIAN AFFAIRS, INC. (Emergency Aid and Health Professions Scholarships)

P.O. Box 268
Sisseton SD 57262
605/698-3998 or 605/698-3787
FAX: 605/698-3316

AMOUNT: $50-$300
DEADLINE(S): MAY 1
FIELD(S): Health professions

Emergency funding program for full-time undergraduates studying in a health field. Based on financial need. Must be at least 1/4 Indian and write a one- to two-page essay on the nature of the emergency need.

Applications available Sept. 1. Send SASE to above location.

1804—BECA FOUNDATION (Alice Newell Joslyn Medical Fund)

310 Via Vera Cruz, Suite 101
San Marcos CA 92069
760/471-5465
FAX: 760/471-9175

AMOUNT: $500-$2,000
DEADLINE(S): MAR 1
FIELD(S): Medicine, Healthcare, Nursing, Dental/Medical Assisting, Physical Therapy

Open to Latino students who live in or attend college in San Diego County, CA, at time of application. For high school seniors and those already in college pursuing undergraduate or graduate education. Based on financial need, scholastic determination, and community/cultural awareness. BECA also provides a mentor to each scholarship recipient.

Send self-addressed, stamped envelope to BECA for an application.

1805—BOYS AND GIRLS CLUBS OF SAN DIEGO (Spence Reese Scholarship Fund)

1761 Hotel Circle So., Ste. 123
San Diego CA 92108
619/298-3520

AMOUNT: $2,000/yr.
DEADLINE(S): MAY 15
FIELD(S): Medicine, Law, Engineering, Political Science

Open to male high school seniors planning a career in one of the above fields. Must be residents of Imperial, Riverside, Orange, San Diego, or Los Angeles counties in California. Boys and Girls Club affiliation NOT required.

$10 application fee. Renewable up to 4 years. Send a self-addressed, stamped envelope to Boys and Girls Club for an application after January 1st.

1806—COLUMBIANA COUNTY PUBLIC HEALTH LEAGUE TRUST FUND (Grants)

P.O. Box 1428
Steubenville OH 43952
740/283-8433
FAX: 740/282-4530

AMOUNT: Varies
DEADLINE(S): FEB 28
FIELD(S): Respiratory Illness, Medicine, Medical Research, Pharmacy, Medical Technology, Physical Therapy, Nursing, Dental Hygiene, Occupational Therapy

Open to undergraduate and graduate Columbiana County, Ohio, residents who are pursuing medical education or research in one of the above fields. Preference given to respiratory illness. Students of veterinary medicine NOT eligible.

Contact Sherrill Schmied for an application.

1807—CYSTIC FIBROSIS FOUNDATION (Research & Training Programs)

6931 Arlington Road
Bethesda MD 20814
301/951-4422 or 800/FIGHT-CF
Internet: www.cff.org

AMOUNT: $55,000/yr. (max.)
DEADLINE(S): Varies
FIELD(S): Cystic Fibrosis Research

Several doctoral/postdoctoral grants for research and training related to cystic fibrosis are available. Senior-level undergraduates planning to pursue graduate training may also apply. Summer programs available.

Contact CFF for an application and/or see website for listing of programs offered.

1808—CYSTIC FIBROSIS FOUNDATION (Student Traineeship Research Grants)

6931 Arlington Road
Bethesda MD 20814
301/951-4422 or 800/FIGHT-CF
Internet: www.cff.org

AMOUNT: $1,500
DEADLINE(S): None
FIELD(S): Cystic Fibrosis Research

Doctoral research grants are to introduce students to research related to cystic fibrosis and to maintain an interest in this area of biomedicine. Must be in or about to enter a doctoral program. Senior-level undergraduates planning to pursue graduate training may also apply. The project's duration should be 10 weeks or more.

Contact CFF for an application and/or see website for listing of programs offered.

1809—EDWARD BANGS KELLEY AND ELZA KELLEY FOUNDATION, INC. (Scholarship Program)

P.O. Drawer M
Hyannis MA 02601-1412
508/775-3117

AMOUNT: $4,000 (max.)
DEADLINE(S): APR 30
FIELD(S): Medicine, Nursing, Health Sciences

Open to residents of Barnstable County, Massachusetts. Scholarships are intended to benefit health and welfare of Barnstable County residents. Awards support study at recognized undergraduate, graduate, and professional institutions. Financial need is considered.

Contact Foundation for an application.

1810—EPILEPSY FOUNDATION OF AMERICA (Behavioral Sciences Student Fellowships)

4351 Garden City Drive
Landover MD 20785-2267
301/459-3700 or 800/EFA-1000
FAX: 301/577-2684
TDD: 800/332-2070
E-mail: postmaster@efa.org
Internet: www.efa.org

AMOUNT: $2,000
DEADLINE(S): FEB 1
FIELD(S): Epilepsy as related to Behavioral Sciences

Three-month fellowships awarded to students in the behavioral sciences for work on an epilepsy study project. For students of vocational rehabilitation counseling. Students propose an epilepsy-related study or training project to be carried out at a US institution of their choice. A preceptor must accept responsibility for supervision of the student and the project.

Contact EFA for an application.

1811—EPILEPSY FOUNDATION OF AMERICA (Health Sciences Student Fellowships)

4351 Garden City Drive
Landover MD 20785-2267
301/459-3700 or 800/EFA-1000
FAX: 301/577-2684
TDD: 800/332-2070
E-mail: postmaster@efa.org
Internet: www.efa.org

AMOUNT: $2,000
DEADLINE(S): FEB 1
FIELD(S): Epilepsy Research

Three-month fellowships awarded to medical and health sciences students for work on an epilepsy study project. The project is carried out at a US institution of the student's choice where there are ongoing programs of research, training, or service in epilepsy. A preceptor must accept responsibility for supervision of the student and the project.

Contact EFA for an application.

1812—FIGHT FOR SIGHT RESEARCH DIVISION OF PREVENT BLINDNESS AMERICA (Student Research Fellowship)

500 E. Remington Road
Schaumburg IL 60173
847/843-2020
FAX: 847/843-8458
E-mail: info@preventblindness.org

AMOUNT: $500/month ($1,500 max.)
DEADLINE(S): MAR 1
FIELD(S): Ophthalmology, Visual Sciences

Stipend open to undergraduates, medical students, or graduate students for full-time eye-related research, usually during the summer months.

Renewable. Contact Prevent Blindness America for an application.

1813—FIRST UNITED METHODIST CHURCH (Robert Stevenson & Doreene E. Cater Scholarships)

302 5th Ave., S.
St. Cloud MN 56301

FAX: 320/251-0878
E-mail: FUMCloud@aol.com

AMOUNT: $100-$300
DEADLINE(S): JUN 1
FIELD(S): Humanitarian & Christian Service: Teaching, Medicine, Social Work, Environmental Studies, etc.

Stevenson Scholarship is open to undergraduate members of the First United Methodist Church of St. Cloud. Cater Scholarship is open to members of the Minnesota United Methodist Conference who are entering the sophomore year or higher of college work. Both require two letters of reference, transcripts, and financial need.

5-6 awards annually. Contact Scholarship Committee for an application.

1814—FORD FOUNDATION/NATIONAL RESEARCH COUNCIL (Howard Hughes Medical Institute Predoctoral Fellowships in Biological Sciences)

2101 Constitution Ave.
Washington DC 20418
202/334-2872
FAX: 202/334-3419
E-mail: infofell@nas.edu
Internet: national-academics.org/osep.fo

AMOUNT: $16,000 stipend + tuition at US institution
DEADLINE(S): NOV 9
FIELD(S): Biochemistry, Biophysics, Epidemiology, Genetics, Immunology, Microbiology, Neuroscience, Pharmacology, Physiology, Virology

Five-year award is open to college seniors and first-year graduate students pursuing a Ph.D. or Sc.D. degree. US citizens/nationals may choose any institution in the US or abroad; foreign students must choose US institution. Based on ability, academic records, proposed study/ research, previous experience, reference reports, and GRE scores.

80 awards annually. See website or contact NRC for an application.

1815—FOUNDATION FOR SEACOAST HEALTH (Scholarship Program)

P.O. Box 4606
Portsmouth NH 03802-4606
603/433-3008
FAX: 603/433-2036
E-mail: ffsh@nh.ultranet.com
Internet: www.nh.ultranet.com/~ffsh

AMOUNT: $1,000-$10,000

DEADLINE(S): FEB 1
FIELD(S): Health-related fields

Open to undergraduate and graduate students pursuing health-related fields of study who are legal residents of the following cities in New Hampshire: Portsmouth, Newington, New Castle, Rye, Greenland, N. Hampton, or these cities in Maine: Kittery, Eliot, or York. Must have resided in the area for at least two years.

Write or check website for details. $150,000 awarded annually; 35 awards given.

1816—HOPI TRIBE (Priority Scholarships)

P.O. Box 123
Kykotsmovi AZ 86039
520/734-2441, ext. 520
800/762-9630
FAX: 520/734-2435

AMOUNT: Varies
DEADLINE(S): JUL 31
FIELD(S): Law, Natural Resources,
    Education, Medicine/Health,
    Engineering, Business

Open to enrolled members of the Hopi Tribe studying in one of the fields listed above, which are considered to be areas of priority interest to the Hopis. Available to college juniors, seniors, and graduate students. Program is to encourage graduates to apply their degrees to Hopi Tribal Goals and Objectives.

Contact Hopi Tribe for an application.

1817—INTERMURAL RESEARCH TRAINING AWARD (Summer Intern Program)

Office of Education, Bldg. 10
Room 1C-129
Bethesda MD 20892
301/496-2427

AMOUNT: Stipend
DEADLINE(S): FEB 1
FIELD(S): Research Training
    (Biomedical Research)

Summer intern program is designed to provide "academically talented" undergraduate, graduate, or medical students a unique opportunity to acquire valuable hands-on research training and experience in the neurosciences.

Write for complete information.

1818—JEWISH VOCATIONAL SERVICE (Academic Scholarship Program)

One S. Franklin Street
Chicago IL 60606

312/357-4500
FAX: 312/855-3282
TTY: 312/855-3282
E-mail: jvschicago@jon.cjfny.org

AMOUNT: $5,000 (max.)
DEADLINE(S): MAR 1
FIELD(S): "Helping" Professions,
    Mathematics, Engineering, Sciences,
    Communications (at Univ IL only),
    Law (certain schools in IL only)

Open to Jewish men and women legally domiciled in the greater Chicago metropolitan area, who are identified as having promise for significant contributions in their chosen careers, and are in need of financial assistance for full-time academic programs in above areas. Must have entered undergraduate junior year in career programs requiring no postgrad education, be in graduate/professional school, or be in a voc-tech training program. Interview required.

Renewable. Contact JVS for an application between December 1st and February 15th.

1819—JUNIATA COLLEGE (Robert Steele Memorial Scholarship)

Financial Aid Office
Huntingdon PA 16652
814/641-3603
FAX: 814/641-3355
E-mail: clarkec@juniata.edu

AMOUNT: $4,000 (max.)
DEADLINE(S): APR 1
FIELD(S): Science, Medical Studies

Open to science/medical students applying to Juniata College. Must demonstrate financial need and fill out government FAFSA form.

Contact Cynthia G. Clarke, Research Specialist, for an application or enrollment information. See your financial aid office for FAFSA.

1820—LUPUS FOUNDATION OF AMERICA, INC. (Finzi Student Summer Fellowship)

1300 Piccard Dr., Suite 200
Rockville MD 20850-4303
800/558-0121 or 301/670-9292
FAX: 301/670-9486
E-mail: LupusInfo@aol.com
Internet: www.lupus.org

AMOUNT: $2,000
DEADLINE(S): FEB 1
FIELD(S): Lupus Erythematosus
    Research

Open to undergraduates, graduates, and postgraduates, but applicants already having college degree are preferred. Research is conducted under the supervision of an established investigator; student is responsible for locating supervisor and lab (must be in US). Projects may be basic, clinical, or psychosocial research and must be related to the causes, treatments, prevention, or cure of lupus.

10 fellowships annually. See website or contact LFA for an application. Notification is in April.

1821—MICROSCOPY SOCIETY OF AMERICA (Undergraduate Research Scholarship)

435 N. Michigan Ave., #1717
Chicago IL 60611-4067
800/538-3672
FAX: 312/644-8557
E-mail: cclark@msa.microscopy.com
Internet: www.msa.microscopy.com

AMOUNT: $2,500 max.
DEADLINE(S): DEC 31
FIELD(S): Microscopy/Microanalysis

For full-time undergraduate juniors and seniors who are US citizens to carry out research projects in above fields. Must submit research proposal and budget as well as a written abstract of results upon completion of research. Must complete research before graduation. Letters of reference and recommendation and curriculum vitae are required with application. Financial need is NOT a factor.

6-10 awards annually. Not renewable. See website or contact Cindy Clark at above address for details.

1822—McDONALD'S/UNITED NEGRO COLLEGE FUND (Scholarships for Medical and Healthcare Students)

312/443-8708

AMOUNT: Full tuition (10); $1,000 (50)
DEADLINE(S): None
FIELD(S): Medicine and Healthcare
    fields

Scholarships for college sophomores attending any of the United Negro College Fund schools and pursuing a career in medicine or related healthcare areas. Must maintain 3.0 GPA and demonstrate participation in community and school activities and financial need.

10 two-year scholarships provide full tuition; 50 scholarship are for $1,000 each. Contact school counselor, UNCF office, or call Burrell Communications at above phone number.

1823—NATIONAL FEDERATION OF THE BLIND (Howard Brown Rickard Scholarship)

805 Fifth Ave.
Grinnell IA 50112
515/236-3366

AMOUNT: $3,000
DEADLINE(S): MAR 31
FIELD(S): Law, Medicine, Engineering, Architecture, Natural Sciences

For legally blind students pursuing or planning to pursue a full-time postsecondary course of study in the US. Based on academic excellence, service to the community, and financial need. Membership NOT required.

1 award annually. Renewable. Contact Mrs. Peggy Elliot, Scholarship Committee Chairman, for an application.

1824—OAK RIDGE INSTITUTE FOR SCIENCE AND EDUCATION (ORISE Education & Training Programs)

P.O. Box 117
Oak Ridge TN 37831-0117
Internet: www.orau.gov/orise/educ.htm

AMOUNT: Varies
DEADLINE(S): Varies
FIELD(S): Engineering, Aeronautics, Computer Science, Technology, Earth Science, Environmental Studies, Biology, Chemistry, Physics, Medical Research

Numerous programs funded by the US Department of Energy are offered for undergraduate students through postgraduate researchers. Includes fellowship and internship opportunities throughout the US. Some have citizenship restrictions. Travel may be included.

See website or write for a catalog of specific programs and requirements.

1825—OKLAHOMA MEDICAL RESEARCH FOUNDATION (Sir Alexander Fleming Scholar Program)

825 Northeast 13th Street
Oklahoma City OK 73104
405/271-7218
800/522-0211 (in-state)

AMOUNT: $2,500 salary + housing
DEADLINE(S): MAR 1
FIELD(S): Sciences

Summer scholarship program (June and July) for Oklahoma students who have completed their junior year of high school through those in their junior year of college at time of application. Excellent academic standing and aptitude in science and math are essential. Students will work in the laboratories of the above organization. Research projects will be selected from: alcoholism/liver disease, arthritis/immunology, carcinogenesis, cardiovascular biology, and more.

Named for the scientist who discovered penicillin and dedicated OMRF in 1949. Contact organization for further information and application forms.

1826—PENINSULA COMMUNITY FOUNDATION (Dr. Mary Finegold Scholarship)

1700 S. El Camino Real, #300
San Mateo CA 94402
650/358-9369
FAX: 650/358-9817

AMOUNT: $1,000
DEADLINE(S): MAR 27 (5 P.M.)
FIELD(S): Sciences

Scholarships for senior girls graduating from high school in Palo Alto, California, who intend to complete a four-year degree in the sciences. Special consideration will be given to girls who have demonstrated a "pioneering" spirit in that they have not been constrained by stereotypical female roles and to those facing financial hardship.

Award was established in the honor of Dr. Mary Finegold who, after completing her medical studies, elected to stay at home until her youngest child was in high school before beginning her medical practice. She was a school physician.

1827—PILOT INTERNATIONAL FOUNDATION (PIF/Lifeline Scholarship)

P.O. Box 5600
Macon GA 31208-5600
Written inquiries

AMOUNT: Varies
DEADLINE(S): MAR 1
FIELD(S): Disabilities/Brain-related Disorders

This program assists ADULT students re-entering the job market, preparing for a second career, or improving their professional skills for an established career. Applicants must be preparing for, or already involved in, careers working with people with disabilities/brain-related disorders. GPA of 3.5 or more is required.

Must be sponsored by a Pilot Club in your home town, or in the city in which your college or university is located. Send a self-addressed, stamped envelope for complete information.

1828—PILOT INTERNATIONAL FOUNDATION (Ruby Newhall Memorial Scholarship)

P.O. Box 5600
Macon, GA 31208-5600
Written inquiries

AMOUNT: Varies
DEADLINE(S): MAR 15
FIELD(S): Disabilities/Brain-related Disorders

For international students who have studied in the US for at least one year, and who intend to return to their home country six months after graduation. Applicants must be full-time students majoring in a field related to human health and welfare, and have a GPA of 3.5 or more.

Applicants must be sponsored by a Pilot Club in their home town, or in the city in which their college or university is located. Send a self-addressed, stamped envelope for complete information.

1829—PILOT INTERNATIONAL FOUNDATION (The Pilot International Scholarship Program)

P.O. Box 5600
Macon GA 31208-5600
Written inquiries

AMOUNT: Varies
DEADLINE(S): MAR 1
FIELD(S): Disabilities/Brain-related Disorders

This program provides assistance to undergraduate students preparing for careers working directly with people with disabilities or training those who will. GPA of 3.5 or greater required.

Applicants must be sponsored by a Pilot Club in their home town, or in the city in which their college or university is located. Send a self-addressed, stamped envelope for complete information.

1830—SRP/NAVAJO GENERATING STATION (Navajo Scholarship)

P.O. Box 850
Page AZ 86040
520/645-6539
FAX: 520/645-7295
E-mail: ljdawave@srp.gov

AMOUNT: Based on need
DEADLINE(S): APR 30
FIELD(S): Engineering, Environmental Studies, Business, Business Management, Health, Education

Scholarships for full-time students who hold membership in the Navajo Tribe and who are pursuing a degree in a field of study recognized as significant to the Navajo Nation, Salt River Project, or the Navajo Generating Station, such as those listed above. Must be junior or senior, have and maintain a GPA of 3.0.

Average of 15 awards per year. Inquire of Linda Dawavendewa at above location.

1831—THE ARC (Research Grants Program in Mental Retardation)

500 E. Border Street, Suite 300
Arlington TX 76010
817/261-6003
FAX: 817/277-3491
E-mail: thearc@metronet.com
Internet: http://www.theArc.org/welcome.html

AMOUNT: Up to $25,000
DEADLINE(S): APR 1
FIELD(S): Prevention, amelioration, or cure of mental retardation

The ARC invites applications from researchers from diverse sources—individuals and universities, hospitals, and professional organizations with research interests.

Contact Dr. Michael Wehmeyer, Assistant Director, Department of Research and Program Services, The ARC, at above address, or Ann Balson.

1832—THE AUGIE J. ALTAR SCHOLARSHIP

7115 W. 91st Street
Bridgeview IL 60455-2048
Write for information

AMOUNT: $500
DEADLINE(S): MAY 31
FIELD(S): Medicine or Agricultural fields

Scholarships for students enrolled or accepted to an accredited college, university, or community college who are of Lithuanian descent and are residents of Illinois. Must be studying in the areas of medicine or agriculture. Financial need considered. Must have and maintain at least a 2.0 GPA.

Send application request to above address with a stamped, self-addressed envelope (SASE).

1833—THE HAN'T FOUNDATION (Quest Award in Micro-Meteorites)

P.O. Box 6694
Coddingtown CA 95406-0694

Written inquiries only

AMOUNT: $2,001
DEADLINE(S): June 5
FIELD(S): Medical Research in Geoscience

Open to full-time undergraduate or graduate students majoring in bio-physical effects of micro-meteorites in all geophysical environments.

Must be ethnic minority and a US citizen. Must have been born on June 5th and demonstrate financial need. Write to the above address for more information.

1834—THE WHITAKER FOUNDATION (Fellowships for Research in Biomedical Engineering)

1700 North Moore Street
Suite 2200
Rosslyn VA 22209
703/528-2430
FAX: 703/528-2431
E-mail: info@whitaker.org
Internet: www.whitaker.org

AMOUNT: $17,500 for 12 months
DEADLINE(S): DEC 10
FIELD(S): Biomedical engineering

Graduate-level fellowships in the field of biomedical engineering.

Contact organization for details.

1835—U.S. DEPT. OF HEALTH & HUMAN SERVICES (Indian Health Service Preparatory Scholarship Program)

Twinbrook Metro Plaza, Suite 100
12300 Twinbrook Pkwy.
Rockville MD 20852
301/443-0234
FAX: 301/443-4815
Internet: www.ihs.gov/Recruitment/DHPS/SP/SBTOC3.asp

AMOUNT: Tuition + fees & monthly stipend of $938
DEADLINE(S): APR 1
FIELD(S): Health Professions, Social Work, or Accounting

Open to Native Americans or Alaska natives who enroll in courses leading to a baccalaureate degree and are preparing for acceptance into programs in the above fields. US citizenship required. Renewable annually with reapplication.

Scholarship recipients must intend to serve the Indian people. They incur a one-year service obligation to the IHS for each year of support for a minimum of two years. Write for complete information.

1836—U.S. DEPT. OF HEALTH & HUMAN SERVICES (Indian Health Service Health Professions Scholarship Program)

Twinbrook Metro Plaza, Suite 100
12300 Twinbrook Pkwy.
Rockville MD 20852
301/443-0234
FAX: 301/443-4815
Internet: www.ihs.gov/Recruitment/DHPS/SP/SBTOC3.asp

AMOUNT: Tuition + fees & monthly stipend of $938
DEADLINE(S): APR 1
FIELD(S): Health Professions, Accounting, Social Work

Open to Native Americans or Alaska natives who are graduate students or college juniors or seniors in a program leading to a career in a field listed above. US citizenship required. Renewable annually with reapplication.

Scholarship recipients must intend to serve the Indian people. They incur a one-year service obligation to the IHS for each year of support for a minimum of two years. Write for complete information.

1837—WASHINGTON STATE HIGHER EDUCATION COORDINATING BOARD (Health Professional Loan Repayment & Scholarship Program)

P.O. Box 43430
Olympia WA 98504-3430
360/753-7850
FAX: 360/753-7808
Internet: www.hecb.wa.gov

AMOUNT: Varies
DEADLINE(S): APR (scholarship); FEB (loan repayment); JUL (loan repayment)
FIELD(S): Healthcare

Scholarships are open to students in accredited undergraduate or graduate healthcare programs leading to eligibility for licensure in Washington state. Must agree to work in designated shortage area for minimum of three years. Loan repayment recipients receive payment from program for purpose of repaying education loans secured while attending program of healthcare training leading to licensure in Washington state. Financial need NOT a factor.

Renewable up to 5 years. Contact Program Manager for a loan repayment application after November 15th and for scholarship application after January 15th.

1838—WOMEN OF THE EVANGELICAL LUTHERAN CHURCH IN AMERICA (The Kahler-Vickers/Raup-Emma Wettstein Scholarships)

8765 West Higgins Road
Chicago IL 60631-4189
800/638-3522, ext. 2747
FAX: 773/380-2419
E-mail: womnelca@elca.org

AMOUNT: $2,000 max.
DEADLINE(S): MAR 1
FIELD(S): Health Professions &
Christian Service

Assists women who are members of the ELCA studying for service in health professions associated with ELCA projects abroad that do not lead to church-certified professions. Must be US citizen and have experienced an interruption of two or more years since completion of high school. Academic records of coursework completed in last five years as well as proof of admission from educational institution are required.

Renewable for an additional year. Contact Faith Fretheim, Program Director, for an application.

1839—ZETA PHI BETA SORORITY EDUCATIONAL FOUNDATION (S. Evelyn Lewis Memorial Scholarship in Medical Health Sciences)

1734 New Hampshire Ave. NW
Washington DC 20009
Internet: www.zpb1920.org/
nefforms.htm

AMOUNT: $500-$1,000
DEADLINE(S): FEB 1
FIELD(S): Medicine, Health Sciences

Open to graduate and undergraduate young women enrolled in a program leading to a degree in medicine or health sciences. Award is for full-time study for one academic year (Fall-Spring) and is paid directly to college/university. Must submit proof of enrollment.

Send self-addressed, stamped envelope to above address between September 1st and December 15th for an application.

MEDICAL TECHNOLOGIES

1840—ALBERT O.J. LANDUCCI, DDS (Dental Assisting Scholarships)

2720 Edison Street
San Mateo CA 94403-2495
650/574-4444
FAX: 650/574-4441
E-mail: e@DrLanducci.com
Internet: www.drlanducci.com

AMOUNT: Varies
DEADLINE(S): Varies
FIELD(S): All fields of study

Awards and scholarships for elementary and high school students who reside in San Mateo County, California, or for those who attend or plan to attend College of San Mateo. Annual scholarships are in four areas: academic excellence, outstanding community and school volunteerism, science and math achievement, and dental assisting.

For more information, contact your school's scholarship representative.

1841—AMERICAN ALLIANCE FOR HEALTH, PHYSICAL EDUCATION, RECREATION & DANCE

1900 Association Drive
Reston VA 20191
703/476-3400 or 800/213-7193
E-mail: webmaster@aahperd.org
Internet: www.aahperd.org

AMOUNT: Varies
DEADLINE(S): Varies
FIELD(S): Health Education, Leisure
and Recreation, Girls and Women in
Sports, Sport and Physical Education,
Dance

This organization has six national sub-organizations specializing in the above fields. Some have grants and fellowships for both individuals and group projects. The website has the details for each group.

Visit website for details or write to above address for details.

1842—AMERICAN ART THERAPY ASSOCIATION (Cay Drachnik Minorities Fund)

1202 Allanson Road
Mundelein IL 60060
708/949-6064
FAX: 708/566-4580

AMOUNT: Varies (for purchase of books only)
DEADLINE(S): JUN 15
FIELD(S): Art Therapy

For ethnic minority group members enrolled in an AATA-approved program. Fund is specifically for the purchase of books. Must demonstrate financial need through letters of reference, copies of financial aid forms, etc.

Contact AATA for an application.

1843—AMERICAN ART THERAPY ASSOCIATION (Gladys Agell Award for Excellence in Research)

1202 Allanson Road
Mundelein IL 60060
708/949-6064
FAX: 708/566-4580

AMOUNT: Varies
DEADLINE(S): JUN 15
FIELD(S): Art Therapy

For AATA student members. Award is designed to encourage student research and goes to the most outstanding project completed within the past year in the area of applied art therapy. Must verify student status in an AATA-approved program. Research project must follow APA guidelines.

Contact AATA for an application.

1844—AMERICAN ASSOCIATION OF MEDICAL ASSISTANTS ENDOWMENT (Maxine Williams Scholarship Fund)

20 N. Wacker Drive, #1575
Chicago IL 60606
312/899-1500

AMOUNT: $1,000
DEADLINE(S): FEB 1; JUN 1
FIELD(S): Medical Assistant

Undergraduate scholarships open to high school graduates who are enrolled or about to be enrolled in a medical assisting program accredited by the CAAHEP.

3 scholarships per year. Renewable. Write for complete information.

1845—AMERICAN DENTAL HYGIENISTS ASSOCIATION INSTITUTE FOR ORAL HEALTH (William E. Motley Scholarship)

444 N. Michigan Ave., Suite 3400
Chicago IL 60611
800/735-4916 or 312/440-8900
FAX: 312/440-8929
Internet: www.adha.org

AMOUNT: $1,000
DEADLINE(S): JUN 1
FIELD(S): Dental Hygiene

Awarded to applicant who has achieved a 4.0 GPA in dental hygiene. Students must be pursuing a bachelor's degree at a four-year accredited institution in the US. Must demonstrate financial need and have completed a minimum one year in a dental hygiene curriculum prior to receiving an award.

1 award annually. Not renewable. Contact Linda Caradine at ADHA for an application.

1846—AMERICAN DENTAL HYGIENISTS ASSOCIATION INSTITUTE FOR ORAL HEALTH (Warner Lambert Joint Oral Hygiene Group Scholarships)

444 N. Michigan Ave., Suite 3400
Chicago IL 60611
800/735-4916 or 312/440-8900
FAX: 312/440-8929
Internet: www.adha.org

AMOUNT: $1,000
DEADLINE(S): JUN 1
FIELD(S): Dental Hygiene

Students must be pursuing a bachelor's degree at a four-year accredited institution in the US. Must have a minimum 3.0 GPA, demonstrate financial need, and have completed a minimum one year in a dental hygiene curriculum prior to receiving an award.

5 awards annually. Not renewable. Contact Linda Caradine at ADHA for an application. Sponsored by Warner Lambert Company.

1847—AMERICAN DENTAL HYGIENISTS ASSOCIATION INSTITUTE FOR ORAL HEALTH (Carol Bauhs Benson Memorial Scholarship)

444 N. Michigan Ave., Suite 3400
Chicago IL 60611
800/735-4916 or 312/440-8900
FAX: 312/440-8929
Internet: www.adha.org

AMOUNT: $1,000
DEADLINE(S): JUN 1
FIELD(S): Dental Hygiene

For students from Minnesota, North Dakota, South Dakota, or Wisconsin. Must be enrolled full-time in a Certificate/Associate Degree Program in the US leading to licensure as a dental hygienist. Must have a minimum 3.0 GPA, demonstrate financial need, and have completed a minimum one year in a dental hygiene curriculum prior to receiving an award.

1 award annually. Not renewable. Contact Linda Caradine at ADHA for an application.

1848—AMERICAN DENTAL HYGIENISTS ASSOCIATION INSTITUTE FOR ORAL HEALTH (Colgate "Bright Smiles, Bright Futures" Minority Scholarships)

444 N. Michigan Ave., Suite 3400
Chicago IL 60611

800/735-4916 or 312/440-8900
FAX: 312/440-8929
Internet: www.adha.org

AMOUNT: $1,250
DEADLINE(S): JUN 1
FIELD(S): Dental Hygiene

Must be enrolled full-time in a Certificate/Associate Degree Program in the US leading to licensure as a dental hygienist. Awarded to members of a minority group currently underrepresented in dental hygiene programs: African Americans, Hispanics, Asians, Native Americans, and males. Must have a minimum 3.0 GPA, demonstrate financial need, and have completed a minimum one year in a dental hygiene curriculum prior to receiving an award.

2 awards annually. Not renewable. Contact Linda Caradine at ADHA for an application. Sponsored by the Colgate Palmolive Company.

1849—AMERICAN DENTAL HYGIENISTS ASSOCIATION INSTITUTE FOR ORAL HEALTH (Oral-B Laboratories Dental Hygiene Scholarships)

444 N. Michigan Ave., Suite 3400
Chicago IL 60611
800/735-4916 or 312/440-8900
FAX: 312/440-8929
Internet: www.adha.org

AMOUNT: $1,000-$1,500
DEADLINE(S): JUN 1
FIELD(S): Dental Hygiene

Awarded to a full-time student at the baccalaureate degree level who demonstrates an intent to encourage professional, excellence and scholarship, promote quality research, and support dental hygiene through public and private education. Must have a minimum 3.5 GPA, demonstrate financial need, attend an accredited US institution, and have completed a minimum one year in a dental hygiene program in the US.

2 awards annually. Not renewable. Contact Linda Caradine at ADHA for an application. Sponsored by Oral-B Laboratories.

1850—AMERICAN DENTAL HYGIENISTS ASSOCIATION INSTITUTE FOR ORAL HEALTH (Dr. Alfred C. Fones Scholarship)

444 N. Michigan Ave., Suite 3400
Chicago IL 60611
800/735-4916 or 312/440-8900
FAX: 312/440-8929
Internet: www.adha.org

AMOUNT: $1,500
DEADLINE(S): JUN 1
FIELD(S): Dental Hygiene Education

Awarded to an applicant in the baccalaureate or graduate degree categories who intends to become a dental hygiene teacher/educator. Must have a minimum 3.0 GPA, demonstrate financial need, attend an accredited four-year US institution, and have completed a minimum one year in a dental hygiene curriculum prior to receiving an award.

1 award annually. Not renewable. Contact Linda Caradine at ADHA for an application.

1851—AMERICAN DENTAL HYGIENISTS ASSOCIATION INSTITUTE FOR ORAL HEALTH (Dr. Harold Hillenbrand Scholarship)

444 N. Michigan Ave., Suite 3400
Chicago IL 60611
800/735-4916 or 312/440-8900
FAX: 312/440-8929
Internet: www.adha.org

AMOUNT: $1,500
DEADLINE(S): JUN 1
FIELD(S): Dental Hygiene

Awarded to an applicant who demonstrates specific academic excellence and outstanding clinical performance. Must have a minimum 3.5 GPA, demonstrate financial need, be working towards a bachelor's dgree at an accredited four-year US institution, and have completed a minimum one year in a dental hygiene curriculum prior to receiving an award.

1 award annually. Not renewable. Contact Linda Caradine at ADHA for an application.

1852—AMERICAN DENTAL HYGIENISTS ASSOCIATION INSTITUTE FOR ORAL HEALTH (ADHA Institute Minority Scholarships)

444 N. Michigan Ave., Suite 3400
Chicago IL 60611
800/735-4916 or 312/440-8900
FAX: 312/440-8929
Internet: www.adha.org

AMOUNT: $1,500
DEADLINE(S): JUN 1
FIELD(S): Dental Hygiene

For students enrolled full-time in a Certificate/Associate Degree Program in the US leading to licensure as a dental hygienist. Must be members of a minority group currently underrepresented in dental hygiene programs: African Americans,

Hispanics, Asians, Native Americans, and males. Must have a minimum 3.0 GPA, demonstrate financial need, and have completed a minimum one year in a dental hygiene curriculum prior to receiving an award.

2 awards annually. Not renewable. Contact Linda Caradine at ADHA for an application.

1853—AMERICAN DENTAL HYGIENISTS ASSOCIATION INSTITUTE FOR ORAL HEALTH (Irene E. Newman Scholarship)

444 N. Michigan Ave., Suite 3400
Chicago IL 60611
800/735-4916 or 312/440-8900
FAX: 312/440-8929
Internet: www.adha.org

AMOUNT: $1,500
DEADLINE(S): JUN 1
FIELD(S): Dental Hygiene

Awarded to an applicant in the baccalaureate or graduate degree categories who demonstrates strong potential in public health or community dental health. Must have a minimum 3.0 GPA, demonstrate financial need, attend an accredited four-year US institution full-time, and have completed a minimum one year in a dental hygiene curriculum prior to receiving an award.

1 award annually. Not renewable. Contact Linda Caradine at ADHA for an application.

1854—AMERICAN DENTAL HYGIENISTS ASSOCIATION INSTITUTE FOR ORAL HEALTH (ADHA Part-Time Scholarship)

444 N. Michigan Ave., Suite 3400
Chicago IL 60611
800/735-4916 or 312/440-8900
FAX: 312/440-8929
Internet: www.adha.org

AMOUNT: $1,500
DEADLINE(S): JUN 1
FIELD(S): Dental Hygiene

For students enrolled part-time in a Certificate/Associate, Baccalaureate, or Graduate Degree program in the US. Must have a minimum 3.0 GPA, demonstrate financial need, and have completed a minimum one year in a dental hygiene program. See application for specific requirements for each degree program.

1 award annually. Not renewable. Contact Linda Caradine at ADHA for an application.

1855—AMERICAN DENTAL HYGIENISTS ASSOCIATION INSTITUTE FOR ORAL HEALTH (Sigma Phi Alpha Undergraduate Scholarship)

444 N. Michigan Ave., Suite 3400
Chicago IL 60611
800/735-4916 or 312/440-8900
FAX: 312/440-8929
Internet: www.adha.org

AMOUNT: $1,000
DEADLINE(S): JUN 1
FIELD(S): Dental Hygiene

For full-time students pursuing a baccalaureate degree or associate degree/certificate in dental hygiene at an accredited US institution. Awarded to an oustanding applicant attending an accredited dental hygiene school with an active chapter of the Sigma Phi Alpha Dental Hygiene Honor Society. Must have a minimum 3.0 GPA, demonstrate financial need, and have completed a minimum one year in a dental hygiene curriculum prior to receiving an award.

1 award annually. Not renewable. Contact Linda Caradine at ADHA for an application.

1856—AMERICAN DENTAL HYGIENISTS ASSOCIATION INSTITUTE FOR ORAL HEALTH (Margaret E. Swanson Scholarship)

444 N. Michigan Ave., Suite 3400
Chicago IL 60611
800/735-4916 or 312/440-8900
FAX: 312/440-8929
Internet: www.adha.org

AMOUNT: $1,500
DEADLINE(S): JUN 1
FIELD(S): Dental Hygiene

For students enrolled full-time in a Certificate/Associate Degree Program in the US leading to licensure as a dental hygienist. Awarded to an applicant who demonstrates exceptional organizational leadership potential. Must have a minimum 3.0 GPA, demonstrate financial need, and have completed a minimum one year in a dental hygiene curriculum prior to receiving an award.

1 award annually. Not renewable. Contact Linda Caradine at ADHA for an application.

1857—AMERICAN DENTAL HYGIENISTS ASSOCIATION INSTITUTE FOR ORAL HEALTH (Rebecca Fisk Scholarship)

444 N. Michigan Ave., Suite 3400
Chicago IL 60611

800/735-4916 or 312/440-8900
FAX: 312/440-8929
Internet: www.adha.org

AMOUNT: $1,000
DEADLINE(S): JUN 1
FIELD(S): Dental Hygiene

For students enrolled full-time in a Certificate/Associate Degree Program in the US leading to licensure as a dental hygienist. Must have a minimum 3.0 GPA, demonstrate financial need, and have completed a minimum one year in a dental hygiene curriculum prior to receiving an award.

1 award annually. Not renewable. Contact Linda Caradine at ADHA for an application.

1858—AMERICAN FOUNDATION FOR THE BLIND (Paul W. Ruckes Scholarship)

11 Penn Plaza, Suite 300
New York NY 10001
212/502-7661
FAX: 212/502-7771
E-mail: juliet@afb.org
Internet: www.afb.org

AMOUNT: $1,000
DEADLINE(S): APR 30
FIELD(S): Engineering, Computer/
Physical/Life Sciences

Open to legally blind and visually impaired undergraduate and graduate students pursuing a degree in one of above fields. Must be US citizen. Must submit written documentation of visual impairment from ophthalmologist or optometrist (need not be legally blind); official transcripts; proof of college/university acceptance; three letters of recommendation; and typewritten statement describing goals, work experience, extracurricular activities, and how monies will be used.

1 award annually. See website or contact Julie Tucker at AFB for an application.

1859—AMERICAN HEALTH INFORMATION MANAGEMENT ASSOCIATION (Barbara Thomas Enterprises Scholarship)

919 N. Michigan, Suite 1400
Chicago IL 60611-1683
312/787-2672, ext. 302
FAX: 312/787-5926
E-mail: juanita@ahima.mhs.
compuserve.com
Internet: http//www.ahima.org

AMOUNT: $5,000
DEADLINE(S): MAY 30

FIELD(S): Health Information
Management, Medical Records,
Health Information Technology

For undergraduates and graduates studying one of the above fields. Must be a single parent accepted to a HIM or technology (HIT) program accredited by the Commission on Accreditation of Allied Health Education programs or to AHIMA's Independent Study Program.

Contact the above address for complete information.

1860—AMERICAN HEALTH INFORMATION MANAGEMENT ASSOCIATION (Foundation of Research and Education in Health Information Management)

919 N. Michigan, Suite 1400
Chicago IL 60611-1683
312/787-2672, ext. 302
FAX: 312/787-5926
E-mail: juanita@ahima.mhs.
compuserve.com
Internet: http//www.ahima.org

AMOUNT: $1,000-$5,000
DEADLINE(S): MAY 30; OCT 20
FIELD(S): Health Information
Management, Medical Records,
Health Information Technology

Loans for undergraduates and graduates studying one of the above fields. US citizenship required.

Contact the above address for complete information.

1861—AMERICAN HEALTH INFORMATION MANAGEMENT ASSOCIATION (Undergraduate Scholarships)

919 N. Michigan Ave., Suite 1400
Chicago IL 60611-1683
312/787-2672, ext. 302
FAX: 312/787-5926
E-mail: juanita@ahima.mhs.
compuserve.com
Internet: http//www.ahima.org

AMOUNT: $1,000-$5,000
DEADLINE(S): MAY 30
FIELD(S): Health Information
Management

Open to undergraduates who have been accepted for admission to a HIM or technology program (HIT) accredited by the Commission on Accreditation of Allied Health Education Programs or accepted to AHIMA's Independent Study Program and successfully completed three individual modules.

Several awards. Write for complete information.

1862—AMERICAN INDIAN SCIENCE AND ENGINEERING SOCIETY (A.T. Anderson Memorial Scholarship)

P.O. Box 9828
Albuquerque NM 87119-9828
505/765-1052
FAX: 505/765-5608
E-mail: scholarships@aises.org
Internet: www.aises.org/scholarships

AMOUNT: $1,000-$2,000
DEADLINE(S): JUN 15
FIELD(S): Medicine, Natural Resources,
Science, Engineering

Open to undergraduate and graduate students who are at least 1/4 American Indian or recognized as member of a tribe. Must be member of AISES ($10 fee), enrolled full-time at an accredited institution, and demonstrate financial need.

Renewable. See website or contact Patricia Browne for an application and/or membership information.

1863—AMERICAN MEDICAL TECHNOLOGISTS (AMT Scholarships)

710 Higgins Road
Park Ridge IL 60068-5765
847/823-5169

AMOUNT: $500
DEADLINE(S): APR 1
FIELD(S): Medical Laboratory
Technology, Medical Assisting, Dental
Assisting, Phlebotomy, Office
Laboratory

Must be a graduate of, or a senior in, an accredited high school (GED okay). Must be enrolled in a school accredited by accrediting agency recognized by US Dept. of Education, or must be enrolled in regionally accredited college/university in the US. Applicant MUST be pursuing one of above careers and should provide evidence of career goals, as well as financial need. Must submit transcripts, two letters of personal reference, and statement of why this career chosen.

5 awards annually. Send a self-addressed, stamped, business-sized envelope to AMT for an application. Recipients announced at AMT National Convention held in mid-summer.

1864—AMERICAN RESPIRATORY CARE FOUNDATION (Jimmy A. Young Memorial Education Recognition Award)

11030 Ables Lane
Dallas TX 75229-4593

972/243-2272
E-mail: info@aarc.org
Internet: www.aarc.org/awards

AMOUNT: $1,000 cash + certificate &
travel to convention
DEADLINE(S): JUN 30
FIELD(S): Respiratory Therapy

Open to undergraduate students of minority origin who are enrolled in an accredited respiratory therapy program. Must have letters of recommendation from program director/senior faculty member and medical director/physician instructor, maintain a minimum 3.0 GPA, and be a US citizen/permanent resident. Must submit original referenced essay on some aspect of respiratory care.

See website or contact Norma Hernandez at ARCF for an application. Selection by September 1st.

1865—AMERICAN RESPIRATORY CARE FOUNDATION (Morton B. Duggan, Jr. Memorial Education Award)

11030 Ables Lane
Dallas TX 75229-4593
972/243-2272
E-mail: info@aarc.org
Internet: www.aarc.org/awards

AMOUNT: $1,000 cash + certificate &
travel to convention
DEADLINE(S): JUN 30
FIELD(S): Respiratory Therapy

Open to undergraduate students enrolled in an accredited respiratory therapy program. Must have letters of recommendation from program director/senior faculty member and medical director/physician instructor, maintain a minimum 3.0 GPA, and be a US citizen/permanent resident. Must submit original referenced essay on some aspect of respiratory care. Preference given to candidates from Georgia and South Carolina; however, nominees will be accepted nationwide.

See website or contact Norma Hernandez at ARCF for an application. Selection by September 1st.

1866—AMERICAN RESPIRATORY CARE FOUNDATION (NBRC/AMP Robert M. Lawrence, MD Education Recognition Award)

11030 Ables Lane
Dallas TX 75229-4593
972/243-2272
E-mail: info@aarc.org

Internet: www.aarc.org/awards

AMOUNT: $2,500 cash + certificate & travel to convention

DEADLINE(S): JUN 30

FIELD(S): Respiratory Therapy

Open to third- and fourth-year students enrolled in an accredited respiratory therapy program leading to a bachelor's degree. Must have letters of recommendation from program director/senior faculty member and medical director/physician instructor, maintain a minimum 3.0 GPA, and be a US citizen/permanent resident. Must submit original referenced paper on some aspect of respiratory care, as well as 1,200-word essay describing how award will assist in reaching goals.

See website or contact Norma Hernandez ARCF for an application. Selection by September 1st.

1867—AMERICAN RESPIRATORY CARE FOUNDATION (NBRC/AMP William W. Burgin, Jr., MD Education Recognition Award)

11030 Ables Lane
Dallas TX 75229-4593
972/243-2272
E-mail: info@aarc.org
Internet: www.aarc.org/awards

AMOUNT: $2,500 cash + certificate & travel to convention

DEADLINE(S): JUN 30

FIELD(S): Respiratory Therapy

Open to second-year students enrolled in an accredited respiratory therapy program leading to an associate's degree. Must have letters of recommendation from program director/senior faculty member and medical director/physician instructor, maintain a minimum 3.0 GPA, and be US citizen/permanent resident. Must submit original referenced paper on some aspect of respiratory care, as well as 1,200-word essay describing how award will assist in reaching goals.

See website or contact Norma Hernandez at ARCF for an application. Selection by September 1st.

1868—AMERICAN SOCIETY FOR CLINICAL LABORATORY SCIENCE (Dorothy Morrison Undergraduate Scholarship)

7910 Woodmont Ave., Suite 530
Bethesda MD 20814
301/657-2768
FAX: 301/657-2909

AMOUNT: $1,000

DEADLINE(S): MAR 1

FIELD(S): Clinical Laboratory Science or Medical Technology

Scholarships for students in the above field enrolled in an approved undergraduate program. Must be in last year of study. US citizenship or permanent US residency required.

Contact address above for complete information. Enclose self-addressed stamped business size envelope. Applications available after Nov. 1.

1869—AMERICAN SOCIETY FOR CLINICAL LABORATORY SCIENCE (Ruth M. French Graduate or Undergraduate Scholarship)

7910 Woodmont Ave., Suite 530
Bethesda MD 20814
301/657-2768
FAX: 301/657-2909

AMOUNT: $1,000

DEADLINE(S): MAR 1

FIELD(S): Clinical Laboratory Science or Medical Technology

Scholarships for students in the above field enrolled in an approved undergraduate or graduate program. Undergrads must be in last year of study. US citizenship or permanent US residency required.

Contact address above for complete information. Enclose self-addressed stamped business size envelope. Applications available after Nov. 1.

1870—AMERICAN SOCIETY FOR CLINICAL LABORATORY SCIENCE (Alpha Mu Tau Undergraduate Scholarship)

7910 Woodmont Ave., Suite 530
Bethesda MD 20814
301/657-2768
FAX: 301/657-2909

AMOUNT: Up to $1,000

DEADLINE(S): MAR 15

FIELD(S): Clinical Laboratory Science, Medical Technology, Clinical Laboratory Technician, Cytotechnology, Histotechnology

Scholarships for undergraduate students in their last year of study in the above fields enrolled in an approved NAACLS accredited program. US citizenship or permanent US residency required.

Contact address above for complete information. Enclose self-addressed stamped business size envelope. Applications available after Nov. 1.

1871—AMERICAN SOCIETY FOR CLINICAL LABORATORY SCIENCE (Forum for Concern of Minorities Scholarship)

7910 Woodmont Ave., Suite 530
Bethesda MD 20814
301/657-2768
FAX: 301/657-2909

AMOUNT: Varies

DEADLINE(S): FEB 15

FIELD(S): Clinical Laboratory Science, Medical Technology, Clinical Laboratory Technology

Scholarships for undergraduate minority students enrolled in an approved NAACLS accredited program in the above fields. Min. 2.5 GPA required. US citizenship or permanent US residency required. Must demonstrate financial need.

Contact address above for complete information. Enclose self-addressed, stamped business size envelope. Applicat-ions available after Nov. 1

1872—AMERICAN SOCIETY OF CLINICAL PATHOLOGISTS (Scholarship Program)

2100 W. Harrison Street
Chicago IL 60612-3798
312/738-1336, ext. 159
E-mail: info@ascp.org

AMOUNT: $1,000

DEADLINE(S): OCT 31

FIELD(S): Cytotechnology, Histologic Technician, Medical Laboratory Technician, Medical Technology

Open to undergraduates in their final clinical year of training in a CAHEA-accredited program in the above fields. Official transcripts and three letters of recommendation are required.

Contact Jennifer Jones at above address.

1873—AMERICAN SOCIETY OF RADIO-LOGIC TECHNOLOGISTS (Isadore N. Stern Scholarship)

15000 Central Ave., SE
Albuquerque NM 87123-3917
505/298-4500
FAX: 505/298-5063
Internet: www.asrt.org

AMOUNT: $1,000

DEADLINE(S): JAN 31

FIELD(S): Radiologic Sciences

For undergraduate and graduate students with a minimum 3.0 GPA. Must have at least one-year membership with ASRT, ARRT registered/unrestricted state license, and must have worked in the radiologic sciences profession for at least one year in the past five years.

4 awards annually. Financial need is NOT a factor. For membership information or an application, contact Renee Lines at the above address.

1874—AMERICAN SPEECH-LANGUAGE-HEARING FOUNDATION (Kala Singh Memorial Fund-International/Minority Student Scholarship)

10801 Rockville Pike
Rockville MD 20852
301/897-5700
FAX: 301/571-0457

AMOUNT: $2,000
DEADLINE(S): JUN 6
FIELD(S): Communication Sciences and Disorders, Speech/Language Pathology, Audiology

Applicants must be international/ethnic minority graduate student studying communication sciences and disorders in the US and demonstrating outstanding academic achievement.

Applications available in February.

1875—AMERICAN SPEECH-LANGUAGE-HEARING FOUNDATION (Leslie Isenberg Fund for Student With Disability)

10801 Rockville Pike
Rockville MD 20852
301/897-5700
FAX: 301/571-0457

AMOUNT: $2,000
DEADLINE(S): JUN 6
FIELD(S): Communication Sciences & Disorders

Open to full-time graduate student with disability enrolled in a communication sciences and disorders program and demonstrating outstanding academic achievement.

Applications available in February.

1876—AMERICAN SPEECH-LANGUAGE-HEARING FOUNDATION (Young Scholars Award for Minority Student)

10801 Rockville Pike
Rockville MD 20852
301/897-5700
FAX 301/571-0457

AMOUNT: $2,000
DEADLINE(S): JUN 6
FIELD(S): Speech/Language Pathology, Audiology

Open to ethnic minorities who are full-time college seniors accepted for graduate

study in speech-language pathology or audiology. Applicants must be US citizens.

Applications available in February.

1877—ARCHBOLD MEDICAL CENTER (Archbold Scholarship/Loan)

Dept. of Education
P.O. Box 1018
Thomasville GA 31799-1018
912/228-2795

AMOUNT: $4,000-$6,000; $500 for technical courses
DEADLINE(S): None specified
FIELD(S): Healthcare fields such as Registered Nurse, Medical Lab, Pharmacy, Physical Therapy, etc.

Open to undergrad and grad students accepted into an accredited healthcare school and within 2 years of completing course work. Student must agree to work at AMC for 3 years following graduation (1 year for tech school students).

Must be Georgia resident. Personal interview required. Repayment is required if recipient fails to work at Archbold for the designated period. Write for complete information.

1878—ARTHUR M. MILLER FUND

P.O. Box 1122
Wichita KS 67201-0004
316/261-4609

AMOUNT: Varies
DEADLINE(S): MAR 31
FIELD(S): Medicine or related fields

Scholarships for Kansas residents for the study of medicine or related fields at accredited institutions.

Send SASE for formal application.

1879—ASSOCIATION ON AMERICAN INDIAN AFFAIRS, INC. (Emergency Aid and Health Professions Scholarships)

P.O. Box 268
Sisseton SD 57262
605/698-3998 or 605/698-3787
FAX: 605/698-3316

AMOUNT: $50-$300
DEADLINE(S): MAY 1
FIELD(S): Health professions

Emergency funding program for full-time undergraduates studying in a health field. Based on financial need. Must be at least 1/4 Indian and write a one- to two-page essay on the nature of the emergency need.

Applications available Sept. 1. Send SASE to above location.

1880—BECA FOUNDATION (Alice Newell Joslyn Medical Fund)

310 Via Vera Cruz, Suite 101
San Marcos CA 92069
760/471-5465
FAX: 760/471-9175

AMOUNT: $500-$2,000
DEADLINE(S): MAR 1
FIELD(S): Medicine, Healthcare, Nursing, Dental/Medical Assisting, Physical Therapy

Open to Latino students who live in or attend college in San Diego County, CA, at time of application. For high school seniors and those already in college pursuing undergraduate or graduate education. Based on financial need, scholastic determination, and community/cultural awareness. BECA also provides a mentor to each scholarship recipient.

Send self-addressed, stamped envelope to BECA for an application.

1881—BOYS AND GIRLS CLUBS OF SAN DIEGO (Spence Reese Scholarship Fund)

1761 Hotel Circle S., Suite 123
San Diego CA 92108
619/298-3520

AMOUNT: $2,000/yr.
DEADLINE(S): MAY 15
FIELD(S): Medicine, Law, Engineering, Political Science

Open to male high school seniors planning a career in one of the above fields. Must be residents of Imperial, Riverside, Orange, San Diego, or Los Angeles counties in California. Boys and Girls Club affiliation NOT required.

$10 application fee. Renewable up to 4 years. Send a self-addressed, stamped envelope to Boys and Girls Club for an application after January 1st.

1882—CALIFORNIA GRANGE FOUNDATION (Deaf Activities Scholarships)

Pat Avila
2101 Stockton Blvd.
Sacramento CA 95817
Written inquiry

AMOUNT: Varies
DEADLINE(S): APR 1
FIELD(S): Course work that will be of benefit to the deaf community

Scholarships for students entering, continuing, or returning to college to pursue studies that will benefit the deaf community.

Write for information after Feb. 1 of each year.

1883—CALIFORNIA PHYSICAL THERAPY FUND (Roy and Roxie Campanella Physical Therapist Professional Education Scholarship Program)

2520 Venture Oaks Way, Ste. 150
Sacramento CA 95833
916/929-2782
FAX: 916/646-5960
E-mail: captfund@ccapta.org
Internet: www.dennis
mc.com/baseball/dtw/dtwcampy.ht
ml-ssi

AMOUNT: $2,000 (max.)
DEADLINE(S): FEB 15
FIELD(S): Physical Therapy

For college seniors attending school in the US; must be a junior at the time of application. Must be currently enrolled in professional portion of physical therapist education program accredited by CAPTE. Must answer: "Why did you choose physical therapy as a profession, and how have your experiences contributed to your sensitivity to peoples of different cultures?" Recommendation from physical therapist required.

Contact CPTF for an application between January 15th & Jan. 31st. Award honors Brooklyn Dodgers' catcher Roy Campanella, who became quadriplegic in auto accident during baseball career.

1884—COLUMBIANA COUNTY PUBLIC HEALTH LEAGUE TRUST FUND (Grants)

P.O. Box 1428
Steubenville OH 43952
740/283-8433
FAX: 740/282-4530

AMOUNT: Varies
DEADLINE(S): FEB 28
FIELD(S): Respiratory Illness, Medicine, Medical Research, Pharmacy, Medical Technology, Physical Therapy, Nursing, Dental Hygiene, Occupational Therapy

Open to undergraduate and graduate Columbiana County, Ohio, residents who are pursuing medical education or research in one of the above fields. Preference given to respiratory illness. Students of veterinary medicine NOT eligible.

Contact Sherrill Schmied for an application.

1885—COMMUNITY FOUNDATION OF WESTERN MASSACHUSETTS (James L. Shriver Scholarship)

1500 Main Street
P.O. Box 15769
Springfield MA 01115

413/732-2858
AMOUNT: $750
DEADLINE(S): APR 15
FIELD(S): Technical Fields

Open to residents of Western Massachusetts to pursue technical careers through college, trade, or technical school. Based on financial need, academic merit, and extracurricular activities. Must submit transcripts and fill out government FAFSA form.

1 award annually. Renewable with reapplication. Contact Community Foundation for an application and your financial aid office for FAFSA. Notification is in June.

1886—COMMUNITY FOUNDATION OF WESTERN MASSACHUSETTS (Nate McKinney Memorial Scholarship)

1500 Main Street
P.O. Box 15769
Springfield MA 01115
413/732-2858

AMOUNT: $1,000
DEADLINE(S): APR 15
FIELD(S): Music, Athletics, Science

Open to graduating seniors of Gateway Regional High School in Huntington, Massachusetts. Recipient must excel academically, demonstrate good citizenship, and have a strong interest in at least two of the following areas: music, science, and athletics. Based on financial need, academic merit, and extracurricular activities. Must submit transcripts and fill out government FAFSA form.

1 award annually. Renewable up to 4 years with reapplication. Contact Community Foundation for an application and your financial aid office for FAFSA. Notification is in June.

1887—CYNTHIA E. AND CLARA H. HOLLIS FOUNDATION

100 Summer Street
Boston MA 02110
Written inquiry

AMOUNT: Varies
DEADLINE(S): APR 1
FIELD(S): Nursing, Social Work, Dental or Medical Technology, and Religion

Scholarships for Massachusetts with preference given to students in the above fields. For undergraduates, graduates, voc-tech, and adult education. Must demonstrate financial need.

Send SASE to Walter E. Palmer, Esq., 35 Harvard Street, Brookline, MA 02146 for application details. Scholarship forms are also available from the rector of All Saints Church, Brookline High School, and St. Mary's High School, all in Brookline, Massachusetts.

1888—EASTER SEAL SOCIETY OF IOWA, INC. (Scholarships & Awards)

P.O. Box 4002
Des Moines IA 50333-4002
515/289-1933

AMOUNT: $400-$600
DEADLINE(S): APR 15
FIELD(S): Physical Rehabilitation, Mental Rehabilitation, and related areas

Open ONLY to Iowa residents who are full-time undergraduate sophomores, juniors, seniors, or graduate students at accredited institutions planning a career in the broad field of rehabilitation. Must indicate financial need and be in top 40% of their class.

6 scholarships per year. Must reapply each year.

1889—EDUCATIONAL AND SCIENTIFIC TRUST OF THE PENNSYLVANIA MEDICAL SOCIETY (Loan Program for Allied Health/Nursing Students)

777 East Park Drive
P.O. Box 8820
Harrisburg PA 17105-8820
717/558-7750, ext. 1257
FAX: 717/558-7818
E-mail: studentloans-trust@pamedsoc.org
Internet: www.pitt.edu/HOME/GHNet/PA_Trust

AMOUNT: Up to $1,500 for bona fide Pennsylvania residents
DEADLINE(S): JUN 1
FIELD(S): Nursing and allied health fields

Open to Pennsylvania residents with demonstrated financial need who are seeking a career in nursing or an allied health field. Must be attending a Pennsylvania institution.

Approx. 200 loans per year. Must be US citizen. Contact above location for complete information.

1890—EDWARD BANGS KELLEY AND ELZA KELLEY FOUNDATION, INC. (Scholarship Program)

P.O. Drawer M
Hyannis MA 02601-1412
508/775-3117

AMOUNT: $4,000 (max.)
DEADLINE(S): APR 30
FIELD(S): Medicine, Nursing, Health
Sciences

Open to residents of Barnstable
County, Massachusetts. Scholarships are
intended to benefit health and welfare of
Barnstable County residents. Awards support study at recognized undergraduate,
graduate, and professional institutions.
Financial need is considered.

Contact Foundation for an application.

1891—EMPIRE COLLEGE (Dean's Scholarship)

3035 Cleveland Ave.
Santa Rosa CA 95403
707/546-4000
FAX: 707/546-4058

AMOUNT: $250-$1,500
DEADLINE(S): APR 15
FIELD(S): Accounting, Secretarial,
Legal, Medical (Clinical &
Administrative), Travel & Tourism,
General Business, Computer
Assembly, Network
Assembly/Administration

Open to high school seniors who plan
to attend Empire College. Must be US citizen.

10 awards annually. Contact Ms. Mary
Farha for an application.

1892—ESPN (Internship Programs)

Human Resources Dept., ESPN, Inc.
ESPN Plaza
Bristol CT 06010
No phone calls.
Internet: espnet.sportszone.com/
editors/studios/97faq.html

AMOUNT: Paid Internships
DEADLINE(S): OCT 1; MAR 1; JUN 1
FIELD(S): Television Industry, Public
Relations, Sports

12-week internships in the spring, summer, and fall for undergraduate
juniors/seniors and graduate students.
Some areas require weekend/evening
hours and a strong knowledge of sports.
Interns receive hourly wages and take part
in many company-sponsored activities.
ESPN does not provide housing for students, but we do try to assist in finding suitable living arrangements once selected.

To apply for internship programs,
please send cover letter and resume to the
above address. If applying to the
Communications Dept., please also
enclose writing samples and send attention
to Diane Lamb.

1893—FELLOWS MEMORIAL FUND (Scholarship Loans)

Pensacola Junior College
1000 College Blvd.
Pensacola FL 32504-8998
904/484-1706

AMOUNT: Individually determined
DEADLINE(S): Varies (Individually
arranged)
FIELD(S): Nursing and Medical
Technology

Loans for students accepted for training
in nursing or in one of the several fields of
medical technology at accredited schools
or colleges. Appropriate for two- or four-
year nursing programs, graduate nursing
study, medical or surgical technology,
anesthesiology, and radiological technology. Must be residents of one of the following Florida counties: Escambia, Santa
Rosa, Okaloosa, or Walton

Loans are interest-free until four
months after graduation. Thereafter,
favorable interest rates will apply with the
total to be paid by the end of eleven years.

1894—FIRST UNITED METHODIST CHURCH (Robert Stevenson & Doreene E. Cater Scholarships)

302 5th Ave., S.
St. Cloud MN 56301
FAX: 320/251-0878
E-mail: FUMCloud@aol.com

AMOUNT: $100-$300
DEADLINE(S): JUN 1
FIELD(S): Humanitarian & Christian
Service: Teaching, Medicine, Social
Work, Environmental Studies, etc.

Stevenson Scholarship is open to undergraduate members of the First United
Methodist Church of St. Cloud. Cater
Scholarship is open to members of the
Minnesota United Methodist Conference
who are entering the sophomore year or
higher of college work. Both require two
letters of reference, transcripts, and financial need.

5-6 awards annually. Contact
Scholarship Committee for an application.

1895—FLORIDA DENTAL HEALTH FOUN-DATION (Dental Assisting Scholarship Program)

1111 E. Tennessee Street
Tallahassee FL 32308
850/681-3629, ext. 119

FAX: 850/681-0116
E-mail: csutherland@
floridadental.org
Internet: www.floridadental.org

AMOUNT: $150-$300/semester
DEADLINE(S): MAY 1; NOV 1
FIELD(S): Dental Assisting

Open to Florida residents of at least
two years who are pursuing undergraduate
study in dental assisting and who have a
minimum 2.5 GPA. Must submit letter
from program director, transcripts, and
financial status.

15-20 awards annually. Renewable.
Contact Cheri Sutherland at FDHF for an
application.

1896—FLORIDA DENTAL HEALTH FOUN-DATION (Dental Hygiene Scholarship Program)

1111 E. Tennessee Street
Tallahassee FL 32308
850/681-3629, ext. 119
FAX: 850/681-0116
E-mail: csutherland@
floridadental.org
Internet: www.floridadental.org

AMOUNT: Varies
DEADLINE(S): MAY 1; NOV 1
FIELD(S): Dental Hygiene

Open to Florida residents of at least
three years who are pursuing undergraduate study in dental hygiene. Must submit
letter from program director, transcripts,
and financial status.

15 awards annually. Renewable.
Contact Cheri Sutherland at FDHF for an
application.

1897—FLORIDA DEPT. OF EDUCATION (Occupational Therapist & Physical Therapist Scholarship Loan Program)

Student Financial Assist.
255 Collins
Tallahassee FL 32399-0400
850/487-0049 or 888/827-2004
E-mail: OSFABF@mail.doe.state.fl.us
Internet: www.firn.edu/doe

AMOUNT: Up to $4,000
DEADLINE(S): APR 15
FIELD(S): Occupational Therapy,
Physical Therapy

Students must enroll full-time in therapist assistant programs, or in therapist programs at the upper division or graduate
level, and declare their intent to be
employed for a minimum of three years as
therapists in Florida public schools. Must

be repaid in cash if the recipient doesn't work full-time in Florida public schools for the required time period.

23 awards annually. Award amount is the cost of education minus other student financial aid, up to $4,000. Contact Florida Department of Education for an application.

1898—FOUNDATION FOR SEACOAST HEALTH (Scholarship Program)

P.O. Box 4606
Portsmouth NH 03802-4606
603/433-3008
FAX: 603/433-2036
E-mail: ffsh@nh.ultranet.com
Internet: www.nh.ultranet.com/~ffsh

AMOUNT: $1,000-10,000
DEADLINE(S): FEB 1
FIELD(S): Health-related fields

Open to undergraduate and graduate students pursuing health-related fields of study who are legal residents of the following cities in New Hampshire: Portsmouth, Newington, New Castle, Rye, Greenland, N. Hampton, or these cities in Maine: Kittery, Eliot, or York. Must have resided in the area for at least two years.

Write or check website for details. $150,000 awarded annually; 35 awards given.

1899—HISPANIC DENTAL ASSOCIATION AND DR. JUAN D. VILLARREAL FOUNDATION (Dental/Dental Hygienist Scholarships)

188 W. Randolph Street, Ste. 1811
Chicago IL 60601-3001
800/852-7921 or 312/577-4013
FAX: 312/577-4013
E-mail: hdassoc@aol.com
Internet: www.hdassoc.org

AMOUNT: $500-$1,000
DEADLINE(S): JUN 15
FIELD(S): Dentistry, Dental Hygiene

Open to Hispanic students pursuing undergraduate study in an accredited Texas dental school.

Contact HDA for an application.

1900—HISPANIC DENTAL ASSOCIATION AND PROCTER & GAMBLE ORAL CARE (Scholarships)

188 W. Randolph Street, Ste. 1811
Chicago IL 60606
800/852-7921 or 312/577-4013

FAX: 312/577-0052
E-mail: hdassoc@aol.com
Internet: www.hdassoc.org

AMOUNT: $500-$1,000
DEADLINE(S): JUN 15
FIELD(S): Dentistry, Dental Hygiene, Dental Assisting, Dental Technician

Open to Hispanic students for undergraduate study in above programs. Based on scholastic achievement, community service, leadership skills, and commitment to improving health in the Hispanic community.

Contact HDA for an application.

1901—HOPI TRIBE (Priority Scholarships)

P.O. Box 123
Kykotsmovi AZ 86039
520/734-2441, ext. 520
800/762-9630
FAX: 520/734-2435

AMOUNT: Varies
DEADLINE(S): JUL 31
FIELD(S): Law, Natural Resources, Education, Medicine/Health, Engineering, Business

Open to enrolled members of the Hopi Tribe studying in one of the fields listed above, which are considered to be areas of priority interest to the Hopis. Available to college juniors, seniors, and graduate students. Program is to encourage graduates to apply their degrees to Hopi Tribal Goals and Objectives.

Contact Hopi Tribe for an application.

1902—INTERNATIONAL ORDER OF THE KING'S DAUGHTERS AND SONS (healthcareers Scholarships)

c/o Mrs. Fred Cannon
Box 1310
Brookhaven MS 39602
Written inquiry

AMOUNT: $1,000 (max.)
DEADLINE(S): APR 1
FIELD(S): Medicine, Dentistry, Nursing, Physical Therapy, Occupational Therapy, Medical Technologies, Pharmacy

Open to students accepted to/enrolled in an accredited US or Canadian four-year or graduate school. R.N. candidates must have completed first year of program; M.D. or D.D.S. candidates must be for at least the second year of medical or dental school; all others must be in at least third year of four-year program. Pre-med students NOT eligible. Must be US or Canadian citizen.

Send self-addressed, stamped envelope, along with a letter stating the field of study and present level, to the Director at above address for an application.

1903—J. HUGH & EARLE W. FELLOWS MEMORIAL FUND (Scholarship Loans)

Pensacola Junior College, President
1000 College Blvd.
Pensacola FL 32504-8998
904/484-1700

AMOUNT: Each is negotiated individually
DEADLINE(S): None
FIELD(S): Medicine, Nursing, Medical Technology, Theology (Episcopal)

Open to bona fide residents of the Florida counties of Escambia, Santa Rosa, Okaloosa, or Walton. For undergraduate study in the fields listed above. US citizenship required.

Loans are interest-free until graduation. Write for complete information.

1904—JEWISH VOCATIONAL SERVICE (Academic Scholarship Program)

One S. Franklin Street
Chicago IL 60606
312/357-4500
FAX: 312/855-3282
TTY: 312/855-3282
E-mail: jvschicago@jon.cjfny.org

AMOUNT: $5,000 (max.)
DEADLINE(S): MAR 1
FIELD(S): "Helping" Professions, Mathematics, Engineering, Sciences, Communications (at Univ IL only), Law (certain schools in IL only)

Open to Jewish men and women legally domiciled in the greater Chicago metropolitan area, who are identified as having promise for significant contributions in their chosen careers, and are in need of financial assistance for full-time academic programs in above areas. Must have entered undergraduate junior year in career programs requiring no postgrad education, be in graduate/professional school, or be in a voc-tech training program. Interview required.

Renewable. Contact JVS for an application between December 1st and February 15th.

1905—JUNIATA COLLEGE (Robert Steele Memorial Scholarship)

Financial Aid Office
Huntingdon PA 16652

814/641-3603
FAX: 814/641-3355
E-mail: clarkec@juniata.edu
AMOUNT: $4,000 (max.)
DEADLINE(S): APR 1
FIELD(S): Science, Medical Studies

Open to science/medical students applying to Juniata College. Must demonstrate financial need and fill out government FAFSA form.

Contact Cynthia G. Clarke, Research Specialist, for an application or enrollment information. See your financial aid office for FAFSA.

1906—MARYLAND HIGHER EDUCATION COMMISSION (Maryland Science and Technology Scholarship Program)

16 Francis Street
Annapolis Park MD 21401
410/974-5370
800/974-1024
E-mail: ssamail@mhec.state.md.us
Internet: http://www.mhec.state.md.us/SSA/stech_qa.htm
AMOUNT: $3,000/yr. (B.A.); $1,000/yr. (A.A.)
DEADLINE(S): None
FIELD(S): Computer Science, Engineering, Technology

Scholarships for college-bound Maryland high school seniors who will major in one of the above fields and who are accepted to an eligible associate or bachelor's degree program in Maryland. Students in the class of 1999 were eligible for the first awards. The deadline was not known at this writing, so check for deadline date. Must agree to work in the state after graduation in a related field, one year for each year of assistance received.

Must maintain a 3.0 GPA.

1907—MARYLAND HIGHER EDUCATION COMMISSION (Physical/Occupational Therapists & Assistants Scholarships)

State Scholarship Admin.
16 Francis Street
Annapolis MD 21401-1781
410/974-5370
AMOUNT: $2,000
DEADLINE(S): JUL 1
FIELD(S): Occupational Therapy, Physical Therapy

Open to Maryland residents who enroll full-time in Maryland postsecondary institutions having approved occupational or physical therapy programs that lead to Maryland licensing as a therapist or assistant.

Recipients agree to one year of service at a public school, state hospital, or other approved site for each year of award. Financial need is NOT a factor.

1908—MARYLAND HIGHER EDUCATION COMMISSION (Tuition Reimbursement of Firefighters & Rescue Squad Members)

State Scholarship Admin.
16 Francis Street
Annapolis MD 21401
410/974-5370
TTY: 800/735-2258
Internet: www.ubalt.edu/www.mhec
AMOUNT: Varies (current resident undergraduate tuition rate at Univ. MD-College Park)
DEADLINE(S): JUL 1
FIELD(S): Firefighting, Emergency Medical Technology

Open to firefighters and rescue squad members who successfully complete one year of coursework in a firefighting or EMT program and a two-year service obligation in Maryland.

Contact MHEC for an application.

1909—MINNESOTA HIGHER EDUCATION SERVICES OFFICE (Health Professions Loan Forgiveness)

1450 Energy Park Drive, #350
St. Paul MN 55108-5265
612/296-3974
FAX: 612/297-8880
E-mail: info@heso.state.mn.us
Internet: www.heso.state.mn.us/
AMOUNT: Varies
DEADLINE(S): None
FIELD(S): Health Professions

Five loan repayment programs for health professionals who agree to serve in federally designated Health Professional Shortage Areas, in designated, underserved urban or rural areas, in licensed nursing homes, or in intermediate care facilities for persons with mental retardation or related conditions.

For details contact Office of Rural Health and Primary Care at 612/282-3838 or 800/366-5424 (Minnesota only).

1910—MISSISSIPPI OFFICE OF STATE STUDENT FINANCIAL AID (healthcare Professions Loan/Scholarship Program)

3825 Ridgewood Road
Jackson MS 39211-6453
601/982-6663
800-327-2980 (free in Miss.)

AMOUNT: $1,500/yr.
DEADLINE(S): JULY 1
FIELD(S): Speech Pathology, Psychology, Occupational Therapy, Physical Therapy, and other allied health programs in critical demand

For Mississippi residents enrolled full-time as juniors or seniors in an accredited training program in Mississippi in the above fields. Student is obligated to serve in the health profession at a state-operated health institution in Mississippi one year for each year's scholarship.

For information and/or application packet, contact above location.

1911—McCORD CAREER CENTER (Level II McCord Medical/Music Scholarship)

Healdsburg High School
1024 Prince Street
Healdsburg CA 95448
707/431-3473
AMOUNT: Varies
DEADLINE(S): APR 30
FIELD(S): Medicine, Music

For graduates of Healdsburg High School who are planning a career in music or medicine. Must be enrolled full-time at a college/university as an undergraduate junior or senior in the fall, or earning an advanced degree in graduate or medical school, or entering into a vocational/certificate program. Transcripts, proof of attendance, and an essay are required.

Contact the McCord Career Center at Healdsburg High School for an application.

1912—McDONALD'S/UNITED NEGRO COLLEGE FUND (Scholarships for Medical and Healthcare Students)

312/443-8708
AMOUNT: Full tuition (10); $1,000 (50)
DEADLINE(S): None
FIELD(S): Medicine and Healthcare fields

Scholarships for college sophomores attending any of the United Negro College Fund schools and pursuing a career in medicine or related healthcare areas. Must maintain 3.0 GPA and demonstrate participation in community and school activities and financial need.

10 two-year scholarships provide full tuition; 50 scholarships are for $1,000 each. Contact school counselor, UNCF office, or call Burrell Communications at above phone number.

1913—NATIONAL ASSOCIATION OF AMERICAN BUSINESS CLUBS (AMBUCS Scholarships for Therapists)

P.O. Box 5127
High Point NC 27262
910/869-2166
FAX: 910/887-8451
E-mail: ambucs@ambucs.com
Internet: www.ambucs.com

AMOUNT: $500-$6,000
DEADLINE(S): APR 15
FIELD(S): Physical Therapy, Music Therapy, Occupational Therapy, Speech-Language Pathology, Audiology, Rehabilitation, Recreation Therapy, and related areas

Open to undergraduate juniors and seniors or graduate students who have good scholastic standing and plan to enter the fields listed above. GPA of 3.0 or better (4.0 scale) and US citizenship required. Must demonstrate financial need.

Renewable. Please include a self-addressed, stamped envelope (SASE); applications are mailed in December; incomplete applications will not be considered.

1914—NATIONAL ATHLETIC TRAINERS' ASSOCIATION (NATA Scholarship Program)

2952 Stemmons Freeway
Dallas TX 75247
214/637-6282
FAX: 214/637-2206

AMOUNT: $2,000
DEADLINE(S): FEB 1
FIELD(S): Athletic Training

Open to student members of NATA who have excellent academic records and have excelled as student athletic trainers. Undergraduates may apply after completion of sophomore year, and graduates may apply after completion of fall semester of their undergraduate senior year. Must have a minimum 3.0 GPA.

Send self-addressed, stamped envelope to NATA for membership information or an application.

1915—NATIONAL HEALTH SERVICE CORPS (NHSC Scholarship Program)

2070 Chain Bridge Rd., Ste. 450
Vienna VA 22182-2536
800/221-9393
Internet: www.bphc.hrsa.dhhs.gov/nhsc

AMOUNT: Full tuition/books/fees/supplies + monthly stipend

DEADLINE(S): MAR
FIELD(S): Family Medicine, General Internal Medicine, General Pediatrics, Obstetrics/Gynecology, Family Nurse Practitioners, Primary Care Physician Assistants, Certified Nurse-Midwives

Must be US citizen attending or enrolled in fully accredited US allopathic/osteopathic medical school, nursing program, or physician assistant program. For each year of support received, you must serve one year in federally designated health professional shortage area of greatest need. Minimum two years service commitment begins upon completion of your residency and/or training.

300 awards annually. Renewable up to 4 years. Contact NHSC for an application.

1916—NATIONAL SOCIETY DAUGHTERS OF THE AMERICAN REVOLUTION (Occupational Therapy Scholarship)

1776 D Street NW
Washington DC 20006-5392
202/628-1776
Internet: www.dar.org

AMOUNT: $500
DEADLINE(S): FEB 15; AUG 15
FIELD(S): Occupational Therapy, Art/Music Therapy, Physical Therapy

For students (US citizens) CURRENTLY ENROLLED in an accredited US school of occupational (includes art and music therapy) or physical therapy. Awards are placed on deposit with college/university. Awards judged on academic excellence, commitment to field of study, and need. No affiliation with DAR required.

Not renewable. See website or send a self-addressed, stamped envelope for an application or more information.

1917—NATIONAL STRENGTH & CONDITIONING ASSN. (Challenge Scholarships)

P.O. Box 38909
Colorado Springs CO 80937-8909
719/632-6722
FAX: 719/632-6722
E-mail: nsca@usa.net
Internet: www.colosoft.com/nsca

AMOUNT: $1,000
DEADLINE(S): MAR 1
FIELD(S): Fields related to body strength & conditioning

Open to National Strength & Conditioning Association members. Awards are for undergraduate or graduate study.

For membership information or an application, write to the above address.

1918—NAVY RECRUITING COMMAND (Armed Forces Health Professions Scholarships)

Commander
801 N. Randolph Street, Code 325
Arlington VA 22203-1991
800/USA-NAVY or 703/696-4926
E-mail: omegahouse@erols.com
Internet: www.navyjobs.com

AMOUNT: $938/month stipend + tuition, fees, books, lab fees, etc.
DEADLINE(S): APR 28
FIELD(S): Medicine, Dentistry, Optometry, Physical Therapy, Pharmacology, healthcare Administration, Industrial Hygiene, etc.

Open to US citizens enrolled or accepted for enrollment in any of the above fields at an accredited institution in the US or Puerto Rico. Must qualify for appointment as a Navy officer and sign a contractual agreement. Must be between the ages of 18 and 36 and have a GPA of at least 3.0.

See website, contact local Navy Recruiting Office, or contact Lieutenant Roger A. House, MPA, CAAMA, Medical Service Corps at above address.

1919—NEW YORK STATE DEPARTMENT OF HEALTH—PRIMARY CARE SERVICE CORPS (Scholarships)

Corning Tower
Room 1084
Empire State Plaza
Albany NY 12237-0053
518/473-7019

AMOUNT: $15,000
DEADLINE(S): APR 3
FIELD(S): Certified Physician Assistant, Nurse Practitioner, Midwife

Open to New York State residents enrolled at, accepted to, or applied at an approved graduate, undergraduate, or certificate course of study. Must be within 24 months of completion of professional training full-time, or within 48 months of completion on a part-time basis.

Contact NY State Dept. of Health for an application.

1920—NEW YORK STATE HIGHER EDUCATION SERVICES CORPORATION (N.Y. State Regents Professional/healthcare Opportunity Scholarships)

Cultural Education Center, Rm. 5C64
Albany NY 12230
518/486-1319
Internet: www.hesc.com

AMOUNT: $1,000-$10,000/yr.
DEADLINE(S): Varies
FIELD(S): Medicine and Dentistry and related fields, Architecture, Nursing, Psychology, Audiology, Landscape Architecture, Social Work, Chiropractic, Law, Pharmacy, Accounting, Speech Language Pathology

For NY state residents who are economically disadvantaged and members of a minority group underrepresented in the chosen profession and attending school in NY state. Some programs carry a service obligation in New York for each year of support. For US citizens or qualifying noncitizens.

Medical/dental scholarships require one year of professional work in NY.

1921—NORTH CAROLINA DEPARTMENT OF PUBLIC INSTRUCTION (Scholarship Loan Program for Prospective Teachers)

301 N. Wilmington Street
Raleigh NC 27601-2825
919/715-1120

AMOUNT: Up to $2,500/yr.
DEADLINE(S): FEB
FIELD(S): Education: Teaching, school psychology and counseling, speech/language impaired, audiology, library/media services

For NC residents planning to teach in NC public schools. At least 3.0 high school GPA required; must maintain 2.5 GPA during freshman year and 3.0 cumulative thereafter. Recipients are obligated to teach one year in an NC public school for each year of assistance. Those who do not fulfill their teaching obligation are required to repay the loan plus interest.

200 awards per year. For full-time students. Applications available in Dec. from high school counselors and college and university departments of education.

1922—NORTH CAROLINA DEPT. OF PUBLIC INSTRUCTION (Teacher Assistant Scholarship Loan)

301 N. Wilmington Street
Raleigh NC 27601-2825
919/715-1120

AMOUNT: Up to $1,200/yr
DEADLINE(S): JAN
FIELD(S): Education: Teaching, School Psychology or Counseling, Speech/Language Impaired, Audiology, llogy, llogy, library/media services

For NC residents employed as K-12 teaching assistants in public schools who wish to pursue teacher licensure. Must either hold a B.A. degree or have completed general college courses prerequisite to admission to degree program and be admitted to an approved teacher education program at a four-year institution. Two-year community college early childhood education program is acceptable.

Must remain employed as teaching assistant while pursuing licensure and teach one year in an NC public school for each year of assistance received. Applications available in Sept. from local school superintendent.

1923—NORTH CAROLINA SOCIETY FOR CLINICAL LABORATORY SCIENCE (Scholarship Award)

1080 19th Place, NW
Hickory NC 28601
828/438-6128

AMOUNT: $300-$700
DEADLINE(S): JUN 1
FIELD(S): Medical Technology, Medical Laboratory Technician

Open to North Carolina residents who have been accepted in an approved clinical laboratory science program. Must meet North Carolina residency requirements.

Renewable. Contact Nancy Shoaf for an application.

1924—OAK RIDGE INSTITUTE FOR SCIENCE AND EDUCATION (ORISE Education & Training Programs)

P.O. Box 117
Oak Ridge TN 37831-0117
Internet: www.orau.gov/orise/educ.htm

AMOUNT: Varies
DEADLINE(S): Varies
FIELD(S): Engineering, Aeronautics, Computer Science, Technology, Earth Science, Environmental Studies, Biology, Chemistry, Physics, Medical Research

Numerous programs funded by the US Department of Energy are offered for undergraduate students through postgraduate researchers. Includes fellowship and internship opportunities throughout the US. Some have citizenship restrictions. Travel may be included.

See website or write for a catalog of specific programs and requirements.

1925—PENINSULA COMMUNITY FOUNDATION (Dr. Mary Finegold Scholarship)

1700 S. El Camino Real, #300
San Mateo CA 94402
650/358-9369
FAX: 650/358-9817

AMOUNT: $1,000
DEADLINE(S): MAR 27 (5 P.M.)
FIELD(S): Sciences

Scholarships for senior girls graduating from high school in Palo Alto, California, who intend to complete a four-year degree in the sciences. Special consideration will be given to girls who have demonstrated a "pioneering" spirit in that they have not been constrained by stereotypical female roles and to those facing financial hardship.

Award was established in the honor of Dr. Mary Finegold who, after completing her medical studies, elected to stay at home until her youngest child was in high school before beginning her medical practice. She was a school physician.

1926—PILOT INTERNATIONAL FOUNDATION (PIF/Lifeline Scholarship)

P.O. Box 5600
Macon GA 31208-5600
Written inquiries

AMOUNT: Varies
DEADLINE(S): MAR 1
FIELD(S): Disabilities/Brain-related Disorders

This program assists ADULT students re-entering the job market, preparing for a second career, or improving their professional skills for an established career. Applicants must be preparing for, or already involved in, careers working with people with disabilities/brain-related disorders. GPA of 3.5 or more is required.

Must be sponsored by a Pilot Club in your home town, or in the city in which your college or university is located. Send a self-addressed, stamped envelope for complete information.

1927—PILOT INTERNATIONAL FOUNDATION (Ruby Newhall Memorial Scholarship)

P.O. Box 5600
Macon, GA 31208-5600
Written inquiries

AMOUNT: Varies
DEADLINE(S): MAR 15
FIELD(S): Disabilities/Brain-related
Disorders

For international students who have studied in the US for at least one year, and who intend to return to their home country six months after graduation. Applicants must be full-time students majoring in a field related to human health and welfare, and have a GPA of 3.5 or more.

Applicants must be sponsored by a Pilot Club in their home town, or in the city in which their college or university is located. Send a self-addressed, stamped envelope for complete information.

1928—PILOT INTERNATIONAL FOUNDATION (The Pilot International Scholarship Program)

P.O. Box 5600
Macon GA 31208-5600
Written inquiries

AMOUNT: Varies
DEADLINE(S): MAR 1
FIELD(S): Disabilities/Brain-related
Disorders

This program provides assistance to undergraduate students preparing for careers working directly with people with disabilities or training those who will. GPA of 3.5 or greater required.

Applicants must be sponsored by a Pilot Club in their home town, or in the city in which their college or university is located. Send a self-addressed, stamped envelope for complete information.

1929—SRP/NAVAJO GENERATING STATION (Navajo Scholarship)

P.O. Box 850
Page AZ 86040
520/645-6539
FAX: 520/645-7295
E-mail: ljdawave@srp.gov

AMOUNT: Based on need
DEADLINE(S): APR 30
FIELD(S): Engineering, Environmental
Studies, Business, Business
Management, Health, Education

Scholarships for full-time students who hold membership in the Navajo Tribe and who are pursuing a degree in a field of study recognized as significant to the Navajo Nation, Salt River Project, or the Navajo Generating Station, such as those listed above. Must be junior or senior, have and maintain a GPA of 3.0.

Average of 15 awards per year. Inquire of Linda Dawavendewa at above location.

1930—STATE STUDENT ASSISTANCE COMMISSION OF INDIANA (Scholarships for Special Education Teachers & Physical/Occupational Therapists)

150 W. Market Street, 5th Fl.
Indianapolis IN 46204
317/232-2350
FAX: 317/232-3260
E-mail: grants@ssaci.in.us
Internet: www.ai.org/ssaci/

AMOUNT: $1,000
DEADLINE(S): Varies (with college)
FIELD(S): Special Education, Physical &
Occupational Therapy

Open to Indiana residents pursuing full-time undergraduate or graduate study in special education or physical or occupational therapy at an Indiana college/university. Must be US citizen, have a minimum 2.0 GPA, and demonstrate financial need.

See website or contact SSACI for an application.

1931—THE ADA ENDOWMENT AND ASSISTANCE FUND, INC. (Allied Dental Health Scholarship-Dental Hygiene)

211 East Chicago Ave.
Chicago IL 60611
312/440-2567

AMOUNT: $1,000
DEADLINE(S): AUG 15
FIELD(S): Dental Hygiene

For students entering second year and currently enrolled in a dental hygiene program accredited by the Commission on Dental Accreditation. Applicants must have an accumulative grade point average of 3.0.

Write to the above address for complete information.

1932—THE ADA ENDOWMENT AND ASSISTANCE FUND, INC. (Allied Dental Health Scholarship-Dental Assisting)

211 East Chicago Ave.
Chicago IL 60611
312/440-2567

AMOUNT: $1,000
DEADLINE(S): SEP 15
FIELD(S): Dental Assisting

Applicants must be entering students enrolled in a dental assisting program accredited by the Commission on Dental Accreditation.

Apply at your school or write to above address for complete information.

1933—THE ADA ENDOWMENTS AND ASSISTANCE FUND, INC. (Allied Dental Health Scholarship-Dental Laboratory Technician)

211 East Chicago Ave.
Chicago IL 60611
312/440-2567

AMOUNT: $1,000
DEADLINE(S): AUG 15
FIELD(S): Dental Laboratory Technician

Applicants must be entering first-year or entering second-year students currently attending or enrolled in a dental laboratory technology program accredited by the Commission on Dental Accreditation. Applicants must have an accumulated grade point average of 2.8 and demonstrate a minimum financial need of $1,000.

Write to the above address for complete infomation.

1934—THE AMERICAN COLLEGE OF PRE-HOSPITAL MEDICINE (Alan R. Klausfelder Memorial Scholarship)

365 Canal Street, Suite 2300
New Orleans LA 70130-1135
800/735-2276
FAX: 800/350-3870

AMOUNT: $4,000
DEADLINE(S): None
FIELD(S): Emergency Medical Services

Scholarships for students enrolled in bachelor of arts programs in emergency medical services outside the US or Canada.

Send self-addressed, stamped envelope to school for application details.

1935—THE AUGIE J. ALTAR SCHOLARSHIP

7115 W. 91st Street
Bridgeview IL 60455-2048
Write for information

AMOUNT: $500
DEADLINE(S): MAY 31
FIELD(S): Medicine or Agricultural fields

Scholarships for students enrolled or accepted to an accredited college, university, or community college who are of Lithuanian descent and are residents of Illinois. Must be studying in the areas of medicine or agriculture. Financial need considered. Must have and maintain at least a 2.0 GPA.

Send application request to above address with a stamped, self-addressed envelope (SASE).

1936—U.S. DEPT. OF HEALTH & HUMAN SERVICES (Indian Health Service Preparatory Scholarship Program)

Twinbrook Metro Plaza, Suite 100
12300 Twinbrook Pkwy.
Rockville MD 20852
301/443-0234
FAX: 301/443-4815
Internet: www.ihs.gov/Recruitment/
DHPS/SP/SBTOC3.asp

AMOUNT: Tuition + fees & monthly
stipend of $938
DEADLINE(S): APR 1
FIELD(S): Health Professions, Social
Work, or Accounting

Open to Native Americans or Alaska natives who enroll in courses leading to a baccalaureate degree and are preparing for acceptance into programs in the above fields. US citizenship required. Renewable annually with reapplication.

Scholarship recipients must intend to serve the Indian people. They incur a one-year service obligation to the IHS for each year of support for a minimum of two years. Write for complete information.

1937—U.S. DEPT. OF HEALTH & HUMAN SERVICES (Indian Health Service Health Professions Scholarship Program)

Twinbrook Metro Plaza, Suite 100
12300 Twinbrook Pkwy.
Rockville MD 20852
301/443-0234
FAX: 301/443-4815
Internet: www.ihs.gov/Recruitment/
DHPS/SP/SBTOC3.asp

AMOUNT: Tuition + fees & monthly
stipend of $938
DEADLINE(S): APR 1
FIELD(S): Health Professions,
Accounting, Social Work

Open to Native Americans or Alaska natives who are graduate students or college juniors or seniors in a program leading to a career in a field listed above. US citizenship required. Renewable annually with reapplication.

Scholarship recipients must intend to serve the Indian people. They incur a one-year service obligation to the IHS for each year of support for a minimum of two years. Write for complete information.

1938—WASHINGTON STATE HIGHER EDUCATION COORDINATING BOARD (Health Professional Loan Repayment & Scholarship Program)

P.O. Box 43430
Olympia WA 98504-3430
360/753-7850
FAX: 360/753-7808
Internet: www.hecb.wa.gov

AMOUNT: Varies
DEADLINE(S): APR (scholarship); FEB
(loan repayment); JUL (loan
repayment)
FIELD(S): Healthcare

Scholarships are open to students in accredited undergraduate or graduate healthcare programs leading to eligibility for licensure in Washington state. Must agree to work in designated shortage area for minimum of three years. Loan repayment recipients receive payment from program for purpose of repaying education loans secured while attending program of healthcare training leading to licensure in Washington state. Financial need NOT a factor.

Renewable up to 5 years. Contact Program Manager for a loan repayment application after November 15th and for scholarship application after January 15th.

1939—WOMEN OF THE EVANGELICAL LUTHERAN CHURCH IN AMERICA (The Kahler-Vickers/Raup-Emma Wettstein Scholarships)

8765 West Higgins Road
Chicago IL 60631-4189
800/638-3522, ext. 2747
FAX: 773/380-2419
E-mail: womnelca@elca.org

AMOUNT: $2,000 max.
DEADLINE(S): MAR 1
FIELD(S): Health Professions &
Christian Service

Assists women who are members of the ELCA studying for service in health professions associated with ELCA projects abroad that do not lead to church-certified professions. Must be US citizen and have experienced an interruption of two or more years since completion of high school. Academic records of coursework completed in last five years as well as proof of admission from educational institution are required.

Renewable for an additional year. Contact Faith Fretheim, Program Director, for an application.

1940—WOMEN'S SPORTS FOUNDATION (Jackie Joyner-Kersee & Zina Garrison Minority Internships)

Eisenhower Park
East Meadow NY 11554
800/227-3988
FAX: 516/542-4716
E-mail: WoSport@aol.com
Internet: www.lifetimetv.com/WoSport

AMOUNT: $4,000-$5,000
DEADLINE(S): Ongoing
FIELD(S): Sports-related fields

Provides women of color an opportunity to gain experience in a sports-related career and interact in the sports community. May be undergraduates, college graduates, graduate students, or women in a career change. Internships are located at the Women's Sports Foundation in East Meadow, New York.

4-6 awards annually. See website or write to above address for details.

1941—ZETA PHI BETA SORORITY EDUCATIONAL FOUNDATION (S. Evelyn Lewis Memorial Scholarship in Medical Health Sciences)

1734 New Hampshire Ave. NW
Washington DC 20009
Internet: www.zpb1920.org/
nefforms.htm

AMOUNT: $500-$1,000
DEADLINE(S): FEB 1
FIELD(S): Medicine; Health Sciences

Open to graduate and undergraduate young women enrolled in a program leading to a degree in medicine or health sciences. Award is for full-time study for one academic year (Fall-Spring) and is paid directly to college/university. Must submit proof of enrollment.

Send self-addressed, stamped envelope to above address between September 1st and December 15th for an application.

NURSING

1942—AIR FORCE RESERVE OFFICER TRAINING CORPS (AFROTC Pre-Health Scholarships)

551 E. Maxwell Blvd.
Maxwell AFB AL 36112-6106
334/953-7783

AMOUNT: Full tuition, lab fees, books, +
$150/month

DEADLINE(S): JUN 15
FIELD(S): Health Professions

For US citizens who are currently enrolled full-time college students, with at least a 3.5 GPA. Must provide personal statement of interest in a career in the medical profession in the uniformed services, as well as three letters of recommendation. Certain courses must be completed by end of junior year.

Contact above address for application packet. The AFHPSP continues your education by providing up to 4 years of medical school to eligible Air Force ROTC Pre-Health cadets.

1943—AMERICAN ASSOCIATION OF CRITICAL CARE NURSES (Educational Advancement Scholarship Program)

101 Columbia
Aliso Viejo CA 92656-1491
800/899-2226
FAX: 949/362-2020
E-mail: aacninfo@aacn.org
Internet: www.aacn.org

AMOUNT: $1,500
DEADLINE(S): MAY 15
FIELD(S): Critical Care Nursing

Open to AACN members who are R.N.'s and are working or have worked in a critical care unit. For undergraduate (junior or senior status) or graduate study at NLA-approved institutions. Should have worked in critical care for one year of the last three and have a minimum 3.0 GPA. Must be US citizen/permanent resident. Financial need NOT a factor.

100 awards annually. Renewable 2 years. At least 20% of awards will go to ethnic minorities. Contact Marilyn Herigstad at AACN for an application.

1944—AMERICAN ASSOCIATION OF NURSE ANESTHETISTS (Educational Loans)

222 S. Prospect Ave.
Park Ridge IL 60068
847/692-7050

AMOUNT: $500-$2,500
DEADLINE(S): None
FIELD(S): Nurse Anesthetist

Loans available to AANA members and associate members enrolled in a school of anesthesia approved by the Council on Accreditation of Nurse Anesthesia Educational Programs. Loans are intended to cover unexpected events of an emergency nature.

Write for membership information or contact the Finance Director for a loan application.

1945—AMERICAN COLLEGE OF NURSE-MIDWIVES FOUNDATION (Scholarship Program)

818 Connecticut Ave. NW, Suite 900
Washington DC 20006
202/728-9865
FAX: 202/728-9897

AMOUNT: Varies
DEADLINE(S): FEB 15
FIELD(S): Nurse-Midwifery

Open to students currently enrolled in ACNM-accredited certificate or graduate nurse-midwifery programs in the US. Student membership in ACNM and completion of one clinical module or semester required.

Contact the directors of nurse-midwifery programs at accredited schools or contact ACNM for membership information and/or an application.

1946—AMERICAN FOUNDATION FOR THE BLIND (Paul W. Ruckes Scholarship)

11 Penn Plaza, Suite 300
New York NY 10001
212/502-7661
FAX: 212/502-7771
E-mail: juliet@afb.org
Internet: www.afb.org

AMOUNT: $1,000
DEADLINE(S): APR 30
FIELD(S): Engineering, Computer/
    Physical/Life Sciences

Open to legally blind and visually impaired undergraduate and graduate students pursuing a degree in one of above fields. Must be US citizen. Must submit written documentation of visual impairment from ophthalmologist or optometrist (need not be legally blind); official transcripts; proof of college/university acceptance; three letters of recommendation; and typewritten statement describing goals, work experience, extracurricular activities, and how monies will be used.

1 award annually. See website or contact Julie Tucker at AFB for an application.

1947—AMERICAN INDIAN SCIENCE AND ENGINEERING SOCIETY (A.T. Anderson Memorial Scholarship)

P.O. Box 9828
Albuquerque NM 87119-9828
505/765-1052
FAX: 505/765-5608

E-mail: scholarships@aises.org
Internet: www.aises.org/scholarships

AMOUNT: $1,000-$2,000
DEADLINE(S): JUN 15
FIELD(S): Medicine, Natural Resources,
    Science, Engineering

Open to undergraduate and graduate students who are at least 1/4 American Indian or recognized as member of a tribe. Must be member of AISES ($10 fee), enrolled full-time at an accredited institution, and demonstrate financial need.

Renewable. See website or contact Patricia Browne for an application and/or membership information.

1948—AMERICAN LEGION-KANSAS (John & Geraldine Hobbie Licensed Practical Nursing Scholarship)

1314 SW Topeka Blvd.
Topeka KS 66612-1886
913/232-9315

AMOUNT: $250
DEADLINE(S): FEB 15
FIELD(S): Licensed Practical Nursing

Open to Kansas residents who have reached the age of 18 before taking the Kansas State Board Examination. Must attend an accredited Kansas school that awards diplomas for LPN.

Contact the Kansas branch of the American Legion for an application.

1949—AMERICAN RED CROSS, SONOMA COUNTY CHAPTER (Nurse Assistant Program Scholarships)

465 Tesconi Circle
Santa Rosa CA 95401-4619
707/577-7600
FAX: 707/577-7621

AMOUNT: Varies
DEADLINE(S): None
FIELD(S): Nurse Assistant Training

Scholarships for a four-week course leading to a certificate as a Nurse Assistant. Must be a resident of Sonoma County, California. Award is based on eligibility and need.

Contact the Sonoma County Chapter of the American Red Cross for an application.

1950—AMERICAN SOCIETY OF PERI-ANESTHESIA NURSES (Scholarships)

6900 Grove Road
Thorofare NJ 08086

609/845-5557
FAX: 609/848-1881
E-mail: aspan@slackinc.com
Internet: www.aspan.org

AMOUNT: $1,000 for degree program; $235 for certification; $500 for conference
DEADLINE(S): JUL 1
FIELD(S): Nursing: postanesthesia, preanesthesia, and ambulatory surgery

Scholarships for nurses aspiring to expertise in the above fields seeking a B.S. or advanced degree in nursing, seeking certification as CPAN or CAPA, or seeking funds for attendance at the ASPAN national conference. Must be a current R.N. and be an active member of ASPAN for the two years prior to application.

Check website or contact organization for further details and requirements.

1951—ARCHBOLD MEDICAL CENTER (Archbold Scholarship/Loan)

Dept. of Education
P.O. Box 1018
Thomasville GA 31799-1018
912/228-2795

AMOUNT: $4,000-$6,000; $500 for technical courses
DEADLINE(S): None specified
FIELD(S): Healthcare fields such as Registered Nurse, Medical Lab, Pharmacy, Physical Therapy, etc.

Open to undergrad and grad students accepted into an accredited healthcare school and within 2 years of completing course work. Student must agree to work at AMC for 3 years following graduation (1 year for tech school students).

Must be Georgia resident. Personal interview required. Repayment is required if recipient fails to work at Archbold for the designated period. Write for complete information.

1952—ARTHUR M. MILLER FUND

P.O. Box 1122
Wichita KS 67201-0004
316/261-4609

AMOUNT: Varies
DEADLINE(S): MAR 31
FIELD(S): Medicine or related fields

Scholarships for Kansas residents for the study of medicine or related fields at accredited institutions.

Send SASE for formal application.

1953—ASSOCIATION ON AMERICAN INDIAN AFFAIRS, INC. (Emergency Aid and Health Professions Scholarships)

P.O. Box 268
Sisseton SD 57262
605/698-3998 or 605/698-3787
FAX: 605/698-3316

AMOUNT: $50-$300
DEADLINE(S): MAY 1
FIELD(S): Health professions

Emergency funding program for full-time undergraduates studying in a health field. Based on financial need. Must be at least 1/4 Indian and write a one- to two-page essay on the nature of the emergency need.

Applications available Sept. 1. Send SASE to above location.

1954—ASSOCIATION OF OPERATING ROOM NURSES (AORN Scholarship Program)

2170 S. Parker Road, Suite 300
Denver CO 80231-5711
303/755-6300
800/755-6304, ext. 8366
FAX: 303/755-4219
E-mail: sstokes@aorn.org
Internet: www.aorn.org

AMOUNT: Tuition & fees
DEADLINE(S): APR 1; OCT 1
FIELD(S): Nursing

Open to students who have been AORN members for at least 12 consecutive months prior to deadline date. Awards support bachelor's, master's, and doctoral degree programs accredited by the NLN or other acceptable accrediting body. For full- or part-time study of nursing or complementary fields in the US. Must have a minimum 3.0 GPA.

Renewable. Contact AORN for an applicaton.

1955—BECA FOUNDATION (Alice Newell Joslyn Medical Fund)

310 Via Vera Cruz, Suite 101
San Marcos CA 92069
760/471-5465
FAX: 760/471-9175

AMOUNT: $500-$2,000
DEADLINE(S): MAR 1
FIELD(S): Medicine, Healthcare, Nursing, Dental/Medical Assisting, Physical Therapy

Open to Latino students who live in or attend college in San Diego County, CA, at time of application. For high school seniors and those already in college pursuing undergraduate or graduate education. Based on financial need, scholastic determination, and community/cultural awareness. BECA also provides a mentor to each scholarship recipient.

Send self-addressed, stamped envelope to BECA for an application.

1956—BUDDHIST COMPASSION RELIEF TZU-CHI FOUNDATION, U.S.A. (Nursing Scholarships)

206 East Palm Ave.
Monrovia CA 91016
626/305-1188
FAX: 626/305-1185
Internet: www.tzuchi.org/usa/english

AMOUNT: $1,000
DEADLINE(S): MAY 31
FIELD(S): Nursing

Scholarships for nursing students who have completed at least the first year of the program and have at least 2.7 GPA. Must demonstrate financial need. Application process includes submitting a 500-word essay on why you think you should receive this scholarship and a description of your family background.

For more details on application requirements, contact organization or access website.

1957—CAREER OPPORTUNITIES FOR YOUTH, INC. (Collegiate Scholarship Program)

P.O. Box 996
Manhattan Beach CA 90266
310/535-4838

AMOUNT: $250 to $1,000
DEADLINE(S): SEP 30
FIELD(S): Engineering, Science, Mathematics, Computer Science, Business Administration, Education, Nursing

For students of Latino/Hispanic background residing in the Southern California area who have completed at least one semester/quarter of study at an accredited four-year university. Must have a cumulative GPA of 2.5 or higher.

Priority will be given to students who demonstrate financial need. Send SASE to above location for details.

1958—CENTER FOR PRIMARY CARE AND RURAL HEALTH-VIRGINIA DEPARTMENT OF HEALTH (Mary Marshall Nursing Scholarships)

1500 E. Main Street, Suite 227
Richmond VA 23219
804/786-4891 or 804/371-4090
FAX: 804/371-0116

AMOUNT: Varies
DEADLINE(S): JUN 30
FIELD(S): Nursing

Applicants must be Virginia residents enrolled as full-time undergraduate or graduate nursing students in Virginia. Must have a minimum 3.0 GPA in required courses. Financial need is considered, and transcripts and letters of recommendation are required. Recipients must agree to engage in full-time nursing in Virginia for one month for every $100 received. If recipient does not fullfill this obligation, award must be repaid with interest.

Renewable. Contact Virginia Department of Health for application packet. Specify which program: Licensed Practical Nurse, Registered Nurse, or Nurse Practitioner, Nurse-Midwife.

1959—COLUMBIANA COUNTY PUBLIC HEALTH LEAGUE TRUST FUND (Grants)

P.O. Box 1428
Steubenville OH 43952
740/283-8433
FAX: 740/282-4530

AMOUNT: Varies
DEADLINE(S): FEB 28
FIELD(S): Respiratory Illness, Medicine, Medical Research, Pharmacy, Medical Technology, Physical Therapy, Nursing, Dental Hygiene, Occupational Therapy

Open to undergraduate and graduate Columbiana County, Ohio, residents who are pursuing medical education or research in one of the above fields. Preference given to respiratory illness. Students of veterinary medicine NOT eligible.

Contact Sherrill Schmied for an application.

1960—COMMUNITY FOUNDATION OF WESTERN MASSACHUSETTS (Deborah Brodeur Foley Memorial Scholarship)

1500 Main Street
P.O. Box 15769
Springfield MA 01115
413/732-2858

AMOUNT: $1,000
DEADLINE(S): APR 15
FIELD(S): Nursing

Open to graduating seniors from Minnechaug Regional High School to pursue full-time study leading to a career in nursing or an allied field. Based on financial need, academic merit, and extracurricular activities. Must submit transcripts and government FAFSA form.

1 award annually. Contact Community Foundation for an application and your financial aid office for FAFSA. Notification is in June.

1961—COMMUNITY FOUNDATION OF WESTERN MASSACHUSETTS (Dean Technical High School Nursing Program Scholarship)

1500 Main Street
P.O. Box 15769
Springfield MA 01115
413/732-2858

AMOUNT: $350
DEADLINE(S): APR 15
FIELD(S): Nursing

Open to students in the nursing program at Dean Technical High School in Holyoke, Massachusetts. Based on financial need, academic merit, and extracurricular activities. Must submit transcripts and government FAFSA form.

1 award annually. Contact Community Foundation for an application and your financial aid office for FAFSA. Notification is in June.

1962—COMMUNITY FOUNDATION OF WESTERN MASSACHUSETTS (Edward C. & Mary Marth Scholarship)

1500 Main Street
P.O. Box 15769
Springfield MA 01115
413/732-2858

AMOUNT: $500
DEADLINE(S): APR 15
FIELD(S): Nursing

Open to graduating seniors from St. Mary's High School in Westfield, Massachusetts, who will be attending college or technical school for nursing or an allied field. Based on financial need, academic merit, and extracurricular activities. Must submit transcripts and government FAFSA form.

1 award annually. Contact Community Foundation for an application and your financial aid office for FAFSA. Notification is in June.

1963—CONNECTICUT LEAGUE FOR NURSING (CLN Scholarships)

P.O. Box 365
Wallingford CT 06492-0365
203/265-4248
FAX: 203/265-5311
E-mail:cln@ct2.nai.net

AMOUNT: $2,000
DEADLINE(S): OCT 15
FIELD(S): Nursing

For Connecticut residents who are US citizens enrolled in nursing education in an NLN accredited Connecticut School of Nursing. Baccalaureate applicants must have completed their third year of a four-year program, and diploma/two-year applicants must have completed their first year of a two-year program.

Contact CLN for an application.

1964—CONNECTICUT LEAGUE FOR NURSING (Nursing Scholarship)

P.O. Box 365
Wallingford CT 06492-0365
Written inquiry

AMOUNT: Varies
DEADLINE(S): OCT 1
FIELD(S): Nursing

Open to residents of Connecticut who are enrolled in an NLN-accredited Connecticut School of Nursing which is a CLN agency member. Bachelor applicants must be seniors; Diploma and Associate applicants must have completed 1st year, R.N. applicants must be entering senior year; graduate students must have completed 20 units.

Write to the above address for complete information.

1965—CUYAHOGA COUNTY MEDICAL FOUNDATION (Scholarship Grant Program)

6000 Rockside Woods Blvd.
Suite 150
Cleveland OH 44131-2352
216/520-1000

AMOUNT: $600-$1,700
DEADLINE(S): JUN 1
FIELD(S): Medicine, Dentistry, Pharmacy, Nursing, Osteopathy

Grants open to residents of Cuyahoga County who are accepted to or enrolled in an accredited professional school in one of the above areas.

Approx 40 awards per year. Write for complete information.

1966—CYNTHIA E. AND CLARA H. HOLLIS FOUNDATION

100 Summer Street
Boston MA 02110
Written inquiry

AMOUNT: Varies
DEADLINE(S): APR 1
FIELD(S): Nursing, Social Work, Dental
or Medical Technology, and Religion

Scholarships for Massachusetts with preference given to students in the above fields. For undergraduates, graduates, voctech, and adult education. Must demonstrate financial need.

Send SASE to Walter E. Palmer, Esq., 35 Harvard Street, Brookline, MA 02146 for application details. Scholarship forms are also available from the rector of All Saints Church, Brookline High School, and St. Mary's High School, all in Brookline, Massachusetts.

1967—DEKALB COUNTY PRODUCERS SUPPLY & FARM BUREAU (Medical Scholarship)

1350 W. Prairie Drive
Sycamore IL 60178
815/756-6361

AMOUNT: Varies
DEADLINE(S): JUNE
FIELD(S): Medical Doctor, Nursing

Applicants (or their parents) must have been voting or associate members of Dekalb County Farm Bureau for at least 2 years prior to application; agree to practice in rural Illinois for 3 years upon completion of training and be a US citizen.

Must have been accepted to or be attending medical school or a nursing program. Write to Virginia Fleetwood at above address for complete information.

1968—DEPARTMENT OF THE ARMY (Armed Forces Health Professions Scholarships)

Attn: RC-HS
1307 Third Ave.
Fort Knox KY 40121
502/626-0367
FAX: 502/626-0923

AMOUNT: Tuition + monthly stipend
DEADLINE(S): None
FIELD(S): Medicine, Osteopathy, Nurse
Anesthetist, Veterinary Medicine,
Optometry, Psychology, Dentistry

Open to health professionals and students participating in a Reserve Service of the US Armed Forces, training in the specialties listed above. Varying lengths of service are required to pay back the stipend. Must be US citizen. Award is based on a competitive process, including GPA. Financial need NOT a factor.

400 awards annually. Contact Major Beecher at above address for an application.

1969—EDUCATIONAL AND SCIENTIFIC TRUST OF THE PENNSYLVANIA MEDICAL SOCIETY (Loan Program for Allied Health/Nursing Students)

777 East Park Drive
P.O. Box 8820
Harrisburg PA 17105-8820
717/558-7750, ext. 1257
FAX: 717/558-7818
E-mail: studentloans-trust@pamedsoc.org
Internet: www.pitt.edu/HOME/GHNet/PA_Trust

AMOUNT: Up to $1,500 for bona fide
Pennsylvania residents
DEADLINE(S): JUN 1
FIELD(S): Nursing and allied health
fields

Open to Pennsylvania residents with demonstrated financial need who are seeking a career in nursing or an allied health field. Must be attending a Pennsylvania institution.

Approx. 200 loans per year. Must be US citizen. Contact above location for complete information.

1970—EDWARD BANGS KELLEY AND ELZA KELLEY FOUNDATION, INC. (Scholarship Program)

P.O. Drawer M
Hyannis MA 02601-1412
508/775-3117

AMOUNT: $4,000 (max.)
DEADLINE(S): APR 30
FIELD(S): Medicine, Nursing, Health
Sciences

Open to residents of Barnstable County, Massachusetts. Scholarships are intended to benefit health and welfare of Barnstable County residents. Awards support study at recognized undergraduate, graduate, and professional institutions. Financial need is considered.

Contact Foundation for an application.

1971—EPILEPSY FOUNDATION OF AMERICA (Behavioral Sciences Student Fellowships)

4351 Garden City Drive
Landover MD 20785-2267
301/459-3700 or 800/EFA-1000
FAX: 301/577-2684
TDD: 800/332-2070
E-mail: postmaster@efa.org
Internet: www.efa.org

AMOUNT: $2,000
DEADLINE(S): FEB 1
FIELD(S): Epilepsy as related to
Behavioral Sciences

Three-month fellowships awarded to students in the behavioral sciences for work on an epilepsy study project. For students of vocational rehabilitation counseling. Students propose an epilepsy-related study or training project to be carried out at a US institution of their choice. A preceptor must accept responsibility for supervision of the student and the project.

Contact EFA for an application.

1972—FELLOWS MEMORIAL FUND (Scholarship Loans)

Pensacola Junior College
1000 College Blvd.
Pensacola FL 32504-8998
904/484-1706

AMOUNT: Individually determined
DEADLINE(S): Varies (Individually
arranged)
FIELD(S): Nursing and Medical
Technology

Loans for students accepted for training in nursing or in one of the several fields of medical technology at accredited schools or colleges. Appropriate for two- or four-year nursing programs, graduate nursing study, medical or surgical technology, anesthesiology, and radiological technology. Must be residents of one of the following Florida counties: Escambia, Santa Rosa, Okaloosa, or Walton

Loans are interest-free until four months after graduation. Thereafter, favorable interest rates will apply with the total to be paid by the end of eleven years.

1973—FIRST UNITED METHODIST CHURCH (Robert Stevenson & Doreene E. Cater Scholarships)

302 5th Ave., S.
St. Cloud MN 56301
FAX: 320/251-0878

E-mail: FUMCloud@aol.com

AMOUNT: $100-$300

DEADLINE(S): JUN 1

FIELD(S): Humanitarian & Christian Service: Teaching, Medicine, Social Work, Environmental Studies, etc.

Stevenson Scholarship is open to undergraduate members of the First United Methodist Church of St. Cloud. Cater Scholarship is open to members of the Minnesota United Methodist Conference who are entering the sophomore year or higher of college work. Both require two letters of reference, transcripts, and financial need.

5-6 awards annually. Contact Scholarship Committee for an application.

1974—FLORIDA DEPT. OF EDUCATION (Nursing Scholarship Program)

Student Financial Assist.
255 Collins
Tallahassee FL 32399-0400
850/487-0049 or 888/827-2004
E-mail: OSFABF@mail.doe.state.fl.us
Internet: www.firn.edu/doe

AMOUNT: $8,000-$12,000

DEADLINE(S): Varies (prior to start of quarter/semester for which assistance is requested)

FIELD(S): Nursing

For full- or part-time students enrolled in the upper division of an approved nursing program leading to a B.S. in nursing, an advanced registered nurse practitioner degree, an associate degree in nursing or a diploma in nursing. Loans must be repaid by working one year in a medically underserved area for each year of assistance received.

Renewable. Contact Florida Department of Education for an application.

1975—FOUNDATION FOR NEONATAL RESEARCH AND EDUCATION (FNRE Scholarships & Grants)

701 Lee Street, Suite 450
Des Plaines IL 60016
847/299-6266
FAX: 847/297-6768
E-mail: CKenner835@aol.com

AMOUNT: up to $1,500 (scholarship); $10,000 (research grant)

DEADLINE(S): Varies

FIELD(S): Nursing

Scholarships are for nurses who want to go back and get further education. Research grants are also available.

3 scholarships and 1 research grant annually. Contact Carole Kenner, President, for more information.

1976—FOUNDATION FOR SEACOAST HEALTH (Scholarship Program)

P.O. Box 4606
Portsmouth NH 03802-4606
603/433-3008
FAX: 603/433-2036
E-mail: ffsh@nh.ultranet.com
Internet: www.nh.ultranet.com/~ffsh

AMOUNT: $1,000-10,000

DEADLINE(S): FEB 1

FIELD(S): Health-related fields

Open to undergraduate and graduate students pursuing health-related fields of study who are legal residents of the following cities in New Hampshire: Portsmouth, Newington, New Castle, Rye, Greenland, N. Hampton, or these cities in Maine: Kittery, Eliot, or York. Must have resided in the area for at least two years.

Write or check website for details. $150,000 awarded annually; 35 awards given.

1977—GOOD SAMARITAN FOUNDATION (Nursing Scholarships)

P.O. Box 271108
Houston TX 77277-1108
Written inquiry

AMOUNT: Varies

DEADLINE(S): None

FIELD(S): Nursing

Open to nursing students at Texas schools who have attained the clinical level of their nursing education. Awards support full-time study in all accredited nursing programs (LVN, Diploma, ADN, R.N., B.S.N.). Must be US citizen or legal resident. Students should apply at least six months before the start of clinical courses.

Renewable. Write for an application form.

1978—HISPANIC NURSES ASSOCIATION (Scholarships)

P.O. Box 12132
Spring TX 77391-2132
713/794-0088
E-mail: info@hispanicnurses.org
Internet: www.hispanicnurses.org/

AMOUNT: Varies

DEADLINE(S): APR 1

FIELD(S): Nursing

Scholarships for nursing students of Hispanic descent who are enrolled for a minimum of nine hours in an accredited Texas

college or university. US citizens or legal US residents. Min. GPA of 2.5 required.

Contact organization for applications and details.

1979—HOPI TRIBE (Priority Scholarships)

P.O. Box 123
Kykotsmovi AZ 86039
520/734-2441, ext. 520
800/762-9630
FAX: 520/734-2435

AMOUNT: Varies

DEADLINE(S): JUL 31

FIELD(S): Law, Natural Resources, Education, Medicine/Health, Engineering, Business

Open to enrolled members of the Hopi Tribe studying in one of the fields listed above, which are considered to be areas of priority interest to the Hopis. Available to college juniors, seniors, and graduate students. Program is to encourage graduates to apply their degrees to Hopi Tribal Goals and Objectives.

Contact Hopi Tribe for an application.

1980—ILLINOIS AMVETS (Sad Sacks Nursing Scholarship)

2200 South Sixth Street
Springfield IL 62703-3496
217/528-4713
FAX: 217/528-9896
E-mail: amvets@warpnet.net
Internet: www.amvets.com

AMOUNT: $500

DEADLINE(S): MAR 1

FIELD(S): Nursing

Must be an Illinois resident who is an undergraduate at, or a high school senior planning to attend, an approved Illinois school of nursing. Must be unmarried, demonstrate financial need, be a child of a veteran, and have a satisfactory academic record. Must also have taken the ACT at time of application. Dependents of deceased or disabled veterans will be given priority.

1 award annually. Renewable. See website or contact Shanna Hughes at above address for more information.

1981—INTERNATIONAL ORDER OF THE KING'S DAUGHTERS AND SONS (healthcareers Scholarships)

c/o Mrs. Fred Cannon
Box 1310
Brookhaven MS 39602

Written inquiry

AMOUNT: $1,000 (max.)

DEADLINE(S): APR 1

FIELD(S): Medicine, Dentistry, Nursing, Physical Therapy, Occupational Therapy, Medical Technologies, Pharmacy

Open to students accepted to/enrolled in an accredited US or Canadian four-year or graduate school. R.N. candidates must have completed first year of program; M.D. or D.D.S. candidates must be for at least the second year of medical or dental school; all others must be in at least third year of four-year program. Pre-med students NOT eligible. Must be US or Canadian citizen.

Send self-addressed, stamped envelope, along with a letter stating the field of study and present level, to the Director at above address for an application.

1982—INTRAVENOUS NURSES SOCIETY (Gardner Foundation Scholarships)

Fresh Pond Square
10 Fawcett Street
Cambridge MA 02138
800/694-0298
FAX: 617/441-3009
www.insl.org/gardner.htm

AMOUNT: $1,000

DEADLINE(S): FEB 27

FIELD(S): Nursing: Intravenous therapy

Scholarships for healthcare professionals wishing to pursue careers in intravenous therapy to promote IV nursing research and educational programs.

Applications are on website as well as through organization.

1983—J. HUGH & EARLE W. FELLOWS MEMORIAL FUND (Scholarship Loans)

Pensacola Junior College, President
1000 College Blvd.
Pensacola FL 32504-8998
904/484-1700

AMOUNT: Each is negotiated individually

DEADLINE(S): None

FIELD(S): Medicine, Nursing, Medical Technology, Theology (Episcopal)

Open to bona fide residents of the Florida counties of Escambia, Santa Rosa, Okaloosa, or Walton. For undergraduate study in the fields listed above. US citizenship required.

Loans are interest-free until graduation. Write for complete information.

1984—JEWISH VOCATIONAL SERVICE (Academic Scholarship Program)

One S. Franklin Street
Chicago IL 60606
312/357-4500
FAX: 312/855-3282
TTY: 312/855-3282
E-mail: jvschicago@jon.cjfny.org

AMOUNT: $5,000 (max.)

DEADLINE(S): MAR 1

FIELD(S): "Helping" Professions, Mathematics, Engineering, Sciences, Communications (at Univ IL only), Law (certain schools in IL only)

Open to Jewish men and women legally domiciled in the greater Chicago metropolitan area, who are identified as having promise for significant contributions in their chosen careers, and are in need of financial assistance for full-time academic programs in above areas. Must have entered undergraduate junior year in career programs requiring no postgrad education, be in graduate/professional school, or be in a voc-tech training program. Interview required.

Renewable. Contact JVS for an application between December 1st and February 15th.

1985—JUNIATA COLLEGE (Robert Steele Memorial Scholarship)

Financial Aid Office
Huntingdon PA 16652
814/641-3603
FAX: 814/641-3355
E-mail: clarkec@juniata.edu

AMOUNT: $4,000 (max.)

DEADLINE(S): APR 1

FIELD(S): Science, Medical Studies

Open to science/medical students applying to Juniata College. Must demonstrate financial need and fill out government FAFSA form.

Contact Cynthia G. Clarke, Research Specialist, for an application or enrollment information. See your financial aid office for FAFSA.

1986—KING COUNTY NURSES ASSOCIATION (Scholarships)

4649 Sunnyside Ave., N., #224
Seattle WA 98103
206/545-0603
FAX: 206/545-3558
E-mail: kcna@kcna.org
Internet: www.kcna.org

AMOUNT: Varies

DEADLINE(S): Varies

FIELD(S): Nursing

Scholarships for nursing students in King County, Washington. One is specifically for R.N.s returning to college, and one is reserved for an ethnic minority student.

Contact above address or website for information.

1987—MARYLAND HIGHER EDUCATION COMMISSION (State Nursing Scholarship and Grant)

State Scholarship Admin.
16 Francis Street
Annapolis MD 21401-1781
410/974-5370
TTY: 800/735-2258
Internet: www.ubalt.edu/www.mhec

AMOUNT: $2,400/year (scholarship); $2,400/year (grant)

DEADLINE(S): MAR 1 (FAFSA); JUN 30 (SSA)

FIELD(S): Nursing

For full- or part-time grad or undergrad study in nursing for Maryland residents. Must have 3.0 or better GPA.

Grant portion requires demonstration of financial need. Renewable. Write for complete information.

1988—MATERNITY CENTER ASSOCIATION (Hazel Corbin Assistance Fund/Stipend Awards)

281 Park Ave. South, 5th Fl.
New York NY 10010
212/777-5000
FAX: 212/777-9320
E-mail: mca birth@aol.com

AMOUNT: $5,000/yr.

DEADLINE(S): AUG 1

FIELD(S): Nurse-Midwifery

For individuals enrolled in ACNM-accredited midwifery certification programs. Grantees are expected to submit annual reports of their accomplishments towards the advancement of midwifery for five years. Must demonstrate academic excellence, financial need, and a commitment to family-centered maternity care.

Write for complete information and application.

1989—McFARLAND CHARITABLE FOUNDATION TRUST (Nursing Scholarships)

Linda Butler, Havana Nat'l Bank
P.O. Box 200
Havana IL 62644

309/543-3361
AMOUNT: $3,000-$20,000
DEADLINE(S): MAY 1
FIELD(S): Registered Nursing

Open to IL residents nursing students. Recipients must agree to return to Havana, IL area to work as R.N. for one year for each year of funding. Written contracts with co-signers are required, and an employment commitment is required prior to award of scholarship. A breach of contract requires repayment with interest from date of each disbursement plus recruitment and replacement costs.

Up to 3 awards per year.

1990—MIDWAY COLLEGE (Institutional Aid Program—Scholarships & Grants)

Financial Aid Office
Midway KY 40347
606/846-4421

AMOUNT: Varies
DEADLINE(S): MAR 1
FIELD(S): Nursing, Paralegal, Education, Psychology, Biology, Equine Studies, Liberal Studies, Business Administration

Scholarships and grants open to women who are accepted for enrollment at Midway College. Awards support undergraduate study in the above areas.

Approx 80 awards per year. Write for complete information.

1991—MINNESOTA HIGHER EDUCATION SERVICES OFFICE (Health Professions Loan Forgiveness)

1450 Energy Park Dr., #350
St. Paul MN 55108-5265
612/296-3974
FAX: 612/297-8880
E-mail: info@heso.state.mn.us
Internet: www.heso.state.mn.us/

AMOUNT: Varies
DEADLINE(S): None
FIELD(S): Health Professions

Five loan repayment programs for health professionals who agree to serve in federally designated Health Professional Shortage Areas, in designated, underserved urban or rural areas, in licensed nursing homes, or in intermediate care facilities for persons with mental retardation or related conditions.

For details contact Office of Rural Health and Primary Care at 612/282-3838 or 800/366-5424 (Minnesota only).

1992—MISSISSIPPI OFFICE OF STATE STUDENT FINANCIAL AID (Nursing Education Loan/Scholarship Program)

3825 Ridgewood Road
Jackson MS 39211-6453
601/982-6663 or 800-327-2980
(toll free in Miss.)
FAX: 601/982-6527

AMOUNT: Up to $6,000/yr.
DEADLINE(S): JUL 1
FIELD(S): Nursing

For registered nurses who have lived in Mississippi at least one year and are enrolled in a nursing program at an accredited Mississippi institution in pursuit of a B.S. degree (R.N. to B.S.N. program). May be juniors, seniors, or graduate students. Also for nurses pursuing Master's and Doctorate degrees.

Scholarships are renewable. Write for complete information.

1993—McCORD CAREER CENTER (Level II McCord Medical/Music Scholarship)

Healdsburg High School
1024 Prince Street
Healdsburg CA 95448
707/431-3473

AMOUNT: Varies
DEADLINE(S): APR 30
FIELD(S): Medicine, Music

For graduates of Healdsburg High School who are planning a career in music or medicine. Must be enrolled full-time at a college/university as an undergraduate junior or senior in the fall, or earning an advanced degree in graduate or medical school, or entering into a vocational/certificate program. Transcripts, proof of attendance, and an essay are required.

Contact the McCord Career Center at Healdsburg High School for an application.

1994—McDONALD'S/UNITED NEGRO COLLEGE FUND (Scholarships for Medical and Healthcare Students)

312/443-8708

AMOUNT: Full tuition (10); $1,000 (50)
DEADLINE(S): None
FIELD(S): Medicine and Healthcare fields

Scholarships for college sophomores attending any of the United Negro College Fund schools and pursuing a career in medicine or related healthcare areas. Must maintain 3.0 GPA and demonstrate participation in community and school activities and financial need.

10 two-year scholarships provide full tuition; 50 scholarships are for $1,000 each. Contact school counselor, UNCF office, or call Burrell Communications at above phone number.

1995—NATIONAL ASSOCIATION OF HISPANIC NURSES (Scholarships)

1501 16th Street NW
Washington DC 20036
202/387-2477
FAX: 202/483-7183
E-mail: nahn@juno.com
Internet: www.incacorp.com/nahn

AMOUNT: Varies
DEADLINE(S): APR 30
FIELD(S): Nursing

Scholarships for nursing students of Hispanic descent enrolled in accredited schools. US citizens or legal US residents. Min. GPA of 3.0 required. Financial need considered.

See website and/or organization for application details.

1996—NATIONAL FEDERATION OF THE BLIND (Howard Brown Rickard Scholarship)

805 Fifth Ave.
Grinnell IA 50112
515/236-3366

AMOUNT: $3,000
DEADLINE(S): MAR 31
FIELD(S): Law, Medicine, Engineering, Architecture, Natural Sciences

For legally blind students pursuing or planning to pursue a full-time postsecondary course of study in the US. Based on academic excellence, service to the community, and financial need. Membership NOT required.

1 award annually. Renewable. Contact Mrs. Peggy Elliot, Scholarship Committee Chairman, for an application.

1997—NATIONAL FOUNDATION FOR LONG-TERM healthcare (James D. Durante Nurse Scholarship Program)

1201 L Street NW
Washington DC 20005-4015
202/842-4444
Hotline Info: 202/898-9352
FAX: 202/842-3860
E-mail: bbride@ahca.org
Internet: www.ahca.org

AMOUNT: $500
DEADLINE(S): MAY 30

FIELD(S): Nursing

Open to LPN and RN students who seek to continue or further their education and are interested in long-term care. Must work in an AHCA-member nursing facility.

20 awards annually. Send a self-addressed, stamped, legal-sized envelope in late winter for an application.

1998—NATIONAL HEALTH SERVICE CORPS (NHSC Scholarship Program)

2070 Chain Bridge Road, Suite 450
Vienna VA 22182-2536
800/221-9393
Internet: www.bphc.hrsa.dhhs.gov/nhsc

AMOUNT: Full tuition/books/fees/
  supplies + monthly stipend
DEADLINE(S): MAR
FIELD(S): Family Medicine, General
  Internal Medicine, General Pediatrics,
  Obstetrics/Gynecology, Family Nurse
  Practitioners, Primary Care Physician
  Assistants, Certified Nurse-Midwives

Must be US citizen attending or enrolled in fully accredited US allopathic/osteopathic medical school, nursing program, or physician assistant program. For each year of support received, you must serve one year in federally designated health professional shortage area of greatest need. Minimum two years service commitment begins upon completion of your residency and/or training.

300 awards annually. Renewable up to 4 years. Contact NHSC for an application.

1999—NATIONAL SOCIETY DAUGHTERS OF THE AMERICAN REVOLUTION (Madeline Pickett Halbert Cogswell Nursing Scholarship)

1776 D Street NW
Washington DC 20006-5392
202/628-1776
Internet: www.dar.org

AMOUNT: $500
DEADLINE(S): FEB 15; AUG 15
FIELD(S): Nursing

For students (US citizens) CURRENTLY ENROLLED in an accredited school of nursing for undergraduate study who are members, eligible for membership, or related to a member of NSDAR, NSCAR (Children of American Revolution), or NSSAR (Sons of American Revolution). Awards are placed on deposit with the US college/university and are based on academic excellence, commitment to field of study, and need.

Not renewable. See website or send a self-addressed, stamped envelope for an application or more information.

2000—NATIONAL SOCIETY DAUGHTERS OF THE AMERICAN REVOLUTION (Caroline Holt Nursing Scholarship)

1776 D Street NW
Washington DC 20006-5392
202/628-1776
Internet: www.dar.org

AMOUNT: $500
DEADLINE(S): FEB 15; AUG 15
FIELD(S): Nursing

Open to undergraduate students (US citizens) enrolled in an accredited nursing school in the US. Awards are placed on deposit with the college/university. Awards judged on academic excellence, commitment to field of study, and need. No affiliation with DAR is required.

Not renewable. See website or send a self-addressed, stamped envelope for an application or more information.

2001—NATIONAL SOCIETY OF THE COLONIAL DAMES IN AMERICA (American Indian Scholarship Awards)

4003 Indian Hills Road
Decatur AL 35603
256/353-7038

AMOUNT: $500-$1,000
DEADLINE(S): None
FIELD(S): Nursing

For American Indians who are high school graduates, enrolled in an accredited school, and recommended by a counselor. Must have passing grades, financial need, and career goals related to the needs of Indian people. Must be US citizen.

16-18 awards annually. Renewable. $3,000 goes unclaimed each year. Contact Mrs. Joe Calvin for an application.

2002—NATIONAL STUDENT NURSES' ASSOCIATION FOUNDATION (Scholarship Program)

555 W. 57th Street, Suite 1327
New York NY 10019
212/581-2211
FAX: 212/581-2368
E-mail: nsna@nsna.org
Internet: www.nsna.org

AMOUNT: $1,000-$2,000
DEADLINE(S): FEB 1
FIELD(S): Nursing

Open to students currently enrolled in state-approved nursing schools or pre-nursing in associate degree, baccalaureate, diploma, generic doctorate, and generic master's programs. Funds available for graduate study ONLY if first degree in nursing. Based on academic achievement, financial need, and involvement in nursing student organizations and community activities related to healthcare. Transcripts required.

$10 application fee. See website, or, beginning in August, send self-addressed, business-sized envelope with 55 cents postage to NSNA for an application. Winners will be notified in March. GRADUATING HIGH SCHOOL SENIORS NOT ELIGIBLE.

2003—NAVAL RESERVE RECRUITING COMMAND (Armed Forces Health Professions Scholarships)

Attn: Code 132
4400 Dauphine Street
New Orleans LA 70146
Written inquiry

AMOUNT: Varies
DEADLINE(S): None specified
FIELD(S): Physicians: Anesthesiology,
  surgical specialties; Nursing:
  Anesthesia, operating room, or
  medical surgical nursing

For health professionals and students participating in a Reserve Service of the US Armed Forces training in the specialties listed above and for undergraduate nursing students. A monthly stipend is paid, and varying lengths of service are required to pay back the stipend.

Navy: above address; OR Army: Headquarters, Dept. of the Army, 5109 Leesburg Pike, Falls Church, VA 22041-3258; OR US Air Force Reserve Personnel Center, ATTN: ARPC SGI, Denver, CO 80280-5000.

2004—NEW YORK STATE DEPARTMENT OF HEALTH—PRIMARY CARE SERVICE CORPS (Scholarships)

Corning Tower, Room 1084
Empire State Plaza
Albany NY 12237-0053
518/473-7019

AMOUNT: $15,000
DEADLINE(S): APR 3
FIELD(S): Certified Physician Assistant,
  Nurse Practitioner, Midwife

Open to New York State residents enrolled at, accepted to, or applied at an approved graduate, undergraduate, or certificate course of study. Must be within 24 months of completion of professional training full-time, or within 48 months of completion on a part-time basis.

Contact NY State Dept. of Health for an application.

2005—NEW YORK STATE HIGHER EDUCATION SERVICES CORPORATION (N.Y. State Regents Professional/healthcare Opportunity Scholarships)

Cultural Education Center, Rm. 5C64
Albany NY 12230
518/486-1319
Internet: www.hesc.com

AMOUNT: $1,000-$10,000/yr.
DEADLINE(S): Varies
FIELD(S): Medicine and Dentistry and related fields, Architecture, Nursing, Psychology, Audiology, Landscape Architecture, Social Work, Chiropractic, Law, Pharmacy, Accounting, Speech lLnguage Pathology

For NY state residents who are economically disadvantaged and members of a minority group underrepresented in the chosen profession and attending school in NY state. Some programs carry a service obligation in New York for each year of support. For US citizens or qualifying noncitizens.

Medical/dental scholarships require one year of professional work in NY.

2006—ODD FELLOWS AND REBEKAHS (Nursing Training Scholarships)

22 Munsey Ave.
Livermore Falls ME 04254
207/897-3173

AMOUNT: $200-$1,000
DEADLINE(S): APR 15
FIELD(S): Nursing

For undergraduate students in an R.N. program enrolled in an accredited Maine school of nursing. Must demonstrate financial need.

20 awards annually. Renewable. Contact Ellen F. Washburn for more information.

2007—OHIO BOARD OF REGENTS (Nurse Education Assistance Loan Program)

State Grants & Scholarships
P.O. Box 182452
Columbus OH 43204
888/833-1133, ext. 46629

FAX: 614/752-5903
E-mail: barbara.closser@sgs.state.oh.us

AMOUNT: $3,000/yr. (max.)
DEADLINE(S): JUN 1
FIELD(S): Nursing

Loans for Ohio residents attending Ohio nursing schools for undergraduate, graduate, or postgraduate study at least half-time. Must be accepted for enrollment in approved pre- or post-licensure LPN/RN nursing program, show evidence of intent to engage in nursing in Ohio after graduation, and maintain good academic standing. Must be US citizen/permanent resident, not be in default or owe refund to federal financial aid program, and demonstrate financial need.

Renewable. Borrowers may be eligible for debt cancellation at 20%/yr. for 4 years if employed in clinical practice of nursing in Ohio. Contact Barbara J. Closser, Program Administrator, for an application.

2008—OHIO LEAGUE FOR NURSING (Grants and Loans)

Student Aid Committee
2800 Euclid Ave., Suite 235
Cleveland OH 44115
216/781-7222

AMOUNT: Varies
DEADLINE(S): MAY 1
FIELD(S): Nursing

Open to nursing students who are residents of Greater Cleveland area (Cuyahoga, Grauga, Lake, Lorain counties) and will agree to work in a healthcare facility in that area for at least a year after graduation. US citizen or legal resident.

20-25 awards per year. Write for complete information.

2009—ONCOLOGY NURSING FOUNDATION (Scholarships, Grants, Awards, & Honors)

501 Holiday Drive
Pittsburgh PA 15220-2749
412/921-7373, ext. 242
FAX: 412/921-6565
E-mail: celia@ons.org

AMOUNT: Varies (with program)
DEADLINE(S): Varies (with program)
FIELD(S): Oncology Nursing

For registered nurses seeking further training or to engage in research in the field of oncology. Various programs range from bachelor's degree level through post-masters and career development. Also honors and awards for oncology nurses who have contributed to professional literature and excellence in their field. Some require ONF membership.

Contact Celia A. Hindes, CFRE, for an application. Notification by early April. Awards are offered by Oncology Nursing Society, Oncology Nursing Foundation, Oncology Nursing Certification Corporation, and Oncology Nursing Press, Inc.

2010—PENINSULA COMMUNITY FOUNDATION (Dr. Mary Finegold Scholarship)

1700 S. El Camino Real, #300
San Mateo CA 94402
650/358-9369
FAX: 650/358-9817

AMOUNT: $1,000
DEADLINE(S): MAR 27 (5 P.M.)
FIELD(S): Sciences

Scholarships for senior girls graduating from high school in Palo Alto, California, who intend to complete a four-year degree in the sciences. Special consideration will be given to girls who have demonstrated a "pioneering" spirit in that they have not been constrained by stereotypical female roles and to those facing financial hardship.

Award was established in the honor of Dr. Mary Finegold who, after completing her medical studies, elected to stay at home until her youngest child was in high school before beginning her medical practice. She was a school physician.

2011—SRP/NAVAJO GENERATING STATION (Navajo Scholarship)

P.O. Box 850
Page AZ 86040
520/645-6539
FAX: 520/645-7295
E-mail: ljdawave@srp.gov

AMOUNT: Based on need
DEADLINE(S): APR 30
FIELD(S): Engineering, Environmental Studies, Business, Business Management, Health, Education

Scholarships for full-time students who hold membership in the Navajo Tribe and who are pursuing a degree in a field of study recognized as significant to the Navajo Nation, Salt River Project, or the Navajo Generating Station, such as those listed above. Must be junior or senior, have and maintain a GPA of 3.0.

Average of 15 awards per year. Inquire of Linda Dawavendewa at above location.

2012—STATE STUDENT ASSISTANCE COMMISSION OF INDIANA (Nursing Scholarship Fund)

150 W. Market Street, Suite 500
Indianapolis IN 46204
317/232-2350
FAX: 317/232-3260
E-mail: grants@ssaci.in.us
Internet: www.ai.org/ssaci

AMOUNT: $5,000 (max.)
DEADLINE(S): Varies (with school)
FIELD(S): Nursing

Open to Indiana residents enrolled at least half-time in an undergraduate nursing program at an Indiana college/university. Must have a minimum 2.0 GPA, be a US citizen, and demonstrate financial need.

275-700 awards annually. Contact SSACI for an application.

2013—THE AUGIE J. ALTAR SCHOLARSHIP

7115 W. 91st Street
Bridgeview IL 60455-2048
Write for information

AMOUNT: $500
DEADLINE(S): MAY 31
FIELD(S): Medicine or Agricultural fields

Scholarships for students enrolled or accepted to an accredited college, university, or community college who are of Lithuanian descent and are residents of Illinois. Must be studying in the areas of medicine or agriculture. Financial need considered. Must have and maintain at least a 2.0 GPA.

Send application request to above address with a stamped, self-addressed envelope (SASE).

2014—TYSON FOUNDATION, INC. (Alabama Scholarship Program)

2210 W. Oaklawn
Springdale AR 72762-6999
501/290-4995

AMOUNT: Varies (according to need)
DEADLINE(S): FEB 28
FIELD(S): Business, Agriculture, Engineering, Computer Science, Nursing

Open to residents of the general areas of Albertville, Ashland, Blountsville, Gadsden, Heflin, or Oxford, Alabama, who are US citizens and live in the vicinity of a Tyson facility. Must be pursuing full-time undergraduate study at an accredited US institution and demonstrate financial need. Must also be employed part-time and/or summers to help fund education.

Renewable up to 8 semesters or 12 trimesters as long as student meets criteria. Contact Tyson Foundation for an application no later than last day of February; deadline to return application is April 20th.

2015—TYSON FOUNDATION, INC. (Arkansas Scholarship Program)

2210 W. Oaklawn
Springdale AR 72762-6999
501/290-4955

AMOUNT: Varies (according to need)
DEADLINE(S): FEB 28
FIELD(S): Business, Agriculture, Engineering, Computer Science, Nursing

Open to Arkansas residents who are US citizens pursuing full-time undergraduate study at an accredited US institution. Must demonstrate financial need and be employed part-time and/or summers to help fund education.

Renewable up to 8 semesters or 12 trimesters as long as student meets criteria. Contact Tyson Foundation for an application no later than last day of February; deadline to return application is April 20th.

2016—TYSON FOUNDATION, INC. (Florida Scholarship Program)

2210 W. Oaklawn
Springdale AR 72762-6999
501/290-4995

AMOUNT: Varies (according to need)
DEADLINE(S): FEB 28
FIELD(S): Business, Agriculture, Engineering, Computer Science, Nursing

Open to residents of the general area of Jacksonville, Florida, who are US citizens and live in the vicinity of a Tyson facility. Must be pursuing full-time undergraduate study in an accredited US institution and demonstrate financial need. Must also be employed part-time and/or summers to help fund education.

Renewable up to 8 semesters or 12 trimesters as long as student meets criteria. Contact Tyson Foundation for an application no later than last day of February; deadline to return application is April 20th.

2017—TYSON FOUNDATION, INC. (Georgia Scholarship Program)

2210 W. Oaklawn
Springdale AR 72762-6999
501/290-4995

AMOUNT: Varies (according to need)
DEADLINE(S): FEB 28
FIELD(S): Business, Agriculture, Engineering, Computer Science, Nursing

Open to residents of the general areas of Cumming, Buena Vista, Dawson, or Vienna, Georgia, who are US citizens and live in the vicinity of a Tyson facility. Must be pursuing full-time undergraduate study in an accredited US institution and demonstrate financial need. Must also be employed part-time and/or summers to help fund education.

Renewable up to 8 semesters or 12 trimesters as long as student meets criteria. Contact Tyson Foundation for an application no later than last day of February; deadline to return application is April 20th.

2018—TYSON FOUNDATION, INC. (Illinois Scholarship Program)

2210 W. Oaklawn
Springdale AR 72762-6999
501/290-4995

AMOUNT: Varies (according to need)
DEADLINE(S): FEB 28
FIELD(S): Business, Agriculture, Engineering, Computer Science, Nursing

Open to residents of the general area of Chicago, Illinois, who are US citizens and live in the vicinity of a Tyson facility. Must be pursuing full-time undergraduate study in an accredited US institution and demonstrate financial need. Must also be employed part-time and/or summers to help fund education.

Renewable up to 8 semesters or 12 trimesters as long as student meets criteria. Contact Tyson Foundation for an application no later than last day of February; deadline to return application is April 20th.

2019—TYSON FOUNDATION, INC. (Indiana Scholarship Program)

2210 W. Oaklawn
Springdale AR 72762-6999
501/290-4995

AMOUNT: Varies (according to need)
DEADLINE(S): FEB 28

FIELD(S): Business, Agriculture, Engineering, Computer Science, Nursing

Open to residents of the general areas of Portland or Corydon, Indiana, who are US citizens and live in the vicinity of a Tyson facility. Must be pursuing full-time undergraduate study at an accredited US institution and demonstrate financial need. Must also be employed part-time and/or summers to help fund education.

Renewable up to 8 semesters or 12 trimesters as long as student meets criteria. Contact Tyson Foundation for an application no later than last day of February; deadline to return application is April 20th.

2020—TYSON FOUNDATION, INC. (Mississippi Scholarship Program)

2210 W. Oaklawn
Springdale AR 72762-6999
501/290-4995

AMOUNT: Varies (according to need)
DEADLINE(S): FEB 28
FIELD(S): Business, Agriculture, Engineering, Computer Science, Nursing

Open to residents of the general areas of Cleveland, Jackson, Forest, or Vicksburg, Mississippi, who are US citizens and live in the vicinity of a Tyson facility. Must be pursuing full-time undergraduate study in an accredited US institution and demonstrate financial need. Must also be employed part-time and/or summers to help fund education.

Renewable up to 8 semesters or 12 trimesters as long as student meets criteria. Contact Tyson Foundation for an application no later than last day of February; deadline to return application is April 20th.

2021—TYSON FOUNDATION, INC. (Missouri Scholarship Program)

2210 W. Oaklawn
Springdale AR 72762-6999
501/290-4995

AMOUNT: Varies (according to need)
DEADLINE(S): FEB 28
FIELD(S): Business, Agriculture, Engineering, Computer Science, Nursing

Open to residents of the general areas of Dexter, Monett, Neosho, Noel, or Sedalia, Missouri, who are US citizens and live in the vicinity of a Tyson facility. Must be pursuing full-time undergraduate study in an accredited US institution and demon-

strate financial need. Must also be employed part-time and/or summers to help fund education.

Renewable up to 8 semesters or 12 trimesters as long as student meets criteria. Contact Tyson Foundation for an application no later than last day of February; deadline to return application is April 20th.

2022—TYSON FOUNDATION, INC. (North Carolina Scholarship Program)

2210 W. Oaklawn
Springdale AR 72762-6999
501/290-4995

AMOUNT: Varies (according to need)
DEADLINE(S): FEB 28
FIELD(S): Business, Agriculture, Engineering, Computer Science, Nursing

Open to residents of the general areas of Creswell, Monroe, Sanford, or Wilkesboro, North Carolina, who are US citizens and live in the vicinity of a Tyson facility. Must be pursuing full-time undergraduate study in an accredited US institution and demonstrate financial need. Must also be employed part-time and/or summers to help fund education.

Renewable up to 8 semesters or 12 trimesters as long as student meets criteria. Contact Tyson Foundation for an application no later than the last day of February; deadline to return application is April 20th.

2023—TYSON FOUNDATION, INC. (Oklahoma Scholarship Program)

2210 W. Oaklawn
Springdale AR 72762-6999
501/290-4995

AMOUNT: Varies (according to need)
DEADLINE(S): FEB 28
FIELD(S): Business, Agriculture, Engineering, Computer Science, Nursing

Open to residents of the general areas of Broken Bow or Stillwell, Oklahoma, who are US citizens and live in the vicinity of a Tyson facility. Must be pursuing full-time undergraduate study in an accredited US institution and demonstrate financial need. Must also be employed part-time and/or summers to help fund education.

Renewable up to 8 semesters or 12 trimesters as long as student meets criteria. Contact Tyson Foundation for an application no later than last day of February; deadline to return application is April 20th.

2024—TYSON FOUNDATION, INC. (Pennsylvania Scholarship Program)

2210 W. Oaklawn
Springdale AR 72762-6999
501/290-4995

AMOUNT: Varies (according to need)
DEADLINE(S): FEB 28
FIELD(S): Business, Agriculture, Engineering, Computer Science, Nursing

Open to residents of the general area of New Holland, Pennsylvania, who are US citizens and live in the vicinity of a Tyson facility. Must be pursuing full-time undergraduate study in an accredited US institution and demonstrate financial need. Must also be employed part-time and/or summers to help fund education.

Renewable up to 8 semesters or 12 trimesters as long as student meets criteria. Contact Tyson Foundation for an application no later than last day of February; deadline to return application is April 20th.

2025—TYSON FOUNDATION, INC. (Tennessee Scholarship Program)

2210 W. Oaklawn
Springdale AR 72762-6999
501/290-4995

AMOUNT: Varies (according to need)
DEADLINE(S): FEB 28
FIELD(S): Business, Agriculture, Engineering, Computer Science, Nursing

Open to residents of the general areas of Shelbyville or Union City, Tennessee, who are US citizens and live in the vicinity of a Tyson facility. Must be pursuing full-time undergraduate study in an accredited US institution and demonstrate financial need. Must also be employed part-time and/or summers to help fund education.

Renewable up to 8 semesters or 12 trimesters as long as student meets criteria. Contact Tyson Foundation for an application no later than last day of February; deadline to return application is April 20th.

2026—TYSON FOUNDATION, INC. (Texas Scholarship Program)

2210 W. Oaklawn
Springdale AR 72762-6999
501/290-4995

AMOUNT: Varies (according to need)
DEADLINE(S): FEB 28

FIELD(S): Business, Agriculture, Engineering, Computer Science, Nursing

Open to residents of the general areas of Carthage, Center, or Seguin, Texas, who are US citizens and live in the vicinity of a Tyson facility. Must be pursuing full-time undergraduate study in an accredited US institution and demonstrate financial need. Must also be employed part-time and/or summers to help fund education.

Renewable up to 8 semesters or 12 trimesters as long as student meets criteria. Contact Tyson Foundation for an application no later than last day of February; deadline to return application is April 20th.

2027—TYSON FOUNDATION, INC. (Virginia Scholarship Program)

2210 W. Oaklawn
Springdale AR 72762-6999
501/290-4995

AMOUNT: Varies (according to need)
DEADLINE(S): FEB 28
FIELD(S): Business, Agriculture, Engineering, Computer Science, Nursing

Open to residents of the general areas of Glen Allen, Harrisonburg, or Temperanceville, Virginia, who are US citizens and live in the vicinity of a Tyson facility. Must be pursuing full-time undergraduate study in an accredited US institution and demonstrate financial need. Must also be employed part-time and/or summers to help fund education.

Renewable up to 8 semesters or 12 trimesters as long as student meets criteria. Contact Tyson Foundation for an application no later than last day of February; deadline to return application is April 20th.

2028—U.S. DEPT. OF HEALTH & HUMAN SERVICES (Indian Health Service Preparatory Scholarship Program)

Twinbrook Metro Plaza, Suite 100
12300 Twinbrook Pkwy.
Rockville MD 20852
301/443-0234
FAX: 301/443-4815
Internet: www.ihs.gov/Recruitment/
DHPS/SP/SBTOC3.asp

AMOUNT: Tuition + fees & monthly stipend of $938
DEADLINE(S): APR 1
FIELD(S): Health Professions, Social Work, or Accounting

Open to Native Americans or Alaska natives who enroll in courses leading to a baccalaureate degree and are preparing for acceptance into programs in the above fields. US citizenship required. Renewable annually with reapplication.

Scholarship recipients must intend to serve the Indian people. They incur a one-year service obligation to the IHS for each year of support for a minimum of two years. Write for complete information.

2029—U.S. DEPT. OF HEALTH & HUMAN SERVICES (Indian Health Service Health Professions Scholarship Program)

Twinbrook Metro Plaza, Suite 100
12300 Twinbrook Pkwy.
Rockville MD 20852
301/443-0234
FAX: 301/443-4815
Internet: www.ihs.gov/Recruitment/
DHPS/SP/SBTOC3.asp

AMOUNT: Tuition + fees & monthly stipend of $938
DEADLINE(S): APR 1
FIELD(S): Health Professions, Accounting, Social Work

Open to Native Americans or Alaska natives who are graduate students or college juniors or seniors in a program leading to a career in a field listed above. US citizenship required. Renewable annually with reapplication.

Scholarship recipients must intend to serve the Indian people. They incur a one-year service obligation to the IHS for each year of support for a minimum of two years. Write for complete information.

2030—USAF RESERVE BONUS PROGRAM

6760 E. Irvington Place, #7000
Denver CO 80280-7000
800-525-0102, ext 231 or 237
DSN 926-6490 or 6484
Commercial: 303/676-6484 or 6490
FAX: 303/676-6164
FAX: DSN: 926-6164
E-mail: spresley@arpcmail.den.disa.mil

AMOUNT: $10,000/yr. for physicians; $3,000/year for Operating Room Nurses
DEADLINE(S): None
FIELD(S): Physicians and nurses in critically needed specialties

A bonus pay program to recruit critically needed medical specialties into the Selected Reserve of the US Air Force.

Direct questions to: Medical Readiness & Incentives Division, SrA Sonja Presley at above location.

2031—USAF RESERVE PERSONNEL CENTER (Armed Forces Health Professionas Scholarships)

6760 E. Irvington Place, #7000
Denver CO 80280-7000
Written inquiry

AMOUNT: Varies
DEADLINE(S): None specified
FIELD(S): Physicans: Anesthesiology, surgical specialties; Nursing: Anesthesia, operating room, or medical surgical nursing

For health professionals and students participating in a Reserve Service of the US Armed Forces training in the specialties listed above and for undergraduate nursing students. A monthly stipend is paid, and varying lengths of service are required to pay back the stipend.

Air Force: above address; Army: Headquarters, Dept. of the Army, 5109 Leesburg Pike, Falls Church, VA 22041-3258; Navy: Naval Reserve Recruiting Command, 4400 Dauphine Street, New Orleans, LA 70146.

2032—VIRGIN ISLANDS BOARD OF EDUCATION (Nursing & Other Health Scholarships)

P.O. Box 11900
St. Thomas VI 00801
809/774-4546

AMOUNT: Up to $1,800
DEADLINE(S): MAR 31
FIELD(S): Nursing, Medicine, Health-related Areas

Open to bona fide residents of the Virgin Islands who are accepted by an accredited school of nursing or an accredited institution offering courses in one of the health-related fields.

This scholarship is granted for one academic year. Recipients may reapply with at least a 'C' average. Write for complete information.

2033—WASHINGTON STATE HIGHER EDUCATION COORDINATING BOARD (Health Professional Loan Repayment & Scholarship Program)

P.O. Box 43430
Olympia WA 98504-3430
360/753-7850

FAX: 360/753-7808
Internet: www.hecb.wa.gov
AMOUNT: Varies
DEADLINE(S): APR (scholarship); FEB (loan repayment); JUL (loan repayment)
FIELD(S): Healthcare

Scholarships are open to students in accredited undergraduate or graduate healthcare programs leading to eligibility for licensure in Washington state. Must agree to work in designated shortage area for minimum of three years. Loan repayment recipients receive payment from program for purpose of repaying education loans secured while attending program of healthcare training leading to licensure in Washington state. Financial need NOT a factor.

Renewable up to 5 years. Contact Program Manager for a loan repayment application after November 15th and for scholarship application after January 15th.

2034—WISCONSIN LEAGUE FOR NURSING, INC. (Scholarship)

2121 East Newport Ave.
Milwaukee WI 53211
414/332-6271
AMOUNT: $500
DEADLINE(S): FEB 28
FIELD(S): Nursing

Open to Wisconsin residents enrolled in a National League for Nursing (NLN)-accredited program in WI. Must be halfway through academic program.

Must have 3.0 or better GPA and demonstrate financial need. Applications are mailed ONLY to NLN-accredited schools in January of each year for distribution to students. Contact your school for application. Specify that you are already in nursing school.

2035—WISCONSIN LEAGUE FOR NURSING, INC. (Scholarships for High School Seniors)

2121 East Newport Ave.
Milwaukee WI 53211
414/332-6271
AMOUNT: $500
DEADLINE(S): FEB
FIELD(S): Nursing

For high school seniors who are Wisconsin residents accepted to a National League for Nursing (NLN)-accredited program in WI. Must demonstrate financial need, scholastic excellence, and leadership potential.

Obtain application from Wisconsin League for Nursing, Inc., c/o Mary Ann Tanner, P.O. Box 107, Long Lake, WI

54542-0107. Specify that you are a high school senior.

2036—WOMEN OF THE EVANGELICAL LUTHERAN CHURCH IN AMERICA (The Kahler-Vickers/Raup-Emma Wettstein Scholarships)

8765 West Higgins Road
Chicago IL 60631-4189
800/638-3522, ext. 2747
FAX: 773/380-2419
E-mail: womnelca@elca.org
AMOUNT: $2,000 max.
DEADLINE(S): MAR 1
FIELD(S): Health Professions & Christian Service

Assists women who are members of the ELCA studying for service in health professions associated with ELCA projects abroad that do not lead to church-certified professions. Must be US citizen and have experienced an interruption of two or more years since completion of high school. Academic records of coursework completed in last five years as well as proof of admission from educational institution are required.

Renewable for an additional year. Contact Faith Fretheim, Program Director, for an application.

2037—WYOMING NURSES ASSOCIATION, INC. (Margaret L. Hageman Scholarships)

1603 Capitol Bldg., Suite 305
Cheyenne WY 82001
Written inquiry
AMOUNT: $1,000/yr. (max.)
DEADLINE(S): Varies
FIELD(S): Nursing

Available to Wyoming students who are in or who will enter a nursing program at any school in Wyoming. Students may also be licensed nurses who are continuing their nursing education. Preference will be given to applicants from Goshen, Converse, or Niobrara counties in Wyoming and to those demonstrating financial need. Must maintain a minimum 3.0 GPA.

Write to above address for an application.

2038—ZETA PHI BETA SORORITY EDUCATIONAL FOUNDATION (S. Evelyn Lewis Memorial Scholarship in Medical Health Sciences)

1734 New Hampshire Ave. NW
Washington DC 20009
Internet: www.zpb1920.org/nefforms.htm

AMOUNT: $500-$1,000
DEADLINE(S): FEB 1
FIELD(S): Medicine; Health Sciences

Open to graduate and undergraduate young women enrolled in a program leading to a degree in medicine or health sciences. Award is for full-time study for one academic year (Fall-Spring) and is paid directly to college/university. Must submit proof of enrollment.

Send self-addressed, stamped envelope to above address between September 1st and December 15th for an application.

NUTRITION

2039—ABBIE SARGENT MEMORIAL SCHOLARSHIP INC. (Scholarships)

295 Sheep Davis Road
Concord NH 03301
603/224-1934
FAX: 603/228-8432
AMOUNT: $400
DEADLINE(S): MAR 15
FIELD(S): Agriculture, Veterinary Medicine, Home Economics

Open to New Hampshire residents who are high school graduates with good grades and character. For undergraduate or graduate study. Must be legal resident of US and demonstrate financial need.

3 annual awards. Renewable with reapplication. Write for complete information.

2040—ADELLE DAVIS FOUNDATION

231 North Grand Ave.
Monrovia CA 91016
818/445-8406
AMOUNT: Varies
DEADLINE(S): Ongoing
FIELD(S): Food Science and Nutrition

Graduate and undergraduate scholarships and research grants for the study of food science and nutrition.

Write to Stephen E. Thurman, Treasurer, at above address, for application information.

2041—AMERICAN ASSOCIATION OF CEREAL CHEMISTS (Undergraduate Scholarships and Graduate Fellowships)

3340 Pilot Knob Road
St. Paul MN 55121-2097
Written inquiry
AMOUNT: $1,000-$2,000 (undergrad);
$2,000-$3,000 (graduate)
DEADLINE(S): APR 1

FIELD(S): Cereal Science/Technology

Open to undergraduate and graduate students majoring or interested in a career in cereal science or technology (incl. baking or related areas) as evidenced by coursework or employment. Undergrads must have completed at least one quarter or semester of college/university work. Strong academic record and career interest important; AACC membership helpful but not necessary. Department head endorsement required. Financial need NOT a factor.

Fields such as culinary arts or dietetics NOT eligible. 30 awards annually. Write for an application.

2042—AMERICAN CULINARY FEDERATION, INC. (Ray & Gertrude Marshall Scholarship Fund)

10 San Bartola Drive
St. Augustine FL 32086
904/824-4468 or 800/624-9458
FAX: 904/825-4758
E-mail: acf@aug.com
Internet: www.acfchefs.org/acf.html

AMOUNT: $500-$1,000
DEADLINE(S): FEB 15; JUN 15; OCT 15
FIELD(S): Culinary Arts

For junior members of the American Culinary Federation enrolled in a postsecondary culinary arts program. Must have been in program for one complete grading period. The fee for a junior/apprentice membership is $55/year.

Contact ACF for membership information and/or an application.

2043—AMERICAN DIETETIC ASSOCIATION (Baccalaureate or Coordinated Program)

216 W. Jackson Blvd.
Chicago IL 60606-6995
312/899-0040
FAX: 312/899-4817
Internet: www.eatright.org/scholelig.html

AMOUNT: $450-$4,500
DEADLINE(S): JAN 15 (Request application by then. Deadline is FEB 13.)
FIELD(S): Dietetics

Open to students who have completed the academic requirements in a CAADE/ADA-accredited or approved college or university program for minumum standing as a junior. Must be US citizen or permanent resident and show promise of value to the profession.

Financial need, professional potential, and scholarship are considerations. Write

to above address or see website for complete information.

2044—AMERICAN DIETETIC ASSOCIATION (Dietetic Internships)

216 W. Jackson Blvd.
Chicago IL 60606-6995
312/899-0040
FAX: 312/899-4817
Internet: www.eatright.org/scholelig.html

AMOUNT: $450-$4,500
DEADLINE(S): JAN 15 (Request application by then. Deadline is FEB 13.)
FIELD(S): Dietetics

Open to students who have applied to a CAADE/ADA-accredited dietetic internship and who show promise of being a valuable contributing member to the profession. US citizenship or permanent residency is required.

Financial need, professional potential, and scholarship are considerations. Write to the above address or see website for complete information.

2045—AMERICAN DIETETIC ASSOCIATION (Dietetic Technician Scholarships)

216 W. Jackson Blvd.
Chicago IL 60606-6995
312/899-0040
FAX: 312/899-4817
Internet: www.eatright.org/scholelig.html

AMOUNT: $450-$4,500
DEADLINE(S): JAN 15 (Request application by then. Deadline is FEB 13.)
FIELD(S): Dietetic Technician

Open to students in their first year of study in a CAADE/ADA-approved dietetic technician program. If selected, student may use the scholarship for study during second year. Must be US citizen or permanent resident and show evidence of leadership and academic ability.

Financial need, professional potential, and scholarship are considerations. Contact above address or see website for complete information.

2046—AMERICAN SOCIETY FOR HEALTHCARE FOOD SERVICE ADMINISTRATORS (Dorothy Killian Scholarship for Undergraduates)

One North Franklin, 31st Fl.
Chicago IL 60606

312/422-3870
AMOUNT: $500 (part-time); $1,000 (full-time)
DEADLINE(S): MAR 1
FIELD(S): Healthcare Food Service Management

Open to undergraduate students at 2- or 4-year colleges.

Contact LeNora Rodriguez at above address for an application.

2047—AMERICAN WINE SOCIETY EDUCATIONAL FOUNDATION (Scholarships and Grants)

1134 West Market Street
Bethlehem PA 18018-4910
610/865-2401 or 610/758-3845
FAX: 610/758-4344
E-mail: lhso@lehigh.edu

AMOUNT: $2,000
DEADLINE(S): MAR 31
FIELD(S): Wine industry professional study: enology, viticulture, health aspects of food and wine, and using and appreciating fine wines

To provide academic scholarships and research grants to students based on academic excellence. Must show financial need and genuine interest in pursuing careers in wine-related fields. For North American citizens, defined as US, Canada, Mexico, the Bahamas, and the West Indies at all levels of education.

Contact L.H. Sperling at above location for application.

2048—FOOD INDUSTRY SCHOLARSHIP FUND OF NEW HAMPSHIRE (Scholarships)

110 Stark Street
Manchester NH 03101-1977
Written inquiry

AMOUNT: $1,000
DEADLINE(S): MAR
FIELD(S): Food Industry

Open to students who are residents of New Hampshire and planning to enter a career in the food industry.

Contact Fund for an application.

2049—GOLDEN GATE RESTAURANT ASSOCIATION (David Rubenstein Memorial Scholarship Foundation Awards)

720 Market Street, Suite 200
San Francisco CA 94102
415/781-5348

AMOUNT: $500-$2,500
DEADLINE(S): MAR 31

FIELD(S): Hotel & Restaurant
Management/Food Science

Open to students who have completed the first semester of college as a foodservice major and have a 2.75 or better GPA (4.0 scale) in hotel and restaurant courses.

7 awards per year. Write for complete information.

2050—ILLINOIS RESTAURANT ASSN. (Scholarship Fund)

200 N. LaSalle Street, Suite 880
Chicago IL 60610-1014
312/787-4000

AMOUNT: Varies
DEADLINE(S): JUN 15
FIELD(S): Food Management, Food Science, Culinary Arts, School-to-Work

Open to Illinois residents for undergraduate study of food service management, culinary arts, food processing, and related subjects at accredited institutions in the US.

Write for complete information.

2051—INSTITUTE OF FOOD TECHNOLOGISTS (Freshman Scholarships)

221 N. LaSalle Street, Suite 300
Chicago IL 60601-1291
312/782-8424
FAX: 313/782-8348
E-mail: info@ift.org

AMOUNT: $1,000-$1,500
DEADLINE(S): FEB 15
FIELD(S): Food Science, Food Technology

Open to scholastically outstanding high school graduates and seniors expecting to graduate from high school. Must be entering college for the first time in an approved program in food science/technology.

25 awards annually. Contact IFT for an application. Applicants notified by April 15th.

2052—INSTITUTE OF FOOD TECHNOLOGISTS (Junior/Senior Scholarships)

221 N. LaSalle Street, Suite 300
Chicago IL 60601-1291
312/782-8424
FAX: 312/782-8348
E-mail: info@ift.org

AMOUNT: $1,000-$2,250
DEADLINE(S): FEB 1
FIELD(S): Food Science, Food Technology

Open to scholastically outstanding sophomores and juniors enrolled in an approved food science/technology program.

64 awards annually. Contact IFT for an application. Applicants notified by April 15th.

2053—INSTITUTE OF FOOD TECHNOLOGISTS (Sophomore Scholarships)

221 N. LaSalle Street, Suite 300
Chicago IL 60601-1291
312/782-8424
FAX: 312/782-8348
E-mail: info@ift.org

AMOUNT: $1,000
DEADLINE(S): MAR 1
FIELD(S): Food Science, Food Technology

Open to scholastically outstanding freshmen with a minimum 2.5 GPA and either pursuing or transferring to an approved program in food science/technology.

23 awards annually. Contact IFT for an application. Applicants notified by April 15th.

2054—INTERNATIONAL ASSOCIATION OF CULINARY PROFESSIONALS FOUNDATION (Scholarships)

304 W. Liberty Street, Suite 201
Louisville KY 40202-3068
502/587-7953
FAX: 502/589-3602
E-mail: emcknight@hdqtrs.com
Internet: www.iacp.com

AMOUNT: $500-$10,000
DEADLINE(S): DEC 1
FIELD(S): Culinary Arts

Culinary scholarships are for basic, continuing, and specialty education courses in the US or abroad. Must have a high school diploma or equivalent by June following deadline. Selection based on merit, foodservice work experience, and financial need. Awards cover partial tuition costs and, occasionally, course-related expenses, such as research, room and board, or travel.

$25 application fee. 60 awards annually. Contact Ellen McKnight, Director of Development, at IACP for an application between June 1st and December 1st.

2055—JOHNSON AND WALES UNIVERSITY (Annual Johnson & Wales University National High School Recipe Contest)

8 Abbott Place
Providence RI 02903

401/598-2345
AMOUNT: $1,000 to $5,000
DEADLINE(S): JAN 31
FIELD(S): Business, Hospitality, Technology, Culinary Arts

For students planning to attend Johnson & Wales University, Providence, Rhode Island.

Write to above address for detailed description.

2056—JOHNSON AND WALES UNIVERSITY (Gilbane Building Company Eagle Scout Scholarship)

8 Abbott Place
Providence RI 02903
401/598-2345

AMOUNT: $1,200
DEADLINE(S): None
FIELD(S): Business, Hospitality, Technology, Culinary Arts

For students attending Johnson & Wales University, Providence, Rhode Island. Must be Eagle Scouts.

Send letter of recommendation and transcript to above address.

2057—JOHNSON AND WALES UNIVERSITY (National High School Entrepreneur of the Year Contest)

8 Abbott Place
Providence RI 02903
401/598-2345

AMOUNT: $1,000 to $10,000
DEADLINE(S): DEC 27
FIELD(S): Business, Hospitality, Technology, Culinary Arts

For students attending Johnson & Wales University, Providence, Rhode Island.

Send for detailed description to above address.

2058—JOHNSON AND WALES UNIVERSITY (Scholarships)

8 Abbott Place
Providence RI 02903
401/598-2345

AMOUNT: $200 to $10,000
DEADLINE(S): None
FIELD(S): Business, Hospitality, Technology, Culinary Arts

For students attending Johnson & Wales University, Providence, Rhode Island.

Renewable for four years. Write for complete information.

2059—KAPPA OMICRON NU (Research/Project Grants)

4990 Northwind Dr., Suite 140
East Lansing MI 48823
517/351-8335

AMOUNT: $500 and $3,500
DEADLINE(S): FEB 15
FIELD(S): Home Economics and related fields

Open to Kappa Omicron Nu members who have demonstrated scholarship, research, and leadership potential. Awards are for home economics research at institutions having strong research programs.

2 grants. Write for complete information.

2060—MONTGOMERY COUNTY ASSOCIATION FOR FAMILY + COMMUNITY EDUCATION (Mary Irene Waters Scholarship Fund)

13011 Margot Drive
Rockville MD 20853
301/942-6086

AMOUNT: 2/$1,000
DEADLINE(S): MAR 31
FIELD(S): Child Care

Open to graduates of Montgomery County, MD high schools or permanent Montgomery County residents.

Write for complete information.

2061—NATIONAL ITALIAN AMERICAN FOUNDATION (GRI/ICIF Culinary Scholarships)

1860 19th Street NW
Washington DC 20009-5599
202/530-5315

AMOUNT: $6,000
DEADLINE(S): MAY 31
FIELD(S): Culinary Arts

For graduates of Italian ancestry who are culinary school graduates. Must meet criteria established by the Italian Culinary Institute for Foreigners and the Gruppo Ristoratori Italiani. For study in Italy.

5 scholarships to be awarded. Before applying, contact Enrico Bazzoni at 718/875-0547 or e-mail at EABChef@aol.com.

2062—NATIONAL RESTAURANT ASSOCIATION EDUCATIONAL FOUNDATION (College Undergraduate Scholarships)

250 S. Wacker Drive, Suite 1400
Chicago IL 60606-5834
800/765-2122, ext. 733
312/715-1010
FAX: 312/715-1362
E-mail: bdejesus@foodtrain.org
Internet: www.edfound.org

AMOUNT: $2,000
DEADLINE(S): MAR 1
FIELD(S): Culinary Arts, Restaurant/Hospitality

For college students pursuing a certificate, associate degree, or bachelor's degree in above fields. Must have a minimum 2.75 GPA and be a US citizen/permanent resident or a non-citizen attending school in US/territories. Must be enrolled a minimum of nine semester hours, have completed first semester, and have at least 750 hours of work experience in the restaurant/hospitality industry.

Applications available January 1st. See website or contact Bridgette de Jesus, Program Coordinator, for more information.

2063—NATIONAL RESTAURANT ASSOCIATION EDUCATIONAL FOUNDATION (High School Seniors Undergraduate Scholarships)

250 S. Wacker Dr., Suite 1400
Chicago IL 60606-5834
800/765-2122, ext. 733
312/715-1010
FAX: 312/715-1362
E-mail: bdejesus@foodtrain.org
Internet: www.edfound.org

AMOUNT: $2,000
DEADLINE(S): MAR 1
FIELD(S): Culinary/Restaurant/ Hospitality Majors

For high school seniors accepted into an undergraduate program in above fields. Must have a minimum 2.75 GPA and be a US citizen/permanent resident or a non-citizen attending school in US/territories. Must have taken a minimum of one foodservice-related course and/or have performed a minimum of 250 hours of restaurant/hospitality work experience. For full-or part-time study.

Applications available January 1st. See website or contact Bridgette de Jesus, Program Coordinator, for more information.

2064—NATIONAL RESTAURANT ASSOCIATION EDUCATIONAL FOUNDATION (Industry Assistance Grants)

250 S. Wacker Drive, Suite 1400
Chicago IL 60606-5834
800/765-2122, ext. 733
312/715-1010
FAX: 312/715-1362
E-mail: bdejesus@foodtrain.org
Internet: www.edfound.org

AMOUNT: $1,000 value*
DEADLINE(S): JUN 1
FIELD(S): Culinary Arts, Restaurant/Hospitality Professionals

For industry professionals who want to further their education and enhance their career opportunities, but are not enrolled as a student in a restaurant/hospitality program. *Includes written materials, videos, and the ServSafe exam (certificate). Must have minimum three years of foodservice supervisory, assistant management, or management experience; be currently employed in the industry; and demonstrate a commitment to the industry. Must be US citizen/resident.

Applications available April 1st. See website or contact Bridgette de Jesus, Program Coordinator, for more information.

2065—NATIONAL RESTAURANT ASSOCIATION EDUCATIONAL FOUNDATION (Teacher Work-Study Grant)

250 S. Wacker Drive, Suite 1400
Chicago IL 60606-5834
800/765-2122, ext. 733
312/715-1010
FAX: 312/715-1362
E-mail: bdejesus@foodtrain.org
Internet: www.edfound.org

AMOUNT: $2,000
DEADLINE(S): FEB 15
FIELD(S): Restaurant and Hospitality Education

For restaurant and hospitality educators/administrators who want to complement classroom time with "hands-on" work experience. Through this program, educators/administrators assume roles as full-time foodservice employees and gain a better understanding of day-to-day restaurant operations. Must be US citizen/permanent resident teaching secondary/postsecondary school within the US and territories.

Renewable after one year, with new work location/experience. See website or contact Bridgette de Jesus, Program Coordinator, for more information.

2066—PENINSULA COMMUNITY FOUNDATION (Dr. Mary Finegold Scholarship)

1700 S. El Camino Real, #300
San Mateo CA 94402
650/358-9369
FAX: 650/358-9817

AMOUNT: $1,000
DEADLINE(S): MAR 27 (5 P.M.)
FIELD(S): Sciences

Scholarships for senior girls graduating from high school in Palo Alto, California, who intend to complete a four-year degree in the sciences. Special consideration will be given to girls who have demonstrated a "pioneering" spirit in that they have not been constrained by stereotypical female roles and to those facing financial hardship.

Award was established in the honor of Dr. Mary Finegold who, after completing her medical studies, elected to stay at home until her youngest child was in high school before beginning her medical practice. She was a school physician.

2067—SCHOOL FOOD SERVICE FOUNDATION (Scholarships)

700 S. Washington Street, Ste. 300
Alexandria VA 22314
703/739-3900 or 800/877-8822
FAX: 703/739-3915
E-mail: lhanley@asfsa.org

AMOUNT: $1,000 (max.)
DEADLINE(S): APR 15
FIELD(S): Food Science, Nutrition, Food Service Management

Must be an ASFSA member and/or the child of an ASFSA member who plans to study in the above field(s). Must express a desire to make school food service a career, be pursuing an undergraduate degree, and have a satisfactory academic record.

Contact ASFSA for an application.

2068—THE ART INSTITUTES INTERNATIONAL (Evelyn Keedy Memorial Scholarship)

300 Sixth Ave., Suite 800
Pittsburgh PA 15222-2598
412/562-9800
FAX: 412/562-9802
E-mail: webadmin@aii.edu
Internet: www.aii.edu

AMOUNT: 2 years full tuition
DEADLINE(S): MAY 1
FIELD(S): Various fields in the creative and applied arts: video production, broadcasting, culinary arts, fashion design, website administration, etc.

Scholarships at 12 different locations nationwide in various fields described above. For graduating high school seniors admitted to an Arts Institutes International School, the New York Restaurant School, or NCPT.

Transcripts, letters of recommendation, and resume must be submitted with application.

See website or contact AII for more information.

2069—THE JAMES BEARD FOUNDATION (Scholarships)

167 W. 12th Street
New York NY 10011
212/675-4984
FAX: 212/645-1438
Internet: www.jamesbeard.org

AMOUNT: Varies
DEADLINE(S): MAR 1
FIELD(S): Culinary studies

Scholarships for students of the culinary arts enrolled in accredited professional programs. Financial need and aptitude are among the criteria.

Applications available in November for the following year. $15 application fee. Write to organization for details.

2070—U.S. DEPT. OF HEALTH & HUMAN SERVICES (Indian Health Service Preparatory Scholarship Program)

Twinbrook Metro Plaza, Suite 100
12300 Twinbrook Pkwy.
Rockville MD 20852
301/443-0234
FAX: 301/443-4815
Internet: www.ihs.gov/Recruitment/DHPS/SP/SBTOC3.asp

AMOUNT: Tuition + fees & monthly stipend of $938
DEADLINE(S): APR 1
FIELD(S): Health Professions, Social Work, or Accounting

Open to Native Americans or Alaska natives who enroll in courses leading to a baccalaureate degree and are preparing for acceptance into programs in the above fields. US citizenship required. Renewable annually with reapplication.

Scholarship recipients must intend to serve the Indian people. They incur a one-year service obligation to the IHS for each year of support for a minimum of two years. Write for complete information.

2071—U.S. DEPT. OF HEALTH & HUMAN SERVICES (Indian Health Service Health Professions Scholarship Program)

Twinbrook Metro Plaza, Suite 100
12300 Twinbrook Pkwy.
Rockville MD 20852

301/443-0234
FAX: 301/443-4815
Internet: www.ihs.gov/Recruitment/DHPS/SP/SBTOC3.asp

AMOUNT: Tuition + fees & monthly stipend of $938.
DEADLINE(S): APR 1
FIELD(S): Health Professions, Accounting, Social Work

Open to Native Americans or Alaska natives who are graduate students or college juniors or seniors in a program leading to a career in a field listed above. US citizenship required. Renewable annually with reapplication.

Scholarship recipients must intend to serve the Indian people. They incur a one-year service obligation to the IHS for each year of support for a minimum of two years. Write for complete information.

2072—U.S. DEPARTMENT OF AGRICULTURE (1890 National Scholars Program)

14th & Independence Ave. SW
Room 301-W, Whitten Bldg.
Washington DC 20250-9600
202/720-6905
E-mail: usda-m@fie.com
Internet: web.fie.com/htdoc/fed/agr/ars/edu/prog/mti/agrpgaak.htm

AMOUNT: Tuition, employment/benefits, use of PC/software, fees, books, room/board
DEADLINE(S): JAN 15
FIELD(S): Agriculture, Food, or Natural Resource sciences

For US citizens, high school grad/GED, GPA 3.0+, verbal/math SAT 1,000+, composite score 21+ ACT, 1st-yr college student, and attend participating school.

34+ scholarships/yr/4 years. Send applications to USDA Liaison Officer at the 1890 Institution of your choice (see Web page for complete list).

2073—UNIVERSITY OF ILLINOIS COLLEGE OF ACES (Jonathan Baldwin Turner Agricultural Merit Scholarship Program)

101 Mumford Hall
1301 W. Gregory Drive
Urbana IL 61801
Written inquiry

AMOUNT: $4,000
DEADLINE(S): Varies (start of high school senior year)
FIELD(S): Agriculture, Nutritional Science

Scholarships in agricultural, food, and human nutritional sciences for outstanding incoming freshmen at the University of Illinois. Must have minimum ACT composite score of 27, equivalent SAT combined scores, or be in the 90th percentile of high school class rank at the end of junior year. Interview required.

60 awards annually. Contact Charles Olson, Assistant Dean, College of Agriculture, for an application.

SCHOOL OF SOCIAL SCIENCE

2074—AMERICAN BAR FOUNDATION (Summer Research Fellowships in Law and Social Science for Minority Undergraduate Students)

750 N. Lake Shore Drive
Chicago IL 60611
312/988-6500
Internet: www.abf-sociolegal.org

AMOUNT: $3,500 stipend
DEADLINE(S): MAR 1
FIELD(S): Social Sciences, Humanities, Law

Summer research opportunity open to sophomore and junior undergraduates who are Native American, African American, Mexican, Puerto Rican, or other minority. Must be US citizen or permanent resident and have at least a 3.0 GPA. Students are assigned a mentor and participate in seminars; must also work at the Foundation's office in Chicago for 35 hours per week for 10 weeks. Essay, transcripts, and letter of recommendation required.

4 awards annually; announced in April. See website or contact ABF for an application.

2075—ASSOCIATION FOR WOMEN IN SCIENCE EDUCATIONAL FOUNDATION (Dr. Vicki L. Schechtman Scholarship)

1200 New York Ave. NW
Suite 650
Washington DC 20005
202/326-8940 or 800/886-AWIS
E-mail: awis@awis.org
Internet: www.awis.org

AMOUNT: $1,000
DEADLINE(S): JAN 16
FIELD(S): Various Sciences and Social Sciences

For female undergraduate students who are US citizens and have a minimum GPA of 3.0. Summary page, essay describ-ing career aspirations, transcripts, proof of matriculation (if available), and two reference letters required with application. Scholarships may be used for tuition, books, housing, research, equipment, etc.

See website or write to above address for an application and more information.

2076—ASSOCIATION FOR WOMEN IN SCIENCE EDUCATIONAL FOUNDATION (Ruth Satter Memorial Award)

1200 New York Ave. NW
Suite 650
Washington DC 20005
202/326-8940 or 800/886-AWIS
E-mail: awis@awis.org
Internet: www.awis.org

AMOUNT: $1,000
DEADLINE(S): JAN 16
FIELD(S): Various Sciences and Social Sciences

Scholarships for female doctoral students who have interrupted their education three years or more to raise a family. Summary page, description of research project, resume, references, transcripts, biographical sketch, and proof of eligibility from department head required. US citizens may attend any graduate institution; non-citizens must be enrolled in US institutions.

See website or write to above address for more information or an application.

2077—BUSINESS & PROFESSIONAL WOMEN'S FOUNDATION (BPW Career Advancement Scholarship Program)

2012 Massachusetts Ave. NW
Washington DC 20036-1070
202/293-1200, ext. 169
FAX: 202/861-0298
Internet: www.bpwusa.org

AMOUNT: $500-$1,000
DEADLINE(S): APR 15
FIELD(S): Biology, Science, Education, Engineering, Social Science, Paralegal, Humanities, Business, Math, Computers, Law, MD, DD

For women (US citizens) aged 25+ accepted into accredited program at US institution (+Puerto Rico & Virgin Islands). Must graduate within 12 to 24 months from the date of grant and demonstrate critical financial need. Must have a plan to upgrade skills, train for a new career field, or to enter/re-enter the job market.

Full- or part-time study. For info see website or send business-sized, self-addressed, double-stamped envelope.

2078—CHRISTIAN A. JOHNSON ENDEAVOR FOUNDATION (Native American Fellows)

Harvard Univ.
79 John F. Kennedy Street
Cambridge MA 02138
617/495-1152
FAX: 617/496-3900
Internet: www.ksg.harvard.edu/hpaied/cjohn.htm

AMOUNT: Varies
DEADLINE(S): MAY 1
FIELD(S): Social Sciences, Government, or program related to Native American studies

Fellowships for students of Native American ancestry who attend a John F. Kennedy School of Government degree program. Applicant, parent, or grandparent must hold membership in a federally or state-recognized tribe, band, or other organized group of Native Americans. Must be commited to a career in American Indian affairs. Awards based on merit and need.

Renewable, based on renomination and availability of funds. To apply, contact John F. Kennedy School of Government at above address.

2079—EAST TEXAS HISTORICAL ASSOCIATION (Ottis Lock Endowment Awards)

P.O. Box 6223
SFA Station
Nacogdoches TX 75962
409/468-2407

AMOUNT: $500
DEADLINE(S): MAY 1
FIELD(S): History, Social Science

Open to residents of East Texas who will be pursuing undergraduate or graduate studies at an East Texas college or university.

Renewable with adequate progress towards degree. Contact East Texas Historical Association for an application.

2080—INSTITUTE FOR HUMANE STUDIES (Humane Studies Fellowship)

4084 University Drive, Suite 101
Fairfax VA 22030-6812
703/934-6920 or 800/697-8799
FAX: 703/352-7535
E-mail: ihs@gmu.edu
Internet: www.theihs.org

AMOUNT: up to $12,000
DEADLINE(S): DEC 31
FIELD(S): Social Sciences, Law,
Humanities, Jurisprudence, Journalism

Awards are for graduate and advanced undergraduate students pursuing degrees at any accredited domestic or foreign school. Based on academic performance, demonstrated interest in classical liberal ideas, and potential to contribute to the advancement of a free society.

90 awards annually. Apply online or contact IHS for an application.

2081—INSTITUTE FOR HUMANE STUDIES (Summer Residential Program)

4084 University Drive, Suite 101
Fairfax VA 22030-6812
703/934-6920 or 800/697-8799
FAX: 703/352-7535
E-mail: ihs@gmu.edu
Internet: www.theihs.org

AMOUNT: All seminar fees: program cost, room/board, materials, and books
DEADLINE(S): MAR 1
FIELD(S): Social Sciences, Humanities, Law, Journalism, Public Policy, Education, Writing

For college students, recent graduates, and graduate students who share an interest in learning and exchanging ideas about the scope of individual rights. One-week and weekend seminars at various campus locations across the US.

Apply online or contact IHS for an application.

2082—NATIONAL COUNCIL FOR THE SOCIAL STUDIES (Grant for the Enhancement of Geographic Literacy)

3501 Newark Street NW
Washington DC 20016
202/966-7840
FAX: 202/966-2061
Internet: www.ncss.org/awards/grants.html

AMOUNT: $2,500
DEADLINE(S): JUL 3
FIELD(S): Social Studies

Grant is co-sponsored by the George F. Cram Company, map publishers. For teachers of any level who present a program to promote and enhance geography education in the schools. Must incorporate the National Geography Standards in "Geography for Life," the "Fundamental Themes in Geography," and appropriate sections of "Expectations of Excellence: Curriculum Standards for Social Studies."

Check website or contact organization for details.

2083—NATIONAL COUNCIL FOR THE SOCIAL STUDIES (Christa McAuliffe Award)

3501 Newark Street NW
Washington DC 20016
202/966-7840
FAX: 202/966-2061
Internet: www.ncss.org/awards/grants.html

AMOUNT: $1,000
DEADLINE(S): MAR 22 (even-numbered years)
FIELD(S): Social Studies

An award for a full-time teacher engaged in teaching social studies (K-12) who submits an abstract (50-150 words) of a proposal describing a unique teaching project. NCSS membership required.

Check website or contact organization for details.

2084—PEW YOUNGER SCHOLARS PROGRAM (Graduate Fellowships)

G-123 Hesburgh Library
University of Notre Dame
Notre Dame IN 46556
219/631-4531
FAX: 219/631-8721
E-mail: Karen.M.Heinig.2@nd.edu
Internet: www.nd.edu/~pesp/pew/PYSPHistory.html

AMOUNT: $13,000
DEADLINE(S): NOV 30
FIELD(S): Social Sciences, Humanities, Theology

Program is for use at any Christian undergraduate school and most seminaries. Check with organization to see if your school qualifies. Apply during senior year. Recipients may enter a competition in which ten students will be awarded a $39,000 ($13,000/yr.) fellowship for three years of dissertation study. For use at top-ranked Ph.D. programs at outstanding universities.

NOT for study in medicine, law, business, performing arts, fine arts, or the pastorate. Check website and/or organization for details.

2085—RESOURCES FOR THE FUTURE (RFF Summer Internship Program)

1616 P Street NW
Washington DC 20036-1400
202/328-5000
E-mail: lewis@rff.org or voigt@rff.org

Internet: www.rff.org
AMOUNT: $375/week
DEADLINE(S): MAR 12
FIELD(S): Social Sciences, Natural Resources, Energy, Environment

Resident-paid summer internships for undergraduate and graduate students for research in the above fields. Divisions are Center for Risk Management, Energy and Natural Resources, and Quality of the Environment. Candidates should have outstanding policy analysis and writing skills. For both US and non-US citizens.

All information is on website. Address inquiries and applications to Sue Lewis (Energy & Natural Resources and Quality of the Environment) or Marilyn Voigt (Center for Risk Management). NO fax submissions.

2086—ROSE HILL COLLEGE (Louella Robinson Memorial Scholarship)

P.O. Box 3126
Aiken SC 29802-3126
800/684-3769
FAX: 803/641-0240
E-mail: rosehill@.edu
Internet: www.rosehill.edu

AMOUNT: $10,000/yr. for four years
DEADLINE(S): Varies
FIELD(S): Liberal Arts and Humanities curricula

For undergraduate residents of Indian River County, Florida, to attend Rose Hill College in Aiken, South Carolina. The school offers a liberal arts education and follows the Great Books curriculum, a program of reading and seminars.

1 annual award. Applicants must meet entry requirements of RHC. Contact above location for details.

2087—ROSE HILL COLLEGE (Scholarships for Children of Eastern Orthodox Priests/Deacons)

P.O. Box 3126
Aiken SC 29802-3126
800/684-3769
FAX: 803/641-0240
E-mail: rosehill@edu
Internet: www.rosehill.edu

AMOUNT: Full scholarship: $10,000/yr. for four years
DEADLINE(S): Varies
FIELD(S): Liberal Arts and Humanities curricula

For undergraduates who are children of Eastern Orthodox Christian priests or deacons to attend Rose Hill College in Aiken,

South Carolina. The school offers a liberal arts education and follows the Great Books curriculum, a program of reading and seminars.

6-10 annual awards. Applicants must meet entry requirements of RHC. Contact above location for details.

2088—ROSE HILL COLLEGE (Scholarships for the Homeschooled)

P.O. Box 3126
Aiken SC 29802-3126
800/684-3769
FAX: 803/641-0240
E-mail: rosehill@rosehill.edu
Internet: www.resehill.edu

AMOUNT: Full scholarship: $10,000/yr. for four years
DEADLINE(S): Varies
FIELD(S): Liberal Arts and Humanities curricula

For undergraduates who have been homeschooled for three of the last five years of their high school education. For use at Rose Hill College in Aiken, South Carolina. The school offers a liberal arts education and follows the Great Books curriculum, a program of reading and seminars. Scholarships will be awarded primarily on the basis of an essay that the student will be asked to write.

4 annual awards. Applicants must meet entry requirements of RHC. Contact above location for details.

2089—SOCIETY FOR THE PSYCHOLOGICAL STUDY OF SOCIAL ISSUES (Applied Social Issues Internship Program)

P.O. Box 1248
Ann Arbor MI 48106-1248
Phone/TTY: 313/662-9130
FAX: 313/662-5607
E-mail: spssi@spssi.org
Internet: www.spssi.org

AMOUNT: $1,500-$2,500
DEADLINE(S): NOV 10
FIELD(S): Social Science & related fields

Internship awards cover research costs, community organizing, summer stipends, etc. Encourages intervention projects, nonpartisan lobbying, applied research, and implementing public policy. Proposals are invited for applying social science principles to social issues, in cooperation with a community, city, or state government organization, public interest group, or other not-for-profit entity. College seniors, graduate students, and first-year postdoctorates may apply.

Contact SPSSI for details. Applications available on website. NO SCHOLARSHIPS AVAILABLE—REQUESTS FOR FINANCIAL AID WILL NOT BE ANSWERED.

2090—THE WALT DISNEY COMPANY (American Teacher Awards)

P.O. Box 9805
Calabasas CA 91372

AMOUNT: $2,500 (36 awards); $25,000 (Outstanding Teacher of the Year)
DEADLINE(S): FEB 15
FIELD(S): Teachers: athletic coach, early childhood, English, foreign language/ESL, general elementary, mathematics, performing arts, physical education/health, science, social studies, visual arts, voc-tech education

Awards for K-12 teachers in the above fields.

Teachers, or anyone who knows a great teacher, can write for applications at the above address.

COMMUNICATIONS

2091—AMERICAN INSTITUTE OF POLISH CULTURE (Scholarships)

1440 79th Street Causeway
Suite 117
Miami FL 33141
305/864-2349
FAX: 305/865-5150
E-mail: info@ampolinstitute.org
Internet: www.ampolinstitute.org

AMOUNT: $1,000
DEADLINE(S): FEB 15
FIELD(S): Journalism, Public Relations, Communications

Awards are to encourage young Americans of Polish descent to pursue the above professions. Can be used for full-time study at any accredited American college. Criteria for selection include achievement, talent, and involvement in public life.

$25 processing fee. Renewable. Send self-addressed, stamped envelope to Mrs. Harriet Irsay for an application.

2092—AMERICAN MEDICAL WRITERS ASSOCIATION (Margaret Mead Journalism Award)

225 Park Ave. S. 17th Fl.
c/o Cohn & Wolfe Healthcare
New York NY 10003

212/598-3600
FAX: 212/598-2812
Internet: www.amwa.org/
Comp.Awards/comp.awards.html

AMOUNT: $1,500
DEADLINE(S): JUL 31
FIELD(S): Journalism

Awards for published print reporting on issues on postmenopausal health.

Two awards: one for a medical professional/trade article and one for a consumer article. Obtain entry form from Heather Rose at above location.

2093—AMERICAN RADIO RELAY LEAGUE FOUNDATION (The PHD ARA Scholarship)

225 Main Street
Newington CT 06111
860/594-0200
FAX: 860/594-0259
Internet: www.arrl.org/

AMOUNT: $1,000
DEADLINE(S): FEB 1
FIELD(S): Journalism; Computer Science; Electronic Engineering

For undergraduate or graduate students who are residents of the ARRL Midwest Division (IA, KS, MO, NE) who hold any class of radio amateur license—or student may be the child of a deceased radio amateur.

1 award annually. Contact ARRL for an application.

2094—AMERICAN WOMEN IN RADIO AND TELEVISION—HOUSTON CHAPTER (Scholarship Program)

P.O. Box 980908
Houston TX 77098
713/662-1363
FAX: 713/662-1398
Internet: www.awrt.org

AMOUNT: $1,000
DEADLINE(S): MAR
FIELD(S): Broadcasting & allied fields

Scholarships are for Houston area college juniors and seniors who are studying broadcasting or an allied field.

Renewable. Contact Kim Scates, AWRT Houston Chapter President, for an application. Awards are made in May.

2095—ASIAN AMERICAN JOURNALISTS ASSOCIATION (AAJA Portland Chapter Scholarships)

1320 SW Broadway
Portland OR 97225
503/412-7021

FAX: 503/297-8804
E-mail: amywang@
news.oregonian.com
Internet: www.aaja.org
AMOUNT: Varies
DEADLINE(S): MAR
FIELD(S): Journalism

For Oregon residents at the high school, undergraduate, or graduate level who are studying journalism or planning on a career in journalism and exhibit interest in Asian American issues. Must be a US citizen. Financial need is NOT a factor.

Not renewable. Contact Amy Wang at above address for an application.

2096—ASIAN AMERICAN JOURNALISTS ASSOCIATION (Scholarships/Internships)

1765 Sutter Street
San Francisco CA 94115-3217
415/346-2051, ext. 300
FAX: 415/346-6343
E-mail: national@aaja.org
Internet: www.aaja.org

AMOUNT: Up to $3,000 (+ travel/lodging/
meals for internships)
DEADLINE(S): APR 1
FIELD(S): Photo, Print, or Broadcast
Journalism

For Asian-American high school seniors, undergraduates, and graduate students enrolled full-time in an accredited college or university. Scholarships/internships require commitment to field of journalism, sensitivity to Asian-American issues as demonstrated by community involvement, journalistic ability, scholastic ability, and financial need.

See website or send self-addressed, 55-cent-stamped envelope to Karen Jaw, Program Coordinator, at above address for application/more information.

2097—ASIAN AMERICAN JOURNALISTS ASSOCIATION—HAWAII CHAPTER (AAJA Scholarship)

P.O. Box 22592
Honolulu HI 96823-2592
808/235-5881, ext. 341
FAX: 808/247-7246
E-mail: NSWCCLCKKE@aol.com

AMOUNT: $750
DEADLINE(S): APR 15
FIELD(S): Journalism

Preference given to Asian-Pacific Islanders for undergraduate college studies. US residency or citizenship required. Cash award. Financial need considered.

2-3 awards annually. Contact Carol Chang, Scholarship Chairman, for an application.

2098—ASSOCIATED PRESS TELEVISION-RADIO ASSOCIATION OF CALIFORNIA/NEVADA (APTRA-Clete Roberts & Kathryn Dettman Memorial Journalism Scholarship Awards)

Rachel Ambrose
221 S. Figueroa Street, #300
Los Angeles CA 90012
213/626-1200
E-mail: rambrose@ap.org

AMOUNT: $1,500
DEADLINE(S): DEC 10
FIELD(S): Broadcast Journalism

Recipients will be students with a broadcast journalism career objective who are enrolled in a California or Nevada college or university. Applicants must complete an entry form and may submit examples of broadcast-related work. Scholarships will be awarded at APTRA's annual awards banquet in March at the Disneyland Hotel in Anaheim, CA.

4 awards annually. Contact Rachel Ambrose at APTRA for an entry form.

2099—ASSOCIATION FOR EDUCATION IN JOURNALISM & MASS COMMUNICATION (Mary A. Gardner Scholarship)

Univ. of South Carolina
LeConte College, Room 121
Columbia SC 29208-0251
803/777-2005

AMOUNT: $300
DEADLINE(S): MAR 23
FIELD(S): News Reporting and/or
Editing

Open to full-time incoming juniors or seniors in a college undergraduate news-editorial program. Must have minimum GPA of 3.0 (on a 4.0 scale). Statement of qualifications/career objectives, biographical narrative (including school/home address/phone), letter of support from professor, official transcript, two letters of recommendation, and copies of clippings/other evidence of journalistic accomplishments required with application.

1 award annually. Send a self-addressed, stamped envelope (SASE) to Jennifer H. McGill, Executive Director, AEJMC, at above address for complete information.

2100—ATLANTA JOURNAL AND CONSTITUTION (Cox Minority Scholarship Program)

72 Marietta Street
Atlanta GA 30303

404/526-5120
AMOUNT: Full four-year tuition
DEADLINE(S): APR 1
FIELD(S): Newspaper Business,
Journalism

Open to undergraduate students who live in the Metro Atlanta, GA area and plan to attend a Georgia university. Students must be US citizens, have a 3.0 GPA, and be a member of a minority group. Students must be interested in the newspaper business.

Write to the above address for complete information.

2101—ATLANTA PRESS CLUB (Journalism Scholarship Awards)

260 14th Street, NW, Suite 300
Atlanta GA 30318
404/57-PRESS
FAX: 404/892-2637
Internet: www.atlpressclub.org

AMOUNT: $1,000
DEADLINE(S): FEB 1
FIELD(S): Journalism

Scholarships for university sophomores and juniors attending school in Georgia. Must be working toward a career in news and aiming to achieve excellence in the field of reporting.

4 awards annually. Not renewable. Contact Amal Bane at the Atlanta Press Club for an application.

2102—BALL STATE UNIVERSITY (David Letterman Telecommunications Scholarship Program)

Dept. of Telecommunications
Muncie IN 47306
317/285-1480
E-mail: finaid@bsu.edu
Internet: www.bsu.edu/students/
finaid/home.html

AMOUNT: Full tuition (1st); 1/2 tuition
(2nd); 1/3 tuition (3rd)
DEADLINE(S): APR 1
FIELD(S): Telecommunications

Open to undergraduate juniors at Ball State who have demonstrated reasonable expectations of becoming professionals in the telecommunications industry. Scholarships are based on creativity; grades are NOT considered. Any creative effort connected with the telecommunications field will be considered.

Contact Ball State for an application or admissions information.

2103—BLUES HEAVEN FOUNDATION, INC. (Muddy Waters Scholarship)

2120 S. Michigan Ave.
Chicago IL 60616
312/808-1286

AMOUNT: $2,000
DEADLINE(S): APR 30
FIELD(S): Music, Music Education, African-American Studies, Folklore, Performing Arts, Arts Management, Journalism, Radio/TV/Film

Scholarship is made on a competitive basis with consideration given to scholastic achievement, concentration of studies, and financial need. Applicant must have full-time enrollment status in a Chicago area college/university in at least their first year of undergraduate studies or a graduate program. Scholastic aptitude, extracurricular involvement, grade point average, and financial need are all considered.

Contact Blues Heaven Foundation, Inc. to receive an application between February and April.

2104—BROADCAST EDUCATION ASSOCI-ATION (Scholarships in Broadcasting)

1771 N Street NW
Washington DC 20036-2891
202/429-5354
E-mail: fweaver@nab.org
Internet: www.beaweb.org

AMOUNT: $1,250-$5,000
DEADLINE(S): JAN 14
FIELD(S): Broadcasting, Radio

For full-time juniors, seniors, and graduate students at BEA Member universities. Applicant should show evidence of superior academic performance and potential to become an outstanding electronic media professional. There should be compelling evidence that applicant possesses high integrity and a well-articulated sense of personal and professional responsibility. Awards exclusively for tuition, student fees, textbooks/supplies, and dorm room and board.

15 awards annually. Not renewable. Contact BEA or your campus faculty for an application no later than December 17th. See website for list of BEA member institutions.

2105—BUCKS COUNTY COURIER TIMES (Summer Internship Program)

8400 Route 13
Levittown PA 19057
215/949-4185, 215/949-4177
E-mail: cper@calkinsnewspapers.com

AMOUNT: $4,380 ($365/wk.)
DEADLINE(S): FEB 1
FIELD(S): News, Business, Feature Reporting

12-week internship for minority students at the *Bucks County Courier Times.* Must be US resident and have car. Financial need NOT a factor.

5 awards annually. Renewable. Contact Carolyn Per at above address for an application.

2106—BUENA VISTA COLLEGE NETWORK (Internships in Film Marketing)

3900 W. Alameda Ave.
Burbank CA 91505-4316
818/567-5000
E-mail: College_Network@
studio.disney.com

AMOUNT: Varies
DEADLINE(S): None
FIELD(S): Fields of study related to the motion picture industry, including marketing and promotion

Internships for full-time college students age 18 and up interested in a career in a facet of the motion picture industry. Must have unlimited access to computer with modem and transportation, be able to work 4-6 hours per week and 2-3 weekends per month. Attend film openings and sneak previews. Evaluate various aspects via an interactive computer system. Compensation ranges from $30 to $60/month. Possible school credit.

Access website by writing "Buena Vista College Network" from Yahoo. Available in most states and parts of Canada. Details, an interactive application, and e-mail access are located on website.

2107—CENTER FOR ENVIRONMENTAL JOURNALISM/UNIVERSITY OF COLORADO AT BOULDER (Ted Scripps Fellowship)

Univ. of Colorado
Macky 201, Campus Box 287
Boulder CO 80309-0287
303/492-0459
FAX: 303/492-0585
E-mail: ackland@spot.colorado.edu
Internet: campuspress.colorado.edu/
cej.html OR
www.scripps.com/foundation

AMOUNT: $27,000 for 9 months
DEADLINE(S): MAR 1
FIELD(S): Print or Broadcast Journalism

Five journalists will be selected to spend the academic year at the University of Colorado at Boulder studying environmental science and policy. For print or broadcast journalists with a minimum of five years professional experience. Can be general assignment reporters, editors, and freelancers.

5 awards annually. May also contact the Scripps Howard Foundation for details: P.O. Box 5380, Cincinnati, OH 45202.

2108—CENTRAL NEWSPAPERS, INC. (Pulliam Journalism Fellowships)

Russell B. Pulliam, Director
P.O. Box 145
Indianapolis IN 46206-0145
317/633-9206
FAX: 317/630-9549

AMOUNT: $5,500 stipend
DEADLINE(S): NOV 15 (early admissions); MAR 1 (final)
FIELD(S): Journalism

Open to recent graduates and to undergraduate seniors who will receive their bachelor's degree between August and June preceding fellowship. Award is for a 10-week work and study internship at one of CNI's newspapers in Indianapolis or Phoenix. Includes sessions with a writing coach and seminars with local and national journalists. Year 2000 Fellowship is June 12th-August 18th.

20 awards annually. Contact Russ Pulliam at CNI for an application.

2109—COX NEWSPAPERS, INC. (Cox Minority Journalism Scholarship)

P.O. Box 105720
Atlanta GA 30348
404/843-5000
FAX: 404/843-7928

AMOUNT: Varies
DEADLINE(S): FEB 19
FIELD(S): Newspaper Industry, Journalism

Open to high school seniors who are racial minorities (African-American, Native American, Asian, Latino) and US citizens, pursuing careers in the newspaper industry. Each year, a Cox-owned newspaper is selected to administer this scholarship; applicants must plan to attend one of the colleges specified by the newspaper.

Contact Cox Newspapers, Inc. for details.

2110—CUBAN AMERICAN NATIONAL FOUNDATION (The Mas Family Scholarships)

7300 NW 35 Terrace
Miami FL 33122
305/592-7768
FAX: 305/592-7889
E-mail canfnet.org
Internet: www.canfnet.org

AMOUNT: Individually negotiated
DEADLINE(S): MAR 15
FIELD(S): Engineering, Business,
  International Relations, Economics,
  Communications, Journalism

For Cuban-American students, graduates and undergraduates, born in Cuba or direct descendants of those who left Cuba. Must be in top 10% of high school class or maintain a 3.5 GPA in college.

10,000 awards/year. Recipients may re-apply for subsequent years. Financial need considered along with academic success, SAT and GRE scores, and leadership potential. Essays and proof of Cuban descent required.

2111—DAYTON FOUNDATION (Larry Fullerton Photojournalism Scholarship)

2100 Kettering Tower
Dayton OH 45423
513/222-0410

AMOUNT: Varies
DEADLINE(S): JAN 31
FIELD(S): Photojournalism

Open to Ohio residents who are full-time undergrad students at an Ohio college, junior college, or school with a structured curriculum and who plan to pursue a photojournalism career. Financial need and personal circumstances are considered.

Portfolio must be submitted following guidelines established by Ohio News Photographers Association. Contact the journalism/photojournalism department at your college for an application.

2112—DOW JONES NEWSPAPER FUND, INC. (Business Reporting Intern Program for Minority Sophomores & Juniors)

P.O. Box 300
Princeton NJ 08543
609/452-2820 or
800/DOWFUND
E-mail: dowfund@wsj.dowjones.com
Internet: www.dj.com/dowfund

AMOUNT: $1,000 + paid summer
  internship

DEADLINE(S): NOV 15
FIELD(S): Journalism, Business
  Reporting, Editing

Summer internships for college sophomores and juniors whose ethnic backgrounds are African-American, Hispanic, Asian, Native American/Eskimo, or Pacific Islanders who will work at daily newspapers as business reporters. Must demonstrate interest in similar career, though journalism major not required. Interns are paid and will attend a 2-week training program. Students returning to full-time studies will receive $1,000 scholarships.

12 awards annually. Applications available from August 15th to November 1st. Contact Dow Jones for an application.

2113—DOW JONES NEWSPAPER FUND, INC. (Newspaper Editing Intern/Scholarship Program)

P.O. Box 300
Princeton NJ 08543-0300
609/452-2820 or
800/DOWFUND
E-mail: dowfund@wsj.dowjones.com
Internet: www.dj.com/dowfund

AMOUNT: $1,000 + paid summer
  internship

DEADLINE(S): NOV 15
FIELD(S): Journalism, Editing

Summer internships for college juniors, seniors, and graduate students to work as copy editors at daily newspapers. Must demonstrate a commitment to a career in journalism, though journalism major not required. Interns are paid by the newspapers for which they work and attend a two-week training program paid for by the Newspaper Fund. Those returning to full-time studies will receive a $1,000 scholarship.

80 awards annually. Applications available from August 15th to November 1st. Contact Dow Jones for an application.

2114—DOW JONES NEWSPAPER FUND, INC. (Online Newspaper Editing Intern/Scholarship Program)

P.O. Box 300
Princeton NJ 08543-0300
609/452-2820
800/DOWFUND
E-mail: dowfund@wsj.dowjones.com
Internet: www.dj.com/dowfund

AMOUNT: $1,000 + paid summer
  internship

DEADLINE(S): NOV 15
FIELD(S): Journalism, Online Editing

Summer internships for college juniors, seniors, and graduate students to work as editors for online newspapers. Must demonstrate a commitment to a career in journalism, though journalism major not required. Interns are paid by the newspapers for which they work and attend a two-week training program paid for by the Newspaper Fund. Those returning to full-time studies will receive a $1,000 scholarship.

12 awards annually. Applications available from August 15th to November 1st. Contact Dow Jones for an application.

2115—DOW JONES NEWSPAPER FUND, INC. (Real-Time Financial News Service Intern/Scholarship Program)

P.O. Box 300
Princeton NJ 08543-0300
609/452-2820
800/DOWFUND
E-mail: dowfund@wsj.dowjones.com
Internet: www.dj.com/dowfund

AMOUNT: $1,000 + paid summer
  internship

DEADLINE(S): NOV 15
FIELD(S): Journalism, Financial
  Journalism, Editing

Summer internship for college juniors, seniors, and graduate students to work as editors and reporters for real-time financial news services. Must demonstrate a commitment to a similar career, though journalism major not required. Interns are paid by the news service for which they work and will attend a two-week training program paid for by the Newspaper Fund. Students returning to full-time studies will receive a $1,000 scholarship.

12 awards annually. Applications available from August 15th to November 1st. Contact Dow Jones for an application.

2116—DOW JONES NEWSPAPER FUND, INC. (Summer Workshops in Journalism for Minority High School Students)

P.O. Box 300
Princeton NJ 08543-0300
609/452-2820
800/DOWFUND
E-mail: dowfund@wsj.dowjones.com
Internet: www.dj.com/dowfund

AMOUNT: $1,000 + paid summer
  internship

DEADLINE(S): NOV 15
FIELD(S): Journalism

Offered at 35+ colleges around the US for high school students interested in journalism and whose ethnic backgrounds are African-American, Pacific Islander, American Indian/Eskimo, Asian, or Hispanic. Ten days of learning to write, report, design, and lay out a newspaper (free). The eight best writers throughout the US of an article relevant to youth will receive a $1,000 scholarship.

Contact Dow Jones for list of which colleges/states are participating.

2117—DULUTH NEWS-TRIBUNE (Native American Internships)

424 West First Street
Duluth MN 55802
800/456-8282 or 218/723-5368
E-mail: newstrib@duluth.infi.net

AMOUNT: $400/week for ten weeks
DEADLINE(S): MAR 30
FIELD(S): Journalism

Ten-week paid internships at the *Duluth News-Tribune*, Duluth, MN, for Native Americans with a journalism or mass communications interest or background.

Contact Holly Gruber at above location for details.

2118—DeVRY INC. (Dean's & Presidential Scholarships)

One Tower Lane
Oakbrook Terrace IL 60181-4624
800/733-3879, ext. 1935
630/571-7700
E-mail: outreach@devry.edu
Internet: www.devry.edu

AMOUNT: $1,000/term (Dean's); Full Tuition (Presidential)
DEADLINE(S): DEC 18; FEB 19; MAR 15
FIELD(S): Accounting, Business Admin, Computers, Electronics Engineering, Telecommunications Management, Electronics Technician

High school seniors who apply to any DeVry Institute are automatically considered for scholarships based on ACT/SAT scores. Presidential scholarships also consider community service, scholastic achievement, extracurricular activities, and essay. Must be US citizen or permanent resident.

Renewable if maintain 3.0 GPA. Number of Dean's Scholarships varies; 2 full-time Presidential awards annually. Contact Brenda Allen, Scholarship Coordinator, for an application.

2119—ELECTRONIC INDUSTRIES FOUNDATION (Scholarship Program)

2500 Wilson Blvd., Suite 210
Arlington VA 22201-3834
703/907-7408
E-mail: mvorac@eia.org

AMOUNT: $5,000
DEADLINE(S): FEB 1
FIELD(S): Electronics, Telecommunications, Electrical Engineering, Industrial Manufacturing, Industrial Engineering, Physics, Electromechanical Technology, Mechanical Applied Sciences

Open to students with disabilities (as defined by Americans with Disabilities Act) who are high school seniors accepted at an accredited four-year college/university. Must be US citizen pursuing studies that lead to career in design, manufacture, or provision of materials, components, products, and services for US high tech, electronics, and communications industries. Based on GPA, goals, activities, need, essay, and letters of recommendation.

Send self-addressed, stamped envelope to EIA for an application. Recipients notified by May 1st; awards paid directly to school.

2120—ESPN (Internship Programs)

Human Resources Dept., ESPN, Inc.
ESPN Plaza
Bristol CT 06010
No phone calls.
Internet: espnet.sportszone.com/editors/studios/97faq.html

AMOUNT: Paid Internships
DEADLINE(S): OCT 1; MAR 1; JUN 1
FIELD(S): Television Industry, Public Relations, Sports

12-week internships in the spring, summer, and fall for undergraduate juniors/seniors and graduate students. Some areas require weekend/evening hours and a strong knowledge of sports. Interns receive hourly wages and take part in many company-sponsored activities. ESPN does not provide housing for students, but we do try to assist in finding suitable living arrangements once selected.

To apply for internship programs, please send cover letter and resume to the above address. If applying to the Communications Dept., please also enclose writing samples and send attention to Diane Lamb.

2121—GEORGIA PRESS EDUCATIONAL FOUNDATION (Scholarships)

3066 Mercer University Dr., Ste. 200
Atlanta GA 30341-4137
770/454-6776
FAX: 770/454-6778
E-mail: mail@gapress.org
Internet: www.gapress.org

AMOUNT: Varies
DEADLINE(S): FEB 1
FIELD(S): Print Journalism

Open to Georgia residents who are high school seniors or undergraduate students attending or planning to attend a college/university in Georgia. Must have interest in print journalism and demonstrate financial need.

22 awards annually. Renewable. Contact Ali Turner for an application.

2122—HILLEL FOUNDATION FOR JEWISH CAMPUS LIFE (Steinhardt Jewish Campus Service Corps)

900 Hilgard Ave.
Los Angeles CA 20036
310/208-5561
E-mail: rweisman@hillel.org
Internet: www.hillel.org

AMOUNT: $19,000
DEADLINE(S): MAR 6
FIELD(S): Student Leadership

Open to college seniors and recent college graduates with leadership skills and ability to create dynamic and innovative engagement strategies designed to reach Jewish college students. Must possess commitment to service; willingness to use time, abilities, and talents to enhance lives of others; and dedication to strengthening Jewish identity among students with whom they work. Corps fellows get to know interests and concerns of students and build programs and activities to match.

100 awards annually. Renewable. See website or contact Rhonda Weisman for an application.

2123—HISPANIC COLLEGE FUND (Scholarships for Hispanic Students)

One Thomas Circle NW, Suite 375
Washington DC 20005
202/296-5400
FAX: 202/296-3774
E-mail: Hispanic.Fund@InternetMCI.com
Internet: http://hispanicfund.org

AMOUNT: Varies
DEADLINE(S): APR 15
FIELD(S): Most college majors leading to a career in business

Scholarships for deserving Hispanic college students pursuing a higher education in a major leading to a business career and who are full-time students at accredited institutions. US citizenship. Must demonstrate financial need.

Contact above organization for details or visit website for application.

2124—INSTITUTE FOR HUMANE STUDIES (Felix Morley Journalism Competition)

4084 University Drive, Suite 101
Fairfax VA 22030-6812
703/934-6920 or 800/697-8799
FAX: 703/352-7535
E-mail: ihs@gmu.edu
Internet: www.theihs.org
AMOUNT: $2,500 (1st prize)
DEADLINE(S): DEC 1
FIELD(S): Journalism/Writing

This competition awards cash prizes to outstanding young writers whose work demonstrates an appreciation of classical liberal principles (i.e., individual rights; their protection through private property, contract, and laws; voluntarism in human relations; and the self-ordering market, free trade, free migration, and peace). Must be full-time students and aged 25 or younger.

Must submit 3-5 articles, editorials, opinion pieces, essays, and reviews published in student newspapers or other periodicals between July 1st and December 1st. See website for complete rules or contact IHS for an entry form.

2125—INSTITUTE FOR HUMANE STUDIES (Humane Studies Fellowship)

4084 University Drive, Suite 101
Fairfax VA 22030-6812
703/934-6920 or 800/697-8799
FAX: 703/352-7535
E-mail: ihs@gmu.edu
Internet: www.theihs.org
AMOUNT: up to $12,000
DEADLINE(S): DEC 31
FIELD(S): Social Sciences, Law,
  Humanities, Jurisprudence, Journalism

Awards are for graduate and advanced undergraduate students pursuing degrees at any accredited domestic or foreign school. Based on academic performance, demonstrated interest in classical liberal

ideas, and potential to contribute to the advancement of a free society.

90 awards annually. Apply online or contact IHS for an application.

2126—INSTITUTE FOR HUMANE STUDIES (Summer Residential Program)

4084 University Drive, Suite 101
Fairfax VA 22030-6812
703/934-6920 or 800/697-8799
FAX: 703/352-7535
E-mail: ihs@gmu.edu
Internet: www.theihs.org
AMOUNT: All seminar fees: program
  cost, room/board, materials, and books
DEADLINE(S): MAR 1
FIELD(S): Social Sciences, Humanities,
  Law, Journalism, Public Policy,
  Education, Writing

For college students, recent graduates, and graduate students who share an interest in learning and exchanging ideas about the scope of individual rights. One-week and weekend seminars at various campus locations across the US.

Apply online or contact IHS for an application.

2127—INTERNATIONAL RADIO AND TELEVISION SOCIETY FOUNDATION (Summer Fellowship Program)

420 Lexington Ave., Suite 1714
New York NY 10170
212/867-6650
FAX: 212/867-6653
Internet: www.irts.org
AMOUNT: Housing, stipend, & travel
DEADLINE(S): NOV 12
FIELD(S): Broadcasting,
  Communications, Sales, Marketing

Nine-week summer fellowship program in New York City is open to outstanding full-time undergraduate juniors and seniors with a demonstrated interest in a career in communications. Financial need NOT a factor.

20-25 awards annually. Not renewable. See website or contact Maria DeLeon-Fisher at IRTS for an application.

2128—INVESTIGATIVE REPORTERS AND EDITORS (Minority Fellowships)

138 Neff Annex
Missouri School of Journalism
Columbia MO 65211
573/882-2042

FAX: 573/882-5431
E-mail: jourire@
  muccmail.missouri.edu
Internet: www.ire.org/resources/
  scholarship/fellowship
AMOUNT: Costs to attend various
  conferences
DEADLINE(S): NOV 1; DEC 15
  (depending on which event)
FIELD(S): Journalism: Investigative

Fellowships for minorities who are either journalism students or employed in the field of journalism to receive financial assistance to attend any of the various conferences of the above organization. Must send clips or audio or visual tape showing your talent as a potential journalist, reference letters, resume, and a goals essay.

Twenty-five fellowships. Application and details are on website and/or contact organization.

2129—INVESTIGATIVE REPORTERS AND EDITORS (Small News Organization Fellowships)

138 Neff Annex
Missouri School of Journalism
Columbia MO 65211
573/882-2042
FAX: 573/882-5431
E-mail: jourire@muccmail.missouri.edu
Internet: www.ire.org/resources/
  scholarship/smallnews/
AMOUNT: Costs to attend various
  conferences
DEADLINE(S): NOV 1; DEC 15
  (depending on which event)
FIELD(S): Journalism: Investigative

Fellowships for reporters producing solid investigative projects in small news organizations to receive financial assistance to attend any of the various conferences of the above organization.

See website and/or contact organization for further information.

2130—INVESTIGATIVE REPORTERS AND EDITORS (The Bennet Scholarship)

138 Neff Annex
Missouri School of Journalism
Columbia MO 65211
573/882-2042
FAX: 573/882-5431
E-mail: jourire@
  muccmail.missouri.edu
Internet: www.ire.org/resources/
  scholarship

AMOUNT: Cost to attend conference
DEADLINE(S): NOV 1
FIELD(S): Journalism: Investigative

Scholarship to send college students to a conference of the above organization. Must be residents of or attending college in Arkansas, Louisiana, Mississippi, and Oklahoma. Must send clips or audio or visual tape showing your talent as a potential journalist, reference letters, resume, and a goals essay.

Application and details are on website and/or contact organization.

2131—IOWA BROADCASTERS ASSOCIATION (Broadcast Scholarship)

P.O. Box 71186
Des Moines IA 50325
515/224-7237

AMOUNT: $3,000
DEADLINE(S): APR 15
FIELD(S): Broadcasting

Open to Iowa high school seniors planning to attend an Iowa college or university in the fall after graduation. Applicants must be Iowa residents planning to study broadcasting. Renewable.

Write to the above address for complete information.

2132—JAPANESE AMERICAN CITIZENS LEAGUE (Kyutaro & Yasuo Abiko Memorial Scholarship)

1765 Sutter Street
San Francisco CA 94115
415/921-5225
FAX: 415/931-4671
E-mail: jacl@jacl.org
Internet: www.jacl.org

AMOUNT: $1,000-$5,000
DEADLINE(S): APR 1
FIELD(S): Agriculture, Journalism

Open to JACL members and their children only. For undergraduate students with an interest in either journalism or agriculture and who are planning to attend a college, university, trade school, business school, or any other institution of higher learning. Must submit personal statement, letters of recommendation, and transcripts. Financial need NOT a factor.

For membership information or an application, send a self-addressed, stamped envelope to above address, stating your level of study. Applications available October 1st through March 20th; recipients notified in July.

2133—JEWISH VOCATIONAL SERVICE (Academic Scholarship Program)

One S. Franklin Street
Chicago IL 60606
312/357-4500
FAX: 312/855-3282
TTY: 312/855-3282
E-mail: jvschicago@jon.cjfny.org

AMOUNT: $5,000 (max.)
DEADLINE(S): MAR 1
FIELD(S): "Helping" Professions,
Mathematics, Engineering, Sciences,
Communications (at Univ IL only),
Law (certain schools in IL only)

Open to Jewish men and women legally domiciled in the greater Chicago metropolitan area, who are identified as having promise for significant contributions in their chosen careers, and are in need of financial assistance for full-time academic programs in above areas. Must have entered undergraduate junior year in career programs requiring no postgrad education, be in graduate/professional school, or be in a voc-tech training program. Interview required.

Renewable. Contact JVS for an application between December 1st and February 15th.

2134—JOHN BAYLISS BROADCAST FOUNDATION (Scholarship)

P.O. Box 221070
Carmel CA 93922
408/624-1536

AMOUNT: $2,500
DEADLINE(S): APR 23
FIELD(S): Radio Broadcasting

Open to undergrads in their junior or senior year and to graduate students who aspire to a career in radio. Applicants should have a 3.0 or better GPA. US citizen or legal resident.

Applications available after Nov. 1. Enclose a self-addressed, stamped envelope for more information. Transcript must be sent with completed application.

2135—JOHN M. WILL JOURNALISM SCHOLARSHIP FOUNDATION (Scholarship)

P.O. Box 290
Mobile AL 36601
334/405-1300

AMOUNT: $2,000-$3,500 (varies)
DEADLINE(S): MAR; APR
FIELD(S): Journalism

Open to full-time students majoring in journalism who are residents of the Alabama counties of Mobile, Baldwin,

Escambia, Clarke, Conecuh, Washington, or Monroe; the Florida counties of Santa Rosa or Escambia; or the Mississippi counties of Jackson or George.

Also open to persons currently employed in journalism who want to take journalism-related training as a full-time student at an accredited college. Write for complete information.

2136—KNTV TELEVISION (Minority Scholarship)

645 Park Ave.
San Jose CA 95110
408/286-1111 or 408/295-5461
Internet: www.kntv.com

AMOUNT: $1,000
DEADLINE(S): APR 15
FIELD(S): Television Broadcasting

Open to Black, Hispanic, Asian/Pacific Islander, or American Indian students who are residents of Santa Clara, Santa Cruz, Monterey, or San Benito counties (Calif.) and attend or plan to attend an accredited four-year institution in California to prepare for a career in television.

Must enroll in at least 12 semester units each semester. Considerations include interest in TV, financial need, community involvement, academics, and career aspirations. Write for complete information.

2137—LOS ANGELES PROFESSIONAL CHAPTER OF SOCIETY OF PROFESSIONAL JOURNALISTS (Bill Farr Scholarship)

SPJ/LA Scholarships
9951 Barcelona Lane
Cypress CA 90630-3759
Written inquiry

AMOUNT: up to $1,000
DEADLINE(S): MAR 1
FIELD(S): Journalism

Open to college juniors, seniors, or graduate students who attend school in Los Angeles, Orange, or Ventura counties in California and are preparing for a career in journalism.

Contact SPJ/LA at above address for an application. Applications available year-round.

2138—LOS ANGELES PROFESSIONAL CHAPTER OF SOCIETY OF PROFESSIONAL JOURNALISTS (Helen Johnson Scholarship)

SPJ/LA Scholarships
9951 Barcelona Lane
Cypress CA 90630-3759

Written inquiry

AMOUNT: up to $1,000

DEADLINE(S): MAR 1

FIELD(S): Broadcast Journalism

Open to college juniors, seniors, or graduate students who reside or attend school in Los Angeles, Ventura, or Orange counties in California and are preparing for a career in broadcast journalism.

Contact SPJ/LA at above address for an application. Applications available year-round.

2139—LOS ANGELES PROFESSIONAL CHAPTER OF SOCIETY OF PROFESSIONAL JOURNALISTS (Ken Inouye Scholarship)

SPJ/LA Scholarships
9951 Barcelona Lane
Cypress CA 90630-3759
Written inquiry

AMOUNT: up to $1,000

DEADLINE(S): MAR 1

FIELD(S): Journalism

Open to ethnic minority students who will be juniors, seniors, or graduate students the following year. Must reside or attend school in Los Angeles, Orange, or Ventura counties in California and be preparing for a career in journalism.

Contact SPJ/LA at above address for an application. Applications available year-round.

2140—LOS ANGELES PROFESSIONAL CHAPTER OF SOCIETY OF PROFESSIONAL JOURNALISTS (Carl Greenberg Prize)

SPJ/LA Scholarships
9951 Barcelona Lane
Cypress CA 90630-3759
Written inquiry

AMOUNT: up to $1,000

DEADLINE(S): MAR 1

FIELD(S): Journalism: Political or
    Investigative Reporting

Open to college juniors, seniors, or graduate students who reside or attend school in Los Angeles, Orange, or Ventura counties in California and are preparing for a career in journalism. Award based on the best published political or investigative report.

Contact SPJ/LA at above address for an application. Applications available year-round.

2141—MARIO MACHADO (American Honda/Mario J. Machado Scholarship)

5750 Briarcliff Road
Los Angeles CA 90068

213/460-4336
FAX: 213/460-4685

AMOUNT: $1,000

DEADLINE(S): Varies

FIELD(S): Communications/Journalism

For high school seniors who attend schools in Los Angeles or Orange county and who plan to pursue a career in communications and/or journalism. For students who would not be able to attend college without it.

Twelve awards per year. Must demonstrate financial need. Write to the above address for complete information.

2142—MEXICAN AMERICAN WOMEN'S NATIONAL ASSOCIATION (MANA) (Rita DiMartino Scholarship in Communication)

1725 K Street NW, Suite 105
Washington DC 20006
202/833-0060
FAX: 202/496-0588
E-mail: HerMANA2@aol.com

AMOUNT: Varies

DEADLINE(S): APR 1

FIELD(S): Communications

For Hispanic female students enrolled in undergraduate or graduate programs in communication at accredited colleges or universities. Must demonstrate financial need and academic achievement. Must be MANA member. There is a $10 application fee.

Send self-addressed, stamped envelope for application for membership and scholarship.

2143—MIAMI INTERNATIONAL PRESS CLUB (Scholarship Program)

c/o Laura Englebright
625 Candia Ave.
Florida Gables FL 33134
305/444-0345

AMOUNT: $500

DEADLINE(S): JUN 1

FIELD(S): Journalism, Communications

South Florida residents (Dade County) who are deserving high school seniors or college students are eligible for these undergraduate scholarships tenable at any accredited college or university.

Renewable. Contact the Scholarship Chair for an application.

2144—NATION INSTITUTE (I.F. Stone Award for Student Journalism)

33 Irving Place, 8th Fl.
New York NY 10003

212/209-5400
E-mail: instinfo@nationinstitute.org
Internet: www.thenation.com/
    institute/masur.htm

AMOUNT: $1,000 cash

DEADLINE(S): SEP 30

FIELD(S): Journalism

Contest is open to all undergraduate students enrolled in a US college. Articles may be submitted by writers themselves or nominated by editors of student publications or faculty members. While entries published in student publications are preferred, all will be considered provided they weren't written as part of regular coursework. Winning article will represent the most outstanding example of student journalism in the tradition of I.F. Stone. May submit 3 entries.

Contact Nation Institute for entry rules.

2145—NATION INSTITUTE (Nation Internship Program)

33 Irving Place, 8th Fl.
New York NY 10003
212/209-5400
E-mail: instinfo@nationinstitute.org
Internet: www.thenation.com/
    institute/masur.htm

AMOUNT: $150/week stipend

DEADLINE(S): NOV 12; MAR 17

FIELD(S): Journalism, Publishing

Full-time internships for college students and recent graduates interested in magazine journalism and publishing. Each applicant evaluated on basis of his/her resume, recommendations, and writing samples. All ages are welcome, though most interns have completed junior year of college. Possible housing and travel grants based on financial need. Internships take place in New York and Washington, DC. Must submit career goals, resume, recommendations, and writing samples.

16 awards annually. Contact Nation Institute for an application.

2146—NATIONAL ASSOCIATION OF BLACK JOURNALISTS (NABJ Scholarship Program)

3100 Taliaferro Hall
University of Maryland
College Park MD 20742-7717
301/405-8500
FAX: 301/405-8555
E-mail: nabj@jmail.umd.edu OR
nabj@nabj.org
Internet: nabj.org

AMOUNT: $2,500
DEADLINE(S): MAR 20
FIELD(S): Journalism: print, photography, radio, television OR planning a career in one of those fields

Minimum of 10 scholarships for African-American undergraduate or graduate students who are accepted to or enrolled in an accredited, four-year journalism program majoring in print, photo, radio, or television journalism OR planning a career in one of those fields. GPA of 2.5 or better (4.0 scale) is required. Also, 2 four-year scholarships are for African-American high school seniors planning to pursue education for a journalism career.

Access website for application forms or contact above location. Write for complete information.

2147—NATIONAL ASSOCIATION OF BLACK JOURNALISTS (NABJ Summer Internships)

3100 Taliaferro Hall
University of Maryland
College Park MD 20742-7717
301/405-8500
FAX: 301/405-8555
E-mail: nabj@jmail.umd.edu OR nabj@nabj.org
Internet: nabj.org

AMOUNT: Varies
DEADLINE(S): DEC 15
FIELD(S): Journalism: print, photography, radio, television OR planning a career in one of those fields

Internships for African-American sophomores, juniors, seniors, and graduate students committed to careers in journalism. Programs are throughout the US Minimum 2.5 GPA required.

Access website for application forms or contact above location for further information. For foreign or US students. Write for complete information.

2148—NATIONAL ASSOCIATION OF HISPANIC JOURNALISTS (NAHJ Scholarship Program)

1193 National Press Bldg.
Washington DC 20045-2100
202/662-7483
FAX: 202/662-7144
Internet: www.nahj.org

AMOUNT: $1,000-$2,000
DEADLINE(S): FEB 25
FIELD(S): Print/Broadcast Journalism, Photojournalism

Open to high school seniors, undergraduates, and graduate students who are committed to a career in print or broadcast journalism or photojournalism. Tenable at two- or four-year schools in the US and its territories. Hispanic ancestry NOT required.

See website or send a self-addressed, stamped envelope to Ana Carrion at NAHJ for an application.

2149—NATIONAL ASSOCIATION OF HISPANIC JOURNALISTS (Newhouse Scholarship Program)

1193 National Press Bldg.
Washington DC 20045-2100
202/662-7483
FAX: 202/662-7144
Internet: www.nahj.org

AMOUNT: $5,000
DEADLINE(S): FEB 25
FIELD(S): Print/Broadcast Journalism, Photojournalism

Open to undergraduate juniors and seniors and graduate students who are committed to pursuing a career in print or broadcast journalism or photojournalism. Awards tenable at accredited institutions in the US and its territories. It is not necessary to be a journalism or broadcast major, and Hispanic ancestry is NOT required.

See website or send a self-addressed, stamped envelope to Ana Carrion at NAHJ for an application.

2150—NATIONAL ASSOCIATION OF WATER COMPANIES—NEW JERSEY CHAPTER (Scholarship)

Elizabethtown Water Co.
600 South Ave.
Westfield NJ 07090
908/654-1234
FAX: 908/232-2719

AMOUNT: $2,500
DEADLINE(S): APR 1
FIELD(S): Business Administration, Biology, Chemistry, Engineering, Communications

For US citizens who have lived in NJ at least 5 years and plan a career in the investor-owned water utility industry in disciplines such as those above. Must be undergrad or graduate student in a 2- or 4-year NJ college or university.

GPA of 3.0 or better required. Contact Gail P. Brady for complete information.

2151—NATIONAL BROADCASTING SOCIETY (Alpha Epsilon Rho Scholarships)

P.O. Box 1058
St. Charles MO 63302-1058
888/NBS-1-COM, ext. 2000

AMOUNT: $500 to $1,000
DEADLINE(S): JAN 1
FIELD(S): Broadcasting

Open ONLY to active student members of NBS-AERho as nominated by local chapters.

Awards are renewable. Contact local NBS-AERho chapter for complete information.

2152—NATIONAL FEDERATION OF PRESS WOMEN (NFPW Communications Contest)

P.O. Box 5556
Arlington VA 22205
800/780-2715
FAX: 703/534-5751
E-mail: Presswomen@aol.com
Internet: www.nfpw.org

AMOUNT: Honorary awards + sweepstakes awards—$250 (1st place), $150 (2nd), $100 (3rd)
DEADLINE(S): FEB 20
FIELD(S): Communications (print/electronic media, public relations, advertising, etc.)

To improve professional skills by recognizing excellence in communicating. The "message" is important—how well it communicates, how it's directed to target audience, how well it achieves objectives. Entrants must be professional, student, or retired members of NFPW. Entries must have been published/broadcast from Nov.-Dec. of preceding year.

$15 entry fee. If you are already a member, contact your state affiliate where you pay dues. If you would like membership information, see website or contact NFPW Headquarters.

2153—NATIONAL FEDERATION OF PRESS WOMEN (NFPW High School Journalism Contest)

P.O. Box 5556
Arlington VA 22205
800/780-2715
FAX: 703/534-5751
E-mail: Presswomen@aol.com
Internet: www.nfpw.org

AMOUNT: $100 (1st prize); plaques for 2nd & 3rd places

DEADLINE(S): FEB 10

FIELD(S): Journalism (Editorial, News, Feature, Sports, Column, Feature Photo, Cartooning, Graphics, Single Page Layout, Review)

Entries must be the work of students enrolled in grades 9-12 during the current school year or the last semester of the senior year for students' work published after the current deadline. Submit two tear sheets (the entire page on which the article or graphic appears) for each entry.

Contact your NFPW state affiliate or see website for official rules.

2154—NATIONAL PRESS CLUB (Ellen Masin Persina Scholarship for Minorities in Journalism)

529 14th St. NW, 13th Fl.
Washington DC 20045
Internet: http://npc.press.org

AMOUNT: $2,500/yr. for 4 yrs.

DEADLINE(S): FEB 1

FIELD(S): Journalism (newspapers, radio, TV, magazine, trade paper)

Scholarships for talented minorities planning to pursue a career in journalism (see above fields). Must provide work samples, an essay, letters of recommendation, etc. Minimum 2.75 GPA required.

Access application from website or address above.

2155—NATIONAL PRESS PHOTOGRAPHERS FOUNDATION (Bob East Scholarship)

3200 Croasdaile Drive, Suite 306
Durham NC 27705
919/383-7246 or 800/289-6772
FAX: 919/383-7261
E-mail: nppa@mindspring.com
Internet: sunsite.unc.edu/nppa/scholarships

AMOUNT: $1,000

DEADLINE(S): MAR 1

FIELD(S): Photojournalism

Must be an undergraduate in the first three and one-half years of college or be planning to pursue graduate work (with proof of acceptance). Academic ability and financial need considered, but primary consideration is portfolio (6+ photos, photo-story counts as one; video journalists should submit a tape with 3 stories). Applicant's school must be in the US or Canada.

1 award annually. See website or contact NPPF for an application/specific details.

2156—NATIONAL PRESS PHOTOGRAPHERS FOUNDATION (Joseph Ehrenreich Scholarships)

3200 Croasdaile Drive, Suite 306
Durham NC 27705
919/383-7246 or 800/289-6772
FAX: 919/383-7261
E-mail: nppa@mindspring.com
Internet: sunsite.unc.edu/nppa/scholarships

AMOUNT: $1,000

DEADLINE(S): MAR 1

FIELD(S): Photojournalism

Must have completed one year at a recognized four-year college/university having courses in photojournalism leading to a bachelor's degree. Must also have at least one-half year of undergraduate schooling remaining at time of award. Aimed at those with journalism potential with little opportunity and great need. Must include portfolio (6+ photos, photo-story counts as one; video journalists must submit tape with 3 stories). Applicant's school must be in US or Canada.

5 awards annually. See website or contact NPPF for an application/specific details.

2157—NATIONAL PRESS PHOTOGRAPHERS FOUNDATION (NPPF Still Scholarship)

3200 Croasdaile Drive, Suite 306
Durham NC 27705
919/383-7246 or 800/289-6772
FAX: 919/383-7261
E-mail: nppa@mindspring.com
Internet: sunsite.unc.edu/nppa/scholarships

AMOUNT: $1,000

DEADLINE(S): MAR 1

FIELD(S): Photojournalism

Must have completed one year at a recognized four-year college/university having courses in photojournalism leading to a bachelor's degree. Must also have at least one-half year of undergraduate schooling remaining at time of award. Aimed at those with journalism potential but with little opportunity and great need. Must submit portfolio of 6+ photos (picture-story counts as one); or for video journalists, tape with 3 stories. Applicant's school must be in US or Canada.

See website or contact NPPF for an application/specific details.

2158—NATIONAL PRESS PHOTOGRAPHERS FOUNDATION (NPPF Television News Scholarship)

3200 Croasdaile Drive, Suite 306
Durham NC 27705
919/383-7246 or 800/289-6772
FAX: 919/383-7261
E-mail: nppa@mindspring.com
Internet: sunsite.unc.edu/nppa/scholarships

AMOUNT: $1,000

DEADLINE(S): MAR 1

FIELD(S): TV News Photojournalism

For students with potential but little opportunity and great need. Must be enrolled in recognized 4-year college/university in US or Canada with courses in TV News Photojournalism leading to bachelor's degree. Must be junior or senior at time award is given. Entry should include video tape with examples of work—no more than 3 complete stories (6 minutes total) with voice narration and natural sound. Letter from professor/advisor and biographical sketch with goals required.

1 award annually. See website or contact NPPF for an application/more information.

2159—NATIONAL PRESS PHOTOGRAPHERS FOUNDATION (Reid Blackburn Scholarship)

3200 Croasdaile Drive, Suite 306
Durham NC 27705
919/383-7246 or 800/289-6772
FAX: 919/383-7261
E-mail: nppa@mindspring.com
Internet: sunsite.unc.edu/nppa/scholarships

AMOUNT: $1,000

DEADLINE(S): MAR 1

FIELD(S): Photojournalism

Must have completed one year at a recognized four-year college/university having courses in photojournalism leading towards a bachelor's degree. Must also have at least one-half year of undergraduate schooling remaining at time of award. Academic ability, aptitude, and financial need are considered. Applicant's school must be in the US or Canada. Portfolio required with entry (6+ photos, picture-story counts as one; video journalists should send a tape of 3 stories).

1 award annually. See website or contact NPPF for an application/specific details.

2160—NATIONAL PRESS PHOTOGRA-PHERS FOUNDATION, KAPPA ALPHA MU (College Photographer of the Year Competition)

Univ. MO School of Journalism
105 Lee Hills Hall
Columbia MO 65211
573/882-4442
E-mail: info@cpoy.org
Internet: www.cpoy.org

AMOUNT: $250-$1,000 +
    plaque/certificate & film
DEADLINE(S): MAR 31
FIELD(S): Photojournalism

Undergraduate or graduate students who have NOT worked two years or more as full-time professional photographers may enter. All entries must have been taken or published for the first time between March 1st & Feb 28th of the current year. First prize includes a 3-month paid internship at the *Dallas Morning News* and a camera as well as above-mentioned prizes. You may enter as many pictures as you like, and there is no entry fee.

See website or contact CPOY Coordinator Catherine Mohesky or CPOY Director David Rees for rules and entry form.

2161—NATIONAL RIGHT TO WORK COMMITTEE (William B. Ruggles Journalism Scholarship)

5211 Port Royal Road, Suite 510
Springfield VA 22151
703/321-9606

AMOUNT: $2,000
DEADLINE(S): MAR 31
FIELD(S): Journalism

Scholarships are open to undergraduate and graduate students majoring in journalism at accredited US institutions of higher learning who exemplify the dedication to principle and high journalistic standards of the late William B. Ruggles.

Write for complete information.

2162—NATIONAL URBAN LEAGUE (Reginald K. Brack, Jr. NULITES Scholarship)

120 Wall Street
New York NY 10005
212/558-5373
Internet: www.nul.org

AMOUNT: Varies
DEADLINE(S): Varies
FIELD(S): Communications, Journalism,
    Publishing, Public Relations,
    Broadcasting

For NULITES graduating from high school with an interest in communications and former NULITES currently in their freshman or sophomore year of college majoring in communications, journalism, or publishing. Must maintain a minimum 3.0 GPA. Scholarships are based on need, merit, community service, and academic achievement. Letter of recommendation from an Urban League affiliate CEO and/or a NULITES Advisor/Youth Development Director/Education Director is required.

Contact your local Urban League or the National Urban League for an application.

2163—NATIVE AMERICAN JOURNALISTS ASSOCIATION (NAJA Scholarships and Internships)

1433 East Franklin Ave., Suite 11
Minneapolis MN 55404
612/874-8833
FAX: 612/874-9007
E-mail: najaut@aol.com
Internet: www.medill.nwu.edu/naja/

AMOUNT: Varies
DEADLINE(S): MAR 31
FIELD(S): Journalism/Communication

Various scholarships and internships in journalism for Native American journalists and students.

Access website or send self-addressed, stamped envelope (SASE) for details.

2164—NEW YORK FINANCIAL WRITERS' ASSOCIATION (Scholarship Program)

P.O. Box 20281
Greeley Square Station
New York NY 10001-0003
800/533-7551

AMOUNT: $3,000
DEADLINE(S): MAR
FIELD(S): Financial Journalism

Open to undergraduate and graduate students enrolled in an accredited college or university in metropolitan New York City and are pursuing a course of study leading to a financial or business journalism career.

Contact NYFWA for an application.

2165—NEW YORK STATE SENATE (Legislative Fellows Program; R. J. Roth Journalism Fellowship; R. A. Wiebe Public Service Fellowship)

NYS Senate Student Programs Office
90 South Swan Street, Room 401
Albany NY 12247

518/455-2611
FAX: 518/432-5470
E-mail: students@senate.state.ny.us

AMOUNT: $25,000 stipend (not a
    scholarship)
DEADLINE(S): MAY (first Friday)
FIELD(S): Political Science, Government,
    Public Service, Journalism, Public
    Relations

One-year programs for US citizens who are grad students and residents of New York state or enrolled in accredited programs in New York state. Fellows work as regular legislative staff members of the office to which they are assigned. The Roth Fellowship is for communications/journalism majors, and undergrads may be considered for this program.

14 fellowships per year. Fellowships take place at the New York State Legislative Office. Write for complete information.

2166—NEW YORK STATE THEATRE INSTITUTE (Internships in Theatrical Production)

155 River Street
Troy NY 12180
518/274-3573
E-mail: nysti@crisny.org
Internet: www.crisny.org/not-for-
    profit/nysti/int.htm

AMOUNT: None
DEADLINE(S): None
FIELD(S): Fields of study related to
    theatrical production, including box
    office and PR

Internships for college students, high school seniors, and educators-in-residence interested in developing skills in above fields. Unpaid, but college credit is earned. Located at Russell Sage College in Troy, NY. Gain experience in box office, costumes, education, electrics, music, stage management, scenery, properties, performance, and public relations. Interns come from all over the world.

Must be associated with an accredited institution. See website for more information. Call Ms. Arlene Leff, Intern Director, at above location. Include your postal mailing address.

2167—ORGANIZATION OF CHINESE AMERICANS (Journalist Award)

1001 Connecticut Avenue NW
Suite 707
Washington DC 20036
202/223-5500
FAX: 202/296-0540

E-mail: oca@ari.net
Internet: www2.ari.net/oca/html/
awards.html
AMOUNT: $500 (1st prize); $300 (2nd);
$200 (3rd)
DEADLINE(S): MAY 1
FIELD(S): Journalism

Given to the journalist with the most enlightening article or series of articles concerning Chinese Americans and/or Asian Americans in English or Chinese. Judged on flow of article, completeness/coverage, accuracy, thoroughness, sensitivity, and depth of understanding of issues concerning Asian Americans.

5 copies of a resume and copies of one or two articles should be sent to the above address.

2168—OUTDOOR WRITERS ASSOCIATION OF AMERICA (Bodie McDowell Scholarship Program)

27 Fort Missoula Rd., Suite 1
Missoula MT 59804
406/728-7434
AMOUNT: $2,000-$3,000
DEADLINE(S): FEB
FIELD(S): Outdoor Communications/
Journalism

This scholarship is open to undergraduate and graduate students interested in writing about outdoor activities, not including organized sports. Acceptable topics include hiking, backpacking, climbing, etc. Availability varies with school participation.

Send self-addressed, stamped envelope to OWAA for an application.

2169—PENNSYLVANIA WOMEN'S PRESS ASSOCIATION (Scholarship)

P.O. Box 152
Sharpsville PA 16150
Written inquiry
Internet: www.regiononline.com/
~pwpa/
AMOUNT: At least $750
DEADLINE(S): APR 20
FIELD(S): Print Journalism

Scholarship for Pennsylvania residents majoring in print journalism in a four-year or graduate-level program in a Pennsylvania college or university. Must be a junior, senior, or graduate. Selection based on proven journalistic ability, dedication to journalism, and general merit.

Write a 500-word essay summarizing your interest in journalism, your career plans, and any other information on why you should receive this scholarship. You may include a statement of financial need. Send transcript copy, clippings of published work (photocopies ok), and list of your brothers and sisters, their ages and educational status. Send to Teresa Spatara at above address.

2170—PEORIA JOURNAL STAR (Newspaper in Education Program)

1 News Plaza
Peoria IL 61643
E-mail: nie@pjstar.com
AMOUNT: $1,000/year for 4 years
DEADLINE(S): Varies
FIELD(S): Reporting, Editing,
Photography, Graphic Design,
Marketing

For Illinois residents only. Open to high school seniors who reside in Bureau, Fulton, Henderson, Knox, LaSalle, Marshall-Putnam, Mason, McDonough, Peoria, Schuyler, Stark, Tazewell, Warren, or Woodford counties in Illinois. Funds can be used for any educational expense, including housing. Financial need is NOT a factor.

Write for complete information, application, and deadline (which is usually in April or May).

2171—PHILADELPHIA COLLEGE OF BIBLE (Scholarships, Grants, and Loans)

Financial Aid Dept.
200 Manor Ave.
Langhorne PA 19047
800/366-0049
Internet: www.pcb.edu
AMOUNT: Varies
DEADLINE(S): Varies
FIELD(S): Fields of study relating to
Christian education

Various scholarships, loans, and grants are available to students attending this undergraduate Bible college in Philadelphia, PA. High school seniors, transfer students, and others may apply. Some programs are for students with outstanding academic achievement, musical talent, or leadership skills. Some are for dependents of Christian workers, missionaries, or alumni. Some are based on financial need.

Access website for details and/or send SASE to school for further information.

2172—PHILLIPS FOUNDATION (Journalism Fellowship Program)

7811 Montrose Road, Suite 100
Potomac MD 208
301/340-2100
FAX: 301/424-0245
Internet: www.phillips.com
AMOUNT: $50,000 (full-time); $25,000
(part-time)
DEADLINE(S): MAR 1
FIELD(S): Journalism

For working print journalists with less than five years of professional experience to complete a one-year writing project supportive of American culture and a free society. Subject matter changes each year.

1 full-time and 2 part-time awards annually. Contact Phillips Foundation for an application.

2173—PRESS CLUB OF DALLAS FOUNDATION (Scholarship)

400 N. Olive
Dallas TX 75201
214/740-9988
AMOUNT: $1,000-$3,000
DEADLINE(S): APR 15
FIELD(S): Journalism and Public
Relations

Open to students who are at least sophomore level in undergraduate studies or working towards a masters degree in the above fields in a Texas college or university. This scholarship is renewable by re-application.

Write to Carol Wortham at the above address for complete information.

2174—QUILL & SCROLL (Edward J. Nell Memorial Scholarship)

Univ. of Iowa School of Journalism &
Mass Communications
Iowa City IA 52242-1528
319/335-5795
AMOUNT: $500
DEADLINE(S): MAY 10
FIELD(S): Journalism

Open to high school seniors who are winners in the National Writing/Photo Contest (deadline Feb. 5th) or Yearbook Excellence Contest (deadline Nov. 1st) sponsored by Quill & Scroll and who plan to enroll in an accredited journalism program. Must be US citizen or legal resident.

Contact your journalism teacher or Quill & Scroll for contest information.

2175—RADIO AND TELEVISION NEWS DIRECTORS FOUNDATION (George Foreman Tribute to Lyndon B. Johnson Scholarship)

1000 Connecticut Ave. NW
Suite 615
Washington DC 20036-5302
202/467-5218
FAX: 202/223-4007
E-mail: danib@rtndf.org
Internet: www.rtndf.org

AMOUNT: $6,000
DEADLINE(S): MAY 3
FIELD(S): Broadcast/Cable Journalism

Any full-time graduate or undergraduate with at least one full year of college remaining may apply. Must be officially enrolled in University of Texas in Austin, be in good standing, and be US citizen. Entry must include 1-3 examples (less than 15 minutes) showing skills on audio/VHS tape, accompanied by scripts and brief statement describing your role in stories, who worked on each one, and what they did. Letter of endorsement and statement explaining career goals required.

1 award annually. See website or contact Dani Browne at RTNDF for an application.

2176—RADIO AND TELEVISION NEWS DIRECTORS FOUNDATION (RTNDF Electronic Journalism Scholarships)

1000 Connecticut Ave. NW
Suite 615
Washington DC 20036-5302
202/467-5218
FAX: 202/223-4007
E-mail: danib@rtndf.org
Internet: www.rtndf.org

AMOUNT: $1,000-$5,000
DEADLINE(S): MAR 2
FIELD(S): Radio/Television Journalism

Several awards for full-time undergraduate and graduate students who are officially enrolled in college and are in good standing. Applicants must have at least one full year of college remaining. All scholarships are paid in semi-annual installments for one year of study. Entries must include 1-3 examples (less than 15 minutes) showing skills on VHS or audio tape, brief description of your role in each story, statement explaining career goals, and letter of endorsement.

15 awards annually. See website or contact Dani Browne at RTNDF for an application.

2177—RADIO AND TELEVISION NEWS DIRECTORS FOUNDATION (RTNDF Minority News Management Internships)

1000 Connecticut Ave. NW
Suite 615
Washington DC 20036-5302
202/467-5218
FAX: 202/223-4007
E-mail: danib@rtndf.org
Internet: www.rtndf.org

AMOUNT: $1,000/month
DEADLINE(S): MAR 1
FIELD(S): Radio/Television Journalism
News Management

Junior or senior undergraduate or graduate minority students (African-American, Asian, Hispanic, Native American) may apply. The 3-month summer internship is full-time for 12 weeks, beginning June 1st. Interns are responsible for own housing/living expenses. Will be assigned to a supervisor and receive hands-on experience in day-to-day management of electronic news. Entry-level internships also available to recent graduates. Essay and letter of endorsement required.

See website or contact Dani Browne at RTNDF for an application.

2178—RADIO AND TELEVISION NEWS DIRECTORS FOUNDATION (RTNDF Fellowships)

1000 Connecticut Ave. NW
Suite 615
Washington DC 20036-5302
202/467-5218
FAX: 202/223-4007
E-mail: danib@rtndf.org
Internet: www.rtndf.org

AMOUNT: $1,000-$2,000
DEADLINE(S): APR 1
FIELD(S): Electronic Journalism

Awards for young journalists in radio or television with 10 years or less experience. Cover letter describing reasons for seeking fellowship and how you intend to use award, letter of recommendation from your news director or general manager, and a script and standard audio cassette/video tape (VHS) of your best work (relevant to fellowship to which you are applying) that is less than 15 minutes are required. Must be US citizen.

6 awards annually. See website or contact Dani Browne at RTNDF for an application.

2179—ROSE HILL COLLEGE (Louella Robinson Memorial Scholarship)

P.O. Box 3126
Aiken SC 29802-3126
800/684-3769
FAX: 803/641-0240
E-mail: rosehill@.edu
Internet: www.rosehill.edu

AMOUNT: $10,000/yr. for four years
DEADLINE(S): Varies
FIELD(S): Liberal Arts and Humanities
curricula

For undergraduate residents of Indian River County, Florida, to attend Rose Hill College in Aiken, South Carolina. The school offers a liberal arts education and follows the Great Books curriculum, a program of reading and seminars.

1 annual award. Applicants must meet entry requirements of RHC. Contact above location for details.

2180—ROSE HILL COLLEGE (Scholarships for Children of Eastern Orthodox Priests/Deacons)

P.O. Box 3126
Aiken SC 29802-3126
800/684-3769
FAX: 803/641-0240
E-mail: rosehill@edu
Internet: www.rosehill.edu

AMOUNT: Full scholarship: $10,000/yr.
for four years
DEADLINE(S): Varies
FIELD(S): Liberal Arts and Humanities
curricula

For undergraduates who are children of Eastern Orthodox Christian priests or deacons to attend Rose Hill College in Aiken, South Carolina. The school offers a liberal arts education and follows the Great Books curriculum, a program of reading and seminars.

6-10 annual awards. Applicants must meet entry requirements of RHC. Contact above location for details.

2181—ROSE HILL COLLEGE (Scholarships for the Homeschooled)

P.O. Box 3126
Aiken SC 29802-3126
800/684-3769
FAX: 803/641-0240
E-mail: rosehill@rosehill.edu
Internet: www.resehill.edu

AMOUNT: Full scholarship: $10,000/yr. for four years
DEADLINE(S): Varies
FIELD(S): Liberal Arts and Humanities curricula

For undergraduates who have been homeschooled for three of the last five years of their high school education. For use at Rose Hill College in Aiken, South Carolina. The school offers a liberal arts education and follows the Great Books curriculum, a program of reading and seminars. Scholarships will be awarded primarily on the basis of an essay that the student will be asked to write.

4 annual awards. Applicants must meet entry requirements of RHC. Contact above location for details.

2182—SAN FRANCISCO CHRONICLE (Chronicle Publishing Company Scholarship)

901 Mission Street
San Francisco CA 94103-2988
415/777-7180
FAX: 415/495-3843
E-mail: logansa@sfgate.com
Internet: www.sfgate.com

AMOUNT: $1,500 + summer job
DEADLINE(S): FEB 28
FIELD(S): Print or Broadcast Journalism

Must be a Bay Area high school senior. Two programs: KRON-TV4 scholarship and summer entry-level job, and *SF Chronicle* scholarship and summer copy clerk job. Official transcripts and letters of recommendation required; samples of work optional. Must answer essay question (up to 500 words, typed, double-spaced), "If you were given the opportunity to cover a story for NewsCenter 4 or for the *SF Chronicle*, what would it be and why?" Financial need NOT a factor.

2 awards annually. Contact Sandy Logan at the *SF Chronicle* for an application.

2183—SCRIPPS HOWARD FOUNDATION (Robert P. Scripps Graphic Arts Scholarships)

312 Walnut Street, P.O. Box 5380
Cincinnati OH 45201-5380
513/977-3847
FAX: 513/977-3800
E-mail: cottingham@scripps.com
Internet: www.scripps.com/foundation

AMOUNT: Varies
DEADLINE(S): Varies
FIELD(S): Newspaper Operations Management

Students must be attending the University of Rochester (NY) and majoring in newspaper operations management.

5 awards annually. Applications are available at the university.

2184—SCRIPPS HOWARD FOUNDATION (Ted Scripps Scholarships & Lecture)

312 Walnut Street, P.O. Box 5380
Cincinnati OH 45201-5380
513/977-3847
FAX: 513/977-3800
E-mail: cottingham@scripps.com
Internet: www.scripps.com/foundation

AMOUNT: $3,000 + medal
DEADLINE(S): Varies
FIELD(S): Journalism

Students must be attending the University of Nevada at Reno and majoring in journalism.

4 awards annually. Applications are available at the university.

2185—SOCIETY FOR TECHNICAL COMMUNICATION (Undergraduate Scholarships)

901 N. Stuart St., Suite 904
Arlington VA 22203-1854
703/522-4114
FAX: 703/522-2075
E-mail: stc@stc-va.org
Internet: www.stc-va.org/scholarships.html

AMOUNT: $2,500
DEADLINE(S): FEB 15
FIELD(S): Technical Communication

Open to full-time undergraduate students who have completed at least one year of study and are enrolled in an accredited 2- or 4-year degree program for career in any area of technical communication: technical writing, editing, graphic design, multimedia art, etc.

Awards tenable at recognized colleges and universities in US and Canada. 14 awards per year—7 undergraduate and 7 graduate. See website and/or write for complete information.

2186—SOCIETY OF BROADCAST ENGINEERS (Harold Ennes Scholarship Fund)

8445 Keystone Crossing, Suite 140
Indianapolis IN 46240-2454
317/253-1640

AMOUNT: $1,000
DEADLINE(S): JUL 1
FIELD(S): Broadcasting

Open to undergraduate students interested in a career in broadcasting. Two references from SBE members are needed to confirm eligibility. Submit a statement of purpose and a brief biography.

Send self-addressed, stamped envelope for application and complete information.

2187—SOCIETY OF PROFESSIONAL JOURNALISTS (Mark of Excellence Awards Competition)

16 South Jackson Street
Greencastle IN 46135-1514
765/653-3333
FAX: 765/653-4631
E-mail: spj@link2000.net
Internet: http://spj.org/prodevelopment/MOE97/moe97/rules.htm

AMOUNT: Varies
DEADLINE(S): JAN 31
FIELD(S): All fields of study

A competition for professional journalists, though journalists may be studying in any field. Awards are for print or broadcast journalism.

See website for details.

2188—SOCIETY OF SATELLITE PROFESSIONALS INTERNATIONAL (SSPI Scholarships)

225 Reinekers Lane, Suite 600
Alexandria VA 22314
703/857-3717
FAX: 703/857-6335
E-mail: neworbit@aol.com
Internet: www.sspi.org

AMOUNT: $1,500 to $4,000
DEADLINE(S): DEC 1
FIELD(S): Satellites as related to communications, domestic and international telecommunications policy, remote sensing, journalism, law, meteorology, energy, navigation, business, government, and broadcasting services

Various scholarships for students studying in the above fields.

Access website for details and applications or send a self-addressed, stamped envelope (SASE) for a complete listing.

2189—SOIL AND WATER CONSERVATION SOCIETY (SWCS Internships)

7515 NE Ankeny Road
Ankeny IA 50021-9764

515/289-2331 or 800/THE-SOIL
FAX: 515/289-1227
E-mail: charliep@swcs.org
Internet: www.swcs.org

AMOUNT: Varies—most are uncompensated
DEADLINE(S): Varies
FIELD(S): Journalism, Marketing, Database Management, Meeting Planning, Public Policy Research, Environmental Education, Landscape Architecture

Internships for undergraduates and graduates to gain experience in the above fields as they relate to soil and water conservation issues. Internship openings vary through the year in duration, compensation, and objective. SWCS will coordinate particulars with your academic advisor.

Contact SWCS for internship availability at any time during the year or see website for jobs page.

2190—SONOMA COUNTY PRESS CLUB (Scholarship)

P.O. Box 4692
Santa Rosa CA 95402
Written inquiry

AMOUNT: $2,000
DEADLINE(S): APR 10
FIELD(S): Journalism

Open to Sonoma County (CA) high school seniors or graduates or students attending either Santa Rosa Junior College or Sonoma State University.

Write for complete information

2191—SPACE COAST CREDIT UNION (Two-Year Scholarships)

Marketing Dept.
P.O. Box 2470
Melbourne FL 32902
Internet: www.sccu.com/scholarship/

AMOUNT: $750/year, two years; $1,000 bonus if go on for Bachelors
DEADLINE(S): APR 15
FIELD(S): Math, Economics, Science, Computer Science, Marketing, Journalism, Political Science

Must be graduating from a high school in Brevard, Volusia, Flagler, or Indian River counties, be a member of SCCU, have a minimum 3.0 GPA, planning to attend a two-year Florida institution of higher education for an associates degree, and be willing to write a 200-word essay on the topic "Why credit unions are valuable to society."

4 annual awards. Students going on to complete a four-year degree could be eligi-

ble for a bonus scholarship of $1,000 for the next two years. For membership information or an application, see our web page or write to the above address.

2192—SPORTS JOURNALISM INSTITUTE (Scholarships/Internships)

Sports Illustrated
1271 Avenue of the Americas
New York NY 10020-1393
212/522-6407
FAX: 212/522-4543
E-mail: sandrite@aol.com

AMOUNT: $500 for 6-week internship
DEADLINE(S): JAN (date varies yearly)
FIELD(S): Print journalism with sports emphasis

10 six-week scholarships for college juniors to support internships in sports journalism. Women and minorities are especially encouraged to apply.

Contact Sandy Baily at above location for details.

2193—THE ART INSTITUTES INTERNATIONAL (Evelyn Keedy Memorial Scholarship)

300 Sixth Ave., Suite 800
Pittsburgh PA 15222-2598
412/562-9800
FAX: 412/562-9802
E-mail: webadmin@aii.edu
Internet: www.aii.edu

AMOUNT: 2 years full tuition
DEADLINE(S): MAY 1
FIELD(S): Various fields in the creative and applied arts: video production, broadcasting, culinary arts, fashion design, website administration, etc.

Scholarships at 12 different locations nationwide in various fields described above. For graduating high school seniors admitted to an Arts Institutes International School, the New York Restaurant School, or NCPT. Transcripts, letters of recommendation, and resume must be submitted with application.

See website or contact AII for more information.

2194—THE CARTER CENTER MENTAL HEALTH PROGRAM (Rosalynn Carter Fellowships for Mental Health Journalism)

One Copenhill
453 Freedom Parkway
Atlanta GA 30307

404/420-5165
FAX: 404/420-5158
E-mail: jgates@emory.edu
Internet: http://www.emory.edu/CARTER_CENTER

AMOUNT: $10,000 + 2 trips to Center
DEADLINE(S): MAY 1
FIELD(S): Print or Broadcast Journalism

5 one-year fellowships for journalists to pursue an individual project related to mental health or mental illness. Must have at least two years of experience in print or broadcast journalism. Fellows are matched with a member of the Advisory Board for mentoring during their fellowship year.

Call or write for application information.

2195—THE CHRONICLE PUBLISHING COMPANY (Scholarship)

P.O. Box 3412
San Francisco CA 94119
Written request

AMOUNT: $1,500
DEADLINE(S): FEB 28
FIELD(S): Journalism

For college-bound high school seniors who reside in the San Francisco Bay Area and plan a career in broadcast or print journalism. Each scholarship includes a 10-week summer job at KRON-TV4 or the *San Francisco Chronicle*.

Contact the company for details.

2196—THE FUND FOR AMERICAN STUDIES (Institutes on Political Journalism; Business & Government Affairs & Comparative Political & Economic Systems)

1526 18th Street NW
Washington DC 20036
202/986-0384 or 800/741-6964
Internet: http://www.dcinternships.com

AMOUNT: Up to $2,975
DEADLINE(S): JAN 31 (early decision); MAR 15 (general application deadline)
FIELD(S): Political Science, Economics, Journalism, Business Administration

The Fund for American Studies, in conjunction with Georgetown University, sponsors summer institutes that include internships, courses for credit, site briefings, and dialogues with policy leaders. Scholarships are available to sophomores and juniors to cover the cost of the program.

Approx 100 awards per year. For Fund's programs only. Call, check website, or write for complete information.

2197—THE FUND FOR INVESTIGATIVE JOURNALISM, INC. (Grants for Journalists)

5120 Kenwood Drive
Annandale VA 22003
703/750-3849
E-mail: fundfij@aol.com
Internet: http://fij.org

AMOUNT: $500 and up
DEADLINE(S): JUN 1; NOV 1
FIELD(S): Journalism

Grants for journalists working outside the protection and backing of major news organizations. Limited to journalists seeking help for investigative pieces involving corruption, malfeasance, incompetence, and societal ills in general as well as for media criticism. No application form. Write a letter outlining the story, what he or she expects to prove, how this will be done, and the sources for the proof.

Include a letter of commitment from an editor or publisher to consider publishing or broadcasting the final product. Check website for details.

2198—THE MODESTO BEE (Scholarship Program for Minority Journalism Students)

P.O. Box 5256
Modesto CA 95352
Written inquiries

AMOUNT: $500
DEADLINE(S): APR 1
FIELD(S): Journalism

Open to seniors graduating from a high school in the *Modesto Bee's* home delivery circulation area. Applicants must have at least a 2.5 GPA and a minority affiliation.

Write to the above address for complete information.

2199—THE NATIONAL ITALIAN AMERI-CAN FOUNDATION (Communications Scholarship)

1860 19th Street NW
Washington DC 20009
202/530-5315

AMOUNT: $2,500
DEADLINE(S): MAY 31
FIELD(S): Journalism or Communications majors

For students of Italian family heritage majoring in journalism or communications. Write a 2- to 3-page typed essay on a family member or a personality you consider: "An Italian American Hero." Also, please submit an essay of your best work.

2 awards given. Also considered are academic merit, financial need, and community service. Write for application and details.

2200—THE PUBLIC RELATIONS SOCIETY OF AMERICA (Multicultural Affairs Scholarship)

33 Irving Place
New York NY 10003-2376
212/995-2230
FAX: 212/995-0757
TDD: 212/254-3464

AMOUNT: $1,500
DEADLINE(S): APR 11
FIELD(S): Communications Studies/ Public Relations

For students whose ethnic backgrounds are African-American, Hispanic, Asian, Native American, Alaskan Native, or Pacific Islander interested in practicing in the career of public relations. Must be a full-time undergraduate student at an accredited four-year college or university, at least a junior, and have a GPA of 3.0 or better.

2 awards given.

2201—THE UNIVERSITY OF NEW MEXICO FOUNDATION (The Kelly Richmond Memorial Fund)

Univ. of New Mexico
Hodgin Hall, 2nd Fl.
Albuquerque NM 87131
Internet: www.ire.org/resources/ scholarship

AMOUNT: Varies
DEADLINE(S): None
FIELD(S): Journalism: Investigative reporting

Scholarship for journalism students at the University of New Mexico to honor Kelly Richmond, an award-winning journalist who died of lung cancer at age 33.

Write for details.

2202—US ENVIRONMENTAL PROTECTION AGENCY—NATIONAL NETWORK FOR ENVIRONMENTAL MANAGEMENT STUDIES (Fellowships)

401 M Street SW, Mailcode 1704
Washington DC 20460
202/260-5283
FAX: 202/260-4095
E-mail: jojokian.sheri@epa.gov
Internet: www.epa.gov/enviroed/ students.html

AMOUNT: Varies
DEADLINE(S): DEC
FIELD(S): Environmental Policies, Regulations, & Law; Environmental Management & Administration; Environmental Science; Public Relations & Communications; Computer Programming & Development

Fellowships are open to undergraduate and graduate students working on research projects in the above fields, either full-time during the summer or part-time during the school year. Must be US citizen or legal resident. Financial need NOT a factor.

85-95 awards annually. Not renewable. See website or contact the Career Service Center of participating universities for an application.

2203—UNITED METHODIST COMMUNI-CATIONS (Leonard Perryman Communications Scholarships)

P.O. Box 320
Nashville TN 37202-0320
615/742-5140
FAX: 615/742-5404
E-mail: scholarships@ umcom.umc.org
Internet: www.umcom.org/ scholarships

AMOUNT: $2,500
DEADLINE(S): MAR 15
FIELD(S): Religious Journalism/Communications

Open to students of Christian faith who are ethnic minority undergraduate juniors and seniors enrolled in accredited US schools of communication or journalism (print, electronic, or audiovisual). Candidates should be pursuing career in religious communication.

2 awards annually. Not renewable. See website or contact Jackie Vaughan at UMC for an application.

2204—UNIVERSITY OF MARYLAND (College of Journalism Scholarships)

Journalism Building, Room 1117
College Park MD 20742-7111
301/405-2399
Internet: www.inform.umd.edu/jour

AMOUNT: $250 to $1,500
DEADLINE(S): FEB 15
FIELD(S): Journalism

Variety of journalism scholarships, prizes, and awards tenable at the University of Maryland. Application forms for all scholarships are available at the address above.

Access website or write for complete information.

2205—UNIVERSITY OF OKLAHOMA—H.H. HERBERT SCHOOL OF JOURNALISM AND MASS COMMUNICATION (Undergraduate Scholarships)

860 Van Vleet Oval, Room 101
Norman OK 73019
405/325-2721

AMOUNT: $5,000/yr.
DEADLINE(S): FEB
FIELD(S): Journalism: Print or broadcast, advertising, electronic media, news communication, professional writing, public relations

For undergraduate students studying in the above fields who plan to attend the University of Oklahoma. Interview is part of acceptance process.

Contact David Dary at above location for details.

2206—UTA ALUMNI ASSOCIATION (Karin McCallum Scholarship)

University of Texas at Arlington
Box 19457
Arlington TX 76019
Internet: www.uta.edu/alumni/scholar.htm

AMOUNT: $250
DEADLINE(S): Varies
FIELD(S): Speech-Communications

Must be a full-time junior or senior at the University of Texas at Arlington. Must submit transcript, professional resume, and letter of recommendation from a Communications professor.

1 award annually. Contact UTA Alumni Association for an application.

2207—UTA ALUMNI ASSOCIATION (Lloyd Clark Scholarship Journalism)

University of Texas at Arlington
Box 19457
Arlington TX 76019
Internet: www.uta.edu/alumni/scholar.htm

AMOUNT: $250
DEADLINE(S): Varies
FIELD(S): Journalism

Must be a full-time junior or higher with at least 15 hours completed at the University of Texas at Arlington and have a commitment to a career in journalism. Must show noticeable academic achievement and evidence of success in journal-

ism. Financial need may be considered. Writing sample required.

1 award annually. Contact UTA Alumni Association for an application.

2208—VANDERBILT UNIVERSITY (Fred Russell-Grantland Rice Scholarship)

2305 West End Ave.
Nashville TN 37203-1700
615/322-2561

AMOUNT: $10,000/year ($40,000 total award)
DEADLINE(S): JAN 1
FIELD(S): Journalism

Four-year scholarship to Vanderbilt University open to high school seniors who want to become a sports writer, have demonstrated outstanding potential in the field, and can meet entrance requirements of Vanderbilt's College of Arts & Science.

Write to Scholarship Coordinator at above address for complete information.

2209—VAUGHAN/NAHWW (Home Workshop Writers Scholarship)

7501 Woodstream Terrace
N. Syracuse NY 13212-1921
Written inquiry

AMOUNT: $2,500
DEADLINE(S): JUN 1
FIELD(S): Do-It-Yourself Journalism or a related technical writing field

Sponsored by the National Association of Home Workshop Writers, this scholarship is for candidates intending to pursue a career in the above field. A 150-word composition on reason and qualifications for applying is required. Must be sponsored by a member of the NAHWW—a member list is included with application.

Send SASE to Frank Burgmeier, Scholarship Coordinator, at above address.

2210—W. EUGENE SMITH MEMORIAL FUND, INC. (Grants)

c/o ICP, 1130 Fifth Ave.
New York NY 10128
212/860-1777
FAX: 212/860-1482

AMOUNT: $20,000; $5,000
DEADLINE(S): JUL 15
FIELD(S): Photojournalism

Career support for photojournalists of any nationality. Must submit a photographic project with a written proposal, illustrated in the humanistic manner of W. Eugene Smith. Financial need NOT a factor.

2 awards annually. Not renewable. Contact Ms. Anna Winand for an application.

2211—WILLIAM RANDOLPH HEARST FOUNDATION (Journalism Awards Program)

90 New Montgomery St., Suite 1212
San Francisco CA 94105
415/543-6033
FAX: 415/243-0760

AMOUNT: $500-$3,000
DEADLINE(S): Varies (OCT-APR)
FIELD(S): Print/Photojournalism, Broadcast News

Journalism awards program offers monthly competitions open to undergraduate college journalism majors who are currently enrolled in one of the 107 participating journalism schools.

6 print journalism, 3 photojournalism, and 4 broadcast news competitions annually. Entry forms and details on monthly contests are available ONLY through the journalism department of participating schools.

2212—WOMEN IN COMMUNICATIONS (Seattle Professional Chapter Scholarships for Washington State Residents)

1412 SW 102nd Street, #224
Seattle WA 98146
206/298-4966

AMOUNT: $600-$1,000
DEADLINE(S): MAR 1
FIELD(S): Communications

Open to Washington state residents who are graduate students or undergraduates in their junior or senior year at a Washington state 4-year college or university. Must be a communications major.

Awards are based on demonstrated excellence in communications, scholastic achievement, and financial need. Write for complete information.

2213—WOMEN ON BOOKS (Scholarships for African-American Women)

879 Rainier Ave., N., Suite A105
Renton WA 98055
206/626-2323

AMOUNT: $1,000
DEADLINE(S): JUN (Mid-month)
FIELD(S): English or Journalism, with intention to pursue a writing career

Scholarships for African-American women pursuing careers in writing. Must major in English or journalism in a four-year university, have a min. GPA of 2.5, and demonstrate financial need.

Write for details.

2214—WOMEN'S SPORTS FOUNDATION (Jackie Joyner-Kersee & Zina Garrison Minority Internships)

Eisenhower Park
East Meadow NY 11554
800/227-3988
FAX: 516/542-4716
E-mail: WoSport@aol.com
Internet: www.lifetimetv.com/WoSport

AMOUNT: $4,000-$5,000
DEADLINE(S): Ongoing
FIELD(S): Sports-related fields

Provides women of color an opportunity to gain experience in a sports-related career and interact in the sports community. May be undergraduates, college graduates, graduate students, or women in a career change. Internships are located at the Women's Sports Foundation in East Meadow, New York.

4-6 awards annually. See website or write to above address for details.

HISTORY

2215—AMERICAN HISTORICAL ASSOCIATION (Michael Kraus Research Award Grant)

400 A Street, SE
Washington DC 20003
202/544-2422
FAX: 202/544-8307
E-mail: aha@theaha.org
Internet: www.theaha.org

AMOUNT: $800
DEADLINE(S): FEB 1
FIELD(S): American Colonial History

For research in American colonial history with particular reference to intercultural aspects of American and European relations. Must be AHA member.

See website or contact AHA for details.

2216—ASSOCIATION FOR WOMEN IN SCIENCE EDUCATIONAL FOUNDATION (Dr. Vicki L. Schechtman Scholarship)

1200 New York Ave. NW
Suite 650
Washington DC 20005
202/326-8940 or 800/886-AWIS
E-mail: awis@awis.org
Internet: www.awis.org

AMOUNT: $1,000

DEADLINE(S): JAN 16
FIELD(S): Various Sciences and Social Sciences

For female undergraduate students who are US citizens and have a minimum GPA of 3.0. Summary page, essay describing career aspirations, transcripts, proof of matriculation (if available), and two reference letters required with application. Scholarships may be used for tuition, books, housing, research, equipment, etc.

See website or write to above address for an application and more information.

2217—ASSOCIATION FOR WOMEN IN SCIENCE EDUCATIONAL FOUNDATION (Ruth Satter Memorial Award)

1200 New York Ave. NW
Suite 650
Washington DC 20005
202/326-8940 or 800/886-AWIS
E-mail: awis@awis.org
Internet: www.awis.org

AMOUNT: $1,000
DEADLINE(S): JAN 16
FIELD(S): Various Sciences and Social Sciences

Scholarships for female doctoral students who have interrupted their education three years or more to raise a family. Summary page, description of research project, resume, references, transcripts, biographical sketch, and proof of eligibility from department head required. US citizens may attend any graduate institution; noncitizens must be enrolled in US institutions.

See website or write to above address for more information or an application.

2218—CENTER FOR 17TH- AND 18TH- CENTURY STUDIES (Fellowships)

UCLA
310 Reyce Hall
Los Angeles CA 90095-1404
310/206-8522
FAX: 310/206-8577
E-mail: c1718cs@humnet.ucla.edu

AMOUNT: $1,000-$18,400
DEADLINE(S): MAR 15
FIELD(S): British Literature/History (17th & 18th Centuries)

Undergraduate stipends, graduate assistantships, and Ahmanson & Getty postdoctoral fellowships are for advanced study and research regarding British literature and history of the 17th and 18th centuries. Tenable at the William Andrews Clark Memorial Library at the University of California, Los Angeles.

Contact the Center for current year's theme and an application.

2219—CHRISTIAN A. JOHNSON ENDEAVOR FOUNDATION (Native American Fellows)

Harvard Univ.
79 John F. Kennedy Street
Cambridge MA 02138
617/495-1152
FAX: 617/496-3900
Internet: www.ksg.harvard.edu/hpaied/cjohn.htm

AMOUNT: Varies
DEADLINE(S): MAY 1
FIELD(S): Social Sciences, Government, or program related to Native American studies

Fellowships for students of Native American ancestry who attend a John F. Kennedy School of Government degree program. Applicant, parent, or grandparent must hold membership in a federally or state-recognized tribe, band, or other organized group of Native Americans. Must be committed to a career in American Indian affairs. Awards based on merit and need.

Renewable, based on renomination and availability of funds. To apply, contact John F. Kennedy School of Government at above address.

2220—EAST TEXAS HISTORICAL ASSOCIATION (Ottis Lock Endowment Awards)

P.O. Box 6223, SFA Station
Nacogdoches TX 75962
409/468-2407

AMOUNT: $500
DEADLINE(S): MAY 1
FIELD(S): History, Social Science

Open to residents of East Texas who will be pursuing undergraduate or graduate studies at an East Texas college or university.

Renewable with adequate progress towards degree. Contact East Texas Historical Association for an application.

2221—HARRY S. TRUMAN LIBRARY INSTITUTE (Harry S. Truman Book Award)

500 W. US Hwy. 24
Independence MO 64050-1798
816/833-0425
FAX: 816/833-2715
E-mail: library@truman.nara.gov
Internet: www.trumanlibrary.org/institut/scholars.htm

AMOUNT: $1,000
DEADLINE(S): JAN 20
FIELD(S): American History: Harry S. Truman or His Era

Award is for the best book written within a two-year period dealing primarily and substantially with some aspect of US history between April 12, 1945 and January 20, 1953, or with the public career of Harry S. Truman. Three copies of each book entered must be submitted.

Awarded only in even-numbered years. See website or contact Book Awards Administrator for guidelines.

2222—HARRY S. TRUMAN LIBRARY INSTITUTE (Undergraduate Student Grant)

500 W. US Hwy. 24
Independence MO 64050-1798
816/833-0425
FAX: 816/833-2715
E-mail: library@truman.nara.gov
Internet: www.trumanlibrary.org/institut/scholars.htm

AMOUNT: $1,000 (max.)
DEADLINE(S): DEC 1
FIELD(S): American History: Harry S. Truman or His Era

For undergraduate students writing a senior thesis on some aspect of life and career of Harry S. Truman or public and foreign policy issues that were prominent during the Truman years. Award is intended to offset expenses for research conducted at Truman Library. Applicants must describe in writing the proposed project and its rationale, and indicate how a research experience at the Truman Library will contribute to applicant's future development.

1 award annually. See website or contact Grants Administrator for an application. Applicants notified of decision within six weeks after deadline.

2223—HILLSDALE COLLEGE (Freedom as Vocation Scholarship)

33 E. College Street
Hillsdale MI 49242-1298
517/437-7341
Internet: www.hillsdale.edu

AMOUNT: Varies
DEADLINE(S): None
FIELD(S): Business, History, Political Science, Economics

Open to Hillsdale College undergraduates who maintain a minimum 3.0 GPA and commit to a series of courses in the above fields. Student must rank in top 20% of class and top 10% of test scores. Must

possess excellent communications, public speaking, and leadership skills and demonstrate outstanding character and citizenship. Financial need NOT a factor.

Renewable. No application process; students are selected. See website for details.

2224—INSTITUTE OF INTERNATIONAL EDUCATION (National Security Education Program-Undergraduate Scholarships)

1400 K St. NW, 6th Floor
Washington DC 20005-2403
202/326-7697
800/618-NSEP (6737)
E-mail: nsep@iie.org
Internet: http://www.iie.org/nsep/

AMOUNT: Varies: up to $8,000/semester
DEADLINE(S): FEB 8
FIELD(S): Open to all majors; preference to applied sciences, engineering, business, economics, math, computer science, international affairs, political science, history, and the policy sciences

For study abroad OUTSIDE the US, Canada, Australia, New Zealand, and Western Europe. For study in areas deemed critical to US national security. Applications available on US campuses from August through early December. Or contact organization for details.

Inquire at above location for details.

2225—JAMES MADISON MEMORIAL FELLOWSHIP (Fellowship for Teachers)

2000 K St. NW
Washington DC 20006
202/653-8700
1-800/525-6928
FAX: 202/653-6045
Internet: www.jamesmadison.com

AMOUNT: $24,000 prorated over study period
DEADLINE(S): MAR 1
FIELD(S): Teaching American History/Government, or Social Studies—concentration on the US Constitution

Fellowships for teachers (senior fellows) in grades 7-12 in the above fields to pursue an M.A. degree. Also for full-time college seniors and grad students (junior fellows). US citizens or US nationals. Fellows are selected from each state and from DC, Puerto Rico, Guam, Virgin Islands, American Samoa, Northern Mariana Islands, and Palau. Program designed to enhance teaching about the US Constitution.

Application is on website or contact: American College Testing, P.O. Box 4030, Iowa City, IA 52243-4030; 800/525-6928
E-mail: Recogprog@ACT-ACT4-PO.act.org

2226—LOUISIANA STATE UNIVERSITY AT SHREVEPORT (Walter O. Bigby Scholarship)

Dean of Liberal Arts
One University Place
Shreveport LA 71115-2399
318/797-5363 or 318/797-5371
FAX: 318/797-5366
E-mail: finaid@pilot.lsus.edu
Internet: www.lsus.edu

AMOUNT: up to $500/semester
DEADLINE(S): Varies
FIELD(S): Political Science, English, History, Law

Recipient must be entering the junior or senior year at LSUS with a major in political science, English, or history; may also be enrolled in some other Liberal Arts degree program if preparing to enter law school.

Contact the Dean's Office in the College of Liberal Arts at LSUS for an application.

2227—NATIONAL FEDERATION OF THE BLIND (Humanities Scholarship)

805 5th Ave.
Grinnell IA 50112
515/236-3366

AMOUNT: $3,000
DEADLINE(S): MAR 31
FIELD(S): Humanities (Art, English, Foreign Languages, History, Philosophy, Religion)

Open to legally blind students pursuing or planning to pursue a full-time postsecondary education in the US. Scholarships are awarded on basis of academic excellence, service to the community, and financial need. Must include transcripts and two letters of recommendation. Membership NOT required.

1 award annually. Renewable. Contact Mrs. Peggy Elliot, Scholarship Committee Chairman, for an application.

2228—NATIONAL ITALIAN AMERICAN FOUNDATION (Rabbi Robert Feinberg Scholarship)

1860 19th Street
Washington DC 20009-5599
202/530-5315

AMOUNT: $1,000
DEADLINE(S): MAY 31
FIELD(S): World War II studies

Open to undergraduate or graduate student of Italian heritage interested in WWII studies. Prepare a 5-page paper on the Italian assistance to Jews in Italy and its occupied territories.

Academic merit, financial need, and community service considered.

2229—NATIONAL SOCIETY DAUGHTERS OF THE AMERICAN REVOLUTION (Enid Hall Griswold Memorial Scholarship)

1776 D Street NW
Washington DC 20006-5392
202/628-1776
Internet: www.dar.org

AMOUNT: $1,000
DEADLINE(S): FEB 15
FIELD(S): History, Political Science, Government, Economics

Open to undergraduate juniors and seniors (US citizens) attending an accredited US college or university. Awards are placed on deposit with school. Awards are judged on academic excellence, commitment to field of study, and need. Affiliation with DAR not required.

Not renewable. See website or send a self-addressed, stamped envelope for an application or more informtion.

2230—NATIONAL SOCIETY DAUGHTERS OF THE AMERICAN REVOLUTION (American History Scholarship)

1776 D Street NW
Washington DC 20006-5392
202/628-1776
Internet: www.dar.org

AMOUNT: $1,000-$2,000
DEADLINE(S): FEB 1
FIELD(S): American History

Open to graduating high school seniors planning to major in American History. Must be US citizen and attend an accredited US college or university. Awards based on academic excellence, commitment to field of study, and need. Affiliation with DAR not necessary. Awards are placed on deposit with school.

Renewable up to four years, with annual transcript review. Scholarships are first judged at the state level. See website or send a self-addressed, stamped envelope for an application or more information.

2231—NATIONAL SPACE CLUB (Dr. Robert H. Goddard Historical Essay Award)

2000 L Street NW, Suite 710
Washington DC 20036-4907
202/973-8661

AMOUNT: $1,000 + plaque
DEADLINE(S): DEC 4
FIELD(S): Aerospace History

Essay competition open to any US citizen on a topic dealing with any significant aspect of the historical development of rocketry and astronautics. Essays should not exceed 5,000 words and should be fully documented. Will be judged on originality and scholarship.

Previous winners not eligible. Send self-addressed, stamped envelope for complete information.

2232—NAVAL HISTORICAL CENTER (Internship Program)

Washington Navy Yard
901 M Street, SE
Washington DC 20374-5060
202/433-6901
FAX: 202/433-8200
E-mail: efurgol@nhc.navy.mil
Internet: www.history.navy.mil

AMOUNT: $400 possible honoraria; otherwise, unpaid
DEADLINE(S): None
FIELD(S): Education, History, Public Relations, Design

Registered students of colleges/universities and graduates thereof are eligible for this program, which must be a minimum of 3 weeks, full- or part-time. Four specialities available: Curator, Education, Public Relations, and Design. Interns receive orientation and assist in their departments, and must complete individual project which contributes to Center. Must submit a letter of recommendation, unofficial transcript, and writing sample of not less than 1,000 words.

Contact Dr. Edward M. Furgol, Curator, for an application.

2233—PHI ALPHA THETA HISTORY HONOR SOCIETY (Nels Andrew N. Cleven Founder's Paper Prize Awards)

6201 Hamilton Blvd., Suite 116
Allentown PA 18106-9691
800/394-8195
FAX: 610/336-4929
E-mail: phialpha@ptd.net

AMOUNT: $150-$250

DEADLINE(S): JUL 1
FIELD(S): History

Open to undergraduate and graduate Phi Alpha Theta members who submit essays on a historical topic. Should combine original historical research on a significant subject, based on source material and manuscripts, if possible, with good English composition and superior style. Must include bibliography. Papers should not exceed 25 typewritten pages in length. Dr. George P. Hammond Prize and Dr. Lynn W. Turner Prize included in this category.

3 awards annually. Contact PAT National Headquarters for guidelines.

2234—PHI ALPHA THETA HISTORY HONOR SOCIETY/WORLD HISTORY ASSOCIATION (World History Paper Prize)

6201 Hamilton Blvd., Suite 116
Allentown PA 18106-9691
800/394-8195
FAX: 610/336-4929
E-mail: phialpha@ptd.net

AMOUNT: $200
DEADLINE(S): JUL 1
FIELD(S): World History

Open to undergraduate and graduate students who submit an essay on world history, which is one that examines any historical issue with global implications. Must be member of either Phi Alpha Theta or the World History Association, and must have composed the paper while enrolled at an accredited college/university during previous academic year (proven by letter from faculty). Bibliography must be included. Papers must be no longer than 25 typewritten pages.

2 awards annually. Contact PAT National Headquarters for guidelines.

2235—ROSE HILL COLLEGE (Louella Robinson Memorial Scholarship)

P.O. Box 3126
Aiken SC 29802-3126
800/684-3769
FAX: 803/641-0240
E-mail: rosehill@.edu
Internet: www.rosehill.edu

AMOUNT: $10,000/yr. for four years
DEADLINE(S): Varies
FIELD(S): Liberal Arts and Humanities curricula

For undergraduate residents of Indian River County, Florida, to attend Rose Hill College in Aiken, South Carolina. The school offers a liberal arts education and follows the Great Books curriculum, a program of reading and seminars.

1 annual award. Applicants must meet entry requirements of RHC. Contact above location for details.

2236—ROSE HILL COLLEGE (Scholarships for Children of Eastern Orthodox Priests/Deacons)

P.O. Box 3126
Aiken SC 29802-3126
800/684-3769
FAX: 803/641-0240
E-mail: rosehill@edu
Internet: www.rosehill.edu

AMOUNT: Full scholarship: $10,000/yr. for four years
DEADLINE(S): Varies
FIELD(S): Liberal Arts and Humanities curricula

For undergraduates who are children of Eastern Orthodox Christian priests or deacons to attend Rose Hill College in Aiken, South Carolina. The school offers a liberal arts education and follows the Great Books curriculum, a program of reading and seminars.

6-10 annual awards. Applicants must meet entry requirements of RHC. Contact above location for details.

2237—ROSE HILL COLLEGE (Scholarships for the Homeschooled)

P.O. Box 3126
Aiken SC 29802-3126
800/684-3769
FAX: 803/641-0240
E-mail: rosehill@rosehill.edu
Internet: www.resehill.edu

AMOUNT: Full scholarship: $10,000/yr. for four years
DEADLINE(S): Varies
FIELD(S): Liberal Arts and Humanities curricula

For undergraduates who have been homeschooled for three of the last five years of their high school education. For use at Rose Hill College in Aiken, South Carolina. The school offers a liberal arts education and follows the Great Books curriculum, a program of reading and seminars. Scholarships will be awarded primarily on the basis of an essay that the student will be asked to write.

4 annual awards. Applicants must meet entry requirements of RHC. Contact above location for details.

2238—SMITHSONIAN INSTITUTION (Minority Student Internship Program)

Fellowships & Grants
955 L'Enfant Plaza, Suite 7000
MRC 902
Washington DC 20560
202/287-3271
FAX: 202/287-3691
E-mail: siofg@ofg.si.edu
Internet: www.si.edu/research+study

AMOUNT: $300/week + possible travel expenses
DEADLINE(S): FEB 15
FIELD(S): Humanities, Environmental Studies, Cultural Studies, Natural History, Earth Science, Art History, Biology, & related fields

Ten-week internships in residence at the Smithsonian for US minority students to participate in research or museum-related activities in above fields. For undergrads or grads with at least a 3.0 GPA. Essay, resume, transcripts, and references required with application. Internships are full-time and are offered for Summer, Fall, or Spring tenures.

Write for application.

2239—SMITHSONIAN INSTITUTION (National Air & Space Museum Verville Fellowship)

National Air and Space Museum
MRC 312
Washington DC 20560
Written inquiry

AMOUNT: $30,000 stipend for 12 months + travel and misc. expenses
DEADLINE(S): JAN 15
FIELD(S): Analysis of major trends, developments, and accomplishments in the history of aviation or space studies

A competitive nine- to twelve-month in-residence fellowship in the above field of study. Advanced degree is NOT a requirement. Contact Fellowship Coordinator at above location.

Open to all nationalities. Fluency in English required.

2240—SONS OF THE REPUBLIC OF TEXAS (Presidio La Bahia Award)

1717 8th Street
Bay City TX 77414
409/245-6644
E-mail: srttexas@srttexas.org
Internet: www.srttexas.org

AMOUNT: $1,200+

DEADLINE(S): SEP 30
FIELD(S): Texas History: Spanish Colonial Period

A competition on the best book, paper, or article that promotes suitable preservation of relics, appropriate dissemination of data, and research into Texas heritage with particular attention to the Spanish Colonial period. Research writings have proved in the past to be the most successful type of entry; however, careful consideration will be given to other literary forms, as well as art, architecture, and archaeological discovery. Entries accepted June-September.

Contact Melinda Williams, SRT Executive Secretary, for a brochure.

2241—SOURISSEAU ACADEMY FOR STATE AND LOCAL HISTORY (Research Grant)

c/o San Jose State University
San Jose CA 95192
408/924-6510 or 408/227-2657

AMOUNT: $500
DEADLINE(S): NOV 1
FIELD(S): California History

Grants are available to support undergraduate and graduate research on California history. Preference to research on Santa Clara County history.

5-10 awards per year are granted for project expences. Write for complete information.

2242—STUDENT CONSERVATION ASSOCIATION (SCA Resource Assistant Program)

P.O. Box 550
Charlestown NH 03603
603/543-1700
FAX: 603/543-1828
E-mail: internships@sca-inc.org
Internet: www.sca-inc.org

AMOUNT: $1,180-$4,725
DEADLINE(S): Varies
FIELD(S): Environment & related fields

Must be 18 and US citizen; need not be student. Fields: Agriculture, archaeology, anthropology, botany, caves, civil/environmental engineering, environmental education, fisheries, forests, herpetology, history, living history/roleplaying, visitor services, landscape architectural/environmental design, paleontology, recreation/resource/range management, trail maintenance/construction, wildlife management, geology, hydrology, library/museums, surveying.

900 positions in US and Canada. Send $1 for postage for application; outside US/Canada, send $20.

2243—THE J. EDGAR HOOVER FOUNDATION

50 Gull Point Road
Hilton Head Island SC 29928
803/671-5020

AMOUNT: $500
DEADLINE(S): Ongoing
FIELD(S): Government, Law Enforcement

Scholarships for the study of government, the promotion of good citizenship, and law enforcement. The foundation strives to safeguard the heritage and freedom of the US, to promote good citizenship through an appreciation of the American form of government, and to combat communism or any other ideology or doctrine opposed to the principles set forth in the US Constitution.

Send letter to Cartha D. De Loach, Chair, at above address.

2244—US INSTITUTE OF PEACE (National Peace Essay Contest)

1200 17th Street NW, Suite 200
Washington DC 20036
202/429-3834
FAX 202/429-6063
E-mail: essay_contest@usip.org
Internet: www.usip.org

AMOUNT: $1,000-$10,000
DEADLINE(S): JAN 26
FIELD(S): Political Science, US History

1,500-word essay contest for high school students on the US response to international conflict. No restrictions as to citizenship/residency.

53 awards annually. Not renewable. See website or contact USIP for specific guidelines.

2245—U.S. MARINE CORPS HISTORICAL CENTER (College Internships)

Building 58
Washington Navy Yard
Washington DC 20374
202/433-3839

AMOUNT: Stipend to cover daily
expenses
DEADLINE(S): None specified
FIELD(S): US Military History, Library
Science, History, Museum Studies

Open to undergraduate students at a college or university that will grant academic credit for work experience as interns at the address above or at the Marine Corps Air-Ground Museum in Quantico, Virginia.

All internships are regarded as beginning professional-level historian, curator, librarian, or archivist positions. Write for complete information.

2246—UTA ALUMNI ASSOCIATION (Pitman-Roberts Endowed Scholarship)

University of Texas at Arlington
Box 19457
Arlington TX 76019
Internet: www.uta.edu/alumni/
scholar.htm

AMOUNT: $325
DEADLINE(S): Varies
FIELD(S): Military Science

Must be a student with 15 hours completed and be currently enrolled in 15 hours at the University of Texas at Arlington; cannot have completed more than four semesters. Must demonstrate outstanding leadership qualities and be currently enrolled in Military Science I or II.

1 award annually. Contact UTA Alumni Association for an application.

LAW

2247—AMERICAN BAR FOUNDATION (Summer Research Fellowships in Law and Social Science for Minority Undergraduate Students)

750 N. Lake Shore Drive
Chicago IL 60611
312/988-6500
Internet: www.abf-sociolegal.org

AMOUNT: $3,500 stipend
DEADLINE(S): MAR 1
FIELD(S): Social Sciences, Humanities,
Law

Summer research opportunity open to sophomore and junior undergraduates who are Native American, African American, Mexican, Puerto Rican, or other minority. Must be US citizen or permanent resident and have at least a 3.0 GPA. Students are assigned a mentor and participate in seminars; must also work at the Foundation's office in Chicago for 35 hours per week for 10 weeks. Essay, transcripts, and letter of recommendation required.

4 awards annually; announced in April. See website or contact ABF for an application.

2248—AMERICAN SOCIETY OF CRIMINOLOGY (Gene Carte Student Paper Competition)

1314 Kinnear Road
Columbus OH 43212-1156

614/292-9207
FAX: 614-292-6767
Internet: asc41@compuserve.com
OR www.asc41.com/cartesp.html

AMOUNT: $300; $150; $100
DEADLINE(S): APR 15
FIELD(S): Criminology, Criminal Justice

Essay competition open to any currently enrolled full-time student at either the undergraduate or graduate level. Papers must be directly related to criminology and may be conceptual and/or empirical and/or be no longer than 7,500 words.

Names and topics of former winners and other information are on website, including address of where to send papers. Or write to organization for details.

2249—ARMENIAN GENERAL BENEVOLENT UNION (Educational Loan Program)

Education Dept.
31 W. 52nd Street
New York NY 10019-6118
212/765-8260
FAX: 212/765-8209/8209
E-mail: agbuny@aol.com

AMOUNT: $5,000 to $7,500/yr.
DEADLINE(S): APR 1
FIELD(S): Law (J.D.) and Medicine
(M.D.)

Loans for full-time students of Armenian heritage pursuing their first professional degrees in law or medicine. Must be attending highly competitive institutions in the US GPA of 3.5 or more required.

Loan repayments begin within 12 months of completion of full-time study and extend 5 to 10 years, depending on the size of the loan. Interest is 3%. Write for complete information.

2250—ASSOCIATION OF CERTIFIED FRAUD EXAMINERS (Scholarships)

The Gregor Building
716 West Ave
Austin TX 78701
800/245-3321 or 512/478-9070
FAX: 512/478-9297
E-mail: acfe@tpoint.net
Internet: www.cfenet.com

AMOUNT: $500
DEADLINE(S): MAY 15
FIELD(S): Accounting and/or Criminal
Justice

Scholarships for full-time graduate or undergraduate students majoring in accounting or criminal justice degree programs. Awards are based on overall academic achievement, three letters of recommendation, and an original 250-word essay explaining why the applicant deserves the award and how fraud awareness will affect his or her professional career development. Also required is a letter of recommendation from a Certified Fraud Examiner or a local CFE Chapter.

Contact organization for applications and further details.

2251—ASSOCIATION OF FORMER AGENTS OF THE US SECRET SERVICE, INC. (Law Enforcement Career Scholarship Program)

P.O. Box 848
Annandale VA 22003-0848
Written inquiry

AMOUNT: Varies
DEADLINE(S): MAY 1
FIELD(S): Law Enforcement, Police Administration

Open to US citizens enrolled in a law enforcement or police administration course in an accredited college or university. Must have completed at least one year of undergraduate study or be a graduate student.

Not renewable. Send self-addressed, stamped, business-sized envelope for an application after September 1st.

2252—BALL STATE UNIVERSITY (Lionel J. Neiman Criminal Justice Scholarship)

Office of Scholarships and
Financial Aid
Muncie IN 47306
765/285-5979
Internet: www.bsu.edu/finaid/
scholars/criminal.html#lionel

AMOUNT: Varies
DEADLINE(S): Varies
FIELD(S): Criminal Justice

Must be full-time student at Ball State University and majoring/minoring in criminal justice. Must have minimum 3.0 GPA and demonstrate financial need. Award is also based on university and community service activities.

Contact the Department of Criminal Justice and Criminology at Ball State University for an application.

2253—BOYS AND GIRLS CLUBS OF SAN DIEGO (Spence Reese Scholarship Fund)

1761 Hotel Circle So., Suite 123
San Diego CA 92108

619/298-3520
AMOUNT: $2,000/yr.
DEADLINE(S): MAY 15
FIELD(S): Medicine, Law, Engineering, Political Science

Open to male high school seniors planning a career in one of the above fields. Must be residents of Imperial, Riverside, Orange, San Diego, or Los Angeles counties in California. Boys and Girls Club affiliation NOT required.

$10 application fee. Renewable up to 4 years. Send a self-addressed, stamped envelope to Boys and Girls Club for an application after January 1st.

2254—BUSINESS & PROFESSIONAL WOMEN'S FOUNDATION (BPW Career Advancement Scholarship Program)

2012 Massachusetts Ave., NW
Washington DC 20036-1070
202/293-1200, ext. 169
FAX: 202/861-0298
Internet: www.bpwusa.org

AMOUNT: $500-$1,000
DEADLINE(S): APR 15
FIELD(S): Biology, Science, Education, Engineering, Social Science, Paralegal, Humanities, Business, Math, Computers, Law, MD, DD

For women (US citizens) aged 25+ accepted into accredited program at US institution (+Puerto Rico & Virgin Islands). Must graduate within 12 to 24 months from the date of grant and demonstrate critical financial need. Must have a plan to upgrade skills, train for a new career field, or to enter/re-enter the job market.

Full- or part-time study. For info see website or send business-sized, self-addressed, double-stamped envelope.

2255—CALIFORNIA HAZARDOUS MATERIALS INVESTIGATORS ASSOCIATION (Scholarships)

1911 Douglas Blvd., Suite 85-167
Roseville CA 95661
Internet: www.chmia.com/
scholarship.html

AMOUNT: $300/class max.
DEADLINE(S): None
FIELD(S): Environmental Law Enforcement

CHMIA provides financial aid to those members who wish to broaden their knowledge and experience for the purpose of becoming more effective in their efforts to enforce environmental laws and regulations. Must be a CHMIA member for a

period of six months before being eligible to receive a scholarship grant. Funds will be awarded for training tuition on a pre-approved reimbursement basis only.

Applications can be completed online. Members should receive notice of whether their scholarship request was approved or disapproved within ten days of application.

2256—COLLEGE MISERICORDIA (Presidential Scholarships)

301 Lake Street
Dallas PA 18612-1098
800/852-7675
Internet: http://miseri.edu/scholar.htm

AMOUNT: Full or part tuition
DEADLINE(S): MAR 1
FIELD(S): Prelaw or the Humanities

Scholarships for incoming freshmen to this co-educational Catholic college in Pennsylvania. High school senior applicants must rank in the upper 20% of their classes and have achieved SAT or ACT scores in the 8th percentile or better.

Obtain applications from the Admissions Office.

2257—CRETE POLICE ASSOCIATION (Law Enforcement Scholarship)

524 W. Exchange Street
Crete IL 60417
Internet: www.spots.ab.ca/~fivestar/
scholarship.html

AMOUNT: $500
DEADLINE(S): Varies
FIELD(S): Law Enforcement

Scholarship is to assist high school seniors, residing in Crete, Illinois, who wish to pursue a career in law enforcement and have been accepted at an accredited college or university. Must show proof of residency (i.e., driver's license) and proof of acceptance at a college/university with a law enforcement related major. All applications must be signed by your high school Dean of Students or school counselor.

See website or contact CPA at above address or your high school counselor for an application.

2258—EARL WARREN LEGAL TRAINING PROGRAM (Shearman & Sterling Scholarship Program)

99 Hudson Street, 16th Fl.
New York NY 10013-2897
Written inquiry
AMOUNT: $10,000
DEADLINE(S): None

FIELD(S): Law

Scholarships for African-American students in their first year of law school. Selected on basis of financial need, academic achievement, career achievement, and personal commitment to the legal profession and public service. Each scholar will be assigned two attorney-mentors available throughout law school career to provide support, counseling, and advice. Each student will also participate in the summer internship programs of LDF and Shearman & Sterling.

2-4 awards annually. Renewable. Grant includes allowance to attend LDF's Civil Rights Institute. Student must request application themselves in writing.

2259—FIREARMS CIVIL RIGHTS LEGAL DEFENSE FUND (Essay Contest for Law Students)

11250 Waples Road
Fairfax VA 22030-7400
703/267-1252
FAX: 703/267-3985

AMOUNT: $5,000; $2,000; $1,000
DEADLINE(S): NOV 30
FIELD(S): Law

Essay competitions for law students who have not been previously admitted to practice law in the US. The 1998 subject was "The Right of the Individual to Keep and Bear Arms as a Federally Protected Right." Papers should be double-spaced and not exceed 30 pages in length, exclusive of endnotes.

Contact organization for detailed information and rules.

2260—H. FLETCHER BROWN FUND (Scholarships)

c/o PNC Bank, Trust Dept.
P.O. Box 791
Wilmington DE 19899
302/429-1186

AMOUNT: Varies
DEADLINE(S): APR 15
FIELD(S): Medicine, Dentistry, Law, Engineering, Chemistry

Open to US citizens born in Delaware and still residing in Delaware. For 4 years of study (undergrad or grad) leading to a degree that enables applicant to practice in chosen field.

Scholarships are based on need, scholastic achievement, and good moral character. Applications available in February. Write for complete information.

2261—H. FLETCHER BROWN TRUST (Scholarships)

222 Delaware Ave., 16th Fl.
Wilmington DE 19899
302/429-1338

AMOUNT: Varies
DEADLINE(S): APR 9
FIELD(S): Chemistry, Engineering, Law, Medicine, Dentistry

Open to financially needy native-born Delaware residents only who are pursuing an undergraduate degree. Must have minimum 1,000 SAT score and rank in upper 20% of class. Interview required.

Send self-addressed, stamped envelope to Donald Drois, Account Administrator, PNC Bank, at above address for an application.

2262—HOPI TRIBE (Priority Scholarships)

P.O. Box 123
Kykotsmovi AZ 86039
520/734-2441, ext. 520
800/762-9630
FAX: 520/734-2435

AMOUNT: Varies
DEADLINE(S): JUL 31
FIELD(S): Law, Natural Resources, Education, Medicine/Health, Engineering, Business

Open to enrolled members of the Hopi Tribe studying in one of the fields listed above, which are considered to be areas of priority interest to the Hopis. Available to college juniors, seniors, and graduate students. Program is to encourage graduates to apply their degrees to Hopi Tribal Goals and Objectives.

Contact Hopi Tribe for an application.

2263—INSTITUTE FOR HUMANE STUDIES (Humane Studies Fellowship)

4084 University Drive, Suite 101
Fairfax VA 22030-6812
703/934-6920 or 800/697-8799
FAX: 703/352-7535
E-mail: ihs@gmu.edu
Internet: www.theihs.org

AMOUNT: up to $12,000
DEADLINE(S): DEC 31
FIELD(S): Social Sciences, Law, Humanities, Jurisprudence, Journalism

Awards are for graduate and advanced undergraduate students pursuing degrees at any accredited domestic or foreign school. Based on academic performance, demonstrated interest in classical liberal ideas, and potential to contribute to the advancement of a free society.

90 awards annually. Apply online or contact IHS for an application.

2264—INSTITUTE FOR HUMANE STUDIES (Koch Summer Fellow Program)

4084 University Drive, Suite 101
Fairfax VA 22030-6812
703/934-6920 or 800/697-8799
FAX: 703/352-7535
E-mail: ihs@gmu.edu
Internet: www.theihs.org

AMOUNT: $1,500 + airfare & housing
DEADLINE(S): MAR 1
FIELD(S): Economics, Politics, Law, Government, Public Policy

For undergraduates and graduates to build skills and gain experience by participating in an 8-week summer internship program. Includes 2 week-long seminars, the internship, and research and writing projects with professionals. College transcripts, essays, and application required. Financial need NOT a factor.

32 awards annually. Not renewable. Apply online or contact IHS for an application.

2265—INSTITUTE FOR HUMANE STUDIES (Summer Residential Program)

4084 University Drive, Suite 101
Fairfax VA 22030-6812
703/934-6920 or 800/697-8799
FAX: 703/352-7535
E-mail: ihs@gmu.edu
Internet: www.theihs.org

AMOUNT: All seminar fees: program cost, room/board, materials, and books
DEADLINE(S): MAR 1
FIELD(S): Social Sciences, Humanities, Law, Journalism, Public Policy, Education, Writing

For college students, recent graduates, and graduate students who share an interest in learning and exchanging ideas about the scope of individual rights. One-week and weekend seminars at various campus locations across the US.

Apply online or contact IHS for an application.

2266—INTER-AMERICAN BAR ASSOCIATION (Writing Competition)

1211 Connecticut Ave. NW
Suite 202
Washington DC 20036

202/393-1217
FAX: 202/393-1241
E-mail: iaba@iaba.org;
www.iaba.org
AMOUNT: $400-$800
DEADLINE(S): FEB 15
FIELD(S): Law

Writing competition for law students on one of the Association's themes. Papers may be prepared in English, Spanish, Portuguese, or French.

Contact organization for details.

2267—INTERNATIONAL ASSN. OF ARSON INVESTIGATORS (John Charles Wilson Scholarship)

300 S. Broadway, Suite 100
St. Louis MO 63102
314/621-1966
AMOUNT: Varies
DEADLINE(S): FEB 15
FIELD(S): Police or Fire Sciences, including Fire Investigation and related subjects

Open to IAAI members, their immediate families, and non-members who are recommended and sponsored by members in good standing. Awards are for undergraduate study in above areas at accredited two- and four-year institutions.

3 awards annually. Transcripts and 500-word essay describing background and goals required. Write to the Executive Director at above address for more information.

2268—JAPANESE AMERICAN CITIZENS LEAGUE (Law Scholarships)

1765 Sutter Street
San Francisco CA 94115
415/921-5225
FAX: 415/931-4671
E-mail: jacl@jacl.org
Internet: www.jacl.org
AMOUNT: $1,000-$5,000
DEADLINE(S): APR 1
FIELD(S): Law

Open to JACL members and their children only. For undergraduate and graduate students pursuing a career in law and planning to attend any accredited institution of higher learning. Must submit personal statement, letters of recommendation, and transcripts.

For membership information or an application, send a self-addressed, stamped envelope to above address, stating your level of study. Applications available

October 1st through March 20th; recipients notified in July.

2269—JEWISH VOCATIONAL SERVICE (Academic Scholarship Program)

One S. Franklin Street
Chicago IL 60606
312/357-4500
FAX: 312/855-3282
TTY: 312/855-3282
E-mail: jvschicago@jon.cjfny.org
AMOUNT: $5,000 (max.)
DEADLINE(S): MAR 1
FIELD(S): "Helping" Professions, Mathematics, Engineering, Sciences, Communications (at Univ IL only), Law (certain schools in IL only)

Open to Jewish men and women legally domiciled in the greater Chicago metropolitan area, who are identified as having promise for significant contributions in their chosen careers, and are in need of financial assistance for full-time academic programs in above areas. Must have entered undergraduate junior year in career programs requiring no postgrad education, be in graduate/professional school, or be in a voc-tech training program. Interview required.

Renewable. Contact JVS for an application between December 1st and February 15th.

2270—LARAMIE COUNTY PEACE OFFICERS' ASSOCIATION (Scholarships)

P.O. Box 5148
Cheyenne WY 82003
Written inquiry
AMOUNT: Varies
DEADLINE(S): APR 1
FIELD(S): Criminal Justice

Available to college sophomores, juniors, and seniors interested in a career in criminal justice who are Laramie County residents and who have a minimum 2.75 GPA. May be used in any public institution in Wyoming.

Renewable. Write to above address for an application.

2271—LOUISIANA STATE UNIVERSITY AT SHREVEPORT (Shreveport Police Memorial Scholarship)

Financial Aid Office
One University Place
Shreveport LA 71115-2399
318/797-5363

FAX: 318/797-5366
E-mail: finaid@pilot.lsus.edu
Internet: www.lsus.edu
AMOUNT: $500/semester
DEADLINE(S): Varies
FIELD(S): Criminal Justice

This one-year award is sponsored by Local No. 75 of the International Union of Police Associations. Recipients must be criminal justice majors at LSUS.

Contact the Student Financial Aid Office at LSUS for an application.

2272—LOUISIANA STATE UNIVERSITY AT SHREVEPORT (Walter O. Bigby Scholarship)

Dean of Liberal Arts
One University Place
Shreveport LA 71115-2399
318/797-5363 or 318/797-5371
FAX: 318/797-5366
E-mail: finaid@pilot.lsus.edu
Internet: www.lsus.edu
AMOUNT: up to $500/semester
DEADLINE(S): Varies
FIELD(S): Political Science, English, History, Law

Recipient must be entering the junior or senior year at LSUS with a major in political science, English, or history; may also be enrolled in some other Liberal Arts degree program if preparing to enter law school.

Contact the Dean's Office in the College of Liberal Arts at LSUS for an application.

2273—MINNESOTA STATE UNIVERSITY AT MANKATO (Korth Scholarship)

PS/LE Department, MSU 7
Mankato MN 56002-8400
507/389-2721
FAX: 507/389-6377
Internet: www.mankato.msus.edu/dept/psle/scholars/korth.html
AMOUNT: $400 (for tuition only)
DEADLINE(S): MAY 1
FIELD(S): Law Enforcement

Scholarships are awarded to high school seniors and undergraduates who attend or plan to attend Minnesota State University at Mankato full-time. Must submit current transcript along with completed application.

Contact the Political Science/Law Enforcement Office, 109 Morris Hall, for an application.

2274—NATIONAL BLACK POLICE ASSOCI-ATION (Alphonso Deal Scholarship Award)

3251 Mt. Pleasant St. NW, 2nd Floor
Washington DC 20010
202/986-2070

AMOUNT: $500
DEADLINE(S): JUN 1
FIELD(S): Law Enforcement, Criminal Justice

Open to minority high school graduates who have been accepted for enrollment in a two- or four-year college. Must have a GPA of 2.5 or better and demonstrate financial need. US citizenship required.

Write for complete information.

2275—NATIONAL FEDERATION OF THE BLIND (Howard Brown Rickard Scholarship)

805 Fifth Ave.
Grinnell IA 50112
515/236-3366

AMOUNT: $3,000
DEADLINE(S): MAR 31
FIELD(S): Law, Medicine, Engineering, Architecture, Natural Sciences

For legally blind students pursuing or planning to pursue a full-time postsecondary course of study in the US. Based on academic excellence, service to the community, and financial need. Membership NOT required.

1 award annually. Renewable. Contact Mrs. Peggy Elliot, Scholarship Committee Chairman, for an application.

2276—NATIONAL ITALIAN AMERICAN FOUNDATION (Assunta Luchetti Martino Scholarship for International Studies)

1860 19th Street NW
Washington DC 20009-5599
202/530-5315

AMOUNT: $1,000
DEADLINE(S): MAY 31
FIELD(S): International Studies

For undergraduates of Italian ancestry who are pursuing degrees in international studies.

Considerations are academic merit, financial need, and community service. Write for application and further information.

2277—NEW YORK STATE HIGHER EDU-CATION SERVICES CORPORATION (N.Y. State Regents Professional/Health Care Opportunity Scholarships)

Cultural Education Center, Rm. 5C64
Albany NY 12230
518/486-1319
Internet: www.hesc.com

AMOUNT: $1,000-$10,000/yr.
DEADLINE(S): Varies
FIELD(S): Medicine and Dentistry and related fields, Architecture, Nursing, Psychology, Audiology, Landscape Architecture, Social Work, Chiropractic, Law, Pharmacy, Accounting, Speech Language Pathology

For NY state residents who are economically disadvantaged and members of a minority group underrepresented in the chosen profession and attending school in NY state. Some programs carry a service obligation in New York for each year of support. For US citizens or qualifying noncitizens.

Medical/dental scholarships require one year of professional work in NY.

2278—OPEN SOCIETY INSTITUTE (Individual Project Fellowships)

400 West 59th Street
New York NY 10019
212/548-0600 or 212/757-2323
FAX: 212/548-4679 or
212/548-4600
Internet: www.soros.org/fellow/
individual.html

AMOUNT: Varies
DEADLINE(S): Varies
FIELD(S): Any field of study related to creating an open society: reliance on the rule of law, the existence of a democratically elected government, a diverse and vigorous civil society, and respect for minorities and minority opinions

Two-year fellowships for use in selected universities in the US for international students. For students/professionals in fields related to environmental policy, legislation, and remediation techniques applicable to their home countries.

To apply, contact the Soros Foundation/Open Society Institute. Further details on website.

2279—PRESIDENT'S COMMISSION ON WHITE HOUSE FELLOWSHIPS

712 Jackson Place NW
Washington DC 20503
202/395-4522
FAX: 202/395-6179
E-mail: almanac@ace.esusda.gov

AMOUNT: Wage (up to GS-14 Step 3; approximately $65,000)
DEADLINE(S): DEC 1
FIELD(S): Public Service, Government, Community Involvement, Leadership

Mid-career professionals spend one year as special assistants to senior executive branch officials in Washington. Highly competitive. Non-partisan; no age or educational requirements. Fellowship year runs September 1 through August 31.

1,200 candidates applying for 11 to 19 fellowships each year. Write for complete information.

2280—RAYMOND J. HARRIS EDUCATION TRUST

P.O. Box 7899
Philadelphia PA 19101-7899
Written inquiry

AMOUNT: Varies
DEADLINE(S): FEB 1
FIELD(S): Medicine, Law, Engineering, Dentistry, or Agriculture

Scholarships for Christian men to obtain a professional education in medicine, law, engineering, dentistry, or agriculture at nine Philadelphia area colleges.

Contact Mellon Bank, N.A. at above location for details and the names of the nine colleges.

2281—ROCKY MOUNTAIN MINERAL LAW FOUNDATION (Law Scholarships)

7039 East 18th Ave.
Denver CO 80200
303/321-8100
FAX: 303/321-7657
E-mail: info@rmmlf.org
Internet: www.rmmlf.org

AMOUNT: $10,000/yr.
DEADLINE(S): Varies
FIELD(S): Law/Natural Resources Law

Scholarships for law students in Foundation Governing Law Schools in the US and Canada pursuing careers in natural resources law.

Access website or contact Carla Sherwood, 303/321-8100, ext. 107 or e-mail sherwood@rmmlf.org at the Foundation for list of participating universities and application information.

2282—ROYAL THAI EMBASSY, OFFICE OF EDUCATIONAL AFFAIRS (Revenue Dept. Scholarships for Thai Students)

1906 23rd Street, NW
Washington DC 20008
202/667-9111 or 202/667-8010
FAX: 202/265-7239

AMOUNT: Varies
DEADLINE(S): APR
FIELD(S): Computer Science (Telecommunications), Law, Economics, Finance, Business Administration

Scholarships for students under age 35 from Thailand who have been accepted to study in the US or UK for the needs of the Revenue Dept., Ministry of Finance. Must pursue any level degree in one of the above fields.

Selections are based on academic records, employment history, and advisor recommendations.

2283—SOCIETY OF SATELLITE PROFESSIONALS INTERNATIONAL (SSPI Scholarships)

225 Reinekers Lane, Suite 600
Alexandria VA 22314
703/857-3717
FAX: 703/857-6335
E-mail: neworbit@aol.com
Internet: www.sspi.org

AMOUNT: $1,500 to $4,000
DEADLINE(S): DEC 1
FIELD(S): Satellites as related to communications, domestic and international telecommunications policy, remote sensing, journalism, law, meteorology, energy, navigation, business, government, and broadcasting services

Various scholarships for students studying in the above fields.

Access website for details and applications or send a self-addressed, stamped envelope (SASE) for a complete listing.

2284—THE AMERICAN ASSOCIATION OF ATTORNEY-CERTIFIED PUBLIC ACCOUNTANTS FOUNDATION (Student Writing Competition)

24196 Alicia Parkway, Suite K
Mission Viejo CA 92691
800/CPA-ATTY
FAX: 714/768-7062

AMOUNT: $250-$1,500
DEADLINE(S): APR 1
FIELD(S): Accounting, Law

Essay contest for accounting and/or law students.

Contact organization for current topics and rules.

2285—THE FEDERAL CIRCUIT BAR ASSOCIATION (George Hutchinson Writing Competition)

Brinks Hofer Gilson & Lione
NBC Tower, Suite 3600
Chicago IL 60611-5599
Internet: http://law.richmond.edu/essaycontests/JUDICIARYhutchinson.htm

AMOUNT: Up to $2,000
DEADLINE(S): JUN 1
FIELD(S): Law

Writing competition for law students on a topic that lies within the procedure, substance, or scope of the jurisdiction of the Federal Circuit Court of Appeals, i.e., patent litigation, Patent and Trademark Office decision, government contract claims, International Trade Commission, Merit Systems Appeals, and Veterans Appeals.

See website or contact organization for details.

2286—THE J. EDGAR HOOVER FOUNDATION

50 Gull Point Road
Hilton Head Island SC 29928
803/671-5020

AMOUNT: $500
DEADLINE(S): Ongoing
FIELD(S): Government, Law Enforcement

Scholarships for the study of government, the promotion of good citizenship, and law enforcement. The foundation strives to safeguard the heritage and freedom of the US, to promote good citizenship through an appreciation of the American form of government, and to combat communism or any other ideology or doctrine opposed to the principles set forth in the US Constitution.

Send letter to Cartha D. De Loach, Chair, at above address.

2287—THE NATIONAL ASSOCIATION OF COUNSEL FOR CHILDREN (Student Essay Competition)

Imhoff Pavilion
1825 Marion Street, Suite 340
Denver CO 80218
303/864-5320
888/828-NACC
E-mail: Advocate@NACCchildlaw.org
Internet: http://naccchildlaw.org

AMOUNT: $100
DEADLINE(S): AUG 3
FIELD(S): Law

Writing competition for law students in the field of children's law. The association welcomes multiple disciplines and endeavors to achieve the well-being of children by promoting multidisciplinary excellence in children's law.

$10 application fee. Contact organization for details.

2288—US CUSTOMS SERVICE (Law Enforcement Explorer Scholarships)

1301 Constitution Ave., Room 3422
Washington DC 20229
Not provided

AMOUNT: $1,000
DEADLINE(S): MAR 15 (local council); MAR 31 (US Customs Service)
FIELD(S): Law Enforcement

For high school seniors who are active in a Law Enforcement Post of the Exploring division of Boy Scouts of America. Must plan to study law enforcement in an accredited college or university.

Send for application through local council or at above address.

2289—US ENVIRONMENTAL PROTECTION AGENCY—NATIONAL NETWORK FOR ENVIRONMENTAL MANAGEMENT STUDIES (Fellowships)

401 M Street SW, Mailcode 1704
Washington DC 20460
202/260-5283
FAX: 202/260-4095
E-mail: jojokian.sheri@epa.gov
Internet: www.epa.gov/enviroed/students.html

AMOUNT: Varies
DEADLINE(S): DEC
FIELD(S): Environmental Policies, Regulations, & Law; Environmental Management & Administration; Environmental Science; Public Relations & Communications; Computer Programming & Development

Fellowships are open to undergraduate and graduate students working on research projects in the above fields, either full-time during the summer or part-time during the school year. Must be US citizen or legal resident. Financial need NOT a factor.

85-95 awards annually. Not renewable. See website or contact the Career Service Center of participating universities for an application.

2290—UNITARIAN UNIVERSALIST ASSN. (Otto M. Stanfield Legal Scholarship)

25 Beacon Street
Boston MA 02144
617/742-2100

AMOUNT: Varies
DEADLINE(S): FEB 15
FIELD(S): Law

Scholarships for law students. Applicants must be Unitarian Universalists.

No phone calls please.

2291—UNIVERSITY OF NEBRASKA AT OMAHA (Paul L. Beck Faculty/Staff Honors Scholarships)

6001 Dodge St., EAB Rm. 103
Omaha NE 68182-0187
402/554-2327
FAX: 402/554-3472
Internet: www.unomaha.edu/
~crimjust/beck.html

AMOUNT: $500 (full-time); $250 (part-time)
DEADLINE(S): FEB 1
FIELD(S): Criminal Justice

Applicants must be students in good standing who have a cumulative GPA of 3.0 or higher. May be resident or non-resident, full-time or part-time, but must be a senior during the term of the award. Recipient may hold no other scholarship during term of the award. Scholarship awarded by a screening committee consisting of the President of the Faculty Senate, the Faculty Senate Student Liaison Representative, and the Director of Financial Aid.

2 awards annually. Contact UNO's Financial Aid Office for an application. The President of the Faculty Senate announces the winners at the annual Honors Convocation.

2292—UNIVERSITY OF SOUTH DAKOTA (Criminal Justice Dept. Scholarships)

414 East Clark Street
Vermillion SD 57069-2390
605/677-5446
E-mail: admiss@usd.edu
Internet: www.usd.edu/cjus/
scholarships.htm#orderofpolice

AMOUNT: Varies

DEADLINE(S): Varies
FIELD(S): Criminal Justice, Political Science, Public Service

The University of South Dakota's Department of Criminal Justice administers 17 different award programs in the above fields. Some require a high GPA and/or financial need, others require an essay or research project.

See website or contact USD for specific details of each award. The Criminal Justice Department gives out an average of $77,000/year to USD students.

2293—UTA ALUMNI ASSOCIATION (John D. Burton Memorial Criminal Justice Scholarship)

University of Texas at Arlington
Box 19457
Arlington TX 76019
Internet: www.uta.edu/alumni/
scholar.htm

AMOUNT: $250
DEADLINE(S): Varies
FIELD(S): Criminal Justice, Urban Affairs

Must be a full-time student at the University of Texas at Arlington and demonstrate financial need. For criminal justice majors, if available; or for urban affairs majors, if no CJ available. Preference given to freshmen and sophomores.

2 awards annually. Contact UTA Alumni Association for an application.

2294—WESTERN SOCIETY OF CRIMINOLOGY (June Morrison Scholarship Fund)

Secretary/Treasurer
7039 Lindero Lane, #2
Rancho Murieta CA 95683
916/354-2980
FAX: 916/354-1389
Internet: www.sonoma.edu/CJA/
WSC/junem00.html

AMOUNT: $75
DEADLINE(S): JAN 31
FIELD(S): Criminology

Provides supplemental funds to support student participation at annual conferences. Students must be WSC members and attend the current year's conference. Conference registration and membership dues must be paid prior to the scholarship being awarded. Entries should not exceed one typewritten double-spaced page and should include the following: name, address, phone, e-mail, school, major,

grad/undergrad, how conference is valuable to you, and faculty sponsor signature.

5 awards annually. Send entries to Judith Embree, Secretary/Treasurer, WSC, at above address. Scholarship winners will be notified in writing by FebrUry 14th.

2295—WESTERN SOCIETY OF CRIMINOLOGY (Student Paper Competition)

Criminal Justice Division
Cal State Univ., 6000 J Street
Sacramento CA 95819-6085
Internet: www.sonoma.edu/CJA/
WSC/WSCstu00.html

AMOUNT: $125 (1st prize); $75 (2nd) + certificates
DEADLINE(S): DEC 15
FIELD(S): Criminology

Any student currently enrolled full- or part-time in an academic program at either the undergraduate or graduate level may enter. All entries must be papers relating to criminology. Papers must be 10 to 20 pages, typewritten, double-spaced on 8 1/2 x 11 white paper, using a standard format for the organization of papers and citations. Two copies must be submitted.

Send your entries to the attention of Dr. Miki Vohryzek-Bolden in the Criminal Justice Division at California State University. Winners will be notified in writing by February 7th.

2296—WOMEN IN DEFENSE (HORIZONS Scholarship Foundation)

NDIA
2111 Wilson Blvd., Suite 400
Arlington VA 22201-3061
703/247-2552
FAX: 703/522-1885
E-mail: dnwlee@moon.jic.com
Internet: www.adpa.org/wid/
horizon/Scholar.htm

AMOUNT: $500+
DEADLINE(S): NOV 1; JUL 1
FIELD(S): Engineering, Computer Science, Physics, Mathematics, Business, Law, International Relations, Political Science, Operations Research, Economics, and fields relevant to a career in the areas of national security and defense

For women who are US citizens, have minimum GPA of 3.25, demonstrate financial need, are currently enrolled at an accredited university/college (full- or part-time—both grads and undergrad juniors/seniors are eligible), and demonstrate interest in pursuing a career related to national security.

Application is online or send SASE, #10 envelope, to Woody Lee, HORIZONS Scholarship Director.

2297—WOMEN PEACE OFFICERS ASSOCI- ATION OF CALIFORNIA (WPOA Scholarship)

39525 Los Alamos Road, Suite A
Murrieta CA 92563
Internet: www.wvmccd.cc.ca.us/
wvmccd/wpoaca/scholar.html

AMOUNT: Varies
DEADLINE(S): Varies
FIELD(S): Law Enforcement

You are eligible to apply for this scholarship if you are a member of WPOA, a child of a WPOA member, or an active Peace Officer in the State of California. Area of study must be related to law enforcement.

For an application, write to WPOA at above address.

2298—WYOMING PEACE OFFICERS ASSO- CIATION (Scholarships for Active or Retired Officers)

1556 Riverbend Drive
Douglas WY 82633
307/358-3617
FAX: 307/358-9603

AMOUNT: $500/semester
DEADLINE(S): JUL 31
FIELD(S): Law Enforcement

Available to active or retired law enforcement officers enrolled in law enforcement at the University of Wyoming or a Wyoming community college. Applicants must complete 12 semester credit hours and maintain at least a "C" average. Scholarship is awarded upon completion of each semester.

4 awards annually. Renewable up to four semesters. Contact Lucille Taylor at WPOA for an application.

2299—WYOMING PEACE OFFICERS ASSO- CIATION (WPOA Scholarships)

1556 Riverbend Drive
Douglas WY 82633
307/358-3617
FAX: 307/358-9603

AMOUNT: $500/semester
DEADLINE(S): JUL 31
FIELD(S): All fields of study; Law
  Enforcement

Available to dependents of active (dues current), lifetime, or deceased WPOA members regardless of field of study or college attended, or students planning to enroll in a law enforcement program at a Wyoming college or university. Applicants must complete 12 semester credit hours and maintain at least a "C" average. Scholarship is awarded upon completion of each semester.

4 awards annually. Renewable up to four semesters. Contact Lucille Taylor at WPOA for an application.

POLITICAL SCIENCE

2300—AIR FORCE RESERVE OFFICER TRAINING CORPS (AFROTC Scholarships)

551 E. Maxwell Blvd.
Maxwell AFB AL 36112-6106
334/953-7783

AMOUNT: Full tuition, books, & fees for
  all 4 years of college
DEADLINE(S): DEC 1
FIELD(S): Science, Engineering,
  Business, Political Science, Psychology,
  Geography, Foreign Studies, Foreign
  Language

Competitive scholarships based on individual merit to high school seniors and graduates who have not completed any full-time college work. Must be a US citizen between the ages of 17-27. Must also have GPA of 2.5 or above, be in top 40% of class, and complete Applicant Fitness Test. Cannot be a single parent. Your college/university must offer AFROTC.

2,300 awards annually. Contact above address for application packet.

2301—AMERICA ISRAEL PUBLIC AFFAIRS COMMITTEE (Internships)

440 First Street NW, Suite 600
Washington DC 20001
202/639-5327
Internet: www.aipac.org

AMOUNT: Internship
DEADLINE(S): SEP 15; DEC 1; JAN 15;
  APR 1
FIELD(S): US-Israel Issues

For highly qualified pro-Israel students for internships in national and regional offices working to strengthen the US-Israel relationship. Interns are expected to return to campus to promote pro-Israel political activity. Cover letter stating interest, resume indicating political experience (student government, etc.) and involvement, one-page typewritten essay about involvement in pro-Israel work on campus, and letter of recommendation from AIPAC campus liaison required.

Contact Steve Bocknek at AIPAC for an application.

2302—AMERICAN BAR FOUNDATION (Summer Research Fellowships in Law and Social Science for Minority Undergraduate Students)

750 N. Lake Shore Drive
Chicago IL 60611
312/988-6500
Internet: www.abf-sociolegal.org

AMOUNT: $3,500 stipend
DEADLINE(S): MAR 1
FIELD(S): Social Sciences, Humanities,
  Law

Summer research opportunity open to sophomore and junior undergraduates who are Native American, African American, Mexican, Puerto Rican, or other minority. Must be US citizen or permanent resident and have at least a 3.0 GPA. Students are assigned a mentor and participate in seminars; must also work at the Foundation's office in Chicago for 35 hours per week for 10 weeks. Essay, transcripts, and letter of recommendation required.

4 awards annually; announced in April. See website or contact ABF for an application.

2303—AMERICAN FEDERATION OF STATE, COUNTY, AND MUNICIPAL EMPLOYEES, AFL-CIO (Jerry Clark Memorial Scholarship)

1625 L Sreet, NW
Washington DC 20036
202/429-1250
FAX 202/429-1272

AMOUNT: $10,000/yr.
DEADLINE(S): JUL 1
FIELD(S): Political Science

For children of active AFSCME members who are college sophomores. Award is for their junior and senior years of college and includes an internship with AFSCME's Political Action Department.

1 award annually. Contact AFSCME Headquarters for an application.

2304—AMERICAN JEWISH COMMITTEE (Harold W. Rosenthal Fellowship)

1156 15th Street, NW Suite 1201
Washington DC 20005
202/785-4200

AMOUNT: $1,800 stipend
DEADLINE(S): FEB
FIELD(S): Political Science, Government
  Service, Foreign Affairs

Open to college seniors and grad students. Fellowship provides opportunity for a student to spend a summer working in the office of a member of Congress or Executive Branch on Foreign Affairs and government service issues. US citizen.

Applications are available from the address above; however, they must be submitted with a recommendation from your dean. Selected fellows will also receive preferential treatment for a European community 3- to 5-week travel study.

2305—ASSOCIATION FOR WOMEN IN SCIENCE EDUCATIONAL FOUNDATION (Dr. Vicki L. Schechtman Scholarship)

1200 New York Ave. NW
Suite 650
Washington DC 20005
202/326-8940 or 800/886-AWIS
E-mail: awis@awis.org
Internet: www.awis.org

AMOUNT: $1,000
DEADLINE(S): JAN 16
FIELD(S): Various Sciences and Social Sciences

For female undergraduate students who are US citizens and have a minimum GPA of 3.0. Summary page, essay describing career aspirations, transcripts, proof of matriculation (if available), and two reference letters required with application. Scholarships may be used for tuition, books, housing, research, equipment, etc.

See website or write to above address for an application and more information.

2306—ASSOCIATION FOR WOMEN IN SCIENCE EDUCATIONAL FOUNDATION (Ruth Satter Memorial Award)

1200 New York Ave. NW
Suite 650
Washington DC 20005
202/326-8940 or 800/886-AWIS
E-mail: awis@awis.org
Internet: www.awis.org

AMOUNT: $1,000
DEADLINE(S): JAN 16
FIELD(S): Various Sciences and Social Sciences

Scholarships for female doctoral students who have interrupted their education three years or more to raise a family. Summary page, description of research project, resume, references, transcripts, biographical sketch, and proof of eligibility from department head required. US citizens may attend any graduate institution; noncitizens must be enrolled in US institutions.

See website or write to above address for more information or an application.

2307—BOYS AND GIRLS CLUBS OF SAN DIEGO (Spence Reese Scholarship Fund)

1761 Hotel Circle S., Suite 123
San Diego CA 92108
619/298-3520

AMOUNT: $2,000/yr.
DEADLINE(S): MAY 15
FIELD(S): Medicine, Law, Engineering, Political Science

Open to male high school seniors planning a career in one of the above fields. Must be residents of Imperial, Riverside, Orange, San Diego, or Los Angeles counties in California. Boys and Girls Club affiliation NOT required.

$10 application fee. Renewable up to 4 years. Send a self-addressed, stamped envelope to Boys and Girls Club for an application after January 1st.

2308—CHRISTIAN A. JOHNSON ENDEAVOR FOUNDATION (Native American Fellows)

Harvard Univ.
79 John F. Kennedy Street
Cambridge MA 02138
617/495-1152
FAX: 617/496-3900
Internet: www.ksg.harvard.edu/hpaied/cjohn.htm

AMOUNT: Varies
DEADLINE(S): MAY 1
FIELD(S): Social Sciences, Government, or program related to Native American studies

Fellowships for students of Native American ancestry who attend a John F. Kennedy School of Government degree program. Applicant, parent, or grandparent must hold membership in a federally or state-recognized tribe, band, or other organized group of Native Americans. Must be committed to a career in American Indian affairs. Awards based on merit and need.

Renewable, based on renomination and availability of funds. To apply, contact John F. Kennedy School of Government at above address.

2309—CONFERENCE OF MINORITY PUBLIC ADMINISTRATORS (Scholarships and Travel Grants)

P.O. Box 3010
Fort Worth TX 76113
817/871-8325
Internet: www.compa.org

AMOUNT: $400 (travel grants); up to $1,500 (academic year)
DEADLINE(S): Varies
FIELD(S): Public Administration/Public Affairs

COMPA offers two academic scholarships, at least five travel grants, and a $1,000 gift to the college that has the largest number of student registrants at its annual conference. Travel grants are for attending the conference. For minorities and women pursuing full-time education in the above fields and committed to excellence in public service and administration in city, county, state, and federal governments.

Contact Edwin Cook at above location for details.

2310—CUBAN AMERICAN NATIONAL FOUNDATION (The Mas Family Scholarships)

7300 NW 35 Terrace
Miami FL 33122
305/592-7768
FAX: 305/592-7889
E-mail canfnet.org
Internet: www.canfnet.org

AMOUNT: Individually negotiated
DEADLINE(S): MAR 15
FIELD(S): Engineering, Business, International Relations, Economics, Communications, Journalism

For Cuban-American students, graduates and undergraduates, born in Cuba or direct descendants of those who left Cuba. Must be in top 10% of high school class or maintain a 3.5 GPA in college.

10,000 awards/year. Recipients may reapply for subsequent years. Financial need considered along with academic success, SAT and GRE scores, and leadership potential. Essays and proof of Cuban descent required.

2311—GENERAL FEDERATION OF WOMEN'S CLUBS OF MASSACHUSETTS (International Affairs Scholarships)

245 Dutton Road, Box 679
Sudbury MA 01776-0679
508/481-3354

AMOUNT: $500
DEADLINE(S): MAR 1
FIELD(S): International Affairs, International Relations

For undergraduate and/or graduate study abroad for legal residents of Massachusetts. Letter of endorsement from sponsoring GFWC of MA club, personal statement of "what I hope to gain from this experience," letter of reference from department head of your major, transcripts, and personal interview required with application.

For further information or an application, send self-addressed, stamped envelope to Sheila E. Shea, Counselor, International Affairs Department, at above address.

2312—HARRY S. TRUMAN SCHOLARSHIP FOUNDATION (Scholarships)

712 Jackson Place, NW
Washington DC 20006-4901
202/395-4831
Internet: www.truman.gov

AMOUNT: $30,000 ($3,000 for senior year + $27,000 for grad studies)
DEADLINE(S): FEB 1
FIELD(S): Public Service, Government

Merit-based awards for those who pursue careers in government or public service and wish to attend graduate/professional school in US or foreign country. Must be full-time junior at four-year institution pursuing bachelor's degree, in upper quarter of class, and US citizen/national. State scholarships available to nominees from each of 50 states, DC, Puerto Rico, and Guam, Virgin Islands, American Samoa, Northern Mariana Islands. Must show community service and leadership.

75-80 awards annually. Applicants must be nominated by their institution. See website or contact Foundation for more information.

2313—HILLSDALE COLLEGE (Freedom as Vocation Scholarship)

33 E. College Street
Hillsdale MI 49242-1298
517/437-7341
Internet: www.hillsdale.edu

AMOUNT: Varies
DEADLINE(S): None
FIELD(S): Business, History, Political Science, Economics

Open to Hillsdale College undergraduates who maintain a minimum 3.0 GPA and commit to a series of courses in the above fields. Student must rank in top 20% of class and top 10% of test scores. Must possess excellent communications, public speaking, and leadership skills, and demonstrate outstanding character and citizenship. Financial need NOT a factor.

Renewable. No application process; students are selected. See website for details.

2314—INSTITUTE FOR HUMANE STUDIES (Humane Studies Fellowship)

4084 University Drive, Suite 101
Fairfax VA 22030-6812
703/934-6920 or 800/697-8799
FAX: 703/352-7535
E-mail: ihs@gmu.edu
Internet: www.theihs.org

AMOUNT: up to $12,000
DEADLINE(S): DEC 31
FIELD(S): Social Sciences, Law, Humanities, Jurisprudence, Journalism

Awards are for graduate and advanced undergraduate students pursuing degrees at any accredited domestic or foreign school. Based on academic performance, demonstrated interest in classical liberal ideas, and potential to contribute to the advancement of a free society.

90 awards annually. Apply online or contact IHS for an application.

2315—INSTITUTE FOR HUMANE STUDIES (Koch Summer Fellow Program)

4084 University Drive, Suite 101
Fairfax VA 22030-6812
703/934-6920 or 800/697-8799
FAX: 703/352-7535
E-mail: ihs@gmu.edu
Internet: www.theihs.org

AMOUNT: $1,500 + airfare & housing
DEADLINE(S): MAR 1
FIELD(S): Economics, Politics, Law, Government, Public Policy

For undergraduates and graduates to build skills and gain experience by participating in an 8-week summer internship program. Includes 2 week-long seminars, the internship, and research and writing projects with professionals. College transcripts, essays, and application required. Financial need NOT a factor.

32 awards annually. Not renewable. Apply online or contact IHS for an application.

2316—INSTITUTE FOR HUMANE STUDIES (Summer Residential Program)

4084 University Drive, Suite 101
Fairfax VA 22030-6812
703/934-6920 or 800/697-8799
FAX: 703/352-7535
E-mail: ihs@gmu.edu
Internet: www.theihs.org

AMOUNT: All seminar fees: program cost, room/board, materials, and books
DEADLINE(S): MAR 1

FIELD(S): Social Sciences, Humanities, Law, Journalism, Public Policy, Education, Writing

For college students, recent graduates, and graduate students who share an interest in learning and exchanging ideas about the scope of individual rights. One-week and weekend seminars at various campus locations across the US.

Apply online or contact IHS for an application.

2317—INSTITUTE OF INTERNATIONAL EDUCATION (National Security Education Program-Undergraduate Scholarships)

1400 K St. NW, 6th Fl.
Washington DC 20005-2403
202/326-7697
800/618-NSEP (6737)
E-mail: nsep@iie.org
Internet: http://www.iie.org/nsep/

AMOUNT: Varies: up to $8,000/semester
DEADLINE(S): FEB 8
FIELD(S): Open to all majors; preference to Applied Sciences, Engineering, Business, Economics, Math, Computer Science, International Affairs, Political Science, History, and the Policy Sciences

For study abroad OUTSIDE the US, Canada, Australia, New Zealand, and Western Europe. For study in areas deemed critical to US national security. Applications available on US campuses from August through early December. Or contact organization for details.

Inquire at above location for details.

2318—JAMES FORD BELL FOUNDATION (Summer Internship Program)

2925 Dean Pkwy., Suite 811
Minneapolis MN 55416
612/285-5435
FAX: 612/285-5437
E-mail: famphiladv@uswest.net

AMOUNT: $4,000 for 3 months
DEADLINE(S): APR 30
FIELD(S): Business/Public Administration, Public Policy, Organization Leadership, Nonprofit Management

Interns spend the summer with organizations selected by the Foundation; the organizations select interns from masters degree programs in above or related fields and college seniors with strong interest in nonprofit work. Internships normally in the Twin Cities area.

Contact Foundation for a list of internship opportunities in February and March only; students should request position list, not an application for the program itself (only organizations apply for the program).

2319—JAMES MADISON MEMORIAL FELLOWSHIP (Fellowship for Teachers)

2000 K Street, NW
Washington DC 20006
202/653-8700
1-800/525-6928
FAX: 202/653-6045
Internet: www.jamesmadison.com

AMOUNT: $24,000 prorated over study period
DEADLINE(S): MAR 1
FIELD(S): Teaching American History/Government, or Social Studies—concentration on the US Constitution

Fellowships for teachers (senior fellows) in grades 7-12 in the above fields to pursue an M.A. degree. Also for full-time college seniors and grad students (junior fellows). US citizens or US nationals. Fellows are selected from each state and from DC, Puerto Rico, Guam, Virgin Islands, American Samoa, Northern Mariana Islands, and Palau. Program designed to enhance teaching about the US Constitution.

Application is on website or contact: American College Testing, P.O. Box 4030, Iowa City, IA 52243-4030; 800/525-6928

E-mail: Recogprog@ACT-ACT4-PO.act.org

2320—JAPANESE AMERICAN CITIZENS LEAGUE (Alice Yuriko Endo Memorial Scholarship)

1765 Sutter Street
San Francisco CA 94115
415/921-5225
FAX: 415/931-4671
E-mail: jacl@jacl.org
Internet: www.jacl.org

AMOUNT: $1,000-$5,000
DEADLINE(S): APR 1
FIELD(S): Public & Social Service

Open to JACL members and their children only. For undergraduate students with an interest in public or social service who are planning to attend a college, university, trade school, business school, or any other institution of higher learning. Preference given to students residing in the Eastern District Council and/or those studying in above fields. Financial need NOT a factor.

For membership information or an application, send a self-addressed, stamped envelope to above address, stating your level of study. Applications available October 1st through March 20th; recipients notified in July.

2321—JAPANESE AMERICAN CITIZENS LEAGUE (Yoshiko Tanaka Memorial Scholarship)

1765 Sutter Street
San Francisco CA 94115
415/921-5225
FAX: 415/931-4671
E-mail: jacl@jacl.org
Internet: www.jacl.org

AMOUNT: $1,000-$5,000
DEADLINE(S): APR 1
FIELD(S): Japanese Language/Culture, US-Japan Relations

Open to JACL members and their children only. For undergraduate students with an interest in Japanese language, culture, or the enhancement of US-Japan relations and who are planning to attend a college, university, trade school, business school, or any other institution of higher learning. Must submit personal statement, letters of recommendation, and transcripts. Financial need NOT a factor.

For membership information or an application, send a self-addressed, stamped envelope to above address, stating your level of study. Applications available October 1st through March 20th; recipients notified in July.

2322—JUNIATA COLLEGE (Baker Peace Scholarship)

Baker Institute
Peace & Conflict Studies
Huntingdon PA 16652-2119
814/641-3265

AMOUNT: $1,000-$2,000
DEADLINE(S): FEB 1
FIELD(S): Peace & Conflict Studies, International Affairs

Open to incoming freshmen at Juniata College who rank in the upper 20% of their high school class, have above-average SAT scores, and demonstrate an interest in peace-related issues. Must submit 1,000-word essay on designated topic, two letters of recommendation, and maintain a minimum 3.0 GPA.

Renewable up to 4 years. Contact Baker Institute for an application.

2323—LOUISIANA STATE UNIVERSITY AT SHREVEPORT (Walter O. Bigby Scholarship)

Dean of Liberal Arts
One University Place
Shreveport LA 71115-2399
318/797-5363 or 318/797-5371
FAX: 318/797-5366
E-mail: finaid@pilot.lsus.edu
Internet: www.lsus.edu

AMOUNT: up to $500/semester
DEADLINE(S): Varies
FIELD(S): Political Science, English, History, Law

Recipient must be entering the junior or senior year at LSUS with a major in political science, English, or history; may also be enrolled in some other Liberal Arts degree program if preparing to enter law school.

Contact the Dean's Office in the College of Liberal Arts at LSUS for an application.

2324—NATIONAL ITALIAN AMERICAN FOUNDATION (Assunta Luchetti Martino Scholarship for International Studies)

1860 19th Street NW
Washington DC 20009-5599
202/530-5315

AMOUNT: $1,000
DEADLINE(S): MAY 31
FIELD(S): International Studies

For undergraduates of Italian ancestry who are pursuing degrees in international studies.

Considerations are academic merit, financial need, and community service. Write for application and further information.

2325—NATIONAL SOCIETY DAUGHTERS OF THE AMERICAN REVOLUTION (Enid Hall Griswold Memorial Scholarship)

1776 D Street NW
Washington DC 20006-5392
202/628-1776
Internet: www.dar.org

AMOUNT: $1,000
DEADLINE(S): FEB 15
FIELD(S): History, Political Science, Government, Economics

Open to undergraduate juniors and seniors (US citizens) attending an accredited US college or university. Awards are placed on deposit with school. Awards are judged on academic excellence, commitment to field of study, and need. Affiliation with DAR not required.

Not renewable. See website or send a self-addressed, stamped envelope for an application or more informtion.

2326—NEW YORK CITY DEPT. CITYWIDE ADMINISTRATIVE SERVICES (Urban Fellows Program)

1 Centre Street, 24th Fl.
New York NY 10007
212/487-5600
FAX: 212/487-5720

AMOUNT: $18,000 stipend
DEADLINE(S): JAN 20
FIELD(S): Public Administration, Urban Planning, Government, Public Service, Urban Affairs

Fellowship program provides one academic year (9 months) of full-time work experience in urban government. Open to graduating college seniors and recent college graduates. US citizenship required.

Write for complete information.

2327—NEW YORK CITY DEPT. OF CITY-WIDE ADMINISTRATIVE SERVICES (Government Scholars Internship Program)

1 Centre Street, 24th Floor
New York NY 10007
212/487-5600
FAX: 212/487-5720

AMOUNT: $3,000 stipend
DEADLINE(S): JAN 13
FIELD(S): Public Administration, Urban Planning, Government, Public Service, Urban Affairs

10-week summer intern program open to undergraduate sophomores, juniors, and seniors. Program provides students with unique opportunity to learn about NY City government. Internships available in virtually every city agency and mayoral office.

Write to New York City Fellowship Programs at above address for complete information.

2328—NEW YORK STATE SENATE (Legislative Fellows Program; R. J. Roth Journalism Fellowship; R. A. Wiebe Public Service Fellowship)

NYS Senate Student Programs Office
90 South Swan Street, Room 401
Albany NY 12247

518/455-2611
FAX: 518/432-5470
E-mail: students@senate.state.ny.us
AMOUNT: $25,000 stipend (not a scholarship)
DEADLINE(S): MAY (first Friday)
FIELD(S): Political Science, Government, Public Service, Journalism, Public Relations

One year programs for US citizens who are grad students and residents of New York state or enrolled in accredited programs in New York state. Fellows work as regular legislative staff members of the office to which they are assigned. The Roth Fellowship is for communications/journalism majors, and undergrads may be considered for this program.

14 fellowships per year. Fellowships take place at the New York State Legislative Office. Write for complete information.

2329—OPEN SOCIETY INSTITUTE (Individual Project Fellowships)

400 West 59th Street
New York NY 10019
212/548-0600 or 212/757-2323
FAX: 212/548-4679 or 212/548-4600
Internet: www.soros.org/fellow/individual.html

AMOUNT: Varies
DEADLINE(S): Varies
FIELD(S): Any field of study related to creating an open society: reliance on the rule of law, the existence of a democratically elected government, a diverse and vigorous civil society, and respect for minorities and minority opinions

Two-year fellowships for use in selected universities in the US for international students. For students/professionals in fields related to environmental policy, legislation, and remediation techniques applicable to their home countries.

To apply, contact the Soros Foundation/Open Society Institute. Further details on website.

2330—PRESIDENT'S COMMISSION ON WHITE HOUSE FELLOWSHIPS

712 Jackson Place NW
Washington DC 20503
202/395-4522
FAX: 202/395-6179

E-mail: almanac@ace.esusda.gov
AMOUNT: Wage (up to GS-14 Step 3; approximately $65,000 in 1995)
DEADLINE(S): DEC 1
FIELD(S): Public Service, Government, Community Involvement, Leadership

Mid-career professionals spend one year as special assistants to senior executive branch officials in Washington. Highly competitive. Non-partisan; no age or educational requirements. Fellowship year runs September 1 through August 31.

1,200 candidates applying for 11 to 19 fellowships each year. Write for complete information.

2331—ROSE HILL COLLEGE (Louella Robinson Memorial Scholarship)

P.O. Box 3126
Aiken SC 29802-3126
800/684-3769
FAX: 803/641-0240
E-mail: rosehill@.edu
Internet: www.rosehill.edu

AMOUNT: $10,000/yr. for four years
DEADLINE(S): Varies
FIELD(S): Liberal Arts and Humanities curricula

For undergraduate residents of Indian River County, Florida, to attend Rose Hill College in Aiken, South Carolina. The school offers a liberal arts education and follows the Great Books curriculum, a program of reading and seminars.

1 annual award. Applicants must meet entry requirements of RHC. Contact above location for details.

2332—ROSE HILL COLLEGE (Scholarships for Children of Eastern Orthodox Priests/Deacons)

P.O. Box 3126
Aiken SC 29802-3126
800/684-3769
FAX: 803/641-0240
E-mail: rosehill@edu
Internet: www.rosehill.edu

AMOUNT: Full scholarship: $10,000/yr. for four years
DEADLINE(S): Varies
FIELD(S): Liberal Arts and Humanities curricula

For undergraduates who are children of Eastern Orthodox Christian priests or deacons to attend Rose Hill College in Aiken, South Carolina. The school offers a liberal arts education and follows the Great Books curriculum, a program of reading and seminars.

6-10 annual awards. Applicants must meet entry requirements of RHC. Contact above location for details.

2333—ROSE HILL COLLEGE (Scholarships for the Homeschooled)

P.O. Box 3126
Aiken SC 29802-3126
800/684-3769
FAX: 803/641-0240
E-mail: rosehill@rosehill.edu
Internet: www.resehill.edu

AMOUNT: Full scholarship: $10,000/yr. for four years
DEADLINE(S): Varies
FIELD(S): Liberal Arts and Humanities curricula

For undergraduates who have been homeschooled for three of the last five years of their high school education. For use at Rose Hill College in Aiken, South Carolina. The school offers a liberal arts education and follows the Great Books curriculum, a program of reading and seminars. Scholarships will be awarded primarily on the basis of an essay that the student will be asked to write.

4 annual awards. Applicants must meet entry requirements of RHC. Contact above location for details.

2334—SOCIETY OF SATELLITE PROFESSIONALS INTERNATIONAL (SSPI Scholarships)

225 Reinekers Lane, Suite 600
Alexandria VA 22314
703/857-3717
FAX: 703/857-6335
E-mail: neworbit@aol.com
Internet: www.sspi.org

AMOUNT: $1,500 to $4,000
DEADLINE(S): DEC 1
FIELD(S): Satellites as related to communications, domestic and international telecommunications policy, remote sensing, journalism, law, meteorology, energy, navigation, business, government, and broadcasting services

Various scholarships for students studying in the above fields.

Access website for details and applications or send a self-addressed, stamped envelope (SASE) for a complete listing.

2335—SOIL AND WATER CONSERVATION SOCIETY (SWCS Internships)

7515 NE Ankeny Road
Ankeny IA 50021-9764

515/289-2331 or 800/THE-SOIL
FAX: 515/289-1227
E-mail: charliep@swcs.org
Internet: www.swcs.org

AMOUNT: Varies—most are uncompensated
DEADLINE(S): Varies
FIELD(S): Journalism, Marketing, Database Management, Meeting Planning, Public Policy Research, Environmental Education, Landscape Architecture

Internships for undergraduates and graduates to gain experience in the above fields as they relate to soil and water conservation issues. Internship openings vary through the year in duration, compensation, and objective. SWCS will coordinate particulars with your academic advisor.

Contact SWCS for internship availability at any time during the year or see website for jobs page.

2336—SPACE COAST CREDIT UNION (Two-Year Scholarships)

Marketing Dept.
P.O. Box 2470
Melbourne FL 32902
Internet: www.sccu.com/scholarship/

AMOUNT: $750/year, two years; $1,000 bonus if go on for Bachelors
DEADLINE(S): APR 15
FIELD(S): Math, Economics, Science, Computer Science, Marketing, Journalism, Political Science

Must be graduating from a high school in Brevard, Volusia, Flagler, or Indian River counties, be a member of SCCU, have a minimum 3.0 GPA, planning to attend a two-year Florida institution of higher education for an associates degree, and be willing to write a 200-word essay on the topic "Why credit unions are valuable to society."

4 annual awards. Students going on to complete a four-year degree could be eligible for a bonus scholarship of $1,000 for the next two years. For membership information or an application, see our web page or write to the above address.

2337—THE FUND FOR AMERICAN STUDIES (Institutes on Political Journalism; Business & Government Affairs & Comparative Political & Economic Systems)

1526 18th Street NW
Washington DC 20036
202/986-0384 or 800/741-6964

Internet: http://www.dcinternships.com

AMOUNT: Up to $2,975
DEADLINE(S): JAN 31 (early decision); MAR 15 (general application deadline)
FIELD(S): Political Science, Economics, Journalism, Business Administration

The Fund for American Studies, in conjunction with Georgetown University, sponsors summer institutes that include internships, courses for credit, site briefings, and dialogues with policy leaders. Scholarships are available to sophomores and juniors to cover the cost of the program.

Approx 100 awards per year. For Fund's programs only. Call, check website, or write for complete information.

2338—THE J. EDGAR HOOVER FOUNDATION

50 Gull Point Road
Hilton Head Island SC 29928
803/671-5020

AMOUNT: $500
DEADLINE(S): Ongoing
FIELD(S): Government, Law Enforcement

Scholarships for the study of government, the promotion of good citizenship, and law enforcement. The foundation strives to safeguard the heritage and freedom of the US, to promote good citizenship through an appreciation of the American form of government, and to combat communism or any other ideology or doctrine opposed to the principles set forth in the US Constitution.

Send letter to Cartha D. De Loach, Chair, at above address.

2339—US INSTITUTE OF PEACE (National Peace Essay Contest)

1200 17th Street NW, Suite 200
Washington DC 20036
202/429-3834
FAX 202/429-6063
E-mail: essay_contest@usip.org
Internet: www.usip.org

AMOUNT: $1,000-$10,000
DEADLINE(S): JAN 26
FIELD(S): Political Science, US History

1,500-word essay contest for high school students on the US response to international conflict. No restrictions as to citizenship/residency.

53 awards annually. Not renewable. See website or contact USIP for specific guidelines.

2340—UNIVERSITY OF SOUTH DAKOTA (Criminal Justice Dept. Scholarships)

414 East Clark Street
Vermillion SD 57069-2390
605/677-5446
E-mail: admiss@usd.edu
Internet: www.usd.edu/cjus/
scholarships.htm#orderofpolice

AMOUNT: Varies
DEADLINE(S): Varies
FIELD(S): Criminal Justice, Political
Science, Public Service

The University of South Dakota's Department of Criminal Justice administers 17 different award programs in the above fields. Some require a high GPA and/or financial need, others require an essay or research project.

See website or contact USD for specific details of each award. The Criminal Justice Department gives out an average of $77,000/year to USD students.

2341—WASHINGTON CROSSING FOUNDATION (National Scholarship Award)

Eugene C. Fish, Esq., Vice Chairman
P.O. Box 503
Levittown PA 19058-0503
215/949-8841
Internet: www.gwcf.org

AMOUNT: $1,000-$10,000
DEADLINE(S): JAN 1
FIELD(S): Government Service, Public
Service

Open to US high school seniors planning a career in government service (local/state/federal). Each interested student is invited to write a typed, double-spaced, one-page essay stating why he/she plans a career in government service, including any inspiration to be derived from the leadership of George Washington in his famous crossing of the Delaware. Tenable at any accredited US college/university. Must be US citizen. Financial need NOT a factor.

6 awards annually. See website or contact GWCF for details.

2342—WOMEN IN DEFENSE (HORIZONS Scholarship Foundation)

NDIA
2111 Wilson Blvd., Suite 400
Arlington VA 22201-3061
703/247-2552
FAX: 703/522-1885
E-mail: dnwlee@moon.jic.com
Internet: www.adpa.org/wid/horizon/
Scholar.htm

AMOUNT: $500+
DEADLINE(S): NOV 1; JUL 1
FIELD(S): Engineering, Computer
Science, Physics, Mathematics,
Business, Law, International Relations,
Political Science, Operations Research,
Economics, and fields relevant to a
career in the areas of national security
and defense

For women who are US citizens, have minimum GPA of 3.25, demonstrate financial need, are currently enrolled at an accredited university/college (full- or part-time—both grads and undergrad juniors/seniors are eligible), and demonstrate interest in pursuing a career related to national security.

Application is online or send SASE, #10 envelope, to Woody Lee, HORIZONS Scholarship Director.

2343—WOODROW WILSON NATIONAL FELLOWSHIP FOUNDATION/US DEPARTMENT OF STATE (FAF/GFAF Foreign Affairs Fellowship Programs)

P.O. Box 2437
Princeton NJ 08543-2437
609/452-7007
FAX: 609/452-0066
E-mail: fafadim@woodrow.org
(undergrad) OR
gfafadim@woodrow.org (grad)
Internet: www.woodrow.org

AMOUNT: Varies
DEADLINE(S): FEB 15
FIELD(S): International Affairs, Foreign
Policy

Prepares students for careers as foreign service officers. FAF program is for undergraduates and includes internships with the State Department and graduate fellowships leading to master's degrees in international affairs. GFAF program is for students planning to enter the first year of graduate school. Must be US citizen.

See website or contact WWNFF for an application.

2344—WOODROW WILSON NATIONAL FELLOWSHIP FOUNDATION/INSTITUTE FOR INTERNATIONAL PUBLIC POLICY (IIPP Fellowships)

CN 5281
Princeton NJ 08543-5281
609/452-7007
FAX: 609/452-0066
E-mail: richard@woodrow.org
Internet: www.woodrow.org

AMOUNT: Varies
DEADLINE(S): Varies
FIELD(S): International Affairs, Foreign
Policy

Open to minorities preparing for careers in international affairs at US colleges/universities. Must apply during sophomore year of college. Program draws from Historically Black Colleges & Universities, the Hispanic Association of Colleges & Universities, and the American Indian Higher Education Consortium.

See website or contact WWNFF for an application.

PSYCHOLOGY

2345—AIR FORCE RESERVE OFFICER TRAINING CORPS (AFROTC Scholarships)

551 E. Maxwell Blvd.
Maxwell AFB AL 36112-6106
334/953-7783

AMOUNT: Full tuition, books, & fees for
all 4 years of college
DEADLINE(S): DEC 1
FIELD(S): Science, Engineering,
Business, Political Science, Psychology,
Geography, Foreign Studies, Foreign
Language

Competitive scholarships based on individual merit to high school seniors and graduates who have not completed any full-time college work. Must be a US citizen between the ages of 17-27. Must also have GPA of 2.5 or above, be in top 40% of class, and complete Applicant Fitness Test. Cannot be a single parent. Your college/university must offer AFROTC.

2,300 awards annually. Contact above address for application packet.

2346—AMERICAN BAR FOUNDATION (Summer Research Fellowships in Law and Social Science for Minority Undergraduate Students)

750 N. Lake Shore Drive
Chicago IL 60611
312/988-6500
Internet: www.abf-sociolegal.org

AMOUNT: $3,500 stipend
DEADLINE(S): MAR 1
FIELD(S): Social Sciences, Humanities,
Law

Summer research opportunity open to sophomore and junior undergraduates who are Native American, African American, Mexican, Puerto Rican, or other minority. Must be US citizen or permanent resident and have at least a 3.0 GPA. Students are assigned a mentor and participate in seminars; must also work at the Foundation's office in Chicago for 35 hours per week for 10 weeks. Essay, transcripts, and letter of recommendation required.

4 awards annually; announced in April. See website or contact ABF for an application.

2347—ASSOCIATION FOR WOMEN IN SCIENCE EDUCATIONAL FOUNDATION (Dr. Vicki L. Schechtman Scholarship)

1200 New York Ave. NW
Suite 650
Washington DC 20005
202/326-8940 or 800/886-AWIS
E-mail: awis@awis.org
Internet: www.awis.org

AMOUNT: $1,000
DEADLINE(S): JAN 16
FIELD(S): Various Sciences and Social Sciences

For female undergraduate students who are US citizens and have a minimum GPA of 3.0. Summary page, essay describing career aspirations, transcripts, proof of matriculation (if available), and two reference letters required with application. Scholarships may be used for tuition, books, housing, research, equipment, etc.

See website or write to above address for an application and more information.

2348—ASSOCIATION FOR WOMEN IN SCIENCE EDUCATIONAL FOUNDATION (Ruth Satter Memorial Award)

1200 New York Ave. NW
Suite 650
Washington DC 20005
202/326-8940 or 800/886-AWIS
E-mail: awis@awis.org
Internet: www.awis.org

AMOUNT: $1,000
DEADLINE(S): JAN 16
FIELD(S): Various Sciences and Social Sciences

Scholarships for female doctoral students who have interrupted their education three years or more to raise a family. Summary page, description of research project, resume, references, transcripts, biographical sketch, and proof of eligibility from department head required. US citizens may attend any graduate institution; non-citizens must be enrolled in US institutions.

See website or write to above address for more information or an application.

2349—DEPARTMENT OF THE ARMY (Armed Forces Health Professions Scholarships)

Attn: RC-HS
1307 Third Ave.
Fort Knox KY 40121
502/626-0367
FAX: 502/626-0923

AMOUNT: Tuition + monthly stipend
DEADLINE(S): None
FIELD(S): Medicine, Osteopathy, Nurse Anesthetist, Veterinary Medicine, Optometry, Psychology, Dentistry

Open to health professionals and students participating in a Reserve Service of the US Armed Forces, training in the specialties listed above. Varying lengths of service are required to pay back the stipend. Must be US citizen. Award is based on a competitive process, including GPA. Financial need NOT a factor.

400 awards annually. Contact Major Beecher at above address for an application.

2350—EASTER SEAL SOCIETY OF IOWA, INC. (Scholarships & Awards)

P.O. Box 4002
Des Moines IA 50333-4002
515/289-1933

AMOUNT: $400-$600
DEADLINE(S): APR 15
FIELD(S): Physical Rehabilitation, Mental Rehabilitation, and related areas

Open only to Iowa residents who are full-time undergraduate sophomores, juniors, seniors, or graduate students at accredited institutions planning a career in the broad field of rehabilitation. Must indicate financial need and be in top 40% of their class.

6 scholarships per year. Must reapply each year.

2351—EPILEPSY FOUNDATION OF AMERICA (Behavioral Sciences Student Fellowships)

4351 Garden City Drive
Landover MD 20785-2267
301/459-3700 or 800/EFA-1000
FAX: 301/577-2684
TDD: 800/332-2070
E-mail: postmaster@efa.org
Internet: www.efa.org

AMOUNT: $2,000
DEADLINE(S): FEB 1

FIELD(S): Epilepsy as related to Behavioral Sciences

Three-month fellowships awarded to students in the behavioral sciences for work on an epilepsy study project. For students of vocational rehabilitation counseling. Students propose an epilepsy-related study or training project to be carried out at a US institution of their choice. A preceptor must accept responsibility for supervision of the student and the project.

Contact EFA for an application.

2352—ESPN (Internship Programs)

Human Resources Dept., ESPN, Inc.
ESPN Plaza
Bristol CT 06010
No phone calls.
Internet: espnet.sportszone.com/editors/studios/97faq.html

AMOUNT: Paid Internships
DEADLINE(S): OCT 1; MAR 1; JUN 1
FIELD(S): Television Industry, Public Relations, Sports

12-week internships in the spring, summer, and fall for undergraduate juniors/seniors and graduate students. Some areas require weekend/evening hours and a strong knowledge of sports. Interns receive hourly wages and take part in many company-sponsored activities. ESPN does not provide housing for students, but we do try to assist in finding suitable living arrangements once selected.

To apply for internship programs, please send cover letter and resume to the above address. If applying to the Communications Dept., please also enclose writing samples and send attention to Diane Lamb.

2353—HISPANIC COLLEGE FUND (Scholarships for Hispanic Students)

One Thomas Circle NW, Suite 375
Washington DC 20005
202/296-5400
FAX: 202/296-3774
E-mail: Hispanic.Fund@Internet MCI.com
Internet: http://hispanicfund.org

AMOUNT: Varies
DEADLINE(S): APR 15
FIELD(S): Most college majors leading to a career in business

Scholarships for deserving Hispanic college students pursuing a higher education in a major leading to a business career and who are full-time students at accredited institutions. US citizenship. Must demonstrate financial need.

Contact above organization for details or visit website for application.

2354—INSTITUTE FOR HUMANE STUDIES (Humane Studies Fellowship)

4084 University Drive, Suite 101
Fairfax VA 22030-6812
703/934-6920 or 800/697-8799
FAX: 703/352-7535
E-mail: ihs@gmu.edu
Internet: www.theihs.org

AMOUNT: up to $12,000
DEADLINE(S): DEC 31
FIELD(S): Social Sciences, Law, Humanities, Jurisprudence, Journalism

Awards are for graduate and advanced undergraduate students pursuing degrees at any accredited domestic or foreign school. Based on academic performance, demonstrated interest in classical liberal ideas, and potential to contribute to the advancement of a free society.

90 awards annually. Apply online or contact IHS for an application.

2355—MIDWAY COLLEGE (Institutional Aid Program—Scholarships & Grants)

Financial Aid Office
Midway KY 40347
606/846-4421

AMOUNT: Varies
DEADLINE(S): MAR 1
FIELD(S): Nursing, Paralegal, Education, Psychology, Biology, Equine Studies, Liberal Studies, Business Administration

Scholarships and grants open to women who are accepted for enrollment at Midway College. Awards support undergraduate study in the above areas.

Approx 80 awards per year. Write for complete information.

2356—MISSISSIPPI OFFICE OF STATE STUDENT FINANCIAL AID (Health Care Professions Loan/Scholarship Program)

3825 Ridgewood Road
Jackson MS 39211-6453
601/982-6663 or 800-327-2980
(free in Miss.)

AMOUNT: $1,500/yr.
DEADLINE(S): JULY 1
FIELD(S): Speech Pathology, Psychology, Occupational Therapy, Physical Therapy, and other allied health programs in critical demand

For Mississippi residents enrolled full-time as juniors or seniors in an accredited training program in Mississippi in the above fields. Student is obligated to serve in the health profession at a state-operated health institution in Mississippi one year for each year's scholarship.

For information and/or application packet, contact above location.

2357—MISSISSIPPI OFFICE OF STATE STUDENT FINANCIAL AID (Psychology Apprenticeship Program)

3825 Ridgewood Road
Jackson MS 39211-6453
601/982-6663 or 800-327-2980
(free in Miss.)

AMOUNT: Up to $1,000/mo. (grads); $500/mo. (undergrads)
DEADLINE(S): APR 1
FIELD(S): Psychology

A stipend/apprenticeship and summer training program for Mississippi residents studying in the field of psychology. Students will be exposed to the professional practice of psychology in a Veterans Affairs Medical Center. Special consideration given to economically, educationally, and/or socially disadvantaged applicants.

Housing and board will be provided by Veterans Affairs Medical Center. Contact above location for details.

2358—NEW YORK STATE HIGHER EDUCATION SERVICES CORPORATION (N.Y. State Regents Professional/Health Care Opportunity Scholarships)

Cultural Education Center, Rm. 5C64
Albany NY 12230
518/486-1319
Internet: www.hesc.com

AMOUNT: $1,000-$10,000/yr.
DEADLINE(S): Varies
FIELD(S): Medicine and Dentistry and related fields, Architecture, Nursing, Psychology, Audiology, Landscape Architecture, Social Work, Chiropractic, Law, Pharmacy, Accounting, Speech Language Pathology

For NY state residents who are economically disadvantaged and members of a minority group underrepresented in the chosen profession and attending school in NY state. Some programs carry a service obligation in New York for each year of support. For US citizens or qualifying noncitizens.

Medical/dental scholarships require one year of professional work in NY.

2359—OPEN SOCIETY INSTITUTE (Individual Project Fellowships)

400 West 59th Street
New York NY 10019
212/548-0600 or 212/757-2323
FAX: 212/548-4679 or 212/548-4600
Internet: www.soros.org/fellow/individual.html

AMOUNT: Varies
DEADLINE(S): Varies
FIELD(S): Any field of study related to creating an open society: reliance on the rule of law, the existence of a democratically elected government, a diverse and vigorous civil society, and respect for minorities and minority opinions

Two-year fellowships for use in selected universities in the US for international students. For students/professionals in fields related to environmental policy, legislation, and remediation techniques applicable to their home countries.

To apply, contact the Soros Foundation/Open Society Institute. Further details on website.

2360—PARAPSYCHOLOGY FOUNDATION (D. Scott Rogo Award for Parapsychological Award)

228 E. 71st Street
New York NY 10021
212/628-1550
FAX: 212/628-1559

AMOUNT: $3,000
DEADLINE(S): APR 15
FIELD(S): Parapsychology

Annual award given to an author working on a manuscript pertaining to the science of parapsychology. A brief synopsis of the proposed contents of the manuscript should be included in the initial application.

Contact Parapsychology Foundation for more information. Recipient notified around May 1st.

2361—PARAPSYCHOLOGY FOUNDATION (Eileen J. Garrett Scholarship)

228 E. 71st Street
New York NY 10021
212/628-1550
FAX: 212/628-1559

AMOUNT: $3,000
DEADLINE(S): JUL 15
FIELD(S): Parapsychology

Open to any undergraduate or graduate student wishing to pursue the academic study of the science of parapsychology. Funding is for study, research, and experimentation only. Applicants must demonstrate previous academic interest in parapsychology. Letters of reference are required from three individuals who are familiar with the applicant's work and/or studies in parapsychology.

Contact Parapsychology Foundation for an application.

2362—PILOT INTERNATIONAL FOUNDATION (PIF/Lifeline Scholarship)

P.O. Box 5600
Macon GA 31208-5600
Written inquiries

AMOUNT: Varies
DEADLINE(S): MAR 1
FIELD(S): Disabilities/Brain-related
Disorders

This program assists ADULT students re-entering the job market, preparing for a second career, or improving their professional skills for an established career. Applicants must be preparing for, or already involved in, careers working with people with disabilities/brain-related disorders. GPA of 3.5 or more is required.

Must be sponsored by a Pilot Club in your home town, or in the city in which your college or university is located. Send a self-addressed, stamped envelope for complete information.

2363—PILOT INTERNATIONAL FOUNDATION (Ruby Newhall Memorial Scholarship)

P.O. Box 5600
Macon, GA 31208-5600
Written inquiries

AMOUNT: Varies
DEADLINE(S): MAR 15
FIELD(S): Disabilities/Brain-related
Disorders

For international students who have studied in the US for at least one year, and who intend to return to their home country six months after graduation. Applicants must be full-time students majoring in a field related to human health and welfare, and have a GPA of 3.5 or more.

Applicants must be sponsored by a Pilot Club in their home town, or in the city in which their college or university is located. Send a self-addressed, stamped envelope for complete information.

2364—PILOT INTERNATIONAL FOUNDATION (The Pilot International Scholarship Program)

P.O. Box 5600
Macon GA 31208-5600
Written inquiries

AMOUNT: Varies
DEADLINE(S): MAR 1
FIELD(S): Disabilities/Brain-related
Disorders

This program provides assistance to undergraduate students preparing for careers working directly with people with disabilities or training those who will. GPA of 3.5 or greater required.

Applicants must be sponsored by a Pilot Club in their home town, or in the city in which their college or university is located. Send a self-addressed, stamped envelope for complete information.

2365—ROSE HILL COLLEGE (Louella Robinson Memorial Scholarship)

P.O. Box 3126
Aiken SC 29802-3126
800/684-3769
FAX: 803/641-0240
E-mail: rosehill@.edu
Internet: www.rosehill.edu

AMOUNT: $10,000/yr. for four years
DEADLINE(S): Varies
FIELD(S): Liberal Arts and Humanities
curricula

For undergraduate residents of Indian River County, Florida, to attend Rose Hill College in Aiken, South Carolina. The school offers a liberal arts education and follows the Great Books curriculum, a program of reading and seminars.

1 annual award. Applicants must meet entry requirements of RHC. Contact above location for details.

2366—ROSE HILL COLLEGE (Scholarships for Children of Eastern Orthodox Priests/Deacons)

P.O. Box 3126
Aiken SC 29802-3126
800/684-3769
FAX: 803/641-0240
E-mail: rosehill@edu
Internet: www.rosehill.edu

AMOUNT: Full scholarship: $10,000/yr.
for four years
DEADLINE(S): Varies
FIELD(S): Liberal Arts and Humanities
curricula

For undergraduates who are children of Eastern Orthodox Christian priests or deacons to attend Rose Hill College in Aiken, South Carolina. The school offers a liberal arts education and follows the Great Books curriculum, a program of reading and seminars.

6-10 annual awards. Applicants must meet entry requirements of RHC. Contact above location for details.

2367—ROSE HILL COLLEGE (Scholarships for the Homeschooled)

P.O. Box 3126
Aiken SC 29802-3126
800/684-3769
FAX: 803/641-0240
E-mail: rosehill@rosehill.edu
Internet: www.resehill.edu

AMOUNT: Full scholarship: $10,000/yr.
for four years
DEADLINE(S): Varies
FIELD(S): Liberal Arts and Humanities
curricula

For undergraduates who have been homeschooled for three of the last five years of their high school education. For use at Rose Hill College in Aiken, South Carolina. The school offers a liberal arts education and follows the Great Books curriculum, a program of reading and seminars. Scholarships will be awarded primarily on the basis of an essay that the student will be asked to write.

4 annual awards. Applicants must meet entry requirements of RHC. Contact above location for details.

2368—SOCIETY FOR THE PSYCHOLOGICAL STUDY OF SOCIAL ISSUES (Applied Social Issues Internship Program)

P.O. Box 1248
Ann Arbor MI 48106-1248
Phone/TTY: 313/662-9130
FAX: 313/662-5607
E-mail: spssi@spssi.org
Internet: www.spssi.org

AMOUNT: $1,500-$2,500
DEADLINE(S): NOV 10
FIELD(S): Social Science & related fields

Internship awards cover research costs, community organizing, summer stipends, etc. Encourages intervention projects, non-partisan lobbying, applied research, and implementing public policy. Proposals are invited for applying social science principles to social issues, in cooperation with a community, city, or state government organization, public interest group, or other not-for-profit entity. College seniors, graduate students, and first-year postdoctorates may apply.

Contact SPSSI for details. Applications available on website. NO SCHOLARSHIPS AVAILABLE—REQUESTS FOR FINANCIAL AID WILL NOT BE ANSWERED.

2369—SOCIETY FOR THE SCIENTIFIC STUDY OF SEXUALITY (Student Research Grant)

P.O. Box 208
Mount Vernon IA 52314-0208
319/895-8407
FAX: 319/895-6203
E-mail: TheSociety@worldnet.att.net
Internet: www.ssc.wisc.edu/ssss

AMOUNT: $750
DEADLINE(S): FEB 1; SEP 1
FIELD(S): Human Sexuality

Open to students doing research in the area of human sexuality. Must be enrolled in a degree-granting program at an accredited institution; can be master's thesis or doctoral dissertation, but this is not a requirement. With application, must submit letter from Department Chairperson stating your status and educational purpose of research, 150-word abstract of proposed research, short biographical sketch, and proposed budget.

3 awards annually. Contact Ilsa Lottes, Ph.D., at SSSS for an application. Recipients announced in November at SSSS annual meeting.

2370—THE ARC (Research Grants Program in Mental Retardation)

500 E. Border Street, Suite 300
Arlington, TX 76010
817/261-6003
FAX: 817/277-3491
E-mail: thearc@metronet.com
Internet: http://www.theArc.org/welcome.html

AMOUNT: Up to $25,000
DEADLINE(S): APR 1
FIELD(S): Prevention, amelioration, or cure of mental retardation

The ARC invites applications from researchers from diverse sources—individuals and universities, hospitals, and professional organizations with research interests.

Contact Dr. Michael Wehmeyer, Assistant Director, Department of Research and Program Services, The ARC, at above address, or Ann Balson.

2371—US DEPARTMENT OF TRANSPORTATION (Dwight D. Eisenhower Transportation Fellowships)

US Dept. of Transportation
Fed. Hwy. Admin.
6300 Georgetown Pike, HHI-20
McLean VA 22101-2296
703/235-0538

AMOUNT: Varies
DEADLINE(S): FEB
FIELD(S): Transportation—such majors as chemistry; materials science; corrosion; civil, chemical, & electronics engineering; structures; human factors; computer science; psychology

Research fellowships for undergrads and grad students at any Dept. of Transportation facility or selected IHE. For three to twelve months. Research must focus on transportation-related research and development in the above fields.

Contact Ilene Payne, Director, Universities and Grants Programs at above location for details.

2372—WOMEN'S SPORTS FOUNDATION (Jackie Joyner-Kersee & Zina Garrison Minority Internships)

Eisenhower Park
East Meadow NY 11554
800/227-3988
FAX: 516/542-4716
E-mail: WoSport@aol.com
Internet: www.lifetimetv.com/WoSport

AMOUNT: $4,000-$5,000
DEADLINE(S): Ongoing
FIELD(S): Sports-related fields

Provides women of color an opportunity to gain experience in a sports-related career and interact in the sports community. May be undergraduates, college graduates, graduate students, or women in a career change. Internships are located at the Women's Sports Foundation in East Meadow, New York.

4-6 awards annually. See website or write to above address for details.

2373—ZETA PHI BETA SORORITY EDUCATIONAL FOUNDATION (Lullelia W. Harrison Scholarship in Counseling)

1734 New Hampshire Ave. NW
Washington DC 20009
Internet: www.zpb1920.org/nefforms.htm

AMOUNT: $500-$1,000
DEADLINE(S): FEB 1
FIELD(S): Counseling

Open to graduate- and undergraduate-level students enrolled in a degree program in counseling. Award is for full-time study for one academic year (Fall-Spring). Must submit proof of enrollment.

Send self-addressed, stamped envelope to above address between September 1st and December 15th for an application.

SOCIOLOGY

2374—AMERICAN BAR FOUNDATION (Summer Research Fellowships in Law and Social Science for Minority Undergraduate Students)

750 N. Lake Shore Drive
Chicago IL 60611
312/988-6500
Internet: www.abf-sociolegal.org

AMOUNT: $3,500 stipend
DEADLINE(S): MAR 1
FIELD(S): Social Sciences, Humanities, Law

Summer research opportunity open to sophomore and junior undergraduates who are Native American, African American, Mexican, Puerto Rican, or other minority. Must be US citizen or permanent resident and have at least a 3.0 GPA. Students are assigned a mentor and participate in seminars; must also work at the Foundation's office in Chicago for 35 hours per week for 10 weeks. Essay, transcripts, and letter of recommendation required.

4 awards annually; announced in April. See website or contact ABF for an application.

2375—ASSOCIATION FOR WOMEN IN SCIENCE EDUCATIONAL FOUNDATION (Dr. Vicki L. Schechtman Scholarship)

1200 New York Ave. NW
Suite 650
Washington DC 20005
202/326-8940 or 800/886-AWIS
E-mail: awis@awis.org
Internet: www.awis.org

AMOUNT: $1,000
DEADLINE(S): JAN 16
FIELD(S): Various Sciences and Social Sciences

For female undergraduate students who are US citizens and have a minimum GPA of 3.0. Summary page, essay describing career aspirations, transcripts, proof of matriculation (if available), and two reference letters required with application. Scholarships may be used for tuition, books, housing, research, equipment, etc.

See website or write to above address for an application and more information.

2376—ASSOCIATION FOR WOMEN IN SCIENCE EDUCATIONAL FOUNDATION (Ruth Satter Memorial Award)

1200 New York Ave. NW
Suite 650
Washington DC 20005
202/326-8940 or 800/886-AWIS
E-mail: awis@awis.org
Internet: www.awis.org

AMOUNT: $1,000
DEADLINE(S): JAN 16
FIELD(S): Various Sciences and Social Sciences

Scholarships for female doctoral students who have interrupted their education three years or more to raise a family. Summary page, description of research project, resume, references, transcripts, biographical sketch, and proof of eligibility from department head required. US citizens may attend any graduate institution; noncitizens must be enrolled in US institutions.

See website or write to above address for more information or an application.

2377—B'NAI B'RITH YOUTH ORGANIZATION (Scholarship Program)

1640 Rhode Island Ave. NW
Washington DC 20036
202/857-6633

AMOUNT: $2,500 per year
DEADLINE(S): Varies (spring)
FIELD(S): Social Work

Open to US citizens of Jewish faith who are first- or second-year grad students attending accredited graduate schools of social work or who are college seniors planning to attend a graduate school of social work.

Must show evidence of good scholarship, interest in working for Jewish agencies, and have knowledge of Jewish communal structure and institutions. Renewable. Write for complete information.

2378—CHRISTIAN A. JOHNSON ENDEAVOR FOUNDATION (Native American Fellows)

Harvard Univ.
79 John F. Kennedy Street
Cambridge MA 02138
617/495-1152
FAX: 617/496-3900
Internet: www.ksg.harvard.edu/
hpaied/cjohn.htm

AMOUNT: Varies
DEADLINE(S): MAY 1
FIELD(S): Social Sciences, Government, or program related to Native American studies

Fellowships for students of Native American ancestry who attend a John F. Kennedy School of Government degree program. Applicant, parent, or grandparent must hold membership in a federally or state-recognized tribe, band, or other organized group of Native Americans. Must be committed to a career in American Indian affairs. Awards based on merit and need.

Renewable, based on renomination and availability of funds. To apply, contact John F. Kennedy School of Government at above address.

2379—COMMUNITY FOUNDATION OF WESTERN MASSACHUSETTS (George H. & Margaret B. McDonnell Family Scholarship)

1500 Main Street
P.O. Box 15769
Springfield MA 01115
413/732-2858

AMOUNT: $1,125
DEADLINE(S): APR 15
FIELD(S): Social Work

Open to Holyoke Catholic High School (MA) graduates pursuing a career in social work or an allied field. Based on financial need, academic merit, and extracurricular activities. Must submit transcripts and fill out government FAFSA form.

1 award annually. Renewable with reapplication. Contact Community Foundation for an application and your financial aid office for FAFSA. Notification is in June.

2380—CONTINENTAL SOCIETY DAUGHTERS OF INDIAN WARS (Scholarship)

Route 2, Box 184
Locust Grove OK 74352
918/479-5670

AMOUNT: $1,000
DEADLINE(S): JUN 15
FIELD(S): Education, Social Work, Social Service

Open to Native American, certified tribal members with plans to work on a reservation. Must be an undergraduate junior or senior accepted to or already attending an accredited college/university, be carrying at least eight semester hours, and have a minimum 3.0 GPA. Must be US citizen and demonstrate financial need.

1 award annually. Renewable. Contact Mrs. Ronald Jacobs for an application.

2381—CYNTHIA E. AND CLARA H. HOLLIS FOUNDATION

100 Summer Street
Boston MA 02110
Written inquiry

AMOUNT: Varies
DEADLINE(S): APR 1
FIELD(S): Nursing, Social Work, Dental or Medical Technology, and Religion

Scholarships for Massachusetts with preference given to students in the above fields. For undergraduates, graduates, voc-tech, and adult education. Must demonstrate financial need.

Send SASE to Walter E. Palmer, Esq., 35 Harvard Street, Brookline, MA 02146 for application details. Scholarship forms are also available from the rector of All Saints Church, Brookline High School, and Street Mary's High School, all in Brookline, Massachusetts.

2382—EASTER SEAL SOCIETY OF IOWA, INC. (Scholarships & Awards)

P.O. Box 4002
Des Moines IA 50333-4002
515/289-1933

AMOUNT: $400-$600
DEADLINE(S): APR 15
FIELD(S): Physical Rehabilitation, Mental Rehabilitation, and related areas

Open only to Iowa residents who are full-time undergraduate sophomores, juniors, seniors, or graduate students at accredited institutions planning a career in the broad field of rehabilitation. Must indicate financial need and be in top 40% of their class.

6 scholarships per year. Must reapply each year.

2383—ESPN (Internship Programs)

Human Resources Dept., ESPN, Inc.
ESPN Plaza
Bristol CT 06010
No phone calls.
Internet: espnet.sportszone.com/
editors/studios/97faq.html

AMOUNT: Paid Internships
DEADLINE(S): OCT 1; MAR 1; JUN 1
FIELD(S): Television Industry, Public Relations, Sports

12-week internships in the spring, summer, and fall for undergraduate juniors/seniors and graduate students. Some areas require weekend/evening hours and a strong knowledge of sports. Interns receive hourly wages and take part in many company-sponsored activities. ESPN does not provide housing for students, but we do try to assist in finding suitable living arrangements once selected.

To apply for internship programs, please send cover letter and resume to the above address. If applying to the Communications Dept., please also enclose writing samples and send attention to Diane Lamb.

2384—FIRST UNITED METHODIST CHURCH (Robert Stevenson & Doreene E. Cater Scholarships)

302 5th Ave., S.
Street Cloud MN 56301
FAX: 320/251-0878
E-mail: FUMCloud@aol.com

AMOUNT: $100-$300
DEADLINE(S): JUN 1
FIELD(S): Humanitarian & Christian Service: Teaching, Medicine, Social Work, Environmental Studies, etc.

Stevenson Scholarship is open to undergraduate members of the First United Methodist Church of Street Cloud. Cater Scholarship is open to members of the Minnesota United Methodist Conference who are entering the sophomore year or higher of college work. Both require two letters of reference, transcripts, and financial need.

5-6 awards annually. Contact Scholarship Committee for an application.

2385—FOUNDATION FOR SEACOAST HEALTH (Scholarship Program)

P.O. Box 4606
Portsmouth NH 03802-4606
603/433-3008
FAX: 603/433-2036
E-mail: ffsh@nh.ultranet.com
Internet: www.nh.ultranet.com/~ffsh

AMOUNT: $1,000-10,000
DEADLINE(S): FEB 1
FIELD(S): Health-related fields

Open to undergraduate and graduate students pursuing health-related fields of study who are legal residents of the following cities in New Hampshire: Portsmouth, Newington, New Castle, Rye, Greenland, N. Hampton, or these cities in Maine: Kittery, Eliot, or York. Must have resided in the area for at least two years.

Write or check website for details. $150,000 awarded annually; 35 awards given.

2386—INSTITUTE FOR HUMANE STUDIES (Humane Studies Fellowship)

4084 University Drive, Suite 101
Fairfax VA 22030-6812
703/934-6920 or 800/697-8799
FAX: 703/352-7535
E-mail: ihs@gmu.edu
Internet: www.theihs.org

AMOUNT: up to $12,000
DEADLINE(S): DEC 31
FIELD(S): Social Sciences, Law, Humanities, Jurisprudence, Journalism

Awards are for graduate and advanced undergraduate students pursuing degrees at any accredited domestic or foreign school. Based on academic performance, demonstrated interest in classical liberal ideas, and potential to contribute to the advancement of a free society.

90 awards annually. Apply online or contact IHS for an application.

2387—INTERNATIONAL ASSOCIATION OF FIRE CHIEFS FOUNDATION (Scholarship Program)

1257 Wiltshire Road
York PA 17403
717/854-9083

AMOUNT: $250-$4,000
DEADLINE(S): AUG 15
FIELD(S): Business and Urban Administration, Fire Science

Open to members of a fire service of a state, county, provincial, municipal, community, industrial, or federal fire department.

Renewable. Write for complete information.

2388—JAMES FORD BELL FOUNDATION (Summer Internship Program)

2925 Dean Pkwy., Suite 811
Minneapolis MN 55416
612/285-5435
FAX: 612/285-5437
E-mail: famphiladv@usweStreetnet

AMOUNT: $4,000 for 3 months
DEADLINE(S): APR 30
FIELD(S): Business/Public Administration, Public Policy, Organization Leadership, Nonprofit Management

Interns spend the summer with organizations selected by the Foundation; the organizations select interns from masters degree programs in above or related fields and college seniors with strong interest in nonprofit work. Internships normally in the Twin Cities area.

Contact Foundation for a list of internship opportunities in February and March ONLY; students should request position list, not an application for the program itself (only organizations apply for the program).

2389—JAPANESE AMERICAN CITIZENS LEAGUE (Alice Yuriko Endo Memorial Scholarship)

1765 Sutter Street
San Francisco CA 94115
415/921-5225
FAX: 415/931-4671
E-mail: jacl@jacl.org
Internet: www.jacl.org

AMOUNT: $1,000-$5,000
DEADLINE(S): APR 1
FIELD(S): Public & Social Service

Open to JACL members and their children only. For undergraduate students with an interest in public or social service who are planning to attend a college, university, trade school, business school, or any other institution of higher learning. Preference given to students residing in the Eastern District Council and/or those studying in above fields. Financial need NOT a factor.

For membership information or an application, send a self-addressed, stamped envelope to above address, stating your level of study. Applications available October 1st through March 20th; recipients notified in July.

2390—JEWISH VOCATIONAL SERVICE (Academic Scholarship Program)

One S. Franklin Street
Chicago IL 60606
312/357-4500
FAX: 312/855-3282
TTY: 312/855-3282
E-mail: jvschicago@jon.cjfny.org

AMOUNT: $5,000 (max.)
DEADLINE(S): MAR 1
FIELD(S): "Helping" Professions, Mathematics, Engineering, Sciences, Communications (at Univ IL only), Law (certain schools in IL only)

Open to Jewish men and women legally domiciled in the greater Chicago metropolitan area, who are identified as having promise for significant contributions in their chosen careers, and are in need of financial assistance for full-time academic programs in above areas. Must have entered undergraduate junior year in career programs requiring no postgrad education, be in graduate/professional school, or be in a voc-tech training program. Interview required.

Renewable. Contact JVS for an application between December 1st and February 15th.

2391—JEWISH WELFARE BOARD (Scholarships)

15 E. 26th Street
New York NY 10010
212/532-4949

AMOUNT: $1,000-$4,000
DEADLINE(S): FEB 1
FIELD(S): Social Work, Adult Education, Early Childhood Education, Health Education, Physical Education, Cultural Studies, Jewish Education

Scholarships for Jewish college juniors or seniors pursuing careers in the above fields. Must be committed to the work of the YMHA, YWHA, or Jewish community centers. Must do a year of field work in a Jewish community center.

Renewable. Contact organization for details.

2392—NEW YORK CITY DEPT. CITYWIDE ADMINISTRATIVE SERVICES (Urban Fellows Program)

1 Centre Street, 24th Fl.
New York NY 10007
212/487-5600
FAX: 212/487-5720

AMOUNT: $18,000 stipend
DEADLINE(S): JAN 20
FIELD(S): Public Administration, Urban Planning, Government, Public Service, Urban Affairs

Fellowship program provides one academic year (9 months) of full-time work experience in urban government. Open to graduating college seniors and recent college graduates. US citizenship required.

Write for complete information.

2393—NEW YORK CITY DEPT. OF CITY-WIDE ADMINISTRATIVE SERVICES (Government Scholars Internship Program)

1 Centre Street, 24th Fl.
New York NY 10007
212/487-5600
FAX: 212/487-5720

AMOUNT: $3,000 stipend
DEADLINE(S): JAN 13
FIELD(S): Public Administration, Urban Planning, Government, Public Service, Urban Affairs

10-week summer intern program open to undergraduate sophomores, juniors, and seniors. Program provides students with unique opportunity to learn about NY City government. Internships available in virtually every city agency and mayoral office.

Write to New York City Fellowship Programs at above address for complete information.

2394—NEW YORK STATE HIGHER EDU-CATION SERVICES CORPORATION (N.Y. State Regents Professional/Health Care Opportunity Scholarships)

Cultural Education Center, Rm. 5C64
Albany NY 12230
518/486-1319
Internet: www.hesc.com

AMOUNT: $1,000-$10,000/yr.
DEADLINE(S): Varies
FIELD(S): Medicine and Dentistry and related fields, Architecture, Nursing, Psychology, Audiology, Landscape Architecture, Social Work, Chiropractic, Law, Pharmacy, Accounting, Speech Language Pathology

For NY state residents who are economically disadvantaged and members of a minority group underrepresented in the chosen profession and attending school in NY state. Some programs carry a service obligation in New York for each year of support. For US citizens or qualifying noncitizens.

Medical/dental scholarships require one year of professional work in NY.

2395—OPEN SOCIETY INSTITUTE (Environmental Management Fellowships)

400 West 59th Street
New York NY 10019
212/548-0600 or 212/757-2323
FAX: 212/548-4679 or
212/548-4600
Internet: www.soros.org/efp.html

AMOUNT: Fees, room, board, living stipend, textbooks, international transportation, health insurance
DEADLINE(S): NOV 15
FIELD(S): Earth Sciences, Natural Sciences, Humanities (exc. language), Anthropology, Sociology, Mathematics, or Engineering

Two-year fellowships for use in selected universities in the US for international students. For students/professionals in fields related to environmental policy, legislation, and remediation techniques applicable to their home countries.

To apply, contact your local Soros Foundation or Open Society Institute. Further details on website.

2396—OPEN SOCIETY INSTITUTE (Individual Project Fellowships)

400 West 59th Street
New York NY 10019
212/548-0600 or 212/757-2323
FAX: 212/548-4679 or
212/548-4600
Internet: www.soros.org/fellow/individual.html

AMOUNT: Varies
DEADLINE(S): Varies
FIELD(S): Any field of study related to creating an open society: reliance on the rule of law, the existence of a democratically elected government, a diverse and vigorous civil society, and respect for minorities and minority opinions

Two-year fellowships for use in selected universities in the US for international students. For students/professionals in fields related to environmental policy, legislation, and remediation techniques applicable to their home countries.

To apply, contact the Soros Foundation/Open Society Institute. Further details on website.

2397—PHILADELPHIA COLLEGE OF BIBLE (Scholarships, Grants, and Loans)

Financial Aid Dept.
200 Manor Ave.
Langhorne PA 19047
800/366-0049
Internet: www.pcb.edu

AMOUNT: Varies
DEADLINE(S): Varies
FIELD(S): Fields of study relating to Christian education

Various scholarships, loans, and grants are available to students attending this undergraduate Bible college in Philadelphia, PA. High school seniors, transfer students, and others may apply. Some programs are for students with outstanding academic achievement, musical talent, or leaderships skills. Some are for dependents of Christian workers, missionaries, or alumni. Some are based on financial need.

Access website for details and/or send SASE to school for further information.

2398—PRESIDENT'S COMMISSION ON WHITE HOUSE FELLOWSHIPS

712 Jackson Place NW
Washington DC 20503
202/395-4522
FAX: 202/395-6179
E-mail: almanac@ace.esusda.gov

AMOUNT: Wage (up to GS-14 Step 3; approximately $65,000)
DEADLINE(S): DEC 1
FIELD(S): Public Service, Government, Community Involvement, Leadership

Mid-career professionals spend one year as special assistants to senior executive branch officials in Washington. Highly competitive. Non-partisan; no age or educational requirements. Fellowship year runs September 1 through August 31.

1,200 candidates applying for 11 to 19 fellowships each year. Write for complete information.

2399—ROSE HILL COLLEGE (Louella Robinson Memorial Scholarship)

P.O. Box 3126
Aiken SC 29802-3126
800/684-3769
FAX: 803/641-0240
E-mail: rosehill@.edu
Internet: www.rosehill.edu

AMOUNT: $10,000/yr. for four years
DEADLINE(S): Varies
FIELD(S): Liberal Arts and Humanities curricula

For undergraduate residents of Indian River County, Florida, to attend Rose Hill College in Aiken, South Carolina. The school offers a liberal arts education and follows the Great Books curriculum, a program of reading and seminars.

1 annual award. Applicants must meet entry requirements of RHC. Contact above location for details.

2400—ROSE HILL COLLEGE (Scholarships for Children of Eastern Orthodox Priests/Deacons)

P.O. Box 3126
Aiken SC 29802-3126
800/684-3769
FAX: 803/641-0240
E-mail: rosehill@edu
Internet: www.rosehill.edu

AMOUNT: Full scholarship: $10,000/yr. for four years
DEADLINE(S): Varies
FIELD(S): Liberal Arts and Humanities curricula

For undergraduates who are children of Eastern Orthodox Christian priests or deacons to attend Rose Hill College in Aiken, South Carolina. The school offers a liberal arts education and follows the Great Books curriculum, a program of reading and seminars.

6-10 annual awards. Applicants must meet entry requirements of RHC. Contact above location for details.

2401—ROSE HILL COLLEGE (Scholarships for the Homeschooled)

P.O. Box 3126
Aiken SC 29802-3126
800/684-3769
FAX: 803/641-0240
E-mail: rosehill@rosehill.edu
Internet: www.resehill.edu

AMOUNT: Full scholarship: $10,000/yr. for four years
DEADLINE(S): Varies
FIELD(S): Liberal Arts and Humanities curricula

For undergraduates who have been homeschooled for three of the last five years of their high school education. For use at Rose Hill College in Aiken, South Carolina. The school offers a liberal arts education and follows the Great Books curriculum, a program of reading and seminars. Scholarships will be awarded primarily on the basis of an essay that the student will be asked to write.

4 annual awards. Applicants must meet entry requirements of RHC. Contact above location for details.

2402—SOCIETY FOR THE PSYCHOLOGICAL STUDY OF SOCIAL ISSUES (Applied Social Issues Internship Program)

P.O. Box 1248
Ann Arbor MI 48106-1248
Phone/TTY: 313/662-9130
FAX: 313/662-5607
E-mail: spssi@spssi.org
Internet: www.spssi.org

AMOUNT: $1,500-$2,500
DEADLINE(S): NOV 10
FIELD(S): Social Science & related fields

Internship awards cover research costs, community organizing, summer stipends, etc. Encourages intervention projects, non-partisan lobbying, applied research, and implementing public policy. Proposals are invited for applying social science principles to social issues, in cooperation with a community, city, or state government organization, public interest group, or other not-for-profit entity. College seniors, graduate students, and first-year postdoctorates may apply.

Contact SPSSI for details. Applications available on website. NO SCHOLARSHIPS AVAILABLE—REQUESTS FOR FINANCIAL AID WILL NOT BE ANSWERED.

2403—THE HEATH EDUCATION FUND (Scholarships for Ministers, Priests, and Missionaries)

Barnett Bank, N.A.
P.O. Box 40200
Jacksonville FL 32203-0200
904/464-2877

AMOUNT: $750-$1,000
DEADLINE(S): JUL 31
FIELD(S): Ministry, Missionary Work, or Social Work

Scholarships to high school graduates from the southeastern US who wish to study in the above fields. Eligible states of residence: Alabama, Florida, Georgia, Kentucky, Louisiana, Maryland, Mississippi, North & South Carolina, Tennessee, Virginia, and West Virginia.

Write to Barnett Bank's Trust Co., N.A., at above address for details and guidelines. Send SASE and letter with brief background of applicant, field of study, religious denomination, and reason for requeStreet Preference to Methodists or Episcopalians.

2404—US DEPARTMENT OF TRANSPORTATION (Dwight D. Eisenhower Transportation Fellowships)

US Dept. of Transportation
Fed. Hwy. Admin.
6300 Georgetown Pike, HHI-20
McLean VA 22101-2296
703/235-0538

AMOUNT: Varies
DEADLINE(S): FEB
FIELD(S): Transportation—such majors as chemistry; materials science; corrosion; civil, chemical, & electronics engineering; structures; human factors; computer science; psychology

Research fellowships for undergrads and grad students at any Dept. of Transportation facility or selected IHE. For three to twelve months. Research must focus on transportation-related research and development in the above fields.

Contact Ilene Payne, Director, Universities and Grants Programs at above location for details.

2405—US DEPT. OF HEALTH & HUMAN SERVICES (Indian Health Service Preparatory Scholarship Program)

Twinbrook Metro Plaza, Suite 100
12300 Twinbrook Pkwy.
Rockville MD 20852
301/443-0234
FAX: 301/443-4815
Internet: www:ihs.gov/Recruitment/
DHPS/SP/SBTOC3.asp

AMOUNT: Tuition + fees & monthly
   stipend of $938
DEADLINE(S): APR 1
FIELD(S): Health Professions, Social
   Work, or Accounting

Open to Native Americans or Alaska natives who enroll in courses leading to a baccalaureate degree and are preparing for acceptance into programs in the above fields. US citizenship required. Renewable annually with reapplication.

Scholarship recipients must intend to serve the Indian people. They incur a one-year service obligation to the IHS for each year of support for a minimum of two years. Write for complete information.

2406—US DEPT. OF HEALTH & HUMAN SERVICES (Indian Health Service Health Professions Scholarship Program)

Twinbrook Metro Plaza, Suite 100
12300 Twinbrook Pkwy.
Rockville MD 20852
301/443-0234
FAX: 301/443-4815
Internet: www.ihs.gov/Recruitment/
DHPS/SP/SBTOC3.asp

AMOUNT: Tuition + fees & monthly
   stipend of $938
DEADLINE(S): APR 1
FIELD(S): Health Professions,
   Accounting, Social Work

Open to Native Americans or Alaska natives who are graduate students or college juniors or seniors in a program leading to a career in a field listed above. US citizenship required. Renewable annually with reapplication.

Scholarship recipients must intend to serve the Indian people. They incur a one-year service obligation to the IHS for each year of support for a minimum of two years. Write for complete information.

2407—WOMEN'S SPORTS FOUNDATION (Jackie Joyner-Kersee & Zina Garrison Minority Internships)

Eisenhower Park
East Meadow NY 11554
800/227-3988
FAX: 516/542-4716
E-mail: WoSport@aol.com
Internet: www.lifetimetv.com/WoSport

AMOUNT: $4,000-$5,000
DEADLINE(S): Ongoing
FIELD(S): Sports-related fields

Provides women of color an opportunity to gain experience in a sports-related career and interact in the sports community. May be undergraduates, college graduates, graduate students, or women in a career change. Internships are located at the Women's Sports Foundation in East Meadow, New York.

4-6 awards annually. See website or write to above address for details.

SCHOOL OF VOCATIONAL EDUCATION

2408—AERO CLUB OF NEW ENGLAND (Aviation Scholarships)

4 Emerson Drive
Acton MA 01720
978/263-7793
E-mail: pattis22@aol.com
Internet: www.acone.org

AMOUNT: $500-$2,000
DEADLINE(S): MAR 31
FIELD(S): Aviation and related fields

Several scholarships with varying specifications for eligibility for New England residents to be used at FAA-approved flight schools in New England states.

Information and applications are on website above.

2409—AIRCRAFT ELECTRONICS ASSOCIATION EDUCATIONAL FOUNDATION (Scholarships)

P.O. Box 1963
Independence MO 64055
816/373-6565
FAX: 816/478-3100
Internet: www.aeaavnews.org

AMOUNT: $1,000-$16,000
DEADLINE(S): Varies
FIELD(S): Avionics, Aircraft Repair

Various scholarships for high school and college students attending post-secondary institutions, including technical schools. Some are for study in Canada or Europe as well as the US.

25 programs. See website or contact AEA for specific details and applications.

2410—AMERICAN ASSOCIATION OF COSMETOLOGY SCHOOLS (ACE Grants)

11811 N. Tatum Blvd., Suite 1085
Phoenix AZ 85028
602/788-1170
FAX: 602/404-8900
E-mail: jim@beautyschools.org
Internet: www.beautyschools.org

AMOUNT: $1,000 (average)
DEADLINE(S): None
FIELD(S): Cosmetology

Grants for US citizens/permanent residents who are accepted to a participating ACE grant school. Must be high school graduate or equivalent. Financial need is NOT a factor.

500+ awards annually. Not renewable. Contact Jim Cox at the American Association of Cosmetology Schools for an application.

2411—AMERICAN BOARD OF FUNERAL SERVICE EDUCATION (ABFSE Scholarships)

38 Florida Ave.
Portland ME 04103
207/878-6530
FAX: 207/797-7686
E-mail: gconnic1@maine.rr.com
Internet: www.abfse.org

AMOUNT: $250-$500
DEADLINE(S): MAR 15; SEP 15
FIELD(S): Funeral Service

Open to US citizens who have completed at least one term of study in an accredited program in funeral service. Applicants must submit IRS form 1040 to demonstrate need.

70 awards annually. Contact the Scholarship Chairman for an application.

2412—AMERICAN FOUNDATION FOR THE BLIND (Paul W. Ruckes Scholarship)

11 Penn Plaza, Suite 300
New York NY 10001
212/502-7661
FAX: 212/502-7771
E-mail: juliet@afb.org
Internet: www.afb.org

AMOUNT: $1,000
DEADLINE(S): APR 30
FIELD(S): Engineering, Computer/
   Physical/Life Sciences

Open to legally blind and visually impaired undergraduate and graduate students pursuing a degree in one of above fields. Must be US citizen. Must submit written documentation of visual impairment from ophthalmologist or optometrist (need not be legally blind); official transcripts; proof of college/university acceptance; three letters of recommendation; and typewritten statement describing goals, work experience, extracurricular activities, and how monies will be used.

1 award annually. See website or contact Julie Tucker at AFB for an application.

2413—AMERICAN FOUNDATION FOR THE BLIND (R.L. Gillette Scholarships)

11 Penn Plaza, Suite 300
New York NY 10001
212/502-7661
FAX: 212/502-7771
E-mail: juliet@afb.org
Internet: www.afb.org

AMOUNT: $1,000
DEADLINE(S): APR 30
FIELD(S): Literature, Music

Open to legally blind women enrolled in a four-year undergraduate degree program in literature or music. Must be US citizen. Must submit evidence of legal blindness; official transcripts; proof of college/university acceptance; three letters of recommendation; performance tape (30 minutes max.) or creative writing sample; and typewritten statement describing educational and personal goals, work experience, extracurricular activities, and how monies will be used.

2 awards annually. See website or contact Julie Tucker at AFB for an application.

2414—AMERICAN HEALTH AND BEAUTY AIDS INSTITUTE (Fred Luster, Sr. Education Foundation Cosmetology Scholarships)

401 North Michigan Ave.
Chicago IL 60611-4267
312/644-6610

AMOUNT: Varies. Scholarships totaling $5,000 presented twice a year.
DEADLINE(S): MAR 15
FIELD(S): Cosmetology

For students enrolled in beauty school and who have completed 300 classroom hours. Must have proven themselves scholastically.

Extracurricular activities, attendance, records, and previous competitions/awards are also taken into consideration.

2415—AMERICAN INSTITUTE OF AERONAUTICS AND ASTRONAUTICS (Undergraduate Scholarships)

1801 Alexander Bell Drive, Suite 500
Reston VA 20191-4344
800/639-AIAA or 703/264-7500
FAX: 703/264-7551
E-mail: custserv@aiaa.org
Internet: www.aiaa.org

AMOUNT: $2,000
DEADLINE(S): JAN 31
FIELD(S): Science, Engineering, Aeronautics, Astronautics

For students who have completed at least one academic semester or quarter of full-time college work in the area of science or engineering encompassed by the technical activities of the AIAA. Must have GPA of at least 3.0, be currently enrolled in accredited college or university. Membership in AIAA not required to apply but must become one before receiving a scholarship award.

Students who receive these awards are eligible for yearly continuation until completion of senior year upon submission of application, career essay, transcripts, and 2 letters of recommendation from college professor.

2416—AMERICAN INSTITUTE OF BAKING (Scholarships)

1213 Bakers Way
Manhattan KS 66502
800/633-5737
FAX: 785/537-1493
E-mail: kembers@aibonline.org
Internet: www.aibonline.org

AMOUNT: $500-$4,000
DEADLINE(S): None
FIELD(S): Baking Industry, Electrical/Electronic Maintenance

Award is to be used towards tuition for a 16- or 10-week course in baking science and technology or maintenance engineering at the Institute. Experience in baking, mechanics, or an approved alternative is required. Awards are intended for people who plan to seek new positions in the baking and maintenance engineering fields.

45 awards annually. Contact AIB for an application.

2417—AMERICAN WELDING SOCIETY (Scholarships)

550 NW LeJeune Road
Miami FL 33126
800/443-9353, ext. 461
305/445-6628

FAX: 305/443-7559
AMOUNT: $2,500-$3,000
DEADLINE(S): JAN 15
FIELD(S): Welding Engineering & Technology

AWS has eight different scholarship programs for US citizens pursuing undergraduate study at an accredited US institution. One program is also for Canadian citizens studying at Canadian institutions. Must be at least 18 years of age with a high school diploma or equivalent and a minimum 2.0 GPA. Some programs require financial need. Must submit two letters of reference, brief biography, transcript, proposed curriculum, and verification of enrollment/employment.

Renewable up to 4 years. Contact AWS for details on specific scholarships. Awards announced in February.

2418—AMERICAN WINE SOCIETY EDUCATIONAL FOUNDATION (Scholarships and Grants)

1134 West Market Street
Bethlehem PA 18018-4910
610/865-2401 or 610/758-3845
FAX: 610/758-4344
E-mail: lhso@lehigh.edu

AMOUNT: $2,000
DEADLINE(S): MAR 31
FIELD(S): Wine industry professional study: enology, viticulture, health aspects of food and wine, and using and appreciating fine wines

To provide academic scholarships and research grants to students based on academic excellence. Must show financial need and genuine interest in pursuing careers in wine-related fields. For North American citizens, defined as US, Canada, Mexico, the Bahamas, and the West Indies at all levels of education.

Contact L.H. Sperling at above location for application.

2419—AVIATION COUNCIL OF PENNSYLVANIA (Scholarships)

3111 Arcadia Ave.
Allentown PA 18103
215/797-1133

AMOUNT: $1,000
DEADLINE(S): JUL 31
FIELD(S): Aviation Maintenance, Aviation Management, or Pilot Training

Scholarships for individuals in the above fields who are residents of Pennsylvania but can attend school outside Pennsylvania.

3 awards yearly.

2420—AVIATION DISTRIBUTORS AND MANUFACTURERS ASSOCIATION INTERNATIONAL (ADMA International Scholarship Fund)

1900 Arch Street
Philadelphia PA 19103-1498
215/564-3484
FAX: 215/564-2175
E-mail: assnhqt@netaxs.com

AMOUNT: Varies
DEADLINE(S): MAR 15
FIELD(S): Aviation Management, Professional Pilot

Open to students seeking a career in aviation management or as a professional pilot. Emphasis may be in general aviation, airway science management, aviation maintenance, flight engineering, or airway a/c systems management.

Applicants must be studying in the aviation field in a four-year school having an aviation program. Write for complete information.

2421—AVIATION INSURANCE ASSOCIATION (Scholarship)

Aviation Technology Department
1 Purdue Airport
West Lafayette IN 47906-3398
954/986-8080

AMOUNT: $1,000
DEADLINE(S): FEB
FIELD(S): Aviation

Scholarships for aviation students who have completed at least 30 college credits, 15 of which are in aviation. Must have GPA of at least 2.5 and be a US citizen.

Write to Professor Bernard Wuile at Purdue University at above address for application and details.

2422—AVIATION MAINTENANCE EDUCATION FUND (AMEF Scholarship Program)

P.O. Box 2826
Redmond WA 98073
206/827-2295

AMOUNT: $250-$1000
DEADLINE(S): None
FIELD(S): Aviation Maintenance Technology

AMEF scholarship program open to any worthy applicant who is enrolled in a federal aviation administration (FAA) certified aviation maintenance technology program.

Write for complete information.

2423—BUSINESS & PROFESSIONAL WOMEN'S FOUNDATION (BPW Career Advancement Scholarship Program)

2012 Massachusetts Ave. NW
Washington DC 20036-1070
202/293-1200, ext. 169
FAX: 202/861-0298
Internet: www.bpwusa.org

AMOUNT: $500-$1,000
DEADLINE(S): APR 15
FIELD(S): Biology, Science, Education, Engineering, Social Science, Paralegal, Humanities, Business, Math, Computers, Law, MD, DD

For women (US citizens) aged 25+ accepted into accredited program at US institution (+Puerto Rico & Virgin Islands). Must graduate within 12 to 24 months from the date of grant and demonstrate critical financial need. Must have a plan to upgrade skills, train for a new career field, or to enter/re-enter the job market.

Full- or part-time study. For info see website or send business-sized, self-addressed, double-stamped envelope.

2424—CALIFORNIA STUDENT AID COMMISSION (Cal Grant C)

P.O. Box 419026
Rancho Cordova CA 95741-9026
916/526-7590
TDD: 916/526-7542
FAX: 916/526-8002
E-mail: custsvcs@csac.ca.gov
Internet: www.csac.ca.gov

AMOUNT: $2,360 max. tuition & fees;
$530 max. books, tools, & equipment
DEADLINE(S): MAR 2
FIELD(S): Occupational/Career Programs

Pays for tuition and training costs in voc-tech programs. Based on financial need and grades. High school seniors and undergraduates who are California residents and planning to attend school in California may apply. Vocational interest and aptitude are considered.

Approximately 1,500 grants annually. Renewable. To apply, submit the FAFSA (800-433-3243). Contact your counselor, financial aid office, or California Student Aid Commission for more information or FAFSA form.

2425—CIVIL AIR PATROL (Dowling Scholarship)

105 S. Hansell Street
Maxwell AFB AL 36112-6332
334/953-5315

AMOUNT: $5,000 (2); $10,000 (2)
DEADLINE(S): JAN 31
FIELD(S): Aviation Technology

Scholarships for students at Dowling College in Long Island, New York, who are pursuing studies in the above field. Must be member of Civil Air Patrol.

Apply through organization above.

2426—CIVIL AIR PATROL (Major Gen. Lucas V. Beau Flight Scholarship)

Civil Air Patrol National HQ
Maxwell AFB AL 36112-6332
334/953-5315

AMOUNT: $2,100
DEADLINE(S): MAR 31
FIELD(S): Ground and Air Training for FAA private pilot licensing

Open to CAP cadets pursuing studies in the above field.

Write for complete information.

2427—CIVIL AIR PATROL (Vocational-Technical Scholarships)

CAP National Headquarters/ETTC
Maxwell Air Force Base
AL 36112-6332
334/953-5315

AMOUNT: $750
DEADLINE(S): JAN 31
FIELD(S): Vocational-Technical Aerospace Studies

Open to CAP members who are qualified and interested in furthering their education in special aerospace courses at accredited vocational-technical institutions.

Write for complete information.

2428—COMMUNITY FOUNDATION OF WESTERN MASSACHUSETTS (James L. Shriver Scholarship)

1500 Main Street
P.O. Box 15769
Springfield MA 01115
413/732-2858

AMOUNT: $750
DEADLINE(S): APR 15
FIELD(S): Technical Fields

Open to residents of Western Massachusetts to pursue technical careers through college, trade, or technical school. Based on financial need, academic merit, and extracurricular activities. Must submit transcripts and fill out government FAFSA form.

1 award annually. Renewable with reapplication. Contact Community Foundation for an application and your financial aid office for FAFSA. Notification is in June.

2429—COOPERATIVE ASSOCIATION OF STATES FOR SCHOLARSHIPS (CASS) (Scholarships)

c/o Commonwealth Liaison
Unit 310 The Garrison
Street Michael BARBADOS
809/436-8754

AMOUNT: Varies
DEADLINE(S): None
FIELD(S): Business Application/
Computer Science

Scholarships for economically disadvantaged deaf youth, ages 17-25, with strong leadership potential and an interest in computer science/business applications. Must be from Barbados, Street Kitts/Nevis, Grenada, Street Vincent, Antigua/ Barbuda, Street Lucia, Dominica, or Jamaica.

Write to E. Caribbean Reg. Coordinator (CASS) at above address.

2430—DeVRY INC. (Dean's & Presidential Scholarships)

One Tower Lane
Oakbrook Terrace IL 60181-4624
800/733-3879, ext. 1935
630/571-7700
E-mail: outreach@devry.edu
Internet: www.devry.edu

AMOUNT: $1,000/term (Dean's); Full
Tuition (Presidential)
DEADLINE(S): DEC 18; FEB 19; MAR
15
FIELD(S): Accounting, Business Admin,
Computers, Electronics Engineering,
Telecommunications Management,
Electronics Technician

High school seniors who apply to any DeVry Institute are automatically considered for scholarships based on ACT/SAT scores. Presidential scholarships also consider community service, scholastic achievement, extracurricular activities, and essay. Must be US citizen or permanent resident.

Renewable if maintain 3.0 GPA. Number of Dean's Scholarships varies; 2 full-time Presidential awards annually. Contact Brenda Allen, Scholarship Coordinator, for an application.

2431—EAA AVIATION FOUNDATION (Scholarship Program)

P.O. Box 3065
Oshkosh WI 54903-3065

920/426-6815
888/EAA-EAA9, 888/322-3229
E-mail: education@eaa.org
Internet: www.eaa.org

AMOUNT: $500-$5,000
DEADLINE(S): MAY 1
FIELD(S): Aviation

Six different scholarship programs open to well-rounded individuals involved in school and community activities as well as aviation. Applicant's academic records should verify his/her ability to complete educational activity for which scholarship is requested. For all but one scholarship, students must major in aviation. Financial need considered in some programs. One scholarship includes tuition, books, fees, etc., at the Fox Valley Technical College in Wisconsin.

Renewable. $5 application fee. Contact EAA for an application (one application covers all of the scholarship programs).

2432—EMPIRE COLLEGE (Dean's Scholarship)

3035 Cleveland Ave.
Santa Rosa CA 95403
707/546-4000
FAX: 707/546-4058

AMOUNT: $250-$1,500
DEADLINE(S): APR 15
FIELD(S): Accounting, Secretarial, Legal,
Medical (Clinical & Administrative),
Travel & Tourism, General Business,
Computer Assembly, Network
Assembly/Administration

Open to high school seniors who plan to attend Empire College. Must be US citizen.

10 awards annually. Contact Ms. Mary Farha for an application.

2433—FOOD INDUSTRY SCHOLARSHIP FUND OF NEW HAMPSHIRE (Scholarships)

110 Stark Street
Manchester NH 03101-1977
Written Inquiry

AMOUNT: $1,000
DEADLINE(S): MAR
FIELD(S): Food industry

Open to students who are residents of New Hampshire and planning to enter a career in the food industry.

Contact Fund for an application.

2434—GEMOLOGICAL INSTITUTE OF AMERICA (GIA Scholarships)

Financial Aid Office
5345 Armada Drive
Carlsbad CA 92008

760/603-4005
FAX: 760/603-4153

AMOUNT: $500-$700
DEADLINE(S): NOV 1
FIELD(S): Gemology

A variety of scholarships offered to US citizens or permanent residents who are at least 17 years of age and are employed in the jewelry industry or who plan to enter the field and enroll in a GIA educational course.

15-20 annual awards. Write for complete information.

2435—GLOBAL AUTOMOTIVE AFTERMARKET SYMPOSIUM (Scholarship)

9140 Ward Parkway, Suite 200
Kansas City MO 64114
Internet: www.aftmkt.com/
associations/AWDA/gass/
scholarshipap

AMOUNT: Varies
DEADLINE(S): MAY 15
FIELD(S): Automotive aftermarket:
various aspects

Scholarship for students pursuing careers in the automotive aftermarket. Must be a graduating senior or have graduated from high school within the past three years. Must be enrolled in a college-level program or a NATEF-accredited automotive technician program.

Application is accessible at above website.

2436—HAYSTACK MOUNTAIN SCHOOL OF CRAFTS (Scholarship Program)

Admissions Office
P.O. Box 518
Deer Isle ME 04627
207/348-2306

AMOUNT: $500-$1,000
DEADLINE(S): MAR 25
FIELD(S): Crafts

Open to technical assistants and work-study students in graphics, ceramics, weaving, jewelry, glass, blacksmithing, fabric, or wood. Tenable for one of the six two- to three-week summer sessions at Haystack Mountain School. One year of graduate study or equivalent experience is required for TA applicants.

Contact Candy Haskell for an application.

2437—HOBART INSTITUTE OF WELDING TECHNOLOGY (Scholarships)

400 Trade Square East
Troy OH 45373

800/332-9448
FAX: 937/332-5200
E-mail: hiwt@welding.org
Internet: www.welding.org
AMOUNT: $4,998
DEADLINE(S): APR 1; AUG 1; DEC 1
FIELD(S): Structural Welding

Open to undergraduates and technical school students in a structural welding program at the Hobart Institute of Welding Technology. Must have graduated from high school within the past seven years, or have obtained a GED equivalent during that time. Based on an essay, grades, and references; financial need NOT a factor.

3 awards annually. Send self-addressed, stamped envelope to Terre Baily for an application.

2438—ILLINOIS PILOTS ASSOCIATION (Scholarships)

46 Apache Lane
Huntley IL 60142
Written request
AMOUNT: $500
DEADLINE(S): APR 1
FIELD(S): Aviation

Scholarships for individuals in aviation who are residents of Illinois and attending a college or university in Illinois.

Write for details.

2439—INTERNATIONAL ASSN. OF ARSON INVESTIGATORS (John Charles Wilson Scholarship)

300 S. Broadway, Suite 100
Street Louis MO 63102
314/621-1966
AMOUNT: Varies
DEADLINE(S): FEB 15
FIELD(S): Police or Fire Sciences, including Fire Investigation and related subjects

Open to IAAI members, their immediate families, and non-members who are recommended and sponsored by members in good standing. Awards are for undergraduate study in above areas at accredited two- and four-year institutions.

3 awards annually. Transcripts and 500-word essay describing background and goals required. Write to the Executive Director at above address for more information.

2440—INTERNATIONAL ASSOCIATION OF FIRE CHIEFS FOUNDATION (Scholarship Program)

1257 Wiltshire Road
York PA 17403
717/854-9083
AMOUNT: $250-$4,000
DEADLINE(S): AUG 15
FIELD(S): Business and Urban Administration, Fire Science

Open to members of a fire service of a state, county, provincial, municipal, community, industrial, or federal fire department.

Renewable. Write for complete information.

2441—INTERNATIONAL FOOD SERVICE EXECUTIVES ASSOCIATION (Worthy Goal Scholarship)

3739 Mykonos Court
Boca Raton FL 33487-1282
561/998-7758
FAX: 561/998-3878
FAX-On-Demand: 954/977-0767
E-mail: hq@ifsea.org
Internet: www.ifsea.org
AMOUNT: $500
DEADLINE(S): FEB 1
FIELD(S): Food Service Management

Undergraduate scholarship for deserving individuals to receive training in food service management. Additional scholarships are available through IFSEA branches.

Renewable by reapplication. Use Fax-On-Demand service or send a self-addressed, stamped envelope to IFSEA for an application.

2442—JAMES F. LINCOLN ARC WELDING FOUNDATION (Scholarships)

22801 Clair Ave.
Cleveland OH 44117-1199
216/481-4300
AMOUNT: Varies
DEADLINE(S): MAY 1 (through JUN 15, depending on program)
FIELD(S): Arc Welding and Engineering Design

Open to high school students, college undergraduates, and graduate students, and to professionals working in the fields of arc welding and engineering design. Various programs are available.

Send self-addressed, stamped envelope to Richard S. Sabo, Executive Director, at above address.

2443—JOHN K. & THIRZA F. DAVENPORT FOUNDATION (Scholarships in the Arts)

20 North Main Street
South Yarmouth MA 02664-3143
508/398-2293
FAX: 508/394-6765
AMOUNT: Varies
DEADLINE(S): JUL 15
FIELD(S): Theatre, Music, Art

For Barnstable County, Massachusetts residents in their last two years of undergraduate or graduate (preferred) study in visual or performing arts. Must demonstrate financial need.

6-8 awards annually. Renewable. Contact Mrs. Chris M. Walsh for more information.

2444—JOHNSON AND WALES UNIVERSITY (Annual Johnson & Wales University National High School Recipe Contest)

8 Abbott Place
Providence RI 02903
401/598-2345
AMOUNT: $1,000 to $5,000
DEADLINE(S): JAN 31
FIELD(S): Business, Hospitality, Technology, Culinary Arts

For students planning to attend Johnson & Wales University, Providence, Rhode Island.

Write to above address for detailed description.

2445—JOHNSON AND WALES UNIVERSITY (Gilbane Building Company Eagle Scout Scholarship)

8 Abbott Place
Providence RI 02903
401/598-2345
AMOUNT: $1,200
DEADLINE(S): None
FIELD(S): Business, Hospitality, Technology, Culinary Arts

For students attending Johnson & Wales University, Providence, Rhode Island. Must be Eagle Scouts.

Send letter of recommendation and transcript to above address.

2446—JOHNSON AND WALES UNIVERSITY (National High School Entrepreneur of the Year Contest)

8 Abbott Place
Providence RI 02903
401/598-2345

AMOUNT: $1,000 to $10,000
DEADLINE(S): DEC 27
FIELD(S): Business, Hospitality, Technology, Culinary Arts

For students attending Johnson & Wales University, Providence, Rhode Island.

Send for detailed description to above address.

2447—JOHNSON AND WALES UNIVERSITY (Scholarships)

8 Abbott Place
Providence RI 02903
401/598-2345

AMOUNT: $200 to $10,000
DEADLINE(S): None
FIELD(S): Business, Hospitality, Technology, Culinary Arts

For students attending Johnson & Wales University, Providence, Rhode Island.

Renewable for four years. Write for complete information.

2448—KANSAS BOARD OF REGENTS (Vocational Scholarship)

700 SW Harrison Street, Suite 1410
Topeka KS 66603-3760
785/296-3518

AMOUNT: $500
DEADLINE(S): NOV; MAR
FIELD(S): Vocational Programs

Available to eligible students enrolled in approved one- or two-year vocational programs at community or technical colleges and some programs at four-year institutions. Applicants must take the vocational exam which is offered at various sites throughout the state on the first Saturday in November and March.

200 awards annually. See your high school or college advisor (or financial aid office) for applications or contact the Board of Regents.

2449—MARYLAND HIGHER EDUCATION COMMISSION (Tolbert Grants)

State Scholarship Admin.
16 Francis Street
Annapolis MD 21401-1781

410/974-5370
TTY: 800/735-2258
Internet: www.ubalt.edu/www.mhec

AMOUNT: $200
DEADLINE(S): Varies
FIELD(S): Vocational-Technical (Private Career Schools)

Open to Maryland residents pursuing full-time study at Maryland private career (vocational-technical) schools. Must be a US citizen/permanent resident and demonstrate financial need. Must file the government FAFSA form. Applicants must be nominated by their schools.

Renewable an additional year. Contact MHEC for nomination procedures, and see your school's financial aid office for the FAFSA form.

2450—MARYLAND HIGHER EDUCATION COMMISSION (Tuition Reimbursement of Firefighters & Rescue Squad Members)

State Scholarship Admin.
16 Francis Street
Annapolis MD 21401
410/974-5370
TTY: 800/735-2258
Internet: www.ubalt.edu/www.mhec

AMOUNT: Varies (current resident undergraduate tuition rate at Univ. MD-College Park)
DEADLINE(S): JUL 1
FIELD(S): Firefighting, Emergency Medical Technology

Open to firefighters and rescue squad members who successfully complete one year of coursework in a firefighting or EMT program and a two-year service obligation in Maryland.

Contact MHEC for an application.

2451—MIDWAY COLLEGE (Institutional Aid Program—Scholarships & Grants)

Financial Aid Office
Midway KY 40347
606/846-4421

AMOUNT: Varies
DEADLINE(S): MAR 1
FIELD(S): Nursing, Paralegal, Education, Psychology, Biology, Equine Studies, Liberal Studies, Business Administration

Scholarships and grants open to women who are accepted for enrollment at Midway College. Awards support undergraduate study in the above areas.

Approx 80 awards per year. Write for complete information.

2452—MINNESOTA AUTOMOBILE DEALERS ASSOCIATION (MADA Scholarships)

277 University Ave. W.
Street Paul MN 55103-2085
612/291-2400
Internet: www.mada.org

AMOUNT: Tuition for one quarter at an accredited Minnesota technical institution
DEADLINE(S): Varies
FIELD(S): Automotive Mechanics, Automotive Body Repair, Parts and Service Management, Automotive Machinist, Automotive Diagnostic Technician

Tuition reimbursement in the above fields of study for students currently enrolled in a Minnesota technical school. Must have completed two quarters of study in the field, be planning to enroll in further study, have maintained an above-average GPA, and be nominated by an instructor or class advisor at a Minnesota technical institution.

Contact instructor, guidance counselor, or check website above for more information.

2453—McCORD CAREER CENTER (Level II McCord Medical/Music Scholarship)

Healdsburg High School
1024 Prince Street
Healdsburg CA 95448
707/431-3473

AMOUNT: Varies
DEADLINE(S): APR 30
FIELD(S): Medicine, Music

For graduates of Healdsburg High School who are planning a career in music or medicine. Must be enrolled full-time at a college/university as an undergraduate junior or senior in the fall, or earning an advanced degree in graduate or medical school, or entering into a vocational/certificate program. Transcripts, proof of attendance, and an essay are required.

Contact the McCord Career Center at Healdsburg High School for an application.

2454—NATIONAL AIR TRANSPORTATION ASSOCIATION FOUNDATION (The Pioneers of Flight Scholarship)

4226 King Street
Alexandria VA 22302
703/845-9000
FAX: 703/845-8176

AMOUNT: $2,500
DEADLINE(S): None
FIELD(S): General aviation

Scholarship for college students who are in the sophomore or junior year at the time of application intending to pursue full-time study at an accredited four-year college or university and can demonstrate an interest in pursuing a career in general aviation.

Must be nominated by an NATA Regular or Associate Member company.

2455—NATIONAL ASSN. OF EXECUTIVE SECRETARIES AND ADMINISTRATIVE ASSISTANTS (Scholarship Award Program)

900 S. Washington Street, Suite G-13
Falls Church VA 22046
Written inquiry

AMOUNT: $250
DEADLINE(S): MAY 31
FIELD(S): Secretarial

Open to postsecondary students working toward a college degree (Associates, Bachelors, Masters) who are NAESAA members or the spouse, child, or grandchild of a member.

Scholarship may be used for Certified Professional Secretary Exam or to buy required books. Write for complete information.

2456—NATIONAL BUSINESS AIRCRAFT ASSOCIATION (Scholarships)

1200 18th Street NW, 2nd Fl.
Washington DC 20036-2598
202/783-9000
FAX: 202/331-8364
E-mail: info@nbaa.org
Internet: lifeofluxury.com/nbaa.html

AMOUNT: $500
DEADLINE(S): OCT 15
FIELD(S): Aviation-related curricula

Valid only for students enrolled at institutions that are NBAA and University Aviation Association (UAA) members. Open to college sophomores, juniors, or seniors who will be continuing in school the following academic year in an aviation-related baccalaureate or graduate program at these specific member institutions. Must be US citizen and have 3.0 or better GPA.

5 awards per year. Write for complete information.

2457—NATIONAL FOUNDATION FOR ADVANCEMENT IN THE ARTS (Arts Recognition and Talent Search)

800 Brickell Ave.
Miami FL 33131
800/970-ARTS or 305/377-1140
FAX: 305/377-1149
Internet: www.nfaa.org

AMOUNT: $100-$3,000
DEADLINE(S): OCT 1
FIELD(S): Creative & Performing Arts

Talent contest for high school seniors and 17- to 18-year-olds in dance, jazz, music, photography, theatre, visual arts, voice, and writing. Except for those applying in Music/Jazz, applicants must be US citizens or permanent residents. May apply in more than one category, but only one financial award will be given to any individual, and a fee is required for each category in which student applies.

$35 application fee ($25 if apply by June 1st); fee may be waived if you are unable to meet this requirement. 400 awards annually. Not renewable. Contact NFAA for an application packet.

2458—NATIONAL GAY PILOTS ASSOCIATION (Pilot Scholarships)

NGPA-EF, P.O. Box 2010-324
South Burlington VT 05407-2010
703/660-3852
24-hr. voice mail: 703/660-3852
Internet: www.ngpa.org

AMOUNT: $1,500
DEADLINE(S): JUL 31
FIELD(S): Pilot training and related fields in aerospace, aerodynamics, engineering, airport management, etc.

Scholarships for tuition or flight training costs for student pilots enrolled at a college or university offering an accredited aviation curriculum in the above fields. Also for flight training costs in a professional pilot training program at any training facility certified by the FAA. Not for training for a Private Pilot license. Send SASE for application or visit website for further instructions.

For gay/lesbian applicants or others who can provide evidence of volunteering in an AIDS organization or in any group that supports the gay/lesbian community and their rights.

2459—NATIONAL SPACE CLUB (Dr. Robert H. Goddard Historical Essay Award)

2000 L Street NW, Suite 710
Washington DC 20036-4907

202/973-8661
AMOUNT: $1,000 + plaque
DEADLINE(S): DEC 4
FIELD(S): Aerospace History

Essay competition open to any US citizen on a topic dealing with any significant aspect of the historical development of rocketry and astronautics. Essays should not exceed 5,000 words and should be fully documented. Will be judged on originality and scholarship.

Previous winners not eligible. Send self-addressed, stamped envelope for complete information.

2460—NEW HAMPSHIRE ELECTRICAL CONTRACTORS ASSOC. (Phil Moran Scholarship Fund)

P.O. Box 1032
Concord NH 03302-1032
603/224-3532
FAX: 603/224-0369

AMOUNT: $1,000
DEADLINE(S): MAY 1
FIELD(S): Electricity (Industrial, Commercial, Residential)

Open to students who reside in New Hampshire and are (or will be) in the top 50% of their high school graduating class. Studies must relate to residential, commercial, or industrial electricity (NOT electronics or electrical engineering). For full-time or part-time study. Must be registered as an apprentice in NH. Must have high school diploma or GED.

Must re-apply each year to renew. Write for complete information.

2461—NINETY-NINES, INC. (Amelia Earhart Memorial Scholarships)

Box 965
7100 Terminal Drive
Oklahoma City OK 73159-0965
800/994-1929 or 405/685-7969
FAX: 405/685-7985
E-mail: 10476.406@compuserve.com
Internet: ninety-nines.org

AMOUNT: Varies
DEADLINE(S): Varies
FIELD(S): Advanced Aviation Ratings

Scholarships for female licensed pilots who are members of the 99s, Inc.

15-20 awards annually. Financial need considered. Contact Lu Hollander at above address for application and/or membership information.

2462—NINETY-NINES, SAN FERNANDO VALLEY CHAPTER/VAN NUYS AIRPORT (Aviation Career Scholarships)

P.O. Box 8160
Van Nuys CA 91409
818/989-0081

AMOUNT: $3,000
DEADLINE(S): MAY 1
FIELD(S): Aviation Careers

For men and women of the greater Los Angeles area pursuing careers as professional pilots, flight instructors, mechanics, or other aviation career specialists. Applicants must be at least 21 years of age and US citizens.

3 awards annually. Send self-addressed, stamped, business-sized envelope to above address for application.

2463—OGLE SCHOOL OF HAIR DESIGN (Scholarships)

2200 West Park Row
Arlington TX 76013
817/461-2500

AMOUNT: Varies
DEADLINE(S): Varies
FIELD(S): Cosmetology

For high school seniors who begin training in the same calendar year they graduate from high school. For use at Ogle facilities in Arlington, Ft. Worth, Hurst, and Dallas, Texas.

Scholarships vary in number and amount based upon the number of applicants and scholarship pool size.

2464—PROFESSIONAL AVIATION MAINTENANCE ASSOCIATION (PAMA Scholarship Fund)

636 Eye Street NW, Suite 300
Washington DC 20001-3736
202/216-9220
FAX: 202/216-9224
E-mail: hq@pama.org
Internet: http://www.pama.org

AMOUNT: $1,000
DEADLINE(S): OCT 31
FIELD(S): Aviation Maintenance

Open to students enrolled in an institution to obtain an airframe and powerplant (A&P) license who have completed 25% of the required curriculum. Must have 3.0 or better GPA, demonstrate financial need, and be recommended by instructor.

Applications to be submitted through student's school. Write for complete information. The application period runs from July 1 through October 31.

2465—PROFESSIONAL AVIATION MAINTENANCE ASSOCIATION (Scholarships)

636 Eye Street NW, Suite 300
Washington DC 20001-3736
202/216-9220
FAX: 202/216-9224
E-mail: hq@pama.org
Internet: http://www.pama.org

AMOUNT: $1,000 per year
DEADLINE(S): OCT 31
FIELD(S): Aviation Maintenance

For students pursuing airframe and powerplant (A&P) technician certification through an FAA Part 147 aviation maintenance technician school. Must have completed 25% of required curriculum and have a 3.0 or better GPA.

Access website or contact above location for more details and application forms, which are accepted between July 1 and Oct. 31.

2466—SOCIETY FOR TECHNICAL COMMUNICATION (Undergraduate Scholarships)

901 N. Stuart Street, Suite 904
Arlington VA 22203-1854
703/522-4114
FAX: 703/522-2075
E-mail: stc@stc-va.org
Internet: www.stc-va.org/scholarships.html

AMOUNT: $2,500
DEADLINE(S): FEB 15
FIELD(S): Technical Communication

Open to full-time undergraduate students who have completed at least one year of study and are enrolled in an accredited 2- or 4-year degree program for career in any area of technical communication: technical writing, editing, graphic design, multimedia art, etc.

Awards tenable at recognized colleges and universities in US and Canada. 14 awards per year—7 undergraduate and 7 graduate. See website and/or write for complete information.

2467—STUDENT CONSERVATION ASSOCIATION (SCA Resource Assistant Program)

P.O. Box 550
Charlestown NH 03603
603/543-1700
FAX: 603/543-1828
E-mail: internships@sca-inc.org
Internet: www.sca-inc.org

AMOUNT: $1,180-$4,725
DEADLINE(S): Varies
FIELD(S): Environment & related fields

Must be 18 and US citizen; need not be student. Fields: Agriculture, archaeology, anthropology, botany, caves, civil/environmental engineering, environmental education, fisheries, forests, herpetology, history, living history/roleplaying, visitor services, landscape architectural/environmental design, paleontology, recreation/resource/range management, trail maintenance/construction, wildlife management, geology, hydrology, library/museums, surveying.

900 positions in US and Canada. Send $1 for postage for application; outside US/Canada, send $20.

2468—THE ART INSTITUTES INTERNATIONAL (Evelyn Keedy Memorial Scholarship)

300 Sixth Ave., Suite 800
Pittsburgh PA 15222-2598
412/562-9800
FAX: 412/562-9802
E-mail: webadmin@aii.edu
Internet: www.aii.edu

AMOUNT: 2 years full tuition
DEADLINE(S): MAY 1
FIELD(S): Various fields in the creative and applied arts: video production, broadcasting, culinary arts, fashion design, website administration, etc.

Scholarships at 12 different locations nationwide in various fields described above. For graduating high school seniors admitted to an Arts Institutes International School, the New York Restaurant School, or NCPT. Transcripts, letters of recommendation, and resume must be submitted with application.

See website or contact AII for more information.

2469—THE FRASCA FAMILY/UNIVERSITY AVIATION ASSOCIATION (The Joseph Frasca Excellence in Aviation Scholarship)

c/o College of Technical Careers
Southern Illinois University
Carbondale IL 62901-6621
618/453-8898

AMOUNT: $500
DEADLINE(S): APR 1 (varies)
FIELD(S): Aviation maintenance or flight training

Scholarships for college juniors or seniors currently enrolled in a University Aviation Association (UAA)-affiliated institution and pursuing a career in one of the above fields. Minimum GPA of 3.0. Must show membership in a flight-related organization.

2 pilot and 2 mechanic awards yearly.

2470—THE WALT DISNEY COMPANY (American Teacher Awards)

P.O. Box 9805
Calabasas CA 91372

AMOUNT: $2,500 (36 awards); $25,000 (Outstanding Teacher of the Year)
DEADLINE(S): FEB 15
FIELD(S): Teachers: athletic coach, early childhood, English, foreign language/ESL, general elementary, mathematics, performing arts, physical education/health, science, social studies, visual arts, voc-tech education
Awards for K-12 teachers in the above fields.

Teachers, or anyone who knows a great teacher, can write for applications at the above address.

2471—US DEPT. OF INTERIOR; BUREAU OF INDIAN AFFAIRS (Adult Education Grants)

1849 C Street NW
MS-3512 MIB
Washington DC 20240-0001
202/208-4871

AMOUNT: Varies
DEADLINE(S): Varies
FIELD(S): Vocational-Technical

Open to Native Americans for job training. Grants for adult vocational training and job placement services for individuals who are unemployed or under-employed.

Applications are available through tribal contract office, area offices, or home agency. Funds for vocational training and job placement only—not for formal degrees.

2472—UNIVERSAL TECHNICAL INSTITUTE (Al Unser National High School Competition)

3002 N. 27th Ave.
Phoenix AZ 85017
800/859-1201
Internet: www.utiedu.com

AMOUNT: Up to $5,000
DEADLINE(S): APR; MAR
FIELD(S): Technical areas, such as auto/truck mechanics or HVAC (heating, ventilation, air conditioning)
Competition for high school seniors pursuing careers as technicians in the above areas. Winners will receive scholarships valued from $1,000 to $5,000 for use at UTI, which has campuses in Arizona, Illinois, and Texas. Awards are based on a written test of technical skills to be taken at various sites in the US Awards also are given to schools by students finishing in the top 10%.

Nearly $400,000 will be awarded in the Auto/Truck competition, and over $100,000 in the HVAC/R competition. Call, check website, or write for details.

2473—VIRGINIA AVIATION AND SPACE EDUCATION FORUM (Scholarships)

5701 Huntsman Road
Sandston VA 23150
800/292-1034
Internet: www.doav.state.va.us/vaocship.htm

AMOUNT: $2,000
DEADLINE(S): FEB 16
FIELD(S): Aviation-related programs

Scholarships for high school seniors planning a career in aviation who are residents of Virginia and who have been accepted and are enrolled in an accredited college. Must have at least a 3.75 GPA.

Contact Betty Wilson at above location or access website for application and details of eligibility requirements.

2474—WHIRLY-GIRLS INC. (International Women Helicopter Pilots Scholarships)

Executive Towers 10-D
207 West Clarendon Ave.
Phoenix AZ 85013
602/263-0190
FAX 602/264-5812

AMOUNT: $4,500
DEADLINE(S): NOV 15
FIELD(S): Helicopter Flight Training

3 scholarships available to licensed women pilots for flight training. 2 are awarded to Whirly-Girls who are helicopter pilots; 1 is awarded to a licensed woman pilot holding a private license (airplane, balloon, or glider).

Applications are available April 15. Write, call, or fax for complete information.

2475—WYOMING TRUCKING ASSOCIATION (Scholarships)

P.O. Box 1909
Casper WY 82602
Written inquiry

AMOUNT: $250-$300
DEADLINE(S): MAR 1
FIELD(S): Transportation Industry

For Wyoming high school graduates enrolled in a Wyoming college, approved trade school, or the University of Wyoming. Must be pursuing a course of study that will result in a career in the transportation industry in Wyoming, including but not limited to: safety, environmental science, diesel mechanics, truck driving, vocational trades, business management, sales management, computer skills, accounting, office procedures, and management.

1-10 awards annually. Write to WYTA for an application.

GENERAL

2476—1ST MARINE DIVISION ASSN. (Scholarship Program)

14325 Willard Road, Suite 107
Chantilly VA 20151-2110
Phone: 703/803-3195
FAX: 703/803-7114

AMOUNT: Varies
DEADLINE(S): Varies
FIELD(S): All fields of study

For dependents of persons who served in the First Marine Division or in a unit attached to or in support of the Division and are deceased from any cause or permanently 100% disabled.

For undergraduate study only. Write for complete information.

2477—37th DIVISION VETERANS ASSOCIATION (Scholarship/Grant)

65 South Front Street, Room 432
Columbus OH 43215
614/228-3788

AMOUNT: Varies
DEADLINE(S): APR 1
FIELD(S): All fields of study

Scholarship/grant open to high school seniors or college students who are direct descendents of 37th Infantry Division veterans who served in World War I, II, or the Korean conflict.

Financial need is a consideration particularly if the father is deceased. 2 scholarships per year. Write for complete information.

2478—A. MARLYN MOYER, JR. SCHOLARSHIP FOUNDATION (Scholarships)

409 Hood Blvd.
Fairless Hills PA 19030
215/943-7400

AMOUNT: Varies
DEADLINE(S): APR 20
FIELD(S): All fields of study

Scholarships for partial support for graduating high school seniors who are enrolling for the first time in colleges, universities, technical schools, nursing schools, and other accredited postsecondary institutions. Must be US citizen and resident of Bucks County, Pennsylvania. Considerations are financial need, academic achievement, activities in school, community, or church.

Contact organization for details.

2479—A.H. BEAN FOUNDATION

c/o First Alabama Bank
2222 Ninth Street
Tuscaloosa AL 35401
Written inquiry

AMOUNT: $200-$600
DEADLINE(S): None given
FIELD(S): All fields of study

Scholarships for Alabama residents who are Christian individuals and are active members of a church, enrolled in a postsecondary educational institution, and recommended for aid by a minister.

Write to Trust Dept. at above location for details. Transcript and minister's recommendation required.

2480—ABBIE M. GRIFFIN EDUCATIONAL FUND (Scholarships)

c/o Winer & Bennett
111 Concord Street
Nashua NH 03060
603/882-5157

AMOUNT: $300-$2,000
DEADLINE(S): MAY 1
FIELD(S): All areas of study

Open only to residents of Merrimack, NH. Awards only to entering freshmen for full-time undergraduate study at an accredited college or university. Based on economic need.

10-15 awards per year. Write for complete information.

2481—ABE AND ANNIE SEIBEL FOUNDATION (Interest-free Educational Loan Fund)

US National Bank
P.O. Box 8210
Galveston TX 77553-8210
409/770-5665 or 409/770-5666

AMOUNT: Up to $3,000 a year
DEADLINE(S): FEB 28
FIELD(S): All fields of study

Open to Texas residents who are US citizens and will be or are enrolled (for at least 12 credit hours per semester) as undergraduate students at a Texas college or university accredited by the Southern Association of Colleges and Schools. Must

maintain 3.0 or better GPA. For study leading to first 4-year degree.

Applications available after Dec. 25. Apply Jan. 1 through Feb. 28. Write for complete information.

2482—ABRAHAM BURTMAN CHARITY TRUST

Burns Bldg.
P.O. Box 608
Dover NH 03820-0608
603/742-2332

AMOUNT: $1,000
DEADLINE(S): MAY 1
FIELD(S): All areas of study

Scholarships for financially needy residents of New Hampshire.

Send SASE to David A. Goodwin at above address for application guidelines.

2483—ADDISON H. GIBSON FOUNDATION (Low-Interest Loans)

One PPG Place, Suite 2230
Pittsburgh PA 15222
412/261-1611
FAX: 412/261-5733

AMOUNT: Varies
DEADLINE(S): None
FIELD(S): Most fields of study

Recipients must have completed at least one full-time year at the college or university from which a B.A. degree will be earned. Student's family home must be in western Pennsylvania, which is determined by an imaginary north-south line drawn through the state at Johnstown, PA. Must be in good academic standing and must demonstrate financial need. Other restrictions may apply.

Do NOT write! Interested/eligible students should telephone the Foundation for more information and to establish residence eligibility.

2484—ADELPHI UNIVERSITY (Various Scholarships)

1 South Ave.
Garden City NY 11530
516/877-3080
Internet: www.adelphi.edu/finaid/awards.html

AMOUNT: Up to $13,500
DEADLINE(S): FEB 15
FIELD(S): All fields of study

Various scholarships for full-time and part-time students at Adelphi University. Must document financial need—fill out a FAFSA form. Must have a 3.0 GPA after

freshman year; some require 3.3 GPA in subsequent years to maintain scholarship.

See website for further information; contact school to apply.

2485—AEROSPACE EDUCATION FOUNDATION (Eagle Plan Grant)

1501 Lee Highway
Arlington VA 22209-1198
800/727-3337, ext. 4880
FAX: 703/247-5853

AMOUNT: $250
DEADLINE(S): Varies
FIELD(S): No field of study specified

For graduates of the Community College of the Air Force pursuing a baccalaureate degree. Must be enlisted personnel—E-4, E-5, E-6, or E-7. Selection committee considers academic achievement, educational goals, leadership, and extracurricular activities.

A one-time grant.

2486—AFS INTERCULTURAL PROGRAMS (International Exchange Student Program)

198 Madison Ave., 8th Floor
New York NY 10016
212/299-9000 or 800/AFS-INFO
FAX: 212/299-9090
Internet: www.afs.org

AMOUNT: Varies
DEADLINE(S): Varies
FIELD(S): Study abroad—all high school subjects

International exchange of high school students for semester or school year. Students live with host families and attend local secondary schools. Students go to and from 50 countries. Scholarship assistance for summer, school year, and semester.

Deadlines are in the fall and spring. 10,000 participants worldwide. Call 800/876-2377; access website or write for complete information.

2487—AGNES T. MAGUIRE TRUST

P.O. Box 91210
Baton Rouge LA 70821-9210
504/332-4011

AMOUNT: Varies
DEADLINE(S): JUL 1
FIELD(S): All fields of study

Student loans for college-bound young women who are residents of Louisiana.

Send letter requesting detailed information after May 1 to Premier Bank, N.A., Trust Dept., at above address.

2488—AID ASSOCIATION FOR LUTHER-ANS (All-College, Vocational/Technical, and Lutheran Campus Scholarships)

4321 N. Ballard Road
Appleton, WI 54919-0001
800/225-5225 (800/CALL-AAL)
E-mail: aalmail@aal.org
Internet: www.aal.org

AMOUNT: $1,000/yr.-$10,000/4 yrs. (All-College); $500 (Voc/Tech); $200-$1,000 (Lutheran Campus)
DEADLINE(S): NOV
FIELD(S): All fields of study

For AAL members seeking post-high school education. An applying student must have an AAL insurance policy or an AAL annuity in his or her name.

For membership information, contact the above address or your local AAL district representative. 2,800 awards annually.

2489—AIR FORCE ACADEMY (Falcon Foundation Scholarships)

3116 Academy Dr., Suite 200
USAF Academy CO 80840-4480
719/333-4096

AMOUNT: $3,000
DEADLINE(S): APR 30
FIELD(S): All areas of study

Scholarships to attend private preparatory schools for students who plan to seek admission to the US Air Force Academy. Open to single students age 17-21 in excellent health and highly motivated to attend the Academy. Must be a US citizen.

100 awards per year. Send a self-addressed stamped envelope for application.

2490—AIR FORCE AID SOCIETY (General Henry H. Arnold Education Grant Program)

1745 Jefferson Davis Hwy., #202
Arlington VA 22202
800/429-9475

AMOUNT: $1,500 freshmen yr. of sons/daughters; $1,000/subsequent yrs.
DEADLINE(S): MAR (Applications available then. Deadline is APR.)
FIELD(S): All fields of study

Open to undergrads who are dependent children of active duty, retired, or deceased members of the US Air Force, spouses of active duty or retired members, or surviving spouses of members who died on active duty or in retired status residing in continental US (lower 48 states) only. US citizenship or legal residency required.

For full-time study at an accredited institution. Must maintain at least a 2.0 GPA. Must reapply each year.

2491—AIR FORCE AID SOCIETY (Voc-Tech Loan Program)

1745 Jefferson Davis Hwy., #202
Arlington VA 22202
800/429-9475

AMOUNT: $1,000 maximum
DEADLINE(S): None specified
FIELD(S): All fields of study in vocational/technical areas

For spouses and children of active duty members at all stateside bases enrolled in vocational/technical programs that increase employment opportunities.

One-time basis only. To be repaid in two years. Upon verification of student's program completion, 25% of the balance will be converted to a grant.

2492—AIR FORCE SERGEANTS' ASSOCIATION (Scholarship Awards Program)

5211 Auth Road
Suitland MD 20746
Internet: amf.org/scholarship.html

AMOUNT: $500-$3,000
DEADLINE(S): APR 15
FIELD(S): All fields of study

Open to single dependent children (under 23) of AFSA members or its auxiliary. For undergraduate study at accredited institutions only. Awards are based on academic excellence.

For application and complete information send self-addressed, stamped ($1.47), 7x10 envelope to AFSA/AMF Scholarship Administrator at above address.

2493—AIR TRAFFIC CONTROL ASSOCIATION INC (Scholarships for Children of Air Traffic Specialists)

2300 Clarendon Blvd., #711
Arlington VA 22201
703/522-5717
FAX: 703/527-7251
E-mail: atca@worldnit.att.net
Internet: www.atca.org

AMOUNT: Varies
DEADLINE(S): MAY 1
FIELD(S): All fields of study

For children (either natural or adopted) of persons serving or having served as air traffic control specialists with either government, US military, or in a private facility in the US. Must be enrolled in an accredited college or university and planning to continue the following year in bachelor's program or higher. Attendance must be equal to at least half-time (6 hours).

Write for complete information.

2494—AIRLINE PILOTS ASSOCIATION (Scholarship Program)

1625 Massachusetts Ave. NW
Washington DC 20036
202/797-4050

AMOUNT: $3,000 per year for up to 4 years
DEADLINE(S): APR 1
FIELD(S): All fields of study

Open to undergraduate sons or daughters of medically retired or deceased pilot members of the Airline Pilots Association. Academic capability and financial need are considered. Renewable for up to 3 years.

Write for complete information ONLY if above qualifications are met.

2495—AIRMEN MEMORIAL FOUNDATION (AFSA/AMF Scholarship Awards Program)

5211 Auth Road
Suitland MD 20746
800/638-0594
Internet: amf.org

AMOUNT: $500-$3,000
DEADLINE(S): APR 15
FIELD(S): All fields of study

Open to unmarried dependent children (under 25) of Air Force enlisted personnel (active or retired) of all components, including Air National Guard and Reserves. For undergraduate study at any accredited academic or trade/technical school.

See website for more information. Send self-addressed, stamped ($1.47) 9x12 envelope to above address for application details. Applications available November 1 through March 31.

2496—ALABAMA COMMISSION ON HIGHER EDUCATION (Scholarships; Grants; Loans; Work Study Programs)

P.O. Box 302000
Montgomery AL 36130-2000
Written inquiry

AMOUNT: Varies
DEADLINE(S): Varies
FIELD(S): All fields of study

The commission administers a number of financial aid programs tenable at postsecondary institutions in Alabama. Some awards are need-based.

Write for the "Financial Aid Sources in Alabama" brochure or contact high school guidance counselor or college financial aid officer.

2497—ALABAMA DEPARTMENT OF VETERANS AFFAIRS (G.I. Dependents Scholarship Program)

P.O. Box 1509
Montgomery AL 36102-1509
334/242-5077

AMOUNT: Varies

DEADLINE(S): Varies (prior to 26th birthday)

FIELD(S): All fields of study

Open to dependent children (under age 26) of veterans who were permanent Alabama residents for at least 1 year prior to active duty and who died as a result of military service or were/are MIAs or POWs or became 20%-100% disabled.

Applicants must be Alabama residents. For attendance at state-supported Alabama institutions as well as vocational training schools. Totally disabled vets who are not original Alabama residents may qualify after 5 years of Alabama residency. Write for complete information.

2498—ALABAMA DEPARTMENT OF VETERANS AFFAIRS (G.I. Dependents Scholarship Program)

P.O. Box 1509
Montgomery AL 36102-1509
334/242-5077

AMOUNT: Varies

DEADLINE(S): None

FIELD(S): All fields of study

Open to wife or widow (not remarried) of veteran who was an Alabama resident for at least 1 year prior to active duty and died as a result of military service, was/is MIA or a POW, or became 20%-100% disabled.

Vets who are not original Alabama residents but have a 100% service-connected disability may qualify after 5 years' residency in Alabama. Awards tenable at state-supported Alabama institutions. Contact Edward H. Minter III at above address for complete information.

2499—ALASKA COMMISSION ON POST-SECONDARY EDUCATION (Student Loan Program; Family Loan Program)

3030 Vintage Blvd.
Juneau AK 99801-7109

907/465-2962

AMOUNT: $8,500 undergraduate; $9,500 graduate

DEADLINE(S): MAY 15

FIELD(S): All areas of study

Open to Alaska residents of at least 1 year. These low-interest loans (8% student; 5% family) support full-time and half-time study at any accredited vocational, undergraduate, or graduate institution.

Up to $8,500 available for vocational or undergraduate study and up to $9,500 for graduate study. Renewable. Write for complete information.

2500—ALASKA COMMISSION ON POST-SECONDARY EDUCATION (State Educational Incentive Grant Program)

3030 Vintage Blvd.
Juneau AK 99801-7109
907/465-6741

AMOUNT: $100 to $1,500

DEADLINE(S): MAY 31

FIELD(S): All fields of study

Open to Alaska residents of at least one year who are accepted to or enrolled in their first undergraduate degree or comparable certificate program at an accredited institution (in-state or out-of-state). Need must be demonstrated.

200 grants per year. Write for complete information.

2501—ALBANY ACADEMY FOR GIRLS (Scholarships)

140 Academy Road
Albany NY 12208
518/463-2201
FAX: 518/463-5096
E-mail: lewisj@albanyacademyforgirls.org

AMOUNT: $3,000/yr. for 4 years + $12,000

DEADLINE(S): DEC 1

FIELD(S): All fields of secondary school study

Scholarship for the school listed above. Based on grades, testing, and recommendations to be admitted; must score well on scholarship exam and essays.

Write for details.

2502—ALBERT BAKER FUND (Student Loans)

5 Third Street, #717
San Francisco CA 94103
415/543-7028

AMOUNT: Up to $3,500

DEADLINE(S): SEP 1

FIELD(S): All fields of study

Open to students who are members of the First Church of Christ Scientist in Boston, MA. Students' residency can be anywhere in the world. For study in the US. Student must have other primary lender and be enrolled in an accredited college or university. Interest rate is 3% below prime.

All students must have co-signer who is a US citizen. Average of 160 awards per year. Write or call for complete information. Applicant must be the one who calls.

2503—ALBERT O.J. LANDUCCI, DDS (Scholarships)

2720 Edison Street
San Mateo CA 94403-2495
650/574-4444
FAX: 650/574-4441
E-mail: e@DrLanducci.com
Internet: www.drlanducci.com

AMOUNT: Varies

DEADLINE(S): Varies

FIELD(S): All fields of study

Awards and scholarships for elementary and high school students who reside in San Mateo County, California, or for those who attend or plan to attend College of San Mateo. Annual scholarships are in four areas: academic excellence, outstanding community and school volunteerism, science and math achievement, and dental assisting.

For more information, contact your school's scholarship representative.

2504—ALBUQUERQUE COMMUNITY FOUNDATION (Financial Aid Program)

P.O. Box 36960
Albuquerque NM 87176
505/883-6240

AMOUNT: Varies

DEADLINE(S): None specified

FIELD(S): All fields of study

A financial aid program for undergraduates attending a four-year college or university. Applicant must be a federal financial aid recipient.

14 awards annually. Renewable. Send self-addressed, stamped envelope to receive application.

2505—ALEXANDER FAMILY EDUCATIONAL FOUNDATION WELFARE TRUST

c/o Nicolas Alexander
802 NE 199th
Portland OR 97233

503/666-9491
AMOUNT: $3,000-$5,000
DEADLINE(S): MAR 1
FIELD(S): All fields of study

Scholarships for residents of Oregon.
Send SASE to above address for formal application.

2506—ALEXANDER GRAHAM BELL ASSOCIATION FOR THE DEAF (School Age Financial Aid Awards)

3417 Volta Place NW
Washington DC 20007-2778
202/337-5220 (voice/TTY)
E-mail: agbell2@aol.com
Internet: www.agbell.org
AMOUNT: Varies
DEADLINE(S): APR 1 (Request application by then. Deadline is MAY 1 postmark.)
FIELD(S): All fields of study

For aural/oral students (aged 6-21) with moderate to profound hearing losses that they acquired before they developed language. Must be registered full-time in an elementary, middle, or high school that enrolls primarily students with normal hearing. Must use speech, residual hearing, and/or speechreading as their primary form of communication.

Request application IN WRITING to the Bell Association's Financial Aid Coordinator; make sure you indicate which program you would like to apply for, and include your name and address on the letter.

2507—ALEXANDER GRAHAM BELL ASSOCIATION FOR THE DEAF (College Scholarship Awards)

3417 Volta Place NW
Washington DC 20007-2778
202/337-5220 (voice/TTY)
E-mail: agbell2@aol.com
Internet: www.agbell.org
AMOUNT: Varies
DEADLINE(S): DEC 1 (Request application by then. Deadline is MAR 15 postmark.)
FIELD(S): All fields of study

For prelingually deaf or hard-of-hearing students who use speech and speechreading to communicate and who are attending or have been admitted to a college or university that primarily enrolls students with normal hearing.

Must have a 60dB or greater hearing loss in the better ear in the speech frequencies of 500, 1000, and 2000 Hz. Application requests must be made IN

WRITING to the Bell Association's Financial Aid Coordinator; make sure you indicate which program you would like to apply for, and include your name and address on your letter.

2508—ALEXANDER GRAHAM BELL ASSOCIATION FOR THE DEAF (Parent Infant Preschool Awards)

3417 Volta Place NW
Washington DC 20007-2778
202/337-5220 (voice/TTY)
E-mail: agbell2@aol.com
Internet: www.agbell.org
AMOUNT: Varies
DEADLINE(S): SEP 1 (Request application by then. Deadline is OCT 1 postmark.)
FIELD(S): All fields of study

Stipends are awarded to parents of infants (younger than 6 years old) who have been diagnosed with moderate to profound hearing losses. May be used to cover expenses associated with early intervention educational and rehabilitative services. The parent or guardian must be committed to an auditory-oral philosophy of education. Family must demonstrate financial need.

Must request application IN WRITING to the Bell Association's Financial Aid Coordinator; make sure you indicate which program you would like to apply for, and include your name and address on the letter.

2509—ALEXANDER SCHOLARSHIP FUND

P.O. Box 719
Evansville IN 47115
812/464-3215
AMOUNT: $2,000
DEADLINE(S): Varies (Set by high school)
FIELD(S): All areas of study

For college-bound high school seniors attending one of three high schools in Posey County, Indiana and who reside in that county.

10 awards. Renewable for three years at $750. Obtain application from high school counselor.

2510—ALL SAINTS' ACADEMY (Financial Aid Awards)

5000 State Road 540 W.
Winter Haven FL 33880
941/293-5980
FAX: 941/294-2819
AMOUNT: $200-$5,000
DEADLINE(S): MAR 1

FIELD(S): All fields of K-12 study

Scholarships for financially needy students in good academic standing at the above K-12 private school.

Contact Debbie Ford at school for details.

2511—ALLIED JEWISH FEDERATION (Charles and Louise Rosenbaum Scholarship Fund)

300 Dahlia Street
Denver CO 80222
Written inquiry
AMOUNT: Varies
DEADLINE(S): MAR 15
FIELD(S): All fields of study

Scholarships for Jewish high school seniors who are residents of Colorado.
Contact above location for details.

2512—AMARILLO AREA FOUNDATION, INC. (Scholarship Program)

801 South Fillmore, #700
Amarillo TX 79101
806/376-4521
FAX: 806/373-3656
E-mail: sylvia@aaf-hf.org
AMOUNT: Varies
DEADLINE(S): APR 1
FIELD(S): All fields of study

Open to graduating high school seniors who live in one of the 26 northernmost counties of the Texas Panhandle.

Renewable. Contact Sylvia Artho, Scholarship Coordinator, for an application or list of eligible counties.

2513—AMERICA'S JUNIOR MISS (Scholarship Competition)

P.O. Box 2786
Mobile AL 36652-2786
334/438-3621
FAX: 334/431-0063
AMOUNT: up to $30,000
DEADLINE(S): Varies (from state to state)
FIELD(S): All fields of study

For college-bound high school senior girls who are US citizens, legal residents of the county and state in which they seek to compete, and have never been married. Must apply your sophomore or junior year. Competition based on judge's interview, creative and performing arts, scholastic achievement, presence and composure, and fitness.

Several scholarships are awarded annually at the local, state, and national levels, totaling approximately $5 million. The 50 winners, one from each state, compete at the Junior Miss pageant in Mobile, Alabama.

2514—AMERICAN ASSOCIATION OF BIO-ANALYSTS (David Birenbaum Scholarship Fund of AAB)

917 Locust Street, Suite 1100
St. Louis MO 63101-1413
314/241-1445
FAX: 314/241-1449
E-mail: aab1445@primary.net

AMOUNT: Varies
DEADLINE(S): Varies
FIELD(S): All fields of study

Open to AAB members, their spouses, and children. Financial need is one of several considerations, including but not limited to, goals, history of acheivements, community involvment, etc.

Write to the above address for complete information.

2515—AMERICAN ASSOCIATION OF UNIVERSITY WOMEN (Foundation for Education—Livermore, Pleasanton, Dublin, Sunol CA)

Scholarship Coordinator
P.O. Box 661
Livermore CA 94551
Written inquiry

AMOUNT: $1,000
DEADLINE(S): MAR 1
FIELD(S): All fields of study

For female residents of Livermore, Pleasanton, Dublin, or Sunol, CA or graduates of a high school in those cities.

3 scholarships to be awarded to juniors or seniors at an accredited 4-year college or university.

2516—AMERICAN ASSOCIATION OF UNIVERSITY WOMEN—HONOLULU BRANCH (Ruth E. Black Scholarship)

1802 Keeaumoku Street
Honolulu HI 96822
808/537-4702

AMOUNT: Varies
DEADLINE(S): MAR 1
FIELD(S): All fields of study

Open to women who are legal residents of Hawaii. For undergraduate study at an accredited college or university in Hawaii. Must demonstrate financial need.

Applications become available October 1st of each year. Contact above address for an application or more information.

2517—AMERICAN CANCER SOCIETY (College Scholarship Program)

1205 E. Saginaw Street
Lansing MI 48906
800/723-0360
Internet: www.gl.cancer.org

AMOUNT: $1,000
DEADLINE(S): APR 15
FIELD(S): All fields of study

For Michigan and Indiana residents who are US citizens and have had a diagnosis of cancer before age 21. Must be an undergraduate under age 21 attending an accredited college/university within Michigan or Indiana. Based on financial need, scholarship, community service, and leadership.

Renewable. Contact ACS's Great Lakes Division for an application packet.

2518—AMERICAN COUNCIL OF THE BLIND (ACB Scholarship Program)

Attn: Holly Fults
1155 15th Street NW, Suite 720
Washington DC 20005
202/467-5081 or 800/424-8666

AMOUNT: $500-$4,000
DEADLINE(S): MAR 1
FIELD(S): All fields of study

Scholarships open to legally blind applicants who have been accepted to or are enrolled in an accredited institution for vocational, technical, undergraduate, graduate, or professional studies. US citizen or legal resident.

25 scholarships awarded. Write for complete information.

2519—AMERICAN EXPRESS SCHOLARSHIP AWARDS PROGRAM

World Financial Center
New York NY 10285-3205

AMOUNT: $1,000-$3,000 per year; also a one-time award of $500 based on academic performance and overall achievement
DEADLINE(S): NOV (Request application by then. Deadline is DEC.)
FIELD(S): All fields of study in an accredited 2 or 4-year undergraduate college or university

For children of American Express employees in US and Canada. Awards based on combination of merit and finan-

cial need. Awards to be paid directly to school.

Renewable annually for a maximum of 4 consecutive years provided recipient's school attendance is uninterrupted and performance is satisfactory.

2520—AMERICAN FEDERATION OF GRAIN MILLERS (Scholarship Program)

4949 Olson Memorial Highway
Minneapolis MN 55422-5199
612/545-0211
FAX: 612/545-5489

AMOUNT: $1,000
DEADLINE(S): DEC 31
FIELD(S): Any field of study

Open to high school members who are members or dependents of members of the American Federation of Grain Millers. Awards will be based on the basis of character, scholastic achievement, an essay, and academic potential.

Write to the above address for complete information.

2521—AMERICAN FEDERATION OF STATE, COUNTY & MUNICIPAL EMPLOYEES, AFL-CIO (AFSCME Family Scholarship)

1625 L Street NW
Washington DC 20036
202/429-1250
800/238-2539
FAX: 202/659-0446

AMOUNT: $2,000 per year for 4 years
DEADLINE(S): DEC 31
FIELD(S): All areas of study

Open to high school seniors who are dependent children of active AFSCME members. Awards for full-time undergraduate study.

Renewable for 4 years.

2522—AMERICAN FEDERATION OF STATE, COUNTY AND MUNICIPAL EMPLOYEES, AFL-CIO (MasterCard Scholarship Award Program)

1625 L Street, NW
Washington DC 20036
800/238-2539
FAX: 202/659-0446

AMOUNT: $500-$4,000
DEADLINE(S): MAY 31
FIELD(S): All fields of study, including vocational/technical

Members must have at least one year of continuous good-standing membership in AFSCME in order for spouses and children to be eligible. Need not be MasterCard holders. Applicant must be accepted into an accredited college or community college or a recognized technical or trade school by June 30.

For application, send a postcard with name, local union number, social security number, and address to: Union MasterCard Scholarship, P.O. Box 9389, Minneapolis, MN 55440-9389.

2523—AMERICAN FEDERATION OF TEACHERS (Robert G. Porter Scholars Program)

555 New Jersey Ave. NW
Washington DC 20001-2079
202/393-7486
FAX: 202/879-4406
E-mail: poconnor@aft.org
Internet: www.aft.org

AMOUNT: $1,000
DEADLINE(S): MAR 31
FIELD(S): All fields of study

Open to members of the American Federation of Teachers seeking continuing education in their fields of study.

3 awards annually. Contact AFT for an application.

2524—AMERICAN FIRE SPRINKLER ASSOCIATION (Scholarship Contest)

12959 Jupiter Road, Suite 142
Dallas TX 75238
214/349-5965
FAX: 343-8898
Internet: www.firesprinkler.org

AMOUNT: Up to $2,500
DEADLINE(S): DEC 5
FIELD(S): Fire safety

A nationwide essay contest for high school seniors. Topic: "How fire sprinklers affect your community." 700-1,000 typed words, double-spaced, 1-inch margins. Regional and nationwide scholarship prizes. Not open to AFSA staff relatives or board members.

Send to "Scholarship Contest" at above location for application.

2525—AMERICAN FOREIGN SERVICE ASSOCIATION (Financial Aid Awards)

2101 E Street NW
Washington DC 20037
202/944-5504

AMOUNT: $500-$2,500
DEADLINE(S): FEB 6
FIELD(S): All fields of study

The American Foreign Service Association offers financial aid scholarships to dependents of US Government Foreign Service employees. Students must be enrolled in undergraduate study at a US college or university.

Write to the above address for complete information.

2526—AMERICAN FOREIGN SERVICE ASSOCIATION (Merit Awards)

2101 E Street NW
Washington DC 20037
202/944-5504

AMOUNT: $1,000
DEADLINE(S): FEB 6
FIELD(S): All fields of study

Open to dependents of US Government Foreign Service employees. Students must be high school seniors.

Write to the above address for complete information.

2527—AMERICAN FOUNDATION FOR THE BLIND (Ferdinand Torres Scholarship)

11 Penn Plaza, Suite 300
New York NY 10001
212/502-7661
FAX: 212/502-7771
E-mail: juliet@afb.org
Internet: www.afb.org

AMOUNT: $1,000
DEADLINE(S): APR 30
FIELD(S): All fields of study

Open to legally blind full-time postsecondary students who present evidence of economic need. Must reside in the US. Preference given to applicants residing in New York City metropolitan area and new immigrants to the US. Must submit evidence of legal blindness; official transcripts; proof of college/university acceptance; evidence of need; three letters of recommendation; proof of residence; and statement of goals, work experience, activities, and how money will be used.

New immigrants should also include country of origin and reason for coming to US. 1 award annually. See website or contact Julie Tucker at AFB for an application.

2528—AMERICAN GI FORUM OF THE US HISPANIC EDUCATION FOUNDATION (Chapter Scholarships)

3301 Mountain Road NW
Albuquerque NM 87104

505/243-7551 or 505/843-8224
FAX: 505/247-2993
Internet: http://www.incacorp.com/agifhef

AMOUNT: Varies
DEADLINE(S): Varies
FIELD(S): All fields of study

Open to Hispanic undergraduate students residing in certain states that have chapters of the above organization. Students must obtain applications from nearest awarding chapter.

Send self-addressed, stamped envelope (SASE) to the above address for complete information.

2529—AMERICAN GI FORUM OF THE US HISPANIC EDUCATION FOUNDATION

3301 Mountain Road NW
Albuquerque NM 87104
505/243-7551 or 505/843-8224
FAX: 505/247-2993
Internet: http://www.incacorp.com/agifhef

AMOUNT: $100-$1,000
DEADLINE(S): Varies
FIELD(S): All fields of study

Open to Hispanic undergraduate students living where AGIF chapters exiStreet Students must seek applications from nearest awarding chapter. Financial need considered.

Send self-address, stamped envelope (SASE) to the above address for complete information.

2530—AMERICAN HEALTH AND BEAUTY AIDS INSTITUTE (Entrepreneurial Leadership Conference)

401 North Michigan Ave.
Chicago IL 60611-4267
312/644-6610

AMOUNT: $100 travel allowance plus conference registration
DEADLINE(S): None specified
FIELD(S): All fields of study

The American Health and Beauty Aids Institute Entrepreneurial Leadership Conference is held each November. Two winners are chosen from each of the 117 Historically Black Colleges and Universities. Winners receive registration plus a $100 travel allowance. Program includes leadership workshops with presidents and key executives from multimillion-dollar African-American-owned hair-care corporations.

11 students will be selected for additional scholarships totaling over $30,000 in scholarship prizes. Submit an essay on entrepreneurship in the black community.

2531—AMERICAN INSTITUTE FOR FOREIGN STUDY (AIFS) (International Scholarships)

102 Greenwich Ave.
Greenwich CT 06830
800/727-2437
E-mail: mjoyce@aifs.org
Internet: www.aifs.org
AMOUNT: $1,000/semester; $500/summer
DEADLINE(S): MAR 15 (summer);
   APR 15 (fall); OCT 15 (spring)
FIELD(S): All fields of study

Scholarship program for undergraduates with at least a 3.0 GPA desiring to spend a semester or summer studying in participating foreign universities. Criteria include leadership potential and extracurricular involvement in multicultural or international issues.

100 semester scholarships and 10 for summer study. Visit website and/or contact above address for details.

2532—AMERICAN INSTITUTE FOR FOREIGN STUDY (AIFS) (International Scholarships for Minorities)

102 Greenwich Ave.
Greenwich CT 06830
800/727-2437
E-mail: mjoyce@aifs.org
Internet: www.aifs.org
AMOUNT: Full program fees +
   transportaiton; or $1,000/semester
DEADLINE(S): APR 15 (fall); OCT 15
   (spring)
FIELD(S): All fields of study

Scholarship program for minority undergraduates with at least a 3.0 GPA desiring to spend a semester or summer studying in participating foreign universities. Criteria include leadership potential and extracurricular involvement in multicultural or international issues. Must be African-American, Asian-American, Native American, Hispanic-American, or Pacific Islander currently enrolled at a US institution.

1 full scholarship and 5 semester scholarships. Visit website and/or contact above address for details.

2533—AMERICAN JEWISH LEAGUE FOR ISRAEL (University Scholarship Fund)

130 E. 59th Street, 14th Fl.
New York NY 10022
212/371-1452
AMOUNT: $1,500
DEADLINE(S): MAY 1
FIELD(S): All fields of study

Open to US citizens of Jewish faith who have been accepted for a year of undergrad or grad study in Israel at Bar Ilan Univ., Ben Gurion Univ., Haifa Univ., Hebrew Univ.-Jerusalem, Technion, Tel Aviv Univ., or Weizmann Institute of Science.

5-6 awards per year. Write for complete information.

2534—AMERICAN JUNIOR BRAHMAN ASSOCIATION (Scholarships)

1313 La Concha Lane
Houston TX 77054-1890
Written inquiry
AMOUNT: Varies
DEADLINE(S): APR 30
FIELD(S): All fields of study

Open to graduating high school seniors who are members of the American Junior Brahman Association who have made outstanding contributions to agriculture and the Brahman industry. For full-time undergraduate study.

Applicants must submit an essay stating why they believe they are deserving of this scholarship. Write for complete information.

2535—AMERICAN LEGION-KANSAS (Dr. "Click" Cowger Scholarship)

1314 SW Topeka Blvd.
Topeka KS 66612-1886
913/232-9315
AMOUNT: $500
DEADLINE(S): JUL 15
FIELD(S): Any field of study

This scholarship is offered to players who have played Kansas American Legion Baseball. It is open to high school seniors, college freshmen, and sophomores. Scholarships must be used at an approved Kansas college, university, or trade school.

Write to above address for complete information.

2536—AMERICAN LEGION (Eagle Scout of the Year Scholarship)

P.O. Box 1055
Indianapolis IN 46206
317/630-1200
FAX: 317/630-1223
Internet: www.legion.org
AMOUNT: $8,000 to winner; $2,000 to
   three 2nd-place winners
DEADLINE(S): MAR 1 (to state or
   dept.); APR 1 (national)
FIELD(S): All fields of study

Scholarship for an Eagle Scout chosen as "The American Legion Eagle Scout of the Year." Recipient will receive scholarship immediately upon high school graduation. Must be an active member of a duly chartered Boy Scout Troop, Varsity Scout Team, or Explorer Post, and the son or grandson of Legionnaire or Auxiliary member. Must have received a Boy Scout religious emblem, demonstrated practical citizenship in church, school, Scouting, and community, and be 15-18.

Apply through American Legion State Headquarters. Contact above location for address liStreet

2537—AMERICAN LEGION-KANSAS (Legion Oratorical Contest)

1314 SW Topeka Blvd.
Topeka KS 66612-1886
913/232-9315
AMOUNT: $1,500 (1st); $500 (2nd); $250
   (3rd); $150 (4th)
DEADLINE(S): Varies
FIELD(S): Any field of study

This oratory contest is for boys or girls attending a Kansas high school.

For complete information write to the above address.

2538—AMERICAN LEGION-KANSAS (Paul Flaherty Athletic Scholarship)

1314 SW Topeka Blvd.
Topeka KS 66612-1886
913/232-9315
AMOUNT: $250
DEADLINE(S): JUL 15
FIELD(S): Any field of study

This scholarship is open to any Kansas boy or girl who has participated in any form of Kansas high school athletics. Scholarship must be used at an approved Kansas college, university, or trade school.

Write to above address for complete information.

2539—AMERICAN LEGION-KANSAS (Ted & Nora Anderson Scholarship Fund; Albert M. Lappin Scholarship; Hugh A. Smith Scholarship)

1314 SW Topeka Blvd.
Topeka KS 66612-1886
913/232-9315

AMOUNT: $500-$1,000
DEADLINE(S): FEB 15
FIELD(S): Any field of study

These scholarships are offered to sons or daughters of Kansas Legion and Auxiliary members. Students must be high school seniors, college freshmen, or sophmores. Scholarships must be at an approved Kansas college, university, or trade school.

Write to the above address for complete information.

2540—AMERICAN LEGION AUXILIARY (Dept. of Minnesota Scholarships)

Dept. of Minnesota
State Veterans Service Building
Street Paul MN 55155
612/224-7634

AMOUNT: $750
DEADLINE(S): MAR 15
FIELD(S): All fields of study

Open to Minnesota residents who are children or grandchildren of US veterans of armed conflicts. Must be high school senior or grad with GPA of 'C' or better, attend Minnesota vocational/business school, college, or university, and demonstrate financial need.

Write for complete information.

2541—AMERICAN LEGION AUXILIARY-KANSAS (Scholarship)

1314 SW Topeka Blvd.
Topeka KS 66612-1886
913/232-1396

AMOUNT: $250 per year (2 years)
DEADLINE(S): APR 1
FIELD(S): Any field of study

This scholarship is open to children, spouses, or unremarried widows of veterans. Applicants must be entering college for the first time. This scholarship can be used only at Kansas schools.

Write to the above address for complete information.

2542—AMERICAN LEGION AUXILIARY, DEPARTMENT OF ALABAMA (Scholarships)

120 North Jackson Street
Montgomery AL 36014-3811

AMOUNT: $850
DEADLINE(S): APR 1
FIELD(S): General fields of study and several for nursing

Applicants must be descendents of veterans serving during a war from WWI to current. Veteran and applicant must be residents of Alabama. Credit given for books, tuition, and board. Submit in handwriting a letter stating qualifications, age, need, etc., with a complete transcript of high school and/or college record. Offered at 13 colleges/universities in Alabama.

40 scholarships to be awarded.

2543—AMERICAN MENSA EDUCATION & RESEARCH FOUNDATION (Scholarships)

3437 West 7th Street, Suite 264
Fort Worth TX 76107
817/332-2600 or 800/666-3672

AMOUNT: $200 to $1,000
DEADLINE(S): JAN 31
FIELD(S): All fields of study

Open to students enrolled for the academic year following the award in a degree program in an accredited American institution of postsecondary education. Applicants must submit an essay describing career, vocational, and academic goals.

Essay should be fewer than 550 words and must be specific rather than general. It MUST be on an official application. Send self-addressed, stamped envelope no later than January 1 for application.

2544—AMERICAN MORGAN HORSE INSTITUTE (Scholarship Program)

P.O. Box 837
Shelburne VT 05482-0519
Written inquiry

AMOUNT: $3,000
DEADLINE(S): MAR 1
FIELD(S): All fields of study

Scholarships for students 21 years or younger who are or will be high school graduates or who hold a GED. Selection based on need, community service, and achievement with horses. Requests for applications MUST include a stamped, self-addressed envelope (SASE).

5 scholarships yearly.

2545—AMERICAN NATIONAL CAN COMPANY (Scholarship Program)

8770 W. Brynmawr Ave., #09-E
Chicago IL 60631
312/399-3000

AMOUNT: $500 to $3,000
DEADLINE(S): MAR 15
FIELD(S): All fields of study

Must be high school senior to apply and the son or daughter of an employee of the American National Can Company with a minimum of 3 years of service.

20 scholarships are available per year. Renewable to 4 years. Write for complete information.

2546—AMERICAN RADIO RELAY LEAGUE FOUNDATION ("You've Got a Friend in Pennsylvania" Scholarship)

225 Main Street
Newington CT 06111
860/594-0200
FAX: 860/594-0259
Internet: www.arrl.org/

AMOUNT: $1,000
DEADLINE(S): FEB 1
FIELD(S): All fields of study

For AARL members who hold a general radio license and are residents of Pennsylvania.

1 award annually. Contact ARRL for an application.

2547—AMERICAN RADIO RELAY LEAGUE FOUNDATION (ARRL Scholarship Honoring Senator Barry Goldwater, K7UGA)

225 Main Street
Newington CT 06111
860/594-0200
FAX: 860/594-0259
Internet: www.arrl.org/

AMOUNT: $5,000
DEADLINE(S): FEB 1
FIELD(S): All fields of study

Open to students who are licensed radio amateurs (at least novice level) and enrolled full-time as a bachelor's or graduate student at a regionally accredited institution.

1 award annually. Contact ARRL for an application.

2548—AMERICAN RADIO RELAY LEAGUE FOUNDATION (Albuquerque Amateur Radio Club Scholarship)

225 Main Street
Newington CT 06111

860/594-0200
FAX: 860/594-0259
Internet: www.arrl.org/
AMOUNT: $500
DEADLINE(S): FEB 1
FIELD(S): All fields of study

Open to radio amateurs holding any class of license and who are residents of New Mexico. For undergraduate study at any institution. Must supply a one-page essay on the role Amateur Radio has played in your life.

1 award annually. Contact ARRL for an application.

2549—AMERICAN RADIO RELAY LEAGUE FOUNDATION (Charles Clarke Cordle Memorial Scholarship)

225 Main Street
Newington CT 06111
860/594-0200
FAX: 860/594-0259
Internet: www.arrl.org/
AMOUNT: $1,000
DEADLINE(S): FEB 1
FIELD(S): All fields of study

For undergraduate or graduate residents of Georgia or Alabama who hold any class of amateur radio license. Must attend school in Georgia or Alabama and have a minimum 2.5 GPA.

1 award annually. Contact ARRL for an application.

2550—AMERICAN RADIO RELAY LEAGUE FOUNDATION (Mary Lou Brown Scholarship)

225 Main Street
Newington CT 06111
860/594-0200
FAX: 860/594-0259
Internet: www.arrl.org/
AMOUNT: $2,500
DEADLINE(S): FEB 1
FIELD(S): All fields of study

Open to residents of the ARRL Northwest Division (AK, ID, MT, OR, WA) who are radio amateurs holding at least a general license. For study leading to a bachelor's degree or higher course of study. Must have GPA of at least 3.0 and a demonstrated interest in promoting the Amateur Radio Service.

Multiple scholarships annually, as income allows. Contact ARRL for an application.

2551—AMERICAN RADIO RELAY LEAGUE FOUNDATION (The New England FEMARA Scholarships)

225 Main Street
Newington CT 06111
860/594-0200
FAX: 860/594-0259
Internet: www.arrl.org/
AMOUNT: $600
DEADLINE(S): FEB 1
FIELD(S): All fields of study

Open to residents of the New England states (ME, NH, VT, MA, CT, RI) who are radio amateurs with a technician license.

Multiple awards annually. Contact ARRL for an application.

2552—AMERICAN RADIO RELAY LEAGUE FOUNDATION (The General Fund Scholarships)

225 Main Street
Newington CT 06111
860/594-0200
FAX: 860/594-0259
Internet: www.arrl.org/
AMOUNT: $1,000
DEADLINE(S): FEB 1
FIELD(S): All fields of study

Open to undergraduate or graduate students holding any level amateur radio license.

Multiple awards annually. Contact ARRL for an application.

2553—AMERICAN RADIO RELAY LEAGUE FOUNDATION (The K2TEO Martin J. Green, Sr. Memorial Scholarship)

225 Main Street
Newington CT 06111
860/594-0200
FAX: 860/594-0259
Internet: www.arrl.org/
AMOUNT: $1,000
DEADLINE(S): FEB 1
FIELD(S): All fields of study

Open to undergraduate or graduate students holding any level amateur radio license. Preference is given to a student ham from a ham family.

1 award annually. Contact ARRL for an application.

2554—AMERICAN RADIO RELAY LEAGUE FOUNDATION (The North Texas Section-Bob Nelson KB5BNU Memorial Scholarship)

225 Main Street
Newington CT 06111
860/594-0200
FAX: 860/594-0259
Internet: www.arrl.org/
AMOUNT: $750
DEADLINE(S): FEB 1
FIELD(S): All fields of study

For radio amateurs with any class of license who are residents of Texas or Oklahoma. Must be enrolled in a full-time degree program, with a minimum 12 credit hours per semester. Character, humanitarianism, and active amateur radio participation are highly important.

Multiple awards annually, when funds support it. Contact ARRL for an application.

2555—AMERICAN RADIO RELAY LEAGUE FOUNDATION (Tom and Judith Comstock Scholarship)

225 Main Street
Newington CT 06111
860/594-0200
FAX: 860/594-0259
Internet: www.arrl.org/
AMOUNT: $1,000
DEADLINE(S): FEB 1
FIELD(S): All fields of study

For a high school senior who holds any class amateur radio license and is accepted at a two- or four-year college. Must be a resident of Texas or Oklahoma.

1 award annually. Contact ARRL for an application.

2556—AMERICAN RADIO RELAY LEAGUE FOUNDATION (The Six Meter Club of Chicago Scholarship)

225 Main Street
Newington CT 06111
860/594-0200
FAX: 860/594-0259
Internet: www.arrl.org/
AMOUNT: $500
DEADLINE(S): FEB 1
FIELD(S): All fields of study

Open to radio amateurs holding any class of license who are students in a post-secondary course of study leading to an undergraduate degree. Must be a resident of Illinois attending any institution in

Illinois (technical school, community college, university). If no qualified Illinois student is found, award is open to remaining ARRL Central Division (Indiana and Wisconsin).

1 award annually. Contact ARRL for an application.

2557—AMERICAN RADIO RELAY LEAGUE FOUNDATION (The Chicago FM Club Scholarships)

225 Main Street
Newington CT 06111
860/594-0200
FAX: 860/594-0259
Internet: www.arrl.org/

AMOUNT: $500
DEADLINE(S): FEB 1
FIELD(S): All fields of study

Open to radio amateurs holding a technician license and who are residents of the FCC Ninth Call District (IN, IL, WI). Students must be in a postsecondary course of study at an accredited 2- or 4-year college or trade school. Must be US citizen or within three months of citizenship.

Multiple awards annually. Contact ARRL for an application.

2558—AMERICAN RADIO RELAY LEAGUE FOUNDATION (The Michael J. Flosi Memorial Scholarship)

225 Main Street
Newington CT 06111
860/594-0200
FAX: 860/594-0259
Internet: www.arrl.org/

AMOUNT: $500
DEADLINE(S): FEB 1
FIELD(S): All fields of study

Open to radio amateurs holding a technician license and who are residents of the FCC Ninth Call District (IN, IL, WI). Must be a high school senior or graduate and be a US citizen or within three months of citizenship.

Multiple awards annually. Contact ARRL for an application.

2559—AMERICAN RADIO RELAY LEAGUE FOUNDATION (The Eugene "Gene" Sallee, W4YFR Memorial Scholarship)

225 Main Street
Newington CT 06111
860/594-0200

FAX: 860/594-0259
Internet: www.arrl.org/

AMOUNT: $500
DEADLINE(S): FEB 1
FIELD(S): All fields of study

Open to radio amateurs holding a technician plus license and who are residents of Georgia. Must have a minimum 3.0 GPA.

1 award annually. Contact ARRL for an application.

2560—AMERICAN SAMOA GOVERNMENT (Financial Aid Program)

Dept. of Education
Office of Student Financial Program
Pago Pago
AMERICAN SAMOA 96799
684/633-5237

AMOUNT: $5,000
DEADLINE(S): APR 30
FIELD(S): All fields of study

Scholarships open to residents of American Samoa. Awards support undergraduate and graduate study at all accredited colleges and universities. Applicants from off islands may be eligible if their parents are citizens of American Samoa.

Approximately 50 awards per year. Renewable. Write for complete information.

2561—AMERICAN SCANDINAVIAN FOUNDATION OF LOS ANGELES (Scholarship Program)

3445 Winslow Drive
Los Angeles CA 90026
213/661-4273

AMOUNT: $1,000
DEADLINE(S): MAR
FIELD(S): All fields of study

Open to full-time upper-level and graduate students at Los Angeles area colleges/universities who exhibit a connection to Scandinavia via life experience, field of study, or heritage.

5 to be awarded. Not renewable.

2562—AMITY INSTITUTE (Internships in the US for Teaching Languages)

10671 Roselle Street, Suite 101
San Diego CA 92121
619/455-6364
FAX: 619/455-6597
E-mail: mail@amity.org
Internet: www.amity.org

AMOUNT: Room & board + small spending allowance
DEADLINE(S): None
FIELD(S): All fields of study

Internships for unmarried native-speakers of Spanish, French, German, Russian, Japanese, and Swahili, aged 20-30, who can teach their languages and customs to students at schools in the US. Teaching is 15 hours/week for either a full academic year (Sept.-June), a semester (5 months), or a quarter (9 weeks). Most assignments are at US high schools in the Midwest region, and some are in elementary schools and colleges.

Must be able to communicate effectively in English. The program is NOT paid employment. Participants must provide their own transportation and $70-$100/month for personal expenses.

2563—AMVETS (National Four-Year Undergraduate Scholarship)

4647 Forbes Blvd.
Lanham MD 20706-4380
301/459-9600
FAX: 301/459-7924

AMOUNT: $1,000 each year for 4 years
DEADLINE(S): APR 15
FIELD(S): All fields of study

Four-year scholarship for graduating high school seniors who are dependents of an American veteran. Must demonstrate academic achievement, show financial need, and demonstrate involvement in extracurricular activities.

Must provide an acceptance letter from a four-year college or university.

2564—AMVETS (National Four-Year Undergraduate Scholarship for Vets)

4647 Forbes Blvd.
Lanham, MD 20706-4380
301/459-9600
FAX: 301/459-7924

AMOUNT: $1,000 each year for 4 years
DEADLINE(S): APR 15
FIELD(S): All fields of study

Four-year scholarship for former members of the US Armed Forces who have exhausted all government financial aid. Must demonstrate academic achievement, show financial need, and demonstrate involvement in extracurricular activities.

Must provide an acceptance letter from a four-year college or university. Write for details.

2565—AN UNCOMMON LEGACY FOUN-DATION, INC. (Scholarships)

150 West 26th Street, Suite 602
New York NY 10001
212/366-6507
FAX: 212/366-4425
Internet: www.uncommonlegacy.org/
scholguidelines.html

AMOUNT: $1,000
DEADLINE(S): MAY 1
FIELD(S): All fields of study

Scholarships for outstanding lesbian undergraduate and graduate full-time students enrolled at accredited colleges or universities in the US Min. GPA 3.0. Must demonstrate commitment or contribution to the lesbian community, demonstrate financial need, and follow required application procedures.

Application is available on website and at the organization. Notification dates occur at different times, according to state of residence.

2566—ANCIENT ORDER UNITED WORK-MEN (Student Memorial Loan Fund)

201 Union Ave. SE, #78
Renton, WA 98059
425/277-1603

AMOUNT: $2,000 maximum
DEADLINE(S): None specified
FIELD(S): All fields of study

Student loan fund open to AOUW members ONLY who have at least sophomore standing at a college or university in the state of Washington.

Write to Carol Benton at above address for complete information.

2567—ANNA AND CHARLES STOCKWITZ FUND FOR EDUCATION OF JEWISH CHIL-DREN (Scholarships)

1600 Scott Street
San Francisco CA 94115
415/561-1226

AMOUNT: $400-$750
DEADLINE(S): Varies
FIELD(S): All fields of study

Scholarships for Jewish undergrads who reside in San Francisco, CA. High school seniors may apply.

Contact above location for complete information.

2568—APPALOOSA YOUTH FOUNDATION (Scholarships)

5070 Highway 8 West
Moscow ID 83843
208/882-5578

AMOUNT: $1,000-$2,000
DEADLINE(S): JUN 10
FIELD(S): All fields of study

Open to members of the Appaloosa Youth Association or the Appaloosa Horse Club, children of Appaloosa Horse Club members, and individuals sponsored by a regional club or racing association.

9 scholarships per year—1 equine related, 8 all areas of study. Renewable. Must demonstrate financial need, number of children, and number of children in college. Contact the Youth Coordinator at address above for complete information.

2569—ARCTIC EDUCATION FOUNDATION (Shareholder Scholarships)

Box 129
Barrow AK 99723
907/852-8633

AMOUNT: Varies according to need
DEADLINE(S): None specified
FIELD(S): All areas of study

Open to Arctic Slope Regional Corporation shareholders and their children. For full-time undergraduate or graduate study at any accredited institution of higher education. Must maintain 2.0 or better GPA and demonstrate financial need.

Available for studies leading to certificates in any type of vocational training. Write for complete information.

2570—ARKANSAS DEPARTMENT OF HIGHER EDUCATION (Arkansas Academic Challenge Scholarship)

114 East Capitol
Little Rock AR 72201-3818
501/371-2050 or 800/54-STUDY
FAX: 501/371-2001
E-mail: finaid@adhe.arknet.edu
Internet: www.arscholarships.com

AMOUNT: $2,500
DEADLINE(S): JUL 1
FIELD(S): All fields of study

For high school seniors who are Arkansas residents planning to attend approved Arkansas public or private colleges/universities. Requires financial need and academic achievement on ACT and in precollegiate or tech preparation core curricula.

See website or contact ADHE for an application. Submit program application no later than October 1st, BUT to ensure payment before the fall term starts, submit application no later than July 1Street

2571—ARKANSAS DEPARTMENT OF HIGHER EDUCATION (Governor's Scholars)

114 East Capitol
Little Rock AR 72201-3818
501/371-2050 or 800/54-STUDY
FAX: 501/371-2001
E-mail: finaid@adhe.arknet.edu
Internet: www.arscholarships.com

AMOUNT: $4,000 for Scholars; Tuition, fees, + room & board for Distinguished Scholars
DEADLINE(S): MAR 1
FIELD(S): All fields of study

For high school seniors who are Arkansas residents attending approved Arkansas public or private colleges/universities. Two kinds of awards: 1) must have at least 27 ACT, 1100 SAT, or 3.60 GPA; and 2) Governor's Distinguished Scholars must have 32 ACT, 1410 SAT, or be a National Merit FinaliStreet Based on academic excellence and leadership, NOT financial need.

Up to 100 Scholar awards annually; ALL Distinguished Scholars will receive awards. See website or contact ADHE for an application.

2572—ARKANSAS DEPARTMENT OF HIGHER EDUCATION (Law Enforcement Officers Dependents' Scholarship)

114 East Capitol
Little Rock AR 72201-3818
501/371-2050 or 800/54-STUDY
FAX: 501/371-2001
E-mail: finaid@adhe.arknet.edu
Internet: www.arscholarships.com

AMOUNT: Waiver for in-state tuition/on-campus room/fees
DEADLINE(S): AUG 1; DEC 1; MAY 1; JUL 1
FIELD(S): All fields of study

For Arkansas residents who are undergraduate dependent children or spouses of persons killed or permanently disabled in the line of duty as a law enforcement officer, fireman, forester, correctional officer, and certain Highway & Transportation Dept. employees. For study at an approved Arkansas public college/university. Limited to 8 semesters or until dependent child becomes 23 years of age, whichever occurs first. Spouses lose eligibility if remarried.

See website or contact ADHE for an application.

2573—ARKANSAS DEPARTMENT OF HIGHER EDUCATION (MIA/KIA Dependents' Scholarship)

114 East Capitol
Little Rock AR 72201-3818
501/371-2050 or 800/54-STUDY
FAX: 501/371-2001
E-mail: finaid@adhe.arknet.edu
Internet: www.arscholarships.com

AMOUNT: Waiver of in-state tuition/on-campus room/fees
DEADLINE(S): AUG 1; DEC 1; MAY 1; JUL 1
FIELD(S): All fields of study

For full-time undergrad/graduate students who are dependent children/spouses of persons who were declared Killed in Action/Missing in Action/Prisoners of War 1960 or after. Must attend approved Arkansas public college/university or technical school. Arkansas residency not required, but parent/spouse must have been resident. Aid to receive bachelor's degree or certification of completion; student may pursue professional degree if undergrad education was not in Arkansas.

See website or contact ADHE for an application.

2574—ARKANSAS DEPARTMENT OF HIGHER EDUCATION (Student Assistance Grants)

114 East Capitol
Little Rock AR 72201-3818
501/371-2050 or 800/54-STUDY
FAX: 501/371-2001
E-mail: finaid@adhe.arknet.edu
Internet: www.arscholarships.com or www.fafsa.ed.gov

AMOUNT: $100-$600
DEADLINE(S): APR
FIELD(S): All fields of study

Need-based awards for Arkansas residents to pursue undergraduate study at Arkansas colleges/universities. Student must enroll full-time and make satisfactory progress. Exact application deadlines are determined by each participating institution. Must be US citizen or permanent resident.

9,500 awards annually. To apply, fill out the Free Application for Federal Student Aid (FAFSA). See above websites, ask your financial aid office, or contact ADHE for a FAFSA form.

2575—ARKANSAS DEPARTMENT OF HIGHER EDUCATION (Second Effort Scholarship)

114 East Capitol
Little Rock AR 72201-3818
501/371-2050 or 800/54-STUDY
FAX: 501/371-2001
E-mail: finaid@adhe.arknet.edu
Internet: www.arscholarships.com

AMOUNT: $1,000
DEADLINE(S): None
FIELD(S): All fields of study

For Arkansas residents who haven't graduated from high school but who have taken the GED and plan to enroll in an Arkansas post-secondary institution. Must have acheived one of the ten highest scores on the Arkansas High School Diploma test during the previous calendar year. *You do not need to apply for this award; ADHE will contact you directly if you have one of the high test scores.*

10 awards annually. Renewable up to 4 years (or equivalent if part-time). See website or contact ADHE for more information.

2576—ARKANSAS SINGLE PARENT SCHOLARSHIP FUND (Scholarships)

614 E. Emma, Suite 119
Springdale AR 72764
501/927-1402
FAX: 501/751-1110
E-mail: jwobser@jtlshop.jonesnet.org
Internet: scholarships-ar-us.org

AMOUNT: up to $600/semester
DEADLINE(S): Varies
FIELD(S): All fields of study

Scholarships are for Arkansas single parents to assist with expenses that would, otherwise, keep them from attending school—childcare, transportation, books, tuition, etc.

Each of the 51 county affiliates has its own set of guidelines; please contact your county's office for details and/or an application. Contact information can be found on the ASPSF website.

2577—ARKANSAS TECH UNIVERSITY (Scholarships)

Office of Admissions
Student Services Bldg., Room 141
Russellville AR 72801

501/968-0343 or 800/582-6953
E-mail: tech.enroll@mail.atu.edu
(for US students) OR
maria.chandle@mail.atu.edu
(international)
Internet: www.atu.edu

AMOUNT: Varies
DEADLINE(S): FEB 15
FIELD(S): All fields of study

Scholarships are available to students planning to attend Arkansas Tech University. Must have a minimum 3.25 GPA. Recipients will have opportunity to participate in early registration.

See website or contact Arkansas Tech for an application.

2578—ARLINE P. PADELFORD SCHOLARSHIP TRUST (Scholarships)

c/o State Street Bank & Trust Co.
P.O. Box 351
Boston MA 02101
617/786-3000

AMOUNT: $600
DEADLINE(S): None specified
FIELD(S): All areas of study

Scholarships for worthy and deserving students at Taunton (MA) High School to pursue college or technical education.

12 scholarships per year. Contact Taunton High guidance counselor for complete information.

2579—ARMENIAN RELIEF SOCIETY OF EASTERN USA, INC. (Grants)

80 Bigelow Ave.
Watertown MA 02172
617/926-3801
FAX: 617/924-7328
E-mail: arser@compuserve.com

AMOUNT: $400-$1,000
DEADLINE(S): APR 1
FIELD(S): All fields of study

Open to undergrad and grad students of Armenian ancestry who are attending an accredited 4-year college or university in the US and have completed at least one semester. Awards based on need, merit, and involvement in Armenian community.

Write to scholarship committee at address above for complete information. Enclose self-addressed, stamped envelope and indicate whether undergrad or grad student.

2580—ARMENIAN STUDENTS' ASSOCIATION OF AMERICA, INC. (Scholarships)

395 Concord Avenue
Belmont MA 02178
617/484-9548

AMOUNT: $500-$2,500
DEADLINE(S): JAN 15
FIELD(S): All fields of study

Applicants must be of Armenian ancestry and be full-time students who plan to attend a four-year, accredited college/university in the US full-time during the next academic year (must have completed or be in the process of completing first year of college or higher). Must demonstrate financial need, have good academic performance, show self help, and participate in extracurricular activities.

30 awards annually. $15 application fee. Contact ASA Scholarship Committee in the fall to request application forms. Deadline for requests is January 15th; completed application package must be returned by March 15th.

2581—ARMY EMERGENCY RELIEF

Dept. of Scholarships
200 Stovall Street
Alexandria VA 22332-0600
Written inquiry
Internet: www.aerhq.org

AMOUNT: Up to $1,500 per year
DEADLINE(S): MAR 1
FIELD(S): All fields of study

Open to unmarried dependent children of active, retired, or deceased members of the US Army. Applicants may not have reached their 22nd birthday before June 1 of the school year that begins the following September. For undergraduate study.

Must submit financial aid form and official high school transcript. Write for complete information.

2582—ARMY ROTC (Scholarships)

Army ROTC Scholarships
Ft. Monroe VA 23651-5238
800/USA-ROTC
Internet: tradoc.army.mil/rotc/indix.html

AMOUNT: $1,500 stipend; $450 books/fees; tiered tuition scholarships up to $12,800
DEADLINE(S): JUL 15 (early cycle); NOV 15 (regular cycle)
FIELD(S): All fields of study

Open to US citizens between the ages of 17 and 27. For undergraduate study at colleges having Army ROTC programs. Must have minimum of 2.5 GPA and SAT score of 850 or ACT score of 19 and meet minimum physical standards.

Renewable yearly. Must be high school graduate. Must have minimum of 920 on SAT or 19 on composite ACT. Must attend an institution with Army ROTC program (more than 600 across the nation). Must meet minimum physical standards. Direct questions to Headquarters, Cadet Command, at above address.

2583—ARTHUR C. & FLORENCE S. BOEHMER FUND (Scholarships)

c/o Rinn & Elliot
P.O. Box 1827
Lodi CA 95241
209/369-2781

AMOUNT: Depends on yearly income
DEADLINE(S): JUN 15 (Applications available MAR 1 to JUN 15)
FIELD(S): Medical

Open to students who are graduates of a high school within the Lodi (San Joaquin County, CA) Unified School District. For undergraduate, graduate, or post-graduate study in the field of medicine at an accredited California institution.

Grade point average of 2.9 or better required. Scholarships are renewable. Write for complete information.

2584—ARTS & ENTERTAINMENT NETWORK (A&E Teacher Grant Competition)

235 East 45th Street
New York NY 10017
212/661-4500

AMOUNT: $1,000 Savings Bond (12); $2,500 Savings Bond (Grand Prize + prizes for the school)
DEADLINE(S): MAR 1
FIELD(S): All fields of study

Awards for teachers of grades 6-12 who have demonstrated how imaginative use of A&E programming results in innovative approaches to classroom instruction. Applicants are to write above a unique classroom project based on an A&E program. Also, a teacher's project can be submitted by a principal, school librarian, or peer teacher.

3 winners in each of four regions: Eastern, Central, Western, and Southern. Contact organization for details.

2585—ASIAN PACIFIC AMERICAN SUPPORT GROUP (Scholarship)

USC, Student Union 410
Los Angeles CA 90089-4851
213/740-4999
FAX: 213/740-5284
E-mail: apass@usc.edu
Internet: www.usc.edu/dept/APASS/

AMOUNT: $1,000-$2,500
DEADLINE(S): MAR 20
FIELD(S): All fields of study

Scholarships for full-time students who have close ties with the Asian Pacific Community. GPA of 3.0 or above required.

15-20 awards per year. Recipients may reapply for second year. Applications available Dec. 2.

2586—ASSOCIATION FOR COMPUTING MACHINERY-WASHINGTON, DC CHAPTER (Undergraduate Scholarship)

1820 Dolley Madison Blvd.
McLean VA 22102
E-mail: charwing@mitre.org
Internet: www.acm.org/chapters/dcacm/scholarships/

AMOUNT: $1,500
DEADLINE(S): MAY 1
FIELD(S): Any field of study involving computer applications

Grant for a candidate enrolled in an undergraduate program at a college or university in Maryland, Virginia, or the District of Columbia in a field involving computers. Must be at least sophomore standing. Applications from students in any academic dept. will be considered.

Access website for details and application or send to Charlotte W. Wales, the MITRE Corp., at above address.

2587—ASSOCIATION ON AMERICAN INDIAN AFFAIRS (Adolph Van Pelt Special Fund for Indian Scholarships)

Box 268
Sisseton SD 57262
605/698-3998 or 605/698-3787
FAX: 605/698-3316

AMOUNT: $500-$800
DEADLINE(S): AUG 1
FIELD(S): Any field of study

For undergraduate or graduate students who demonstrate a financial need and can prove (with certificate) that they are at least 1/4 Indian in a federally recognized tribe. Students must submit an essay describing educational goals and two letters of recommendation.

Award is renewable and increases with each year. Send SASE to above address for complete information and an application.

2588—ASSOCIATION ON AMERICAN INDIAN AFFAIRS, INC. (Displaced Homemakers Scholarships)

Box 268
Sisseton SD 57262
605/698-3998 or 605/698-3787
FAX: 605/698-3316

AMOUNT: Varies
DEADLINE(S): SEP 1
FIELD(S): Any field of study

For mid-life homemakers (female or male) who are unable to fill their educational goals. Scholarship will augment the usual and expected financial sources of educational money to assist those students with childcare, transportation, and some living expenses. Must demonstrate special financial needs as heads of households, single parents, or as displaced homemakers.

Must be at least 1/4 Indian blood from a federally recognized tribe and submit a one- or two-page essay outlining your life experience. Send SASE to above address for complete information.

2589—ASSOCIATION OF THE SONS OF POLAND (Scholarship Program)

333 Hackensack Street
Carlstadt NJ 07072
201/935-2807

AMOUNT: $1,000 Scholarship; $100 Achievement Award
DEADLINE(S): MAY 14
FIELD(S): All fields of study

Open to high school students who have been members of the Association of the Sons of Poland for at least 2 years and are insured by the association. Must be entering an accredited college in September of the year of high school graduation.

Must be US citizen. Write for complete information.

2590—ASTRAEA NATIONAL LESBIAN ACTION FOUNDATION (Margot Karle Scholarship)

116 E. 16th Street, 7th Fl.
New York NY 10003
212/529-8021

AMOUNT: $500
DEADLINE(S): FEB 15; AUG 15
FIELD(S): All fields of study

Must demonstrate financial need and a high degree of community involvement.

Available ONLY to undergrads enrolled in the City University of New York system.

2591—ATHEISTS OF FLORIDA, INC. (Mark Twain Scholarship Fund)

P.O. Box 3893
Ft. Pierce FL 34948-3893
FAX: 561/465-6402
E-mail: AthALFLE@aol.com

AMOUNT: $500 (1st & 2nd places); $300 (3rd & 4th)
DEADLINE(S): DEC 31
FIELD(S): Most fields of study

Promotes and assists the postsecondary education of qualified young Americans in their chosen discipline within the fields of the Arts & Humanities, Applied Arts, Education, Science, Social Sciences, Mathematics, Engineering, or Law. Applicants must be of a Freethinking persuasion, against all efforts to impose superstitious religious teachings and interpretations on society and anything that inhibits freedom. Must be full-time bachelors degree students. Essay required.

Contact the Mark Twain Scholarship Fund for an application and yearly essay topic. Recipients notified by February 28th.

2592—AURORA FOUNDATION (Scholarships)

111 W. Downer Place
Aurora IL 60506-6112
630/896-7800

AMOUNT: Varies
DEADLINE(S): Varies
FIELD(S): All fields of study

Scholarships are administered by this Foundation for residents of the Greater Aurora Area, including the Tri-Cities and Kendall County, Illinois.

Write or call for details.

2593—AUSTIN CHILDREN'S EDUCATIONAL OPPORTUNITY FOUNDATION

111 Congress, Suite 3000
Austin TX 78701
512/472-0153
FAX: 512/310-1688
E-mail/Internet: austinceo@aol.com

AMOUNT: Up to half of tuition—up to $1,000/yr.
DEADLINE(S): None
FIELD(S): All fields of study

Scholarships for children who are residents of Travis County, Texas, ages 6-14 (as of Sept. 1 of the school year) attending any school. Family must qualify for the federal school lunch program guidelines.

Contact Jane Kilgore at above location. First come, first served. Renewable for 3 years.

2594—AUTOMOTIVE HALL OF FAME, INC. (Scholarship Program)

P.O. Box 1727
Midland MI 48641-1727
517/631-5760
FAX: 517/631-0524

AMOUNT: $250-$2,000
DEADLINE(S): JUN 30
FIELD(S): All fields of study

Open to full-time undergraduate college students who have a sincere interest in pursuing an automotive career upon graduation from college. Must be at least a sophomore when scholarship is granted, but freshmen may send in application.

16-24 awards per year. Renewable with reapplication. Write for complete information.

2595—AVON LATINA MODEL OF THE YEAR (Competition)

Rules Requests
1251 Sixth Ave.
New York NY 10020-1196
800/FOR-AVON

AMOUNT: Up to $15,000 in educational awards and modeling fees and gifts
DEADLINE(S): FEB 15
FIELD(S): All fields of study

For Hispanic females between the ages of 17 and 25 who are "intelligent, poised, and beautiful."

Send self-addressed, stamped envelope for application and official rules.

2596—AYN RAND INSTITUTE (Anthem Contest)

Use website
Internet: www.aynrand.org/contests

AMOUNT: $1,000 (first place); $200 (10 second); $100 (20 third)
DEADLINE(S): APR 1
FIELD(S): All fields of study

Open to high school 9th and 10th graders. Cash awards for essays on Ayn Rand's novelette *Anthem*. Awards are to encourage analytical thinking and writing excellence and introduce young people to the novelette's philosophical meaning.

Access website or contact your English teacher or guidance counselor for details.

2597—AYN RAND INSTITUTE (Fountainhead Essay Contest)

Use website
E-mail: essay@aynrand.org
Internet: www.aynrand.org/contests

AMOUNT: $10,000 (first); $2,000 (5 second); $1,000 (10 third)
DEADLINE(S): APR 15
FIELD(S): All fields of study

Essay competition open to high school juniors and seniors. Contest is to encourage analytical thinking and writing excellence and to introduce students to the philosophic and psychological meaning of Ayn Rand's novel *The Fountainhead*.

16 awards per year. All instructions are on website, including mailing instructions for finished essays.

2598—B & L EDUCATIONAL FOUNDATION

2111 Northridge Drive NE
Grand Rapids MI 49505
616/364-8499

AMOUNT: $200-$2,000
DEADLINE(S): JUL 1; DEC 24
FIELD(S): All fields of study

Scholarships for individuals who are residents of, or attending schools in, Michigan or Arizona.

Send SASE to above address for formal application and details.

2599—BAPTIST GENERAL CONVENTION OF TEXAS (Scholarships)

333 N. Washington Street, Suite 371
Dallas TX 75246-1798
214/828-5131

AMOUNT: Varies
DEADLINE(S): Varies
FIELD(S): All fields of study

Scholarships for college-bound high school seniors and undergraduates who are members of the Baptist Church and also an ethnic minority. Must attend or plan to attend a Baptist college.

Send SASE for details.

2600—BARNABAS MINISTRIES OF SHREVEPORT

4451 Charter Point Blvd.
Jacksonville FL 32211-1027
318/227-1313

AMOUNT: Varies
DEADLINE(S): Ongoing

FIELD(S): All fields of study

Scholarships and assistance to financially needy residents of the state of Louisiana.

Send letter to Dr. John Sullivan, Trustee, at above address.

2601—BARNARD COLLEGE PRE-COLLEGE PROGRAMS (Grants for Summer in New York)

Columbia University
3009 Broadway
New York NY 10027-6598
212/854-8866
FAX: 212/854-8867
E-mail: pcp@barnard.columbia.edu
Internet: www.barnard.columbia.edu/pcp

AMOUNT: $200-$800 towards program cost
DEADLINE(S): APR 19
FIELD(S): All fields of study

A summer pre-college program at Barnard College in New York City (June 27-July 31) for high school students who are intellectually prepared for college-level work and will have completed the 10th or 11th grade by start of program. Grants are offered only on the basis of financial need. Selection based on strong high school records, recommendations, and involvement in extracurricular activities.

Cost is $3,295 for residential students and $1,990 for commuters. The grant would offset part of this. Write to above address for booklet describing program which also contains application forms.

2602—BASIN ELECTRIC POWER COOPERATIVE (Scholarship Program)

Human Resources
1717 E. Interstate Ave.
Bismark ND 58501
800/242-2372

AMOUNT: $1,000
DEADLINE(S): MAR 14
FIELD(S): All fields of study

Available to children of full-time employees of Basin Electric Power Cooperative and its subsidiaries, and the children of member-system employees and consumers. Must be a student who is enrolled or planning to enroll in a full-time graduate or undergraduate course of study at an accredited two-year or four-year college, university, or vocational/technical school.

20 awards annually. Contact Basin Electric's Human Resources Division for an application.

2603—BEATRICE AND FRANCIS THOMPSON SCHOLARSHIP FUND (Scholarship)

Ms. Diane Duffy
Co-trustee/Secretary
417 Summit Ave.
Oradell NJ 07649
Written inquiry only

AMOUNT: $2,000 to $4,000
DEADLINE(S): NOV 1 (for spring semester); MAR 1 (for fall semester)
FIELD(S): All areas of study

Open to undergraduate or voc-tech students whose parents are both deceased. Applicants should have a 2.5 or better GPA. Financial need is a consideration. Renewable.

Open to US citizens who are Pennsylvania and New Jersey residents only.

2604—BECA FOUNDATION (General Scholarship Fund)

310 Via Vera Cruz, Suite 101
San Marcos CA 92069
760/471-5465
FAX: 760/471-9175

AMOUNT: $500-$1,000
DEADLINE(S): APR 4
FIELD(S): All fields of study

Scholarships for Latino students who are high school graduates or seniors in a North San Diego County high school and entering college in the fall. Can be used for any field of study anywhere in the US. BECA also provides role models for Latino students by assigning a mentor to each scholarship recipient.

Send self-addressed, stamped envelope (SASE) to address above for details.

2605—BECA FOUNDATION (The Daniel Gutierrez Memorial General Scholarship Fund)

310 Via Vera Cruz, Suite 101
San Marcos CA 92069
760/471-5465
FAX: 760/471-9175

AMOUNT: $250-$500
DEADLINE(S): APR 4
FIELD(S): All fields of study

Scholarships for Latino students who are high school graduates or graduating seniors in a San Diego County high school and entering college in the fall. Can be used for any field of study anywhere in the US. BECA also provides role models for

Latino students by assigning a mentor to each scholarship recipient.

Send self-addressed, stamped envelope (SASE) to address above for details.

2606—BEDDING PLANTS FOUNDATION, INC. (BPI Family Member Scholarship)

P.O. Box 280
East Lansing MI 48826-0280
517/333-4617
FAX: 517/333-4494
E-mail: BPFI@aol.com
Internet: www.bpfi.org

AMOUNT: $1,000
DEADLINE(S): MAY 15
FIELD(S): All fields of study

Open to graduate and undergraduate students at an accredited university in the US or Canada who are majoring in any field. Must be a child, parent, or spouse of a current member of Bedding Plants International. Cash award, with checks issued jointly in name of recipient and college/institution he or she will attend for current year. Must submit references and transcripts.

1 award annually. See website or send printed self-addressed mailing label (or self-addressed, stamped envelope) to BPFI after January 1st for an application. Recipient will be notified.

2607—BEMENT EDUCATIONAL GRANTS COMMITTEE (Diocese of Western Massachusetts Undergraduate Grants)

37 Chestnut Street
Springfield MA 01103
413/737-4786

AMOUNT: Up to $750
DEADLINE(S): FEB 1
FIELD(S): All fields of study

Undergraduate grants for unmarried students who are active Episcopalians in the Diocese of Western Massachusetts. High GPA. Financial need. Interview required as arranged.

60-70 awards per year. Apply after Nov. 1. Renewable with reapplication. Send SASE for complete information.

2608—BIA HIGHER EDUCATION/ HOPI SUPPLEMENTAL GRANT

P.O. Box 123
Kykotsmovi AZ 86039
520/734-2441, ext. 520
800/762-9630
FAX: 520/734-2435

AMOUNT: Varies
DEADLINE(S): JUL 31 (fall); NOV 30 (spring); APR 30 (summer)
FIELD(S): All fields of study

For enrolled members of the Hopi Tribe pursuing associate, baccalaureate, graduate, or post-graduate degrees. Minimum 2.0 GPA required. Grant is a supplemental source of financial aid for eligible students.

Financial need is primary consideration.

2609—BILLY BARTY FOUNDATION (Evelyn Barty Scholarship Awards Programs)

929 W. Olive Ave., Suite C
Burbank CA 91506
818/953-5410

AMOUNT: $2,000 per applicant
DEADLINE(S): JUL 15
FIELD(S): All fields of study

Open to undergraduates who are 4 feet 10 inches and under (or who are related to someone of this stature). Must be a US citizen studying in the continental US. Financial need, leadership, and scholarship are award criteria.

8-15 awards per year. Renewable. Write for complete information.

2610—BLACKFEET HIGHER EDUCATION PROGRAM (BIA Grant)

P.O. Box 850
Browning MT 59417
406/338-7539

AMOUNT: $2,500-$3,000
DEADLINE(S): MAR 1
FIELD(S): All fields of study

Open to enrolled members of the Blackfeet Tribe for undergraduate or vocational education.

Write to the above address for complete information.

2611—BLINDED VETERANS ASSOCIATION (Kathern F. Gruber Scholarship Program)

477 H Street NW
Washington DC 20001-2694
800/669-7079 or 202/371-8880
FAX: 202/371-8258

AMOUNT: $1,000-$2,000
DEADLINE(S): APR 17
FIELD(S): All areas of study

Open to children and spouses of blinded veterans. The vet must be legally blind, either service or non-service connected.

Must be accepted or already enrolled full-time in a college or vocational school and be a US citizen.

8 scholarships of $2,000 and 2 of $1,000. Write for complete information.

2612—BOB JONES UNIVERSITY (Rebate Program)

1700 Wade Hampton Blvd.
Greenville SC 29614
864-242-5100
FAX: 800-232-9258, ext 2085

AMOUNT: $2,000-1st year; $1,000-2nd year
DEADLINE(S): Varies (beginning of semester)
FIELD(S): All areas of study

Bob Jones University is a private, Christian-oriented college which offers vocational, technical, and academic programs. The financial aid program requires that the student participate in a work program for at least 7 hours/week.

Renewable at $1,000. US citizenship required.

2613—BOETTCHER FOUNDATION (Scholarships)

600 17th Street, Suite 2210 South
Denver CO 80202
303/534-1938

AMOUNT: Tuition + $2,800 stipend
DEADLINE(S): FEB 1
FIELD(S): All fields of study

Open to Colorado residents presently in the top 7% of their high school class who have been accepted as an incoming freshman at a Colorado college or university. Minimim ACT score 27; SAT 1100. US citizen.

40 awards per year. Write for complete information or consult your high school counselor.

2614—BONNEVILLE TRANSLOADERS, INC. (Scholarship)

642 South Federal
Riverton WY 82501
Written inquiry

AMOUNT: $1,000
DEADLINE(S): MAY 1
FIELD(S): All fields of study

Available to high school graduates of Fremont or Sweetwater counties in Wyoming.

Write to above address for an application.

2615—BOY SCOUTS OF AMERICA (National Eagle Scout Scholarships)

1325 West Walnut Hill Lane
P.O. Box 152079
Irving TX 75015-2079
972/580-2431

AMOUNT: Varies
DEADLINE(S): FEB 28
FIELD(S): All fields of study

For college-bound high school seniors currently registered in the Boy Scouts of America who have been granted the Eagle Scout Award. Must document leadership ability in Scouting and a strong record of participation of activities outside of scouting.

Not for two-year or technical schools. Send SASE to above location for application.

2616—BOY SCOUTS OF AMERICA-DR. HARRY BRITENSTOOL SCHOLARSHIP COMMITTEE (Greater New York City Councils Scholarship Fund)

345 Hudson Street
New York NY 10014-4588
212/242-1100, ext. 271

AMOUNT: Varies
DEADLINE(S): JUN 1
FIELD(S): All fields of study

Undergraduate scholarships for students who have been at one time registered with the Greater New York councils, Boy Scouts of America, or employed by that organization. Must show academic excellence, financial need, and study at least 24 credit hours during the school year. US citizens only.

Must submit essay on "What Scouting has meant to me."

2617—BOYS AND GIRLS CLUB OF VENTURA (Emma Nylen Scholarship)

1440 N. Olive Street
Ventura CA 93001
805/641-5585
FAX: 805/639-0180

AMOUNT: $100-$1,000
DEADLINE(S): Varies (end of March, beginning of April)
FIELD(S): All fields of study

Scholarships for residents of Ventura County who are full-time students and who have at least a "C" average. US citizenship.

20-60 annual awards. Must reapply to renew.

2618—BREWER FOUNDATION, INC.

3819 Woodlawn Road
Rocky Mount NC 27804
919/443-1333

AMOUNT: Varies
DEADLINE(S): None specified
FIELD(S): All fields of study

Scholarships for higher education to residents of North Carolina.

Contact Joseph B. Brewer, Jr., President, at foundation listed above for current application deadline and procedures.

2619—BRITISH AMERICAN EDUCATIONAL FOUNDATION (Scholars' Program)

P.O. Box 33
Larchmont NY 10538
914/834-2064
E-mail: study@baef.org
Internet: www.baef.org

AMOUNT: up to $5,000
DEADLINE(S): MAY 1
FIELD(S): Wide variety limited by British 'A' level offerings at each school

Open to American high school seniors who are 18 or younger and want to spend a year at an independent boarding school in the United Kingdom prior to entering college in either the UK or US. Must have financial need.

See website or contact Stephen Bauer for complete information.

2620—BUCK INSTITUTE FOR EDUCATION (American Revolution Bicentennial Scholarships)

Marie Kanarr
18 Commercial Blvd.
Novato CA 94949
415/883-0122

AMOUNT: $500 to $2,000
DEADLINE(S): MAR 31
FIELD(S): All fields of study

For Marin County students who have been county residents since Sept. 1 of the year prior to submitting an application. Scholarships tenable at accredited colleges, universities, and vocational or trade programs.

Contact high school or college counselor or send self-addressed, stamped envelope with inquiry to organization for complete information.

2621—BUDDHIST COMPASSION RELIEF TZU-CHI FOUNDATION, U.S.A. (Scholarships)

206 East Palm Ave.
Monrovia CA 91016
626/305-1188
FAX: 626/305-1185
Internet: www.tzuchi.org/usa/english

AMOUNT: $1,000
DEADLINE(S): MAY 31
FIELD(S): All fields of study

Scholarships for college-bound high school seniors (at least 3.8 GPA) and college students (at least 3.5 GPA). Must demonstrate financial need. Application process includes submitting a 500-word essay on why you think you should receive this scholarship and a description of your family background.

For more details on application requirements, contact organization or access website.

2622—BUREAU OF MAINE VETERANS SERVICES (Veterans Dependents Educational Benefits)

117 State House Station
Augusta ME 04333-0117
207/626-4464 or 800/345-0116
FAX: 207/626-4471

AMOUNT: Tuition Waiver
DEADLINE(S): None
FIELD(S): All fields of study

For undergraduates, aged 16-21, to attend any state of Maine supported university or technical college. Must be a dependent (child or spouse) of 100% permanently disabled or deceased veteran. Veteran must have entered service from Maine or have lived in Maine at least five years preceding application. Financial need NOT a factor.

Renewable. Contact Leslie Breton at above address for an application.

2623—BUTTE CREEK FOUNDATION

1350 E. Lassen Ave., No. 2
Chico CA 95926
530/895-1512

AMOUNT: Varies
DEADLINE(S): Ongoing
FIELD(S): All fields of study

Scholarships for residents of California.

Apply by letter to John Burghardt, President and Secretary, at above address.

2624—C. BASCOM SLEMP FOUNDATION (Scholarships)

Star Bank, NA
P.O. Box 5208
Cincinnati OH 45201
513/762-8878

AMOUNT: $2,000
DEADLINE(S): OCT 1
FIELD(S): All fields of study

Open ONLY to residents of Lee or Wise counties in Virginia. For undergraduate study.

30 awards per year. Write for complete information.

2625—C. G. FULLER FOUNDATION (Scholarships)

NationsBank of SC
P.O. Box 448
Columbia SC 29202-9972
803/925-5879

AMOUNT: $2,000
DEADLINE(S): MAR 31
FIELD(S): All fields of study

Open to South Carolina residents who are high school seniors and will enroll in an accredited undergraduate college or university in South Carolina. Must be a US citizen and have at least a 3.0 grade point average (4.0 scale).

Approx 10 awards per year. Write to Pamela S. Postal for complete information.

2626—CABRILLO CIVIC CLUBS OF CALIFORNIA (Scholarships)

2376 Caminito Seguro
San Diego CA 92107
619/224-7534

AMOUNT: $400
DEADLINE(S): APR 1
FIELD(S): All fields of study

Open to California high school seniors of Portuguese descent who have a grade point average of 3.5 or better. For undergraduate study at two- or four-year college. US citizen or permanent resident.

56 to 60 awards per year. Write for complete information.

2627—CALIF/HAWAII ELKS MAJOR PROJECT, INC. (Undergraduate Disabled Student Scholarships)

5450 E. Lamona
Fresno CA 93727
818/963-1636

AMOUNT: $2,000; $1,000
DEADLINE(S): MAR 15
FIELD(S): All fields of study

Open to Calif/Hawaii students who are disabled and are enrolled in a school program that will help enable the student to be independent. US citizenship is required.

An interview with a chairman of an Elks lodge is mandatory. Documentation by physician of the student's disability is required. Write to the above address for complete information.

2628—CALIFORNIA CHICANO NEWS MEDIA ASSOCIATION (Joel Garcia Memorial Scholarship)

c/o USC School of Journalism;
3716 S. Hope Street, Room 301
Los Angeles CA 90007-4344
213/743-2440
FAX: 213/744-1809
E-mail: info@ccnma.org
Internet: www.ccnma.org

AMOUNT: $250-$2,000
DEADLINE(S): APR 2
FIELD(S): Journalism, News Media

For full-time high school senior, undergraduate, or graduate Latino students who are either California residents or plan to attend an accredited college/university in California. Awards based on commitment to above fields, scholastic achievement, community awareness, and financial need. Autobiographical essay explaining goals, two reference letters, official transcripts, and samples of work must be submitted with completed application. No faxed materials accepted.

See website or contact Julio Moran, Executive Director, for an application/more information.

2629—CALIFORNIA COLLEGE DEMOCRATS (Internships)

See website
Internet: www.collegedems.org

AMOUNT: Varies
DEADLINE(S): None
FIELD(S): All fields of study

Internships available for various California Democratic office holders, candidates for office, and for several organizations, especially those working on environmental issues.

See website for list of statewide openings, which constantly changes. Some offer pay. Possible credit through your university.

2630—CALIFORNIA CORRECTIONAL PEACE OFFICERS ASSOCIATION (Joe Harper Scholarship Foundation)

755 Riverpoint Drive, Suite 200
West Sacramento CA 95605-1634
Written inquiry

AMOUNT: Varies
DEADLINE(S): APR 30
FIELD(S): All fields of study, scholastic or vocational

For active members, retired members, or immediate family members of current or deceased members of the California Correctional Peace Officers Association. Applicants will be judged on academic achievement, school activities, financial need, and community service.

Renewable if college GPA is maintained at 3.5. For scholastic or vocational field. Contact location above for complete information.

2631—CALIFORNIA DEPARTMENT OF VETERANS AFFAIRS (College Fee Waiver Program)

1227 'O' Street
Sacramento CA 95814
916/653-2573 or 800/952-5626
Internet: www.ns.net/cadva/

AMOUNT: Tuition and fee waiver
DEADLINE(S): None
FIELD(S): All fields of study

For spouses and children of military and California National Guard veterans who (as a result of military service) are disabled or died of service-related injuries. Awards are for study at California state universities, University of California campuses, and California community colleges.

Call, write, or visit website for information about this and other programs offered by the California Department of Veterans Affairs.

2632—CALIFORNIA GOVERNOR'S COMMITTEE FOR EMPLOYMENT OF DISABLED PERSONS (Hal Connolly Scholar-Athlete Award)

P.O. Box 826880, MIC 41
Sacramento CA 94280-0001
916/654-8055
TDD: 916/654-9820

AMOUNT: $1,000
DEADLINE(S): FEB 28
FIELD(S): All fields of study

Must have competed during high school in varsity level or equivalent athletics and have a disabilty. Academic and athletic histories must demonstrate the qualities of leadership and accomplishment. Minimum 2.8 GPA. Age 19 or under.

6 awards—3 to females and 3 to males. Must be a California resident; write for more information.

2633—CALIFORNIA GRANGE FOUNDATION (Scholarships)

Pat Avila
2101 Stockton Blvd.
Sacramento CA 95817
Written inquiry

AMOUNT: Varies
DEADLINE(S): APR 1
FIELD(S): All fields of study

Four scholarship programs for members of the California Grange or their dependents. Some are for high school seniors, and others are for students already enrolled in college.

Write for information after Feb. 1 of each year.

2634—CALIFORNIA JUNIOR MISS PROGRAM (Scholarships & Awards)

P.O. Box 729
Windsor CA 95492
707/837-1900
Internet: www.ajm.org/california

AMOUNT: Up to $15,000
DEADLINE(S): Varies
FIELD(S): All fields of study

Competition open to girls in their junior year of high school who are US citizens and California residents. Winner receives a $15,000 college scholarship; runners-up share up to $30,000 in awards. For undergraduate or graduate study.

Apply before or early in junior year of high school. Award can be used for books, fees, and tuition at any college in the world. Write to Ms. Katy Gillwood at above address for complete information, or visit website.

2635—CALIFORNIA MASONIC FOUNDATION (General and Special Fund Scholarship Programs)

1111 California Street
San Francisco CA 94108-2284
415/776-7000
Info. line: 415/292-9196
FAX: 415/776-0483

AMOUNT: Varies
DEADLINE(S): JAN 31
FIELD(S): All fields of study

Undergraduate scholarships open to California residents accepted to or enrolled in accredited colleges or technical schools in the US. No religious or membership requirements. Must be US citizen.

Special funds have been established with various restrictive conditions. Send SASE (self-addressed, stamped envelope) to Judy Liang at above address.

2636—CALIFORNIA STUDENT AID COMMISSION (Cal Grant A)

P.O. Box 419026
Rancho Cordova CA 95741-9026
916/526-7590
TDD: 916/526-7542
FAX: 916/526-8002
E-mail: custsvcs@csac.ca.gov
Internet: www.csac.ca.gov

AMOUNT: Up to $3,600
DEADLINE(S): MAR 2
FIELD(S): All fields of study

Based on financial need and grades. Helps pay for tuition and fees at four-year colleges. High school seniors and undergraduates who are California residents and planning to attend college in California may apply; if you plan on attending a community college first, you can reserve your award until time of transfer.

Approximately 19,000 grants annually. Renewable. To apply, submit the FAFSA (800-433-3243). Contact your counselor, financial aid office, or California Student Aid Commission for more information or FAFSA form.

2637—CALIFORNIA STUDENT AID COMMISSION (Cal Grant B)

P.O. Box 419026
Rancho Cordova CA 95741-9026
916/526-7590
TDD: 916/526-7542
FAX: 916/526-8002
E-mail: custsvcs@csac.ca.gov
Internet: www.csac.ca.gov

AMOUNT: $1,400 max. living allowance; $3,600 max. tuition
DEADLINE(S): MAR 2
FIELD(S): All fields of study

Provides a living allowance for very low-income students. California residents who are high school seniors or undergraduates planning to attend school in California may apply. Grant for first-year students usually limited to assisting with living expenses (books, supplies, transportation). When renewed, can be used for tuition and fees. Selection based on finan-

cial need, grades, and disadvantaged background.

Approximately 19,000 grants annually. Renewable. To apply, submit the FAFSA (800-433-3243). Contact your counselor, financial aid office, or California Student Aid Commission for more information or FAFSA form.

2638—CALIFORNIA STUDENT AID COMMISSION (Law Enforcement Dependents Scholarships—LEPD)

P.O. Box 419026
Rancho Cordova CA 95741-9026
916/526-7590
TDD: 916/526-7542
FAX: 916/526-8002
E-mail: custsvcs@csac.ca.gov
Internet: www.csac.ca.gov

AMOUNT: $100-$9,036/year
DEADLINE(S): None given
FIELD(S): All fields of study

Need-based grant to dependents/spouses of California peace officers (Hwy Patrol/marshals/sheriffs/police), specified CA Dept. of Corrections and CA Youth Authority employees, and firefighters employed by public entities who have been killed or totally disabled in the line of duty. If you receive a Cal Grant, your LEPD will match your Cal Grant award. Receiving LEPD will not prevent you from receiving Cal Grant or any other grant/fee waiver.

Renewable up to four years. For more information, contact the California Student Aid Commission.

2639—CALIFORNIA STUDENT AID COMMISSION (Robert C. Byrd Honors Scholarships)

P.O. Box 419029
Rancho Cordova CA 95741-9029
916/526-8250
TDD: 916/526-7542
FAX: 916/526-8002
E-mail: custsvcs@csac.ca.gov
Internet: www.csac.ca.gov

AMOUNT: up to $1,500/yr.
DEADLINE(S): APR 30
FIELD(S): All fields of study

A federally funded program administered by the California Student Aid Commission designed to recognize exceptionally able students who show promise of continued academic excellence. Scholarships are awarded solely on the basis of merit; GPA, SAT, & ACT scores considered.

Renewable up to four years. Each California public and private secondary school may nominate up to 2 applicants. Contact your high school scholarship coordinator to apply.

2640—CALIFORNIA TABLE GRAPE COMMISSION (California Table Grape Field Worker Scholarship Program)

P.O. Box 27320
Fresno CA 93729-7320
209/447-8350
FAX: 209/447-9184
E-mail: info@tablegrape.com
Internet: www.tablegrape.com

AMOUNT: $12,000 and $5,000
DEADLINE(S): APR 1
FIELD(S): All fields of study

Scholarships for undergraduates in a four-year college program who worked in the California table grape fields, or whose families did so, during the previous year. US citizenship required.

Two $12,000 scholarships, plus one $5,000 vocational scholarship.

2641—CALIFORNIA TEACHERS ASSOCIATION (CTA Scholarships for Dependent Children)

P.O. Box 921
Burlingame CA 94011-0921
650/697-1400
E-mail: scholarships@cta.org
Internet: www.cta.org

AMOUNT: $2,000
DEADLINE(S): FEB 15
FIELD(S): All fields of study

For undergraduate students who are dependents of an active, retired-life, or deceased California Teachers Association member. Financial need is NOT considered.

25 awards annually. Contact the Human Rights Department at above address between October and February for an application.

2642—CALLEJO-BOTELLO FOUNDATION CHARITABLE TRUST

4314 North Central Expressway
Dallas TX 75206
214/741-6710

AMOUNT: Varies
DEADLINE(S): APR 23
FIELD(S): All areas of study

Scholarships for students planning to attend educational institutions in Texas.

Send SASE to William F. Callejo, Trustee, at above address.

2643—CAMP FOUNDATION (Scholarship Grants)

P.O. Box 813
Franklin VA 23851
804/562-3439

AMOUNT: $4,000 (1); $2,500 (6)
DEADLINE(S): MAR 1
FIELD(S): All fields of study

Open to graduating high school seniors in the city of Franklin and the counties of Isle of Wight and Southampton, Virginia, or to residents of these areas who graduated from high school elsewhere. For undergraduate study.

These awards are made locally—NOT on a nationwide basis. Only those who meet residency requirements should write for complete information.

2644—CAMPBELL HALL SCHOOL (Scholarships)

4533 Laurel Canyon Blvd.
North Hollywood CA 91607
818/980-7280
FAX: 818/505-5319
E-mail: powerse@campbellhall.org
Internet: www.campbellhall.org

AMOUNT: Up to full tuition
DEADLINE(S): FEB 1
FIELD(S): All fields of study

Financial aid for students who meet admissions criteria to this Episcopalian day school serving grades K-12 in California. Must demonstrate financial need.

30 awards yearly. Contact school for details.

2645—CANNON SCHOOL (Scholarships)

5801 Poplar Tent Road
Concord NC 28027
704/786-8171
FAX: 708/788-7779
E-mail: rsnyder@cannonschool.org
Internet: www.cannonschool.org

AMOUNT: $500-$5,000
DEADLINE(S): None
FIELD(S): All fields of secondary school study

Financial aid to attend this private K-12 school in North Carolina.

20 annual awards. Renewable. Must demonstrate financial need. Admission is competitive.

2646—CAPE CANAVERAL CHAPTER RETIRED OFFICERS ASSOC. (Scholarships)

P.O. Box 254708
Patrick AFB FL 32925-4708

Written inquiry
AMOUNT: $2,000/yr.
DEADLINE(S): MAR 31
FIELD(S): All fields of study

Open ONLY to Brevard County, Florida, residents who have completed at least three semesters at any accredited four-year college in the US and are descendants or dependents of active duty or retired military personnel. Must be US citizen.

Awards renewable for one year. Send #10 SASE to the Scholarship Committee (address above) for complete information.

2647—CARBON POWER AND LIGHT, INC. (Scholarships)

Box 579
Saratoga WY 82331-0579
Written inquiry

AMOUNT: $1,000
DEADLINE(S): Varies
FIELD(S): All fields of study

Available to high school seniors from the area served by Carbon Power and Light. May be used at any accredited college, university, or technical school.

6 awards annually. See your school's financial aid office or write to above address for an application.

2648—CARGILL (Scholarship Program for Rural America)

P.O. Box 5650
Minneapolis MN 55440-5650
612/742-6201

AMOUNT: $1,000
DEADLINE(S): FEB 15
FIELD(S): All fields of study

Open to high school seniors who are from a family whose livelihood is at least 50% derived from farming. Applicant must be US citizen planning to attend a US school of higher education—either 2- or 4-year college or university or vocational-technical school.

250 awards. Write to Gladys Tripp at the address above for complete information.

2649—CARL AND VIRGINIA JOHNSON DAY TRUST

108 West Madison
Yazoo City MS 39194-1018
601/746-4901

AMOUNT: Varies
DEADLINE(S): JUL 4 (for Fall loans); NOV (Thanksgiving day for Spring loans)

FIELD(S): All fields of study

Interest-free student loans for residents of Mississippi who are under 25 years old and attend Mississippi schools.

Approximately 100 loans per year. Write to Carolyn Johnson at above location for details.

2650—CASCADE POLICY INSTITUTE (Independence Essay Competition)

813 SW Alder, Suite 450
Portland OR 97205
503/242-0900
FAX: 503/242-3822
E-mail: ESSAY@CascadePolicy.org
Internet: www.CascadePolicy.org

AMOUNT: $1,000
DEADLINE(S): MAR
FIELD(S): All fields of study

Essay competition open to Oregon high school-age students attending a private, public, or homeschool. Subject is "Exploring the Foundations of Freedom."

Up to 5 awards annually. Contact Kurt T. Weber for details.

2651—CASSNER FOUNDATION (Scholarship Program)

835 S. High Street
Hillsboro OH 45133
937/393-3426
FAX: 937-393-8428

AMOUNT: $1,500/yr.
DEADLINE(S): MAR 31
FIELD(S): All fields of study

For high school seniors in Highland County, Ohio.

4 annual awards. Renewable for four years.

2652—CATHOLIC AID ASSN. (College Tuition Scholarship Program)

3499 N. Lexington Ave.
Street Paul MN 55126
612/490-0170

AMOUNT: $300-$500
DEADLINE(S): MAR 15
FIELD(S): All fields of study

Open to Catholic Aid Association members (insurance or annuity) of at least 2 years. Must be entering freshman or sophomore year in an accredited college, university, or tech school.

Write for complete information.

2653—CATHOLIC DIOCESE OF KANSAS CITY-Street JOSEPH—CENTRAL CITY SCHOOL FUND (Scholarships)

P.O. Box 419037
Kansas City MO 64141-6037
816/756-1850
FAX: 816/756-0878
Internet: www.diocese-kcsj.org

AMOUNT: Tuition
DEADLINE(S): None
FIELD(S): All fields of study

Provides educational support in the Central City Schools for the children of the urban core of Kansas City. Grades K-12.

Applicants need not be Catholic. Contact above location for details.

2654—CDR. WILLIAM S. STUHR SCHOLARSHIP FUND

1200 Fifth Ave., Apt. 9-D
New York NY 10029
Written inquiry

AMOUNT: $1,125 per year for 4 years
DEADLINE(S): Varies (according to service—usually FEB 1)
FIELD(S): All fields of study

For high school seniors who are dependents of active duty or retired career members of one of five branches of the armed services. For study at an accredited 4-year college only.

Applicants should be in top 10% of their class and demonstrate leadership ability and financial need. Send self-addressed, stamped envelope (business size) for information.

2655—CENTRAL SCHOLARSHIP BUREAU (Interest-free Loans)

1700 Reisterstown Road, #220
Baltimore MD 21208
410/415-5558

AMOUNT: $500-$8,000 (max. through grad school)
DEADLINE(S): JUN 1; DEC 1
FIELD(S): All fields of study

Interest-free loans for residents of metropolitan Baltimore area who have exhausted all other available avenues of funding. Aid is offered for study at any accredited undergrad or graduate institution.

Awards are made on a non-competitive basis to anyone with a sound educational plan. 125 loans per year. Must apply first through government and school. Write for complete information.

2656—CEO AMERICA (School Choice Scholarships)

901 McClean, Suite 802
Bentonville AR 72712
501/273-6957
FAX: 501/273-9362
E-mail: tdwilli@ceoamerica.org
Internet: www.ceoamerica.org

AMOUNT: Varies
DEADLINE(S): Varies
FIELD(S): All fields of study

Tuition assistance for K-12 students to attend private schools. Typically for low-income families meeting federal free/reduced lunch guidelines. Residence and eligibility requirements vary from program to program.

Contact Troy Williamson for details.

2657—CHAIRSCHOLARS FOUNDATION, INC. (Scholarships)

16101 Carancia Lane
Odessa FL 33556-3278
813/920-2737
Internet: www.chairscholars.org

AMOUNT: $3,000
DEADLINE(S): None
FIELD(S): All fields of study

Scholarships for high school seniors or college freshmen confined to wheelchairs or who are otherwise physically challenged. Must demonstrate financial need, satisfactory academic past performance, and some degree of past community service. Must sign contract to remain drug-free and crime-free.

3 annual awards. Send name, address, age, and sex to the above address to begin application process.

2658—CHARLES COOPER INDUSTRIAL SCHOOL

Chittenden Trust Co.
401 Main Street
Bennington VT 05201
Written inquiry

AMOUNT: Not specified
DEADLINE(S): None specified
FIELD(S): All areas of study

Student loans for higher education for Vermont residents.

Write to Loraine B. Smith at above address for application information.

2659—CHARLES H. BOND TRUST

P.O. Box 1861
Boston MA 02105

Written inquiry

AMOUNT: Varies

DEADLINE(S): APR 15

FIELD(S): All fields of study

Scholarship to high school seniors who are residents of Massachusetts and will be attending college the following year.

Renewable upon approval of transcript. Send SASE to Sharon Driscoll, Trust Officer, The First National Bank of Boston, at above address.

2660—CHARLES I. AND EMMA J. CLAPP SCHOLARSHIP FUND

c/o First of America Bank
110 East Allegan Street
Otsego MI 49078
Written inquiry

AMOUNT: Varies

DEADLINE(S): Ongoing

FIELD(S): All fields of study

Interest-free student loans to non-drinkers. Female applicants must, in addition, be nonsmokers.

Contact Jim Yankoviak, Trust Officer, at above address for details.

2661—CHARLES J. HUGHES FOUNDATION

P.O. Box 1498
Pagosa Springs CO 81147
970/264-2228

AMOUNT: Varies

DEADLINE(S): Ongoing

FIELD(S): All fields of study

Scholarships to students with learning disabilities who live in Colorado.

Apply by letter outlining financial need. Contact Terrence P. Allie, President, at above location.

2662—CHARLESTON SCIENTIFIC AND CULTURAL EDUCATIONAL FUND

P.O. Box 190011
Charleston SC 29419-9011
803/723-2000

AMOUNT: Varies

DEADLINE(S): JUN 1

FIELD(S): All areas of study

Grants to natives of South Carolina for scientific, cultural, or educational pursuits in Charleston, SC.

Apply to Wade H. Logan III, P.O. Box 848, Charleston, SC 29402 for detailed information.

2663—CHAROTAR PATIDAR SAMAJ (Sardar Patel Scholarships)

4767 Dunbarton Drive
Orlando FL 32817
407/671-2447 or 704/364-5225
FAX: 704/364-6684
E-mail: patidar@tgate.com
Internet: patidar.net

AMOUNT: $1,000 (4); $201 (5)

DEADLINE(S): OCT 20 (of senior yr. in high school)

FIELD(S): All fields of study

This organization is a private group of people from the State of Gujarat, India, who are US residents. The group strives to unite all Patel familes in the US and assist with educational expenses. Applicants must apply during senior year in high school, have a minimum GPA of 3.5, min. SAT score of 1100 or ACT of 25. An essay is required.

Print application from website and/or contact Mrs. Meena Patel at above address for details.

2664—CHATHAM COLLEGE (Merit Scholarship Program)

Office of Admissions
Woodland Road
Pittsburgh PA 15232
412/365-1290

AMOUNT: Up to $10,000 per year

DEADLINE(S): None

FIELD(S): All fields of study

Women only. Awards open to entering first-year and transfer students accepted at Chatham College. Selection based on past academic performance.

Renewable for up to 4 years. Contact Office of Admissions for details.

2665—CHAUTAUQUA REGION COMMUNITY FOUNDATION INC. (Scholarships)

21 E. Third Street, Suite 301
Jamestown NY 14701
716/661-3390

AMOUNT: $100-$2,000

DEADLINE(S): JUN 1 (college freshmen); JUL 15 (college students)

FIELD(S): All fields of study

Numerous scholarships with varying requirements open ONLY to students living in the vicinity of Jamestown, NY. Preference to students in 12 school districts in Southern Chautauqua County. For full-time study.

Write for complete information.

2666—CHEROKEE NATION (Higher Education Need-based Grant Program)

P.O. Box 948
Tahlequah OK 74465
918/456-0671

AMOUNT: Varies

DEADLINE(S): APR 1

FIELD(S): All areas of study

Grants available to members of the Cherokee Nation of Oklahoma. Awards are tenable at accredited undergraduate 2-year and 4-year colleges and universities in the US US citizenship required. Students must be eligible for Pell grants.

500 awards per year. Write for complete information.

2667—CHESTNUT HILL ACADEMY (Scholarships and Financial Aid)

500 W. Willow Grove Ave.
Philadelphia PA 19118
215/247-4700
FAX: 215/242-4055
E-mail: admissions@cha.k12pa.us
Internet: www.cha.k12.pa.us

AMOUNT: Varies (up to 100% of demonstrated need)

DEADLINE(S): DEC (early)

FIELD(S): All fields of K-12 study

Varying degrees of financial aid available at this independent day school for boys in Philadelphia, PA. Specific programs are available for students of color entering grades 4-7 or 9-11 as well as for all students for grades K-12 (up to 100% for grades 6-12).

Criteria relate to group exam, interview, and recommendations.

2668—CHEYENNE AND ARAPAHO TRIBES OF OKLAHOMA (Scholarships)

P.O. Box 38
Concho OK 73022
405/262-0345 or 800/247-4612
FAX: 405/262-0745

AMOUNT: Based on unmet need and availability of funds

DEADLINE(S): JUN 1 (1st semester); NOV 1 (2nd semester); APR 1 (summer semester)

FIELD(S): All fields of study

For enrolled members of the Cheyenne-Arapaho Tribes of Oklahoma enrolled at the Concho agency. Must be certified to be at least 1/4 or more degree Cheyenne-Arapaho Indian, be a high school graduate or GED recipient, and in need of financial aid. For grads and under-grads. Summer and part-time students may be considered.

Write to Cheyenne-Arapaho Education Department at above address for details.

2669—CHINESE AMERICAN CITIZENS ALLIANCE FOUNDATION

1055 Wilshire Blvd., Suite 1210
Los Angeles CA 90017-2494
213/250-5515

AMOUNT: $1,000
DEADLINE(S): JUL 31
FIELD(S): All fields of study

Scholarships for students of Chinese ancestry who are entering their junior year at colleges and universities in the Southern California area.

Awards based primarily on scholastic achievement, but consideration is also given to community and extracurricular activities.

2670—CHINESE CHRISTIAN HERALD CRUSADES (Chinese Collegiate Merit Scholarship for New York Schools)

Dr. Timothy Kok C. Tam
48 Allen Street
New York NY 10002
212/334-2033

AMOUNT: Up to $1,500
DEADLINE(S): JUL 31
FIELD(S): All fields of study

Open to Chinese students who are NOT US citizens and who are attending a school within a 100-mile radius of New York City.

2 undergraduate and 2 graduate awards each year. Write for complete information.

2671—CHINESE PROFESSIONAL CLUB OF HOUSTON (Scholarship Program)

5411 Queensloch Drive
Houston TX 77096-4027
713/729-8816

AMOUNT: $500-$1,000
DEADLINE(S): NOV 15
FIELD(S): All fields of study

For high school seniors of Chinese descent who reside in the greater Houston (Texas) metropolitan area. For study at an accredited college or university in the US.

10-16 awards yearly. Dollar amount and number of scholarships vary each year. NOT renewable. Write for complete information.

2672—CHOCTAW NATION OF OKLAHOMA HIGHER EDUCATION PROGRAM (Grants)

Drawer 1210
Durant OK 74702-1210
405/924-8280 or 800/522-6170
FAX: 405/924-1267

AMOUNT: Up to $1,600/yr.
DEADLINE(S): MAR 15
FIELD(S): All fields of study leading to a degree

For enrolled members of the Choctaw Nation of Oklahoma who are undergraduates or graduates. Must be seeking at least an Associate of Arts degree. Priority is given undergrads depending on availability of funds. For use at accredited colleges or universities.

Must submit copies of Certificate of Degree of Indian Blood and Tribal Membership cards showing Choctaw descent, photo, and transcripts. Apply between Jan. 1 and March 15. For renewal must reapply each year.

2673—CHRIST SCHOOL (Scholarships)

500 Christ School Road
Arden NC 28704
828/684-6232, ext. 18
FAX: 828/684-2745
E-mail: cdunnigan@christschool.org
Internet: www.christschool.org

AMOUNT: $500-$20,000
DEADLINE(S): MAR 1
FIELD(S): All fields of study

Scholarships available to attend this independent, coeducational school which includes grades 8 through 12.

Renewable depending on performance. Contact school for details.

2674—CHRISTIAN RECORD SERVICES INC. (Scholarships)

4444 South 52nd Street
Lincoln NE 68516
402/488-0981
TDD: 402/488-1902
FAX: 402/488-7582
E-mail: 74617.236@compuserve.com
Internet: www.tagnet.org/crs/scholar.htm

AMOUNT: $500 to $1,000
DEADLINE(S): APR 1
FIELD(S): All fields of study

Undergraduate scholarships available to legally blind students to secure training that will enable independence and self-support. An international service. In Canada,

address is: 1300 King Street East, Suite 119, Oshawa, ON L1H 8N9 (905/436-7102).

Application is on website and is accepted between Nov. 1 and April 1 for use during the fall term of the following year.

2675—CHUNG KUN AI FOUNDATION

P.O. Box 1559
Honolulu HI 96805
Written inquiry

AMOUNT: $2,000
DEADLINE(S): Ongoing
FIELD(S): All areas of study

Scholarships to financially needy residents of Hawaii with a GPA of at least 2.8.

Contact Samuel S. Chung, Trustee, at above address for application procedures.

2676—CITIZEN'S SCHOLARSHIP FOUNDATION OF AMERICA (CIGNA Foundation Scholarship)

One Liberty Place
1650 Market Street
Philadelphia PA 19192-1540
215/761-3444

AMOUNT: $1,000-$3,000
DEADLINE(S): MAR 15
FIELD(S): All fields of study

Open to children of employees of CIGNA companies; employees must work at least 20 hours a week, and have been employed for at least one year. Applicants must be unmarried and under the age of 23.

Applications should be requested by phone at the above phone number.

2677—CITIZEN'S SCHOLARSHIP FOUNDATION OF AMERICA, INC. (The Chrysler Corporation Fund Scholarship Program)

P.O. Box 297
Street Peter MN 56082
800/537-4180

AMOUNT: $1,000-$5,000
DEADLINE(S): FEB 15
FIELD(S): All fields of study

For children of regular, full-time employees, retirees, and deceased employees of Chrysler Corporation and its US-based subsidiaries. Application can be made during the senior year of high school. High school graduates age 21 or under may also apply.

125 awards per year. Renewable. Financial need is considered. Write to the above address for complete information.

2678—CITIZENS SCHOLARSHIP FOUNDATION OF GUERNSEY COUNTY (Dollars for Scholars)

P.O. Box 811
Cambridge OH 43725
740/439-3558

AMOUNT: Varies
DEADLINE(S): JUN 1
FIELD(S): All fields of study

For residents of Guernsey County, Ohio, who are pursuing undergraduate studies. Must have graduated from one of the following high schools: Cambridge, Meadowbrook, Buckeye Trail, Newcomerstown, John Glenn, Bishop Rosecrans, Guernsey-Noble Career Center, Muskingum-Perry Career Center, or Guernsey County ABLE/GED Center. US citizenship NOT required.

Approx. 280 awards annually. Renewable up to four years. Financial need must be demonstrated. Contact Melody Greathouse at above address for an application/more information.

2679—CITIZENS' SCHOLARSHIP FOUNDATION OF WAKEFIELD, INC. (Scholarships)

467 Main Street
P.O. Box 321
Wakefield MA 01880
781/245-4890
FAX: 781/245-6761

AMOUNT: $300-$2,000
DEADLINE(S): MAR 15
FIELD(S): All fields of study

For full-time students (undergrads, graduates, voc-tech, continuing ed, etc.) who are residents of Wakefield, Massachusetts. Must demonstrate financial need.

300+ awards annually. Renewable with reapplication. Contact Lynne P. Zervas at above address or visit Wakefield High School's Guidance Office for an application.

2680—COCA-COLA SCHOLARS FOUNDATION (Scholarship)

P.O. Box 442
Atlanta GA 30301-0442
800/306-COKE

AMOUNT: $1,000-$5,000 (per year for 4 years)
DEADLINE(S): OCT 31
FIELD(S): All areas of study

Open to college-bound high school seniors who are involved in school leadership, civic, and other extracurricular activities. Award is based on merit, academic achievement, and motivation to succeed. Students must live in a participating area.

Call or write to the above address for complete information.

2681—COLLEGE BOUND STUDENT OF THE YEAR (Contest)

2071 Clove Road, Suite 206
Staten Island NY 10304
Internet: www.collegebound.net/contests/soy99.html

AMOUNT: $1,500 + various prizes, including personal computer
DEADLINE(S): MAY 15
FIELD(S): All fields of study

For outstanding high school students planning to attend college. Write a typed, 300- to 500-word essay about the event or experience that motivated you to pursue a college education.

2 winners annually; 25 runners-up also receive prizes. Send a self-addressed, stamped envelope to above address for an application. Or complete the application and essay online, and mail a copy of your most recent transcript to the above address. Winners announced June 15th.

2682—COLLEGE FOUNDATION INC. (Federal PLUS Loans Under NC Federal Family Education Loan Program)

2100 Yonkers Road
P.O. Box 12100
Raleigh NC 27605
919/821-4771 or 888/234-6400
E-mail: info@cfi-nc.org
Internet: www.cfi-nc.org

AMOUNT: Difference between cost of attending and other financial aid received
DEADLINE(S): Varies
FIELD(S): All fields of study

For parent of student who is dependent (by Federal definition) and enrolled in eligible US college. If the student is at a college not in NC, borrower must be legal NC resident. Parent does not have to demonstrate need but must NOT have "adverse credit history." Must meet nationwide Federal PLUS Loans requirements.

Approximately 2,600 loans per year. Must reapply each year. Write for complete information and an application.

2683—COLLEGE FOUNDATION INC. (North Carolina Federal Family Education Loan Program; Stafford Loans—Subsidized & Unsubsidized—and PLUS Loans)

2100 Yonkers Road
P.O. Box 12100
Raleigh NC 27605
919/821-4771 or 888/CFI-6400
E-mail: info@cfi-nc.org
Internet: www.cfi-nc.org

AMOUNT: $2,625 and up
DEADLINE(S): Varies
FIELD(S): All fields of study

Open to US citizens who are legal residents of NC enrolled in an eligible in-state or out-of-state college or an out-of-state student attending an eligible NC college. Must meet nationwide eligibility requirements of Stafford loans. Must complete and file the Free Application for Federal Student Aid (FAFSA).

Approximately 56,000 loans per year. Financial need must be established for subsidized loan. New loan application is required yearly. Write for complete information.

2684—COLLEGE FOUNDATION INC. (North Carolina's Federal Family Education Loan Program)

2100 Yonkers Road
P.O. Box 12100
Raleigh NC 27605
919/821-4771 or 888/234-6400
E-mail: info@cfi-nc.org
Internet: www.cfi-nc.org

AMOUNT: Varies
DEADLINE(S): Varies
FIELD(S): All fields of study

For North Carolina students attending eligible institutions of higher education and vocational schools in state or out of state, and for out-of-state students attending eligible institutions of higher education and vocational schools in North Carolina.

Write for complete information and application.

2685—COLLEGE FOUNDATION INC. (North Carolina Student Incentive Grant)

2100 Yonkers Road
P.O. Box 12100
Raleigh NC 27605
919/821-4771 or 888/234-6400
E-mail: info@cfi-nc.org
Internet: www.cfi-nc.org

AMOUNT: $200 to $1,500
DEADLINE(S): MAR 15
FIELD(S): All fields of study

Undergraduate grants to students who are US citizens, North Carolina residents, and attending or planning to attend college in North Carolina. Must demonstrate substantial financial need and maintain satisfactory academic progress. Must complete and file the Free Application for Federal Student Aid (FAFSA).

Approximately 4,300 grants per year. Renewable to a maximum of 5 years of undergraduate study.

2686—COLLEGE MISERICORDIA (Honor Scholarships)

301 Lake Street
Dallas PA 18612-1098
800/852-7675
Internet: http://miseri.edu/scholar.htm

AMOUNT: Full or part tuition
DEADLINE(S): MAR 1
FIELD(S): All fields of study

Scholarships for incoming freshmen and transfer students to this coeducational Catholic college in Pennsylvania. Must have attained outstanding academic records. For undergraduates and graduate students.

Renewable until graduation provided minimum GPAs are maintained. GPA requirements are outlined in the scholarship notification letter. Obtain applications from the Admissions Office.

2687—COLLEGE OF MARIN FOUNDATION (Disabled Students Program)

835 College Ave.
Kentfield CA 94904-2590
415/485-9406
FAX: 415/457-4791

AMOUNT: $300
DEADLINE(S): MAR 15
FIELD(S): All fields of study

Open to undergraduate students enrolled in or planning to enroll in the disabled students program at the College of Marin. Must be a US citizen and demonstrate financial need.

3 awards annually. Not renewable. Contact Marie McCarthy at the C.O.M. Foundation for an application.

2688—COLLEGE OF SAINT ELIZABETH (Scholarships)

2 Convent Road
Morristown NJ 07960

973/290-4000
Internet: www.st-elizabeth.edu

AMOUNT: Varies
DEADLINE(S): Varies
FIELD(S): All fields of study

Various scholarships available for use at this private Catholic college for females in New Jersey.

Check website and/or write for details.

2689—COLLEGE OF Street FRANCIS (Various Scholarship/Grant Programs)

500 Wilcox Street
Joliet IL 60435
815/740-3360
Internet: www.stfrancis.edu

AMOUNT: Varies
DEADLINE(S): Varies
FIELD(S): All fields of study

Scholarships and grants for students at Street Francis College at all levels—incoming freshmen and transfers, undergraduates, and graduates. Some are tied to certain requirements, such as athletics, biology, academic achievement, financial need, minority group, leadership, choir participation, and community activities.

See website and/or contact college for details on financial aid.

2690—COLORADO MASONS BENEVOLENT FUND ASSOCIATION (Scholarship Program)

1130 Panorama Drive
Colorado Springs CO 80904
719/471-9587

AMOUNT: Up to $20,000 over four years
DEADLINE(S): MAR 15
FIELD(S): All fields of study

Open to seniors in Colorado public high schools who plan to attend a Colorado college or university. Must be Colorado resident but Masonic affiliation is not required. Need is considered but is not paramount.

Applications are mailed early in November to all Colorado public schools. Contact Colorado schools. DO NOT write address above.

2691—COLORADO ROCKY MOUNTAIN SCHOOL (Scholarships)

1493 County Road 106
Carbondale CO 81623
970/963-2562
FAX: 970/963-9865
E-mail: crms@crms.org

Internet: www.crms.org

AMOUNT: Tuition
DEADLINE(S): None given
FIELD(S): All areas

Scholarship for tuition at this private secondary school in Colorado, grades 9-12. Awards based on financial need.

45 awards yearly.

2692—COLORADO STATE UNIVERSITY (First-Generation Award)

Financial Aid Office
Administration Annex
Fort Collins CO 80523-8024
970/491-6321

AMOUNT: $3,100
DEADLINE(S): APR 1
FIELD(S): All areas of study

Award is open to students whose parents have never received a bachelor's degree. Students must be accepted for full-time study at CSU in a program leading to a bachelor's degree. Must demonstrate financial need.

Colorado residents ONLY. Write for complete information.

2693—COLUMBUS SCHOOL FOR GIRLS (Scholarships)

56 S. Columbia Ave.
Columbus OH 43209
614/252-0781
FAX: 614/252-0571
E-mail: schec_th@csg.capital.edu
Internet: www.csg.capital.edu

AMOUNT: Varies
DEADLINE(S): APR 1
FIELD(S): All fields of study

Scholarships available to attend this independent school for girls which includes elementary and high school. Awards based on family's financial need.

Renewable. Contact school for details.

2694—COMMITTEE ON INSTITUTIONAL COOPERATION (Summer Research Opportunities Program)

302 E. John Street, Suite 1705
Champaign IL 61820-5698
800/457-4420 or 217/265-8005
FAX: 217/244-7127
E-mail: aeprice@uiuc.edu
Internet: www.cic.uiuc.edu

AMOUNT: $2,500 stipend + room, board, & travel
DEADLINE(S): JAN 28

FIELD(S): All fields of study

To interest talented undergrad minorities in academic careers and enhance preparation for grad study through research with faculty mentors. African Americans, Mexican Americans, Puerto Ricans, and other Latinos who are sophomores or juniors are eligible. Must devote full-time to program during 8- to 10-week summer session. Need transcripts and recommendations.

See website or contact Anne Price, CIC Secretary, for application. Session at CIC campus (U Chicago, U IL, IN U, U IA, U MI, MI State, U MN, Northwestern, OH State, PA State, Purdue, or U WI).

2695—COMMONWEALTH OF VIRGINIA DEPARTMENT OF VETERANS' AFFAIRS (War Orphans Education Program)

270 Franklin Rd. SW, Room 1012
Poff Federal Building
Roanoke VA 24011-2215
703/857-7104

AMOUNT: Tuition + required fees
DEADLINE(S): None
FIELD(S): All fields of study

Open to surviving/dependent children (aged 16-25) of US military personnel who were/are Virginia residents and as a result of war/armed conflict are deceased, disabled, prisoners of war, or missing in action.

Must attend a state-supported secondary or postsecondary educational institution to pursue any vocational, technical, undergraduate, or graduate program. Write for complete information.

2696—COMMUNITY FOUNDATION OF GREATER LORAIN COUNTY (Various Scholarship Programs)

1865 N. Ridge Road E., Suite A
Lorain OH 44055
216/277-0142
FAX: 216/277-6955

AMOUNT: Varies
DEADLINE(S): Varies
FIELD(S): All fields of study

For residents of Lorain County, Ohio. Various programs, ranging from opportunities for high school seniors through doctoral programs. Dollar amounts vary as do deadlines.

Contact the organization above for details.

2697—COMMUNITY FOUNDATION OF SARASOTA COUNTY (Scholarship Funds)

P.O. Box 49587
Sarasota FL 34230-6587
941/955-3000
Internet: www.communityfoundation.com

AMOUNT: Varies
DEADLINE(S): MAR 3 (postmark)
FIELD(S): All fields of study

The Foundation manages several scholarships, some for high school seniors and others for students already attending college. Some are for specific areas of study, and some are general. Most are for residents of Charlotte, Manatee, or Sarasota counties in Florida.

Contact the above organization for a detailed list of scholarship opportunities.

2698—COMMUNITY FOUNDATION OF WESTERN MASSACHUSETTS (Albert Steiger Memorial Scholarships)

1500 Main Street
P.O. Box 15769
Springfield MA 01115
413/732-2858

AMOUNT: $2,500
DEADLINE(S): APR 15
FIELD(S): All fields of study

Open to graduating seniors of Central High School in Springfield, Massachusetts. Based on financial need, academic merit, and extracurricular activities. Must submit transcripts and fill out government FAFSA form.

2-4 awards annually. Renewable with reapplication. Contact Community Foundation for an application and your financial aid office for FAFSA. Notification is in June.

2699—COMMUNITY FOUNDATION OF WESTERN MASSACHUSETTS (Arrighi Memorial Scholarship)

1500 Main Street
P.O. Box 15769
Springfield MA 01115
413/732-2858

AMOUNT: $2,400
DEADLINE(S): APR 15
FIELD(S): All fields of study

Open to residents of Greenfield, Massachusetts, for full-time undergraduate, graduate, trade, or professional school. Based on financial need, academic merit, and extracurricular activities. Must submit transcripts and fill out government FAFSA form.

1-2 awards annually. Renewable with reapplication. Contact Community Foundation for an application and your financial aid office for FAFSA. Notification is in June.

2700—COMMUNITY FOUNDATION OF WESTERN MASSACHUSETTS (African-American Achievement Scholarships)

1500 Main Street
P.O. Box 15769
Springfield MA 01115
413/732-2858

AMOUNT: $2,500-$3,000
DEADLINE(S): APR 15
FIELD(S): All fields of study

Open to African-American residents of Hampden, Hampshire, and Franklin counties, Massachusetts, who attend or plan to attend a four-year college full-time. These are loans that can be repaid by demonstrating community service. Based on financial need, academic merit, and extracurricular activities. Must submit transcripts and fill out government FAFSA form.

5 awards annually. Renewable with reapplication. Contact Community Foundation for an application and your financial aid office for FAFSA. Notification is in June.

2701—COMMUNITY FOUNDATION OF WESTERN MASSACHUSETTS (Anthony & Madeline Sampson Kapinos Scholarships)

1500 Main Street
P.O. Box 15769
Springfield MA 01115
413/732-2858

AMOUNT: $1,200
DEADLINE(S): APR 15
FIELD(S): All fields of study

Open to graduates of Chicopee High School in Massachusetts to assist with continuing their education. Based on financial need. Must submit transcripts and fill out government FAFSA form.

2 awards annually. Renewable with reapplication. Contact Community Foundation for an application and your financial aid office for FAFSA. Notification is in June.

2702—COMMUNITY FOUNDATION OF WESTERN MASSACHUSETTS (Charles F. Warner Loans)

1500 Main Street
P.O. Box 15769
Springfield MA 01115
413/732-2858

AMOUNT: $250

DEADLINE(S): APR 15

FIELD(S): All fields of study

Interest-free loans are open to residents of Springfield, Massachusetts, to pursue full-time undergraduate or graduate study. Based on financial need, academic merit, and extracurricular activities. Must submit transcripts and fill out government FAFSA form.

4-5 awards annually. Renewable with reapplication. Contact Community Foundation for an application and your financial aid office for FAFSA. Notification is in June.

2703—COMMUNITY FOUNDATION OF WESTERN MASSACHUSETTS (Carlos B. Ellis Scholarships)

1500 Main Street
P.O. Box 15769
Springfield MA 01115
413/732-2858

AMOUNT: $200-$1,000

DEADLINE(S): APR 15

FIELD(S): All fields of study

Open to members and graduates of Commerce High School in Massachusetts to continue their education. Based on financial need, academic merit, and extracurricular activities. Must submit transcripts and fill out government FAFSA form.

9 awards annually. Renewable with reapplication. Contact Community Foundation for an application and your financial aid office for FAFSA. Notification is in June.

2704—COMMUNITY FOUNDATION OF WESTERN MASSACHUSETTS (Clarence H. Matteson Scholarships)

1500 Main Street
P.O. Box 15769
Springfield MA 01115
413/732-2858

AMOUNT: $1,125

DEADLINE(S): APR 15

FIELD(S): All fields of study

Open to residents of Greenfield, Massachusetts, with a high scholastic ability to pursue full-time education beyond high school (college, graduate, or postgraduate studies). Based on financial need, academic merit, and extracurricular activities. Must submit transcripts and fill out government FAFSA form.

5-8 awards annually. Renewable with reapplication. Contact Community Foundation for an application and your financial aid office for FAFSA. Notification is in June.

2705—COMMUNITY FOUNDATION OF WESTERN MASSACHUSETTS (C. Kenneth Sanderson Scholarship)

1500 Main Street
P.O. Box 15769
Springfield MA 01115
413/732-2858

AMOUNT: $5,000

DEADLINE(S): APR 15

FIELD(S): All fields of study

Open to top graduates of Monson High School in Massachusetts to assist with college tuition. Based on financial need, academic merit, and extracurricular activities. Must submit transcripts and fill out government FAFSA form.

1 award annually. Renewable with reapplication. Contact Community Foundation for an application and your financial aid office for FAFSA. Notification is in June.

2706—COMMUNITY FOUNDATION OF WESTERN MASSACHUSETTS (Deerfield Plastics/Barker Family Fund)

1500 Main Street
P.O. Box 15769
Springfield MA 01115
413/732-2858

AMOUNT: $3,750

DEADLINE(S): APR 15

FIELD(S): All fields of study

Open to children of Deerfield Plastics employees who wish to pursue full-time undergraduate or graduate study. Based on financial need, academic merit, and extracurricular activities. Must submit transcripts and fill out government FAFSA form.

5 awards annually. Renewable with reapplication. Contact Community Foundation for an application and your financial aid office for FAFSA. Notification is in June.

2707—COMMUNITY FOUNDATION OF WESTERN MASSACHUSETTS (Dr. Jeffrey A. Ferst Valedictorian Memorial Scholarship)

1500 Main Street
P.O. Box 15769
Springfield MA 01115
413/732-2858

AMOUNT: $2,000-$3,500

DEADLINE(S): APR 15

FIELD(S): All fields of study

Awarded annually to the valedictorian of Westfield High School in Massachusetts.

1 award annually. Contact Community Foundation for details.

2708—COMMUNITY FOUNDATION OF WESTERN MASSACHUSETTS (Donald A. & Dorothy F. Axtell Grant Scholarships)

1500 Main Street
P.O. Box 15769
Springfield MA 01115
413/732-2858

AMOUNT: $500-$1,000

DEADLINE(S): APR 15

FIELD(S): All fields of study

Open to Protestant residents of Hampshire County, Massachusetts, for full-time undergraduate or graduate study. Based on financial need, academic merit, and extracurricular activities. Must submit transcripts and fill out government FAFSA form.

2-4 awards annually. Renewable with reapplication. Contact Community Foundation for an application and your financial aid office for FAFSA. Notification is in June.

2709—COMMUNITY FOUNDATION OF WESTERN MASSACHUSETTS (First National Bank of Amherst Centennial Educational Scholarships)

1500 Main Street
P.O. Box 15769
Springfield MA 01115
413/732-2858

AMOUNT: $600

DEADLINE(S): APR 15

FIELD(S): All fields of study

Open to students from Northampton, Hadley, Amherst, UMass, Amherst College, and Hampshire College in Massachusetts to pursue full-time undergraduate or graduate study. Based on financial need, academic merit, and extracurricular activities. Must submit transcripts and fill out government FAFSA form.

6 awards annually. Renewable with reapplication. Contact Community Foundation for an application and your financial aid office for FAFSA. Notification is in June.

2710—COMMUNITY FOUNDATION OF WESTERN MASSACHUSETTS (Frank W. Jendrysik, Jr. Memorial Scholarship)

1500 Main Street
P.O. Box 15769
Springfield MA 01115
413/732-2858

AMOUNT: $1,000

DEADLINE(S): APR 15

FIELD(S): All fields of study

Open to residents of Chicopee, Holyoke, and Springfield, Massachusetts, to pursue full-time undergraduate or graduate study. Based on financial need, academic merit, and extracurricular activities. Must submit transcripts and fill out government FAFSA form.

1 award annually. Renewable with reapplication. Contact Community Foundation for an application and your financial aid office for FAFSA. Notification is in June.

2711—COMMUNITY FOUNDATION OF WESTERN MASSACHUSETTS (Frederick W. Porter Scholarships)

1500 Main Street
P.O. Box 15769
Springfield MA 01115
413/732-2858

AMOUNT: $650
DEADLINE(S): APR 15
FIELD(S): All fields of study

Open to graduates of Greenfield High School in Massachusetts to pursue full-time undergraduate or graduate study. Based on financial need, academic merit, and extracurricular activities. Must submit transcripts and fill out government FAFSA form.

2 awards annually. Renewable with reapplication. Contact Community Foundation for an application and your financial aid office for FAFSA. Notification is in June.

2712—COMMUNITY FOUNDATION OF WESTERN MASSACHUSETTS (Gertrude & William C. Hill Scholarships)

1500 Main Street
P.O. Box 15769
Springfield MA 01115
413/732-2858

AMOUNT: $600-$1,450
DEADLINE(S): APR 15
FIELD(S): All fields of study

Open to graduates of Central High School in Springfield, Massachusetts, to obtain a college education. Preference given to those majoring in liberal arts. Based on financial need, academic merit, and extracurricular activities. Must submit transcripts and fill out government FAFSA form.

7 awards annually. Renewable with reapplication. Contact Community Foundation for an application and your financial aid office for FAFSA. Notification is in June.

2713—COMMUNITY FOUNDATION OF WESTERN MASSACHUSETTS (Horace Hill Scholarships)

1500 Main Street
P.O. Box 15769
Springfield MA 01115
413/732-2858

AMOUNT: $750
DEADLINE(S): APR 15
FIELD(S): All fields of study

Open to children and grandchildren of the members of the Springfield Newspapers' 25-Year Club to pursue full-time undergraduate or graduate study. Based on financial need, academic merit, and extracurricular activities. Must submit transcripts and fill out government FAFSA form.

4 awards annually. Renewable with reapplication. Contact Community Foundation for an application and your financial aid office for FAFSA. Notification is in June.

2714—COMMUNITY FOUNDATION OF WESTERN MASSACHUSETTS (James W. Colgan Loan Fund)

1500 Main Street
P.O. Box 15769
Springfield MA 01115
413/732-2858

AMOUNT: $1,500-$2,000
DEADLINE(S): APR 15
FIELD(S): All fields of study

Interest-free loans are open to residents of Massachusetts for the past five years to pursue full-time undergraduate study. Based on financial need, academic merit, and extracurricular activities. Must submit transcripts, copy of parents' and applicant's Federal Income Tax Return and W-2 form, and three letters of reference for first-time applicants. Must fill out government FAFSA form.

250 loans annually. Renewable with reapplication. Send self-addressed, stamped envelope to Community Foundation for an application and contact your financial aid office for FAFSA. Notification is in June.

2715—COMMUNITY FOUNDATION OF WESTERN MASSACHUSETTS (Jeffrey I. Glaser, M.D. Memorial Scholarship)

1500 Main Street
P.O. Box 15769
Springfield MA 01115
413/732-2858

AMOUNT: $500

DEADLINE(S): APR 15
FIELD(S): All fields of study

Open to a graduating Longmeadow High School (Longmeadow, MA) senior who has distinguished himself or herself on the swim team and academically. Based on financial need, academic merit, and extracurricular activities. Must be nominated by your school and fill out government FAFSA form.

1-2 awards annually. Contact Community Foundation for details and your financial aid office for FAFSA. Notification is in June.

2716—COMMUNITY FOUNDATION OF WESTERN MASSACHUSETTS (Jane A. Korzeniowski Memorial Scholarship)

1500 Main Street
P.O. Box 15769
Springfield MA 01115
413/732-2858

AMOUNT: $350
DEADLINE(S): APR 15
FIELD(S): All fields of study

Open to Chicopee, Massachusetts, residents who attend or plan to attend college for full-time graduate or undergraduate study. Based on financial need, academic merit, and extracurricular activities. Must submit transcripts and fill out government FAFSA form.

1 award annually. Renewable with reapplication. Contact Community Foundation for an application and your financial aid office for FAFSA. Notification is in June.

2717—COMMUNITY FOUNDATION OF WESTERN MASSACHUSETTS (James Z. Naurison Scholarships)

1500 Main Street
P.O. Box 15769
Springfield MA 01115
413/732-2858

AMOUNT: $750-$1,000
DEADLINE(S): APR 15
FIELD(S): All fields of study

Open to residents of Hampden, Hampshire, Franklin, and Berkshire counties, Massachusetts, and Enfield and Suffield, Connecticut. For graduates and undergraduates to pursue full-time study. Based on financial need, academic merit, and extracurricular activities. Must submit transcripts and fill out government FAFSA form.

425 awards annually. Renewable up to 4 years with reapplication. Contact Community Foundation for an application and your financial aid office for FAFSA. Notification is in June.

2718—COMMUNITY FOUNDATION OF WESTERN MASSACHUSETTS (Jessie M. Law Scholarships)

1500 Main Street
P.O. Box 15769
Springfield MA 01115
413/732-2858

AMOUNT: $600-$1,450
DEADLINE(S): APR 15
FIELD(S): All fields of study

Open to residents of Hamden County, Massachusetts, to pursue full-time undergraduate or graduate study. Based on financial need, academic merit, and extracurricular activities. Must submit transcripts and fill out government FAFSA form.

7 awards annually. Renewable with reapplication. Contact Community Foundation for an application and your financial aid office for FAFSA. Notification is in June.

2719—COMMUNITY FOUNDATION OF WESTERN MASSACHUSETTS (John P. & James F. Mahoney Memorial Scholarships)

1500 Main Street
P.O. Box 15769
Springfield MA 01115
413/732-2858

AMOUNT: $1,000
DEADLINE(S): APR 15
FIELD(S): All fields of study

Open to residents of Hampshire County, Massachusetts, who will be attending college or vocational school full-time at the graduate or undergraduate level. Based on financial need, academic merit, and extracurricular activities. Must submit transcripts, two letters of reference from teachers, and fill out government FAFSA form. One-page essay on personal ambition, future plans, and why you would be an appropriate recipient required.

14 awards annually. Renewable with reapplication. Contact Community Foundation for an application and your financial aid office for FAFSA. Notification is in June.

2720—COMMUNITY FOUNDATION OF WESTERN MASSACHUSETTS (Kimber Richter Family Scholarship)

1500 Main Street
P.O. Box 15769
Springfield MA 01115
413/732-2858

AMOUNT: $500

DEADLINE(S): APR 15
FIELD(S): All fields of study

Open to students of the Baha'i faith who attend or plan to attend college full-time at the undergraduate or graduate level. Must be resident of Western Massachusetts. Based on financial need, academic merit, and extracurricular activities. Must submit transcripts and fill out government FAFSA form.

1 award annually. Renewable with reapplication. Contact Community Foundation for an application and your financial aid office for FAFSA. Notification is in June.

2721—COMMUNITY FOUNDATION OF WESTERN MASSACHUSETTS (Kenneth B. & Adeline J. Graves Scholarships)

1500 Main Street
P.O. Box 15769
Springfield MA 01115
413/732-2858

AMOUNT: $2,500
DEADLINE(S): APR 15
FIELD(S): All fields of study

Open to residents of Granby, Massachusetts, to pursue full-time undergraduate or graduate study. Based on financial need, academic merit, and extracurricular activities. Must submit transcripts and fill out government FAFSA form.

10 awards annually. Renewable with reapplication. Contact Community Foundation for an application and your financial aid office for FAFSA. Notification is in June.

2722—COMMUNITY FOUNDATION OF WESTERN MASSACHUSETTS (Louis W. & Mary S. Doherty Scholarships)

1500 Main Street
P.O. Box 15769
Springfield MA 01115
413/732-2858

AMOUNT: $4,000
DEADLINE(S): APR 15
FIELD(S): All fields of study

Open to students from Hampden, Hampshire, and Franklin counties in Massachusetts who attend or plan to attend college full-time. Based on financial need, academic merit, and extracurricular activities. Must submit transcripts and fill out government FAFSA form.

8-10 awards annually. Renewable with reapplication. Contact Community Foundation for an application and your

financial aid office for FAFSA. Notification is in June.

2723—COMMUNITY FOUNDATION OF WESTERN MASSACHUSETTS (Latino Scholarships)

1500 Main Street
P.O. Box 15769
Springfield MA 01115
413/732-2858

AMOUNT: $250-$500
DEADLINE(S): APR 15
FIELD(S): All fields of study

Open to Latino residents of Holyoke, Massachusetts, who are graduating high school seniors who demonstrate academic promise and are community service oriented. Based on financial need, academic merit, and extracurricular activities. Must submit transcripts and fill out government FAFSA form.

5 awards annually. Renewable with reapplication. Contact Community Foundation for an application and your financial aid office for FAFSA. Notification is in June.

2724—COMMUNITY FOUNDATION OF WESTERN MASSACHUSETTS (Lucius H. Tarbell & Dorothy J. Tarbell Scholarships)

1500 Main Street
P.O. Box 15769
Springfield MA 01115
413/732-2858

AMOUNT: $600-$3,000
DEADLINE(S): APR 15
FIELD(S): All fields of study

Open to students of Western New England College in Massachusetts to pursue full-time undergraduate or graduate study. Based on financial need, academic merit, and extracurricular activities. Must submit transcripts and fill out government FAFSA form.

2 awards annually. Renewable with reapplication. Contact Community Foundation for an application and your financial aid office for FAFSA. Notification is in June.

2725—COMMUNITY FOUNDATION OF WESTERN MASSACHUSETTS (Lena A. Tucker Scholarships)

1500 Main Street
P.O. Box 15769
Springfield MA 01115
413/732-2858

AMOUNT: $200-$2,000
DEADLINE(S): APR 15

FIELD(S): All fields of study

Open to Springfield students from the High School of Commerce and Putnam Vocational-Technical High School in Massachusetts to pursue college education. Based on financial need, academic merit, and extracurricular activities. Must submit transcripts and fill out government FAFSA form.

25 awards annually. Renewable with reapplication. Contact Community Foundation for an application and your financial aid office for FAFSA. Notification is in June.

2726—COMMUNITY FOUNDATION OF WESTERN MASSACHUSETTS (Maury Ferriter Memorial Scholarship)

1500 Main Street
P.O. Box 15769
Springfield MA 01115
413/732-2858

AMOUNT: $500
DEADLINE(S): APR 15
FIELD(S): All fields of study

Open to full-time undergraduate or graduate students from Holyoke Catholic High School, Amherst College, or Georgetown Law School. Based on financial need, academic merit, and extracurricular activities. Must submit transcripts and fill out government FAFSA form.

1 award annually. Renewable with reapplication. Contact Community Foundation for an application and your financial aid office for FAFSA. Notification is in June.

2727—COMMUNITY FOUNDATION OF WESTERN MASSACHUSETTS (Margaret J. Hyland Scholarships)

1500 Main Street
P.O. Box 15769
Springfield MA 01115
413/732-2858

AMOUNT: $1,900
DEADLINE(S): APR 15
FIELD(S): All fields of study

Open to undergraduates and graduates pursuing full-time study at the University of Massachusetts who have been Holyoke residents for ten years or longer. Preference given to financially needy students of the Roman Catholic faith. Based on financial need, academic merit, and extracurricular activities. Must submit transcripts and fill out government FAFSA form.

33 awards annually. Renewable with reapplication. Contact Community Foundation for an application and your

financial aid office for FAFSA. Notification is in June.

2728—COMMUNITY FOUNDATION OF WESTERN MASSACHUSETTS (Mt. Sugarloaf Lodge Memorial Scholarships)

1500 Main Street
P.O. Box 15769
Springfield MA 01115
413/732-2858

AMOUNT: $350-$700
DEADLINE(S): APR 15
FIELD(S): All fields of study

Open to students from Frontier Regional High School in Massachusetts to pursue full-time undergraduate or graduate study. Based on financial need, academic merit, and extracurricular activities. Must submit transcripts and fill out government FAFSA form.

2-3 awards annually. Renewable with reapplication. Contact Community Foundation for an application and your financial aid office for FAFSA. Notification is in June.

2729—COMMUNITY FOUNDATION OF WESTERN MASSACHUSETTS (Permelia A. Butterfield Scholarship)

1500 Main Street
P.O. Box 15769
Springfield MA 01115
413/732-2858

AMOUNT: $2,000-$4,000
DEADLINE(S): APR 15
FIELD(S): All fields of study

Open to residents of Athol, Erving, New Salem, Wendell, Orange, Shutesbury, and Franklin counties, Massachusetts to pursue full-time undergraduate or graduate study. Preference goes to the support and education of orphan children (students with one or no living parent or those deprived of parental care). Based on financial need, academic merit, and extracurricular activities. Must submit transcripts and fill out government FAFSA form.

1 award annually. Renewable with reapplication. Contact Community Foundation for an application and your financial aid office for FAFSA. Notification is in June.

2730—COMMUNITY FOUNDATION OF WESTERN MASSACHUSETTS (Ruth L. Brocklebank Memorial Scholarships)

1500 Main Street
P.O. Box 15769
Springfield MA 01115
413/732-2858

AMOUNT: $2,000
DEADLINE(S): APR 15
FIELD(S): All fields of study

Open to African-American students from the Springfield Public School System high schools to attend college. Based on financial need, academic merit, and extracurricular activities. Must submit transcripts and fill out government FAFSA form.

7 awards annually. Renewable with reapplication. Contact Community Foundation for an application and your financial aid office for FAFSA. Notification is in June.

2731—COMMUNITY FOUNDATION OF WESTERN MASSACHUSETTS (Sarah & Abraham Milstein Scholarships)

1500 Main Street
P.O. Box 15769
Springfield MA 01115
413/732-2858

AMOUNT: $150
DEADLINE(S): APR 15
FIELD(S): All fields of study

Awarded annually to the valedictorian and salutatorian of Westfield High School in Massachusetts.

2 awards annually. Contact Community Foundation for details.

2732—COMMUNITY FOUNDATION OF WESTERN MASSACHUSETTS (Stanley Ciejek, Sr. Scholarships)

1500 Main Street
P.O. Box 15769
Springfield MA 01115
413/732-2858

AMOUNT: $1,000
DEADLINE(S): APR 15
FIELD(S): All fields of study

Open to residents of Hampden, Hampshire, and Franklin counties, Massachusetts to pursue full-time undergraduate or graduate study at a Massachusetts institute of higher education. Based on financial need, academic merit, and extracurricular activities. Must submit transcripts and fill out government FAFSA form.

4 awards annually. Renewable with reapplication. Contact Community Foundation for an application and your financial aid office for FAFSA. Notification is in June.

2733—COMMUNITY FOUNDATION OF WESTERN MASSACHUSETTS (Stuart D. Mackey Scholarship)

1500 Main Street
P.O. Box 15769
Springfield MA 01115
413/732-2858

AMOUNT: $500-$1,000
DEADLINE(S): APR 15
FIELD(S): All fields of study

Open to graduates of East Longmeadow High School in Massachusetts who have strong academic records to pursue full-time undergraduate or graduate study. Based on financial need, academic merit, and extracurricular activities. Must submit transcripts and fill out government FAFSA form.

1-2 awards annually. Renewable with reapplication. Contact Community Foundation for an application and your financial aid office for FAFSA. Notification is in June.

2734—COMMUNITY FOUNDATION OF WESTERN MASSACHUSETTS (Springfield Teachers' Club Scholarships)

1500 Main Street
P.O. Box 15769
Springfield MA 01115
413/732-2858

AMOUNT: Varies
DEADLINE(S): APR 15
FIELD(S): All fields of study

Open to graduates of Springfield high schools to obtain further education. Based on financial need, academic merit, and extracurricular activities. Must submit transcripts and fill out government FAFSA form.

Renewable with reapplication. Contact Community Foundation for an application and your financial aid office for FAFSA. Notification is in June.

2735—COMMUNITY FOUNDATION OF WESTERN MASSACHUSETTS (Wilcox-Ware Scholarships)

1500 Main Street
P.O. Box 15769
Springfield MA 01115

413/732-2858

AMOUNT: $300-$1,200
DEADLINE(S): APR 15
FIELD(S): All fields of study

Open to graduates of Mohawk Regional High School in Massachusetts who reside in Buckland, Shelburne, Colrain, or contiguous towns to pursue undergraduate or graduate study. Based on financial need, academic merit, and extracurricular activities. Must submit transcripts and fill out government FAFSA form.

22 awards annually. Renewable with reapplication. Contact Community Foundation for an application and your financial aid office for FAFSA. Notification is in June.

2736—CONGRESS OF MINNESOTA RESORTS (Scholarships)

HC 05 Box 374
Park Rapids MN 56470
888/761-4245

AMOUNT: $500
DEADLINE(S): MAR 15
FIELD(S): All fields of study

Open to undergraduate students who are dependents of three-year members of the Congress of Minnesota Resorts. Members should have a current good standing membership.

2 awards are given. Write to the above address for complete information.

2737—CONGRESSIONAL HISPANIC CAUCUS INSTITUTE, INC. (Summer Internship Program)

504 C Street, NE
Washington DC 20002
800/EXCEL-DC or 202/543-1771
E-mail: comments@chci.org
Internet: www.chci.org

AMOUNT: Stipend, round-trip transportation, & housing
DEADLINE(S): FEB
FIELD(S): All fields of study

Two-month stay in DC (June-Aug) to gain first-hand knowledge of how government works. College-bound high school seniors and currently enrolled undergraduates (except college seniors) are eligible. Must be Hispanic and have a minimum 3.0 GPA, excellent written and oral communication skills, active interest/participation in community affairs, a solid work ethic, and leadership potential. Must be US citizen/permanent resident or have student work visa.

30 students reflecting the diversity of the Hispanic community are selected each summer. See website or contact CHCI for an application.

2738—CONNECTICUT DEPT. OF HIGHER EDUCATION (State Scholastic Achievement Grant)

61 Woodland Street
Hartford CT 06015-2391
860/566-2618
TDD: 860/566-3910
Internet: http://www/lib.uconn.edu/ConnState/HigherEd/dhe.htm

AMOUNT: Up to $2,000
DEADLINE(S): FEB 15
FIELD(S): All fields of study

Open to Connecticut high school seniors and graduates who ranked in top 20% of their high school class or scored above 1,200 on SAT. For undergraduate study at a Connecticut college or at colleges in states that have reciprocity agreements with Connecticut. US citizenship or legal residency required.

3,000 awards per year. Write for complete information.

2739—CONNECTICUT DEPT. OF HIGHER EDUCATION (Student Financial Aid Programs)

61 Woodland Street
Hartford CT 06105-2391
860/566-2618
TDD: 860/566-3910

AMOUNT: Varies (programs differ)
DEADLINE(S): Varies (programs differ)
FIELD(S): All fields of study

Various state and federal programs providing financial aid to Connecticut students. Programs include tuition waivers for veterans and senior citizens, work study programs, loans, scholarships, and grants.

Most programs emphasize financial need. Write for brochure listing programs and application information.

2740—CONVERSE COUNTY 4-H FOUNDATION (Scholarships)

Extension Office
107 N. 5th
Douglas WY 82633
Written inquiry

AMOUNT: Varies
DEADLINE(S): JAN
FIELD(S): All fields of study

Available to former Converse County 4-H program members who have completed at least three years of active 4-H club work and are currently enrolled in an institution of higher education. Eligible students may apply as often as they wish. Priority consideration is given to first-time applicants. Scholarships are for use during the Spring semester.

Write to the Converse County Extension Office for an application.

2741—COOPER WOOD PRODUCTS FOUNDATION, INC.

P.O. Box 489
Rocky Mount VA 24151
Written inquiry

AMOUNT: Varies
DEADLINE(S): MAY 1
FIELD(S): All areas of study

Scholarships and loans for Virginia residents who intend to remain in Virginia after completion of education.

Write to Joyce Aldridge, Executive Secretary, at above address for application requirements.

2742—COUNCIL OF CITIZENS WITH LOW VISION INTERNATIONAL (CCLVI Telesensory Scholarship)

1400 N. Drake Road
Kalamazoo MI 49006
616/381-9566

AMOUNT: $1,000
DEADLINE(S): APR 15
FIELD(S): All fields of study

Open to undergraduate or graduate students who are vision impaired but NOT legally blind and who have a GPA of 3.0 or better.

4 awards per year. Write for complete information.

2743—COUNCIL ON INTERNATIONAL EDUCATIONAL EXCHANGE (Bailey Minority Student Scholarships)

205 E. 42nd Street
New York NY 10017-5706
212/822-2600
888/COUNCIL
FAX: 212/822-2699
E-mail: Info@ciee.org
Internet: http://www.ciee.org

AMOUNT: $500
DEADLINE(S): APR 1 (for summer, fall, and academic year programs); NOV 1 (for spring programs)

FIELD(S): Any field of study—international exchange program

For study, work, volunteer, and home-stay programs anywhere in the world except: Australia, Canada, Europe, Israel, Japan, Korea, New Zealand, Russia, Singapore, or the United States.

Send SASE for details.

2744—CRESTAR BANK (Trivia Contest)

Student Lending Division
P.O. Box 27172
Richmond VA 23261-7172
E-mail: crestar@student-loans.com
Internet: www.student-loans.com

AMOUNT: up to $1,000
DEADLINE(S): Varies
FIELD(S): All fields of study

Annual scholarship contest to promote student loan web page. Open to students enrolled at accredited US colleges and universities. Prizes awarded to students with the highest number of correctly answered questions.

Three $1,000 awards, three $500 awards, ten $100 book awards, ten $50 book awards, and 100 merchandise awards. Contest must be done online.

2745—CRYSTAL SPRINGS UPLANDS SCHOOL (Financial Aid)

400 Uplands Drive
Hillsborough CA 94010
415/342-4175
Internet: www.csus.com

AMOUNT: Varies
DEADLINE(S): Varies
FIELD(S): All fields of study

This independent school in San Mateo County, California, offers educational programs for grades 6-12. The school seeks students who are athletes, artists, performers, activists, thinkers, and comedians. Financial aid is available.

Contact school for details.

2746—CUBAN AMERICAN TEACHERS' ASSN. (Scholarships)

Dr. Albert C. Del Calvo
12037 Peoria Street
Sun Valley CA 91352
818/768-2669

AMOUNT: $300-$1,000
DEADLINE(S): APR 1
FIELD(S): All fields of study

Open to high school students of Cuban descent who live in Los Angeles County,

CA and plan to continue their education at the college level. Applicants should have at least a "B" average and speak acceptable Spanish.

30 annual awards. Applicants must demonstrate an interest in their cultural heritage. Write for complete information.

2747—CYMDEITHAS GYMREIG/PHILADELPHIA (Scholarships)

Daniel Williams, Ysg., Hen Dy Hapus
367 S. River Street
Wilkes-Barre PA 18702
Written inquiry only

AMOUNT: $500 to $1,500
DEADLINE(S): MAR 1
FIELD(S): All fields of study

Open to undergrads of Welsh descent who live within 150 miles of Philadelphia or plan to enroll in a college within that area. Must prove Welsh descent and be active in a Welsh organization or church or participate in Welsh activities.

Must be US citizen or legal resident. 5 to 6 awards per year. Renewable. Send SASE to Daniel E. Williams, Ysg., Cymdeithas Gymreig/Philadelphia (at the above address) for application and complete information.

2748—D. D. HACHAR CHARITABLE TRUST FUND (Undergraduate Scholarships)

Laredo National Bank, Trustee
P.O. Box 59
Laredo TX 78042-0059
956/723-1151, ext. 2670

AMOUNT: Varies
DEADLINE(S): APR (last Friday)
FIELD(S): All areas of study

Open to residents of Laredo (Webb County), Texas. Scholarships available for undergraduate study. College freshmen and sophomores must maintain minimum 2.0 GPA; juniors and seniors at least 2.5 GPA. Must be enrolled full-time.

Annual family income cannot exceed $60,000. US citizenship or legal residency required. Write for complete information.

2749—DANISH SISTERHOOD OF AMERICA (Scholarship Program)

8004 Jasmine Blvd.
Port Richey FL 34668-3224
Written inquiry only

AMOUNT: Varies
DEADLINE(S): Varies
FIELD(S): Continuing Education

Open to Danish Sisterhood of America members in good standing (and their children) who are attending approved schools. One-year or longer membership required. Awards are based on high academic achievement.

Write to National Vice President & Scholarship Chair Elizabeth K. Hunter at above address for complete information.

2750—DATATEL SCHOLARS FOUNDATION (Angelfire Scholarships)

4375 Fair Lakes Court
Fairfax VA 22033
703/968-9000
E-mail: scholars@datatel.com
Internet: www.datatel.com/scholars.htm

AMOUNT: $700-$2,000—based on tuition costs
DEADLINE(S): FEB 15
FIELD(S): All fields of study

Scholarships for part- or full-time students, both undergraduates and graduates. Must be: a military veteran of the Vietnam War; or a child or spouse of a military veteran of the Vietnam War; or a Vietnamese, Cambodian, or Laotian refugee who entered the United States between 1964 and 1975. Nationalization is not a requirement. For use at a higher learning institution selected from one of Datatel's more than 400 client sites.

Apply through the institution's Financial Aid or Scholarship office, which may nominate up to 2 students. Or contact organization for details.

2751—DATATEL SCHOLARS FOUNDATION (Datatel Scholarships)

4375 Fair Lakes Court
Fairfax VA 22033
703/968-9000
E-mail: scholars@datatel.com
Internet: www.datatel.com/scholars.htm

AMOUNT: $700-$2,000—based on tuition costs
DEADLINE(S): FEB 15
FIELD(S): All fields of study

Scholarships for part- or full-time students, both undergraduates and graduates. For use at a higher learning institution selected from one of Datatel's more than 400 client sites.

Apply through the institution's Financial Aid or Scholarship office, which may nominate up to 2 students. Or contact organization for details.

2752—DAUGHTERS OF PENELOPE (Undergraduate Scholarships)

1909 Q Street NW, Suite 500
Washington DC 20009
202/234-9741
FAX: 202/483-6983

AMOUNT: $500, $1,000, and $1,500
DEADLINE(S): JUN 20
FIELD(S): All fields of study

Open to female undergraduates of Greek descent who are members of Daughters of Penelope or Maids of Athena or the daughter of a member of Daughters of Penelope or Order of AHEPA. Academic performance and need are main considerations.

Renewable. For membership information or an application, write to the above address.

2753—DAUGHTERS OF THE AMERICAN REVOLUTION (American Indians Scholarship)

Mrs. Lyle A. Ross
3738 South Mission Drive
Lake Havasu City AZ 86406-4250
Written inquiry

AMOUNT: $500
DEADLINE(S): JUL 1; NOV 1
FIELD(S): All fields of study

Open to Native Americans, both youth and adults, striving to get an education. Funds help students of any tribe in any state based on need, academic achievement, and ambition.

Send SASE to above address for complete information.

2754—DAUGHTERS OF THE AMERICAN REVOLUTION (DAR Schools' Scholarships)

1776 D Street NW
Washington DC 20006-5392
202/628-1776
Internet: www.dar.org

AMOUNT: $1,000-$2,000
DEADLINE(S): Varies
FIELD(S): All fields of study

For graduates of Kate Duncan Smith (in AL) or Tamassee (in SC) DAR Schools. Applications are through the respective school scholarship committees; awards are made in June. Includes Idamae Cox Otis Scholarship, Longman-Harris Scholarship, and Mildred Louise Brackney Scholarship.

Renewable. Contact individual schools for more information. Send self-addressed, stamped envelope to DAR for info about their other scholarships (DAR affiliation not required).

2755—DAUGHTERS OF THE CINCINNATI (Scholarship Program)

122 East 58th Street
New York NY 10022
212/319-6915

AMOUNT: Varies
DEADLINE(S): MAR 15
FIELD(S): All fields of study

Open to high school seniors who are daughters of commissioned officers (active, retired, or deceased) in the US Army, Navy, Air Force, Marine Corps, or Coast Guard. For undergraduate study at any accredited four-year institution.

Awards based on need and merit. Include parent's rank and branch of service when writing for application or further information.

2756—DAUGHTERS OF UNION VETERANS OF THE CIVIL WAR (Grand Army of the Republic Living Memorial Scholarship)

503 South Walnut
Springfield IL 62704
Written inquiry, postmarked by FEB 1 (MUST include SASE)

AMOUNT: $200
DEADLINE(S): APR 30
FIELD(S): All fields of study

Open to LINEAL descendants of a union veteran of the Civil War. Must be a junior or senior in college, in good scholastic standing, of good moral character, and have a firm belief in the US form of government.

For complete information send us a self-addressed, stamped envelope and PROOF of direct lineage to a Civil War union veteran (military record). 3 to 4 awards per year.

2757—DAVID WASSERMAN SCHOLARSHIP FUND INC. (Award Program)

Adirondack Center
4722 State Hwy. 30
Amsterdam NY 12010
Written inquiry

AMOUNT: $300 per year
DEADLINE(S): APR 15
FIELD(S): All fields of study

Open to bona fide residents of Montgomery County, NY who are pursuing an undergraduate degree and are US citizens.

20-25 awards per year. Renewable. Write for information and applications.

2758—DAVIS-ROBERTS SCHOLARSHIP FUND INC. (Scholarships to DeMolays & Job's Daughters)

P.O. Box 1974
Cheyenne WY 82003
307/632-0491

AMOUNT: $350
DEADLINE(S): JUN 15
FIELD(S): All fields of study

Open to Wyoming residents who are or have been a DeMolay or a Job's Daughter in the state of Wyoming. Scholarships for full-time undergraduate study. Financial need is a consideration. US citizenship required.

12-14 awards annually. Renewable. Write for complete information.

2759—DAYTON-MONTGOMERY COUNTY SCHOLARSHIP PROGRAM

348 W. First Street
Dayton OH 45402
937/262-5338

AMOUNT: $300-$1,500
DEADLINE(S): APR 15
FIELD(S): All fields of study

Open to students who are Dayton and Montgomery county (OH) residents and graduating from a participating high school. Financial need must exiStreet

Write to the above address for complete information.

2760—DELLA M. BAILEY INDIAN SCHOLARSHIP TRUST

c/o First National Bank
P.O. Box 1007
Fairfield IA 52556
515/472-4121

AMOUNT: Varies
DEADLINE(S): Ongoing
FIELD(S): All fields of study

Scholarships for students of Native-American parentage.

Write to Melva Dahl at above address for application.

2761—DELTA GAMMA FOUNDATION

3250 Riverside Drive
P.O. Box 21397
Columbus OH 43221-0397
614/481-8169

AMOUNT: $1,000-$2,500
DEADLINE(S): MAR 1; APR 1
FIELD(S): All fields of study

Scholarships, fellowships, and loans open to Delta Gamma members and their dependents. Awards may be used for undergraduate or graduate study.

Approx 60 awards per year. Contact the Grants & Loans chairman, address above, for complete information.

2762—DELTA PHI EPSILON EDUCATIONAL FOUNDATION

734 West Port Plaza, Suite 271
Street Louis MO 63146
314/275-2626
FAX: 314/275-2655
E-mail: ealper@conentric.net
Internet: www.dphie.org

AMOUNT: Varies
DEADLINE(S): APR 1 (undergrads); APR 15 (grads)
FIELD(S): All fields of study

Scholarships for women students who are members or daughters or granddaughters of members of Delta Phi Epsilon sorority.

Applications available in January. Write or e-mail Ellen Alper, Executive Director, at above address.

2763—DeMOLAY FOUNDATION INC. (Scholarships)

10200 N. Executive Hills Blvd.
Kansas City MO 64153
816/891-8333
FAX: 816/891-9062
Internet: www.demolay.org

AMOUNT: $1,500
DEADLINE(S): APR 1
FIELD(S): Dental or Medical fields

For undergraduate freshmen or sophomores with a 2.0 GPA or better. DeMolay membership is required. Considerations are leadership, academic achievement, and goals.

3 grants per year. Write for complete information.

2764—DENISON UNIVERSITY (Financial Aid)

Nancy Hoover, Director
Office of Financial Aid
Granville OH 43023
614/587-6279
800/DENISON
Internet: www.denison.edu

AMOUNT: Varies
DEADLINE(S): Varies
FIELD(S): All fields of study

Denison University offers opportunities for students to receive financial assistance, including grants and loans, from various sources in addition to merit-based scholarships.

Renewable for four years after re-evaluation. See website and/or contact Financial Aid Office for further information.

2765—DENISON UNIVERSITY (Honors Program)

Prof. Anthony J. Lisska
Honors Program
Gilpatrick House, Box M
Granville OH 43023
614/587-6573
Internet: www.denison.edu

AMOUNT: Varies
DEADLINE(S): Varies
FIELD(S): All fields of study

Denison University offers an Honors Program for high-performing incoming freshmen and transfer students. Applicants will be most competitive if they are in the top 10 of graduating class, have an ACT of 28 or higher, and a combined SAT of 1230. After their first year, students with a 3.4 GPA not already enrolled in the program will receive invitations to participate. Certain scholarships are available only to students in the Honors Program.

See website for details or send letter of inquiry to Prof. Lisska for further information.

2766—DENISON UNIVERSITY (Merit-Based Scholarships)

Admissions Office
Granville OH 43023
800/DENISON
E-mail: admissions@denison.edu
Internet: www.denison.edu

AMOUNT: Varies
DEADLINE(S): Varies
FIELD(S): All fields of study

Denison University offers more than 200 academic scholarships for first-year students. Some are related to specific fields of study, some are for National Merit Scholars, some are tied to certain high schools, and some are for minority students. All require excellence in academic achievement, and some are based on personal merit combined with financial need. See web page under "Scholarships" for liStreet

Renewable for four years if stipulated GPA is maintained. Contact Admissions Office for information on merit-based scholarships.

2767—DEPARTMENT OF VETERANS AFFAIRS (Survivors and Dependents Educational Assistance Program)

810 Vermont Ave. NW
Washington DC 20420
800/827-1000

AMOUNT: $404 per month for full-time study
DEADLINE(S): Varies
FIELD(S): All fields of study

Educational support for children (aged 18-26) and spouses/widows of veterans who are 100% disabled or deceased due to military service or are classified currently as prisoner of war or missing in action. Training in approved institution.

Spouses are eligible up to 10 years after determination of eligibility. Contact the nearest VA office for complete information.

2768—DESCENDANTS OF THE SIGNERS OF THE DECLARATION OF INDEPENDENCE (Scholarship Grant)

609 Irving Ave.
Deale MD 20751
Written inquiry only

AMOUNT: Average $1,100
DEADLINE(S): MAR 15
FIELD(S): All areas of study

Undergrad and grad awards for students who are DSDI members (proof of direct descent of signer of Declaration of Independence necessary, STUDENT MUST BE A MEMBER OF DSDI before he/she can apply). Write to Scholarship Chairman at the above address for membership. Must be full-time student accepted or enrolled in a recognized US four-year college or university.

Applicants for membership must provide proof of direct, lineal descendancy from a Signer. Enclose stamped, self-addressed envelope.

2769—DEXTER G. JOHNSON EDUCATIONAL AND BENEVOLENT TRUST (Student Loans)

P.O. Box 26663
Oklahoma City OK 73125
Written inquiry

AMOUNT: Varies
DEADLINE(S): Ongoing
FIELD(S): All fields of study

Educational loans for financially needy residents of Oklahoma for study at Oklahoma high schools, vocational schools, and Oklahoma State University, Oklahoma City University, or the University of Oklahoma. Preference given to physically disabled students.

Write to Betty Crews at above address for application details.

2770—DISABLED AMERICAN VETERANS AUXILIARY (DAVA Student Loans)

3725 Alexandria Pike
Cold Spring KY 41076
606/441-7300

AMOUNT: Up to $1,000 for 4 years
DEADLINE(S): APR 25
FIELD(S): All fields of study

Open to citizens of US who have been accepted by an institution of higher education and are children whose living mother is a life member of DAV Auxiliary or (if mother is deceased) father is a life member of at least 1 year. Must be a full-time student with a minimum of 12 credit hours and maintain at least a 2.0 GPA.

40-42 loans per year. Renewable. Write for complete information.

2771—DISCOVER CARD TRIBUTE AWARD (Scholarship)

American Association of
School Administrators
P.O. Box 9338
Arlington VA 22219
703/875-0708

AMOUNT: $1,000-$20,000
DEADLINE(S): JAN
FIELD(S): Any field of study

Open to high school juniors whose freshman and sophomore GPA was at least 2.75. This scholarship can be used for any type of accredited training, licensing, or certification program or for any accredited degree program. Applicants must have achievement in 4 of these 5 areas: Special talent, leadership, obstacles overcome, community service, unique endeavors.

Total of 9 scholarships available in each of the 50 states: 3 Gold—$2,500 each; 3 Silver—$1,500 each; 3 Bronze—$1,000 each. The State Gold Tribute Award recipients are automatically entered to compete for 9 national scholarships: state scholarships, 9 national scholarships: 3 Gold—$20,000; 3 Silver—$15,000; 3 Bronze—$10,000. Write to Shirley Keller for complete information.

2772—DISTRICT OF COLUMBIA (State Student Incentive Grant Program)

2100 M. L. King Jr. Ave. SE
Suite 401
Washington DC 20020
202/727-3688
FAX: 202/727-2739
Internet: www.Ci.Washington.DC.US

AMOUNT: Varies
DEADLINE(S): JUN 27
FIELD(S): All undergrad majors and 1st yr. of M.A. program. NOT for Law & Medicine

Open to US citizens or legal residents who have lived in DC for at least 15 consecutive months, have at least a 2.0 GPA, can demonstrate financial need, and are enrolled in an eligible US institution.

Renewable scholarships for undergraduate study. Must have high school diploma or equivalent. Write for complete information.

2773—DIXIE YARNS FOUNDATION, INC. (George West Scholarship Fund)

P.O. Box 751
Chattanooga TN 37401
423/493-7267

AMOUNT: Varies
DEADLINE(S): FEB 1
FIELD(S): All fields of study

Open only to children of employees of Dixie Yarns, Inc. for undergraduate study.

Write to the above address for complete information.

2774—DODD & DOROTHY L. BRYAN FOUNDATION (Interest-Free Loans)

P.O. Box 6287
4 N. Main, Suite 407
Sheridan WY 82801
307/672-9102

AMOUNT: $4,000
DEADLINE(S): JUL 15
FIELD(S): All fields of study

These "interest free" loans are available to undergraduate, graduate, and post-graduate students who live in one of these six counties: Sheridan, WY, Johnson, WY, Campbell, WY, Rosebud, MT, Big Horn, MT, or Powder River, MT. Applicants must demonstrate financial need.

Write to the above address for complete information.

2775—DOG WRITERS' EDUCATIONAL TRUST (Scholarships)

Mary Ellen Tarman
P.O. Box E
Hummelstown PA 17036-0199
Written inquiries only

AMOUNT: Varies
DEADLINE(S): DEC 31
FIELD(S): All fields of study

For college students who have participated in organized activities with dogs or whose parents or other close relatives have done so.

Scholarships support undergraduate or graduate study. Send SASE to above location for complete information.

2776—DOLPHIN SCHOLARSHIP FOUNDATION (Scholarships)

1683 Dillingham Blvd.
Norfolk Naval Station
Norfolk VA 23511
757/451-3660
FAX: 757/489-8578

AMOUNT: $2,500/year
DEADLINE(S): APR 15
FIELD(S): All fields of study

For high school or college dependent children of current or former members of the US Navy Submarine Force who qualified in submarines and served in the force for at least 5 years or for Navy members who served at least 6 years in direct support of the Submarine Force or died in active duty.

25 awards/year. For students seeking B.A. or B.S. degree. Financial need is a consideration. Renewable for 4 years. Send SASE (business size) for complete information.

2777—DRY CREEK NEIGHBORS CLUB (Scholarships)

Contact your senior advisor

AMOUNT: Varies
DEADLINE(S): APR 15
FIELD(S): All fields of study

Scholarships are awarded to graduating seniors from Healdsburg and Geyserville High Schools in California.

3 awards annually. Contact your high school for an application.

2778—DURACELL/NATIONAL SCIENCE TEACHERS ASSOCIATION (Scholarship Competition)

1840 Wilson Blvd.
Arlington VA 22201-3000
888/255-4242
E-mail: duracell@nsta.org

AMOUNT: $500 to $20,000 in Savings Bonds
DEADLINE(S): NOV 13
FIELD(S): All fields of study

Design competition open to all US students in grades 6 through 12 who create and build an original working device powered by one or more Duracell batteries. 100 awards given. The teachers of the six top winners will each receive $2,000 in gift certificates for computers and accessories. All entrants will receive a gift and a certificate.

Official entry forms are available from science teachers or by writing to NSTA at the address above. Write for complete information. For technical questions, e-mail Gordon Isleib at DFZM70A@prodigy.com OR Mark Yeary at: mbyeary@gte.net

2779—EARTHWATCH STUDENT CHALLENGE AWARDS (High School Student Research Expeditions)

P.O. Box 9104
Watertown MA 02272-9104
800/776-0188 or 617/926-8200
FAX: 617/926-8532
E-mail: drobbins@earthwatch.org
Internet: www.earthwatch.org/

AMOUNT: Travel/Living expenses
DEADLINE(S): NOV 12
FIELD(S): All fields of study

Awards for high school sophomores, juniors, and seniors, especially those gifted in the arts and humanities. Awardees will have an intimate look at the world of science and state-of-the-art technology. Teams of 6 to 8 students from across the US will spend 2 to 3 weeks at sites in North or Central America. Must be at least age 16 by June 15 during year of program.

Students must be nominated by a teacher in their school. Write or visit website for further information. Interested students may submit the name and school address of a high school teacher whom they would like to receive a brochure.

2780—EAST LONGMEADOW SCHOLARSHIP FOUNDATION FUND (Scholarships)

Box 66
East Longmeadow MA 01028
413/732-2858

AMOUNT: Varies
DEADLINE(S): APR 15
FIELD(S): All fields of study

Open to residents of East Longmeadow, Massachusetts, to pursue undergraduate or graduate study.

Contact Scholarship Fund at above address for an application or the Community Foundation of Western Massachusetts at above phone number for details.

2781—EASTER SEAL SOCIETY OF IOWA, INC. (James L. & Lavon Madden Mallory Annual Disability Scholarship Program)

P.O. Box 4002
Des Moines IA 50333-4002
515/289-1933

AMOUNT: $1,000
DEADLINE(S): APR 15
FIELD(S): All fields of study

Open ONLY to Iowa residents with a permanent disability who are graduating high school seniors. Award supports undergraduate study at a recognized college or university.

Write for complete information.

2782—EASTERN ORTHODOX COMMITTEE ON SCOUTING (Scholarship)

862 Guy Lombardo Ave.
Freeport NY 11520
516/868-4050
FAX: 516/868-4052

AMOUNT: $1,000 & $500
DEADLINE(S): APR 15
FIELD(S): All fields of study

Open to Boy or Girl Scouts who have received an Eagle or Gold Award and are seniors in high school. Students must be of the Eastern Orthodox religion and be US citizens and studying in the US.

Write to the above address for complete information.

2783—EBELL OF LOS ANGELES SCHOLARSHIP PROGRAM

743 S. Lucerne Blvd.
Los Angeles CA 90005-3707
213/931-1277

AMOUNT: $2,000 ($200/month for 10 months)

DEADLINE(S): MAY 1

FIELD(S): All fields of study

For Los Angeles County residents who are undergraduate sophomores, juniors, or seniors enrolled in a Los Angeles County college or university. Must be a US citizen. GPA of 3.25 must be maintained for renewal.

50-60 awards per year. Financial need is a consideration. Students must contact Ebell of Los Angeles for an application.

2784—EBERHARDT I. FOR SCHOLARSHIP FOUNDATION

One Mellon Bank Center
Pittsburgh PA 15230-9897
Written inquiries

AMOUNT: Varies

DEADLINE(S): MAY 15

FIELD(S): All fields of study

Scholarships for residents of Pennsylvania who attend colleges and universities in Pennsylvania.

Contact college financial aid officer for current application guidelines.

2785—ECKMANN FOUNDATION

12730 Carmel Country Road
Suite 120
San Diego CA 92130
Written inquiry

AMOUNT: Varies

DEADLINE(S): MAY 1

FIELD(S): All fields of study

Scholarships for individuals pursuing a Christian education and are residents of California.

Write to Helen L. Eckmann, Director, at above address.

2786—EDUCATION ASSISTANCE CORPORATION (Federal Family Education Loan Program)

115 First Ave., SW
Aberdeen SD 57401
605/225-6423

AMOUNT: Varies

DEADLINE(S): None

FIELD(S): All fields of study

Loans for South Dakota residents enrolled in eligible schools on at least a half-time basis. Must be a US citizen or national or eligible non-resident (see federal guidelines).

Renewable. Write for an application and complete information.

2787—EDUCATIONAL CREDIT MANAGEMENT CORPORATION (Loan Programs for Virginia Students)

411 E. Franklin Street, Suite 300
Richmond VA 23219-2243
804/644-6400 or 888/775-ECMC
FAX: 804/344-6743
E-mail: mellyson@ecmc.org

AMOUNT: Varies

DEADLINE(S): None

FIELD(S): All fields of study

Various loan programs open to students enrolled in approved institutions. Eligibility governed by ECMC and federal regulations.

Contact college financial aid office or write to address above for complete information.

2788—EDUCATIONAL COMMUNICATIONS SCHOLARSHIP FOUNDATION (College Scholarship Award)

721 McKinley Road
P.O. Box 5002
Lake Forest IL 60045-5002
847/295-6650 or 847/295-3072
E-mail: scholars@ecsf.org

AMOUNT: $1,000

DEADLINE(S): MAY 31

FIELD(S): All fields of study

The Foundation will award 50 scholarships of $1,000 each. College students with a grade point average of B+ or better who are US citizens may compete.

Requests for applications must be made by March 15. Write to the above address for complete information.

2789—EDUCATIONAL COMMUNICATIONS SCHOLARSHIP FOUNDATION (High School Scholarship Award)

721 N. McKinley Road
P.O. Box 5012
Lake Forest IL 60045-5012
847/295-6650
FAX: 847/295-3972
E-mail: scholars@ecsf.org

AMOUNT: $1,000

DEADLINE(S): MAR 15 (Request application by then. Deadline is JUN 1.)

FIELD(S): All fields of study

Open to current high school students who are US citizens and have taken the SAT or ACT examination. Awards based on GPA, achievement test scores, leadership, work experience, essay, and financial need.

200 scholarships per year. For complete information, write, fax, or e-mail above location. Include name, home address, current year in high school, and approximate grade point average.

2790—EDWARDS SCHOLARSHIP FUND (Undergraduate and Graduate Scholarships)

10 Post Office Square So., Suite 1230
Boston MA 02109
617/426-4434

AMOUNT: $250 to $5,000

DEADLINE(S): MAR 1

FIELD(S): All fields of study

Open ONLY to Boston residents under age 25 who can demonstrate financial need, scholastic ability, and good character. For undergraduate or graduate study but undergrads receive preference. Family home must be within Boston city limits.

Applicants must have lived in Boston from at least the beginning of their junior year in high school. Metropolitan Boston is NOT included.

2791—EL PASO COMMUNITY FOUNDATION (Scholarships)

201 East Main, Suite 1616
El Paso TX 79901
915/533-4020
FAX: 915/532-0716

AMOUNT: Varies

DEADLINE(S): Varies

FIELD(S): All fields of study

Various scholarships for residents of El Paso County, Texas.

Contact organization for details.

2792—ELIE WIESEL FOUNDATION FOR HUMANITY (Prize in Ethics Essay Contest)

450 Lexington Ave., Suite 1920
New York NY 10017
212/450-9295
FAX: 212/450-8299

AMOUNT: $500-$5,000

DEADLINE(S): JAN 23

FIELD(S): All fields of study

Essay contest open to full-time students in their junior or senior year at accredited four-year colleges or universities in the United States. Themes could be such ideas as ethics based on a personal experience, "Why are we here?" or "How are we to meet our ethical obligations?"

5 annual prizes. Send SASE for complete information by Dec. 19.

2793—ELMER O. AND IDA PRESTON EDUCATIONAL TRUST (Scholarships)

801 Grand Ave., Suite 3700
Des Moines IA 50309
515/243-4191

AMOUNT: $500-$700
DEADLINE(S): Varies
FIELD(S): All fields of study

Scholarships for male students, undergraduates and graduates, who are members of a Protestant church, are residents of Iowa, and attending any college in the state of Iowa.

Renewable. 35 awards. Contact organization for details.

2794—EMANUEL STERNBERGER EDUCATIONAL FUND (Interest-Free Loan Program)

P.O. Box 1735
Greensboro NC 27402
910/275-6316

AMOUNT: $1,000 (1st year) & $2,000 (subsequent years if funds are available); maximum $5,000
DEADLINE(S): MAR 31
FIELD(S): All fields of study

Open to North Carolina residents who are entering their junior or senior year of college or are graduate students. Considerations include grades, economic situation, references, and credit rating.

Personal interview is required. Can be used at any college or university. Write for complete information.

2795—ENGLISH-SPEAKING UNION (Lucy Dalbiac Luard Scholarship)

16 E. 69th Street
New York NY 10021
212/879-6800

AMOUNT: Full tuition and expenses
DEADLINE(S): NOV
FIELD(S): All fields of study

Open to students attending a United Negro College or Howard or Hampton University. Full scholarship to spend undergraduate junior year at a university in England. US citizen.

Application must be made through student's college or university. Information and applications are sent each fall to the Academic Dean/VP for Academic Affairs at participating schools.

2796—EPILEPSY FOUNDATION (Camperships)

4351 Garden City Drive
Landover MD 20785-2267
800/EFA-1000 or 301/459-3700
FAX: 301/577-4941
E-mail: info@efa.org

AMOUNT: $250 (for cost of camp)
DEADLINE(S): Varies
FIELD(S): All fields of study

A program for children with epilepsy to attend summer camp for a week. Helps build self-esteem, independence, and a network of friends by letting kids with seizures meet other kids with the same condition.

Contact Summer Camperships Coordinator for details.

2797—ETHEL AND EMERY FAST SCHOLARSHIP FOUNDATION, INC.

12620 Rolling Road
Potomac MD 20854
301/762-1102

AMOUNT: Varies
DEADLINE(S): Ongoing
FIELD(S): All fields of study

Scholarships for graduate and undergraduate Native Americans who have successfully completed one year of postsecondary studies and are full-time students.

Write or phone above location for application procedures.

2798—ETHEL N. BOWEN FOUNDATION (Scholarships)

P.O. Box 1559
Bluefield WV 24701-1559
304/325-8181

AMOUNT: Varies
DEADLINE(S): APR 30
FIELD(S): All fields of study

Undergraduate and occasional graduate scholarships open to residents of southern West Virginia and southwest Virginia.

20-25 awards per year. Send self-addressed, stamped envelope for complete information.

2799—ETHICAL CULTURE FIELDSTON SCHOOL (Financial Aid and Loans)

33 Central Park West
New York NY 10023
212/874-5205
FAX: 212/501-8973

Internet: www.EDFS.ORG
AMOUNT: Varies
DEADLINE(S): Varies
FIELD(S): All fields of study

Need-based scholarships and low-interest loans available to attend this independent, coeducational school which includes preschool through high school. Must submit documentation indicating financial need.

Must apply at time of admission. Contact school for details.

2800—EVEREG-FENESSE MESROBIAN-ROUPINIAN EDUCATIONAL SOCIETY, INC.

4140 Tanglewood Court
Bloomfield Hills MI 48301
Written inquiry

AMOUNT: Varies
DEADLINE(S): DEC 15
FIELD(S): All fields of study

Scholarships for students attending Armenian day schools, and for full-time undergraduate or graduate students of Armenian descent attending colleges and universities. Participating chapters of the society are New York/New Jersey, California, and Detroit, Michigan.

Applications available from designated local chapter representatives.

2801—EVERGREEN STATE COLLEGE (Scholarships)

Dean of Enrollment Services
Olympia WA 98505
206/866-6000, ext. 6310

AMOUNT: Varies
DEADLINE(S): FEB 1
FIELD(S): All fields of study

Variety of scholarships open to new or currently enrolled students at Evergreen State College, Olympia, Washington. Some awards are limited to specific ethnic groups; others require demonstration of financial need. All require enrollment at Evergreen.

Write to Evergreen College to request a scholarship brochure.

2802—FEDERAL EMPLOYEE EDUCATION AND ASSISTANCE FUND (OK Scholarship Fund)

8441 W. Bowles Ave., Suite 200
Littleton CO 80123-9501
303/933-7580
FAX: 303/933-7587

E-mail: feeahq@aol.com
Internet: www.feea.org
AMOUNT: Full tuition
DEADLINE(S): None
FIELD(S): All fields of study

FEEA will provide a full college education to all the children who lost a parent in the Oklahoma City Bombing. By the time the program ends in 2018, over 200 children will have received a complete college education, including the six preschoolers from the daycare center who survived the bombing.

Contact FEEA for details.

2803—FEDERAL EMPLOYEE EDUCATION AND ASSISTANCE FUND (FEEA Scholarship Program)

8441 W. Bowles Ave., Suite 200
Littleton CO 80123-9501
303/933-7580
FAX 303/933-7587
E-mail: feeahq@aol.com
Internet: www.feea.org
AMOUNT: $300-$1,500
DEADLINE(S): MAY 8
FIELD(S): All fields of study

Open to current civilian federal and postal employees (with at least 3 yrs. service) and dependent family members enrolled or planning to enroll in a 2-year, 4-year, or graduate-degree program. Must have minimum 3.0 GPA, and an essay is required. Involvement in extracurricular/community activities is considered.

See website or send a business-sized, self-addressed, stamped envelope for an application between January and May. Notification mailed by August 31Street

2804—FEDERAL EMPLOYEE EDUCATION AND ASSISTANCE FUND (NARFE Scholarship Program)

8441 W. Bowles Ave., Suite 200
Littleton CO 80123-9501
800/627-3394 or 303/933-7580
FAX: 303/933-7587
E-mail: feeahq@aol.com
Internet: www.feea.org
AMOUNT: Varies
DEADLINE(S): Varies
FIELD(S): All fields of study

FEEA, along with the National Association of the Retired Federal Employees (NARFE), offers scholarships to the children and grandchildren of federal retirees who are NARFE members.

Send a self-addressed, stamped envelope to FEEA for an application, or contact NARFE at above 800 number.

2805—FEDERATION OF JEWISH AGENCIES OF GREATER PHILADELPHIA (Foreman Fleisher Fund)

226 S. 16th Street, 13th Fl.
Philadelphia PA 19102
215/585-5491
AMOUNT: Varies
DEADLINE(S): Ongoing
FIELD(S): All fields of study

Scholarships for Jewish women who seek professional education.

Contact Frances W. Freedman at above address for more information.

2806—FEILD CO-OPERATIVE ASSOCIATION (Mississippi Resident Loans)

P.O. Box 5054
Jackson MS 39296-5054
601/939-9295
AMOUNT: $2,000 per calendar year (12 months)
DEADLINE(S): MAY (apply at any time)
FIELD(S): All fields of study

Open ONLY to Mississippi residents who are undergraduate juniors and seniors and graduate students with satisfactory academic standing. Demonstrate evidence of need and promise of financial responsibility. US citizenship or legal residency required.

These are loans—NOT scholarships. Loans are renewable. Write for complete information.

2807—FERN BROWN MEMORIAL FUND

P.O. Box 1
Tulsa OK 74193
918/586-5594
AMOUNT: Varies
DEADLINE(S): Ongoing
FIELD(S): All fields of study

Scholarships for residents of Oklahoma.
Send SASE to Mike Bartel, V.P., Liberty Bank & Trust Co. of Tulsa, NA, at above address.

2808—FIRST CATHOLIC SLOVAK LADIES ASSOCIATION (College Scholarships)

24950 Chagrin Blvd.
Beachwood OH 44122-5634

800/464-4642 or 216/464-8015
FAX: 216/464-8717
AMOUNT: $1,000
DEADLINE(S): MAR 1
FIELD(S): All fields of study

For full-time undergraduate or graduate students who have been members of FCSLA for at least three years and who will attend an accredited institution in the US or Canada. Must submit transcripts, autobiographical statement, and wallet-size photo with application. Award must be used for tuition. Financial need is NOT a factor.

80 awards annually. Not renewable, though undergraduate recipients may reapply as graduate students. Contact the Receptionist at above address for an application.

2809—FIRST CATHOLIC SLOVAK LADIES ASSOCIATION (High School Scholarships)

24950 Chagrin Blvd.
Beachwood OH 44122-5634
800/464-4642 or 216/464-8015
FAX: 216/464-8717
AMOUNT: $500
DEADLINE(S): MAR 1
FIELD(S): All fields of study

Must have been a member of FCSLA for at least three years and be planning on attending a private or Catholic accredited high school in the US or Canada. With application, must submit transcripts, wallet-sized photo, and a written report (250 words) on "What this high school scholarship will do for me." Award must be used for tuition. Financial need is NOT a factor.

16 awards annually. Not renewable, though recipients may reapply as undergraduate and graduate students. Contact the Receptionist at above address for an application.

2810—FIRST CAVALRY DIVISION ASSOCIATION (Scholarships)

302 N. Main
Copperas Cove TX 76522
Written inquiry
AMOUNT: $600 per year up to 4 years max
DEADLINE(S): None specified
FIELD(S): All fields of study

Awards to children of soldiers who died or were declared 100% disabled from injuries while serving with the 1st Cavalry Division during and since the Vietnam War or during Desert Storm.

If death occurred after 3/1/80 deceased parent must have been an Association member and serving with the division at the time of death. Send self-addressed stamped envelope for complete information.

2811—FIRST CITIZENS FOUNDATION, INC.

P.O. Box 1377
Smithfield NC 27577-1377
Written inquiry

AMOUNT: Varies
DEADLINE(S): Varies
FIELD(S): All fields of study

Scholarships to students in North Carolina in financial distress for educational purposes in accredited trade schools, colleges, and universities.

Contact above location for deadline information and application.

2812—FIRST COMMERCIAL BANK (Regions/National Advisory Board Scholarship)

400 West Capitol
Little Rock AR 72201
501/371-7012
FAX: 501/371-6525

AMOUNT: Varies
DEADLINE(S): Varies
FIELD(S): All fields of study

Scholarship winners will be chosen from a list of eligible Arkansas high school seniors who are National Merit semi-finalists, meet the academic credentials, and intend on attending an Arkansas college or university.

This list will be provided to us by the National Merit Scholarship Corporation, and we will NO LONGER ACCEPT APPLICATIONS DIRECTLY FROM STUDENTS.

2813—FIRST UNITED METHODIST CHURCH STUDENT LOAN PROGRAM (Stephen McCready Fund)

c/o First United Methodist Church
1126 E. Silver Springs Blvd.
Ocala FL 34470

AMOUNT: Varies
DEADLINE(S): MAY 1
FIELD(S): All areas of study

College loans available to undergraduate students. Preference given to theological students or those who intend to enter into full-time religious work. Preference

also given to residents of Marion County, Florida.

20 to 25 annual loans. Must reapply each year.

2814—FLEET RESERVE ASSOCIATION (Scholarships and Awards)

FRA Scholarship Administrator
125 N. West Street
Alexandria VA 22314
708/683-1400 or 800/424-1120

AMOUNT: Approximately $500
DEADLINE(S): APR 15
FIELD(S): All areas of study

Open to children/spouses of Fleet Reserve Association members. Dependents of retired or deceased members also may apply. For undergraduate study. Awards based on financial need, scholastic standing, character, and leadership qualities.

'Dependent child' is defined as unmarried, under 21, or under 23 if currently enrolled in college. Write for complete information.

2815—FLORENCE EVANS BUSHEE FOUNDATION, INC. (Scholarships)

One Beacon Street
Boston MA 02108
617/573-0100
FAX: 617/227-4420

AMOUNT: Varies
DEADLINE(S): MAY 1
FIELD(S): All fields of undergraduate study

Open to undergraduate college students who reside ONLY in the Massachusetts towns of Byfield, Newbury, Newburyport, Rowley, or West Newbury OR who are graduates of Newburyport High School or Triton Regional School (up to 5 years after graduation).

Approx 125 grants per year. Write for complete information.

2816—FLORIDA AIR ACADEMY SCHOLARSHIP FUND, INC.

1950 South Academy Drive
Melbourne FL 32901
Written inquiry

AMOUNT: Varies
DEADLINE(S): Ongoing
FIELD(S): All fields of study

Scholarships for residents of Florida. Write to above location for details.

2817—FLORIDA DEPT. OF EDUCATION (Bright Futures Scholarship Program)

Student Financial AssiStreet
255 Collins
Tallahassee FL 32399-0400
850/487-0049 or 888/827-2004
E-mail: OSFABF@mail.doe.state.fl.us
Internet: www.firn.edu/doe

AMOUNT: Varies
DEADLINE(S): APR 1
FIELD(S): All fields of study

A lottery-funded scholarship to reward Florida high school graduates who demonstrate high academic achievement and enroll in eligible Florida postsecondary institutions. This program has three award levels, each of which has different academic criteria and award amounts. The top-ranked scholar from each county will receive an additional award of up to $1,500.

70,000+ awards annually. Contact your high school guidance counselor or Florida Department of Education for specific details.

2818—FLORIDA DEPT. OF EDUCATION (Florida Student Assistance Grants)

Student Financial AssiStreet
255 Collins
Tallahassee FL 32399-0400
850/487-0049 or 888/827-2004
E-mail: OSFABF@mail.doe.state.fl.us
Internet: www.firn.edu/doe

AMOUNT: $200-$1,500
DEADLINE(S): Varies (Spring)
FIELD(S): All fields of study

Need-based grant program for full-time undergraduate students attending eligible public or private Florida institutions. Must be US citizens, Florida residents, and be enrolled in eligible academic degree programs. Must also submit the FAFSA form (available online at www.fafsa.ed.gov).

40,000+ awards annually. Renewable. Forms (including FAFSA) available from your school's financial aid office, or contact Florida Department of Education. Actual deadline varies with each participating institution.

2819—FLORIDA DEPT. OF EDUCATION (Florida Work Experience Program)

Student Financial AssiStreet
255 Collins
Tallahassee FL 32399-0400
850/487-0049 or 888/827-2004

E-mail: OSFABF@mail.doe.state.fl.us
Internet: www.firn.edu/doe

AMOUNT: Varies

DEADLINE(S): Varies (established by each institution)

FIELD(S): All fields of study

Employment program to introduce undergraduate students who demonstrate financial need to work experiences that will complement and reinforce their educational and career goals. Must be enrolled at least half-time, be in good standing at an eligible Florida institution, and meet residency requirements for state student aid. Must submit the FAFSA (available online at www.fafsa.ed.gov).

458 awards annually. Applications (as well as the FAFSA) are available from the financial aid office at participating institutions.

2820—FLORIDA DEPT. OF EDUCATION (Jose Marti Scholarship Challenge Grant Fund)

Student Financial AssiStreet
255 Collins
Tallahasee FL 32399-0400
850/487-0049 or 888/827-2004
E-mail: OSFABF@mail.doe.state.fl.us
Internet: www.firn.edu/doe

AMOUNT: $2,000

DEADLINE(S): APR 1

FIELD(S): All fields of study

A need-based scholarship for students of Hispanic culture who were born in, or who have a natural parent who was born in Mexico, Spain, South America, Central America, or the Caribbean. Must apply as a high school senior or as a graduate student and have a minimum unweighted GPA of 3.0. Must enroll full-time, be a US citizen or eligible non-citizen, and be a Florida resident. Must also submit the FAFSA (available online at www.fafsa.ed.gov).

98 awards annually. Renewable. Forms (including FAFSA) available from your school's financial aid office or contact Florida Department of Education.

2821—FLORIDA DEPT. OF EDUCATION (Limited Access Competitive Grant)

Student Financial AssiStreet
255 Collins
Tallahassee FL 32399-0400
850/487-0049 or 888/827-2004
E-mail: OSFABF@mail.doe.state.fl.us
Internet: www.firn.edu/doe

AMOUNT: Varies

DEADLINE(S): Varies (established by each institution)

FIELD(S): All fields of study

Provides enrollment opportunities for Florida residents who are community college graduates or transfer students from state universities, and who enroll in one of the designated limited access programs at eligible private colleges/universities in Florida. Priority given to Florida residents who graduated from Florida high schools or community colleges. Award amount is 50% of the state's cost per academic year to fund an undergrad's postsecondary education.

700+ awards annually. Applications available from the financial aid office at the private institution you plan to attend.

2822—FLORIDA DEPT. OF EDUCATION (Mary McLeod Bethune Scholarship)

Student Financial AssiStreet
255 Collins
Tallahasee FL 32399-0400
850/487-0049 or 888/827-2004
E-mail: OSFABF@mail.doe.state.fl.us
Internet: www.firn.edu/doe

AMOUNT: $3,000/academic year

DEADLINE(S): Varies (established by each institution)

FIELD(S): All fields of study

A need-based scholarship for high school seniors who have at least a 3.0 GPA, who will attend Florida A&M University, Bethune-Cookman College, Edward Walters College, or Florida Memorial College, and who meet residency requirements for receipt of state student aid.

180 awards annually. Applications are available from the financial aid offices at the four participating institutions.

2823—FLORIDA DEPT. OF EDUCATION (Rosewood Family Scholarship Fund)

Student Financial AssiStreet
255 Collins
Tallahassee FL 32399-0400
850/487-0049 or 888/827-2004
E-mail: OSFABF@mail.doe.state.fl.us
Internet: www.firn.edu/doe

AMOUNT: Up to $4,000

DEADLINE(S): APR 1

FIELD(S): All fields of study

Need-based scholarship for undergraduate students who are descendants of affected African-American Rosewood families and who are enrolled full-time in eligible programs at state universities, pub-lic community colleges, or public postsecondary vocational-technical schools in Florida. Other minority undergraduate students will be considered for awards if funds remain available after awarding Rosewood descendants. Must fill out FAFSA (available online at www.fafsa.ed.gov).

25 awards annually. Award is amount of tuition and fees for up to 30 credit hours, not to exceed $4,000. For an application, contact Florida Department of Education.

2824—FLORIDA DEPT. OF EDUCATION (Scholarships for Children of Deceased or Disabled Veterans)

Student Financial AssiStreet
255 Collins
Tallahassee FL 32399-0400
850/487-0049 or 888/827-2004
E-mail: OSFABF@mail.doe.state.fl.us
Internet: www.firn.edu/doe

AMOUNT: Tuition + fees for the academic year

DEADLINE(S): APR 1

FIELD(S): All fields of study

For dependent children of deceased or 100% disabled veterans, or for children of servicemen classified as POW or MIA for attendance at eligible public or private institutions. Residency requirements vary.

215 awards annually. Applications are available from Florida Department of Education or from Florida Department of Veterans' Affairs, P.O. Box 31003, Street Petersburg, FL 33731-8903.

2825—FLORIDA DEPT. OF EDUCATION (William L. Boyd IV Florida Resident Access Grant)

Student Financial AssiStreet
255 Collins
Tallahassee FL 32399-0400
850/487-0049 or 888/827-2004
E-mail: OSFABF@mail.doe.state.fl.us
Internet: www.firn.edu/doe

AMOUNT: Varies

DEADLINE(S): Varies (established by each institution)

FIELD(S): All fields of study

Provides tuition assistance for Florida residents who are full-time undergraduate students attending eligible private non-profit Florida colleges or universities. Financial need is NOT considered.

23,000+ awards annually. Applications available from the financial aid office at the private institution you plan to attend.

2826—FLORIDA DEPT. OF EDUCATION/US DEPT. OF EDUCATION (Robert C. Byrd Honors Scholarship Program)

Student Financial AssiStreet
255 Collins
Tallahassee FL 32399-0400
850/487-0049 or 888/827-2004
E-mail: OSFABF@mail.doe.state.fl.us
Internet: www.firn.edu/doe

AMOUNT: Varies
DEADLINE(S): APR 15
FIELD(S): All fields of study

For outstanding Florida high school seniors. Must be Florida resident (may have graduated from out-of-state school) and may attend any public or private non-profit postsecondary school and enroll for a course of study at least one year in length. Recipients must be nominated by their high school; each high school can nominate one student.

1,200 awards annually. Applications available from your high school guidance counselor.

2827—FLORIDA STATE DEPT. OF EDUCATION (Seminole/Miccosukee Indian Scholarships)

Student Financial AssiStreet
255 Collins
Tallahassee FL 32399-0400
850/487-0049 or 888/827-2004
E-mail: OSFABF@mail.doe.state.fl.us
Internet: www.firn.edu/doe

AMOUNT: Varies (determined by respective tribe)
DEADLINE(S): Varies (established by tribe)
FIELD(S): All fields of study

For Seminole and Miccosukee Indians of Florida who are enrolled as full-time or part-time undergraduate or graduate students at eligible Florida institutions.

23 awards annually. Applications available from each tribe's Higher Education Committee or contact Florida Department of Education.

2828—FLORIDA STATE UNIVERSITY (Online Scholar Challenge)

P.O. Box 2400
Tallahassee FL 32306-2400
850/644-2913
Internet: www.fsu.edu

AMOUNT: 4-years full tuition at FSU

DEADLINE(S): Varies (registration opens in March & is limited to the first 2,500 teams)
FIELD(S): All fields of study

This is an online information scavenger hunt, which pits high school juniors and seniors against one another in seeking information and answering tough questions on a wide variety of topics through LEXIS-NEXIS Academic Universe. Qualifying rounds are conducted on the Internet. The five top-scoring teams (a team may have 1 or 2 students) and their chaperones will receive all-expense-paid trips to FSU in June for the finals.

See website or call Fran Conaway at above number for details. For admissions information, write to above address.

2829—FOND DU LAC RESERVATION (Scholarhip/Grants Program)

105 University Road
Cloquet MN 55720
218/879-4691

AMOUNT: Up to $3,000/year
DEADLINE(S): Varies
FIELD(S): All fields of study

For tribally enrolled members of the Fond du Lac Reservation who plan to pursue postsecondary education, including vocational schools in accredited higher education institutions. Must apply for all financial aid available and submit an education plan. Will assist out-of-state education for those attending colleges but not vocational schools.

Contact Bonnie Wallace, Career Education Specialist, at above address.

2830—FOND REV. EDMOND GELINAS, INC. (Scholarships)

603 Stark Lane
Manchester NH 03102-8515
Written inquiry

AMOUNT: Varies
DEADLINE(S): JUL 1
FIELD(S): All fields of study

Scholarships to students in New Hampshire who are Catholic and of French or Canadian ancestry.

Write for application details.

2831—FOOTACTION USA (Hooked on Sports)

7880 Bent Branch Drive, #100
Irving TX 75063-6019

AMOUNT: $10,000; $2,000
DEADLINE(S): JAN 15

FIELD(S): All fields of study

Open to high school seniors planning to attend college in the US Must have GPA of 2.0 or better and be involved in some type of athletics (high school program, city/metro organization, individual sport, etc.). US citizenship required.

30 awards per year. Financial need must be demonstrated. Write for complete information.

2832—FOUNDATION FOR AMATEUR RADIO (Scholarships)

6903 Rhode Island Ave.
College Park MD 20740
Written inquiry

AMOUNT: Varies each year
DEADLINE(S): JUN 1
FIELD(S): All fields of study

Program open to active, licensed, radio amateurs ONLY. Since this specialized program changes so much each year, the Foundation annually places announcements with complete eligibility requirements in the amateur radio magazines.

To determine your eligibility look for announcements in magazines such as *QST, CQ, 73, Worldradio*, etc. Write for complete information.

2833—FOUNDATION FOR EXCEPTIONAL CHILDREN (Infinitec Scholarship Award)

1920 Association Drive
Reston VA 20191
703/264-3507
Internet: www.cec.sped.org/fd/scholapp.htm

AMOUNT: $500 & $1,000
DEADLINE(S): FEB 1
FIELD(S): All fields of study

Undergraduate awards for students with disabilities who use augmentative communication devices or other technology-based alternative to oral communication.

Financial need considered. Must be entering freshman. Application and further information are at above website or write for complete information.

2834—FOUNDATION FOR EXCEPTIONAL CHILDREN (Stanley E. Jackson Scholarship Awards)

1920 Association Drive
Reston VA 20191
703/264-3507
Internet: www.cec.sped.org/fd/scholapp.htm

AMOUNT: $500

DEADLINE(S): FEB 1

FIELD(S): All fields of study

Undergraduate awards in 4 categories—1. Students with disabilities. 2. Ethnic minority students with disabilities. 3. Gifted/talented students with disabilities. 4. Ethnic minority gifted/talented with disabilities.

Apply in one category only. Financial need considered. Must be entering freshman. Application and further information are at above website or write for complete information.

2835—FOUNDATION NORTHWEST SCHOLARSHIP FUNDS (Eileen M. Hutchison Scholarship Fund)

1501 Riverview Road
P.O. Box 297
St. Peter MN 56082
800/537-4180

AMOUNT: Varies

DEADLINE(S): MAR 10

FIELD(S): All fields of study

For residents of Bonner County, Idaho, who are high school seniors or graduates. Academic achievement is the primary factor for selection. Students must have maintained a 3.5 GPA through the last two semesters of their education.

Renewals subject to reapplication.

2836—FOUNDATION NORTHWEST SCHOLARSHIP FUNDS (Ren H. Rice Scholarship Fund)

1505 Riverview Road
P.O. Box 297
Street Peter MN 56082
800/537-4180

AMOUNT: Varies

DEADLINE(S): MAR 10

FIELD(S): All fields of study

For applicants who are physically disabled youth or youth who were permanent or temporary wards of Washington State at their 18th birthdays or at their high school graduations. Must attend a postsecondary institution in the state of Washington.

Preference will be given to children who have lived in institutions. Contact Scholarship Management Services, CSFA, at above location for details.

2837—FOURTH TUESDAY (Pat Hoban Memorial Scholarship)

1387 Oxford Road NE, Suite 801
Atlanta GA 30307
770/662-4353

E-mail: 4thtues@lambda.net
Internet: www.lambda.net/~4thtues/Schol.html

AMOUNT: $1,000

DEADLINE(S): Varies

FIELD(S): All fields of study

Scholarship for an Atlanta area lesbian attending an institution of higher education. Fourth Tuesday is a nonprofit professional social networking organization for lesbians.

Contact organization for details.

2838—FRANCIS OUIMET SCHOLARSHIP FUND

190 Park Road
Weston MA 02193
617/891-6400

AMOUNT: $500-$4,500

DEADLINE(S): DEC 1

FIELD(S): All fields of study

Undergraduate needs-based scholarships for residents of Massachusetts who have worked as golf caddies, in pro shops, or as course superintendents of operations in Massachusetts for three years. Must work at a golf course.

263 awards. Renewable. Contact Bob Donovan at above address.

2839—FRANKLIN LINDSAY STUDENT AID FUND

P.O. Box 550
Austin TX 78789-0001
512/479-2645

AMOUNT: Up to $3,000 per year

DEADLINE(S): Varies

FIELD(S): All fields of study

Loans for undergraduate and graduate students who have completed at least one year of college attending Texas colleges or universities.

Send SASE for brochure to Texas Commerce Bank-Austin, Trust Div., at above address. May reapply in subsequent years for up to $9,000 per student provided the recipient maintains at least a "C" average.

2840—FRANKS FOUNDATION FUND

P.O. Box 3168, Trust Div.
Portland OR 97208-3168
503/275-4456

AMOUNT: Varies

DEADLINE(S): JUN 15

FIELD(S): All fields of study

Student loans to high school students residing in Oregon.

Applications accepted between June 1 and Jun 15. Write to United States National Bank of Oregon at above address.

2841—FRED A. BRYAN COLLEGIATE STUDENTS FUND (Trust Fund Scholarships)

Norwest Bank Indiana, NA
12 W. Jefferson Blvd.
South Bend IN 46601
219/237-3314

AMOUNT: $1,400-$1,600

DEADLINE(S): MAR 1

FIELD(S): All fields of study

Open to male graduates of South Bend, Indiana, high schools with preference to those who are or have been Boy Scouts. For undergraduate study at a recognized college or university. Financial need must be demonstrated. US citizenship required.

Renewable for up to 4 years. Write for complete information.

2842—FRED B. & RUTH B. ZIGLER FOUNDATION (Scholarships)

P.O. Box 986
324 Broadway
Jennings LA 70546
318/824-2413

AMOUNT: $1,250 per semester

DEADLINE(S): MAR 10

FIELD(S): All areas of study

Scholarships open to graduating seniors at Jefferson Davis Parish (LA) high schools. Awards are tenable at recognized colleges and universities.

10-18 scholarships per year. Renewable for up to 4 years. Write for complete information.

2843—FULLER E. CALLAWAY FOUNDATION (Hatton Lovejoy Scholarship)

209 Broome Street
La Grange GA 30240
706/884-7348

AMOUNT: $3,600 per school year

DEADLINE(S): FEB 15

FIELD(S): All fields of study

Open to high school graduates who have lived in Troup County, GA for at least two years and rank in the upper 25 percent of their class.

10 scholarships per year. Write for complete information.

2844—FUND FOR EDUCATION AND TRAINING (FEAT Loans)

1930 Connecticut Ave. NW
Washington DC 20009
202/483-2220
FAX: 202/483-1246

AMOUNT: $2,500
DEADLINE(S): None
FIELD(S): All fields of study

For male non-registrants of the Selective Service for undergraduate or graduate study, as well as career support. Financial need is NOT a factor.

Renewable. Contact Fran Donelan at above address for an application.

2845—GABRIEL J. BROWN TRUST (Loan Program)

112 Avenue E. West
Bismarck ND 58501-3662
701/223-5916

AMOUNT: Varies
DEADLINE(S): JUN 15
FIELD(S): All fields of study

Student loans for needy residents of North Dakota. Must have attended college for four semesters or six quarters or have acquired 48 credits. Students at Bismarck State College, Medcenter One College of Nursing, or the University of Mary may have attended only two semesters or three quarters or have acquired 24 credits. Must demonstrate financial need.

Interest rate is 6% per year. Send SASE for application guidelines.

2846—GABRIEL J. BROWN TRUST (Trust Loan Fund)

112 Avenue E. West
Bismarck ND 58501-3662
701/223-5916

AMOUNT: $1,000-4,000
DEADLINE(S): JUN 15
FIELD(S): All fields of study

Special low-interest loans (6%) open to residents of North Dakota who have completed at least 2 years of undergraduate study at a recognized college or university and have a 2.5 or better GPA. US citizen.

Approximately 75 loans per year. Renewable. Write for complete information.

2847—GATES MILLENNIUM SCHOLARS PROGRAM (Scholarships for High School Seniors)

8260 Willow Oaks Corporate Drive
Fairfax VA 22031-4511
877/690-4677
Internet: www.gmsp.org

AMOUNT: Varies
DEADLINE(S): FEB 1
FIELD(S): All fields of study

High school principals, teachers, and counselors may nominate high school seniors who are African Americans, Native Americans, Hispanic Americans, or Asian Americans planning to enter college. Based on academic performance in math & science, commitment to academic study, involvement in community service & school activities, potential for leadership, and financial need. Must submit transcripts and letters of recommendation. Must be US citizen with a minimum 3.3 GPA.

Application materials available November 1st; scholars will be notified in May. Funded by the Bill & Melinda Gates Foundation, and administered by the United Negro College Fund.

2848—GATES MILLENNIUM SCHOLARS PROGRAM (Scholarships for College Students)

8260 Willow Oaks Corporate Drive
Fairfax VA 22031-4511
877/690-4677
Internet: www.gmsp.org

AMOUNT: Varies
DEADLINE(S): FEB 1
FIELD(S): All fields of study

College presidents, professors, and deans may nominate undergraduates who are African Americans, Native Americans, Hispanic Americans, or Asian Americans enrolled in college. Based on academic performance in math, science, and education; commitment to academic study; involvement in community service and school activities; potential for leadership; career goals; and financial need. Must submit transcripts and letters of recommendation. Must be US citizen with a minimum 3.3 GPA.

Application materials available November 1st; scholars will be notified in May. Funded by the Bill & Melinda Gates Foundation, and administered by the United Negro College Fund.

2849—GATEWAY EDUCATIONAL TRUST (Scholarships)

7716 Forsyth Blvd.
Street Louis MO 63105-1810
314/721-1375
FAX: 314/721-1857
E-mail: afer2@aol.com

AMOUNT: up to $1,000 (1/2 tuition)
DEADLINE(S): None
FIELD(S): All fields of study

Scholarships/tuition assistance for K-4th grade students who are residents of Street Louis, Missouri, and/or who plan to attend private school in Street Louis. Household income must meet requirements for federal school lunch program.

Renewable for three years. Contact Irene M. Allen, Executive Director, for more information.

2850—GENERAL EDUCATIONAL FUND, INC.

P.O. Box 8490
Burlington VT 05402
Written inquiry

AMOUNT: Varies
DEADLINE(S): JUN 14
FIELD(S): All fields of study

Undergraduate scholarships for financially needy graduates of high schools in Vermont for study in the US.

Write to The Merchants Trust Co. for details; however, applications are made through Vermont Student Assistance Corp.

2851—GENERAL FEDERATION OF WOMEN'S CLUBS OF MASSACHUSETTS (Edith Folsom Hall Scholarships)

245 Dutton Road
P.O. Box 679
Sudbury MA 01776-0679
508/229-2023

AMOUNT: $500
DEADLINE(S): MAR 1
FIELD(S): All fields of study

For young women high school graduates (or GED receivers) who have been accepted by Mount Ida College. Must have completed application to Mount Ida College and completed application form in duplicate sent to chairman in order to apply.

Several scholarships annually. For more information or an application, send self-addressed, stamped envelope to Marilyn Perry, Scholarship Chairman, at above address. For more information on Mt. Ida College, call 617/928-4500. Or write to 777 Dedham Street, Newton Centre, MA 02159.

2852—GENERAL FEDERATION OF WOM-EN'S CLUBS OF MASSACHUSETTS (Partial Scholarship to Fisher College)

245 Dutton Road
Box 679
Sudbury MA 01776-0679
508/229-2023

AMOUNT: $600
DEADLINE(S): MAR 1
FIELD(S): All fields of study

For a young woman high school graduate with credits acceptable to Admittance Committee of school as well as indication of financial need. Must have completed admission form to Fisher College, completed financial aid form processed through College Scholarship Service, and completed application form in duplicate sent to chairman in order to apply.

1 scholarship annually. For more information or an application, send self-addressed, stamped envelope to Marilyn Perry, Scholarship Chairman, at above address. For more info on Fisher College, call 617/236-8800. Or write to 118 Beacon Street, Boston, MA 02116.

2853—GEORGE ABRAHAMIAN FOUNDA-TION (Scholarships for Rhode Island Armenians)

945 Admiral Street
Providence RI 02904
401/831-2887

AMOUNT: $600-$900
DEADLINE(S): SEP 1
FIELD(S): All areas of study

Open to undergraduate and graduate students who are US citizens of Armenian ancestry and live in Rhode Island, are of good character, have the ability to learn, and can demonstrate financial need. Must be affiliated with an Armenian Church and attend or plan to attend college in Rhode Island. Min. GPA of 3.0 required.

Renewable. Write for complete information.

2854—GEORGE BIRD GRINNELL AMERI-CAN INDIAN CHILDREN'S FUND (Schulyer M. Meyer, Jr. Scholarship Award)

11602 Montague Ct.
Potomac MD 20854
301/424-2440
FAX: 301/424-8281
E-mail: Grinnell_Fund@MSN.com

AMOUNT: $1,000/yr. (max.)
DEADLINE(S): JUN 1

FIELD(S): All fields of study

Open to Native American students enrolled in undergraduate or graduate programs at two- or four-year institutions. Must be American Indian/Alaska Native (documented with Certified Degree of Indian Blood), be enrolled in college/university, be able to demonstrate commitment to serving community or other tribal nations, and document financial need.

Renewable. Contact Dr. Paula M. Mintzies, President, for an application after January 1Street

2855—GEORGE E. ANDREWS TRUST (George E. Andrews Scholarship)

Trust Dept., Blackhawk State Bank
P.O. Box 719
Beloit WI 53512-0179
608/364-8914

AMOUNT: $2,500 or more
DEADLINE(S): FEB 15
FIELD(S): All fields of study

Open to seniors at high schools in the City of Beloit, Town of Beloit, or Town of Turtle, Rock County, Wisconsin. Awards based on scholastic standing, financial need, moral character, industriousness, and other factors.

To assist and encourage a worthy, needy, and industrious student by defraying the student's expense for the first year of college.

2856—GEORGE GROTEFEND SCHOLAR-SHIP FUND (Grotefend Scholarship)

1644 Magnolia Ave.
Redding CA 96001
916/225-0227

AMOUNT: $150-$400
DEADLINE(S): APR 20
FIELD(S): All fields of study

Scholarships open to applicants who completed all 4 years of high school in Shasta County, California. Awards support all levels of study at recognized colleges and universities.

300 awards per year. Write for complete information.

2857—GEORGE SCHOOL (Scholarship)

Box 4000
Newtown PA 18940
215/579-6500
FAX: 215/579-6549
E-mail: admissions@
georgeschoolpvt.k12pa.us

Internet: www.georgeschool.pvt.
k12pa.us

AMOUNT: $10,000
DEADLINE(S): MAR 1
FIELD(S): All fields of study

Scholarships for this coed independent Quaker high school in Newton, Pennsylvania. Both boarding and day school. Students come from all over the US and 31 countries. 4 scholarships are based on academics (3.5+ GPA), community service, leadership, and citizenship. Others are based on financial need.

Contact school for details.

2858—GEORGE T. WELCH (Scholarships)

Baker Boyer Bank, Trust Dept.
P.O. Box 1796
Walla Walla WA 99362-0353
509/525-2000

AMOUNT: Up to $2,500 (amount varies)
DEADLINE(S): MAR 1
FIELD(S): All fields of study

Open ONLY to US citizens who reside in Walla Walla County, Washington, and have graduated from a Walla Walla high school.

Approximately 45 awards per year. Contact Holly T. Howard at address above for complete information.

2859—GEORGE W. AND ANNE A. HOOVER SCHOLARSHIP FUND (Student Loans)

2-16 South Market Street
P.O. Box 57
Selinsgrave PA 17870
717/374-4252

AMOUNT: $2,500/yr. for two-yr. schools;
$5,000/yr. for four-year schools
DEADLINE(S): None specified
FIELD(S): All fields of study

Student loans to individuals to attend colleges or universities.

Send self-addressed, stamped envelope to above address for details.

2860—GEORGIA BOARD OF REGENTS (Scholarships)

244 Washington Street SW
Atlanta GA 30334
404/656-2272

AMOUNT: $500 for junior college; $750
for 4-year college; $1,000 for grad
school students
DEADLINE(S): Varies
FIELD(S): All areas of study

Must be legal Georgia resident enrolled or accepted in an institution of the university system of GA. Must be in upper 25% of class (based on high school and SAT scores) and demonstrate financial need.

DO NOT contact the GA Board of Regents above; contact the appropriate school for complete information.

2861—GEORGIA STUDENT FINANCE COMMISSION (HOPE Scholarships)

2082 East Exchange Place
Tucker GA 30084
770/414-3085 (metro Atlanta)
800/546-HOPE (toll-free in Georgia)
Internet: www.gsfc.org/gsfc/apphope.htm

AMOUNT: Varies
DEADLINE(S): Varies (end of spring term)
FIELD(S): All fields of study

The HOPE Scholarship Program (Helping Outstanding Pupils Educationally) is funded by the Georgia Lottery for Education. Program details are subject to change. For use at all Georgia colleges, universities, and technical institutes.

Applicants must complete the Free Application for Federal Student Aid (FAFSA) form. Contact the financial aid office at the public or private institution you plan to attend. High school students should check with counselor for eligibility requirements.

2862—GERBER REWARDS (Scholarship Drawings)

P.O. Box 651
Street Petersburg FL 33731-0651
800/376-BABY
Internet: www.gerber.com

AMOUNT: Up to $250,000
DEADLINE(S): JUL; DEC
FIELD(S): All fields of study

Drawing for parents of a child up to 24 months. Purchase at least 16 Gerber food products, remove and save the UPC labels, and receive a game piece with a toll-free number.

Check the website or 800 number above for details.

2863—GERONIMO CORPORATION, INC. (William B. Klusty Memorial Scholarship Fund for Native Americans)

206 Zion Road
Salisbury MD 21804

Internet: www.geronimo.org/scholarship

AMOUNT: $1,000
DEADLINE(S): Varies (2nd Friday of the fall quarter)
FIELD(S): All fields of study

Scholarships for Native American students, both undergraduate and graduate. Criteria are previous academic work, community involvement, career goals, leadership ability, financial need, and an explanation as to why the students should receive a scholarship (as explained in a 250-word, typed essay). Submit proof of Native American heritage. Must have 3.5 GPA.

Access website or contact organization for application.

2864—GETCOLLEGE.COM (Strivers Scholarships)

1400 Allendale Road, Suite 1
West Palm Beach FL 33405
Internet: www.getcollege.com/scholarship-strivers.html

AMOUNT: $2,000
DEADLINE(S): APR 1
FIELD(S): All fields of study

Open to US high school seniors who plan to enroll in a full-time undergraduate course of study at an accredited two- or four-year US college/university. Must be a US citizen or eligible non-citizen, have a GPA of 2.7 to 3.3, and have a combined SAT score of 950-1100. Must submit essay (up to 500 words) on why you are going to college, and household income cannot exceed $50,000/year.

6 awards annually (2 are restricted to Palm Beach County, FL, residents). Renewable up to 3 years with minimum 3.2 GPA. See website or write to above address for details. Recipients notified by May 16th.

2865—GHIDOTTI FOUNDATION (Scholarships)

Wells Fargo Private Banking Group
P.O. Box 2511
Sacramento CA 95812
916/440-4433

AMOUNT: Not specified
DEADLINE(S): None given
FIELD(S): All areas of study

Open to graduates of public or private high schools located within the boundaries of Nevada County, California.

Write for complete information.

2866—GILL Street BERNARD'S SCHOOL (Financial Aid)

P.O. Box 604
Gladstone NJ 07934
908/234-1611
FAX: 908/719-8865

AMOUNT: Varies
DEADLINE(S): Varies
FIELD(S): All fields of study

A need-based merit scholarship for students in grades 7-12 at this private secondary, college preparatory school in New Jersey.

Renewable.

2867—GLAMOUR MAGAZINE (Top Ten College Women Competition)

350 Madison Ave.
New York NY 10017
800/244-GLAM
E-mail: ttcw@Glamour.com

AMOUNT: $1,000
DEADLINE(S): JAN 31
FIELD(S): All fields of study

Scholarships for female college juniors attending accredited four-year colleges in the US. Winners have an opportunity to meet with top women professionals in their fields of study and national recognition in *Glamour* magazine. Winners are recognized in the October issue every year. Considered are community activities, leadership ability, academic achievement, and unique and inspiring goals.

Applications available through university financial aid or student affairs offices or by e-mail above.

2868—GLASS, MOLDERS, POTTERY, PLASTICS & ALLIED WORKERS INTERNATIONAL UNION (Scholarship Program)

P.O. Box 607
Media PA 19063
610/565-5051

AMOUNT: $2,500 per year for 4 years
DEADLINE(S): NOV 1
FIELD(S): All fields of study

Open to dependent children of union members. Applicants must rank in the top 1/4 of high school senior class. Children of international union officers are NOT eligible. Awards tenable at accredited undergraduate colleges and universities.

Write for complete information.

2869—GLENDALE COMMUNITY FOUNDATION (Scholarships)

P.O. Box 313
Glendale CA 91209-0313
818/241-8040
Internet: www.cwore.com/gcf/

AMOUNT: Varies
DEADLINE(S): Varies
FIELD(S): All fields of study

Scholarships through this Foundation for needy students who are residents of Glendale, La Canada Flintridge, La Crescenta, Montrose, or Verdugo City, California.

Contact organization for details.

2870—GLENLYON-NORFOLK SCHOOL (Entrance Scholarships)

801 Bank Street
Victoria BC CANADA V85 4A8
250/370-6801
FAX: 250/370-6838
E-mail: gns@islandnet.com
Internet: www.islandnet.com~gns/

AMOUNT: $1,000 max.
DEADLINE(S): FEB 1
FIELD(S): All fields of study

For students applying to this university preparatory private school in grades 8-12 with a high academic standing (86%), and a demonstrated interest in co-curricular activities. If not a Canadian student, student authorization is required. Financial need NOT a factor.

8-10 awards annually. Renewable. See website or write to above address for more information.

2871—GLORIA FECHT MEMORIAL SCHOLARSHIP FUND

402 W. Arrow Hwy., #10
San Dimas CA 91773
619/562-0304
FAX: 619/562-4116
E-mail: rlmtswingle@msn.com

AMOUNT: $2,000-$3,000
DEADLINE(S): MAR 1
FIELD(S): All areas of study

For undergraduate and graduate females, who are residents of Southern California, have a 3.0 GPA, and an interest in golf. Must demonstrate financial need.

Renewable. 30 awards per year. For an application, write to the above address.

2872—GOLDIE GIBSON SCHOLARSHIP FUND (Student Loans)

1601 S.E. Harned Drive
Bartlesville OK 74006
918/333-5268

AMOUNT: Varies
DEADLINE(S): Ongoing
FIELD(S): All fields of study

Student loans for residents of Oklahoma.

Renewable. Write to Ruth Andrews, Secretary-Treasurer, for application information.

2873—GOLF COURSE SUPERINTENDENTS ASSOCIATION OF AMERICA (Legacy Awards)

1421 Research Park Drive
Lawrence KS 66049-3859
785/832-3678
FAX: 785/832-3665
E-mail: psmith@gcsaa.org
Internet: www.gcsaa.org

AMOUNT: $1,500
DEADLINE(S): APR 15
FIELD(S): All fields of study (except golf course management)

Available to the children and grandchildren of GCSAA members who have been an active member for five or more consecutive years. The student must be studying a field UNRELATED to golf course management. Must be enrolled full-time at an accredited institution of higher learning, or in the case of high school seniors, must be accepted at such institution for the next academic year.

See website or contact Pam Smith at GCSAA for an application.

2874—GRACE EDWARDS SCHOLARSHIP FUND (Scholarships)

10 Post Office Square, Suite 1230
Boston MA 02109
Written inquiry

AMOUNT: Varies
DEADLINE(S): MAR 1
FIELD(S): All fields of study

Scholarships for legal residents of Boston, Massachusetts. Must be under age 25 and demonstrate academic excellence and need.

Renewable for up to six years.

2875—GRAHAM-FANCHER SCHOLARSHIP TRUST

149 Josephine Street, Suite A
Santa Cruz CA 95060-2798
408/423-3640

AMOUNT: Varies
DEADLINE(S): MAY 1
FIELD(S): All fields of study

Open to graduating seniors from high schools in Northern Santa Cruz County, California. School and community activities and financial need are considerations.

10 awards annually. Applications accepted only through school scholarship committee at school attended by applicant.

2876—GRAND LODGE OF ILLINOIS (Illinois Odd Fellow-Rebekah Scholarship Award)

P.O. Box 248
305 North Kickapoo Street
Lincoln IL 62656
217/735-2561

AMOUNT: Varies
DEADLINE(S): DEC 1 (application request); MAR 1 (completed application)
FIELD(S): All fields of study

Illinois residents. Scholarships for undergraduate study. Applicants must use the official Odd Fellow-Rebekah scholarship form, submit official transcript of latest grades, and demonstrate need. US citizenship required.

Write to address above for complete information and application forms.

2877—GRAND LODGE OF MASONS OF WYOMING (Scholarships)

Grand Secretary
P.O. Box 459
Casper WY 82602
Written inquiry

AMOUNT: $750
DEADLINE(S): MAY 1
FIELD(S): All fields of study

Available to undergraduate students who are residents of Wyoming. Must submit an original application form; copies are not acceptable.

30 awards annually. Write to above address for an application.

2878—GRAPHIC COMMUNICATIONS INTERNATIONAL UNION (GCIU-A.J. DeAndrade Scholarship Awards Program)

1900 L Street NW
Washington DC 20036-5080
202/462-1400
FAX: 331-9516

AMOUNT: $2,000 (payable $500 per year)
DEADLINE(S): FEB 15
FIELD(S): All areas of study

Open to citizens of the US or Canada who are graduating high school seniors to be graduated in January or June of the current school year and recent high school graduates who, by Sept. 1, will not have completed more than a half-year of college. Must be dependents of Graphic Communications International Union members.

10 awards per year. Write for complete information.

2879—GRAY FOUNDATION (Scholarship Program)

1712 Corby Ave.
Santa Rosa, CA 95407
707/544-7409

AMOUNT: $2,000
DEADLINE(S): MAR 31
FIELD(S): Any field of study

The Gray Foundation offers scholarships for undergraduate study to Sonoma County high school graduates, or those from Middletown HS in Lake County, or GED certificate receivers of Sonoma County, California. Applicants must complete the FAFSA form.

Write to the above address for complete information.

2880—GREATER SPRINGFIELD CHAMBER OF COMMERCE (Women's Partnership Scholarship Fund)

1350 Main Street, 3rd Fl.
Springfield MA 01103
413/732-2858

AMOUNT: Varies
DEADLINE(S): APR 15
FIELD(S): All fields of study

Open to women 25 years or older in the greater Springfield area attending any accredited college for an associate or baccalaureate degree.

Contact Chamber of Commerce at above address for an application or the Community Foundation of Western Massachusetts at above phone number for details.

2881—GUIDEPOSTS MAGAZINE (Young Writers Contest)

16 E. 34th Street
New York NY 10016
212/251-8100

AMOUNT: $1,000-$8,000 + electric typewriters
DEADLINE(S): DEC 1
FIELD(S): All fields of study

Open to any high school junior or senior (US or foreign citizen) who writes an original 1,200-word personal experience story (in English) in which the writer's faith in God played a role. Stories should be true and written in the first person.

Scholarship prizes are not redeemable in cash, not transferable, and must be used within five years after high school graduation. Send SASE for details.

2882—GUSTAVUS ADOLPHUS COLLEGE (Andrew Thorson Scholarships)

Office of Admission
800 West College Ave.
Street Peter MN 56082
507/933-7676 or 800/GUSTAVUS
E-mail: admission@gustavus.edu
Internet: www.gustavus.edu/

AMOUNT: Up to $3,000
DEADLINE(S): MAR 1
FIELD(S): All fields of study

Scholarships tenable at Gustavus Adolphus College, Street Peter, Minnesota, for students who come from a farm family or rural area or in a town of fewer than 2,000 people, or who attend a school with a graduating class of fewer than 100 students. Financial need considered.

Contact college for details.

2883—GUSTAVUS ADOLPHUS COLLEGE (Congregational Scholarship Matching Program)

Office of Admission
800 West College Ave.
Street Peter MN 56082
507/933-7676 or 800/GUSTAVUS
E-mail: admission@gustavus.edu
Internet: www.gustavus.edu/

AMOUNT: Up to $1,000
DEADLINE(S): MAR 1
FIELD(S): All fields of study

Scholarships tenable at Gustavus Adolphus College, Street Peter, Minnesota, for students whose home church congregation has provided scholarship funding in amounts of up to $1,000. This program will match this at a rate of 1.5 times each scholarship dollar. Congregational scholarships from any denomination will be matched.

Contact college for details.

2884—GUSTAVUS ADOLPHUS COLLEGE (National Merit College-Sponsored Scholarships)

Office of Admission
800 West College Ave.
Street Peter MN 56082
507/933-7676 or 800/GUSTAVUS
E-mail: admission@gustavus.edu
Internet: www.gustavus.edu/

AMOUNT: $750-$2,000
DEADLINE(S): None
FIELD(S): All fields of study

Scholarships tenable at Gustavus Adolphus College, Street Peter, Minnesota, for students selected as finalists in the Naitonal Merit Scholarship competition and who designate Gustavus as their first-choice college.

Renewable. Amount of award is based on need. Contact college for details.

2885—GUSTAVUS ADOLPHUS COLLEGE (Partners in Scholarship)

Office of Admission
800 West College Ave.
Street Peter MN 56082
507/933-7676 or 800/GUSTAVUS
E-mail: admission@gustavus.edu
Internet: www.gustavus.edu/

AMOUNT: $7,500/yr.
DEADLINE(S): APR 15
FIELD(S): All fields of study

Scholarships tenable at Gustavus Adolphus College, Street Peter, Minnesota, for students who rank at or near the top of their high school graduating class, have composite test scores of at least 32 on the ACT or 1400 on the SAT, and intend to pursue a graduate degree after Gustavus.

Renewable yearly if GPA of 3.25 is maintained. Contact college for details.

2886—GUSTAVUS ADOLPHUS COLLEGE (Trustee Scholarships)

Office of Admission
800 West College Ave.
Street Peter MN 56082
507/933-7676 or 800/GUSTAVUS
E-mail: admission@gustavus.edu
Internet: www.gustavus.edu/

AMOUNT: $1,000-$5,000/yr.
DEADLINE(S): APR 15

FIELD(S): All fields of study

Scholarships tenable at Gustavus Adolphus College, Street Peter, Minnesota, for students who have shown academic achievement in high school as measured by the difficulty of courses taken, grades earned, and standardized test scores.

Renewable yearly if GPA of 3.0 is maintained. Contact college for details.

2887—H. T. EWALD FOUNDATION (Scholarship Awards)

15175 E. Jefferson Ave.
Grosse Pointe MI 48230
313/821-1278

AMOUNT: $400 to $2,500
DEADLINE(S): APR 1
FIELD(S): All fields of study

Open to residents of the metropolitan Detroit (MI) area who will be entering college as freshmen. Awards are available for up to 4 years of undergraduate work. Based on financial need, academic achievement, and extracurricular activities.

10 to 18 awards per year. Write for complete information.

2888—H.G. AND A.G. KEASBEY MEMORIAL FOUNDATION

One Logan Square, Suite 2000
Philadelphia PA 19103-6993
Written inquiry

AMOUNT: Varies
DEADLINE(S): Varies
FIELD(S): All areas of study

Scholarships to individuals primarily for study in the United Kingdom.

Contact Geraldine J. O'Neill, Executive Secretary, at above address for application guidelines.

2889—HAGGAR CLOTHING COMPANY (Haggar Foundation Scholarship Program)

P.O. Box 311370
Denton TX 76203-1370
940/565-2302
FAX: 940/565-2738
E-mail: bonner@unt.edu

AMOUNT: $4,000/yr.
DEADLINE(S): APR 30
FIELD(S): All fields of study

Open to an immediate relative of an employee of the Haggar Clothing Co. Applicants must be studying in the US.

Renewable for up to four years. Write to the above address for complete information.

2890—HARNESS HORSEMEN INTERNATIONAL FOUNDATION (J. L. Hauck Memorial Scholarship Fund)

14 Main Street
Robbinsville NJ 08691
609/259-3717

AMOUNT: $4,000
DEADLINE(S): JUN 1
FIELD(S): All fields of study

Open to sons and daughters of Harness Horseman International Assn. members. Scholarship supports undergraduate study at any recognized college or university.

Renewable. Write for complete information.

2891—HARNESS TRACKS OF AMERICA (Scholarship)

4640 East Sunrise, Suite 200
Tucson AZ 85718
520/529-2525
FAX 520/529-3235

AMOUNT: $3,000
DEADLINE(S): JUN 15
FIELD(S): All fields of study

Applicants MUST be children of licensed harness racing drivers, trainers, breeders, or caretakers (including retired or deceased) or young people actively engaged in harness racing. For study beyond the high school level.

5 scholarships per year for 1 year each awarded on the basis of merit and financial need. No student may be awarded more than 2 separate yearly scholarships. Write for complete information.

2892—HARRY E. & FLORENCE W. SNAYBERGER MEMORIAL FOUNDATION (Grant Award)

c/o Pennsylvania National Bank & Trust Company
Trust Dept.
Center & Norwegian
Pottsville PA 17901-7150
717/622-4200

AMOUNT: Varies
DEADLINE(S): FEB
FIELD(S): All fields of study

Applicants must be residents of Schuylkill County, PA. Scholarships given based on college expense need.

Contact trust clerk Carolyn Bernatonis for complete information.

2893—HARVARD UNIVERSITY—NIEMAN FOUNDATION (Fellowships for Journalists)

Walter Lippmann House
One Francis Ave.
Cambridge MA 02138
617/495-2237
FAX 617/495-8976
E-mail: nieman@harvard.edu
Internet: www.Nieman.harvard.edu/nieman.html

AMOUNT: $25,000 stipend + tuition
DEADLINE(S): JAN 31 (American journalists); MAR 1 (foreign journalists)
FIELD(S): All fields of study

Must be full-time staff or freelance journalist working for the news or editorial dept. of newspaper, news service, radio, TV, or magazine of broad public interest and must have at least 3 years of professional experience in the media and must be fluent in English.

Consists of an academic year of non-credit study. Approximately 24 fellowships awarded annually. Fellows design their own course of study. Write for complete information.

2894—HARVARD/RADCLIFFE OFFICE OF ADMISSIONS AND FINANCIAL AID (Scholarships; Grants; Loans & Work Study Programs)

Byerly Hall, 3rd floor
8 Garden Street
Cambridge MA 02138
617/495-1581

AMOUNT: Varies
DEADLINE(S): None
FIELD(S): All fields of study

Needs-based funds available to all who are admitted and can show proof of need.

Applicants must be accepted for admission to Harvard/Radcliffe before they will be considered for funding. Many factors other than family income are considered. Write for complete information.

2895—HATTIE M. STRONG FOUNDATION (No-interest Loans)

1620 Eye Street NW, Room 700
Washington DC 20006
202/331-1619
FAX: 202/466-2894

AMOUNT: Up to $3,000
DEADLINE(S): MAR 31 (applications available JAN 1)

FIELD(S): All fields of study

Open to US undergraduate and graduate students in their last year of study in the US or abroad. Loans are made solely on the basis of individual merit. There is no interest and no collateral requirement. US citizen or permanent resident. Repayment terms are based upon monthly income after graduation and arranged individually.

Financial need is a consideration. Approximately 240 awards per year. For complete information send SASE and include personal history, school attended, subject studied, date expected to complete studies, and amount of funds needed.

2896—HAUSS-HELMS FOUNDATION, INC. (Grant Program/Scholarships)

P.O. Box 25
Wapakoneta OH 45895
419/738-4911

AMOUNT: Varies
DEADLINE(S): APR 15
FIELD(S): All fields of study

Undergraduate scholarships open to residents of Auglaize or Allen county, Ohio, who are recommended by their high school principal, a responsible faculty member, or their guidance counselor. US citizen.

195 scholarships per year. Renewable with reapplication. Write and include SASE for complete information.

2897—HAVENS FOUNDATION, INC.

25132 Oakhurst, Suite 210
Spring TX 77386
Written inquiry

AMOUNT: Varies
DEADLINE(S): Ongoing
FIELD(S): All fields of study

Undergraduate scholarships primarily for residents of Texas.

Write to Joe Havens, President, at above location for detail.

2898—HAWAII COMMUNITY FOUNDATION

900 Fort Street Mall, Suite 1300
Honolulu HI 96813
808/556-5570
FAX: 808/521-6286

AMOUNT: Varies
DEADLINE(S): Varies
FIELD(S): All areas of study

Several different scholarship programs, each having its own criteria. Some are for specific college majors, others for specific

ethnic groups, and others for specific high schools and colleges or geographic areas.

Send to the organization above for a listing of the programs.

2899—HEBREW IMMIGRANT SOCIETY (HIAS Scholarship Program)

333 Seventh Ave.
New York NY 10001-5004
212/613-1358
FAX: 212/629-0921
Internet: www.hias.org

AMOUNT: $1,500
DEADLINE(S): MAR 15
FIELD(S): All fields of study

Open to refugees and asylees who were assisted by HIAS and who arrived in the US during or after 1985. For high school seniors planning to pursue postsecondary education or students already enrolled in undergraduate or graduate study who will continue the following year. Must have completed one year of study at a US school, be a US resident, and demonstrate financial need.

100+ awards annually. Not renewable. See website or send a self-addressed, stamped, business-sized envelope to Phoebe Lewis for an application.

2900—HEBRON ACADEMY (Scholarships)

P.O. Box 309
Hebron ME 04238
207/966-2100
FAX: 207/966-1111
E-mail: addmissions@
mail.hebronacademy.pvt.k12.me.us

AMOUNT: $500 to $14,000
DEADLINE(S): None
FIELD(S): All fields of secondary school study

Scholarships for students admitted to Hebron Academy in Hebron, Maine, a private college-prep secondary school.

Send SASE for details. Financial need must be demonstrated.

2901—HERBERT HOOVER PRESIDENTIAL LIBRARY ASSOCIATION (Uncommon Student Award)

P.O. Box 696
West Branch IA 52245
319/643-5327
FAX: 319/643-2391
E-mail: info@hooverassoc.org
Internet: www.hooverassoc.org

AMOUNT: $500; $5,000

DEADLINE(S): MAR 31
FIELD(S): All fields of study

For Iowa high school juniors to use for their undergraduate college studies. Financial need is NOT a factor.

15 $500 awards and 3 $5,000 awards annually. Not renewable. Contact Patricia Hand at above address for an application.

2902—HERBERT LEHMAN EDUCATION FUND (Scholarships)

99 Hudson Street, Suite 1600
New York NY 10013-2897
Written inquiry

AMOUNT: $2,000
DEADLINE(S): APR 30
FIELD(S): All fields of study

Open to African-American high school graduates planning to begin undergraduate study at a four-year institution having a below-average enrollment of African-Americans. Must be US citizen and have outstanding potential, as evidenced by high school academic records, test scores, personal essays, community/school involvement, and educational goals. Must demonstrate financial need.

25-40 awards annually. Renewable. Requests for application forms must be in writing and requested by the applicant—include education to date, educational and career goals, planned college, and why assistance is being requested. Applications available November 30th-February 15th.

2903—HERMAN O. WEST FOUNDATION (Scholarship)

101 Gordon Drive
Lionville PA 19341-0645
610/594-2945

AMOUNT: Up to $2,500/yr.
DEADLINE(S): FEB 28
FIELD(S): All fields of study

Must be a high school senior entering college in the fall of the same year. Open to dependents of full-time employees of The West Company. This scholarship is for undergraduate study in any area of study. Selection is based on academic achievement, extracurricular activities, and/or community service.

7 awards annually; renewable. Write to the above address for complete information.

2904—HERSCHEL C. PRICE EDUCATIONAL FOUNDATION (Grants Program)

P.O. Box 412
Huntington WV 25708

304/529-3852

AMOUNT: $250 to $2,500 per semester
DEADLINE(S): OCT 1; APR 1
FIELD(S): All fields of study

Scholarships for students who are residents of West Virginia in attendance at WV institutions at the undergraduate level. Some graduate awards are available. US citizen.

Write for complete information.

2905—HISPANIC SCHOLARSHIP FUND (Scholarships)

One Sansome Street, Suite 1000
San Francisco CA 94104
415/445-9930
877-HSF-INFO, ext. 33
FAX: 415/445-9942
E-mail: info@hsf.net
Internet: www.hsf.net

AMOUNT: $500-$2,500
DEADLINE(S): OCT 15
FIELD(S): All fields of study

HSF scholarships are available to students who are of Hispanic background (at least half), are US citizens/permanent residents, have earned at least 15 undergraduate credits from an accredited college, have a minimum GPA of 2.5, and are enrolled in and attending college full-time (undergraduates min. 12 credits/term; graduate students min. 6 credits/term).

See website or send business-sized, self-addressed stamped envelope to HSF for an application.

2906—HOLY CROSS HIGH SCHOOL (Scholarships/Financial Aid)

587 Oronoke Road
Waterbury CT 06708
203/757-9248
FAX: 203/757-3423
E-mail: info@holycrosshs-ct.com

AMOUNT: Up to $2,500
DEADLINE(S): Varies
FIELD(S): All fields of study

A private, Catholic high school in Connecticut. The two students who score the highest on the Entrance Exam receive renewable $2,500 scholarships. Financial aid grants avaliable based strictly on need. Students can also work part-time. Eighth-graders can apply for local sources of financial aid.

Contact school for details.

2907—HOPI PRIVATE HIGH SCHOOL SCHOLARSHIP

P.O. Box 123
Kykotsmovi AZ 86039
520/734-2441, ext. 520
800/762-9630
FAX: 520/734-2435

AMOUNT: Varies
DEADLINE(S): JUL 31
FIELD(S): All fields of study

For enrolled members of the Hopi Tribe to encourage achievement of a high level of academic excellence in accredited private high schools. Entering freshmen must have a GPA of 3.5; continuing students must have GPA of 3.2.

2 awards. Academic merit is primary consideration.

2908—HOPI SCHOLARSHIP

P.O. Box 123
Kykotsmovi AZ 86039
520/734-2441, ext. 520
800/762-9630
FAX: 520/734-2435

AMOUNT: Varies
DEADLINE(S): JUL 31
FIELD(S): All fields of study

For enrolled members of the Hopi Tribe pursuing associate, baccalaureate, graduate, or post-graduate degrees. Minimum 3.0 GPA (3.2 for graduates). Entering freshmen must be in the top 10% of graduating class or score min. of 21 on ACT or 930 on SAT; undergrads must have and maintain 3.0 GPA.

Academic merit is primary consideration.

2909—HORACE MANN COMPANIES (Scholarship Program)

P.O. Box 20490
Springfield IL 62708
217/789-2500
Internet: www.horacemann.com

AMOUNT: $20,000 (1); $4,000 (5); $1,000 (10)
DEADLINE(S): FEB 28 (postmark)
FIELD(S): All fields of study

For college-bound high school seniors whose parent or legal guardian is employed by a US public school district or public college or university. Must have a 3.0 or better GPA and score at least 23 on the ACT or 1,100 on the SAT. Essay, transcript, activities, and letters of recommendation considered. Scholarships are awarded directly to the college/university of each recipient's choice for tuition, fees, and other educational expenses.

16 awards annually. Renewable each year of college provided a GPA of at least 2.0 is maintained. Financial need is NOT a factor. Visit website for application and complete information or contact your local Horace Mann representative.

2910—HORACE MANN SCHOOL (Scholarships)

231 W. 246th Street
Riverdale NY 10471
718/548-4000
FAX: 718/548-0689
E-mail: admission@horacemann.org
Internet: www.horacemann.org

AMOUNT: Varies
DEADLINE(S): FEB 1
FIELD(S): All fields of study

Scholarships available to attend this independent, coeducational school that includes nursery through twelfth grade. Students must qualify by submitting a form from School and Student Service for Financial Aid (SSS) and other documentation indicating financial need.

270 annual awards. Renewable, but must reapply. Contact school for details.

2911—HORACE SMITH FUND (Loans)

P.O. Box 3034
1441 Main Street
Springfield MA 01101
413/739-4222

AMOUNT: Varies
DEADLINE(S): JUN 15 (college students); JUL 1 (high school)
FIELD(S): All areas of study

Open to graduates of Hampden County, MA secondary schools for undergraduate or graduate study. Financial need is of primary importance. Applications available after April 1. No interest if paid back within a year after the student completes his/her education.

Renewable. Write for complete information.

2912—HORACE SMITH FUND (Walter S. Barr Scholarships)

Box 3034
Springfield MA 01101
413/739-4222

AMOUNT: Varies
DEADLINE(S): DEC 31
FIELD(S): All fields of study

For members of the senior classes of Agawam, Chicopee, East Longmeadow, Longmeadow, Ludlow, Springfield, West Springfield, and Wilbraham high schools in Massachusetts. Based on school records, college entrance exams, general attainments, and financial needs.

Applications available after Sept. 15 in the guidance offices of the schools listed above.

2913—HORATIO ALGER ASSOCIATION (Scholarships)

99 Canal Center Plaza
Alexandria VA 22314
703/684-9444
FAX: 703/548-3822
E-mail: horatioaa@aol.com
Internet: www.horatioalger.com

AMOUNT: Tuition, room & board, textbooks
DEADLINE(S): Varies
FIELD(S): All fields of study involving service to others

A scholarship program for college-bound high school seniors combined with leadership and civic education training through participation in the National Scholars Conference. Must be committed to use their college degrees in service to others. Applicants must participate in one of the more than 100 Youth Seminars held across the country in order to be eligible for the scholarships.

The organization focuses on young people who have faced and triumphed over exceptional hardships. Send SASE to above address for details on seminar participation. Visit website for more information.

2914—HOWARD AND MAMIE NICHOLS SCHOLARSHIP TRUST (Scholarships)

Wells Fargo Bank
Trust Dept.
5262 N. Blackstone
Fresno CA 93710
Written inquiries only

AMOUNT: Varies
DEADLINE(S): FEB 28
FIELD(S): All fields of study

Open to graduates of Kern County, California, high schools for full-time undergraduate or graduate study at a post-secondary institution. Must demonstrate financial need and have a 2.0 or better GPA.

Approximately 100 awards per year. Renewable with reapplication. Write for complete information.

2915—HOYT FOUNDATION (May Emma Hoyt Scholarship)

P.O. Box 788
New Castle PA 16103
724/652-5511
FAX: 724/654-8413

AMOUNT: Varies
DEADLINE(S): JUN 15
FIELD(S): All fields of study

Open to residents of Lawrence County, Pennsylvania, for undergraduate study. There are no restrictions on the choice of a college.

Renewable. $150,000 given annually, number of awards varies. Contact Jaimie L. Kopp, Secretary, at above address for an application.

2916—HUALAPAI TRIBAL COUNCIL (Scholarship Program)

P.O. Box 179
Peach Springs AZ 86434
520/769-2216

AMOUNT: Up to $2,500/semester
DEADLINE(S): Varies
FIELD(S): All areas of study

Scholarships are offered to Native Americans only with priority given to members of the Hualapai Tribe. Must be enrolled as a student full-time and maintain passing grades. US citizenship required.

Apply four weeks before each semester. Write to Sheri K. Yellowhawk at above address for complete information.

2917—HUMBOLDT AREA FOUNDATION (Scholarships)

P.O. Box 99
Bayside CA 95524
707/442-2993
FAX: 707/442/3811
E-mail: hafound@northcoaStreetcom
Internet: www.northcoaStreetcom/~hafound

AMOUNT: Varies
DEADLINE(S): Varies
FIELD(S): All fields of study

Scholarships through this Foundation for needy students who are residents of Humboldt County, California.

Contact organization for details.

2918—IDAHO STATE BOARD OF EDUCATION (Idaho Governor's Scholarship)

P.O. Box 83720
Boise ID 83720-0037

208/334-2270
AMOUNT: $3,000
DEADLINE(S): JAN 31
FIELD(S): Vocational/Technical areas

For use in a vocational/technical school in Idaho. Requires GPA of 3.0 or above.

15-20 scholarships awarded. Renewable.

2919—IDAHO STATE BOARD OF EDUCATION (Paul Fowler Memorial Scholarship)

LBJ Building, Room 307
P.O. Box 83720
Boise ID 83720-0037
208/334-2270

AMOUNT: $3,000
DEADLINE(S): JAN 31
FIELD(S): Academic fields of study

Open to Idaho residents who are graduating seniors from Idaho high schools and who are US citizens. For undergraduate study at recognized colleges and universities. Must submit ACT score and class ranking.

2 scholarships awarded.

2920—IDAHO STATE BOARD OF EDUCATION (State of Idaho Scholarship)

P.O. Box 83720
Boise ID 83720-0037
208/334-2270

AMOUNT: $2,700
DEADLINE(S): JAN 31
FIELD(S): All fields of study: 75% academic, 25% vocational

Open to seniors graduating from Idaho high schools. ACT score and rank in class information needed.

20-25 to be awarded. Renewable.

2921—ILLINOIS AMVETS (Scholarships)

2200 South Sixth Street
Springfield IL 62703-3496
217/528-4713
FAX: 217/528-9896
E-mail: amvets@warpnet.net
Internet: www.amvets.com

AMOUNT: $500-$1,000
DEADLINE(S): MAR 1
FIELD(S): All fields of study

Various scholarships for Illinois residents who are unmarried high school seniors and are children of a veteran. Must have taken the ACT at time of application and must demonstrate financial need.

40 awards annually. Renewable. See website or contact Shanna Hughes at above address for more information.

2922—ILLINOIS DEPARTMENT OF THE AMERICAN LEGION (Scholarships)

P.O. Box 2910
Bloomington IL 61702-2910
309/663-0361

AMOUNT: $1,000
DEADLINE(S): MAR 15
FIELD(S): All fields of study

Scholarships for high school seniors who are sons and daughters of Illinois American Legion members. Awards are tenable at recognized undergraduate colleges, universities, and vocational or nursing schools. US citizenship required. Academic achievement and financial need considered.

20 scholarships per year. Write for complete information.

2923—ILLINOIS DEPARTMENT OF THE AMERICAN LEGION (Boy Scout Scholarships)

P.O. Box 2910
Bloomington IL 61702-2910
309/663-0361

AMOUNT: $1,000 and four $200 runner-up awards
DEADLINE(S): APR 15
FIELD(S): All fields of study

Scholarships for high school seniors who are Boy Scouts or Explorer Scouts and are Illinois residents. Must write a 500-word essay on Legion's Americanism and Boy Scout programs. US citizenship required. Academic achievement and financial need considered.

Contact local Boy Scout Office or Legion Boy Scout Chairman at the above address for complete application information.

2924—ILLINOIS DEPARTMENT OF THE AMERICAN LEGION (Oratorical Contest)

P.O. Box 2910
Bloomington IL 61702-2910
309/663-0361

AMOUNT: Prizes range from $75 to $1,600
DEADLINE(S): JAN (Contest begins)
FIELD(S): All fields of study

Scholarships for high school students, grades 9-12, who are state and regional winners in the American Legion's speech contests for Illinois residents. Winners can go on to national level.

Contact local American Legion Post or Headquarters listed above for details.

2925—ILLINOIS DEPARTMENT OF THE AMERICAN LEGION (Essay Contest)

P.O. Box 2910
Bloomington IL 61702-2910
309/663-0361

AMOUNT: $50 to $75
DEADLINE(S): FEB 12
FIELD(S): All fields of study

Scholarship awards for high school students, grades 9-12, who are winners in the American Legion's Americanism Essay Contest for Illinois residents. Must write a 500-word essay on a selected topic.

Contact local American Legion Post or Legion Headquarters, P.O. Box 1426, Bloomington, IL 61702, for details.

2926—ILLINOIS STUDENT ASSISTANCE COMMISSION (Grants for Descendents of Police, Fire, or Correctional Officers)

1755 Lake Cook Road
Deerfield IL 60015-5209
800/899-ISAC
Internet: www.isac1.org

AMOUNT: Tuition and fees
DEADLINE(S): None
FIELD(S): All fields of study

Grants Illinois post-secondary students who are descendants of police, fire, and correctional personnel killed or disabled in the line of duty.

30 annual awards. Apply at end of academic year. Illinois residency and US citizenship required. Access website or write for complete information.

2927—ILLINOIS STUDENT ASSISTANCE COMMISSION (Illinois Incentive for Access)

1755 Lake Cook Road
Deerfield IL 60015-5209
800/899-ISAC
Internet: www.isac1.org

AMOUNT: Up to $500
DEADLINE(S): JUN
FIELD(S): All fields of study

This program provides eligible Illinois first-time freshmen a one-time grant for use at approved Illinois institutions. Applicants must fill out FAFSA.

19,000 annual awards. Illinois residency and US citizenship required. Write for complete information.

2928—ILLINOIS STUDENT ASSISTANCE COMMISSION (Illinois National Guard Grant)

1755 Lake Cook Road
Deerfield IL 60015-5209
800/899-ISAC
Internet: www.isac1.org

AMOUNT: Tuition and fees—average $1,350
DEADLINE(S): SEP 15
FIELD(S): All fields of study

Grants for qualified personnel of the Illinois National Guard attending public universities and community colleges.

2,500 annual awards. Illinois residency and US citizenship required. Access website or write for complete information.

2929—ILLINOIS STUDENT ASSISTANCE COMMISSION (Illinois Veterans' Grant)

1755 Lake Cook Road
Deerfield IL 60015-5209
800/899-ISAC
Internet: www.isac1.org

AMOUNT: Tuition and fees—average $1,350
DEADLINE(S): Varies
FIELD(S): All fields of study

Grants for veterans of the US Armed Forces attending public universities and community colleges.

150,000 annual awards. Illinois residency and US citizenship required. Apply three months after end of term. Write for complete information.

2930—ILLINOIS STUDENT ASSISTANCE COMMISSION (Merit Recognition Scholarship)

1755 Lake Cook Road
Deerfield IL 60015-5209
800/899-ISAC
Internet: www.isac1.org

AMOUNT: $1,000
DEADLINE(S): JUN 15
FIELD(S): All fields of study

Scholarships to recognize Illinois high school seniors who are in the top 2.5% of their high school class and who will attend approved Illinois institutions or a US service academy. Illinois residency and US citizenship required.

Access website or write for complete information.

2931—ILLINOIS STUDENT ASSISTANCE COMMISSION (Monetary Award Program)

1755 Lake Cook Road
Deerfield IL 60015-5209
800/899-ISAC
Internet: www.isac1.org

AMOUNT: Tuition and fees up to $4,320
DEADLINE(S): JUN 1 (continuing students); OCT 1 (new students)
FIELD(S): All fields of study

This program is Illinois's primary need-based grant program. Awards are provided for tuition and fees for eligible students at approved Illinois institutions. Applicants must fill out FAFSA.

130,000 annual awards. Illinois residency and US citizenship required. Write for complete information.

2932—INDEPENDENCE FEDERAL SAVINGS BANK (Federal Family Education Loans)

1900 L Street NW, Suite 700
Washington DC 20036-5001
800/733-0473 or 202/626-0473
FAX: 202/775-4533
E-mail: ifsb@aol.com
Internet: www.ifsb.com

AMOUNT: up to $8,500
DEADLINE(S): None
FIELD(S): All fields of study

Loans are open to US citizens or legal residents who are undergraduate or graduate students accepted to or enrolled in a school approved by the US Department of Education. Includes Federal Subsidized/Unsubsidized Stafford Loans and Federal Parent Loans (PLUS). Financial need considered for some loans. Repayment begins six months after graduation or when student withdraws/stops attending school at least half time.

Contact IFSB for an application.

2933—INSTITUTE FOR THE INTERNATIONAL EDUCATION OF STUDENTS (Scholarships)

223 West Ohio Street
Chicago IL 60610-4196
800/995-2300
312/944-1750
FAX: 312/944-1448
E-mail: info@iesa.broad.org
Internet: iesabroad.org

AMOUNT: Varies
DEADLINE(S): APR 1 (fall semester & full-year students); OCT 1 (spring semester students)
FIELD(S): All fields of study

IES offers many scholarships for studying abroad in various countries; some are based on academic merit, and some are based on financial need. The organization wants to encourage students with a variety of interests and abilities and who represent a wide range of social and economic backgrounds to study abroad.

The website is quite comprehensive and includes application forms, scholarship lists, and descriptions of what is available country-by-country. If you do not have Web access, contact IES for the necessary materials.

2934—INTERNATIONAL ALLIANCE OF THEATRICAL STAGE EMPLOYEES AND MOVING PICTURE MACHINE OPERATORS (Richard F. Walsh Foundation)

1515 Broadway, Suite 601
New York NY 10036
212/730-1770

AMOUNT: $1,750
DEADLINE(S): DEC 31
FIELD(S): All fields of study

Scholarship is offered to high school seniors who are children of members in good standing. Awards are based on transcripts, SAT scores, and letter(s) of recommendation from clergy or teacher.

Award renewable for 4 years. Write for complete information.

2935—INTERNATIONAL ASSN. OF BRIDGE STRUCTURAL AND ORNAMENTAL IRON WORKERS (John H. Lyons Scholarship Program)

1750 New York Ave. NW, Suite 400
Washington DC 20006
202/383-4800

AMOUNT: $2,500 per year maximum
DEADLINE(S): MAR 31
FIELD(S): All areas of study

Must be children of members or deceased members in good standing at the time of death. Applicants must rank in the upper half of high school graduating class. For undergraduate study in US or Canada. Must be a senior in high school.

Scholarships will be awarded for one year and may be renewed for three academic years. Write for complete information.

2936—INTERNATIONAL ASSOCIATION OF FIRE FIGHTERS (W.H. "Howie" McClennan Scholarship)

1750 New York Ave. NW
Washington DC 20006-5395
202/737-8484

AMOUNT: $2,500
DEADLINE(S): FEB 1
FIELD(S): All fields of study

Scholarship for sons, daughters, and legally adopted children of fire fighters who were members in good standing of the International Association of Fire Fighters and died in the line of duty.

Write to the above address for complete information.

2937—INTERNATIONAL BILL ONEXIOCA II (Founders Memorial Award)

911 Bartlett Place
Windsor CA 95492
Written inquiry only

AMOUNT: $2,500
DEADLINE(S): JAN 31
FIELD(S): All fields of study

Annual award in memory of Hernesto K. Onexioca/founder. Anyone with the legal surname of Onexioca who is not a relative of Onexioca by blood or marriage and was born on Jan. 1 is eligible to apply.

All inquiries MUST include proof of name and birth date. Those without such proof will NOT be acknowledged.

2938—INTERNATIONAL BROTHERHOOD OF TEAMSTERS (Scholarship Fund)

25 Louisiana Ave. NW
Washington DC 20001
202/624-8735

AMOUNT: $1,000-$1,500/yr.
DEADLINE(S): DEC 15
FIELD(S): All fields of study

Open to high school seniors who are dependent children of Teamster members. For students in top 20% of their class with excellent SAT/ACT scores. Must be US or Canadian citizen and demonstrate financial need.

25 awards annually. Renewable. Contact the Teamsters for an application.

2939—INTERNATIONAL LADIES GARMENT WORKERS UNION (National College Award Program)

1710 Broadway
New York NY 10019

212/265-7000

AMOUNT: $350 annually; renewable for up to four years
DEADLINE(S): JAN 31
FIELD(S): All fields of study

Open to sons or daughters of union members who have been members in good standing for at least 2 years. Applications accepted only from high school seniors.

10 scholarships per year. Write for complete information.

2940—INTERNATIONAL SOCIETY FOR CLINICAL LABORATORY TECHNOLOGY (David Birenbaum Scholarship Fund)

917 Locust Street, Suite 1100
Street Louis MO 63101-1413
314/241-1445

AMOUNT: Varies
DEADLINE(S): JUL 15
FIELD(S): All fields of study

Open to ISCLT members, and their spouses and dependent children. Requires graduation from an accredited high school or equivalent.

Write for complete information.

2941—INTERNATIONAL UNION OF BRICK-LAYERS AND ALLIED CRAFTSMEN (Harry C. Bates Merit Scholarship Program)

815 15th Street NW
Washington, DC 20005
202/783-3788

AMOUNT: $500 to $2,000 per year up to 4 years
DEADLINE(S): OCT (PSAT tests)
FIELD(S): All areas of study

Open to natural or legally adopted children of current, retired, or deceased BAC members. Competition is administered by National Merit Scholarship Corp. which conducts PSAT/NMSQT during October of student's junior year of high school.

Applicants must be national merit semifinalists. Award tenable at any accredited university or community college the student attends full-time. Write for complete information.

2942—INTERNATIONAL UNION OF ELEC-TRONIC, ELECTRICAL, SALARIES, MACHINE, & FURNITURE WORKERS—IEU (J. B. Carey, D. J. Fitzmaurice, & W. H. Bywater Scholarships)

1126 16th Street, NW
Washington DC 20036-4866

202/296-1200

AMOUNT: $1,000—JBC (9 awards); $2,000—DJF (1); $3,000—WHB (1)
DEADLINE(S): APR 15
FIELD(S): All fields of study

Programs open to undergraduate dependents of union members. JBC scholarships support undergraduate study for one year in all fields of study. DJF scholarship supports undergraduate study for one year in engineering only. WHB scholarship available only to children of elected union officials.

Contact local union representative for complete information.

2943—IOWA AMERICAN LEGION (Boy Scout of the Year Contest Scholarship)

720 Lyon Street
Des Moines IA 50309
515/282-5068

AMOUNT: $2,000
DEADLINE(S): FEB 1
FIELD(S): All fields of study

Open to Iowa Boy Scouts who have received the Eagle Scout award. Scholarship is given based on scout's outstanding service to his religious institution, school, and community. For undergraduate study at an Iowa college or university.

Write for complete information.

2944—IOWA AMERICAN LEGION (Oratorical Contest Scholarship)

720 Lyon Street
Des Moines IA 50309
515/282-5068

AMOUNT: $2,000 (1st prize); $600 (2nd); $400 (3rd)
DEADLINE(S): DEC 1
FIELD(S): All fields of study

Speech Contest based on the US Constitution open to Iowa high school students in the 9th through 12th grades. Prizes are in the form of scholarships to attend a college or university in Iowa.

Write for complete information.

2945—IOWA COLLEGE STUDENT AID COMMISSION (Federal Stafford Loan Program; Federal PLUS Loans)

200 Tenth Street, 4th Fl.
Des Moines IA 50309-3609
515/281-3501

AMOUNT: $2,625-$4,000 undergraduate; $7,500 graduate
DEADLINE(S): None

FIELD(S): All fields of study

Loans open to Iowa residents enrolled in or attending approved institutions. Must be US citizens or legal residents and demonstrate need.

Write for complete information.

2946—IOWA COLLEGE STUDENT AID COMMISSION (Iowa Tuition Grant Program)

200 Tenth Street, 4th Fl.
Des Moines IA 50309-3609
515/281-3501

AMOUNT: $3,400
DEADLINE(S): JUN 2
FIELD(S): All fields of study

Open to Iowa residents enrolled or planning to enroll as undergraduates at eligible privately supported colleges or universities, business schools, or hospital nursing programs in Iowa. Must demonstrate need.

US citizen or legal resident. 10,140 grants per year. Renewable. Write for complete information.

2947—IOWA COLLEGE STUDENT AID COMMISSION (State of Iowa Scholarships)

200 Tenth Street, 4th Fl.
Des Moines IA 50309-3609
515/281-3501

AMOUNT: $400
DEADLINE(S): NOV 1
FIELD(S): All fields of study

Open to Iowa high school seniors who are in the top 15% of their class and plan to attend an eligible Iowa college or university. Considerations include ACT or SAT composite test scores; GPA and class rank. US citizenship required.

3,000 scholarships per year. Contact your counselor or write to address above for complete information.

2948—IOWA COMMISSION OF VETERANS AFFAIRS (War Orphans Educational Scholarship Aid)

Camp Dodge
7700 NW Beaver Drive
Johnston IA 50131
800/VET-IOWA or 515/242-5331
FAX: 515/242-5659

AMOUNT: Up to $600 per year
DEADLINE(S): None specified
FIELD(S): All fields of study

Resident of Iowa for at least 2 years prior to application. Child of parent who died in or as a result of military service during wartime. Also eligible are orphnas of National Guardsmen and other members of Reserve Components who died performing duties ordered by appropriate Federal or State authorities. High school graduate or equivalent. Attend a postsecondary institution in Iowa.

Renewable. Write for complete information.

2949—IOWA FEDERATION OF LABOR AFL-CIO (Annual Scholarship Program)

2000 Walker Street, Suite A
Des Moines IA 50317
515/262-9571

AMOUNT: $1,500
DEADLINE(S): MAR 28
FIELD(S): All areas of study

Competition based on essay. Open only to Iowa high school seniors.

Write for complete information.

2950—ITALIAN AMERICAN CHAMBER OF COMMERCE OF CHICAGO (Scholarships)

30 S. Michigan Ave., Suite 504
Chicago IL 60603
312/553-9137
FAX: 312/553-9142
E-mail: chicago@italchambers.net
Internet: www.italchambers.net/chicago

AMOUNT: $1,000
DEADLINE(S): MAY 31
FIELD(S): All fields of study

For students of Italian ancestry who are residents of one of the following Illinois counties: Cook, DuPage, Kane, Lake, Will, or McHenry. Must be a full-time student between last year in high school and last year of a fully accredited four-year college/university. Must have a minimum GPA of 3.5. Good moral character and scholastic achievement are the basic criteria for the award.

Not renewable. Applicants will be notified by November 1Street Contact Leonora or Frank at above address for an application.

2951—ITALIAN CATHOLIC FEDERATION INC. (College Scholarships for High School Seniors)

675 Hegenberger Road, #110
Oakland CA 94621
888/ICF-1924

AMOUNT: $400-$1,000
DEADLINE(S): MAR 15

FIELD(S): All fields of study

Open to graduating high school seniors of Italian ancestry and Catholic faith. Winners may attend any accredited institution. Limited to students who live in states where the federation is located (California, Nevada, and Illinois) and be US citizens.

Minimum GPA of 3.0 (4.0 scale). 200 scholarships per year. Send stamped self-addressed envelope to address above for further information.

2952—J. WOOD PLATT CADDIE SCHOLARSHIP TRUST (Scholarships)

Drawer 808
Southeastern PA 19399
215/687-2340

AMOUNT: Up to $9,000
DEADLINE(S): MAY 1
FIELD(S): All fields of study

Open to high school seniors and undergraduate students who have served as a caddie at a Golf Association of Philadelphia member club, have financial need, and have capability to successfully complete their undergraduate degree.

Renewable. Write for complete information.

2953—J.H. BAKER SCHOLARSHIP FUND (Student Loans)

c/o Tom Dechant, CPA
P.O. Box 280
La Crosse KS 67548
913/222-2537

AMOUNT: $2,000 per year
DEADLINE(S): JUL 15
FIELD(S): All undergrad fields of study

For graduates of high schools in the Kansas counties of Rush, Barton, Ellis, Ness, and Pawnee. Must be under 25 years of age. Selection is based on academic performance, character, ability, and need.

Contact address above for complete information.

2954—JACKQUELINE ELVIRA HODGES JOHNSON FUND, INC. (Scholarships)

P.O. Box 12393
Street Petersburg FL 33733
813/867-9567

AMOUNT: Varies
DEADLINE(S): APR 1; OCT 1
FIELD(S): All fields of study

Open to undergraduate cancer survivors who are US citizens or permanent residents. Must be a college-bound high

school senior or undergraduate enrolled in postsecondary study and demonstrate financial need. GPA minimum: 2.5.

Write to above address for complete information.

2955—JACKQUELINE ELVIRA HODGES JOHNSON FUND, INC. (Scholarship)

P.O. Box 1442
Walterboro SC 29488
803/538-8640

AMOUNT: Varies
DEADLINE(S): APR 1
FIELD(S): All fields of study

This scholarship is for cancer survivors and residents of South Carolina who are college-bound high school seniors or students enrolled in postsecondary study. Must demonstrate financial need and have at least a 3.0 GPA

Write to the above address for complete information.

2956—JACKSONVILLE STATE UNIVERSITY

Financial Aid Office
Jacksonville AL 36265
Written inquiry

AMOUNT: Varies
DEADLINE(S): MAR 15
FIELD(S): All fields of study

Numerous scholarship programs tenable at Jacksonville State University, Alabama, in all subject areas and with various restrictions concerning residency, year in school, major, etc.

Write to above address for complete listing and application.

2957—JACKSONVILLE UNIVERSITY (Scholarships & Grants Programs)

Director
Student Financial Assistance
Jacksonville FL 32211
904/745-7060

AMOUNT: Varies
DEADLINE(S): JAN 1
FIELD(S): All areas of study

Jacksonville University offers numerous scholarships, grants-in-aid, service awards, and campus employment. Financial need is not necessarily a consideration. Early applications are advised.

Candidates must apply for admission and for financial aid. 100 awards per year for study at Jacksonville University. Write for complete information.

2958—JAMES A. & JULIET L. DAVIS FOUNDATION, INC. (Scholarship)

P.O. Box 2027
Hutchinson KS 67504-2027
316/663-5021

AMOUNT: Varies
DEADLINE(S): None given
FIELD(S): All fields of study

Candidates are selected from the top 15% of the graduating class and are awarded scholarships on basis of demonstrating superior academic performance, citizenship, and financial need.

Scholarships are for four years of undergraduate study. Contact W.Y. Chalfant at address above for information.

2959—JAMES F. BYRNES FOUNDATION

P.O. Box 9596
Columbia SC 29290
803/254-9325

AMOUNT: $2,500
DEADLINE(S): FEB 15
FIELD(S): All fields of study

Undergraduate scholarships for young South Carolina residents who are high school seniors, college freshmen or sophomores, and whose parent or parents are deceased. Must be seeking B.S. or B.A. degree—not for technical education or associate degrees. GPA 2.5 or above. Must indicate qualities of character, ability, and enterprise.

Renewable for four years. Program also provides counseling, social events, a retreat, and awards luncheon. Involvement in the Byrnes Scholarship Program is expected. Phone or write to Jean P. Elton, Executive Secretary, at above address for details.

2960—JAMES G. K. McCLURE EDUCATIONAL AND DEVELOPMENT FUND (Western North Carolina Scholarships)

11 Sugar Hollow Road
Fairview NC 28730
704/628-2114

AMOUNT: $300 to $1,500
DEADLINE(S): MAY 15
FIELD(S): All fields of study

Open to students residing in western North Carolina who are entering the freshman class of a North Carolina college or university. Financial need is a consideration.

Write for complete information.

2961—JAMES M. HOFFMAN SCHOLARSHIP (Undergraduate Scholarship)

Southtrust Bank Asset Mngmt. Co.
P.O. Box 1000
Anniston AL 36202
205/238-1000, ext. 338

AMOUNT: Varies
DEADLINE(S): MAR 1
FIELD(S): All fields of study

For high school seniors attending schools in Calhoun County, Alabama. For undergraduate study at accredited colleges and universities. Must submit copies of parents' W-2 forms.

Write to attention of William K. Priddy for complete information.

2962—JAMES P. AND RUTH C. GILLROY FOUNDATION, INC.

100 East 42nd Street, Suite 1020
New York NY 10017
212/697-2710

AMOUNT: $1,250/semester; $2,500/yr.
DEADLINE(S): Varies (two months prior to date payment is due to the college)
FIELD(S): All fields of study

Undergraduate scholarships primarily for residents of the five boroughs of the City of New York.

Contact Edmund C. Grainger, Jr., President, at above location for details.

2963—JAMES Z. NAURISON SCHOLARSHIP FUND

1500 Main Street
P.O. Box 15769
Springfield MA 01115
413/732-2858

AMOUNT: $400-$2,000
DEADLINE(S): MAR 15
FIELD(S): All fields of study

Open to undergraduate and graduate students who are residents of the Massachusetts counties of Berkshire, Franklin, Hampden, or Hampshire or of the cities of Suffield or Enfield, CT. Awards based on financial need and academic record. Must fill out FAFSA and send a copy with your application, along with transcript(s).

Renewable up to four years. Approximately 300 awards per year. Self-addressed, stamped envelope must accompany request for application.

2964—JAPANESE AMERICAN CITIZENS LEAGUE (Abe & Esther Hagiwara Student Aid Award)

1765 Sutter Street
San Francisco CA 94115
415/921-5225
FAX: 415/931-4671
E-mail: jacl@jacl.org
Internet: www.jacl.org

AMOUNT: $1,000-$5,000
DEADLINE(S): APR 1
FIELD(S): All fields of study

Open only to JACL members and their children who demonstrate severe financial need. For undergraduate and graduate students planning to attend a college, university, trade school, business school, or any other institution of higher learning. Purpose is to provide financial assistance to a student who otherwise would have to delay or terminate his/her education due to lack of financing. Must submit personal statement, letters of recommendation, and transcripts.

For membership information or an application, send a self-addressed, stamped envelope to above address, stating your level of study. Applications available October 1st through March 20th; recipient notified in July.

2965—JAPANESE AMERICAN CITIZENS LEAGUE (Entering Freshmen Awards)

1765 Sutter Street
San Francisco CA 94115
415/921-5225
FAX: 415/931-4671
E-mail: jacl@jacl.org
Internet: www.jacl.org

AMOUNT: $1,000-$5,000
DEADLINE(S): MAR 1
FIELD(S): All fields of study

Open to JACL members and their children only. For entering freshmen planning to attend a college, university, trade school, business school, or any other institution of higher learning. Must submit personal statement, letters of recommendation, and transcript.

For membership information or an application, send a self-addressed, stamped envelope to above address, stating your level of study. Applications available October 1st through February 20th; recipients notified in July.

2966—JAPANESE AMERICAN CITIZENS LEAGUE (Undergraduate Awards)

1765 Sutter Street
San Francisco CA 94115
415/921-5225
FAX: 415/931-4671
E-mail: jacl@jacl.org
Internet: www.jacl.org

AMOUNT: $1,000-$5,000
DEADLINE(S): APR 1
FIELD(S): All fields of study

Open to JACL members and their children only. For undergraduate students planning to attend a college, university, trade school, business school, or any other institution of higher learning. Must submit personal statement, letters of recommendation, and transcripts.

For membership information or an application, send a self-addressed, stamped envelope to above address, stating your level of study. Applications available October 1st through March 20th; recipients notified in July.

2967—JAYCEE WAR MEMORIAL SCHOLARSHIP PROGRAM

P.O. Box 7
Tulsa OK 74102
800/JAYCEES
Internet: www.usjaycees.org/education/scholarships.htm

AMOUNT: $1,000 (25); $5,000 (1)
DEADLINE(S): MAR 1
FIELD(S): All fields of study

Open to US citizens who are enrolled in or accepted for admission to a college or university. Must possess academic potential and leadership traits. Financial need must be demonstrated.

Applications available ONLY between July 1 and February 1. Send self-addressed, stamped, business-size envelope and $5 application fee to JWMF, Dept. 94922, Tulsa, OK 74194-0001.

2968—JEANNETTE RANKIN FOUNDATION (Competitive Awards)

P.O. Box 6653
Athens GA 30604
Written inquiry

AMOUNT: $1,000
DEADLINE(S): MAR 1
FIELD(S): All fields of study

Open to women aged 35 or older accepted or enrolled in a certified program of voc-tech training or an undergrad pro-gram (NOT for grad study or 2nd undergrad degree). US citizenship is required. Financial need is major factor in selection.

Include business-size SASE; state sex, age, and level of study or training.

2969—JEWISH FAMILY AND CHILDREN'S SERVICES (Anna and Charles Stockwitz Children and Youth Fund)

1600 Scott Street
San Francisco CA 94115
415/561-1226

AMOUNT: $5,000 per year (student loans)
DEADLINE(S): None
FIELD(S): All fields of study

Loans and grants open to undergrads who are US permanent residents or citizens. Must be of the Jewish faith and age 25 or less. Must reside in San Francisco, San Mateo, Santa Clara, Marin, or Sonoma counties. Loan repayment is flexible; interest is approx. 80% of current prime.

Grant applicants must demonstrate financial need. Loan applicants must show ability to repay. Contact local JFCS office for complete information.

2970—JEWISH FAMILY AND CHILDREN'S SERVICES (College Loan Fund)

1600 Scott Street
San Francisco CA 94115
415/561-1226

AMOUNT: $5,000 maximum (student loan)
DEADLINE(S): None
FIELD(S): All fields of study

Open to worthy college students of the Jewish faith with limited resources but with a demonstrated ability to repay. Must be US permanent resident and living in San Francisco, San Mateo, Santa Clara, Marin, or Sonoma counties, California.

Guarantors or co-makers are required but not collateral. Repayment terms flexible; interest usually set at 80% of current prime rate. Contact local JFCS office for forms and complete information.

2971—JEWISH FAMILY AND CHILDREN'S SERVICES (Fogel Loan Fund)

1600 Scott Street
San Francisco CA 94115
415/561-1226

AMOUNT: Varies
DEADLINE(S): None
FIELD(S): All fields of study

Loans to help individuals of all ages for college or vocational studies and for personal, business, or professional purposes. Applicant must be a US permanent resident of Jewish faith and have a sound plan for repayment.

Must be a resident of San Francisco, San Mateo, Santa Clara, Marin, or Sonoma counties, California. Guarantor or co-makers required but no collateral is needed. Contact JFCS office for complete information.

2972—JEWISH FAMILY AND CHILDREN'S SERVICES (Jacob Rassen Memorial Scholarship Fund)

1600 Scott Street
San Francisco CA 94115
415/561-1226

AMOUNT: Up to $2,000
DEADLINE(S): None
FIELD(S): Study trip to Israel

Open to Jewish students under age 22 who demonstrate academic achievement and financial need and the desire to enhance Jewish identity and increase knowledge of and connection to Israel. Must be US permanent resident.

The opportunity to travel and study in Israel. Must reside in San Francisco, San Mateo, Santa Clara, Marin, or Sonoma counties in California. Contact local JFCS office for forms and complete information.

2973—JEWISH FAMILY AND CHILDREN'S SERVICES (Stanley Olson Youth Scholarship Fund)

1600 Scott Street
San Francisco CA 94115
415/561-1226

AMOUNT: Up to $2,500
DEADLINE(S): None
FIELD(S): All fields of study (preference to liberal arts majors)

Open to undergrad or grad students of Jewish faith who are 25 or younger, have demonstrated academic achievement and financial need, and have been accepted for enrollment in a college or university. Must be US permanent resident.

Must reside in San Francisco, San Mateo, Santa Clara, Marin, or Sonoma counties, California. Contact local JFCS office for applications and complete information.

2974—JEWISH FAMILY AND CHILDREN'S SERVICES (Vivienne Camp College Scholarship Fund)

1600 Scott Street
San Francisco CA 94115
415/561-1226

AMOUNT: $3,500 per year
DEADLINE(S): None
FIELD(S): All fields of study

Open to students of Jewish faith for undergrad or vocational study. Must be US permanent resident and have demonstrated academic achievement, financial need. Must be broad-based in extracurricular activities and community involvement.

Must have been accepted to a California college or vocational school and reside in San Francisco, San Mateo, Santa Clara, Marin, or Sonoma counties in California. Contact local JFCS office for forms and complete information.

2975—JEWISH SOCIAL SERVICE AGENCY OF METROPOLITAN WASHINGTON (Morton A. Gibson Memorial Scholarship)

6123 Montrose Road
Rockville MD 20852
301/881-3700

AMOUNT: $2,500
DEADLINE(S): JUN 1
FIELD(S): All fields of study

Open to current high school seniors who have performed significant volunteer service in the local Jewish community or for a Jewish organization. Must be admitted to an accredited 4-year undergrad degree program in the US and be residents of the Washington DC metropolitan area.

Volunteer service, financial need, and academic achievement are considered. 2 grants per year. Write for complete information.

2976—JEWISH SOCIAL SERVICE AGENCY OF METROPOLITAN WASHINGTON (Loan Fund)

6123 Montrose Road
Rockville MD 20852
301/881-3700

AMOUNT: Up to $2,000
DEADLINE(S): Ongoing
FIELD(S): All fields of study

Open to Jewish applicants 18 or older who are within eighteen months of completing an undergraduate or graduate degree or a vocational training program and are residents of the Washington metropolitan area. No-interest loan based on financial need.

A one-time award. US citizen or permanent resident who will seek citizenship. Recipient must agree to a stipulation to pay $50 per month within three months after graduation. Write for complete information.

2977—JEWISH SOCIAL SERVICE AGENCY OF METROPOLITAN WASHINGTON (Max and Emmy Dreyfuss Undergraduate Scholarship)

6123 Montrose Road
Rockville MD 20852
301/881-3700

AMOUNT: Up to $3,500/year
DEADLINE(S): JUN 1
FIELD(S): All fields of study

Open to Jewish undergraduates no older than 30 who are enrolled in an accredited undergraduate four-year degree program and are from the Washington metropolitan area. Special consideration is given to refugees.

Renewable upon reapplication for four years. Awards based on financial need. Call Scholarship and Loan Coordinator at above number to request application.

2978—JEWISH SOCIAL SERVICE AGENCY OF METROPOLITAN WASHINGTON (Jeanette Siegel Memorial Scholarship)

6123 Montrose Road
Rockville MD 20852
301/881-3700

AMOUNT: One full tuition or two partial tuitions/yr.
DEADLINE(S): APR 25
FIELD(S): All fields of study for grades 4-12

For students no younger than fourth grade in a Jewish primary or secondary day school who would be unable to attend a Jewish school without a scholarship. Refugees will be given preference. Must be residents of the Washington DC metropolitan area.

A fund of last resort—it is not intended to duplicate funds available from other sources. Names of candidates are to be submitted by the Jewish day schools by April 25. Candidates should not apply directly to JSSA.

2979—JEWISH VOCATIONAL SERVICE (JVS) (Community Scholarship Fund)

5700 Wilshire Blvd., Suite 2303
Los Angeles CA 90036
213/761-8888, ext. 122
FAX: 213/761-8850

AMOUNT: Up to $2,000
DEADLINE(S): APR 15 (March 1 for application requests)
FIELD(S): All fields of study

For undergraduate students who are sophomores or higher, graduate or professional students, or students pursuing vocational training. Must be Jewish permanent residents of Los Angeles County, California with financial need, US citizens or permanent residents, and are in a full-time course of study in an accredited institution.

Renewable annually. Preference given to students in California schools. Call or write for application.

2980—JOHN C. CHAFFIN EDUCATIONAL FUND (Scholarships and Loans Programs)

100 Walnut Street
Newtonville MA 02160
617/552-7652

AMOUNT: Scholarships: $500/semester; Loans: $600/semester
DEADLINE(S): None given
FIELD(S): All fields of study

Open only to graduates of Newton North and Newton South High Schools in Newton, Massachusetts. Preference to students enrolling in four-year accredited undergraduate programs; trustees may also support those attending less than four-year degree and non-degree granting school provided they are accredited schools.

Approximately 30 awards per year. Renewable to a maximum of $2,000 for scholarships and $4,800 for loans. Loans begin to accrue 6% interest rate six months after graduation. Write for complete information.

2981—JOHN EDGAR THOMSON FOUNDATION (Grants)

201 South 18th Street, Suite 318
Philadelphia PA 19103
Phone/FAX: 215/545-6083

AMOUNT: Monthly stipend
DEADLINE(S): None
FIELD(S): All fields of study

Financial assistance for females from infancy through age 22 whose deceased parent was a railroad worker. Support ends at age 18 if daughter does not seek higher education. The cause of death need not be work-related. The daughter must live in the home of the surviving parent, except while living at a college campus. Eligibility is dependent upon the daughter and parent remaining unmarried. Financial need considered.

The Foundation also provides special health care benefits to the daughter. Contact Sheila Cohen, Director, for more information.

2982—JOHN GYLES EDUCATION FUND (Scholarships)

P.O. Box 4808
712 Riverside Drive
Fredericton, New Brunswick
E3B 5G4 CANADA
506/459-7460

AMOUNT: $3,000 (max.)
DEADLINE(S): APR 1; JUN 1; NOV 15
FIELD(S): All fields of study

Financial assistance for full-time post-secondary students who are citizens of either the US or Canada. Minimum GPA of 2.7 required. Criteria other than strictly academic ability and financial need are considered.

To receive application, please send ONLY a stamped (US 33 cents)*, business-sized (#10), self-addressed envelope to The Secretary at above address.

*US postage acceptable due to use of international mail services.

2983—JOHN T. HALL TRUST

P.O. Box 4655
Atlanta GA 30302-4655
Written inquiry

AMOUNT: Varies
DEADLINE(S): Ongoing
FIELD(S): All areas of study

Student loans to residents of Georgia for undergraduate and graduate education.

Write to Miss Dale Welch, c/o SunTrust Bank, Atlanta, at above address for application details.

2984—JOHN T. HOGAN MEMORIAL FOUNDATION

60 State Street
Boston MA 02109
Written inquiry

AMOUNT: Varies
DEADLINE(S): MAR 31
FIELD(S): All fields of study

Undergraduate scholarships to residents of New England. Preference is given to residents of Massachusetts and New Hampshire.

Send SASE to Samuel Dennis, Trustee, c/o Hale and Dorr, at above address for application guidelines.

2985—JOHN WOOLMAN SCHOOL (Financial Aid Program)

13075 Woolman Lane
Nevada City CA 95959
530/273-3183
FAX: 530/273-9028
E-mail: jwsadmit@nccn.net
Internet: www.pacificnet.~woolman/

AMOUNT: Up to $10,000
DEADLINE(S): AUG 1
FIELD(S): All fields of study

Needs-based scholarships for students accepted at this coed, college preparatory boarding school in Nevada City, CA. Must demonstrate financial need based on application and recent IRS 1040 form. The school is associated with the Friends, or Quaker, religion.

18 new awards yearly. Renewable. Contact school for details. Also, a $500 needs-based scholarship for children or relatives of school's alumni.

2986—JOHN WOOLMAN SCHOOL (Native American Scholarship Program)

13075 Woolman Lane
Nevada City CA 95959
530/273-3183
FAX: 530/273-9028
E-mail: jwsadmit@nccn.net
Internet: www.pacificnet.~woolman/

AMOUNT: $500-$5,000
DEADLINE(S): JUN 1
FIELD(S): All fields of study

Needs-based scholarships for Native American students accepted at this coed, college preparatory boarding school in Nevada City, CA. Must demonstrate financial need. The school is associated with the Friends, or Quaker, religion.

1-2 awards yearly. Renewable. Contact school for details.

2987—JOHNSON AND WALES UNIVERSITY (Gaebe Eagle Scout Scholarships)

8 Abbott Place
Providence RI 02903
401/598-1000

AMOUNT: $300
DEADLINE(S): APR 30

FIELD(S): All fields of study

Open to undergraduate freshmen who have been accepted at Johnson and Wales University. Must be Eagle Scout who has received a religious award of his faith.

All eligible freshmen receive award of $300. Write for complete information.

2988—JOHNSON CONTROLS FOUNDATION (Scholarship Program)

5757 N. Green Bay Ave., X-34
Milwaukee WI 53201
414/228-2296

AMOUNT: $1,750 per year ($7,000 over 4 yrs.)
DEADLINE(S): FEB 1
FIELD(S): All areas of study

Eligibility for scholarships limited to children of employees of Johnson Controls Inc. Must be in upper 30% of high school graduating class and must maintain standards in college for renewal. Scholarships for full-time study only.

US citizenship required. Write for complete information.

2989—JUNIATA COLLEGE (Church of the Brethren Scholarships)

Financial Aid Office
Huntingdon PA 16652
814/641-3603
FAX: 814/641-3355
E-mail: clarkec@juniata.edu

AMOUNT: $5,000 (max.)
DEADLINE(S): APR 1
FIELD(S): All fields of study

Open to Church of the Brethren members in various geographic areas who are applying to Juniata College. Must fill out government FAFSA form.

Contact Cynthia G. Clarke, Research Specialist, for an application or enrollment information. See your financial aid office for FAFSA.

2990—JUNIATA COLLEGE (Frederick & Mary F. Beckley Scholarship Fund)

Financial Aid Office
Huntingdon PA 16652
814/641-3603
FAX: 814/641-3355
E-mail: clarkec@juniata.edu

AMOUNT: $700-$1,000
DEADLINE(S): None
FIELD(S): All fields of study

Open to needy left-handed students who have junior or senior standing at Juniata College.

Contact Cynthia G. Clarke, Research Specialist, for an application or enrollment information.

2991—JUNIATA COLLEGE (Friendship Scholarships)

Financial Aid Office
Huntingdon PA 16652
814/641-3603
FAX: 814/641-3355
E-mail: clarkec@juniata.edu

AMOUNT: $2,000
DEADLINE(S): MAR 15
FIELD(S): All fields of study

Open to international students applying to Juniata College.

Contact Cynthia G. Clarke, Research Specialist, for an application or enrollment information.

2992—JUNIATA COLLEGE (Sam Hayes, Jr. Scholarship)

Financial Aid Office
Huntingdon PA 16652
814/641-3603
FAX: 814/641-3355
E-mail: clarkec@juniata.edu

AMOUNT: $1,500 (max.)
DEADLINE(S): APR 1
FIELD(S): All fields of study

Open to Pennsylvania 4H and FFA members who are applying to Juniata College. Must demonstrate financial need and fill out government FAFSA form.

Contact Cynthia G. Clarke, Research Specialist, for an application or enrollment information. See your financial aid office for FAFSA.

2993—JUNIOR LEAGUE OF NORTHERN VIRGINIA (Scholarships)

7921 Jones Branch Drive, #320
McLean VA 22102
703/893-0258

AMOUNT: $500 to $2,000
DEADLINE(S): DEC 15
FIELD(S): All fields of study

Open to women who are 23 years old or more and accepted to or enrolled in an accredited college or university as an undergraduate student in northern Virginia unless the course is not offered at a northern Virginia school. Must be resident of Northern Virginia, a US citizen, and demonstrate financial need.

8-10 awards per year. Write for complete information.

2994—KAISER FOUNDATION, INC.

90 13th Street
Wheatland WY 82201
307/322-2026

AMOUNT: $1,000
DEADLINE(S): MAY 1
FIELD(S): All fields of study

Scholarships for high school students who are residents of Wyoming.

Write to Edward W. Hunter, Executive Director, at above address.

2995—KANSAS AMERICAN LEGION (Scholarships)

1314 SW Topeka Blvd.
Topeka KS 66612
Written inquiry

AMOUNT: $150-$1,000
DEADLINE(S): FEB 15; JUL 15
FIELD(S): All fields of study

Variety of scholarships and awards for Kansas residents to attend Kansas colleges, universities, or trade schools. Some are limited to Legion members and/or designated fields of study.

Write for complete information.

2996—KANSAS BOARD OF REGENTS (Ethnic Minority Scholarship)

700 SW Harrison Street, Suite 1410
Topeka KS 66603-3760
785/296-3518

AMOUNT: Up to $1,500/yr.
DEADLINE(S): APR 1
FIELD(S): All fields of study

For financially needy, academically competitive students who are Kansas residents and are American Indian/Alaskan Native, Asian/Pacific Islander, Black, or Hispanic. Priority given to high school seniors. Must have one of the following: ACT 21/SAT 816, GPA 3.0, high school rank of upper 33%, completion of Regents Recommended Curriculum, selection by National Merit Corporation in any category, or selection by College Board as a Hispanic Scholar. Must complete the FAFSA.

$10 application fee. Renewable for 4 years (5 years if a 5-yr. program). Contact Kansas Board of Regents for an application. See your financial aid office for the FAFSA.

2997—KANSAS BOARD OF REGENTS (Kansas Comprehensive Grants)

700 SW Harrison Street, Suite 1410
Topeka KS 66603-3760

785/296-3518
FAFSA: 800/433-3243
Internet: www.fafsa.ed.gov

AMOUNT: $200-$2,500 (private); $100-$1,100 (public)
DEADLINE(S): APR 1
FIELD(S): All fields of study

Available to needy Kansas residents enrolled full-time at the seventeen private colleges/universities located in Kansas, the six public universities, and Washburn University. The Kansas Legislature provides limited assistance to financially needy students. To be considered, you must complete and submit the FAFSA, listing one or more eligible colleges in Step 5.

1 in 5 eligible students are funded annually. See website or contact your financial aid office for a copy of the FAFSA.

2998—KANSAS BOARD OF REGENTS (Kansas State Scholarship)

700 SW Harrison Street, Suite 1410
Topeka KS 66603-3760
785/296-3518

AMOUNT: Up to $1,000
DEADLINE(S): MAY 15
FIELD(S): All fields of study

Assists financially needy students in top 20-40% of Kansas high school graduates who are designated as Kansas Scholars. Applicants must have received a letter of designation in their senior year of high school. Must have taken ACT Assessment between April of sophomore year and December of senior year, AND complete Regents Recommended Curriculum. The 7th semester GPA and curriculum data will be provided by high school official by March. Must complete the FAFSA.

Renewable. Contact Kansas Board of Regents for an application. See your financial aid office for the FAFSA.

2999—KANSAS COMMISSION ON VETERANS' AFFAIRS (Scholarships)

700 SW Jackson Street, #701
Topeka KS 66603
913/296-3976

AMOUNT: Free tuition and fees in state-supported institutions
DEADLINE(S): Varies
FIELD(S): All areas of study

Open to dependent child of person who entered US military service as a resident of Kansas and was prisoner of war, missing, or killed in action or died as a result of service-connected disabilities incurred during service in Vietnam.

Application must be made prior to enrollment. Renewable to maximum of 12 semesters. Write for complete information.

3000—KANSAS STATE UNIVERSITY FOUNDATION (Various Scholarships)

Office of Student Financial Assistance
104 Fairchild Hall
Manhattan KS 66506-1104
785/532-6420
FAX: 785/532-7628
E-mail: ksusfa@ksu.edu
Internet: www.found.ksu.edu/
Schshps/Sch-txt.htm

AMOUNT: Varies
DEADLINE(S): Varies
FIELD(S): All fields of study

More than 1,300 scholarships are administered by the KSU Foundation for students attending KSU at either the Manhattan or Salina campus.

Salina campus address: Office of Student Financial Assistance, 223 College Center, Salina, KS 67401; Phone: 785/826-2638

FAX: 785/826-2936
E-mail: Hheter@mail.sal.ksu.edu.
Website above is the same for Salina.

3001—KAPPA SIGMA ENDOWMENT FUND (Scholarship/Leadership Awards Program)

P.O. Box 5643
Charlottesville VA 22907
804/295-3193
FAX: 804/296-9557
E-mail: Mic@imh.kappasigma.org

AMOUNT: $250-$1,250
DEADLINE(S): OCT 15
FIELD(S): All fields of study

Undergraduate awards are for members of Kappa Sigma fraternity. Based on scholarship, leadership, GPA, and activities. Financial need NOT a factor.

Not renewable. Contact Mitchell B. Wilson for an application.

3002—KENNEDY FOUNDATION (Scholarships)

P.O. Box 27296
Denver CO 80227
303/933-2435

AMOUNT: Approx. $1,000
DEADLINE(S): JUN 30
FIELD(S): All fields of study

Scholarships for Colorado residents attending colleges or universities.

Send SASE to Jacqueline Kennedy, Vice President, at above location for application information.

3003—KENTUCKY CENTER FOR VETERANS AFFAIRS (Benefits for Veterans' Dependents, Spouses, & Widows)

545 S. 3rd Street, Room 123
Louisville KY 40202
502/595-4447
FAX: 502/595-4448

AMOUNT: Varies
DEADLINE(S): None
FIELD(S): All fields of study

Kentucky residents. Open to dependent children, spouses, and non-remarried widows of permanently and totally disabled war veterans who served during periods of federally recognized hostilities or who were MIA or a POW.

Veteran must be a resident of KY or, if deceased, a resident at time of death.

3004—KENTUCKY HIGHER EDUCATION ASSISTANCE AUTHORITY (College Access Program [CAP] Grant)

1050 US 127 South, Suite 102
Frankfort KY 40601-4323
502-564-7990 or 800/928-8926

AMOUNT: $246 to $490 per semester
DEADLINE(S): MAR 15 (priority date)
FIELD(S): All fields of study

Open to Kentucky residents who are US citizens or legal residents enrolled or planning to enroll at least half-time in a 2- or 4-year undergrad (or voc-tech) program at an eligible Kentucky institution.

Renewable with reapplication. Write for complete information.

3005—KENTUCKY HIGHER EDUCATION ASSISTANCE AUTHORITY (Student Loan Program)

1050 US 127 South, Suite 102
Frankfort KY 40601-4323
502/564-7990 or 800/928-8926

AMOUNT: $2,625 to $18,500 (amount varies according to academic standing and whether student is dependent or independent)
DEADLINE(S): Varies
FIELD(S): All fields of study

Open to US citizens or legal residents enrolled or accepted for enrollment (on at least a half-time basis) at an eligible post-secondary educational institution.

Write for complete information.

3006—KEY BANK OF CENTRAL MAINE FOUNDATION

P.O. Box 1054
Augusta ME 04330
Written inquiry

AMOUNT: Varies
DEADLINE(S): Ongoing
FIELD(S): All fields of study

Scholarships for individuals to attend Maine colleges and universities.

Send SASE to Key Bank of Maine at above address.

3007—KITTIE M. FAIREY EDUCATIONAL FUND

P.O. Box 1465
Taylors SC 29687-1465
803/765-3677

AMOUNT: Varies
DEADLINE(S): MAR 15
FIELD(S): All fields of study

Scholarships for residents of South Carolina attending four-year colleges or universities in SC.

Write to Sandra Lee, Director, at above address.

3008—KNIGHTS OF COLUMBUS (Canadian Scholarship Program)

P.O. Drawer 1670
New Haven CT 06507-0901
203/772-2130, ext. 224
FAX: 203/773-3000

AMOUNT: $1,500 maximum
DEADLINE(S): MAY 1
FIELD(S): All areas of study

Open to daughters/sons of Knights of Columbus members in good standing who are Canadian citizens and will be entering their first year of a Canadian university program that will lead to a baccalaureate degree.

12 scholarships per year. Renewable for each year of undergraduate study if satisfactory progress is made. Write for complete information.

3009—KNIGHTS OF COLUMBUS (Fourth Degree Pro Deo & Pro Patria Scholarships)

P.O. Box 1670
New Haven CT 06507-0901
203/772-2130, ext. 332
FAX: 203/773-3000

AMOUNT: $1,500
DEADLINE(S): MAR 1
FIELD(S): All fields of study

Open to students enrolling in the freshman class in a Catholic college who can show evidence of satisfactory academic performance. Must be a member or dependent of a Knights of Columbus member or dependent of a Columbian Squires member in good standing or of a deceased member.

62 scholarships per year; 50 at any Catholic college and 12 at the Catholic University of America in Washington DC. Renewable up to 4 years.

3010—KNIGHTS OF COLUMBUS (Francis P. Matthews and John E. Swift Educational Trust Scholarship)

P.O. Drawer 1670
New Haven CT 06507
203/772-2130, ext. 332
FAX: 203/773-3000

AMOUNT: Varies
DEADLINE(S): None specified
FIELD(S): All fields of study

Open to children of Knights of Columbus members who died in military service or became totally and permanently disabled from causes directly connected with a period of conflict or from duties as a policeman or fireman.

For undergraduate studies at a Catholic college. Unspecified number of awards per year. Write for complete information.

3011—KNIGHTS OF COLUMBUS (Squires Scholarship Program)

P.O. Drawer 1670
New Haven CT 06507
203/772-2130

AMOUNT: $1,500
DEADLINE(S): MAR 1
FIELD(S): All areas of study

Open to students entering their freshman year at a Catholic college who are members in good standing of the Columbian Squires and have demonstrated academic excellence.

Renewable up to four years. Write for complete information.

3012—KNIGHTS TEMPLAR EDUCATIONAL FOUNDATION (Special Low-Interest Loans)

5097 N. Elston, Suite 101
Chicago IL 60630-2460
312/777-3300

AMOUNT: $6,000 maximum per student
DEADLINE(S): Varies
FIELD(S): All fields of study

Special low-interest loans (5% fixed rate). No payments while in school. Interest and repayments start after graduation or when you leave school. Open to voc-tech students or junior/senior undergraduate students or graduate students.

US citizen or legal resident. Request information from Charles R. Neumann (Grand Recorder-Secretary). Call or write to your state's grand commandery for proper application.

3013—KOOMRUIAN EDUCATION FUND

3333 South Beaudry Ave., Box 16
Los Angeles, CA 90017-1466
Written inquiry

AMOUNT: Varies
DEADLINE(S): None specified
FIELD(S): All fields of study

Scholarships to students of Armenian descent residing in California.

Send SASE to Bank of America at above location.

3014—KOSCIUSZKO FOUNDATION (Tuition Scholarships)

15 East 65th Street
New York NY 10021-6595
212/734-2130
FAX: 212/628-4552
Internet: www.kosciuszkofoundation.org/grants/tuitapp.htm

AMOUNT: $1,000-$5,000
DEADLINE(S): JAN 16
FIELD(S): All fields of study

Open to full-time graduate students of Polish descent who are US citizens or permanent US residents. Some scholarships are available for juniors and seniors.

There is a nonrefundable $25 application fee. Candidates who are at least associate members of the Foundation are exempt from the application fee. Application is on website. Write or access website for complete information.

3015—LARAMIE COUNTY FARM BUREAU (Scholarships)

206 Main Street, Box 858
Pine Bluffs WY 82082-0858
Written inquiry

AMOUNT: $300
DEADLINE(S): MAY 1
FIELD(S): All fields of study

Available to needy high school seniors and college students whose parents have been members of Laramie County Farm Bureau for more than one year and who

are current members. Award may be used at any institution of postsecondary education. Interviews will be done by appointment.

3 awards annually. Write to above address for an application.

3016—LEADERS IN FURTHERING EDUCATION (LIFE Unsung Hero Program Scholarships)

252 Ocean Blvd.
Manalapan FL 33462
561/547-9307
FAX: 561/585-3235
E-mail: life@life-edu.org
Internet: www.life-edu.org

AMOUNT: $10,000 for recipient's college tuition, books, housing; $2,500 to the charity with which they are involved; $2,500 to their high school
DEADLINE(S): DEC 15
FIELD(S): All fields of study

Scholarships for high school students (grades 9-12) who are residents of Palm Beach County, Florida, who engage in volunteer community service. Service must have been carried out for at least the past two years. GPA of 2.5 must be maintained.

Contact organization or access website for details.

3017—LEGACY SOCCER FOUNDATION, INC./LEVER BROTHERS (Endowed Scholarships)

P.O. Box 3481
Winter Park FL 32790
407/263-8285
FAX: 407/740-8406
Internet: www.legacysoc.org

AMOUNT: Varies
DEADLINE(S): Varies
FIELD(S): All fields of study

Scholarships for Florida residents of either Brevard, Orange, Osceola, Seminole, or Volusa counties. Must be a US citizen with a high school GPA of at least 2.5. Must graduate in top 1/3 of class and have played organized soccer for two out of past five years. Must meet financial aid requirements of the institution. Tenable at institutions in those same five counties.

Contact financial aid office at either Brevard Community College Foundation, Florida Tech, Seminole Community College, Valencia Community College Foundation, or Univ. of Central Florida for more information.

3018—LEON L. GRANOFF FOUNDATION

P.O. Box 2148
Gardena CA 90247-0148
Written inquiry

AMOUNT: Varies
DEADLINE(S): Varies
FIELD(S): All fields of study

Undergraduate scholarships for California residents to attend California colleges and universities.

Renewable provided recipients maintain at least a 3.25 GPA. Contact foundation for current application deadline and procedures.

3019—LEON M. JORDAN SCHOLARSHIP AND MONUMENT FUND

Box 15544
Kansas City MO 64106
Written inquiry

AMOUNT: Varies
DEADLINE(S): Varies
FIELD(S): All fields of study

Scholarships to residents of Missouri.

Write to Alexander Ellison, Treasurer, Advisory Committee, at above address for application details.

3020—LEONARD H. BULKELEY SCHOLARSHIP FUND (Scholarship Grants)

c/o R. N. Woodworth, Treasurer
17 Crocker Street
New London CT 06320
860/447-1461

AMOUNT: $1,000 (approximately)
DEADLINE(S): APR 1
FIELD(S): All fields of study

Open ONLY to residents of New London, CT, for undergraduate study in an accredited college or university. Must demonstrate financial need.

Write for complete information.

3021—LEOPOLD SCHEPP FOUNDATION (Undergraduate Awards)

551 Fifth Ave., Suite 3000
New York NY 10176-2597
212/986-3078

AMOUNT: Up to $7,500
DEADLINE(S): Not given
FIELD(S): All fields of study

Undergraduates should write detailing their education to date, year in school, length of course of study, vocational goal, financial need, age, citizenship, and availability for interview in New York City.

Approximately 200 new awards per year. Recipients may reapply for subsequent years. Applicants should already be in college and not older than 30. High school seniors may NOT apply. Print or type name and address. Send SASE with above information for application.

3022—LLOYD D. SWEET SCHOLARSHIP FOUNDATION (Scholarships)

Box 638 (Attn: Academic year)
Chinook MT 59523
406/357-2236

AMOUNT: Varies
DEADLINE(S): MAR 2
FIELD(S): All fields of study

Scholarships open to graduates of Chinook (MT) High School. Awards are for full-time undergraduate or graduate study at accredited colleges and universities in the US.

Approximately 75 awards per year. Write for complete information.

3023—LOS MOLINOS UNIFIED SCHOOL DISTRICT (S. R. Pritchett Scholarship Fund)

District Superintendent
P.O. Box 609
Los Molinos CA 96055
916/384-7900
FAX: 916/384-1534

AMOUNT: Not specified
DEADLINE(S): APR 15
FIELD(S): All fields of study

Undergraduate scholarships open only to current year graduates of high school in the Vina area of Tehama County, CA.

Write for complete information.

3024—LOU AND LUCIENNE BRIGHTMAN SCHOLARSHIP

94 Pleasant Street
Malden MA 02148
Written inquiry

AMOUNT: Varies
DEADLINE(S): JUN 1
FIELD(S): All areas of study

Scholarships for college-bound high school seniors who are residents of Maine.

Renewable. Send SASE to Robert M. Wallask, V.P., Eastern Bank & Trust Co., at above address.

3025—LOUISIANA DEPT. OF VETERANS AFFAIRS (Awards Program)

Capitol Station
P.O. Box 94095

Baton Rouge LA 70804
504/922-0500
FAX 504/922-0511

AMOUNT: Varies
DEADLINE(S): Varies
FIELD(S): All fields of study

Louisiana resident. Open to children (aged 16-25) and widows/spouses of deceased/disabled (100%) war veterans who were Louisiana residents for at least 1 year prior to service. For undergraduate study at state supported schools in Louisiana.

Approximately 200 awards per year. Renewable up to 4 years. Write for complete information.

3026—LOUISIANA OFFICE OF STUDENT FINANCIAL ASSISTANCE (Tuition Opportunity Program for Students-Opportunity Award)

P.O. Box 91202
Baton Rouge LA 70821-9202
800/259-5626, ext. 1012
FAX: 504/922-0790
Internet: http://www.osfa.state.la.us

AMOUNT: Tuition waver at a LA public school or average public school tuition at an LAICU private school
DEADLINE(S): JUN 1
FIELD(S): All fields of study

Must apply as a first-time freshman within 4 semesters of graduation from an approved LA high school. Must have 2.5 GPA, the prior year's state average on the ACT (min. 19), and completion of 16.5 units of the core curriculum. For use at Louisiana public colleges, universities, or technical schools and member schools of the Louisiana Association of Independent Colleges and Universities.

Apply by completing the Free Application for Federal Student Aid (FAFSA).

3027—LOUISIANA OFFICE OF STUDENT FINANCIAL ASSISTANCE (Tuition Opportunity Program for Students-Performance Award)

P.O. Box 91202
Baton Rouge LA 70821-9202
800/259-5626, ext. 1012
FAX: 504/922-0790
Internet: http://www.osfa.state.la.us

AMOUNT: Tuition waver at a LA public school + $400, or average public school tuition + $400 at an LAICU private school

DEADLINE(S): JUN 1

FIELD(S): All fields of study

Must accept as an undergraduate by the fourth semester following graduation from an approved LA high school. Must rank in top 5% of class, have 3.5 high school GPA, and ACT composite score of 23. If college has been attended, a GPA of 3.0 is required.

Apply by completing the Free Application for Federal Student Aid (FAFSA).

3028—LOUISIANA OFFICE OF STUDENT FINANCIAL ASSISTANCE (Tuition Opportunity Program for Students-Honors Award)

P.O. Box 91202
Baton Rouge LA 70821-9202
1-800/259-5626, ext. 1012
FAX: 504/922-0790
Internet: http://www.osfa.state.la.us

AMOUNT: Tuition waver at a LA public school + $800, or average public school tuition + $800 at an LAICU private school

DEADLINE(S): JUN 1

FIELD(S): All fields of study

Must accept award as an undergraduate by the fourth semester following graduation from an approved LA high school. Must have 3.5 high school GPA, ACT composite score of 27, and completion of core curriculum. If college has been attended, a GPA of 3.0 is required.

Apply by completing the Free Application for Federal Student Aid (FAFSA).

3029—LOUISIANA STATE UNIVERSITY AT SHREVEPORT (LSUS Academic Scholarship)

Financial Aid Office
One University Place
Shreveport LA 71115-2399
318/797-5363
FAX: 318/797-5366
E-mail: finaid@pilot.lsus.edu
Internet: www.lsus.edu

AMOUNT: Tuition & fees +$400 for books & supplies

DEADLINE(S): DEC 1

FIELD(S): All fields of study

This may be a one-year or a four-year award. Student must be a Louisiana resident, a high school graduate/equivalent (or a senior in high school), have at least a 28 composite score on the ACT (which must be taken in October to have the results on

file with LSUS by December 1st deadline), and must have a minimum 3.5 GPA.

Contact your high school counselor or the Student Financial Aid Office at LSUS for an application. Awards are made by the end of February.

3030—LOUISIANA STATE UNIVERSITY AT SHREVEPORT (LSUS Foundation Scholarship)

Financial Aid Office
One University Place
Shreveport LA 71115-2399
318/797-5363
FAX: 318/797-5366
E-mail: finaid@pilot.lsus.edu
Internet: www.lsus.edu

AMOUNT: $300-$750/semester

DEADLINE(S): DEC 1; MAR

FIELD(S): All fields of study

Student must be an entering freshman with at least a 20 ACT composite score and minimum 3.0 cumulative GPA or be a transfer student with at least 48 credit hours and a 3.5 or higher college GPA. Entering freshmen awards are for up to eight semesters, and transfer student awards range from two to four semesters.

High school students should submit the LSUS scholarship application by December 1st of senior year. Transfer students should send a letter of application to the Financial Aid Office with an official college transcript of all coursework by the March prior to the fall semester they are entering.

3031—LOUISIANA STATE UNIVERSITY AT SHREVEPORT (LSUS Alumni Association Scholarship)

Financial Aid Office
One University Place
Shreveport LA 71115-2399
318/797-5363
FAX: 318/797-5366
E-mail: finaid@pilot.lsus.edu
Internet: www.lsus.edu

AMOUNT: $1,000/yr.

DEADLINE(S): FEB 1

FIELD(S): All fields of study

This four-year award is for entering freshmen with at least a 3.2 cumulative high school GPA (grades 9-11) and a 25 or higher composite score on the ACT. To retain scholarship, the recipient must complete at least 12 hours credit and make at least a 3.0 GPA average each semester. Must apply during senior year of high school.

Contact your high school counselor or the Student Financial Aid Office at LSUS for an application.

3032—LUBBOCK AREA FOUNDATION, INC. (Scholarships)

1655 Main Street, #209
Lubbock TX 79401
806/762-8061
FAX: 806/762-8551
E-mail: lubaf@worldnet.att.net

AMOUNT: Varies

DEADLINE(S): Varies

FIELD(S): All fields of study

Several scholarships are administered by this Foundation for residents of the Lubbock, Texas, area. Some are for graduates of specific high schools, some are for use at specific institutions, and one is for women age 50+.

Contact organization for specifics.

3033—LUCY E. MEILLER EDUCATIONAL TRUST

P.O. Box 13888
Roanoke VA 24038
Written inquiry

AMOUNT: $3,000

DEADLINE(S): Ongoing

FIELD(S): All fields of study

Scholarships for financially needy residents of Virginia to attend colleges and universities.

Apply through the financial aid office at the Virginia college or university or contact Perry Gorham, Crestar Bank, at above address for details.

3034—LULAC (LEAGUE OF UNITED LATIN AMERICAN CITIZENS) (National Scholarship Fund)

1133 20th Street NW, Suite 750
Washington DC 20036
202/408-0060
FAX: 202/408-0064
Internet: www.lulac.org/

AMOUNT: Varies

DEADLINE(S): Varies

FIELD(S): All fields of study

Open to high school seniors, undergraduate, and graduate college students of Hispanic origin. Some are for specific fields of study such as business or engineering, and some have certain GPA requirements.

See high school counselor or send self-addressed, stamped envelope for complete information. Application and e-mail info is also on website.

3035—LULAC NATIONAL EDUCATIONAL SERVICE CENTER, INC.
(Hispanic/Burlington Northern Santa Fe Foundation American Scholarship Program)

1133 20th Street NW, Suite 750
Washington DC 20036
202/408-0060
FAX: 202/408-0064
Internet: www.lulac.org/

AMOUNT: Varies
DEADLINE(S): MAR 31
FIELD(S): All fields of study

Open to college-bound high school seniors and undergraduate students who are Hispanic US citizens or legal residents. Preference is given to students living in states where Burlington Northern Santa Fe Corporation operates: CO, AZ, KS, MN, MT, ND, NM, OD, OR, SD, WA, and San Bernardino, CA.

Write to the above address or contact high school counselor for complete information.

3036—LUTHERAN BROTHERHOOD
(Stafford Student Loans)

625 Fourth Ave. South
Minneapolis MN 55415
800/328-7168

AMOUNT: $2,625-$8,500
DEADLINE(S): None
FIELD(S): All fields of study

Loans open to Lutheran students on a first-come, first-served basis who have been accepted for admission by an eligible higher education institution and are making satisfactory progress. Must meet federal requirements.

Contact address above for complete information.

3037—LUTHERAN BROTHERHOOD
(Undergraduate Scholarships)

625 Fourth Ave., South
Minneapolis MN 55415
800/328-7168

AMOUNT: $500-$2,000
DEADLINE(S): JAN 15
FIELD(S): All fields of study

Open to Lutheran Brotherhood members. Recipients are chosen by an independent panel of judges on the basis of scholastic achievement (minimum high

school GPA of 3.25), school/community involvement, and future plans.

$500 award for public school; $1,000 award for private non-Lutheran school; $2,000 award for Lutheran school. Renewable. For membership information or an application, write to the above address.

3038—LYONS CLUB OF RAWLINS (K. Craig Williams Memorial Scholarship)

Rawlins High School
Guidance Office
Rawlins WY 82301
307/328-9288

AMOUNT: $250-$600
DEADLINE(S): APR 15
FIELD(S): All fields of study

Available to current year Rawlins High School graduates. Award may be used at any accredited postsecondary institution.

1 award annually. Applications are available from the Rawlins High School Guidance Office.

3039—LaFETRA OPERATING FOUNDATION (Fellowships for Training of Volunteers Abroad)

1221 Preservation Park Way, #100
Oakland CA 94612-1216
510/763-9206
FAX: 510/763-9290
E-mail: fellowship@lafetra.org
Internet: www.lafetra.org

AMOUNT: Stipend for internship + travel & program costs
DEADLINE(S): DEC 18
FIELD(S): All fields of study

An internship in SF Bay Area, CA, to learn skills in volunteering, and a fellowship for living and working in another country. Open to persons of color, individuals who demonstrate financial need, and adult professionals in various fields. Applicants from the Bay Area are preferred because housing/transportation for SF training cannot be provided for persons outside that area, but those who can provide their own housing/transportation in SF are welcome to apply.

See website or contact above address for an application/more information.

3040—MADDEN BROTHERS (Goshen County Community Scholarships)

Route 1, Box 360
Torrington WY 82240
307/532-7079

AMOUNT: $300
DEADLINE(S): Varies
FIELD(S): All fields of study

Available to recent graduates of a Goshen County (WY) high school who will be attending any college, university, or trade school, and entering as freshmen. Participation in 4-H or FFA activities will be considered but is not mandatory.

3 awards annually. Contact Madden Brothers for an application.

3041—MAINE AMERICAN LEGION, PAST COMMANDERS CLUB (James V. Day Scholarship)

P.O. Box 545
Union ME 04862
Not given

AMOUNT: Not specified
DEADLINE(S): MAY 1
FIELD(S): All fields of study in accredited college or vocational or technical school

Open to students in the graduating class of their high schools. Parent must be a current member of an American Legion Post in the Department of Maine. Must be of good character and have demonstrated that he/she believes in the American way of life.

Application requires 300-word essay describing student's objectives for furthering education.

3042—MAINE COMMUNITY FOUNDATION (Scholarship Program)

P.O. Box 148
Ellsworth ME 04605
207/667-9735

AMOUNT: Varies
DEADLINE(S): Varies
FIELD(S): Varied fields of study

All scholarships are available to Maine residents only. The Maine Community Foundation offers over 80 scholarships, covering a wide range of fields of study. Interested applicants should contact the MCF for a complete listing of its scholarships and an application.

Write to Nancy Eveld, Scholarship Coordinator, at the above address for complete information.

3043—MAINE STUDENT INCENTIVE SCHOLARSHIP PROGRAM

One Weston Court
119 State House Station
Augusta ME 04333

800/228-3734
Internet: www.famemaine.com

AMOUNT: Up to $1,000

DEADLINE(S): MAY 1 (receipt date of FAFSA)

FIELD(S): All fields of study

Open to Maine residents attending regional accredited colleges in AK, CT, DC, DE, MA, MD, NH, PA, RI, or VT. Awards are for full-time undergraduate study.

8,000 awards per year. Application is the Free Application for Federal Student Aid (FAFSA) available in your college financial aid office.

3044—MAINE VETERAN'S SERVICES (Grants for Dependents)

State House Station 117
Augusta ME 04333-0117
207/626-4464 or 800/345-0116

AMOUNT: Free tuition at state-supported Maine schools

DEADLINE(S): None

FIELD(S): All fields of study

For Maine residents who are children or stepchildren (ages 16-21 and high school graduates) or spouses (or widows) of military veterans who are totally disabled due to service or who died in service or as a result of service. Tenable at all branches of the University of Maine System, all State of Maine Vocational Technical Colleges, and Maine Maritime Academy at Castine.

Veteran must have lived in Maine at time of entering service or for 5 years prior to application. Write for complete information.

3045—MAKARIOS SCHOLARSHIP FUND, INC. (Scholarships)

13 East 40th Street
New York NY 10016
212/696-4590 or 800/775-7217

AMOUNT: Varies

DEADLINE(S): MAY 5

FIELD(S): All fields of study

For students from Cyprus with valid student visas who are pursuing studies in an accredited United States college or university on a full-time basis. Includes Theodore & Wally Lappas Award and Thomas & Elaine Kyrus Endowment.

Financial need determines award. Applications must be typewritten and include various documents—please write or call for complete information.

3046—MAMIE ADAMS MEMORIAL AWARD

4126 Pocahontas Drive
Baytown TX 77521
713/421-2915
FAX: 713/421-2915

AMOUNT: $1,000/yr.

DEADLINE(S): APR 30

FIELD(S): All fields of study

A scholarship for a high school senior planning to attend college in the fall or for undergraduate college students enrolled at a 2- or 4-year institution. Min. 2.5 GPA required. Preference given to students who have demonstrated consistency and improvement in their scholastic records.

1 award. Can apply between Feb. 1 and April 30. Write or call for detailed eligibility requirements. Key qualification is to show improvement in academic standing.

3047—MARCH OF DIMES BIRTH DEFECTS FOUNDATION/KMART CORPORATION (Youth Leadership Scholarships)

1275 Mamaroneck Avenue
White Plains NY 10605
888-MODIMES or 914/997-4456
E-mail: EducationServices@
modimes.org
Internet: www.modimes.org

AMOUNT: $2,500

DEADLINE(S): APR 30

FIELD(S): All fields of study

Scholarships for college-bound high school seniors planning to pursue a degree at an accredited US postsecondary institution. For youths who have exhibited qualities of excellence in volunteer service and leadership, particularly in a program that improves the health of babies. Must have a minimum 3.0 GPA. Transcripts and letters of reference from two adults (a volunteer supervisor and a teacher) are required.

10 awards annually. See website or contact March of Dimes for an application.

3048—MARIE L. ROSE HUGUENOT SOCIETY OF AMERICA (Scholarships)

122 East 58th Street
New York NY 10022
212/755-0592
FAX: 212/317-0676

AMOUNT: $1,800/yr.

DEADLINE(S): JUN 1

FIELD(S): All fields of study

For American undergraduates who submit proof of descent from a Huguenot who emigrated from France and either settled in what is now the US or left France for countries other than America before 1787. Only students approved by one of the participating colleges may apply; no application sent directly to the Huguenot Society will be considered. Financial need is NOT a factor.

25 awards annually. Renewable. Contact your school's financial aid office for an application or contact Dorothy Kimball at above address for a list of participating colleges/universities.

3049—MARIN EDUCATION FUND (Asian Scholarship Fund)

1010 B Street, Suite 300
San Rafael CA 94901
415/459-4240
FAX: 415/459-0527

AMOUNT: $500 to $2,000

DEADLINE(S): MAR 31

FIELD(S): All fields of study

For students who have been residents of Marin or Sonoma counties in California, for at least one year. Must have one biological parent of Asian ancestry; proof may be requested. Scholarships based on outstanding achievement, demonstrated community responsibility and service, leadership, and financial need. Must be attending an accredited or state-approved school and enrolled in a full-time, undergraduate academic program leading to a degree.

10 awards annually. May be attending an educational institution outside of Marin or Sonoma counties provided applicant has satisfied the one-year residency requirement.

3050—MARIN EDUCATIONAL FUND (Undergraduate Scholarship Program)

1010 B Street, Suite 300
San Rafael CA 94901
415/459-4240

AMOUNT: $800-$2,000

DEADLINE(S): MAR 2

FIELD(S): All fields of study

Open to Marin County (CA) residents only for undergraduate study in 2- or 4-year colleges and for fifth-year teaching credentials. Must be enrolled at least half-time and demonstrate financial need.

Write for complete information.

3051—MARINE CORPS SCHOLARSHIP FOUNDATION (Scholarships to Sons and Daughters of Marines)

P.O. Box 3008
Princeton NJ 08543-3008
800/292-7777 or 609/921-3534
FAX: 609/452-2259
E-mail: mcsf@marine-scholars.org
Internet: www.marine-scholars.org

AMOUNT: $500-$2,500
DEADLINE(S): APR 1
FIELD(S): Any field of study

The Marine Corps Scholarship Foundation offers scholarships to undergraduates who are sons and daughters of current or former Marines. Special consideration is given to an applicant whose parent was killed or wounded in action. Applicants must be seniors or high school graduates or be enrolled in an accredited college or vocational school. Parents combined income cannot exceed $42,000.

Financial need considered. Application requests are available at the above website or by mail. No phone requests.

3052—MARINE CORPS TANKERS ASSOCIATION (John Cornelius Memorial Scholarship)

1112 Alpine Heights Road
Alpine CA 91901-2814
619/445-8423

AMOUNT: $1,500+
DEADLINE(S): MAR 15
FIELD(S): All fields of study

Must be a survivor, a dependent, or under legal guardianship of a Marine Tanker—active duty, reserve, retired, or honorably discharged—who served in a Marine Tank unit OR be a Marine or Navy Corpsman who personally qualifies in the foregoing. Must be a member of MCTA, or will join. May apply as a high school senior, undergraduate, or graduate student. Letters of recommendation, transcripts, and personal narrative required with application.

12 awards annually. Renewable with reapplication. Notification by the end of April. Contact Phil Morell, Scholarship Chairman, for an application.

3053—MARION BRILL SCHOLARSHIP FOUNDATION, INC. (Undergraduate Scholarships)

97 West Street
P.O. Box 420
Ilion NY 13357
315/895-7771

AMOUNT: $100-$500
DEADLINE(S): JAN 15
FIELD(S): All fields of study

Undergraduate scholarships open to residents of Ilion (Herkimer County), NY who graduated from Ilion Central School District. Must demonstrate financial need to satisfaction of screening committee. FAFSA form required.

Write for complete information.

3054—MARK R. FUSCO FOUNDATION

P.O. Box 9618
New Haven CT 06535
203/777-7451

AMOUNT: Varies
DEADLINE(S): Ongoing
FIELD(S): All fields of study

Scholarships for students who are residents of Connecticut for all academic fields. Acceptance based on academic record, SAT/ACT scores, financial need, and recommendations from instructors.

Write to Paul Morris, Secretary-Treasurer, at above address.

3055—MARY E. HODGES FUND

222 Tauton Ave.
East Providence RI 02914-4556
401/435-4650

AMOUNT: Varies
DEADLINE(S): MAY 1
FIELD(S): All fields of study

Scholarships for students who have a Rhode Island Masonic affiliation or who have been residents of Rhode Island for at least five years.

Send SASE to John M. Faulhaber, Secretary, at above address for details.

3056—MARY INSTITUTE AND SAINT LOUIS COUNTRY DAY SCHOOL (Financial Aid)

101 North Warson Road
St. Louis MO 63124
314/995-7367
FAX: 314/872-3257
E-mail: jhall@micds.pvt.k12.mo.us
Internet: micds.pvt.k12.mo.us

AMOUNT: Tuition
DEADLINE(S): None
FIELD(S): All fields of secondary school study

Financial aid for this coed private school, grades K-12, in Street Louis, MO. The aid is for the secondary level.

Access website for information about the school. Renewable yearly. Must demonstrate financial need.

3057—MARY M. AARON MEMORIAL TRUST (Scholarships)

1190 Civic Center Blvd.
Yuba City CA 95997
Written inquiry

AMOUNT: $500 to $1,000
DEADLINE(S): MAR 15
FIELD(S): All areas of study

Open to any needy student from Sutter County, California, attending an accredited 2-year (approx. $500) or 4-year (approx. $1,000) California college or university. Grants based mainly on financial need. Grades and activities are not considered as significant.

Write for complete information.

3058—MARYLAND HIGHER EDUCATION COMMISSION (Delegate Scholarships)

State Scholarship Admin.
16 Francis Street
Annapolis MD 21401-1781
410/974-5370
TTY: 800/735-2258

AMOUNT: Varies: $200 minimum
DEADLINE(S): Varies
FIELD(S): All fields of study

For Maryland residents who are undergraduate or graduate students in Maryland (or out-of-state with a unique major). Must be US citizen.

Duration is up to 4 years; 2-4 scholarships per district. Also for full- or part-time study at certain private career schools and diploma schools of nursing. Write to your delegate for complete information.

3059—MARYLAND HIGHER EDUCATION COMMISSION (Educational Assistance Grant)

State Scholarship Admin.
16 Francis Street
Annapolis MD 21401-1781
410/974-5370
TTY: 800/735-2258

AMOUNT: $200-$3,000
DEADLINE(S): MAR 1 (via FAFSA)
FIELD(S): All areas of study

Open to Maryland residents for full-time undergraduate study at a Maryland degree-granting institution or hospital school of nursing. Financial need must be demonstrated.

Renewable with reapplication for up to 3 years. Write for complete information.

3060—MARYLAND HIGHER EDUCATION COMMISSION (Edward T. Conroy Memorial Scholarships)

State Scholarship Admin.
16 Francis Street
Annapolis MD 21401-1781
410/974-5370
TTY: 800/735-2258

AMOUNT: Up to $3,800 for tuition and mandatory fees
DEADLINE(S): JUL 15
FIELD(S): All fields of study

For sons and daughters of persons 100% disabled or killed in the line of military duty who were Maryland residents at the time of disability or death, to sons and daughters of MIAs or POWs, and to sons, daughters, and un-remarried spouses of public safety employees disabled or killed in the line of duty. Also for 100% disabled public safety employees.

For undergraduate or graduate study, full- or part-time, in an MD institution. Write for complete information.

3061—MARYLAND HIGHER EDUCATION COMMISSION (Guaranteed Access Grant)

State Scholarship Admin.
16 Francis Street
Annapolis MD 21401-1781
410/974-5370
TTY: 800/735-2258
Internet: www.ubalt.edu/www.mhec

AMOUNT: $8,000 (max.)
DEADLINE(S): MAR 1
FIELD(S): All fields of study

For Maryland high school seniors who have completed high school in Maryland with a GPA of at least 2.5. Must have completed a college preparatory or an articulated tech prep program.

Must demonstrate financial need. Write for complete information.

3062—MARYLAND HIGHER EDUCATION COMMISSION (Senatorial Scholarship Program)

State Scholarship Admin.
16 Francis Street
Annapolis MD 21401-1781
410/974-5370
TTY: 800/735-2258

AMOUNT: $400-$2,000
DEADLINE(S): MAR 1 (via FAFSA)

FIELD(S): All fields of study

Open to Maryland residents for undergrad or grad study at MD degree-granting institutions, certain private career schools, nursing diploma schools in Maryland. For full- or part-time study. SAT or ACT required for some applicants.

Students with unique majors or with impaired hearing may attend out of state. Duration is 1-4 years with automatic renewal until degree is granted. Senator selects recipients. Write for complete information.

3063—MASSACHUSETTS BOARD OF HIGHER EDUCATION (Public Service Grant)

Office of Student Financial Assistance
330 Stuart Street, 3rd Fl.
Boston MA 02116
617/727-9420

AMOUNT: Varies with school (covers tuition; not fees)
DEADLINE(S): MAY 1
FIELD(S): All fields of study

Open to permanent Massachusetts residents who are the child or deceased police/fire/corrections officer killed in line of duty or child of deceased veteran whose death was service-related.

Write for complete information.

3064—MASSACHUSETTS BOARD OF HIGHER EDUCATION (Veterans Tuition Exemption Program)

Office of Student Financial Assistance
330 Stuart Street, 3rd Fl.
Boston MA 02116
617/727-9420

AMOUNT: Tuition exemption
DEADLINE(S): None
FIELD(S): All areas of study

Open to military veterans who are permanent residents of Massachusetts. Awards are tenable at Massachusetts postsecondary institutions.

Contact veterans agent at college or address above for complete information.

3065—MASSACHUSETTS COMPANY (The M. Geneva Gray Scholarship Fund)

Trust Dept.
125 High Street
Boston MA 02110
617/556-2335

AMOUNT: Up to $1,000
DEADLINE(S): MAR 1
FIELD(S): All fields of study

Open to undergraduate students who are MA residents and are unable to qualify for financial aid due to high parental income. Family must have more than one child to educate. Income between $25,000 and $50,000.

There are no academic requirements other than enrollment and good standing. Send a self-addressed, stamped envelope for an application and list of instructions.

3066—MASSACHUSETTS OFFICE OF STUDENT FINANCIAL ASSISTANCE (National Guard Tuition Waiver)

330 Stuart Street, 3rd Fl.
Boston MA 02116
617/727-9420

AMOUNT: Tuition waiver
DEADLINE(S): None
FIELD(S): All areas of study

Program open to undergraduate students who are enrolled at a Massachusetts public college or university and are active members of the Massachusetts National Guard or the Massachusetts Air National Guard.

Contact the veterans office at your college or address above for complete information.

3067—MASSACHUSETTS OFFICE OF STUDENT FINANCIAL ASSISTANCE (General Scholarship Program)

330 Stuart Street, 3rd Fl.
Boston MA 02116
617/727-9420

AMOUNT: $250-$2,500
DEADLINE(S): MAY 1
FIELD(S): All fields of study

Open to permanent residents of Massachusetts. Awards are for undergraduate study at accredited colleges and universities in Massachusetts. Must complete FAFSA by May 1.

40,000-50,000 awards per year. Write for complete information.

3068—MAY THOMPSON HENRY TRUST

P.O. Box 3448
Enid OK 73702
405/233-3535

AMOUNT: Varies
DEADLINE(S): Ongoing
FIELD(S): All fields of study

Scholarships for students attending state-supported Oklahoma colleges and universities.

Contact Stella Knowles, Trust Officer, at Central National Bank & Trust Co., at above location for details.

3069—McDONALD'S RESTAURANTS OF WEST NEW YORK (BOMAC Scholarship Award)

c/o Stern Advertising
6265 Sheridan Drive
Bldg. A, Suite 216
Amherst NY 14221
716/631-2476
FAX: 716/631-5317

AMOUNT: $500
DEADLINE(S): Varies
FIELD(S): All fields of study

Open to employees of McDonald's who are high school seniors living in West New York—the McDonald's you are employed at must belong to the co-op of 66 restaurants that oversees this award. This scholarship is to be used for postsecondary study.

20 awards annually. Contact your store manager to see if your McDonald's belongs to this co-op.

3070—McCURDY MEMORIAL SCHOLARSHIP FOUNDATION (McCurdy Scholarship)

134 West Van Buren Street
Battle Creek MI 49017
616/962-9591

AMOUNT: $1,000
DEADLINE(S): MAR 31
FIELD(S): All fields of study

Must be a resident of Calhoun County, Michigan. Program is for undergraduate students.

7 scholarships per year. Renewable with reapplication and satisfactory grades. Write for complete information.

3071—McDONALD'S (Golden Arches Scholarships)

See your local McDonald's
    Tri-State restaurant
Internet: www.archingintoeducation.
com/

AMOUNT: $1,000
DEADLINE(S): MAR 31
FIELD(S): All fields of study

New York Tri-State residents (NYC, Long Island & specific counties in CT & NJ) planning to attend their first year of college are eligible. Must be a US citizen or permanent resident, have a cumulative GPA of 3.0 or above, possess a record of community service and/or employment, plan to enroll as a full-time undergraduate student at an accredited two- or four-year college/university, and demonstrate financial need.

100 awards annually. Pick up an application in your local New York, New Jersey, or Connecticut McDonald's.

3072—McDONALD'S (RMHC/HACER Scholarship Program)

Kroc Drive
Oak Brook IL 60523
800/736-5219
Internet: www.mcdonalds.com/
community/education/scholarships/
hacer/index.html

AMOUNT: $1,000+
DEADLINE(S): FEB 1
FIELD(S): All fields of study

For college-bound Hispanic students who have a demonstrated record of academic achievement, financial need, and community involvement. Must be US citizen or permanent resident and live in District of Columbia, Puerto Rico, or one of the following states: AZ, CA, CO, CT, DE, FL, IL, IN, MD, MA, NJ, NM, NY, OK, PA, RI, TX, VA, WV, WI, or WY. Essay, transcripts, SAT/ACT scores, and letters of recommendation required with application.

Not renewable. Applications are available from your local participating McDonald's restaurant or high school counselor, or call the RMHC/HACER hotline above.

3073—McDONALD'S (UNCF New York Tri-State Scholarships)

See your local McDonald's
    Tri-State restaurant
Internet: www.archingintoeducation.
com/

AMOUNT: $1,000; $10,000
DEADLINE(S): MAR 31
FIELD(S): All fields of study

New York Tri-State residents (NYC, Long Island & specific counties in CT & NJ) who are planning to attend a United Negro College Fund institution are eligible.

50 $1,000 awards annually; 1 $10,000 award for a student demonstrating outstanding academic merit. Pick up an application in your local New York, New Jersey, or Connecticut McDonald's.

3074—MERCANTILE BANK OF TOPEKA (Claude & Ina Brey Memorial Endowment Fund)

c/o Trust Dept.
P.O. Box 192
Topeka KS 66601

913/291-1118
AMOUNT: $500
DEADLINE(S): APR 15
FIELD(S): All fields of study

Scholarships open to fourth-degree Kansas Grange members. Awards tenable at recognized undergraduate colleges and universities. US citizen.

8 awards per year. Renewable. For complete information write to Marlene Bush, P.O. Box 186, Melvern, KS 66510.

3075—METHODIST LADIES' COLLEGE (Scholarships)

207 Barkers Road Kew
Melbourne Victoria 3101
AUSTRALIA
+61 (3) 9274 6333
FAX: +61 (3) 9819 2345
E-mail: college@mlc.vic.edu.au
Internet: www.www.mic.vic.edu.au

AMOUNT: Varies
DEADLINE(S): Varies
FIELD(S): All fields of study

Various scholarships at this pre-kindergarten-grade 12 boarding school for girls in Melbourne, Australia. Scholarships are for students in grades 7-12. Some are for music students. Selection is based on scholarship test results, school grade results, and interview. Some are based on financial need. Although the school is rooted in the Methodist church, girls from all religious and ethnic backgrounds are welcome. For citizens or permanent residents of Australia.

Approximately 33 awards yearly, full- or half-scholarships. Contact school for details.

3076—METROPOLITAN MILWAUKEE ASSOCIATION OF COMMERCE (Scholarships)

756 N. Milwaukee Street
Milwaukee WI 53202
Not given

AMOUNT: Up to $3,500/yr.
DEADLINE(S): MAY 1
FIELD(S): All fields of study

Must be a graduate of a Milwaukee Public High School with a 90% cumulative attendance rate. Must have a cumulative GPA of 2.5 or better, demonstrate financial need, and attend the University of Wisconsin at Milwaukee full-time.

Apply through your high school guidance counselor or by contacting MMAC, Education & Scholarship Programs, at above address.

3077—MEXICAN AMERICAN BUSINESS AND PROFESSIONAL SCHOLARSHIP ASSOCIATION (Scholarship Program)

P.O. Box 22292
Los Angeles CA 90022
Written inquiry only

AMOUNT: $100-$1,000
DEADLINE(S): MAY 1 (postmark)
FIELD(S): All fields of study

Open to Los Angeles County residents who are of Mexican-American descent and are enrolled full-time in an undergraduate program. Awards are based on financial need and past academic performance.

Send self-addressed, stamped envelope (SASE) with request for complete information.

3078—MEXICAN AMERICAN WOMEN'S NATIONAL ASSOCIATION (MANA) (Raquel Marquez Frankel Scholarship Fund)

1725 K Street NW, Suite 105
Washington DC 20006
202/833-0060
FAX: 202/496-0588
E-mail: HerMANA2@aol.com

AMOUNT: $200-$1,000
DEADLINE(S): APR 1
FIELD(S): All fields of study

For Hispanic female students enrolled in undergraduate or graduate programs at accredited colleges or universities. Must demonstrate financial need and academic achievement. Must be MANA member. There is a $10 application fee.

Send self-addressed, stamped envelope for application for membership and scholarship.

3079—MICHIGAN COMMISSION ON INDIAN AFFAIRS; MICHIGAN DEPT. OF CIVIL RIGHTS (Tuition Waiver Program)

201 N. Washington Sq., Suite 700
Lansing MI 48933
517/373-0654

AMOUNT: Tuition (only) waiver
DEADLINE(S): Varies (8 weeks prior to class registration)
FIELD(S): All areas

Open to any Michigan resident who is at least 1/4 North American Indian (certified by their tribal nation) and willing to attend any public Michigan community college, college, or university.

Award is for all levels of study and is renewable. Must be Michigan resident for at least 12 months before class registration. Write for complete information.

3080—MICHIGAN ELKS ASSOCIATION CHARITABLE GRANT FUND

43904 Lee Ann Lane
Canton MI 48187
Written inquiry

AMOUNT: Varies
DEADLINE(S): JAN 20
FIELD(S): All fields of study

Scholarships to physically disabled students who are residents of Michigan.

Contact local Elks Lodge for application information.

3081—MICHIGAN GUARANTY AGENCY (Stafford and PLUS Loans)

P.O. Box 30047
Lansing MI 48909
800/642-5626
FAX: 517/335-6703

AMOUNT: Varies
DEADLINE(S): None
FIELD(S): All fields of study

Guaranteed student loans available to students or parents of students who are Michigan residents enrolled in an eligible institution.

Write for complete information.

3082—MICHIGAN HIGHER EDUCATION ASSISTANCE AUTHORITY (Michigan Competitive Scholarships)

Office of Scholarships and Grants
P.O. Box 30462
Lansing MI 48909
517/373-3394

AMOUNT: $100-$1,200
DEADLINE(S): FEB 21 (for freshmen)
FIELD(S): All fields of study (except BRE degree)

Open to US citizens who have lived in Michigan at least a year and are enrolled at least half time in an eligible Michigan college. Must demonstrate financial need and submit ACT scores.

Scholarships renewable. Applicants must file the FAFSA form. Fact sheets are available from high school counselors. Write for complete information.

3083—MICHIGAN HIGHER EDUCATION ASSISTANCE AUTHORITY (Michigan Tuition Grants)

Office of Scholarships and Grants
P.O. Box 30462
Lansing MI 48909

517/373-3394

AMOUNT: $100-$2,450
DEADLINE(S): Varies
FIELD(S): All fields of study (except BRE degree)

Open to Michigan residents enrolled at least half time at independent nonprofit Michigan institutions (list available from above address). Both undergraduate and graduate students who can demonstrate financial need are eligible.

Grants renewable. Applicants must file the FAFSA form. Write for complete information.

3084—MICHIGAN VETERANS TRUST FUND (Tuition Grant Program)

611 West Ottawa, 3rd Floor
Lansing MI 48913
517/373-3130

AMOUNT: Up to $2,500/year
DEADLINE(S): None
FIELD(S): All areas of study

Open to Michigan residents of at least 12 months preceding enrollment who are aged 16-26 and are children of Michigan veterans killed in action or who later died or were totally disabled due to a service-connected cause.

Renewable for 36 months. Grants are for undergraduate study at Michigan post-secondary schools. Write for complete information.

3085—MIDWEST STUDENT EXCHANGE PROGRAM (Tuition Reduction)

Minnesota Higher Education Service
1450 Energy Park Drive, #350
Street Paul MN 55108-5265
612/626-8288
FAX: 612/626-8290

AMOUNT: Up to $2,500 tuition reduction
DEADLINE(S): FEB 1
FIELD(S): All fields of study

At least 10% reduction in out-of-state tuition for residents of Kansas, Michigan, Minnesota, Missouri, and Nebraska who attend participating institutions in those same states.

Contact your high school counselor or the Office of Admissions at the college you plan to attend for a list of participating institutions. When applying to a college, mark prominently on the form that you seek admission as a MSEP student.

3086—MILITARY ORDER OF THE PURPLE HEART (Sons, Daughters, and Grandchildren Scholarship Program)

National Headquarters
5413-B Backlick Road
Springfield VA 22151
703/642-5360
FAX: 703/642-2054

AMOUNT: $1,000 per year (4 years maximum)
DEADLINE(S): MAR 15
FIELD(S): All fields of study

Open to children and grandchildren of Military Order of Purple Heart Members or Purple Heart Recipients. For full-time study at any level by US citizen or legal resident. Must demonstrate academic achievement and financial need.

Renewable for up to 4 years provided a 3.5 GPA is maintained. $5 processing fee. Write for complete information.

3087—MINNESOTA HIGHER EDUCATION SERVICES OFFICE (Minnesota Indian Scholarship Program)

Indian Education
1819 Bemidji Ave.
Bemidji MN 56601
218/755-2926

AMOUNT: Average $1,450/year
DEADLINE(S): None
FIELD(S): All fields of study

For Minnesota residents who are one-fourth or more Indian ancestry and members of or elgible for membership in a tribe. Must be high school graduates or GED recipients and be accepted by an approved college, university, or vocational school in Minnesota, and approved by the Minnesota Indian Scholarship Committee. Apply as early as possible before starting your post-high school program.

Indian students also must apply to federally funded grant programs, including the Pell Grant Program, their respective tribal agency, and the Minnesota Grant Program. Contact Joe Aitken at the above location.

3088—MINNESOTA HIGHER EDUCATION SERVICES OFFICE (Scholarships, Grants, Loans, and Work-Study Programs)

1450 Energy Park Drive, #350
Street Paul MN 55108-5265
612/296-3974
FAX: 612/297-8880
E-mail: info@heso.state.mn.us
Internet: www.heso.state.mn.us/

AMOUNT: Varies
DEADLINE(S): None specified
FIELD(S): All fields of study

Grants, scholarships, and loans for Minnesota residents to attend colleges and universities. Includes summer programs at college campuses for grades 7-12. Most programs require attendance at Minnesota institutions. High school juniors and seniors should begin planning ahead. Special programs for minorities, health fields, veterans and their dependents, and reciprocity for out-of-state tuition in certain other states.

Send for booklet "Focus on Financial Aid" at above address and/or check website.

3089—MINNESOTA HIGHER EDUCATION SERVICES OFFICE (Summer Scholarships for Academic Enrichment)

1450 Energy Park Drive, #350
Street Paul MN 55108-5265
612/296-3974
FAX: 612/297-8880
E-mail: info@heso.state.mn.us
Internet: www.heso.state.mn.us/

AMOUNT: Up to $1,000
DEADLINE(S): Varies
FIELD(S): All academic subjects

For Minnesota students in grades 7-12 to attend eligible summer academic programs sponsored by Minnesota postsecondary schools—University of Minnesota campuses, state universities, community colleges, private colleges, and technical colleges. Must be US citizen or permanent resident, hold at least a "B" average for the most recent term, or have a "B" average in the subject area of the enrichment course, and demonstrate financial need (based on parents' income).

Deadline dates vary depending on the program. Contact above address for list of participating postsecondary institutions.

3090—MINNESOTA STATE DEPARTMENT OF VETERANS AFFAIRS (Deceased Veterans' Dependents Scholarships)

Veterans Service Bldg.
20 W. 12th, 2nd Fl.
Street Paul MN 55155-2079
612/296-2562

AMOUNT: Tuition + $350
DEADLINE(S): None
FIELD(S): All fields of study

Open to 2-year (or more) residents of Minnesota who are sons/daughters of veterans killed in service or who died as a result of a service-caused condition. Parent must have been a resident of Minnesota at time of entry into service. Must be US citizen/legal resident and an undergraduate planning to attend a Minnesota college/university.

Renewable. Contact the Minnesota State Department of Veterans Affairs for an application.

3091—MINNESOTA STATE DEPARTMENT OF VETERANS AFFAIRS (Veterans Grants)

Veterans Service Bldg.
20 W. 12th, 2nd Fl.
Street Paul MN 55155-2079
612/296-2562

AMOUNT: $350
DEADLINE(S): None
FIELD(S): All fields of study

Open to veterans who were residents of Minnesota at the time of their entry into the armed forces of the US and were honorably discharged after having served on active duty for at least 181 consecutive days. Must be US citizen/legal resident and planning to attend an accredited institution in Minnesota. Must also have time remaining on federal education period and have exhausted through use any federal educational entitlement. Must demonstrate financial need.

Contact the Minnesota State Department of Veterans Affairs for an application.

3092—MINNESOTA TEAMSTERS JOINT COUNCIL NO.32 (Scholarship Awards)

Education Committee
3001 University Ave. SE
Minneapolis MN 55414
612/331-6767

AMOUNT: $2,000
DEADLINE(S): APR 30
FIELD(S): All fields of study

Open to graduating seniors of Minnesota high schools who are dependent children of members or deceased members of MN Teamsters Joint Council No 32. For study at any MN college or university or voc-tech institute. Must have 3.0 or better GPA.

Applications available from members' local unions.

3093—MINNIE PEARL SCHOLARSHIP PROGRAM

1817 Patterson Street
Nashville TN 37203
800/545-HEAR (Voice/TDD)

AMOUNT: $2,000 (or amount of tuition, whichever is less)
DEADLINE(S): FEB 15
FIELD(S): All fields of study

Open to mainstream high school seniors with a significant bi-lateral hearing loss, a 3.0 or better GPA, and who are enrolled in or have been accepted by an accredited college, university, or tech school. For full-time study. US citizens only.

Number of awards varies each year. Renewable throughout college career. Write for complete information.

3094—MISS HALL'S SCHOOL (Berkshire County Scholarships)

492 Holmes Road
Pittsfield MA 01201
413/499-1300
FAX: 413/448-2994
E-mail: info@misshalls.com
Internet: www.mishalls.com

AMOUNT: $5,000
DEADLINE(S): MAR 2
FIELD(S): All fields of study

Miss Hall's is a private girls' prep high school (grades 9-12) in Massachusetts. It is both a boarding and day school. Scholarship applicants must be entering 9th or 10th grade and be residents of Berkshire County, Massachusetts. US citizenship.

Contact Elaine Cooper at above location for further information. Applicants considered on academic record, interview, and essays.

3095—MISSISSIPPI OFFICE OF STATE STUDENT FINANCIAL AID (Law Enforcement Officers and Firemen Scholarship Program)

3825 Ridgewood Road
Jackson MS 39211-6453
601/982-6570 or 800-327-2980
(free in Miss.)

AMOUNT: Tuition; room; required fees
DEADLINE(S): None specified
FIELD(S): All areas of study

Open to children, stepchildren, or spouse of Mississippi law enforcement officers or full-time firemen who were fatally

injured or were totally disabled while on duty. Children must be under age 23.

Tuition-free scholarships for 8 semesters at any state-supported college or university in Mississippi. Write for complete information.

3096—MISSISSIPPI OFFICE OF STATE STUDENT FINANCIAL AID (Southeast Asia POW/MIA Scholarship Program)

3825 Ridgewood Road
Jackson MS 39211-6453
601/982-6570 or 800-982-6663
(free in Miss.)

AMOUNT: Tuition; room; required fees
DEADLINE(S): None specified
FIELD(S): All areas of study

Open to dependent children of military veterans formerly or currently listed as missing in action in Southeast Asia or as prisoners of war as a result of military action against the US Naval Vessel Pueblo.

Tuition-free scholarships for 8 semesters at any state-supported Mississippi college or university. Write for complete information.

3097—MOBIL CORPORATION (Desert Storm Scholarship Program)

3225 Gallows Road
Fairfax VA 22037-0001
Written inquiry only

AMOUNT: Varies
DEADLINE(S): Varies (with institution)
FIELD(S): All fields of study

Open to veterans of Operation Desert Shield/Desert Storm, their spouses, and their children. The spouses and children of those who died in the operations receive highest priority. For full-time undergraduate study leading to a bachelor's degree.

Scholarships are renewable and available at 20 US colleges and universities. Financial need is a consideration. Write for list of participating schools and complete information.

3098—MOBILITY INTERNATIONAL USA (Travel-Study Program for People With Disabilities)

P.O. Box 10767
Eugene OR 97440
541/343-1284 (VOICE/TDD)
FAX: 541/343-6812
E-mail: info@miusa.org
Internet: www.miusa.org

AMOUNT: Varies

DEADLINE(S): Varies
FIELD(S): All fields of study.

Travel and study opportunities worldwide for people with disabilities.

3099—MODERN WOODMEN OF AMERICA (Fraternal College Scholarship Program)

1701 First Avenue
Rock Island IL 61201
Written inquiry only

AMOUNT: $500-$2,000
DEADLINE(S): JAN 1
FIELD(S): All fields of study

Open to high school seniors who have been beneficial members of Modern Woodmen for at least two years and are in the upper half of their graduating class. For use at any accredited four-year college in the US.

36 awards per year renewable for four years. Write for complete information.

3100—MONGOLIA SOCIETY (Dr. Gombojab Hangin Memorial Scholarship)

Indiana Univ.
322 Goodbody Hall
Bloomington IN 47405
812/855-4078
FAX: 812/855-7500
E-mail: MONSOC@Indiana.edu

AMOUNT: $2,500
DEADLINE(S): JAN 1
FIELD(S): All fields of study

Open to students of Mongolian heritage (defined as an individual of Mongolian ethnic orgins who is a citizen of Mongolia, the People's Republic of China, or the former Soviet Union) to pursue studies in the US Award does not include transportation from recipient's country to US nor does it include room and board at university. Upon conclusion of the award year, recipient must write a report of his/her activities that resulted from receipt of the scholarship.

Recipient will receive scholarship monies in one lump sum after enrollment in the scholarship holder's institution in the US Write for complete information.

3101—MONTANA UNIVERSITY SYSTEM (Indian Fees Waiver Program)

2500 Broadway
P.O. Box 203101
Helena MT 59620
406/444-6594

AMOUNT: Waiver of registration and incidental fees

DEADLINE(S): None

FIELD(S): All fields of study

One-fourth or more Indian blood and Montana residency for at least 1 year before enrolling in Montana University System required. Financial need must be demonstrated.

Each unit of the Montana University System makes its own rules governing selection. 500 waivers per year. Write for complete information.

3102—MONTANA UNIVERSITY SYSTEM (Montana State Student Incentive Grants)

2500 Broadway
P.O. Box 203101
Helena MT 59620
406/444-6594

AMOUNT: Up to $600

DEADLINE(S): None

FIELD(S): All fields of study

Open to Montana residents who are full-time undergraduate students attending accredited schools in Montana. Must demonstrate need.

1,150 awards per year. Contact financial aid office of the school you plan to attend as these grants are decentralized.

3103—MORRIS SCHOLARSHIP FUND (Scholarships for Minorities in Iowa)

206 6th Ave., Suite 900
Des Moines IA 50309-4018
515/282-8192
FAX: 515/282-9117
E-mail: morris@assoc-mgmt.com
Internet: www.assoc-mgmt.com/users/morris/morris.html

AMOUNT: Varies

DEADLINE(S): FEB 1

FIELD(S): All fields of study

Program to provide financial assistance, motivation, and counseling for minority students pursuing higher education. Awards are based on academic achievement, community service, and financial need. Preference is given to Iowa residents attending an Iowa-based college or university.

Contact organization or check website for details.

3104—MOSTARS/MISSOURI DEPARTMENT OF HIGHER EDUCATION (Charles Gallagher Student Financial Assistance Program)

3515 Amazonas Drive
Jefferson City MO 65018

800/473-6757 or 573/751-3940
FAX: 573/751-6635
Internet: www.mocbhe.gov

AMOUNT: $100-$1,500

DEADLINE(S): APR 1

FIELD(S): All fields of study (except Theology & Divinity)

Grants are open to Missouri residents who are US citizens pursuing undergraduate studies full-time at eligible Missouri institutions. Must fill out the government FAFSA form and check that you want information released to the state. Must demonstrate financial need.

Renewable with reapplication. See website or contact MOSTARS Information Center for details.

3105—MOSTARS/MISSOURI DEPARTMENT OF HIGHER EDUCATION ("Bright Flight" Academic Scholarship Program)

3515 Amazonas Drive
Jefferson City MO 65018
800/473-6757 or 573/751-3940
FAX: 573/751-6635
Internet: www.mocbhe.gov

AMOUNT: $2,000

DEADLINE(S): JUL 31

FIELD(S): All fields of study (except Theology & Divinity)

Scholarships are for Missouri residents who are US citizens accepted to or enrolled at eligible Missouri institutions. Must be pursuing undergraduate studies and have a composite ACT or SAT score in top 3 percent. Apply for fall term immediately following graduation from high school or obtaining GED.

Renewable yearly as an undergraduate. See website or contact MOSTARS Information Center for an application.

3106—MOSTARS/MISSOURI DEPARTMENT OF HIGHER EDUCATION (Marguerite Ross Barnett Memorial Scholarship)

3515 Amazonas Drive
Jefferson City MO 65018
800/473-6757 or 573/751-3940
FAX: 573/751-6635
Internet: www.mocbhe.gov

AMOUNT: Varies

DEADLINE(S): JUL 31

FIELD(S): All fields of study (except Theology & Divinity)

Scholarship is open to Missouri residents who are pursuing undergraduate studies at eligible Missouri institutions. Must be attending school at least half-time

but less than full-time. Compensated for employment at least 20 hours per week. Must demonstrate financial need.

Renewable with reapplication. See website or contact MOSTARS Information Center for details.

3107—MOTHER JOSEPH ROGAN MARYMOUNT FOUNDATION (Grant and Loan Programs)

c/o NationsBank
P.O. Box 14737
Street Louis MO 63101
314/391-6248

AMOUNT: $400 to $750

DEADLINE(S): MAY 1

FIELD(S): All fields of study

Grants and loans for students who are US citizens, live in the metropolitan Street Louis area, and are entering or enrolled in a high school, vocational/technical school, college, or university.

Applications are NOT accepted. Grants and loans are awarded by the administration and faculty of various Street Louis schools. Please do not send inquiries to this address. Contact your school for more information.

3108—MOUNT SAINT JOSEPH ACADEMY (Partial Scholarships)

120 West Wissahickon Ave.
Flourtown PA 19031
215/233-3177
Internet: mciunix.mciu.k12.pa.us/~msjaweb/Mount_web_page.html

AMOUNT: Partial tuition—varies

DEADLINE(S): OCT 31

FIELD(S): All fields of study

A private Catholic high school (grades 9-12) for girls in Pennsylvania. Partial scholarships available for academic ability, musical ability, and art talent. Also, one is for a high-ranking African American student and one for a daughter, granddaughter, or niece of an alumna.

3109—McCURDY MEMORIAL SCHOLARSHIP FOUNDATION (Emily Scofield Scholarship Fund)

134 West Van Buren Street
Battle Creek MI 49017
616/962-9591

AMOUNT: $100-$1,000

DEADLINE(S): MAR 31

FIELD(S): All areas of study

Scholarships for residents of Calhoun County, Michigan. Must be undergraduate.

4-5 scholarships per year. Renewable with reapplication and satisfactory grades. Write for complete information.

3110—McDONALD'S HISPANIC AMERICAN COMMITMENT TO EDUCATIONAL RESOURCES PROGRAM (Scholarships for High School Seniors)

One Sansome Street, Suite 1000
San Francisco CA 94104
800/736-5219 or 415/445-9930
FAX: 415/445-9942
E-mail: info@nhsf.org
Internet: www.nhsf.org

AMOUNT: $1,000 (more in certain areas)
DEADLINE(S): MAR 1
FIELD(S): All fields of study

For college-bound Hispanic high school seniors who are US citizens or permanent residents. Available in certain counties in 21 states throughout the US Designated counties are at above Internet site.

Inquire of high school counselor, local McDonald's manager, the above 800 number, or the National Hispanic Scholarship Fund at above location. Not renewable. Refer to RMHC/HACER program (Ronald McDonald House Charities/Hispanic American Commitment to Educational Resources).

3111—McDONOGH SCHOOL (Scholarships)

P.O. Box 380
Owings Mills MD 21117-0380
410/581-4719
FAX: 410/581-4777
Internet: www.mcdonogh@
mcdonogh.com

AMOUNT: Partial tuition
DEADLINE(S): DEC 15
FIELD(S): All fields of study

Need-based scholarships with a merit component for students admitted to this private, independent school in Maryland. Grades 5-12. For US citizens.

Renewable if need is determined.

3112—NAACP NATIONAL OFFICE (Agnes Jones Jackson Scholarship)

4805 Mount Hope Drive
Baltimore MD 21215
401/358-8900

AMOUNT: $1,500 undergrads; $2,500 grads

DEADLINE(S): APR 30
FIELD(S): All areas of study

Undergraduates must have GPA of 2.5+; graduates must possess 3.0 GPA. Applicants must be NAACP members and must be under the age of 25 by Apr. 30.

Send legal-size, self-addressed, stamped envelope to address above for application and complete information.

3113—NAACP NATIONAL OFFICE (Roy Wilkins Scholarship)

4805 Mount Hope Drive
Baltimore MD 21215
401/358-8900

AMOUNT: $1,000
DEADLINE(S): APR 30
FIELD(S): All fields of study

Open to graduating high school seniors who are members of the NAACP. Applicants must have at least a 2.5 (C+) grade point average.

Write for complete information. Include a legal-size, self-addressed, stamped envelope.

3114—NATIONAL ALLIANCE FOR EXCELLENCE, INC. (National Scholarship Competition)

20 Thomas Ave.
Shrewsbury NJ 07702
732/747-0028
E-mail: info@excellence.org
Internet: www.excellence.org

AMOUNT: $1,000-$5,000
DEADLINE(S): None
FIELD(S): All fields of study

National competition for merit-based scholarships, based entirely on talent and ability, NOT financial need. Students receive awards in presentation ceremonies with governors, senators, and other leaders. Must be US citizen attending or planning to attend college full-time. Four categories: Academic (must have minimum 3.7 GPA), Technological Innovations, Visual Arts (send 20 examples), and Performing Arts (send VHS of performance). Some require letters of recommendation.

$5 application fee required. See website for application form and complete eligibility, or write to above address.

3115—NATIONAL AMPUTATION FOUNDATION (Scholarships)

38-40 Church Street
Malverne NY 11565

516/887-3600 or 516/887-3667

AMOUNT: $125 per year
DEADLINE(S): None
FIELD(S): All fields of study

Open to high school seniors with major limb amputations. Awards support undergraduate full-time study at any recognized college or university.

24 awards per year. Write for complete information.

3116—NATIONAL ART MATERIALS TRADE ASSOCIATION (NAMTA Scholarships)

10115 Kincey Ave., Suite 260
Huntersville NC 28078
704/948-5554
E-mail: scholarships@namta.org

AMOUNT: $1,000
DEADLINE(S): MAR 1
FIELD(S): All fields of study

Open to undergraduate and graduate students who are employees or relatives of employees of a NAMTA member firm. Based on financial need, grades, activities, interests, and career goals.

Contact NAMTA for an application.

3117—NATIONAL ASSOCIATION OF NEGRO BUSINESS AND PROFESSIONAL WOMENS CLUB (Scholarships)

1806 New Hampshire Ave. NW
Washington DC 20009-3208
202/483-4206
FAX: 462-7253
Internet: www.afrika.com

AMOUNT: $1,000
DEADLINE(S): MAR 31 (request applications Sept. 1-Dec. 31)
FIELD(S): All fields of study

Scholarships for college-bound graduating high school seniors and first-year college students. US citizenship or permanent residency required. For males or females of any ethnic background.

10 national awards and 750 awards by local clubs. Send self-addressed, stamped envelope with request application (if not, requests will not be answered!).

3118—NATIONAL ASSOCIATION OF SECONDARY SCHOOL PRINCIPALS (National Honor Society Scholarships)

1904 Association Drive
Reston VA 22091
800/253-7746

AMOUNT: $1,000
DEADLINE(S): FEB 1

FIELD(S): All fields of study

Open to National Honor Society Members. Each chapter nominates two seniors to compete for scholarships at the national level.

250 scholarships per year. Contact your NHS chapter high school principal, or guidance counselor for complete information.

3119—NATIONAL ASSOCIATION OF SECONDARY SCHOOL PRINCIPALS (Wendy's High School Heisman Award)

1904 Association Drive
Reston VA 22091
800/253-7746

AMOUNT: Trip to New York City for December Heisman awards ceremony plus grants for schools of winners
DEADLINE(S): SEP (early)
FIELD(S): All fields of study

Award recognizes scholarship, citizenship, and athletic ability. Schools may nominate two seniors, one male and one female. Twelve national finalists will visit New York City and two finalists will be named the Wendy's High School Heisman Award winners. Winners' schools will receive grants of up to $3,000.

Contact your high school principal.

3120—NATIONAL ASSOCIATION OF SECONDARY SCHOOL PRINCIPALS (Century III Leaders Program)

1904 Association Drive
Reston VA 22091
800/253-7746

AMOUNT: Not specified
DEADLINE(S): NOV
FIELD(S): All fields of study

Program recognizes outstanding high school seniors who have a good academic record, are involved in school and community activities, and have an awareness of world events. Application process includes a two-page projection written by school winners concerning a problem America will face in its third century as a nation. A current events exam is also given.

Funds total $142,000 for awards. Funded by Sylvan Learning Centers. Ask your high school principal for application materials or contact above location.

3121—NATIONAL ASSOCIATION TO ADVANCE FAT ACCEPTANCE—THE NEW ENGLAND CHAPTER (NAAFA Scholarship Program)

P.O. Box 1820
Boston MA 02205

781/986-2232
AMOUNT: $500
DEADLINE(S): MAY 1
FIELD(S): All fields of study

This scholarship is offered to any fat or large-sized college-bound high school senior student in the New England states. Students will be required to complete an application.

Send SASE to Sharon Irinms at the above address for complete information.

3122—NATIONAL BAPTIST CONVENTION USA, INC. (Scholarships)

356 E. Boulevard
Baton Rouge LA 70802
Written inquiry

AMOUNT: $1,000
DEADLINE(S): Varies
FIELD(S): All fields of study

Scholarships for college-bound high school seniors and undergraduates who are active members of a church of the National Baptist Convention.

Send SASE for details.

3123—NATIONAL BURGLAR & FIRE ALARM ASSOCIATION (NBFAA/Security Dealer Youth Scholarship Program)

7101 Wisconsin Ave., #901
Bethesda MD 20814
301/907-3202
FAX: 301/907-7897
E-mail: staff@alarm.org
Internet: www.alarm.org

AMOUNT: $6,500 (Nat'l, 1st prize),
$3,500 (2nd); $1,000 (State, 1st prize),
$500 (2nd)
DEADLINE(S): JUN 1
FIELD(S): All fields of study

Must be the child of active-duty police or fire personnel and living in a state that has NBFAA chartered state association. Award is for high school seniors and is based on academic achievement, community & extracurricular activities, and an essay describing "How (their) Father, Mother, or Guardian Helps Us Secure Our Community." Each state chapter has own contest, and winners are automatically entered in national competition.

Contact local NBFAA chapter, or write to above address for application. Participating states include WA, NC, CA, GA, IN, PA, NJ, CT, and VA.

3124—NATIONAL COLLEGIATE ATHLETIC ASSOCIATION (Grants to undergraduates who have exhausted institutional financial aid opportunity)

6201 College Blvd.
Overland Park KS 66211
913/339-1906

AMOUNT: Tuition, board & room, books, and fees
DEADLINE(S): MAY 1 (postmark)
FIELD(S): All fields of study

Open to NCAA student athletes who have received but exhausted institutional eligibility for athletics-related financial aid and are within 30 semester hours (45 quarter hours) of graduation. Financial information will be required.

Application and documentation must be submitted by student's director of athletics. Must have GPA of 2.0 or better. Write for complete information.

3125—NATIONAL COLLEGIATE ATHLETIC ASSOCIATION (Walter Byers Postgraduate Scholarship)

6201 College Blvd.
Overland Park KS 66211
913-339-1906

AMOUNT: $12,500
DEADLINE(S): JAN (Mid)
FIELD(S): All fields of study

Open to NCAA student-athletes who are graduating seniors or graduates with a GPA of 3.5 or better and have been accepted into a graduate-degree program at an accredited nonprofit educational institution. Must be in final year of athletics eligibility at the institution from which they received their degree. For full-time study.

Award goes to one male and one female student athlete. Must be nominated by faculty athletics representative.

3126—NATIONAL COUNCIL OF JEWISH WOMEN—GREATER BOSTON SECTION (Amelia Greenbaum/Rabbi Marshall Lifson Scholarship Program)

831 Beacon Street
Newton Centre MA 02159
617/783-9660

AMOUNT: $400 maximum
DEADLINE(S): APR 30
FIELD(S): All fields of study

Open to Jewish women who are residents of Boston (or vicinity) and attend a Massachusetts college or university as an undergraduate. Must demonstrate financial need. Priority is given to those returning to school after a five-year absence or more.

Write for complete information.

3127—NATIONAL DO SOMETHING LEAGUE (Community Project Awards)

423 West 55th Street, 8th Fl.
New York NY 10019
212/523-1175
FAX: 212/582-1307
E-mail: grants@dosomething.org;
www.dosomething.org
AMOUNT: Up to $500; $10,000; $100,000
DEADLINE(S): MAR 1; JUL 1; NOV 1
FIELD(S): All fields of study, plus
community activities

Grants and awards program funds young leaders up to age 30 to transform their ideas into community-building action programs. Three sections: Elem. K-6, Secondary, 7-12, and Campus. Grants are up to $500. "Brick" awards are $100,000 (1) and $10,000 (9). Individuals and groups may apply.

Call or visit website above for details and online applications for either grant or award.

3128—NATIONAL FALLEN FIREFIGHTERS FOUNDATION (Scholarship Program)

P.O. Drawer 498
Emmitsburg MD 21727
301/447-1365
FAX: 301/447-1645
E-mail: firehero@erols.com
Internet: www.firehero.org/
scholars.htm
AMOUNT: Varies
DEADLINE(S): APR 1
FIELD(S): All fields of study

For spouse or child of fallen firefighter who met criteria for inclusion on National Fallen Firefighters Memorial in MD. Children must be under age 30. Applicant must have high school diploma/equivalency and be pursuing undergraduate, graduate, or job skills training at an accredited university, college, or community college, either full- or part-time. Minimum 2.0 GPA and 2 letters of recommendation required; extracurricular activities and special circumstances considered.

Contact NFFF for an application.

3129—NATIONAL FEDERATION OF THE BLIND (American Action Fund Scholarship)

805 Fifth Ave.
Grinnell IA 50112
515/236-3366
AMOUNT: $10,000
DEADLINE(S): MAR 31
FIELD(S): All fields of study

Applicants must be legally blind and pursuing or planning to pursue a full-time postsecondary course of study in the US. Based on academic excellence, service to the community, and financial need. Membership NOT required. Given by the American Action Fund for Blind Children and Adults.

1 award annually. Renewable. Contact Mrs. Peggy Elliot, Scholarship Committee Chairman, for an application.

3130—NATIONAL FEDERATION OF THE BLIND (E.U. Parker Scholarship)

805 Fifth Ave.
Grinnell IA 50112
515/236-3366
AMOUNT: $3,000
DEADLINE(S): MAR 31
FIELD(S): All fields of study

For legally blind students pursuing or planning to pursue a full-time postsecondary course of study in the US. Based on academic excellence, service to the community, and financial need. Membership NOT required.

1 award annually. Renewable. Contact Mrs. Peggy Elliot, Scholarship Committee Chairman, for an application.

3131—NATIONAL FEDERATION OF THE BLIND (Hermione Grant Calhoun Scholarship)

805 Fifth Ave.
Grinnell IA 50112
515/236-3366
AMOUNT: $3,000
DEADLINE(S): MAR 31
FIELD(S): All fields of study

Open to legally blind female undergraduate or graduate students pursuing or planning to pursue a full-time postsecondary course of study in the US. Based on academic excellence, service to the community, and financial need. Membership NOT required.

1 award annually. Renewable. Contact Mrs. Peggy Elliot, Scholarship Committee Chairman, for an application.

3132—NATIONAL FEDERATION OF THE BLIND (Kuchler-Killian Memorial Scholarship)

805 Fifth Ave.
Grinnell IA 50112
515/236-3366
AMOUNT: $3,000
DEADLINE(S): MAR 31
FIELD(S): All fields of study

Open to legally blind students pursuing or planning to pursue a full-time postsecondary course of study in the US. Based on academic excellence, service to the community, and financial need. Membership NOT required.

1 award annually. Renewable. Contact Mrs. Peggy Elliot, Scholarship Committee Chairman, for an application.

3133—NATIONAL FEDERATION OF THE BLIND (Melva T. Owen Memorial Scholarship)

805 Fifth Ave.
Grinnell IA 50112
515/236-3366
AMOUNT: $4,000
DEADLINE(S): MAR 31
FIELD(S): All fields of study

Open to legally blind students for all postsecondary areas of study directed towards attaining financial independence. Excludes religion and those seeking only to further their general and cultural education. For full-time study in the US. Based on academic excellence, service to the community, and financial need. Membership NOT required.

1 award annually. Renewable. Contact Mrs. Peggy Elliot, Scholarship Committee Chairman, for an application.

3134—NATIONAL FEDERATION OF THE BLIND (Mozelle and Willard Gold Memorial Scholarship)

805 Fifth Ave.
Grinnell IA 50112
515/236-3366
AMOUNT: $3,000
DEADLINE(S): MAR 31
FIELD(S): All fields of study

Open to legally blind students pursuing or planning to pursue a full-time postsecondary course of study in the US. Based on academic excellence, service to the community, and financial need. Membership NOT required.

1 award annually. Renewable. Contact Mrs. Peggy Elliot, Scholarship Committee Chairman, for an application.

3135—NATIONAL FEDERATION OF THE BLIND (NFB General Scholarships)

805 Fifth Ave.
Grinnell IA 50112
515/236-3366

AMOUNT: $3,000-$4,000
DEADLINE(S): MAR 31
FIELD(S): All fields of study

Open to legally blind students pursuing or planning to pursue a full-time postsecondary course of study in the US. Based on academic excellence, service to the community, and financial need. Membership NOT required. One of the awards will be given to a person working full-time who is attending or planning to attend a part-time course of study that will result in a new degree and broader opportunities in present or future work.

15 awards annually (2 for $4,000, 13 for $3,000). Renewable. Contact Mrs. Peggy Elliot, Scholarship Committee Chairman, for an application.

3136—NATIONAL FOREST FOUNDATION (Firefighters' Scholarship Fund)

1099 14th Street NW, Suite 5600W
Washington DC 20005
202/501-2473
FAX: 202/219-6585
Internet: www.nffweb.org/

AMOUNT: $500-$3,000
DEADLINE(S): MAY 15
FIELD(S): All fields of study

This fund provides for the continued education of firefighters or the dependants of firefighters who have been significantly disabled or killed in the line of duty fighting forest fires after January 1, 1980. These individuals must be employed by the Forest Service, Department of Interior, or state firefighting agencies. The scholarships go to those seeking admission to a college, university, or trade/technical school.

Contact NFF for an application. Award announcements made by June 30th.

3137—NATIONAL FOSTER PARENT ASSOCIATION, INC. (The Benjamin Eaton Scholarship Fund)

9 Dartmoor Drive
Crystal Lake IL 60014

800/557-5238 or 815/455-2527
FAX: 815/455-1527
E-mail: nfpais@mc.net
Internet: www.nfpainc.org

AMOUNT: $1,000
DEADLINE(S): MAR 31
FIELD(S): All fields of study

Scholarships for college-bound or voc-tech-school-bound high school seniors who are foster children at the time of application. Also for birth or adopted children of persons who are foster parents. In both cases, foster parents must be members of the National Foster Parent Association.

3 awards each year for foster children, and one each for birth or adopted children of foster parents.

3138—NATIONAL HORSESHOE PITCHERS ASSOCIATION (Junior Scholar Pitcher Program)

3085 76th Street
Franksville WI 53124
414/835-9108

AMOUNT: $250
DEADLINE(S): None
FIELD(S): All fields of study

Open to students who compete in a horseshoe pitching league and are 18 or younger.

Write to the above address for complete information.

3139—NATIONAL ITALIAN AMERICAN FOUNDATION (Agnes E. Vaghi Cornaro Scholarship)

1860 19th Street NW
Washington DC 20009-5599
202/530-5315

AMOUNT: $2,000
DEADLINE(S): MAY 31
FIELD(S): All fields of study

Open to Italian-American undergraduate women who submit a 3-page, double-spaced essay on a famous Italian-American woman.

Also considered are academic merit, financial need, and community service.

3140—NATIONAL ITALIAN AMERICAN FOUNDATION (Alyce M. Cafaro Scholarship)

1860 19th Street NW
Washington DC 20009-5599
202/530-5315

AMOUNT: $5,000
DEADLINE(S): MAY 31

FIELD(S): Any field of study

Open to undergraduates of Italian ancestry from Ohio.

Considerations are academic merit, financial need, and community service. Write for application and further information.

3141—NATIONAL ITALIAN AMERICAN FOUNDATION (Alex and Henry Recine Scholarships)

1860 19th Street NW
Washington DC 20009-5599
202/530-5315

AMOUNT: $2,500
DEADLINE(S): MAY 31
FIELD(S): All fields of study

Open to undergraduates of Italian ancestry who are residents of the state of New York.

Financial need, academic merit, and community service are considered.

3142—NATIONAL ITALIAN AMERICAN FOUNDATION (Angela Scholarship)

1860 19th Street NW
Washington DC 20009-5599
202/530-5315

AMOUNT: $2,500
DEADLINE(S): MAY 31
FIELD(S): Any field of study

For entering freshmen students of Italian ancestry with an exemplary academic record showing social responsibilities during high school. Must be willing to intern at the NIAF for one semester.

Write for application information. Financial need also considered.

3143—NATIONAL ITALIAN AMERICAN FOUNDATION (Antonio and Felicia Marinelli Scholarships)

1860 19th Street NW
Washington DC 20009-5599
202/530-5315

AMOUNT: $1,000
DEADLINE(S): MAY 31
FIELD(S): Any field of study

For undergraduate American students of Italian ancestry accepted at the American University of Rome. Applicants must write a 2- to 3-page typed essay on a family member or personality he/she considers to be "An Italian American Hero."

4 awards to be given. Academic merit, financial need, and community service are considered. Contact Maria Enrico at 301/977-2250 or 202/331-8327 for application information.

3144—NATIONAL ITALIAN AMERICAN FOUNDATION (Daniel Stella Scholarship)

1860 19th Street NW
Washington DC 20009-5599
202/530-5315

AMOUNT: $1,000
DEADLINE(S): MAY 31
FIELD(S): All fields of study

For graduate or undergraduate students of Italian ancestry who have Cooley's Anemia disease.

Financial need, scholastic merit, and community service are considered.

3145—NATIONAL ITALIAN AMERICAN FOUNDATION (Dr. William L. Amoroso, Jr. Scholarship)

1860 19th Street NW
Washington DC 20009-5599
202/530-5315

AMOUNT: $1,000
DEADLINE(S): MAY 31
FIELD(S): Any field of study

For undergraduate American students of Italian ancestry accepted at the American University of Rome.

Academic merit, financial need, and community service are considered. Call Maria Enrico at 301/977-2250 for details.

3146—NATIONAL ITALIAN AMERICAN FOUNDATION (Frank De Pietro Memorial Scholarship)

1860 19th Street NW
Washington DC 20009-5599
202/530-5315

AMOUNT: Varies ($14,000 for numerous scholarships)
DEADLINE(S): MAY 31
FIELD(S): All fields of study

For current or entering freshmen students of Italian ancestry at Harvey Mudd College, California.

Numerous awards. Academic merit, financial need, and community service considered. Contact Barbara Bergman at 909/621-8384.

3147—NATIONAL ITALIAN AMERICAN FOUNDATION (Guido-Zerilli-Marimo Scholarships)

1860 19th Street NW
Washington DC 20009-5599
202/530-5315

AMOUNT: $1,000

DEADLINE(S): MAY 31
FIELD(S): All fields of study

Open to undergraduate or graduate students at New York University who are of Italian heritage.

3 awards. Evidence of financial need, academic merit, and community service to be submitted with application.

3148—NATIONAL ITALIAN AMERICAN FOUNDATION (John A. Volpe Scholarship)

1860 19th Street NW
Washington DC 20009-5599
202/530-5315

AMOUNT: $1,000
DEADLINE(S): MAY 31
FIELD(S): All fields of study

For undergraduate students of Italian ancestry who live in the New England area.

Financial need, community service, and academic merit are considered.

3149—NATIONAL ITALIAN AMERICAN FOUNDATION (Joe Tangaro Athletic Scholarship)

1860 19th Street NW
Washington DC 20009-5599
202/530-5315

AMOUNT: $2,500
DEADLINE(S): MAY 31
FIELD(S): Any field of study

Open to high school seniors of Italian ancestry residing in Street Louis, MO, who excel in athletics.

Also considered are academic merit, financial need, and community service.

3150—NATIONAL ITALIAN AMERICAN FOUNDATION (John and Anne Parente/NIAF Matching Scholarship)

1860 19th Street NW
Washington DC 20009-5599
202/530-5315

AMOUNT: $2,000
DEADLINE(S): MAY 31
FIELD(S): All fields of study

For undergraduate students of Italian ancestry attending King's College in Wilkes-Barre, PA. Write a 2- to 3-page essay on a family member or a personality you consider: "An Italian American Hero."

Also considered are academic merit, financial need, and community service. Contact organization for application and details.

3151—NATIONAL ITALIAN AMERICAN FOUNDATION (Johnson and Wales Governor Christopher Del Sesto/NIAF Scholarship)

1860 19th Street NW
Washington DC 20009-5599
202/530-5315

AMOUNT: $2,000
DEADLINE(S): MAY 31
FIELD(S): All fields of study

For freshmen students of Italian ancestry attending Johnson and Wales University, Rhode Island.

Financial need, academic merit, and community service considered. Contact Richard Tarantino at 401/598-1072.

3152—NATIONAL ITALIAN AMERICAN FOUNDATION (Louis J. Salerno, M.D. Memorial Scholarship)

1860 19th Street NW
Washington DC 20009-5599
202/530-5315

AMOUNT: $2,000
DEADLINE(S): MAY 31
FIELD(S): Art history

For undergraduate American students of Italian ancestry wishing to attend the American University of Rome and who are pursuing studies in art history.

Academic merit, financial need, and community service are considered. Contact Maria Enrico at 202/331-8327 or 301/977-2250.

3153—NATIONAL ITALIAN AMERICAN FOUNDATION (Marija Bileta Scholarship)

1860 19th Street NW
Washington DC 20009-5599
202/530-5315

AMOUNT: $1,000
DEADLINE(S): MAY 31
FIELD(S): Any field of study

Open to undergraduates of Italian ancestry.

Considerations are academic merit, financial need, and community service. Write for application and further information.

3154—NATIONAL ITALIAN AMERICAN FOUNDATION (NIAF/NOIAW Cornaro Scholarship)

1860 19th Street NW
Washington DC 20009-5599
202/530-5315

AMOUNT: $1,000
DEADLINE(S): MAY 31
FIELD(S): All areas of study

For female undergraduate and graduate students with Italian ancestry. Prepare a 3-page, double-spaced paper on a current issue of concern for Italian American women or a famous Italian American woman.

3 awards. Financial need, academic merit, and community service are considered.

3155—NATIONAL ITALIAN AMERICAN FOUNDATION (NIAF/Sacred Heart University Matching Scholarship)

1860 19th Street NW
Washington DC 20009-5599
202/530-5315

AMOUNT: $2,000
DEADLINE(S): MAY 31
FIELD(S): All fields of study

Open to undergraduates of Italian heritage who attend Sacred Heart University in Fairfield, Connecticut.

Also considered are academic merit, financial need, and community service. Write for application and details.

3156—NATIONAL ITALIAN AMERICAN FOUNDATION (NIAF/FIERI National Matching Scholarship)

1860 19th Street NW
Washington DC 20009-5599
202/530-5315

AMOUNT: $1,000
DEADLINE(S): MAY 31
FIELD(S): All fields of study

Open to undergraduates of Italian heritage currently enrolled or entering college. FIERI is a national organization of students and young professionals proud of their Italian heritage. Write a 2- to 3-page typed essay on a family member or a personality you consider: "An Italian American Hero."

Also considered are academic merit, financial need, and community service. Write for application and details.

3157—NATIONAL ITALIAN AMERICAN FOUNDATION (O. Mike Marinelli Scholarship)

1860 19th Street NW
Washington DC 20009-5599
202/530-5315

AMOUNT: $2,000

DEADLINE(S): MAY 31
FIELD(S): Any field of study

For undergraduate American students of Italian ancestry attending Nova University, Florida.

Community service, scholastic merit, and financial need are considered.

3158—NATIONAL ITALIAN AMERICAN FOUNDATION (O. Mike Marinelli Scholarship)

1860 19th Street NW
Washington DC 20009-5599
202/530-5315

AMOUNT: $1,000
DEADLINE(S): MAY 31
FIELD(S): All fields of study

For undergraduate students of Italian ancestry attending Barry University, Florida.

Financial need, scholastic merit, and community service are considered.

3159—NATIONAL ITALIAN AMERICAN FOUNDATION (Robert J. Di Pietro Scholarship)

1860 19th Street NW
Washington DC 20009-5599
202/530-5315

AMOUNT: $1,000
DEADLINE(S): MAY 31
FIELD(S): Any field of study

For undergraduate and graduate students of Italian ancestry age 25 or under. Include essay of 400-600 words on how applicant intends to use his/her ethnicity throughout his/her chosen field of education to preserve and support this ethnicity throughout life. Submit 4 copies with name and title of essay on each.

2 awards given. Academic merit, financial need, and community service also considered.

3160—NATIONAL ITALIAN AMERICAN FOUNDATION (Silvio Conte Internship)

1860 19th Street NW
Washington DC 20009-5599
202/530-5315

AMOUNT: $1,000
DEADLINE(S): MAY 31
FIELD(S): All fields of study

For undergraduate and graduate students of Italian descent interested in interning for one semester on Capitol Hill in Washington DC. Applicant must provide a letter of acceptance from a congres-

sional office. Student is expected to write a 2- to 3-page double-spaced, typed paper on the importance of this experience to his/her career.

Academic merit, community service, and financial need considered.

3161—NATIONAL ITALIAN AMERICAN FOUNDATION (Study Abroad Scholarships)

1860 19th Street NW
Washington DC 20009-5599
202/530-5315

AMOUNT: $2,000
DEADLINE(S): MAY 31
FIELD(S): Any field of study

For undergraduate or graduate students of Italian ancestry wishing to study in Italy. Programs are available at the American University of Rome and John Cabot University. Must show letter of acceptance.

Academic merit, community service, and financial need are considered. 5 awards given.

3162—NATIONAL ITALIAN AMERICAN FOUNDATION (West Virginia Italian Heritage Festival Scholarships)

1860 19th Street NW
Washington DC 20009-5599
202/530-5315

AMOUNT: $3,500 total
DEADLINE(S): MAY 31
FIELD(S): Any field of study

For students entering college or already enrolled who are of Italian ancestry and reside in West Virginia.

Financial need, community service, and academic merit are considered.

3163—NATIONAL MAKE IT YOURSELF WITH WOOL COMPETITION (Scholarship/Awards)

P.O. Box 175
Lavina MT 59046
406/636-2731

AMOUNT: Various awards including $2,000 scholarship
DEADLINE(S): Varies (with state)
FIELD(S): All fields of study

Sewing, knitting, and crocheting competition open to students who make a wool garment from a current pattern. Fabric must contain at least 60% wool. Awards tenable at any recognized college or university.

Teenagers and older pay an entry fee of $10; preteens pay $5. State winners advance to national competition. Write for complete information.

3164—NATIONAL MERIT SCHOLARSHIP CORPORATION (National Achievement Scholarship Program)

1560 Sherman Ave., Suite 200
Evanston IL 60201
847/866-5100

AMOUNT: Varies
DEADLINE(S): Varies
FIELD(S): All fields of study

For Black American high school students to use for undergraduate studies. Must take the PSAT/NMSQT in the proper high school year (usually junior year). Financial need NOT required.

700 awards annually. Renewable. See school counselor for a PSAT/NMSQT Student Bulletin. The Achievement Program will contact students to be recognized through their schools.

3165—NATIONAL ROOFING FOUNDATION (Scholarship Program)

CSFA, 1505 Riverview Road
P.O. Box 297
Street Peter MN 56082
800/537-4180 or 847/299-1183
FAX: 847/299-1183
E-mail: NRCA@nrca.net
Internet: www.nrca.net

AMOUNT: $1,000/yr.
DEADLINE(S): JAN 31
FIELD(S): All fields of study

Open to employees, immediate family members of employees, or immediate family members of NRCA contractor members. Must be high school seniors/graduates who plan to enroll or are already enrolled in full-time undergraduate course of study at accredited 2- or 4-year college, university, or voc-tech school. Based on academic record, potential to succeed, leadership, school/community activities, honors, work experience, goals, and references. Financial need NOT a factor.

Renewable up to 4 years with minimum C+ GPA. Contact NRF for an application.

3166—NATIONAL RURAL EDUCATION ASSOCIATION (Essay Contest)

Colorado State University
Educ. Bldg., Room 230
Ft. Collins CO 80523-1588

970/491-7022
FAX: 970/491-1317
E-mail: jnewlin@lamar.colostate.edu
Internet: www.colostate.edu/
Orgs/NREA/

AMOUNT: $250 (gr. 3-5); $500 (gr. 6-9); $500 (high school)
DEADLINE(S): JUN 30 (postmark)
FIELD(S): All fields of study

Essay contest for students in grades 3 to 12 who attend a rural school. Topic: "How can schools and communities work together to improve rural school?" For grades 3-5, 250 words; for grades 6-12, 500 words. Must be written in ink or typed double-spaced on one side of the paper only. No names or school names should appear in the essay itself—use a cover sheet. Only 5 entries from each school.

For details, contact Dr. Joe Newlin, Exec. Director, NREA Headquarters, at above address.

3167—NATIONAL SCIENCE TEACHERS ASSOCIATION (Space Science Student Involvement Program)

1840 Wilson Blvd.
Arlington VA 22201-3000
703/243-7100

AMOUNT: Trips to NASA centers for students and teachers
DEADLINE(S): None specified
FIELD(S): Science, Math, Technology, and Art related to space science exploration

For students in grades 3-12 and their teachers to incorporate the above fields into space science exploration. Specific themes for each grade level.

For US students and teachers to win trips to NASA center, internships with NASA scientists, Space Camp scholarships, medals, ribbons, certificates, and recognition at the National Space Science symposium in Washington, DC.

3168—NATIONAL SCIENCE TEACHERS ASSOCIATION (Toshiba/NSTA ExploraVision Awards)

1840 Wilson Blvd.
Arlington VA 22201-3000
703/243-7100 or 800/EXPLOR-9
E-mail: exploravision@nsta.org
Internet: www.nsta.org/programs/
exploravision.shtml

AMOUNT: Up to $10,000 in US Savings Bonds, plus gifts for teachers and parents and all participants

DEADLINE(S): FEB 3
FIELD(S): Students working in teams of three or four envision what a form of technology today would be like in 20 years.
Write to above location for details.

3169—NATIONAL SLOVAK SOCIETY (Peter V. Rovnianek Scholarship Fund)

2325 E. Carson Street
Pittsburgh PA 15203
412/488-1890

AMOUNT: Varies
DEADLINE(S): MAY 1
FIELD(S): All fields of study

Open to deserving and needy high school seniors enrolling in 2- or 4-year colleges, universities, or trade schools. Applicants must have been a beneficial member of the society for at least 2 years before applying.

Write for complete information.

3170—NATIONAL SOCIETY DAUGHTERS OF THE AMERICAN REVOLUTION (Lillian and Arthur Dunn Scholarship)

1776 D Street NW
Washington DC 20006-5392
202/628-1776
Internet: www.dar.org

AMOUNT: $1,000
DEADLINE(S): FEB 15
FIELD(S): All fields of study

Open to graduating high school seniors (US citizens) whose MOTHERS are current DAR members. Must be planning to attend US college/university; awards are placed on deposit with school. Awards judged on academic excellence and need.

Renewable up to four years, with annual transcript review; outstanding students may apply for an additional four years as needed for continuing study. See website or send a self-addressed, stamped envelope for an application or more information.

3171—NATIONAL SOCIETY DAUGHTERS OF THE AMERICAN REVOLUTION (Margaret Howard Hamilton Scholarship)

1776 D Street NW
Washington DC 20006-5392
202/628-1776
Internet: www.dar.org

AMOUNT: $1,000
DEADLINE(S): FEB 15
FIELD(S): All fields of study

For a graduating high school senior who has been accepted into the Jones Learning Center, University of the Ozarks. Applications must be requested directly from the Learning Center upon acceptance into this program for learning disabled students. Awards are placed on deposit with the school and are based on academic excellence and need. No affiliation with DAR required.

Renewable up to four years, with annual transcript review. For information on DAR's other scholarships, see website or send a self-addressed, stamped envelope.

3172—NATIONAL SOCIETY OF THE SONS OF THE AMERICAN REVOLUTION (Eagle Scout Scholarship)

1000 S. Fourth Street
Louisville KY 40203
502/589-1776

AMOUNT: $5,000 (1st); $1,000 (2nd)
DEADLINE(S): DEC 31
FIELD(S): All fields of study

Open to the current class of Eagle Scouts who passed their board of review between July 1 and the following June 30 of each year. College plans DO NOT have to be complete in order to receive the cash scholarships.

An essay of 500 words or less on a patriotic theme is required. Contact your local SAR Eagle Scout Chairman for complete information.

3173—NATIONAL TWENTY AND FOUR (Memorial Scholarships)

6000 Lucerne Ct., #2
Mequon WI 53092
Written inquiry

AMOUNT: Up to $500/yr.
DEADLINE(S): MAY 1
FIELD(S): All areas of study

Open to members and children, grandchildren, or great-grandchildren of women who are members of the Twenty and Four, Honor Society of Women Legionnaires. Also for descendents of deceased former members. Must be between the ages of 16 and 25. For use at a school, college, university, or vocational institution beyond high school. Selection is based on financial need, scholastic standing, and school activities.

Write to "National Aide" for complete information ONLY if above qualifications are met.

3174—NATIONAL WELSH-AMERICAN FOUNDATION (Exchange Scholarship Program)

24 Carverton Road
Trucksville PA 18708

717/696-6923

AMOUNT: Up to $5,000
DEADLINE(S): MAR 1
FIELD(S): All fields of study

Open to US citizens of Welsh descent who are enrolled in undergraduate or graduate degree programs at recognized US institutions. For study of Welsh-oriented subjects at a college in Wales.

Welsh family ties are required. Write for complete information.

3175—NATIONS BANK TRUST DEPT. (Minne L. Maffett Scholarship Trust)

P.O. Box 831515
Dallas TX 75283
214/559-6476

AMOUNT: $50-$1,000
DEADLINE(S): APR 1
FIELD(S): All fields of study

Open to US citizens who graduated from Limestone County, Texas high schools. Scholarships for full-time study at an accredited Texas institution.

30 scholarships per year. Write to Debra Hitzelberger, vice president and trust officer, at address above for complete information.

3176—NATIVE SONS OF THE GOLDEN WEST (Annual High School Public Speaking Contest)

414 Mason Street, Room 300
San Francisco CA 94102
415/566-4117

AMOUNT: $600-$2,000
DEADLINE(S): DEC 1
FIELD(S): California History

Public speaking competition open to California high school students under age 20. Speeches should be 7-9 minutes in length and may be on any subject related to California's past or present.

District eliminations take place in February and March; finals are in May. Write for complete information.

3177—NATRONA COUNTY EDUCATION ASSOCIATION (Scholarships)

851 Werner Ct., Suite 105
Casper WY 82601
Written inquiry

AMOUNT: $500
DEADLINE(S): MAR 1
FIELD(S): All fields of study

Available to graduating high school seniors from Natrona County, Wyoming,

high schools. Parents must be NCEA members or retired NCEA members who are currently WEA members.

Write to the NCEA Scholarship Committee for an application.

3178—NAVY SUPPLY CORPS FOUNDATION (Scholarships)

1425 Prince Ave.
Athens GA 30606-2205
706/354-4111

AMOUNT: $2,000
DEADLINE(S): FEB 15
FIELD(S): All fields of study

For dependent sons/daughters of Navy Supply Corps Officers (including Warrant) & Supply Corps associated enlisted ratings on active duty, in reserve status, retired-with-pay, or deceased. For undergraduate study at accredited 2-yr/4-yr colleges. 3.0 GPA for high school/college required.

Approx 50 awards per year. Send SASE for complete information.

3179—NAVY WIVES CLUBS OF AMERICA (Scholarship Foundation)

Barbara Stead, NWCA Director
3848 Old Colony Circle
Virginia Beach VA 23452
757/340-2088

AMOUNT: $1,000
DEADLINE(S): MAR 15
FIELD(S): All fields of study

Open to dependents of enlisted members of the US Navy, Marine Corps, or Coast Guard who are on active duty, retired with pay, or deceased. For undergraduate study. Must demonstrate financial need.

Applicants must be previously approved for admission to an accredited school. 29 awards per year. Send self-addressed, stamped business-size envelope for complete information.

3180—NAVY-MARINE CORPS RELIEF SOCIETY (Battleship IOWA Memorial Fund and USS STARK Memorial Fund)

801 N. Randolph Street, Suite 1228
Arlington VA 22203-1978
703/696-4960

AMOUNT: Varies
DEADLINE(S): None specified
FIELD(S): All areas of study

Limited to children and widows of deceased crewmembers of the USS IOWA who perished as a result of the April 19, 1989 turret explosion and the USS STARK crewmembers who perished as a result of the Persian Gulf missile attack May 17, 1987.

3181—NAVY-MARINE CORPS RELIEF SOCIETY (Children of Deceased Servicemembers)

801 N. Randolph Street, Suite 1228
Arlington VA 22203-1978
703/696-4960

AMOUNT: Varies
DEADLINE(S): None specified
FIELD(S): All fields of study

Grants or interest-free loans for children of a servicemember who died on active duty. Amount determined on a case-by-case basis.

Write for more information.

3182—NAVY-MARINE CORPS RELIEF SOCIETY (Children of Deceased Servicemembers)

801 N. Randolph Street, Suite 1228
Arlington VA 22203-1978
703/696-4960

AMOUNT: Varies
DEADLINE(S): None specified
FIELD(S): All fields of study

Grants to children of servicemembers who died in retired status or on active duty.
Write for more information.

3183—NAVY-MARINE CORPS RELIEF SOCIETY (E.P. Travers Scholarship)

801 N. Randolph Street, Suite 1228
Arlington VA 22203-1978
703/696-4960

AMOUNT: $2,000
DEADLINE(S): None given
FIELD(S): All fields of study

Undergraduate scholarship for dependent children of active duty or retired servicemembers and spouses of active duty servicemembers of the US Marines or US Navy. GPA must be no less that 2.0.
Renewable up to four years.

3184—NAVY-MARINE CORPS RELIEF SOCIETY (E.P. Travers Loan)

801 N. Randolph Street, Suite 1228
Arlington, VA 22203-1978
703/696-4960

AMOUNT: Minimum loan: $500;
    maximum loan: $3,000

DEADLINE(S): OCT 15
FIELD(S): All fields of study.

Loan for parents of an undergraduate student who is a dependent of an active duty or retired member of the US Marines or US Navy or spouse of an active member. Minimum GPA: 2.0.

Must be repaid in 24 months by allotment of pay.

3185—NAVY-MARINE CORPS RELIEF SOCIETY (Spouse Tuition Aid Program)

801 N. Randolph Street, Suite 1228
Arlington VA 22203-1978
703/696-4960

AMOUNT: Up to 50% of tuition for on-base education programs, up to a maximum of $300 per undergraduate term, or $350 per graduate term, and $1,500 per academic year
DEADLINE(S): None specified
FIELD(S): Any field of study

For spouses of active US Navy or Marine personnel and who reside overseas with the active duty servicemember. Applicant need not be a full-time student.

Administered locally by an NMCRS Auxiliary.

3186—NAVY-MARINE CORPS RELIEF SOCIETY (Tuition Assistance Program/GI Bill)

801 N. Randolph Street, Suite 1228
Arlington VA 22203-1978
703/696-4960

AMOUNT: To be determined
    individually
DEADLINE(S): None specified
FIELD(S): All fields of study

Loans to cover all or a portion of the servicemember's cost under the Navy Department's Tuition Assistance Program. Also loans to allow enrollment under the GI Bill if education benefits from the Veteran's Administration are untimely. Apply at one of the Society's field offices.
Write for details.

3187—NAVY-MARINE CORPS RELIEF SOCIETY (USS TENNESSEE Scholarship Fund)

801 N. Randolph Street, Suite 1228
Arlington VA 22203-1978
703/696-4960

AMOUNT: $1,000/yr.
DEADLINE(S): None specified
FIELD(S): Any field of study

Limited to dependent children of active duty personnel assigned to or previously assigned to duty aboard the USS TENNESSEE.
Write for details.

3188—NEGRO EDUCATIONAL EMERGENCY DRIVE (NEED Scholarship Program)

643 Liberty Ave., 17th Fl.
Pittsburgh PA 15222
412/566-2760

AMOUNT: $100 to $1,000
DEADLINE(S): APR 30
FIELD(S): All areas of study

Pennsylvania residency and US citizenship required. Open to black students with a high school diploma or GED who reside in Allegheny, Armstrong, Beaver, Butler, Washington, or Westmoreland counties.

400 scholarships per year. Renewable.
Write for complete information.

3189—NELLIE MAE (Student Loans)

50 Braintree Hill Park, Suite 300
Braintree MA 02184-1763
617/849-1325 or 800/634-9308

AMOUNT: Up to cost of education less
    financial aid
DEADLINE(S): None specified
FIELD(S): All fields of study

Variety of loans available for undergraduate and graduate study at accredited degree-granting colleges or universities. Varied repayment and interest rate options. Savings programs for on-time repayments.
Write for complete information.

3190—NETTIE MILLHOLLON EDUCATIONAL TRUST ESTATE (Student Loans)

309 West Saint Anna Street
P.O. Box 79782
Stanton TX 79782
915/756-2261

AMOUNT: Varies
DEADLINE(S): JUL 1 (for Fall); JAN 2
    (for Spring)
FIELD(S): All fields of study

Student loans for financially needy Texas residents under 25 years of age. Financial need, character, evidence of ability, and desire to learn and further one's education, and unavailability of other financial resources are all considered. At least 2.5 GPA required.

Send SASE to above address for details.

3191—NEVADA DEPARTMENT OF EDUCATION (Robert C. Byrd Honors Scholarship)

700 E. Fifth Street
Carson City NV 89701
702/687-9228

AMOUNT: $1,121 (varies)
DEADLINE(S): None specified (Must have taken SATI/ACT by JAN 1)
FIELD(S): All fields of study

For Nevada high school seniors with 3.5 GPA or higher, 25 or higher on ACT, or 1000 or higher on SATI.

Inquire through school counselor or office listed above.

3192—NEVADA DEPARTMENT OF EDUCATION (Student Incentive Grant Program)

700 E. Fifth Street
Carson City NV 89701
702/687-9228

AMOUNT: Varies
DEADLINE(S): Varies
FIELD(S): All fields of study

Student incentive grants available to Nevada residents enrolled in eligible Nevada institutions. For both graduate and undergraduate study.

Application must be made through the financial aid office of eligible participating institutions.

3193—NEW BEDFORD PORT SOCIETY-LADIES BRANCH (Limited Scholarship Grant)

15 Johnny Cake Hill
New Bedford MA 02740
Written inquiry only

AMOUNT: $300-$400
DEADLINE(S): MAY 1
FIELD(S): All areas of study

Open to residents of greater New Bedford, MA, who are descended from seafarers such as whaling masters and other fishermen. For undergrad and marine biology studies.

Renewable. Write for complete information.

3194—NEW ENGLAND BOARD OF HIGHER EDUCATION (New England Regional Student Program)

45 Temple Place
Boston MA 02111
617/357-9620

AMOUNT: Tuition reduction (varies)

DEADLINE(S): Varies
FIELD(S): All fields of study

Under this program New England residents may attend public colleges and universities in other New England states at a reduced tuition rate for certain majors that are not available in their own state's public institutions.

Write to the above address for complete information.

3195—NEW HAMPSHIRE HIGHER EDUCATION ASSISTANCE FOUNDATION (Federal Family Education Loan Program)

4 Barrell Court
P.O. Box 877
Concord NH 03302-0877
800/525-2577, ext. 119
603/225-6612

AMOUNT: Varies
DEADLINE(S): None
FIELD(S): All fields of study

Open to New Hampshire residents pursuing a college education in or out of state and to non-residents who attend a New Hampshire college or university. US citizenship required.

Also provides scholarship searches, career searches, college searches, and individual counseling to parents and prospective college students (all free of charge). Interested students/parents may call or write to above address.

3196—NEW JERSEY DEPT. OF HIGHER EDUCATION (Educational Opportunity Fund Grants)

Office of Student Assistance
CN 540
Trenton NJ 08625
609/588-3230
800/792-8670 in NJ
TDD: 609/588-2526

AMOUNT: $200-$2,100 undergrads; $200-$4,150 graduate students
DEADLINE(S): Varies
FIELD(S): All areas of study

Must be New Jersey resident for at least 12 months prior to application. Grants for economically and educationally disadvantaged students. For undergraduate or graduate study in New Jersey. Must demonstrate need and be US citizen or legal resident.

Grants renewable. Write for complete information.

3197—NEW JERSEY DEPT. OF HIGHER EDUCATION (Public Tuition Benefits Program)

Office of Student Assistance
CN 540
Trenton NJ 08625
609/588-3230
800/792-8670 in NJ
TDD: 609/588-2526

AMOUNT: Actual cost of tuition
DEADLINE(S): OCT 1; MAR 1
FIELD(S): All areas of study

Open to New Jersey residents who are dependents of emergency service personnel and law officers killed in the line of duty in NJ. For undergraduate study in NJ US citizenship or legal residency required.

Renewable. Write for complete information.

3198—NEW JERSEY DEPT. OF MILITARY & VETERANS AFFAIRS (Veterans Tuition Credit Program)

Eggert Crossing Road
CN340, Attn: DVL6S
Trenton NJ 08625-0340
609/530-6961
800/624-0508 in NJ

AMOUNT: $400 (full-time); $200 (half-time)
DEADLINE(S): OCT 1; MAR 1
FIELD(S): All fields of study

Open to US military veterans who served between Dec. 31, 1960 and May 7, 1975 and were residents of New Jersey for one year prior to application or were NJ residents at time of induction or discharge. Proof of residency is required.

Applies to all levels of study. Write for complete information.

3199—NEW JERSEY DEPT. OF MILITARY & VETERANS AFFAIRS (POW/MIA Dependents Grants)

Eggert Crossing Road
CN 340, Attn: DCUA-FO
Trenton NJ 08625-0340
609/530-6961
800/624-0508 in NJ

AMOUNT: Full tuition
DEADLINE(S): OCT 1; MAR 1
FIELD(S): All fields of study

For New Jersey residents who are dependent children of US military personnel who were officially declared POW or MIA after Jan 1, 1960. Grants will pay undergraduate tuition at any accredited public or independent college/university in NJ.

Write for complete information.

3200—NEW JERSEY STATE GOLF ASSOC. (Caddie Scholarships)

P.O. Box 6947
Freehold NJ 07728
973/338-8334

AMOUNT: $800—$2,500
DEADLINE(S): MAY 1
FIELD(S): All fields of study

Open to students who have served as a caddie at a New Jersey golf club which is a member of the NJ state golf association. For full-time undergraduate study at an accredited college or university.

Awards are based on scholastic achievement, financial need, SAT scores, character, and length of service as a caddie. 40+ new awards per year. Renewable for 3 additional years. Write for complete information.

3201—NEW JERSEY TESOL-BE (Postsecondary Scholarship)

c/o Irma Lorenz
138 Bentley Drive
Mt. Laurel NJ 08054
800/95EBESL

AMOUNT: $750
DEADLINE(S): APR 1
FIELD(S): All fields of study

Open to New Jersey high school seniors who are bilingual and English as a second language students.

Write to the above address for further information.

3202—NEW MEXICO COMMISSION ON HIGHER EDUCATION (Student Incentive Grant)

P.O. Box 15910
Santa Fe NM 87506-5910
505/827-7383
FAX: 505/827-7393
E-mail: highered@che.state.nm.us
Internet: www.nmche.org

AMOUNT: $600 average
DEADLINE(S): Varies
FIELD(S): All fields of study

Open to New Mexico residents who are undergraduates attending public and selected private, nonprofit, postsecondary institutions in New Mexico. Must be enrolled at least half-time.

Renewable. Approximately 12,000 grants per year. Contact college financial aid office for deadlines and other information.

3203—NEW MEXICO FARM AND LIVE-STOCK BUREAU (Memorial Scholarships)

P.O. Box 20004
Las Cruces NM 88004-9004

505/532-4702
FAX: 505/532-4710
E-mail: nmflb@zianet.com

AMOUNT: Varies
DEADLINE(S): MAY 1
FIELD(S): All fields of study

Available to members of New Mexico Farm & Livestock Bureau families for one year of continuing education at an institution of their choice. Must be a resident of New Mexico and have a minimum 2.5 GPA. Transcripts, two letters of recommendation, and a recent photograph for publicity purposes are required. Financial need NOT a factor.

5 awards annually. Renewable through reapplication. Contact Missy Aguayo at NMFLB for an application.

3204—NEW MEXICO TECH (Freshmen and Transfer Student Scholarships)

CS Box M-801, Leroy Place
Socorro NM 87801
505/835-5333

AMOUNT: $1,750-$5,000
DEADLINE(S): MAR 1
FIELD(S): All fields of study

Various scholarship programs for entering freshmen and transfer students to New Mexico Tech. Also for graduating high school seniors who are winners at the NM Science and Engineering Fair or at NM Science Olympiad.

Write to above address for details.

3205—NEW MEXICO TECH (Scholarships for Non-resident Students)

CS Box M-801, Leroy Place
Socorro NM 87801
505/835-5333

AMOUNT: $700
DEADLINE(S): MAR 1
FIELD(S): All fields of study

Scholarship for non-residents of New Mexico planning to attend New Mexico Tech. Priority given to transfer students. Non-resident part of tuition is waived. GPA required: 3.0 freshmen; 3.5 college transfers.

Renewable up to four years. Contact above location for details.

3206—NEW MEXICO TECH (Transfer Student Scholarship)

CS Box M-801, Leroy Place
Socorro NM 87801
505/835-5333

AMOUNT: $3,500/yr.

DEADLINE(S): MAR 1
FIELD(S): All fields of study

Scholarships for transfer students to New Mexico Tech with GPA of 3.5 or better. Renewable for up to three years.

3207—NEW MEXICO VETERANS' SERVICE COMMISSION (Scholarship Program)

P.O. Box 2324
Santa Fe NM 87503
505/827-6300

AMOUNT: Full tuition + $300
DEADLINE(S): None
FIELD(S): All fields of study

Open to New Mexico residents (aged 16-26) who are son or daughter of person who was killed in action or died as a result of military service in the US Armed Forces during a period of armed conflict.

Veteran must have been NM resident at time of entry into service and must have served during a period of armed conflict. Approx 13 full tuition scholarships for undergrads per year. Write for complete information.

3208—NEW YORK STATE EDUCATION DEPT. (Awards, Scholarships, and Fellowships)

Bureau of NEOP/UATEA/Scholarships
Room 1076 EB
Albany NY 12234
518/486-1319
FAX: 518/486-5346

AMOUNT: Varies
DEADLINE(S): Varies
FIELD(S): All fields of study

Various state and federal programs administered by the NY State Education Department open to residents of New York state. One year's NY residency immediately preceding effective date of award is required.

Write for complete information.

3209—NEW YORK STATE HIGHER EDUCATION SERVICES CORPORATION (Robert C. Byrd Honors Scholarship)

HESC, Student Information
Albany NY 12255
518/486-1319
Internet: www.hesc.com

AMOUNT: $1,500/yr.
DEADLINE(S): None
FIELD(S): All fields of study

For NY state academically talented high school seniors who plan to attend any approved institution of higher education in the United States.

For more information on other state and federal student financial aid programs, write to above address.

3210—NEW YORK STATE HIGHER EDU-CATION SERVICES CORPORATION (Memorial Scholarships for Families of Deceased Police Officers and Firefighters)

HESC, Student Information
Albany NY 12255
518/486-1319
Internet: www.hesc.com

AMOUNT: Varies
DEADLINE(S): None
FIELD(S): All fields of study

Scholarships for NY state children and spouses of deceased police officers, firefighters, and volunteer firefighters who died as the result of injuries sustained in the line of duty.

Complete a Free Application for Federal Student Aid (FAFSA) and the New York State Tuition Assistance Program (TAP) application to apply.

3211—NEW YORK STATE HIGHER EDU-CATION SERVICES CORPORATION (Vietnam Veterans and Persian Gulf Veterans Tuition Awards)

HESC, Student Information
Albany NY 12255
518/486-1319
Internet: www.hesc.com

AMOUNT: $500 (part-time); $1,000 (full-time). Total awards cannot exceed $10,000.
DEADLINE(S): MAY 1
FIELD(S): All fields of study

Scholarships for NY residents who are veterans of either the Vietnam War or the Persian Gulf War (Desert Storm/Desert Shield). For voc-/tech. training, undergraduate, and graduate study. Contact a local County Veterans' Service Agency or the NY State Division of Veterans' Affairs for details.

Complete a Free Application for Federal Student Aid (FAFSA) and the New York State Tuition Assistance Program (TAP) application to apply.

3212—NEW YORK STATE HIGHER EDU-CATION SERVICES CORPORATION (Tuition Assistance Program [TAP] and Aid for Part-Time Study [APTS])

HESC, Student Information
Albany NY 12255
518/486-1319
Internet: www.hesc.com

AMOUNT: Varies
DEADLINE(S): MAY 1 (TAP)
FIELD(S): All fields of study

Grants for students at all levels, including some for part-time study.

Contact above location for details of these and other New York state programs.

3213—NEW YORK STATE SENATE (Undergraduate Session Assistants Program)

NYS Student Programs Office
90 South Swan, Room 401
Albany NY 12247
518/455-2611
FAX: 518-432-5470
E-mail: students@senate.state.ny.us

AMOUNT: $2,800 stipend
DEADLINE(S): OCT (last Friday)
FIELD(S): All fields of study

Open to talented undergraduates (except freshmen) who want first-hand experience at the New York state legislature. Need a good academic record. All majors may apply. Must be enrolled in a college or university in New York state. US citizenship. Must demonstrate keen writing skills and have the recommendation and support of on-campus faculty.

Contact Dr. Russell J. Williams at above location for complete information.

3214—NICHOLL SCHOLARSHIPS (Undergraduate and Graduate Scholarships)

P.O. Box HM 1179
Hamilton HM EX Bermuda
441/295-2244

AMOUNT: BD$15,000
DEADLINE(S): JUN 15
FIELD(S): All fields of study

Open to Bermuda residents with at least 5 years of schooling in Bermuda who are at least 18 and not more than 24 years old as of September 1 of year of application. For undergrad or graduate study at accredited universities in British Commonwealth countries or the US.

4 awards per year; renewable up to 4 years. Write for complete information.

3215—NON-COMMISSIONED OFFICERS ASSOCIATION (Scholarships)

P.O. Box 33610
San Antonio TX 78265-3610
512/653-6161

AMOUNT: $900-$1,000
DEADLINE(S): MAR 31
FIELD(S): All fields of study

Undergraduate and vocational training scholarships open to children and spouses of members of the Non-Commissioned Officers Association. Children of members must be under age 25 to receive initial grants.

35 awards per year. Full-time students who maintain at least a 3.0 GPA may reapply each year for scholarship renewal. Write for complete information.

3216—NORRIS BURSARY SCHOLARSHIP FUND

431 Alhambra Circle
Miami FL 33134-4901
305/266-3333

AMOUNT: $1,000
DEADLINE(S): Ongoing
FIELD(S): All fields of study

Scholarships for residents of Florida for undergraduate study at an accredited college or trade school.

Send SASE to Matthew Slepin, Trustee, at above address.

3217—NORTH CAROLINA ASSOCIATION OF EDUCATORS (Martin Luther King, Jr., Scholarship)

P.O. Box 27347
Raleigh NC 27611
Written inquiry

AMOUNT: Varies
DEADLINE(S): FEB 1
FIELD(S): All fields of study

For college-bound North Carolina high school seniors. Children of NCAE members will be considered firStreet Other selection criteria are character, personality, and scholastic achievement.

Number and amount of scholarships are determined by the funds received from fund-raising efforts of the organization. Send SASE to the state NCAE office at above address, Martin Luther King, Jr., Scholarship Committee, for application.

3218—NORTH CAROLINA DEPARTMENT OF PUBLIC INSTRUCTION (Scholarship Loan Program for Prospective Teachers)

301 N. Wilmington Street
Raleigh NC 27601-2825
919/715-1120

AMOUNT: $1,110/year
DEADLINE(S): FEB
FIELD(S): All fields of study

For North Carolina high school seniors with GPAs of at least 3.0 and SATs of 900+. For use at four-year institutions.

160 awards. Renewable up to four years.

3219—NORTH CAROLINA DIVISION OF SERVICES FOR THE BLIND (Rehabilitation Assistance for Visually Impaired)

309 Ashe Ave.
Raleigh NC 27606
919/733-9700

AMOUNT: Tuition + fees; books & supplies
DEADLINE(S): None
FIELD(S): All areas of study

Open to North Carolina residents who are legally blind or have a progressive eye condition that may result in blindness (thereby creating an impediment for the individual) and who are undergrad or grad students at a NC school.

Write for complete information.

3220—NORTH CAROLINA DIVISION OF VETERANS AFFAIRS (Dependents Scholarship Program)

325 N. Salisbury Street, Suite 1065
Raleigh NC 27603
919/733-3851

AMOUNT: $1,500 to $3,000 (private college); tuition & fees + room & board (public college)
DEADLINE(S): MAY 31
FIELD(S): All fields of study

Undergraduate scholarships open to children of veterans who died as a result of wartime service or were disabled; POW; MIA; or received pension from the VA. Veteran entered service as NC resident or applicant NC resident since birth.

Awards tenable at private and public colleges in North Carolina. 350-400 awards per year. Renewable up to 4 years. Write for complete information.

3221—NORTH CAROLINA STATE EDUCATION ASSISTANCE AUTHORITY (Student Financial Aid for North Carolinians)

P.O. Box 2688
Chapel Hill NC 27515
919/549-8614

AMOUNT: Varies
DEADLINE(S): Varies
FIELD(S): All fields of study

The state of NC, private NC organizations, and the federal government fund numerous scholarships, grants, work-study, and loan programs for North Carolina residents at all levels of study.

The NC State Education Assistance Authority annually publishes a financial aid booklet describing in detail various programs for North Carolina residents. A copy is available free to undergrads who plan to attend a school in NC.

3222—NORTH CAROLINA STATE UNIVERSITY (John Gatling Scholarship Program)

2119 Pullen Hall, Box 7342
Raleigh NC 27695
919/515-3671
FAX: 919/515-6021
E-mail: pat_lee@ncsu.edu

AMOUNT: $8,000 per year
DEADLINE(S): FEB 1
FIELD(S): All fields of study

If you were born with surname of "Gatlin" or "Gatling," this program will provide $8,000 toward the cost of attending NC State Univ. as an undergraduate provided you meet NC State Univ. entrance and transfer requirements. US citizenship.

Award is renewable each year if you study full time (24 or more credits per year) and maintain at least 2.0 GPA. Contact the NCSU merit awards program coordinator at address above for complete information.

3223—NORTH CAROLINA DEPT. OF PUBLIC INSTRUCTION (Challenge Scholars Program)

301 N. Wilmington Street
Raleigh NC 27601-2825
919/715-1120

AMOUNT: Counseling and technical skills enrichment
DEADLINE(S): FEB
FIELD(S): Teaching

An incentive program for NC students in low-wealth and low-performing/warning status school systems to choose teaching as a career objective. To be chosen from 9th, 10th, and 11th grades, they will be afforded every means of support possible by the local education agency in which they are enrolled, such as information and skills necessary to gain admission to an institution of higher education to later become employed in public schools in NC.

Applications are available in December for local educational agency superintendents.

3224—NORTH CROSS SCHOOL (Scholarships)

4254 Colonial Ave.
Roanoke VA 24018
540-989-6641
FAX: 540/989-7299
Internet: www.NorthCross.org

AMOUNT: $1,500-$3,000
DEADLINE(S): JUN 1 (merit)
FIELD(S): All fields of study

Grants for students attending this independent, nonprofit, nonsectarian K-12 college preparatory school in Roanoke, Virginia. Two programs: merit scholarships (2) are based on academics and testing; need-based scholarships (50) are for students demonstrating financial need.

No deadline for scholarships based on need. Contact school for details.

3225—NORTH DAKOTA INDIAN SCHOLARSHIP PROGRAM (Scholarships)

State Capitol Building
600 East Blvd., 10th Fl.
Bismarck ND 58505
701/328-2960

AMOUNT: $700-$2,000
DEADLINE(S): JUL 15
FIELD(S): All fields of study

Open to North Dakota residents who have at least 1/4 Indian blood or are enrolled members of a North Dakota tribe. Awards are tenable at recognized undergraduate colleges and universities in North Dakota. US citizenship required.

100-150 scholarships per year. Renewable. Write for complete information.

3226—NORTH DAKOTA STUDENT FINANCIAL ASSISTANCE AGENCY (Grants)

State Capitol
600 East Blvd., 10th Fl.
Bismarck ND 58505
701/328-4114

AMOUNT: Up to $600

DEADLINE(S): APR 15

FIELD(S): All fields of study

Open to residents of North Dakota for undergraduate study at colleges and universities in North Dakota. Must be citizen or legal US resident.

2,400 awards per year. Renewable. Write for complete information.

3227—NORTHEASTERN LOGGERS ASSOCIATION, INC. (Scholarship Contest)

P.O. Box 69
Old Forge NY 13420-0069
315/369-3078
FAX: 315/369-3736
E-mail: nela@telenet.net

AMOUNT: $500

DEADLINE(S): APR 1

FIELD(S): All fields of study

Scholarship awards for families of individual members or employees of Industrial and Associate Members of the Northeastern Loggers' Association. Open to high school seniors, students in two-year associate degree of technical school programs, or juniors or seniors in four-year B.A. programs. Must prepare a 1,000-word essay on "What it means to grow up in the forest industry." Essay must be typed and will be about four pages double-spaced.

Send for official application form and return with essay and grade transcript/report card data before April 1.

3228—NORTHWEST DANISH FOUNDATION (Scholarships)

Scandinavian Dept.
Univ. of Washington
318 Raitt Hall, Box 353420
Seattle WA 98195-3420
206/543-0645 or 206/543-6084

AMOUNT: $250

DEADLINE(S): MAR 15

FIELD(S): All fields of study

Scholarship for students of Danish descent or married to someone of Danish descent. Must be residents of Washington or Oregon. May be used for study in the US or in Denmark.

Contact Professor Marianne Stecher-Hanson at above address or phone numbers or the Foundation at 206/523-3263.

3229—NUCLEAR AGE PEACE FOUNDATION (Lena Chang Scholarship Awards)

1187 Coast Village Road, Suite 123
Santa Barbara CA 93108-2794

805/965-3443
FAX: 805/568-0466
E-mail: wagingpeace@napf.org
Internet: www.wagingpeace.org

AMOUNT: $2,500

DEADLINE(S): JUL 1

FIELD(S): All fields of study

For ethnic minority students enrolled in an accredited college or university in undergraduate or graduate studies who can demonstrate financial need and academic excellence.

Write a typed, double-spaced essay (not to exceed three pages) on ways to achieve peace in the Nuclear Age and how you hope to contribute to that end. Also send separately two letters of recommendation (at least one from a college instructor and not from relatives) and a college transcript copy. Send SASE for official application form.

3230—OAKWOOD FRIENDS SCHOOL (Scholarships)

515 South Road
Poughkeepsie NY 12601
914/462-4200
FAX: 914/462-4251
E-mail: admissions@o-f-s.org
Internet: www.o-f-s.org

AMOUNT: $8,000 or up to 70% tuition

DEADLINE(S): MAR

FIELD(S): All fields of study

Two scholarship programs for new Oakwood upper school students (grades 9-12), and one for current Oakwood upper school students. Must be US citizen. Awards each have one or more of the following criteria: community service, recommendations, personal interview, academic achievement, scholarly potential, good academic/social standing, written exam, scores from standardized testing, and essays. Financial need NOT a factor.

1 award per program annually. Renewable. Contact Cynthia L. Pope, Director of Admissions, for more information.

3231—OHEF SHOLOM TEMPLE (Sarah Cohen Scholarship Fund)

530 Raleigh Ave.
Norfolk VA 23507
757/625-4295
FAX: 757/625-3762

AMOUNT: Varies

DEADLINE(S): Varies

FIELD(S): All areas of study

Open to residents of Norfolk, VA who have high academic standing and a marked potential for service to the community.

Apply before the end of the spring semester. For undergraduate study at a recognized college or university that grants a degree. Must show financial need. Write for complete information.

3232—OHIO AMERICAN LEGION (Scholarship)

4060 Indianola Ave.
Columbus OH 43214
614/268-7072
FAX: 614/268-3048
E-mail: ohlegion@netwalk.com

AMOUNT: $1,500

DEADLINE(S): APR 15

FIELD(S): All areas of study

Open to students with at least a 3.5 GPA or composite score of 25 on the ACT if a high school senior. Applicants must be direct descendants of Legionnaires, direct descendants of deceased Legionnaires, and/or surviving spouses or children of deceased or disabled US military persons.

Must reapply for renewable. Write to the above address for complete information.

3233—OHIO BOARD OF REGENTS (Ohio Academic Scholarship Program)

State Grants & Scholarships Dept.
P.O. Box 182452
Columbus OH 43218-2452
888/833-1133 or 614/752-9536
FAX: 614/752-5903

AMOUNT: $2,000/yr. for up to 4 years

DEADLINE(S): FEB 23

FIELD(S): All fields of study

Open to seniors at chartered Ohio high schools who are Ohio residents and intend to be enrolled as full-time undergraduate students in eligible Ohio institutions of higher education.

1,000 awards per year. Scholarships are automatically renewable for up to four years of undergraduate study provided satisfactory progress is made. Apply through high school guidance office.

3234—OHIO BOARD OF REGENTS (Ohio Instructional Grant Program)

State Grants & Scholarship Dept.
P.O. Box 182452
Columbus OH 43218-2452
888/833-1133 or 614/466-7420

FAX: 614-752-5903
AMOUNT: $288-$4,296
DEADLINE(S): OCT 1
FIELD(S): All fields of study

For Ohio residents enrolled full-time in an eligible Ohio or Pennsylvania institution of higher education. Must be in a good academic standing and demonstrate financial need. Based on family income and number of dependents in the family.

90,000 renewable grants per year. Benefits are restricted to the student's instructional and general fee charges. Apply by completing the FAFSA form.

3235—OHIO BOARD OF REGENTS (Ohio Student Choice Grant)

State Grants & Scholarships Dept.
P.O. Box 182452
Columbus OH 43218-2452
888/833-1133 or 614/644-7420
FAX: 614/752-5903

AMOUNT: Varies
DEADLINE(S): Ongoing
FIELD(S): All fields of study

For Ohio residents enrolled as full-time undergraduate students at an eligible private nonprofit Ohio college or university. Assists in narrowing the tuition gap between the state's public and private non-profit colleges and universities.

23,000 awards per year renewable for a maximum of 5 years. Write for complete information.

3236—OHIO BOARD OF REGENTS (Regents Graduate/Professional Fellowship Program)

State Grants & Scholarships Dept.
P.O. Box 182452
Columbus OH 43218-2452
888/833-1133 or 614/644-7420
FAX: 614/752-5903

AMOUNT: $3,500/yr. for up to 2 years
DEADLINE(S): None specified
FIELD(S): All fields of study

For holders of B.A. degrees who enroll for graduate school or professional study at participating Ohio colleges and universities.

Contact a college financial aid administrator, the university's graduate school, or the above location for details.

3237—OHIO BOARD OF REGENTS (Robert C. Byrd Honors Scholarship Program)

State Grants & Scholarships Dept.
P.O. Box 182452
Columbus OH 43218-2452

888/833-1133 or 614/644-7420
FAX: 614/752-5903

AMOUNT: Varies
DEADLINE(S): MAR (second Friday)
FIELD(S): All fields of study

Open to seniors who demonstrate outstanding academic achievement in high school. Based on class rank, grades, test scores, and participation in leadership activities. At least one scholarship is awarded in each congressional district.

Renewable for up to four years of undergraduate study provided satisfactory progress is made. Apply through high school Guidance Office.

3238—OHIO BOARD OF REGENTS (War Orphans Scholarship Program)

State Grants & Scholarships Dept.
P.O. Box 182452
Columbus OH 43218-2452
888/833-1133 or 614/466-7420
FAX: 614/752-5903

AMOUNT: Full tuition at public schools;
equivalent amount at private schools
DEADLINE(S): JUL 1
FIELD(S): All areas of study

For Ohio residents who are dependents of veterans who served during war and as a result is now severely disabled or deceased. Must be enrolled for full-time undergraduate study at an Ohio institution.

Varies per year. Contact above address, high school guidance offices, veterans service offices, and college financial aid offices for complete information.

3239—OHIO UNIVERSITY (Charles Kilburger Scholarship)

Asst. Dir. of Student Services
1570 Granville Pike
Lancaster OH 43130
614/654-6711

AMOUNT: Tuition
DEADLINE(S): FEB 1
FIELD(S): All fields of study

Scholarship open to seniors graduating from a Fairfield County (Ohio) high school who will enroll at Ohio University-Lancaster for at least two years. For undergraduate study only. US citizenship required.

Applications available ONLY from Fairfield County, OH high school counselors. Must demonstrate financial need.

3240—OLDFIELDS SCHOOL (Grants and Loans)

P.O. Box 697
Glencoe MD 21152-0697

410/472-4800
FAX: 410/472-6839
E-mail: admissions@
Oldfields.pvtk12.md.us
Internet: www.school.com/Oldfields

AMOUNT: Varies
DEADLINE(S): FEB 10
FIELD(S): All fields of study, grades 8-12

Grants and loans for needy students enrolled in the private 8-12 school in Maryland listed above.

Contact school for details.

3241—ONEIDA HIGHER EDUCATION (Various Fellowships, Internships, and Scholarships)

P.O. Box 365
Oneida WI 54155
920/869-4333
800/236-2214, ext. 4333
FAX: 910/869-4039

AMOUNT: Varies with program
DEADLINE(S): APR 15 (fall term);
OCT 1 (spring term); MAY 1 (summer term)
FIELD(S): All fields of study

For enrolled members of the Oneida Tribe of Indians of Wisconsin. Several programs are offered for all levels of study in various fields, including internships, emergency funding, and special scholarships for economics and business majors and those in the hotel/restaurant management field.

Some programs list deadline dates different from those above. Send for descriptive brochure.

3242—OPERATING ENGINEERS LOCAL UNION NO. 3 (IUOE Scholarship Program)

1620 South Loop Road
Alameda CA 94502
510/748-7400

AMOUNT: Up to $3,000
DEADLINE(S): MAR 1
FIELD(S): All areas of study

Open to dependent children of members of IUOE Local No. 3 who are high school seniors with at least a 3.0 GPA. Awards tenable at recognized undergraduate colleges and universities. US citizenship required.

Write for complete information.

3243—ORDER OF THE EASTERN STAR (Grand Chapter of California Scholarships)

870 Market Street, Suite 722
San Francisco CA 94102-2996

Written inquiry
Internet: www.oescal.org

AMOUNT: $250-$500 (2-year college);
$500-$1,000 (4-year college)

DEADLINE(S): MAR 15

FIELD(S): All fields of study, including
vocational/technical/special religious

Open to all California residents who are accepted to or enrolled in California colleges, universities, or trade schools and have at least a 3.5 GPA (4.0 scale). Must demonstrate financial need and be US citizen.

Access website for application or send SASE to Mrs. Shirley Orth, Grand Secretary, address above, for complete information.

3244—OREGON CREDIT UNION LEAGUE EDUCATIONAL FOUNDATION (Lois M. Hartley Benefit Scholarship)

P.O. Box 1900
Beaverton OR 97075
800/688-6098, ext. 240
E-mail: jimh@nwcunet.org

AMOUNT: $4,000

DEADLINE(S): MAR 31

FIELD(S): All fields of study

Open to any member of an Oregon credit union who is currently enrolled in an undergraduate program at an accredited institution and has some form of hearing impairment.

1 award annually. Award announced in May. Contact your credit union or Jim Hier at above address for an application.

3245—OREGON DEPARTMENT OF VETERANS' AFFAIRS (Educational Aid for Oregon Veterans)

700 Summer Street NE, Suite 150
Salem OR 97310-1270
800/692-9666 or 503/373-2085

AMOUNT: $35 to $50 per month

DEADLINE(S): None

FIELD(S): All fields of study

For veterans on active duty during the Korean War, June 25, 1950 to Jan. 31, 1955, or who received a campaign or expeditionary medal or ribbon awarded by the Armed Forces of the United States for services after June 30, 1958. Must be resident of Oregon and US citizen with a qualifying military service record at time of application. For study in an accredited Oregon school.

Write for complete information.

3246—OREGON STATE SCHOLARSHIP COMMISSION (Federal Family Education Loan Program)

1500 Valley River Drive, #100
Eugene OR 97401
800/452-8807, 503/687-7400
Internet: www.teleport.com~ossc

AMOUNT: $2,625-$6,635 undergrad;
$8,500-$18,500 graduate (annual maximum)

DEADLINE(S): None specified

FIELD(S): All fields of study

Open to US citizens or permanent residents who are attending an eligible Oregon institution and to Oregon residents attending any eligible institution outside of Oregon at least half-time.

Write or visit website for complete information.

3247—OREGON STATE SCHOLARSHIP COMMISSION (Oregon Need Grants)

1500 Valley River Drive, #100
Eugene OR 97401
503/687-7400

AMOUNT: $906-$1,584

DEADLINE(S): APR 1

FIELD(S): All areas of study

Open to Oregon residents enrolled full-time in any 2- or 4-year nonprofit college or university in Oregon. Must be US citizen or legal resident and demonstrate financial need.

It is not necessary to take SAT/ACT for need grants. 22,000 awards and grants per year. Renewable. Write for complete information.

3248—OREGON STATE SCHOLARSHIP COMMISSION (Private Scholarship Programs Administered by the Commission)

1500 Valley River Drive, #100
Eugene OR 97401
503/687-7395

AMOUNT: $250-$3,000

DEADLINE(S): MAR 1

FIELD(S): All fields of study

100 different private scholarship programs are administered by the Commission and are for Oregon residents only. Some are tied to a specific field and/or level of study but in general they are available to all levels and fields of study.

Dependent students must have parents residing in Oregon. Independent students must live in Oregon for 12 months prior to

Sept. 1 of the academic year for which the application is made. For complete information send a 55-cent, stamped, self-addressed #10 business-sized envelope to the above address.

3249—ORGANIZATION OF AMERICAN STATES (Leo S. Rowe Pan American Fund)

1889 F Street NW, Second Fl.
Washington DC 20006
202/458-6208

AMOUNT: Up to US $5,000/yr.

DEADLINE(S): None

FIELD(S): All fields of study

No-interest loans for undergrad and grad students from member countries of the Organization of American States who are studying or wish to study in the US.

Must be within two years of completing degree or research. Loan repayable within five years of completion of studies. Write for complete details.

3250—ORGANIZATION OF CHINESE AMERICANS (Avon College Scholarship)

1001 Connecticut Ave. NW
Suite 707
Washington DC 20036
202/223-5500
VOICE MAIL: 202/223-5523
FAX: 202/296-0540
E-mail: oca@ari.net
Internet: www2.ARI.NET/OCA

AMOUNT: $1,000

DEADLINE(S): MAY 1

FIELD(S): All fields of study

For Asian Pacific American women who will be entering their first year of college. Must be US citizen or permanent resident.

10-15 one-year awards. Check website for application data and/or send SASE to above address. Awardee must write a paper at the end of her first year in college describing her college experience as an Asian Pacific American woman.

3251—ORGANIZATION OF CHINESE AMERICANS (National Essay Contest)

1001 Connecticut Ave. NW
Suite 707
Washington DC 20036
202/223-5500
FAX: 202/296-0540
E-mail: oca@ari.net
Internet: www2.ARI.NET/OCA

AMOUNT: $400, $200, and $100

DEADLINE(S): MAY 1
FIELD(S): All fields of study

An essay contest for Asian American high school students (grades 9-12). Topic: "What can you do in your community to prevent or decrease anti-Asian violence?" 800 to 1,000 words in English, typed on 8-1/2" by 11" white bond paper, double-spaced with full references and bibliography where applicable. Must be US citizen or permanent resident.

3 winners. Send SASE for complete details to above address.

3252—ORPHAN FOUNDATION OF AMERICA (Scholarship Program)

380 Maple Ave West, Suite LL5
Vienna VA 22180
Written inquiries only
AMOUNT: $800-$2,500
DEADLINE(S): MAY 1
FIELD(S): All areas of study

Program open to orphans or youth in foster care at the age of 18 who have not been adopted. Awards tenable at any recognized undergraduate or vocational school in the US. Must be US citizens or legal resident.

50+ scholarships per year. Renewable with reapplication. Send self-addressed, stamped envelope for application and information.

3253—OTTO A. HUTH SCHOLARSHIP FUND

P.O. Box 30100
Reno NV 89520
702/334-5846
AMOUNT: Varies
DEADLINE(S): Varies (prior to college semester)
FIELD(S): All areas of study

Scholarships to financially needy high school seniors who are orphans and who are residents of Nevada.

Write to Barbara Van de Mark at above address for application.

3254—OUTDOOR WRITERS ASSOCIATION OF AMERICA (Youth Contest Writing Award)

22155 E. College Ave.
State College PA 16801
814/234-1011
AMOUNT: $1,000
DEADLINE(S): JAN 31
FIELD(S): All fields of study

Writing contest for high school students to sharpen their abilities to communicate the outdoor experience. All articles must be published before entering conteStreet

Contact Eileen King, Executive Assistant, at the above address for complete information.

3255—P.L.A.T.O. JUNIOR EDUCATION LOAN

205 Van Buren Street, Suite 200
Herndon VA 20170
888/PLATO-JR or 703/709-8100
FAX: 703/904-1541
E-mail: kittor@servus.com
Internet: www.platojr.com
AMOUNT: $1,500-$15,000 per year
DEADLINE(S): None
FIELD(S): All fields of study

Education loans for parents of students in kindergarten-12th grade private schools. Must be US citizen or permanent resident, earn minimum of $15,000 annually, and have a good credit history. Co-applicants allowed.

Renewable. Unlimited funding available. Financial need is NOT a factor.

3256—PADGETT BUSINESS SERVICES (Scholarship Program)

160 Hawthorne Park
Athens GA 30606
800/723-4388
AMOUNT: $500
DEADLINE(S): MAR 1
FIELD(S): All fields of study

This scholarship is open to dependents of small business owners who employ less than 20 individuals, own at least 10% of the stock or capital in the business, and are active in the day-to-day operations of the organization. Applicants must be graduating high school seniors planning on attending an accredited postsecondary institution.

For more information or an application, please contact your local Padgett office or call the phone number listed above.

3257—PARENTS AND FRIENDS OF LESBIANS AND GAYS—PFLAG CINCINNATI (Scholarships)

P.O. Box 19634
Cincinnati OH 45219
513/721-7900
AMOUNT: $500
DEADLINE(S): APR 15
FIELD(S): All fields of study

Scholarships for students who are gay, lesbian, bisexual, and transgender. Can be high school senior, undergraduate, or graduate student. Applications from students in the Cincinnati area will have preference.

Contact organization for details.

3258—PARENTS WITHOUT PARTNERS (International Scholarship)

401 N. Michigan Ave.
Chicago IL 60611-4267
312/644-6610
AMOUNT: Varies
DEADLINE(S): MAR 15
FIELD(S): All fields of study

Open to dependent children (up to 25 years of age) of Parents Without Partners members. Can be a graduating high school senior or college student. For undergraduate study at trade or vocational school, college, or university.

Write for complete information (send postage-paid envelope).

3259—PARENTS, FAMILIES, AND FRIENDS OF LESBIANS AND GAYS—NEW ORLEANS CHAPTER (Scholarships)

P.O. Box 15515
New Orleans LA 70175
504/895-3936
E-mail: lhpeebles@aol.com
Internet: www.gayneworleans.org/pflag/
AMOUNT: Varies
DEADLINE(S): FEB 17
FIELD(S): All fields of study

Scholarships for self-identified gay and lesbian students pursuing college degrees. For residents of Louisiana.

Application materials are at website (which also features great music!). Contact organization for details.

3260—PARENTS, FAMILIES, AND FRIENDS OF LESBIANS AND GAYS—SAN JOSE/PENINSULA CHAPTER (Scholarships)

690-57 Persian Drive
Sunnyvale CA 94089
408/745-1736 or 408/269-8418
FAX: 408/745-6063
E-mail: BobPhoto@webtv.net
Internet: www.pflag.org
(follow links to San Jose/Peninsula Chapter)
AMOUNT: $1,000
DEADLINE(S): APR 10
FIELD(S): All fields of study

Scholarships for college-bound gay and lesbian high school seniors in public, private, or parochial high schools. For residents of San Mateo or Santa Clara counties in California. Also for students who have demonstrated support for justice and equality for gay, lesbian, and bisexual persons in their community.

For use at two- or four-year college, university, or business/technical school, full- or part-time. Contact organization for details.

3261—PARENTS, FAMILIES, AND FRIENDS OF LESBIANS AND GAYS—ATLANTA (Scholarships)

P.O. Box 8482
Atlanta GA 31106
770/662-6475
FAX: 404/864-3639
E-mail: mcjcatl@mindspring.com

AMOUNT: Varies
DEADLINE(S): APR 1
FIELD(S): All fields of study

Scholarships for college-bound gay, lesbian, or bisexual high school seniors, undergraduates, graduates, or postgraduates who are either Georgia residents or attend or will attend a college or university in Georgia. Part-time students considered for reduced awards.

Renewable. Contact organization for details.

3262—PARENTS, FAMILIES, AND FRIENDS OF LESBIANS AND GAYS (PFLAG)—NORTH BAY CHAPTER (Scholarships)

P.O. Box 2626
Petaluma CA 94953-2626
707/762-0107
Internet: www.pflag-nb.org/scholarship/app-schol.html

AMOUNT: Varies
DEADLINE(S): APR 12
FIELD(S): All fields of study

Scholarships for college-bound high school seniors in some way involved in the struggle against prejudice and discrimination against lesbian, gay, bisexual, and transgendered people. Must be graduating from a high school in Marin, Napa, or Sonoma counties in California between Jan. and June. Amounts vary according to donations to organization.

A typewritten essay, not to exceed 500 words, is required. Topic: Describe the way(s) in which you have been involved in the struggle against prejudice and homophobia. Why is discrimination against les-

bian, gay, bisuxual, and transgendered people a concern of all citizens? For more instructions and application form, access website. Use of official form is required.

3263—PARKE-DAVIS (Epilepsy Scholarship Award)

c/o IntraMed
1633 Broadway, 25th Fl.
New York NY 10019
800/292-7373

AMOUNT: $3,000
DEADLINE(S): MAR 1
FIELD(S): All fields of study

For high school seniors and undergraduates on medication for and undergoing treatment for epilepsy. Must be US citizen. Transcripts, short essay, and two letters of recommendation required with application.

16 awards annually. Contact Jeffrey Tarnoff, Program Director, for more information (212/969-2544). Applications available in November; decisions made by June 1Street

3264—PARTNERS ADVANCING VALUES IN EDUCATION (PAVE) (Scholarships for K-12 Private/Parochial School Students in Milwaukee, WI)

1434 W. State Street
Milwaukee WI 53233
414/342-1505
FAX: 414/342-1513
Internet: www.pave.org

AMOUNT: Half of tuition
DEADLINE(S): None
FIELD(S): All fields of study in K-12 schools

Scholarships for students from kindergarten through high school for use at any of 112 private or parochial schools in Milwaukee, WI. Pays half the tuition for needy families who meet the criteria established for the federal school lunch program. Must be residents of Milwaukee, WI.

School may require service work by families to assist with tuition program. Apply through your school of choice.

3265—PAUL AND MARY HAAS FOUNDATION (Scholarship Grants)

P.O. Box 2928
Corpus Christi TX 78403
512/887-6955

AMOUNT: $1,000 per semester
DEADLINE(S): Varies (initially fall of high school senior year)

FIELD(S): All fields of study

Program open to high school seniors who are Corpus Christi, Texas, residents. Awards support full-time pursuit of first undergraduate degree.

Approximately 50 awards per year. Must prove financial need. Write for complete information.

3266—PAUL O. AND MARY BOGHOSS-IAN FOUNDATION

One Hospital Trust Plaza
Providence RI 02903
401/278-8752

AMOUNT: $500-$2,500
DEADLINE(S): MAY 1
FIELD(S): All fields of study

Scholarships for residents of Rhode Island.

Write c/o The Rhode Island Hospital Trust National Bank at above address for details and application.

3267—PENINSULA COMMUNITY FOUNDATION (African-American Scholarship Fund)

1700 S. El Camino Real, #300
San Mateo CA 94402
650/358-9369
FAX: 650/358-9817

AMOUNT: $5,000
DEADLINE(S): MAR 27 (5 P.M.)
FIELD(S): All fields of study

Scholarship for African-American graduating high school seniors of a high school in San Mateo County or Northern Santa Clara County (Daly City to Mountain View), California. Must have GPA of at least 2.5. Award contingent upon acceptance at a California community college, state university, or branch of the University of California.

Program was designed to assist a motivated African-American student who otherwise would be unable to attend college.

3268—PENINSULA COMMUNITY FOUNDATION (Crain Educational Grants Program)

1700 S. El Camino Real, #300
San Mateo CA 94402
650/358-9369
FAX: 650/358-9817

AMOUNT: Up to $5,000
DEADLINE(S): MAR 27 (5 P.M.)
FIELD(S): All fields of study

Scholarships for students who have graduated from or are current high school seniors of a public or private high school in San Mateo County or Santa Clara County, California. Must be US citizen, have financial need, have demonstrated community involvement over a period of years, and maintain a GPA of at least 3.0. For full-time enrollment in an accredited two- or four-year college, university, or vocational school in the US.

Program was established to enable worthy high school graduates to pursue courses of study that they would otherwise by unable to follow due to limited financial means.

3269—PENINSULA COMMUNITY FOUNDATION (Curry Award for Girls and Young Women)

1700 S. El Camino Real, #300
San Mateo CA 94402
650/358-9369
FAX: 650/358-9817

AMOUNT: $500
DEADLINE(S): MAR 27 (5 P.M.)
FIELD(S): All fields of study

Awards for young women, age 16 to 26, who have attended a high school in San Mateo County, California. Must need financial support to re-enter a post-secondary school, community college, university, or vocational school. Award is to help women who have dropped out of school for reasons beyond their control or have undergone unusual hardships to remain in school.

Awards are for one year, but recipients may reapply.

3270—PENINSULA COMMUNITY FOUNDATION (Ruppert Educational Grant Program)

1700 S. El Camino Real, #300
San Mateo CA 94402
650/358-9369
FAX: 650/358-9817

AMOUNT: Up to $1,000
DEADLINE(S): MAR 27 (5 P.M.)
FIELD(S): All fields of study

Grants for current graduating seniors of a high school in San Mateo County, California. Must be US citizen, have financial need. Grants are awarded for an accredited two- or four-year college, university, or trade school.

Program is designed for students who show academic promise but who are not likely to receive other scholarships because of lower GPAs. Awards are for one time only. "Late bloomers" are encouraged to apply.

3271—PENINSULA COMMUNITY FOUNDATION (Scholarship Fund for Gay/Lesbian Asian Students)

1700 S. El Camino Real, #300
San Mateo CA 94402
650/358-9369
FAX: 650/358-9817

AMOUNT: $2,000-$12,000
DEADLINE(S): MAR 27 (5 P.M.)
FIELD(S): All fields of study

Scholarships for gay/lesbian high school seniors graduating from San Mateo County, California, public or private high schools. Applicants must be US citizens of Asian descent. Financial need and academic promise are considered. For use at accredited colleges and universities or voc-tech schools.

The Fund's donor understands the abandonment, alienation, and loneliness a gay or lesbian person may experience in today's social, economic, and political environment.

3272—PENNSYLVANIA DEPARTMENT OF MILITARY AFFAIRS—BUREAU OF VETERANS AFFAIRS (Scholarships)

Fort Indiantown Gap
Annville PA 17003-5002
717/861-8904 or 717/861-8910
FAX: 717/861-8589

AMOUNT: Up to $500/term ($4,000 for 4 years)
DEADLINE(S): None
FIELD(S): All areas of study

Open to children of military veterans who died or were totally disabled as a result of war, armed conflict, or terrorist attack. Must have lived in Pennsylvania for 5 years prior to application, be age 16-23, and demonstrate financial need.

70 awards per year. Renewable. For study at Pennsylvania schools. Must be US citizen. Write for complete information.

3273—PENNSYLVANIA HIGHER EDUCATION ASSISTANCE AGENCY (Robert C. Byrd Honors Scholarship Program)

P.O. Box 8114
Harrisburg PA 17105-8114
717/720-2850

AMOUNT: Determined yearly by the federal government
DEADLINE(S): MAY 1
FIELD(S): All fields of study

Open to PA high school seniors in the top 5 percent of their graduating class with a 3.5 or better GPA and an SAT score of 1200 or higher. Must be US citizen and have been accepted for enrollment in an institution of higher education.

Renewable to a maximum of four years. Write for complete information.

3274—PERRY & STELLA TRACY SCHOLARSHIP FUND (Scholarships)

Wells Fargo Private Banking Group
P.O. Box 2511
Sacramento CA 95812
916/440-4449

AMOUNT: Varies $350-$750
DEADLINE(S): None given
FIELD(S): All areas of study

Open to applicants who are graduates of El Dorado County high schools and have resided in El Dorado County, CA for at least 2 years. Awards are tenable at recognized undergraduate colleges and universities.

Approximately 125 awards per year. Renewable. Contact high school counselor for complete information. DO NOT contact Wells Fargo.

3275—PETER BLOSSER STUDENT LOAN FUND

P.O. Box 6160
Chillicothe OH 45601-6160
614/773-0043

AMOUNT: $2,000 max/yr.
DEADLINE(S): None
FIELD(S): All areas of study

A student loan for students who have been residents of Ross County, Ohio, for at least three years, have a minimum GPA of 2.0, graduated from a Ross County high school, or received a GED in the state of Ohio. To be used at an institution in Ross County.

Renewable up to $8,000. 15-40 annual loans. Contact Marie Rosebrook at above address for details.

3276—PFLAG/H.A.T.C.H. (Scholarship Fund)

P.O. Box 53796
Houston TX 77052-3796
713/867-9020
FAX: 281/440-1902
E-mail: PatRickey@aol.com

AMOUNT: $500-$2,500
DEADLINE(S): FEB 26
FIELD(S): All fields of study

For undergraduate/voc-tech students from the Greater Houston Metropolitan Area. Students must be gay or lesbian and be between the ages of 17-26. Financial need is NOT a factor.

10-15 awards annually. Renewable for four years with at least a "C" average. Contact Pat Rickey at above address for an application.

3277—PHI KAPPA THETA NATIONAL FOUNDATION (Scholarship Program)

c/o Scott Bova
3901 W. 86th Street, Suite 425
Indianapolis IN 46265
317/872-9934

AMOUNT: $1,500 maximum
DEADLINE(S): APR 30
FIELD(S): All fields of study

Undergraduate scholarships for members of Phi Kappa Theta, a men's social fraternity. Applications are sent to all chapters; extras are available at national office. Not available to high school or graduate students.

Renewable. 5 scholarships annually. Financial need is a consideration but is relative to the other applicants. Write for complete information.

3278—PHI THETA KAPPA INTERNATIONAL HONOR SOCIETY (Guistwhite Scholar Program)

P.O. Box 13729
Jackson MS 39236
800/946-9995, ext. 966
E-mail: williawm@PhiThetaKappa.jackson.ms.us
Internet: www.phithetakappa.jackson.ms.us/pub/gw/gwapp97.txt

AMOUNT: Varies
DEADLINE(S): MAY 31
FIELD(S): All fields of study

For active members of Phi Theta Kappa who are pursuing an associates degree and who plan on continuing their education at an accredited senior institution. Minimum GPA of 3.5 is required, and student must be at junior level at time of transfer. Letters of recommendation, typed application, official transcript, college registrar's certification form, and student essay required.

Alternate address: 460 Briarwood Drive, Suite 415, Jackson, MS 39206. 10 Guistwhite Scholars receive commemorative medal cash stipend ($125/academic term). 10 Finalists receive certificate and cash award.

3279—PHILIPS NORTH AMERICA CORPORATION (Scholarship Program)

100 East 42nd Street
New York NY 10017
212/850-5000

AMOUNT: $2,500; $500-$1,500
DEADLINE(S): JAN (Apply in JAN. Deadline is MAR 1.)
FIELD(S): All areas of study

Open to dependent children of Philips North America employees. Applicants must be high school seniors who expect to graduate during the current year. Considerations include academic record, SAT or ACT scores, and biographical questionnaire.

52 awards per year. Financial need is considered except for two $3,500 awards that are merit-based only. Participation in extracurricular activities and sports are considered. Write for complete information.

3280—PHILLIPS EXETER ACADEMY (Financial Aid: Grants and Loans)

20 Main Street
Exeter NH 03833
603/777-3637
FAX: 603/777-4399
E-mail: pmahoney@exeter.edu
Internet: www.exeter.edu

AMOUNT: $1,000-$22,000
DEADLINE(S): JAN 31
FIELD(S): All fields of secondary school study

Financial aid to attend this private boarding high school, which also includes in-town students. Encompasses grades 9-12 and one "postgraduate" year, equivalent to grade 13. Academic excellence is a prerequisite. International student body.

150 annual awards. Must demonstrate financial need. Admission is competitive.

3281—PICKETT & HATCHER EDUCATIONAL FUND INC. (Loans)

P.O. Box 8169
Columbus GA 31908-8169
706/327-6586

AMOUNT: $16,000 max
DEADLINE(S): Varies
FIELD(S): All fields of study EXCEPT Law, Medicine, and Ministry

Open to US citizens who are legal residents of and attend colleges located in the southeastern portion of the US. Must enroll in four-year program of study in

four-year college. Loans are not made for graduate or voc-tech studies.

Write for applications and complete information in January preceding academic year in which loan is needed. May not have other educational loans.

3282—PINE BLUFFS AREA CHAMBER OF COMMERCE (Scholarship)

P.O. Box 486
Pine Bluffs WY 82082-0486
Written inquiry

AMOUNT: $300
DEADLINE(S): Varies
FIELD(S): All fields of study

Available to a graduate of Pine Bluffs High School to attend any accredited college, trade, or technical school in the US. Award is based on need, aptitude, academic, and overall performance. Must submit an essay on plans to help community in which student will live.

1 award annually. Not renewable. Write to above address for an application.

3283—PORTSMOUTH HIGH SCHOOL (George C. Cogan Scholarship)

50 Alumni Circle
Portsmouth NH 03801
603/436-7100
FAX: 603/427-2320

AMOUNT: Varies
DEADLINE(S): APR 15
FIELD(S): All fields of study

For male graduates of Portsmouth (New Hampshire) High School or Street Thomas Aquinas High School (in Dover, NH) who were residents in Portsmouth, NH for at least four years prior to graduation. For undergraduate study. Financial need is NOT a factor.

15 awards annually. Renewable for three more years of undergraduate work. Send proof of residency and high school transcripts (including date of graduation) to Sonya Desjardins at above address.

3284—PORTUGUESE CONTINENTAL UNION (Scholarships)

899 Boylston Street
Boston MA 02115
617/536-2916

AMOUNT: Varies
DEADLINE(S): MAR 31
FIELD(S): All areas of study

Open to members of the Portuguese Continental Union of the US with at least one-year membership in good standing and who plan to enroll or are enrolled in any accredited college or university.

Financial need is a consideration. Write for complete information.

3285—POWER STUDENTS NETWORK (Scholarship)

c/o Imagine Media
150 North Hill Drive, Suite 40
Brisbane CA 94005
Internet: www.powerstudents.com

AMOUNT: $1,000
DEADLINE(S): MAR 15
FIELD(S): All fields of study

High school students and undergraduates may apply. Awards may only be used to finance your education at an accredited college, junior college, community college, technical school, or university.

See website to request application or send a self-addressed, stamped envelope to above address. If you sign up online you will receive a free Power Students Network Survival Kit and access to exclusive admissions, financial aid, and college success articles. With your application you must submit your transcript and an essay on a topic of your choice (less than four pages).

3286—PRESBYTERIAN CHURCH (USA.) (Appalachian Scholarship)

100 Witherspoon Street
Louisville KY 40202-1396
502/569-5760
E-mail: MariaA@ctr.pcusa.org
Internet: www.pcusa.org/highered

AMOUNT: $100-$1,500
DEADLINE(S): JUL 1
FIELD(S): All fields of study

For undergraduate residents of the Appalachian areas of Kentucky, North Carolina, Tennessee, Virginia, and West Virginia. Must be US citizens or permanent residents, demonstrate financial need, and be members of the Presbyterian Church (U.S.A.). Nontraditional-age students with no previous college experience are encouraged to apply.

Renewable. Contact Maria Alvarez at above address for more information.

3287—PRESBYTERIAN CHURCH (USA.) (Native American Education Grant)

100 Witherspoon Street
Louisville KY 40202-1396
502/569-5760

E-mail: MariaA@ctr.pcusa.org
Internet: www.pcusa.org/highered

AMOUNT: $200-$2,500
DEADLINE(S): JUN 1
FIELD(S): All fields of study

For Native Americans and Alaska Natives pursuing full-time post-secondary education. Must be members of the Presbyterian Church (U.S.A.), be US citizens or permanent residents, and demonstrate financial need.

Renewable. Contact Maria Alvarez at above address for more information.

3288—PRESBYTERIAN CHURCH (USA.) (National Presbyterian College Scholarship)

100 Witherspoon Street
Louisville KY 40202-1396
502/567-5745
E-mail: KSmith@ctr.pcusa.org
Internet: www.pcusa.org/highered

AMOUNT: $500-$1,400
DEADLINE(S): DEC 1
FIELD(S): All fields of study

Scholarships for full-time incoming freshmen at one of the participating colleges related to the Presbyterian Church (USA.). Applicants must be superior high school seniors and members of the Presbyterian Church. Must be US citizen or permanent resident and demonstrate financial need. Must take the SAT/ACT exam no later than December 15th of senior year.

Renewable. Application and brochure available after September 1Street Contact Kathy Smith at above address for more information.

3289—PRESBYTERIAN CHURCH (USA.) (Samuel Robinson Award)

100 Witherspoon Street
Louisville KY 40202-1396
502/569-5745
E-mail: KSmith@ctr.pcusa.org
Internet: www.pcusa.org/highered

AMOUNT: $1,000
DEADLINE(S): APR 1
FIELD(S): All fields of study

For undergraduate juniors and seniors enrolled full-time in one of the colleges related to the Presbyterian Church. Applicants must successfully recite the answers to the Westminster Shorter Catechism and write a 2,000-word original essay on a related assigned topic.

20-30 awards per year. Not renewable. Contact Kathy Smith at above address for more information.

3290—PRESBYTERIAN CHURCH (USA.) (Service Program)

100 Witherspoon Street
Louisville KY 40202-1396
502/567-5745
E-mail: FrancesC@ctr.pcusa.org
Internet: www.pcusa.org/highered

AMOUNT: $1,500
DEADLINE(S): APR 1
FIELD(S): All fields of study

Provides undergraduate students with an opportunity to pay a portion of their educational expenses through service in various school, church, or community projects. Applicants must be in 2nd or 3rd year of full-time study, be recommended by campus pastor or chaplain of college/university, and complete 250 hours of community service. Money must be repaid if service project is not completed by graduation or discontinuation of studies.

Not renewable. Contact Frances Cook at above address for more information.

3291—PRESBYTERIAN CHURCH (USA.) (Student Opportunity Scholarship)

100 Witherspoon Street
Louisville KY 40202-1396
502/567-5745
E-mail: MariaA@ctr.pcusa.org
Internet: www.pcusa.org/highered

AMOUNT: $100-$1,400
DEADLINE(S): APR 1
FIELD(S): All fields of study

Designed to assist racial ethnic undergraduate students (African American, Alaska Native, Asian American, Hispanic American, Native American) to finance their undergraduate education. Applicants must be US citizens/permanent residents who are high school seniors and members of the Presbyterian Church (USA.). Must demonstrate financial need.

Renewable. Applications available after February 1Street Contact Maria Alvarez at above address for more information.

3292—PRESBYTERIAN CHURCH (USA.) (Undergraduate/Graduate Loan Programs)

100 Witherspoon Street
Louisville KY 40202-1396
502/569-5735
E-mail: FrancesC@ctr.pcusa.org
Internet: www.pcusa.org/highered

AMOUNT: $200-$7,000/year

DEADLINE(S): None
FIELD(S): All fields of study

Loans open to members of the Presbyterian Church (USA.) who are US citizens or permanent residents. For full-time undergraduate or graduate study at an accredited college/university. No interest while in school; repayment begins six months after graduation or discontinuation of studies. Must demonstrate financial need, be in good academic standing, and give evidence of financial reliability.

Renewable. May apply for maximum amount in final year of study if have not previously borrowed. Contact Frances Cook at above address for more information.

3293—PRIDE FOUNDATION & GREATER SEATTLE BUSINESS ASSOCIATION (Scholarships for Gays & Lesbians)

1122 E. Pike Street, Suite 1001
Seattle WA 98122-3934
206/323-3318
800/735-7287 (outside Seattle area)
FAX: 206/323-1017
E-mail: giving@pridefoundation.org
Internet: www.pridefoundation.org

AMOUNT: Up to $3,500
DEADLINE(S): MAR 1
FIELD(S): All fields of study

A variety of scholarships for gay, lesbian, bisexual, and transgender youth and adults who reside in Washington, Oregon, Idaho, Montana, or Alaska. For all levels of postsecondary education—community college, four-year college, or vocational training. Some require financial need.

Check website and/or write to organization for details. Applications available Nov. 1.

3294—PRINCE GEORGE'S CHAMBER OF COMMERCE FOUNDATION (Scholarship)

4601 Presidents Drive, Suite 230
Lanham MD 20706
301/731-5000

AMOUNT: Full tuition at Maryland schools; partial tuition at out-of-state schools
DEADLINE(S): MAY 15
FIELD(S): All fields of study

Open to residents of Prince George's County, MD, for undergraduate study. Must be US citizen. Financial need is a consideration.

Write for complete information.

3295—PROFESSIONAL BOWLERS ASSOCIATION (Billy Welu Memorial Scholarship)

Young American Bowling Alliance
5301 S. 76th Street
Greendale WI 53129
Written inquiry

AMOUNT: $1,000
DEADLINE(S): MAY 15
FIELD(S): All fields of study

The scholarship is designed to assist undergraduate students who are enrolled in college and are current members of a college ABS, WIBC, or YABA league.

The aim of the PBA is to support and promote the sport of bowling. Send self-addressed, stamped #10 envelope to above address.

3296—PROFESSIONAL HORSEMEN'S SCHOLARSHIP FUND, INC.

c/o Mrs. Ann Grenci
204 Old Sleepy Hollow Road
Pleasantville NY 10570
561/694-6893 (Nov.-Apr.)
914/769-1493 (May-Oct. 15)

AMOUNT: Up to $1,000
DEADLINE(S): MAY 1
FIELD(S): All areas of study

For members or dependents of members of the Professional Horsemen's Association. Awards can be used for college or trade school.

Up to 10 awards annually. Write to Mrs. Ann Grenci at above address for complete information.

3297—PUBLIC EMPLOYEES ROUNDTABLE (Public Service Scholarships)

P.O. Box 44801
Washington DC 20026-4801
202/401-4344
Internet: http://www.patriot.net/users/permail

AMOUNT: $500 (part-time); $1,000 (full-time)
DEADLINE(S): MAY 15
FIELD(S): All fields of study

Open to graduate students and undergraduate sophomores, juniors, and seniors who are planning a career in government service at the local, state, or federal level. Minimum of 3.5 cumulative GPA. Preference to applicants with some public service work experience (paid or unpaid).

10 to 15 awards per year. Applications available as of February 1. Send self-addressed, stamped envelope (SASE) for application and details. OR print out application on website and mail it to organization. NOTE: Above address may change, so check website for current address!

3298—REALTY FOUNDATION OF NEW YORK (Scholarship Program)

551 Fifth Ave., Suite 1105
New York NY 10176-0166
212/697-3943

AMOUNT: Varies
DEADLINE(S): Varies
FIELD(S): All fields of study

Open to Realtors and their children or employees of real estate firms and their children. The student or his/her parent are required to be employed in the real estate industry in Metropolitan New York.

Write to the above address for complete information.

3299—RECORDING FOR THE BLIND (Marion Huber Learning Through Listening Awards)

20 Roszel Road
Princeton NJ 08540
609/452-0606
FAX: 609/520-7990

AMOUNT: $2,000 and $6,000
DEADLINE(S): FEB 1
FIELD(S): Any field of study

Awards for college-bound high school seniors with specific learning disabilities registered with RFB&D for at least one year prior to the filing deadline, who have an overall GPA of "B" or above, based on grades 10-12, and plan to continue formal education beyond high school at either a two- or four-year college or a vocational school.

Academic achievement and service to others through extracurricular activities considered. Contact above address for details.

3300—RECORDING FOR THE BLIND (Mary P. Oenslager Scholastic Achievement Awards)

20 Roszel Road
Princeton NJ 08540
609/452-0606
FAX: 609/520-7990

AMOUNT: $1,000; $2,000; $6,000
DEADLINE(S): FEB 1
FIELD(S): All fields of study

Open to legally or totally blind college students registered with RFB&D for at least one year prior to the filing deadline, who have received or will receive a bachelor's degree from a 4-year college or university in the United States or its terrorities, and who have a 3.0 GPA or better.

Bachelor's degree must be received between July 1 of year preceding application deadline date and June 30 of year of application deadline date. Write for complete information.

3301—RED RIVER VALLEY FIGHTER PILOTS ASSOCIATION (River Rats Scholarship Grant Programs)

P.O. Box 1551
North Fork CA 93643
559/877-5000
FAX: 559/877-5001
E-mail: AFBridger@aol.com
Internet: www.eos.net/rrva

AMOUNT: $500-$3,500
DEADLINE(S): MAY 15
FIELD(S): All fields of study

For a) immediate dependents (spouse/children) of any member of US Armed Forces who is listed in KIA/MIA status from any combat situation involving our military since 8/64; b) immediate dependents of military aircrew members killed as result of performing aircrew duties during non-combat mission; c) immediate dependents of current/deceased RRVA-members in good standing; and d) grandchildren of qualifying military relative. Must be US citizen/permanent resident.

15-40 awards annually. Renewable. Based on need, achievement, and activities. See website or contact Al Bache, Executive Director, for an application.

3302—RESERVE OFFICERS ASSOCIATION OF THE UNITED STATES (Henry J. Reilly Memorial Scholarships for Undergraduates)

One Constitution Ave. NE
Washington DC 20002-5655
202/479-2200 or 800/809-9448
FAX: 202/479-0416
E-mail:
71154.1267@compserve.com

AMOUNT: $500
DEADLINE(S): Varies (applications available in FEB)
FIELD(S): All fields of study

Must be active or associate members of ROA or ROAL, or be children or grand-

children, aged 26 or younger, of members. Children of deceased members eligible if under age 21. For full-time study at a four-year college/university. Must have minimum 3.3 high school GPA and 3.0 college GPA. 500-word (handwritten) essay on career goals, leadership qualities, and SAT/ACT scores required. Spouses not eligible unless they are members.

75 awards annually. Contact Ms. Mickey Hagen for an application—please specify your grade level.

3303—RESERVE OFFICERS ASSOCIATION OF THE UNITED STATES (Henry J. Reilly Memorial Scholarships for Graduates)

One Constitution Ave. NE
Washington DC 20002-5655
202/479-2200 or 800/809-9448
FAX: 202/479-0416
E-mail: 71154.1267@compserve.com

AMOUNT: $500
DEADLINE(S): Varies (applications available in FEB)
FIELD(S): All fields of study

Must be active or associate members of ROA who are graduate students at a regionally accredited US college/university. Must be enrolled in at least two courses (if you are employed full-time, you may be eligible if enrolled in only one course) and have a minimum 3.2 GPA. Must demonstrate leadership qualities—letter of recommendation from military or civilian "reporting senior" is required, as well as two letters in regards to academic ability and curriculum vitae.

35 awards annually. Contact Ms. Mickey Hagen for an application—please specify your grade level. Undergrad program for ROA/ROAL members also available.

3304—RHODE ISLAND HIGHER EDUCATION ASSISTANCE AUTHORITY (Loan Program; PLUS Loans)

560 Jefferson Blvd.
Warwick RI 02886
401/736-1160

AMOUNT: Up to $5,500 for undergrads & up to $8,500 for graduates (subsidized); up to $5,000 for undergrads & up to $10,000 for graduates (unsubsidized)
DEADLINE(S): None specified
FIELD(S): All fields of study

Open to Rhode Island residents or non-residents attending an eligible school. Must be US citizen or legal resident and be

enrolled at least half-time. Rhode Island residents may attend schools outside the state.

Must demonstrate financial need. Write for current interest rates and complete information.

3305—RHODE ISLAND HIGHER EDUCATION ASSISTANCE AUTHORITY (Undergraduate Grant & Scholarship Program)

560 Jefferson Blvd.
Warwick RI 02886
407/736-1100

AMOUNT: $250-$2,000
DEADLINE(S): MAR 1
FIELD(S): All fields of study

Open to Rhode Island residents who are enrolled or planning to enroll at least 1/2 time in a program that leads to a degree or certificate at the postsecondary, undergraduate level. Grant is limited to eligible schools in the US, Canada, and Mexico.

Must demonstrate financial need, cost of education minus estimated Pell Grant minus expected family contribution equal need (must have at least $1,000 in financial need). Write for complete information.

3306—RICHARD E. MERWIN INTERNATIONAL AWARD

P.O. Box 6694
Coddingtown CA 95406-0694
Written inquiry only

AMOUNT: $1,000
DEADLINE(S): AUG 18
FIELD(S): All fields of study

Must reside in the US, and attend a school in Europe. Scholarships based on a 400-word essay on how to expand intercultural activity for study. Must have been born in Europe and desire to study there after living in the US.

For undergraduate or graduate study. Write for complete information.

3307—RIPON COLLEGE (Academic Tuition Scholarships)

Admissions Office
300 Seward Street
P.O. Box 248
Ripon WI 54971
920/748-8102 or 800/94-RIPON
E-mail: admbinfo@ripon.edu
Internet: www.ripon.edu

AMOUNT: $5,000-$18,000/yr.
DEADLINE(S): MAR 1
FIELD(S): All fields of study

Open to entering first-year students at Ripon College. Must have minimum 3.2 GPA and ACT score of at least 24 or SAT score of at least 1110. Interview may be required.

Renewable. Contact Office of Admission for an application.

3308—RISING STAR INTERNSHIPS (Internships and Part-Time Employment for Students)

1904 Hidden Point Road
Annapolis MD 21401
410/974-4783
E-mail: webmaster@rsinternships.com
Internet: www.rsinternships.com

AMOUNT: Varies
DEADLINE(S): None
FIELD(S): All fields

A website containing opportunities for internships and part-time student employment nationwide. The search is free, but there is a charge for students to post a resume. Organizations offering opportunities can do so for free for one month, but must pay $10 per month thereafter. Many vocational areas are available.

Most internships are unpaid.

3309—ROTARY FOUNDATION OF ROTARY INTERNATIONAL (Ambassadorial Scholarships)

1 Rotary Center
1560 Sherman Ave.
Evanston IL 60201-3698
847/866-3000
FAX: 847/328-8554
E-mail: sheynina@riorc.mhs.
compuserve.com
Internet: www.rotary.org

AMOUNT: Varies—Up to $23,000/yr.
DEADLINE(S): Varies (with local Rotary Club)
FIELD(S): All fields of study

International travel/study opportunity for individuals of all ages who are citizens of a country in which there is a Rotary Club; must have completed at least two years of university coursework or equivalent professional experience. For as short a time as three months to three years.

1,300 annual awards. Contact local Rotary Club for deadlines and application submissions. Deadlines can be as early as March and as late as July 15. Check website above for details.

3310—ROTARY FOUNDATION OF ROTARY INTERNATIONAL (Grants for University Teachers)

1 Rotary Center
1560 Sherman Ave.
Evanston IL 60201-3698
847/866-3000
FAX: 847/328-8554
E-mail: sheynina@riorc.mhs.
compuserve.com
Internet: www.rotary.org

AMOUNT: Varies—Up to $20,000
DEADLINE(S): Varies (with local Rotary Club)
FIELD(S): All fields of study

An opportunity for university teachers to teach at a university in a low-income country. Grants are for either three to five months (US$10,000) or six to ten months (US$20,000). Must be a citizen of a country where there is a Rotary Club.

Rotarians and their relatives are eligible as well as non-Rotarians. Contact local Rotary Club for deadlines and application submissions. Check website for further information.

3311—ROYAL A. & MILDRED D. EDDY STUDENT LOAN TRUST FUND; LOUISE I. LATSHAW STUDENT LOAN TRUST FUND (Student Loans)

NBD Bank Trust Dept.
8585 Broadway, Suite 396
Merriville IN 46410
Written inquiry

AMOUNT: $2,000/year
DEADLINE(S): Ongoing
FIELD(S): All fields of study

Loan fund available to undergraduate juniors and seniors who are US citizens. Two credit-worthy co-signers are required. Interest rate is 10%, and payments must begin five months after graduation. For study in the US only.

Write to above address for complete information.

3312—ROYAL NEIGHBORS OF AMERICA (Fraternal Scholarships)

230 16th Street
Rock Island IL 61201
309/788-4561

AMOUNT: $500 to $2,000 a year for 4 years
DEADLINE(S): DEC 1
FIELD(S): All areas of study

Open to high school seniors who are RNA members of at least 2 years and in the upper quarter of their class. Awards tenable by US citizens at recognized undergrad colleges and universities.

22 non-renewable $500 scholarships for freshman year only and 10 national scholarships that are renewable for 4 years. Write for complete information.

3313—ROYAL NEIGHBORS OF AMERICA (Non-traditional Scholarship)

230 16th Street
Rock Island IL 61201
309/788-4561
FAX: 309/788-9234

AMOUNT: $1,000
DEADLINE(S): DEC 1
FIELD(S): All areas of study

For those who have been RNA members for at least two years and are 25 years of age or older.

10 awards per year. Contact Betty Walsh at above address/number.

3314—ROYAL NORWEGIAN EMBASSY (May 8th Memorial Fund)

2720 34th Street NW
Washington DC 20008
202/333-6000

AMOUNT: Food & lodging; tuition is free
DEADLINE(S): MAR 15
FIELD(S): None specified

Scholarship commemorating 25th anniversary of Liberation of Norway for one year's residence at a Norwegian Folk High School. No formal credits, not college; objective is to prepare young people for everyday life in the community.

Must be between 18 and 22 years of age; your country must be among those selected for this year's bursaries. Other restrictions apply. Write for complete information.

3315—RURITAN NATIONAL FOUNDATION (Grant and Loan Program)

P.O. Box 487
Dublin VA 24084
703/674-9441

AMOUNT: Varies—minimum grant $200; minimum loan $500
DEADLINE(S): APR 1
FIELD(S): All fields of study

Grants and loans for postsecondary education. Applicant must be recommended by two active Ruritans. Clubs are located in 25 states.

Financial need, character, scholarship, academic promise, and desire for further education are considered.

3316—SACHS FOUNDATION (Scholarship Program)

90 S. Cascade Ave., Suite 1410
Colorado Springs CO 80903
719/633-2353
AMOUNT: $3,000 (undergrad); $4,000 (graduate)
DEADLINE(S): FEB 15
FIELD(S): All fields of study

Open to African-American residents of Colorado who are high school graduates, US citizens, have a 3.4 or better GPA, and can demonstrate financial need. For undergrad study at any accredited college or university. Very few graduate grants are awarded.

Approximately 50 scholarships per year. Renewable if 2.5 or better GPA is maintained. Grants are for up to 4 years in duration. Write for complete information.

3317—SACRAMENTO SCOTTISH RITE OF FREEMASONRY (Charles M. Goethe Memorial Scholarship)

P.O. Box 19497
Sacramento CA 95819-0497
916/452-5881
AMOUNT: Varies
DEADLINE(S): JUN 10
FIELD(S): All fields of study

For any field of study but preference is to students majoring in eugenics or biological sciences. Grants are limited to students who are members or senior members of the Order of DeMolay.

Also open to children of members or deceased members of a California Masonic Lodge. Write for complete information.

3318—SACRED HEART ACADEMY (Merit Scholarship)

200 Strawberry Hill Ave.
Stamford CT 06102
203/323-3173
FAX: 203/975-7804
E-mail: sacred.heart.academy@snet.com
AMOUNT: $1,500
DEADLINE(S): DEC
FIELD(S): All fields of study

Scholarships at a private secondary school. Must take Dec. or March exam the year before entering 9th grade. Top scorers are awarded scholarships renewable for 4 years, dependent upon maintaining a 3.2 GPA. Also, financial aid is available based on need determined by application with W-2 forms.

3 merit scholarships; number of recipients varies for financial aid.

3319—SAINT ANTHONY OF PADUA SCHOOL (Tuition Assistance)

906 Jenkins Street
Endicott NY 13760
607/754-0875
Internet: home.stny.lrun.com/stanthony's/index/html
AMOUNT: Varies
DEADLINE(S): Varies
FIELD(S): All fields of study

Tuition assistance for this private Catholic school for children in grades K-4 in Endicott, NY.

Check website or write for details.

3320—SAINT JOHN'S PREPARATORY SCHOOL (President's Scholarship)

P.O. Box 4000
Collegeville MN 56321
320/363-3321
FAX: 320/363-3513
E-mail: admitprep@csbsju.edu
Internet: www.csbs.edu/sjprep
AMOUNT: $800/yr.
DEADLINE(S): APR 1
FIELD(S): All fields of study

Academic scholarship for a student at this independent high school who has demonstrated an interest in academics, athletics, and community service. Must be US citizen or permanent resident.

Renewable for 4 years. Contact school for details.

3321—SAINT MARK'S SCHOOL (Financial Aid)

25 Marlbourough Road
P.O. Box 9105
Southborough MA 01772
508/786-6112
FAX: 508/786-6120
AMOUNT: Up to $25,000
DEADLINE(S): JAN
FIELD(S): All fields of study

Street Mark's is a private college prep high school (grades 9-12) in Massachusetts. Financial aid applicants must be strong candidates for admission and demonstrate financial need. US citizenship.

Contact Jim Barker at above location for further information.

3322—SAINT MARY'S EPISCOPAL SCHOOL (Financial Aid)

60 North Perkins
Memphis TN 38117
901/537-1405
FAX: 901/4682-3809
E-mail: lwilliam@stmarysschool.org
Internet: www.stmarysschool.org
AMOUNT: Varies
DEADLINE(S): FEB 10
FIELD(S): All fields of study

Financial aid programs based on need are available at this K-12 Episcopalian girls' day school in Memphis, Tennessee.

Contact school for details. For financial aid application, contact School and Student Services for Financial Aid, P.O. Box 6657, Princeton, NJ 08511-6657.

3323—SAMUEL LEMBERG SCHOLARSHIP LOAN FUND INC. (Scholarships-Loans)

60 East 42nd Street, Suite 1814
New York NY 10165
Written inquiry
AMOUNT: Up to $5,000 per academic year
DEADLINE(S): APR 1
FIELD(S): All fields of study

Special no-interest scholarship-loans open to Jewish men and women pursuing any undergraduate, graduate, or professional degree. Recipients assume an obligation to repay their loans within 10 years after the completion of their studies.

Write for complete information.

3324—SAN FRANCISCO INDEPENDENT SCHOLARS (Star and Step Scholarships)

755 Sansome Street, Suite 450
San Francisco CA 94111
415/561-4607
FAX: 415/561-4606
E-mail: aweeks@pacificresearch.org
Internet: www.pacificresearch.org
AMOUNT: $2,000
DEADLINE(S): JAN 15
FIELD(S): All fields of study

Step scholarships are for 8th graders in public schools in San Francisco who wish to apply to a private or parochial high school. Star scholarships are for middle school and high school students who are homeschooled and who wish to design or enroll in an independent study program within state laws. Must be resident of San Francisco. Essays, transcripts, etc., are considered.

Renewable. See website or contact Alison Weeks, Program Director, for an application. Applicants also eligible for Johns Hopkins SFIS Partner Award.

3325—SAN FRANCISCO STATE UNIVERSITY (Over-60 Program)

Admissions Office
1600 Holloway Ave.
San Francisco CA 94132
415/338-2037

AMOUNT: Admissions & registration fees waiver
DEADLINE(S): None
FIELD(S): All fields of study

Open to California residents over 60 years of age who have lived in the state for at least one year by September 20th. Must meet the university's regular admissions standards. Total cost is $3.50 per semester.

Write Admissions Office for complete information.

3326—SAN FRANCISCO UNIVERSITY HIGH SCHOOL (Financial Aid Grants)

3065 Jackson Street
San Francisco CA 94115
415/447-3100
FAX: 415/447-5801
Internet: www.sfuhs.pvt.k12.ca.us

AMOUNT: $100 to full tuition
DEADLINE(S): JAN 19
FIELD(S): All fields of study

Financial aid for students admitted to this independent, coed high school (9-12) in San Francisco, California. Must demonstrate financial need.

90 awards yearly. Contact website and/or school for more information.

3327—SAN JOSE STATE UNIVERSITY (Scholarships)

Financial Aid Office
One Washington Square
San Jose CA 95192-0036
408/924-6095
FAX: 408/924-6089
E-mail: ellioja@sjsuvm1.sjsu.edu

AMOUNT: $100 to $2,000 (based on GPA)
DEADLINE(S): MAR 15
FIELD(S): All fields of study

Students must have established a GPA at SJSU based on the successful completion of at least 8 graduate or 12 undergraduate units prior to filing an application. Incoming freshmen/transfer students not

eligible. Must attend full-time and have filled out the FAFSA (however, foreign nationals are eligible to apply). Financial need considered.

300-500 awards annually. Contact Janet M. Elliot, Counselor, for an application. Note: Students should contact their department majors for information on any departmental scholarships that may be available.

3328—SAN MATEO COUNTY FARM BUREAU (Scholarship)

765 Main Street
Half Moon Bay CA 94019
415/726-4485

AMOUNT: Varies
DEADLINE(S): APR 1
FIELD(S): All areas of study

Open to entering college freshmen and continuing students who are members of the San Mateo County Farm Bureau or the dependent child of a member.

Write for complete information.

3329—SANTA ROSA JUNIOR COLLEGE (Business and Community Scholarships)

Barnett Hall, #1284
1501 Mendocino Ave.
Santa Rosa CA 95401-4395
707/527-4740
E-mail: merle_martin@garfield.santarosa.edu
Internet: www.santarosa.edu/scholarship

AMOUNT: Varies
DEADLINE(S): MAR 1
FIELD(S): Varies

For students attending Santa Rosa Junior College, Santa Rosa, CA. Applications are at SRJC Scholarship Office, Barnett Hall, Rm. 1284. The Resource Center works with more than 175 different businesses and community organizations. Awards are based on various criteria. For high school seniors, students already attending SRJC pursuing A.A. degree or units necessary to transfer to a four-year institution, and for voc-tech students. Amounts and deadlines vary.

Contact SRJC scholarship office for details.

3330—SANTA ROSA JUNIOR COLLEGE (Doyle Scholarship Program)

Barnett Hall, #1284
1501 Mendocino Ave.
Santa Rosa CA 95401-4395

707/527-4740
E-mail: merle_martin@garfield.santarosa.edu
Internet: www.santarosa.edu/scholarship

AMOUNT: $650-$1,300
DEADLINE(S): MAR 1
FIELD(S): All fields of study

For students attending Santa Rosa Junior College, Santa Rosa, CA. Applications through the SRJC Scholarship Office, Barnett Hall, Rm. 1284. Awards are based on scholastic achievement. For high school seniors, students already attending SRJC pursuing A.A. degree or units necessary to transfer to a four-year institution, and for students planning to complete one of the Occupational Certificate programs. US citizenship or permanent residency.

Financial need may determine award amount but is not required to receive a Doyle Scholarship. See website for details and/or contact SRJC Scholarship Office. Applications available from Jan. 4 through March 1.

3331—SANTA ROSA JUNIOR COLLEGE (SRJC Foundation Scholarships)

Barnett Hall, #1284
1501 Mendocino Ave.
Santa Rosa CA 95401-4395
707/527-4740
E-mail: merle_martin@garfield.santarosa.edu
Internet: www.santarosa.edu/scholarship

AMOUNT: Varies
DEADLINE(S): MAR 1
FIELD(S): All fields of study

For continuing students at Santa Rosa Junior College, Santa Rosa, CA, who have completed at least 12 units at SRJC (GPA 2.5 or +) and for students with at least 56 transferable units transferring to a four-year institution during the upcoming academic year (GPA 3.0 or +). Applications through the SRJC Scholarship Office, Barnett Hall, Rm. 1284. Various awards—completing one application will put you in the running for more than 200 different scholarships.

See website for details and/or contact SRJC Scholarship Office. Applications available from Jan. 4 through March 1.

3332—SARA LEE CORPORATION (Nathan Cummings Scholarship Program)

Three First National Plaza
Chicago IL 60602-4260

312/726-2600

AMOUNT: $500-$2,000/year
DEADLINE(S): JAN 1 (junior year)
FIELD(S): All areas of study

Scholarships for high school juniors who are the natural or legally adopted children of regular full-time employees of a Sara Lee Corporation. Children of retired and deceased employees are also eligible. Must take SAT/National Merit Scholarship Qualifying Test on Oct. of junior year. See guidance counselor for test information.

Scholarship continues as long as student continues to remain in good scholastic and disciplinary standing.

3333—SARA LEE CORPORATION (Nathan Cummings Scholarship Program)

350 Albert Street, Suite 600
Ottawa, Ontario K1R 1B1
CANADA
613/563-1236
FAX: 613/563-9745

AMOUNT: $1,500
DEADLINE(S): JUNE 1
FIELD(S): All fields of study

Scholarships for dependent children, including adopted children, stepchildren, and wards in legal guardianship of regular active full-time employees of Sara Lee Corporation and its Canadian divisions. Children of deceased and retired employees also are eligible. For use at recognized Canadian university-transfer colleges.

For study in a full-time program leading to a degree. Write to Awards Division, Association of Universities and Colleges of Canada, at above address.

3334—SARA'S WISH FOUNDATION (Scholarships)

23 Ash Lane
Amherst MA 01002
413/256-0914
FAX: 413/253-3338
E-mail: info@saraswish.org
Internet: saraswish.org

AMOUNT: Varies
DEADLINE(S): None
FIELD(S): All fields of study

Scholarships for individuals who share Sara Schewe's zest for life, love of adventure, and zeal to excel. Sara was killed in a bus accident in India while on a student tour. The scholarship is for students dedicated to community service, who actively participate in creative pursuits, and who will be advocates for safe travel conditions.

3335—SCHERING/KEY ("Will to Win" Asthma Athlete Scholarship)

2000 Galloping Hill Road
Kenilworth NJ 07033
800-558-7305

AMOUNT: $1,000 (Bronze-5); $5,000 (Silver-4); $10,000 (Gold-1)
DEADLINE(S): MAR 31
FIELD(S): All fields of study

For high school seniors and undergrads with asthma who have achieved both excellence in competitive sports and a superior high school academic record. Must be accepted to a regionally accredited US college and pursue a bachelor's degree.

In addition to the scholarship, Silver and Gold Award winners will be invited to an all-expenses-paid Awards Weekend. Write for application.

3336—SCHOLARSHIP FOUNDATION OF Street LOUIS (Interest-free Loan Program)

8215 Clayton Road
Street Louis MO 63117
314/725-7990

AMOUNT: Up to $3,000
DEADLINE(S): APR 15
FIELD(S): All areas except ministry

Residents of the St. Louis area who are high school graduates and who can demonstrate financial need. Loans are interest-free. Six years to repay following graduation.

Loans are renewable up to a maximum of $15,000 per person provided student is in good academic standing and continues to show need. Write for complete information.

3337—SCHOOL FOR INTERNATIONAL TRAINING (College Semester Abroad and Other Scholarships Related to International Education)

Kipling Road
P.O. Box 676
Brattleboro VT 05302-0676
800/336-1616
FAX: 802/258-3500
E-mail: info@sit.edu
Internet: www.worldlearning.org/sit/financial.html

AMOUNT: $500-$2,500
DEADLINE(S): Varies

FIELD(S): All fields of study

Several scholarships are available through this organization for studying abroad or for training others in international relations areas. Some are for teachers, some are for undergraduates, some are for former Peace Corps volunteers and other similar organizations, and some are for majors in fields such as international business management, foreign language and ESL teachers, etc.

Contact organization for detailed information concerning all of their programs.

3338—SCOTTISH RITE FOUNDATION OF WYOMING (Scholarships)

College Office of Student Financial Aid 1820 Capitol Ave.
Cheyenne WY 82001
Written inquiry

AMOUNT: $1,000
DEADLINE(S): JUN 1
FIELD(S): All fields of study

Available to full-time college sophomores of Scottish ancestry who have completed at least 30 credit hours with a minimum 2.0 GPA. Applicants must be graduates of a Wyoming high school or hold a GED certificate obtained through a Wyoming community college or the University of Wyoming.

3 awards annually. Write to above address for an application.

3339—SCREAMING POLITICIANS (Scholarship Essay Contest)

4720 Vineland Ave., Suite 300
North Hollywood CA 91602
Internet: www.ScreamingPoliticians.com/scholar.html

AMOUNT: $1,000
DEADLINE(S): JUL 4
FIELD(S): All fields of study

For high school/college student who most clearly writes a one-page interpretation of what they think Screaming Politicians' feelings, emotions, and thoughts are in a pre-selected song—1999's topic was "Shame." Must be US resident. High school students must plan on attending college/university following high school. Essay must be typed, double-spaced on legal-size paper and in English. Must be stapled to entry form. LAST name and last 4 digits of SSN must be on each page.

1 award annually. 2 copies of essay must be mailed in flat, 9x12 envelope. See website to hear song and apply online. Or send self-addressed, stamped envelope for entry form.

3340—SCREEN ACTORS GUILD FOUNDATION (John L. Dales Scholarship Fund)

5757 Wilshire Blvd.
Los Angeles CA 90036-3600
213/549-6610

AMOUNT: Varies—Determined annually
DEADLINE(S): APR 30
FIELD(S): All areas of study

Scholarships open to SAG members with at least five years' membership or dependent children of members with at least eight years' membership. Awards are for any level of undergraduate, graduate, or post-graduate study at an accredited institution.

Financial need is a consideration. Renewable yearly with reapplication. Write for complete information.

3341—SEABEE MEMORIAL SCHOLARSHIP ASSOCIATION, INC. (Scholarships)

P.O. Box 6574
Silver Spring MD 20916
301/871-3172
E-mail: smsa@erols.com
Internet: www.seabee.org

AMOUNT: $2,000
DEADLINE(S): APR 15
FIELD(S): All fields of study

Undergraduate scholarships open to children and grandchildren (NOT great grandchildren) of regular, reserve, retired, or deceased officers or enlisted members who have served or who are now serving with the Seabees or the Naval Civil Engineer Corps. US citizenship required.

70 awards per year. Renewable up to 4 years. See website or write to above address for complete information.

3342—SEAFARERS' WELFARE PLAN (Charlie Logan Scholarship Program for Seamen)

5201 Auth Way
Camp Springs MD 20746
301/899-0675

AMOUNT: $6,000-$15,000
DEADLINE(S): APR 15
FIELD(S): All areas of study

Open to seaman who has no less than 2 years of actual employment on vessels of companies signatory to the seafarers' welfare plan. Must have had 125 days employment in previous calendar year.

Renewable up to 2 years. Write for complete information.

3343—SEAFARERS' WELFARE PLAN (Charlie Logan Scholarship Program for Dependents)

5201 Auth Way
Camp Springs MD 20746
301/899-0675

AMOUNT: $15,000
DEADLINE(S): APR 15
FIELD(S): All areas of study

Open to dependent children of seaman who has been employed for at least 3 years by a contributor to seafarer's welfare plan. Student must be H.S. (or equiv) grad in upper 1/3 of class, unmarried, and under 19 years of age.

Write for complete information and restrictions.

3344—SELBY FOUNDATION (Direct Scholarship Program)

1800 Second Street, Suite 750
Sarasota FL 34236
941/957-0442

AMOUNT: $1,000-$2,500
DEADLINE(S): MAR 1
FIELD(S): All fields of study (preference for Technology, Science, and Math majors)

For undergraduate study by residents of Sarasota or Manatee Counties, Florida, who are attending an accredited college full-time and have a GPA of 3.0 or better. Must demonstrate financial need and be a US citizen.

Write for complete information.

3345—SEMINOLE TRIBE OF FLORIDA (Higher Education Awards)

6073 Stirling Road
Hollywood FL 33024
305/584-0400, ext. 154

AMOUNT: None specified
DEADLINE(S): APR 15; JUL 15; NOV 15
FIELD(S): All areas of study

Open to enrolled members of the Seminole Tribe of Florida or to those eligible to become a member. For undergraduate or graduate study at an accredited college or university.

Awards renewable. Write for complete information.

3346—SENECA NATION HIGHER EDUCATION (Scholarships and Grants)

P.O. Box 231
Salamanca NY 14779

716/945-1790
FAX: 716/945-7170

AMOUNT: Varies
DEADLINE(S): JUL 15; DEC 31; MAY 20
FIELD(S): All fields of study

Open to enrolled members of the Seneca Nation of Indians who are New York residents in need of funding for post-secondary education and are accepted in accredited degree programs. May be used toward associate's, bachelor's, master's, or doctor's degrees.

65-75 awards per year. Must demonstrate financial need. Write for complete information.

3347—SERB NATIONAL FOUNDATION (Scholarships)

One Fifth Ave.
Pittsburgh PA 152222
800/538-SERB or 412/642-SERB
FAX: 642-1372
E-mail: snf@serbnatlfed.org
Internet: serbnatlfed.org/benefits.htm

AMOUNT: Varies
DEADLINE(S): Varies (spring)
FIELD(S): All fields of study

Scholarships for students of Serbian ancestry attending postsecondary institutions in the US Must have been members of the organization for at least two years.

Contact above organization for details.

3348—SERTOMA FOUNDATION INTERNATIONAL (Scholarships for Students With Hearing Loss)

1912 East Meyer Blvd.
Kansas City MO 64132-1174
Phone & TTY: 816/333/8300
FAX: 816/333-4320

AMOUNT: $1,000
DEADLINE(S): MAY 1
FIELD(S): All fields of study

For students with a documented hearing loss who are entering or continuing students at universities or colleges in the US or Canada pursuing four-year bachelor's degrees. Must have at least 3.2 GPA or at least 85% in all high school and college classes.

Renewable up to four times; however, student must submit a new application and compete with other students each year. To apply, starting in October send #10 SASE to "$1,000 Scholarships" at above address.

3349—SERVICE EMPLOYEES INTERNATIONAL UNION (Scholarship Program)

1313 L Street, NW
Washington DC 20005
800/846-1561 or 202/842-0046
Internet: seiu.org.com

AMOUNT: $1,000 and $3,000
DEADLINE(S): MAR (mid-month)
FIELD(S): All fields of study

Scholarships open to Service Employees International Union members (in good standing) and their dependent children. Awards can be used at a community college or trade/tech school or to continue education at a 4-year college or university.

20 awards per year. Write for complete information.

3350—SHOSHONE HIGHER EDUCATION PROGRAM (Shoshone Tribal Scholarship)

P.O. Box 628
Fort Washakie WY 82514
Written inquiry

AMOUNT: Varies
DEADLINE(S): Varies
FIELD(S): All fields of study

Available to high school graduates who are enrolled members of the Wind River Shoshone Tribe and may be used at any public institution in Wyoming. Applicants must have a financial need analysis completed by the college financial aid office. New applicants should forward to the agency a letter of acceptance from a post-secondary institution, a transcript or GED certificate, and a letter stating a proposed course of full-time study and plans upon receiving a degree.

Renewable. Write to above address for an application at least six weeks prior to beginning of school year.

3351—SICO FOUNDATION (Scholarships)

Scholarships Coordinator
Mount Joy PA 17552
Not given

AMOUNT: $1,000 per year
DEADLINE(S): FEB 15
FIELD(S): All fields of study

Open to high school seniors residing in the state of Delaware or the Pennsylvania counties of Adams, Berks, Chester, Cumberland, Dauphin, Delaware, Lancaster, Lebanon, or York.

Also available to residents of New Jersey counties of Atlantic, Cape May, Cumberland, Gloucester, and Salem and to residents of Cecil County, Maryland. Write for complete information.

3352—SIDNEY H. AND MARY L. LANGILLE GRAY FAMILY SCHOLARSHIP FUND TRUST

125 High Street
Boston MA 02110-2713
800/842-6512

AMOUNT: $1,000
DEADLINE(S): MAY 15
FIELD(S): All fields of study

Scholarships for undergraduate study for residents of Massachusetts who are members of middle-income ($15,000-$32,000) families who have several children to educate. The purpose is to assist students whose parental income is too high to qualify for other aid yet not sufficient to pay for all of their children's tuition.

Send SASE to PNC Bank, New England, Trust Dept., at above address for application.

3353—SIDNEY-SHELBY COUNTY YMCA (Lee E. Schauer Memorial Scholarship)

300 E. Parkwood
Sidney OH 45365
937/492-9134
FAX: 937/492-4705
E-mail: y5175@bright.net
Internet: www.bright.net/~y5175

AMOUNT: $5,000
DEADLINE(S): Varies
FIELD(S): All fields of study

Scholarship is for a college-bound high school senior who is a member of the Sidney-Shelby County YMCA for at least three years prior to application. Must have a minimum 2.5 GPA, demonstrate Christian values and leadership, be involved in sports or fitness activities, and volunteer at the Y or in the community. Scholarship must "make a significant difference" to recipient. Financial need NOT a factor.

1 award annually. Renewable for four years. Contact Barbara Sperl at YMCA for an application.

3354—SIGNET CLASSIC SCHOLARSHIP ESSAY COMPETITION

Penguin USA
375 Hudson Street
New York NY 10014
Internet: www.penguinputnam.com/academic/essay

AMOUNT: $1,000
DEADLINE(S): APR 15
FIELD(S): For all fields of study

Essay contest for high school juniors and seniors on a work of classic literature chosen by Signet Classic, publisher of literary works. Contact company or check website for next year's subject and deadline. Must be submitted by a high school English teacher on behalf of the student. Each teacher may submit one junior and one senior essay.

For US citizens or permanent residents. 5 winners. Winning students' schools will also receive a Signet Classic library for their school valued at $1,700.

3355—SIKH EDUCATION AID FUND (Scholarships and Interest-free Loans)

P.O. Box 140
Hopewell VA 23860
804/541-9290
FAX: 804/452-1270
Internet: ASP@MABOLI.COM

AMOUNT: $400-$3,000
DEADLINE(S): JUN 20
FIELD(S): All fields of study

Open to undergraduate, graduate, and post-graduate students who are either followers of the Sikh faith or pursuing Sikh studies and are US citizens. Recipient must maintain acceptable performance in academic programs to retain loan.

Write to the above address for complete information.

3356—SKY PEOPLE HIGHER EDUCATION (Northern Arapaho Tribal Scholarship)

P.O. Box 8480
Ethete WY 82520
Written inquiry

AMOUNT: Varies
DEADLINE(S): Varies
FIELD(S): All fields of study

Scholarships are available to high school graduates who are enrolled members of the Northern Arapaho Tribe and may be used at any public institution in Wyoming. New applicants should forward to the agency a letter of acceptance from a postsecondary institution, a high school transcript or GED certificate, and a letter stating a proposed course of full-time study and plans upon receiving a degree. Applications should be made at least six weeks prior to school year.

Renewable. Contact above address for an application.

3357—SOCIETY OF DAUGHTERS OF THE US ARMY (Scholarships)

7717 Rock Ledge Ct.
Springfield VA 22152
Written inquiry

AMOUNT: $1,000
DEADLINE(S): MAR 1 (to receive application); MAR 31 (completed application)
FIELD(S): All fields of study

Open to daughters, step-, and grand-daughters of commissioned officers of the US Army who are on active duty, are retired, or who died on active duty, or after eligible retirement. Must demonstrate financial need and merit.

Approximately 8 scholarships per year. Renewable. Include qualifying parent's name, rank, Social Security number, and dates of service. Send self-addressed stamped envelope and a pre-paid postal card between November 1 and March 1.

3358—SOCIETY OF THE FIRST DIVISION FOUNDATION (Scholarships)

5 Montgomery Ave.
Erdenheim PA 19038
Written inquiry

AMOUNT: $750 per year (4 years maximum)
DEADLINE(S): JUN 1
FIELD(S): All fields of study

Open to high school seniors who are the children or grandchildren of soldiers who served in the US Army 1st Infantry division. Award based on scholastic achievements, career objectives, and essay. For undergrad study at 2- or 4-year college.

Write for complete information. Include a self-addressed, stamped envelope for an application.

3359—SONOMA STATE UNIVERSITY (Scholarship Program)

Scholarship Office
1801 East Cotati Ave.
Rohnert Park CA 94928
707/664-2261

AMOUNT: $250-$2,500
DEADLINE(S): MAR 1
FIELD(S): All fields of study

Student must be an applicant or full-time student of Sonoma State University and have a 3.0 GPA or higher. Some financial need must be demonstrated. Average of 300 awards given annually.

Contact Kay Ashbrook at above address for details.

3360—SONS OF ITALY FOUNDATION (National Leadership Grants)

219 E Street, NE
Washington DC 20002
202/547-2900 or 202/547-5106

AMOUNT: $2,000 to $5,000
DEADLINE(S): FEB 28
FIELD(S): All fields of study

National leadership grant competition is open to any full-time student of Italian heritage studying at an accredited college or university. For undergraduate or graduate study.

Write for complete information. Also contact local and state lodges for information regarding scholarships offered to members and their children.

3361—SONS OF NORWAY FOUNDATION (Astrid G. Cates Scholarship Fund)

1455 West Lake Street
Minneapolis MN 55408
Written inquiry

AMOUNT: $250 to $750
DEADLINE(S): MAR 1
FIELD(S): All fields of study

Applicants must be between the ages of 17-22 and be CURRENT members of Sons of Norway or children or grandchildren of current Sons of Norway members. Must demonstrate financial need.

Write for complete information.

3362—SONS OF THE AMERICAN REVOLUTION (Joseph S. Rumbaugh Historical Oration Contest)

1000 South 4th Street
Louisville KY 40203
Written inquiry

AMOUNT: $2,000 (1st prize); $1,000 (2nd prize); $500 (3rd prize)
DEADLINE(S): FEB 1
FIELD(S): All fields of study

Oratory competition for high school sophomores, juniors, and seniors who submit an original 5- to 6-minute oration on a personality, event, or document of the American Revolutionary War and how it relates to the US today.

Oration must be delivered from memory without props or charts. Applicants must be US citizens. Write for complete information.

3363—SONS OF THE REPUBLIC OF TEXAS (Texas History Essay Contest)

1717 8th Street
Bay City TX 77414
409/245-6644

AMOUNT: $3,000; $2,000; $1,000
DEADLINE(S): FEB 3
FIELD(S): All fields of study

An essay contest for high school seniors on the historical period of the Republic of Texas (1836-1846). Authors of the three essays judged to be the winners will receive the above prizes. Check with organization for current year's topic. Only one essay judged best in each high school may be submitted.

Contact Melinda Williams, SRT Executive Secretary, at above location for complete information.

3364—SOROPTIMIST FOUNDATIONS (Soroptimist International of the Americas—Youth Citizenship Award)

Two Penn Center Plaza, Suite 1000
Philadelphia PA 19102-1883
215/557-9300
FAX: 215/568-5200
E-mail: siahq@omni.voicenet.com

AMOUNT: $1,250 (54 awards); $2000 (1)
DEADLINE(S): DEC 15 (of senior year)
FIELD(S): All fields of study

Award of merit open to outstanding high school seniors who have demonstrated service in the home, school, and community. Applications available from participating Soroptimist clubs.

54 regional US awards and 17 in other countries/territories within the limits of Soroptimist International of the Americas. Applications available from participating Soroptimist clubs. Contact local club or send SASE to SIA at above address for complete information.

3365—SOROPTIMIST FOUNDATIONS (Soroptimist International of the Americas—Women's Opportunity Awards)

Two Penn Center Plaza, Suite 1000
Philadelphia PA 19102-1883
215/557-9300
FAX: 568-5200
E-mail: siahq@omni.voicenet.com

AMOUNT: $3,000-$5,000 (54 awards); $10,000 (1 award)
DEADLINE(S): DEC 15
FIELD(S): All fields of study

Open to mature women heads of households furthering their skills/training to upgrade employment status. Preference to voc-tech training or undergrad degree completion. Not available for grad work. Must document financial need.

54 regional US awards; 17 in other countries/territories within the territorial limits of Soroptimist International of the Americas. Contact local club or send SASE to SIA (Attn: Women's Opportunity Award) at above address for complete information.

3366—SOUTH CAROLINA GOVERNOR'S OFFICE; DIVISION OF VETERANS AFFAIRS (Tuition Assistance for Children of Certain War Veterans)

1205 Pendleton Street
Columbia SC 29201
803/255-4317
FAX: 803/255-4257

AMOUNT: Tuition waiver
DEADLINE(S): None
FIELD(S): All fields of study

For children of veterans who were legal residents of South Carolina at time of entry into military service and who (during service) were MIA, POW, killed in action, totally disabled, or died of disease, as rated by the Veterans Administration, and/or who is a recipient of the Medal of Honor.

South Carolina residency and US citizenship required. For undergraduate study at South Carolina state-supported schools. Write for complete information.

3367—SOUTH CAROLINA STUDENT LOAN CORPORATION

P.O. Box 21487
Columbia SC 29221
803/798-0916
Internet: www.slc.sc.edu

AMOUNT: Varies
DEADLINE(S): Varies
FIELD(S): All areas of study

Open to South Carolina residents who are US citizens or eligible non-citizens. Must be enrolled or accepted for enrollment at an eligible postsecondary school. Amount of loan determined by cost of school and financial need.

Interest is variable, not to exceed at 8.25%. Loan must be renewed annually. Write or visit website for complete information.

3368—SOUTH CAROLINA TUITION GRANTS COMMITTEE (Higher Education Tuition Grants Program)

P.O. Box 12159
Keenan Bldg., 1st Fl.
Columbia SC 29211-2159
803/734-1200

AMOUNT: Up to $3,260
DEADLINE(S): None specified
FIELD(S): All fields of study

Open to residents of South Carolina who are accepted to or enrolled in eligible private, postsecondary institutions in South Carolina. Must demonstrate financial need and academic merit. US citizenship or legal residency required.

Approximately 8,000 grants per year. Renewable. Contact financial aid office or write to address above for complete information.

3369—SOUTH DAKOTA DEPARTMENT OF EDUCATION AND CULTURAL AFFAIRS (Robert Byrd Honors Scholarship)

700 Governors Drive
Pierre SD 57501-2291
605/773-3134
FAX: 605/773-6139

AMOUNT: $1,110
DEADLINE(S): MAY 1
FIELD(S): All fields of study

Must have ACT score of 24 or above, GPA 3.5+, no final grade below a "C" in 4 years of English, math and science, 3 years of social studies and 2 years of foreign language, or 2 years of computer science.

Renewable for 4 years. Contact Roxie Thielen at above address.

3370—SOUTH DAKOTA DIVISION OF VETERANS AFFAIRS (Aid to Veterans)

500 E. Capitol Ave.
Pierre SD 57501-5070
605/773-3269
FAX: 605/773-5380

AMOUNT: Free tuition in state-supported schools
DEADLINE(S): None specified
FIELD(S): All fields of study

Open to veterans (as defined by SDCL) who are residents of SD, were honorably discharged (as defined by SDCL), have exhausted their GI Bill, and have no other federal educational benefits available.

One-month free tuition for every month of qualified service. Benefit must be used within 20 years of cessation of hostilities or 6 years from discharge (whichever is later). Write for complete stipulations and information.

3371—SOUTH DAKOTA DIVISION OF VETERANS AFFAIRS (Aid to Dependents of Deceased Veterans)

500 E. Capitol Ave.
Pierre SD 57501-5070
605/773-3269
FAX: 605/773-5380

AMOUNT: Free tuition in state-supported schools
DEADLINE(S): None specified
FIELD(S): All fields of study

Open to residents of SD under 25 years of age who are children of veterans who were residents of SD at least 6 months immediately prior to entry into active service and who died from any cause while in the service of the US armed forces.

Must attend a state-supported college or university in SD. Write for complete information.

3372—SOUTH DAKOTA DIVISION OF VETERANS AFFAIRS (Aid to Dependents of Prisoners of War or Missing in Action)

500 E. Capitol Ave.
Pierre SD 57501-5070
605/773-3269
FAX: 605/773-5380

AMOUNT: 8 semesters or 12 quarters of free tuition and mandatory fees, other than subsistence expenses, in a state-supported institution
DEADLINE(S): None specified
FIELD(S): All fields of study, including technical or vocational

Open to children born before or during the period of time a parent served as a prisoner of war or was declared missing in action OR legally adopted OR in the legal custody of the parent prior to and during the time the parent served as a POW or was MIA OR the spouse of a POW or MIA. Once qualified, the return of the qualifying veteran will not remove any provisions or benefits.

No state benefits are available if equal or greater federal benefits are available; state benefits can supplement any lesser benefits from federal sources.

3373—SOUTHWESTERN UNIVERSITY (Scholarships and Grants)

1001 E. University Ave.
Georgetown TX 78626

512/863-6511 (main) or
512/863-1200 or
800/252-3166 (admissions)
Internet: www.southwestern.edu

AMOUNT: Varies
DEADLINE(S): JAN 15
FIELD(S): All fields of study

Both merit-based and need-based scholarships and awards are available through this undergraduate, United Methodist-related, liberal arts college in Georgetown, TX. Some are subject-related, i.e., awards in vocal and instrumental music, theatre, and art. Funds are also available for students planning careers within the church and for dependents of United Methodist clergy. SAT, ACT, GPAs, and need are all considered.

See website for further details; contact university for latest and complete information.

3374—SPRINGSIDE SCHOOL (Grants)

8000 Cherokee Street
Philadelphia PA 19118
215/247-7007
FAX: 215/247-7308

AMOUNT: $500-$12,690
DEADLINE(S): MAR 1
FIELD(S): All fields of study

Grants for students attending this independent K-12 college preparatory school for girls in Philadelphia, Pennsylvania.

100 annual awards. Must demonstrate financial need.

3375—Street DAVID'S SOCIETY (Scholarship)

3 West 51 Street
New York NY 10019
212/422-5480

AMOUNT: $500-$2,500
DEADLINE(S): JUN 1
FIELD(S): All fields of study

Scholarships for college students who are either of Welsh heritage, attending a Welsh school, or studying Welsh culture and/or language. For graduates or undergraduates.

Approximately 12 awards per year. Renewable.

3376—STANFORD UNIVERSITY (Dofflemyer Honors Eagle Scout Scholarship)

Financial Aid Office
Stanford University
322 Old Union
Stanford CA 94305-3021

650/723-3058

AMOUNT: Varies
DEADLINE(S): MAY 31
FIELD(S): All areas of study

Open to Eagle Scouts who have been admitted to and plan to attend, or currently attend, Stanford. Financial need considered.

Write for complete information.

3377—STANHOME INC. (Stanhome Scholarship Program)

333 Western Ave.
Westfield MA 01085
413/562-3631, ext. 254

AMOUNT: $2,000 to $10,000
DEADLINE(S): DEC 31
FIELD(S): All fields of study

Open to children of full-time or regular part-time Stanhome associates or participating affiliated companies.

For undergrad study at any state-accredited degree-granting college or nurses' training program. Write for complete information.

3378—STATE COLLEGE AND UNIVERSITY SYSTEMS OF WEST VIRGINIA—CENTRAL OFFICE (WV Higher Education Grant Program)

1018 Kanawha Blvd. E. Suite 700
Charleston WV 25301-2827
304/558-4614
FAX: 304/558-4622
E-mail: long@scusco.WVnet.edu
Internet: www.scusco.WVNET.edu

AMOUNT: $350 to $2,348
DEADLINE(S): JAN 1; MAR 1
FIELD(S): All areas of study

Open to high school grads who have lived in WV for one year prior to application and are enrolled full-time as an undergrad in an approved WV or PA educational institution. Must be US citizen and demonstrate financial need.

Approximately 8,000 grants per year. Renewable up to 8 semesters. Write for complete information.

3379—STATE FARM COMPANIES FOUNDATION (Scholarships for Dependents)

One State Farm Plaza, SC-3
Bloomington IL 61710-0001
309/766-2039/2161
E-mail: Jill.Jones.A3RI@statefarm.com
Internet: www.statefarm.com

AMOUNT: Varies
DEADLINE(S): Varies
FIELD(S): All fields of study

Scholarships are for high school seniors who are legal dependents of full-time State Farm agents, employees, or retirees. Winners are selected by the National Merit Scholarship Corporation on the basis of test scores, academic record, extracurricular activities, personal essay, and counselor recommendation.

100 awards annually. Contact Jill Jones at above address for more information.

3380—STATE OF NEW JERSEY OFFICE OF STUDENT ASSISTANCE (Edward J. Bloustein Distinguished Scholars Program)

CN 540
Trenton NJ 08625
609/588-3230
800/792-8670 in NJ
TDD: 609/588-2526

AMOUNT: $1,000 per year for 4 years
DEADLINE(S): OCT 1
FIELD(S): All areas of study

Open to New Jersey residents who are academically outstanding high school students planning to attend a NJ college or university. US citizenship or legal residency required.

Students may not apply directly to the program. Applications must be made through the high school. Contact guidance counselor or address above for complete scholarship information.

3381—STATE OF NEW JERSEY OFFICE OF STUDENT ASSISTANCE (Tuition Aid Grants)

CN 540
Trenton NJ 08625
609/588-3230
800/792-8670 in NJ
TDD: 609/588-2526

AMOUNT: $760-$5,570
DEADLINE(S): Varies
FIELD(S): All areas of study

For students who have been New Jersey residents for at least 12 months and who are or intend to be enrolled as full-time undergraduate in any college, university, or degree-granting postsecondary institution in NJ. US citizen or legal resident.

Grants renewable. Write to Office of Student Assistance for complete information.

3382—STATE OF NEW JERSEY OFFICE OF STUDENT ASSISTANCE (Garden State Scholarships)

CN 540
Trenton NJ 08625
609/588-3230
800/792-8670 in NJ
TDD: 609/588-2526

AMOUNT: $500 per year for 4 years
DEADLINE(S): OCT 1
FIELD(S): All areas of study

Must be a resident of New Jersey for at least 12 months prior to receiving award. For undergraduate study in NJ. Demonstrate scholastic achievement and need. US citizen or legal resident.

Renewable. Students may not apply directly to the program. Contact high school guidance couselor or address above for complete information.

3383—STATE OF NEW JERSEY OFFICE OF STUDENT ASSISTANCE (NJClass Loan Program)

CN 540
Trenton NJ 08625
609/588-3200
800/35-NJ-LOAN
TDD: 609/588-2526

AMOUNT: May not exceed cost of attendance minus other financial assistance
DEADLINE(S): None specified
FIELD(S): All areas of study

For US citizens or legal residents who are NJ residents. Must be enrolled at least half-time at an approved school making satisfactory academic progress towards a degree. Repayment is 15 years from date of first disbursement. Various options available.

Apply at least two months prior to need. Write for complete information.

3384—STATE STUDENT ASSISTANCE COMMISSION OF INDIANA (Higher Education & Freedom of Choice Grants)

150 W. Market Street, Suite 500
Indianapolis IN 46204
317/232-2350

AMOUNT: $500-$7,412
DEADLINE(S): MAR 2
FIELD(S): All fields of study

Open to Indiana residents who are accepted to or enrolled in eligible Indiana institutions as full-time undergraduate students. US citizen or legal resident.

Approx 56,000 grants per year. Grants are based on financial need. Students must complete the Free Application for Federal Student Aid (FAFSA). No other application is required. Write for complete information.

3385—STATE STUDENT ASSISTANCE COMMISSION OF INDIANA (Robert C. Byrd Honors Scholarships)

150 W. Market Street, 5th Fl.
Indianapolis IN 46204
317/232-2350
FAX: 317/232-3260
E-mail: grants@ssaci.in.us
Internet: www.ai.org/ssaci/

AMOUNT: $1,110
DEADLINE(S): APR 24
FIELD(S): All areas of study

For Indiana high school seniors with GPA of 3.0 or better for use at a not-for-profit private or public institution in the US. US citizenship required.

144 annual awards. Score of 1300 on SAT or 65 on ACT required.

3386—STEPHEN M. PRICE FOUNDATION (Aviation Training Scholarships for Youth)

4251 University Blvd. S., Suite 301
Jacksonville FL 32216
904/636-9585
FAX: 904/636-5282
Internet: www.smpf.org

AMOUNT: Tuition and training
DEADLINE(S): Varies
FIELD(S): Pilot training and airplane maintenance and repair

"Young Aviators" program for boys and girls, age 14-16, who are economically disadvantaged and reside in the area of Jacksonville, Florida. Two years of ground school classroom and flight training. Students must maintain 2.5 GPA in school subjects, observe certain dress codes, abstain from all illegal substances, and perform community service projects. Training will lead to a private pilot's license.

Contact organization for details.

3387—STEPHEN T. MARCHELLO SCHOLARSHIP FOUNDATION (Scholarships)

1170 E. Long Place
Littleton CO 80122
303/798-0406
E-mail: FMarchello@ntr.net

AMOUNT: $2,500
DEADLINE(S): MAR 15

FIELD(S): All fields of study

Undergraduate scholarships are available to survivors of childhood cancer. Must be resident of Colorado or Arizona, but will open to other states as funding permits. Applicants must have a minimum 2.7 GPA. Letter from doctor or place of treatment is required. Financial need NOT a factor.

Renewable. Send a self-addressed, stamped envelope to Franci Marchello for an application.

3388—STEVEN KNEZEVICH TRUST (Grants)

100 E. Wisconsin Ave., Suite 1020
Milwaukee WI 53202
414/271-6364

AMOUNT: $100 to $800
DEADLINE(S): NOV 1
FIELD(S): All areas of study

Undergraduate and graduate grants for students of Serbian descent. Must establish evidence of ancestral heritage. It is common practice for students to be interviewed in Milwaukee prior to granting the award.

Address inquiries to Stanley Hack. Include self-addressed stamped envelope.

3389—STUDENT AID FOUNDATION, INC. (Loans)

2520 E. Piedmont Rd., Suite F-180
Marietta GA 30062
770/973-7077
FAX: 770/973-2220

AMOUNT: $2,500/yr. (undergrad); $3,000/yr. (graduate)
DEADLINE(S): APR 15
FIELD(S): All fields of study

Low-interest loans for women who are residents of Georgia or out-of-state women attending a Georgia school. Grades, financial need, personal integrity, and sense of responsibility are considerations.

70 loans annually. Renewable with re-application. Send a self-addressed, stamped envelope for an application.

3390—STUDENT LOAN GUARANTEE FOUNDATION OF ARKANSAS (SLGFA Loans)

219 South Victory Street
Little Rock AR 72201-1884
800/622-3446 or 501/372-1491
FAX: 501/688-7675

E-mail: slgfa@org

Internet: www.slgfa.org

AMOUNT: $2,625 (1st year); $3,500 (2nd); $5,500 (3rd & 4th); $8,500 (graduate)

DEADLINE(S): Varies

FIELD(S): All fields of study

Loans open to eligible borrowers using a SLGFA participating lender. Must be US citizen and either an Arkansas resident or planning to study in Arkansas. For undergraduate or graduate study leading to a degree or certificate.

Contact SLGFA for an application.

3391—SUBURBAN CABLE (Scholarships)

P.O. Box 989

Oaks PA 19456-0989

610/650-1000

FAX: 610/650-1131

E-mail: ljavens@suburban.com

AMOUNT: $1,000-$3,500

DEADLINE(S): MAR 1

FIELD(S): All fields of study

Scholarships for high school seniors in the counties of Pennsylvania, New Jersey, and Delaware living in the Suburban Cable viewing area.

50 awards. Contact above address for detailed information.

3392—SUDBURY FOUNDATION ATKINSON SCHOLARSHIP PROGRAM

278 Old Sudbury Road

Sudbury MA 01776

978/443-0849

AMOUNT: Up to $5,000 per year

DEADLINE(S): NOV 1

FIELD(S): All fields of study

Open to Lincoln-Sudbury High School (MA) graduating seniors or dependents of Sudbury residents for postsecondary studies, including vocational training.

Must demonstrate financial need. Academic and non-academic factors are considered in evaluating candidates.

3393—SUNKIST GROWERS INC. (A.W. Bodine-Sunkist Memorial Scholarship)

P.O. Box 7888

Van Nuys CA 91409

818/379-7510

AMOUNT: $2,000-$3,000

DEADLINE(S): APR 30

FIELD(S): All fields of study

Open to California and Arizona undergraduates who come from an agricultural background and are in need of financial assistance. Must have a 3.0 GPA.

Write for complete information.

3394—SWISS BENEVOLENT SOCIETY OF CHICAGO (Scholarship Fund)

6440 N. Bosworth Ave.

Chicago IL 60626

Written inquiry

AMOUNT: $750 to $2,500

DEADLINE(S): NOV 15 (Request application then. Deadline is FEB 28.)

FIELD(S): All areas of study

Undergraduate scholarships open to Swiss nationals or those of proven Swiss descent who are permanent residents of Illinois or Southern Wisconsin and accepted to or enrolled in accredited colleges or universities. Minimum 3.5 GPA required.

Swiss students studying in the USA on a student or visitor's visa are NOT eligible. Write for complete information.

3395—SWISS BENEVOLENT SOCIETY OF SAN FRANCISCO (Clement & Frieda Amstutz Fund Scholarship)

c/o Swiss Consulate General

456 Montgomery Street, Suite 1500

San Francisco CA 94104-1233

415/788-2272

AMOUNT: Varies

DEADLINE(S): MAY 15

FIELD(S): All fields of study

Undergrad scholarships at US colleges open to Swiss nationals who have lived within a 150-mile radius of the San Francisco City Hall for 3 years prior to application date. Applicant must have applied for admission to any institution of higher learning in the US (community colleges and trade schools excluded).

Number of awards varies each year. Write for complete information.

3396—SYNOD OF THE NORTHEAST (Wurffel/Sills Student Loan Program)

5811 Heritage Landing Drive

E. Syracuse NY 13057-9360

800/585-5881

FAX: 315/446-3708

AMOUNT: Varies

DEADLINE(S): APR 1

FIELD(S): All fields of study

Interest-free loans are open to Presbyterians who are undergraduates or seminary students. Must show need for funds by completing application and required worksheet/forms.

Renewable. Contact Synod of the Northeast for an application.

3397—TAILHOOK FOUNDATION (Scholarship Fund)

9696 Business Park Ave.

San Diego CA 92131

619/689-9223

FAX: 619/578-8839

E-mail: thookassn@aol.com

AMOUNT: $1,000

DEADLINE(S): JUL 1

FIELD(S): All fields of study

Scholarships for students at all levels whose parent was or is serving in any branch of military service on an aircraft carrier. Must be US citizen and enrolled in or attending a four-year college or university.

5 awards per year. May reapply for renewal.

3398—TALBOTS (Women's Scholarship Fund)

175 Beal Street

Hingham MA 02043

781/749-7600

FAX: 781/741-4369

Internet: www.talbots.com

AMOUNT: Varies

DEADLINE(S): MAR 3

FIELD(S): All fields of study

Open to women returning to college to complete their undergraduate degrees. Must be US citizen/permanent resident.

55 awards annually. Applications available November 15th through March 3rd at all US Talbots stores. Recipients announced by July.

3399—TALL CLUBS INTERNATIONAL (Kae Sumner Einfeldt Scholarship Award)

P.O. Box 1964

Bloomfield NJ 07003-1964

888/I-M-TALL-2

Internet: www.tall.org

AMOUNT: $1,000

DEADLINE(S): Varies

FIELD(S): All fields of study

Scholarships for unusually tall college-bound high school seniors (girls—5'10", boys—6'2"). Must apply through regional clubs or members-at-large. Tall Clubs also has a group for teens called "Skywriters"— a way to meet pen pals who are also tall. To e-mail: TCI-skywriters@tall.org.

Several scholarships available. Contact organization for location of your nearest Tall Club. Send self-addressed, stamped envelope (SASE) for information.

3400—TARGET STORES (Target All-Around Scholarships)

Citizen's Scholarship Foundation
1505 Riverview Road
Street Peter MN 56082-0480
800/316-6142
Internet: www.target.com

AMOUNT: $1,000-$10,000
DEADLINE(S): NOV 1
FIELD(S): All fields of study

Open to well-rounded high school graduates and current college students who volunteer in their communities. Must be US resident under the age of 24.

1,800 awards annually. See website or contact your local Target store for an application.

3401—TARGET STORES (Target Teachers Scholarships)

Citizen's Scholarship Foundation
1505 Riverview Road
Street Peter MN 56082-0480
800/316-6142
Internet: www.target.com

AMOUNT: $500-$1,500
DEADLINE(S): NOV 1
FIELD(S): All fields of study

Open to teachers and school administrators to further their education through classes, seminars, and other staff development opportunites.

1,800 awards annually (2 per store) + 96 District Teacher Scholarships annually. See website or contact your local Target store for an application.

3402—TEEN MAGAZINE (Miss Teenage America Program)

6420 Wilshire Blvd., 15th Floor
Los Angeles CA 90048
323/782-2950

AMOUNT: $10,000
DEADLINE(S): SEP 15
FIELD(S): All fields of study

Open to young women between the ages of 12 and 18. Candidates are judged on scholastic achievement, individual accomplishment, community service, poise, appearance, and personality. Competition is held in Los Angeles, CA.

Write for complete information.

3403—TEKTRONIX FOUNDATION (Scholarship for Dependent Children of Tektronix Employees)

P.O. Box 1114
Grass Valley CA 95945-1114
503/685-4030

AMOUNT: $4,000
DEADLINE(S): MAR 15
FIELD(S): All fields of study

Open to dependents of Tektronix employees who are high school seniors planning to attend a US college or university.

Contact Max Palmer, Scholarship Coordinator, at above address for an application.

3404—TENNESSEE STUDENT ASSISTANCE CORPORATION (Ned McWherter Scholars Program)

Parkway Towers, Suite 1900
404 James Robertson Parkway
Nashville TN 37243-0820
615/741-1346 or 800/342-1663

AMOUNT: $6,000 for max. of 4 yrs.
DEADLINE(S): FEB 15
FIELD(S): Any field of study

Scholarships for entering freshmen with at least a 3.5 high school GPA and an ACT of 29 or SAT in the top 5% nationally. Must be a resident of Tennessee AND must attend an eligible Tennessee institution.

Renewable for 4 years. Contact your high school guidance office or the address above in December for an application.

3405—TENNESSEE STUDENT ASSISTANCE CORPORATION (Robert C. Byrd Honors Scholarship Program)

Parkway Towers, Suite 1950
404 James Robertson Parkway
Nashville TN 37243-0820
615/741-1346 or 800/342-1663

AMOUNT: $1,500
DEADLINE(S): APR 1
FIELD(S): Any field of study at an accredited postsecondary institution

For Tennessee high school seniors or GED students, the award must be utilized in the same year of graduation. Students must have achieved a 3.5 GPA or have an average GED score of 57. Students with at least a 3.0 GPA and an ACT or SAT in the top quartile nationally may also apply.

Contact the high school guidance office or the above address for more information.

3406—TERESA F. HUGHES TRUST

Hawaiian Community Foundation
900 Fort Street Mall, Suite 1300
Honolulu HI 96813
808/566-5570

AMOUNT: Varies
DEADLINE(S): Ongoing
FIELD(S): All fields of study

Scholarships to financially needy Hawaiian residents who are orphans, half-orphans, social orphans (neglected or abused), and children born out-of-wedlock, for preschool, summer programs, private school, and college.

Write to Hawaiian Community Foundation at above address for details.

3407—TEXAS A&M UNIVERSITY (Academic Excellence Awards)

Student Financial Aid Dept.
College Station TX 77843-1252
409/845-3236/3987

AMOUNT: $500-$1,500
DEADLINE(S): MAR 1
FIELD(S): All fields of study

Open to full-time undergraduate and graduate students at Texas A&M University. Awards are intended to recognize and assist students who are making excellent scholastic progress, campus and community activities, leadership positions, and work experience.

Approximately 600 awards per year. Awards granted for one year. Applications are available at the student financial aid office during January and February.

3408—TEXAS A&M UNIVERSITY (Opportunity Award Scholarship)

Student Financial Aid Office
College Station TX 77843-1252
409/845-3236/3987

AMOUNT: $500- $2,500
DEADLINE(S): JAN 15
FIELD(S): All fields of study

Scholarships to Texas A&M University for college freshmen with outstanding high school records. Selection based on leadership ability, character, SAT scores, activities, and high school record. US citizen or permanent resident.

Recipients from outside Texas receive a waiver on non-resident tuition. Contact financial aid office for complete information.

3409—TEXAS A&M UNIVERSITY (President's Achievement Award Scholarship and Aggie Spirit Award Scholarship)

Office of Honors Programs & Academic Scholarships
College Station TX 77843-1252
409/845-1957

AMOUNT: President's: $3,000/yr.; Aggies: $1,000/yr.
DEADLINE(S): JAN 8
FIELD(S): All fields of study

This competitive academic scholarship program provides 4-year scholarships for African-American and Hispanic high school seniors who will be attending Texas A&M University. For US citizens or permanent residents. Must maintain 2.5 GPA to remain in good scholarship standing.

Recipients from outside Texas receive a waiver of non-resident tuition.

3410—TEXAS A&M UNIVERSITY (President's Endowed Scholarship; Lechner Scholarship; McFadden Scholarship)

Office of Honors Programs & Academic Scholarships
College Station TX 77843-1252
409/845-1957

AMOUNT: $2,000-$3,000 per year over 4 years
DEADLINE(S): JAN 8
FIELD(S): All fields of study

For high school seniors who will be attending Texas A&M. Must score 1300 or higher on SAT (or equivalent of 30 on ACT) and rank in the top 10% of high school graduating class or are National Merit Scholarship semi-finalists.

US citizenship or legal residency required. Non-Texans qualify for a waiver on non-resident tuition.

3411—TEXAS A&M UNIVERSITY (Scholarships, Grants, and Loans)

Division of Student Affairs
College Station TX 77843-1252
409/845-3236/3987

AMOUNT: Varies
DEADLINE(S): Varies
FIELD(S): All fields of study

Texas A&M University offers several scholarship and loan programs. They are awarded on the basis of academic criteria and/or combinations of financial need, campus/community activities, leadership positions, and work experience. Some are for minorities, teacher candidates, cadets, and Texas high school class valedictorians. Applicants do not have to be prior Texas residents and should begin inquiries as high school seniors.

Send to above location for comprehensive information.

3412—TEXAS ELECTRIC COOPERATIVES INC. (Ann Lane Homemaker Scholarship)

P.O. Box 9589
Austin TX 78766-9589
512/454-0311

AMOUNT: $1,000
DEADLINE(S): MAR 1
FIELD(S): Home Economics

Open to Texas residents who are graduating high school seniors and active members of a local Future Homemakers of America chapter. Award tenable at accredited undergraduate colleges or universities. Must be US citizen.

Write for complete information.

3413—TEXAS HIGHER EDUCATION COORDINATING BOARD (Scholarships, Grants, and Loans)

Capitol Station
P.O. Box 12788
Austin TX 78711-2788
512/427-6340 or 800/242-3062
TDD: 800/735-2988

AMOUNT: Varies
DEADLINE(S): Varies (with program)
FIELD(S): All fields of study

Open to students attending Texas institutions. Numerous state-administered student financial aid programs (including scholarships, grants, and loans) are offered.

Contact your school's financial aid office or write to the address above for the booklet "Financial Aid for Texas Students" which describes all programs in detail.

3414—THE AMERICAN LEGION, DEPARTMENT OF MAINE (Daniel E. Lambert Memorial Scholarship)

P.O. Box 900
Waterville ME 04903-0900
None given

AMOUNT: Not specified
DEADLINE(S): MAY 1
FIELD(S): All fields of study in an accredited college or vocational technical school

Open to students showing evidence of being enrolled in or attending an accredited school. Must be of good character and have demonstrated that he/she believes in the American way of life.

Parent must be a veteran.

3415—THE AMERICAN LEGION, DEPT. OF SOUTH CAROLINA (Robert E. David Children's Scholarship Fund)

P.O. Box 11355
Columbia SC 29211
803/799-1992
FAX: 803/771-9831

AMOUNT: $500
DEADLINE(S): MAY 1
FIELD(S): All fields of study

Open to undergraduates in any area of study who are residents of South Carolina. Must have a relative who is a member of the American Legion in South Carolina. Financial statement and copies of state and federal tax returns must be submitted with application.

5-10 awards annually. Renewable—must reapply each year. Write to above address for complete information.

3416—THE AU EDUCATION FOUNDATION FOR CHINESE

499 East Taylor Street
San Jose CA 95112
Written inquiry

AMOUNT: $1,000
DEADLINE(S): MAR 1
FIELD(S): All fields of study

For California high school seniors of Chinese descent with Chinese family names. Three categories: 1) high achievers with financial need (10); 2) foreign students with financial need (5); 3) exceptionally high achievers based on merit alone (5).

20 awards. Send SASE to above location for details.

3417—THE AUGUSTUS SOCIETY (Scholarships)

P.O. Box 28255
Las Vegas NV 89126
Written inquiry

AMOUNT: $1,500
DEADLINE(S): None
FIELD(S): All fields of study

College scholarships for students of Italian-American ancestry who are residents of Clark County, Nevada. Considerations are need and ability.

Contact organization for details.

3418—THE BARKER FOUNDATION, INC.

P.O. Box 328
Nashua NH 03061-0328
Written inquiry

AMOUNT: Varies
DEADLINE(S): None specified
FIELD(S): All fields of study

Undergraduate scholarships for residents of New Hampshire.

Financial need, academic performance, and recommendations are all considered. Send SASE to above location for details.

3419—THE BRYN MAWR SCHOOL (Grants)

109 West Melrose Ave.
Baltimore MD 21210
410/323-8800
FAX: 410/377-8963
E-mail: @brynmawr.pvt.k12.md.us
Internet:
www.brynmawr.pvt.k12.md.us

AMOUNT: Varies
DEADLINE(S): JAN 15
FIELD(S): All fields of study

Grants for girls in a private school in Baltimore, MD, in grades K-12. Must be US citizen or permanent resident. Must demonstrate financial need.

Renewable, but must reapply each year.

3420—THE BUFFETT FOUNDATION

222 Keiwit Plaza
Omaha NE 68131
402/451-6011

AMOUNT: Tuition and fees for Nebraska state colleges and universities; $500 per semester at other institutions
DEADLINE(S): APR 15; OCT 15
FIELD(S): All areas of study

Scholarships for financially needy residents of Nebraska.

Must demonstrate financial need. Send SASE to Allen Greenberg, c/o Devon Buffett, P.O. Box 4508, Decatur, IL 62525; 402/451-6011.

3421—THE CAMBRIDGE SCHOOL OF WESTON (Scholarships)

Georgian Road
Weston MA 02193
781/642-8650
FAX: 781-899-3870
E-mail: adm@csw.org

Internet: www.csw.org
AMOUNT: Up to full tuition
DEADLINE(S): FEB 10
FIELD(S): All fields of study

Need-based, work-study tuition scholarships for this private high school in Massachusetts. For US citizens.

60 annual awards. Renewable. Contact Arnold J. Klingenberg at above location.

3422—THE CHARTER FUND

370 17th Street, Suite 5300
Denver CO 80202
303/572-1727

AMOUNT: Varies
DEADLINE(S): Varies
FIELD(S): All areas of study

Scholarships to Colorado high school seniors.

Write or phone Cindy Kennedy at above location after Feb. 1 requesting application.

3423—THE COLORADO SPRINGS SCHOOL (K-12 Scholarships)

21 Broadmoor Ave.
Colorado Springs CO 80906
719/475-9747
FAX: 719/475-9864

AMOUNT: Up to $2,500
DEADLINE(S): Varies
FIELD(S): All fields of study

Scholarships and other financial aid available for students at this independent, private school in Colorado Springs. A day school for all grades K-12 as well as a boarding school for grades 9-12.

Contact above location for details.

3424—THE CULTURAL SOCIETY, INC.

200 West 19th Street
Panama City FL 32045
Written inquiry

AMOUNT: Varies
DEADLINE(S): Ongoing
FIELD(S): All areas of study

Scholarship for Muslim students.

Write to Dr. Yahya Abdul Rahim, President, at above address for application requirements.

3425—THE CYPRUS CHILDREN'S FUND, INC. (Scholarship Endowment)

13 East 40th Street
New York NY 10016

212/696-4590 or 800/775-7217
AMOUNT: Varies
DEADLINE(S): MAY 5
FIELD(S): All fields of study

To students of Greek or Greek Cypriot origin. Applicants can be US residents, US citizens, or citizens of Greece or Cyprus. May be pursuing studies in accredited college or university in the US, Greece, or Cyprus.

1 scholarship annually. Financial need determines award. Applications must be typewritten and include various documents—please write or call for complete information.

3426—THE DAVID AND DOVETTA WILSON SCHOLARSHIP FUND (Scholarships)

115-67 237th Street
Elmont NY 11003
800/759-7512 or 516/285-4573
FAX: 516/285-8532
E-mail: DAWSF4@aol.com
Internet: www.wilsonfund.org

AMOUNT: $1,000
DEADLINE(S): MAR 1
FIELD(S): All fields of study

Scholarships for college-bound high school seniors who are US citizens and selected for their academic achievement and involvement in community and religious activities. Recipients pursuing careers in the social sciences, education, public service, and journalism can receive additional awards.

$20 application fee. To receive a list of the last 9 winners, send SASE to above address. 9 annual awards. Financial need a consideration.

3427—THE E. PERRY AND GRACE BEATTY MEMORIAL FOUNDATION

P.O. Box 450
Youngstown OH 44501
Written inquiry

AMOUNT: $1,000
DEADLINE(S): Ongoing
FIELD(S): All fields of study

Scholarships for residents of Ohio.

Write to National City Bank, Northeast, at above address for current guidelines.

3428—THE EDDIE G. ROBINSON FOUNDATION (Scholarships)

18310 Redriver Dawn
San Antonio TX 78259
Phone/FAX: 210/495-3313

E-mail: erob@txdirect.net

AMOUNT: Up to $5,000

DEADLINE(S): DEC 31

FIELD(S): All fields of study

Scholarships for Louisiana college-bound 8th graders and high school seniors who demonstrate leadership, academic, and/or athletic skills. Additionally, one scholarship is for students with demonstrated financial need. The awards for 8th graders will be held in an account for later use in college. Recipients must attend accredited institutions.

Contact organization for details.

3429—THE EDMUND F. MAXWELL FOUNDATION (Scholarships)

P.O. Box 22537
Seattle WA 98122-0537
E-mail: admin@maxwell.org
Internet: www.maxwell.org

AMOUNT: $3,500

DEADLINE(S): APR 30

FIELD(S): All fields of study

Scholarships for entering freshmen who reside in Western Washington and plan to attend accredited independent colleges or universities. Combined SAT scores of over 1200 required. Must demonstrate financial need, ability, aptitude, and a promise of useful citizenship.

Applicants are required to write an essay of up to 500 words describing an event or person you feel "has changed or significantly impacted your life."

3430—THE EDUCATION RESOURCES INSTITUTE (Parent Loans for Elementary and Secondary Education—PLEASE)

P.O. Box 312
Boston MA 02117-0312
800/255-8374
FAX: 888/329-8374
Internet: teri.org

AMOUNT: $500-$20,000/yr. ($80,000 max. total)

DEADLINE(S): None

FIELD(S): All fields of study

Elementary and secondary students enrolled at TERI-approved, private institutions are eligible for a PLEASE loan. To qualify, parents or other creditworthy individuals must have established, satisfactory credit history; sufficient current income of at least $1,500/month to meet current liabilities; and stable residence and employment history. At least one applicant must be US citizen or permanent resident, and have been residing in the US for the previous two years.

Low interest rates. Allows up to 10 years for repayment, depending on amount borrowed. Repayment begins within 45 days after funds are dispersed (at least $50/month). No prepayment penalty. Contact Customer Service for more information.

3431—THE FALMOUTH INSTITUTE SCHOLARSHIP

3702 Pender Drive, Suite 300
Fairfax VA 22030-6066
703/641-9100

AMOUNT: $1,000

DEADLINE(S): MAY 1

FIELD(S): Any field of study

The Falmouth Institute will award a $1,000 scholarship to a Native American high school student planning to attend a two- or four-year accredited school of higher education. The award will be determined by academic achievement and financial need. Proof of tribal enrollment and high school transcripts will be required for the application.

Write to Jeffrey S. Marciano at the above address for complete information.

3432—THE FLINN FOUNDATION (Flinn Scholarships)

3300 N. Central Ave., Suite 2300
Phoenix AZ 85012-2513
602/274-9000
FAX: 602/274-3194
E-mail: fscholars@enet.net

AMOUNT: $40,000 value (total for four years)

DEADLINE(S): NOV 1

FIELD(S): All fields of study

A full scholarship for students who have been accepted at Arizona State University, Northern Arizona University, or the University of Arizona. Highly competitive. For US citizens and legal residents of Arizona for two years prior to the application deadline. Must have at least a 3.5 GPA and rank in the top 5 percent of high school class. Merit is the only factor considered, which includes academic assessment and personal achievement.

20 awards yearly. Includes two travel-study experiences abroad. Must submit progress reports and evidence of participation in campus activities for renewals.

3433—THE FOUNDATION OF THE Street ANDREW'S SOCIETY OF PHILADELPHIA (Study-Abroad Scholarships)

620 Golf Club Road
Newtown Square PA 19073
Written inquiry

AMOUNT: Varies

DEADLINE(S): Varies

FIELD(S): All areas of study

Scholarships for US citizens of Scottish descent who are from the Philadelphia, Pennsylvania, area who wish to spend their junior year abroad.

Write to organization for details.

3434—THE FRANK H. & EVA BUCK FOUNDATION (Frank H. Buck Scholarships)

P.O. Box 5610
Vacaville CA 95696
707/446-7700

AMOUNT: Tuition, books, room & board

DEADLINE(S): DEC 1

FIELD(S): All fields of study

Open to unique students (from the 9th grade forward) who have an overwhelming motivation to succeed in all endeavors. Preference is given to residents of Solano, Napa, Yolo, Sacramento, San Joaquin, and Contra Costa counties. Renewable.

For students in private secondary schools and specialized trade schools as well as universities and college. Applications available in mid-Sept; apply by Dec. 1.

3435—THE GERBER FOUNDATION (Scholarship Program)

5 So. Division Ave.
Fremont MI 49412
616/924-3175

AMOUNT: $1,500/yr.

DEADLINE(S): MAR 31

FIELD(S): All areas of study

Undergraduate scholarship for dependents of a Gerber Products Company associate. Must have GPA of 2.0 or above.

Renewable for three years. Contact above location for details.

3436—THE GRAND RAPIDS FOUNDATION (Edwin F. Doyle Scholarship)

209-C Waters Bldg.
161 Ottawa Ave. NW
Grand Rapids MI 49503-2703

616/454-1751
FAX: 616/454-6455

AMOUNT: Varies
DEADLINE(S): APR 3
FIELD(S): All fields of study

Grants are available for seniors graduating from Lowell High School, Kent County, Michigan.

Apply through the Director of Student Services at Lowell High School.

3437—THE GRAND RAPIDS FOUNDATION (Lavina Laible Scholarship)

209-C Waters Bldg.
161 Ottawa Ave. NW
Grand Rapids MI 49503-2703
616/454-1751
FAX: 616/454-6455

AMOUNT: Varies
DEADLINE(S): APR 3
FIELD(S): All fields of study

Grants are available to Grand Rapids Community College women students transferring to the University of Michigan for their junior year.

Apply through the Financial Aid Office of Grand Rapids Community College.

3438—THE GRAND RAPIDS FOUNDATION (Scholarships)

209-C Waters Bldg.
161 Ottawa Ave. NW
Grand Rapids MI 49503-2703
616/454-1751
FAX: 616/454-6455

AMOUNT: Varies
DEADLINE(S): APR 3
FIELD(S): All fields of study

Must be Kent County resident for at least 3 years and have 3.0 or better GPA. Can be part- or full-time students at a local Grand Rapids area college or a full-time student at a college of their choice in Michigan, excluding the seven local colleges listed.

Send SASE to above address for complete information.

3439—THE HARLEY SCHOOL (Grants)

1981 Clover Street
Rochester NY 14618
716/442-1770
FAX: 716/442-5758

AMOUNT: Varies
DEADLINE(S): MAR 15
FIELD(S): All fields of study

Need-based grants available to attend this independent, coeducational school which includes kindergarten through 12th grade. Must submit documentation indicating financial need.

125-130 annual grants. Renewable. Must maintain an overall "C" average. Contact school for details.

3440—THE HELLENIC FOUNDATION

P.O. Box 7224
York PA 17405
Written inquiry

AMOUNT: Tuition, books, and living expenses
DEADLINE(S): Ongoing
FIELD(S): All fields of study

Scholarships to financially needy residents of Pennsylvania for attendance at colleges and universities.

Write to John F. Grove, Jr., Trustee, at above location for details. Include information regarding academic records, recommendaitons, and statement of financial need.

3441—THE HORIZONS FOUNDATION (Joseph Towner Fund for Gay and Lesbian Families)

870 Market Street, #1155
San Francisco CA 94102
415/398-2333

AMOUNT: $500/term
DEADLINE(S): JUN 15
FIELD(S): All fields of study

Scholarships for postsecondary students who have at least one lesbian or gay parent residing in one of the following Bay Area counties: Alameda, Contra Costa, Marin, San Francisco, San Mateo, Santa Clara, Napa, Sonoma, and Solano.

Must have 2.5 GPA or better.

3442—THE HUDSON SCHOOL (Scholarships)

506 Park Ave.
Hoboken NJ 07030
201/659-8335
FAX: 201/222-3669
E-mail: Hudson@Hudsonet.com

AMOUNT: $500-$5,000
DEADLINE(S): MAR 15
FIELD(S): All fields of study

Scholarships available to attend this independent, coeducational school which includes grades 5 through 12. Students must qualify by scoring at or above 90th percentile on admission test, present a

school transcript, and letters of recommendation that indicate their ability to handle a vigorous program of studies, a passion for the arts and sciences, and good character. Financial need considered.

50-60 annual awards. Renewable depending on performance. Contact school for details.

3443—THE JACKIE ROBINSON FOUNDATION (Scholarships)

3 West 35th Street
New York NY 10001-2204
212/290-8600
Internet: www.jackierobinson.org/
Scholar/Prog/Src/lower.html

AMOUNT: $5,000/yr. for 4 years
DEADLINE(S): APR 1
FIELD(S): All fields of study

Scholarships for college-bound high school seniors who are members of a minority group. Program also includes personal and career counseling on a year-round basis, assistance obtaining summer jobs, and permanent employment after graduation. Financial need, leadership potential, high academic achievement, and satisfactory SAT or ACT scores required.

Contact organization for details and/or check website.

3444—THE JANICE AND BEN GROMET FUND FOR DISADVANTAGED CHILDREN

900 Fort Street Mall, Suite 1300
Honolulu HI 96813
808/955-5544

AMOUNT: Varies
DEADLINE(S): Varies
FIELD(S): All fields of study

Scholarships for financially needy residents of Hawaii who have graduated from Hawaii high schools. Academic achievement, financial need, special talents, and results of personal interview are all considered.

Renewable. Write to Charles Rolles, President, through Hawaii Community Foundation at above address for application deadline and other details.

3445—THE JERUSALEM FELLOWSHIPS (Internships in Israel for Leaders)

2124 Broadway, Suite 244
New York NY 10023
800/FELLOWS
E-mail: jf@aish.edu
Internet: www.jerusalemfellowships.org

AMOUNT: $3,500 and up
DEADLINE(S): Varies
FIELD(S): All fields of study

Program for young Jewish student leaders to deepen their understanding of the people of and explore the land of Israel. Open to all Jewish students; however, additional and more valuable scholarships are available in Alabama and the Southeastern United States through the Ruttenberg Foundation of Birmingham, AL. Additional programs available at Rutgers, Cornell, Penn State, U of Georgia, Emory, Tulane, and U of Alabama.

Check website for details. Applications available online or at above location; $25 application fee.

3446—THE KIMBO FOUNDATION

1245 Howard Street
San Francisco CA 94103
415/522-5100

AMOUNT: $1,000
DEADLINE(S): JUN 1
FIELD(S): All fields of study

Scholarships for financially needy students of Korean descent residing in California. For use at four-year colleges and universities. High school seniors and current undergraduates may apply.

Application process includes essay in English or Korean. Program is announced in the *Korea Central Daily* paper in March or April every years. Send SASE to Mr. Yeon Taek, *Korea Central Daily,* at above address for details.

3447—THE KISKI SCHOOL (Financial Aid)

1888 Brett Lane
Saltsburg PA 15681
724/639-8467
FAX: 724/639-8467

AMOUNT: Up to $19,000
DEADLINE(S): APR 1
FIELD(S): All fields of study

Financial aid to attend this private college preparatory secondary school, grades 9-12. Award is based on family's financial need. US citizenship required.

Renewable. Contact school for details.

3448—THE KNOTT SCHOLARSHIP FUNDS (Scholarships)

Street Mary's Seminary & University
5400 Roland Ave.
Baltimore MD 21210-1929
410/323-4300

AMOUNT: Full tuition
DEADLINE(S): None specified
FIELD(S): All fields of study

Open to Catholic students to attend Catholic parish elementary or Catholic secondary school in Baltimore (city) or the counties of Baltimore, Carroll, Frederick, Harford, Anne Arundel, or Howard, or one of the 3 Catholic colleges in Maryland. Residency in the Archdiocese of Baltimore is required. Scholarships based primarily on outstanding academic achievement.

Student involvement in church, school, and community taken into account. Send business-sized, self-addressed stamped envelope for information, stating level of education.

3449—THE KOREAN AMERICAN SCHOLARSHIP FOUNDATION (Scholarships)

P.O. Box 486
Pacific Palisades CA 90272
310/459-4080
Internet: www.kasf.org

AMOUNT: Up to $1,000
DEADLINE(S): JAN 31
FIELD(S): All fields of study

Scholarships for students of Korean descent who are US citizens or permanent residents.

Send SASE to Scholarship Committee at above address or visit website.

3450—THE MADEIRA SCHOOL (Scholarships)

8328 Georgetown Road
McLean VA 22102
703/556-8273
FAX: 703/821-2845
E-mail: admissions@madeira.org
Internet: www.madeira.org

AMOUNT: Varies
DEADLINE(S): FEB 15
FIELD(S): All fields of study

Need-based and merit scholarships available to freshman and sophomore girls attending this independent girls college preparatory school which encompasses grades 9-12. Although scholarships are for boarding students, the institution also operates as a day school.

Renewable. Contact school for details.

3451—THE MILLER SCHOOL OF ALBEMARLE (Grants)

1000 Samuel Miller Loop
Charlottesville VA 22903

804/823-4805
FAX: 804/823-6617
E-mail: jim@millerschool.org
Internet: www.millerschool.org

AMOUNT: Average $4,500
DEADLINE(S): JUN 1
FIELD(S): All fields of study

Financial aid is available for needy students attending this independent school in Virginia which includes 5-12. The school has both boarding and day students.

35-45 annual awards. Student population is approximately 110.

3452—THE NATIONAL HEMOPHILIA FOUNDATION (Kevin Child Scholarship)

116 W. 32nd Street, 11th Fl.
New York NY 10001
212/328-3700 or 800/42-HANDI
FAX: 212/328-3799
E-mail: info@hemophilia.org
Internet: www.hemophilia.org

AMOUNT: $1,000
DEADLINE(S): JUL 3
FIELD(S): All fields of study

Scholarships for college students with a bleeding disorder (hemophilia, etc.) through HANDI (Hemophilia and AIDS/HIV Network for the Dissemination of Information).

Contact HANDI at above location for applications.

3453—THE NATIONAL ITALIAN AMERICAN FOUNDATION (Capital Area Regional Scholarship)

1860 19th Street NW
Washington DC 20009
202/530-5315

AMOUNT: $1,000
DEADLINE(S): MAY 31
FIELD(S): For all areas of study

For students of Italian family heritage residing in Maryland, Virginia, West Virginia, or Washington DC. Write a 2- to 3-page typed essay on a family member or a personality you consider: "An Italian American Hero." For undergraduates.

Write for application and details. 4 awards given. Also considered are academic merit, financial need, and community service.

3454—THE NATIONAL ITALIAN AMERICAN FOUNDATION (Italian Regional Scholarship)

1860 19th Street NW
Washington DC 20009

202/530-5315
AMOUNT: $1,000
DEADLINE(S): MAY 31
FIELD(S): For all areas of study

For undergraduate students of Italian family heritage accepted at Italian universities for courses offering credits toward their undergraduate degrees. Write a 2- to 3-page typed essay on a family member or a personality you consider: "An Italian American Hero."

Academic merit, financial need, and community service. Contact organization for application details.

3455—THE NATIONAL ITALIAN AMERICAN FOUNDATION (Lower Mid-Atlantic Regional Scholarship)

1860 19th Street NW
Washington DC 20009
202/530-5315

AMOUNT: $1,000
DEADLINE(S): MAY 31
FIELD(S): For all areas of study

For students of Italian family heritage residing in Pennsylvania, Southern New Jersey (including Trenton), and Delaware.

Considered are academic merit, financial need, and community service.

3456—THE NATIONAL ITALIAN AMERICAN FOUNDATION (Mid-America Regional Scholarship)

1860 19th Street NW
Washington DC 20009
202/530-5315

AMOUNT: $1,000
DEADLINE(S): MAY 31
FIELD(S): For all areas of study

For students of Italian family heritage residing in Iowa, Missouri, Arkansas, Oklahoma, Kansas, Nebraska, or Colorado. Write a 2- to 3-page typed essay on a family member or a personality you consider: "An Italian American Hero." For undergraduates.

Considered are academic merit, financial need, and community service.

3457—THE NATIONAL ITALIAN AMERICAN FOUNDATION (Mid-Pacific Regional Scholarship)

1860 19th Street NW
Washington DC 20009
202/530-5315

AMOUNT: $1,000
DEADLINE(S): MAY 31

FIELD(S): For all areas of study

For students of Italian family heritage residing in Northern California, Northern Nevada (Reno), Utah, Guam, and Hawaii. Write a 2- to 3-page typed essay on a family member or a personality you consider: "An Italian American Hero." For undergraduates.

Considered are academic merit, financial need, and community service.

3458—THE NATIONAL ITALIAN AMERICAN FOUNDATION (New England Regional Scholarship)

1860 19th Street NW
Washington DC 20009
202/530-5315

AMOUNT: $1,000
DEADLINE(S): MAY 31
FIELD(s): For all areas of study

For undergraduate students of Italian heritage residing in Maine, Vermont, New Hampshire, Massachusetts, Rhode Island, or Connecticut. Write a 2- to 3-page typed essay on a family member or a personality you consider: "An Italian American Hero."

Considered are academic merit, financial need, and community service.

3459—THE NATIONAL ITALIAN AMERICAN FOUNDATION (North Central Regional Scholarship)

1860 19th Street NW
Washington DC 20009
202/530-5315

AMOUNT: $1,000
DEADLINE(S): MAY 31
FIELD(S): For all areas of study

For undergraduate students of Italian family heritage residing in Ohio, Kentucky, Indiana, Illinois, Wisconsin, Michigan, Minnesota, South Dakota, and North Dakota. Write a 2- to 3-page typed essay on a family member or a personality you consider: "An Italian American Hero."

Considered are academic merit, financial need, and community service.

3460—THE NATIONAL ITALIAN AMERICAN FOUNDATION (North Regional Scholarship)

1860 19th Street NW
Washington DC 20009
202/530-5315

AMOUNT: $1,000
DEADLINE(S): MAY 31

FIELD(S): For all areas of study

For students of Italian family heritage residing in Washington state, Oregon, Idaho, Montana, Wyoming, and Alaska. Write a 2- to 3-page typed essay on a family member or a personality you consider: "An Italian American Hero." For undergraduates.

Considered are academic merit, financial need, and community service.

3461—THE NATIONAL ITALIAN AMERICAN FOUNDATION (Street Anselm's College Scholarship)

1860 19th Street NW
Washington DC 20009
202/530-5315

AMOUNT: $5,000
DEADLINE(S): MAY 31
FIELD(S): For all areas of study

For undergraduate students of Italian heritage entering Street Anselm's College, New Hampshire. For students who are NOT residents of New England, Maine, Vermont, New Hampshire, Massachusetts, Rhode Island, or Connecticut.

Considered are academic merit, financial need, and community service. Tenable ONLY at Street Anselm's College.

3462—THE NATIONAL ITALIAN AMERICAN FOUNDATION (Southeast Regional Scholarship)

1860 19th Street NW
Washington DC 20009
202/530-5315

AMOUNT: $1,000
DEADLINE(S): MAY 31
FIELD(S): For all areas of study

For students of Italian family heritage residing in North Carolina, South Carolina, Georgia, and Florida. Write a 2- to 3-page typed essay on a family member or a personality you consider: "An Italian American Hero." For undergraduates.

4 awards given. Also considered are academic merit, financial need, and community service.

3463—THE NATIONAL ITALIAN AMERICAN FOUNDATION (South Central Regional Scholarship)

1860 19th Street NW
Washington DC 20009
202/530-5315

AMOUNT: $1,000
DEADLINE(S): MAY 31

FIELD(S): For all areas of study

For students of Italian family heritage residing in Alabama, Mississippi, Tennessee, Louisiana, and Texas. Write a 2- to 3-page typed essay on a family member or a personality you consider: "An Italian American Hero." For undergraduates.

4 awards given. Also considered are academic merit, financial need, and community service.

3464—THE NATIONAL ITALIAN AMERICAN FOUNDATION (Southwest Regional Scholarship)

1860 19th Street NW
Washington DC 20009
202/530-5315

AMOUNT: $1,000
DEADLINE(S): MAY 31
FIELD(S): For all areas of study

For undergraduates of Italian family heritage residing in Southern California, Southern Nevada (Las Vegas), Arizona, and New Mexico. Write a 2- to 3-page typed essay on a family member or a personality you consider: "An Italian American Hero."

4 awards given. Also considered are academic merit, financial need, and community service.

3465—THE NATIONAL ITALIAN AMERICAN FOUNDATION (Upper Mid-Atlantic Regional Scholarship)

1860 19th Street NW
Washington DC 20009
202/530-5315

AMOUNT: $1,000
DEADLINE(S): MAY 31
FIELD(S): For all areas of study

For students of Italian family heritage residing in New York or Northern New Jersey (north of Trenton). Write a 2- to 3-page typed essay on a family member or a personality you consider: "An Italian American Hero." For undergraduates.

4 awards given. Also considered are academic merit, financial need, and community service.

3466—THE OVERLAKE SCHOOL (Scholarships)

20301 NE 108th
Redmond WA 98053-7499
425/868-1000
FAX: 425/868-6770
E-mail: mkrauss@overlade.org

Internet: www.overlake.org
AMOUNT: Varies
DEADLINE(S): FEB 1
FIELD(S): All fields of study

Financial aid for students already accepted and enrolled at this independent, nondenominational 5-12 college preparatory school in the state of Washington. Must demonstrate financial need.

65 awards yearly. Contact school for details.

3467—THE PARKERSBURG AREA COMMUNITY FOUNDATION (Scholarships)

501 Avery Street
Parkersburg WV 26102
304/428-4438
FAX: 304/428-1200
E-mail: pkbgcomfdn@
alpha.wvup.wvnet.edu

AMOUNT: Varies
DEADLINE(S): Varies
FIELD(S): All fields of study

This Foundation administers more than 40 different scholarship funds. Many are for high school seniors at specific area high schools; others are for dependents of employees of certain companies or are for specific subject areas.

Contact organization for details.

3468—THE PAUL & DAISY SOROS FELLOWSHIPS FOR NEW AMERICANS (Graduate Fellowships)

400 West 59th Street
New York NY 10019
212/547-6926
FAX: 212/548-4623
E-mail: pdsoros_fellows@sorosny.org
Internet: www.pdsoros.org

AMOUNT: $20,000/yr. + 1/2 tuition
DEADLINE(S): NOV 30
FIELD(S): All fields of study leading to a graduate degree

Two-year graduate-level fellowships for "New Americans"—1) holds a Green Card, or 2) is a naturalized US citizen, or 3) is the child of two naturalized citizens. Must hold a B.A. degree or be in final year of undergraduate study and be at least 20 but not older than 30 years of age. Must be pursuing a graduate degree in any professional or scholarly discipline, including the Fine and Performing Arts. For use only in the US.

30 awards per year. Applications and details are available from college academic advisors, the Internet, or the organization (see location/website).

3469—THE RETIRED OFFICERS ASSOCIATION (TROA Scholarship Fund)

201 North Washington Street
Alexandria VA 22314-2539
800/245-8762
E-mail: edassist@troa.org
Internet: www.troa.org

AMOUNT: $3,000
DEADLINE(S): MAR 1
FIELD(S): All fields of study

Interest-free loans for full-time undergraduate study. Students must be under age 24, never-married dependent sons and daughters of TROA members, or unmarried dependent sons and daughters of active-duty, reserve, National Guard, and retired enlisted personnel. Students must have a minimum 3.0 GPA. Awards are based on scholastic ability, potential, character, leadership, and financial need. To be used for educational (including living) expenses only.

Renewable for five years. Loan recipients may also be considered for grants. See website or contact TROA for an application.

3470—THE SUMMIT COUNTRY DAY SCHOOL (Financial Aid)

2161 Grandin Road
Cincinnati OH 45208
513/871-4700
FAX: 513/533-5373

AMOUNT: Varies
DEADLINE(S): FEB 20
FIELD(S): All fields of study

Financial aid to attend this private college preparatory secondary school, grades 9-12. Award is based on family's financial need. US citizenship or permanent residency required.

Renewable. Contact school for details.

3471—THE UPS FOUNDATION (The George D. Smith Scholarship Program)

55 Glenlake Parkway NE
Atlanta GA 30328
404/828-6374

AMOUNT: $500-$2,000
DEADLINE(S): FEB
FIELD(S): All fields of study

For high school seniors planning to attend business schools, vocational-technical schools, associate-degree programs, or 4-year colleges. Students must be children of United Parcel Service employees.

Contact local human resources department at UPS for an application and additional information.

3472—THE UPS FOUNDATION (The James E. Casey Scholarship Program)

55 Glenlake Parkway NE
Atlanta GA 30328
404/828-6374

AMOUNT: $2,000-$6,000
DEADLINE(S): DEC
FIELD(S): All fields of study

Open to children of United Parcel Service employees. Students must be attending a four-year degree program. Applicants must provide PSAT scores.

Contact local UPS human resources department for application and complete information.

3473—THE URBAN SCHOOL OF SAN FRANCISCO (Financial Aid)

1563 Page Street
San Francisco CA 94117
415/626-2919
FAX: 415/626-1125
E-mail: jbeam@urban.pvt.k12.ca.us

AMOUNT: $1,000-$5,000
DEADLINE(S): JAN 19
FIELD(S): All fields of secondary school study

Financial aid based on need for students accepted at this private high school in San Francisco.

Contact school for details.

3474—THE WASIE FOUNDATION (Scholarship Program)

US Bank Place, Suite 4700
601 2nd Ave. South
Minneapolis MN 55402
612/332-3883
FAX: 612/332-2440

AMOUNT: $1,000-$14,000
DEADLINE(S): MAR 1
FIELD(S): All fields of study

Scholarships for high school students, college undergraduates, and graduate students of Polish descent who are enrolled in specified private high schools and colleges in Minnesota. Approx. 70 awards per year.

Applicants must be full-time students who can demonstrate financial need. Applications available Sept. 1 in financial aid offices of the institutions. Contact organization for list of schools.

3475—THE WILLIAM LOEB MEMORIAL FUND

P.O. Box 9555
Manchester NH 03108
603/668-4321
800/562-8218, ext. 506

AMOUNT: Varies
DEADLINE(S): MAR 15
FIELD(S): All fields of study

Scholarships for high school seniors who have been New Hampshire residents for at least two years for attendance at colleges, universities, and voc-tech schools. Prime consideration is given to those who demonstrate initiative, involvement, and a high degree of volunteerism in community and school activities. Not based on GPA or financial need.

Send letter, typed and double-spaced, to Jeanne Tancrede, Educational Grants, at above address stating why you feel you deserve a scholarship and how you will better yourself and New Hampshire through the use of the scholarship.

3476—THE WINSTON SCHOOL (The Mary Eggemeyer Fund Grants)

5707 Royal Lane
Dallas TX 75229
214/691-6950
FAX: 214/691-1509
E-mail: amy_smith@winston-sch.org
Internet: www.winston-school.org

AMOUNT: $1,000
DEADLINE(S): JUL 1
FIELD(S): All fields of study

The Winston School enrolls students from grades 1 through 12 who demonstrate average- to above-average intelligence with a diagnosed learning difference.

The grant is for first-time students new to the school.

3477—THIRD MARINE DIVISION ASSOCIATION (Scholarships)

P.O. Box 634
Inverness FL 34451
Written inquiry

AMOUNT: $500-$2,400
DEADLINE(S): APR 15
FIELD(S): All fields of study

Undergrad scholarships for dependent children of USMC and USN personnel who died as a result of service in Vietnam or the Southeast Asia Operations, OR Desert Shield and Desert Storm as a result of service with the 3rd Marine Division.

Also open to children of Association members (living or dead) who held membership 2 years or more. Must demonstrate financial need. Awards renewable. Write for complete information.

3478—THOMAS J. WATSON FOUNDATION (The Thomas J. Watson Fellowship Program)

217 Angell Street
Providence RI 02906-2120
401/274-1952

AMOUNT: $18,000 single; $25,000 with accompanying financial & legal dependent
DEADLINE(S): NOV 1
FIELD(S): All fields of study

Open to graduating seniors at the 48 US colleges on the foundation's roster. Fellowship provides for one year of independent study and travel abroad immediately following graduation.

Candidates must be nominated by their college. Up to 60 awards per year. Write for list of participating institutions and complete information.

3479—TOWSON STATE UNIVERSITY (Scholarship & Award Programs)

Scholarship Office
Towson MD 21252
410-830-2654

AMOUNT: Varies
DEADLINE(S): Varies
FIELD(S): All fields of study

Numerous scholarship and award programs available to entering freshmen and to graduate and transfer students attending Towson State University.

Write for scholarships and awards booklet which describes each program in detail. Awards are for Towson State University students only.

3480—TOZER FOUNDATION (Scholarships)

104 N. Main Street
Stillwater MN 55082
Written inquiry

AMOUNT: Varies
DEADLINE(S): Varies
FIELD(S): All fields of study

Available to students from Pine, Kanabec, and Washington counties in Minnesota for four years of undergraduate studies.

Write to above address for an application.

3481—TRANSPORT WORKERS UNION OF AMERICA (Michael J. Quill Scholarship Fund)

80 West End Ave.
New York NY 10023
212/873-6000

AMOUNT: $1,200
DEADLINE(S): MAY 1
FIELD(S): All fields of study

Open to high school seniors (under 21) who are dependents of TWU members in good standing or of a deceased member who was in good standing at time of death. Dependent brothers or sisters of members in good standing also may apply.

15 scholarships per year. Renewable up to 4 years. Write for complete information.

3482—TREACY COMPANY (Scholarship)

P.O. Box 1700
Helena MT 59624
406/442-3632

AMOUNT: $400/yr.
DEADLINE(S): JUN 15
FIELD(S): All areas of study

For college freshmen and sophomores who reside in Montana, North or South Dakota, or Idaho.

Approximately 50 awards. Contact James O'Connell at above location for details.

3483—TRI-STATE GENERATION AND TRANSMISSION ASSOCIATION (Scholarships)

12076 Grant Street
P.O. Box 33695
Denver CO 80233
303/452-6111

AMOUNT: $500
DEADLINE(S): Varies
FIELD(S): All fields of study

Available to children of Tri-State Generation and Transmission member-system employees or consumers.

2 awards annually. Write to above address for an application.

3484—TRIDENT ACADEMY (Scholarships)

1455 Wakendaw Road
Mt. Pleasant SC 29464
843/884-3494
FAX: 843/884-1483
E-mail: adminis@bellsouth.net
Internet: www.tridentacademy.com

AMOUNT: $1,000-$3,000

DEADLINE(S): JUL 1
FIELD(S): All fields of study

Need-based scholarships for students attending this independent K-12 school in South Carolina for students with diagnosed learning disabilities.

Contact school for details.

3485—TRINITY UNIVERSITY (Various Scholarships)

Financial Aid Office
715 Stadium Drive
San Antonio TX 78212-7200
800/TRINITY or 210/736-8315
Internet: www.trinity.edu/departments/admissions/faid.html

AMOUNT: Up to $10,000
DEADLINE(S): Varies
FIELD(S): All fields of study

Various scholarships and other forms of financial aid based on merit, need, or a combination of these, for students at this private college in San Antonio, TX, which has Presbyterian roots. SAT, ACT, and GPA scores are all considered. Some are specifically for certain subject area, such as music. Music scholarships are based on an audition in person or by tape—for majors or non-majors (up to $2,000/yr.).

See website for scholarship list and how to apply for financial aid and when. Contact the Office of Admissions for application details.

3486—TRINITY-PAWLING SCHOOL (Scholarships/Grants)

300 Route 22
Pawling NY 12564
914/855-4825
FAX: 914/855-3816
E-mail: admit@tps.k12.ny.us
Internet: www.tps.k12.ny.us

AMOUNT: Varies
DEADLINE(S): FEB 15
FIELD(S): All fields of study

Scholarships and grants are available at this independent, college preparatory school for boys, grades 7-12, in Pawling, New York. Must demonstrate financial need.

35 annual awards. Send for information.

3487—TUITION GRANT PROGRAM ADJUTANT GENERAL'S DEPARTMENT (Ohio National Guard Tuition Grant Program)

Adj. Gen. Dept., Attn AGOH-TG
2825 W. Granville Road
Columbus OH 43235

614/889-7143

AMOUNT: Public schools: 60% of tuition; for private schools: 60% of avg. state school fees
DEADLINE(S): NOV 1; FEB 1; APR 1
FIELD(S): All fields of study

Open to undergraduate residents of Ohio with an enlisted obligation of six years in the Ohio National Guard. Provides 12 quarter or 8 semester hours.

Write to the tuition grant office at above address for complete information.

3488—TULANE UNIVERSITY (Scholarships & Fellowships)

Admissions Office
New Orleans LA 70118
504/865-5731
Internet: www.tulane.edu

AMOUNT: Varies
DEADLINE(S): Varies
FIELD(S): All areas of study

Numerous need-based and merit-based scholarship and fellowship programs for undergraduate and graduate study at Tulane University. There is also an honors program for outstanding students accepted for enrollment at Tulane.

Write for complete information.

3489—TWO/TEN INTERNATIONAL FOOTWEAR FOUNDATION (Scholarship Program)

56 Main Street
Watertown MA 02172
617/923-4500 or 800/346-3210

AMOUNT: $200 to $2,000
DEADLINE(S): JAN 15
FIELD(S): All fields of study

Open to children of footwear, leather, and allied industry workers (employed a minimum of 1 year) or to students employed a minimum of 500 hours in one of the above industries. Must be high school senior or within 4 years of graduation.

200-250 awards annually. For full-time undergrad study at 2- or 4-year college, voc-tech, or nursing school. Financial need and superlative academic achievement must be demonstrated. Renewable if criteria continue to be met. Write for complete information.

3490—TY COBB EDUCATIONAL FOUNDATION (Undergraduate Scholarship Program)

P.O. Box 725
Forest Park GA 30051

Written inquiry

AMOUNT: Varies
DEADLINE(S): MAY
FIELD(S): All fields of study

For Georgia residents who have completed at least one academic year in an accredited college with a 'B' grade average. Must demonstrate financial need.

Renewable with reapplication and completion of 45 quarter or 30 semester credit hours. Write for complete information.

3491—TYLENOL (Scholarship Fund)

1505 Riverview Road
P.O. Box 88
Street Peter MN 56082
215/233-8505

AMOUNT: $10,000; $1,000
DEADLINE(S): JAN 17
FIELD(S): All fields of study

Open to US residents who will be attending an undergraduate course of study in the fall at an accredited two- or four-year college, university, or voc-tech school. This includes students currently enrolled in an undergraduate course of study and have one or more years of school remaining. Must demonstrate leadership in community and school activities.

510 awards annually (10 $10,000 & 500 $1,000). See local drug store or contact Citizen's Scholarship Foundation at above address for an application.

3492—U.N.I.T.E. (Philadelphia-South Jersey District Council Scholarship Awards)

Education Director
35 S. 4th Street
Philadelphia PA 19106
215/351-0750

AMOUNT: $1,000 per year
DEADLINE(S): APR 15 (to return application)
FIELD(S): All fields of study

Open to high school students or graduates within 2 years who are children of Philadelphia-South Jersey District Council members of UNITE, International Ladies Garment Workers Union (for at least 2 years) or to children of members who have died within the last 2 years.

Students currently enrolled in college are NOT eligible to apply.

3493—US AIR FORCE ACADEMY (Academy Appointment)

HQ USAFA/RRS (Admissions Office)
2304 Cadet Drive, Suite 200
USAF Academy CO 80840-5025

800/443-9226 or 9267
Internet: www.usafa.edu/rr/

AMOUNT: Full tuition & all costs + salary
DEADLINE(S): JAN 31
FIELD(S): All fields of study

Appointment is for a 4-year undergraduate degree followed by a commission as a second lieutenant in the USAF. Recipients are obligated to five years of active duty. Must be US citizen between the ages of 17 and 22, unmarried, and with no dependents.

Nomination is required for appointment. Essay, interview, and SAT/ACT scores required. Write for information on obtaining nomination and for detailed admission requirements.

3494—US DEPARTMENT OF STATE (Internships)

Recruitment Division
P.O. Box 9317
Arlington VA 22219
Written inquiry

AMOUNT: Varies—unpaid and paid internships
DEADLINE(S): NOV 1; MAR 1; JUL 1
FIELD(S): All fields of study

Internships during summer, fall, or spring through the US Department of State. Some assignments are in the US; some are abroad. Most are unpaid.

Write to organization for application and other details.

3495—US DEPT OF INTERIOR; BUREAU OF INDIAN AFFAIRS (Higher Education Grant Programs)

1849 C Street NW, MS-3512 MIB
Washington DC 20240-0001
202/208-4871
Internet: www.doi.giv/bia

AMOUNT: Varies depending on need
DEADLINE(S): Varies
FIELD(S): All areas of study

Open to enrolled members of Indian tribes or Alaskan native descendants eligible to receive services from the Secretary of the Interior. For study leading to associate's, bachelor's, or graduate degree.

Must demonstrate financial need. Contact home agency, area office, tribe, BIA office, or financial aid office at chosen college. Check website for details, including address and phone numbers of area offices nationwide.

3496—US DEPT OF INTERIOR; BUREAU OF INDIAN AFFAIRS (Higher Education Grant Programs-Northern Calif. & Nevada)

Western Nevada Agency
1677 Hot Springs Road
Carson City NV 89707
702/887-3515
FAX: 702/887-0496
Internet: www.doi.giv/bia

AMOUNT: Varies depending on need
DEADLINE(S): JUL 15; DEC 15
FIELD(S): All areas of study

Open to enrolled members of Indian tribes or Alaskan native descendants eligible to receive services from the Secretary of the Interior who reside in Northern California or Nevada. For study leading to associate's, bachelor's, graduate degrees, or adult education.

Must demonstrate financial need. Contact home agency, area office, tribe, or BIA office. Check website for details, including address and phone numbers of area offices nationwide.

3497—US DEPT. OF EDUCATION (Robert C. Byrd Honors Scholarship Program)

600 Independence Ave. SW
Portals Bldg., Room CY-80
Washington DC 20202-5335
202/260-3394
FAX: 202/401-7532
E-mail: Darlene_Collins@ed.gov

AMOUNT: Up to $1,500/year
DEADLINE(S): Varies (by state)
FIELD(S): All fields of study

Open to outstanding high school seniors who graduate in the same academic year the award is being made or who have a GED and who have applied to or been accepted by an institution of higher education. Must be US citizen or permanent resident.

Available for up to four years of study. State educational agencies receive funding from the US Dept. of Education. Apply through your state board of education or contact school counselor for complete information.

3498—US MARINE CORPS (Naval Reserve Officer Training Corps [NROTC])

College Scholarship Program
801 N. Randolph Street
Arlington VA 22203-9933
800/MARINES

Internet: www.marines.com

AMOUNT: Full scholarship + $150/mo.

DEADLINE(S): DEC 1

FIELD(S): All fields of study

Open to US citizens who are high school seniors or graduates. Requires a four- or eight-year enlistment, qualifying scores on SAT or ACT, and physical qualification by Marine Corps standards.

Renewable yearly.

3499—US SPACE CAMP FOUNDATION (Space Camp, Space Academy, Advanced Space Academy)

P.O. Box 070015
Huntsville AL 35807-7015
800/63-SPACE
Internet: www.spacecamp.com

AMOUNT: Full- or part-tuition

DEADLINE(S): DEC 1; JUN 1 (essays due)

FIELD(S): For all fields of study

Full- or partial-tuition scholarships to Space Camp and related events for deserving students currently attending fourth through twelfth grades. Based on essay competition. The five-day camps are located in California, Florida, and Alabama. An opportunity to learn about and participate in experiences related to our space program and aeronautics.

Call phone number above for scholarship applications, which are available from Oct. 1 to May 1.

3500—UNICO NATIONAL, INC. (Various Scholarships)

72 Burroughs Place
Bloomfield NJ 07003
973/748-9144
FAX: 973/748-9576
E-mail: unico@uniconat.com
Internet: www.uniconat.com

AMOUNT: Varies

DEADLINE(S): Varies

FIELD(S): All fields of study

Scholarship program for Americans of Italian ancestry. Programs are administered through various state chapters.

Contact national organization above to locate state chapters; then contact state chapter for application details.

3501—UNITE (Duchessi-Sallee Scholarship)

1710 Broadway
New York NY 10019

212/265-7000

AMOUNT: $1,000

DEADLINE(S): MAR 15

FIELD(S): All fields of study

3 winners are selected each year for scholarships to any 2-year or 4-year degree-granting college. Awards are made ONLY to incoming freshmen who are the daughter or son of a union member in good standing for 2 years or more.

Scholarship is renewable for one additional year. Write for complete information.

3502—UNITED CHURCH OF CHRIST—SPECIAL HIGHER EDUCATION PROGRAM (Commission for Racial Justice)

700 Prospect Ave.
Cleveland OH 44115-1100
216/736-3786

AMOUNT: $500-$2,000

DEADLINE(S): Varies

FIELD(S): All fields of study

Scholarships for undergraduates who are members of the United Church of Christ and who are members of a minority ethnic group. Considered are essay, extracurricular activities, and personal and career goals.

Renewable. Contact organization for details.

3503—UNITED DAUGHTERS OF THE CONFEDERACY (Scholarships)

Business Office, Memorial Bldg.
328 North Blvd.
Richmond VA 23220-4057
804/355-1636
FAX: 804/353-1396
Internet: www.hsv.tis.nit/~maxs/UDC/index.html

AMOUNT: $800 to $1,000

DEADLINE(S): FEB 15

FIELD(S): All fields of study

Various programs for descendants of worthy Confederate veterans. Applicants who are collateral descendants must be active members of the United Daughters of the Confederacy or of the Children of the Confederacy and MUST be sponsored by a UDC chapter.

Most awards for undergraduate study. For complete information send self-addressed, stamped #10 envelope (SASE) to address above or contact the education director in the division where you reside. Division addresses are on Internet site.

3504—UNITED FEDERATION OF TEACHERS (Albert Shanker College Scholarship Fund)

260 Park Ave. South
New York NY 10010
212/529-2110
FAX: 212/533-2704

AMOUNT: $1,000/yr.

DEADLINE(S): DEC 15

FIELD(S): All fields of study

Open to New York City residents who attend New York City public high schools. Scholarships support undergraduate study at recognized colleges and universities. Financial need and academic standing are considerations.

Students are eligible in the year they graduate. Approximately 250 awards per year. Renewable. Write for complete information.

3505—UNITED FOOD & COMMERCIAL WORKERS INTERNATIONAL UNION (UFCW Scholarship Program)

1775 K Street NW
Washington DC 20006
201/223-3111

AMOUNT: $1,000 per year for 4 years

DEADLINE(S): DEC 31

FIELD(S): All fields of study

Open to UFCW members or high school seniors who are children of members. Applicants must meet certain eligibility requirements. Awards for full-time study only.

7 awards per year. Contact Douglas H. Dority, president, address above for complete information.

3506—UNITED FOOD & COMMERCIAL WORKERS UNION—UFCW LOCAL 555 (L. Walter Derry Scholarship Fund)

P.O. Box 23555
Tigard OR 97223
503/684-2822
FAX: 503/620-3816

AMOUNT: $1,900 (any field) + up to $2,500 (labor relations)

DEADLINE(S): MAY 14

FIELD(S): All fields of study

Members of Local 555 in good standing for at least 1 year prior to application deadline are eligible to apply, or sponsor their child or spouse. Confidential questionnaire, high school & college transcripts, and 3 personal references required. May be used at any accredited college/university, technical/vocational, or junior/community college for any course of study. Additional award in field of labor relations available; submit 500-word essay on plans, with application.

6 awards annually (5 in any field; 1 in labor relations). Contact Larry A. Weirich, Chairman, Scholarship Committee, for an application.

3507—UNITED METHODIST CHURCH (Scholarship and Loan Program)

P.O. Box 871
Nashville TN 37202-0871
615/340-7346
FAX: 615/340-7367
E-mail: jimnose@umhighered.org
Internet: www.gbhem.org
AMOUNT: Varies
DEADLINE(S): JUN 1
FIELD(S): All fields of study

Scholarships and loans for undergraduates and graduate students. Most graduate scholarships are limited to theology, higher education administraiton, or older adults changing careers. Must have been a full and active member of a United Methodist church for at least one year. US citizenship/permanent residency required. Minimum GPA of 2.5 required.

Check with financial aid dept. at your United Methodist college, the chairperson of your annual conference board of Higher Education and campus Ministry, or the address above for application details.

3508—UNITED NEGRO COLLEGE FUND (Scholarships)

8260 Willow Oaks Corporate Drive
Fairfax VA 22031
703/205-3400 or 800/331-2244
Internet: www.uncf.org
AMOUNT: Varies
DEADLINE(S): Varies
FIELD(S): All areas of study

Scholarships available to students who enroll in one of the 39 United Negro College Fund member institutions. Financial need must be established through the financial aid office at a UNCF college.

For information and a list of the UNCF campuses, write to the address above.

3509—UNITED PAPERWORKERS INTER-NATIONAL UNION (Scholarship Program)

P.O. Box 1475
Nashville TN 37202

615/834-8590
AMOUNT: $1,000
DEADLINE(S): MAR 15
FIELD(S): All fields of study

Scholarships open to high school seniors who are sons or daughters of paid-up union members of at least one year. Awards tenable at accredited undergraduate colleges & universities. Must be US or Canadian citizen.

22 awards per year. Recipients are asked to take at least one labor course during their college career. Financial need is a consideration. Write for complete information.

3510—UNITED STUDENT AID FUNDS INC. (Guaranteed Student Loan Program; PLUS Loans)

1912 Capital Ave., #320
Cheyenne WY 82001
307/635-3259
AMOUNT: $2,625 to $5,500
(undergrads); $8,500 (grads)
DEADLINE(S): None
FIELD(S): All fields of study

Low-interest loans are available to Wyoming residents who are citizens or permanent residents of the US and enrolled at least half-time in school. Must demonstrate financial need.

Write for complete information.

3511—UNIVERSITY OF BRIDGEPORT (Undergraduate Scholarships & Grants)

600 University Ave.
Bridgeport CT 06601
203/576-4212 or 800/EXCEL-UB
FAX: 203/576-4051
E-mail: stephen_healey@msn.com
Internet: www.bridgeport.edu
AMOUNT: Varies
DEADLINE(S): Varies
FIELD(S): All fields of study, especially Religion

Undergraduate grants and other award programs are available to both US and international students. Some are merit-based; others are need-based. All majors are considered; however, World Religions applicants stand a very good chance, as it's a relatively new program.

100 full tuition awards + several other awards annually. Renewable for four years with satisfactory academic progress. Contact Stephen Healey, Director, World Religions Program, at the University of Bridgeport.

3512—UNIVERSITY OF CALIFORNIA AT BERKELEY (Undergraduate Scholarships)

Sproul Hall, Room 210
Berkeley CA 94720
510/642-3175
Internet: www.berkeley.edu
AMOUNT: Varies
DEADLINE(S): Varies
FIELD(S): All fields of study

Various scholarships are available to students at UC Berkeley on the basis of academic achievement and financial need. To be considered for scholarships that require financial need, student must have filled out the government FAFSA form.

2,500 awards annually. Entering students should fill out the UC Application for Undergraduate Admissions & Scholarships, and continuing UCB students should complete a UC Berkeley Scholarship Data Sheet (SDS). See your financial aid office for the FAFSA form.

3513—UNIVERSITY OF MICHIGAN (Scholarships and Merit Programs for Undergraduates)

2011 Student Activities Building
Ann Arbor MI 48109-1316
734/763-6600
E-mail: financial.aid@umich.edu
AMOUNT: Varies
DEADLINE(S): MAR 1
FIELD(S): All fields of study

A wide variety of scholarships and merit programs for undergraduates. Michigan residency NOT required. Send for brochure: "A Guide to Scholarships and Merit Programs for Undergraduates" at the Office of Financial Aid at above address. Requirements vary. Entering freshmen will be automatically considered for most programs. Some scholarships are for out-of-state students.

Equal consideration is given to students admitted to the University before February 1 and apply for financial aid by March 1.

3514—UNIVERSITY OF MISSOURI, ROLLA (The Distinguished Scholars Program for Non-Missouri Residents)

G-1 Parker Hall
1870 Miner Circle
Rolla MO 65409-1060
573/341-4282 or 800/522-0938
FAX: 573/341-4274

E-mail: umroll@umr.edu

Internet: www.umr.edu/~enrol/
scholarnonmo.html

AMOUNT: $1,000-$5,000 reduced non-resident fees

DEADLINE(S): FEB 1

FIELD(S): All fields of study

Tuition reduction for out-of-state students at the University of Missouri, Rolla. Top students are automatically considered when they submit the Undergraduate Application for Admission, Financial Aid & Scholarships.

Renewable provided student completes 24 credit hours/year and maintains a 2.5 cumulative GPA.

3515—UNIVERSITY OF NEBRASKA AT LINCOLN (Regents, David, Davis, National Merit, and Departmental Scholarships)

16 Administration Bldg.
Lincoln NE 68588-0411
401/472-2030

AMOUNT: Varies

DEADLINE(S): JAN 15 (preceding fall semester)

FIELD(S): All fields of study

Open to Nebraska high school graduates who have taken the ACT or SAT and sent scores to University of Nebraska, Lincoln. Variety of scholarships available—some for minorities, some based on financial need, and various other requirements.

By applying for admission by Jan. 15 of the preceding fall semester, submitting the need supplement (optional) and the activities resume (optional), the student is competing for approximately 1,500 other individual scholarship programs at UNL. Write for complete information.

3516—UNIVERSITY OF NEW MEXICO (Amigo and Amigo Transfer Scholarships)

Mesa Hall, Room 3020
Albuquerque NM 87131
505/277-6090
FAX: 505/277-5325
E-mail: schol@unm.edu
Internet: www.unm.edu//~schol/
schol.html

AMOUNT: Waiver of out-of-state tuition + $100/semester

DEADLINE(S): JAN 10; AUG 15

FIELD(S): All fields of study

The University of New Mexico offers awards to non-New Mexico residents who are new freshmen or transfer students. Must be US citizen or permanent resident.

Contact Scholarships Office (address above) for complete information.

3517—UNIVERSITY OF NEW MEXICO (Scholarships)

Mesa Hall, Room 3019
Albuquerque NM 87131
505/277-6090
FAX: 505/277-5325
E-mail: schol@unm.edu
Internet: www.unm.edu//
~schol/schol.html

AMOUNT: Varying amounts to $8,000

DEADLINE(S): DEC 1 (Regents & Presidential); FEB 1 (UNM Scholars)

FIELD(S): All fields of study

The University of New Mexico awards to eligible first-time freshmen more than 1,000 scholarships from six major scholarship programs. Considerations include extracurricular activities and personal statement. Must be US citizen or permanent resident.

Contact Scholarships Office (address above) for complete information.

3518—UNIVERSITY OF OXFORD— SOMERVILLE COLLEGE (Janet Watson Bursary)

Somerville College
College Secretary
Oxford OX2 6HD UNITED KINGDOM
1865-270629/19
FAX: 1865-270620

AMOUNT: 3,500 pounds sterling for each of 2 years

DEADLINE(S): MAR 2

FIELD(S): All fields of study

Bursary is offered for US citizens who are graduate students wishing to read for a further degree at the University of Oxford in England. Renewable for a second year.

Write for complete information.

3519—UNIVERSITY OF WINDSOR (Undergraduate Scholarships)

Student Awards Office
Windsor Ontario N9B 3P4 CANADA
519/253-4232

AMOUNT: Approximately $600

DEADLINE(S): MAY 31; DEC 31

FIELD(S): All fields of study

Open to students who are graduates of a US high school, have superior grades, and wish to study at Windsor University in Ontario, Canada. In-course awards are available to those who are already enrolled. Students must complete all admissions requirements.

Renewable for three years if qualifying average is maintained. Write for complete information and a catalog of available undergraduate scholarships.

3520—U.S. COAST GUARD MUTUAL ASSISTANCE (Adm. Roland Student Loan Program)

2100 2nd Street SW
Washington DC 20593-0001
202/267-1683

AMOUNT: Up to $2,700 per year (undergrads); $7,500 (grads)

DEADLINE(S): None specified

FIELD(S): All areas of study

For members and dependents of Coast Guard Mutual Assistance members who are enrolled at least half-time in an approved postsecondary school.

Loans renewable for up to four years. Must reapply annually. Write for complete information.

3521—U.S. DEPARTMENT OF DEFENSE (Student Educational Employment Program)

Alicia Pfenniger, US Army TARDEC
Armament RD&E Center (ARDEC)
ATTN: AMSTA-AR-TDD
Picatinny Arsenal NJ 07908-5000
973/724-3437
Internet: www.acq.osd.mil/ddre/
edugate/s-aindx.html

AMOUNT: Paid employment while in school

DEADLINE(S): None specified

FIELD(S): All fields of study

US citizens. Student Career Experience assigns work to students that relates to their career goals or interests. Includes benefits and can't interfere with academic studies. Noncompetitive conversion to permanent position if requirements met. Student temporary employment is yearly, and the nature of the student's duties doesn't have to be related to academic/career goals. No opportunity for conversion.

Salary from $13,113 to $25,025. Appointment to career experience may not extend beyond 120 days after completion of education and work-study requirements. Students who discontinue their education are disqualified.

3522—U.S. DEPT OF VETERANS AFFAIRS (Vocational Rehabilitation)

810 Vermont Ave. NW (28)
Washington DC 20420

VA regional office in each state or 800-827-1000

AMOUNT: Tuition; books; fees; equipment; subsistence allowance

DEADLINE(S): Varies (Within 12 years from date of notification of entitlement to VA comp)

FIELD(S): All fields of study

Open to US military veterans disabled during active duty, honorably discharged & in need of rehab services to overcome an employment handicap. At least a 20% disability comp rating (or 10% with a serious employment handicap) required.

Program will provide college, trade, technical, on-job or on-farm training (at home or in a special rehab facility if vet's disability requires). Contact nearest VA office for complete information.

3523—U.S. SUBMARINE VETERANS OF WWII (Scholarship Program)

Norfolk Naval Station
1683 Dillingham Blvd.
Norfolk VA 23511
757/451-3660
FAX 757/489-8578

AMOUNT: $1,750/year

DEADLINE(S): APR 15

FIELD(S): All fields of study

For children of paid-up regular members of US submarine veterans of WWII. Applicant must be an unmarried high school senior or have graduated from high school no more than 4 years prior to applying and be under the age of 24.

List those submarines in which your sponsor served during WWII and include sponsor's membership card number when requesting application.

3524—USA TODAY (All-USA Academic Team Award)

1000 Wilson Blvd.
Arlington VA 22229
703/276-5890

AMOUNT: $2,500 + 2-page newspaper article

DEADLINE(S): FEB 21 (postmark)

FIELD(S): All fields of study

Competition open to outstanding high school students nominated by a teacher. Considerations are nominee's academic record, creativity, leadership, and independent scholarly/artistic work which must be described and judged for competition.

Independent endeavor may be in art, music, literature, poetry, scientific research, history, community service, or public affairs. 20 awards per year. Write for complete information.

3525—UTA ALUMNI ASSOCIATION (African-American Endowed Scholarship)

University of Texas at Arlington
Box 19457
Arlington TX 76019
Internet: www.uta.edu/alumni/scholar.htm

AMOUNT: $350

DEADLINE(S): Varies

FIELD(S): All fields of study

Must be a full-time sophomore or higher in good standing at the University of Texas at Arlington. Must have demonstrated financial need and success and be of African-American descent.

1 award annually. Contact UTA Alumni Association for an application.

3526—UTA ALUMNI ASSOCIATION (Frankie S. Hansell Endowed Scholarship)

University of Texas at Arlington
Box 19457
Arlington TX 76019
Internet: www.uta.edu/alumni/scholar.htm

AMOUNT: $1,000

DEADLINE(S): Varies

FIELD(S): All fields of study

For undergraduate or graduate students at the University of Texas at Arlington. Must be US citizen and demonstrate financial need. Preference is given to females.

3 awards annually. Contact UTA Alumni Association for an application.

3527—UTA ALUMNI ASSOCIATION (Hispanic Scholarship)

University of Texas at Arlington
Box 19457
Arlington TX 76019
Internet: www.uta.edu/alumni/scholar.htm

AMOUNT: $250

DEADLINE(S): Varies

FIELD(S): All fields of study

For students of Hispanic origin who attend full-time with at least 15 hours completed at the University of Texas at Arlington. Must have a minimum 2.5 GPA, be in good standing, and demonstrate financial need, leadership ability, and potential for success. Transcripts and letter stating financial need are required.

1 award annually. Contact UTA Alumni Association for an application.

3528—UTA ALUMNI ASSOCIATION (Simmons-Blackwell Endowed Scholarship)

University of Texas at Arlington
Box 19457
Arlington TX 76019
Internet: www.uta.edu/alumni/scholar.htm

AMOUNT: $300

DEADLINE(S): Varies

FIELD(S): All fields of study

Must be a first-generation college student with less than 90 hours and attend the University of Texas at Arlington. Must have demonstrated financial need and a minimum 2.5 GPA. Letter outlining career goals is required.

1 award annually. Contact UTA Alumni Association for an application.

3529—UTA ALUMNI ASSOCIATION (Student Foundation Sophomore Scholarship)

University of Texas at Arlington
Box 19457
Arlington TX 76019
Internet: www.uta.edu/alumni/scholar.htm

AMOUNT: $250

DEADLINE(S): Varies

FIELD(S): All fields of study

Must be a sophomore enrolled in at least nine hours at the University of Texas at Arlington. Must demonstrate financial need and have a minimum 2.75 GPA.

1 award annually. Contact UTA Alumni Association for an application.

3530—UTAH STATE BOARD OF REGENTS (State Student Incentive Grants)

355 W. North Temple, #3 Triad
Suite 550
Salt Lake City UT 84180-1205
801/321-7188 or 800/418-2551
Internet: www.utah-student-assiStreetorg

AMOUNT: $2,500

DEADLINE(S): Varies (Contact school's financial aid office.)

FIELD(S): All fields of study

Open to Utah residents attending eligible Utah schools who have substantial financial need. Grants are intended to enable such students to continue their studies. US citizen or legal resident.

Awards are made through the financial aid office at each eligible institution.

3531—UTILITY WORKERS UNION OF AMERICA (Private Utility Workers Union of America Scholarship Program Award)

815 16th Street NW
Washington DC 20006
202/347-8105

AMOUNT: $500-$2,000 per year
DEADLINE(S): JAN 1 (of junior year in high school)
FIELD(S): All fields of study

Scholarships are for sons and daughters of utility workers union members in good standing. Winners are selected from the group of high school juniors who take the national merit scholarship exams.

2 four-year scholarships awarded annually. Write for complete information.

3532—VALENCIA COMMUNITY COLLEGE FOUNDATION (Scholarships)

P.O. Box 3028
Orlando FL 32802-3028
407/317-7950
FAX: 407/317-7956
E-mail: Valencia3@aol.com
Internet: http://www.valencia.org/scholar.html

AMOUNT: Varies
DEADLINE(S): Varies
FIELD(S): All fields of study

The Valencia Community College Foundation lists numerous financial aid programs. The listed website is comprehensive.

Access website or write to foundation for list of financial aid programs.

3533—VENTURE CLUBS OF THE AMERIC-AS (Student Aid Awards)

Two Penn Center Plaza, Suite 1000
Philadelphia PA 19102-1883
215/557-9300
FAX: 215/568-5200
E-mail: siahq@voicenet.com

AMOUNT: $2,500 and $5,000
DEADLINE(S): DEC 31
FIELD(S): All fields of study

Awards for young, physically disabled individuals in need of further education who are between 15 and 40 years old. A Venture Club is an organization for young business and professional women sponsored by Soroptimist International of the Americas. The major selection criteria are financial need and the capacity to profit from further education.

Applicants should contact the nearest Venture Club or Soroptimist Club for application or send self-addressed, stamped envelope (SASE) to above address. Allow plenty of time before deadline date for application to be returned to the nearest local club.

3534—VERMONT STUDENT ASSISTANCE CORPORATION (Incentive Grants for Undergraduates)

P.O. Box 2000
Winooski VT 05404-2601
802/655-9602 or 800/642-3177
TDD: 800/281-3341
FAX: 802/654-3765
Internet: www.vsac.org

AMOUNT: $500-$6,800
DEADLINE(S): None
FIELD(S): All fields of study

Open to Vermont residents enrolled full-time at approved postsecondary institutions. Must meet need teStreet Award amounts depend on expected family contribution, Pell Grant eligibility, and institution attended.

Contact VSAC for an application.

3535—VERMONT STUDENT ASSISTANCE CORPORATION (Part-Time Grant)

P.O. Box 2000
Winooski VT 05404-2601
802/655-9602 or 800/642-3177
TDD: 800/281-3341
FAX: 802/654-3765
Internet: www.vsac.org

AMOUNT: $250-$5,100
DEADLINE(S): None
FIELD(S): All fields of study

Open to Vermont residents pursuing part-time undergraduate study in a degree, diploma, or certificate program. Must be taking fewer than 12 credit hours, have not received a bachelor's degree, and meet need teStreet Award amounts depend on number of credit hours taken.

2,600 awards annually. Contact VSAC for an application.

3536—VETERANS OF FOREIGN WARS/V.F.W. LADIES AUXILIARY (M.J. "Mel" Ornelas Memorial Scholarships)

4432 E. 7th
Cheyenne WY 82001
Written inquiry

AMOUNT: $100
DEADLINE(S): Varies
FIELD(S): All fields of study

Available to graduating high school seniors who are children or grandchildren of members of the Veterans of Foreign Wars or the V.F.W. Ladies Auxiliary. Applicants must have a minimum 2.5 GPA, write a letter of application, and a 200-word essay on: "Serving the Dead While Helping the Living—What the V.F.W. Motto Means to Me." Certification of GPA as well as of V.F.W. membership from Post commander or Auxiliary president required.

2 awards annually (one to a man & one to a woman). To apply, send above materials to Sandy Ross.

3537—VETERANS OF FOREIGN WARS OF THE UNITED STATES (Voice of Democracy Audio-Essay Scholarship Contest)

VFW Bldg., 406 W. 34th Street
Kansas City MO 64111
816/968-1117
FAX: 816/968-1157
E-mail: harmer@vfw.org
Internet: www.vfw.org

AMOUNT: $1,000 to $20,000
DEADLINE(S): NOV 1
FIELD(S): Scholarship awards for all fields of study

Open to 10th, 11th, and 12th graders in public, private, and parochial high schools. Contestants will be judged on their treatment of an annual theme. They may not refer to themselves, their schools, states, or cities, etc., as a means of identification.

55 national awards per year. Foreign exchange students not eligible. Contact local VFW post or high school for details.

3538—VIKKI CARR SCHOLARSHIP FOUNDATION (Scholarships)

P.O. Box 5126
Beverly Hills CA 90210
Written inquiry

AMOUNT: Up to $3,000
DEADLINE(S): APR 15
FIELD(S): All fields of study

Open to Latino residents of California and Texas between the ages of 17 and 22. Awards are for undergrad study at accredited colleges and universities. No US citizenship requirement.

5-10 awards per year. Applications available Jan 1. Send SASE for complete information to California address above or Texas address: P.O. Box 780968, San Antonio, TX 78278.

3539—VILLA MADONNA ACADEMY (Scholarships)

2500 Amsterdam Road
Villa Hills KY 41017
Internet: www.iglou.com/vma/

AMOUNT: Varies: $500-$5,000
DEADLINE(S): Varies
FIELD(S): All fields of study

Partial scholarships for males and females at this private, Catholic (Benedictine) high school in Kentucky. Several different financial aid programs, including those based on academic ability, need, leadership and service, and accomplishments. One is for sons or daughters of alumni.

A college prep school. Contact school for details.

3540—VINCENT L. HAWKINSON FOUNDATION FOR PEACE AND JUSTICE (Scholarship Award)

Grace University Lutheran Church
324 Harvard Street SE
Minneapolis MN 55414
612/331-8125

AMOUNT: Approx. $1,500 (varies)
DEADLINE(S): APR 30
FIELD(S): All fields of study

Scholarships for students who either reside in or attend college in one of the following states: Minnesota, Iowa, Wisconsin, North Dakota, or South Dakota. Must have demonstrated a commitment to peace and justice through study, internships, or projects that illustrate their commitment. For undergraduates, graduates, or M.A. candidates.

2 awards. Contact organization for details.

3541—VIRGIN ISLANDS BOARD OF EDUCATION (Exceptional Children Scholarship)

P.O. Box 11900
Street Thomas VI 00801
809/774-4546

AMOUNT: $2,000
DEADLINE(S): MAR 31
FIELD(S): All fields of study

Open to bona fide residents of the Virgin Islands who suffer from physical, mental, or emotional impairment and have demonstrated exceptional abilities and the need of educational training not available in Virgin Islands schools.

NOT for study at the college level. Write for complete information.

3542—VIRGIN ISLANDS BOARD OF EDUCATION (Territorial Scholarship Grants)

P.O. Box 11900
Street Thomas VI 00801
809/774-4546

AMOUNT: $1,000-$3,000
DEADLINE(S): MAR 31
FIELD(S): All fields of study

Grants open to bona fide residents of the Virgin Islands who have a cumulative GPA of at least 'C' and are enrolled in an accredited institution of higher learning.

300-400 loans and grants per year. Renewable provided recipient maintains an average of 'C' or better. Loans are also available. Write for complete information.

3543—VIRGINIA MILITARY INSTITUTE (Scholarships)

Financial Aid Office
Lexington VA 24450-0304
540/464-7213
FAX: 540/464-7629

AMOUNT: Varies
DEADLINE(S): Varies
FIELD(S): All fields of study

Scholarships are available to attend this four-year, coeducational, undergraduate university in Lexington, Virginia. Awards include ROTC Scholarships, State Cadetships, and the Institute Scholars Program. Must complete government FAFSA form as well as the VMI financial aid form found in the admissions packet.

Contact VMI for descriptions of programs and details of the school.

3544—VIRGINIA SMITH SCHOLARSHIP TRUST (Scholarships)

632 West 13th Street
Merced CA 95340
209/381-6604

AMOUNT: Varies
DEADLINE(S): MAY 1
FIELD(S): All fields of study

Scholarships for students who attended a public high school in the City of Merced, California, for at least three years. Must have 60 units and/or junior status, and must have applied for admission to a public or private institution of higher learning, excluding community colleges, in the State of California. GPA of at least 2.8 required. Financial need considered.

Contact Mrs. Eleanor Giebeler at above location.

3545—VIRGINIA STATE COUNCIL OF HIGHER EDUCATION (Tuition Assistance Grant Program)

James Monroe Bldg.
101 N. 14th Street
Richmond VA 23219
804/786-1690
E-mail: fainfo@schev.edu

AMOUNT: Up to $2,000
DEADLINE(S): JUL 31
FIELD(S): All fields of study except Theology

Open to Virginia residents who are full-time undergraduate, graduate, or professional students at eligible private colleges and universities in Virginia. Must be working in first degree. Late applications may be considered if funds are available.

Contact the financial aid office at the college you plan to attend.

3546—VIRGINIA STATE COUNCIL OF HIGHER EDUCATION (College Scholarship Assistance Program)

James Monroe Bldg.
101 N. 14th Street
Richmond VA 23219
804/786-1690
E-mail: fainfo@schev.edu

AMOUNT: $400 to $5,000
DEADLINE(S): Varies
FIELD(S): All fields of study except Religion

Open to Virginia residents who are undergraduate students with at least 6 credit hours at eligible Virginia colleges and universities. May not be used for religious training or theological education.

Write for complete information or contact your institution's financial aid office.

3547—VIRGINIA STATE COUNCIL OF HIGHER EDUCATION (Undergraduate Student Financial Assistance "Last Dollar" Program)

James Monroe Bldg.
101 N. 14th Street
Richmond VA 23219
804/786-1690
E-mail: fainfo@schev.edu

AMOUNT: Ranges from $400 to the cost of full-time tuition and fees
DEADLINE(S): Varies (with each school)
FIELD(S): All areas of study

"Last dollar" is a need-based program designed to assist minority Virginia students to attend Virginia public colleges or universities. Minorities include Black, Native American, Asian/Pacific Islander, and Hispanic. Must be a Virginia resident.

Contact the financial aid office at your college or university.

3548—VIRGINIA STATE COUNCIL OF HIGHER EDUCATION (Virginia Transfer Grant Program)

James Monroe Bldg.
101 N.14th Street
Richmond VA 23219
804/786-1690
E-mail: fainfo@schev.edu

AMOUNT: Up to full tuition and fees
DEADLINE(S): Varies (check with financial aid office)
FIELD(S): All fields of study

For minority students who enroll in one of the Commonwealth's 13 historically white colleges or universities and all transfer students at Norfolk State and Virginia State Universities. Applicants must qualify for entry as first-time transfer students.

Contact college financial aid office for complete information.

3549—WAL-MART FOUNDATION (Sam Walton Scholarship)

702 SW 8th Street
Bentonville AR 72716-8071
501/277-1905
FAX: 501/273-6850

AMOUNT: $1,000
DEADLINE(S): None
FIELD(S): All fields of study

For a college-bound high school senior in each community where a Wal-Mart store is operating. An informational packet and scholarship applications will be available through your high school guidance counselor in January.

Deadline is early spring. Applications available through your guidance counselor or at your local Wal-Mart store only.

3550—WAL-MART FOUNDATION SCHOLARSHIPS (Distribution Center Scholarships)

702 SW 8th Street
Bentonville AR 72716-8071
501/277-1905
FAX: 501/273-6850

AMOUNT: $2,500 payable over 4 years
DEADLINE(S): MAY 1
FIELD(S): All fields of study

Open to Wal-Mart associates who work for a Distribution Center. ACT, SAT, counselor recommendations, transcripts,

class rank, community activities, leadership, and financial need will be considered.

2 scholarships will be awarded in each unit that has been operating for at least one year. Contact the distribution Personnel Manager for complete information.

3551—WAL-MART FOUNDATION SCHOLARSHIPS (Wal-Mart Associate Scholarship)

702 SW 8th Street
Bentonville AR 72716-8071
501/273-1905
FAX: 501/273-6850

AMOUNT: $1,000
DEADLINE(S): MAR 1
FIELD(S): All fields of study

Open to high school seniors who work for Wal-Mart and to those associates' children ineligible for the Walton Foundation Scholarship due to length of employment or not working full-time. Applications available at local store in January or call or write above location.

ACT, SAT, transcripts, class rank, community activities, leadership, and financial need are considered.

3552—WAL-MART FOUNDATION SCHOLARSHIPS (Walton Foundation Scholarship)

702 SW 8th Street
Bentonville, AR 72716-8071
501/273-1905
FAX: 501/273-6850

AMOUNT: $6,000 over 4 years
DEADLINE(S): MAR 1
FIELD(S): All fields of study

Open to college-bound high school seniors who are dependents of Wal-Mart associates who are employed full-time (28 hours/week or more) for one year as of March 1. Applications are available in January at local store or you can call the Wal-Mart Foundation.

70 awards. Write to the above address for complete information.

3553—WASHINGTON HIGHER EDUCATION COORDINATING BOARD (American Indian Endowed Scholarship)

P.O. Box 43430
Olympia WA 98504-3430
360/753-7850

AMOUNT: $1,000
DEADLINE(S): MAY 15
FIELD(S): All fields of study

For undergraduate and graduate Native American students who are residents of Washington state. The purpose is to create

an educational opportunity for American Indians to attend and graduate from higher education institutions in the state of Washington. Interest earned from the endowment is used each year to award scholarships to financially needy, resident, American Indian students.

Awards are renewable. Amounts dependent upon endowment earnings. Applications are available in the spring from above address.

3554—WASHINGTON HIGHER EDUCATION COORDINATING BOARD (Washington State Educational Opportunity Grant)

P.O. Box 43430
Olympia WA 98504-3430
360/753-7850

AMOUNT: $2,500
DEADLINE(S): JUN 1
FIELD(S): All fields of study

Open to financially needy, placebound residents of Washington state residing in one of 14 certain counties. Awards tenable at eligible Washington colleges and universities. For upper division (juniors and seniors) students.

In 1996-97, 400 such grants were awarded. Applications available after January 1. For details, write to above address.

3555—WASHINGTON HIGHER EDUCATION COORDINATING BOARD (Washington State Need Grant)

P.O. Box 43430
Olympia WA 98504-3430
360/753-7850

AMOUNT: Varies
DEADLINE(S): None specified
FIELD(S): All fields of study

Open to financially needy residents of Washington state who attend participating institutions.

For details, write to above address.

3556—WASHINGTON HIGHER EDUCATION COORDINATING BOARD (Washington Scholars)

P.O. Box 43430
Olympia WA 98504-3430
360/753-7850

AMOUNT: Varies
DEADLINE(S): None specified
FIELD(S): All fields of study

For 3 high school seniors in each legislative district in Washington state. High school principals nominate the top one percent of the graduating senior class based upon academic accomplishments, leadership, and community service.

To encourage outstanding students to attend Washington public and independent colleges and universities. For details, write to above address.

3557—WASHINGTON INTERNATIONAL SCHOOL (Scholarships)

3100 Macomb Street NW
Washington DC 20008-3324
202/243-1815
FAX: 202/243-1807
E-mail: admiss@wis.edu
Internet: www.wis.edu

AMOUNT: Tuition assistance
DEADLINE(S): JAN 15 (admission); FEB 15 (financial aid)
FIELD(S): All fields of study (K-12)

Financial assistance towards tuition for this independent, coed day school that enrolls 685 students, nursery-12, in Washington DC. The students represent 90 different countries; faculty and staff come from 25 countries. Multi-lingual opportunities. Applicants must be currently enrolled or newly admitted.

Renewable. No merit-based or athletic scholarships—financial need must be documented. 10-12% of the student body receives financial assistance; all families must pay some portion of tuition and fees.

3558—WASHINGTON STATE HIGHER EDUCATION COORDINATING BOARD (Aid to Blind Students)

P.O. Box 43430
Olympia WA 98504-3430
360/753-7845
FAX: 360/753-7808

AMOUNT: $200
DEADLINE(S): Varies
FIELD(S): All fields of study

Small grant is available to needy blind students who are Washington state residents. Recipients are reimbursed for special equipment, services, and books and supplies required because of their visual impairment.

Contact Program Manager for an application.

3559—WASHINGTON STATE PTA (Financial Grant Foundation)

2003 65th Ave. West
Tacoma WA 98466-6215

253/565-2153
FAX: 253/565-7753
E-mail: wapta@wastatepta.org
Internet: www.wastatepta.org

AMOUNT: $1,000 (4-yr. schools); $500 (2-yr. schools)
DEADLINE(S): MAR 2
FIELD(S): All fields of study

Open to Washington state residents. Grant program is designed to assist Washington state high school seniors and graduates who will be entering freshmen at an accredited college or university, community college, voc-tech school, or other accredited school. Applicants need not be current graduates. Financial need is primary consideration.

Check with high school counselor or contact above location for complete information.

3560—WASHINGTON TRUST BANK (Herman Oscar Schumacher College Fund Trust)

Trust Dept., P.O. Box 2127
Spokane WA 99210-2127
509/353-4150

AMOUNT: $500
DEADLINE(S): OCT 1
FIELD(S): All fields of study

Scholarships for male residents of Spokane County, Washington. Preference given to orphans. Must have completed at least one full year at an accredited school of higher education as a full-time student.

25 annual awards. Must reapply for renewal.

3561—WASHINGTON WATER POWER (Mindpower Generation Scholarship Program)

Tower Bldg.
1809 Seventh Ave., Suite 600
Seattle WA 98101
206/623-4494
Internet: www.wwpco.com/minpowr.html

AMOUNT: $1,500
DEADLINE(S): MAR 14
FIELD(S): All fields of study

Various scholarships offered to seniors graduating from high schools in WWP's service areas in Eastern Washington or Northern Idaho. Must be accepted to certain participating 2- or 4-year colleges in the same service area. Must have a min. GPA of 2.5. Applicants must write an essay in addition to other requirements. Rules are on website listed above.

Recipients may apply during their sophomore years for other WWP-sponsored scholarships. Apply to: Mindpower Scholarship Selection Committee, Independent Colleges of Washington, Inc.

3562—WELLESLEY COLLEGE (Fellowships for Wellesley Graduates & Graduating Seniors)

Center for Work & Service
106 Central Street
Wellesley MA 02481-8203
781/283-3525
FAX: 781/283-3674
E-mail: fellowships@bulletin.wellesley.edu
Internet: www. wellesley.edu/CWS/step2/fellow.html

AMOUNT: $1,200-$50,000
DEADLINE(S): JAN 3
FIELD(S): All fields of study

Numerous fellowship programs open to Wellesley College graduating seniors and Wellesley College graduates. For graduate study or research at institutions in the US or abroad. Awards are based on merit and need.

See website or send self-addressed, stamped envelope to Rose Crawford, Secretary to the Committee on Extramural Graduate Fellowships & Scholarships, for an application and information on specific fellowships.

3563—WEST VIRGINIA DIVISION OF VETERANS' AFFAIRS (War Orphans Education Program)

1321 Plaza East, Suite 101
Charleston WV 25301
304/558-3661

AMOUNT: $400 to $500/year/waiver of tuition
DEADLINE(S): JUL 15; DEC 1
FIELD(S): All areas of study

Open to surviving children (aged 16-23) of deceased veterans whose active duty service in armed forces of the US involved hostile action. Student must have been a resident of West Virginia for one year prior to initial application. Death of parent must have occurred on active duty OR if subsequent to discharge, death must have been the result of a disability incurred during such wartime service.

Awards tenable at any state-supported high school, college, or university. Write for complete information.

3564—WESTERN GOLF ASSOCIATION/EVANS SCHOLARS FOUNDATION (Caddie Scholarships)

1 Briar Road
Golf IL 60029
847/724-4600

AMOUNT: Full tuition & housing
DEADLINE(S): NOV 1
FIELD(S): All fields of study

Open to US high school seniors in the top 25% of their class who have served as a caddie at a WGA member club for at least 2 years. Outstanding personal character and financial need are considerations.

Applications are accepted after completion of junior year in high school (between July 1 and November 1). 200 awards per year; renewable for 4 years. Contact your local country club or write to address above for complete information.

3565—WESTERN SUNBATHING ASSOCIATION (Scholarships)

P.O. Box 1168-107
Studio City CA 91604
E-mail: WSANUDE@delphi.com
Internet: www.wsanude.com

AMOUNT: $1,000
DEADLINE(S): APR 1
FIELD(S): All fields of study

Open to students who have been, or whose parents have been, members of WSA for at least three years. Must be high school seniors or currently enrolled full- or part-time in an accredited postsecondary school. Must be less than 27 years of age and have a minimum 2.5 GPA. Based on academic records, leadership, and potential for growth. Financial need NOT a factor.

2 awards annually. Renewable. Contact Oliver Ellsworth at WSA for an application. Applicants notified by June 1st, and funds are forwarded directly to student's school. WSA is a region of the American Association for Nude Recreation.

3566—WESTOVER SCHOOL (Mandeville Teachers' Daughters Scholarship)

Whittemore Road, P.O. Box 847
Middlebury CT 06762-0847
203/758-2423
FAX: 203/577-4588
E-mail: admission@
westover.pvt.k12.cut.us
Internet: http//:www.westover.pvt.
k12.ct.us

AMOUNT: Full tuition/room/board
DEADLINE(S): FEB 1
FIELD(S): All fields of study—college
preparatory

Scholarships for high school girls (9-12) to attend Westover School, a private preparatory boarding school in Middlebury, CT. For entering students who are daughters of teachers. The teacher must be the primary family provider.

2 awards per year. Selections are based on demonstrated high motivation for learning and outstanding personal qualities.

3567—WESTRIDGE SCHOOL (Financial Aid)

324 Madeline Drive
Pasadena CA 91105-3309
626/799-1153
FAX: 626/799-9236
E-mail: CChan@westridge.org
Internet: www.westridge.org

AMOUNT: Varies
DEADLINE(S): FEB 6
FIELD(S): All fields of study

Financial aid for students already accepted and enrolled at this independent school for girls, grades 4-12, in Pasadena, California. Must demonstrate financial need.

60-70 awards yearly. Contact school for details.

3568—WHEATLAND COMMUNITY SCHOLASTIC FUND, INC. (Scholarships)

1250 Oak Street
Wheatland WY 82201
Written inquiry

AMOUNT: Varies
DEADLINE(S): Varies
FIELD(S): All fields of study

Available to graduates of Wheatland High School in Wyoming.

Write to Mr. Marvin L. Dunham at above address for an application.

3569—WHEATLAND R.E.A. (Scholarships)

P.O. Box 1209
2154 South Rd.
Wheatland WY 82201
Written inquiry

AMOUNT: $200
DEADLINE(S): MAR 1
FIELD(S): All fields of study

Available to undergraduate students in any major, whose parents reside within the Wheatland REA service area and who plan to attend the University of Wyoming or a Wyoming community college.

2 awards annually. Write to above address for an application.

3570—WHITTIER COLLEGE (John Greenleaf Whittier Scholars Program)

13406 E. Philadelphia Street
Whittier CA 90608
562/907-4238
FAX: 562/907-4870
E-mail: admission@whittier.edu
Internet: www.whittier.edu

AMOUNT: $2,000
DEADLINE(S): FEB 1
FIELD(S): All fields of study

GPA, SAT or ACT, and class rank are all considered in determining award eligibility and amount.

Write above address for complete information.

3571—WILLIAM BRADLEY SCHOLARSHIP FOUNDATION INC. (William Bradley Scholarship)

125 Ozark Drive
Crystal City MO 63019-1703
314/937-2570

AMOUNT: $600
DEADLINE(S): APR 1
FIELD(S): All fields of study

Open to graduating seniors of Crystal City High School, Festus High School, or Street Pius X High School in Jefferson County, Missouri. Must rank in the top 10 percent of class.

Renewable. Write for complete information.

3572—WILLIAM F. COOPER SCHOLARSHIP

c/o First Union National Bank-CMG
P.O. Box 9947
Savannah GA 31412
912/944-2154

AMOUNT: $1,000-$1,500 annually
DEADLINE(S): MAY 15
FIELD(S): All fields of study EXCEPT
Law, Theology, or Medicine (Nursing acceptable)

Undergraduate scholarships for women based on financial need and GPA. Must be Georgia resident; first preference is for women who live in Chatham County.

15-20 yearly. Renewable.

3573—WILLIAM H. CHAPMAN FOUNDATION (Scholarships)

P.O. Box 1321
New London CT 06320
203/443-8010

AMOUNT: $200-$1,150
DEADLINE(S): APR 1
FIELD(S): All fields of study

Open ONLY to residents of New London County, CT. Awards support full-time undergraduate study at accredited colleges and universities. US citizenship or legal residency required. Must demonstrate financial need.

Approximately 100 awards per year. Renewable with reapplication. Write for complete information.

3574—WILLIAM RANDOLPH HEARST FOUNDATION (US Senate Youth Program)

90 New Montgomery Street
Suite 1212
San Francisco CA 94105-4504
415/543-4057 or 800/841-7048
FAX: 415/243-0760

AMOUNT: $2,000 + all-expenses-paid week in Washington
DEADLINE(S): Varies
FIELD(S): All fields of study

Open to any high school junior or senior who is serving as an elected student body officer at a US high school. Student receives a week's stay in Washington as guest of the Senate, and the scholarship is presented during the visit. Student must become a candidate for a degree at an accredited US college/university within two years of high school graduation, pledging to include courses in government or related subjects to his or her undergraduate program.

2 students are selected from each state and the District of Columbia. Contact your high school principal or the William Randolph Hearst Foundation for an application.

3575—WINDHAM FOUNDATION INC. (Scholarships)

P.O. Box 70
Grafton VT 05146
802/843-2211

AMOUNT: $500-$1,500
DEADLINE(S): APR 1
FIELD(S): All fields of study

Program is open ONLY to students who are residents of Windham County, Vermont. Scholarships are tenable at recognized undergraduate colleges and universities.

Approximately 400 awards per year. Renewable up to 4 years. Write for complete information.

3576—WINONA PUBLIC SCHOOLS (Community Education Scholarships)

Lincoln School
654 Huff Street
Winona MN 55987
507/454-9450
Internet: www.winonanet.com/schools

AMOUNT: Varies
DEADLINE(S): None
FIELD(S): All fields of study

Scholarships for all ages in the community education section of this school district. Includes programs for pre-school, K-12, and adult education in a variety of fields (computers, languages, arts, etc.). Also parent training.

Write or call for complete information.

3577—WISCONSIN DEPARTMENT OF VETERANS AFFAIRS (Deceased Veterans' Survivors Economic Assistance Loan/Education Grants)

P.O. Box 7843
Madison WI 53703-7843
608/266-1311 or 800/947-8387
Internet: badger.state.wi.us/agencies/dva

AMOUNT: Varies
DEADLINE(S): None specified
FIELD(S): All areas of study

Open to surviving spouses (who have not remarried) of deceased eligible veterans and to the minor dependent children of the deceased veterans. Must be residents of Wisconsin at the time of application.

Approximately 5,700 grants and loans per year. Contact a Wisconsin veterans' service officer in your county of residence for complete information.

3578—WISCONSIN DEPARTMENT OF VETERANS AFFAIRS (Veterans Personal Loan/Education Grants)

P.O. Box 7843
Madison WI 53703-7843
608/266-1311 or 800/947-8387
Internet: badger.state.wi.us/agencies/dva

AMOUNT: $10,000 maximum
DEADLINE(S): None specified
FIELD(S): All areas of study

For veterans (as defined in Wisconsin Statute 45.35.5) who are living in Wisconsin

at the time of application. There are limitations on income.

Approximately 5,700 grants and loans per year. Write for complete information.

3579—WISCONSIN HIGHER EDUCATION AIDS BOARD (Student Financial Aid Program)

P.O. Box 7885
Madison WI 53707
608/267-2206
FAX: 608/267-2808

AMOUNT: Varies
DEADLINE(S): VAries
FIELD(S): All fields of study

Board administers a variety of state and federal programs available to Wisconsin residents enrolled at least half-time and who maintain satisfactory academic record. Most require demonstration of financial need.

Write for complete information.

3580—WOMEN OF THE EVANGELICAL LUTHERAN CHURCH IN AMERICA (The Amelia Kemp Scholarship)

8765 West Higgins Road
Chicago IL 60631-4189
800/638-3522, ext. 2747
FAX: 773/380-2419
E-mail: womnelca@elca.org

AMOUNT: $2,000 max.
DEADLINE(S): MAR 1
FIELD(S): All fields of study

Assists women of color who are members of the ELCA studying in undergraduate, graduate, professional, or vocational courses of study leading to a career other than a church-certified profession. Must be US citizen and have experienced an interruption of two or more years since completion of high school. Academic records of coursework completed in last five years as well as proof of admission from educational institution are required.

Renewable for an additional year. Contact Faith Fretheim, Program Director, for an application.

3581—WOMEN OF THE EVANGELICAL LUTHERAN CHURCH IN AMERICA (The Cronk Memorial, First Triennium Board, General, Mehring, Paepke, Piero/Wade/Wade & Edwin/Edna Robeck Scholarships)

8765 West Higgins Road
Chicago IL 60631-4189
800/638-3522, ext. 2747

FAX: 773/380-2419
E-mail: womnelca@elca.org

AMOUNT: $2,000 max.
DEADLINE(S): MAR 1
FIELD(S): All fields of study

Assists women who are members of ELCA in undergraduate, graduate, professional, and vocational courses of study not leading to a church-certified profession. Must be US citizen and have experienced an interruption of two or more years since completion of high school. Academic records of coursework completed in last five years as well as proof of admission to educational institution are required.

Renewable an additional year. Contact Faith Fretheim, Program Director, for an application.

3582—WOMEN'S SPORTS FOUNDATION (AQHA Female Equestrian Award)

Eisenhower Park
East Meadow NY 11554
800/227-3988
FAX: 516/542-4716
E-mail: WoSport@aol.com
Internet: www.lifetimetv.com/WoSport

AMOUNT: $2,000
DEADLINE(S): FEB 1
FIELD(S): All fields of study

Honors an outstanding female equestrian and rewards her for her accomplishments as a horsewoman and as an athlete. For female equestrians with national ranking and competition who exhibit leadership, sportsmanship, and commitment to the sport and its athletes.

1 award annually. Awarded in March. See website or write to above address for details.

3583—WOMEN'S SPORTS FOUNDATION (Linda Riddle/SMGA Endowed, Gart Sports Sportmart, & Mervyn's WSF College Scholarships)

Eisenhower Park
East Meadow NY 11554
800/227-3988
FAX: 516/542-4716
E-mail: WoSport@aol.com
Internet: www.lifetimetv.com/WoSport

AMOUNT: $1,500 (Linda); $5,000 (Gart); $1,000 (Mervyn's)
DEADLINE(S): NOV 20; DEC 11; APR 17
FIELD(S): All fields of study

These scholarships provide female high school student-athletes with a means to continue their athletic participation as well as their college education. For Linda Riddle award, must be high school senior (athlete) who will be pursuing full-time course of study at 2- or 4-year accredited school in the Fall. For Gart Sports & Mervyn's awards, must be high school senior who has participated in one or more interscholastic sports and is attending college in the Fall.

3-5 Linda Riddle, 8 Gart Sports, & 100 Mervyn's awards annually. See website or write to above address for details.

3584—WOMEN'S SPORTS FOUNDATION (Ocean Spray Travel & Training Grants)

Eisenhower Park
East Meadow NY 11554
800/227-3988
FAX: 516/542-4716
E-mail: WoSport@aol.com
Internet: www.lifetimetv.com/WoSport

AMOUNT: Up to $1,500 (individual); up to $3,000 (team)
DEADLINE(S): NOV 15
FIELD(S): All fields of study

Provides financial assistance to aspiring female athletes and teams for coaching, specialized training, equipment, and/or travel. Must have regional and/or national ranking or successful competitive records, and have the potential to achieve higher performance levels and rankings. High school and college/university varsity and/or rec. teams are NOT eligible.

20 individual grants & 8 team grants annually. Awards made in February. See website or write to above address for details.

3585—WOMEN'S WESTERN GOLF FOUNDATION (Scholarships)

c/o Mrs. Richard Willis
393 Ramsay Road
Deerfield IL 60015
Written inquiry

AMOUNT: $2,000 per year
DEADLINE(S): APR 15
FIELD(S): All fields of study

Open to female high school seniors having high academic achievement, financial need, and an involvement with the sport of golf. Golf skill is NOT a criterion. For undergraduate study at any accredited four-year institution. US citizens.

15 awards per year. Renewable if a "B" average is maintained. Write for complete information.

3586—WORLD OF KNOWLEDGE (Today & Tomorrow Scholarship Program)

P.O. Box 4146
Winter Park FL 32793
888/953-7737
Internet: www.worldofknowledge.org

AMOUNT: $2,000
DEADLINE(S): JAN 30
FIELD(S): All fields of study

Open to college-bound high school seniors in San Francisco, CA, or Middlesex County, NJ. To apply, submit Entry Form and write a 900- to 1,100-word essay on "Contrast Your Immigrant Ancestors' Life in America Compared with Your Life Today."

20 awards annually. See website or contact World of Knowledge for an application. Funded by the ICM/AT&T Association Loyalty Program.

3587—WYOMING ASSOCIATION OF FUTURE HOMEMAKERS OF AMERICA (FHA/HERO Scholarship)

LCCC-B105
400 E. College Drive
Cheyenne WY 82007
307/778-4312

AMOUNT: $400
DEADLINE(S): Varies
FIELD(S): All fields of study

Available to high school seniors, college freshmen, and college sophomores who are/were members of FHA/HERO in Wyoming or who completed one Family and Consumer Sciences course at a Wyoming high school. Applicants must submit a 100-word essay relating their FHA/HERO membership to their declared college major. May be used at any Wyoming institution of postsecondary education.

1 award annually. Contact Marci Altman at the Wyoming FHA for an application.

3588—WYOMING DEPARTMENT OF CORRECTIONS (Wayne Martinez Memorial Scholarships)

P.O. Box 393
Rawlins WY 82301
307/324-2622

AMOUNT: Varies
DEADLINE(S): Varies
FIELD(S): All fields of study

Available to employees and children of employees of the Wyoming Department of Corrections.

Write to above address, attention: application request, or call Amee Medina at above number for an application.

3589—WYOMING DEPARTMENT OF EDU-CATION (Douvas Memorial Scholarship)

Hathaway Building
Cheyenne WY 82002
Written inquiry

AMOUNT: $500
DEADLINE(S): Varies
FIELD(S): All fields of study

Available to high school seniors or others between the ages of 18 and 22 who are first-generation Americans and Wyoming residents. May be used at any Wyoming public institution of higher education.

1 award annually. Write to Jim Lendino at above address for an application.

3590—WYOMING DEPARTMENT OF VET-ERANS AFFAIRS (War Orphans Scholarships)

2360 E. Pershing Blvd.
Cheyenne WY 82001
Written inquiry

AMOUNT: Tuition & mandatory fees
DEADLINE(S): Varies
FIELD(S): All fields of study

Available to a limited number of orphans of Wyoming war veterans and children of Wyoming service people who are listed officially in the military records of the US as being a prisoner of war or missing in action as a result of the Korean or Vietnam conflicts. Eligibility will be verified by the Department of Veterans Affairs.

Write to above address for an application.

3591—WYOMING FARM BUREAU FEDER-ATION (Dodge Merit Award)

Box 1348
Laramie WY 82073
Written inquiry

AMOUNT: $500
DEADLINE(S): MAR 1
FIELD(S): All fields of study

Available to a student from a Wyoming Farm Bureau family. May be used at any public institution of postsecondary education in Wyoming.

2 awards annually. Applications are available from each county Farm Bureau or from the above address.

3592—WYOMING FEDERATION OF WOM-EN'S CLUBS (Mary N. Brooks Education Fund—Boys)

316 Hwy. 14A East
Lovell WY 82431
307/548-2860

AMOUNT: $500
DEADLINE(S): MAR 1
FIELD(S): All fields of study

Available to a boy who is a recent graduate of a Wyoming high school. Award may be used at any Wyoming institution of postsecondary education.

Contact Mrs. Delsa H. Asay at WFWC for an application.

3593—WYOMING FEDERATION OF WOM-EN'S CLUBS (Mary N. Brooks Education Fund—Daughters & Granddaughters)

316 Hwy. 14A East
Lovell WY 82431
307/548-2860

AMOUNT: $500
DEADLINE(S): MAR 1
FIELD(S): All fields of study

Available to a daughter or granddaughter of WFWC member in good standing attending any Wyoming institution of higher education.

Contact Mrs. Delsa H. Asay at above address for an application.

3594—WYOMING REPUBLICAN FOUNDA-TION (Scholarships)

P.O. Box 416
Laramie WY 82020
Written inquiry

AMOUNT: Varies
DEADLINE(S): MAR 1
FIELD(S): All fields of study

Available to any student at the University of Wyoming or a Wyoming community college. Full-time enrollment required.

Write to above address for an application. Award is provided by Republican donors statewide.

3595—WYOMING STUDENT LOAN COR-PORATION (Leadership Scholarship)

P.O. Box 209
Cheyenne WY 82003-0209
Written inquiry

AMOUNT: $500/semester
DEADLINE(S): MAR 15
FIELD(S): All fields of study

For Wyoming residents who are first-year, first-time students attending Wyoming postsecondary institutions. Applicants must submit a letter of recommendation, an official transcript, and a typed, 500-word autobiographical essay. Must also submit a resume or a list of activity information. Minimum 2.5 GPA required for renewal.

6 awards annually. Renewable up to eight semesters of undergraduate work. Write to the WSLC Scholarship Committee for an application.

3596—YOUNG AMERICAN BOWLING ALLIANCE (Alberta E. Crowe Star of Tomorrow Scholarship)

5301 S. 76th Street
Greendale WI 53129
Written inquiry

AMOUNT: $4,000 per year
DEADLINE(S): JAN 15
FIELD(S): Any field of study

Open to women who are amateur bowlers and members in good standing with WIBC or YABA. Must be at most age 22 or younger preceding Jan. 15. Must be a senior in high school or attending college.

Send #10 SASE to above address for complete information.

3597—YOUNG AMERICAN BOWLING ALLIANCE (Al Thompson Junior Bowler Scholarship)

5301 S. 76th Street
Greendale WI 53129
Written inquiry

AMOUNT: $1,500/$1,000
DEADLINE(S): JUN 15
FIELD(S): All fields of study

Open to high school seniors who are good standing members with ABC, YABA or WIBC. Students must carry at least a 2.5 GPA. Applicant must also carry a current season average of 170 (females) and 190 (males).

Write to the above address for complete information.

3598—YOUNG AMERICAN BOWLING ALLIANCE (Chuck Hall Star of Tomorrow Scholarship)

5301 S. 76th Street
Greendale WI 53129
Written inquiry

AMOUNT: $4,000
DEADLINE(S): JAN 15
FIELD(S): Any field of study

Open to male students who are amateur bowlers and members in good standing with ABC or YABA. Students must be age 21 or younger before deadline. Must be a senior in high school or attending college.

Send #10 SASE to above address for complete information.

3599—YOUTH FOR UNDERSTANDING INTERNATIONAL EXCHANGE (Congress-Bundestag Youth Exchange Program)

3501 Newark Street NW
Washington DC 20016-3199
800/TEENAGE
Internet: www.yfu.org

AMOUNT: Not specified
DEADLINE(S): NOV 12
FIELD(S): All fields of study

Full-year scholarship to study in Germany open to any high school sophomore or junior having a 3.0 or better GPA (4.0 scale). Students attend a German high school and live with a host family. There is no language requirement.

Must be US citizen. 300 scholarships per year. Write/call for complete information.

3600—YOUTH FOR UNDERSTANDING INTERNATIONAL EXCHANGE (Congress-Bundestag Senior Program)

3501 Newark Street NW
Washington DC 20016-3199
800/TEENAGE
Internet: www.yfu.org

AMOUNT: Not specified
DEADLINE(S): DEC 15
FIELD(S): All fields of study

Full-year scholarship to study in Germany after high school graduation. Open to any high senior with a 3.0 or better GPA (4.0 scale). Students attend a German high school and live with a host family. There is no language requirement.

10 merit-based awards are given. Must be US citizen. 300 scholarships per year. Write/call for complete information.

3601—YOUTH FOR UNDERSTANDING INTERNATIONAL EXCHANGE (Face of America)

3501 Newark Street NW
Washington DC 20016-3199
800/TEENAGE
Internet: www.yfu.org

AMOUNT: Domestic and international travel, insurance, + $150 spending money
DEADLINE(S): JAN 1
FIELD(S): All fields of study

A nationwide competition for 40 minority students to spend the summer in select countries living with a host family. Students must have at least a 2.0 GPA, and family income must not exceed $55,000. Recipients must pay $650 program contribution.

Write/call for complete information.

3602—YOUTH FOR UNDERSTANDING INTERNATIONAL EXCHANGE (Finland-US Senate Youth Exchange)

3501 Newark Street NW
Washington DC 20016-3199
800/TEENAGE
Internet: www.yfu.org

AMOUNT: Partial program expenses
DEADLINE(S): OCT
FIELD(S): All fields of study

Merit scholarships for 2 high school juniors from each of these states: CA, FL, MA, MI, MN, OR, and WA for study in Finland during the summer months. A GPA of 3.2 (4.0 scale) is required. Must be US citizen. Must pay $500 toward program.

2 students are selected from each of the seven participating states. Contact above location for details.

3603—YOUTH FOR UNDERSTANDING INTERNATIONAL EXCHANGE (Future Homemakers of America/Kikkoman Corp. Scholarships)

3501 Newark Street NW
Washington DC 20016-3199
800/TEENAGE
Internet: www.yfu.org

AMOUNT: Partial program expenses
DEADLINE(S): DEC
FIELD(S): All fields of study

For members of Future Homemakers of America (in partnership with Kikkoman Corp.). Merit-based scholarships for high school students who wish to go overseas to Japan for a summer (6 weeks).

20 annual awards. For membership information or further details, contact above location.

3604—YOUTH FOR UNDERSTANDING INTERNATIONAL EXCHANGE (Mazda National Scholarships)

3501 Newark Street NW
Washington DC 20016-3199
800/TEENAGE
Internet: www.yfu.org

AMOUNT: Partial program expenses
DEADLINE(S): NOV
FIELD(S): All fields of study

Merit scholarships for summer program in Japan living with a host family for US high school students with GPA of 2.0 or better (4.0 scale).

Contact above location for details. YFU does not offer scholarships for college students.

3605—YOUTH FOR UNDERSTANDING INTERNATIONAL EXCHANGE (Scholarship Programs)

3501 Newark Street NW
Washington DC 20016-3199
800/TEENAGE
Internet: www.yfu.org

AMOUNT: Program expenses
DEADLINE(S): OCT (Applications available then. Deadline is JAN.)
FIELD(S): All fields of study

Scholarships for high school students who wish to go overseas for a summer or for a school year. Some are corporate-sponsored and for dependents of employees of 60+ corporations, some are for specific countries only, and some are for students from specific states or cities/counties.

Parents of interested students should check with their personnel office at work to see if their firm is a participant. Call above number for brochure.

3606—YOUTH FOUNDATION, INC. (Study-Abroad Scholarships)

36 West 44th Street
New York NY 10036
Written inquiry

AMOUNT: Varies
DEADLINE(S): Varies
FIELD(S): All areas of study

This organization offers scholarships for an undergraduate's Junior Year Abroad. Selection is based on character, need, scholastic achievement, objective, motivation, potential for leaderships, and good citizenship.

Write for details.

3607—ZETA PHI BETA SORORITY EDUCATIONAL FOUNDATION (General Undergraduate Scholarships)

1734 New Hampshire Ave. NW
Washington DC 20009
Internet: www.zpb1920.org/nefforms.htm

AMOUNT: $500-$1,000
DEADLINE(S): FEB 1
FIELD(S): All fields of study

Open to undergraduate college students and graduating high school seniors planning to enter college in the Fall. Award is for full-time study for one academic year (Fall-Spring) and is paid directly to college/university to be applied for tuition or appropriate fees. Must submit proof of enrollment/university acceptance.

Send self-addressed, stamped envelope to above address between September 1st and December 15th for an application.

Helpful Publications

3608—"ACE" ANY TEST

AUTHOR: Ron Fry, ISBN 1-56414-460-7
  Career Press, Inc.
  3 Tice Road, P.O. Box 687
  Franklin Lakes NJ 07417
  800/CAREER-1 or 201/848-0310
  FAX: 201/848-1727
  Internet: www.careerpress.com
COST: $8.99

Walks test-takers through successful test preparation, including reading for maximum retention, researching the teacher's test-giving history, and "psyching up" for test day. 128 pages.

3609—"EDUTRAX" QUARTERLY NEWSLETTER

AUTHOR:
  National Scholarship Research
    Service
  2280 Airport Blvd.
  Santa Rosa CA 95403
  707/546-6777
  FAX: 707/546-6785
  E-mail: nsrs@metro.net
COST: $35 (annual subscription)

Provides incisive and comprehensive guidance on what to be, where to go to school, how to get in, and how to pay for it—plus timely articles on important developments in the education arena.

3610—PERSONAL COUNSELING SERVICE BY DAN CASSIDY AND HIS PROFESSIONAL STAFF

AUTHOR: Daniel J. Cassidy and various
    professionals
  National Scholarship Research
    Service (NSRS) & International
    (ISRS)
  5577 Skylane Blvd., Suite 6A
  Santa Rosa CA 95403
  707/546-6777
  FAX: 707/546-6785
  E-mail: nsrs@aol.com
COST: Averages $250.00 to $500.00
  depending on services chosen. Phone or personal counseling is available at $65 per hour.

NSRS & ISRS personal counseling service helping you decide 1) What to be, 2) Where to go, 3) How to get in, and 4) How to pay for it.

3611—101 GREAT ANSWERS TO THE TOUGHEST INTERVIEW QUESTIONS

AUTHOR: Ron Fry, ISBN 1-56414-464-X
  Career Press, Inc.
  3 Tice Road, P.O. Box 687
  Franklin Lakes NJ 07417
  800/CAREER-1 or 201/848-0310
  FAX: 201/848-1727
  Internet: www.careerpress.com
COST: $11.99

For part-time job seekers or those seeking permanent careers, this guide includes overview of the interviewing process and covers the full range of possible interview topics—everything from "Why are you thinking of leaving your current job?" to "When can you start?" 224 pages.

3612—101 GREAT RESUMES

AUTHOR: Editors, ISBN 1-56414-201-9
  Career Press, Inc.
  3 Tice Road, P.O. Box 687
  Franklin Lakes NJ 07417
  800/CAREER-1 or 201/848-0310
  FAX: 201/848-1727
  Internet: www.careerpress.com
COST: $9.99

Covers the greatest range of formats, personal situations, and careers. 216 pages.

3613—270 WAYS TO PUT YOUR TALENT TO WORK IN THE HEALTH FIELD

  National Health Council
  1730 M Street NW, Suite 500
  Washington DC 20036
  202/785-3910
  E-mail: info@nhcouncil.org
  Internet: www.nhcouncil.org
COST: $15.00

A resource book containing career information on various health fields.

3614—A CAREER GUIDE TO MUSIC EDUCATION

AUTHOR: Written by Barbara Payne
  Music Educators National Conference
  1806 Robert Fulton Drive
  Reston VA 20191
  703/860-4000
  Internet: http://www.menc.org
COST: Free (available only on Internet at above website)

A comprehensive guide to careers in music, how to find a job, prepare a resume, etc.

3615—A GUIDE TO AVIATION EDUCATION RESOURCES

AUTHOR: Booklet #EP-1996-11-354-HQ
  National Coalition for Aviation
    Education
  P.O. Box 28086
  Washington DC 20038
  Internet: www2.db.erau.edu/~ncae/
COST: Free

A comprehensive directory of organizations related to aviation training: governmental, industrial, labor, etc. Lists sources of training and scholarships in various allied fields and includes addresses, phone numbers, e-mail addresses, and website locations. A great resource for education and funding for this field!

3616—A TEACHER'S GUIDE TO FELLOWSHIPS AND AWARDS

AUTHOR: Lists financial aid sources for
    teachers in many fields.
  Massachusetts Dept. of Education
  350 Main Street
  Malden MA 02148-5123
  781/388-3300
  Internet: www.doe.mass.edu/
    doedocs/tgfatoc.html
COST: Free

Available on website: www.doe.mass.edu/doedocs/tgfatoc.html

3617—ABCs OF FINANCIAL AID (Montana Financial Aid Handbook)

AUTHOR: Montana Guaranteed Student
    Loan Program
  Montana Guaranteed Student
    Loan Program
  2500 Broadway
  Helena MT 59620-3101
  406/444-6594 or
  800/537-7508
COST: Free

Describes educational costs and financial aid available in Montana for Montana residents or those attending school in Montana only. It covers application and award procedures and financial aid programs.

3618—ACADEMIC YEAR ABROAD

AUTHOR: Sara J. Steen, Editor
Institute of International Education
IIE Books, 809 United Nations Plaza
New York NY 10017-3580
COST: $44.95 + $5 handling

Provides information on more than 2,350 postsecondary study programs outside the US.

3619—ADVENTURE CAREERS

AUTHOR: Alex Hiam & Susan Angle, ISBN 1-56414-175-6
Career Press, Inc.
3 Tice Road, P.O. Box 687
Franklin Lakes NJ 07417
800/CAREER-1 or 201/848-0310
FAX: 201/848-1727
Internet: www.careerpress.com
COST: $11.99

This comprehensive source for information about completely different and decidedly unroutine career paths is packed with practical how-to's, lists of contacts, and first-hand experiences. 288 pages.

3620—AFL-CIO GUIDE TO UNION-SPONSORED SCHOLARSHIPS

AUTHOR: AFL-CIO Department of Education
AFL-CIO
815 16th Street NW
Washington DC 20006
COST: Free to union members; $3.00 non-union

Comprehensive guide for union members and their dependent children. Describes local, national, and international union-sponsored scholarship programs. Includes a bibliography of other financial aid sources.

3621—AMERICAN INSTITUTE OF ARCHITECTS INFORMATION POSTER AND BOOKLET

AUTHOR: AIA
American Institute of Architects
1735 New York Ave. NW
Washington DC 20006
COST: Free

Provides list of accredited professional programs and scholarship information.

3622—ANIMATION SCHOOL DIRECTORY

AUTHOR: AWN
Animation World Network
6525 Sunset Blvd., Garden Suite 10
Hollywood CA 90028

323/468-2554
FAX: 323/464-5914
E-mail: sales@awn.com
Internet: www.awn.com
COST: $24.99 (+$3 shipping US; $5 Canada/Mexico; $8 other)

Reference guide to over 400 animation-related schools and educational institutions from 34 different countries. Free version is available online; however, the deluxe edition contains special information, such as interviews, articles, links, and recommendations. May order online.

3623—ANNUAL REGISTER OF GRANT SUPPORT

AUTHOR: Reed Reference Publishing
Reed Reference Publishing Company
121 Chanlon Road
New Providence NJ 07974
908-464-6800
COST: $199.95 + 7% shipping/handling + state sales tax

Annual reference book found in most major libraries. Details thousands of grants for research that are available to individuals and organizations.

3624—ART CALENDAR

AUTHOR: Barbara L. Dougherty, Publisher
P.O. Box 199
Upper Fairmount MD 21867-0199
410/651-9150
FAX: 410/651-5313
E-mail: barbdoug@dmv.com
Internet: www.artcalendar.com
COST: $32.00/one year

Monthly publication contains articles of interest to artists including listings of grants, fellowships, exhibits, etc. Annual edition lists opportunities without deadlines. Access website for more information. Sample copy of monthly is available for $5.

3625—BARRON'S GUIDE TO LAW SCHOOLS

AUTHOR: Barron's College Division
ISBN 0-8120-9558-8
Barron's Educational Series Inc.
250 Wireless Blvd.
Hauppauge NY 11788
800/645-3476 or 516/434-3311
Internet: www.barronseduc.com
COST: $14.95

Comprehensive guide covering more than 200 ABA-approved American law schools. Advice on attending law school.

3626—BASIC FACTS ON STUDY ABROAD

AUTHOR: IIE
Institute of International Education
IIE Books, 809 United Nations Plaza
New York NY 10017
COST: Free

Brochure offering essential information on planning for undergraduate and graduate study outside the US.

3627—BETTER GRAMMAR IN 30 MINUTES A DAY

AUTHOR: Constance Immel & Florence Sacks, ISBN 1-56414-204-3
Career Press, Inc.
3 Tice Road, P.O. Box 687
Franklin Lakes NJ 07417
800/CAREER-1 or 201/848-0310
FAX: 201/848-1727
Internet: www.careerpress.com
COST: $9.99

Here's help for anyone who has something to say or write but has difficulty doing so in standard English. It features thorough coverage of key areas of grammar, clear explanations with a minimum of grammatical terms, and in an abundant variety of exercises. 252 pages.

3628—BETTER SENTENCE WRITING IN 30 MINUTES A DAY

AUTHOR: Dianna Campbell, ISBN 1-56414-203-5
Career Press, Inc.
3 Tice Road, P.O. Box 687
Franklin Lakes NJ 07417
800/CAREER-1 or 201/848-0310
FAX: 201/848-1727
Internet: www.careerpress.com
COST: $9.99

Features clear discussions of rules and strategies for good writing, concise explanations with a minimum of grammatical terms, and an abundant variety of exercises, from filling-in-the-blanks to joining short sentences into longer and more graceful combinations. 224 pages.

3629—BETTER SPELLING IN 30 MINUTES A DAY

AUTHOR: Harry H. Crosby & Robert W. Emery, ISBN 1-56414-202-7
Career Press, Inc.
3 Tice Road, P.O. Box 687
Franklin Lakes NJ 07417

800/CAREER-1 or 201/848-0310
FAX: 201/848-1727
Internet: www.careerpress.com
COST: $9.99

Features diagnostic exercises that allow readers to identify their weak spelling areas, thorough coverage of key areas of phonics, a focus on the most commonly misspelled words, ample opportunity for proofreading practice, and clear explanations with a minimum of difficult terms. 224 pages.

3630—BETTER VOCABULARY IN 30 MINUTES A DAY

AUTHOR: Edie Schwager,
ISBN 1-56414-247-7
Career Press, Inc.
3 Tice Road, P.O. Box 687
Franklin Lakes NJ 07417
800/CAREER-1 or 201/848-0310
FAX: 201/848-1727
Internet: www.careerpress.com
COST: $9.99

Offers a comprehensive method for adding a more impressive list of words to your everyday speech and learning how to use them effortlessly and accurately. 192 pages.

3631—BIG BOOK OF MINORITY OPPORTUNITIES

AUTHOR: ISBN 0-89434-204-5
Garrett Park Press
P.O. Box 190
Garrett Park MD 20896
301/946-2553
COST: $39.00; $35.00 prepaid

Hundreds of attractive financial aid, career guidance, internship, and occupation information programs have been developed by colleges & universities, foundations, federal & state agencies, professional & trade associations, and others to help minorities meet their educational & career goals. Over 3,500 sources are listed with information provided on scholarships, fellowships, & other financial aid in various fields of study. 636 pages.

3632—BIG BOOK OF OPPORTUNITIES FOR WOMEN

AUTHOR: ISBN 0-89434-183-9
Garrett Park Press
P.O. Box 190
Garrett Park MD 20896
301/946-2553
COST: $39.00; $35.00 prepaid

Hundreds of attractive financial aid, career guidance, internship, and occupation information programs have been developed by colleges & universities, foundations, federal & state agencies, professional & trade organizations, and others to help women meet their educational & career goals. Over 3,500 sources are listed with information on scholarships, fellowships, & other financial aid in various areas of study. 455 pages.

3633—BUILDING A GREAT RESUME

AUTHOR: Kate Wendleton,
ISBN 1-56414-433-X
Career Press, Inc.
3 Tice Road, P.O. Box 687
Franklin Lakes NJ 07417
800/CAREER-1 or 201/848-0310
FAX: 201/848-1727
Internet: www.careerpress.com
COST: $12.99

Learn how to turn your resume into a marketing piece that presents you just the way you want a prospective employer to see you. Includes scores of sample resumes and case studies as it takes you through the entire process of developing a resume that's right for you. 192 pages.

3634—BARTENDING

AUTHOR: Call or e-mail for shipping quote and/or information on the Book version.
Complete World Bartending Guide (CD-Rom; Book also available)
c/o Bar Biz
2245 E. Colorado Blvd., Suite 104
Pasadena CA 91107-6921
800/615-6888
888/303-5145 (International)
Internet: www.barbiz.com/bartend.htm
COST: $29.95 + shipping via UPS

Over 2,400 drink recipes, glassware database for each recipe, pop-up video tips from professional bartenders, powerful search engine allows you to look up recipes by key words or ingredients, wine database and tips for which wines go well with meals, over one hour of video instruction, and 200+ non-alcohol recipes.

3635—CARE AND FEEDING OF YOUR BRAIN

AUTHOR: Kenneth Giuffre, MD,
ISBN 1-56414-380-5

Career Press, Inc.
3 Tice Road, P.O. Box 687
Franklin Lakes NJ 07417
800/CAREER-1 or 201/848-0310
FAX: 201/848-1727
Internet: www.careerpress.com
COST: $16.99

Explains why many functions of the brain that are seemingly uncontrollable and unpredictable are in fact readily affected by the things we eat, drink, smoke, and swallow. Describes how brain and body work together on a physical level and how our diet and environment can be altered to improve how we think and what we feel. 224 pages.

3636—CAREER GUIDE FOR SINGERS

AUTHOR: Mary McDonald
OPERA America
1156 15th St. NW, Suite 810
Washington DC 20005-1704
202/293-4466
FAX 202/393-0735
E-mail: Frontdesk@operaam.org
COST: $45.00 non-members; $25.00 members

Directory of producing organizations, institutes, and workshops for advanced training, degree-granting educational institutions with opera/performance degrees, and major opera workshops, competitions, and grants. A resource for aspiring artists seeking opportunities in the opera field. Entries include casting policies, repertoire, and audition/application procedures, along with other pertinent information.

3637—CAREER PRESS CATALOG

Career Press, Inc.
3 Tice Road, P.O. Box 687
Franklin Lakes NJ 07417
800/CAREER-1 or 201/848-0310
FAX: 201/848-1727
Internet: www.careerpress.com
COST: Free

Career Press offers a variety of helpful publications in scholastic, professional, and general interest areas.

3638—CAREERS WITHOUT COLLEGE: CARS

AUTHOR: ISBN 0-7689-0265-7
Peterson's, Inc.
P.O. Box 2123
Princeton NJ 08543-2123
800/225-0261

FAX: 609/924-5338
Internet: www.petersons.com
COST: $7.96

Helps you gear up for your career in the auto industry. Find out about skills and training, salary, benefits, promotions, and more. Features interviews with experts in the field. Learn how to make it as a CAD Specialist, Car Salesperson, Service Technician, Claims Representative, or Electronics Specialist. 142 pages.

3639—CFKR CAREER MATERIALS CATALOG

AUTHOR: CFKR

CFKR Career Materials
11860 Kemper Road, #7
Auburn CA 95603
800/525-5626 or 530/889-2357
FAX 916/889-0433
E-mail: cfkr@cfkr.com
Internet: www.cfkr.com
COST: Free

A catalog of printed materials, software, and videotapes covering career planning, college financing, and college test preparation. Includes materials applicable to all ages—from the primary grades through graduate school.

3640—CHALLENGE IN AGRICULTURE

American Farm Bureau Federation
225 Touhy Ave.
Park Ridge IL 60068
312/399-5700
COST: Free

Scholarship listings, career opportunities, and web page directory regarding careers and research in various agricultural fields.

3641—CHRONICLE CAREER INDEX

AUTHOR: CGP, ISBN #1-55631-243-1
Chronicle Guidance Publications
66 Aurora Street, P.O. Box 1190
Moravia NY 13118-1190
800/622-7284 or 315/497-0330
FAX: 315/497-3359
Internet: www.chronicleguidance.com
COST: $14.25 + $1.43 shipping/handling
(Order #502CI)

Listings of career and vocational materials for students and counselors. Describes over 500 sources of publications and audio-visual materials. 90 pages.

3642—CHRONICLE FINANCIAL AID GUIDE

AUTHOR: CGP

Chronicle Guidance Publications
66 Aurora Street, P.O. Box 1190
Moravia NY 13118-1190
800/622-7284 or 315/497-0330
FAX: 315/497-3359
Internet: www.chronicleguidance.com
COST: $24.98 + shipping/handling

Annual guide containing information on financial aid programs offered nationally and regionally by public and private organizations. Programs support study for high school seniors, college undergraduates, graduates, and adult learners. 330 pages.

3643—CHRONICLE FOUR-YEAR COLLEGE DATABOOK

AUTHOR: CGP, ISBN #1-55631-292-X
Chronicle Guidance Publications
66 Aurora Street, P.O. Box 1190
Moravia NY 13118-1190
800/622-7284 or 315/497-0330
FAX: 315/497-3359
Internet: www.chronicleguidance.com
COST: $24.99 + shipping/handling
(Order #502CM4)

Reference book in two sections. "Majors" section lists 2,160 institutions offering 760 majors classified by CIP. "Charts" section contains information and statistics on each of the schools. 372 pages.

3644—CHRONICLE TWO-YEAR COLLEGE DATABOOK

AUTHOR: CGP, ISBN #1-55631-293-8
Chronicle Guidance Publications
66 Aurora Street, P.O. Box 1190
Moravia NY 13118-1190
800/622-7284 or 315/497-0330
FAX: 315/497-3359
COST: $24.97 plus shipping/handling
(Order #502CM2)

Reference book in two sections. "Majors" section lists 2,432 institutions offering 760 certificate/diploma, associate, and transfer programs. "Charts" section contains comprehensive information and statistics on each institution. 372 pages.

3645—CHRONICLE VOCATIONAL SCHOOL MANUAL

AUTHOR: CGP, ISBN #1-55631-285-7
Chronicle Guidance Publications
66 Aurora Street, P.O. Box 1190
Moravia NY 13118-1190
800/622-7284 or 315/497-0330
FAX: 315/497-3359
Internet: www.chronicleguidance.com
COST: $24.96 + 10% shipping/handling

More than 3,400 accredited vocational and technical schools and over 920 programs of study. Charts format gives statistical data on institutions listed alphabetically by state. Extensive cross-references.

3646—COLLEGE ATHLETIC SCHOLARSHIP GUIDE

AUTHOR: WSF

Women's Sports Foundation
Eisenhower Park
East Meadow NY 11554
800/227-3988
FAX: 516/542-4716
E-mail: WoSport@aol.com
Internet: www.lifetimetv.com/WoSport
COST: Free (1st copy; 2-100 copies $.10 ea, 100+ $.05 ea)

A listing of over 10,000 college athletic scholarships for women as well as a "game plan for success" with suggestions on how to go about a scholarship search. Updated annually. 32 pages.

3647—COLLEGE BOUND FAMILY LIBRARY & SUPPORT PACKAGE

AUTHOR: Various professional authors
National Scholarship Research
    Service (NSRS) & International
    (ISRS)
5577 Skylane Blvd., Suite 6A
Santa Rosa CA 95403
707/546-6781
FAX: 707/546-6785
E-mail: nsrs@aol.com
COST: $199.95 (plus shipping & handling)

Includes Occupational Outlook Handbook, Guide to 4-Year Colleges, Complete Preparation for the SAT, Dan Cassidy's Worldwide College & Graduate Scholarship Directories, How to Win a Sports Scholarship, and much more (11 items in all).

3648—COLLEGE DEGREES BY MAIL & MODEM

AUTHOR: John Bear, Ph.D. & Mariah
Bear, M.A., ISBN 1-58008-109-6
Ten Speed Press
P.O. Box 7123
Berkeley CA 94707
800/841-BOOK or 510/559-1600
FAX: 510/559-1629
E-mail: order@tenspeed.com
Internet: www.tenspeed.com
COST: $12.95 + $4.50 shipping

With the rise of Internet-based education, distance learning has never been hotter. You really can earn a fully accredited degree (undergraduate or graduate) in a wide range of fields without ever leaving your home. This guide is updated every year and provides full information on the top 100 distance-learning schools worldwide, including chapters on getting credit from life experience and how to tell the good schools from the bad. 216 pages.

3649—COLLEGE FINANCIAL AID EMERGENCY KIT

AUTHOR: Joyce Lain Kennedy and
Dr. Herm Davis
Sun Features Inc.
Box 368
Cardiff CA 92007
760/431-1660
COST: $6.95 (includes postage and
handling)

40-page booklet filled with tips on how to meet tuition and room and board costs. It tells what is available, whom to ask, and how to ask.

3650—COLLEGE FINANCIAL AID FOR DUMMIES

AUTHOR: Joyce Lain Kennedy and
Dr. Herm Davis, ISBN 0-7645-5049-7
Also in bookstores.
College Financial Aid for Dummies
IDG Books Worldwide, Inc.
919 E. Hillsdale Blvd., Suite 400
Foster City CA 94404
800/762-2974
Internet: www.dummies.com
COST: $19.99

This book is a major new guide to understanding the financial aid maze. Useful for high school and college students and also for adults returning to school.

3651—COLLEGE IS POSSIBLE

Coalition of America's Colleges and
Universities
Internet: www.collegeispossible.org
COST: Free (online)

An online resource guide for parents, students, and education professionals, containing information on preparing for college, choosing the right college, and paying for college.

3652—COLLEGE READY REPORT: THE FIRST STEP TO COLLEGE

AUTHOR: Student Resources, Inc.
Student Resources, Inc.
260 Maple Avenue
Barrington RI 02806
800/676-2900
COST: $100

Students and parents fill out a questionnaire to receive an individualized report with valuable college information. This includes a quick reference to the twelve colleges that most closely match the student's profile, along with admissions selections guides, detailed summaries of the schools, and estimated costs and financial aid planning.

3653—COLLEGE SMARTS—THE OFFICIAL FRESHMAN HANDBOOK

AUTHOR: Joyce Slayton Mitchell,
ISBN 0-912048-92-1
Garrett Park Press
P.O. Box 190
Garrett Park MD 20896
301/946-2553
COST: $10.95

Cogent advice for the college freshman. Covers such practical subjects as what things to take, coping with dorm life/your roommate, registration, fraternity/sorority rush, and even your laundry. Advice is practical and to the point.

3654—COLLEGE SURVIVAL INSTRUCTION BOOK

AUTHOR: Steve Mott & Susan Lutz,
ISBN 1-56414-248-5
Career Press, Inc.
3 Tice Road, P.O. Box 687
Franklin Lakes NJ 07417
800/CAREER-1 or 201/848-0310
FAX: 201/848-1727
Internet: www.careerpress.com
COST: $6.99

Filled with tips, advice, suggestions, and secrets for making your college life more interesting and rewarding. 128 pages.

3655—COLLEGES WITH PROGRAMS FOR STUDENTS WITH LEARNING DISABILITIES OR ATTENTION DEFICIT DISORDER

AUTHOR: ISBN 1-56079-853-X
Peterson's, Inc.
P.O. Box 2123
Princeton NJ 08543-2123
800/225-0261
FAX: 609/924-5338
Internet: www.petersons.com
COST: $26.36

A bonus CD-ROM guides you to find the assistance and accommodations for your specific requirements at more than 1,000 two- and four-year colleges in the US and Canada. Students with learning disabilities or Attention Deficit Disorder can find out what's available for them with full descriptions of special services and programs on campus. 669 pages.

3656—COOPERATIVE EDUCATION COLLEGE ROSTER

AUTHOR: NCCE
National Commission for
Cooperative Education
360 Huntington Ave., 384CP
Boston MA 02115-5096
617/373-3770
FAX: 617/373-3463
E-mail: ncce@lynx.neu.edu
Internet: www.co-op.edu
COST: Free

Explains what co-op education is, details its advantages, and lists colleges and universities that offer co-op education programs in which industry becomes a partner in education.

3657—CREATIVE GUIDE TO RESEARCH

AUTHOR: Robin Rowland,
ISBN 1-56414-442-9
Career Press, Inc.
3 Tice Road, P.O. Box 687
Franklin Lakes NJ 07417
800/CAREER-1 or 201/848-0310
FAX: 201/848-1727
Internet: www.careerpress.com
COST: $16.99

Guide for students, professionals, and others pursuing research, describing how to find what you need, online or offline.

3658—CULINARY SCHOOLS

AUTHOR: ISBN 0-7689-0127-8

Peterson's, Inc.
P.O. Box 2123
Princeton NJ 08543-2123
800/225-0261
FAX: 609/924-5338
Internet: www.petersons.com

COST: $19.96

Leading chefs and cooking school directors stir up the pot to guide you through this unique guide of complete listings of professional culinary programs at two- and four-year colleges and culinary institutes. Easy-to-use profiles and additional resources add the right spice. 380 pages.

3659—DAN CASSIDY'S GUIDE TO PRIVATE SECTOR KINDERGARTEN-12TH GRADE (K-12) SCHOLARSHIPS

AUTHOR: Daniel J. Cassidy
National Scholarship Research
Service (NSRS) & International
(ISRS)
5577 Skylane Blvd., Suite 6A
Santa Rosa CA 95403
707/546-6777
FAX: 707/546-6785
E-mail: nsrs@aol.com

COST: $20 (includes shipping)

A 50-page booklet of scholarships for elementary and secondary private schools with introduction on how to apply. Note: Due to the fairly new nature of this subject, many awards are based for particular cities, states, and schools.

3660—DAN CASSIDY'S GUIDE TO TRAVEL GRANTS

AUTHOR: Daniel J. Cassidy
National Scholarship Research
Service (NSRS) & International
(ISRS)
5577 Skylane Blvd., Suitte 6A
Santa Rosa CA 95403
707/546-6777
FAX: 707/546-6785
E-mail: nsrs@aol.com

COST: $20 (includes shipping)

A guide to finding funds for traveling for research, sabbaticals, and/or personal enrichment.

3661—DEBT-FREE GRADUATE: HOW TO SURVIVE COLLEGE WITHOUT GOING BROKE

AUTHOR: Murray Baker,
ISBN 1-56414-472-0
Career Press, Inc.
3 Tice Road, P.O. Box 687
Franklin Lakes NJ 07417
800/CAREER-1 or 201/848-0310
FAX: 201/848-1727
Internet: www.careerpress.com

COST: $13.99

Tells students how they can stay out of debt by taking simple and easy measures, while still having the time of their lives at college. Includes how to get a great summer job and make it pay; how to negotiate with a bank—and win; how to find affordable student housing; how to eat, drink, and be merry on a budget; how to graduate without a huge student debt; and how to cut costs with bills. 320 pages.

3662—DIRECTORY OF ACCREDITED INSTITUTIONS

AUTHOR: ACICS
Accrediting Council for Independent
Colleges and Schools
750 1st Street NE, Suite 980
Washington DC 20002
202/336-6780
Internet: www.acics.org

COST: Free (and is also on website)

Annual directory containing information on more than 650 institutions offering business or business-related career programs and accredited by ACICS.

3663—DIRECTORY OF FINANCIAL AIDS FOR MINORITIES

AUTHOR: Gail A. Schlachter &
R. David Weber, ISBN 0-918276-28-4
Reference Service Press
5000 Windplay Drive, Suite 4
El Dorado Hills CA 95762
916/939-9620

COST: $47.50 + $4.00 shipping

Describes over 2,000 scholarships, fellowships, grants, loans, awards, and internships set aside for American minorities and minority organizations. Covers all levels of study. 666 pages.

3664—DIRECTORY OF FINANCIAL AID FOR STUDENTS OF ARMENIAN DESCENT

AUTHOR: Armenian Assembly of
America
Armenian Assembly of America
122 'C' Street NW, Suite 350
Washington DC 20001
201/393-3434
Internet: www.geocities.org/
CollegePark/4042/finaid.html

COST: Free

The Armenian Assembly prepares this annual booklet that describes numerous scholarship, loan, and grant programs available from sources in the Armenian community. Available online.

3665—DIRECTORY OF FINANCIAL AIDS FOR WOMEN

AUTHOR: Gail A. Schlachter,
ISBN 0-918276-27-6
Reference Service Press
5000 Windplay Drive, Suite 4
El Dorado Hills CA 95762
916/939-9620

COST: $45.00 + $4.00 shipping

Contains over 1,500 descriptions of scholarships, fellowships, grants, loans, awards, and internships set aside for women and women's organizations. Covers all levels of study. 498 pages. Cloth.

3666—DIRECTORY OF MEMBER SCHOOLS

Association of Independent Schools
in New England
100 Grossman Drive, Suite 301
Braintree MA 02184
800/886-2323
Internet: www.aisne.org

COST: Free

A directory of independent schools in five New England states; includes preschool through postgraduate schools and both day and boarding programs. Some are coed, and others are for a single sex. Some are religious, and some are for students with learning disabilities. Access Internet for a list and/or call for more information.

3667—DIRECTORY OF NATIONAL INFORMATION SOURCES ON DISABILITIES (7th Edition)

AUTHOR: NARIC

National Rehabilitation Information Center
1010 Wayne Ave., Suite 800
Silver Spring MD 20910-5633
800/346-2742 or 301/562-2400
TTY: 301/495-5626
FAX: 301/562-2401
E-mail: naricinfo@kra.com
Internet: www.naric.com/naric
COST: $5.00

Two-volume directory inventories public/federal/private resources at the national level that offer information and/or direct services to people with disabilities & people involved in educating, training, or helping people with disabilities.

3668—DIRECTORY OF POSTSECONDARY EDUCATIONAL RESOURCES IN ALASKA

AUTHOR: ACPE

Alaska Commission on
Postsecondary Education
3030 Vintage Blvd.
Juneau AK 99801
907/465-2962 or 800/441-2962
COST: Free

Comprehensive directory of postsecondary institutions and programs in Alaska plus information on state and federal grants, loans, and scholarships for Alaska residents (those who have lived in Alaska for two years).

3669—DIRECTORY OF RESEARCH GRANTS

AUTHOR: Oryx, ISBN 1-57356-095-2
Pages: 1,232. Published 1999

Oryx Press
P.O. Box 33889
Phoenix AZ 85067-3889
Internet: www.oryxpress.com
COST: $135.00

Annual reference book found in most major libraries. Provides current data on funds available from foundations, corporations, and state/local organizations, as well as from federal sources, for research projects in medicine, physical/social sciences, arts, humanities, and education. More than 5,900 sources.

3670—DIRECTORY OF TECHNICAL SCHOOLS, COLLEGES, AND UNIVERSITIES OFFERING COURSES IN GRAPHIC COMMUNICATIONS

AUTHOR: NSTF

National Scholarship Trust Fund of
the Graphic Arts

200 Deer Run Road
Sewickley PA 15153-2600
412/741-6860
FAX: 412/741-2311
E-mail: nstf@gatf.org
Internet: www.gatf.org
COST: Free

A listing of accredited institutions that offer degrees in graphic arts and related fields.

3671—DIRECTORY OF UNDERGRADUATE POLITICAL SCIENCE FACULTY

AUTHOR: Patricia Spellman

American Political Science Association
1527 New Hampshire Ave. NW
Washington DC 20036-1206
202/483-2512
FAX: 202/483-2657
E-mail: apsa@apsanet.org
Internet: www.apsanet.org
COST: $25 (APSA members) + $4 shipping; $40 (non-members) + $6 shipping

Directory listing nearly 600 separate political science departments in the US and Canada. Includes department names, addresses, telephone numbers, names, and specializations of faculty members.

3672—DOLLARS FOR COLLEGE: THE QUICK GUIDE TO SCHOLARSHIPS, FELLOWSHIPS, LOANS, AND OTHER FINANCIAL AID PROGRAMS FOR . . .

Garrett Park Press
P.O. Box 190
Garrett Park MD 20896
301/946-2553
COST: $7.95 each or $60 for set of all twelve booklets (+ $1.50 for shipping no matter how many are ordered)

User-friendly series of 12 booklets pinpoints awards in areas of particular concern to students: Art, Music, Drama; Business & Related Fields; The Disabled; Education; Engineering; Journalism & Mass Communications; Law; Liberal Arts—Humanities & Social Science; Medicine, Dentistry, & Related Fields; Nursing & Other Health Fields; Science; and Women In All Fields. Booklets are revised every 18 months, and each cites from 300 to 400 programs. 70-90 pages each.

3673—EDITOR & PUBLISHER JOURNALISM AWARDS AND FELLOWSHIPS DIRECTORY

Editor & Publisher
11 West 19th Street
New York NY 10011

212/675-4380
E-mail: edpub@mediainfo.com
Internet: www.mediainfo.com/store/awards.htm
COST: $8.00

A source of information for awards, fellowships, grants, and scholarships for journalism students and professionals. Also available as a pullout section of the December issue of *Editor & Publisher* magazine. Both national and international awards.

3674—EDUCATION AND TRAINING PROGRAMS IN OCEANOGRAPHY AND RELATED FIELDS

AUTHOR: Marine Technology Society

Marine Technology Society
1828 L Street NW, Suite 906
Washington DC 20036
COST: $6 shipping/handling

A guide to current marine degree programs and vocational instruction available in the marine field. Consolidates and highlights data needed by high school students as well as college students seeking advanced degrees.

3675—EDUCATIONAL LEADERSHIP, EDUCATION UPDATE, & CURRICULUM UPDATE

AUTHOR: ASCD

Association for Supervision and
Curriculum Development
1703 N. Beauregard Street
Alexandria VA 22311-1714
800/933-ASCD or
703/578-9600, ext. 2
COST: $49 for membership

Membership includes eight issues of *Educational Leadership*, giving you case studies of successful programs, interviews with experts, and features by educators & administrators in the field. Also included are eight issues of *Education Update*, advising you of significant trends affecting education, networking opportunities, and the newest resources & ASCD services. The quarterly newsletter, *Curriculum Update*, also included, examines current, major issues in education.

3676—EEO BIMONTHLY

AUTHOR: Timothy M. Clancy,
Executive Editor
CASS Recruitment Publications Inc.
1800 Sherman Place, Suite 300
Evanston IL 60201
708/475-8800
FAX 708/475-8807
COST: $42.00/Year

Bimonthly publication containing detailed career opportunity profiles on American companies; geographic employer listings and occupational index.

3677—ENCYCLOPEDIA OF ASSOCIATIONS—Vol. 1

AUTHOR: ISBN 0-8103-7945-7
Gale Research Inc.
835 Penobscot Bldg.
Detroit MI 48226
800/223-GALE, 313/961-2242
COST: $415.00

An outstanding research tool. 3-part set of reference books found in most major libraries. Contains detailed information on over 22,000 associations, organizations, unions, etc. Includes name and key word index.

3678—EVERYDAY MATH FOR THE NUMERICALLY CHALLENGED

AUTHOR: Audrey Carlan,
ISBN 1-56414-355-4
Career Press, Inc.
3 Tice Road, P.O. Box 687
Franklin Lakes NJ 07417
800/CAREER-1 or 201/848-0310
FAX: 201/848-1727
Internet: www.careerpress.com
COST: $11.99

Presents real-life math in an understandable format that actually makes math enjoyable, practical, and useful. Written for everyone—even if you'd just love to balance your checkbook the first time through. 160 pages.

3679—EXPLORING CAREERS IN MUSIC

AUTHOR: Paul Bjorneberg,
ISBN 0-940796-86-4
Music Educators National Conference
1806 Robert Fulton Drive
Reston VA 20191
COST: $13.25/$10.60 for MENC members

Informative booklet geared toward young people that discusses careers in the performing arts, music education, the music business, recording industry, and allied fields.

3680—FEDERAL BENEFITS FOR VETERANS & DEPENDENTS (S/N 051-000-00212-1)

AUTHOR: Veterans Administration
Superintendent of Documents
US Government Printing Office
Washington DC 20402

COST: $5.50

94-page booklet containing details of all Federal benefit programs available to veterans and their dependents.

3681—FELLOWSHIP GUIDE TO WESTERN EUROPE

AUTHOR: Gina Bria Vescori, Editor
Council for European Studies
Columbia University
International Affairs Bldg. 807-807A
New York NY 10027
212/854-4172
FAX: 212/854-8808
E-mail: ces@columbia.edu
Internet: www.europanet.org
COST: $8.00 (prepaid—check to
Columbia Univ.)

This booklet is intended to assist US students in finding funds for European travel and study in the social sciences and humanities.

3682—FINANCIAL AID FOR MINORITIES

Garrett Park Press
P.O. Box 190
Garrett Park MD 20896
301/946-2553
COST: $5.95 each or $30 for set of all six
booklets

Several booklets with hundreds of sources of financial aid for minorities. When ordering, please specify which of the following you are interested in: Students of Any Major; Business & Law; Education; Journalism & Mass Communications; Health Fields; or Engineering & Science. Booklets average 80 pages in length, and each lists between 300 and 400 different sources of aid.

3683—FINANCIAL AID FOR THE DISABLED AND THEIR FAMILIES

AUTHOR: Gail Ann Schlachter and
R. David Weber
Reference Service Press
5000 Windplay Drive, Suite 4
El Dorado Hills CA 95762
916/939-9620
COST: $38.50 + $4.00 shipping

Contains descriptions of 900 scholarships, fellowships, grants, loans, awards, and internships set aside for the disabled and their families. Covers all levels of study. 310 pages.

3684—FINANCIAL AID FOR VETERANS; MILITARY PERSONNEL & THEIR FAMILIES

AUTHOR: Gail Ann Schlachter and
R. David Weber
Reference Service Press
5000 Windplay Drive, Suite 4
El Dorado Hills CA 95762
916/939-9620
COST: $38.50 + $4 shipping

Contains over 950 descriptions of scholarships, fellowships, grants, loans, awards, and internships set aside for veterans, military personnel, and their families. Covers all levels of study. 300 pages.

3685—FINANCIAL AID INFORMATION FOR PHYSICIAN ASSISTANT STUDENTS

American Academy of Physician
Assistants
950 North Washington Street
Alexandria VA 22314
708/836-2272
COST: Free

A comprehensive listing of scholarships, traineeships, grants, loans, and related publications related to the physician assistant field of study.

3686—FINANCIAL AID RESOURCE GUIDE- #17.97

National Clearinghouse for
Professions in Special Education
The Council for Exceptional Children
1920 Association Drive
Reston VA 20191-1589
800-641-7824 or 703/264-9476
TTY: 703/264-9480
FAX: 703/264-1637
E-mail: ncpse@cec.sped.org
Internet: www.cec.sped.org/ncpse.htm
COST: Free

General information on finding financial assistance for students preparing for careers in special education and related services.

3687—FINANCIAL ASSISTANCE FOR LIBRARY & INFORMATION STUDIES

AUTHOR: ALA
American Library Association
Office for Library Personnel
Resources
50 E. Huron Street
Chicago IL 60611-2795
312/280-4282
FAX: 312/280-3256

Internet: www.ala.org
COST: $4.00 for postage/handling

An excellent summary of fellowships, scholarships, grants-in-aid, loan funds, and other financial assistance for library education. Published each fall for the following year.

3688—FINDING MONEY FOR COLLEGE

AUTHOR: John Bear, Ph.D. & Mariah Bear, M.A., ISBN 1-58008-117-7
Ten Speed Press
P.O. Box 7123
Berkeley CA 94707
800/841-BOOK or 510/559-1600
FAX: 510/559-1629
E-mail: order@tenspeed.com
Internet: www.tenspeed.com
COST: $8.95 + $4.50 shipping

Contains hundreds of listings with complete information, including names & addresses, as well as bonus chapters covering unconventional techniques of lowering tuition. Special sections cover grants based on gender, race or ethnic background, religion, and physical or learning disabilities. 168 pages.

3689—FISKE GUIDE TO COLLEGES

AUTHOR: New York Times Books, ISBN 812-92534-1
Times Books
400 Hahn Road
Westminster MD 21157
COST: $18.00

Describes the top-rated 265 out of 2,000 possible four-year schools in the US. They are rated for academics, social life, and quality of life.

3690—FLORIDA STUDENT FINANCIAL AID—FACT SHEETS

AUTHOR: Florida Department of Education
Florida Department of Education
Office of Financial Assistance
State Programs
255 Collins
Tallahassee FL 32399-0400
850/487-0049 or 888/827-2004
E-mail: OSFABF@mail.doe.state.fl.us
Internet: www.firn.edu/doe
COST: Free

Booklet containing information on Florida grants, scholarships, and teacher programs.

3691—FLY BUCKS

2280 Airport Blvd.
Santa Rosa, CA 95403
707/546-6777
FAX: 707/546-6785
COST: $20 (includes shipping)

A 30-page booklet containing over 80 sources of funding for education in aeronautics, aviation, aviation electronics, aviation writing, space science, aviation maintenance technology, and vertical flight.

3692—FUNDING A COLLEGE EDUCATION

AUTHOR: Alice Drum & Richard Kneedler
Harvard Business School Publishing
Attn: Customer Service
60 Harvard Way
Boston MA 02163
617/495-6117
COST: $14.95 + S/H

An insider's guide, written by two college administrators and college students, to the essentials of college financial aid. It will help you sort through facts and forms to secure financial aid for your child's college education, at the right school for him/her.

3693—FUTURE AIRLINE PILOTS STARTER KIT

AUTHOR: AIR, Inc.
Aviation Information Resources, Inc.
1001 Riverdale Court
Atlanta GA 30337
800/247-2777 or 800/AIR APPS
E-mail: cmobly@airpps.com
Internet: www.airapps.com
COST: $69.95

200-page career planning manual for prospective airline pilots with zero to 1,000 hours. Created by experienced pilots, this kit is filled with pilot training options, certificates, ratings, and medical requirements from private pilot through jet-type ratings. It guides you through the process of choosing a flight school and financing your flight training.

3694—GED—THE KEY TO YOUR FUTURE

AUTHOR: American Council on Education
GED Testing Service of the American Council on Education
One Dupont Circle NW
Washington DC 20036
202/939-9490
COST: Free

If you or someone you know left high school before graduation, this free brochure will explain what the GED tests are and how they provide the opportunity to earn a high school equivalency diploma.

3695—GET ORGANIZED

AUTHOR: Ron Fry, ISBN 1-56414-461-5
Career Press, Inc.
3 Tice Road, P.O. Box 687
Franklin Lakes NJ 07417
800/CAREER-1 or 201/848-0310
FAX: 201/848-1727
Internet: www.careerpress.com
COST: $8.99

Teaches you how to create your "ideal study environment" by using simple time-management tips to develop to-do lists, daily schedules, monthly calendars, and project boards. Includes electronic and online planning tools. 128 pages.

3696—GET SMART FAST

AUTHOR: Sondra Geoffrion
Access Success Associates
6565 Camino Caseta
Goleta CA 93117
805/964-7030
COST: $6.95 + $2.50 US postage ($4.00 foreign postage). California residents add sales tax.

Your grades will improve dramatically with this 61-page handbook for academic success which explains how to master the art of studying, discovering what will be tested, preparing for and taking tests strategically, etc.

3697—GETTING INTERVIEWS

AUTHOR: Kate Wendleton, ISBN 1-56414-448-8
Career Press, Inc.
3 Tice Road, P.O. Box 687
Franklin Lakes NJ 07417
800/CAREER-1 or 201/848-0310
FAX: 201/848-1727
Internet: www.careerpress.com
COST: $12.99

Guide for job hunters, career changers, consultants, and freelancers that tells you how to find out whom you should be talking to and how to get those people to meet with you. 192 pages.

3698—GETTING STARTED IN THE MUSIC BUSINESS

Texas Music Office
P.O. Box 13246
Austin TX 78711
512/463-6666
FAX: 512/463-4114
E-mail: music@governor.state.tx.us
Internet: www.governor.state.tx.us/music/tmlp_intro.htm
COST: Free Online Information

This online guide for musicians in Texas provides short-answer reference to the basic legal and business practices associated with the music industry. Links to many informative sites.

3699—GIFTED & TALENTED EDUCATION

Prufrock Press
P.O. Box 8813
Waco TX 76714-8813
800/998-2208 or 254/756-3337
FAX: 800/240-0333 or
254/756-3339
Internet: www.prufrock.com
COST: Varies

This catalog is filled with books for teachers and parents of gifted and talented children.

3700—GIFTED CHILD QUARTERLY

AUTHOR: See website or contact NAGC for information on specific helpful publications for parents of gifted children.
National Association for Gifted Children
1707 L Street NW, Suite 550
Washington DC 20036
202/785-4268
Internet: www.nagc.org
COST: Associate Membership is $25; Full Membership (including newsletter) is $50; Various publications also available

An organization of parents, educators, other professionals, and community leaders who unite to address the unique needs of all children and youth with demonstrated gifts and talents as well as those who may be able to develop their talent potential with appropriate educational experiences.

3701—GOVERNMENT ASSISTANCE ALMANAC

AUTHOR: J. Robert Dumouchel,
ISBN 0-7808-0061-3
OmniGraphics Inc.
2500 Penobscot Bldg.
Detroit MI 48226
313/961-1340
COST: $135.00

Comprehensive guide to more than $834 billion worth of federal programs available to the American public. Contains 825 pages and 1,370 entries detailing programs of benefit to students, educators, researchers, and consumers.

3702—GRANTS AND AWARDS AVAILABLE TO AMERICAN WRITERS

AUTHOR: ISBN 0-934638-15-2
Pen American Center
568 Broadway
New York NY 10012-3225
212/334-1660
FAX: 212/334-2181
E-mail: pen@echonyc.com
COST: $15 (+ tax if NY resident); + shipping charges for international airmail

More than 1,000 awards listed for poets, journalists, playwrights, etc., including American as well as international grants (including residencies at writers' colonies). Order by mail or fax only. 267 pages.

3703—GRANTS, FELLOWSHIPS, AND PRIZES OF INTEREST TO HISTORIANS

AUTHOR: AHA
American Historical Association
400 A Street, SE
Washington DC 20003
202/544-2422
FAX: 202/544-8307
E-mail: aha@theaha.org
Internet: www.theaha.org
COST: $8.00 AHA members; $10.00 non-members

Offering information on more than 450 funding sources—from undergraduate scholarships to postdoctoral fellowships and awards for written work and publications—the AHA's annual guide can help individuals find funding to begin or continue a research project or degree program. Includes suggestions for writing successful grant proposals and a bibliography of other sources for grant, fellowship, and prize information. 226 pages.

3704—GREAT BIG BOOK OF HOW TO STUDY

AUTHOR: Ron Fry, ISBN 1-56414-423-2
Career Press, Inc.
3 Tice Road, P.O. Box 687
Franklin Lakes NJ 07417
800/CAREER-1 or 201/848-0310
FAX: 201/848-1727
Internet: www.careerpress.com
COST: $15.95

More than 400 pages of useful information and advice, written in a direct, motivational style that will help students regain the confidence they need to succeed in school. 448 pages.

3705—GREAT LITTLE BOOK ON PERSONAL ACHIEVEMENT

AUTHOR: Brian Tracy,
ISBN 1-56414-283-3
Career Press, Inc.
3 Tice Road, P.O. Box 687
Franklin Lakes NJ 07417
800/CAREER-1 or 201/848-0310
FAX: 201/848-1727
Internet: www.careerpress.com
COST: $6.99

Inspiration for anyone who wants to build wealth into the 21st century, attain a fulfilling personal life, and meet high career goals. 128 pages. Other "Great Little Books" include *Mastering Your Time*, *Motivational Minutes*, *Peak Performance Woman*, and *Wisdom*.

3706—GUIDANCE MANUAL FOR THE CHRISTIAN HOME SCHOOL

AUTHOR: David & Laurie Callihan,
ISBN 1-56414-452-6
Career Press, Inc.
3 Tice Road, P.O. Box 687
Franklin Lakes NJ 07417
800/CAREER-1 or 201/848-0310
FAX: 201/848-1727
Internet: www.careerpress.com
COST: $22.99

Guide to preparing home school students for college or career, giving parents information they need to successfully mentor their children in grades 7 through 12 toward adulthood. 264 pages.

3707—GUIDE TO SOURCES OF INFORMATION ON PARAPSYCHOLOGY

AUTHOR: Eileen J. Garrett Library
Parapsychology Foundation
228 E. 71st Street
New York NY 10021
212/628-1550
FAX: 212/628-1559
COST: $3.00

An annual listing of sources of information on major parapsychology organizations, journals, books, and research.

3708—HANDBOOK OF PRIVATE SCHOOLS

AUTHOR: ISBN #0-87558-135-8

Porter Sargent Publishers Inc.
11 Beacon Suite, Suite 1400
Boston MA 02108
617/523-1670

COST: $85.00 + $2.74 postage and handling

Annual reference book found in most major libraries. Describes in detail 1700 American elementary and secondary private schools. 1,396 pages.

3709—HIGHER EDUCATION PROGRAMS

AUTHOR: Catalog available in hard copy, also. Check with organization for ordering information and price.
Presbyterian Church (U.S.A.)
100 Witherspoon Street
Louisville KY 40202-1396
Internet: www.theology.org/highed/catalog.html

COST: Free (on Internet)

An extensive online list of financial aid sources from undergraduate through postgraduate study for theology students in most, not all, religious groups. NOT limited to Presbyterians. Includes Protestant, Catholic, and Jewish sources. Many are not designated for specific groups. Some are for women and ethnic minorities. E-mail can be sent from the website.

3710—HOMESCHOOLING ALMANAC

AUTHOR: Mary & Michael Leppert
Prima Publishing
P.O. Box 1260BK
Rocklin CA 95677
916/632-4400
Internet: www.primalifestyles.com

COST: $24.95

This all-encompassing guide includes more than 900 educational products, such as books/magazines, software, videos, games, crafts, science kits, prepackaged curricula, cybersources, methods, etc. Provides state-by-state breakdown of legal requirements, support groups, and organizations.

3711—HOW TO FIND OUT ABOUT FINANCIAL AID

AUTHOR: Gail Ann Schlachter
Reference Service Press
5000 Windplay Drive, Suite 4
El Dorado Hills CA 95762
916/939-9620

COST: $37.50 + $4.00 shipping

A comprehensive guide to more than 700 print and online directories that identify over $21 billion in financial aid available to undergraduates, graduate students, and researchers.

3712—HOW TO STUDY

AUTHOR: Ron Fry, ISBN 1-56414-456-9
Career Press, Inc.
3 Tice Road, P.O. Box 687
Franklin Lakes NJ 07417
800/CAREER-1 or 201/848-0310
FAX: 201/848-1727
Internet: www.careerpress.com

COST: $12.99

Includes how to create a work environment, excel in class, use the library, do research online, and more. 224 pages.

3713—HOW TO WIN A SPORTS SCHOLARSHIP 1999 Edition

AUTHOR: ISBN 1-884309-04-6 (soft cover)
Hastings Communications
P.O. Box 14927
Santa Rosa CA 95402
707/579-3479

COST: $19.95 + $3.00 S/H (CA residents add $1.49 tax)

Easy-to-use workbook teaches high school athletes and their families a step-by-step process for winning sports scholarships. Special section for women athletes. 250 pages.

3714—IMPROVE YOUR MEMORY

AUTHOR: Ron Fry, ISBN 1-56414-459-3
Career Press, Inc.
3 Tice Road, P.O. Box 687
Franklin Lakes NJ 07417
800/CAREER-1 or 201/848-0310
FAX: 201/848-1727
Internet: www.careerpress.com

COST: $8.99

For high school students, college students, and anyone seeking to improve his or her memory power. Learn the essential principles of memory to help you increase your ability to retain what you read, perform better on tests, or just remember where you last put your car keys. 128 pages.

3715—IMPROVE YOUR READING

AUTHOR: Ron Fry, ISBN 1-56414-458-5
Career Press, Inc.
3 Tice Road, P.O. Box 687
Franklin Lakes NJ 07417

800/CAREER-1 or 201/848-0310
FAX: 201/848-1727
Internet: www.careerpress.com

COST: $8.99

Presents a practical way to increase what you learn from texts, notes, and resources. Whether reading texts or your own notes, you'll learn effective reading comprehension skills required for success in high school, college, and throughout life. 128 pages.

3716—IMPROVE YOUR WRITING

AUTHOR: Ron Fry, ISBN 1-56414-457-7
Career Press, Inc.
3 Tice Road, P.O. Box 687
Franklin Lakes NJ 07417
800/CAREER-1 or 201/848-0310
FAX: 201/848-1727
Internet: www.careerpress.com

COST: $8.99

Presents all the elements important to turning in an excellent research paper. This step-by-step walk-through includes selecting a topic, library research, developing an outline, writing from the first to final draft, proofreading, online research, and more. 128 pages.

3717—INDEX OF MAJORS & GRADUATE DEGREES

AUTHOR: CBP, ISBN #0-87447-592-9
The College Board Publications
Two College Way
Forrester Center WV 25438
800/323-7155
FAX: 800/525-5562
Internet: www.collegeboard.org

COST: $18.95 + $4 + applicable tax

Describes over 600 major programs of study at 3,200 undergraduate and graduate schools. Also lists schools that have religious affiliations, special academic programs, and special admissions procedures. 695 pages.

3718—INSIDER'S GUIDE TO MEDICAL SCHOOLS

AUTHOR: ISBN 0-7689-0203-7
Peterson's, Inc.
P.O. Box 2123
Princeton NJ 08543-2123
800/225-0261
FAX: 609/924-5338
Internet: www.petersons.com

COST: $17.56

Get the inside scoop on admissions, the curriculum, the student body, and campus life from students at 138 medical schools. Plus valuable tips on getting into and preparing for medical school. 480 pages.

3719—INTERNATIONAL JOBS

AUTHOR: Eric Kocher
  Perseus Books
  1 Jacob Way
  Reading MA 01867
COST: $16.00

The 5th edition provides everything you need to navigate complex international job market (including websites).

3720—INFORMATION ON THE PHYSICIAN ASSISTANT PROFESSION

AUTHOR: Write to address for
  information.
  American Academy of Physician
    Assistants
  950 North Washington Street
  Alexandria VA 22314-1552
  703/836-2272
  FAX: 703/684-1924
  E-mail: aapa@aapa.org
  Internet: www.aapa.org
COST: Free

A pamphlet describing the profession of physican assistant—what to study and where to go to school, the salaries, and the specialties.

3721—INFORMATIONAL BROCHURE

AUTHOR: A valuable, free resource for
  parents of elementary and secondary
  school-aged girls whether in private or
  public schools.
  The National Coalition of
    Girls Schols
  228 Main Street
  Concord MA 01742
  978/287-4485
  FAX: 978/287-6014
  E-mail: ncgs@ncgs.org
  Internet: http://www.ncgs.org
COST: Free

A free brochure listing member schools in 23 states, Washington DC, New Zealand, Canada, and Australia, of the Coalition. Many of them have financial aid programs. The brochure also contains valuable information about the issues related to the education of girls. Schools are also listed on the website.

3722—INTERNATIONAL FORESTRY AND NATURAL RESOURCES

AUTHOR: Hard copies no longer
  available; please feel free to download
  and print your own copy.
  United States Department of
    Agriculture (A Guide to
    Grants, Fellowships, and
    Scholarships in International
    Forestry and Natural Resources)
  P.O. Box 96090
  Washington DC 20090-6090
  Internet: http://www.fs.fed.us/
    people/gf/gf00.htm

An online guide to grants, fellowships, and scholarships in international forestry and natural resources.

3723—JOB OPPORTUNITIES FOR THE BLIND (JOB)

AUTHOR: JOB offers the only recorded
  (audio cassette) job magazine in the
  US, along with over 40 other
  publications (most on cassette; some in
  print for employer education).
  National Federation of the Blind
  1800 Johnson Street
  Baltimore MD 21230
  800-638-7518 or 301-659-9314
COST: Free

JOB is operated by the NFB in partnership with the US Dept. of Labor. It offers a free recorded job magazine, other publications, and a national reference service to blind job seekers on all aspects of looking for work, to employers, and to those assisting blind persons.

3724—JOURNALISM AND MASS COMMUNICATIONS ACCREDITATION

AUTHOR: Also see website.
  Accrediting Council on Education in
    Journalism and Mass
    Communications
  Stauffer-Flint Hall
  University of Kansas School of
    Journalism
  Lawrence KS 66045
  785/864-5225
  FAX: 785/864-5225
  E-mail: sshaw@kuhub.cc.ukans.edu
  Internet: www.ukans.edu/~acejmc
COST: $1.00

Comprehensive listing of colleges and universities with accredited journalism and mass communications programs. Also listed are numerous related professional organizations, many of which offer scholarships, internships, etc.

3725—JOURNALISM AND MASS COMMUNICATION DIRECTORY

AUTHOR: AEJMC
  Association for Education in
    Journalism & Mass
    Communications
  Univ. of SC
  LeConte College, Room 121
  Columbia SC 29208-0251
COST: $25.00 US; $35.00 foreign

Annual directory listing more than 350 schools and departments of journalism and mass communication, information on national funds, fellowships, foundations, and collegiate and scholastic services. More than 3,000 individual members.

3726—JOURNALIST'S ROAD TO SUCCESS: A Career and Scholarship Guide

AUTHOR: DJNF
  Dow Jones Newspaper Fund
  P.O. Box 300
  Princeton NJ 08543-0300
  800/DOW-FUND
  E-mail: newsfund@wsj.dowjones.com
  Internet: www.dj.com/newsfund
COST: $3.00 (prepaid check/money
  order)

Comprehensive source book for high school and college students who are interested in journalism careers. Intended to help students choose colleges that offer the best combination of academic programs, practical experience, and scholarships. Updated yearly, the Guide tells students how to prepare for a newspaper career, lists more than 400 colleges that offer news-editorial journalism majors, and lists hundreds of scholarships for the study of news-editorial journalism.

3727—LANGUAGE LIAISON PROGRAM DIRECTORY

  Language Liaison
  1610 Woodstead Ct., Suite 130
  The Woodlands TX 77380
  281/367-7302 or 800/284-4448
  FAX: 281/367-4498
  E-mail: learn@launguageliaison.com
  Internet: www.languageliaison.com
COST: Free

Want to learn another language? Learn it like a native in the country where it is spoken. New programs start every week year-round from two weeks to a year long. Programs are open to students, teachers, executives, teens, seniors, families, and leisure travelers. Includes activities, excursions, and homestays. See website for details on this program as well as various language tools.

3728—LAST-MINUTE COLLEGE FINANCING

AUTHOR: Daniel J. Cassidy,
ISBN 1-56414-468-2
National Scholarship Research
Service
5577 Skylane Blvd., Suite 6A
Santa Rosa CA 95403
707/546-6777
FAX: 707/546-6785
E-mail: nsrs@msn.com
Internet: www.800headstart.com
COST: $20

Whether your child starts college in 15 years or next semester, this helpful guide answers such questions as, "How do I get the money together in time?" "How do I locate quality low-cost colleges?" and "How do I find sources of financial aid that I may have overlooked?" 128 pages.

3729—LAST-MINUTE INTERVIEW TIPS

AUTHOR: Brandon Toropov,
ISBN 1-56414-240-X
Career Press, Inc.
3 Tice Road, P.O. Box 687
Franklin Lakes NJ 07417
800/CAREER-1 or 201/848-0310
FAX: 201/848-1727
Internet: www.careerpress.com
COST: $7.99

Gives you all the tips, tricks, and techniques you need to ace an interview with little preparation and win the job. 128 pages.

3730—LAST-MINUTE RESUMES

AUTHOR: Brandon Toropov,
ISBN 1-56414-354-6
Career Press, Inc.
3 Tice Road, P.O. Box 687
Franklin Lakes NJ 07417
800/CAREER-1 or 201/848-0310
FAX: 201/848-1727
Internet: www.careerpress.com
COST: $9.99

Quickly takes you step by step through the whole resume-preparation process, from self-evaluation to powerful resume models to add drama and excitement to your application. 160 pages.

3731—LAST-MINUTE STUDY TIPS

AUTHOR: Ron Fry, ISBN 1-56414-238-8
Career Press, Inc.
3 Tice Road, P.O. Box 687
Franklin Lakes NJ 07417
800/CAREER-1 or 201/848-0310
FAX: 201/848-1727
Internet: www.careerpress.com
COST: $7.99

Guide to help students with study habits. 128 pages.

3732—LESKO'S SELF-HELP BOOKS

AUTHOR: Matthew Lesko
Information USA, Inc.
P.O. Box E
Kensington MD 20895
800/955-7693 or 301/924-0556
FAX: 301/929-8907
Internet: www.lesko.com
COST: Varies

A variety of self-help books on "free stuff." Author gives information on free government information, expert advice, and money. See website or contact publisher for a list of titles.

3733—LIFE AFTER DEBT

AUTHOR: Bob Hammond,
ISBN 1-56414-421-6
Career Press, Inc.
3 Tice Road, P.O. Box 687
Franklin Lakes NJ 07417
800/CAREER-1 or 201/848-0310
FAX: 201/848-1727
Internet: www.careerpress.com
COST: $14.99

Attacks the causes of debt and how to solve credit problems. Also provides addresses/phone numbers of consumer credit services, state banking authorities, and other resources to get you on your way to financial stability, regardless of income. 256 pages.

3734—LIST OF SCHOLARSHIPS AND AWARDS IN ELECTRICAL, ELECTRONICS, AND COMPUTER ENGINEERING

IEEE-USA Computer Society
1828 L Street NW, Suite 1202
Washington DC 20036-5104
202/371-1013
FAX: 202/778-0884
Internet: www.ieeeusa.org
COST: Free

A source of information containing a multitude of scholarships in the above fields, including application information.

3735—MAKING A DIFFERENCE—CAREER OPPORTUNITIES IN DISABILITY-RELATED FIELDS

AUTHOR: The ARC
The ARC, National Headquarters
P.O. Box 1047
Arlington TX 76004
817/261-6003
817/277-0553 (TDD)
COST: $10.00 (includes S/H)

A handbook of over 50 professions that serve people with disabilities. Includes career overview, employment settings, populations served, and salary/educational/certification requirements.

3736—MAKING IT THROUGH COLLEGE

AUTHOR: PSC
Professional Staff Congress
25 W. 43rd Sreet, 5th Fl.
New York NY 10036
COST: $1.00

Handy booklet containing information on coping with competition, getting organized, study techniques, solving work overloads, and more. 14 pages.

3737—MAKING THE MOST OF YOUR COLLEGE EDUCATION

AUTHOR: Marianne Ragins (Order
MMC-999dsc)
The Scholarship Workshop
P.O. Box 176
Centreville VA 20122
912/755-8428
Internet: www.scholarshipworkshop.com
COST: $10.95 + $3 shipping & handling

This book shows you how to pack your college years with career-building experiences that can lead to graduate and professional schools clamoring to admit you; how to write an impressive professional resume; and how to gain keen entrepreneurial skills, an investment portfolio, and multiple job offers. Offers information on securing internships, travel opportunities, managing your money, using the Internet to your advantage, and other helpful advice.

3738—MASTER MATH

AUTHOR: Debra Anne Ross
Career Press, Inc.
3 Tice Road, P.O. Box 687
Franklin Lakes NJ 07417

800/CAREER-1 or 201/848-0310
FAX: 201/848-1727
Internet: www.careerpress.com
COST: $12.99 each

Four books focusing on mathematical principles that establish a solid foundation and help students move on to more advanced topics. Specify which book when ordering: Algebra, Basic Math & Pre-Algebra, Calculus, or Pre-Calculus & Geometry.

3739—MEDICAL SCHOOL ADMISSION REQUIREMENTS

AUTHOR: Cynthia T. Bennett
Association of American Medical
Colleges
2450 N Street, NW
Washington DC 20037-1126
202/828-0400
FAX: 202/828-1125
COST: $25 + $5 shipping

Contains admission requirements of accredited medical schools in the US and Canada.

3740—MEDICINE—A CHANCE TO MAKE A DIFFERENCE

AUTHOR: AMA
American Medical Association
Order Processing
515 N. State Street
Chicago IL 60610
COST: $5.00 + $4.95 shipping/handling
(pkg. of 10 brochures)

For college students considering a career in medicine. Answers questions about the profession and medical education, including prerequisites, admission requirements, and choosing a medical school.

3741—MITCHELL EXPRESS—THE FAST TRACK TO THE TOP COLLEGES

AUTHOR: Joyce Slayton Mitchell,
ISBN 1-880774-03-8
Garrett Park Press
P.O. Box 190
Garrett Park MD 20896
301/946-2553
COST: $15.00

A college catalog-sized directory describing 270 of America's most popular colleges. It profiles the colleges and provides information on admissions, financial aid, and campus life. 269 pages.

3742—MUSIC SCHOLARSHIP GUIDE (3rd Edition)

AUTHOR: Sandra V. Fridy,
ISBN 1-56545-050-7
Music Educators National Conference
1806 Robert Fulton Drive
Reston VA 20191
COST: $33.00 ($26.40 MENC members)

Lists over 2,000 undergraduate music scholarships in more than 600 public and private educational institutions (colleges & universities) in the United States and Canada, including eligibility requirements, application deadlines, and contact information.

3743—NATIONAL DIRECTORY OF COLLEGE ATHLETICS (Men's and Women's Editions)

AUTHOR: Kevin Cleary,
Editor/Publisher
Collegiate Directories Inc.
P.O. Box 450640
Cleveland OH 44145
COST: $29.95 (men's edition)—$23.95
(women's edition)

Comprehensive directory of college athletic programs in the US and Canada. Revised for each new school year.

3744—NATIONAL DIRECTORY OF CORPORATE GIVING

AUTHOR: TFC, ISBN 0-87954-400-7
Foundation Center (The)
79 Fifth Ave., 16th Street
New York NY 10003
212/620-4230
COST: $199.50 (including shipping/
handling)

Book profiles 2,000 programs making contributions to nonprofit organizations. A valuable tool to assist grant seekers in finding potential support.

3745—NEED A LIFT? (49th edition-2000 Issue)

The American Legion
Attn: National Emblem Sales
P.O. Box 1050
Indianapolis IN 46206
888/453-4466 or 317/630-1200
FAX: 317/630-1223
Internet: www.legion.org
COST: $3.00 (pre-paid only)

Outstanding guide to federal and state government-related financial aid as well as private sector programs. Contains information on the financial aid process (how, when, and where to start), and addresses for scholarship, loan, and career information. 150 pages.

3746—NEWSPAPERS, DIVERSITY & YOU

AUTHOR: DJNF
Dow Jones Newspaper Fund
P.O. Box 300
Princeton NJ 08543-0300
800/DOW-FUND
E-mail: newsfund@wsj.dowjones.com
Internet: www.dj.com/newsfund
COST: Free

Information on grants, scholarships, and internships specifically for minority high school and college students, along with articles written by professional journalists of color.

3747—OCCUPATIONAL OUTLOOK HANDBOOK

AUTHOR: US Dept. of Labor Bureau of
Statistics; 1998-99
CFKR Career Materials
11860 Kemper Road, #7
Auburn CA 95603
800/525-5626 or 916/889-2357
FAX: 800/770-0433 or
916/889-0433
E-mail: cfkr@cfkr.com
Internet: www.cfkr.com
COST: $17.95 (soft cover); $20.95 (hard
cover)

Annual publication designed to assist individuals in selecting appropriate careers. Describes approximately 250 occupations in great detail and includes current and projected job prospects for each. A great resource for teachers and counselors. Versions for grades 5-12 and related activity books also available. 508 pages.

3748—OFF TO COLLEGE

Guidance Research Group
Order Fulfillment Dept. 98-RSCH
P.O. Box 931
Montgomery AL 36101

COST: $3.00

An excellent annual booklet in magazine form that helps incoming freshmen prepare for success in college living through personal essays concerning a variety of campus experiences.

3749—OFFICIAL STUDY GUIDE FOR THE CLEP EXAMINATIONS

AUTHOR: CBP, ISBN 0-87447-595-3
The College Board Publications
Two College Way
Forrester Center WV 25438
800/323-7155
FAX: 800/525-5562
Internet: www.collegeboard.org
COST: $18.00

Official guide to College Level Examination Program (CLEP) tests from the actual sponsors of the tests. Contains sample questions and answers, advice on how to prepare for tests, which colleges grant credit for CLEP, and more. 500 pages.

3750—ONLINE STUDY ABROAD DIREC-TORY

AUTHOR: Website is associated with the University of Minnesota
International Study and Travel Center
48 Coffman Union
300 Washington Ave. SE
Minneapolis MN 55455
612/626-ISTC
FAX: 612/626-0979
E-mail: istc@tc.umn.edu
Internet: www.istc.umn.edu/default.html
COST: Free

An easy-to-access database of opportunities for studying abroad. The subheading "Hot Spots" leads you to a great resource of overseas opportunities. Click on "Scholarships" on the opening page for a list of study opportunities all over the world for which there is financial aid available.

3751—ORDER FORM FOR BOOK LIST ON THEATRE-WRITING CAREERS

Theatre Directories
P.O. Box 510
Dorset VT 05251-0510
802/867-2223
FAX: 802/867-2223
Internet: http://genghis.com/theatre.htm
COST: Free pamphlet/directory of books

A pamphlet listing books on training programs for careers in theatre and playwriting.

3752—PARALEGAL

AUTHOR: Barbara Bernardo,
ISBN 1-56079-894-7
Peterson's, Inc.
P.O. Box 2123
Princeton NJ 08543-2123
800/225-0261
FAX: 609/924-5338
Internet: www.petersons.com
COST: $13.56

A practicing paralegal spells out how to get into this career that offers excellent pay and great opportunities. 224 pages.

3753—PERSPECTIVES: AUDITION ADVICE FOR SINGERS

AUTHOR: Various leaders in the opera field
OPERA America
1156 15th Street NW, Suite 810
Washington DC 20005-1704
202/293-4466
FAX 393-0735
E-mail: Frontdesk@operaam.org
COST: $15/non-members; $10/members

A collection of personal observations from professionals who want to help singers perpare for and perform winning auditions. Features 27 valuable essays from general directors, artistic administrators, training program directors, artist managers, stage directors, teachers, established singers, and university and conservatory directors.

3754—PERSPECTIVES: THE SINGER/MAN-AGER RELATIONSHIP

AUTHOR: Various leaders in the opera field
OPERA America
1156 15th Street NW, Suite 810
Washington DC 20005-1704
202/293-4466
FAX 393-0735
E-mail: Frontdesk@operaam.org
COST: $15 nonmembers; $12 members

Features essays by leaders in the field about artist managers and their roles and responsibilities in identifying and advancing the careers of aspiring singers. Opera professionals, including artist managers, singers, and opera company casting representatives share experiences and give insights to the most frequently asked questions.

3755—PETERSON'S FOUR-YEAR COLLEGES

AUTHOR: ISBN 0-7689-0194-4
Peterson's, Inc.
P.O. Box 2123
Princeton NJ 08543-2123
800/225-0261
FAX: 609/924-5338
Internet: www.petersons.com
COST: $21.56

Begin your college search by exploring accurate, current, and impartial profiles of 2,000 accredited colleges and universities. Find out about specific academic programs, campus life, and athletics. QuickFind college search indexes and charts speed your search. The bonus CD-ROM provides in-depth college descriptions. Get a head start with SAT and ACT practice tests. 3,176 pages.

3756—PETERSON'S PRIVATE SECONDARY SCHOOLS

AUTHOR: ISBN 0-7689-0186-3
Peterson's, Inc.
P.O. Box 2123
Princeton NJ 08543-2123
800/225-0261
FAX: 609/924-5338
Internet: www.petersons.com
COST: $23.96

Explore 1,500 accredited day, boarding, religious, military, junior boarding, and special needs schools worldwide. School profiles cover programs, cost & financial aid, facilities, and student life. 1,451 pages.

3757—PETERSON'S SPORTS SCHOLAR-SHIPS AND ATHLETIC PROGRAMS

AUTHOR: ISBN 1-56079-830-0
Peterson's, Inc.
P.O. Box 2123
Princeton NJ 08543-2123
800/225-0261
FAX: 609/924-5338
Internet: www.petersons.com
COST: $19.96

This is a college-by-college, sport-by-sport guide that covers 32 men's and women's sports. 872 pages.

3758—PETERSON'S TWO-YEAR COLLEGES

AUTHOR: ISBN 0-7689-0195-2
Peterson's, Inc.
P.O. Box 2123
Princeton NJ 08543-2123
800/225-0261

FAX: 609/924-5338
Internet: www.petersons.com
COST: $19.96

Get all the details on 1,600 junior and community colleges in the US and Canada, including programs offered, tuition, and financial aid. 811 pages.

3759—PHARMACY SCHOOL ADMISSION REQUIREMENTS

AUTHOR: AACP
American Association of Colleges of Pharmacy
Office of Student Affairs
1426 Prince Street
Alexandria VA 22314
703/739-2330
COST: $25.00 prepaid plus $3.00 shipping and handling.

100-page booklet containing comparative information charts along with the general history of accredited pharmacy programs and current admission requirements.

3760—PING AMERICAN COLLEGE GOLF GUIDE

AUTHOR: Dean W. Frischknecht
Dean Frischknecht Publishing
P.O. Box 1179
Hillsboro OR 97123
503/648-1333
Internet: www.collegegolf.com
COST: $11.95

Alphabetical listing by state of two- and four-year colleges with intercollegiate golf programs. Includes scholarship and financial aid information, resumes, ratings, and scores. 304 pages. Updated annually.

3761—PLANNING FOR A DENTAL EDUCATION

AUTHOR: AADS
American Association of Dental Schools
1625 Massachusetts Ave. NW
Washington DC 20036-2212
COST: Free

Brochure discusses dentistry as a career and offers advice on planning for a dental education.

3762—POWER STUDY TO UP YOUR GRADES AND GPA

AUTHOR: Sondra Geoffrion

Access Success Associates
6565 Camino Caseta
Goleta CA 93117
805/964-7030
COST: $4.95 each + $2.50 US postage ($4.00 foreign postage). California residents add sales tax.

One of five excellent booklets explaining techniques to discover what will be tested, cut study time in half, prepare thoroughly, write essays, and take tests. Other titles cover math, English, social studies, and science. Please specify which title you would like when ordering.

3763—PHYSICIAN ASSISTANT PROGRAMS DIRECTORY

SpecWorks
810 South Bond Street
Baltimore MD 21231
800/708-7581
FAX: 410/558-1410
COST: $35.00

A catalog of physician assistant educational programs, including addresses, admissions procedures and requirements, course outlines, length of program, university and institutional affiliations, tuition, and sources of financial assistance.

3764—POUR MAN'S FRIEND: A GUIDE AND REFERENCE FOR BAR PERSONNEL

AUTHOR: John C. Burton,
ISBN 0-9624625-0-0
Aperitifs Publishing
1731 King Street
Santa Rosa CA 95404
707/523-1611
COST: $14.95 + shipping

Includes comprehensive bartending techniques, ways to achieve top industry standards with current regulations and guidelines.

3765—PUBLIC RELATIONS CAREERS BOOKLET; WHERE TO STUDY

Public Relations Society of America
33 Irving Place
New York NY 10003
COST: $3.50 (public relations booklet); $5.00 (where to study)

3766—REPAIR YOUR OWN CREDIT

AUTHOR: Bob Hammond,
ISBN 1-56414-308-2
Career Press, Inc.
3 Tice Road, P.O. Box 687
Franklin Lakes NJ 07417

800/CAREER-1 or 201/848-0310
FAX: 201/848-1727
Internet: www.careerpress.com
COST: $8.99

Reveals the unethical and illegal secrets of the credit repair industry from an insider's point of view and explains how you can restore your own credit. 128 pages.

3767—RESOURCE PAPERS, NEWSLETTER ARTICLE REPRINTS, AND OTHER PUBLICATIONS FOR INDIVIDUALS WITH DISABILITIES

AUTHOR: Write for a list of HEATH publications, price list, and order form; materials also available at website
American Council on Education/ Heath Resource Center
One Dupont Circle, Suite 800
Washington DC 20036-1193
202/939-9320 (Voice/TTY)
FAX: 202/833-4760
E-mail: HEATH@ACE.NCHE.EDU
Internet: www.ACENET.edu
Gopher: //bobcat-ace.nche.edu
COST: Varies

Serves as an information exchange about educational support services, policies, procedures, adaptations, and opportunities at American campuses, vocational-technical schools, and other postsecondary education and training.

3768—SCHOLARSHIP LIST SERVICE

AUTHOR: Contact organization for details. Can register online at website
National Foundation for Advancement in the Arts
800 Brickell Ave., Suite 500
Miami FL 33131
800/970-ARTS or 305/377-1147
FAX: 305/377-1149
E-mail: nfaa@nfaa.org
Internet: www.nfaa.org
COST: Varies

A list of higher education institutions that offer opportunities for scholarships and financial aid to students in the arts. Available via e-mail address above.

3769—SCHOLARSHIPS & LOANS FOR NURSING EDUCATION

AUTHOR: National League for Nursing,
ISBN #0-88737-730-0
Jones and Bartlett Publishers
40 Tall Pine Drive
Sudbury MA 01776
800/832-0034

FAX: 978/443-8000
E-mail: info@jbpub.com
Internet: www.jbpub.com
COST: $18.75 + $4.50 postage/handling

Information on all types of scholarships, awards, grants, fellowships, and loans for launching or continuing your career in nursing. 125 pages. Other books available: *NLN State-Approved Schools of Nursing* ($39.95) and *Nursing: The Career of a Lifetime* ($22.50).

3770—SELECTED FINANCIAL AID REFERENCES FOR STUDENTS WITH DISABILITIES-#107.96

National Clearinghouse for
   Professions in Special Education
The Council for Exceptional Children
1920 Association Drive
Reston VA 20191-1589
800-641-7824 or 703/264-9476
TTY: 703/264-9480
FAX: 703/264-1637
E-mail: ncpse@cec.sped.org
Internet: www.cec.sped.org/ncpse.htm
COST: Free

A list of specific sources of financial assistance for students with disabilities preparing for careers in special education and related services, such as physical therapy, occupational therapy, speech-language pathology, and others.

3771—SELECTED FINANCIAL AID RESOURCES FOR INDIVIDUALS FROM CULTURALLY/ETHNICALLY DIVERSE BACKGROUNDS-#104.96

National Clearinghouse for
   Professions in Special Education
The Council for Exceptional Children
1920 Association Drive
Reston VA 20191-1589
800-641-7824 or 703/264-9476 or
TTY: 703/264-9480
FAX: 703/264-1637
E-mail: ncpse@cec.sped.org
Internet: www.cec.sped.org/ncpse.htm
COST: Free

A list of specific sources of financial assistance for minority students preparing for careers in special education and related services, such as physical therapy, occupational therapy, speech-language pathology, and others.

3772—SELECTED FINANCIAL AID RESOURCES FOR RELATED SERVICES-#103.97

National Clearinghouse for
   Professions in Special Education
The Council for Exceptional Children
1920 Association Drive
Reston VA 20191-1589
800-641-7824 or 703/264-9476
TTY: 703/264-9480
FAX: 703/264-1637
E-mail: ncpse@cec.sped.org
Internet: www.cec.sped.org/ncpse.htm
COST: Free

A list of specific sources of financial assistance for students preparing for careers in services related to special education, such as physical therapy, occupational therapy, speech-language pathology, and others.

3773—SELECTED FINANCIAL AID RESOURCES FOR SPECIAL EDUCATION-#102.97

National Clearinghouse for
   Professions in Special Education
The Council for Exceptional Children
1920 Association Drive
Reston VA 20191-1589
800-641-7824 or 703/264-9476
TTY: 703/264-9480
FAX: 703/264-1637
E-mail: ncpse@cec.sped.org
Internet: www.cec.sped.org/ncpse.htm
COST: Free

A list of specific sources of financial assistance for students preparing for careers in special education and related services.

3774—SMART WOMAN'S GUIDE TO CAREER SUCCESS

AUTHOR: Janet Hauter,
   ISBN 1-56414-056-3
Career Press, Inc.
3 Tice Road, P.O. Box 687
Franklin Lakes NJ 07417
800/CAREER-1 or 201/848-0310
FAX: 201/848-1727
Internet: www.careerpress.com
COST: $11.95

Identifies the obstacles that most often cause women to bump their heads on the glass ceilings, walls, and doors. 160 pages.

3775—SMART WOMAN'S GUIDE TO INTERVIEWING AND SALARY NEGOTIATION

AUTHOR: Julie Adair King,
   ISBN 1-56414-206-X
Career Press, Inc.
3 Tice Road, P.O. Box 687
Franklin Lakes NJ 07417
800/CAREER-1 or 201/848-0310
FAX: 201/848-1727
Internet: www.careerpress.com
COST: $12.99

Covers the entire interview process, job applications, employment tests (including drug tests), evaluating job offers, negotiating your best deal, accepting or declining an offer, and how to ask for a raise—and get it. 224 pages.

3776—SMART WOMAN'S GUIDE TO RESUMES AND JOB HUNTING

AUTHOR: Julie Adair King & Betsy
   Sheldon, ISBN 1-56414-205-1
Career Press, Inc.
3 Tice Road, P.O. Box 687
Franklin Lakes NJ 07417
800/CAREER-1 or 201/848-0310
FAX: 201/848-1727
Internet: www.careerpress.com
COST: $9.99

Walks the reader through the resume-creating process step by step (including career worksheets & sample resumes). Addresses other key career issues of interest to women, including breaking through the glass ceiling and other gender barriers, commanding a fair salary, networking to find hidden job opportunities, using "power language," and more. 216 pages.

3777—SPANISH ABROAD

AUTHOR: See website for details.
Spanish Abroad, Inc.
6520 N. 41st Street
Paradise Valley AZ 852253
888/722-7623 (toll-free US &
   Canada) or 602/947-4652
FAX: 602/840-1545
E-mail: info@spanishabroad.com
Internet: www.spanishabroad.com
COST: Varies

This website is a vast source of opportunities for Spanish immersion programs in many countries around the world. Included is a page that has a list of financial aid and scholarships for this purpose.

3778—STANFORD HOME STUDY GUIDE FOR SAT SUCCESS

AUTHOR: Company guarantees a 100-point SAT score increase. Visit website computer requirements and to print out order form.

Stanford Testing Systems, Inc.
206 N. Washington Street, Suite 320
Alexandria VA 22314
800/233-4728
FAX: 703/836-8710
E-mail: sales@testprep.com
Internet: www.testprep.com

COST: $150.00 + $15. shipping/handling

A software program that provides extensive preparation for the SAT tests. Includes a two-year personal license and toll-free telephone support, and free software upgrades for two years. Available on 3.5" disks for MAC and IBM PC. Provides real SAT practice exams. NOT A BOOK.

3779—STATE RESOURCE SHEETS

National Clearinghouse for
    Professions in Special Education
The Council for Exceptional Children
1920 Association Drive
Reston VA 20191-1589
800-641-7824 or 703/264-9476
TTY: 703/264-9480
FAX: 703/264-1637
E-mail: ncpse@cec.sped.org
Internet: www.cec.sped.org/ncpse.htm

COST: Free

A list of sources of financial assistance in specific states for students preparing for careers in special education and related services, such as physical therapy, occupational therapy, speech-language pathology, and others. When ordering, specify the state or states in which you attend or may attend college.

3780—STUDENT FINANCIAL AID AND SCHOLARSHIPS AT WYOMING COLLEGES

AUTHOR: UW

University of Wyoming
Office of Student Financial Aid
P.O. Box 3335
Laramie WY 82071-3335
307/766-2116
FAX: 307/766-3800

COST: Free

Describes postsecondary student aid and scholarship programs that are available to Wyoming students. Booklets can be obtained at all Wyoming high schools and colleges.

3781—STUDENT GUIDE—FINANCIAL AID FROM THE US DEPARTMENT OF EDUCATION

AUTHOR: US Department of Education

Federal Student Aid Information Center
P.O. Box 84
Washington DC 20044
800/4-FEDAID or 800/433-3243

COST: Free

Lists qualifications and sources of information for federal grants, loans, and work-study programs.

3782—STUDY ABROAD

AUTHOR: UNESCO

United Nations Educational,
    Scientific and Cultural Organization
Bernan Associates, UNESCO Agent
4611-F Assembly Drive
Lanham MD 20706

COST: $29.95 + postage/handling

Printed in English, French, & Spanish, this volume lists 3,700 international study programs in all academic and professional fields in more than 124 countries. Also available on CD-ROM.

3783—SUMMER FUN—LEARNING PROGRAMS

AUTHOR: ISBN 0-7689-0188-X

Peterson's, Inc.
P.O. Box 2123
Princeton NJ 08543-2123
800/225-0261
FAX: 609/924-5338
Internet: www.petersons.com

COST: $7.96

Includes detailed listings of summer learning camps and programs, advice on how to pick the right program, secrets to handling homesickness, firsthand experiences from other kids, and more. 230 pages.

3784—SUMMER ON CAMPUS: COLLEGE EXPERIENCES FOR HIGH SCHOOL STUDENTS

AUTHOR: ISBN #0-87447-526-0

College Board Publications
45 Columbus Ave.
New York NY 10023
800/323/7155
FAX: 212/713-8143

COST: $15

Comprehensive information on more than 450 academic summer programs at over 350 institutions nationwide. 3,211 pages. Paperbound.

3785—TAFT CORPORATE GIVING DIRECTORY

AUTHOR: ISBN 0-914756-79-6

Taft Group
12300 Twinbrook Pkwy., Suite 520
Rockville MD 20852-1607
800/877-8238

COST: $375.00

This reference book is found in most major libraries. It contains comprehensive information on over 500 foundations sponsored by top corporations. 859 pages.

3786—TARGETING THE JOB YOU WANT

AUTHOR: Kate Wendleton
    ISBN 1-56414-449-6

Career Press, Inc.
3 Tice Road, P.O. Box 687
Franklin Lakes NJ 07417
800/CAREER-1 or 201/848-0310
FAX: 201/848-1727
Internet: www.careerpress.com

COST: $12.99

Includes strategies and tips that can help people figure out what they want to do with their lives. Readers learn to develop job targets, become industry leaders, discover new opportunities, and network more quickly and efficiently. 224 pages.

3787—TEN STEPS IN WRITING THE RESEARCH PAPER

AUTHOR: Roberta Markman, Peter Markman, and Marie Waddell

Barron's Educational Series Inc.
250 Wireless Blvd.
Hauppauge NY 11788
800/645-3476
Internet: www.barronseduc.com

COST: $9.95, ISBN 08120-1868-10

Arranged to lead the student step-by-step through the writing of a research paper—from finding a suitable subject to checking the final copy. Easy enough for the beginner, complete enough for the graduate student. 177 pages.

3788—TEXAS MUSIC INDUSTRY DIRECTORY

State of Texas, Music Office
P.O. Box 13246
Austin TX 78711
512/463-4114

FAX: 512/463-4114
E-mail: music@governor.state.tx.us
Internet: www.governor.state.tx.us/
music
COST: $18.00

A publication of the Texas Governor's Office that lists more than 8,000 Texas music business contacts, including events, classical music, books, and Texas colleges offering music and music business courses. Could be a valuable resource to anyone considering a career in the business of music. 424 pages.

3789—THE BUNTING & LYON BLUE BOOK: PRIVATE INDEPENDENT SCHOOLS

AUTHOR: ISBN 0-913094-51-X
Bunting & Lyon, Inc.
238 North Main Street
Wallingford CT 06492
203/269-3333
FAX: 203/269-5697
E-mail: BandLBluBK@aol.com
Internet: www.acadia.net/
bunting_lyon/
COST: $100 + postage

A comprehensive directory of independent elementary and secondary schools in the US and abroad. Access Internet for an online search and/or more information. A counseling service (for which there is a charge) is also available. 1,122 listings; 656 pages.

3790—THE CARE BOOK (College Aid Resources for Education)

AUTHOR: ISBN 0-9656724-0-9
National College Scholarship
Foundation, Inc. (NCSF)
16728 Frontenac Terrace
Rockville MD 20855
301/548-9423
FAX: 301/548-9453
E-mail: ncsfdn@aol.com
COST: $29.95

This publication was developed to be a hands-on daily reference for counselors as well as for families. It assists counselors and students to have a quick reference to find stats on a college and to compare college costs, enrollments, form requirements, etc. Includes a CD-ROM money planner.

3791—THE CAREER ATLAS

AUTHOR: Gail Kuenstler, Ph.D., ISBN
1-56414-225-6
Career Press, Inc.
3 Tice Road, P.O. Box 687
Franklin Lakes NJ 07417

800/CAREER-1 or 201/848-0310
FAX: 201/848-1727
Internet: www.careerpress.com
COST: $12.99

Details education and experience requirements for 400 career paths within 40 occupational areas. 256 pages.

3792—THE COLLEGE GUIDE FOR PARENTS

AUTHOR: ISBN 0-87447-474-4
College Board Publications
45 Columbus Ave.
New York NY 10023
800/323/7155
FAX: 212/713-8143
COST: $14

Helps parents guide their teenagers through the entire college admission process, from taking the right courses to applying for financial aid. 200 pages. Paperbound.

3793—THE COLLEGE HANDBOOK

AUTHOR: CBP, ISBN 0-87447-590-2
College Board Publications
Two College Way
Forrester Center WV 25438
800/323-7155
FAX: 800/525-5562
Internet: www.collegeboard.org
COST: $25.95 + 5. shipping/handling +
applicable sales tax

Describes in detail more than 3,200 two- and four-year undergraduate institutions in the US Includes information on admission requirements, costs, financial aid, majors, activities, enrollment, campus life, and more. 1,600 pages. Also available on Windows CD-ROM.

3794—THE FOUNDATION DIRECTORY

AUTHOR: ISBN 0-87954-449-6 (soft
cover); 0-87954-484-8 (hard cover)
The Foundation Center
79 Fifth Ave.
New York NY 10003
800/424-9836
COST: $160.00 soft cover; $185.00 hard
cover; + $4.50 shipping by UPS

Authoritative annual reference book found in most major libraries. Contains detailed information on over 6,300 of America's largest foundations. Indexes allow grantseekers, researchers, etc., to quickly locate foundations of interest.

3795—THE GUERRILLA GUIDE TO MASTERING STUDENT LOAN DEBT

AUTHOR: Anne Stockwell,
ISBN 0-06-273435-0
HarperCollins Publishers
2275 Hidalgo Ave.
Los Angeles CA 90039
323/664-4323
COST: US $14; CANADA $20 (plus
tax/shipping)

Identifies which loans are best for you and explains how to repay them once you're in debt. Includes advice from loan officers, legislators, collection agents, and students.

3796—THE MEMORY KEY

AUTHOR: Dr. Fiona McPherson, ISBN
1-56414-470-4
Career Press, Inc.
3 Tice Road, P.O. Box 687
Franklin Lakes NJ 07417
800/CAREER-1 or 201/848-0310
FAX: 201/848-1727
Internet: www.careerpress.com
COST: $12.99

Practical, easy-to-use handbook helps students with study skills and anyone dealing with information overload, shedding light on how memory works and what you need to do to achieve memory improvement.

3797—THE NATIONAL DIRECTORY OF INTERNSHIPS

AUTHOR: ISBN 0-536-01123-0
National Society for Experiential
Education
Simon & Schuster
5550 W. 74th Street
Indianapolis IN 46268
877/587-4666 (Simon & Schuster)
919/787-3263 (NSEE)
FAX: 919/787-3381
E-mail: info@nsee.org
Internet: www.nsee.org/
COST: $29.95 ($24.95 NSEE members) +
$5.59 shipping

Lists thousands of internships in over 85 fields in government, nonprofit, and corporate settings. Includes work and service opportunities for college, graduate, and high school students, as well as those not in school, mid-career professionals, and retired people. Indexed by name of organization, geographic locations, and field of interest. 722 pages. Order from toll-free Simon & Schuster Custom Publishing number or access website for order form.

3798—THE SCHOLARSHIP WATCH

National Academy of American
  Scholars
1249 S. Diamond Bar Blvd., #325
Diamond Bar CA 91765-4122
Internet: www.naas.org
COST: $25/yr.

A newsletter printed biannually containing extensive information about scholarship sources and techniques for acquiring financial aid.

3799—THE VINCENT/CURTIS EDUCATIONAL REGISTER

Vincent/Curtis
224 Clarendon Street, Suite 40
Boston MA 02116
617/536-0100
FAX: 617/536-8098
Internet: www.vincentcurtis.com
COST: Free

A directory of 1,000 private K-12 schools and camps for students age 8 through 18. Access Internet for an online search and/or call or write for book. A counseling service (for which there is a charge) is also available.

3800—THEIR WORLD

AUTHOR: NCLD
  National Center for Learning
    Disabilities
  381 Park Ave. S., Suite 1401
  New York NY 10016
  212/545-7510
  FAX: 212/545-9665
  Internet: www.ncld.org
COST: $6.00

This annual magazine offers a wide range of practical material to benefit the millions of children and adults with learning disabilities, and their families as well as educators and other helping professionals.

3801—THERE ARE NO LIMITS

AUTHOR: Danny Cox,
  ISBN 1-56414-340-6
  Career Press, Inc.
  3 Tice Road, P.O. Box 687
  Franklin Lakes NJ 07417
  800/CAREER-1 or 201/848-0310
  FAX: 201/848-1727
  Internet: www.careerpress.com
COST: $24.99

Helps students and others develop a plan for achieving goals, written for anyone who wants to make a change in his or her personal or professional life. 256 pages.

3802—TOP SECRET EXECUTIVE RESUMES

AUTHOR: Steven Provenzano,
  ISBN 1-56414-431-3
  Career Press, Inc.
  3 Tice Road, P.O. Box 687
  Franklin Lakes NJ 07417
  800/CAREER-1 or 201/848-0310
  FAX: 201/848-1727
  Internet: www.careerpress.com
COST: $14.99

Presents the writing and most effective use of cover letters; executive networking; preparation and format of reference, support materials, and salary information sheets; using the Internet to expand your search; and more than 150 pages of sample resumes covering most major professions. 256 pages.

3803—UAA-102 COLLEGIATE AVIATION GUIDE

AUTHOR: Gary W. Kiteley, Executive
  Director
  University Aviation Association
  3410 Skyway Drive
  Auburn AL 36830-6444
  334/844-2434
  FAX: 334/844-2432
  E-mail: uaa@auburn.edu
COST: $30 non-members (+$4 S&H); $20
  members (+$4 S&H)

Guide to college-level aviation study. Detailed state-by-state listings of aviation programs offered by US colleges and universities.

3804—UAA-116 COLLEGIATE AVIATION SCHOLARSHIP LISTING

AUTHOR: Gary W. Kiteley, Executive
  Director
  University Aviation Association
  3410 Skyway Drive
  Auburn AL 36830-6444
  334/844-2434
  FAX: 334/844-2432
  E-mail: uaa@auburn.edu
COST: $8 members (+$4 S&H); $15 non-
  members (+$4 S&H)

This guide includes a listing of financial aid sources, methods of applying for general purpose aid, and a listing of aviation scholarships arranged by broad classification.

3805—ULTIMATE HIGH SCHOOL SURVIVAL GUIDE

AUTHOR: Julianne Dueber,
  ISBN 0-7689-0241-X
  Peterson's, Inc.
  P.O. Box 2123
  Princeton NJ 08543-2123
  800/225-0261
  FAX: 609/924-5338
  Internet: www.petersons.com
COST: $11.96

Includes helpful information on getting along with teachers, dealing with pressure, preventing intimidation, taking tests, managing time, making friends, and developing creativity. This guide is packed with caring "reality therapy" for improving skills and building confidence. 292 pages.

3806—VACATION STUDY ABROAD

AUTHOR: Sara J.Steen, Editor
  Institute of International Education
  IIE Books, 809 United Nations Plaza
  New York NY 10017-3580
COST: $39.95 + $5 shipping and handling

Guide to some 1,800 summer or short-term study-abroad programs sponsored by US colleges, universities, private institutions, and foreign institutions. 400 pages.

3807—WHAT COLOR IS YOUR PARACHUTE?

AUTHOR: Richard N. Bolles,
  ISBN 1-58008-123-1
  Ten Speed Press
  P.O. Box 7123
  Berkeley CA 94707
  800/841-BOOK or 510/559-1600
  FAX: 510/559-1629
  E-mail: order@tenspeed.com
  Internet: www.tenspeed.com
COST: $16.95 + $4.50 shipping

Step-by-step career planning guide now in its 30th Anniversary Edition. Highly recommended for anyone who is job hunting or changing careers. Contains valuable tips on assessing your skills, writing resumes, and handling job interviews. 368 pages.

3808—WHERE THE JOBS ARE

AUTHOR: Joyce Hadley Copeland,
  ISBN 1-56414-422-4
  Career Press, Inc.
  3 Tice Road, P.O. Box 687
  Franklin Lakes NJ 07417
  800/CAREER-1 or 201/848-0310
  FAX: 201/848-1727

Internet: www.careerpress.com
COST: $13.99

An in-depth look at today's job market reveals more about the most current trends and the hottest industries that offer the greatest career opportunities. 320 pages.

3809—WINNING SCHOLARSHIPS FOR COLLEGE—AN INSIDER'S GUIDE

AUTHOR: Marianne Ragins (Order
    Code: DSC999)
The Scholarship Workshop
P.O. Box 176
Centreville VA 20122
912/755-8428
Internet: www.scholarshipworkshop.
com
COST: $12.95 + $3 shipping & handling

Author Marianne Ragins, winner of more than $400,000 in scholarship funds, proves that it's not always those with the best grades or highest SAT scores who win scholarships. You'll see that rigorous research efforts, involvement in extracurricular activities, leadership potential, and special talents all combine to determine your chances of securing aid for college. Tips on using the Internet, scholarly resumes, selling yourself, test-taking tips, and writing essays.

3810—WORLD DIRECTORY OF MEDICAL SCHOOLS

AUTHOR: WHO
World Health Organization
(1211 Geneva 27, Switzerland)
WHO Publication Center
49 Sheridan Ave.
Albany NY 12210
COST: $35 (shipping/handling included)

Comprehensive book that describes the medical education programs and schools in each country. Arranged in order by country or area.

3811—WRITE YOUR WAY TO A HIGHER GPA

AUTHOR: Randall S. Hansen, Ph.D. &
    Katherine Hansen, ISBN 0-89815-903-2
Ten Speed Press
P.O. Box 7123
Berkeley CA 94707
800/841-BOOK or 510/559-1600
FAX: 510/559-1629
E-mail: order@tenspeed.com

Internet: www.tenspeed.com
COST: $11.95 + $4.50 shipping

This book tells how any student can use writing skills to get the highest grade possible in any class. Special focus on the Internet and other new resources. 240 pages.

3812—WRITING CONTESTS FOR LAW STUDENTS

AUTHOR: Compiled at the Cecil C.
    Humphreys School of Law at the
    University of Memphis.
University of Memphis
Internet: www.people.memphis.edu/
    ~law/contests.html
COST: Free

Comprehensive list of writing contests on various topics for law students.

3813—WHERE THERE'S A WILL THERE'S AN "A" TO GET BETTER GRADES IN COLLEGE (OR HIGH SCHOOL)

Olney "A" Seminars
P.O. Box 686
Scottsdale AZ 85252-0686
800/546-3883
Internet: www.wheretheresawill.com
COST: $44.95

Videotape seminars on how to get better grades.

3814—YOUR CAREER IN THE COMICS

AUTHOR: Lee Nordling; Publisher:
    Andrews McMeel Publishing
Newspaper Features Council, Inc.
22 Byfield Lane
Greenwich CT 06830
COST: $9.95 + $3 postage + $1
    packaging/handling

Detailed information on the business of being a professional cartoonist for newspapers. Learn from the artists and professionals themselves how cartoon syndication works.

Career Information

3815—

ACCOUNTING/NET
600 Stewart Street, Suite 1101
Seattle WA 98101
206/441-8285
FAX: 206/441-8385
E-mail: counselor@
accountingstudents.com
Internet: www.accountingstudents.
com/toolbox/index.html

3816—Accounting (Career Information)

AMERICAN INSTITUTE OF
CERTIFIED PUBLIC ACCOUNTANTS
1211 Avenue of the Americas
New York NY 10036-8775
212/596-6200
FAX: 212/596-6213
Internet: www.aicpa.org

3817—Accounting (Career Information)

NATIONAL SOCIETY OF PUBLIC
ACCOUNTANTS
1010 North Fairfax Street
Alexandria VA 22314-1574
703/549-6400
FAX: 703/549-2984
Internet: www.nsacct.org

3818—Accounting (Career Information)

INSTITUTE OF MANAGEMENT
ACCOUNTANTS
10 Paragon Drive
Montvale NJ 07645
201/573-9000

3819—Actuarial Science (Career Information)

SOCIETY OF ACTUARIES
475 N. Martingale Road, Suite 800
Schaumburg IL 60173-2226
847/706-3509
FAX: 847/706-3599

3820—Acupuncture/Oriental Medicine & Drug/Alcoholism Recovery (Career Information)

NATIONAL ACUPUNCTURE
DETOXIFICATION ASSOCIATION
3220 N Street NW, Suite 275
Washington DC 20007

503/222-1362
FAX: 503/228-4618
E-mail: AcuDetox@aol.com
Internet: www.healthy.net/pan/pa/
acupuncture/nada/nadamain.htm

3821—Acupuncture/Oriental Medicine (Career Information)

NATIONAL ACUPUNCTURE AND
ORIENTAL MEDICINE ALLIANCE
14637 Starr Road SE
Olalla WA 98359
206/851-6896
FAX: 206/851-6883
Internet: www.healthy.net/pan/pa/
acupuncture/naoma.htm

3822—Acupuncture/Oriental Medicine (Career Information)

CALIFORNIA SOCIETY FOR
ORIENTAL MEDICINE (CSOM)
12926 Riverside Drive, #B
Sherman Oaks CA 91423
FAX: 818/981-2766
Internet: www.quickcom.net/csom/

3823—Advertising (Career Information)

AMERICAN ADVERTISING
FEDERATION
Education Services
1101 Vermont Ave. NW, Suite 500
Washington DC 20005-6306

3824—Aeronautics (Career Information)

AMERICAN INSTITUTE OF
AERONAUTICS AND
ASTRONAUTICS
(Student Programs Department)
1801 Alexander Bell Drive, Suite 500
Reston VA 20191-4344
800/NEW-AIAA or 703/264-7500
FAX: 703/264-7551
Internet: www.aiaa.org

3825—Aerospace Education (Career Information)

AEROSPACE EDUCATION
FOUNDATION
1501 Lee Highway
Arlington VA 22209-1198

800/727-3337, ext. 4880
FAX: 703/247-5853
E-mail: aefstaff@aef.org

3826—Agricultural & Biological Engineering (Career Information)

ASAE SOCIETY FOR ENGINEERING
IN AGRICULTURAL FOOD AND
BIOLOGICAL SYSTEMS
2950 Niles Road
St. Joseph MI 49085

3827—Agriculture (Career Information)

AMERICAN FARM BUREAU
FEDERATION ("There's a New
Challenge In Agriculture")
Public Policy Division
225 Touhy Ave.
Park Ridge IL 60068
847/685-8848
FAX: 847/685-8969
E-mail: susan@fb.com

3828—Agronomy; Crops; Soils; Environment (Career Information)

AMERICAN SOCIETY OF
AGRONOMY
677 S. Segoe Road
Madison WI 53711
608/273-8080
FAX: 608/273-2021

3829—Air Force (Career Information)

AIR FORCE OPPORTUNITY CENTER
P.O. Box 3505
Capitol Heights MD 20791

3830—Air Force Academy/AFROTC (Career Information)

DIRECTOR OF SELECTIONS
HQ USAFA/RRS
2304 Cadet Drive, Suite 200
USAF Academy CO 80840-5025
Internet: www.usafa.edu/rr/

3831—Airline (Career Information)

AIR TRANSPORT ASSOCIATION
OF AMERICA
1301 Pennsylvania Ave. NW
Suite 1100
Washington DC 20004-1707

3832—Airline Industry (Career Information)

AVIATION INFORMATION
RESOURCES (AIR, Inc.)
1001 Riverdale Ct.
Atlanta GA 30337-6005
800/AIR-APPS or 770/996-5424
FAX: 770/996-5547 or
800/AIR-FAXS

3833—Animal Science (Career Information)

NATIONAL ASSOCIATION OF
ANIMAL BREEDERS (NAAB)
401 Bernadette Drive
P.O. Box 1033
Columbia MO 65205
573/445-4406 or 573/445-9541
FAX: 573/446-2279
E-mail: naab-css.org

3834—Animation (Career Information)

WOMEN IN ANIMATION (WIA)
P.O. Box 17706
Encino CA 91416
E-mail: info@women.in.animation.org
Internet: women.in.animation.org

3835—Anthropology (Career Information)

AMERICAN ANTHROPOLOGICAL
ASSOCIATION
4350 N. Fairfax Drive, Suite 640
Arlington VA 22203-1620
703/528-1902
FAX: 703/528-3546
Internet: www.ameranthassn.org

3836—Appraising (Career Information)

AMERICAN SOCIETY OF
APPRAISERS
P.O. Box 17265
Washington DC 20041

3837—Apprenticeship (Career Information)

US DEPT OF LABOR
BUREAU OF APPRENTICESHIP
AND TRAINING
200 Constitution Ave. NW
Room N-4649
Washington DC 20210

3838—Archaeology (Career Information)

ARCHAEOLOGICAL INSTITUTE
OF AMERICA
Boston University
656 Beacon Street
Boston MA 02215-2006
617/353-9361
FAX: 617/353-6550
E-mail: aia@bu.edu
Internet: www.archaeological.org

3839—Architecture (Career Information)

AMERICAN ARCHITECTURAL
FOUNDATION (AIA/AAF
Scholarship Program)
1735 New York Ave., NW
Washington DC 20006-5292
202/626-7511
FAX: 202/626-7420
E-mail: felberm@aiamail.aia.org

3840—Astronomy & Astrophysics (Career Information for Women)

HARVARD-SMITHSONIAN CENTER
FOR ASTROPHYSICS
Publication Dept., MS-28
60 Garden Street
Cambridge MA 02138
617/495-7461

3841—Astronomy (Career Information)

AMERICAN ASTRONOMICAL
SOCIETY
2000 Florida Ave. NW, Suite 400
Washington DC 20009
202/328-2010
FAX: 202/324-2560
E-mail: aas@aas.org
Internet: www.aas.org

3842—Audiology; Speech Pathology (Career Information)

AMERICAN SPEECH-LANGUAGE-
HEARING ASSOCIATION
10801 Rockville Pike
Rockville MD 20852

3843—Automotive Engineering (Career Information)

SOCIETY OF AUTOMOTIVE
ENGINEERS (SAE)
400 Commonwealth Drive
Warrendale PA 15096-0001

724/772-4047
E-mail: connie@sae.org
Internet: www.sae.org

3844—Aviation (Career Information)

AIRCRAFT OWNERS AND PILOTS
ASSOCIATION
421 Aviation Way
Frederick MD 21701
301/695-2160
FAX: 301/695-2375
E-mail: Janette.prince@aopa.org
Internet: www.aopa.org

3845—Aviation (Career Information)

AVIATION DISTRIBUTORS AND
MANUFACTURERS ASSOCIATION
1900 Arch Street
Philadelphia PA 19103-1498
215/564-3484
FAX: 215/564-2175
E-mail: assnhqt@netaxs.com

3846—Aviation (Career Information)

GENERAL AVIATION
MANUFACTURERS ASSOCIATION
1400 K Street NW, Suite 801
Washington DC 20005
202/637-1378
FAX: 202/842-4063
E-mail: bmikula@generalaviation.org
Internet: www.generalaviation.org

3847—Aviation Maintenance (Career Information)

PROFESSIONAL AVIATION
MAINTENANCE ASSOCIATION
636 Eye Street NW, Suite 300
Washington DC 20001-3736
202/216-9220
FAX: 202/216-9224
E-mail: hq@pama.org
Internet: www.pama.org

3848—Bartending (Career Information)

PROFESSIONAL BARTENDING
SCHOOLS OF AMERICA
888/4-BARKIT
Internet: www.pbsa.com/info.html

3849—Bartending (Career Information)

BARTENDERS' SCHOOL OF
SANTA ROSA
1731 King Street
Santa Rosa CA 95404
707/523-1611

3850—Biologist (Career Information)

AMERICAN INSTITUTE OF
BIOLOGICAL SCIENCES
1444 Eye Street NW, Suite 200
Washington DC 20005
202/628-1500, ext. 281

3851—Biotechnology (Career Information)

BIOTECHNOLOGY INDUSTRY
ORGANIZATION
1625 K Street NW, Suite 1100
Washington DC 20006
202/857-0244

3852—Broadcast News (Career Information)

RADIO AND TELEVISION NEWS
DIRECTORS ASSOCIATION
1000 Connecticut Ave. NW
Suite 615
Washington DC 20036-5302
202/659-6510
FAX: 202/223-4007
E-mail: michellet@rtndf.org
Internet: www.rtndf.org

3853—Broadcasting (Career Information)

AMERICAN WOMEN IN RADIO &
TELEVISION
c/o Lauren Kravetz
1001 Pennsylvania Ave., 6th Floor
Washington DC 20004
202/624-7283
FAX: 202/624-7222
Internet: www.awrt.org

3854—Careers in the Public Life (Information)

NATIONAL ASSOCIATION OF
SCHOOLS OF PUBLIC AFFAIRS
AND ADMINISTRATION
1120 G Street NW, Suite 730
Washington DC 20005-3801
E-mail: info@naspaa.org
Internet: www.naspaa.org/
publicservicecareers

3855—Cartooning (Career Information)

NEWSPAPER FEATURES COUNCIL
22 Byfield Lane
Greenwich CT 06830-3446

3856—Cartooning (Career Information)

NATIONAL CARTOONISTS
SOCIETY
10 Columbus Circle, Suite 1620
New York NY 10019
Internet: www.reuben.org

3857—Chemical Engineering (Career Information)

AMERICAN INSTITUTE OF
CHEMICAL ENGINEERS
Communications Dept.
345 E. 47th Street
New York NY 10017-2395
Internet: www.aiche.org/careers/

3858—Chiropractics (Career/College Information)

AMERICAN CHIROPRACTIC
ASSOCIATION
1701 Clarendon Blvd.
Arlington VA 22209
800/377-8397 or 703/276-8800
FAX: 703/243-2593

3859—Chiropractics (Career/School Information)

INTERNATIONAL CHIROPRACTORS
ASSOCIATION
1110 N. Glebe Road, Suite 1000
Arlington VA 22201

3860—Civil Engineering (Career Information)

AMERICAN SOCIETY OF CIVIL
ENGINEERS
1801 Alexander Bell Drive
Reston VA 20191-4400
800-548-ASCE or 703/295-6000
FAX: 703/295-6333
E-mail: student@asce.org
Internet: www.asce.org

3861—Clinical Chemist (Career Information)

AMERICAN ASSOCIATION FOR
CLINICAL CHEMISTRY
2101 L Street NW, Suite 202
Washington DC 20037-1526
800/892-1400
FAX: 202/892-1400
E-mail: educatn@aacc.org
Internet: www.aacc.org

3862—College Information

CALIFORNIA COMMUNITY
COLLEGES
1107 Ninth Street
Sacramento CA 95814

3863 —College Information

UNIVERSITY OF CALIFORNIA
SYSTEM
300 Lakeside Drive, 17th Fl.
Oakland CA 94612-3550

3864—College Information

CALIFORNIA STATE UNIVERSITY
SYSTEM
400 Golden Shore, #318
Long Beach CA 90802-4275

3865—College Information

ASSOCIATION OF INDEPENDENT
COLLEGES AND UNIVERSITIES
1100 11th Street, Suite 205
Sacramento CA 95814

3866—Computer Science (Career Information)

IEEE COMPUTER SOCIETY
1828 L Street NW, Suite 1202
Washington DC 20036-5104
202/371-1013
FAX: 202/778-0884
Internet: www.ieeeusa.org.usab

3867—Computer Science (Career Information)

ASSOCIATION FOR COMPUTING
MACHINERY
1515 Broadway, 17th Fl.
New York NY 10036
800/342-6626 or 212/626-0500
FAX: 212/944-1318
Internet: www.acm.org/membership/
career/

3868—Construction (Career Information)

ASSOCIATED GENERAL
CONTRACTORS OF AMERICA
1957 E Street NW
Washington DC 20006

3869—Cosmetology (Career Information)

AMERICAN ASSOCIATION OF
COSMETOLOGY SCHOOLS
11811 N. Tatum Blvd., Suite 1085
Phoenix AZ 85028
602/788-1170
FAX: 602/404-8900
E-mail: jim@beautyschools.org
Internet: www.beautyschools.org

3870—Crafts (Career Information)

AMERICAN CRAFT COUNCIL
LIBRARY
72 Spring Street
New York NY 10012
212/274-0630
FAX: 212/274-0650

3871—Creative Writing (Career Information)

NATIONAL WRITERS
ASSOCIATION
3140 S. Peoria, PMB 295
Aurora CO 80014
303/751-7844
FAX: 303/751-8593
E-mail: sandywrter@aol.com
Internet: www.nationalwriters.com

3872—Culinary Arts (Career Information)

AMERICAN CULINARY
FEDERATION, INC.
10 San Bartola Drive
Augustine FL 32086
904/824-4460 or 800/624-9458

3873—Data Processing Management (Career Information)

ASSOCIATION OF INFORMATION
TECHNOLOGY PROFESSIONALS
315 S. Northwest Highway
Suite 200
Park Ridge IL 60068-4278

3874—Dental Assistant (Career Information)

AMERICAN DENTAL ASSISTANTS
ASSOCIATION
203 N. LaSalle Street, Suite 1320
Chicago IL 60601
312/541-1550 or 800/733-2322

3875—Dental Laboratory Technology (Career Information)

NATIONAL ASSOCIATION OF
DENTAL LABORATORIES
8201 Greensboro Drive, Suite 300
McLean VA 22102
703/610-9035

3876—Dental Profession (Career Information)

ADA ENDOWMENT AND
ASSISTANCE FUND INC.
211 E. Chicago Ave.
Chicago IL 60611

3877—Dentistry; Dental Hygiene; Dental Lab Technology (Career Information)

FLORIDA DENTAL HEALTH
FOUNDATION
1111 E. Tennessee Street
Tallahassee FL 32308
850/681-3629, ext. 119
FAX: 850/681-0116
E-mail: csutherland@floridadental.org
Internet: www.floridadental.org

3878—Dietitian (Career Information)

AMERICAN DIETETIC
ASSOCIATION (ADA)
Attn: Networks Team
216 W. Jackson Blvd.
Chicago IL 60606-6995
800/877-1600, ext. 4897
FAX: 312/899-0008
E-mail: network@eatright.org
Internet: www.eatright.org

3879—Disabled (Career Information)

THE ARC
P.O. Box 1047
Arlington TX 76004

3880—Drama/Acting (Career Information)

SCREEN ACTORS GUILD
5757 Wilshire Blvd.
Los Angeles CA 90036-3600
213/954-1600

3881—Education (Career Information)

AMERICAN FEDERATION OF
TEACHERS
Public Affairs Dept.
555 New Jersey Ave. NW
Washington DC 20001-2079
202/879-4400
Internet: www.aft.org/pr/teaching.htm

3882—Electrical Engineering (Career Information)

INSTITUTE OF ELECTRICAL AND
ELECTRONICS ENGINEERS—
US ACTIVITIES
1828 L Street NW, Suite 1202
Washington DC 20036-5104

3883—Engineering (Program/Career Information)

JUNIOR ENGINEERING TECHNICAL
SOCIETY, INC. (JETS)
1420 King Street, Suite 405
Alexandria VA 22314
Internet: www.ASEE.org/JETS

3884—Engineering (Career Information)

NATIONAL SOCIETY OF
PROFESSIONAL ENGINEERS
1420 King Street
Alexandria VA 22314
703/684-2830

3885—Entomology (Career Information)

ENTOMOLOGICAL SOCIETY OF
AMERICA
9301 Annapolis Road
Lanham MD 20706-3115
301/731-4535
FAX: 301/731-4538
E-mail: esa@entsoc.org
Internet: www.entsoc.org

3886—Environmental (Career/Studies Information)

US ENVIRONMENTAL PROTECTION
AGENCY
Office of Communications,
Education, and Public Affairs
Environmental Education Division
401 M Street SW
Washington DC 20460

3887—FBI (Career Information)

FEDERAL BUREAU OF
INVESTIGATION
Office of Public &
Congressional Affairs
Washington DC 20535
Internet: www.fbi.gov

3888—Family & Consumer Science (Career Information)

AMERICAN ASSOCIATION OF
FAMILY AND CONSUMER
SCIENCES
1555 King Street
Alexandria VA 22314-2752
703/706-4600
FAX: 703/706-4663
E-mail: info@aafcs.org
Internet: www.aafcs.org

3889—Fashion Design (Educational Information)

FASHION INSTITUTE OF
TECHNOLOGY
Seventh Ave. @ 27th Street
New York NY 10001-5992
800/GO-TO-FIT or 212/217-7684
E-mail: FITinfo@sfitva.cc.fitsuny.edu
Internet: www.fitnyc.suny.edu

3890—Fire Service (Career Information)

NATIONAL FIRE PROTECTION
ASSN. (Public Fire Protection)
1 Batterymarch Park
P.O. Box 9101
Quincy MA 02269-9101

3891—Fisheries (Career/University Information)

AMERICAN FISHERIES SOCIETY
5410 Grosvenor Lane, Suite 110
Bethesda MD 20814-2199

3892—Floristry (Career Information)

SOCIETY OF AMERICAN FLORISTS
1601 Duke Street
Alexandria VA 22314

3893—Food & Nutrition Service (Career Information)

US DEPT OF AGRICULTURE
FOOD AND NUTRITION SERVICE
Personnel Division, Room 620
1301 Park Center Drive
Alexandria VA 22302

3894—Food Service (Career Information)

NATIONAL RESTAURANT
ASSOCIATION EDUCATIONAL
FOUNDATION
250 S. Wacker Drive, Suite 1400
Chicago IL 60606-5834
800/765-2122, ext. 733
312/715-1010
FAX: 312/715-1362
E-mail: bdejesus@foodtrain.org
Internet: www.edfound.org

3895—Foreign Service Officer (Career Information)

US DEPT. OF HEALTH
RECRUITMENT DIVISION
P.O. Box 9317, Rosslyn Station
Arlington VA 22219
703/875-7165
FAX: 703/875-7243

3896—Forest Service (Career Information)

US DEPT. OF AGRICULTURE
14th & Independence Ave.
Room 801 RPE
Washington DC 20250

3897—Forestry (Career Information ONLY)

SOCIETY OF AMERICAN
FORESTERS
5400 Grosvenor Lane
Bethesda MD 20814-2198

3898—Funeral Director (Career Information)

NATIONAL FUNERAL DIRECTORS
ASSOCIATION
11121 W. Oklahoma Ave.
Milwaukee WI 53227-0641
800/228-6332 or 414/541-2500
FAX: 541-2500
E-mail: nfda@nfda.org
Internet: www.nfda.org

3899—Gemology (Career Information)

GEMLINES.COM
1524 NW 52nd Street
Seattle WA 98107
FAX: 978/477-8361
E-mail: gemlines@yahoo.com
Internet: www.gemlines.com

3900—Geography (Career Information)

ASSOCIATION OF AMERICAN
GEOGRAPHERS
1710 16th Street NW
Washington DC 20009-3198
202/234-1450
FAX: 202/234-2744
E-mail: gaia@aag.org
Internet: www.aag.org

3901—Geological Sciences (Career Information)

GEOLOGICAL SOCIETY OF
AMERICA
3300 Penrose Place, P.O. Box 9140
Boulder CO 80301-9140
303/447-2020
FAX: 303/447-1133
E-mail: educate@geosociety.org
Internet: www.geosociety.org/
educate/career.htm

3902—Geological Sciences (Career Information)

AMERICAN GEOLOGICAL
INSTITUTE
4220 King Street
Alexandria VA 22302
703/379-2480
FAX: 703/379-7563
E-mail: ehr@agiweb.org
Internet: www.agiweb.org

3903—Geophysics (Career Information)

AMERICAN GEOPHYSICAL UNION
2000 Florida Ave. NW
Washington DC 20009
202/462-6900 or 800/966-2481
FAX: 202/328-0566
Internet: www.agu.org

3904—Graphic Arts (Career Information)

AMERICAN INSTITUTE OF
GRAPHIC ARTS
164 Fifth Ave.
New York NY 10010

3905—Graphic Communications (Career/Education Information)

EDUCATION COUNCIL OF THE
GRAPHIC ARTS INDUSTRY
1899 Preston White Drive
Reston VA 20191

703/648-1768
FAX: 703/620-0994

3906—Heating & Air Conditioning Engineer (Career Information)

REFRIGERATION SERVICE
ENGINEERS SOCIETY
1666 Rand Road
Des Plaines IL 60016-3552
708/297-6464
FAX: 847-297-5038
E-mail: rses@starnetinc.com
Internet: www.rses.org

3907—Homeopathic Medicine (Career Information)

NATIONAL CENTER FOR
HOMEOPATHY
801 North Fairfax Street, Suite 306
Alexandria VA 22314
703/548-7790
FAX: 703/548-7792
E-mail: nchinfo@igc.apc.org
Internet: www.healthy.net/nch/

3908—Homeopathic Medicine (Career Information)

HOMEOPATHIC EDUCATIONAL
SERVICES
2124B Kittredge Street
Berkeley CA 94704
510/649-0294
FAX: 510/649-1955
Internet: www.homeopathic.com/
ailments/hesdent.htm

3909—Horticulture (Career Information)

AMERICAN ASSOCIATION OF
NURSERYMEN
1250 'I' Street NW
Washington DC 20005

3910—Hospital Administration (Career Information)

AMERICAN COLLEGE OF HEALTH
CARE EXECUTIVES
One N. Franklin Street, Suite 1700
Chicago IL 60606-3491

3911—Hotel Management (Career Information)

AMERICAN HOTEL FOUNDATION
1201 New York Ave. NW
Suite 600
Washington DC 20005

3912—Illuminating Engineering (Career Information)

ILLUMINATING ENGINEERING
SOCIETY OF NORTH AMERICA
120 Wall Street, 17th Fl.
New York NY 10005

3913—Insurance (Career Information)

COLLEGE OF INSURANCE
101 Murray Street
New York NY 10007
212/962-4111
FAX: 212/964-3381
Internet: www.tci.edu

3914—Journalism (Career Information)

AMERICAN SOCIETY OF
NEWSPAPER EDITORS
11690B Sunrise Valley Drive
Reston VA 20191-1409
703/453-1122
FAX: 703/453-1133
E-mail: asne@asne.org
Internet: www.asne.org

3915—Law (Career Information Booklet)

AMERICAN BAR ASSOCIATION
750 N. Lake Shore Drive
Chicago IL 60611

3916—Law Librarianship (Career Information)

AMERICAN ASSOCIATION OF
LAW LIBRARIES
53 W. Jackson Blvd., Suite 940
Chicago IL 60604
312/939-4764
FAX: 312/431-1097
E-mail: aallhq@aall.org;
www.aallnet.org

3917—Learn to Fly (Career Information)

NATIONAL AIR TRANSPORTATION
ASSOCIATION
4226 King Street
Alexandria VA 22302
800/I CAN FLY

3918—Learning Disabled (Education/Career Information)

LEARNING DISABILITIES ASSN. OF
AMERICA
4156 Library Road
Pittsburgh PA 15234
412/341-1515

3919—Management (Career Information)

AMERICAN MANAGEMENT
ASSOCIATION
1601 Broadway
New York NY 10019-7420
212/903-8161
FAX: 212/903-8171
E-mail: cust_serv@amanet.org
Internet: www.amanet.org

3920—Massage Therapy (Career Information)

AMERICAN MASSAGE THERAPY
ASSOCIATION (AMTA)
820 Davis Street, Suite 100
Evanston IL 60201-4444
847/864-0123
FAX: 847/864-1178
Internet: www.amtamassage.org

3921—Mathematical Sciences (Career Information)

MATHEMATICAL ASSOCIATION
OF AMERICA
P.O. Box 90973
Washington DC 20090
800/331-1622

3922—Mathematics Teacher (Career Information)

NATIONAL COUNCIL OF
TEACHERS OF MATHEMATICS
1906 Association Drive
Reston VA 22091-1593
703/620-9840
FAX: 703/476-2970
E-mail: vwilliams@nctm.org
Internet: www.nctm.org

3923—Mechanical Engineering (Career Information)

AMERICAN SOCIETY OF
MECHANICAL ENGINEERS
3 Park Ave.
New York NY 10016-5990
212/591-8131
FAX: 212/591-7143
E-mail: malaven@asme.org
Internet: www.asme.org

3924—Medical Laboratory Technology (Career Information)

AMERICAN SOCIETY OF CLINICAL PATHOLOGISTS
Careers
2100 W. Harrison
Chicago IL 60612

3925—Medical Records (Career Information)

AMERICAN HEALTH INFORMATION MANAGEMENT ASSOCIATION
919 N. Michigan Ave., Suite 1400
Chicago IL 60611

3926—Medicine (Career Information)

AMERICAN MEDICAL ASSOCIATION
515 N. State Street
Chicago IL 60610

3927—Metallurgy & Materials Science (Career Information)

ASM FOUNDATION FOR EDUCATION & RESEARCH
Student Outreach Program
Materials Park OH 44073

3928—Microbiology (Career Information)

AMERICAN SOCIETY FOR MICROBIOLOGY (Office of Education & Training)
1325 Massachusetts Ave. NW
Washington DC 20005
202/942-9283

3929—Motion Picture (Career Information)

SOCIETY OF MOTION PICTURE AND TELEVISION ENGINEERS
595 W. Hartsdale Ave.
White Plains NY 10607
914/761-1100

3930—Music Therapy (Career Information)

NATIONAL ASSN. FOR MUSIC THERAPY
8455 Colesville Road, Suite 1000
Silver Spring MD 20910

301/589-3300
FAX: 301/589-5175

3931—Naturopathic Medicine (Career Information)

AMERICAN ASSOCIATION OF NATUROPATHIC PHYSICIANS
601 Valley Street, Suite 105
Seattle WA 98109
206/298-0126
FAX: 206/298-0129
E-mail: 74602.3715@ compuserve.com
Internet: healer.infinite.org/ Naturopathic.Physician/Welcome.html

3932—Naval Architecture (Career Information)

SOCIETY OF NAVAL ARCHITECTS AND MARINE ENGINEERS
601 Pavonia Ave.
Jersey City NJ 07306

3933—Naval/Marine Engineering (Career Information)

SOCIETY OF NAVAL ARCHITECTS AND MARINE ENGINEERS
601 Pavonia Ave.
Jersey City NJ 07306

3934—Newspaper Industry (Career Information)

NEWSPAPER ASSN. OF AMERICA
1921 Gallows Road #4
Vienna VA 22182-3900

3935—Nurse Anesthetist (Career Information)

AMERICAN ASSOCIATION OF NURSE ANESTHETISTS
222 S. Prospect Ave.
Park Ridge IL 60068-4001
708/692-7050

3936—Nursing (Career Information)

NATIONAL LEAGUE FOR NURSING
61 Broadway, 33rd Fl.
New York NY 10006
800/669-1656 or 212/363-5555
FAX: 212/812-0393
E-mail: custhelp@nln.org
Internet: www.nln.org

3937—Oceanography & Marine Science (Career Information)

MARINE TECHNOLOGY SOCIETY
1828 L Street NW, Suite 906
Washington DC 20036
202/775-5966

3938—Operations Research & Management Science (Career Information)

INSTITUTE FOR OPERATIONS RESEARCH AND THE MANAGEMENT SCIENCES (INFORMS)
P.O. Box 64794
Baltimore MD 21264-4794
800/4INFORMS
FAX: 410/684-2963
E-mail: informs@informs.org
Internet: www.informs.org/Edu/ Career/booklet.html

3939—Optometry (Career Information)

NATIONAL OPTOMETRIC ASSOCIATION
P.O. Box F
E. Chicago IN 46312
219/398-1832
FAX: 219/398-1077

3940—Optometry (Career Information)

AMERICAN OPTOMETRIC ASSOCIATION
243 N. Lindbergh Blvd.
St. Louis MO 63141-7881
314/991-4100
FAX: 314/991-4101
Internet: www.opted.org

3941—Osteopathic Medicine (Career Information)

AMERICAN OSTEOPATHIC ASSOCIATION
Dept. of Predoctoral Education
142 East Ontario
Chicago IL 60611
800/621-1773, ext. 7401

3942—Paleontology (Career Information)

PALEONTOLOGICAL SOCIETY
P.O. Box 1897
Lawrence KS 66044-8897

Internet: www.uic.edu/orgs/
paleo/homepage.html

3943—Pathology as Career in Medicine (Career Information Brochure)

INTERSOCIETY COMMITTEE ON
PATHOLOGY INFORMATION
9650 Rockville Pike
Bethesda MD 20814-3993
301/571-1880
FAX: 301/571-1879

3944—Pediatrics (Career Information)

AMERICAN ACADEMY OF
PEDIATRICS
141 NW Point Blvd.
P.O. Box 927
Elk Grove Village IL 60009

3945—Petroleum Engineering (Career Information)

SOCIETY OF PETROLEUM
ENGINEERS
P.O. Box 833836
Richardson TX 75083-3836
972/952-9315
FAX: 972/952-9435
E-mail: twhipple@spelink.spe.org
Internet: www.spe.org

3946—Pharmacology (Career Information)

AMERICAN SOCIETY FOR
PHARMACOLOGY &
EXPERIMENTAL THERAPEUTICS INC.
9650 Rockville Pike
Bethesda MD 20814-3995

3947—Pharmacy (Career Information)

AMERICAN ASSOCIATION OF
COLLEGES OF PHARMACY
Office of Student Affairs
1426 Prince Street
Alexandria VA 22314
703/739-2330

3948—Pharmacy (Career Information)

AMERICAN FOUNDATION FOR
PHARMACEUTICAL EDUCATION
One Church Street, Suite 202
Rockville MD 20850

3949—Pharmacy (School Information Booklet)

AMERICAN COUNCIL ON
PHARMACEUTICAL EDUCATION
311 W. Superior, #512
Chicago IL 60610
312/664-3575
FAX: 312/664-4652

3950—Physical Therapy (Career Information)

AMERICAN PHYSICAL
THERAPY ASSN.
1111 N. Fairfax Street
Alexandria VA 22314-1488
703/684-2782
FAX: 703/684-7343
Internet: www.apta.org

3951—Physician Assistant (Career Information)

AMERICAN ACADEMY OF
PHYSICIAN ASSISTANTS
950 North Washington Street
Alexandria VA 22314-1552
703/836-2272
FAX: 703/684-1924
E-mail: aapa@aapa.org
Internet: www.apa.org

3952—Physics (Career Information)

AMERICAN INSTITUTE OF PHYSICS
STUDENTS
One Physics Ellipse
College Park MD 20740-3843
301/661-9404

3953—Podiatry (Career Information)

FUND FOR PODIATRIC MEDICAL
EDUCATION
9312 Old Georgetown Road
Bethesda MD 20814-1698
301/581-9200
FAX: 301/530-2752

3954—Precision Machining Technology (Career Information)

NATIONAL TOOLING AND
MACHINING ASSN.
9300 Livingston Road
Ft. Washington MD 20744

3955—Psychiatry (Career Information)

AMERICAN PSYCHIATRIC ASSN.,
DIVISION OF PUBLIC AFFAIRS
1400 K Street NW
Washington DC 20005

3956 —Psychology (Career Information)

AMERICAN PSYCHOLOGICAL
ASSOCIATION
750 First Street NE
Washington DC 20002-4242
202/336-6027
FAX: 202/336-6012
E-mail: mfp@apa.org
Internet: www.apa.org

3957—Public Administration (Career Information)

AMERICAN SOCIETY FOR PUBLIC
ADMINISTRATION
1120 G Street NW, Suite 700
Washington DC 20005-3801
E-mail: info@aspanet.org
Internet: www.aspanet.org

3958—Radiologic Technology (Career Information)

AMERICAN SOCIETY OF
RADIOLOGIC TECHNOLOGISTS
(ASRT)
15000 Central Ave., SE
Albuquerque NM 87123-3917
505/298-4500
FAX: 505/298-5063
Internet: www.asrt.org

3959—Range Management (Career Information)

SOCIETY FOR RANGE
MANAGEMENT
1839 York Street
Denver CO 80206
303/355-7070
FAX: 303/355-5059
E-mail: srmden@ix.netcom.com
Internet: srm.org

3960—Rehabilitation Counseling (Career Information)

NATIONAL REHABILITATION
COUNSELING ASSN.
8807 Sudley Road, #102
Manassas VA 22110-4719

3961—Respiratory Therapy (Career Information)

AMERICAN RESPIRATORY CARE FOUNDATION
11030 Ables Lane
Dallas TX 75229-4593
972/243-2272
E-mail: info@aarc.org
Internet: www.aarc.org

3962—Safety Engineering (Career Information)

AMERICAN SOCIETY OF SAFETY ENGINEERS
1800 E. Oakton Street
Des Plaines IL 60018-2187
847/699-2929

3963—School Administration (Career Information)

AMERICAN ASSOCIATION OF SCHOOL ADMINISTRATORS
1801 North Moore Street
Arlington VA 22209-1813
Internet: www.aasa.org

3964—Science Teacher (Career Information)

NATIONAL SCIENCE TEACHERS ASSN.
Attn: Office of Public Information
1840 Wilson Blvd.
Arlington VA 22201
703/243-7100

3965—Secretary/Office Professional (Career Information)

PROFESSIONAL SECRETARIES INTERNATIONAL—THE ASSOCIATION FOR OFFICE PROFESSIONALS
10502 NW Ambassador Drive
Kansas City MO 64195-0404
816/891-6600
FAX: 816-891-9118
E-mail: service@psi.org
Internet: www.gvi.net/psi

3966—Social Work (Career Information)

NATIONAL ASSN. OF SOCIAL WORKERS
750 First Street NE, Suite 700
Washington DC 20002

202/408-8600
FAX: 202/336-8310

3967—Sociology (Career Information)

AMERICAN SOCIOLOGICAL ASSOCIATION
1722 N Street NW
Washington DC 20036
202/833-3410
FAX: 202/785-0146
E-mail: apap@asanet.org
Internet: www.asanet.org

3968—Soil Conservation (Career Information)

SOIL & WATER CONSERVATION SOCIETY
7515 NE Ankeny Road
Ankeny IA 50021-9764
515/289-2331 or 800/THE-SOIL
FAX: 515/289-1227
E-mail: charliep@secs.org
Internet: www.swcs.org

3969—Special Education Teaching (Career Information)

NATIONAL CLEARINGHOUSE FOR PROFESSIONS IN SPECIAL EDUCATION
The Council for Exceptional Children
1920 Association Drive
Reston VA 20191-1589
800/641-7824 or 703/264-9476
TTY: 703/264-9480
FAX: 703/264-1637
E-mail: ncpse@cec.sped.org
Internet: www.cec.sped.org/ncpse.htm

3970—Speech & Hearing Therapy (Career Information—send SASE)

ALEXANDER GRAHAM BELL ASSOCIATION FOR THE DEAF
3417 Volta Place NW
Washington DC 20007-2778
202/337-5220 (voice/TTY)
E-mail: Agbell2@aol.com
Internet: www.agbell.org

3971—Truckdriving (Career Information)

LAYOVER.COM
800/361-3081
FAX: 717/859-1524
E-mail: info@layover.com

Internet: www.layover.com

3972—Truckdriving (Career Information)

AMERICAN TRUCKING ASSOCIATIONS
2200 Mill Road
Alexandria VA 22314-4677
703/838-1700
Internet: www.trucking.org

3973—U.S. Navy Officer (Career Information)

US NAVAL ACADEMY
Candidate Guidance Office
Annapolis MD 21402
800/638-9156

3974—U.S. Navy/Marine Corps (Career Information)

US NAVAL ACADEMY
Candidate Guidance
117 Decatur Road
Annapolis MD 21402-5018

3975—U.S. Navy/Marine Corps (Career Information)

NAVY AND MARINE CORPS ROTC COLLEGE SCHOLARSHIPS BULLETIN
Navy Recruiting Command, Code 314
801 N. Randolph Street
Arlington VA 22203-1991
800/USA-NAVY
Internet: www.navyjobs.com

3976—U.S. Army (Career Information)

US MILITARY ACADEMY
Director of Admissions
606 Thayer Road
West Point NY 10996

3977—U.S. Coast Guard (Career Information)

US COAST GUARD ACADEMY
Director of Admissions
31 Mohegan Ave.
New London CT 06320
FAX: 860/701-6700

3978—Urban Planning (Career Information)

AMERICAN PLANNING ASSOCIATION
122 South Michigan Ave., Suite 1600
Chicago IL 60605
312/431-9100
FAX: 312/431-9985

3979— Veterinarian (Career Information)

AMERICAN VETERINARY MEDICAL ASSOCIATION
1931 N. Meacham Road, Suite 100
Schaumburg IL 60173

3980—Water Management (Career Information)

WATER ENVIRONMENT FEDERATION
Internet: www.wef.org

3981—Welding Technology (Career Information)

HOBART INSTITUTE OF WELDING TECHONOLOGY
Trade Square East
Troy OH 45373
513/332-5215
FAX 513/332-5200
E-mail: hiwt@welding.org
Internet: www.welding.org

3982—Women Pilots (Career Information)

THE NINETY-NINES, INC.
7100 Terminal Drive, Box 965
Oklahoma City OK 73159
405/685-7969
FAX: 405/685-7985

3983—Women in Airport Management (Career Information)

AIRPORTS COUNCIL INTERNATIONAL—NORTH AMERICA
1775 K Street NW, Suite 500
Washington DC 20006
202/293-8500
FAX: 202/331-1362

3984—Writing (Career Information)

KIDZWRITE
To subscribe, send message:
subscribe KidzWrite
E-mail Subscription:
majordomo@userhome.com

3985—Youth Leadership (Career Information)

BOYS & GIRLS CLUBS OF AMERICA
1230 W. Peachtree Street NW
Atlanta GA 30309

3986—Youth Leadership (Career Information)

BOY SCOUTS OF AMERICA
National Eagle Scout Assn., S220
1325 W. Walnut Hill Lane
P.O. Box 152079
Irving TX 75015
972/580-2431

Alphabetical Index

"ACE" ANY TEST 3608
"EDUTRAX" QUARTERLY NEWSLETTER 3609
Personal Counseling Service by Dan Cassidy and his professional staff. 3610
101 GREAT ANSWERS TO THE TOUGHEST INTERVIEW QUESTIONS 3611
101 GREAT RESUMES 3612
1ST MARINE DIVISION ASSN. (Scholarship Program) 2476
270 WAYS TO PUT YOUR TALENT TO WORK IN THE HEALTH FIELD 3613
37th DIVISION VETERANS ASSOCIATION (Scholarship/Grant) 2477
A CAREER GUIDE TO MUSIC EDUCATION 3614
A GUIDE TO AVIATION EDUCATION RESOURCES 3615
A TEACHER'S GUIDE TO FELLOWSHIPS AND AWARDS 3616
A. MARLYN MOYER, JR. SCHOLARSHIP FOUNDATION (Scholarships) 2478
A.H. BEAN FOUNDATION 2479
ABBIE M. GRIFFIN EDUCATIONAL FUND (Scholarships) 2480
ABBIE SARGENT MEMORIAL SCHOLARSHIP INC. (Scholarships) 1249, 1712, 2039
ABCs OF FINANCIAL AID (Montana Financial Aid Handbook) 3617
ABE AND ANNIE SEIBEL FOUNDATION (Interest-free Educational Loan Fund) 2481
ABRAHAM BURTMAN CHARITY TRUST 2482
ACADEMIC YEAR ABROAD 3618
ACADEMY OF MOTION PICTURE ARTS AND SCIENCES (Student Academy Awards) 874, 957
ACADEMY OF VOCAL ARTS (Scholarships) 1060
ACCOUNTING/NET 3815
ACCOUNTING/NET (Account for Your Future Scholarship Program) 41
ACL/NJCL NATIONAL LATIN EXAM (Scholarships) 1036
ADA ENDOWMENT AND ASSISTANCE FUND INC. 3876
ADDISON H. GIBSON FOUNDATION (Low-Interest Loans) 2483
ADELLE DAVIS FOUNDATION 2040
ADELPHI UNIVERSITY (Athletic Grants) 199
ADELPHI UNIVERSITY (Talent Awards) 875, 1061
ADELPHI UNIVERSITY (Various Scholarships) 2484
ADVENTURE CAREERS 3619
AERO CLUB OF NEW ENGLAND (Aviation Scholarships) 472, 2408
AEROSPACE EDUCATION FOUNDATION 3825
AEROSPACE EDUCATION FOUNDATION (Eagle Plan Grant) 2485
AFL-CIO GUIDE TO UNION-SPONSORED SCHOLARSHIPS 3620
AFS INTERCULTURAL PROGRAMS (International Exchange Student Program) 2486
AGNES T. MAGUIRE TRUST 2487
AID ASSOCIATION FOR LUTHERANS (All-College, Vocational/Technical, and Lutheran Campus Scholarships) 2488
AIR FORCE ACADEMY (Falcon Foundation Scholarships) 2489
AIR FORCE AID SOCIETY (General Henry H. Arnold Education Grant Program) 2490
AIR FORCE AID SOCIETY (Voc-Tech Loan Program) 2491
AIR FORCE OPPORTUNITY CENTER 3829
AIR FORCE RESERVE OFFICER TRAINING CORPS (AFROTC Scholarships) 42, 301, 473, 512, 562, 588, 656,
. . . . .701, 775, 832, 1037, 1331, 1471, 1563,
. . . . .1594, 1648, 1713, 1942, 2300, 2345
AIR FORCE SERGEANTS' ASSOCIATION (Scholarship Awards Program) 2492
AIR TRAFFIC CONTROL ASSOCIATION INC. (Scholarship Awards Program) 474, 475, 2493
AIR TRANSPORT ASSOCIATION OF AMERICA 3831
AIRCRAFT ELECTRONICS ASSOCIATION EDUCATIONAL FOUNDATION (Scholarships) 43, 476, 2409
AIRCRAFT OWNERS AND PILOTS ASSOCIATION 3844
AIRLINE PILOTS ASSOCIATION (Scholarship Program) 2494

AIRMEN MEMORIAL FOUNDATION (AFSA/AMF Scholarship Awards Program) 2495
AIRPORTS COUNCIL INTERNATIONAL (Scholarships) 44
AIRPORTS COUNCIL INTERNATIONAL-NORTH AMERICA 3983
AIRPORTS COUNCIL INTERNATIONAL-NORTH AMERICA (Commissioners Roundtable Scholarship Program) 45
ALABAMA COMMISSION ON HIGHER EDUCATION (Scholarships; Grants; Loans; Work Study Programs) 2496
ALABAMA DEPARTMENT OF VETERANS AFFAIRS (GI Dependents Scholarship Program) 2497, 2498
ALASKA COMMISSION ON POSTSECONDARY EDUCATION (Alaska Teacher Scholarship Loan Program) 200, 2499, 2500
ALASKA VISITORS ASSOCIATION (Various Scholarships) 46
ALBANY ACADEMY FOR GIRLS (Scholarships) 2501
ALBERT BAKER FUND (Student Loans) 2502
ALBERT O.J. LANDUCCI, DDS (Dental Assisting Scholarships) 1840
ALBERT O.J. LANDUCCI, DDS (Scholarships) 2503
ALBUQUERQUE COMMUNITY FOUNDATION (Financial Aid Program) 2504
ALCOHOLIC BEVERAGE MEDICAL RESEARCH FOUNDATION (Grants for Alcohol Research) 1795
ALEXANDER FAMILY EDUCATIONAL FOUNDATION WELFARE TRUST 2505
ALEXANDER GRAHAM BELL ASSOCIATION FOR THE DEAF (School Age Financial Aid Awards) . . .2506, 2507, 2508, 3970
ALEXANDER SCHOLARSHIP FUND 2509
ALL SAINTS' ACADEMY (Financial Aid Awards) 2510
ALLIANCE FOR YOUNG ARTISTS AND WRITERS, INC./AMERICAN
    MUSEUM OF NATURAL HISTORY (Young Naturalist Awards) 833, 876, 958, 1228, 1250, 1332, 1394, 1433, 1456, 1520
ALLIED JEWISH FEDERATION (Charles and Louise Rosenbaum Scholarship Fund) 2511
ALPHA KAPPA ALPHA SORORITY INC. (AKA/PIMS Summer Youth Mathematics & Science Camp) 1472, 1595
ALPHA MU GAMMA NATIONAL OFFICE (Goddard/Indovina/Krakowski Scholarships) 1038
ALVIN M. BENTLEY FOUNDATION (Scholarship Program) 877, 959, 1062, 1473
AMARILLO AREA FOUNDATION, INC. (Scholarship Program) 2512
AMELIA MAGAZINE (Creative Writing Contest) 960
AMERICA ISRAEL PUBLIC AFFAIRS COMMITTEE (Internships) 2301
AMERICA'S JUNIOR MISS (Scholarship Competition) 2513
AMERICAN ACADEMY OF PEDIATRICS 3944
AMERICAN ACADEMY OF PHYSICIAN ASSISTANTS 3951
AMERICAN ACCORDION MUSICOLOGICAL SOCIETY (Contest) 1063
AMERICAN ADVERTISING FEDERATION 3823
AMERICAN ALLIANCE FOR HEALTH, PHYSICAL EDUCATION, RECREATION & DANCE 47, 201, 1064, 1841
AMERICAN ANTHROPOLOGICAL ASSOCIATION 3835
AMERICAN ARCHITECTURAL FOUNDATION (AIA/AAF Scholarship Program) 3839
AMERICAN ART THERAPY ASSOCIATION (Cay Drachnik Minorities Fund) 1842, 1843
AMERICAN ASSOCIATION FOR CLINICAL CHEMISTRY 3861
AMERICAN ASSOCIATION OF ADVERTISING AGENCIES, INC. (Multicultural Advertising Internship Program) 48, 49
AMERICAN ASSOCIATION OF AIRPORT EXECUTIVES (Scholarships) 50
AMERICAN ASSOCIATION OF BIOANALYSTS (David Birenbaum Scholarship Fund of AAB) 2514
AMERICAN ASSOCIATION OF CEREAL CHEMISTS (Undergraduate Scholarships and Graduate Fellowships) 2041
AMERICAN ASSOCIATION OF COLLEGES OF PHARMACY (PHARMLOAN Program) 1714, 3947
AMERICAN ASSOCIATION OF COSMETOLOGY SCHOOLS (ACE Grants) 2410, 3869
AMERICAN ASSOCIATION OF CRITICAL CARE NURSES (Educational Advancement Scholarship Program) 1943
AMERICAN ASSOCIATION OF FAMILY AND CONSUMER SCIENCES 3888
AMERICAN ASSOCIATION OF HISPANIC CERTIFIED PUBLIC ACCOUNTANTS (Scholarships) 51
AMERICAN ASSOCIATION OF LAW LIBRARIES 3916
AMERICAN ASSOCIATION OF MEDICAL ASSISTANTS ENDOWMENT (Maxine Williams Scholarship Fund) 1844
AMERICAN ASSOCIATION OF NATUROPATHIC PHYSICIANS 3931
AMERICAN ASSOCIATION OF NURSERYMEN 3909
AMERICAN ASSOCIATION OF NURSE ANESTHETISTS (Educational Loans) 1944, 3935
AMERICAN ASSOCIATION OF SCHOOL ADMINISTRATORS 3963
AMERICAN ASSOCIATION OF TEACHERS OF FRENCH (National French Contest) 834, 835, 1039, 1040, 1041

AMERICAN ASSOCIATION OF UNIVERSITY WOMEN—HONOLULU BRANCH
(Tweet Coleman Aviation Scholarship) 477, 2515, 2516
AMERICAN ASSOCIATION OF WOMEN DENTISTS (Gillette Hayden Memorial Foundation) 1715
AMERICAN ASTRONOMICAL SOCIETY 3841
AMERICAN ASTRONAUTICAL SOCIETY (Donald K. "Deke" Slayton Memorial Scholarship) 478
AMERICAN BAR ASSOCIATION 3915
AMERICAN BAR FOUNDATION (Summer Research Fellowships in Law and
Social Science for Minority Undergraduate Students) 812, 836, 2074, 2247, 2302, 2346, 2374
AMERICAN BOARD OF FUNERAL SERVICE EDUCATION (ABFSE Scholarships) 2411
AMERICAN CANCER SOCIETY (College Scholarship Program) 2517
AMERICAN CATHOLIC HISTORICAL ASSOCIATION (John Gilmary Shea Prize) 1188, 1189
AMERICAN CHEMICAL SOCIETY (Minority Scholars Program) 702, 1564
AMERICAN CHIROPRACTIC ASSOCIATION 3858
AMERICAN COLLEGE OF HEALTH CARE EXECUTIVES 3910
AMERICAN COLLEGE OF MEDICAL PRACTICE EXECUTIVES (ACMPE Scholarships) 1716
AMERICAN COLLEGE OF NURSE-MIDWIVES FOUNDATION (Scholarship Program) 1945
AMERICAN CONGRESS ON SURVEYING AND MAPPING
(AAGS Joseph F. Dracup Scholarship Award, Nettie Dracup Memorial
Scholarship, & Berntsen International Scholarship in Surveying) 1333, 1334, 1335, 1336, 1337, 1338, 1339, 1340, 1341
AMERICAN CONSULTING ENGINEERS COUNCIL (Scholarships) 302
AMERICAN COUNCIL OF THE BLIND (ACB Scholarship Program) 2518
AMERICAN COUNCIL ON PHARMACEUTICAL EDUCATION 3949
AMERICAN CRAFT COUNCIL LIBRARY 3870
AMERICAN CULINARY FEDERATION, INC. 3872
AMERICAN CULINARY FEDERATION, INC. (Ray & Gertrude Marshall Scholarship Fund) 2042
AMERICAN DENTAL ASSISTANTS ASSOCIATION 3874
AMERICAN DENTAL HYGIENISTS ASSOCIATION INSTITUTE FOR ORAL HEALTH
(William E. Motley Scholarship) 1845, 1846, 1847, 1848, 1849, 1850,
. . . . .1851, 1852, 1853, 1854, 1855, 1856, 1857
AMERICAN DIETETIC ASSOCIATION (ADA) 3878
AMERICAN DIETETIC ASSOCIATION (Baccalaureate or Coordinated Program) 2043
AMERICAN DIETETIC ASSOCIATION (Dietetic Internships) 2044
AMERICAN DIETETIC ASSOCIATION (Dietetic Technician Scholarships) 2045
AMERICAN EXPRESS SCHOLARSHIP AWARDS PROGRAM 2519
AMERICAN FARM BUREAU FEDERATION ("There's a New Challenge in Agriculture") 3827
AMERICAN FEDERATION OF GRAIN MILLERS (Scholarship Program) 2520
AMERICAN FEDERATION OF STATE, COUNTY, AND MUNICIPAL EMPLOYEES, AFL-CIO
(Jerry Clark Memorial Scholarship) 2303, 2521, 2522
AMERICAN FEDERATION OF TEACHERS 3881
AMERICAN FEDERATION OF TEACHERS (Robert G. Porter Scholars Program) 2523
AMERICAN FIRE SPRINKLER ASSOCIATION (Scholarship Contest) 2524
AMERICAN FISHERIES SOCIETY 3891
AMERICAN FOREIGN SERVICE ASSOCIATION (Financial Aid Awards) 2525, 2526
AMERICAN FOUNDATION FOR AGING RESEARCH (Fellowship Program) 1796
AMERICAN FOUNDATION FOR PHARMACEUTICAL EDUCATION
(First-Year Graduate Scholarship Program) 1717, 1718, 3948
AMERICAN FOUNDATION FOR THE BLIND (Delta Gamma Foundation Memorial Scholarship) 202, 203, 303, 589,
. . . . .961, 1065, 1066, 1229, 1342,
. . . . .1434, 1474, 1521, 1565, 1649,
. . . . .1719, 1797, 1858, 1946, 2412, 2413, 2527
AMERICAN FOUNDATION FOR VISION AWARENESS (Education/Research Grants) 1720, 1721
AMERICAN GEOLOGICAL INSTITUTE 3902
AMERICAN GEOLOGICAL INSTITUTE (AGI Minority Geoscience Scholarships) 1343, 1435, 1566
AMERICAN GEOPHYSICAL UNION 3903
AMERICAN GI FORUM OF THE U.S. HISPANIC EDUCATION FOUNDATION (Chapter Scholarships) 2528, 2529

AMERICAN GUILD OF ORGANISTS (National Competition in Organ Improvisation) 1067, 1068, 1069

AMERICAN HEALTH AND BEAUTY AIDS INSTITUTE
  (Fred Luster, Sr. Education Foundation Scholarships for College-Bound High School Seniors) 1, 52, 304, 1567, 2414, 2530

AMERICAN HEALTH INFORMATION MANAGEMENT ASSOCIATION
  (Barbara Thomas Enterprises Scholarship) 1859, 1860, 1861, 3925

AMERICAN HEART ASSOCIATION (Helen N. and Harold B. Shapira Scholarship) 1650

AMERICAN HISTORICAL ASSOCIATION (Beveridge Family Teaching Prize for K-12 Teaching) .187

AMERICAN HISTORICAL ASSOCIATION (Eugene Asher Distinguished Teaching Award for Postsecondary Teaching) 188

AMERICAN HISTORICAL ASSOCIATION (Michael Kraus Research Award Grant) 2215

AMERICAN HOTEL FOUNDATION 3911

AMERICAN HOTEL FOUNDATION (American Express Card Scholarship Program) 53

AMERICAN HOTEL FOUNDATION (Arthur J. Packard Memorial Scholarship Competition) 54

AMERICAN HOTEL FOUNDATION (Ecolab Scholarship Program) 55

AMERICAN HOTEL FOUNDATION (Hyatt Hotel Fund for Minority Lodging Management Students) 56

AMERICAN INDIAN SCIENCE AND ENGINEERING SOCIETY (Burlington Northern Santa Fe
  Pacific Foundation Scholarships) 2, 189, 204, 305, 306, 703,
  . . . . .1230, 1344, 1345, 1395, 1396,
  . . . . .1436, 1475, 1476, 1522, 1568,
  . . . . .1651, 1722, 1723, 1798, 1862, 1947

AMERICAN INSTITUTE FOR FOREIGN STUDY (AIFS) (International Scholarships) 2531, 2532

AMERICAN INSTITUTE OF AERONAUTICS AND ASTRONAUTICS (Undergraduate Scholarships) 479, 1596, 2415, 3824

AMERICAN INSTITUTE OF ARCHITECTS/AMERICAN ARCHITECTURAL FOUNDATION
  (Scholarship Program) 513, 514, 515

AMERICAN INSTITUTE OF ARCHITECTS/AMERICAN HOSPITAL ASSOCIATION (AIA/AHA Fellowships in Health
  Facilities Planning and Design) 516

AMERICAN INSTITUTE OF ARCHITECTS INFORMATION POSTER AND BOOKLET 3621

AMERICAN INSTITUTE OF ARCHITECTS, NEW YORK CHAPTER
  (Haskell Awards for Student Architectural Journalism) 517, 518, 519, 878

AMERICAN INSTITUTE OF BAKING (Scholarships) 2416

AMERICAN INSTITUTE OF BIOLOGICAL SCIENCES 3850

AMERICAN INSTITUTE OF CERTIFIED PUBLIC ACCOUNTANTS
  (Undergraduate Minority Scholarships Program) 57, 3816

AMERICAN INSTITUTE OF CHEMICAL ENGINEERS
  (Donald F. Othmer Sophomore Academic Excellence Award) 704, 705, 706, 707, 708, 3857

AMERICAN INSTITUTE OF GRAPHIC ARTS 3904

AMERICAN INSTITUTE OF PHYSICS STUDENTS 3952

AMERICAN INSTITUTE OF POLISH CULTURE (Scholarships) 58, 2091

AMERICAN INTERCONTINENTAL UNIVERSITY (Emilio Pucci Scholarships) 59, 879

AMERICAN INTERCONTINENTAL UNIVERSITY (One-Year Tuition Scholarship) 880

AMERICAN JEWISH COMMITTEE (Harold W. Rosenthal Fellowship) 2304

AMERICAN JEWISH LEAGUE FOR ISRAEL (University Scholarship Fund) 2533

AMERICAN JUNIOR BRAHMAN ASSOCIATION (Ladies of the ABBA Scholarship) 1251, 2534

AMERICAN LEGION-KANSAS (Dr. "Click" Cowger Scholarship) 2535

AMERICAN LEGION (Eagle Scout of the Year Scholarship) 2536

AMERICAN LEGION-KANSAS (John & Geraldine Hobbie Licensed Practical Nursing Scholarship) 1948

AMERICAN LEGION-KANSAS (Legion Oratorical Contest) 2537

AMERICAN LEGION-KANSAS (Music Committee Scholarship) 1070

AMERICAN LEGION (National High School Oratorical Contest) 962

AMERICAN LEGION-KANSAS (Paul Flaherty Athletic Scholarship) 2538

AMERICAN LEGION-KANSAS (Ted & Nora Anderson Scholarship Fund;
  Albert M Lappin Scholarship; Hugh A. Smith Scholarship) 2539

AMERICAN LEGION AUXILIARY (Dept. of Minnesota Scholarships) 2540

AMERICAN LEGION AUXILIARY (Health Care Scholarships) 1724

AMERICAN LEGION AUXILIARY (Past Presidents Parley Healthcare Scholarship) 1725

AMERICAN LEGION AUXILIARY-KANSAS (Scholarship) 2541

AMERICAN LEGION AUXILIARY, DEPARTMENT OF ALABAMA (Scholarships) 2542

AMERICAN MANAGEMENT ASSOCIATION 3919
AMERICAN MANAGEMENT ASSOCIATION INTERNATIONAL
    (Operation Enterprise—Business Leadership Training for Young Adults) 60
AMERICAN MASSAGE THERAPY ASSOCIATION—AMTA 3920
AMERICAN MEDICAL ASSOCIATION 3926
AMERICAN MEDICAL TECHNOLOGISTS (AMT Scholarships) 1863
AMERICAN MEDICAL WRITERS ASSOCIATION (Margaret Mead Journalism Award) 2092
AMERICAN MENSA EDUCATION & RESEARCH FOUNDATION (Scholarships) 2543
AMERICAN METEOROLOGICAL SOCIETY (AMS/Industry/Government Graduate Fellowships) 1346
AMERICAN METEOROLOGICAL SOCIETY (AMS/Industry Minority Scholarships) 1347
AMERICAN METEOROLOGICAL SOCIETY (AMS/Industry Undergraduate Scholarships) 1348, 1349
AMERICAN METEOROLOGICAL SOCIETY (Father James B. Macelwane Award) 1350
AMERICAN MORGAN HORSE INSTITUTE (Scholarship Program) 2544
AMERICAN MOTHERS, INC. (Gertrude Fogelson Cultural and Creative Arts Awards) 881, 963, 1071
AMERICAN MUSEUM OF NATURAL HISTORY (Research Experiences for Undergraduates) 1523
AMERICAN NATIONAL CAN COMPANY (Scholarship Program) 2545
AMERICAN NUCLEAR SOCIETY (John & Muriel Landis Scholarships) 709
AMERICAN NUCLEAR SOCIETY (Undergraduate Scholarships) 710
AMERICAN OPTOMETRIC ASSOCIATION 3940
AMERICAN ORNITHOLOGISTS' UNION (AOU Student Research Awards) 1524
AMERICAN OSTEOPATHIC ASSOCIATION 3941
AMERICAN PHYSIOLOGICAL SOCIETY (Porter Physiology Development Program) 1525
AMERICAN PHYSICAL SOCIETY (Scholarships for Minority Undergraduate Students in Physics) 1597
AMERICAN PHYSICAL THERAPY ASSN. 3950
AMERICAN PLANNING ASSOCIATION 3978
AMERICAN PLANNING ASSOCIATION (Minority Scholarship and Fellowship Programs) 61, 520, 1397
AMERICAN POMOLOGICAL SOCIETY (U.P. Hedrick Awards) 1252
AMERICAN PSYCHOLOGICAL ASSOCIATION 3956
AMERICAN PSYCHIATRIC ASSN., DIVISION OF PUBLIC AFFAIRS 3955
AMERICAN PUBLIC TRANSIT ASSOCIATION (Transit Hall of Fame Scholarships) 62
AMERICAN RADIO RELAY LEAGUE FOUNDATION
    (The Henry Broughton, K2AE Memorial Scholarship) 307, 590, 657, 658, 659, 660, 661, 662, 663,
    . . . . .664, 665, 666, 667, 668, 669, 670, 671, 1477,
    . . . . .2093, 2546, 2547, 2548, 2549, 2550, 2551, 2552,
    . . . . .2553, 2554, 2555, 2556, 2557, 2558, 2559
AMERICAN RED CROSS—SONOMA COUNTY CHAPTER (Nurse Assistant Program Scholarships) 1949
AMERICAN RESPIRATORY CARE FOUNDATION 3961
AMERICAN RESPIRATORY CARE FOUNDATION
    (Jimmy A. Young Memorial Education Recognition Award) 1864, 1865, 1866, 1867
AMERICAN SAMOA GOVERNMENT (Financial Aid Program) 2560
AMERICAN SCANDINAVIAN FOUNDATION OF LOS ANGELES (Scholarship Program) 2561
AMERICAN SOCIOLOGICAL ASSOCIATION 3967
AMERICAN SOCIETY FOR CLINICAL LABORATORY SCIENCE
    (Dorothy Morrison Undergraduate Scholarship) 1726, 1727, 1728, 1729, 1868, 1869, 1870, 1871
AMERICAN SOCIETY FOR ENOLOGY AND VITICULTURE (Scholarship) 1526
AMERICAN SOCIETY FOR HEALTHCARE FOOD SERVICE ADMINISTRATORS
    (Dorothy Killian Scholarship for Undergraduates) 2046
AMERICAN SOCIETY FOR MICROBIOLOGY (ASM Faculty Fellowship Program) 1527, 1528, 1529, 3928
AMERICAN SOCIETY FOR PHARMACOLOGY & EXPERIMENTAL THERAPEUTICS INC. 3946
AMERICAN SOCIETY FOR PUBLIC ADMINISTRATION 3957
AMERICAN SOCIETY OF AGRONOMY 3828
AMERICAN SOCIETY OF APPRAISERS 3836
AMERICAN SOCIETY OF CIVIL ENGINEERS (Arthur S. Tuttle Memorial Scholarship) 563, 564, 565, 566, 3860
AMERICAN SOCIETY OF CLINICAL PATHOLOGISTS (Scholarship Program) 1872, 3924
AMERICAN SOCIETY OF CRIMINOLOGY (Gene Carte Student Paper Competition) 2248

AMERICAN SOCIETY OF ENGINEERS OF INDIAN ORIGIN
(Undergraduate Scholarship Programs) 308, 521, 591, 672, 776, 1351, 1398

AMERICAN SOCIETY OF HEATING, REFRIGERATION, AND AIR-CONDITIONING ENGINEERS
(ASHRAE Scholarship Program) 711, 712, 713

AMERICAN SOCIETY OF INTERIOR DESIGNERS EDUCATIONAL FOUNDATION
(Yale R. Burge Competition) 882, 883, 884, 885

AMERICAN SOCIETY OF MECHANICAL ENGINEERS
(ASME Student Loans) 777, 778, 779, 780, 781, 782, 783, 784, 785, 3923

AMERICAN SOCIETY OF NAVAL ENGINEERS (ASNE Scholarships) 309

AMERICAN SOCIETY OF NEWSPAPER EDITORS 3914

AMERICAN SOCIETY OF PERIANESTHESIA NURSES (Scholarships) 1950

AMERICAN SOCIETY OF RADIOLOGIC TECHNOLOGISTS (Isadore N. Stern Scholarship) 1873, 3958

AMERICAN SOCIETY OF SAFETY ENGINEERS 3962

AMERICAN SOCIETY OF TRAVEL AGENTS (ASTA) FOUNDATION (Student Scholarships) 63

AMERICAN SOCIETY OF WOMEN ACCOUNTANTS (Scholarships) 64

AMERICAN SPEECH-LANGUAGE-HEARING ASSOCIATION 3842

AMERICAN SPEECH-LANGUAGE-HEARING FOUNDATION
(Kala Singh Memorial Fund-International/Minority Student Scholarship) 205, 1730, 1799, 1874

AMERICAN SPEECH-LANGUAGE-HEARING FOUNDATION
(Leslie Isenberg Fund for Student With Disability) 206, 1731, 1800, 1875

AMERICAN SPEECH-LANGUAGE-HEARING FOUNDATION
(Young Scholars Award for Minority Student) 207, 1732, 1801, 1876

AMERICAN STRING TEACHERS ASSOCIATION (ASTA) (Solo Competitions) 1072

AMERICAN SYMPHONY ORCHESTRA LEAGUE (Music Assistance Fund) 1073

AMERICAN TRUCKING ASSOCIATIONS (Career Information) 3972

AMERICAN VETERINARY MEDICAL ASSOCIATION 3979

AMERICAN VETERINARY MEDICAL FOUNDATION (AVMA Auxiliary Student Loan Fund) 1733

AMERICAN WATER RESOURCES ASSOCIATION (Richard A. Herbert Memorial Scholarships) 714, 1352, 1437

AMERICAN WELDING SOCIETY (Scholarships) 715, 2417

AMERICAN WINE SOCIETY EDUCATIONAL FOUNDATION (Scholarships and Grants) 1530, 2047, 2418

AMERICAN WOMEN IN RADIO & TELEVISION 3853

AMERICAN WOMEN IN RADIO AND TELEVISION—HOUSTON CHAPTER (Scholarship Program) 2094

AMITY INSTITUTE (Internships in the US for Teaching Languages) 2562

AMVETS (National Four-Year Undergraduate Scholarship) 2563, 2564

AN UNCOMMON LEGACY FOUNDATION, INC. (Scholarships) 2565

ANCIENT ORDER UNITED WORKMEN (Student Memorial Loan Fund) 2566

ANIMATION SCHOOL DIRECTORY 3622

ANNA AND CHARLES STOCKWITZ FUND FOR EDUCATION OF JEWISH CHILDREN (Scholarships) 2567

ANNUAL REGISTER OF GRANT SUPPORT 3623

AOPA AIR SAFETY FOUNDATION (Mcallister & Burnside Scholarships) 480

APICS EDUCATION AND RESEARCH FOUNDATION (Donald W. Fogarty International Student Paper Competition) 65

APPALOOSA YOUTH FOUNDATION (Scholarships) 2568

APPRAISAL INSTITUTE EDUCATION TRUST (Scholarships) 66

ARCHAEOLOGICAL INSTITUTE OF AMERICA 3838

ARCHBOLD MEDICAL CENTER (Archbold Scholarship/Loan) 1734, 1877, 1951

ARCTIC EDUCATION FOUNDATION (Shareholder Scholarships) 2569

ARKANSAS DEPARTMENT OF HIGHER EDUCATION
(Emergency Secondary Education Loan) 208, 209, 210, 2570, 2571, 2572, 2573, 2574, 2575

ARKANSAS SINGLE PARENT SCHOLARSHIP FUND (Scholarships) 2576

ARKANSAS TECH UNIVERSITY (Scholarships) 2577

ARLINE P. PADELFORD SCHOLARSHIP TRUST (Scholarships) 2578

ARMED FORCES COMMUNICATIONS AND ELECTRONICS ASSOCIATION
(General Emmett Paige Scholarships for Military Personnel, Veterans, and Their Dependents) 592, 593, 594, 673,
. . . . .674, 675, 1598, 1599, 1600

ARMENIAN GENERAL BENEVOLENT UNION (Educational Loan Program) 1652, 2249

ARMENIAN RELIEF SOCIETY OF EASTERN USA, INC. (Grants) 2579
ARMENIAN STUDENTS' ASSOCIATION OF AMERICA, INC. (Scholarships) 2580
ARMY EMERGENCY RELIEF 2581
ARMY ROTC (Scholarships) 2582
AROMANDO FAMILY EDUCATIONAL FOUNDATION (Aromando & Mauriello Memorial Awards) 211
ART CALENDAR 3624
ART INSTITUTE OF SOUTHERN CALIFORNIA (Scholarships) 886
ARTHUR & DOREEN PARRETT SCHOLARSHIP TRUST FUND (Scholarships) 310, 1353, 1531, 1569, 1653, 1735
ARTHUR C. & FLORENCE S. BOEHMER FUND (Scholarships) 2583
ARTHUR M. MILLER FUND 1654, 1736, 1802, 1878, 1952
ARTS & ENTERTAINMENT NETWORK (A&E Teacher Grant Competition) 2584
ARTS MANAGEMENT P/L (Miles Franklin Literary Award) 964
ASAE SOCIETY FOR ENGINEERING IN AGRICULTURAL FOOD AND BIOLOGICAL SYSTEMS 3826
ASIAN AMERICAN JOURNALISTS ASSOCIATION (AAJA Portland Chapter Scholarships) 2095, 2096
ASIAN AMERICAN JOURNALISTS ASSOCIATION—HAWAII CHAPTER (AAJA Scholarship) 2097
ASIAN PACIFIC AMERICAN SUPPORT GROUP (Scholarship) 2585
ASIFA (Helen Victoria Haynes World Peace Storyboard & Animation Contest) 887
ASM FOUNDATION FOR EDUCATION & RESEARCH 3927
ASM INTERNATIONAL FOUNDATION (Undergraduate Scholarships) 786
ASSOCIATED BUILDERS AND CONTRACTORS SCHOLARSHIP PROGRAM 567
ASSOCIATED GENERAL CONTRACTOR'S EDUCATION AND RESEARCH FOUNDATION
    (Horowitz/Heffner Scholarships for Graduate Students) 568, 569
ASSOCIATED GENERAL CONTRACTORS OF AMERICA 3868
ASSOCIATED MALE CHORUSES OF AMERICA (Scholarships) 1074
ASSOCIATED PRESS TELEVISION-RADIO ASSOCIATION OF CALIFORNIA/NEVADA
    (APTRA-Clete Roberts & Kathryn Dettman Memorial Journalism Scholarship Awards) 2098
ASSOCIATED WESTERN UNIVERSITIES, INC. (AWU Undergraduate Student Fellowships) 311, 312, 481, 482, 522,
    ....523, 570, 571, 595, 596, 676, 677,
    ....716, 717, 787, 788, 1478, 1479, 1532,
    ....1533, 1570, 1571, 1601, 1602
ASSOCIATION FOR COMPUTING MACHINERY 3867
ASSOCIATION FOR COMPUTING MACHINERY (Listing of Internships & Summer Jobs) 597, 678
ASSOCIATION FOR COMPUTING MACHINERY-WASHINGTON, DC CHAPTER (Undergraduate Scholarship) 2586
ASSOCIATION FOR EDUCATION AND REHABILITATION OF THE BLIND AND VISUALLY IMPAIRED
    (William and Dorothy Ferrell Scholarship) 212, 213
ASSOCIATION FOR EDUCATION IN JOURNALISM & MASS COMMUNICATION (Mary A. Gardner Scholarship) 2099
ASSOCIATION FOR LIBRARY & INFORMATION SCIENCE EDUCATION (Alise Research Grants Program) 965
ASSOCIATION FOR RETARDED CITIZENS (Brazoria County Scholarships) 214
ASSOCIATION FOR WOMEN IN PSYCHOLOGY/AMERICAN PSYCHOLOGICAL ASSOCIATION DIVISION 35
    (Annual Student Research Prize) 837
ASSOCIATION FOR WOMEN IN SCIENCE EDUCATIONAL FOUNDATION
    (Dr. Vicki L. Schechtman Scholarship) 67, 68, 313, 314, 598, 599, 838, 839, 966, 967,
    ....1190, 1191, 1354, 1355, 1457, 1458, 1534, 1535,
    ....1572, 1573, 1603, 1604, 1737, 1738, 2075, 2076,
    ....2216, 2217, 2305, 2306, 2347, 2348, 2375, 2376
ASSOCIATION FOR WOMEN VETERINARIANS (Student Scholarship) 1739
ASSOCIATION OF AMERICAN GEOGRAPHERS 3900
ASSOCIATION ON AMERICAN INDIAN AFFAIRS, INC.
    (Emergency Aid and Health Professions Scholarships) 1655, 1740, 1803, 1879, 1953, 2587, 2588
ASSOCIATION OF CERTIFIED FRAUD EXAMINERS (Scholarships) 69, 2250
ASSOCIATION OF FORMER AGENTS OF THE U.S. SECRET SERVICE, INC.
    (Law Enforcement Career Scholarship Program) 2251
ASSOCIATION OF INDEPENDENT COLLEGES AND UNIVERSITIES 3865
ASSOCIATION OF INFORMATION TECHNOLOGY PROFESSIONALS 3873
ASSOCIATION OF OPERATING ROOM NURSES (AORN Scholarship Program) 1954
ASSOCIATION OF THE SONS OF POLAND (Scholarship Program) 2589

ASTRAEA NATIONAL LESBIAN ACTION FOUNDATION (Margot Karle Scholarship) 2590

AT&T BELL LABORATORIES (Summer Research Program for Minorities & Women) 315, 600, 679, 718, 789, 1605

ATHEISTS OF FLORIDA, INC. (Mark Twain Scholarship Fund) 2591

ATLANTA JOURNAL AND CONSTITUTION (Cox Minority Scholarship Program) 2100

ATLANTA PRESS CLUB (Journalism Scholarship Awards) 2101

AUBURN UNIVERSITY SCHOOL OF FORESTRY (Various Scholarships) 1356

AURORA FOUNDATION (Scholarships) 2592

AUSTIN CHILDREN'S EDUCATIONAL OPPORTUNITY FOUNDATION 2593

AUTOMOTIVE HALL OF FAME, INC. (Scholarship Program) 2594

AVIATION COUNCIL OF PENNSYLVANIA (Scholarships) 483, 2419

AVIATION DISTRIBUTORS AND MANUFACTURERS ASSOCIATION INTERNATIONAL
 (ADMA International Scholarship Fund) 70, 484, 2420, 3845

AVIATION INFORMATION RESOURCES (AIR, Inc.) 3832

AVIATION INSURANCE ASSOCIATION (Scholarship) 485, 2421

AVIATION MAINTENANCE EDUCATION FUND (AMEF Scholarship Program) 2422

AVON LATINA MODEL OF THE YEAR (Competition) 2595

AYN RAND INSTITUTE (Anthem Contest) 2596

AYN RAND INSTITUTE (*Atlas Shrugged* Essay Contest for Undergraduate Business Students) 71

AYN RAND INSTITUTE (*Fountainhead* Essay Contest) 2597

B & L EDUCATIONAL FOUNDATION 2598

B'NAI B'RITH YOUTH ORGANIZATION (Scholarship Program) 2377

B.M. WOLTMAN FOUNDATION (Lutheran Scholarships for Students of the Ministry and Teaching) 215, 1192

BAJA CALIFORNIA LANGUAGE COLLEGE (Spanish Language Immersion Contest) 1042

BALL STATE UNIVERSITY (David Letterman Telecommunications Scholarship Program) 2102

BALL STATE UNIVERSITY (Lionel J. Neiman Criminal Justice Scholarship) 2252

BALTIMORE OPERA STUDIO (Apprenticeship) 1075

BAPTIST GENERAL CONVENTION OF TEXAS (Scholarships) 2599

BARNABAS MINISTRIES OF SHREVEPORT 2600

BARNARD COLLEGE PRE-COLLEGE PROGRAMS (Grants for Summer in New York) 2601

BARNUM FESTIVAL (Jenny Lind Competition for Sopranos) 1076

BARRON'S GUIDE TO LAW SCHOOLS (12th Edition) 3625

BARRY GOLDWATER SCHOLARSHIP AND EXCELLENCE IN EDUCATION FOUNDATION
 (Scholarships) 316, 719, 1231, 1606

BARTENDERS' SCHOOL OF SANTA ROSA 3849

BASIC FACTS ON STUDY ABROAD 3626

BASIN ELECTRIC POWER COOPERATIVE (Scholarship Program) 2602

BEATRICE AND FRANCIS THOMPSON SCHOLARSHIP FUND (Scholarship) 2603

BECA FOUNDATION (Alice Newell Joslyn Medical Fund) 1656, 1741, 1804, 1880, 1955

BECA FOUNDATION (General Scholarship Fund) 2604

BECA FOUNDATION (The Daniel Gutierrez Memorial General Scholarship Fund) 2605

BEDDING PLANTS FOUNDATION, INC. (Harold Bettinger Memorial Scholarship) 3, 4, 72, 73, 74, 1253, 1254,
. . . . .1255, 1256, 1257, 1258, 1259, 1260,
. . . . .1261, 1262, 1263, 1264, 1265, 2606

BEMENT EDUCATIONAL GRANTS COMMITTEE (Diocese of Western Massachusetts Undergraduate Grants) 2607

BETTER GRAMMAR IN 30 MINUTES A DAY 3627

BETTER SENTENCE WRITING IN 30 MINUTES A DAY 3628

BETTER SPELLING IN 30 MINUTES A DAY 3629

BETTER VOCABULARY IN 30 MINUTES A DAY 3630

BEVERLY HILLS THEATRE GUILD (Julie Harris Playwright Award Competition) 968

BFGOODRICH (Collegiate Inventors Program) (BFG-CIP) 1480

BIA HIGHER EDUCATION/HOPI SUPPLEMENTAL GRANT 2608

BIG BOOK OF MINORITY OPPORTUNITIES 3631

BIG BOOK OF OPPORTUNITIES FOR WOMEN 3632

BILLY BARTY FOUNDATION (Evelyn Barty Scholarship Awards Programs) 2609

BINNEY & SMITH INC.-LIQUITEX (Liquitex Student Paint Exchange) 888
BIOTECHNOLOGY INDUSTRY ORGANIZATION 3851
BLACKFEET HIGHER EDUCATION PROGRAM (BIA Grant) 2610
BLINDED VETERANS ASSOCIATION (Kathern F. Gruber Scholarship Program) 2611
BLUES HEAVEN FOUNDATION, INC. (Muddy Waters Scholarship) 75, 216, 840, 889, 969, 1077, 2103
BOB JONES UNIVERSITY (Rebate Program) 2612
BOETTCHER FOUNDATION (Scholarships) 2613
BONNEVILLE TRANSLOADERS, INC. (Scholarship) 2614
BOSTON SAFE DEPOSIT & TRUST CO. (Blanche E. Colman Awards) 890, 1078
BOY SCOUTS OF AMERICA 3986
BOY SCOUTS OF AMERICA (National Eagle Scout Scholarships) 2615
BOY SCOUTS OF AMERICA-DR. HARRY BRITENSTOOL SCHOLARSHIP COMMITTEE
   (Greater New York City Councils Scholarship Fund) 2616
BOYS & GIRLS CLUBS OF AMERICA 3985
BOYS AND GIRLS CLUBS OF SAN DIEGO (Spence Reese Scholarship Fund) 317, 1657, 1742, 1805, 1881, 2253, 2307
BOYS AND GIRLS CLUB OF VENTURA (Emma Nylen Scholarship) 2617
BREWER FOUNDATION, INC. 2618
BRITISH AMERICAN EDUCATIONAL FOUNDATION (Scholars' Program) 2619
BROADCAST EDUCATION ASSOCIATION (Scholarships in Broadcasting) 2104
BROOKHAVEN WOMEN IN SCIENCE (Renate W. Chasman Scholarship) 318, 572, 601, 680, 720, 790,
   ....1357, 1438, 1536, 1574, 1607
BUCK INSTITUTE FOR EDUCATION (American Revolution Bicentennial Scholarships) 2620
BUCKS COUNTY COURIER TIMES (Summer Internship Program) 2105
BUDDHIST COMPASSION RELIEF TZU-CHI FOUNDATION, U.S.A. (Nursing Scholarships) 1956, 2621
BUENA VISTA COLLEGE NETWORK (Internships in Film Marketing) 76, 891, 970, 1079, 2106
BUILDING A GREAT RESUME 3633
BUREAU OF MAINE VETERANS SERVICES (Veterans Dependents Educational Benefits) 2622
BUSINESS & PROFESSIONAL WOMEN'S FOUNDATION
   (BPW Career Advancement Scholarship Program) 5, 77, 78, 190, 217, 319, 320, 602, 813, 1481,
   ....1537, 1608, 1658, 1743, 1744, 2077, 2254, 2423
BUTTE CREEK FOUNDATION 2623
Bartending 3634
C. BASCOM SLEMP FOUNDATION (Scholarships) 2624
C. G. FULLER FOUNDATION (Scholarships) 2625
CABRILLO CIVIC CLUBS OF CALIFORNIA (Scholarships) 2626
CALIF/HAWAII ELKS MAJOR PROJECT,INC. (Undergraduate Disabled Student Scholarships) 2627
CALIFORNIA ASSOCIATION OF REALTORS (CAR Scholarship Foundation) 79
CALIFORNIA CHICANO NEWS MEDIA ASSOCIATION (Joel Garcia Memorial Scholarship) 2628
CALIFORNIA COMMUNITY COLLEGES 3862
CALIFORNIA COLLEGE DEMOCRATS (Internships) 2629
CALIFORNIA COLLEGE OF ARTS & CRAFTS (Scholarships) 892
CALIFORNIA CORRECTIONAL PEACE OFFICERS ASSOCIATION (Joe Harper Scholarship Foundation) 2630
CALIFORNIA DEPARTMENT OF VETERANS AFFAIRS (College Fee Waiver Program) 2631
CALIFORNIA FARM BUREAU SCHOLARSHIP FOUNDATION (Scholarships) 1266
CALIFORNIA GOVERNOR'S COMMITTEE FOR EMPLOYMENT OF DISABLED PERSONS
   (Hal Connolly Scholar-Athlete Award) 2632
CALIFORNIA GRANGE FOUNDATION (Deaf Activities Scholarships) 218, 1745, 1882
CALIFORNIA GRANGE FOUNDATION (Scholarships) 2633
CALIFORNIA HAZARDOUS MATERIALS INVESTIGATORS ASSOCIATION (Scholarships) 2255
CALIFORNIA JUNIOR MISS PROGRAM (Scholarships & Awards) 2634
CALIFORNIA LIBRARY ASSOCIATION (Reference Service Press Fellowship) 971, 972
CALIFORNIA MASONIC FOUNDATION (General and Special Fund Scholarship Programs) 2635
CALIFORNIA PHYSICAL THERAPY FUND (Roy and Roxie Campanella Physical Therapist Professional
   Education Scholarship Program) 1883

CALIFORNIA SCHOOL LIBRARY ASSOCIATION (Leadership for Diversity Scholarship) 219

CALIFORNIA SOCIETY FOR ORIENTAL MEDICINE (CSOM) 3822

CALIFORNIA STUDENT AID COMMISSION
 (Assumption Program of Loans for Education—APLE) 220, 221, 2424, 2636, 2637, 2638, 2639

CALIFORNIA STATE UNIVERSITY SYSTEM 3864

CALIFORNIA TABLE GRAPE COMMISSION (California Table Grape Field Worker Scholarship Program) 2640

CALIFORNIA TEACHERS ASSOCIATION (CTA Scholarships for Members) 222, 2641

CALIFORNIA TEACHERS ASSOCIATION (L. Gordon Bittle Memorial Scholarships) 223

CALIFORNIA TEACHERS ASSOCIATION (Martin Luther King, Jr. Memorial Scholarship) 224

CALLEJO-BOTELLO FOUNDATION CHARITABLE TRUST 2642

CAMP FOUNDATION (Scholarship Grants) 2643

CAMPBELL HALL SCHOOL (Scholarships) 2644

CANNON SCHOOL (Scholarships) 2645

CAPE CANAVERAL CHAPTER RETIRED OFFICERS ASSOC. (Scholarships) 2646

CARBON POWER AND LIGHT, INC. (Scholarships) 2647

CARE AND FEEDING OF YOUR BRAIN 3635

CAREER GUIDE FOR SINGERS 3636

CAREER OPPORTUNITIES FOR YOUTH, INC. (Collegiate Scholarship Program) 6, 80, 225, 321, 603, 1232, 1482, 1957

CAREER PRESS CATALOG 3637

CAREERS WITHOUT COLLEGE: CARS 3638

CARGILL (Scholarship Program for Rural America) 2648

CARL AND VIRGINIA JOHNSON DAY TRUST 2649

CAS/SOCIETY OF ACTUARIES (Minority Recruiting Program) 81

CASCADE POLICY INSTITUTE (Independence Essay Competition) 2650

CASSNER FOUNDATION (Scholarship Program) 2651

CATHOLIC AID ASSN. (College Tuition Scholarship Program) 2652

CATHOLIC DIOCESE OF KANSAS CITY-ST. JOSEPH—CENTRAL CITY SCHOOL FUND (Scholarships) 2653

CATHOLIC LIBRARY ASSOCIATION (World Book, Inc., Award) 973

CDR. WILLIAM S. STUHR SCHOLARSHIP FUND 2654

CENEX FOUNDATION SCHOLARSHIP PROGRAM (Agricultural Studies) 1267, 1268

CENTER FOR 17TH- AND 18TH-CENTURY STUDIES (Fellowships) 841, 974, 2218

CENTER FOR ENVIRONMENTAL JOURNALISM/UNIVERSITY OF COLORADO AT BOULDER
 (Ted Scripps Fellowship) 2107

CENTER FOR PRIMARY CARE AND RURAL HEALTH-VIRGINIA DEPARTMENT OF HEALTH
 (Mary Marshall Nursing Scholarships) 1958

CENTRAL NEWSPAPERS, INC. (Pulliam Journalism Fellowships) 2108

CENTRAL SCHOLARSHIP BUREAU (Interest-free Loans) 2655

CEO AMERICA (School Choice Scholarships) 2656

CFKR CAREER MATERIALS CATALOG 3639

CHAIRSCHOLARS FOUNDATION, INC. (Scholarships) 2657

CHALLENGE IN AGRICULTURE 3640

CHAMBER MUSIC AMERICA (Gruber Foundation Award/Heidi Castleman Award for Excellence
 in Chamber Music Teaching) 1080

CHARLES COOPER INDUSTRIAL SCHOOL 2658

CHARLES E. SAAK TRUST (Educational Grants) 191, 1746

CHARLES H. BOND TRUST 2659

CHARLES I. AND EMMA J. CLAPP SCHOLARSHIP FUND 2660

CHARLES J. HUGHES FOUNDATION 2661

CHARLESTON SCIENTIFIC AND CULTURAL EDUCATIONAL FUND 2662

CHAROTAR PATIDAR SAMAJ (Sardar Patel Scholarships) 2663

CHATHAM COLLEGE (Merit Scholarship Program) 2664

CHATHAM COLLEGE (Minna Kaufmann Ruud Fund) 1081

CHAUTAUQUA INSTITUTION (Scholarships) 814

CHAUTAUQUA LAKE FISHING ASSOCIATION (Scholarship) 1399

CHAUTAUQUA REGION COMMUNITY FOUNDATION INC. (Scholarships) 2665
CHEROKEE NATION (Higher Education Need-based Grant Program) 2666
CHESTNUT HILL ACADEMY (Scholarships and Financial Aid) 2667
CHEYENNE AND ARAPAHO TRIBES OF OKLAHOMA (Scholarships) 2668
CHICAGO TRIBUNE (Heartland Prizes) 975
CHICAGO TRIBUNE (Nelson Algren Awards) 976
CHINESE AMERICAN CITIZENS ALLIANCE FOUNDATION 2669
CHINESE CHRISTIAN HERALD CRUSADES (Chinese Collegiate Merit Scholarship for New York Schools) 2670
CHINESE PROFESSIONAL CLUB OF HOUSTON (Scholarship Program) 2671
CHOCTAW NATION OF OKLAHOMA HIGHER EDUCATION PROGRAM (Grants) 2672
CHOPIN FOUNDATION OF THE UNITED STATES, INC. (Scholarship Program for Young Pianists) 1082
CHRIST SCHOOL (Scholarships) 2673
CHRISTIAN A. JOHNSON ENDEAVOR FOUNDATION (Native American Fellows) 842, 2078, 2219, 2308, 2378
CHRISTIAN CHURCH-DISCIPLES OF CHRIST (Katherine J. Schutze Memorial and Edwin G. &
  Lauretta M. Michael Scholarship) 1193, 1194, 1195
CHRISTIAN RECORD SERVICES INC. (Scholarships) 2674
CHRONICLE CAREER INDEX 3641
CHRONICLE FINANCIAL AID GUIDE 3642
CHRONICLE FOUR-YEAR COLLEGE DATABOOK 3643
CHRONICLE TWO-YEAR COLLEGE DATABOOK 3644
CHRONICLE VOCATIONAL SCHOOL MANUAL 3645
CHUNG KUN AI FOUNDATION 2675
CITIZEN'S SCHOLARSHIP FOUNDATION OF AMERICA (CIGNA Foundation Scholarship) 2676, 2677
CITIZENS SCHOLARSHIP FOUNDATION OF GUERNSEY COUNTY (Dollars For Scholars) 2678
CITIZENS' SCHOLARSHIP FOUNDATION OF WAKEFIELD, INC. (Scholarships) .2679
CIVIL AIR PATROL (CAP Undergraduate Scholarships) 226, 322, 815, 1483
CIVIL AIR PATROL (Casaday-Elmore Ministerial Scholarship) 1196
CIVIL AIR PATROL (Col. Louisa Spruance Morse CAP Scholarship) 486
CIVIL AIR PATROL (Dowling Scholarship) 2425
CIVIL AIR PATROL (Major Gen. Lucas V. Beau Flight Scholarship) 487, 2426
CIVIL AIR PATROL (Vocational-Technical Scholarships) 2427
CLAYFOLK (Ellice T. Johnston Scholarship) 893
CLEM JAUNICH EDUCATION TRUST (Scholarships) 1197, 1659
CLUB MANAGERS ASSOCIATION OF AMERICA 82
COALITION FOR THE ADVANCEMENT OF JEWISH EDUCATION (Abraham A. Spack Fellowship) 843
COCA-COLA SCHOLARS FOUNDATION (Scholarship) 2680
COLBURN-PLEDGE MUSIC SCHOLARSHIP FOUNDATION (Scholarships for Texas String Instrument Students) 1083
COLLEGE ATHLETIC SCHOLARSHIP GUIDE 3646
COLLEGE BOUND FAMILY LIBRARY & SUPPORT PACKAGE 3647
COLLEGE BOUND STUDENT OF THE YEAR (Contest) 2681
COLLEGE DEGREES BY MAIL & MODEM 3648
COLLEGE FINANCIAL AID EMERGENCY KIT 3649
COLLEGE FINANCIAL AID FOR DUMMIES 3650
COLLEGE FOUNDATION INC (Federal PLUS Loans Under NC Federal Family Education Loan Program) 2682
COLLEGE FOUNDATION INC. (North Carolina Federal Family Education Loan Program; Stafford Loans—
  Subsidized & Unsubsidized—and PLUS loans) 2683, 2684, 2685
COLLEGE IS POSSIBLE 3651
COLLEGE MISERICORDIA (Honor Scholarships) 2686
COLLEGE MISERICORDIA (Presidential Scholarships) 816, 2256
COLLEGE OF INSURANCE 3913
COLLEGE OF INSURANCE (Scholars Award Program) 83
COLLEGE OF MARIN FOUNDATION (Disabled Students Program) 2687
COLLEGE OF SAINT ELIZABETH (Scholarships) 2688
COLLEGE OF ST. FRANCIS (Various Scholarship/Grant Programs) 2689

COLLEGE READY REPORT: THE FIRST STEP TO COLLEGE 3652
COLLEGE SMARTS—THE OFFICIAL FRESHMAN HANDBOOK 3653
COLLEGE SURVIVAL INSTRUCTION BOOK 3654
COLLEGES WITH PROGRAMS FOR STUDENTS WITH LEARNING DISABILITIES OR
    ATTENTION DEFICIT DISORDER 3655
COLORADO MASONS BENEVOLENT FUND ASSOCIATION (Scholarship Program) 2690
COLORADO ROCKY MOUNTAIN SCHOOL (Scholarships) 2691
COLORADO SOCIETY OF CPAs EDUCATIONAL FOUNDATION (Scholarships for High School Seniors) . . .84, 85, 86, 87, 88
COLORADO STATE UNIVERSITY (First-Generation Award) 2692
COLUMBIA UNIVERSITY (Joseph H. Bearns Prize in Music) 1084
COLUMBIANA COUNTY PUBLIC HEALTH LEAGUE TRUST FUND (Grants) 1660, 1747, 1806, 1884, 1959
COLUMBUS SCHOOL FOR GIRLS (Scholarships) 2693
COMMITTEE ON INSTITUTIONAL COOPERATION (Summer Research Opportunities Program) 2694
COMMONWEALTH OF VIRGINIA DEPARTMENT OF VETERANS' AFFAIRS (War Orphans Education Program) 2695
COMMUNITY FOUNDATION OF GREATER LORAIN COUNTY (Various Scholarship Programs) 2696
COMMUNITY FOUNDATION OF SARASOTA COUNTY (Scholarship Funds) 2697
COMMUNITY FOUNDATION OF WESTERN MASSACHUSETTS (Joseph Bonfitto Scholarship) 89, 227, 323, 573, 721,
    . . . . .894, 1085, 1358, 1439, 1484,
    . . . . .1609, 1885, 1886, 1960, 1961, 1962,
    . . . . .2379, 2428, 2698, 2699, 2700, 2701, 2702,
    . . . . .2703, 2704, 2705, 2706, 2707, 2708, 2709, 2710,
    . . . . .2711, 2712, 2713, 2714, 2715, 2716, 2717, 2718, 2719,
    . . . . .2720, 2721, 2722, 2723, 2724, 2725, 2726, 2727,
    . . . . .2728, 2729, 2730, 2731, 2732, 2733, 2734, 2735
COMMUNITY FOUNDATION SILICON VALLEY (Valley Scholars Program) 324, 1233, 1485, 1610
CONFERENCE OF MINORITY PUBLIC ADMINISTRATORS (Scholarships and Travel Grants) 90, 2309
CONGRESS OF MINNESOTA RESORTS (Scholarships) 2736
CONGRESSIONAL HISPANIC CAUCUS INSTITUTE, INC. (Summer Internship Program) .2737
CONNECTICUT DEPT. OF HIGHER EDUCATION (State Scholastic Achievement Grant) 2738, 2739
CONNECTICUT LEAGUE FOR NURSING (CLN Scholarships) 1963, 1964
CONSULTING ENGINEERS AND LAND SURVEYORS OF CALIFORNIA (CELSOC Undergraduate Scholarships) 325
CONSULTING ENGINEERS COUNCIL OF NEW JERSEY (Louis Goldberg Scholarship Fund) 326, 1359
CONTEMPORARY RECORD SOCIETY (CRS Competitions) 1086
CONTINENTAL SOCIETY DAUGHTERS OF INDIAN WARS (Scholarship) 192, 228, 2380
CONTRACT MANAGEMENT INSTITUTE (Scholarships) 91
CONVERSE COUNTY 4-H FOUNDATION (Scholarships) 2740
COOPER WOOD PRODUCTS FOUNDATION, INC. 2741
COOPERATIVE ASSOCIATION OF STATES FOR SCHOLARSHIPS (CASS) (Scholarships) 92, 604, 2429
COOPERATIVE EDUCATION COLLEGE ROSTER 3656
COUNCIL FOR BASIC EDUCATION (Arts Education Fellowships) 895, 977, 1087
COUNCIL OF CITIZENS WITH LOW VISION INTERNATIONAL (CCLVI Telesensory Scholarship) 2742
COUNCIL ON INTERNATIONAL EDUCATIONAL EXCHANGE (Bailey Minority Student Scholarships) 2743
COX NEWSPAPERS, INC. (Cox Minority Journalism Scholarship) 2109
CREATIVE GUIDE TO RESEARCH 3657
CRESTAR BANK (Trivia Contest) 2744
CRETE POLICE ASSOCIATION (Law Enforcement Scholarship) 2257
CRYSTAL SPRINGS UPLANDS SCHOOL (Financial Aid) 2745
CUBAN AMERICAN NATIONAL FOUNDATION (The Mas Family Scholarships) 7, 93, 327, 2110, 2310
CUBAN AMERICAN TEACHERS' ASSN. (Scholarships) 2746
CULINARY SCHOOLS 3658
CURTIS INSTITUTE OF MUSIC (Tuition Scholarships) 1088
CUYAHOGA COUNTY MEDICAL FOUNDATION (Scholarship Grant Program) 1661, 1748, 1965
CYMDEITHAS GYMREIG/PHILADELPHIA (Scholarships) 2747
CYNTHIA E. AND CLARA H. HOLLIS FOUNDATION 1198, 1887, 1966, 2381
CYSTIC FIBROSIS FOUNDATION (Research & Training Programs) 1807

CYSTIC FIBROSIS FOUNDATION (Student Traineeship Research Grants) 1808
D. D. HACHAR CHARITABLE TRUST FUND (Undergraduate Scholarships) 2748
DAN CASSIDY'S GUIDE TO PRIVATE SECTOR KINDERGARTEN-12TH GRADE (K-12) SCHOLARSHIPS 3659
DAN CASSIDY'S GUIDE TO TRAVEL GRANTS 3660
DANISH SISTERHOOD OF AMERICA (Scholarship Program) 2749
DATATEL SCHOLARS FOUNDATION (Angelfire Scholarships) 2750
DATATEL SCHOLARS FOUNDATION (Datatel Scholarships) 2751
DAUGHTERS OF PENELOPE (Undergraduate Scholarships) 2752
DAUGHTERS OF THE AMERICAN REVOLUTION (American Indians Scholarship) 2753, 2754
DAUGHTERS OF THE CINCINNATI (Scholarship Program) 2755
DAUGHTERS OF UNION VETERANS OF THE CIVIL WAR
   (Grand Army of the Republic Living Memorial Scholarship) 2756
DAVID WASSERMAN SCHOLARSHIP FUND Inc. (Award Program) 2757
DAVIS-ROBERTS SCHOLARSHIP FUND INC. (Scholarships to DeMolays & Job's Daughters) 2758
DAYTON FOUNDATION (Larry Fullerton Photojournalism Scholarship) 2111
DAYTON-MONTGOMERY COUNTY SCHOLARSHIP PROGRAM 2759
DEBT-FREE GRADUATE: HOW TO SURVIVE COLLEGE WITHOUT GOING BROKE 3661
DECA (Harry A. Applegate Scholarships) 94
DEKALB COUNTY PRODUCERS SUPPLY & FARM BUREAU (Medical Scholarship) 1662, 1967
DELLA M. BAILEY INDIAN SCHOLARSHIP TRUST 2760
DELTA GAMMA FOUNDATION 2761
DELTA OMICRON (Triennial Composition Competition for Solo Piano 1089
DELTA OMICRON INTERNATIONAL MUSIC FRATERNITY
   (Triennial Composition Competition for Sacred Choral Anthem for Three- or Four-Part Voices) 1090
DELTA PHI EPSILON EDUCATIONAL FOUNDATION 2762
DEMOLAY FOUNDATION INC. (Scholarships) 2763
DEMONSTRATION OF ENERGY-EFFICIENT DEVELOPMENTS (DEED Scholarship Program) 1360
DENISON UNIVERSITY (Financial Aid) 2764
DENISON UNIVERSITY (Honors Program) 2765
DENISON UNIVERSITY (Merit-Based Scholarships) 2766
DEPARTMENT OF THE ARMY (Armed Forces Health Professions Scholarships) 1663, 1749, 1968, 2349
DEPARTMENT OF VETERANS AFFAIRS (Survivors and Dependents Educational Assistance Program) 2767
DESCENDANTS OF THE SIGNERS OF THE DECLARATION OF INDEPENDENCE (Scholarship Grant) 2768
DEXTER G. JOHNSON EDUCATIONAL AND BENEVOLENT TRUST (Student Loans) 2769
DIRECTOR OF SELECTIONS 3830
DIRECTORY OF ACCREDITED INSTITUTIONS 3662
DIRECTORY OF FINANCIAL AIDS FOR MINORITIES 3663, 3664, 3665
DIRECTORY OF MEMBER SCHOOLS 3666
DIRECTORY OF NATIONAL INFORMATION SOURCES ON DISABILITIES (7th Edition) 3667
DIRECTORY OF POSTSECONDARY EDUCATIONAL RESOURCES IN ALASKA 3668
DIRECTORY OF RESEARCH GRANTS 3669
DIRECTORY OF TECHNICAL SCHOOLS, COLLEGES, AND UNIVERSITIES OFFERING COURSES IN
   GRAPHIC COMMUNICATIONS 3670
DIRECTORY OF UNDERGRADUATE POLITICAL SCIENCE FACULTY 3671
DISABLED AMERICAN VETERANS AUXILIARY (DAVA Student Loans) 2770
DISCOVER CARD TRIBUTE AWARD (Scholarship) 2771
DISTRICT OF COLUMBIA (State Student Incentive Grant Program) 2772
DISTRICT OF COLUMBIA COMMISSION ON THE ARTS & HUMANITIES (Grants) 896, 978, 1091
DIXIE COLLEGE (Music Scholarships) 1092
DIXIE YARNS FOUNDATION, INC. (George West Scholarship Fund) 2773
DODD & DOROTHY L. BRYAN FOUNDATION (Interest-Free Loans) 2774
DOG WRITERS' EDUCATIONAL TRUST (Scholarships) 2775
DOLLARS FOR COLLEGE: THE QUICK GUIDE TO SCHOLARSHIPS, FELLOWSHIPS, LOANS, AND OTHER
   FINANCIAL AID PROGRAMS FOR... 3672

DOLPHIN SCHOLARSHIP FOUNDATION (Scholarships) 2776

DOW JONES NEWSPAPER FUND, INC.
  (Business Reporting Intern Program for Minority Sophomores & Juniors) 2112, 2113, 2114, 2115, 2116

DRY CREEK NEIGHBORS CLUB (Scholarships) 2777

DULUTH NEWS-TRIBUNE (Native American Internships) 2117

DUMBARTON OAKS (The Bliss Prize Fellowship in Byzantine Studies) 844

DURACELL/NATIONAL SCIENCE TEACHERS ASSOCIATION (Scholarship Competition) 2778

DeVRY INC. (Dean's & Presidential Scholarships) 95, 605, 681, 722, 2118, 2430

EAA AVIATION FOUNDATION (Scholarship Program) 96, 488, 2431

EARL WARREN LEGAL TRAINING PROGRAM (Shearman & Sterling Scholarship Program) .2258

EARTHWATCH STUDENT CHALLENGE AWARDS (High School Student Research Expeditions) 2779

EAST LONGMEADOW SCHOLARSHIP FOUNDATION FUND (Scholarships) 2780

EAST OHIO CONFERENCE BOARD OF ORDAINED MINISTRY (Ministerial Student Grants) .1199

EAST TEXAS HISTORICAL ASSOCIATION (Ottis Lock Endowment Awards) 2079, 2220

EAST-WEST CENTER (Undergraduate and Graduate Fellowships for Pacific Islanders) 845

EASTER SEAL SOCIETY OF IOWA, INC. (Scholarships & Awards) 229, 1888, 2350, 2382, 2781

EASTERN KENTUCKY UNIVERSITY (Music Scholarships) 1093

EASTERN ORTHODOX COMMITTEE ON SCOUTING (Scholarship) 2782

EBELL OF LOS ANGELES SCHOLARSHIP PROGRAM 2783

EBERHARDT I. FOR SCHOLARSHIP FOUNDATION 2784

ECKMANN FOUNDATION 2785

EDITOR & PUBLISHER JOURNALISM AWARDS AND FELLOWSHIPS DIRECTORY 3673

EDUCATION AND TRAINING PROGRAMS IN OCEANOGRAPHY AND RELATED FIELDS 3674

EDUCATION ASSISTANCE CORPORATION (Federal Family Education Loan Program) 2786

EDUCATION COUNCIL OF THE GRAPHIC ARTS INDUSTRY 3905

EDUCATIONAL AND SCIENTIFIC TRUST OF THE PENNSYLVANIA MEDICAL SOCIETY
  (Loan Program for Allied Health/Nursing Students) 1889, 1969

EDUCATIONAL CREDIT MANAGEMENT CORPORATION (Loan Programs for Virginia Students) 2787

EDUCATIONAL COMMUNICATIONS SCHOLARSHIP FOUNDATION (College Scholarship Award) 2788, 2789

EDUCATIONAL LEADERSHIP, EDUCATION UPDATE, & CURRICULUM UPDATE 3675

EDWARD AND ANNA RANGE SCHMIDT CHARITABLE TRUST (Grants & Emergency Financial Assistance) . . .1361, 1400

EDWARD BANGS KELLEY AND ELZA KELLEY FOUNDATION, INC. (Scholarship Program) . . .1664, 1750, 1809, 1890, 1970

EDWARDS SCHOLARSHIP FUND (Undergraduate and Graduate Scholarships) 2790

EEO BIMONTHLY 3676

EL PASO COMMUNITY FOUNDATION (Scholarships) 2791

ELECTRONIC INDUSTRIES FOUNDATION (Scholarship Program) 682, 723, 791, 1611, 2119

ELIE WIESEL FOUNDATION FOR HUMANITY (Prize in Ethics Essay Contest) 2792

ELMER O. & IDA PRESTON EDUCATIONAL TRUST (Grants & Loans) 1200

ELMER O. AND IDA PRESTON EDUCATIONAL TRUST (Scholarships) 2793

EMANUEL STERNBERGER EDUCATIONAL FUND (Interest-Free Loan Program) 2794

EMPIRE COLLEGE (Dean's Scholarship) 8, 97, 1891, 2432

ENCYCLOPEDIA OF ASSOCIATIONS—Vol. 1 3677

ENGLISH-SPEAKING UNION (Lucy Dalbiac Luard Scholarship) 2795

ENTOMOLOGICAL SOCIETY OF AMERICA (Stan Beck Fellowship) 1538, 1539, 3885

EPILEPSY FOUNDATION (Camperships) 2796

EPILEPSY FOUNDATION OF AMERICA (Behavioral Sciences Student Fellowships) 1665, 1810, 1811, 1971, 2351

ESPN (Internship Programs) 98, 1892, 2120, 2352, 2383

ETHEL AND EMERY FAST SCHOLARSHIP FOUNDATION, INC. 2797

ETHEL N. BOWEN FOUNDATION (Scholarships) 2798

ETHICAL CULTURE FIELDSTON SCHOOL (Financial Aid and Loans) 2799

ETUDE MUSIC CLUB OF SANTA ROSA (Music Competition for Instrumentalists) 1094, 1095

EVEREG-FENESSE MESROBIAN-ROUPINIAN EDUCATIONAL SOCIETY, INC. 2800

EVERGREEN STATE COLLEGE (Scholarships) 2801

EVERYDAY MATH FOR THE NUMERICALLY CHALLENGED 3678

EXPLORERS CLUB (Youth Activity Fund) 1234
EXPLORING CAREERS IN MUSIC 3679
FASHION GROUP INTERNATIONAL OF GREATER WASHINGTON DC (Scholarships) 99, 897
FASHION INSTITUTE OF TECHNOLOGY 3889
FASHION INSTITUTE OF TECHNOLOGY (Scholarships) 898
FEDERAL BENEFITS FOR VETERANS & DEPENDENTS (S/N 051-000-00212-1) 3680
FEDERAL BUREAU OF INVESTIGATION 3887
FEDERAL EMPLOYEE EDUCATION AND ASSISTANCE FUND (OK Scholarship Fund) 2802, 2803, 2804
FEDERAL HIGHWAY ADMINISTRATION, DEPT OF TRANSPORTATION (Grants for Research Fellowships) 9
FEDERATION OF JEWISH AGENCIES OF GREATER PHILADELPHIA (Foreman Fleisher Fund) 2805
FEILD CO-OPERATIVE ASSOCIATION (Mississippi Resident Loans) 2806
FELLOWS MEMORIAL FUND (Scholarship Loans) 1893, 1972
FELLOWSHIP GUIDE TO WESTERN EUROPE 3681
FELLOWSHIP OF UNITED METHODISTS IN MUSIC AND WORSHIP ARTS (Scholarships) 1096, 1201
FERN BROWN MEMORIAL FUND 2807
FIGHT FOR SIGHT RESEARCH DIVISION OF PREVENT BLINDNESS AMERICA (Student Research Fellowship) 1812
FINANCE AUTHORITY OF MAINE (Teachers for Maine) 230
FINANCIAL AID FOR MINORITIES 3682
FINANCIAL AID FOR THE DISABLED AND THEIR FAMILIES 3683
FINANCIAL AID FOR VETERANS; MILITARY PERSONNEL & THEIR FAMILIES 3684
FINANCIAL AID INFORMATION FOR PHYSICIAN ASSISTANT STUDENTS 3685
FINANCIAL AID RESOURCE GUIDE-#17.97 3686
FINANCIAL ASSISTANCE FOR LIBRARY & INFORMATION STUDIES 3687
FINDING MONEY FOR COLLEGE 3688
FIREARMS CIVIL RIGHTS LEGAL DEFENSE FUND (Essay Contest for Law Students) .2259
FIRST CATHOLIC SLOVAK LADIES ASSOCIATION (College Scholarships) 2808, 2809
FIRST CAVALRY DIVISION ASSOCIATION (Scholarships) 2810
FIRST CITIZENS FOUNDATION, INC. 2811
FIRST COMMERCIAL BANK (Regions/National Advisory Board Scholarship) 2812
FIRST UNITED METHODIST CHURCH (Grannis-Martin Educational Foundation Fund) 1202, 1401, 1666, 1751,
. . . . .1813, 1894, 1973, 2384
FIRST UNITED METHODIST CHURCH STUDENT LOAN PROGRAM (Stephen McCready Fund) 2813
FISKE GUIDE TO COLLEGES 3689
FITZGERALD TRUST FUND (Scholarships) 1203
FLEET RESERVE ASSOCIATION (Scholarships and Awards) 2814
FLORENCE EVANS BUSHEE FOUNDATION, INC. (Scholarships) 2815
FLORIDA AIR ACADEMY SCHOLARSHIP FUND, INC. 2816
FLORIDA DENTAL HEALTH FOUNDATION 3877
FLORIDA DENTAL HEALTH FOUNDATION (Dental Assisting Scholarship Program) 1895, 1896
FLORIDA DEPARTMENT OF STATE—ARTS COUNCIL (Individual Artists' Fellowships) 899, 979, 1097
FLORIDA DEPT. OF EDUCATION (Ethics In Business Scholarship Program) 100, 231, 1897, 1974, 2817, 2818,
. . . . .2819, 2820, 2821, 2822, 2823, 2824, 2825
FLORIDA DEPT. OF EDUCATION/U.S. DEPT. OF EDUCATION (Robert C. Byrd Honors Scholarship Program) 2826
FLORIDA FEDERATION OF GARDEN CLUBS, INC. (FFGC Scholarships for College Students) 524, 525, 1269, 1270,
. . . . .1362, 1363, 1402, 1403,
. . . . .1440, 1441, 1540, 1541
FLORIDA RURAL REHABILITATION SCHOLARSHIP 1271
FLORIDA STATE DEPT. OF EDUCATION (Seminole/Miccosukee Indian Scholarships) 2827
FLORIDA STATE UNIVERSITY (Online Scholar Challenge) 2828
FLORIDA STUDENT FINANCIAL AID—FACT SHEETS 3690
FLY BUCKS 3691
FOND DU LAC RESERVATION (Scholarhip/Grants Program) 2829
FOND REV. EDMOND GELINAS, INC. (Scholarships) 2830
FOOD INDUSTRY SCHOLARSHIP FUND OF NEW HAMPSHIRE (Scholarships) 2048, 2433

FOOTACTION USA (Hooked on Sports) 2831

FORD FOUNDATION/NATIONAL RESEARCH COUNCIL
(Howard Hughes Medical Institute Predoctoral Fellowships in Biological Sciences) 1542, 1575, 1752, 1814

FOREST ROBERTS THEATRE (Mildred & Albert Panowski Playwriting Award) 980

FORT COLLINS SYMPHONY ASSOCIATION (National Young Artist Competition) 1098

FOUNDATION FOR AMATEUR RADIO (Scholarships) 2832

FOUNDATION FOR EXCEPTIONAL CHILDREN (Minigrant Awards for Teachers) 232, 2833, 2834

FOUNDATION FOR NEONATAL RESEARCH AND EDUCATION (FNRE Scholarships & Grants) 1975

FOUNDATION FOR SEACOAST HEALTH (Scholarship Program) 1667, 1753, 1815, 1898, 1976, 2385

FOUNDATION FOR TECHNOLOGY EDUCATION (Hearlihy/FTE Grant) 233, 234, 235

FOUNDATION NORTHWEST SCHOLARSHIP FUNDS (Eileen M. Hutchison Scholarship Fund) 2835, 2836

FOUNDATION OF FLEXOGRAPHIC TECHNICAL ASSOCIATION (Flexographic Scholarship) .900

FOURTH TUESDAY (Pat Hoban Memorial Scholarship) 2837

FRANCIS NATHANIEL AND KATHERYN PADGETT KENNEDY FOUNDATION
(Scholarships for Southern Baptists) 236, 1204

FRANCIS OUIMET SCHOLARSHIP FUND 2838

FRANKLIN LINDSAY STUDENT AID FUND 2839

FRANKS FOUNDATION FUND 2840

FRAUNHOFER CENTER FOR RESEARCH IN COMPUTER GRAPHICS
(Student & Scholar Exchange Programs) 606, 607, 683, 684

FRED A. BRYAN COLLEGIATE STUDENTS FUND (Trust Fund Scholarships) 2841

FRED B. & RUTH B. ZIGLER FOUNDATION (Scholarships) 2842

FREEDOM FROM RELIGION FOUNDATION (Student Essay Contest) 237, 817, 981, 1205, 1235, 1486

FUKUNAGA SCHOLARSHIP FOUNDATION (Scholarships) 101

FULLER E. CALLAWAY FOUNDATION (Hatton Lovejoy Scholarship) 2843

FUND FOR EDUCATION AND TRAINING (FEAT Loans) 2844

FUND FOR PODIATRIC MEDICAL EDUCATION 3953

FUNDING A COLLEGE EDUCATION 3692

FUTURE AIRLINE PILOTS STARTER KIT 3693

GABRIEL J. BROWN TRUST (Loan Program) 2845

GABRIEL J. BROWN TRUST (Trust Loan Fund) 2846

GAMMA THETA UPSILON INTERNATIONAL GEOGRAPHIC HONOR SOCIETY
(Buzzard, Richason, & Maxfield Presidents Scholarships) 1364

GARDEN CLUB OF AMERICA (CGA Awards for Summer Environmental Studies) 1404

GARDEN CLUB OF AMERICA (Frances M. Peacock Scholarship) 1405

GARDEN CLUB OF AMERICA (Katharine M. Grosscup Scholarships) 1272

GATES MILLENIUM SCHOLARS PROGRAM (Scholarships for High School Seniors) 2847, 2848

GATEWAY EDUCATIONAL TRUST (Scholarships) 2849

GED—THE KEY TO YOUR FUTURE 3694

GEMLINES.COM 3899

GEMOLOGICAL INSTITUTE OF AMERICA (GIA Scholarships) 2434

GENERAL AVIATION MANUFACTURERS ASSOCIATION 3846

GENERAL EDUCATIONAL FUND, INC. 2850

GENERAL FEDERATION OF WOMEN'S CLUBS OF MASSACHUSETTS
(Newtonville Woman's Club Scholarship) 238, 901, 902, 1099, 1100, 2311, 2851, 2852

GENERAL LEARNING COMMUNICATIONS (DuPont Challenge Science Essay Awards Program) 328, 724, 982, 1487

GEOLOGICAL SOCIETY OF AMERICA 3901

GEORGE ABRAHAMIAN FOUNDATION (Scholarships for Rhode Island Armenians) 2853

GEORGE BIRD GRINNELL AMERICAN INDIAN CHILDREN'S FUND (Al Qoyawayma Award) 329, 903, 1101, 1488, 2854

GEORGE E. ANDREWS TRUST (George E. Andrews Scholarship) 2855

GEORGE GROTEFEND SCHOLARSHIP FUND (Grotefend Scholarship) 2856

GEORGE HARDING SCHOLARSHIP FUND 102

GEORGE MASON UNIVERSITY (Associated Writing Programs Award Series; St. Martin's Press Award) 983

GEORGE MASON UNIVERSITY (Mary Roberts Rinehart Awards) 984

GEORGE SCHOOL (Scholarship) 2857

GEORGE T. WELCH (Scholarships) 2858
GEORGE W. AND ANNE A. HOOVER SCHOLARSHIP FUND (Student Loans) 2859
GEORGE WASHINGTON UNIVERSITY (Maud E. McPherson Scholarship) 985
GEORGIA BOARD OF REGENTS (Scholarships) 2860
GEORGIA LIBRARY ASSOCIATION ADMINISTRATIVE SERVICES (Hubbard Scholarship Fund) 986
GEORGIA PRESS EDUCATIONAL FOUNDATION (Scholarships) 2121
GEORGIA STUDENT FINANCE COMMISSION (HOPE Scholarships) 2861
GERBER REWARDS (Scholarship Drawings) 2862
GERBER SCIENTIFIC, INC. (H. Joseph Gerber Vision Scholarship Program) 330, 608, 1236, 1489, 1612
GERONIMO CORPORATION, INC. (William B. Klusty Memorial Scholarship Fund for Native Americans) 2863
GET ORGANIZED 3695
GET SMART FAST 3696
GETCOLLEGE.COM (Strivers Scholarships) 2864
GETTING INTERVIEWS 3697
GETTING STARTED IN THE MUSIC BUSINESS 3698
GHIDOTTI FOUNDATION (Scholarships) 2865
GIFTED & TALENTED EDUCATION 3699
GIFTED CHILD QUARTERLY 3700
GILL ST. BERNARD'S SCHOOL (Financial Aid) 2866
GLAMOUR MAGAZINE (Top Ten College Women Competition) 2867
GLASS, MOLDERS, POTTERY, PLASTICS & ALLIED WORKERS INTERNATIONAL UNION (Scholarship Program) 2868
GLENDALE COMMUNITY FOUNDATION (Scholarships) 2869
GLENLYON-NORFOLK SCHOOL (Entrance Scholarships) 2870
GLENN MILLER BIRTHPLACE SOCIETY (Scholarship Program) 1102
GLOBAL AUTOMOTIVE AFTERMARKET SYMPOSIUM (Scholarship) 725, 2435
GLORIA FECHT MEMORIAL SCHOLARSHIP FUND 2871
GOLDEN GATE RESTAURANT ASSOCIATION (David Rubenstein Memorial Scholarship Foundation Awards) 103, 2049
GOLDEN STATE MINORITY FOUNDATION (College Scholarships) 104
GOLDIE GIBSON SCHOLARSHIP FUND (Student Loans) 2872
GOLF COURSE SUPERINTENDENTS ASSOCIATION OF AMERICA (GCSAA Essay Contest) 1273, 1274, 1275, 2873
GONSTEAD CHIROPRACTIC EDUCATIONAL TRUST 1754
GOOD SAMARITAN FOUNDATION (Nursing Scholarships) 1977
GOVERNMENT ASSISTANCE ALMANAC (9th edition) 3701
GOVERNMENT FINANCE OFFICERS ASSOCIATION (Frank L. Greathouse Government Accounting Scholarship) 105
GRACE EDWARDS SCHOLARSHIP FUND (Scholarships) 2874
GRAHAM FOUNDATION FOR ADVANCED STUDIES IN THE FINE ARTS (Research Grants) 526
GRAHAM-FANCHER SCHOLARSHIP TRUST 2875
GRAND AVENUE PRESBYTERIAN CHURCH (Davis Foute Eagleton Memorial Student Loan Fund) 1206
GRAND LODGE OF ILLINOIS (Illinois Odd Fellow-Rebekah Scholarship Award) 2876
GRAND LODGE OF MASONS OF WYOMING (Scholarships) 2877
GRANTS AND AWARDS AVAILABLE TO AMERICAN WRITERS 3702
GRANTS, FELLOWSHIPS, AND PRIZES OF INTEREST TO HISTORIANS 3703
GRAPHIC COMMUNICATIONS INTERNATIONAL UNION (GCIU-A.J. DeAndrade Scholarship Awards Program) 2878
GRASS VALLEY GROUP, INC. SCHOLARSHIP FOUNDATION 106
GRAY FOUNDATION (Scholarship Program) 2879
GREAT BIG BOOK OF HOW TO STUDY 3704
GREAT LAKES COMMISSION (Carol A. Ratza Memorial Scholarship) 685
GREAT LITTLE BOOK ON PERSONAL ACHIEVEMENT 3705
GREATER SPRINGFIELD CHAMBER OF COMMERCE (Women's Partnership Scholarship Fund) 2880
GUIDANCE MANUAL FOR THE CHRISTIAN HOME SCHOOL 3706
GUIDE TO SOURCES OF INFORMATION ON PARAPSYCHOLOGY 3707
GUIDEPOSTS MAGAZINE (Young Writers Contest) 2881
GUSTAVUS ADOLPHUS COLLEGE (Anderson Theatre and Dance Scholarships) 1103, 2882
GUSTAVUS ADOLPHUS COLLEGE (Congregational Scholarship Matching Program) 2883

GUSTAVUS ADOLPHUS COLLEGE (National Merit College-Sponsored Scholarships) 2884
GUSTAVUS ADOLPHUS COLLEGE (Partners in Scholarship) 2885
GUSTAVUS ADOLPHUS COLLEGE (The Jussi Bjorling Music Scholarships) 1104
GUSTAVUS ADOLPHUS COLLEGE (Trustee Scholarships) 2886
H. FLETCHER BROWN FUND (Scholarships) 331, 1576, 1668, 1755, 2260
H. FLETCHER BROWN TRUST (Scholarships) 332, 1577, 1669, 1756, 2261
H. T. EWALD FOUNDATION (Scholarship Awards) 2887
H.G. AND A.G. KEASBEY MEMORIAL FOUNDATION 2888
H.H. HARRIS FOUNDATION 792
HACH SCIENTIFIC FOUNDATION (Chemistry Scholarships) 1578
HAGGAR CLOTHING COMPANY (Haggar Foundation Scholarship Program) 2889
HANDBOOK OF PRIVATE SCHOOLS 3708
HARNESS HORSEMEN INTERNATIONAL FOUNDATION (J. L. Hauck Memorial Scholarship Fund) 2890
HARNESS TRACKS OF AMERICA (Scholarship) 2891
HARRY E. & FLORENCE W. SNAYBERGER MEMORIAL FOUNDATION (Grant Award) 2892
HARRY S. TRUMAN LIBRARY INSTITUTE (Harry S. Truman Book Award) 2221, 2222
HARRY S. TRUMAN SCHOLARSHIP FOUNDATION (Scholarships) 2312
HARVARD UNIVERSITY—NIEMAN FOUNDATION (Fellowships for Journalists) 2893
HARVARD-SMITHSONIAN CENTER FOR ASTROPHYSICS 3840
HARVARD/RADCLIFFE OFFICE OF ADMISSIONS AND FINANCIAL AID
    (Scholarships; Grants; Loans & Work Study Programs) 2894
HATTIE M. STRONG FOUNDATION (No-interest Loans) 2895
HAUSS-HELMS FOUNDATION, INC. (Grant Program/Scholarships) 2896
HAVENS FOUNDATION, INC. 2897
HAWAII COMMUNITY FOUNDATION 2898
HAYSTACK MOUNTAIN SCHOOL OF CRAFTS (Scholarship Program) 904, 2436
HEBREW IMMIGRANT SOCIETY (HIAS Scholarship Program) 2899
HEBRON ACADEMY (Scholarships) 2900
HENRY P. BRIDGES MINISTERS' TRUST (Scholarships) 1207
HERBERT HOOVER PRESIDENTIAL LIBRARY ASSOCIATION (Uncommon Student Award) 2901
HERBERT LEHMAN EDUCATION FUND (Scholarships) 2902
HERMAN O. WEST FOUNDATION (Scholarship) 2903
HERSCHEL C. PRICE EDUCATIONAL FOUNDATION (Grants Program) 2904
HIGHER EDUCATION PROGRAMS 3709
HILLEL FOUNDATION FOR JEWISH CAMPUS LIFE (Steinhardt Jewish Campus Service Corps) 846, 2122
HILLSDALE COLLEGE (Freedom as Vocation Scholarship) 10, 107, 2223, 2313
HISPANIC COLLEGE FUND (Scholarships for Hispanic Students) 108, 527, 609, 686, 726, 2123, 2353
HISPANIC DENTAL ASSOCIATION AND DR. JUAN D. VILLARREAL FOUNDATION
    (Dental/Dental Hygienist Scholarships) 1757, 1899
HISPANIC DENTAL ASSOCIATION AND PROCTER & GAMBLE ORAL CARE (Scholarships) 1758, 1900
HISPANIC NURSES ASSOCIATION (Scholarships) 1978
HISPANIC SCHOLARSHIP FUND (Scholarships) 2905
HOBART INSTITUTE OF WELDING TECHNOLOGY (Scholarships) 727, 2437, 3981
HOLY CROSS HIGH SCHOOL (Scholarships/Financial Aid) 2906
HOME FASHION PRODUCTS ASSN. (Home Textile Surface Design Competition) 905
HOMEOPATHIC EDUCATIONAL SERVICES 3908
HOMESCHOOLING ALMANAC 3710
HOPI PRIVATE HIGH SCHOOL SCHOLARSHIP 2907
HOPI SCHOLARSHIP 2908
HOPI TRIBE (Priority Scholarships) 11, 109, 193, 239, 333, 574, 687, 728, 793,
    ....1237, 1670, 1759, 1816, 1901, 1979, 2262
HORACE MANN COMPANIES (Scholarship Program) 2909
HORACE MANN SCHOOL (Scholarships) 2910
HORACE SMITH FUND (Loans) 2911

HORACE SMITH FUND (Walter S. Barr Scholarships) 2912
HORATIO ALGER ASSOCIATION (Scholarships) 2913
HORTICULTURAL RESEARCH INSTITUTE (Timothy Bigelow Scholarship) 1276
HOSPITALITY FINANCIAL AND TECHNOLOGY PROFESSIONALS (Scholarships) 110
HOW TO FIND OUT ABOUT FINANCIAL AID 3711
HOW TO STUDY 3712
HOW TO WIN A SPORTS SCHOLARSHIP 1999 Edition 3713
HOWARD AND MAMIE NICHOLS SCHOLARSHIP TRUST (Scholarships) 2914
HOWARD UNIVERSITY (Debbie Allen & Phylicia Rashad's Dr. Andrew Allen Creative Arts Scholarship) 1105
HOYT FOUNDATION (May Emma Hoyt Scholarship) 2915
HUALAPAI TRIBAL COUNCIL (Scholarship Program) 2916
HUBBARD FARMS CHARITABLE FOUNDATION 1277, 1406, 1543
HUMBOLDT AREA FOUNDATION (Scholarships) 2917
IDAHO STATE BOARD OF EDUCATION (Idaho Governor's Scholarship) .2918, 2919, 2920
IEEE COMPUTER SOCIETY 3866
IEEE COMPUTER SOCIETY (Lance Stafford Larson Student Scholarship) 610
IEEE COMPUTER SOCIETY (Richard Merwin Student Scholarship) 611, 688
IEEE COMPUTER SOCIETY (Upsilon Pi Epsilon Student Award) 612
ILLINOIS AMVETS (Sad Sacks Nursing Scholarship) 1980
ILLINOIS AMVETS (Scholarships) 2921
ILLINOIS ARTS COUNCIL (Artists Fellowship Awards) 906, 987, 1106
ILLINOIS CONGRESS OF PARENTS AND TEACHERS (Illinois PTA Scholarships) 240
ILLINOIS DEPARTMENT OF THE AMERICAN LEGION (Scholarships) 2922, 2923, 2924, 2925
ILLINOIS PILOTS ASSOCIATION (Scholarships) 489, 2438
ILLINOIS RESTAURANT ASSN. (Scholarship Fund) 2050
ILLINOIS STUDENT ASSISTANCE COMMISSION
  (David A. DeBolt Teacher Shortage Scholarship Program) 241, 242, 243, 2926, 2927, 2928, 2929, 2930, 2931
ILLUMINATING ENGINEERING SOCIETY OF NORTH AMERICA
  (Robert W. Thunen Memorial Scholarships) 334, 3912
IMPROVE YOUR MEMORY 3714
IMPROVE YOUR READING 3715
IMPROVE YOUR WRITING 3716
INDEPENDENCE FEDERAL SAVINGS BANK (Federal Family Education Loans) 2932
INDEPENDENT ACCOUNTANTS INTERNATIONAL EDUCATIONAL FOUNDATION, INC. (Robert Kaufman Memorial
  Scholarship Award) 111
INDEX OF MAJORS & GRADUATE DEGREES 3717
INDIANA STATE UNIVERSITY (Music Scholarships) 1107
INDIANA UNIVERSITY SCHOOL OF MUSIC (Music Scholarships) 1108
INSIDER'S GUIDE TO MEDICAL SCHOOLS 3718
INSTITUT D'ETUDES FRANCAISES D'AVIGNON/BRYN MAWR COLLEGE
  (Scholarships for Summer Study in Avignon, France) 847, 1043
INSTITUTE FOR HUMANE STUDIES (Koch Summer Fellow Program) 112, 113, 244, 818, 819, 848, 988, 989, 1208, 2080,
  . . . . .2081, 2124, 2125, 2126, 2263, 2264, 2265, 2314,
  . . . . .2315, 2316, 2354, 2386
INSTITUTE FOR OPERATIONS RESEARCH AND THE MANAGEMENT SCIENCES
  (INFORMS Summer Internship Directory) 114, 613, 689, 729, 1613, 3938
INSTITUTE FOR THE INTERNATIONAL EDUCATION OF STUDENTS (Scholarships) 2933
INSTITUTE OF ELECTRICAL & ELECTRONICS ENGINEERS (Charles Le Geyt Fortescue Fellowship) 690
INSTITUTE OF ELECTRICAL AND ELECTRONICS ENGINEERS—US ACTIVITIES 3882
INSTITUTE OF FOOD TECHNOLOGISTS (Freshman Scholarships) 2051, 2052, 2053
INSTITUTE OF INDUSTRIAL ENGINEERS (Dwight D. Gardner Scholarship and A.O. Putnam Scholarship) 730, 731, 732
INSTITUTE OF INTERNATIONAL EDUCATION
  (National Security Education Program-Undergraduate Scholarships) 115, 335, 614, 1044, 1109, 1365, 1407, 1614, 2224, 2317
INSTITUTE OF MANAGEMENT ACCOUNTANTS 3818
INSTITUTE OF MANAGEMENT ACCOUNTANTS (National Scholarship Program) 116

INTER-AMERICAN BAR ASSOCIATION (Writing Competition) 2266

INTERMURAL RESEARCH TRAINING AWARD (Summer Intern Program) 1817

INTERNATIONAL ALLIANCE OF THEATRICAL STAGE EMPLOYEES AND MOVING PICTURE MACHINE
   OPERATORS (Richard F. Walsh Foundation) 2934

INTERNATIONAL ASSN. OF ARSON INVESTIGATORS (John Charles Wilson Scholarship) 2267, 2439

INTERNATIONAL ASSN. OF BRIDGE STRUCTURAL AND ORNAMENTAL IRON WORKERS
   (John H. Lyons Scholarship Program) 2935

INTERNATIONAL ASSOCIATION OF CULINARY PROFESSIONALS FOUNDATION (Scholarships) 2054

INTERNATIONAL ASSOCIATION OF FIRE CHIEFS FOUNDATION (Scholarship Program) 117, 2387, 2440, 2936

INTERNATIONAL BILL ONEXIOCA II (Founders Memorial Award) 2937

INTERNATIONAL BROTHERHOOD OF TEAMSTERS (Scholarship Fund) 2938

INTERNATIONAL CHIROPRACTORS ASSOCIATION 3859

INTERNATIONAL COMPETITION FOR SYMPHONIC COMPOSITION (Premio Citta Di Trieste) 1110

INTERNATIONAL FOOD SERVICE EXECUTIVES ASSOCIATION (Worthy Goal Scholarship) 2441

INTERNATIONAL JOBS 3719

INTERNATIONAL LADIES GARMENT WORKERS UNION (National College Award Program) 2939

INTERNATIONAL ORDER OF THE ALHAMBRA (Undergraduate Scholarship Grant) 245, 1671, 1760, 1902, 1981

INTERNATIONAL RADIO AND TELEVISION SOCIETY FOUNDATION (Summer Fellowship Program) 118, 2127

INTERNATIONAL READING ASSOCIATION (Albert J. Harris Award) .246, 247, 248, 249, 250

INTERNATIONAL SOCIETY FOR CLINICAL LABORATORY TECHNOLOGY
   (David Birenbaum Scholarship Fund) 2940

INTERNATIONAL SOCIETY OF WOMEN AIRLINE PILOTS (ISA International Career Scholarship) . . .490, 491, 492, 493, 494

INTERNATIONAL TRUMPET GUILD (Conference Scholarships) 1111

INTERNATIONAL UNION OF BRICKLAYERS AND ALLIED CRAFTSMEN
   (Harry C. Bates Merit Scholarship Program) 2941

INTERNATIONAL UNION OF ELECTRONIC, ELECTRICAL, SALARIES, MACHINE, &
   FURNITURE WORKERS—IEU (J. B. Carey, D. J. Fitzmaurice, & W. H. Bywater Scholarships) 2942

INTERSOCIETY COMMITTEE ON PATHOLOGY INFORMATION 3943

INTRAVENOUS NURSES SOCIETY (Gardner Foundation Scholarships) 1982

INVESTIGATIVE REPORTERS AND EDITORS (Minority Fellowships) 2128, 2129, 2130

IOWA AMERICAN LEGION (Boy Scout of the Year Contest Scholarship) 2943

IOWA AMERICAN LEGION (Oratorical Contest Scholarship) 2944

IOWA BROADCASTERS ASSOCIATION (Broadcast Scholarship) 2131

IOWA COLLEGE STUDENT AID COMMISSION (Federal Stafford Loan Program; Federal PLUS Loans) 2945, 2946, 2947

IOWA COMMISSION OF VETERANS AFFAIRS (War Orphans Educational Scholarship Aid) 2948

IOWA FEDERATION OF LABOR AFL-CIO (Annual Scholarship Program) 2949

IOWA PHARMACY FOUNDATION 1761

IOWA SCHOOL OF LETTERS (The John Simmons Short Fiction Award) 990

IRISH AMERICAN CULTURAL INSTITUTE (Irish Way Scholarships) 849

ITALIAN AMERICAN CHAMBER OF COMMERCE OF CHICAGO (Scholarships) 2950

ITALIAN CATHOLIC FEDERATION INC. (College Scholarships for High School Seniors) 2951

Information on the Physician Assistant Profession 3720

Informational Brochure 3721

International Forestry and Natural Resources 3722

J. HUGH & EARLE W. FELLOWS MEMORIAL FUND (Scholarship Loans) 1209, 1672, 1903, 1983

J. WOOD PLATT CADDIE SCHOLARSHIP TRUST (Scholarships) 2952

J.H. BAKER SCHOLARSHIP FUND (Student Loans) 2953

JACQUELINE ELVIRA HODGES JOHNSON FUND, INC. (Scholarships) 2954, 2955

JACKSONVILLE STATE UNIVERSITY 2956

JACKSONVILLE UNIVERSITY (Scholarships & Grants Programs) 2957

JACOB'S PILLOW DANCE FESTIVAL (Scholarships) 1112

JAMES A. & JULIET L. DAVIS FOUNDATION, INC. (Scholarship) 2958

JAMES F. BYRNES FOUNDATION 2959

JAMES F. LINCOLN ARC WELDING FOUNDATION (Scholarships) 733, 2442

JAMES FORD BELL FOUNDATION (Summer Internship Program) 119, 2318, 2388

JAMES G. K. MCCLURE EDUCATIONAL AND DEVELOPMENT FUND (Western North Carolina Scholarships) 2960

JAMES M. HOFFMAN SCHOLARSHIP (Undergraduate Scholarship) 2961

JAMES MADISON MEMORIAL FELLOWSHIP (Fellowship for Teachers) .194, 251, 850, 2225, 2319

JAMES P. AND RUTH C. GILLROY FOUNDATION, INC. 2962

JAMES Z. NAURISON SCHOLARSHIP FUND 2963

JAPANESE AMERICAN CITIZENS LEAGUE (Yoshiko Tanaka Memorial Scholarship) 851, 907, 991, 1045, 1113, 1278,
. . . . .1279, 1280, 2132, 2268, 2320, 2321,
. . . . .2389, 2964, 2965, 2966

JAYCEE WAR MEMORIAL SCHOLARSHIP PROGRAM 2967

JC PENNEY (Scholarship Program) 12, 120

JEANNETTE RANKIN FOUNDATION (Competitive Awards) 2968

JEWISH FAMILY AND CHILDREN'S SERVICES (Anna and Charles Stockwitz Children and Youth Fund) 2969, 2970,
. . . . .2971, 2972, 2973, 2974

JEWISH FEDERATION OF METROPOLITAN CHICAGO
(Academic Scholarship Program for Studies in the Sciences) 336, 1238, 1490, 1615

JEWISH SOCIAL SERVICE AGENCY OF METROPOLITAN WASHINGTON
(Morton A. Gibson Memorial Scholarship) 2975, 2976, 2977, 2978

JEWISH VOCATIONAL SERVICE (Academic Scholarship Program) .252, 1544, 1579, 1616, 1673, 1762,
. . . . .1818, 1904, 1984, 2133, 2269, 2390

JEWISH VOCATIONAL SERVICE (E.E. Grosmann/I.S. Joseph Scholarship Program) 852

JEWISH VOCATIONAL SERVICE (JVS) (Community Scholarship Fund) 2979

JEWISH VOCATIONAL SERVICE (Recruitment Scholarship) 853

JEWISH WELFARE BOARD (Scholarships) 253, 854, 2391

JIMMIE ULLERY CHARITABLE TRUST (Scholarship Grant) 1210

JOB OPPORTUNITIES FOR THE BLIND (JOB) 3723

JOHN BAYLISS BROADCAST FOUNDATION (Scholarship) 2134

JOHN C. CHAFFIN EDUCATIONAL FUND (Scholarships and Loans Programs) 2980

JOHN EDGAR THOMSON FOUNDATION (Grants) 2981

JOHN GYLES EDUCATION FUND (Scholarships) 2982

JOHN K. & THIRZA F. DAVENPORT FOUNDATION (Scholarships in the Arts) 908, 1114, 2443

JOHN M. WILL JOURNALISM SCHOLARSHIP FOUNDATION (Scholarship) 2135

JOHN T. HALL TRUST 2983

JOHN T. HOGAN MEMORIAL FOUNDATION 2984

JOHN WOOLMAN SCHOOL (Financial Aid Program) 2985

JOHN WOOLMAN SCHOOL (Native American Scholarship Program) 2986

JOHNSON AND WALES UNIVERSITY
(Annual Johnson & Wales University National High School Recipe Contest) 13, 121, 337, 615, 2055, 2444

JOHNSON AND WALES UNIVERSITY (Gaebe Eagle Scout Scholarships) 2987

JOHNSON AND WALES UNIVERSITY (Gilbane Building Company Eagle Scout Scholarship) 14, 122, 338, 616, 2056, 2445

JOHNSON AND WALES UNIVERSITY (National High School Entrepreneur of the Year Contest) . .15, 123, 339, 617, 2057, 2446

JOHNSON AND WALES UNIVERSITY (Scholarships) 16, 124, 340, 618, 2058, 2447

JOHNSON CONTROLS FOUNDATION (Scholarship Program) 2988

JOSEPH BLAZEK FOUNDATION (Scholarships) 341, 1491

JOURNALISM AND MASS COMMUNICATIONS ACCREDITATION 3724

JOURNALISM AND MASS COMMUNICATION DIRECTORY 3725

JOURNALIST'S ROAD TO SUCCESS: A Career and Scholarship Guide 3726

JULIUS AND ESTHER STULBERG COMPETITION, INC. (International String Competition) 1115

JUNIATA COLLEGE (Anna Groninger Smith Memorial Scholarship) 17

JUNIATA COLLEGE (Baker Peace Scholarship) 855, 2322

JUNIATA COLLEGE (Church of the Brethren Scholarships) 2989

JUNIATA COLLEGE (Frederick & Mary F. Beckley Scholarship Fund) 2990

JUNIATA COLLEGE (Friendship Scholarships) 2991

JUNIATA COLLEGE (Information Technology Scholarships) 619

JUNIATA COLLEGE (Robert Steele Memorial Scholarship) 1492, 1674, 1763, 1819, 1905, 1985

JUNIATA COLLEGE (Sam Hayes, Jr. Scholarship) 2992

JUNIOR ENGINEERING TECHNICAL SOCIETY INC (JETS) 3883
JUNIOR LEAGUE OF NORTHERN VIRGINIA (Scholarships) 2993
KAISER FOUNDATION, INC. 2994
KANSAS AMERICAN LEGION (Scholarships) 2995
KANSAS BOARD OF REGENTS (Kansas Teacher Scholarship) 254, 2448, 2996, 2997, 2998
KANSAS COMMISSION ON VETERANS' AFFAIRS (Scholarships) 2999
KANSAS STATE UNIVERSITY FOUNDATION (Various Scholarships) 3000
KAPPA OMICRON NU (Research/Project Grants) 2059
KAPPA SIGMA ENDOWMENT FUND (Scholarship/Leadership Awards Program) 3001
KARLA SCHERER FOUNDATION (Scholarships) 125
KENNEDY FOUNDATION (Scholarships) 3002
KENTUCKY CENTER FOR VETERANS AFFAIRS (Benefits for Veterans' Dependents, Spouses, & Widows) 3003
KENTUCKY HIGHER EDUCATION ASSISTANCE AUTHORITY (College Access Program [CAP] Grant) 3004, 3005
KEY BANK OF CENTRAL MAINE FOUNDATION 3006
KIDZWRITE 3984
KING COUNTY NURSES ASSOCIATION (Scholarships) 1986
KITTIE M. FAIREY EDUCATIONAL FUND 3007
KNIGHTS OF COLUMBUS (Canadian Scholarship Program) 3008
KNIGHTS OF COLUMBUS (Fourth Degree Pro Deo & Pro Patria Scholarships) 3009
KNIGHTS OF COLUMBUS (Francis P. Matthews and John E. Swift Educational Trust Scholarship) 3010
KNIGHTS OF COLUMBUS (Squires Scholarship Program) 3011
KNIGHTS TEMPLAR EDUCATIONAL FOUNDATION (Special Low-Interest Loans) 3012
KNTV TELEVISION (Minority Scholarship) 2136
KOOMRUIAN EDUCATION FUND 3013
KOREAN-AMERICAN SCIENTISTS AND ENGINEERS ASSOCIATION (KSEA Scholarships) 342, 1239, 1493, 1675
KOSCIUSZKO FOUNDATION (Chopin Piano Competition) 1116
KOSCIUSZKO FOUNDATION (Marcella Sembrich Voice Competition) 1117
KOSCIUSZKO FOUNDATION (Study/Research Programs for Americans in Poland) 856
KOSCIUSZKO FOUNDATION (Tuition Scholarships) 3014
LADIES AUXILIARY TO THE VETERANS OF FOREIGN WARS OF THE UNITED STATES
  (Young American Creative Patriotic Art Awards) 909
LADIES OF NORTHANTS (Scholarship) 734
LAND IMPROVEMENT FOUNDATION FOR EDUCATION (Scholarship) 1408
LANDSCAPE ARCHITECTURE FOUNDATION (Edward D. Stone Jr. & Associates Minority Scholarship) 528
LANDSCAPE ARCHITECTURE FOUNDATION (Edith H. Henderson Scholarship) 529
LANDSCAPE ARCHITECTURE FOUNDATION (Harriett Barnhart Wimmer Scholarship) 530
LANDSCAPE ARCHITECTURE FOUNDATION (Hawaii Chapter/The David T. Woolsey Scholarship) 531
LANDSCAPE ARCHITECTURE FOUNDATION (LAF/CLASS Fund Scholarships) 532, 1281
LANDSCAPE ARCHITECTURE FOUNDATION (Raymond E. Page Scholarship) 533
LANDSCAPE ARCHITECTURE FOUNDATION (Thomas P. Papandrew Scholarship) 534
LANDSCAPE ARCHITECTURE FOUNDATION (The Rain Bird Company Scholarship) .535
LANDSCAPE ARCHITECTURE FOUNDATION (William J. Locklin Scholarship) 536
LANGUAGE LIAISON PROGRAM DIRECTORY 3727
LARAMIE COUNTY FARM BUREAU (Scholarships) 3015
LARAMIE COUNTY PEACE OFFICERS' ASSOCIATION (Scholarships) 2270
LAST-MINUTE COLLEGE FINANCING 3728
LAST-MINUTE INTERVIEW TIPS 3729
LAST-MINUTE RESUMES 3730
LAST-MINUTE STUDY TIPS 3731
LAYOVER.COM 3971
LEADERS IN FURTHERING EDUCATION (LIFE Unsung Hero Program Scholarships) 3016
LEARNING DISABILITIES ASSN OF AMERICA 3918
LEGACY SOCCER FOUNDATION, INC./LEVER BROTHERS (Endowed Scholarships) 3017
LEON L. GRANOFF FOUNDATION 3018

LEON M. JORDAN SCHOLARSHIP AND MONUMENT FUND 3019

LEONARD H. BULKELEY SCHOLARSHIP FUND (Scholarship Grants) 3020

LEOPOLD SCHEPP FOUNDATION (Undergraduate Awards) 3021

LESKO'S SELF-HELP BOOKS 3732

LIBERACE FOUNDATION FOR THE PERFORMING AND CREATIVE ARTS (Scholarship Fund) 910, 1118

LIEDERKRANZ FOUNDATION, INC. (Scholarship Awards) 1119

LIFE AFTER DEBT 3733

LIGHT WORK (Artist-in-Residence Program) 911

LIST OF SCHOLARSHIPS AND AWARDS IN ELECTRICAL, ELECTRONICS, AND COMPUTER ENGINEERING 3734

LLOYD D. SWEET SCHOLARSHIP FOUNDATION (Scholarships) 3022

LOREN L. ZACHARY SOCIETY FOR THE PERFORMING ARTS
  (National Vocal Competition for Young Opera Singers) 1120

LOS ANGELES COUNCIL OF BLACK PROFESSIONAL ENGINEERS (Al-Ben Scholarship) 343, 495, 537, 575, 620,
  ....691, 735, 794, 1617

LOS ANGELES PROFESSIONAL CHAPTER OF SOCIETY OF PROFESSIONAL JOURNALISTS
  (Bill Farr Scholarship) 2137, 2138, 2139, 2140

LOS MOLINOS UNIFIED SCHOOL DISTRICT (S. R. Pritchett Scholarship Fund) 3023

LOU AND LUCIENNE BRIGHTMAN SCHOLARSHIP 3024

LOUISIANA DEPT. OF VETERANS AFFAIRS (Awards Program) 3025

LOUISIANA OFFICE OF STUDENT FINANCIAL ASSISTANCE
  (Tuition Opportunity Program for Students-Teachers Award) 195, 255, 1366, 1409, 1442, 1545, 1580, 1618, 3026, 3027, 3028

LOUISIANA STATE UNIVERSITY AT SHREVEPORT (College of Business Administration Scholarships) 126, 621, 992,
  ....993, 1367, 1581, 1619,
  ....1676, 2226, 2271, 2272, 2323, 3029, 3030, 3031

LUBBOCK AREA FOUNDATION, INC. (Scholarships) 3032

LUCY E. MEILLER EDUCATIONAL TRUST 3033

LULAC (LEAGUE OF UNITED LATIN AMERICAN CITIZENS) (National Scholarship Fund) 3034

LULAC NATIONAL EDUCATIONAL SERVICE CENTER, INC
  (Hispanic/Burlington Northern Santa Fe Foundation American Scholarship Program) 3035

LUPUS FOUNDATION OF AMERICA, INC. (Finzi Student Summer Fellowship) 1820

LUSO-AMERICAN EDUCATION FOUNDATION (General Scholarships) 1046

LUTHERAN BROTHERHOOD (Stafford Student Loans) 3036

LUTHERAN BROTHERHOOD (Undergraduate Scholarships) 3037

LYONS CLUB OF RAWLINS (K. Craig Williams Memorial Scholarship) 3038

LaFETRA OPERATING FOUNDATION (Fellowships for Training of Volunteers Abroad) 3039

MADDEN BROTHERS (Goshen County Community Scholarships) 3040

MAINE AMERICAN LEGION, PAST COMMANDERS CLUB (James V. Day Scholarship) 3041

MAINE COMMUNITY FOUNDATION (Scholarship Program) 3042

MAINE STUDENT INCENTIVE SCHOLARSHIP PROGRAM 3043

MAINE VETERAN'S SERVICES (Grants for Dependents) 3044

MAKARIOS SCHOLARSHIP FUND, INC. (Scholarships) 3045

MAKING A DIFFERENCE—CAREER OPPORTUNITIES IN DISABILITY-RELATED FIELDS 3735

MAKING IT THROUGH COLLEGE 3736

MAKING THE MOST OF YOUR COLLEGE EDUCATION 3737

MAMIE ADAMS MEMORIAL AWARD 3046

MARCH OF DIMES BIRTH DEFECTS FOUNDATION/KMART CORPORATION (Youth Leadership Scholarships) 3047

MARIE L. ROSE HUGUENOT SOCIETY OF AMERICA (Scholarships) 3048

MARIN EDUCATION FUND (Asian Scholarship Fund) 3049

MARIN EDUCATIONAL FUND (Undergraduate Scholarship Program) 3050

MARINE CORPS SCHOLARSHIP FOUNDATION (Scholarships to Sons and Daughters of Marines) 3051

MARINE CORPS TANKERS ASSOCIATION (John Cornelius Memorial Scholarship) 3052

MARINE TECHNOLOGY SOCIETY 3937

MARIO MACHADO (American Honda/Mario J. Machado Scholarship) 2141

MARION BRILL SCHOLARSHIP FOUNDATION, INC. (Undergraduate Scholarships) 3053

MARK R. FUSCO FOUNDATION 3054

MARTIN MUSICAL SCHOLARSHIP FUND (Scholarships) 1121

MARY E. HODGES FUND 3055

MARY GONTER AND SARA O'BRIEN SCHOLARSHIP FOUNDATION 1211

MARY INSTITUTE AND SAINT LOUIS COUNTRY DAY SCHOOL (Financial Aid) 3056

MARY M. AARON MEMORIAL TRUST (Scholarships) 3057

MARYLAND ASSOCIATION OF CERTIFIED PUBLIC ACCOUNTANTS EDUCATIONAL FOUNDATION
  (Scholarship Program) 127

MARYLAND HIGHER EDUCATION COMMISSION
  (Sharon Christa McAuliffe Critical Shortage Teacher Program) 256, 344, 496, 576, 622, 692, 736, 795, 1494,
  . . . . .1546, 1582, 1906, 1907, 1908, 1987, 2449, 2450,
  . . . . .3058, 3059, 3060, 3061, 3062

MASSACHUSETTS BOARD OF HIGHER EDUCATION (Public Service Grant) 3063, 3064

MASSACHUSETTS COMPANY (The M. Geneva Gray Scholarship Fund) 3065

MASSACHUSETTS OFFICE OF STUDENT FINANCIAL ASSISTANCE (National Guard Tuition Waiver) 3066, 3067

MASTER MATH 3738

MATERNITY CENTER ASSOCIATION (Hazel Corbin Assistance Fund/Stipend Awards) 1988

MATHEMATICAL ASSOCIATION OF AMERICA 3921

MAY THOMPSON HENRY TRUST 3068

McCORD CAREER CENTER (Level II McCord Medical/Music Scholarship) 1128, 1679, 1766, 1911, 1993, 2453

McCURDY MEMORIAL SCHOLARSHIP FOUNDATION (McCurdy Scholarship) 3070

McCURDY MEMORIAL SCHOLARSHIP FOUNDATION (Emily Scofield Scholarship Fund) 3109

McDONALD'S RESTAURANTS OF WEST NEW YORK (BOMAC Scholarship Award) 3069

McDONALD'S (Golden Arches Scholarships) 3071

McDONALD'S (GospelFest Music Scholarships) 1122

McDONALD'S (RMHC/HACER Scholarship Program) 3072

McDONALD'S (UNCF New York Tri-State Scholarships) 3073

McDONALD'S HISPANIC AMERICAN COMMITMENT TO EDUCATIONAL RESOURCES PROGRAM
  (Scholarships For High School Seniors) 3110

McDONALD'S/UNITED NEGRO COLLEGE FUND (Scholarships for Medical and Healthcare Students) 1680, 1767,
  . . . . .1822, 1912, 1994

McDONOGH SCHOOL (Scholarships) 3111

McFARLAND CHARITABLE FOUNDATION TRUST (Nursing Scholarships) 1989

MEDICAL SCHOOL ADMISSION REQUIREMENTS 3739

MEDICINE—A CHANCE TO MAKE A DIFFERENCE 3740

MEMORIAL FOUNDATION FOR JEWISH CULTURE (International Scholarship Program for Community Service) . . .857, 858

MEMPHIS COLLEGE OF ART (Portfolio Awards) 912

MERCANTILE BANK OF TOPEKA (Claude & Ina Brey Memorial Endowment Fund) 3074

MERCYHURST COLLEGE D'ANGELO SCHOOL OF MUSIC (Young Artists Competition) 1123, 1124

METHODIST LADIES' COLLEGE (Scholarships) 3075

METROPOLITAN MILWAUKEE ASSOCIATION OF COMMERCE (Scholarships) 3076

METROPOLITAN MUSEUM OF ART (Internships) 913

METROPOLITAN OPERA ASSOCIATION (National Council Auditions) 1125

MEXICAN AMERICAN BUSINESS AND PROFESSIONAL SCHOLARSHIP ASSOCIATION (Scholarship Program) 3077

MEXICAN AMERICAN GROCERS ASSOCIATION (Scholarships) 128

MEXICAN AMERICAN WOMEN'S NATIONAL ASSOCIATION (MANA)
  (Rita DiMartino Scholarship in Communication) 2142, 3078

MIAMI INTERNATIONAL PRESS CLUB (Scholarship Program) 2143

MICHIGAN AGRI-BUSINESS ASSOCIATION EDUCATIONAL TRUST FUND 1282

MICHIGAN COMMISSION ON INDIAN AFFAIRS; MICHIGAN DEPT OF CIVIL RIGHTS (Tuition Waiver Program) . . .3079

MICHIGAN ELKS ASSOCIATION CHARITABLE GRANT FUND 3080

MICHIGAN GUARANTY AGENCY (Stafford and PLUS Loans) 3081

MICHIGAN HIGHER EDUCATION ASSISTANCE AUTHORITY (Michigan Competitive Scholarships) 3082, 3083

MICHIGAN VETERANS TRUST FUND (Tuition Grant Program) 3084

MICROSCOPY SOCIETY OF AMERICA (Undergraduate Research Scholarship) 1821

MICROSOFT CORPORATION (National Minority and/or Women's Technical Scholarships) 623, 693, 1620

MICROSOFT CORPORATION (Summer Internships) 624, 694, 1621

MIDWAY COLLEGE (Institutional Aid Program—Scholarships & Grants) 129, 257, 820, 1283, 1547, 1990, 2355, 2451

MIDWEST ROOFING CONTRACTORS ASSOCIATION (Construction Industry Scholarships) 577

MIDWEST STUDENT EXCHANGE PROGRAM (Tuition Reduction) 3085

MILITARY ORDER OF THE PURPLE HEART (Sons, Daughters, and Grandchildren Scholarship Program) 3086

MINERALOGICAL SOCIETY OF AMERICA (MSA Grant for Research in Crystallography) 1368, 1369

MINISTRY OF EDUCATION OF THE REPUBLIC OF CHINA (Scholarships for Foreign Students) 859

MINNESOTA AUTOMOBILE DEALERS ASSOCIATION (MADA Scholarships) 737, 2452

MINNESOTA HIGHER EDUCATION SERVICES OFFICE
  (Assistance for Farm Families) 1284, 1677, 1909, 1991, 3087, 3088, 3089

MINNESOTA STATE ARTS BOARD (Grants Program) 914, 994, 1126

MINNESOTA STATE DEPARTMENT OF VETERANS AFFAIRS (Deceased Veterans' Dependents Scholarships) 3090, 3091

MINNESOTA STATE UNIVERSITY AT MANKATO (Korth Scholarship) 2273

MINNESOTA TEAMSTERS JOINT COUNCIL NO.32 (Scholarship Awards) 3092

MINNIE PEARL SCHOLARSHIP PROGRAM 3093

MISS HALL'S SCHOOL (Berkshire County Scholarships) 3094

MISSISSIPPI OFFICE OF STATE STUDENT FINANCIAL AID
  (William Winter Teacher Education Program) .258, 1764, 1765, 1910, 1992, 2356, 2357, 3095, 3096

MISSOURI STATE MEDICAL FOUNDATION (Medical School Low-interest Loans) 1678

MITCHELL EXPRESS—THE FAST TRACK TO THE TOP COLLEGES 3741

MOBIL CORPORATION (Desert Storm Scholarship Program) 3097

MOBILITY INTERNATIONAL USA (Travel-Study Program for People With Disabilities) 3098

MODERN WOODMEN OF AMERICA (Fraternal College Scholarship Program) 3099

MONGOLIA SOCIETY (Dr. Gombojab Hangin Memorial Scholarship) 3100

MONTANA UNIVERSITY SYSTEM (Indian Fees Waiver Program) 3101

MONTANA UNIVERSITY SYSTEM (Montana State Student Incentive Grants) 3102

MONTGOMERY COUNTY ASSOCIATION FOR FAMILY + COMMUNITY EDUCATION
  (Mary Irene Waters Scholarship Fund) 2060

MORRIS SCHOLARSHIP FUND (Scholarships for Minorities in Iowa) 3103

MOSTARS/MISSOURI DEPARTMENT OF HIGHER EDUCATION
  (Charles Gallagher Student Financial Assistance Program) 3104, 3105, 3106

MOTHER JOSEPH ROGAN MARYMOUNT FOUNDATION (Grant and Loan Programs) 3107

MOUNT SAINT JOSEPH ACADEMY (Partial Scholarships) 3108

MUSIC ACADEMY OF THE WEST (Scholarships) 1127

MUSIC SCHOLARSHIP GUIDE (3rd Edition) 3742

NAACP NATIONAL OFFICE (Agnes Jones Jackson Scholarship) 3112

NAACP NATIONAL OFFICE (NAACP Willems Scholarship) 345, 1583, 1622

NAACP NATIONAL OFFICE (NAACP/Department of Energy Scholarship) .346, 1410, 1584, 1623

NAACP NATIONAL OFFICE (Roy Wilkins Scholarship) 3113

NAACP NATIONAL OFFICE (Sutton Education Scholarship) 259

NATION INSTITUTE (I.F. Stone Award for Student Journalism) 2144

NATION INSTITUTE (Nation Internship Program) 2145

NATIONAL ACADEMY FOR NUCLEAR TRAINING (Undergraduate Scholarships and Graduate Fellowships) 738

NATIONAL ACTION COUNCIL FOR MINORITIES IN ENGINEERING-NACME, INC. (Scholarships) 347

NATIONAL ACUPUNCTURE AND ORIENTAL MEDICINE ALLIANCE 3821

NATIONAL ACUPUNCTURE DETOXIFICATION ASSOCIATION 3820

NATIONAL AIR TRANSPORTATION ASSOCIATION 3917

NATIONAL AIR TRANSPORTATION ASSOCIATION FOUNDATION (The Pioneers of Flight Scholarship) 130, 497, 2454

NATIONAL ALLIANCE FOR EXCELLENCE, INC. (National Scholarship Competition) 3114

NATIONAL AMPUTATION FOUNDATION (Scholarships) 3115

NATIONAL ART MATERIALS TRADE ASSOCIATION (NAMTA Scholarships) 3116

NATIONAL ASSN. FOR MUSIC THERAPY 3930

NATIONAL ASSN. OF EXECUTIVE SECRETARIES AND ADMINISTRATIVE ASSISTANTS
  (Scholarship Award Program) 2455

NATIONAL ASSN. OF SOCIAL WORKERS 3966

NATIONAL ASSOCIATION OF AMERICAN BUSINESS CLUBS (AMBUCS Scholarships for Therapists) 260, 1913
NATIONAL ASSOCIATION OF ANIMAL BREEDERS (NAAB) 3833
NATIONAL ASSOCIATION OF BLACK JOURNALISTS (NABJ Scholarship Program) 2146, 2147
NATIONAL ASSOCIATION OF DENTAL LABORATORIES 3875
NATIONAL ASSOCIATION OF HISPANIC JOURNALISTS (NAHJ Scholarship Program) 2148, 2149
NATIONAL ASSOCIATION OF HISPANIC NURSES (Scholarships) 1995
NATIONAL ASSOCIATION OF NEGRO BUSINESS AND PROFESSIONAL WOMENS CLUB (Scholarships) 3117
NATIONAL ASSOCIATION OF PASTORAL MUSICIANS (Scholarships) 1129
NATIONAL ASSOCIATION OF PLUMBING-HEATING-COOLING CONTRACTORS
 (NAPHCC Educational Foundation Scholarship Program) 739
NATIONAL ASSOCIATION OF SCHOOLS OF PUBLIC AFFAIRS AND ADMINISTRATION 3854
NATIONAL ASSOCIATION OF SECONDARY SCHOOL PRINCIPALS
 (National Honor Society Scholarships) 3118, 3119, 3120
NATIONAL ASSOCIATION OF TEACHERS OF SINGING (Artist Awards Competition) 1130
NATIONAL ASSOCIATION OF WATER COMPANIES—NEW JERSEY CHAPTER
 (Scholarship) 131, 578, 740, 796, 1548, 1585, 2150
NATIONAL ASSOCIATION OF WOMEN IN CONSTRUCTION (Founders' Scholarship Foundation Awards) 579
NATIONAL ASSOCIATION TO ADVANCE FAT ACCEPTANCE-THE NEW ENGLAND CHAPTER
 (NAAFA Scholarship Program) 3121
NATIONAL ATHLETIC TRAINERS' ASSOCIATION (NATA Scholarship Program) 1914
NATIONAL BAPTIST CONVENTION USA, INC. (Scholarships) 3122
NATIONAL BLACK POLICE ASSOCIATION (Alphonso Deal Scholarship Award) 2274
NATIONAL BROADCASTING SOCIETY (Alpha Epsilon Rho Scholarships) 2151
NATIONAL BURGLAR & FIRE ALARM ASSOCIATION (NBFAA/Security Dealer Youth Scholarship Program) 3123
NATIONAL BUSINESS AIRCRAFT ASSOCIATION (Scholarships) 498, 2456
NATIONAL CARTOONISTS SOCIETY 3856
NATIONAL CENTER FOR HOMEOPATHY 3907
NATIONAL CLEARINGHOUSE FOR PROFESSIONS IN SPECIAL EDUCATION
 (Various Financial Aid Sources) 261, 3969
NATIONAL COLLEGIATE ATHLETIC ASSOCIATION
 (NCAA Ethnic Minority and Women's Enhancement Program) 262, 3124, 3125
NATIONAL COUNCIL FOR THE SOCIAL STUDIES (Grant for the Enhancement of Geographic Literacy) 1370, 2082, 2083
NATIONAL COUNCIL OF FARMER COOPERATIVES (Undergraduate Awards & Scholarships) 1285
NATIONAL COUNCIL OF JEWISH WOMEN—GREATER BOSTON SECTION
 (Amelia Greenbaum/Rabbi Marshall Lifson Scholarship Program) 3126
NATIONAL COUNCIL OF STATE GARDEN CLUBS, INC. (Scholarships) 538, 1286
NATIONAL COUNCIL OF TEACHERS OF MATHEMATICS 3922
NATIONAL CUSTOMS BROKERS & FORWARDERS ASSN OF AMERICA INC (NCBFAA Scholarship) 132
NATIONAL DAIRY SHRINE (Dairy Student Recognition Program Scholarship Awards) 1287
NATIONAL DIRECTORY OF COLLEGE ATHLETICS (Men's and Women's Editions) 3743
NATIONAL DIRECTORY OF CORPORATE GIVING 3744
NATIONAL DO SOMETHING LEAGUE (Community Project Awards) 3127
NATIONAL ENDOWMENT FOR THE ARTS (Visual Artists Fellowships) 915, 995
NATIONAL ENVIRONMENTAL HEALTH ASSOCIATION (NEHA/AAS Scholarship) 1411, 1768
NATIONAL FALLEN FIREFIGHTERS FOUNDATION (Scholarship Program) 3128
NATIONAL FEDERATION OF MUSIC CLUBS COMPETITIVE AWARDS PROGRAM (Student Awards) 1131
NATIONAL FEDERATION OF PRESS WOMEN (NFPW Communications Contest) 2152, 2153
NATIONAL FEDERATION OF STATE POETRY SOCIETIES (Edna Meudt Memorial Scholarship Fund) 996
NATIONAL FEDERATION OF THE BLIND (Educator of Tomorrow Award) 263, 348, 349, 539, 540,
 . . . . .625, 821, 916, 997, 1047, 1212, 1371, 1681,
 . . . . .1769, 1823, 1996, 2227, 2275, 3129, 3130,
 . . . . .3131, 3132, 3133, 3134, 3135
NATIONAL FFA FOUNDATION (College & Voc/Tech School Scholarship Program) 1288
NATIONAL FIRE PROTECTION ASSN. (Public Fire Protection) 3890
NATIONAL FOREST FOUNDATION (Firefighters' Scholarship Fund) 3136

NATIONAL FOSTER PARENT ASSOCIATION, INC. (The Benjamin Eaton Scholarship Fund) 3137
NATIONAL FOUNDATION FOR ADVANCEMENT IN THE ARTS
  (Arts Recognition and Talent Search) 917, 918, 998, 1132, 2457
NATIONAL FOUNDATION FOR LONG-TERM HEALTH CARE (James D. Durante Nurse Scholarship Program) 1997
NATIONAL FUNERAL DIRECTORS ASSOCIATION 3898
NATIONAL GAY PILOTS ASSOCIATION (Pilot Scholarships) 499, 2458
NATIONAL GUILD OF COMMUNITY SCHOOLS OF THE ARTS (Young Composers Awards) 1133
NATIONAL HEALTH SERVICE CORPS (NHSC Scholarship Program) 1682, 1915, 1998
NATIONAL HORSESHOE PITCHERS ASSOCIATION (Junior Scholar Pitcher Program) 3138
NATIONAL ITALIAN AMERICAN FOUNDATION (George L. Graziado Fellowship for Business) 18, 19, 133, 134, 135,
  . . . . .136, 137, 138, 350, 541, 822, 823,
  . . . . .860, 861, 862, 919, 920, 921, 1048, 1049,
  . . . . .1134, 1135, 1136, 1137, 1138, 1240, 1289, 1495, 2061,
  . . . . .2228, 2276, 2324, 3139, 3140, 3141, 3142, 3143, 3144,
  . . . . .3145, 3146, 3147, 3148, 3149, 3150, 3151, 3152, 3153,
  . . . . .3154, 3155, 3156, 3157, 3158, 3159, 3160, 3161, 3162
NATIONAL JUNIOR CLASSICAL LEAGUE (Scholarships) 999
NATIONAL LEAGUE FOR NURSING 3936
NATIONAL LEAGUE OF AMERICAN PEN WOMEN, INC. (Scholarships for Mature Women) 922, 1000, 1139
NATIONAL MAKE IT YOURSELF WITH WOOL COMPETITION (Scholarship/Awards) 3163
NATIONAL MERIT SCHOLARSHIP CORPORATION (National Achievement Scholarship Program) 3164
NATIONAL OPTOMETRIC ASSOCIATION 3939
NATIONAL ORCHESTRAL INSTITUTE (School of Music Scholarship) 1140
NATIONAL PRESS CLUB (Ellen Masin Persina Scholarship for Minorities in Journalism) 2154
NATIONAL PRESS PHOTOGRAPHERS FOUNDATION (Bob East Scholarship) 2155, 2156, 2157, 2158, 2159
NATIONAL PRESS PHOTOGRAPHERS FOUNDATION, KAPPA ALPHA MU
  (College Photographer of the Year Competition) 2160
NATIONAL REHABILITATION COUNSELING ASSN. 3960
NATIONAL RESTAURANT ASSOCIATION EDUCATIONAL FOUNDATION
  (College Undergraduate Scholarships) 2062, 2063, 2064, 2065, 3894
NATIONAL RIGHT TO WORK COMMITTEE (William B. Ruggles Journalism Scholarship) 2161
NATIONAL ROOFING FOUNDATION (Scholarship Program) 3165
NATIONAL RURAL EDUCATION ASSOCIATION (Essay Contest) 3166
NATIONAL SCHOOL SUPPLY AND EQUIPMENT ASSOCIATION-EDUCATION EXCELLENCE FOUNDATION
  (Be Your Best! Teacher Scholarships) 264
NATIONAL SCHOLARSHIP TRUST FUND OF THE GRAPHIC ARTS (Scholarships & Fellowships) 923
NATIONAL SCIENCE TEACHERS ASSN 3964
NATIONAL SCIENCE TEACHERS ASSOCIATION (Teacher Award Programs) 1496, 3167, 3168
NATIONAL SCULPTURE SOCIETY (Alex J. Ettl Grant) 924
NATIONAL SCULPTURE SOCIETY (Young Sculptor Awards Competition) 925
NATIONAL SLOVAK SOCIETY (Peter V. Rovnianek Scholarship Fund) 3169
NATIONAL SOCIETY DAUGHTERS OF THE AMERICAN REVOLUTION
  (Enid Hall Griswold Memorial Scholarship) 139, 1916, 1999, 2000, 2229, 2230, 2325, 3170, 3171
NATIONAL SOCIETY OF ACCOUNTANTS SCHOLARSHIP FOUNDATION
  (NSA Annual Awards) 140, 141
NATIONAL SOCIETY OF BLACK ENGINEERS (Scholarships) 351, 500, 542, 580, 626, 695, 741, 797
NATIONAL SOCIETY OF PROFESSIONAL ENGINEERS 3884
NATIONAL SOCIETY OF PUBLIC ACCOUNTANTS 3817
NATIONAL SOCIETY OF THE COLONIAL DAMES IN AMERICA (American Indian Scholarship Awards) 2001
NATIONAL SOCIETY OF THE SONS OF THE AMERICAN REVOLUTION (Eagle Scout Scholarship) 3172
NATIONAL SPACE CLUB (Dr. Robert H. Goddard Scholarship) 352, 353, 501, 502, 1497, 1498, 2231, 2459
NATIONAL SPEAKERS ASSOCIATION (NSA Scholarship) 1001
NATIONAL SPEAKERS ASSOCIATION (Outstanding Professor Awards) 1002
NATIONAL STONE ASSOCIATION (NSA Quarry Engineering Scholarships) 798
NATIONAL STONE ASSN./AMERICAN SOCIETY OF LANDSCAPE ARCHITECTS (Student Competition) 543

NATIONAL STRENGTH & CONDITIONING ASSN. (Challenge Scholarships) 265, 1770, 1917

NATIONAL STUDENT NURSES' ASSOCIATION FOUNDATION (Scholarship Program) 2002

NATIONAL TECHNICAL ASSOCIATION, INC.
   (Scholarship Competitions for Minorities and Women in Science and Engineering) 354, 1499, 1624

NATIONAL TOOLING AND MACHINING ASSN 3954

NATIONAL TOURISM FOUNDATION (NTF Scholarships) 142

NATIONAL TWENTY AND FOUR (Memorial Scholarships) 3173

NATIONAL URBAN LEAGUE (Reginald K. Brack, Jr. NULITES Scholarship) 2162

NATIONAL URBAN LEAGUE, INC. (Duracell/NUL Scholarship/Intern Program for Minority Students) 143, 355, 742

NATIONAL WELSH-AMERICAN FOUNDATION (Exchange Scholarship Program) 3174

NATIONAL WRITERS ASSOCIATION 3871

NATIONAL WRITERS ASSOCIATION FOUNDATION (Scholarship) 1003

NATIONS BANK TRUST DEPT (Minne L. Maffett Scholarship Trust) 1683, 3175

NATIVE AMERICAN JOURNALISTS ASSOCIATION (NAJA Scholarships and Internships) 2163

NATIVE AMERICAN SCHOLARSHIP FUND, INC. (Scholarships) 20, 196, 266, 356, 627, 1500, 1625

NATIVE SONS OF THE GOLDEN WEST (Annual High School Public Speaking Contest) 3176

NATRONA COUNTY EDUCATION ASSOCIATION (Scholarships) 3177

NAVAL HISTORICAL CENTER (Internship Program) 144, 197, 267, 926, 1459, 2232

NAVAL RESERVE RECRUITING COMMAND (Armed Forces Health Professions Scholarships) 1684, 2003

NAVY AND MARINE CORPS ROTC COLLEGE SCHOLARSHIPS BULLETIN 3975

NAVY RECRUITING COMMAND (Armed Forces Health Professions Scholarships) 743, 1685, 1771, 1918

NAVY SUPPLY CORPS FOUNDATION (Scholarships) 3178

NAVY WIVES CLUBS OF AMERICA (Scholarship Foundation) 3179

NAVY-MARINE CORPS RELIEF SOCIETY
   (Battleship IOWA Memorial Fund and USS STARK Memorial Fund) 3180, 3181, 3182, 3183, 3184, 3185, 3186, 3187

NCSU PULP & PAPER FOUNDATION (Scholarships) 744

NEED A LIFT? (49th edition-2000 Issue) 3745

NEGRO EDUCATIONAL EMERGENCY DRIVE (NEED Scholarship Program) 3188

NELLIE MAE (Student Loans) 3189

NETTIE MILLHOLLON EDUCATIONAL TRUST ESTATE (Student Loans) 3190

NEVADA DEPARTMENT OF EDUCATION (Robert C. Byrd Honors Scholarship) 3191

NEVADA DEPT. OF EDUCATION (Student Incentive Grant Program) 3192

NEW BEDFORD PORT SOCIETY- LADIES BRANCH (Limited Scholarship Grant) 3193

NEW ENGLAND BOARD OF HIGHER EDUCATION (New England Regional Student Program) 3194

NEW HAMPSHIRE ELECTRICAL CONTRACTORS ASSOC. (Phil Moran Scholarship Fund) 2460

NEW HAMPSHIRE HIGHER EDUCATION ASSISTANCE FOUNDATION (Federal Family Education Loan Program) 3195

NEW JERSEY DEPT. OF HIGHER EDUCATION (Educational Opportunity Fund Grants) 3196, 3197

NEW JERSEY DEPT. OF MILITARY & VETERANS AFFAIRS (Veterans Tuition Credit Program) 3198, 3199

NEW JERSEY STATE GOLF ASSOC. (Caddie Scholarships) 3200

NEW JERSEY STATE OPERA (Cash Awards) 1141

NEW JERSEY STATE OPERA (International Vocal Competition) 1142

NEW JERSEY TESOL-BE (Postsecondary Scholarship) 3201

NEW MEXICO COMMISSION ON HIGHER EDUCATION (Student Incentive Grant) 3202

NEW MEXICO FARM AND LIVESTOCK BUREAU (Memorial Scholarships) 3203

NEW MEXICO TECH (Freshmen and Transfer Student Scholarships) 3204

NEW MEXICO TECH (Scholarships for Non-resident Students) 3205

NEW MEXICO TECH (Transfer Student Scholarship) 3206

NEW MEXICO VETERANS' SERVICE COMMISSION (Scholarship Program) 3207

NEW YORK CITY DEPT. CITYWIDE ADMINISTRATIVE SERVICES (Urban Fellows Program) 145, 544, 2326, 2392

NEW YORK CITY DEPT. OF CITYWIDE ADMINISTRATIVE SERVICES
   (Government Scholars Internship Program) 146, 545, 2327, 2393

NEW YORK FINANCIAL WRITERS' ASSOCIATION (Scholarship Program) 2164

NEW YORK STATE DEPARTMENT OF HEALTH—PRIMARY CARE SERVICE CORPS (Scholarships) 1919, 2004

NEW YORK STATE EDUCATION DEPT. (Awards, Scholarships, and Fellowships) 3208

NEW YORK STATE HIGHER EDUCATION SERVICES CORPORATION
  (N.Y. State Regents Professional/Health Care Opportunity Scholarships) 147, 357, 546, 1686, 1772, 1920,
  . . . . .2005, 2277, 2358, 2394, 3209, 3210, 3211, 3212
NEW YORK STATE SENATE (Legislative Fellows Program;
  R. J. Roth Journalism Fellowship; R. A. Wiebe Public Service Fellowship) 148, 2165, 2328
NEW YORK STATE SENATE (Undergraduate Session Assistants Program) 3213
NEW YORK STATE THEATRE INSTITUTE (Internships in Theatrical Production) 149, 268, 927, 1004, 1143, 2166
NEWSPAPER ASSN OF AMERICA 3934
NEWSPAPER FEATURES COUNCIL 3855
NEWSPAPERS, DIVERSITY & YOU 3746
NICHOLL SCHOLARSHIPS (Undergraduate and Graduate Scholarships) 3214
NINETY-NINES, INC. (Amelia Earhart Memorial Scholarships) 503, 2461
NINETY-NINES, SAN FERNANDO VALLEY CHAPTER/VAN NUYS AIRPORT
  (Aviation Career Scholarships) 150, 504, 2462
NON-COMMISSIONED OFFICERS ASSOCIATION (Scholarships) 3215
NORRIS BURSARY SCHOLARSHIP FUND 3216
NORTH AMERICAN DIE CASTING ASSOCIATION (David Laine Memorial Scholarships) 745
NORTH CAROLINA ASSOCIATION OF EDUCATORS (Mary Morrow Scholarships) 269, 3217
NORTH CAROLINA DEPARTMENT OF PUBLIC INSTRUCTION
  (Scholarship Loan Program for Prospective Teachers) 270, 271, 1005, 1006, 1773, 1774, 1921, 1922, 3218
NORTH CAROLINA DEPT. OF PUBLIC INSTRUCTION (Challenge Scholars Program) 3223
NORTH CAROLINA DIVISION OF SERVICES FOR THE BLIND (Rehabilitation Assistance for Visually Impaired) 3219
NORTH CAROLINA DIVISION OF VETERANS AFFAIRS (Dependents Scholarship Program) .3220
NORTH CAROLINA SOCIETY FOR CLINICAL LABORATORY SCIENCE (Scholarship Award) 1923
NORTH CAROLINA STATE EDUCATION ASSISTANCE AUTHORITY (Student Financial Aid for North Carolinians) 3221
NORTH CAROLINA STATE UNIVERSITY (Thomas Jefferson Scholarship in Agriculture & Humanities) 824, 1290, 3222
NORTH CROSS SCHOOL (Scholarships) 3224
NORTH DAKOTA DEPARTMENT OF TRANSPORTATION (Grants) 581
NORTH DAKOTA INDIAN SCHOLARSHIP PROGRAM (Scholarships) 3225
NORTH DAKOTA STUDENT FINANCIAL ASSISTANCE AGENCY (Grants) 3226
NORTHEASTERN LOGGERS ASSOCIATION, INC. (Scholarship Contest) 3227
NORTHERN NEW JERSEY UNIT-HERB SOCIETY OF AMERICA (Scholarship) 1291, 1549
NORTHWEST DANISH FOUNDATION (Scholarships) 3228
NORTHWEST PHARMACISTS COALITION (Prepharmacy Scholarships) 1775
NORWEGIAN INFORMATION SERVICE (Norwegian Emigration Fund of 1975) 863
NORWICH JUBILEE ESPERANTO FOUNDATION (Travel Grants) 1050
NUCLEAR AGE PEACE FOUNDATION (Lena Chang Scholarship Awards) 3229
OAK RIDGE INSTITUTE FOR SCIENCE AND EDUCATION
  (ORISE Education & Training Programs) 358, 505, 582, 628, 746, 1372, 1412, 1550, 1586, 1626, 1824, 1924
OAKWOOD FRIENDS SCHOOL (Scholarships) 3230
OCCUPATIONAL OUTLOOK HANDBOOK 3747
ODD FELLOWS AND REBEKAHS (Nursing Training Scholarships) 2006
OFF TO COLLEGE 3748
OFFICE OF NAVAL RESEARCH (NSAP—Naval Science Awards Program) 359, 1373, 1443, 1501
OFFICIAL STUDY GUIDE FOR THE CLEP EXAMINATIONS 3749
OGLE SCHOOL OF HAIR DESIGN (Scholarships) 2463
OHEF SHOLOM TEMPLE (Sarah Cohen Scholarship Fund) 3231
OHIO AMERICAN LEGION (Scholarship) 3232
OHIO BOARD OF REGENTS (Nurse Education Assistance Loan Program) 2007
OHIO BOARD OF REGENTS (Ohio Academic Scholarship Program) 3233
OHIO BOARD OF REGENTS (Ohio Instructional Grant Program) 3234
OHIO BOARD OF REGENTS (Ohio Student Choice Grant) 3235
OHIO BOARD OF REGENTS (Regents Graduate/Professional Fellowship Program) 3236
OHIO BOARD OF REGENTS (Robert C. Byrd Honors Scholarship Program) 3237
OHIO BOARD OF REGENTS (War Orphans Scholarship Program) 3238

OHIO LEAGUE FOR NURSING (Grants and Loans) 2008
OHIO UNIVERSITY (Charles Kilburger Scholarship) 3239
OKLAHOMA MEDICAL RESEARCH FOUNDATION (Sir Alexander Fleming Scholar Program) 1502, 1551, 1587, 1627,
. . . . .1687, 1776, 1825
OLDFIELDS SCHOOL (Grants and Loans) 3240
OMAHA SYMPHONY GUILD (International New Music Competition) 1144
ONCOLOGY NURSING FOUNDATION (Scholarships, Grants, Awards, & Honors) 2009
ONEIDA HIGHER EDUCATION (Various Fellowships, Internships, and Scholarships) 3241
ONLINE STUDY ABROAD DIRECTORY 3750
OPEN SOCIETY INSTITUTE (Environmental Management Fellowships) 583, 747, 799, 825, 1241, 1292, 1374, 1413,
. . . . .1444, 1552, 1588, 1628, 2395
OPEN SOCIETY INSTITUTE (Individual Project Fellowships) 864, 2278, 2329, 2359, 2396
OPERA AMERICA (Fellowship Program) 151, 1145
OPERATING ENGINEERS LOCAL UNION NO. 3 (IUOE Scholarship Program) 3242
ORCHESTRA SONOMA GUILD (Scholarship) 1146
ORDER OF THE EASTERN STAR (Grand Chapter of California Scholarships) 3243
OREGON AFL-CIO (Scholarship Contest) 152
OREGON CREDIT UNION LEAGUE EDUCATIONAL FOUNDATION (Lois M. Hartley Benefit Scholarship) 3244
OREGON DEPARTMENT OF VETERANS' AFFAIRS (Educational Aid for Oregon Veterans) 3245
OREGON PTA (Teacher Education Scholarships) 272
OREGON STATE SCHOLARSHIP COMMISSION (Federal Family Education Loan Program) 3246, 3247, 3248
OREGON STATE SCHOLARSHIP COMMISSION GRANTS DIVISION (Ben Selling Student Loan Fund) 1213
ORGAN HISTORICAL SOCIETY (E. Power Biggs Fellowship) 1147
ORGANIZATION OF AMERICAN STATES (Leo S. Rowe Pan American Fund) 3249
ORGANIZATION OF CHINESE AMERICANS (Journalist Award) 2167, 3250, 3251
ORPHAN FOUNDATION OF AMERICA (Scholarship Program) 3252
OTTO A. HUTH SCHOLARSHIP FUND 3253
OUR WORLD-UNDERWATER SCHOLARSHIP SOCIETY (Scholarship & Internships) 1445
OUTDOOR WRITERS ASSOCIATION OF AMERICA (Bodie McDowell Scholarship Program) 2168, 3254
Order form for book list on theatre/writing careers 3751
P.L.A.T.O. JUNIOR EDUCATION LOAN 3255
PACIFIC PRINTING AND IMAGING ASSOCIATION (Scholarships) 928
PADGETT BUSINESS SERVICES (Scholarship Program) 3256
PALEONTOLOGICAL SOCIETY 3942
PARALEGAL 3752
PARAPSYCHOLOGY FOUNDATION (D. Scott Rogo Award for Parapsychological Award) 2360
PARAPSYCHOLOGY FOUNDATION (Eileen J. Garrett Scholarship) 2361
PARENTS AND FRIENDS OF LESBIANS AND GAYS—PFLAG CINCINNATI (Scholarships) 3257
PARENTS WITHOUT PARTNERS (International Scholarship) 3258
PARENTS, FAMILIES, AND FRIENDS OF LESBIANS AND GAYS-NEW ORLEANS CHAPTER
(Scholarships) 3259, 3260, 3261, 3262
PARKE-DAVIS (Epilepsy Scholarship Award) 3263
PARTNERS ADVANCING VALUES IN EDUCATION (PAVE)
(Scholarships for K-12 Private/Parochial School Students in Milwaukee, WI) 3264
PAUL AND MARY HAAS FOUNDATION (Scholarship Grants) 3265
PAUL O. AND MARY BOGHOSSIAN FOUNDATION 3266
PENINSULA COMMUNITY FOUNDATION (African-American Scholarship Fund) 3267
PENINSULA COMMUNITY FOUNDATION (Bobette Bibo Gugliotta Memorial Scholarship for Creative Writing) 1007
PENINSULA COMMUNITY FOUNDATION (Crain Educational Grants Program) 3268
PENINSULA COMMUNITY FOUNDATION (Curry Award for Girls and Young Women) 3269
PENINSULA COMMUNITY FOUNDATION (Dr. James L. Hutchinson and Evelyn Ribbs Hutchinson Scholarship Fund) 1688
PENINSULA COMMUNITY FOUNDATION (Dr. Mary Finegold Scholarship) .1242, 1293, 1375, 1414,
. . . . .1446, 1460, 1503, 1553, 1589, 1629,
. . . . .1689, 1777, 1826, 1925, 2010, 2066
PENINSULA COMMUNITY FOUNDATION (Ruppert Educational Grant Program) 3270

PENINSULA COMMUNITY FOUNDATION (Scholarship Fund for Gay/Lesbian Asian Students) 3271
PENN STATE UNIVERSITY—COLLEGE OF EARTH & MINERAL SCIENCES (Scholarships) 1376, 1415
PENNSYLVANIA DEPARTMENT OF MILITARY AFFAIRS—BUREAU OF VETERANS AFFAIRS (Scholarships) 3272
PENNSYLVANIA HIGHER EDUCATION ASSISTANCE AGENCY (Robert C. Byrd Honors Scholarship Program) 3273
PENNSYLVANIA WOMEN'S PRESS ASSOCIATION (Scholarship) 2169
PEORIA JOURNAL STAR (Newspaper in Education Program) 2170
PERRY & STELLA TRACY SCHOLARSHIP FUND (Scholarships) 3274
PERSPECTIVES: AUDITION ADVICE FOR SINGERS 3753
PERSPECTIVES: THE SINGER/MANAGER RELATIONSHIP 3754
PETER BLOSSER STUDENT LOAN FUND 3275
PETERSON'S FOUR-YEAR COLLEGES 3755
PETERSON'S PRIVATE SECONDARY SCHOOLS 3756
PETERSON'S SPORTS SCHOLARSHIPS AND ATHLETIC PROGRAMS 3757
PETERSON'S TWO-YEAR COLLEGES 3758
PEW YOUNGER SCHOLARS PROGRAM (Graduate Fellowships) 826, 1214, 2084
PFLAG/H.A.T.C.H. (Scholarship Fund) 3276
PHARMACY SCHOOL ADMISSION REQUIREMENTS 3759
PHI ALPHA THETA HISTORY HONOR SOCIETY (Nels Andrew N. Cleven Founder's Paper Prize Awards) 2233, 2234
PHI DELTA KAPPA (Scholarship Grants for Prospective Educators) 273
PHI DELTA KAPPA, INC. (Scholarship Grants for Prospective Educators) 274
PHI KAPPA THETA NATIONAL FOUNDATION (Scholarship Program) 3277
PHI THETA KAPPA INTERNATIONAL HONOR SOCIETY (Guistwhite Scholar Program) 3278
PHILADELPHIA COLLEGE OF BIBLE (Scholarships, Grants, and Loans) 275, 1148, 1215, 2171, 2397
PHILIPS NORTH AMERICA CORPORATION (Scholarship Program) 3279
PHILLIPS EXETER ACADEMY (Financial Aid: Grants and Loans) 3280
PHILLIPS FOUNDATION (Journalism Fellowship Program) 2172
PHYSICIAN ASSISTANT FOUNDATION (Scholarships, Traineeships, & Grants) 1778
PI LAMBDA THETA (Distinguished Student Scholar Award for Education Majors) 276
PI LAMBDA THETA (Thelma Jean Brown Classroom Teacher Award) 277
PICKETT & HATCHER EDUCATIONAL FUND INC. (Loans) 3281
PILOT INTERNATIONAL FOUNDATION (PIF/Lifeline Scholarship) 278, 1690, 1827, 1926, 2362
PILOT INTERNATIONAL FOUNDATION (Ruby Newhall Memorial Scholarship) 279, 1691, 1828, 1927, 2363
PILOT INTERNATIONAL FOUNDATION (The Pilot International Scholarship Program) 280, 1692, 1829, 1928, 2364
PINE BLUFFS AREA CHAMBER OF COMMERCE (Scholarship) 3282
PING AMERICAN COLLEGE GOLF GUIDE 3760
PITTSBURGH NEW MUSIC ENSEMBLE (Harvey Gaul Composition Contest) 1149
PIXAR ANIMATION STUDIOS (Summer Internships) 929
PLANNING FOR A DENTAL EDUCATION 3761
PLAYWRIGHTS' CENTER (Jerome Fellowships) 1008
PLAYWRIGHTS' CENTER (Many Voices Residency & Collaboration Grants Programs) 1009
PLAYWRIGHTS' CENTER (McKnight Advancement Grant) 1010
PLAYWRIGHTS' CENTER (McKnight Fellowships) 1011
PLAYWRIGHTS' CENTER (PlayLabs) 1012
POETRY SOCIETY OF AMERICA (George Bogin Memorial Award) 1013, 1014, 1015, 1016
PORTSMOUTH HIGH SCHOOL (George C. Cogan Scholarship) 3283
PORTUGUESE CONTINENTAL UNION (Scholarships) 3284
POWER STUDENTS NETWORK (Scholarship) 3285
POWER STUDY TO UP YOUR GRADES AND GPA 3762
PRESBYTERIAN CHURCH (U.S.A.) (Loan Program for Theological Studies) 1216, 1693, 3286, 3287,
....3288, 3289, 3290, 3291, 3292
PRESIDENT'S COMMISSION ON WHITE HOUSE FELLOWSHIPS 153, 2279, 2330, 2398
PRESS CLUB OF DALLAS FOUNDATION (Scholarship) 154, 2173
PRIDE FOUNDATION & GREATER SEATTLE BUSINESS ASSOCIATION (Scholarships for Gays & Lesbians) 3293
PRINCE GEORGE'S CHAMBER OF COMMERCE FOUNDATION (Scholarship) 3294

PRINCESS GRACE FOUNDATION-USA (Dance Scholarships) 1150
PRINCESS GRACE FOUNDATION-USA (Drama Scholarships and Fellowships) 1151
PRINCESS GRACE FOUNDATION-USA (Grants for Young Playwrights) 1017
PRINCESS GRACE FOUNDATION-USA (Scholarships for Senior and Graduate Thesis Film Productions) 930
PROFESSIONAL AVIATION MAINTENANCE ASSOCIATION (PAMA Scholarship Fund) 2464, 2465
PROFESSIONAL BARTENDING SCHOOLS OF AMERICA 3848
PROFESSIONAL BOWLERS ASSOCIATION (Billy Welu Memorial Scholarship) 3295
PROFESSIONAL GROUNDS MANAGEMENT SOCIETY (Anne Seaman Memorial Scholarships) 1294
PROFESSIONAL HORSEMEN'S SCHOLARSHIP FUND, INC. 3296
PROFESSIONAL SECRETARIES INTERNATIONAL-THE ASSOCIATION FOR OFFICE PROFESSIONALS 3965
PUBLIC EMPLOYEES ROUNDTABLE (Public Service Scholarships) 3297
PURDUE UNIVERSITY (Freshman Scholarship Awards of Excellence) 1295, 1377
PHYSICIAN ASSISTANT PROGRAMS DIRECTORY 3763
POUR MAN'S FRIEND: A GUIDE AND REFERENCE FOR BAR PERSONNEL 3764
Professional Aviation Maintenance Association 3847
Public Relations Careers booklet: 3.50; Where to Study: $5.00. 3765
QUILL & SCROLL (Edward J. Nell Memorial Scholarship) 2174
RADIO AND TELEVISION NEWS DIRECTORS ASSOCIATION 3852
RADIO AND TELEVISION NEWS DIRECTORS FOUNDATION
  (George Foreman Tribute to Lyndon B. Johnson Scholarship) 2175, 2176, 2177, 2178
RAGDALE FOUNDATION (Frances Shaw Fellowship) 1018
RAYMOND J. HARRIS EDUCATION TRUST 360, 1296, 1694, 1779, 2280
REAL ESTATE EDUCATORS ASSN. (REEA—Harwood Scholarship Program) 155
REALTY FOUNDATION OF NEW YORK (Scholarship Program) 3298
RECORDING FOR THE BLIND (Marion Huber Learning Through Listening Awards) 3299, 3300
RED RIVER VALLEY FIGHTER PILOTS ASSOCIATION (River Rats Scholarship Grant Programs) 3301
REFRIGERATION SERVICE ENGINEERS SOCIETY EDUCATIONAL FOUNDATION
  (J.W. Harris Company Scholarship) 748, 3906
REPAIR YOUR OWN CREDIT 3766
RESERVE OFFICERS ASSOCIATION OF THE UNITED STATES
  (Henry J. Reilly Memorial Scholarships for Undergraduates) 3302, 3303
RESOURCES FOR THE FUTURE (RFF Summer Internship Program) 1243, 1378, 1416, 2085
RHODE ISLAND HIGHER EDUCATION ASSISTANCE AUTHORITY (Loan Program; PLUS Loans) 3304, 3305
RHYTHM & HUES STUDIOS (Computer Graphics Scholarship) 931
RICHARD E. MERWIN INTERNATIONAL AWARD 3306
RIPON COLLEGE (Academic Tuition Scholarships) 3307
RIPON COLLEGE (Performance/Recognition Tuition Scholarships) 932, 1019, 1152
RISING STAR INTERNSHIPS (Internships and Part-Time Employment for Students) 3308
ROBERT SCHRECK MEMORIAL FUND (Grants) 361, 547, 1217, 1590, 1695, 1780
ROBOTIC INDUSTRIES ASSOCIATION (RIA Robotics Scholarship Competition) 362, 629, 749, 800
ROCKY MOUNTAIN COAL MINING INSTITUTE (Scholarships) 801
ROCKY MOUNTAIN MINERAL LAW FOUNDATION (Law Scholarships) 2281
ROSE HILL COLLEGE (Louella Robinson Memorial Scholarship) 827, 933, 1020, 1218, 1461, 2086, 2179, 2235, 2331, 2365, 2399
ROSE HILL COLLEGE (Scholarships for Children of Eastern Orthodox Priests/Deacons) 828, 934, 1021, 1219, 1462, 2087,
  . . . . .2180, 2236, 2332, 2366, 2400
ROSE HILL COLLEGE (Scholarships for the Homeschooled) 829, 935, 1022, 1220, 1463, 2088, 2181, 2237, 2333, 2367, 2401
ROTARY FOUNDATION OF ROTARY INTERNATIONAL (Ambassadorial Scholarships) 3309, 3310
ROYAL A. & MILDRED D. EDDY STUDENT LOAN TRUST FUND;
  LOUISE I. LATSHAW STUDENT LOAN TRUST FUND (Student Loans) 3311
ROYAL NEIGHBORS OF AMERICA (Fraternal Scholarships) 3312, 3313
ROYAL NORWEGIAN EMBASSY (May 8th Memorial Fund) 3314
ROYAL THAI EMBASSY, OFFICE OF EDUCATIONAL AFFAIRS
  (Revenue Dept. Scholarships for Thai Students) 156, 630, 696, 2282
RURITAN NATIONAL FOUNDATION (Grant and Loan Program) 3315
Resource papers, newsletter article reprints, and other publications for individuals with disabilities 3767

SACHS FOUNDATION (Scholarship Program) 3316

SACRAMENTO ASSOCIATION OF REALTORS (Scholarship) 157

SACRAMENTO SCOTTISH RITE OF FREEMASONRY (Charles M. Goethe Memorial Scholarship) 3317

SACRED HEART ACADEMY (Merit Scholarship) 3318

SAINT ANTHONY OF PADUA SCHOOL (Tuition Assistance) 3319

SAINT JOHN'S PREPARATORY SCHOOL (President's Scholarship) 3320

SAINT MARK'S SCHOOL (Financial Aid) 3321

SAINT MARY'S EPISCOPAL SCHOOL (Financial Aid) 3322

SAMUEL LEMBERG SCHOLARSHIP LOAN FUND INC. (Scholarships-Loans) 3323

SAN ANGELO SYMPHONY SOCIETY (Sorantin Young Artist Award) 1153

SAN DIEGO AEROSPACE MUSEUM (Bill Gibbs Scholarship) 363, 506, 1244, 1297, 1379, 1417,
. . . .`1447, 1464, 1504, 1554, 1591, 1630

SAN DIEGO COUNTY COW-BELLES (Memorial Scholarship) 1298

SAN FRANCISCO CHRONICLE (Chronicle Publishing Company Scholarship) .2182

SAN FRANCISCO CONSERVATORY OF MUSIC (Various Scholarships) 1154

SAN FRANCISCO FOUNDATION (James D. Phelan Art Awards) 936, 1023

SAN FRANCISCO FOUNDATION (Joseph Henry Jackson Literary Award) 1024

SAN FRANCISCO INDEPENDENT SCHOLARS (Star and Step Scholarships) .3324

SAN FRANCISCO STATE UNIVERSITY (Over-60 Program) 3325

SAN FRANCISCO UNIVERSITY HIGH SCHOOL (Financial Aid Grants) 3326

SAN JOSE STATE UNIVERSITY (Scholarships) 3327

SAN MATEO COUNTY FARM BUREAU (Scholarship) 3328

SANTA BARBARA FOUNDATION (Mary & Edith Pillsbury Foundation Scholarships) 1155

SANTA BARBARA FOUNDATION (Pillsbury/Fahlman Music Scholarship Program) 1156

SANTA ROSA JUNIOR COLLEGE (Business and Community Scholarships) 3329

SANTA ROSA JUNIOR COLLEGE (Doyle Scholarship Program) 3330

SANTA ROSA JUNIOR COLLEGE (SRJC Foundation Scholarships) 3331

SARA LEE CORPORATION (Nathan Cummings Scholarship Program) .3332, 3333

SARA'S WISH FOUNDATION (Scholarships) 3334

SCHERING/KEY ("Will to Win" Asthma Athlete Scholarship) 3335

SCHOLARSHIP FOUNDATION OF ST. LOUIS (Interest-free Loan Program) .3336

SCHOLARSHIP LIST SERVICE 3768

SCHOLARSHIPS & LOANS FOR NURSING EDUCATION 3769

SCHOLARSHIPS FOR EXCELLENCE IN AGRICULTURE 1299

SCHOOL FOOD SERVICE FOUNDATION (Scholarships) 2067

SCHOOL FOR INTERNATIONAL TRAINING (College Semester Abroad and Other Scholarships Related
to International Education) 3337

SCIENCE SERVICE (Intel International Science & Engineering Fair) 364, 1505, 1631

SCIENCE SERVICE (Intel Science Talent Search) 365, 1506, 1632

SCOTTISH RITE FOUNDATION OF WYOMING (Scholarships) 3338

SCREAMING POLITICIANS (Scholarship Essay Contest) 3339

SCREEN ACTORS GUILD 3880

SCREEN ACTORS GUILD FOUNDATION (John L. Dales Scholarship Fund) .3340

SCRIPPS HOWARD FOUNDATION (Charles M. Schulz Award) 937

SCRIPPS HOWARD FOUNDATION (Robert P. Scripps Graphic Arts Scholarships) 2183

SCRIPPS HOWARD FOUNDATION (Ted Scripps Scholarships & Lecture) 2184

SEABEE MEMORIAL SCHOLARSHIP ASSOCIATION, INC. (Scholarships) .3341

SEAFARERS' WELFARE PLAN (Charlie Logan Scholarship Program for Seamen) 3342, 3343

SEASPACE (Scholarships) 1448

SELBY FOUNDATION (Direct Scholarship Program) 3344

SELECTED FINANCIAL AID REFERENCES FOR STUDENTS WITH DISABILITIES-#107.96 3770

SELECTED FINANCIAL AID RESOURCES FOR INDIVIDUALS FROM CULTURALLY/
ETHNICALLY DIVERSE BACKGROUNDS-#104.96 . . . . .3771, 3772, 3773

SEMINOLE TRIBE OF FLORIDA (Higher Education Awards) 3345

SENECA NATION HIGHER EDUCATION (Scholarships and Grants) 3346
SERB NATIONAL FOUNDATION (Scholarships) 3347
SERTOMA FOUNDATION INTERNATIONAL (Scholarships for Students With Hearing Loss) 3348
SERVICE EMPLOYEES INTERNATIONAL UNION (Scholarship Program) 3349
SHOSHONE HIGHER EDUCATION PROGRAM (Shoshone Tribal Scholarship) 3350
SICO FOUNDATION (Scholarships) 3351
SIDNEY H. AND MARY L. LANGILLE GRAY FAMILY SCHOLARSHIP FUND TRUST 3352
SIDNEY-SHELBY COUNTY YMCA (Lee E. Schauer Memorial Scholarship) 3353
SIGNET CLASSIC SCHOLARSHIP ESSAY COMPETITION 3354
SIKH EDUCATION AID FUND (Scholarships and Interest-free Loans) 3355
SKIDMORE COLLEGE (Filene Music Scholarships) 1157
SKIDMORE COLLEGE (Merit Scholarships in Math and Science) 1245, 1507, 1633
SKIDMORE, OWINGS & MERRILL FOUNDATION (Architecture Traveling Fellowship Program) 548, 549, 938
SKY PEOPLE HIGHER EDUCATION (Northern Arapaho Tribal Scholarship) 3356
SMART WOMAN'S GUIDE TO CAREER SUCCESS 3774
SMART WOMAN'S GUIDE TO INTERVIEWING AND SALARY NEGOTIATION 3775
SMART WOMAN'S GUIDE TO RESUMES AND JOB HUNTING 3776
SMITHSONIAN INSTITUTION (Cooper-Hewitt, National Design Museum-Mark Kaminski
   Summer Internship) 550, 551, 552, 939, 940, 941, 1465, 1466
SMITHSONIAN INSTITUTION (Minority Student Internship Program) 865, 942, 1380, 1418, 1467, 1555, 2238
SMITHSONIAN INSTITUTION (National Air & Space Museum Verville Fellowship) 507, 1381, 1592, 1634, 2239
SMITHSONIAN INSTITUTION (Native American Internship Program) 866
SMITHSONIAN INSTITUTION ENVIRONMENTAL RESEARCH CENTER
   (Work/Learn Program in Environmental Studies) 1419
SOCIETY FOR IMAGING SCIENCE AND TECHNOLOGY (Raymond Davis Scholarship) 750
SOCIETY FOR MARINE MAMMALOGY (The Emily B. Shane Award) 1556
SOCIETY FOR RANGE MANAGEMENT 3959
SOCIETY FOR RANGE MANAGEMENT (Masonic Range Science Scholarship) 1300, 1382, 1420
SOCIETY FOR SOFTWARE QUALITY (Grant-In-Aid Essay Contest) 631
SOCIETY FOR TECHNICAL COMMUNICATION (Undergraduate Scholarships) 943, 2185, 2466
SOCIETY FOR THE PSYCHOLOGICAL STUDY OF SOCIAL ISSUES
   (Applied Social Issues Internship Program) 2089, 2368, 2402
SOCIETY FOR THE SCIENTIFIC STUDY OF SEXUALITY (Student Research Grant) 2369
SOCIETY OF ACTUARIES 3819
SOCIETY OF AMERICAN FLORISTS 3892
SOCIETY OF AMERICAN FORESTERS 3897
SOCIETY OF AUTOMOTIVE ENGINEERS (Calvin College/James Bosscher/SAE Scholarship) 366
SOCIETY OF AUTOMOTIVE ENGINEERS (Cedarville College/SAE Scholarship) 367
SOCIETY OF AUTOMOTIVE ENGINEERS (Cornell Univ/McMullin Dean's Scholar/SAE Scholarship) 368
SOCIETY OF AUTOMOTIVE ENGINEERS (Embry-Riddle Aeronautical Univ/SAE Scholarship) 369
SOCIETY OF AUTOMOTIVE ENGINEERS (Gannon Univ/SAE Scholarship) 370
SOCIETY OF AUTOMOTIVE ENGINEERS (Geneva College/SAE Scholarship) 371
SOCIETY OF AUTOMOTIVE ENGINEERS (Grand Valley State Univ/Padnos/SAE Scholarship) 372
SOCIETY OF AUTOMOTIVE ENGINEERS (IUPUI/SAE Scholarship) 373
SOCIETY OF AUTOMOTIVE ENGINEERS (Illinois Institute of Technology/SAE Scholarship) 374
SOCIETY OF AUTOMOTIVE ENGINEERS (Iowa State Univ/SAE Scholarship) 375
SOCIETY OF AUTOMOTIVE ENGINEERS (Kansas State Univ/SAE Scholarship) 376
SOCIETY OF AUTOMOTIVE ENGINEERS (Kettering Univ/SAE Scholarship) 377
SOCIETY OF AUTOMOTIVE ENGINEERS (LaFayette College/SAE Scholarship) 378
SOCIETY OF AUTOMOTIVE ENGINEERS (Mankato State Univ/SAE Scholarship) .751
SOCIETY OF AUTOMOTIVE ENGINEERS (Mercer Univ/SAE Scholarship) 379
SOCIETY OF AUTOMOTIVE ENGINEERS (Michigan State Univ/SAE Scholarship) 752, 802
SOCIETY OF AUTOMOTIVE ENGINEERS (Miami Univ/Ken Shinn/SAE Scholarship) 753
SOCIETY OF AUTOMOTIVE ENGINEERS (Murray State Univ/SAE Scholarship) 754

SOCIETY OF AUTOMOTIVE ENGINEERS (New York Institute of Technology/SAE Scholarship) 380
SOCIETY OF AUTOMOTIVE ENGINEERS (Oakland Univ/SAE Scholarship) 381
SOCIETY OF AUTOMOTIVE ENGINEERS (Ohio State Univ/Motorsports Team/SAE Scholarship) 382
SOCIETY OF AUTOMOTIVE ENGINEERS (Oklahoma State Univ (CEAT)/SAE Scholarship) .383
SOCIETY OF AUTOMOTIVE ENGINEERS (Parks College of St. Louis Univ/SAE Scholarship) 384
SOCIETY OF AUTOMOTIVE ENGINEERS (Penn State Erie-Behrend College/SAE Scholarship) 385, 386
SOCIETY OF AUTOMOTIVE ENGINEERS (Pittsburgh State Univ/SAE Scholarship) 755
SOCIETY OF AUTOMOTIVE ENGINEERS (Purdue Univ/Dean's Engineering Scholar/SAE Scholarship) 387
SOCIETY OF AUTOMOTIVE ENGINEERS (Rochester Institute of Technology/SAE Scholarship) 388
SOCIETY OF AUTOMOTIVE ENGINEERS (SAE) 3843
SOCIETY OF AUTOMOTIVE ENGINEERS (SAE Long-Term Member Sponsored Scholarships) 389
SOCIETY OF AUTOMOTIVE ENGINEERS (SAE Undesignated Engineering Scholarships) 390
SOCIETY OF AUTOMOTIVE ENGINEERS (SUNY-Stony Brook/SAE Scholarship) 391
SOCIETY OF AUTOMOTIVE ENGINEERS (SUNY-Alfred/Vernon Gleasman/SAE Scholarship) 392
SOCIETY OF AUTOMOTIVE ENGINEERS (SUNY-New Paltz/SAE Scholarship) 393
SOCIETY OF AUTOMOTIVE ENGINEERS (Stevens Institute of Technology/SAE Scholarship) 394
SOCIETY OF AUTOMOTIVE ENGINEERS (Univ Alaska Fairbanks/SAE Scholarship) 395, 396
SOCIETY OF AUTOMOTIVE ENGINEERS (Univ Evansville/John R. Tooley/SAE Scholarship) 397
SOCIETY OF AUTOMOTIVE ENGINEERS (Univ Florida/Dean's Engineering Scholar/SAE Scholarship) 398
SOCIETY OF AUTOMOTIVE ENGINEERS (Univ Illinois-Chicago/SAE Scholarship) 756
SOCIETY OF AUTOMOTIVE ENGINEERS (Univ Pittsburgh/SAE Scholarship) 399
SOCIETY OF AUTOMOTIVE ENGINEERS (Univ Southern California/SAE Scholarship) 400
SOCIETY OF AUTOMOTIVE ENGINEERS (Univ Texas-Austin/SAE Scholarship) 401, 402
SOCIETY OF AUTOMOTIVE ENGINEERS (Univ Wisconsin-Milwaukee/Sundstrand/SAE Scholarship) 803
SOCIETY OF AUTOMOTIVE ENGINEERS (Wayne State Univ/College of Engineering/Dean's/SAE Scholarship) 403
SOCIETY OF AUTOMOTIVE ENGINEERS (Washington Univ/SAE Scholarship) 404
SOCIETY OF AUTOMOTIVE ENGINEERS (Western Michigan Univ/SAE Scholarship) 405
SOCIETY OF AUTOMOTIVE ENGINEERS (West Virginia Univ/SAE Scholarship) 406
SOCIETY OF AUTOMOTIVE ENGINEERS (Wichita State Univ/SAE Scholarship) 407
SOCIETY OF AUTOMOTIVE ENGINEERS (Widener Univ/SAE Scholarship) 408
SOCIETY OF AUTOMOTIVE ENGINEERS (Wright State Univ/SAE Scholarship) 409
SOCIETY OF AUTOMOTIVE ENGINEERS (Yanmar/SAE Scholarship) 410
SOCIETY OF BIOLOGICAL PSYCHIATRY (Ziskind-Somerfield Research Award) 1696
SOCIETY OF BROADCAST ENGINEERS (Harold Ennes Scholarship Fund) 2186
SOCIETY OF DAUGHTERS OF THE U.S. ARMY (Scholarships) 3357
SOCIETY OF EXPLORATION GEOPHYSICISTS (SEG) FOUNDATION (Scholarships) 1383
SOCIETY OF HISPANIC PROFESSIONAL ENGINEERS FOUNDATION (SHPE Scholarships) 411, 1508
SOCIETY OF MANUFACTURING ENGINEERING EDUCATION FOUNDATION (Scholarships& Fellowship) 757
SOCIETY OF MECHANICAL ENGINEERS-WYOMING SECTION
 (Coates-Wolff-Russell Memorial Mining Industry Scholarships) 804
SOCIETY OF MOTION PICTURE AND TELEVISION ENGINEERS 3929
SOCIETY OF NAVAL ARCHITECTS AND MARINE ENGINEERS 3932, 3933
SOCIETY OF PETROLEUM ENGINEERS 3945
SOCIETY OF PETROLEUM ENGINEERS (Gus Archie Memorial Scholarship) 412
SOCIETY OF PHYSICS STUDENTS (SPS Scholarships) 1635
SOCIETY OF PROFESSIONAL JOURNALISTS (Mark of Excellence Awards Competition) 2187
SOCIETY OF SATELLITE PROFESSIONALS INTERNATIONAL (SSPI Scholarships) 21, 758, 805, 1384, 2188, 2283, 2334
SOCIETY OF THE FIRST DIVISION FOUNDATION (Scholarships) 3358
SOCIETY OF WOMEN ENGINEERS (3M Company Scholarships) 413
SOCIETY OF WOMEN ENGINEERS (Admiral Grace Murray Hopper Scholarships) 632
SOCIETY OF WOMEN ENGINEERS (Anne Maureen Whitney Barrow Memorial Scholarship) 414
SOCIETY OF WOMEN ENGINEERS (B.K. Krenzer Memorial Re-entry Scholarship) 415
SOCIETY OF WOMEN ENGINEERS (Central Intelligence Agency Scholarship) 416
SOCIETY OF WOMEN ENGINEERS (Chrysler Corporation Re-entry Scholarship) 417, 418, 419

SOCIETY OF WOMEN ENGINEERS (Chevron Scholarships) 420

SOCIETY OF WOMEN ENGINEERS (David Sarnoff Research Center Scholarship) 421

SOCIETY OF WOMEN ENGINEERS (Dorothy Lemke Howarth Scholarships) 422

SOCIETY OF WOMEN ENGINEERS (GTE Foundation Scholarships) 423

SOCIETY OF WOMEN ENGINEERS (General Electric Fund Scholarships) 424

SOCIETY OF WOMEN ENGINEERS (General Motors Foundation Scholarships) 425

SOCIETY OF WOMEN ENGINEERS (Ivy Parker Memorial Scholarship) 426

SOCIETY OF WOMEN ENGINEERS (Judith Resnick Memorial Scholarship) 427

SOCIETY OF WOMEN ENGINEERS (Lillian Moller Gilbreth Scholarship) 428

SOCIETY OF WOMEN ENGINEERS (Lockheed-Martin Corporation Scholarships) 429

SOCIETY OF WOMEN ENGINEERS (Lockheed-Martin Fort Worth Scholarships) 430

SOCIETY OF WOMEN ENGINEERS (MASWE Memorial Scholarships) 431

SOCIETY OF WOMEN ENGINEERS (Microsoft Corporation Scholarships) 633

SOCIETY OF WOMEN ENGINEERS (Nalco Foundation Scholarship) 759

SOCIETY OF WOMEN ENGINEERS (Northrop Corporation Founders Scholarship) 432

SOCIETY OF WOMEN ENGINEERS (Northrop Grumman Scholarships) 433

SOCIETY OF WOMEN ENGINEERS (Olive Lynn Salembier Scholarship) 434

SOCIETY OF WOMEN ENGINEERS (Rockwell Corporation Scholarships) 435

SOCIETY OF WOMEN ENGINEERS (Stone & Webster Scholarships) 436

SOCIETY OF WOMEN ENGINEERS (TRW Foundation Scholarships) 437

SOCIETY OF WOMEN ENGINEERS (United Technologies Corporation Scholarships) 438

SOCIETY OF WOMEN ENGINEERS (Westinghouse/Bertha Lamme Scholarships) 439

SOIL & WATER CONSERVATION SOCIETY 3968

SOIL AND WATER CONSERVATION SOCIETY (SWCS Internships) 158, 553, 1301, 1302, 1303, 1385,
....1421, 1422, 1423, 2189, 2335

SOLOMON R. GUGGENHEIM MUSEUM (Internship Programs) 944

SONOMA COUNTY PRESS CLUB (Scholarship) 2190

SONOMA STATE UNIVERSITY (Scholarship Program) 3359

SONS OF ITALY FOUNDATION (National Leadership Grants) 3360

SONS OF NORWAY FOUNDATION (Astrid G. Cates Scholarship Fund) 3361

SONS OF NORWAY FOUNDATION (King Olav V Norwegian-American Heritage Fund) ...867, 868

SONS OF THE AMERICAN REVOLUTION (Joseph S. Rumbaugh Historical Oration Contest) 3362

SONS OF THE REPUBLIC OF TEXAS (Presidio La Bahia Award) 2240, 3363

SOPHIA SCHNITMAN EDUCATIONAL FOUNDATION (Scholarship) 830

SOROPTIMIST FOUNDATIONS (Soroptimist International of the Americas—Youth Citizenship Award) 3364, 3365

SOURISSEAU ACADEMY FOR STATE AND LOCAL HISTORY (Research Grant) 2241

SOUTH CAROLINA FARM BUREAU FOUNDATION (Scholarships) 1304

SOUTH CAROLINA GOVERNOR'S OFFICE; DIVISION OF VETERANS AFFAIRS
(Tuition Assistance for Children of Certain War Veterans) 3366

SOUTH CAROLINA STUDENT LOAN CORPORATION 3367

SOUTH CAROLINA TUITION GRANTS COMMITTEE (Higher Education Tuition Grants Program) 3368

SOUTH DAKOTA DEPARTMENT OF EDUCATION AND CULTURAL AFFAIRS
(Robert Byrd Honors Scholarship) 3369

SOUTH DAKOTA DIVISION OF VETERANS AFFAIRS (Aid to Veterans) 3370, 3371, 3372

SOUTHEAST MISSOURI STATE UNIVERSITY (Constance Rowe French Scholarship) 1051, 1052, 1053

SOUTHERN ILLINOIS UNIVERSITY (Music Scholarships) 1158

SOUTHWESTERN UNIVERSITY (Scholarships and Grants) 3373

SPACE COAST CREDIT UNION (Four-Year Scholarships) 159, 634

SPACE COAST CREDIT UNION (Two-Year Scholarships) 160, 635, 1509, 1636, 2191, 2336

SPANISH ABROAD 3777

SPECIAL LIBRARIES ASSOCIATION (SLA Scholarship Program) 1025

SPORTS JOURNALISM INSTITUTE (Scholarships/Internships) 2192

SPRINGSIDE SCHOOL (Grants) 3374

SRP/NAVAJO GENERATING STATION (Navajo Scholarship) 22, 161, 281, 440, 1424, 1697, 1781, 1830, 1929, 2011

ST. DAVID'S SOCIETY (Scholarship) 3375

STANFORD HOME STUDYGUIDE FOR SAT SUCESS 3778

STANFORD UNIVERSITY (Dofflemyer Honors Eagle Scout Scholarship) 3376

STANFORD YOUTH ENVIRONMENTAL SCIENCE PROGRAM (SYESP Summer Residence Program) 1425

STANHOME INC. (Stanhome Scholarship Program) 3377

STANLEY DRAMA AWARD (Playwriting/Musical Awards Competition) 1026

STATE COLLEGE AND UNIVERSITY SYSTEMS OF WEST VIRGINIA—CENTRAL OFFICE
(WV Higher Education Grant Program) 3378

STATE FARM COMPANIES FOUNDATION (Exceptional Student Fellowship) 162, 636, 1637

STATE FARM COMPANIES FOUNDATION (Scholarships for Dependents) 3379

STATE OF NEW JERSEY OFFICE OF STUDENT ASSISTANCE
(Edward J. Bloustein Distinguished Scholars Program) 3380, 3381, 3382, 3383

STATE RESOURCE SHEETS 3779

STATE STUDENT ASSISTANCE COMMISSION OF INDIANA
(Scholarships for Special Education Teachers & Physical/Occupational Therapists) 282, 283, 1930, 2012, 3384, 3385

STEPHEN M. PRICE FOUNDATION (Aviation Training Scholarships for Youth) 3386

STEPHEN T. MARCHELLO SCHOLARSHIP FOUNDATION (Scholarships) 3387

STEVEN KNEZEVICH TRUST (Grants) 3388

STUDENT AID FOUNDATION, INC. (Loans) 3389

STUDENT CONSERVATION ASSOCIATION (SCA Resource Assistant Program) 163, 554, 584, 760, 1027, 1159, 1305,
. . . . .1386, 1426, 1449, 1468, 1557, 2242, 2467

STUDENT FINANCIAL AID AND SCHOLARSHIPS AT WYOMING COLLEGES 3780

STUDENT GUIDE—Financial Aid from the U.S. Department of Education 3781

STUDENT LOAN GUARANTEE FOUNDATION OF ARKANSAS (SLGFA Loans) 3390

STUDY ABROAD 3782

SUBURBAN CABLE (Scholarships) 3391

SUCCESSFUL FARMING-BAYER CORPORATION (Crop Protection Scholarships) 1306

SUDBURY FOUNDATION ATKINSON SCHOLARSHIP PROGRAM 3392

SUMMER FUN—LEARNING PROGRAMS 3783

SUMMER ON CAMPUS: COLLEGE EXPERIENCES FOR HIGH SCHOOL STUDENTS .3784

SUNKIST GROWERS INC (A.W. Bodine-Sunkist Memorial Scholarship) 3393

SUZUKI ASSOCIATION OF THE AMERICAS (Music Teacher Scholarships) 1160

SWISS BENEVOLENT SOCIETY OF CHICAGO (Scholarship Fund) 3394

SWISS BENEVOLENT SOCIETY OF SAN FRANCISCO (Clement & Frieda Amstutz Fund Scholarship) 3395

SYNOD OF THE NORTHEAST (Wurffel/Sills Student Loan Program) 3396

TAFT CORPORATE GIVING DIRECTORY 3785

TAILHOOK FOUNDATION (Scholarship Fund) 3397

TALBOTS (Women's Scholarship Fund) 3398

TALL CLUBS INTERNATIONAL (Kae Sumner Einfeldt Scholarship Award) 3399

TARGET STORES (Target All-Around Scholarships) 3400

TARGET STORES (Target Teachers Scholarships) 3401

TARGETING THE JOB YOU WANT 3786

TAU BETA PI ASSOCIATION, INC. (Undergraduate Scholarships) 441

TECHNOLOGY STUDENT ASSOCIATION (Scholarships for Future Teachers) 284

TEEN MAGAZINE (Miss Teenage America Program) 3402

TEKTRONIX FOUNDATION (Scholarship for Dependent Children of Tektronix Employees) 3403

TEN STEPS IN WRITING THE RESEARCH PAPER 3787

TENNESSEE STUDENT ASSISTANCE CORPORATION (TSAC Minority Teaching Fellows Program) 285, 286, 3404, 3405

TERESA F. HUGHES TRUST 3406

TEXAS A&M UNIVERSITY (Academic Excellence Awards) 3407

TEXAS A&M UNIVERSITY (Opportunity Award Scholarship) 3408

TEXAS A&M UNIVERSITY (President's Achievement Award Scholarship and Aggie Spirit Award Scholarship) 3409

TEXAS A&M UNIVERSITY (President's Endowed Scholarship; Lechner Scholarship; McFadden Scholarship) 3410

TEXAS A&M UNIVERSITY (Scholarships, Grants, and Loans) 3411

TEXAS ELECTRIC COOPERATIVES INC. (Ann Lane Homemaker Scholarship) 3412

TEXAS HIGHER EDUCATION COORDINATING BOARD (Scholarships, Grants, and Loans) 3413

TEXAS MUSIC INDUSTRY DIRECTORY 3788

TEXAS SOCIETY OF PROFESSIONAL ENGINEERS (Scholarships) 442, 1246, 1469, 1510, 1638

THE ADA ENDOWMENT AND ASSISTANCE FUND, INC. (Minority Dental Student Scholarship) . . .1782, 1783, 1931, 1932, 1933

THE ALISA FLATOW MEMORIAL FUND (Scholarships for the Study of the Jewish Religion in Israel) 869

THE AMERICAN ASSOCIATION OF ATTORNEY-CERTIFIED PUBLIC ACCOUNTANTS FOUNDATION
   (Student Writing Competition) 164, 2284

THE AMERICAN ASSOCIATION OF TEACHERS OF ARABIC (Translation Contest) 1054

THE AMERICAN CLASSICAL LEAGUE (Ed Phinney Commemorative Scholarship) 287, 870, 1055, 1056

THE AMERICAN COLLEGE OF PREHOSPITAL MEDICINE (Alan R. Klausfelder Memorial Scholarship) 1934

THE AMERICAN LEGION, DEPT. OF MARYLAND, INC. (Scholarship Program) 1511, 1639, 3414, 3415

THE ARC 3879

THE ARC (Research Grants Program in Mental Retardation) 288, 1831, 2370

THE ART INSTITUTES INTERNATIONAL (Evelyn Keedy Memorial Scholarship) 165, 761, 945, 2068, 2193, 2468

THE ASCAP FOUNDATION (Morton Gould Young Composer Awards) 1161

THE AU EDUCATION FOUNDATION FOR CHINESE 3416

THE AUGIE J. ALTAR SCHOLARSHIP 1307, 1558, 1698, 1784, 1832, 1935, 2013

THE AUGUSTUS SOCIETY (Scholarships) 3417

THE BAGBY FOUNDATION FOR THE MUSICAL ARTS, INC. (Musical Study Grants) 1162

THE BARKER FOUNDATION, INC. 3418

THE BRYN MAWR SCHOOL (Grants) 3419

THE BUFFETT FOUNDATION 3420

THE BUNTING & LYON BLUE BOOK: PRIVATE INDEPENDENT SCHOOLS 3789

THE CAMBRIDGE SCHOOL OF WESTON (Scholarships) 3421

THE CARE BOOK (College Aid Resources for Education) 3790

THE CAREER ATLAS 3791

THE CARTER CENTER MENTAL HEALTH PROGRAM (Rosalynn Carter Fellowships for Mental Health Journalism) 2194

THE CENTER FOR CROSS-CULTURAL STUDY (Tuition Awards for Study in Sevill, Spain) 871, 1057

THE CHARTER FUND 3422

THE CHRONICLE PUBLISHING COMPANY (Scholarship) 2195

THE COLLEGE GUIDE FOR PARENTS 3792

THE COLLEGE HANDBOOK 3793

THE COLORADO SPRINGS SCHOOL (K-12 Scholarships) 3423

THE COUNCIL FOR EXCEPTIONAL CHILDREN (Black Caucus Scholarship) 289, 290

THE CULTURAL SOCIETY, INC. 3424

THE CYPRUS CHILDREN'S FUND, INC. (Scholarship Endowment) 3425

THE DAVID AND DOVETTA WILSON SCHOLARSHIP FUND (Scholarships) 3426

THE DONNA REED FOUNDATION (National Scholarships) 1163

THE DONNA REED FOUNDATION (Performing Arts Scholarships for Iowa High School Seniors) 1164, 1165

THE E. PERRY AND GRACE BEATTY MEMORIAL FOUNDATION 3427

THE EDDIE G. ROBINSON FOUNDATION (Scholarships) 3428

THE EDMUND F. MAXWELL FOUNDATION (Scholarships) 3429

THE EDUCATIONAL AND SCIENTIFIC TRUST OF THE PENNSYLVANIA MEDICAL SOCIETY
   (Loan Program for Pennsylvania Medical School Students) 1699, 1700

THE EDUCATION RESOURCES INSTITUTE (Parent Loans for Elementary and Secondary Education—PLEASE) 3430

THE ELECTRICAL WOMEN'S ROUND TABLE INC. (Julia Kiene & Lyle Mamer Fellowships) 697

THE FALMOUTH INSTITUTE SCHOLARSHIP 3431

THE FEDERAL CIRCUIT BAR ASSOCIATION (George Hutchinson Writing Competition) 2285

THE FLINN FOUNDATION (Flinn Scholarships) 3432

THE FLUOR FOUNDATION (Fluor Daniel Engineering Scholarship Program) 443

THE FOUNDATION DIRECTORY 3794

THE FOUNDATION OF THE ST. ANDREW'S SOCIETY OF PHILADELPHIA (Study-Abroad Scholarships) 3433

THE FRANK H. & EVA BUCK FOUNDATION (Frank H. Buck Scholarships) 3434

THE FRASCA FAMILY/UNIVERSITY AVIATION ASSOCIATION
(The Joseph Frasca Excellence in Aviation Scholarship) 508, 2469
THE FUND FOR AMERICAN STUDIES (Institutes on Political Journalism; Business &
Government Affairs & Comparative Political & Economic Systems) 166, 2196, 2337
THE FUND FOR INVESTIGATIVE JOURNALISM, INC. (Grants for Journalists) 2197
THE GERBER FOUNDATION (Scholarship Program) 3435
THE GRAND RAPIDS FOUNDATION (Economic Club of Grand Rapids Scholarship) .23
THE GRAND RAPIDS FOUNDATION (Edwin F. Doyle Scholarship) 3436
THE GRAND RAPIDS FOUNDATION (Grand Rapids Combined Theatre Scholarship Fund) 1166
THE GRAND RAPIDS FOUNDATION (Lavina Laible Scholarship) 3437
THE GRAND RAPIDS FOUNDATION (Mathilda Gallmeyer Scholarship) 946
THE GRAND RAPIDS FOUNDATION (Mildred E. Troske Music Scholarship) 1167
THE GRAND RAPIDS FOUNDATION (Paul Collins Scholarship) 947
THE GRAND RAPIDS FOUNDATION (Scholarships) 3438
THE GUERRILLA GUIDE TO MASTERING STUDENT LOAN DEBT 3795
THE HAN'T FOUNDATION (Quest Award in Micro-Meteorites) 1833
THE HARLEY SCHOOL (Grants) 3439
THE HEATH EDUCATION FUND (Scholarships for Ministers, Priests, and Missionaries) 1221, 2403
THE HELLENIC FOUNDATION 3440
THE HORIZONS FOUNDATION (Joseph Towner Fund for Gay and Lesbian Families) 3441
THE HUDSON SCHOOL (Scholarships) 3442
THE INTERNATIONAL SOCIETY FOR OPTICAL ENGINEERING (Scholarships and Grants) 762
THE J. EDGAR HOOVER FOUNDATION 2243, 2286, 2338
THE JACKIE ROBINSON FOUNDATION (Scholarships) 3443
THE JAMES BEARD FOUNDATION (Scholarships) 2069
THE JANICE AND BEN GROMET FUND FOR DISADVANTAGED CHILDREN 3444
THE JERUSALEM FELLOWSHIPS (Internships in Israel for Leaders) 3445
THE JOHN F. KENNEDY CENTER FOR THE PERFORMING ARTS (Awards, Fellowships, and Scholarships) 1028, 1168
THE JOHNS HOPKINS UNIVERSITY APPLIED PHYSICS LAB (APL Summer Employment Program) 444
THE KIMBO FOUNDATION 3446
THE KISKI SCHOOL (Financial Aid) 3447
THE KNOTT SCHOLARSHIP FUNDS (Scholarships) 3448
THE KOREAN AMERICAN SCHOLARSHIP FOUNDATION (Scholarships) 3449
THE KUN SHOULDER REST, INC. (Listing of Music Competitions) 1169
THE MADEIRA SCHOOL (Scholarships) 3450
THE MEMORY KEY 3796
THE MILLER SCHOOL OF ALBEMARLE (Grants) 3451
THE MODESTO BEE (Scholarship Program for Minority Jounalism Students) 2198
THE MR. HOLLAND'S OPUS FOUNDATION (Solo Program: Musical Instruments for Individuals) 1170
THE NATIONAL ASSOCIATION OF COUNSEL FOR CHILDREN (Student Essay Competition) 2287
THE NATIONAL ASSOCIATION OF NEGRO MUSICIANS, INC. (Scholarship Competitions) 1171, 1172
THE NATIONAL DIRECTORY OF INTERNSHIPS 3797
THE NATIONAL HEMOPHILIA FOUNDATION (Kevin Child Scholarship) 3452
THE NATIONAL ITALIAN AMERICAN FOUNDATION (Communications Scholarship) 2199, 3453, 3454, 3455, 3456,
. . . . .3457, 3458, 3459, 3460, 3461,
. . . . .3462, 3463, 3464, 3465
THE NINETY-NINES, INC. 3982
THE OVERLAKE SCHOOL (Scholarships) 3466
THE PARKERSBURG AREA COMMUNITY FOUNDATION (Scholarships) 3467
THE PAUL & DAISY SOROS FELLOWSHIPS FOR NEW AMERICANS (Graduate Fellowships) 3468
THE PUBLIC RELATIONS SOCIETY OF AMERICA (Multicultural Affairs Scholarship) 2200
THE RETIRED OFFICERS ASSOCIATION (TROA Scholarship Fund) 3469
THE ROOTHBERT FUND, INC. (Scholarships and Grants) 291
THE SCHOLARSHIP WATCH 3798

THE SOCIETY OF TRIBOLOGISTS AND LUBRICATION ENGINEERS (Scholarships and Fellowships) 763

THE SUMMIT COUNTRY DAY SCHOOL (Financial Aid) 3470

THE UNIVERSITY OF NEW MEXICO FOUNDATION (The Kelly Richmond Memorial Fund) 2201

THE UPS FOUNDATION (The George D. Smith Scholarship Program) 3471

THE UPS FOUNDATION (The James E. Casey Scholarship Program) 3472

THE URBAN SCHOOL OF SAN FRANCISCO (Financial Aid) 3473

THE VINCENT/CURTIS EDUCATIONAL REGISTER 3799

THE WALT DISNEY COMPANY (American Teacher Awards) 292, 948, 1029, 1058, 1173, 1512, 1640, 2090, 2470

THE WASIE FOUNDATION (Scholarship Program) 3474

THE WHITAKER FOUNDATION (Fellowships for Research in Biomedical Engineering) .1834

THE WILLIAM LOEB MEMORIAL FUND 3475

THE WINSTON SCHOOL (The Mary Eggemeyer Fund Grants) 3476

THEIR WORLD 3800

THELONIOUS MONK INSTITUTE OF JAZZ (International Jazz Trumpet Competition) .1174, 1175

THERE ARE NO LIMITS 3801

THERESA CORTI FAMILY AGRICULTURAL TRUST (Scholarship Program) 1308

THIRD MARINE DIVISION ASSOCIATION (Scholarships) 3477

THOMAS J. WATSON FOUNDATION (The Thomas J. Watson Fellowship Program) 3478

TOP SECRET EXECUTIVE RESUMES 3802

TOWSON STATE UNIVERSITY (Scholarship & Award Programs) 3479

TOZER FOUNDATION (Scholarships) 3480

TRANSPORT WORKERS UNION OF AMERICA (Michael J. Quill Scholarship Fund) 3481

TRANSPORTATION CLUBS INTERNATIONAL (Charlotte Woods Memorial Scholarship) 167, 168, 169, 170, 171, 172

TRAVEL AND TOURISM RESEARCH ASSOCIATION (Awards for Projects) 173

TREACY COMPANY (Scholarship) 3482

TRI-STATE GENERATION AND TRANSMISSION ASSOCIATION (Scholarships) 3483

TRIDENT ACADEMY (Scholarships) 3484

TRINITY UNIVERSITY (Various Scholarships) 3485

TRINITY-PAWLING SCHOOL (Scholarships/Grants) 3486

TUITION GRANT PROGRAM ADJUTANT GENERAL'S DEPARTMENT
   (Ohio National Guard Tuition Grant Program) 3487

TULANE UNIVERSITY (Scholarships & Fellowships) 3488

TWO/TEN INTERNATIONAL FOOTWEAR FOUNDATION (Scholarship Program) 3489

TY COBB EDUCATIONAL FOUNDATION (Undergraduate Scholarship Program) 3490

TYLENOL (Scholarship Fund) 3491

TYSON FOUNDATION, INC. (Alabama Scholarship Program) 24, 445, 637, 1309, 2014

TYSON FOUNDATION, INC. (Arkansas Scholarship Program) 25, 446, 638, 1310, 2015

TYSON FOUNDATION, INC. (Florida Scholarship Program) 26, 447, 639, 1311, 2016

TYSON FOUNDATION, INC. (Georgia Scholarship Program) 27, 448, 640, 1312, 2017

TYSON FOUNDATION, INC. (Illinois Scholarship Program) 28, 449, 641, 1313, 2018

TYSON FOUNDATION, INC. (Indiana Scholarship Program) 29, 450, 642, 1314, 2019

TYSON FOUNDATION, INC. (Mississippi Scholarship Program) 30, 31, 451, 452, 643, 644, 1315, 1316, 2020, 2021

TYSON FOUNDATION, INC. (North Carolina Scholarship Program) 32, 453, 645, 1317, 2022

TYSON FOUNDATION, INC. (Oklahoma Scholarship Program) 33, 454, 646, 1318, 2023

TYSON FOUNDATION, INC. (Pennsylvania Scholarship Program) 34, 455, 647, 1319, 2024

TYSON FOUNDATION, INC. (Tennessee Scholarship Program) 35, 36, 456, 457, 648, 649, 1320, 1321, 2025, 2026

TYSON FOUNDATION, INC. (Virginia Scholarship Program) 37, 458, 650, 1322, 2027

U.N.I.T.E. (Philadelphia-South Jersey District Council Scholarship Awards) 3492

UAA-102 COLLEGIATE AVIATION GUIDE 3803

UAA-116 COLLEGIATE AVIATION SCHOLARSHIP LISTING 3804

ULTIMATE HIGH SCHOOL SURVIVAL GUIDE 3805

UNCF/MERCK SCIENCE INITIATIVE (Undergraduate Science Research Scholarship Awards) 1388, 1428, 1450,
. . . . .1515, 1559, 1593, 1644

UNICO NATIONAL, INC. (Various Scholarships) 3500

UNITARIAN UNIVERSALIST ASSN. (Marion Barr Stanfield Art Scholarship) 831
UNITARIAN UNIVERSALIST ASSOCIATION (Musicians' Network Scholarships) 949, 1031, 1176
UNITARIAN UNIVERSALIST ASSN. (Otto M. Stanfield Legal Scholarship) 2290
UNITE (Duchessi-Sallee Scholarship) 3501
UNITED AGRIBUSINESS LEAGUE (UAL Scholarship Program) 1323
UNITED CHURCH OF CHRIST—SPECIAL HIGHER EDUCATION PROGRAM (Commission for Racial Justice) 3502
UNITED DAUGHTERS OF THE CONFEDERACY (Scholarships) 3503
UNITED FEDERATION OF TEACHERS (Albert Shanker College Scholarship Fund) 3504
UNITED FOOD & COMMERCIAL WORKERS INTERNATIONAL UNION (UFCW Scholarship Program) 3505
UNITED FOOD & COMMERCIAL WORKERS UNION—UFCW LOCAL 555 (L. Walter Derry Scholarship Fund) 3506
UNITED METHODIST CHURCH (Ernest and Eurice Miller Bass Scholarship Fund) 1222
UNITED METHODIST CHURCH (Scholarship and Loan Program) 3507
UNITED METHODIST CHURCH (Youth Ministry—Richard S. Smith Scholarship) 1223, 1224
UNITED METHODIST COMMUNICATIONS (Leonard Perryman Communications Scholarships) 2203
UNITED NEGRO COLLEGE FUND (Scholarships) 3508
UNITED PAPERWORKERS INTERNATIONAL UNION (Scholarship Program) 3509
UNITED STATES DEPARTMENT OF AGRICULTURE (1890 National Scholars Program) 177, 1247, 1324, 1389,
....1429, 1451, 1560, 1788, 2072
UNITED STUDENT AID FUNDS INC. (Guaranteed Student Loan Program; Plus Loans) 3510
UNIVERSAL TECHNICAL INSTITUTE (Al Unser National High School Competition) 766, 2472
UNIVERSITY FILM & VIDEO ASSOCIATION (Carole Fielding Student Grants) 950, 1032, 1177
UNIVERSITY FILM AND VIDEO FOUNDATION (Eastman Scholarship Program) 951
UNIVERSITY OF ALABAMA AT BIRMINGHAM (Theatre Scholarships) 1178
UNIVERSITY OF BRIDGEPORT (Undergraduate Scholarships & Grants) 3511
UNIVERSITY OF CALIFORNIA-DAVIS (Brad Webb Scholarship Fund) 1561
UNIVERSITY OF CALIFORNIA AT BERKELEY (Undergraduate Scholarships) 3512
UNIVERSITY OF CALIFORNIA SYSTEM 3863
UNIVERSITY OF CONNECTICUT (BRIDGE Pratt & Whitney Scholarships) 462
UNIVERSITY OF ILLINOIS AT URBANA-CHAMPAIGN (Lydia E. Parker Bates Scholarship) 556, 952, 1179
UNIVERSITY OF ILLINOIS COLLEGE OF ACES (Jonathan Baldwin Turner Agricultural Merit
   Scholarship Program) 1325, 2073
UNIVERSITY OF MAINE PULP & PAPER FOUNDATION (Pulp & Paper Foundation Scholarships) 767
UNIVERSITY OF MARYLAND (College of Journalism Scholarships) 2204
UNIVERSITY OF MARYLAND (John B. & Ida Slaughter Endowed Scholarship in Science,
   Technology, & the Black Community) 463, 768, 873, 1516
UNIVERSITY OF MICHIGAN (Scholarships and Merit Programs for Undergraduates) 3513
UNIVERSITY OF MINNESOTA COLLEGE OF AGRICULTURE (Scholarship Program) 1326
UNIVERSITY OF MISSOURI ROLLA (The Distinguished Scholars Program for Non-Missouri Residents) 3514
UNIVERSITY OF NEBRASKA AT LINCOLN (Regents, David, Davis, National Merit, and Departmental Scholarships) 3515
UNIVERSITY OF NEBRASKA AT OMAHA (Paul L. Beck Faculty/Staff Honors Scholarships) 2291
UNIVERSITY OF NEW MEXICO (Amigo and Amigo Transfer Scholarships) 3516, 3517
UNIVERSITY OF NORTH TEXAS (Merchandising and Hospitality Scholarships) 178, 293, 953, 1180
UNIVERSITY OF OKLAHOMA—H.H. HERBERT SCHOOL OF JOURNALISM AND
   MASS COMMUNICATION (Undergraduate Scholarships) 179, 2205
UNIVERSITY OF OXFORD—SOMERVILLE COLLEGE (Janet Watson Bursary) 3518
UNIVERSITY OF ROCHESTER (Mildred R. Burton Summer Study Grants/Scholarships for Summer Language Study) 1059
UNIVERSITY OF SAN FRANCISCO McLAREN SCHOOL OF BUSINESS (Laura D. Sypin Memorial Scholarship) 198
UNIVERSITY OF SOUTH DAKOTA (Criminal Justice Dept. Scholarships) 2292, 2340
UNIVERSITY OF TEXAS AT EL PASO (Music Scholarships) 1181
UNIVERSITY OF UTAH COLLEGE OF PHARMACY (Departmental Scholarships) 1789, 1790
UNIVERSITY OF WINDSOR (Undergraduate Scholarships) 3519
UNIVERSITY OF WYOMING (Superior Students in Education Scholarship) 294
UNIVERSITY SYSTEM OF WEST VIRGINIA (Health Sciences Scholarship Program) 1704
U.S. AIR FORCE ACADEMY (Academy Appointment) 3493

U.S. COAST GUARD ACADEMY 3977

U.S. COAST GUARD MUTUAL ASSISTANCE (Adm. Roland Student Loan Program) 3520

U.S. CUSTOMS SERVICE (Law Enforcement Explorer Scholarships) 2288

U.S. DEPARTMENT OF DEFENSE (CO-OP Program-CECOM Research, Development, & Engineering Center-ADO) 464, 3521

U.S. DEPARTMENT OF DEFENSE (High School Apprenticeship Program) .459, 460, 1513, 1514, 1641, 1642

U.S. DEPARTMENT OF DEFENSE-NATIONAL SECURITY AGENCY
(Director's Summer Program) 1643

U.S. DEPARTMENT OF STATE (Internships) 3494

U.S. DEPARTMENT OF TRANSPORTATION (Dwight D. Eisenhower Transportation Fellowships) 174, 461, 555, 585,
. . . . .698, 764, 806, 2371, 2404

U.S. DEPT. OF AGRICULTURE 3896

U.S. DEPT. OF AGRICULTURE; FOOD AND NUTRITION SERVICE 3893

U.S. DEPT. OF EDUCATION (Robert C. Byrd Honors Scholarship Program) 3497

U.S. DEPT. OF HEALTH; RECRUITMENT DIVISION 3895

U.S. DEPT. OF HEALTH & HUMAN SERVICES (Indian Health Service Preparatory Scholarship Program) 175, 176,
. . . . .651, 1701, 1702, 1703,
. . . . .1785, 1786, 1787, 1835, 1836, 1936, 1937,
. . . . .2028, 2029, 2070, 2071, 2405, 2406

U.S. DEPT. OF INTERIOR; BUREAU OF INDIAN AFFAIRS (Adult Education Grants) 2471

U.S. DEPT. OF INTERIOR; BUREAU OF INDIAN AFFAIRS (Higher Education Grant Programs) 3495, 3496

U.S. DEPT. OF LABOR; BUREAU OF APPRENTICESHIP AND TRAINING 3837

U.S. DEPT. OF VETERANS AFFAIRS (Vocational Rehabilitation) 3522

U.S. ENVIRONMENTAL PROTECTION AGENCY 3886

U.S. ENVIRONMENTAL PROTECTION AGENCY—NATIONAL NETWORK FOR
ENVIRONMENTAL MANAGEMENT STUDIES (Fellowships) .652, 765, 1387, 1427, 2202, 2289

U.S. INSTITUTE OF PEACE (National Peace Essay Contest) 872, 1030, 2244, 2339

U.S. MARINE CORPS (Naval Reserve Officer Training Corps-NROTC) 3498

U.S. MARINE CORPS HISTORICAL CENTER (College Internships) 1033, 1470, 2245

U.S. MILITARY ACADEMY 3976

U.S. NAVAL ACADEMY 3973, 3974

U.S. SPACE CAMP FOUNDATION (Space Camp, Space Academy, Advanced Space Academy) 3499

U.S. SUBMARINE VETERANS OF WWII (Scholarship Program) 3523

USA TODAY (All-USA Academic Team Award) 3524

USAF RESERVE BONUS PROGRAM 1705, 2030

USAF RESERVE PERSONNEL CENTER (Armed Forces Health Professionas Scholarships) 1706, 2031

UTA ALUMNI ASSOCIATION (African-American Endowed Scholarship) 3525

UTA ALUMNI ASSOCIATION (Daniel Kauth Scholarship) 180

UTA ALUMNI ASSOCIATION (Frankie S. Hansell Endowed Scholarship) 3526

UTA ALUMNI ASSOCIATION (Hispanic Scholarship) 3527

UTA ALUMNI ASSOCIATION (John D. Burton Memorial Criminal Justice Scholarship) 2293

UTA ALUMNI ASSOCIATION (Karin McCallum Scholarship) 2206

UTA ALUMNI ASSOCIATION (Lloyd Clark Scholarship Journalism) 2207

UTA ALUMNI ASSOCIATION (Pitman-Roberts Endowed Scholarship) 2246

UTA ALUMNI ASSOCIATION (Simmons-Blackwell Endowed Scholarship) 3528

UTA ALUMNI ASSOCIATION (Student Foundation Sophomore Scholarship) 3529

UTA ALUMNI ASSOCIATION (Sue & Art Mosby Scholarship Endowment in Music) 1182

UTAH STATE BOARD OF REGENTS (State Student Incentive Grants) 3530

UTAH STATE OFFICE OF EDUCATION (T.H. Bell Teaching Incentive Loan Program) 295

UTILITY WORKERS UNION OF AMERICA (Private Utility Workers Union of America Scholarship Program Award) 3531

V.M. EHLERS MEMORIAL FUND, INC. 1430

VACATION STUDY ABROAD 3806

VALENCIA COMMUNITY COLLEGE FOUNDATION (Scholarships) 3532

VANDERBILT UNIVERSITY (Fred Russell-Grantland Rice Scholarship) 2208

VAUGHAN/NAHWW (Home Workshop Writers Scholarship) 2209

VENTURE CLUBS OF THE AMERICAS (Student Aid Awards) 3533

VERMONT STUDENT ASSISTANCE CORPORATION (Incentive Grants for Undergraduates) 3534, 3535

VERTICAL FLIGHT FOUNDATION (Scholarships) 509

VETERANS OF FOREIGN WARS/V.F.W. LADIES AUXILIARY (M.J. "Mel" Ornelas Memorial Scholarships) 3536

VETERANS OF FOREIGN WARS OF THE UNITED STATES (Voice of Democracy Audio-Essay Scholarship Contest) ...3537

VIKKI CARR SCHOLARSHIP FOUNDATION (Scholarships) 3538

VILLA MADONNA ACADEMY (Scholarships) 3539

VINCENT L. HAWKINSON FOUNDATION FOR PEACE AND JUSTICE (Scholarship Award) 3540

VIOLET R. AND NADA V. BOHNETT MEMORIAL FOUNDATION 1225

VIRGIN ISLANDS BOARD OF EDUCATION (Music Scholarships) 1183, 1707, 2032, 3541, 3542

VIRGINIA AIRPORT OPERATORS COUNCIL (VAOC Aviation Scholarship Award) 510

VIRGINIA AVIATION AND SPACE EDUCATION FORUM (Scholarships) 511, 2473

VIRGINIA BAPTIST MISSION BOARD (Virginia Baptist Ministerial Undergraduate Student Loans) 1226

VIRGINIA MILITARY INSTITUTE (Scholarships) 3543

VIRGINIA MUSEUM OF FINE ARTS (Fellowships) 954

VIRGINIA SMITH SCHOLARSHIP TRUST (Scholarships) 3544

VIRGINIA STATE COUNCIL OF HIGHER EDUCATION (Tuition Assistance Grant Program) 3545, 3546, 3547, 3548

W. EUGENE SMITH MEMORIAL FUND, INC. (Grants) 2210

W.E. UPJOHN INSTITUTE FOR EMPLOYMENT RESEARCH (Grant) 181

WAL-MART FOUNDATION (Sam Walton Scholarship) 3549

WAL-MART FOUNDATION SCHOLARSHIPS (Distribution Center Scholarships) 3550

WAL-MART FOUNDATION SCHOLARSHIPS (Wal-Mart Associate Scholarship) 3551

WAL-MART FOUNDATION SCHOLARSHIPS (Walton Foundation Scholarship) 3552

WAMSO (Young Artist Competition) 1184

WASHINGTON CROSSING FOUNDATION (National Scholarship Award) 2341

WASHINGTON HIGHER EDUCATION COORDINATING BOARD
    (American Indian Endowed Scholarship) 3553, 3554, 3555, 3556

WASHINGTON INTERNSHIPS FOR STUDENTS OF ENGINEERING (Summer Internships) 465, 466

WASHINGTON INTERNATIONAL SCHOOL (Scholarships) 3557

WASHINGTON PULP & PAPER FOUNDATION (Scholarship Program) 769

WASHINGTON STATE HIGHER EDUCATION COORDINATING BOARD
    (Health Professional Loan Repayment & Scholarship Program) 1708, 1709, 1791, 1792, 1837, 1938, 2033, 3558

WASHINGTON STATE PTA (Financial Grant Foundation) 3559

WASHINGTON TRUST BANK (Herman Oscar Schumacher College Fund Trust) 3560

WASHINGTON WATER POWER (Mindpower Generation Scholarship Program) 3561

WATER ENVIRONMENT FEDERATION 3980

WATER ENVIRONMENT FEDERATION (Student Paper Competition) 770, 1390, 1431, 1452

WAVERLY COMMUNITY HOUSE INC. (F. Lammot Belin Arts Scholarships) 557, 955, 1034, 1185

WAYNE RESA (Scholarships) 296

WEBB INSTITUTE (Naval Architecture Scholarships) 558, 807

WELLESLEY COLLEGE (Fellowships for Wellesley Graduates & Graduating Seniors) 3562

WEST VIRGINIA DIVISION OF VETERANS' AFFAIRS (War Orphans Education Program) 3563

WEST VIRGINIA SOCIETY OF ARCHITECTS/AMERICAN INSTITUTE OF ARCHITECTS (Scholarships) 559

WESTERN GOLF ASSOCIATION/EVANS SCHOLARS FOUNDATION (Caddie Scholarships) 3564

WESTERN SOCIETY OF CRIMINOLOGY (June Morrison Scholarship Fund) 2294, 2295

WESTERN SUNBATHING ASSOCIATION (Scholarships) 3565

WESTOVER SCHOOL (Mandeville Teachers' Daughters Scholarship) 3566

WESTRIDGE SCHOOL (Financial Aid) 3567

WHAT COLOR IS YOUR PARACHUTE? 3807

WHEATLAND COMMUNITY SCHOLASTIC FUND, INC. (Scholarships) 3568

WHEATLAND R.E.A. (Scholarships) 3569

WHERE THE JOBS ARE 3808

WHIRLY-GIRLS INC. (International Women Helicopter Pilots Scholarships) 2474

WHITTIER COLLEGE (John Greenleaf Whittier Scholars Program) 3570

WHITTIER COLLEGE (Talent Scholarship) 956, 1186

WILLIAM BRADLEY SCHOLARSHIP FOUNDATION INC. (William Bradley Scholarship) 3571
WILLIAM F. COOPER SCHOLARSHIP 3572
WILLIAM H. CHAPMAN FOUNDATION (Scholarships) 3573
WILLIAM M. GRUPE FOUNDATION, INC. (Scholarships) 1517
WILLIAM RANDOLPH HEARST FOUNDATION (Journalism Awards Program) 2211, 3574
WILSON ORNITHOLOGICAL SOCIETY (Fuertes, Nice, & Stewart Grants) 1562
WINDHAM FOUNDATION INC. (Scholarships) 3575
WINNING SCHOLARSHIPS FOR COLLEGE—AN INSIDER'S GUIDE 3809
WINONA PUBLIC SCHOOLS (Community Education Scholarships) 3576
WISCONSIN CONGRESS OF PARENTS AND TEACHERS INC. (Brookmire-Hastings Scholarships) 297
WISCONSIN DEPARTMENT OF VETERANS AFFAIRS
    (Deceased Veterans' Survivors Economic Assistance Loan/Education Grants) 3577, 3578
WISCONSIN FARM BUREAU FOUNDATION (Scholarship Program) 1327
WISCONSIN HIGHER EDUCATION AIDS BOARD (Student Financial Aid Program) 3579
WISCONSIN LEAGUE FOR NURSING, INC. (Scholarship) 2034, 2035
WITTENBERG UNIVERSITY (Music Scholarship Funds) 1187
WOMAN'S SEAMEN'S FRIEND SOCIETY OF CONNECTICUT, INC. (Scholarships) 1453
WOMEN GROCERS OF AMERICA (Mary Macey Scholarships) 38
WOMEN IN ANIMATION (WIA) 3834
WOMEN IN COMMUNICATIONS (Seattle Professional Chapter Scholarships for Washington State Residents) 2212
WOMEN IN DEFENSE (HORIZONS Scholarship Foundation) 39, 182, 467, 653, 1645, 2296, 2342
WOMEN OF THE EVANGELICAL LUTHERAN CHURCH IN AMERICA ...183, 1227, 1710, 1793, 1838, 1939, 2036, 3580, 3581
WOMEN ON BOOKS (Scholarships for African-American Women) 1035, 2213
WOMEN PEACE OFFICERS ASSOCIATION OF CALIFORNIA (WPOA Scholarship) 2297
WOMEN'S AUXILIARY TO THE AMERICAN INSTITUTE OF MINING METALLURGICAL &
    PETROLEUM ENGINEERS (WAAIME Scholarship Loan Fund) 771, 808, 1391
WOMEN'S SPORTS FOUNDATION (AQHA Female Equestrian Award) 3582
WOMEN'S SPORTS FOUNDATION (Jackie Joyner-Kersee &
    Zina Garrison Minority Internships) 184, 298, 1940, 2214, 2372, 2407
WOMEN'S SPORTS FOUNDATION (Linda Riddle/SMGA Endowed, Gart Sports Sportmart, &
    Mervyn's WSF College Scholarships) 3583
WOMEN'S SPORTS FOUNDATION (Ocean Spray Travel & Training Grants) 3584
WOMEN'S WESTERN GOLF FOUNDATION (Scholarships) 3585
WOODROW WILSON NATIONAL FELLOWSHIP FOUNDATION/
    U.S. DEPARTMENTS OF COMMERCE AND AGRICULTURE (Fellowships) 40, 468, 1328, 1392, 1518, 1646, 2343, 2344
WOODS HOLE OCEANOGRAPHIC INSTITUTION (Summer Student Fellowship) 1454
WOODS HOLE OCEANOGRAPHIC INSTITUTION
    (Traineeships in Oceanography for Minority Group Undergraduates) 469, 1248, 1393, 1455, 1519, 1647
WORCESTER COUNTY HORTICULTURE SOCIETY (WCHS Scholarship) 1329
WORLD DIRECTORY OF MEDICAL SCHOOLS 3810
WORLD OF KNOWLEDGE (Today & Tomorrow Scholarship Program) 3586
WRITE YOUR WAY TO A HIGHER GPA 3811
WRITING CONTESTS FOR LAW STUDENTS 3812
WYOMING ASSOCIATION OF FUTURE HOMEMAKERS OF AMERICA (FHA/HERO Scholarship) 3587
WYOMING CROP IMPROVEMENT ASSOCIATION (Scholarship) 1330
WYOMING DEPARTMENT OF CORRECTIONS (Wayne Martinez Memorial Scholarships) 3588
WYOMING DEPARTMENT OF EDUCATION (Douvas Memorial Scholarship) 3589
WYOMING DEPARTMENT OF VETERANS AFFAIRS (War Orphans Scholarships) 3590
WYOMING FARM BUREAU FEDERATION (Dodge Merit Award) 3591
WYOMING FEDERATION OF WOMEN'S CLUBS (Mary N. Brooks Education Fund-Boys) 3592, 3593
WYOMING MINING ASSOCIATION (Scholarships) 809
WYOMING NURSES ASSOCIATION, INC. (Margaret L. Hageman Scholarships) 2037
WYOMING PEACE OFFICERS ASSOCIATION (Scholarships for Active or Retired Officers) 2298, 2299
WYOMING REPUBLICAN FOUNDATION (Scholarships) 3594
WYOMING STUDENT LOAN CORPORATION (Leadership Scholarship) 3595

WYOMING TRUCKING ASSOCIATION (Scholarships) 185, 772, 1432, 2475

WHERE THERE'S A WILL THERE'S AN "A" TO GET BETTER GRADES IN COLLEGE (or High School) 3813

XEROX TECHNICAL MINORITY SCHOLARSHIP (School-Year Tuition) 470, 471, 560, 561, 586, 587,
. . . . .654, 655, 699, 700, 773, 774, 810, 811

Y'S MEN INTERNATIONAL—US AREA (Alexander Scholarship Loan Fund) 186, 299

YOUNG AMERICAN BOWLING ALLIANCE (Alberta E. Crowe Star of Tomorrow Scholarship) 3596, 3597, 3598

YOUR CAREER IN THE COMICS 3814

YOUTH FOR UNDERSTANDING INTERNATIONAL EXCHANGE
(Congress Bundestag Youth Exchange Program) 3599, 3600, 3601, 3602, 3603, 3604, 3605

YOUTH FOUNDATION, INC. (Study-Abroad Scholarships) 3606

ZETA PHI BETA SORORITY EDUCATIONAL FOUNDATION
(Isabel M. Herson Scholarship in Education) 300, 1711, 1794, 1839, 1941, 2038, 2373, 3607

Notes

Notes

Notes

Notes

Notes

Notes

Notes

Notes

Notes

Notes

Notes

Notes

Notes